Política

Política

Nuevomexicanos and American Political Incorporation, 1821–1910

PHILLIP B. GONZALES

University of Nebraska Press • Lincoln & London

© 2016 by the Board of Regents of the University of Nebraska

Acknowledgments for the use of copyrighted material appear on page xxi, which constitutes an extension of the copyright page.

All rights reserved
Manufactured in the United States of America

♾

Library of Congress Cataloging-in-Publication Data
Names: Gonzales, Felipe, 1946– author.
Title: Política: nuevomexicanos and American political incorporation, 1821–1910 / Phillip B. Gonzales.
Description: Lincoln: University of Nebraska Press, 2016.
Includes bibliographical references and index.
Identifiers: LCCN 2016003752
ISBN 9780803284654 (hardback)
ISBN 9780803288294 (mobi)
ISBN 9780803288287 (epub)
ISBN 9780803288300 (pdf)
Subjects: LCSH: New Mexico—Politics and government—1848–1950. | Mexican Americans—New Mexico—Politics and government—19th century. | Hispanic Americans—New Mexico—Politics and government—19th century. | Mexican-American Border Region—Historiography. | BISAC: HISTORY / United States / State & Local / Southwest (AZ, NM, OK, TX). | POLITICAL SCIENCE / History & Theory. | SOCIAL SCIENCE / Sociology / General.
Classification: LCC F801 .G66 2016 | DDC 978.9/04—dc23 LC record available at https://lccn.loc.gov/2016003752

Set in Minion Pro by M. Scheer.

*Dedicado a la memoria de mi padre,
el hijo de Nuevo México,
Benerito Domingo Gonzales*

The history of New Mexico is, perhaps, to an uncommon degree the history of her politicians.

—MARALYN BUDKE

Contents

List of Illustrations xi
List of Maps xii
List of Tables xii
Preface xiii
Acknowledgments xxi
Introduction 1

Part 1. Initializing Annexation
Chapter 1. Nuevomexicano Politics and Society on the Eve of the American Conquest 43
Chapter 2. Bloodless and Bloody Conquests, 1846–1847 85
Chapter 3. Integrative Conquest, 1847–1848 139

Part 2. Política in the Ante Bellum
Chapter 4. A Budding Binary, 1848–1852 207
Chapter 5. Mexican Democratic Party, 1853–1854 249
Chapter 6. American Democratic Party, 1854–1859 299

Part 3. Party Modalities in the Time of Civil War
Chapter 7. Low Tide in the Partisan Divide, 1861 355
Chapter 8. Republican Toehold and the Partisan Normal, 1861–1863 379
Chapter 9. Bosque Redondo and the Rise of José Francisco Chávez, 1863–1865 429

Part 4. Political Agonism under Reconstruction
Chapter 10. Party Definitions of the Colonizer, 1865–1867 . . . 491
Chapter 11. *Política Judaica e Literaria* 549
Chapter 12. A Contest for the Ages, 1867–1868 611

Part 5. Arriving
Chapter 13. Republican Party Debut, 1867–1868 643
Chapter 14. Steady Republicans, Hazy Democrats, 1869 691
Chapter 15. Realized Political Parties, 1869–1871 725
Conclusions 785

Appendixes 807
Notes 849
Bibliography 991
Index 1021

Illustrations

1. Palace of the Governors, Santa Fe, New Mexico 44
2. Palace of the Governors, watercolor, 1866. 45
3. Gen. Manuel Armijo, ca. 1840 91
4. Brig. Gen. Stephen Watts Kearny, capture of
   Santa Fe, 1846. 106
5. S. W. Kearny, from an original daguerreotype 107
6. Charles Bent, governor of New Mexico 1846–47 127
7. Donaciano Vigil, governor of New Mexico 1847–48 141
8. James Silas Calhoun, governor of New Mexico 1851–52 . . 212
9. William Carr Lane, governor of New Mexico, 1852 254
10. José M. Gallegos, 1872 270
11. Santa Fe Plaza and cathedral before installation of
    clock, 1866 274
12. Archbishop Jean Baptiste Lamy and St. Francis Cathedral
    as originally planned 275
13. Santa Fe, July 20, 1866 276
14. Tomás Cabeza de Baca, ca. 1860–89 278
15. Miguel Antonio Otero I 301
16. Henry Connelly, governor of New Mexico, 1861–66 368
17. José Francisco Perea, New Mexico delegate to United States
    Congress, 1863–65 404
18. Plaza looking west, Santa Fe, New Mexico, 1866 405
19. Brevet Brig. Gen. J. H. Carleton, Santa Fe, New Mexico,
    1866 432
20. Bosque Redondo era Indian captives at Fort Sumner,
    New Mexico, ca. 1864–68 433
21. Sutler's Store at Fort Union, New Mexico, ca. 1866. 440

22. José Francisco Chaves [sic], at-large district member, U.S. House of Representatives 482
23. Robert B. Mitchell, governor of New Mexico, ca. 1869. . . 510
24. Don Trinidad Alarid, ca. 1890 513
25. Taoseños, 1881 526
26. Augustine De Marle and Charles P. Clever, 1860. 552
27. Maj. José D. Sena, Albuquerque, New Mexico, ca. 1880 . . 589
28. William Breeden. 649
29. Don José Leandro Perea, ca. 1860 733
30. Kirby Benedict. 753

Maps

1. Geopolitical districts (*partidos*) defined in the Mexican period for New Mexico and surrounding area 59
2. Map of Texas and the countries adjacent, 1844 94
3. Precinct stops along the nineteenth-century campaign trail in elections for delegate to Congress. 339

Tables

1. Delegates to Congress, New Mexico Territory, 1851–1882 . . 5
2. Ratio of Nuevomexicanos in political office in the homeland counties, 1848–1906 7
3. Majority vote by county, delegate for Congress, 1863 . . . 423
4. Official returns for delegate to Congress, 1863 and 1865 . . 484
5. Official vote for delegate to Congress, New Mexico Territory, 1871. 780
6. Delegates to Congress from the Territory of New Mexico, 1884–1912 794

Preface

The tiny El Rito Campus of the Northern New Mexico College bristled with *Historias de Nuevo México*/Histories of New Mexico conference activities. In the crisp air of the El Rito autumn of 2013, participants spoke to, represented, and performed portions of the Nuevomexicano, indigenous tribal, and Euroamerican (white) contributions to New Mexico culture. For the Native American and Nuevomexicano representations particularly, the focal resolve involved the preservation of tradition.

In the perspective of the Nuevomexicanos (Mexican American natives of New Mexico), the declared attachment was to *herencia* and the active devotion to *querencia*. *Herencia*, literally "heritage," harks back to an agrarian base with origins in the Spanish colonization of the region, a base that evolved through a Mexican period and survived as the United States took possession of what became the American Southwest. *Querencia* figures as the beloved culture of the homeland, linked here to a distinct bioregional place identity. However, for proponents today, querencia leaves wistful nostalgia and romantic memory behind, acting instead to defend Nuevomexicano material culture and village tradition, maintaining community survival as a matter of collective well-being against the ravages of externally driven modernity (including a debilitating heroin problem among village dwellers) and overriding colonial structures.

Such themes as the communal land grants, the wisdom of everyday life in rural aridity, a unique folk spiritualism, and the *acequia* system of horticulture form the stuff of reverential querencia in the outlands of northern New Mexico. In this light an arresting juxtaposition appeared in the conference setting. It was that *Historias de Nuevo México* held its sessions in a venue named Jaramillo Hall and convened its plenary in Cutting Hall.

Nuevomexicanos have been engaged in conventional Western-style politics for a very long time, yet that heritage is generally not counted among the elements of querencia. For one thing, politicians have appeared in the region whose commitment to herencia has gone lacking, and in the politics of querencia this is seen as a reprehensible cultural betrayal. Moreover, "politics" has a way of appearing contaminated on its own; the effect, perhaps, of compromise, horse-trading, and the ambitious player. How, then, to reconcile the original portraits of both Jaramillo and Cutting hanging on the central spaces of honor in a deep site of northern New Mexico herencia?

A native of El Rito, Venceslao Jaramillo was born in 1875 on a *rancho* off the El Rito village. He attended Notre Dame elementary school in Indiana, followed by a Jesuit boarding school in Denver. Even as he embarked on a political career as an adult, he became a successful rancher and stock-raiser, straight in the tradition of his father, and an El Rito merchant. He served in both chambers of the territorial assembly before New Mexico became a state, as chair of the Territorial Republican Central Committee as New Mexico was becoming a state, followed by a stint as Río Arriba County collector and treasurer. Working his connections with the territorial legislator from his district, Jaramillo succeeded in brokering the territorial government for the creation of the Spanish American Normal School at El Rito in 1909, an institution that in its initial phase trained teachers to serve in isolated Nuevomexicano schools, later evolving to its present extension of the Northern New Mexico College in the nearby town of Española.

Bronson Cutting was a New York Brahmin who moved to Santa Fe in 1910. Cutting rapidly rose as a celebrity in New Mexico's bourgeois society, but his first love was politics. A dyed-in-the-wool Progressive, he engaged with whatever conservative politics he encountered in the state, supporting candidates whom he considered progressive in their leanings, purchasing the daily Santa Fe *New Mexican* to further the causes of the late Progressive Era. He proved effective in bolstering his favorites and sinking his enemies. In 1928, New Mexico U.S. Senator Andrieus Jones passed away, and in acknowledgment of the New Yorker's personal power, Governor A. W. Hockenhull appointed Cutting to fill the vacancy left by Jones.

In this whole trajectory Cutting endeared himself to the Nuevomexicanos in particular, and it was they who formed his base of power. Their undying allegiance from both urban and rural areas of the state garnered for him a level of representative power he did not seek as a personal ambition. All the while, he became a significant support for their right to political and civic inclusion. Cutting's ghost haunts El Rito for the visitations the senator paid to that and many of the other northern New Mexico villages, in which he earned the undying affection of the common folk, much as John F. Kennedy would later in the century. Moreover, at his death, the Cutting will bequeathed $150,000 to the El Rito campus when it was the Spanish-American Normal School.

The lesson, of course, is that good things can come out of politics. Indeed, New Mexico localities commonly take pride in a prodigal person's fruitful public career, regarding it as their own accomplishment. For those communities that have been marginalized compared to the well-endowed American mainstream, the politician's presence in the field of politics can carry value, more so if a voice is raised on behalf of the disadvantaged.

The honoring of Jaramillo and Cutting on the campus at El Rito reflects a kind of public service querencia. And it is more than a still-life scene. The memories are active. Current community residents go before the advisory board of the Northern New Mexico College and the Rio Arriba County Commission proposing that the El Rito facility be renamed for Jaramillo.

The political rise of Cutting and Jaramillo occurred at a time when "politics" really meant something to Nuevomexicanos. Politics saturated their communities. Nuevomexicano coalescence as a political force manifested itself not only within particular communities but across the entire state. Nuevomexicanos voted with a clear ethnic voice, considered vital by the political parties. Not that the group formed a single bloc: the American system of political competition generally does not permit holistic unity for major social or ethnic segments. What did arise was a certain Nuevomexicano-identified enthusiasm for the frays of the popular election, for government generally, and for public administration. It was a distinct political culture, and the people relished it.

An underlying intent of the present work is to reveal the obscured roots of the Nuevomexicano political herencia, and by the time the account ends, to suggest how a political history deserves a place in the temple of Nuevomexicano querencia. A strong political patrimony rightfully belongs to a substantial readership that cares deeply about New Mexico and its storied past. Many among the Nuevomexicanos today hold close the images, personages, and events of the ancestral homeland, considering these their heritage particularly. My hope is that the honoring of their political ancestors will emerge as a viable product of the chapters to follow. It applies as well to a substantial portion of the non-Nuevomexicano readership, those who hold abiding affection for New Mexico's rich ethno-cultural legacy, in which their ancestors may have participated.

The book's purpose will thus have fallen short if it fails to respond to the "disciplinary" requisites of public readerships, and to bundle in stories that reflect "their" history, even as their relationships to the past are capable of changing. Many will not agree with particular views, interpretations, or descriptions expressed herein, and a balk or two may arise at what may appear as the public washing of some in-house laundry. But as I have come to realize through many years in the study of New Mexico, the open contentions over the interpretations of the past, capable of exploding onto the public stage at a moment's notice, are themselves integral patches of New Mexico's historical quilt. They are also forceful motivators, if sometimes negative inspirations, for keeping our shared sense of New Mexico's rich chronicle alive.

From the academic perch, my dive into the stormy political waters of New Mexico's territorial period was taken from the platform of a prior interest I had developed in New Mexico's politics during the couple of decades after it became a state in 1912. In that work, in which both Cutting and Jaramillo figured, I labored to comprehend the roles that the Nuevomexicanos played in the political development of their consolidating state. What stood out as I began to perceive this complex was the heavy stamp of the established political parties. The dynamics of party organization and mobilization molded Nuevomexicanos into fierce partisan loyalists. The very cultural identity of Nuevomexicanos intertwined with their commitment or opposition to the Democratic and Republican parties and/or the factions within those organizations. The more clearly that political connection emerged from the primary sources, the stronger grew the compulsion to know of the origins of the link between the Nuevomexicanos as a group and the American tradition of party organization, membership, leadership, and militancy.

Working backward from 1912, my first forays bore frustration. Unfortunately, no authoritative or sufficiently precise research had even documented the establishment of the American political parties in New Mexico, let alone in specific relation to the Nuevomexicanos. In the daunting prospect, I came to realize that the initial Nuevomexicano-American party associations lay deep in New Mexico's territorial waters. To examine these associations, it emerged as necessary to navigate the channels of archival collections, micro-reeled newspapers, government reports, administrative records, and shelves of published materials. Wading through the sources generated a rising tide of fragmentary references to Nuevomexicanos and political party activity.

I succeeded, finally, in identifying certain critical events that led to the formation of the Democratic and Republican parties during New Mexico's territorial period. As I did, it was gratifying to realize that the parties would not have germinated in New Mexico, and could not have developed to their twentieth-century incarnations, without the involvement and contributions of the very Nuevomexicanos who had animated my whole inquiry to begin with.

The enmeshing of Nuevomexicanos and the American political parties could have served as the core of a regional chronicle, and indeed that story threads through the narrative in emotion-filled electoral campaigns; the machinations of factional formation and confrontation; the rise and fall of charismatic, tough-minded, proven, and blundering politicians; a parade of intrigues descending from Washington DC and other points east; and various protest outbreaks and minor collective movements.

In bringing strategic events and vivid characters to life, some grist for New Mexico's historical mills is provided. One challenge is leveled at facile generalizations that have been made regarding the life of the political parties in New Mexico, including erroneous conclusions about Nuevomexicano political participation. Another is offered to researchers' claims about which elements within the Nuevomexicano populace were the real beneficiaries of the American political system in the nineteenth century. Also up for reconsideration is Manifest Destiny and its impact on the Nuevomexicanos. How New Mexico related to a succession of national political eras forms an area of review, to include successive presidential regimes, the Civil War, and Reconstruction. In this regard I have sought to inspire a clearer understanding of how these historical dynamics figured into the partisanship of territorial New Mexico for the first couple of decades of its existence and how New Mexico's internal politics helped shape national contours.

Descending in search of the story of when and how the American political parties took hold in New Mexico, I arrived at the very moment in which New Mexico became a part of the United States. At this point a greater set of questions emerged, principally involving the imperial conquest and national incorporation of the Nuevomexicanos by the United States. It became necessary to ask how the appearance and development of the party system fit into that whole situational mystery.

The discipline of sociology has an eminently rightful claim on the events and sociopolitical patterns associated with New Mexico's transfer from an extension of the Mexican Republic to the periphery of the United States. In the need to make choices for framing the interpretation of findings, sociologists have amassed an impressive body of research and publications on the subject of regions that have been impacted by invading national forces. In matching the historical materials coming before me with the themes, theories, and concepts of the discipline, the more general problematic and possibilities of a case study emerged.

Particular themes from the sociological corpus guide the chronology. The application to political parties and other aspects of republican government exposes core processes of Nuevomexicano incorporation, integration and exclusion, inter- and intra-ethnic relations and social change, colonialism, and liberalism—and all of it in relation to the political development of a U.S. territory. All political dances occur against a backdrop of significant social change. Both the dominant "colonizing" sector and the conquered subalterns make their moves in the contextual waltz. It could have been no different in New Mexico. The United States had to contend with different manifestations of agency by its new denizens. At stake for the Nuevomexicanos were the exigencies of their relationship to the central government as well as their evolving sense of themselves as natives in their conquered homeland. Nuevomexicano identity had much to do with waves of Euroamerican settlers, short-term residents, and administrative agents as well as the U.S. states themselves, each bringing or injecting evolving policies, decisions, and conflicts into the arena.

In working to track down facts, individuals, patterns, and especially key relationships, the narrative ground expanded, as a proper survey of New Mexican territorial politics called for the context of the American political system itself, especially as it related to the federal territory. Without the conceptions of political scientists, the result would have been a rather more ragged rendering of territorial administration and institutional development. Certainly a political science perspective on the modern "political party" appeared necessary, together with a consideration of party formation and change in the United States. Essays by political scientists also helped deal with such matters as the U.S. approach to international treaty making, the congressional formation of territories, the theory of the conventional politician's career, the factors typically influencing voting among the American electorate, and especially the process of territories becoming states prior to the 1920s.

Yet the social sciences, formally speaking, are not the only bounded fields I have needed in order to satisfy the interpretive demands of the excavated materials. Viewpoints from the history of American politics and from accounts of the development of republican institutions in the United States are also applied. I found it necessary as well to draw on the likes of cultural and literary studies, textual analysis, and a biblical scholar or two. The trick for a narrative presentation was to sketch in the academic eddies without disrupting the flow of the chronological stream. Hopefully nonspecialists can sail on to a revealed portrait of New Mexico's territorial politics, Nuevomexicanos within them, and ethno-racial dynamics in American history.

Acknowledgments

Thanks go to two journals for permission to reproduce portions of three of my articles: "New Mexico Statehood and Political Inequality: The Case of Nuevomexicanos" (*New Mexico Historical Review* 90, no. 1 [2015]: 31–52); "Mexican Party, American Party, Democratic Party: Establishing the American Political Party in New Mexico, 1848–1853" (*New Mexico Historical Review* 88, no. 3 [2013]: 253–85); and "Struggle for Survival: The Hispanic Land Grants of New Mexico" (*Agricultural History* 77, no. 2 [2003]: 293–324).

I owe debts of gratitude for the research assistance provided for this project by the staff members at the Center for Southwest Research and Special Collections at the University of New Mexico, including Nancy Brown-Martinez, Christopher Geherin, Francesca Glaspell, Ellen Price, Suzanne Schadl, Samuel Sisneros, Mary Alice Tsosie, and the dearly departed Ann Massmann; also Rachel Adler at the New Mexico State Archives and Research Center. Erika Derkas, Edward Gonzales, Velia C. Silva, Bryan Turo, and Melina Vizcaino provided valuable primary investigation. Translations from Spanish texts are mine unless otherwise indicated, and minor adjustments were made in quoted text for grammar, accepted usage, and diacritical marks; personal names varying across sources have been adjusted for consistency in the text but are given in the endnotes as used in the sources. As the reader will come to realize, Spanish language texts, found especially in the bilingual weekly newspapers of the era, have provided crucial material for the innovative account bounding through the chapters. Anthony Cárdenas-Rotullo and A. Gabriel Meléndez helped with the translations of particularly difficult Spanish-language sources. Funds, time, and other resources enabling the research process came from the Center for Regional Studies at the University of New Mexico, directed by Tobías Durán; the Sociology Department at the University of New Mexico, chaired by Richard Wood; the Office of Dean of the College of Arts and Sciences at the University of New Mexico, headed by Brenda Claiborne at the outset and then by Mark Peceny; and the staff of the School of Public Administration, especially Angela Kamman and Gene Henley.

Among those who read portions of the draft and provided important commentary, key criticism, relevant references, and kind encouragement, I am especially grateful to Durwood Ball, Tobías Durán, Laura Gómez, Davíd Montejano, Mary Louise Pratt, Rosina A. Solano, and Carlos Vélez-Ibáñez. John Nieto-Phillips and David Holtby critiqued the entire draft manuscript with valuable interest. It's amazing how much mileage one can derive from conversation with the right knowledgeable person. Valuable tips were provided to me by Kyra Ellis-Moore, Robert Fiala, Doug McAdam, Joan B. Moore, Renato Rosaldo, Joseph P. Sánchez, and Gerald Vizenor. Students and faculty members at the University of New Mexico, Northern New Mexico College, and the University of California, Los Angeles, who heard me present some of the book's material offered penetrating and thought-provoking questions and suggestions. Joan B. Moore made possible my participation at the *Historias de Nuevo México*/Histories of New Mexico event at the Northern New Mexico College, while Vilma Ortiz and Casandra Salgado did the host honors at UCLA. Matthew Bokovoy, my editor at the University of Nebraska Press, committed excellent substantive, editorial, and logistical guidance for the production of this work. In addition, I thank Matt for allowing me to convey the long string of stories that I have included in this book. Sally Antrobus enhanced the text overall with her expert reading knowledge and keen eye for textual wrinkles. I received important technical support from Mark Montoya and Marisa Montoya provided strong moral support, for which I am eternally grateful.

Jennifer Moore devoted the utmost in review, care, and companionship. Her close scrutiny of my chicken scratches were nothing short of inspirational. Thank you, Jenny, for being there and keeping me going to the end.

Política

Introduction

Lt. Col. George A. McCall returned from a brief sojourn in Washington DC to his army unit in New Mexico in mid-1849. McCall described the local color in his report to headquarters: he found politics "the rage, engrossing the attention of all classes of people" when he arrived back in Santa Fe.[1] McCall's allusion reads intriguingly when placed in its temporal circumstance. New Mexico did not even belong to the United States the year before and had been a territory of the Republic of Mexico until February 1848. The Treaty of Guadalupe Hidalgo that concluded the brutal two-year American invasion of Mexico empowered the United States to take permanent possession of New Mexico, California, and most of the Southwest. The process of establishing American institutions on the nineteenth-century frontier of western North America would be drawn out. Yet many contemporary observers of daily life in New Mexico such as McCall immediately witnessed the energetic, American-style political scene that teemed with public events and expressed public objections to American military rule. Contests among citizen groups over whether New Mexico should become a regular state or a federal territory, and heated local elections not too long afterward, opened up a vital political culture after 1848 and, not known practically at all, a fundamental phase in the political development of one of the states of the American Union.

McCall also referred to the remarkable fact of politics absorbing "all classes of people." By this time a motley collection of American and European immigrants had settled in New Mexico. The newcomers such as fur trappers, trail merchants, land speculators, soldiers of fortune, and exiled thieves had been present, or had moved in and out, for a decade or more. Others decided to remain after participating in the American military occupation of New Mexico in 1846. More people arrived by order of Washington DC to help administer this newest acquisition of empire. At the same time, however, McCall implied another kind of diversity found in political rage; the very Mexican natives of New Mexico whom the United States had just absorbed.

The political involvement of Nuevomexicanos at this juncture in North American history should not be denied. There is a sense in which it was not supposed to have happened. One way of appreciating its significance is through the lens of what is commonly called colonialism or, in cases like New Mexico, "internal colonialism." Internal colonialism refers to a set of unequal social relations between conquerors and the people of preexisting local communities in a region that has been forcibly taken from a neighboring country; "forced" annexation, as I call it. Historically internal colonialism often resulted in highly deleterious effects on conquered subjects. When it did not result in massacres of civilian populations, the invader's domination could still arise as starkly oppressive.[2] In some prominent instances of internal colonialism worldwide, the conquering overseers imposed wholesale segregation, turning the natives into a proletariat in the colonial project of extracting the natural resources of the annexed lands. The sociologist Michael Hechter calls such a condition the "cultural division of labor."[3]

The conquest of New Mexico was violent and swift, and as researchers point out, Nuevomexicanos were placed in a colonial situation by virtue of the common process of forced annexation, and while Nuevomexicano actors did not use these particular terms, it is clear that they understood the colonial character of their subordinations to American power, as we shall see.[4] In Laura Gómez's framing, Nuevomexicanos were placed within a stratified racial order within the new American territory, positioned below common Euroamerican settlers, with Native Americans and blacks situated below them. The United States held the new imperial order together through the racializing force of Manifest Destiny. Yet it seems that at the cessation of military hostilities and for several decades afterward, the New Mexico case resulted in a qualified form of colonial domination, than, say, the cultural division of labor. Gómez characterizes the American conquest of Nuevomexicanos as an episode where they became integral to a system of "power-sharing" with Euroamericans. Gómez focuses on the power-sharing that emerged in the territorial judicial domain. Mexicans were "essentially excluded from the most powerful positions in the [judicial] system," Gómez emphasizes, those of judge, prosecutor, and defense lawyer. Euroamericans, as elected and appointed officials outside New Mexico, controlled judicial and prosecutorial appointments, which they reserved for members of their own racial group during this era." It posed a kind of "glass ceiling" on Mexican participation in the system. Yet Gómez notes that Mexicans formed the great majority of the *petit* jurors, constantly deciding on the legal fates of Euroamerican defendants.[5]

The clue behind McCall's allusion points to Nuevomexicano-Euroamerican power-sharing as it arose more widely in the New Mexico Territory's political system. The United States conquered Nuevomexicanos through military coercion, but the latter realized substantial participation in the American polity from the start. The significant participation of Nuevomexicanos in the U.S. territorial system recasts histories of both nineteenth-century American expansion and Mexican Americans in the territories acquired by the United States during the war with Mexico. The Nuevomexicano experience during the early territorial period is critical to a general understanding of the internal and external workings of colonialism in North America and forced annexation as a process of producing ethnoracial segmentation in societal development.

To Illustrate

Delving into the 1867 election for territorial delegate to Congress from New Mexico can help illustrate the quality and quantity of Nuevomexicano political incorporation after the American conquest of the Southwest. The position of delegate to Congress formed the primary link between residents and the nation's capital in the American system of territorial administration. The territorial delegate was given a seat in the House of Representatives "with the right of speaking, but not of voting."[6] The delegate's influence could be considerable in gaining appropriations for his constituents and influencing patronage appointments to his territory. Who would hold the post was determined by popular election. The New Mexico contest featured two candidates with different heritage origins.

The Nuevomexicano, José Francisco Chávez, hailed from Valencia County, and his family's wealth and social prominence went back to the Spanish colonial period. His opponent, Charles P. Clever, had emigrated in 1850 from Cologne, Prussia. The Chávez-Clever bout flared into a close campaign through partisan rancor and name calling. Election officials tabulated the votes from the territory's nine counties, and the territorial governor handed the certificate of election to Clever. However, Chávez accused his opponent's supporters of fraudulently ejecting votes for him at several of the territory's polling stations, enough to deny him his majority. As a result Chávez filed to contest the election. The U.S. House of Representatives Committee on Territories agreed to hear his appeal. Lawyers for each candidate began a process of evidence gathering to support their cases. The legal teams interrogated nearly two dozen witnesses in a handful of New Mexico communities. Precinct poll judges were chief among those to testify. Typical among them was one Jesús María Baca y Salazar, an election poll official in Santa Fe County.

The roles of Chávez, Baca, and Clever in the 1867 election reflected Nuevomexicano participation in the territory's developing political system. Chávez at the time was actually the incumbent delegate to Congress (or as close to an incumbent as the rules for the term of a territorial delegate allowed at the time), having won the post two years before. He was not the only one among Nuevomexicanos. Three others had already occupied the post, one of them for three terms. Starting in 1853 the pressure to nominate Nuevomexicanos to run for the post of delegate derived from the substantial *mexicano* majority of New Mexico's electorate.

Table 1 shows that Chávez won his contest with Clever, and it illustrates a major portion of what significant Nuevomexicano political involvement meant for the period covered in this book. In seventeen elections for territorial delegate up to 1882 a Nuevomexicano won the office thirteen times. Of eleven separate individuals who took the election, nine were Nuevomexicano. Ten elections pitted Nuevomexicanos against fellow Nuevomexicanos. Nuevomexicano political popularity appears in three individuals who served for more than one term as delegate.

Table 1. Delegates to Congress, New Mexico Territory, 1851–1882*

Year Elected	Winner	Loser(s)
1851	Richard H. Weightman	S. Messervy, A. W. Reynolds
1853	+José Manuel Gallegos	William Carr Lane
1855	+Miguel A. Otero	+José Manuel Gallegos
1857	+Miguel A. Otero	Spruce M. Baird
1859	+Miguel A. Otero	+José Manuel Gallegos
1861	John S. Watts	+Diego Archuleta
1863	+Francisco Perea	+José Manuel Gallegos
1865	+J. Francisco Chávez	+Francisco Perea
1867	+J. Francisco Chávez	Charles P. Clever
1869	+J. Francisco Chávez	+Vicente Romero
1871	+José Manuel Gallegos	+J. Francisco Chávez, +Jose D. Sena
1873	Stephen B. Elkins	+Jose Manuel Gallegos
1875	Stephen B. Elkins	+Pedro Valdez
1876	+Trinidad Romero	+Pedro Valdez
1879	+Mariano S. Otero	+R. Benito Baca
1880	+Tranquilino Luna	+Miguel A. Otero
1882	+Francisco A. Manzanares	+Tranquilino Luna

* Note that in 1849, when New Mexico was not yet an incorporated territory, a convention went through the motions of electing a Euroamerican delegate and a Nuevomexicano alternate. + Indicates a Nuevomexicano candidate.

Previous to becoming delegate to Congress, Chávez also served a term in the territorial legislature. The American federal system granted to its territories the right of electing a legislative assembly similar to those of the regular states. For three decades after 1850 Nuevomexicanos comprised 72 percent of all members of the territorial council and a similar average of 75 percent majority of the territorial house of representatives.[7]

Nuevomexicano political participation arose still more comprehensively. The political career of Baca hints at widespread Nuevomexicano placement in elected and appointed office on county and local levels. Baca was a forty-seven-year-old native of Santa Fe who served as a poll judge in the 1867 election. He was also at that time a local justice of the peace. A lawyer in the contest investigation asked him about his competency to serve as a poll official. Baca affirmed in a translation from the Spanish:[8] "Ever since the Territory has been annexed to the United States, I have been a partisan and worker in the elections held in this Territory." Baca revealed under cross-examination that he had attended to elections in his county "from 1850 up to this time." He disclosed his service, "for five or six years," as sheriff of Santa Fe County.[9] Scores of Nuevomexicanos like Baca managed the polling booths throughout the territory at every election. They performed necessary duties to conduct the elections, including appointing clerks of election and swearing them into office, keeping the polls open from nine in the morning to six in the evening, publicly counting the votes once the poll closed, and reporting the results to the probate judge.[10]

The sheer list of offices filled by Nuevomexicanos beyond the precinct impresses as well. Baca had been a county probate judge (who appointed poll judges), a county sheriff, and a local justice of the peace. Mexicans developed such a profile by stepping onto their public squares. The distribution of Nuevomexicanos in county offices is suggested in table 2. County records were more consistently maintained after 1870, and data is spotty for brief intervals. The figures nevertheless convey the broad front of Nuevomexicano participation in local government in seven of the ten counties that encompassed the historic New Mexican districts. In counties like San Miguel, Mora, Taos, and Guadalupe, where the Nuevomexicano population majority appeared dramatic, their presence in local office was inevitable. Even in those counties with larger Euroamerican populations—Bernalillo, Santa Fe, and Socorro—the machinery of local governance would have had difficulty functioning without Nuevomexicano involvement.

Table 2. Ratio of Nuevomexicanos in political office in the homeland counties, 1848–1906

	Bernalillo	San Miguel	Taos	Socorro	Santa Fe	Mora	Guadalupe	Margins
Probate clerk	9/15*	15/17	21/25	14/16	25/37	12/15	5/6	101/131 77%
Probate judge	12/12	20/20	20/28	19/24	33/38	20/24	6/7	130/153 85%
Sheriff	11/12	17/17	25/30	8/13	20/33	13/16	7/7	101/128 79%
Treasurer	6/11	17/17	no data	5/10	14/19	4/10	7/7	53/74 71%
Assessor	7/8	9/10	no data	6/8	9/10	9/10	5/6	45/52 87%
Co. Comm.	22/33	28/36	37/50	31/53	20/52	43/51	18/21	199/296 67%
Co. Total	67/91 74%	93/105 89%	103/133 77%	83/124 67%	121/189 64%	101/126 80%	48/54 88%	

* Dates are not inclusive in all counties, nor continuous in any county. The unit of observation is term of office, or reelection, based on Spanish surname. Probate judge includes prefects. Treasurer includes collector. Data from Anderson, *History of New Mexico*, 2: 525–26, 580–81, 594–95, 611–12, 632–34, 649–50, 816.

To Frame, Perchance Explain

Gómez claims that the American colonizers "permitted" power-sharing for three principal reasons. One was demographic and involved the pragmatic need for Americans to run a federal unit. Mexicans comprised the clear majority of the population, and so American conquerors had no "viable alternative" but to allow them a share in the governing of the vast jurisdiction. The American military proved inadequate to institute martial law, and too few Americans arrived to implement a civil government, this argument goes. The Mexicans thus filled in for the ongoing functioning of the territorial apparatus.[11]

The inclusion of Nuevomexicanos in American institutions in Gómez's view also served Euroamerican ends by "legitimizing their governance after an initial violent occupation."[12] I take the liberty of bringing this claim within the scope of what critical scholars call the general theory of "hegemonic colonialism." In hegemonic colonialism, the conquering force succeeds in the project of institutionalizing newly acquired territory into its expanding social system by getting the conquered natives to accept their forced annexation with a minimum of resistance. The successful extraction of legitimation means a "consent to colonialism." The willing submission to subordination eases the extension of sociopolitical, economic, and cultural dominion over the territory. In this frame, Nuevomexicanos would have accepted the American conquest, distracted (not to say deluded) from continuing the order of violent resistance that many of them mounted against the occupying army at the start of the U.S.-Mexico War.[13]

Gómez's third claim holds that the Nuevomexicano upper class went along with the conquest because it benefited them specifically. José Francisco Chávez, his extended family, and the rest of the vernacular *rico* class of New Mexico would have worked out a power-sharing arrangement according to this interpretation to stay above the lower-class Nuevomexicanos (and Indians and blacks). They thus retained the power to control the political process and keep their material advantages as they had in Mexican days by collaborating with Euroamerican officials.[14] The hegemonic view of indirect rule also applies here. A subaltern set of native aristocrats do relatively well for themselves by mediating between the lower and higher racial strata. The majority remains in conditions of underdevelopment, not least because the strategy of hegemony includes racialized projects to control the populace.[15]

I found these points—concerning the demographic pressure to include Mexicans in territorial government, a contingent need to legitimate the conquest in the face of any native consternation over it, and the self-interested roles played by the Nuevomexicano elite—providing a partial account of Nuevomexicano substantial politics. What must be reckoned with, I argue, is political development in the territory structured by greater political and ideological forces. In scouring the political ground of territorial New Mexico through various types of documents, what I found remarkable was the extent to which Nuevomexicanos invoked the lexicon of classic Enlightenment liberalism in their attempts to procure civic equality and political leverage for themselves. Political actors marshaled the codes of informed political involvement alongside Euroamericans, including "the people," "the citizen," democracy, the public, the voter, reason, individual liberty, group equality, civil rights, universal rights, natural rights, church and state, and science. Even the category of "government," in its Lockean form as a protector of the life, liberty, and property of the citizens, received its recognition in the remote territory. The government attained a sacrosanct and benevolent quality at this time, equivalent to the "nation" itself, a political historian observes. To assail government in the nineteenth century "meant to attack American society itself and the principles for which it stood."[16]

Nuevomexicanos refrained from launching an attack of this kind after an initial bout of violent resistance to conquest and once they were securely ensconced within the American state. What stood out for me, then, is how they absorbed or appropriated the liberal world view that encased the political systems of the West throughout the late eighteenth and most of the nineteenth centuries. Indeed, as I see it, Nuevomexicanos were swept into the American polity on a distinct interweave of liberalism, imperial expansion, and internal colonialism, a combination that forms the basis for interpreting their political experience in the wake of the U.S. conquest of their territory.

Controversy characterizes the study of what classic liberalism and the Enlightenment were about and what they stood for.[17] But as Immanuel Wallerstein makes clear in his latest installment on the history of the world system, the tenets, principles, and organizations of

Enlightenment liberalism did reign triumphant in the chief capitalist societies from the end of the eighteenth century through most of the nineteenth century.[18] The roots of Enlightenment thought lay in what Jonathan Israel sees were the radical ideas presaging a "'revolution of the mind.'" The intellectual transformation brought a "huge cultural shift, the essential revolution that preceded the [French, British, and American] revolutions of fact." He writes: "What proved to be the great strength of the Radical Enlightenment was that it was an ideological system that answered to long-standing and intrinsic grievances and needs of large portions of society, especially but by no means only on the European side of the Atlantic." The "decisive phase in the rise of democracy, individual liberty, and egalitarian values to centrality within the Western World's value system [was] clearly the period from immediately prior to the American Revolution, say from around 1770, down to 1789." Liberal reform philosophy, in moderate and revolutionary forms, defined the shifting trends in western political and civic systems.[19] An oft-cited indicator was the Marquis de Lafayette's "world-shattering" Declaration of the Rights of Man and of the Citizen (1789).[20]

An "unprecedented surge" of egalitarian literature in the 1770s to 1790s spurred the leading intellectual lights of the original thirteen colonies to adopt European liberalism. The founders and their successors keyed into the principles of Machiavellian liberal and Kantian radical philosophy and the English Revolution. They influenced the course of liberalism as in the lending hand Thomas Jefferson gave to Lafayette's Declaration. They reinterpreted and innovated Enlightenment principles for application to their particular contexts, such as the American Revolution.[21] American intellectuals declared opposition to monarchical despotism and hereditary aristocracy in their absolute and enlightened forms. Thomas Paine's *The Rights of Man* (1791) circulated a famous defense of the French Revolution against its conservative critics.[22]

Nuevomexicanos, then, traded in the tongue of liberalism because it disseminated the currency for enacting the politics of their epoch and, quite important, because they believed in the basic principles its coinages represented. But how did it come about, and what did it mean for their American annexation experience? As we study the Enlightenment, Trish Loughran, among others, cautions that we not "remain objects... rather than critics of it."[23] Through the lens of hegemonic colonialism one would be led to argue that the adoption of the liberal Weltanshauung by Nuevomexicanos reflected but a false belief in its promises of democracy, equality, and liberty if it turned out that they remained shackled in ethnoracial colonialism. Much of the scholarship on Western empire critiques "liberal imperialism"; that is, the use of liberal ideas as justification for a claimed mission of civilizing backward peoples and cultures while fundamentally aiming for rule over, or exploitation of, native groups.[24]

That said, what I found in nineteenth-century New Mexico leads me to see the relation between classic liberalism and Nuevomexicano political participation in two lights. As Richard Schermerhorn has pointed out, social change can produce either centripetal or centrifugal outcomes for race and ethnic relations. In the centripetal pathway, the superordinate element actually desires the minority's incorporation, wants it to become a part of their society, while members of the minority have the same goal. Centrifugal goals, on the other hand, enforce separation and solidify sociopolitical dominance on the part of the conquering element, whether or not the minority would want it.[25] In this formulation, it is "an empirical question," as they say. I see *centripetal colonialism* as having emerged in New Mexico; a tension, that is, between effective enough inclusion and centrifugal effects.

With regard to centripety, it is important to note that American liberalism constituted its own theory and expectation of social integration, or at least it held that the integration of outside groups was both necessary and possible. Accordingly, it should be a valid step to put that theory to its test. In fact, this is what we do when we point out the contradiction between liberal tenets of equality and the finding of widespread social inequality. Much of the critique of liberal imperialism turns on overseas empire, the case of India in the British Empire regarded as a prime instance. I contend that Nuevomexicanos encountered a centripetal greeting when they were taken into the United States through a process of *continental liberalism*. Continental liberalism turns on the idea of the United States having integrated its own self on the basis of a liberal and universalist plan from its origins in the thirteen colonies and as it moved outward. The theorist of empire Uday Singh Mehta notes that Tocqueville made "the continental expanse of America the point of departure for his reflections on democracy in America."[26] In one of the ways the insightful French observer encapsulated the point, Tocqueville wrote: "In democratic centuries the extreme mobility of men and their impatient desires make them constantly change place, and make the inhabitants of different countries mingle together, and see and hear each other, and borrow from each other. So it is not only the members of the same nation who become similar; nations themselves assimilate, and all together form in the eye of the beholder nothing more than a vast democracy in which each citizen is a people."[27]

The expectation of cross-national incorporation appeared in the very process of annexing Nuevomexicanos, and for some actors at the time even before, as I seek to demonstrate. Continental liberalism provided the platform for substantial political participation at least for the first half of the term that New Mexico existed as an American territory. Circumstantially, it was enabled by the fact that New Mexico became part of the United States through a kind of incidental annexation. That is, the territory was not the apple of the American imperialist's gaze over Mexican lands, shiny like California. Prior research has failed to discern how comprehensively liberalism impacted nineteenth-century Nuevomexicanos. American liberalism proved instrumental for guiding and facilitating Nuevomexicano political inclusion. The coursing of not only liberal ideology but liberal governing entities cut the operative factor for opening, sustaining, and shaping the intimate experience of joint Nuevomexicano-Euroamerican political action and power-sharing as New Mexico adjusted to a new national environment.

Given the foundational adoption of the Enlightenment in the formation of the American polity, three interrelated trends can be seen to have informed continental liberalism as it overcame New Mexico: (a) the establishment of liberal governmental and administrative mechanisms; (b) promotion of the ideal of incorporating foreign elements; and (c) the geographic diffusion of liberalism by agents of continental expansion.

First, American statesmen favored what the Enlightenment put forth as the battery of liberal necessities to reform society. A secular, rational state, the belief held, needed to be separated from religion. Statecraft should support the common interest of society and civil rights. Democratic egalitarianism, personal liberty, and tolerance arose as essential values. The "nobility of reason" and "virtue" were seen as the basis of "progress" and morality. The importance of education for the masses to free them from credulity, superstition, and ignorance rose to prominence.[28]

Classic liberalism specified mechanisms to implement progressive ideals. The "fundamentals of political life" in the United States prioritized representative government, private property, free markets, constitutionalism, and the rule of law in order to secure individual rights and liberties.[29] American liberalism took distinctive shape around an enhanced conception of republican government to promote the "general good" and the life of a free society.[30] Republicanism became a "secular faith for Americans," one historian notes, which enlivened politics with fresh and vital force.[31] Republican identity rested on the break from the politically usurping British crown. The appeal of the republic lay in the idea of the individual's sovereignty. Citizens gathered in the public sphere "to engage in self-governance" through the exercise of free speech, political action, and representation.[32] American liberalism recast the Enlightenment parliament into the people's "legislature," a secular entity dedicated to virtuous government and pulled from the grip of an executive. This institution was considered to represent the general will and to serve the needs and interests of all "on an equal basis" and to help promote "a true republican spirit." American liberalism laid great stress on universal primary education to enlighten the masses for involvement in the domain of the republic based on superior laws while allowing individual citizens to indulge in quests for their happiness.[33]

It is crucial to acknowledge the extent to which American liberalism identified with a spirit of societal integration. Philosophical liberalism rested on an ideal of individual and group inclusion. Quite importantly, inclusion was prescriptive in American liberalism, beyond mere ideology. It originated in the fact that the United States incorporated peripheral and lower-class elements of the eastern regions into a united nation and, as confirmed in the Declaration of Independence, it claimed the right to naturalize foreign immigrants, even though the effective process led to the enhancement of American racial whiteness. The Declaration of Independence was founded on the principles of "one people," "all men created equal," and the assumption that "all people have a right to a properly constituted government."[34] The "liberal government foundation" encoded in the Declaration of Independence, the U.S. Constitution, and the *Federalist Papers* claimed the capacity to integrate foreign elements, at least those of a western lineage (as distinct from the African and tribal native). The United States set out boasting of its capacity to bring out-groups (freshly incorporated populations) into its civic and political folds. The principles of the central value system, eventually encoded in the *American Creed* authored by William Tyler Page, proved compelling for minorities seeking integration.[35]

As Anatol Lieven writes, "American civic nationalism, which has done much to embody liberal principle, has been central both to the assimilation over the centuries of huge numbers of immigrants and to America's eventual transition from Herrenvolk [yeoman farmer] democracy [prior to the first half of the twentieth century] to civilizational empire." The American Creed helped prevent the country's "immensely disparate and sometimes morally absolutist social, cultural, religious and ethnic groups from flying apart" and allowed people from disparate cultures to live together without coercion. "Even most American dissidents throughout history have sincerely phrased their protests not as a rejection of the American Creed as such," Lieven notes, "but rather, as a demand that Americans, or American governments, return to a purer form of the Creed or to a more faithful adherence to it."[36]

Twentieth-century liberal academics added their concepts to the canon of the United States as a liberal and integrative social system. A prior generation of historians, under influence of Tocqueville, implied continental liberalism. In the nineteenth-century U.S. expansion toward the Pacific coast, pioneering Americans established the "settler society." Frederick Jackson Turner's famous thesis of the peopling of the western United States advanced the notion of the frontier breeding democratic nationalism. American pioneers looked to the federal government to adopt needed measures such as land management and, as we shall see, statehood. They mingled with people from other states and societies, perceived the particular attributes of various social groups, "and then [considered] them all countrymen, or all of 'a people.'"[37] In a related and significant point, one political historian called the federally incorporated territories in the nineteenth century "seedbeds of democracy," a point elaborated in the introduction to part 2 of this book.[38]

Liberal social scientists, who generated what can be called "integration theory," emphasized the diffusion of modern institutions. For them, an important consideration was the encounter with "pre-modern" or "traditional" communities. Traditional culture was generally branded as "authoritarian," anti-democratic, or otherwise lacking in the values of social equality, democracy, and enlightened citizenship. Extensive modernity took foreign elements out of their ancient cultures, economies, and politics, so it was imagined. The virtue of modern structures lay in their being large scale, bureaucratic, scientific, secular, law respecting, market driven, and innovative. These powerful instruments of incorporation took in groups within pre-modern regions that would otherwise be locked out of the modern political order. Integration theory considers the extension of civic citizenship a turning point of political development. The granting of "popular sovereignty" to individual members of the enlightened state did much to draw in foreign subjects, according to the theory. Universal citizenship spurred democracy. The liberal "sovereignty" of the individual member of the enlightened state would prove attractive to outsiders. Annexed locals would readily accept the benefits of modern society if it meant liberation from the strictures of their stagnant communities with their tradition-bound hierarchies. Peripheral groups would learn to love the modern political system as their own.[39]

Some scholars argue that the colonized experience of the Mexicans in the nineteenth century United States had nothing to do with what European immigrants underwent. The Germans, Irish, Italians, Poles, and others from Europe may have been subject to racialized treatment upon their arrival to the eastern shore but were ultimately provided with opportunity to assimilate into the American mainstream and to "become white."[40] The incorporation of "colonized minorities" including Mexicans (along with blacks, indigenes, Puerto Ricans, and Pacific Islanders) involved social segregation, oppression, and exclusion from liberal institutions through extended racism, the decimation of traditional culture, concentrated labor exploitation, and administrative/political control.[41]

Considerable merit lies in the immigrant-colonized distinction. It should be recognized, however, how greatly the patterns of territorial and group incorporation varied. As the political theorist David Leopold points out in relation to the work of Michael Freeden about the historical development of liberalism, it did not reflect a "single reassuring story of all conquering progress." Rather, "multiple narratives" obtained. Advances made in some areas were "accompanied by significant deformations and distortions elsewhere."[42] Carey McWilliams suggested the context of multiple narratives for the annexed Mexicans of the Southwest in his notion of the "broken border." The Spanish empire and the Mexican state failed to consolidate the far northern outposts of Texas, California, and New Mexico. The United States took possession of their homelands in episodes of forced annexation and the Tejanos, Californios, and Nuevomexicanos underwent distinct experiences of incorporation and societal integration in effective isolation from one another.[43]

Californios enjoyed an initial time of privileged political status following their American incorporation. Soon a powerful wave of capitalist immigration from the states shunted them from meaningful participation in what quickly became the State of California's institutional and governing framework. Euroamericans undercut continental liberalism by passing laws specifically designed to exclude Mexicans from political and civic participation and deliberately intimidated Californios to prevent them from conducting election campaigns. Neither did the national political parties do the Californios any good. The openly racist Democrats presented a distinct threat to Californios. Republicans could do little to combat it. The overrun Californios were left to assume political roles in limited localities, the process of liberal integration having minimal effect in the entire experience.[44]

Texas Mexicans participated in the electoral politics of Lone Star Republic after 1836 but saw decline as the new nation developed.[45] Texas was made a state of the American union in 1845, a year before the American invasion of Mexico. Its Mexican residents did not fall under the terms of the Treaty of Guadalupe Hidalgo if they were technically born in Mexico. The treaty granted citizenship to the former citizens of Mexico in New Mexico and California if they wanted it, but the Mexico-born Tejanos were not citizens. Fifty-three percent of the Tejano males twenty-one years of age and older were not American-born in 1850 and therefore not qualified to vote. This order of disfranchisement was exacerbated by the lack of literacy among the citizen Mexicans and the residential segregation of Euroamericans, which prevented their Mexicanization. An active Know-Nothing party challenged the Democratic Party in the San Antonio elections of 1854 and 1856, using xenophobic and anti-Catholic rhetoric to foster discontent among incumbent politicians and, once in office, doing away with Spanish-language public resources. Texas Mexicans formed significant portions of the electorate prior to the Civil War, although they failed to defeat white Americans who undermined majority Mexican tickets without effective political organization and mobilization. Euroamericans arrived by the 1860s to take over the political machines from Tejano elites in the heavily populated Tejano districts. It forced the decline, though not the disappearance, of Mexican power.[46]

In actuality, Nuevomexicanos underwent a similar decline of power at the hands of large-scale Euroamerican movement into their territory, but it was not set into motion until the 1880s, as noted in the conclusion to this work. It was the earlier frontier period of American annexation that provided an object lesson in fruitful if difficult liberal inclusion. As we shall see, some key experience in liberal governance carried over from the Mexican period to affect Nuevomexicano politics significantly in the American territorial period. Much of the enlightened republicanism in the United States diffused at the hands of Euroamerican settlers and from voices on the national stage. A parallel diffusion of continental liberalism moved out from the more powerful northern European countries to peripheral regions of Europe in the long eighteenth century. What happened in that case also occurred in the American West, the connections between Enlightenment and government reform emerging by turns "tenuous and robust, explicit and subterranean."[47]

Nuevomexicanos in their variant were taken into the United States on a crest of liberal diffusion. Sociologist Thomas Hall points out that the United States acted as a strong incorporative power in the Southwest compared to the weaker control the Spanish crown and the Mexican Republic exercised over New Mexico, California, and somewhat in Texas. The American takeover altered the relations of culture groups and affected local alliances and patterns of production in both cooperative and conflict directions, and it is important not to neglect the cooperative experiences.[48] If the principles of civic, public, and political development in the United States spoke in terms of universal inclusion, their application varied from region to region and among ethnoracial sets. The failures in relation to Tejanos, Californios, Native Americans, blacks, and women were stunning.[49] Yet the Mexicans in their regional settings along the U.S.-Mexico border presented confounding experiences. That of Nuevomexicano males in the nineteenth century reveals a certain probability of effective impact at the hands of the institutions and ideologies of American liberalism.

It is important to take note of another comparison. The United States took both Mexicans and the first nations of the New Mexico–centric Southwest in the same fell swoop. The political annexation of Nuevomexicanos occurred on a different plane from that of the several thousands of Native Americans because of conditions inherent in tribal culture and the American federal definition of "Indian." Tribes were placed in a special American Indian administrative jurisdiction of the central government. Guided in part by article 1, section 8 of the U.S. Constitution, the indigenous communities fell outside the U.S. republican system. Nuevomexicanos, in contrast, were channeled directly into the conventional American political machinery embodied in the typical federal territory.[50] The American territory constituted an abbreviated republican institution to be sure, but for Nuevomexicanos it included sufficient degrees of liberal extension to permit socialization into the devices of American politics.

Theoretical mechanisms, policies, applied concepts, and ideological expressions have their histories. The practice of republicanism in the United States took form according to circumstance, region, and culture area. Actors cast their local politics "in their own images."[51] The chapters herein focus on how American republicanism and modern liberalism set up and guided the process of Nuevomexicano political participation during the initial decades of New Mexico's annexation. The basics of liberal diffusion and American idealism impacted New Mexico before the outbreak of war between the United States and Mexico. It explains both the willingness and ability of Nuevomexicanos to engage the American polity as it made its way to their communities. The very occupation of New Mexico imported civic, administrative, and representational mechanisms from the American corpus of republican government before the eyes of a sufficiently informed and receptive Nuevomexicano audience.

The diffusion of American citizenship to Nuevomexicanos at war's end opened up significant channels of political access as provided by a U.S. territory. If the extension of this status had not occurred, the experience of American annexation would have turned out very differently for Nuevomexicanos. The very popular election that permitted José Francisco Chávez to run for delegate to Congress represented a critical mechanism for Nuevomexicano political incorporation. Popular elections have been "many things in many different ages," it has been observed—"surrogates for battle, festivals of acclamation, ritualistic searches for truth (like a criminal trial), mechanisms for holding leaders accountable, or simply the least bad mechanisms for switching from one set of rulers to another."[52] The popular election for Nuevomexicanos of the nineteenth century formed a reliable barometer of their political incorporation. Elections slotted them into civic and political positions in the American government structure. They enabled the means to engage *realpolitik,* such as that which lay behind the Chávez-Clever race for delegate to Congress, a truly dramatic event, as we shall come to see.

The core procedure in this book for tying together the threads of liberal incorporation of Nuevomexicanos traces the drawn-out journey regional politicos embarked upon to establish a working two-party system for the New Mexico Territory. Twentieth-century integration theory recognized political parties as "the main instruments" of modern liberalism in constitutional orders, performing the functions of ideology in "binding the community together" and "organizing the role personalities of the maturing individual." The more hard-nosed assessment regards the party simply as the "essential gateway to the exercise of power, or at any rate for influencing it."[53] Yet the case of the U.S. incorporation of Nuevomexicanos gives sufficient reason to go along with the liberal thesis of the "party of integration," up to a point. As suffrage spawned the democratic election, it necessitated the freedom of citizens to disagree. The Western party in such a context became the "most articulate form of modern political organization."[54] It was an instrument for "aggregating opinions."[55] The liberal view regarded the legitimate party as the principal agent for politically integrating the citizenry of a modern state. In its simplest form, parties integrated because they were the means for getting people into office. Elites designed the party to win voter support. Opportunity for citizen engagement opened up as party chiefs organized public opinion, communicated demands to the centers of power and decision making, articulated to followers the sense and meaning of the broader community, and developed a leadership corps. Parties in developing democracies sustained popular roles in government decision making. They facilitated the voting process, connected localities to centers, established coalitions, and mobilized popular support.[56] The party of integration smoothed out the barriers of difference. It bridged populations, kept pace with the shifting needs of society and economy, and supplied essential two-way interaction between tradition-oriented masses and change-oriented elites.[57] Integration parties translated the demands and desires of outsiders from particularistic or parochial standards into civic, universal, and national norms. They sent interpretations of government policy "out and down through an unofficial communications network" and made official actions meaningful, acceptable, legitimate, and binding.[58]

The importance of the integrative party was recognized in history. Stephen A. Douglas looked over the Illinois political landscape in the 1830s in search of the means for enabling citizens to exercise power over government. He realized the need of the masses "to organize into parties." Without them the people would be left "ignorant and dispersed." Douglas envisioned the party uniting the masses and informing them of the "best ideas and people so that their equality would be maintained." He helped promote the party as the "best means to see to it that the in-egalitarian instincts of would-be aristocrats were thwarted."[59]

As we shall see, the manifest political incorporation of Nuevomexicanos pivoted on the preeminent goal actors derived to have a system of party contention for the territory, one worthy of American standards. In this lay the core active mechanism of political incorporation. The story of New Mexico establishing a permanent two-party political system climaxes in 1871, which was the year when clearly defined Republican and Democratic parties went after each other. This milestone represented the permanent integration of Nuevomexicano involvement in American politics. The tale begins while the territory still belonged to Mexico, before the United States conquered and took possession of the Southwest. Certain Mexicans and Euroamericans formed the elemental groups that would go on to assume a partisan character in the American period. The dynamic of partisan opposition bore through the two-year (1846–48) military occupation of New Mexico by the United States. The pattern coincided with the principal division among Nuevomexicanos: those who collaborated with the conquest versus those who physically resisted it at the cost of lives on both sides. The occupation favored the collaborators, of course, and they were facilitating American political incorporation even before the war ended.

The two factions stayed alive after the war. New Mexicans built upon the two groups from the start of the territorial period, going on to compete with all the ferocity of formally organized parties. These proto-parties, as they should be seen, formed the units for stabilizing the political development on the frontier, serving therefore as the key mechanisms of integration in the process of Nuevomexicano political incorporation. As the names listed in appendix 1 indicate, the memberships of the two factions remained remarkably stable. The few defections from one to the other that did occur reflected but a common incident in the American version of binary partyism, but also generated immediate reaction from the abandoned organization, which reinforces the point about the significance of maintaining party cohesion. A sustained tendency toward factional contention fired Nuevomexicanos up to pitch into the process of party building for the sake of their self-defined interests, their public survival, and the goal of obtaining resources for their home community.

Biennial elections and yearly legislative sessions fueled a system of quasi-party contention. The two-year electoral schedule and the desire to stand in closer relation to the political center in Washington DC compelled the citizens of New Mexico to hammer out a working factional contention. The electoral process fostered the territory's political development, compelling the factions to act like parties by convening nominating conventions and putting forth territorial and local tickets. The factions competed for the right to establish a Democratic Party in the 1850s. It was a critically important step in institutionalizing a factional polarization. That contention was interrupted by the Civil War. One faction stayed loyal to a nominal Democratic Party; the other came under the influence of Republicans who filtered into the territory. Both regional and national issues stoked partisanship among acting party militants. The proposal to convert New Mexico into a state of the union became an issue of partisan debate every time a statehood movement raised its head.

In a situation of colonialism, the partisan division could well have corresponded to the two major ethnoracial groups, but the drive to form a party system came to involve a liberal cross-ethnic consensus among Nuevomexicanos and those Euroamericans who settled into the territory, moved in and out, and acted to influence matters from the outside. Popular suffrage tied into the classic liberal requirement that native and incoming agents engage in positive interpersonal contact.[60] A signature mark on the political annexation of Nuevomexicanos involved the deep and abiding alliances they forged with members of the Euroamerican settler class. The departure from the segregationist model of internal colonialism could not be more striking, while belying the rigidity of a hegemonic race hierarchy. The European immigrant Charles Clever would not have been a contender for delegate in 1867 without the voluntary endorsement of Nuevomexicanos who hooked into his particular faction. Conversely significant, Clever negotiated strong bonds with Nuevomexicanos who helped spearhead his campaign at the local level. By the same token, Chávez's powerful candidacy relied on Euroamericans who buoyed his chances for victory with money, press support, and efforts to mobilize the vote for him. The ties among Nuevomexicanos and Euroamerican settlers throughout New Mexico's territorial period proved an extraordinarily distinctive feature of this instance of conquest and formal annexation.

National political events, trends, and developments contributed mightily to the efforts of New Mexicans to institutionalize a legitimate two-party system. The tenets of American civic nationalism and political governance were not simply activated by principles and policies of sociopolitical and economic integration. A special mechanism of liberal diffusion is implied. New Mexicans responded to the ideological and action fallout of such major political phases as the shifting platforms of the national political parties, the politics of slavery and the Sectional Crisis, the Lincoln presidency, the Civil War, and Reconstruction. Euroamericans provided strategic leadership for translating the national issues, campaigns, and candidates to regional relevance. Journalists and others associated with the developing press of the territory played fundamental roles in New Mexico's political development.

The political scientist Jack Holmes notes that by the turn of the twentieth century Nuevomexicanos racked up a strong political record in communities whose voters developed a "highly organized, stable, and competitive two-party politics at the village as well as precinct and county levels."[61] The territorial level can be added to this generalization. Nuevomexicanos kneaded a distinct political culture defined by party loyalty and the volatility of the electoral seasons. Nuevomexicano politics contributed to the process of establishing a tradition of contention between permanently organized Republican and Democratic parties. That event in 1871 signified a triumph for the territory's efforts at organizing its political arena and for the goal of becoming a recognized property of the national domain. Driving the close-cropped narrative in the chapters is how citizen-denizens got to this plateau. The competitive ordeal was embedded in citizen deliberation of social issues in a sequence of interrelated episodes. The blow-by-blow account traces in a brutal chronology the political incorporation of the Nuevomexicanos as embodied in tightly knit social interactions among Nuevomexicanos and Euroamericans and among elements within each group. Nuevomexicano *nativos* did not simply go along for the ride. They exercised necessary agency in what became an interactively organic process of pushing toward a functioning party system.

Greater American and Enlightenment liberalism pulsed through intensified competition between the territory's two core political factions. Research into nineteenth-century New Mexico has begun to perceive the importance of liberal doctrine in Nuevomexicano lives. David Correia points out in relation to the Spanish and Mexican land grants that they "shared liberal notions of private property and even understood land grant common property in terms consistent with Lockean-derived liberal theory."[62] Nuevomexicanos understood what liberalism meant as a legacy of their membership in the Mexican state. A key measure of political integration post-1848 involved Nuevomexicanos adopting the liberal idiom for themselves in a system of factional squabbles. The contentions turned on the consideration of relevant questions for the territory, like whether citizens should push for regular statehood for their province or leave it as a federal territory until the proper time came to realize statehood. Liberal measures even hooked into the policy debates about how to deal with the war dimensions in the presence of plains tribes (Navajo, Apache, Ute, Comanche, Kiowa).

After the annexation of New Mexico a definite public discourse emerged brimming with the linguistics of liberalism and political party. The terminology of American republicanism became part and parcel of the fights for office and spoils of territorial governance. Politicians worked for the interests of their faction on the basis of tropes from American and Enlightenment liberalism. They were often expressed as shibboleths or platitudes. Even so, they struck significantly in the brave new world of politics being established on formerly foreign ground. The point applies in relation to the Euroamericans who came into New Mexico bent on hauling American republicanism to the frontier. Speeches, editorials, opinion pieces, and letters to compatriots and sundry leaders prove the point. Euroamericans resorted to liberal thought processes not only to legitimize their presence in a foreign land but to establish a modernist claim to improving the politics of traditional New Mexico through a system of party competition.

New Mexico went through an increasing attachment to the American administrative structure after 1848, and as it did, Nuevomexicano compatriots voiced concern for their interests. We shall see their fluency in liberal/Enlightenment vocabulary sounding out in the Spanish language, reflecting what Benedict Anderson and Sally Engle Merry mean by "vernacularization," nineteenth-century subjects in a peripheral or semi-peripheral area translating in print and public speech the concepts of nationalism and human rights designed in dominant international centers and shaped to fit their regional circumstances and priorities.[63] Nuevomexicanos vernacularized American liberalism as part of their integral participation in a factional framework. Close and extensive examination of their works (and those of Euroamericans as well) affords a certain hermeneutic reading of their activated politics in the New Mexico Territory and allows us to comprehend clearly such matters as their claim of the right to participate in what was deemed an advanced liberal state. Defining the priority of membership in American government took precedence over Mexico's less advanced brand of liberalism. Nuevomexicano oratorical method carried self-interested strategy, particularly if the group was going to be able to stand alongside their Euroamerican counterparts in the competitions of a developing political arena. The ability to sing the refrains of liberalism proved vital to those who either inherited or pined for leadership among the Nuevomexicano populace. Their political survival and ascendance required that they hang with the competitive discourse of the liberal field.

Citizen voices in New Mexico played in the key of liberalism not only to affirm membership in a modern state. Liberal speechcraft proved the means for Nuevomexicanos to recruit adherents at election time. Here was where some cross-class integration took place. Upper-class Nuevomexicanos forged political ties with elements stratified below them. Other exigencies demanded a liberal translation, including the need to combat an opposing faction over certain policies and sustaining their candidate against the charges of political enemies. Nuevomexicanos drew extensively from the liberal repertoire and not just as mimes of the American puppeteer.

Nuevomexicanos learned to construct the verbal weaponry to wound symbolically the character of political opponents and to slay their chances and opportunities. A politician worthy of the name stood by the virtues of the Enlightenment for the worth of the nation's civics. The logical step had him painting an enemy with the gravest anti-, pre-, or nonliberal brush possible, declaring him "despotic" and "tyrannical," just as the framers of the Declaration of Independence condemned the monarch of Great Britain, but in more typically American terms as "conspiratorial," "factional," "egotistical," and the like. The charges by self-declared champions of liberalism flew in both directions on both sides of what emerged as the major political divide in the territory. The entire enterprise of liberalism and American nationality found expression through the alchemy of the Spanish language. An aspect of American political pluralism was necessitated. Nuevomexicanos translated liberal rhetorical devices into their traditional cultural and literary repertoire for dissemination to partisan constituencies. Included were such forms as the imaginative *diálogo,* the *décima,* Iberian-derived scriptural allusions, the songs of the *trovador,* and other Hispanic verse forms.

The Declaration of Independence and classic integration theory promoted the goal of powerful economic development. In time, Western imperial ideologues and integration academics laid faith in the ability of capitalism to bring wealth, employment, and production to geographical outbacks. This too had its discursive touch-point in the context of territorial New Mexico's under-development. A sensitive issue turned on which of the two major "parties" had the better ideas and personnel for equipping the territory's economic growth. The resulting give-and-take projected economic modernization in terms of hoped-for regional increases in productive capacity and the recruitment of outside investors and employers. How Nuevomexicanos fit into these remedies arose strategically as a point of debate among Euroamerican and Nuevomexicano spokespersons.

Nuevomexicanos did not simply engage their conquest and colonization. They answered to the question demanded by the historian Raul Coronado: "How did Latinos become modern" in what became the American Southwest?[64] In New Mexico they did so largely by deriving their distinctive discursive formations progressively within American political development. In seeking to generate solidarity for their faction, or stand in opposition to their enemies, they authored their own publicly disseminated political scripts. They named the names of allies and opponents and provided interpretations of their collective past and alternative destinies under the American flag.

What merits credibility at the outset, then, is the legitimation Nuevomexicanos handed to the American liberal framework. That José Francisco Chávez and Jesús María Baca y Salazar so readily accepted the U.S. government signifies an annexed populace perceiving sufficient benefit from American nationality to embrace it as part of their longer political strategy. Nuevomexicanos may have had little choice but to submit to American state power and little alternative but to express commitment to the American ideals to ensure their public survival. Were they to be asked, they would claim their right and privilege to do so.

To be sure, the expansion of advanced liberalism encountered its test in clashes with lesser structures in the form of "tradition." The sort of obstacle classic integration theory anticipated wended its way to territorial New Mexico. The major instances involved a pre-modern form of Catholicism that had been in place in the New Mexico region for a century and a half at least and the need of liberal authority to address Mexico's system of indentured labor and Indian captivity and slavery as they all carried over onto the American polity. The contradiction arose in the process of Nuevomexicanos needing to rationalize ancient forms of labor exploitation against what was projected as a colonial assault on traditional culture.

Many of the manifest claims of diffusion and inclusion expressed by modernization theory and American nationalism were borne out in the annexation of Nuevomexicanos. A veritable grab-bag of mechanisms, verbal tools, governing principles, electoral processes, administrative rules, and republican norms are available for interpretation and framing of their experience. The momentum toward an integrative political party stood on the most structurally solid ground. Certain conditions were necessary for it all to transpire. The effectiveness of Nuevomexicano politics was fostered precisely by demographic restrictions on the volume of Euroamerican migration to the territory, as Gómez and others emphasize.

In spite of the centripetal dimensions in the annexation of Nuevomexicanos, the expansion of liberalism was not determinative. Rather, it formed a "historically contingent process of constructing, spreading and legitimating the institutions and values of modernity."[65] The notion of "inclusion" should not imply a "true opening up" or process of "authentic recognition," as Jeffery Alexander emphasizes. The term "incorporation" refers to the "possibility of closing the gap between stigmatized [or foreign] categories of persons . . . and the utopian promises that in principle regulate civil life, principles that imply equality, solidarity, and respect among members of society."[66] It does not equate to what American civic discourse, greatly influenced by the civil rights movement, has meant by the ideal of "integration" as equality. Integration was not to be taken for granted; inclusion needed to be struggled for. The introduction of monolithic democratic systems in foreign and annexed lands resulted in discrete or partial states of an ostensible process of establishing liberal institutions, customs, and values.[67]

As such, limits shrank the extension of liberal benefits to Nuevomexicanos, and it is appropriate to classify them as colonial in nature. The idea of *integrative colonialism* means to capture the ambition of integration with equality even as the New Mexico Territory constituted a racialized colonial enterprise. Most obvious was the structural inequality born of the fact that the offices of first rank in the federal territory were filled by appointment in Washington in a system of national patronage. This condition was suffered by all citizens in the territory. It formed one of the bases for Nuevomexicanos and Euroamericans to share in a major grievance delivered to Washington: the lack of the home rule that would come with the appointment of New Mexico residents rather than patronage hacks. But Nuevomexicanos were super-colonized on the basis of race. Of 256 top officials appointed to rule for 60 years following New Mexico's designation as a federal territory, 28 were Nuevomexicanos. One historian calls it a pattern of "token representation."[68]

A tendency toward bias worked against Nuevomexicanos within local political arenas. The territorial system of governance included an appointed governor who had the power to veto laws passed by the legislature. The process worked against Nuevomexicanos in particular in those instances when the governor negated measures specifically designed to serve the majority Nuevomexicano populace. The barrier had its reinforcement at the federal level. Congress retained the power to cancel laws passed by the territorial assembly, curtailing Nuevomexicano self-government.[69] Representation in public office suffered in particular. "Many officeholders of local importance, especially district attorneys, were appointed by the territorial governor," a researcher notes. "*Americanos* [Euroamericans] held these positions. Only one territorial governor bore a Spanish surname, and no native New Mexican served as district judge, surveyor general or secretary of the territory. Governors chose some *mexicanos* for territorial offices, but even in local appointments native New Mexicans did not receive recognition in proportion to their numbers."[70] Out of 150 people appointed to territorial boards, 15 were Nuevomexicanos, a consistent ratio of ten to one in favor of Euroamericans.[71]

A more direct form of racialized colonialism obtained. The United States extended the jewels of liberal republicanism and democracy to the Nuevomexicanos from a position of supreme power, what W. E. B. Dubois called "democratic despotism."[72] The American anti-imperialist president of Stanford University, David Starr Jordan, called it "imperial democracy." Jordan helped popularize the notion of imperial democracy in his 1899 book criticizing the United States' imperial war with Spain. It questioned the pride the United States felt in knowing that its agents spread around the world the fruits and virtues of the most advanced brand of liberalism that had ever been created. Anglo-Saxons thought themselves the rescuers of inferior natives unable to govern themselves. They felt the responsibility in their military aggression to provide the world with their valued institutions and democracy. Jordan indicted this attitude because he did not believe it possible to instill democracy in backward peoples through military force. He did not relegate the American conquest of Mexico to imperial democracy. Jordan believed that America had not "floated its flag over Chapultepec." The United States did not take over the entire country and attempt to impose institutions on it. It had, through nonwarlike "permeation," aided in the development of Mexico by widening its influence economically.[73]

Jordan erred in his historical interpretation. Imperial democracy, while not called that in the 1840s, arose as an ideological force during the American mobilization against Mexico and afterward. The American attitude of democratic superiority is what permeated the conquest of New Mexico. Imperial democracy aggravated and competed with liberal integration. It was seen in those Euroamericans who attempted to apply the liberal tool to mold the backward Mexicans into modern shape, lecturing them on how to conduct themselves according to the expectations of the bourgeois American.

Jordan's critique of imperial democracy was the work of xenophobes. Xenophobism and race distinction contributed independently to a diverse platform of liberal domination in territorial New Mexico. Carol A. Horton points out that race in the United States has been "instrumental in creating some of the nation's most radically democratic forms of liberal politics, which emphasize the inclusion of the disfranchised, the importance of socioeconomic equity, and more recently, the value of cultural diversity." At the same time historically distinct "limits" held back the realization of American liberalism's promise. The very structures of liberalism heralded by American pride contained the transformative impact of race on American politics and society. The liberal contours of racial identity go "beyond formally defined racial issues such as non discrimination or affirmative action," to qualify and sometimes impede the inclusion of disparate groups in the dominant institutions of the society, Horton points out.[74] The annexation of a foreign, culturally different populace was destined to produce problems of ethnoracial conflict, including the belief by many a Euroamerican settler that, in fact, it was not recommended that the enlightened United States incorporate such a lowly apparition as the mixed-blood Mexican.

It is in the interlacing of liberal inclusionary aspirations and the racially based hegemonic demons that the meaningful nineteenth-century political incorporation of the Nuevomexicanos comes into focus. Nuevomexicano resistance to subordination occurred as part and parcel of the integration process and the drive to establish a bone fide political party system. It appeared in the very names of the key factions that are at the heart of the drama to be told. The colonial stranger appeared to the Nuevomexicano eye in many a Euroamerican guise: dictatorial governor, supercilious military officer, hate-filled soldier, patronizing lone-wolf citizen, crusading bishop, contemptuous judge, Anglo-Saxon nationalist chiming in from the East Coast, and know-it-all newspaperman. Euroamericans often joined in the protest of their countryman's prejudices. Animosities grew intensely. It is commonplace for the high emotions of collective action to drop social protest off the deep end into the pool of non- or anti-liberal rationalism. It happened among the territorial Nuevomexicanos. The ringing, misbegotten anti-Semitism they launched in a particularly heated election could have derailed the train of liberalism they had been riding. It proved a temporary manifestation and counted in its own way as an indicator of Nuevomexicano public power seeking to counter a perceived colonial threat.

If the issues of domination were serious, the challenges to them were equally biting. At that, political confrontation was confined within the liberal frame that facilitated the Mexican entry into the American polity to begin with. The inherent goal of widespread solidarity would have strengthened the resistance of the conquered and perhaps established a politics outside the formal operations of mainstream political processes. Liberal republicanism gave hope for the resolution of social problems at the same time that the antagonistic nature of American politics, particularly the value of loyalty to one's party, undercut unity among Nuevomexicanos qua Nuevomexicano. Resistance posited the ideal of cultural pluralism to pursue as the alternative to the classic liberal expectation of pure, individualistic assimilation and Anglo-Saxon conformity. It was an explicit debate that served to harden the oppositional frames of factional contenders.

The linear saga in the chapters marks the tracks of Nuevomexicano political incorporation interlaid with the grooves and ruts of consensus-and-conflict, cross-ethnic coalition, ethnoracial dominance, and the inexorable importation of liberal American meaning into a swath of formerly Mexican soil. The struggle that Nuevomexicano natives and Euroamerican settlers put up to become as fully integrated as possible into the U.S. nationality is conducted in the light of major constraints, succeeding significantly but only in part. Arising along the way are observations about the character and history of American politics; Nuevomexicanos' contributions to the sociology of change; and the imprint of their active engagement as American political beings.

1

Initializing Annexation

Students of social change have long argued that whether friendly or unfriendly social relations will ensue between groups from different nationalities locked in initial race-and-culture contact depends on the extent to which their respective cultures and social institutions resemble each other. Natives are more apt to accept modernizing imperialism if they perceive significant similarities of its institutions and their own. The more they have in common, the thesis goes, the greater the likelihood of positive interaction and mutual adaptation. In the formal language of one researcher, "When the ethos of the superordinates has values common to those in the ethos of the subordinates, integration (coordination of objectives) will be facilitated." The greater the clash of incompatibilities, on the other hand, the greater the chances for difficulties of mutually agreeable integration, failed consensus, and native rejection of the incoming system and its representatives.[1]

Classic modernization theory tended to draw a sharp, either-or contrast between "traditional" culture—clustered in village, tribe, clan, or pre-industrial empire—and Western institutions. In this view traditional societies exhibited hardened status hierarchies, ancient agricultural methods, and religiously dictated customs. Modern society evinced democracy, industry, and science. It was from such a dualistic approach that Howard Roberts Lamar, the senior historian of the territorial Southwest, characterized pre-American New Mexico. According to Lamar, the Spanish *adelantado* (official pioneer) Juan de Oñate led a hardy band of colonizers in 1598 in establishing the province of *Nuevo Méjico* as a "feudal" society under the crown of Spain. The Pueblo peoples revolted in 1680, killing off or banishing the Spanish settlers because the colonial rulers forced them into labor and disrespected their religion. Diego de Vargas reconquered New Mexico for Spain in 1692, and in this interpretation he reinstituted a feudal society but without the *encomienda* system of forced labor. And feudal did New Mexico remain through its time as a member of the Mexican Republic.[2] The sociologist Thomas Hall disputes this as having little to do with actual social structure. Hall indicts the notion of a feudal New Mexico as masking the considerable change that had occurred in two hundred years prior to the American annexation. The attribution "feudal," in his opinion, is a way for Euroamerican scholars to diminish Nuevomexicanos as backward, lacking "enlightened," "progressive," or "advanced" qualities.[3]

Hall has the edge here. New Mexico underwent significant change in the time between Spain's colonization and the takeover by the United States. Hall and other scholars suggest that the "modern-tradition" distinction in the study of social change is not always easy to make, for nuance is apt to apply in many instances.[4] Much of what New Mexico looked like in the nineteenth century stemmed from conditions in Mexico generally. The United States and Mexico were both modernizing societies in the nineteenth century. One way of comparing the two countries is by degree of development or modernization. The United States manifested powerful development. One reason had to do with its underlying nationhood. A core Anglo-Saxon identity pulled together a powerful "republic of white men."[5] One can add that it was a white man's capitalism that engendered American economic dynamism. "Since 1800," it has been noted, "the United States had undergone rapid and sweeping economic transformations. During the early decades of the nineteenth century Americans feverishly built roads, bridges, canals, telegraph lines, railways and steam engines. By the 1820s the country was beginning a period of frantic urbanization and mechanized industries were thriving."[6]

Mexico by contrast remained in a mercantile mode. It struggled in part because of an economically unfriendly topography. Industrialization barely pulsed, and exports of bullion plummeted.[7] Total incomes skyrocketed 1,270.4 percent in the United States between 1800 and 1860, while in Mexico they declined by 10.5 percent. Poverty abounded throughout Mexico after its independence from Spain.[8]

Another hallmark of Mexican social change in the early nineteenth century concerned political instability. The movement for independence from Britain in the thirteen American colonies turned on a fundamental ideological unity around European liberal principles. Enlightenment ideas held sway after independence as well. The central government permitted southern slavery and confirmed the rapacious grabbing of Indian lands. Yet the politics of the core American nation emerged "assertive and robust" with "broad agreement on the essential [liberal] principle that sovereignty resided—or at least should rightly reside—with the people."[9] Moreover, the United States remained more consistently consolidated in its republican, federated, and bureaucratic structure, which fed its expansionist power.

Mexico won its independence by virtue of "an odd alliance between conservatives and revolutionaries." Creole conservatives and Spanish military officers joined the independence movement out of disenchantment with Spain, which had returned to absolute rule after rescinding an enlightened monarchy. The liberal ideologues in the fight for independence, stood behind civic citizenship, secular rights, representation by deputies, equality under the law, and legitimacy of the state by popular acclaim.[10]

A fractured political field took Mexico through a series of executives. The first government went not to the liberals who instigated the break with Spain but to conservative creoles who established a regency. Agustín Cosme Damián de Iturbide y Arámburu, who led the military securing of Mexico City to cap the revolt, became constitutional emperor. The Plan de Iguala guaranteed a constitutional monarchy, social equality for all, and a Catholic national religion. The monarchy disdained the impoverished masses and indigenous folk, however.[11]

The Iturbide government lasted two years. An argument broke out among ideologically contending factions over who was, in fact, the true author of Independence. Decades of severe political conflict followed with factions fighting over what kind of political philosophy and structure to convene for Mexico. Liberals, known as *puros* (pure ones), followed in the affect of the Enlightenment to vie for a system of federal autonomy for the provincial units, free trade, secularism, civilian control of the military, and public education. *Conservados* favored state centralism and a state religion, some continuing to call for a monarchy. The moderates (*moderados*) went for democratic centralism and, like the puros, called for reduction in military and church influence in the affairs of state while mistrusting left liberalism. A failure of loyal opposition produced a three-way cleavage. Opportunistic cross-alliances cut the politics of Mexico in assassinations, coups d'état, uprisings, and recrimination.[12]

The precarious Mexican government slogged through a series of distinct chief executives after the constitutional monarchy, including an empire, a provisional government, a federal republic, a centralized state system, a dictatorship, and a central government again. The centralist Constitution of 1835–1836 reconfigured all the Mexican states and territories to departments, including New Mexico, under the fundamental *Siete Leyes Constitucionales* (Seven Constitutional Laws).[13] A strong conservative constitution, the 1842 *Bases Orgánicas,* granted disproportionate power to the wealthy while slighting civil rights for citizens.[14]

Mexico City supervised the provinces up to the 1840s with considerable difficulty. Federal revenues flowed meagerly. Several of the Mexican territories either threatened or attempted to break away in secession.[15] Geopolitically, nineteenth-century Mexico resembled what experts on nationalism call a pre-industrial "agrarian society." The provinces in the classic agrarian empire were largely left alone to become what Ernest Gellner calls "sub-communities." Such communities had the capacity to reproduce themselves without much help from the center. They enabled themselves to do "on a smaller scale anything done by the larger unit."[16] Such societies were structured like wheels. Their major communication routes joined into "only one place," the capital.[17] Mexico up to the mid-1840s resembled a state-centered agrarian society struggling to consolidate itself. The provincial areas farthest from Mexico City carried on much like Gellnerian subsocieties—nonmanufacturing entities, reliant on ranching and small-scale husbandry, mostly fending for themselves on rough terrain with primitive nation-building resources, including poor communications facilities, and lacking railroads, the telegraph, and craftsmanship.[18] Multiple "spokes" extended out from New Mexico with varying degrees of firmness. An administrative line extended to the national capital; ecclesiastical and judicial ones linked up to Durango; a military authority connected to Chihuahua; and a commercial market cut through *el norte grande,* the northern provinces, down to Chihuahua, Aguascalientes, Querétaro, Guadalajara, and Mexico City.[19]

Old customs survived and tied into modernizing trends under such a formation. The characteristic legacy of the Spanish dominion of the mid-southern American continent saw "the ghosts of a surviving past [returned] from a place out of time or a different temporality to haunt and disturb the historical present." The past and present, or in liberal terms modernization and tradition, were "not necessarily successive" in this social structure. Rather, they "coexisted as uneven temporalities."[20] Much of "traditional" New Mexican society thus reflected continuations of the past having little counterpart in the United States, where in other respects the preexisting social structure had some strategic things in common with the more comprehensively modern American state and values.

How New Mexico's institutional framework and sociocultural structures operated at the zero point of the U.S. invasion prophesied much of how Nuevomexicanos would respond to the American occupation and how their experience of American incorporation would shape up. The points around which the original New Mexican and U.S. polities and societies compared and contrasted set precursors for the Nuevomexicano experience of sociopolitical incorporation. Chapter 1 suggests the chronological depth to eventual Nuevomexicano political incorporation into the United States through a political, social, economic, and cultural portrait of New Mexico when it was a department of Mexico. A telling picture of New Mexican society prior to the American occupation unfolds based on the Journal of the Assembly of New Mexico, newspaper accounts coming out of Santa Fe, and published historical works. It was a place where the preexisting social structure had much in common with the expanding American social system and in which much differed. New Mexico, following its national model, consisted of a hybrid liberal modernity, contrasted to the more forthright and comprehensively developed American version.

It makes sense theoretically as well that national communities should affect each other for being continental neighbors. Issues of cultural congruence, over contact among foreigners, and about modernizing diffusion can arise in the would-be colony before the process of annexation is set into motion. It all came into play in the case of New Mexico. Key connections established between Mexicans and Americans prior to the war of 1846 greatly complicated the forced annexation of Nuevomexicanos. Cross-national relations established between peripatetic Americans and Mexican homelanders provided the seedlings for what would blossom into the major factional parties to govern the political process of American New Mexico.

Chapters 2 and 3 go on to cover the action-packed American occupation of New Mexico. An American army prepared to invade New Mexico in August 1846 following the U.S. declaration of war with Mexico. A fearful assault portended a rupture in Nuevomexicano national belonging. Overwhelming American power and its potential for imposing a blanket of foreign domination over the Mexican section evidenced itself from the beginning.

The case proved complex. Political scientist Mark Peceny notes that no state has more consistently proclaimed its adherence to a vision of democracy and free market for the world than the United States, and at the same time no state other than the United States has worked harder to promote it by coercing others to adopt liberal institutions "at the point of bayonets," as it were. A penchant for proudly imposing the American system of politics appeared in the twentieth century when, of ninety-three military interventions in foreign countries, thirty-three involved attempts to implant its political framework through the use of force.[21] In truth, the first experiment in democracy promotion by the United States through saber-rattling and invasion occurred at the midpoint of the nineteenth century in the occupation of northern Mexico. It was in New Mexico that the diffusion of liberalism at the point of bayonets was the most pointedly focused and had its real-life effects and consequences.

The promotion of democracy via bayonets is coercive virtually by definition, yet the process can take shape in any number of forms. Patriotic resistance to foreign invasion would be a natural response. On the other hand, even when democracy and liberal institutions are forcibly presented, natives have been known to accept them "not just because [they are] being imposed by a more powerful state, but because they find [them] persuasive and compelling."[22] For any given case the question arises of how well the imposition of liberalism takes. Much may well depend on the fit between the imported institutions and the political establishment of the invaded territory.

It follows for the phenomenon of collaboration to arise. The "elite pact" involving would-be antagonists can facilitate the transition to a workable or more advanced democracy.[23] An "elite settlement" legitimates a conquest and provides key assistance to the practical organization of the new regime.[24] Collaboration produced what David Montejano means by a "peace structure" in the American conquest of the former Mexican territories, a "general postwar arrangement that allows the victors to maintain law and order without the constant use of force."[25] "Collaboration" carries the dark tones of Nazi-occupied Europe.[26] But as John Breuilly points out, networks of collaboration have occurred in quite varied contexts with different consequences not only for "domination or westernization" or beyond the narrow interests of collaborators. They have proved central to an understanding of national expansion and colonial situations.[27]

Chapters 2 and 3 revisit the U.S. invasion of New Mexico with an eye to its liberal-integrative and colonial-destructive manifestations. Original documents and published studies provide a window for a preview of integrative colonialism. The brief occupation of New Mexico unfolded rife with contradiction. Threats of terror and the crushing of native resistance accompanied a liberal integrative face legitimated by key elements of the conquered.

The invading commander informed his mission of forcibly appropriating New Mexico with a plan to incorporate the native Mexicans into his own political system. Sociologist T. K. Oomen's notion of "replicative colonialism" helps to explain how it could have happened naturally. In "retreatist" colonialism ("insularist" may be a better description), colonizers withdraw to form their own makeshift community in the colony. Imperialists in replicative colonialism seek to reproduce, or transplant, their home society. Colonizers in replicative colonialism strive to bring the colonized into their "same field of historicity."[28]

Oomen cites the New World (the Americas, Australia) as a setting where replicative colonialism obtained, although he does not examine it historically. It is clear that nineteenth-century American expansion involved a grand effort by pioneer settlers to reproduce on the frontier the institutional and cultural matrices they had known at home.[29] Oomen suggests that they would have done so with the centripetal intent of bringing the native subjects into their sphere of operation. The general who was charged with annexing New Mexico started such a process. At the tip of his bayonet sat the aim of sweeping Nuevomexicanos into the liberal state of which he saw himself an emissary. His occupying project produced armed resistance on one hand and, on the other, Nuevomexicano collaboration. The agents of these responses corresponded to the factional divisions that had emerged in the preconquest years. Remarkably, American republican governance and the political integration of Nuevomexicanos arose as part of the military occupation itself. The very currents of military dominance served to stage Nuevomexicano leaders for eventual participation in the politics of an incorporated territory.

CHAPTER ONE

Nuevomexicano Politics and Society on the Eve of the American Conquest

New Mexico in the early 1840s operated politically as a department of the Republic of Mexico. The official structure of the New Mexico Department had some equivalencies to the American territory while displaying important differences. Both were founded on a legal-rational framework, itself a hallmark of liberal modernity.[1] Governance headquarters were seated in a regional capital, Santa Fe. A governor (*jefe político*) was appointed by the Mexican president just as the American president appointed the governor of the U.S. territory. The governor occupied his seat of office in the historic Palace of the Governors on the Santa Fe Plaza. Nuevomexicanos enforced the right to select the departmental governor from among their own ranks. Small chance of that happening in the American territory, where the president tended to reserve the appointment as a patronage reward to one who had supported his election or worked for their shared party. The New Mexico governor appointed an executive staff, including the secretary (department deputy), collector of special taxes (revenues derived from interstate and international commerce), and director of internal revenue. An important executive duty involved the granting of common lands to individuals and groups of family petitioners.[2]

The New Mexico Department included a legislative assembly (*asamblea de diputación departamental*) just like the American territory. Historically it was granted by the Mexican Congress to satisfy citizen demands for relative autonomy and to counterpose the extensive powers of the governor.[3] An 1843 congressional decree mandated an eleven-member asamblea for departments, with a minimum of seven allowed. A minimum age of twenty-five was required to be a member. Historian Joseph Sánchez describes the duties of the assembly as "establishing taxes with congressional approval, regulating spending, and appointing necessary employees.

FIG. 1. *Palace of the Governors, Santa Fe, New Mexico*, ca. 1865–70, United States Army Signal Corps. The palace housed the headquarters of New Mexico's departmental and territorial governor, and there were rooms where the territorial council and house of representatives met until the 1880s, when a legislative building was constructed. Courtesy Palace of the Governors Photo Archives, New Mexico History Museum/Digitized Collection Archives (NMHM/DCA), negative #009099.

The asamblea regulated the acquisition, alienation, and exchange of property with legislation in accordance with colonization laws. Attending to the departmental infrastructure was a priority, and the asamblea provided for opening and maintaining roads. Among the many responsibilities of the asamblea were the promotion of public instruction, the recruitment and maintenance of the army, and the establishment of municipal corporations."[4] The assembly journals reveal additional duties: organizing town judiciaries; deciding on district seats; settling disputes over assembly membership; and setting forth the organization of municipal laws and regulations according to the *Bases Orgánicas*. "Congress retained the right to review and, if need be, annul legislation or actions by the asambleas," Sánchez notes, identical to the American territorial system.[5]

Juan Gómez-Quiñones characterizes politics in the far northern regions of Mexico as "Mexican Republicanism on the Frontera."[6] In

FIG. 2. *Watercolor illustration of the Palace of the Governors, Santa Fe, New Mexico*, 1866, by Anthony Kellner, 5th Infantry, U.S. Army's Ninth Military Department (New Mexico Territory). Courtesy Palace of the Governors Photo Archives, NMHM/DCA, negative #074473.

contrast to what prevailed in the American territory, New Mexico did not have a system of popular elections. *Vocales* (assemblymen) were selected in an indirect election by members of the *junta electoral* (electoral body), who came from the ranks of propertied men and were appointed by the governor by district. Replacements were elected by the outgoing session in staggered terms.[7] Deputies met on a weekly basis during a term.[8] Traveling from far-flung settlements to attend sessions in Santa Fe was no easy journey, yet assemblymen stood committed to what they deemed the "sacred duty" of representing the interests of the people.[9] Vocales were supposed to be paid for their service, as in the American system. The department treasury was generally insufficient to provide full or steady salaries. Gifts and the appropriation of public resources, including land, often served as remuneration.[10]

Both the U.S. territory and the Mexican department sent a delegate to represent them in the halls of Congress in the national capital.[11] Governor Melgares convened in 1821 without authorization of any national office forty electors to name a seven-member provincial council tasked with creating the congressional delegate position.[12] A brief hiatus in filling the post followed.[13] The large land holder Rafael

Sarracino assumed it in 1830.[14] The centralist 1835 Constitution sought to give the weak position some teeth. The delegate's primary duties came to lie as counsel to the governor and assembly.[15] The governor during the department's last electoral meeting under the Mexican flag named three individuals to a commission so that they could appoint the next regular delegate to the assembly and his substitute as well as five new members and three alternates.[16]

The Mexican state strove to effect regional attachment to the national center. According to Joseph Sánchez, Nuevomexicanos in 1821 "had scant understanding, and cared little, about the meaning of a republic." It began to sink in after the nascent Mexican government disseminated a decree throughout the country to celebrate independence. Governor Facundo Melgares received an order from the national capital in December 1821 for him and other New Mexico officials to take an oath of allegiance to independent Mexico. Nuevomexicanos put on a fittingly enthusiastic commemoration. Speakers at the Santa Fe Plaza praised the Three Guarantees of the Revolution—Religion, Union, and Independence—under cloth bunting and the national flag. The *alcaldías* (mayorships) swore loyalty to Mexico. Santa Feans celebrated the coronation of Iturbide as emperor of the Mexican regency. In two months they were hailing the triumph of the republicans and a constitutional government.[17] Nuevomexicanos celebrated the fifteenth anniversary of Mexican Independence as well.[18]

The Three Powers: Ricos, Officers, and Priests

Three distinct sectors controlled New Mexico's governance by the 1840s. The power of each derived from the Revolt of 1837. The Mexican department had less autonomy than a territory, much less a state.[19] A significant tension arose from the fact that Mexico remained a "country of regions," while the United States managed its territories on the model of Great Britain's sustained bureaucratic administration of the colonies.[20] Mexico's chronic political instability, weak economy, and primitive communications subverted effective oversight of the periphery.[21] While villagers held tight to familial and local ties, an "exaggerated regionalism" joined to the divisions of race and class to form one of the country's "most intractable problems during its early decades."[22] Mexican histories quote a *moderado*'s contemporary lament that "there has not been, nor could there have been, a national spirit, for there is no nation."[23]

The Santa Fe asamblea received a steady stream of official notices regarding political affairs in Mexico.[24] The departments of Puebla, Oaxaca, and Yucatan threatened or mounted secessionist movements while Sonora persisted in virtual civil war. More prosperous states fought off central control as well.[25] The administration of the moderate liberal President Joaquín Herrera resisted the trend in the 1830s of moving toward national centralism. In Santa Fe *El Payo* (the Rustic) *de Nuevo Méjico* praised Herrera and assailed the deposed President Santa Anna "as the chief of a party founded on vice, prostitution and brigandage." The paper pledged to reproduce official communications of the "supreme general government." It would support the politics of autonomy of the departments by publishing the reports of their honorable assemblies, prefectures, and courts. The proclamations showed how to promote "liberty, equality, individual guaranties and the division of powers."[26]

Nuevomexicanos favored political autonomy in the face of irregular funding from the central government for running the department.[27] Department officials received sparse salaries for their public service.[28] Lack of resources kept the military from adequately protecting the villages at times of battle with surrounding tribal bands.[29] Resentment of the national Congress grew because it turned a deaf ear to New Mexico's claims for greater self-governance. The assembly asked to retain more of the public rents.[30] It also petitioned for the privilege of waiving fees for export products, both to no avail.[31] Modest requests for special appropriations to manage public lands were rejected. The assembly cautioned the treasurer to economize.[32] Father Antonio José Martínez's 1831 appeal to the national Congress pointed to the assembly's lack of capacity to deal with regional problems and complained of the vague definition of the separation of powers among the governor, the assembly, and local governments. The barrister and territorial judicial assessor, Antonio Barreiro, lamented the power of the assembly as "null and insignificant."[33]

The Mexican Congress renewed a centralist constitution in 1835. The powers of states were abrogated and department councils mandated to report directly to the Congress. Tension between national and regional loyalties broke out painfully in New Mexico in 1837.[34]

The president appointed as governor of New Mexico a native of Mexico City, violating the custom since 1827 of Nuevomexicanos choosing their own governor. Governor Albino Pérez had orders to bring the department under tighter central control, and he complied by replacing the assembly with an advisory council, ordering prefects to report to him, imposing various taxes, and effecting other executive controls. Bishop José Antonio Laureano de Zubiría, headquartered in Durango, was enjoined to reinforce centralization, which he did by extracting coin from parishioners. An 1837 federal decree gave additional power to jefes político.[35] Pérez sparked resistance when he had an alcalde arrested for not obeying a reversal of his decision in a court case. A crowd liberated the alcalde from his jail cell and fled to a mountain stronghold.[36]

Three to six thousand lower-class Mexicans, military officers, Pueblo Indians, and large land owners moved on Pérez. The so-called Chimayó Revolt flared for over three weeks. The rebellion had "religious overtones" as grassroots Catholics attacked priests who had raised the costs of saving souls by enforcing church fees and regulating burials.[37] The outbreak led to the assassination of Governor Pérez, his cabinet, and collaborators. Former Taos alcalde and militia lieutenant colonel Pablo Montoya led Taos area resisters. Two other Montoyas, Abad and Desiderio, and Truchas *nativo* Antonio Vigil sent circulars to mobilize communities. A rebel *pronunciamiento* swore to "God and the Nation and the Faith of Jesus Christ" that the land would be defended "to the last drop of blood." Rebel forces appointed José Gonzales governor of the revolutionary government; they negated Pérez's Department Plan with its onerous taxes; and they called their autonomous district a *cantón*.[38]

The triumphant coalition soon split apart. Anti-centralists called for a complete break from the national government. Moderates pressed for a program of fair representation in Mexico City. Liberals favored reinstatement of the federalist constitution of 1824 with popular elections. Some sentiment was expressed for having the United States annex New Mexico.[39] The rebel government randomly jailed persons not actively opposed to Pérez. Priests were forced to bury people in the church edifice in violation of an edict against it. A counterrevolutionary movement coalesced in the Río Abajo below the capital of Santa Fe. The Plan of Tomé called for the restoration of order and loyalty to the Constitution and its laws. A Río Abajo public figure was appointed commander of the movement. A "Liberating Army," joined by outside military aid, acted as agent of the Mexican state and guarantor "of the national constitutional order." The restored department command moved to put down the Chimayó Revolt.[40]

Those who actively opposed the revolt established political dominance over New Mexico. The moderado Manuel Armijo became governor and mopped up remnants of the rebellion. The final encounter occurred on January 27, 1838, at the Battle of La Cañada. José Gonzales was captured and executed. Rebel leaders were executed by decapitation.[41] The revolt failed to dislodge Mexican centralization. Historian Andrés Reséndez convincingly argues that as a result of the Chimayó Revolt the boundaries of three ruling sectors became more clearly defined than before. Their members composed the minority of New Mexican society who could read and write. They were in this regard New Mexico's version of what specialists in Spanish American history call *los letrados*, a special learned class of men whose literacy empowered them to interpret and manipulate the written word "on behalf of the masses."[42]

An aristocracy of large land owners, the vernacular *rico* class, which made up 5 percent of the population, held primary economic power in the department.[43] The basis of rico wealth lay in the wide expanses of pasturage, primarily in the river-bottom Río Abajo (southern) district with some such pockets in the northern Río Arriba district where Santa Fe sat. Rico *rancheros* raised cattle, horses, and mules, although sheep constituted the basis of their wealth. Profits from mutton (not wool) may hardly have compared to American advantages from livestock, but they made for a stratified order in New Mexico.[44] Rico families held title to large land parcels received originally as personal grants for military and administrative service to the crown and the later Mexican government. An expanded demand for sheep and their products at the turn of the nineteenth century, spurred by the fiscal and market policies of the Mexican-Bourbon reforms, supported rico class consolidation. Large-scale sheep owners drove their stock to the Mexican interior and occasionally to California by 1800. Sheep operations expanded from 1821 to 1846. Thousands of head were driven biannually to markets in Durango and the mining districts of Chihuahua and Zacatecas. Sheep formed a general economic staple well before 1846, often the medium of exchange and payments.[45] The personal resources of the landed gentry were indispensable to the support of the departmental administration.[46]

Politically, the ricos and their allies in the military constituted the Nuevomexicano version of Mexico's *hombres de bien* (men of goodwill, men of good breeding, well-born men). The *hombre de bien* category originated among Mexico City's rising middle class. Hombres de bien were men of means who rose to political dominance in the centralist decade of 1835–46. They posed as ideal citizens of Mexico, each the kind of "gentleman" that "the electorate was always urged to vote for by all parties in every election campaign." Such a man was typically white, a property owner, in a profession that permitted investment capital or professional employment. Hombres de bien upheld the Catholic faith but favored secular elections and believed that election to public office should be restricted to their civilized class of property owners or to those above a certain income level.[47] They desired economic growth and valued political stability, social harmony, the rule of law, social order, and public morality. In this vein, they helped dismantle the federal republic of 1824 because of its chaotic mass-based support.[48] They opposed the 1840 Mexico City movement to restore federalism once it appeared as a bloody "caldron" with criminals committing acts of vandalism.[49] Hombres de bien leaned toward a moderate variety of liberalism. Much like moderados, they claimed to stand above the rabble "mob."[50]

Upper-class Nuevomexicanos represented the typical hombre de bien ideologically.[51] In an essay published in 1848, Capt. Donaciano Vigil used the term to mean New Mexico's "men of higher quality."[52] Consistent with both moderado and conservative outlooks, New Mexico's hombres de bien who participated in the 1837 counterrevolution condemned the Chimayó Revolt for its disrespect of the Mexican state and its ruthless violence.[53] Governor Manuel Armijo entrenched himself into what Reséndez calls New Mexico's "political demiurge."[54] Armijo publicly condemned the tumultuous factions that in "anarchy, ruin, and desolation, shatter[ed] the national unity to which we [in New Mexico] are tied in sweet obedience to a free, paternal, and magnanimous government which fortunately leads us." In stressing social order, Armijo proclaimed that fraud and deceit could never prevail "against truth and justice," for "the people ought to be undeceived by error and be certain of the constitutional laws that raised this territory to the rank of department, which puts it equal in pleasures and rights with the rest of the republic." Armijo charged the rebels with "maliciously and falsely" opposing Pérez's taxes "to satisfy villainous and invidious passions working for private interest." He declared in favor of the central state, emphasizing that the taxes authorized by law would "positively prohibit abuses . . . being a particular attribution of the only supreme legislative power that has the faculty of doing so when the necessities of the country demand it."[55] Armijo thus dismissed the homeland identity of autonomy that motivated the Chimayó Revolt.

Other hombres de bien who had participated in the events of the Chimayó Revolt went on to greater prominence, including Vicente Sánchez Vergara, former governor Francisco Sarracino, and the liberal hombre de bien Antonio José Otero. Otero, New Mexico's congressional representative under the liberal President Herrera, distinguished himself in service to revising the constitution of the republic and in other ways, having "worked, and effected reforms in the administration of the offices of his country."[56] Some hombres de bien were merchants, including Ambrosio Armijo of Alburquerque.[57] Bernalillo merchant Francisco Perea, Santa Fe trader José Chávez y Castillo, and leading ranchers Miguel Antonio Otero I, Juan Perea, and Vicente Martínez stood among New Mexico's hombres de bien.

A military presence provided a second source of political leadership. A Western military tradition dated in New Mexico to Spanish colonial days. New Mexico was made a military *comandancia* separate from Chihuahua in 1839. In 1846 the few troops in the department were employed primarily in Santa Fe "in sustaining the authorities and in keeping order among the inhabitants," one historian notes. "Due to their number and the deterioration of most of their equipment, even if the troops were free from this service, they would not be able to defend more than the place where they live." The lack of a strong military fortification was a principal reason for New Mexico's underdevelopment.[58]

The army detachment of the Mexican Republic included a commandant and disbursing officer. Inefficient resources from the central government limited a regular military unit and made for unsteady salaries.[59] Yet Nuevomexicanos were drawn to the military by avocation and because a regionalized military officer could rise to *caudillo* (boss, or jefe) over a militia and community following. Rafael Chacón began his training in a Chihuahua military school in the 1830s in preparation for entering the national army and served as a teenage cadet under General Armijo.[60] José María Chávez's military roots lay in the late Spanish period as a lieutenant in the militia, battalion captain, and adjutant for King Ferdinand VII. He earned promotion to colonel and military inspector of the Abiquiú–Ojo Caliente–El Rito frontier and led eleven regular campaigns against Indians, five as commander in chief.[61]

Adding to a military tradition, an important civilian militia had existed in New Mexico since colonial days. The first companies were headquartered in Santa Fe and Alburquerque with expansions to Taos and San Miguel. Serving under their own officers at their own expense, militiamen mounted principally in the periodic warfare with Plains tribes and proved important in repelling the 1841 attempt by Texas to invade and capture New Mexico.[62]

The military and militia officer corps consolidated into a power group in the wake of the Chimayó Revolt. Some members shared in the hombre de bien sector. Donaciano Vigil stood out in this regard. Captain Vigil had served as the assassinated Governor Pérez's treasurer. He became New Mexico's secretary to the general commandancy in Chihuahua and served twice in the department assembly and in various local posts.[63] The rough-hewn jefe Col. Diego Archuleta was not of pure hombre de bien stock, but he did serve as a delegate to the general Congress in Mexico City and a term in the office of department lieutenant governor.[64] Some militia officers joined in the attack on Governor Pérez. More of them collaborated with and defended the central government. The embattled governor left the loyalist Lt. Col. José María Ronquillo in control of the capital when it became necessary to confront the insurgents in the field. Ronquillo marched out to stop the main body of rebels as they approached Santa Fe.[65]

The Catholic Church afforded a third fount for established power in pre-American New Mexico. A tradition of priests participating in political affairs marked a clear departure from American practice. Protestant Christianity formed the orthodoxy of religious truth in the United States. Seven of the original thirteen colonies established one or another denomination as their official religion. A trend toward church-state separation evolved out of a diversity of Christian denominations. An evangelical revival in the mid-eighteenth century expanded the range to include Anglicans, Congregationalists, Baptists, Quakers, Presbyterians, Lutherans, Huguenots, and Dutch and German Reformed Church members besides Catholics and Jews. Protestant sects competed bitterly for the title of the one true Christian institution, as if they constituted separate religions. A plethora of Christian representation among delegates pressed the Continental Congress of 1774 to assume a position of religious tolerance while effectively preventing the rise of a dominant political church. A second evangelical awakening further eroded religion's connection to government. The American Revolution endorsed the Enlightenment's faith in liberty of conscience. The American Constitution laid down a clear separation of church and state. Religion and politics were to be kept apart and individual rights protected regardless of religious or nonreligious affiliation. All of the American states disestablished their official churches by 1833.[66] Congress did not outlaw or prohibit clergymen from serving in Congress, but by the 1840s society generally disapproved of it.[67]

In Mexico no other faith could compete with Roman Catholicism in meeting the spiritual needs of a national space. Spain consolidated its empire with the king as head of both state and church. Spanish colonialism in the western hemisphere turned on the "religious conquest" of indigenous nations. Bishops commonly served as viceroys. In the disenchantment that set Spanish America against Castilian rulers, Catholic clerics returned to Thomist Scholasticism and participated in the debates regarding modernity and national sovereignty. A developing ecclesiastical-civil conflict toward the end of the colonial period led the crown to reduce Church power. Church officials and clergy continued to exert influence nonetheless. Key clerics joined in the wars of Mexican independence. The independence struggle adopted the standard of the Virgin of Guadalupe as its symbol and protector. Church power passed into post-Independence Mexico. The Iturbide regency elevated the Church to an emblem of Mexican sovereignty. The 1824 republican constitution ordained Catholicism as the country's official religion and awarded the Church special legal privileges. It owned one-half to two-thirds of the country's real property, becoming the largest land-owner next to the government, with revenue estimated to be five times that of the state.[68]

The Church could not serve as "a national dominant class," and its power did not go unchallenged. A protracted discourse, exacerbated by an economy teetering on collapse, debated the Church's proper political place. The canonist Church demanded state protection of its religious monopoly and civil privileges. Conservative allies pushed to keep it the national religion. Radical liberals blamed the Church for the country's woes, pushed for its excision from the public square, and demanded nationalization of its wealth. Moderates called for a regal control over Church administration, much as Spain had developed. These positions contended within and among the executive, congressional, and state levels of government. Conservative and liberal presidencies dealt with the issue of the Church's proper public role. In one view a strident anti-clericalism proved "the crippling feature of life in Mexico."[69] Still, every constitution up to the 1850s acknowledged Catholicism as the one religion meriting state sanction.[70] The Church's place in the Mexican nation was reflected in *Dios y Libertad* (God and Liberty), the official stamp for signing off on official correspondence among civil officers from the president to the obscure Nuevomexicano clerk.[71]

The Church began in the northern *provincias* in the late eighteenth century with Franciscan Indian missionization. As the order declined at the turn of the nineteenth century, Independence led to the secularization of the missions. The New Mexico assembly secularized the main churches of the department in the 1820s. New Mexico had no bishopric of its own. The chief church authority existed in the vicar forane, who reported to the bishop in Durango. The first *vicario* sought to expel the Franciscans working at some of the Pueblo missions. Nine friars and two priests gave mass, and many churches lay in ruin. Concerted steps were taken to firm the Church's regional extensions in conjunction with the new centralizing government in the 1830s. Bishop Zubiría reasserted the vatical structure for the Catholic outpost, assigning several priests to New Mexico and appointing Father Juan Felipe Ortiz the curate, and later vicar, of Santa Fe. Ortiz, a "scion of one of the most prominent New Mexican families and a former student in the seminary of Durango," became the bishop's "most trusted ally in the difficult task of restoring the influence of the diocesan church in New Mexico." Ortiz was in place at the time of the American occupation of New Mexico.[72]

The Nuevomexicanos who were trained to become priests in the interior of Mexico and at the seminary in Durango during the centralist decade stood out for their Mexican patriotism, although on a track separate from that of the hombres de bien.[73] The erudite Antonio José Martínez was ordained in Durango in 1822. His career training earned him "an unbounded admiration for the most famous *Presbitero* of his day, don José Miguel Hidalgo," the first hero of revolutionary Mexico, who was executed by the Spanish six years before Martínez went to Durango. Martínez pledged loyalty to the new liberal constitution of 1824.[74] He delivered a sermon at the fifteen-year celebration of Mexican independence, evoking the Virgin of Guadalupe in praise of Mexico's independence and calling Father Hidalgo a liberator whose "eminent" legacy endured in his "worthy companions, apostles of our freedom."[75]

The clergy, among the most literate Nuevomexicanos and following Mexican tradition, were qualified to hold public office.[76] Padre Martínez served prior to the 1837 Revolt in the office of territorial deputy (secretary) and as a member of the department assembly.[77] The curate of Santa Fe and future New Mexico vicar Juan Felipe Ortiz served as the province's deputy to Congress at the time that the revolt broke out.[78] Liberal hombres de bien politically persecuted prominent priests during the Chimayó Revolt, which drove them deeper into political activity. Martínez, who had joined the Tomé movement, played a critical role in quieting the people, issuing warnings that their rebellious activity made New Mexico vulnerable to American imperial designs. He afterward came to serve as a member of the assembly in 1845 and 1846.[79]

The Church grew into one of the three primary chains of command in New Mexico after the Chimayó Revolt. It rivaled the civil administration and the military "in influence, wealth, geographic reach, and hierarchical and centralizing impulses."[80] Clergymen contended with lay politicians over their commitments to the national political framework. The Martínez protégé Padre José Manuel Gallegos complained in 1843 that there was insufficient love of the Republic in New Mexico, "even among those in authority."[81] New Mexico had fourteen secular (diocesan, non-Franciscan) priests in 1845 under the vicar general in Santa Fe.[82] Their power was enhanced as the people relied on the clergy as much as civil officers to adjudicate personal disputes.[83]

The presbyter José Francisco Leyva was appointed interim representative to Congress in 1845 on the death of Mariano Chávez.[84] Father Gallegos, Vicar Ortiz, and Monsignor Martínez received votes for the assembly later that year. The pastors Gallegos, Martínez, and Leyva were among the seven vocales selected by the electoral junta to serve in the first departmental assembly with a term of office of four years.[85]

On the eve of the American occupation, then, hombre de bien Antonio José Otero served as New Mexico's representative in the national council of Mexico. Vicente Sánchez Vergara, a leader in the suppression of the Chimayó Revolt, stood by as the delegate's alternate. Vocales in the departmental assembly included the priests (*hombres de Dios*, as it were) Antonio José Martínez, José Manuel Gallegos, and José Francisco Leyva, but representatives were primarily hombres de bien: Tomás Ortiz, Juan Perea and Felipe Sena. Capt. Donaciano Vigil, Juan Cristóbal Armijo, Serafín Ramirez, Vicente Martínez, and Santiago Armijo filled in as *suplentes* (alternates). Augustín Durán served as department treasurer. Governor Manuel Armijo, Secretary Juan Bautista y Vigíl, and Lieutenant Governor Diego Archuleta occupied the executive offices. These were the governance functionaries in place at the time of Gen. Stephen Watts Kearny's invasion of New Mexico in August 1846.[86]

The assembly continued in the aftermath of the Chimayó Revolt to balance national attachments and New Mexico's embedded claim to autonomy, members expressing a desire to have their governor selected from the assembly's list of nominees.[87] The Journal of the Assembly of New Mexico shows Nuevomexicano politicians requesting guarantee of the appointment of New Mexicans to federal jobs and military offices, asking for the authority to run their independent treasury, and affirming the need to have the New Mexico military commandancy be made independent of Chihuahua. The self-identifier *hijo del país* (native son) reinforced the demand for autonomy as it did among Californios who developed their society in semi-isolation.[88] Nuevomexicanos maintained a strong identity as hijos del país. Its modern etymology *país* commonly denotes "country." However, its historically traditional usage signified "'region, kingdom, or province.'"[89] The term *nativo* had its purpose as well, Nuevomexicanos issuing stern requests to Mexico City for nativos, that is, *los Nuevo Mejicanos*, to run the department.[90]

Spotty Print Culture

New Mexico's newspaper efforts never flourished, in contradistinction to the vibrant press in the United States and the formidable print culture of interior Mexico. A small hand press arrived in Santa Fe in 1834. There are varying accounts of by whom and how it was brought. One legend has it arriving in the cargo of the trader Josiah Gregg, who owned or ordered it and sold it to assembly secretary Ramón Abreu.[91] Another has Abreu bringing it from Mexico for service of the department.[92] Antonio Barreiro put out the first New Mexico newspaper for four weeks in August and November 1834, giving it the tellingly liberal name *El Crepúsculo de la Libertad* (The Dawn of Liberty). Padre Martínez took the press to Taos in November 1835 for his "unflagging efforts" on behalf of his seminary students and the population. Martínez donated it to the Taos community and invited literary contributions. An orthography notebook became the first published text in New Mexico. A primer, a speller, a numbers and syntax booklet, prayer books, matrimonial procedures, and a pamphlet of moral sayings were widely distributed at Martínez's expense.[93]

Accounts have Martínez introducing the press and publishing to Capt. Donaciano Vigil in 1842, and Martínez ran the weekly *La Verdad* (The Truth) for a time. The press moved back to Santa Fe in 1844, where it was used for putting out *La Verdad* under Governor Mariano Chávez. Assemblyman Vigil proposed that the governor start a new paper at government expense so as to publicize the measures enacted by departmental authorities. Padre Martínez, it appears, arranged in 1845 with the American merchant James Magoffin for the department to purchase a press so as to publish official government announcements and proceedings. Governor Chávez agreed, and three months after *La Verdad* closed, *El Payo de Nuevo Méjico*, billed as the "Official Newspaper of the Department of New Mexico under the Government of Mexico," put out several issues.[94]

Robust Local Governance

The department assembly decreed three New Mexico *prefecturas* (districts) in 1844: the Central, Northern, and Southwestern. *Alcaldías* (townships of over a thousand) were governed by an *ayuntamiento* (local council). Santa Fe, Santa Cruz de la Cañada, Alburquerque, Tomé, and Taos were the main alcaldías. A judicial code comparable to the American system of justice set forth civil and criminal laws in the alcaldía. New Mexico was partitioned into two major civil districts: the Río Arriba (northern highlands from La Cienega and Santa Fe north) and the Río Abajo (southern lowland, or middle section of modern New Mexico, from Peña Blanca to Socorro; the far southern section that would sit on the future U.S.-Mexico border would not be integrated with the other two until the middle of the nineteenth century). Each had a prefecture who reported to the governor, and seven smaller district courts served the populace.[95]

The important position of *alcalde mayor* was a locally elected official whose array of responsibilities differed from that of any U.S. local officer.[96] This official served as magistrate in charge of the *corte de primaria instancia* (court of first instance), where criminal and civil cases were litigated. The *corte de segunda instancia* constituted a district court of appeals. That the alcalde and ayuntamiento were locally elected was considered an important mark of the people's sovereignty, "cultivating . . . a sense of belonging to [the] particular province." It also meant that the unsalaried alcalde was subject to the political and military government. His court did not have a jury, he himself handing down judicial decisions.[97]

The alcalde's duties involved keeping order, issuing licenses, serving as trade inspector, and holding the power of confiscating private property as payment of fines. The *juezes de letra* constituted a kind of supreme court. The *juezes de paz* (justices of the peace) were locally elected magistrates of junior and senior status, to whom the alcaldes eventually reported. All foreigners and natives residing outside Santa Fe were required to report to the alcalde within three days of arrival. Justices of the peace were charged with making a complete list of the inhabitants, punishing *drones* (idle ones), and suppressing the vices of immorality and gambling. The Mexican constitution provided for an appointed prefect and subprefects, to serve four years, and a federal receiver of public funds. Municipalities could require licenses and impose fees for various enterprises, including dances, saloons, and gambling establishments.[98]

Two post offices operated in New Mexico, one in Santa Fe, which served as the control center of the department postal system, and another at Tomé in the Río Abajo. The mail went out to Chihuahua twice a month, a thirteen-day trip. New laws and other official notices to the various ministries generally took thirty-three days to arrive in Mexico City. A response typically took two months to arrive, good weather permitting.[99]

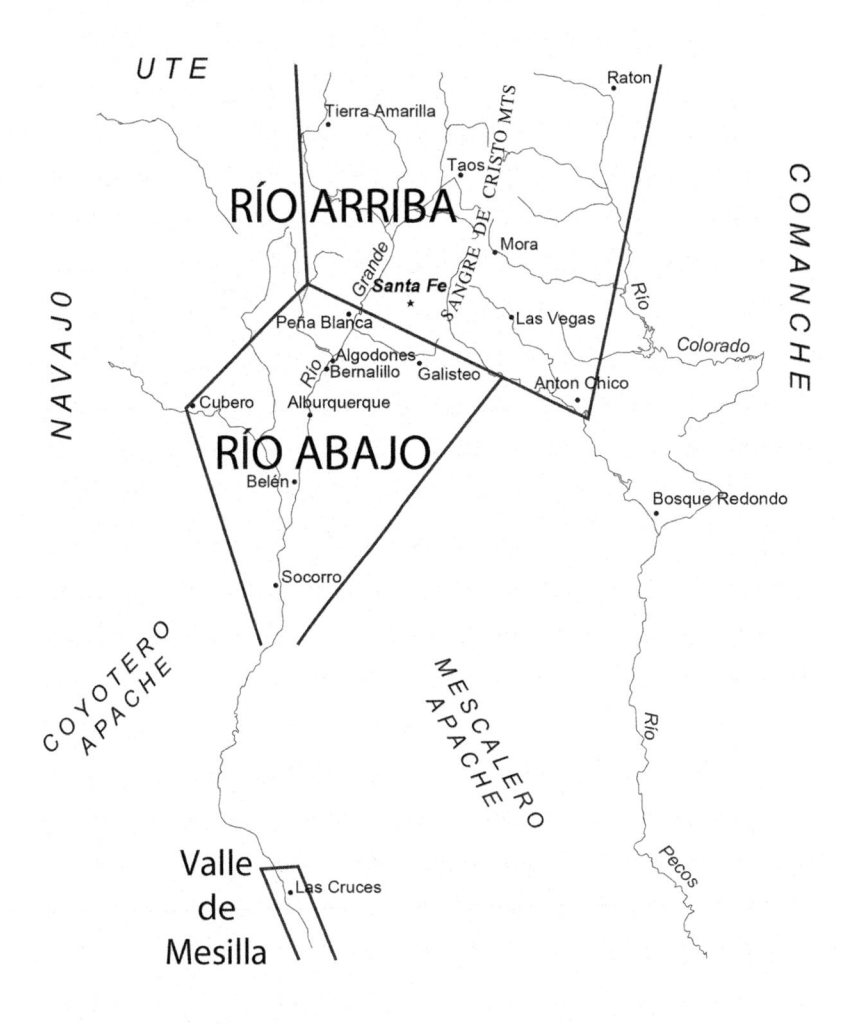

MAP 1. Geopolitical districts (*partidos*) defined in the Mexican period for New Mexico. The bold lines are not official borders. They are intended here only to embrace the extent of Nuevomexicano settlements in early to mid-territorial period. The Las Vegas area is placed in Río Arriba based on political affiliations. Adapted from Giovanni Banfi/Map of New Mexico/Thinkstock (with the assistance of Mark Montoya).

Education, Barely

Scant schooling appeared in New Mexico and the priests dominated it. While nineteen parish schools were noted in 1827, dwindling diocesan resources left only a few still operating by the 1840s.[100] Padre Antonio José Martínez opened schools in Taos and Abiquiú for the training of future priests. Martínez kept a seminary preparatory school open for most of the last twenty years of the Mexican period. Several of his pupils went on to the priesthood.[101] Martínez protégé José Manuel Gallegos, from a large land-owning family, enrolled in the Durango seminary, where his close association with Bishop Zubiría bestirred his nationalism.[102]

The legislative assembly held responsibility for constituting public schools. The goal of public education existed in New Mexico, the institution hardly at all. A primary school law was passed in 1822 and one for secondary schools in 1823. Plans for free schools were to be developed at the local level. Trinidad Barceló, superintendent of education under Governor Antonio Narbona, forwarded a set of Ten Regulations on Education to Taos as prescribed by the Mexican government, which the Taos Village Council endorsed.[103] The assembly journal for 1830 reveals valiant attempts to institute and maintain common schools. Another director of education set forth qualifications for a preceptor, a kind of teacher-superintendent.[104] Success in establishing public schools was modest at best, and regulating truancy proved virtually impossible. New Mexico's congressional deputy closed the schools for lack of funds in 1834. Governors lamented the sad state of education in the late Mexican period and made some attempt to construct schools.[105] An 1840 census found eighteen teachers in New Mexico who were not necessarily connected to a school.[106]

The few "select" schools that existed were run by "subscription." Parents of the landed elite paid teachers to educate their children in small classroom settings. English language instruction was sometimes provided.[107] Parents commonly educated their young at home.[108] The intellectually gifted, informed, and philosophical Donaciano Vigil had no formal schooling but was taught to read and write by his father, who also taught the children of neighbors. Vigil had "the most intimate knowledge of the Spanish and Mexican real property law," which served him well in his position of military secretary under Governor Armijo. Vigil knew more than any other Nuevomexicano about American institutions through sheer personal study, an hombre de bien befitted.[109] Father Martínez furthered his education by joining the seminary in Durango, where he fostered his "love for letters." Three members of the Ortiz family—Juan Felipe, Fernando and Rafael—were homeschooled in the late Mexican period.[110] The priests, starting with the missionaries and followed by the secularists, took responsibility for educating upper-class youth.[111] The experience of Diego Archuleta shows that some, especially if ambitious for an education, could go to the Durango seminary without the intent of becoming a priest.[112]

Agrarian Hard Life

The economy of northern Mexico developed after independence from Spain in the expansion of cattle and sheep husbandry and land settlement.[113] Yet as already noted, extremes of wealth and poverty characterized Mexico. Money in New Mexico circulated from the salary of the governor's office and the small garrison of soldiers in Santa Fe.[114] Village economy relied on irrigated agriculture, sheep and cattle, handicraft production including the weaving of *jergas* (wool rugs), hunting, trade with the Plains Indians for furs and hides, and the cultivation of wine grapes and making of *aguardiente* (brandy).[115]

New Mexico's terrain set limits on economic development. Soils of the region, described as "poor and barren," or "too rough and sterile," provided little surplus forage for the development of animal industry or large-scale farming.[116] The wide Río Abajo river bottoms from Peña Blanca south to the Socorro area were productive, but as a visitor remarked, the want of fuel made "even that best district unattractive." Col. George McCall estimated that while 124,760 acres were under cultivation, another 303,240 acres of cultivable land went vacant. Little timber was to be had except at high elevations. Indigenous fruits were modest and were not given concentrated cultivation. Little development of mining had recently occurred, and in 1850 at least mine localities were largely unknown, although McCall saw promise in mining to provide for the future wealth and development of the area. An American observer commented on the lack of industriousness: "There are myriads of wild fowl—geese, brant, sand-cranes; the people seem never even to molest them!"[117]

Importantly, as one American asserted, the "incursions and marauding of the Indians" had "destroyed any enterprise the people ever had." From the Mexican perspective, the main nemeses were the Navajo, who raided settlements from the west; Jicarilla Apaches descending from the north; Mescalero Apaches stealthing up from the south; Utes from the northwest; and Comanches entering from the east. The complaint of raiding serving to curtail Mexican and Pueblo horticulture and ranching, or keeping them stagnant, would be commonly expressed until the 1880s.[118]

Popular Elements

Poverty prevailed in New Mexico. One observer remarked on how "very little [was] being required, apparently, to feed the people upon."[119] A town appeared to another in "a ruinous and dilapidated appearance, and no doubt has seen better days."[120] Debt peonage was responsible for much of this. Americans likened it to a worsened condition of slavery.[121] The expanded sheep market and management of large flocks brought about the *partido* system. Owners contracted sheep out to individuals or families in return for additional sheep at the end of the mating season. Many formerly indebted *peónes* entered into partido contracts. Other *partidarios* were liberated from social ties in neighboring villages.[122] The partido ossified into a hardened class distinction. Owners freed from managing livestock augmented their wealth by other means, such as grape cultivation for high-demand wine.[123] But the need for a medium of exchange in cash-poor New Mexico pushed the peónes themselves to dependence on the *patrón* (boss-owner). The peón put himself at risk of lifelong bondage for a small debt without provisions of support for infirmity or old age by putting up private collateral to guarantee repayment.[124] A peón partidario incurred other potential dangers. Plains tribes stepped up their raiding toward the end of the Mexican period, killing and stealing livestock. Many herders absorbed "immense losses" and could not repay their advances. They fell into debt, facilitated by the increased flow of cash into the local economy.[125] Many a peón lived on the private land of the patrón, or in communities on grants to *empresarios*, which were large holdings that individuals received for their close association with the governor. The empresario allowed lower-class settlers to establish communities, two hundred families being the guide, a system that fostered paternalism and the ritual observance of privilege.[126]

It is difficult to tell what portion of the population consisted of peón debtors. One officer of the American army reported in the 1850s that they constituted "the most numerous *class*" (emphasis his).[127]

Ernest Gellner defines agrarian society in part by its social segmentation. "Economic classes tend to be separated," he notes.[128] A distinct segment known as the *poblador* (yeoman small-holder) class existed in New Mexico apart from the patrón-peón relation. The pobladores derived from the Spanish crown's need to hold off the incursions of other foreign empires. New Mexico served as an anchor for a claim to territories flung hundreds of miles in all directions from the main towns along the Río Grande. Poblador families staked out ranching and farming settlements across the high mountains from Santa Fe northward. Settlers fortified themselves into the designated *plaza* (town square) to hold off the constant threat of Indian raids.[129]

Pobladores, also known as *vecinos* (citizen neighbors), secured title to their lands by petitioning for a communal land grant. The communal grant, the vernacular *merced,* survived as a Spanish colonial institution. Individual families received plots along the river where they built homes and cultivated crops for domestic usage. Owners in a system of customary partible inheritance treated their home lots as private property and could sell them. The tract extending out from the settlement, often involving thousands of acres, belonged to no individual. The open pasturage was reserved for all the heirs of the particular grant, and as communal property, could not be sold.[130] Compared to the American system of private real estate, the communal grant was "a study in contrasts," as one historian puts it.[131] Hundreds of land grants were awarded in New Mexico during its colonial and Mexican periods. Many were made permanent by displacing tribal communities from their ancestral homes.[132] In all, more than nine million acres of commons came into being. Over sixty community grants, involving millions of acres, were active in New Mexico in the 1840s.[133]

Not all poblador communities were formed through communal grants, which reflected in a way Gellner's point regarding class differentiation in the agrarian society. *Empresario* grants were outlying lands awarded to individuals in exchange for an agreement to settle two hundred families and establish a colony to prevent foreign encroachment on the province. The empresario retained title to the land and could sell parcels for cash. He or she had to reconvey title to at least two hundred individuals if the grant was not to be abandoned. Empresarios were awarded in both the Río Arriba and Río Abajo.[134] Also reflecting Gellnerian segmentation, Mexican land tenure supported private property. Private real estate was acquired by privatizing communal Pueblo and vecino grants or by occupying the open domain.[135]

Some pobladores were made beholden by the 1840s to upper-class land holders in partido contracts.[136] They engaged in buffalo hunting and trade with several of the mobile tribes in the Río Arriba and eastern plains sections.[137] Predominant poblador economics rested on subsistence farming and livestock husbandry.[138] American observers regarded the farming methods of the pobladores as acutely premodern. A commonly heard refrain concerned the old-fashioned implements used to eke out the yield of small and irregular parcels. The contemporary observer Lewis H. Garrard noted the plows "of the primitive kind—the same as those used by the Egyptians thousands of years ago—being but the fork of a small tree, with only one handle."[139] More ungenerous witnesses attributed a "natural indolence" to the common folk and shook their heads at Mexican refusal to work beyond acquiring the pittance necessary to survive or gamble away.[140]

Economic segmentation affected vecino pobladores. Some village niches specialized in crops that others did not. Newer villages in the lower plains depended more on livestock than on crops. The rancho villages were originally economically self-sufficient. As currency and goods increased through the covered-wagon trails, some folk rose from subsistence farmers to patrón employers or loaners of money. The traditional communal system continued in some communities, while in others an internal class distinction arose, especially in the high plains adjacent to the middle Río Grande region, which tended to foster larger private ranching enterprises apart from the smaller, defensively oriented and corporate communities in the higher elevations. Neighboring villages were sometimes unequally divided between a patrón class in one and a larger, poorer laboring element in another, although families from both stocked land with their herds.[141] A marked class hierarchy appeared in the larger settlements such as Alburquerque, Santa Fe, and Tomé.[142]

Socioeconomic complexity also stemmed from multiple relations with the numerous original nations. The Mexican economy throughout the eighteenth century and into the Mexican period emerged suffused with the exchange of livestock, women, and children, involving Comanche, Ute, Apache, Navajo, Kiowa, and other nonsedentary groups. The system of exchange, necessary for frontier survival, had both military and mercantile aspects. Theft and retaliatory raids resulted in the violent taking of captives to be used as slaves on all sides—ricos, pobladores, and Indians. On the other hand, sheep, cattle, horses, women, and children were sold in a frontier market. New Mexico officials negotiated peace settlements with the Comanches to establish friendly trade relations, opening up important economic activity among pobladores and egalitarian economic relations among the villages. The practices expanded to include the Navajo in the "pastoral borderlands" west of the main Río Abajo settlements in the Valencia community. Mutual raiding by Indians and Mexicans formed a constant feature of life on the frontier. James F. Brooks calls it as much of a "cultural exchange" as the trade of resources.[143]

A lower-order class of domestic servants sprang from this redistribution. Slavery was abolished in Mexico in 1824, but New Mexico's servitude amounted to a chattel system, given the ability to purchase and sell captives.[144] Women and children pulled from their tribal cultures became permanent members of poblador and rico households. An American observed, "I arrived at breakfast time at the straggling village of Valencia, and went to the house of Señor Otero. . . . It was Sunday morning; I encountered first an Indian slave woman, carrying to the chamber of a young man, on a silver salver, chocolate and sponge cake, which they take at rising."[145]

Captives not sold off or stolen often assimilated into the cultural base of the vecino and rico settlements. Captured or ransomed Plains Indians outside vecino and rico domiciles constituted an identifiable segment, the famed *genízaros*. Genízaros were Indians captured in battle or acquired through market exchange. Their status was quite low in a quasi-caste order. In the debt peonage between 1700 and 1880 "some five thousand members of plains or pastoral Indian groups entered New Mexican society as *indios de rescate* [rescued Indians], *indios genízaros*, *criados* [servants] or *huerfanos* [orphans] primarily through the artifice of 'ransom' by colonial purchase. Ostensibly the development of ransom would be retired by ten to twenty years of service to the redeemers, after which these individuals would become vecinos." In practice "these people appear to have experienced their bondage on a continuum that ranged from near slavery to familial incorporation, but few shed the stigma of servility."[146]

Original genízaros lived in segregated sections in the Plaza de los Jarales near Belen and the Barrio de Analco in Santa Fe. Some families resided alongside vecino neighbors in Ranchos de Taos and San Juan de los Caballeros. Groups of genízaros received land grants in time near Belen, Ranchos de Taos, Las Trampas, Abiquiú, Ojo Caliente, San Miguel de Carnué, San José de las Huertas, Socorro, San Miguel del Vado, and Anton Chico. These settlements made for buffers on the frontier between the plains bands and the villages in the Río Grande Valley. Genízaros petitioned for their own places, as land acquisition opened a route out from under the rule of the upper classes. They organized to protest incursions on their communal lands by colonial *estancieros* (estate holders). Groups from these elements were converted into military units for use in the constant "raiding and revenge" pattern of interaction with some of the Indians, participating at times in the capture of slaves.[147]

Genízaro racial and cultural distinctiveness eroded in the Mexican period, when much of the Nuevomexicano populace became more uniform. The cultural economy of captives and women and children ransomed across cultural borders contributed to the process of *mestizaje*. European and Indian bloodlines churned out a complex, albeit marginal, hybrid cultural formation.[148] The warring and peaceful exchange of women and children continued between Nuevomexicanos and tribes up to the 1870s. The crossing of individuals from the latter to the former sustained a genízaro demographic, indicated by one estimate of 3.2 percent of the settled population in 1860 being Navajo slave captives.[149]

Cultural Segmentation

Complex pre-industrial social formations endowed with complicated divisions of labor were "in a way confirmed or even sanctified, by great cultural diversity," Gellner notes. Linguistic, sartorial, gastronomic, ritual, and doctrinal variety abounded. People expressed and recognized their identity "in these idiosyncratic features of their social station."[150] New Mexico's cultural fabric evinced a Gellnerian cultural segmentation.

Rico families enjoyed domestic insularity. American arrivals noted their relatively fancy domiciles in the Río Abajo. The one-story "mansions" were thickly plastered and whitewashed *haciendas* with spacious courtyards, apartments, storerooms, offices, and "provision for all the requirements of the family, the farm, and for trade."[151] Rico families and professional men mostly were generally literate. Archives such as the Donaciano Vigil Papers at the New Mexico State Records Center and Archives show private letter writing among themselves. Gellner states that the "overwhelming" majority of the population in pre-industrial agrarian society lived as agricultural producers, possessing "neither the means nor the need for literacy, or for the art of abstract communication." Only those of the higher strata, and not all of them, were able to use language in an abstract manner. In agro-literate society, "literate high cultures co-exist with illiterate low or folk cultures."[152]

The high literate/low nonliterate distinction held though not so starkly among pastoral Nuevomexicanos. Members of the economic elite had their family libraries, while illiteracy prevailed in the rest of the population.[153] Villagers kept written documents for business such as petitioning for grants of commons and to establish communities when their old ones grew overpopulated.[154] Handwritten records dating from colonial times were staples for all kinds of administrative functions, including the keeping of legal standards for the all-important land grants and the minutes of the territorial assembly.[155] Curates and missionaries dealt in documents, but no lawyers practiced and magistrates often could not read.[156]

Mexican intellectuals and political leaders, like so many other national liberation movements, sought to establish their nationhood by casting off identification with their erstwhile colonial master. New Mexico joined Mexico in 1827 in banning Spaniards from living in the territory, clergy included.[157] Certain exemptions to the expulsion probably obtained. Mexico's pluralism and embryonic national identity resulted in remnants of *hispanidad*, identification with the old Iberian or Spanish creole line, persisting in various parts of Mexico long after national independence.[158] "Spaniard" did not disappear as a self-identifier among the economic elites and political officials of New Mexico. Capt. Donaciano Vigil asked the 1846 assembly to request from the central Mexican government arms and munitions so that the "Spanish race"—that is, the "descendants of the ancient discoverers and conquerors of this immense continent," who had "not degenerated in New Mexico"—could protect itself from increasing Indian depredations.[159]

The identity of being "Mexican" predominated in the populace after Mexico's national independence. The elements lower than the reigning upper class rooted their social identities in "family relations, one's native community, one's class," and a "unique" dynamic of Pueblo-Spanish ethnic relations at the village level.[160]

An important religious distinction held in lower poblador culture. A lay brotherhood called Los Hermanos Piadosa de Nuestro Padre Jesus Nazareno took root shortly before or after 1800 among the hamlets and villages of northern New Mexico. Los Hermanos represented the peasant version of the *cofradía* Latin American institution, a local "factor of unity," as it has been described, "because it congregated the populace around the cult of the patron saint of the community." In New Mexico, they were popularly called *penitentes* for their flagellant practices during Holy Week. The brotherhood's origins are debated. Some researchers favor a Third Order of St. Francis explanation; others see it the result of diffusion from Latin America; still others consider it an indigenous innovation.[161] Local chapters organized on the *morada* (chapel) flourished in the context of a distant church and parish system.[162] Once independent Mexico expelled the European-born clergy, a shortage of church resources resulted in inadequate spiritual services to the village folk. The brotherhood became a community force and an instrument of protection in far-flung settlements, providing necessary religious and mutual aid.[163] Church and other authorities in greater Latin America often attacked the cofradías for their alleged indiscretions and for standing outside the religious hierarchy. And so it was that the bishopric of Durango condemned and prohibited the Nuevomexicano Hermanos prior to the American conquest. Bishop Zubiría sought to repress the striking penitential devotions as violations of church decorum. The bishop applauded Father Antonio José Martínez's efforts to curtail the "excesses of body and soul" in the Taos area. Zubiría censured the *hermandad* for acting without ideological legitimacy, but he failed to eradicate it.[164]

It bespoke Gellnerian differentiation that not all village men belonged to Los Hermanos. Strict requirements for recruitment and membership obtained.[165] Not all Nuevomexicano villages had moradas or were "solidly penitente."[166] Penitential rites required specialized knowledge of Passion plays. Two subregional variations shaped brotherhood membership. More moradas existed in the villages of the rugged Río Arriba high country than the gentler Río Abajo flatlands. And the order was "strongest in the more isolated areas of the older core of Hispanic settlements," even in the Río Arriba.[167]

New Mexico's agrarian upper class shared little culture with the lower orders. The men from wealthier families "seem rarely to have joined the brotherhood." The Río Abajo had fewer moradas. Priests could more readily access its parishes. The brotherhood was a strong indication of poblador social independence. The peón class of sheepherders and servants under control of the rico patrones labored in a dependent state, preventing their integration into the activities of the brotherhood with their oppositional attitude toward authority.[168]

Standard priestly duties reinforced religious differentiation. Mass and confession tended to be restricted to the more concentrated areas such as Santa Cruz, Santa Fe, Abiquiú, San Miguel, Alburquerque, and Tomé. The parish differed organizationally from the morada particularly as the new Republic secularized the provincial missions and replaced the Franciscans with nonsectarian priests.[169] It is important, finally, that, even as the moradas spread after 1800, they tended to remain heavily localized within their disparate ecological settings. No central organization to administer all the chapters would come into being until the twentieth century.[170]

Economic, Cultural, and Liberal Diffusions

In the two decades prior to its U.S. annexation, "traditional" New Mexico underwent what historians call the "Americanization of the Far Mexican Frontier," the "Americanization of New Mexico," and New Mexico's "Conquest by Merchants."[171] Mexican New Mexico was in a manner of speaking elongated toward the United States. The United States had been developing according to its "integrative revolution" since 1787.[172] It thus embarked on a broad, seemingly inexorable, movement westward.[173] It doubled its territorial holdings twenty years after achieving independence and expanded its land base to three times its original size by the mid-1800s.[174] The Mexican republic aided and abetted American expansion by removing Spain's protectionist policies, liberalizing its immigration laws (partly to quiet the American passion for taking Texas), and opening its borders to international trade.[175]

What it meant for Nuevomexicano and American relations proved dialectical. Friendly, mutually accommodating interactions, freshly consensual on the order of liberal necessity, developed on one hand. On the other, sectors of Nuevomexicanos put up bright social and conflictive boundaries with what they saw as ugly *gringos*.

Contact within Consensus

The easy arrival of American citizens, European immigrants, and French-Canadian entrepreneurs amounted to what one historian calls an "invasion."[176] Indeed, New Mexico and its surrounds constituted what the critical theorist Mary Louise Pratt calls a "contact zone"; that is, a social space "where disparate cultures meet, clash, and grapple with each other." Pratt points out that contact zones often involved "highly asymmetrical relations of domination and subordination," but they also brought relations of social accord into being. In the New Mexican contact zone of the early nineteenth century, many a male outsider came to stay. The Mexican Colonization Decree, which was meant to have foreigners remain rather than extract natural resources and leave, eased immigrant settlement and naturalization.[177] The first American petition for Mexican naturalization appeared in 1824.[178] Some 550 strangers were resident in the department in 1846. Many lived on ranches, assisted by Mexican federal law that permitted them to own over 4,000 acres for farming and livestock.[179]

Marriage with Mexican women enabled Americans and other foreigners to gain control of millions of acres of land by inheriting the real estate belonging to the families of their wives, by petitioning for land grants with Nuevomexicano intermediaries, and by speculation.[180] The New Mexican officials shifted their spatial strategy after 1821 with the opening of the Santa Fe Trail. Multiterm governor Manuel Armijo awarded large parcels to American and Canadian settlers.[181] The American settler-speculator C. John Furnier put in a request to the departmental assembly in 1845 for a special court to protect mining interests in the department. Assemblymen passed the measure, and the governor applauded the effort of Americans to "foment the spirit of enterprise in all its branches in relation to the riches of the land."[182]

Americans came in for "Latinization" as one historian puts it.[183] The

Colonization Decree required permanent settlers to convert to Catholicism. Many of those seeking homes in New Mexico were Catholic, mostly of French and Canadian origin, ready to enter into religious affairs. Non-Catholic Euroamerican immigrants generally remained on the religious sidelines.[184]

Mexico's northern frontier underwent a market revolution on the back of immigration. Overland merchants were gladdened by the news of Mexico accepting free trade with the United States. New Mexico Governor Facundo Melgares informed William Becknell, known as the "father" of the Santa Fe trade, of his desire to cooperate in commerce, which up to that time had been a trickle.[185] American wagons supplied New Mexico with merchandise, Taos nativos favoring their quality and low prices. The Robidoux brothers brought the first Missouri train of merchandise into Fernandez de Taos in 1822, a year after the customs office was established in Santa Fe. In 1824 the first large train of merchandise arrived in Santa Fe. Henry Colews & Bro. established the first American Mercantile House there in 1826. Twenty more Americans opened business houses in Taos, Santa Fe, San Miguel del Bado, Anton Chico, and other locales.[186]

The process of setting up a frontier trade went through fits and starts, sometimes because of Euroamerican racial prejudice against Mexicans, called "Spaniards."[187] Americans who had lived in New Mexico for a time finalized mercantile posts in the Taos area, and trade soon took off. Mexico welcomed it, for an economic debacle caused national expenditures earmarked for the northern departments to fall by 1.5 million pesos.[188] Some 1,500 trailblazers arduously carried $1.5 million in merchandise in 700 wagons to markets at the end of the Santa Fe Trail between 1826 and 1835. By the 1830s, one historian notes, "scores of fur trappers had already discovered Taos and were dealing with its inhabitants in a rapidly developing profitable business."[189] The $15,000 value of merchandise imported to New Mexico in 1822 doubled in two years and doubled again by 1826. It expanded thirtyfold to half a million dollars in two decades. New Mexico's economy, according to Reséndez, was "radically" affected by the opening of the Santa Fe Trail as it steadily "gravitated toward the orbit of the expanding American economy." The shift accelerated the passage from sheep husbandry and subsistence farming to a "dramatic reorientation toward the United States."[190]

Bent's Fort, established in 1830 by the Taos traders Charles Bent, William Bent, and Ceran St. Vrain, stood on the southeast plain of Colorado like a bold American temple. Massively filled with the necessities to support the trading system, it was a "citadel in the wilderness," a hub of market operations into New Mexico, Wyoming, Utah, Colorado, Arizona, Texas, Oklahoma, Kansas, and Nebraska. Bent's Fort played host to an assortment of fur trappers, Taos traders, government officials, Missouri mountain men, Mexicans, and Great Plains and New Mexico Indians.[191] A small group of newcomers, their partnerships extending from Bent's Fort into Taos and Santa Fe, came into control of New Mexico's incipient commercial system, including the Bent Brothers, St. Vrain, and David Waldo. By 1846 Waldo had generated a million dollars of merchandise and netted a profit of $400,000 by outfitting 375 wagons, using 1,700 mules and 2,000 oxen, and employing 500 men.[192]

It would be very important for coming international events that entrepreneurial Nuevomexicanos got in on the economic revolution. They had sent representatives for an official visit to St. Louis in 1821 to see about bringing the trade to their homeland. Governor Bartolomé Baca's caravan, carrying $1,500 worth of goods, hit the trail. Euroamerican and especially French domination of the commercial line was soon matched by a Nuevomexicano movement. The overland trade provided an expanded source of goods for Mexican merchants to trade in California and interior Mexico by the end of the 1830s. An initially fluctuating volume of shipments expanded after 1839. Ninety sophisticated caravans moved to the eastern industrial centers and back to Mexico in 1844.[193]

New Mexico *paisanos* became engrossed in the "spirit of mercantile capitalism," as Donaciano Vigil recalled. Nuevomexicanos came to control various branches of the regional trading system.[194] No better example of congruence between foreign entities exists than that between the rico livestock business and American frontier capitalism. By the 1840s New Mexico imposed a charge of $500 on each wagon entering Santa Fe. "This added expense encouraged traders to use larger wagons and to establish friendlier relations with local officials."[195] Reséndez analyzes the customs receipts for 1843 and finds Nuevomexicanos undermining the virtual monopoly of the foreign-born merchants on exports to Mexico. Mexicans "shrewdly" made the transition from "land-based, sheep-raising enterprises to the world of international and domestic trade." The New Mexico Department gained rights from the federal government to export its products duty free in 1845 for another ten years. By 1846 prominent nativo families regularly drove their own covered wagon trains filled with Mexican products to the United States, establishing stores and warehouses with superior American goods for New Mexico provision and wholesaling American products farther south into Mexico. The traditional base of rico wealth—sheep running, peón exploitation, civil taxation, and limited mining—expanded with development of the Santa Fe trade. Mexican residents of the frontier "no longer found themselves at the terminus but at the crossroads of new trading routes originating in Louisiana and Missouri and began participating as international merchants in their own right."[196]

Legion did certain family names become as emblems of Nuevomexicano commercialism. Among the illustrious, the sons of Tomás Chávez y Castillo took large caravans of goods to the United States and drove thousands of sheep south to interior Mexico. Antonio José Otero and his kin imported merchandise from the United States and sold sheep in Mexico. Three-time governor Manuel Armijo combined sheep exporting to northern Mexico with the sale of domestic and foreign goods.[197]

Market revolution was hastened by the fact that it took about six weeks for a Missouri wagon train to reach Santa Fe, a much shorter time than for one to arrive from interior Mexico with its inferior and more expensive goods.[198] The shift raised the economic fortunes of those below the sheep oligarchs. Conductors who transported and handled shipments leveraged earnings to become owners themselves. Muleteers, packers, tailors, and seamstresses profited from the circulation of goods.[199] Opportunity for establishing footholds in the freighting business fell to military officers, lending them mobility and capacity for accumulation based on the covered wagon trade and other entrepreneurial activities.[200] Capt. Donaciano Vigil and Lt. Col. Mariano Chávez exploited the Santa Fe trade to boost their modest and undependable military salaries.[201] Lodging, restaurant, and entertainment businesses sprang up. The expanding saloon business made a remarkable woman, Gertrudis Barceló, one of the wealthiest persons in the entire department in both cash and property.[202] One historian notes that the financial records of Manuel Álvarez "give testimony to the social status of their sex in Mexico's northern province. Not only were women allowed to negotiate their own business and receive credit, some of them were literate enough to record their own dealings." That they "crossed social and sexual barriers"—that is, the constraints of narrow domestic roles and patriarchal norms of honor and virtue in traditional Mexico—offers testimony to the effects of this trend of economic modernization.[203]

In addition, revenues for the departmental administration augmented. Import revenues supplied nearly 70 percent of the departmental budget by the 1830s.[204] As earlier noted, New Mexico levied a $500 duty on each U.S. wagon load in the early 1840s. The American traders disparaged Governor Armijo as a corrupt tyrant, alleging that he arbitrarily imposed the fee without regard to the size or value of the goods. Research finds that corruption "quickly dominated the system, and by the 1840s an 'understanding' had been reached: the fee was divided into three parts, one for the government, one for the customs official, and the last retained by the trader."[205] The levy brought anywhere from $81,000 to half a million dollars a year to the public coffers, making it clear why Armijo sought to monopolize the Santa Fe trade.[206] The duties on precious metals, mules, buffalo rugs, furs, and wool exported to the United States provided other revenues.[207] "The continuance of the trade was a necessity for the very existence of the government of New Mexico," notes one observer, "since its officials and employees were paid largely out of the funds derived from the duties and fees collected from the Santa Fe traders." Commerce receipts also supported New Mexico's soldiers.[208]

The availability of hard currency and loads of dry goods began to institute a "new ethic: materialism." The shops that newly bedecked the Santa Fe and Taos plazas, mostly American-kept, encouraged a desire for consumables. An assortment of miscellaneous and cheap household items appeared, associated with a new industrialism—cotton goods, cutlery, and light hardware; "glassware; medicines; hardware such as nails, needles, screws, brass, iron, chisels, files, hatchets, saws, and locks and chains; coffee grinders; guns, knives, swords; items of clothing such as caps and hats, aprons, shoes; finished dry goods and assortments of groceries."[209] Alcohol and new medicines became fashionable, the latter spurred by the American concern over the lack of medical services on the frontier. Americans brought French champagne and imported wines and set up distilleries with advanced methods of production.[210] Not only did the trade provide employment to Mexicans as traders and freighters; it opened the villages to new forms of economic exchanges, providing desired consumer goods "while stimulating a secondary set of economic activities in the service areas (i.e., food, services and supplies)." Lewis Garrard's modernist eye foresaw the American plows imported by the store of St. Vrain & Co. teaching the Mexican farmers to learn "something from these models."[211]

A key measure of cross-national social consensus flowered from market aggrandizement. Arrival of American trade caravans proved festive affairs. The spectacles of products and foreigners caused a "great deal of bustle and excitement among the natives," the pioneer merchant Josiah Gregg witnessed. Merchandising encouraged socialization. Nuevomexicanos could have pulled inward in the face of foreign agents. Instead they found financial considerations a stronger bond than national affinity. The relatively free ability to associate closely with the United States followed from New Mexico's de facto autonomy and the prior commercial experience of wealthy land owners. "It is small wonder that minds on both sides of the great prairies were stimulated," a historian notes. "As Mexican commercial ventures expanded in cooperation with traders from the United States, the interests of the Mexican and American mercantile groups began to merge," claims another. The saloon of Gertrudis Barceló, with its constant offerings of gambling and *fandangos* (dances), proved a micro contact zone unto itself. As historian Deena González notes, Barceló did more than accommodate foreigners by inviting them to gamble. "She furthered their adjustment to Santa Fé by bringing them into a setting that required their presence and money. At the saloon, the men were introduced to Spanish-Mexican music, habits, and humor. They could judge the locals firsthand and could observe a community's values and habits through this single activity. After they had a few drinks, their initial fears and prejudices gradually yielded to the relaxed, sociable atmosphere of the gambling hall."[212]

Americanization also impacted literacy. Arrivals brought cargos of books, some for themselves, others to sell. It is said that Josiah Gregg brought more than a thousand. Well-to-do families began to acquire impressive libraries and to read widely. In no small part did this reflect the replication of a certain American cultural domain, the "assumptions and aspirations of a whole society" that pioneers brought to the rural West.[213]

The impact of the market revolution served to "rivet" New Mexico to the American economy. Reséndez points to a contributing cause, the common "disjuncture" in Latin American frontier regions between market and state. The Mexican political system failed to develop centralized control over an expanding capitalism, the source of which was the United States.[214]

Diffusion and liberal consensus resonated in the reception that key Nuevomexicanos gave Americans. Many ordinary and well-to-do Mexicans favored *norteamericanos*. The officers and soldiers of the New Mexican and American military commands proved cordial in their assignments as guardians of the merchant trade wagons. Mexicans made friends of Maj. Bennet Riley and Capt. Philip St. George Cooke, and each left his mark on New Mexico society. Col. Antonio Viscarra and Pvt. Santiago Abreu sustained working and social relationships with Americans. That Capt. Donaciano Vigil particularly came to know many an American settler and trader would prove vital in the American conquest.[215]

Compared to Mexican federal agents, local government representatives were "far more supportive of fluid and open relations" with the United States. "Frontier officials not only had to take into account the wishes of a native elite that understood perfectly well the importance of liberal commercial and immigration policies, but also had to accommodate an increasingly prominent foreign-born community whose economic prosperity translated into commensurate political muscle." New Mexico authorities invested heavily in the trade, dating from Governor Bartolomé Baca in the early 1820s and the governors and treasurers of the 1830s to Manuel Armijo, the governor who would be in office at the time of the American invasion. As they benefited from Mexico's economic liberalism, their financial interest in the trade included partnerships with Americans in the driving of export wagons to the United States. Governor Armijo reportedly "learned to respect the power and ability of the American people."[216]

Social relations went deeper still. Classic liberalism regards intermarriage a significant facilitator of cross-ethnic communication, establishing complementary habits for modern forms of sociation.[217]

An American's union with a Mexican woman facilitated personal acceptance in Mexican society. In one report, 239 Euroamerican men were married to Nuevomexicanas in 1850, about 2 percent of Mexican women who intermarried.[218] Rebecca Craver's path-breaking work finds 90 percent of the cross marriages involving individuals "of modest circumstances" who embarked on family life on the New Mexico frontier in obscurity.[219] Ordinary Nuevomexicanos became accustomed to the presence of the proverbial gringo. Some of the 10 percent that involved women from rico families became politically strategic liaisons. Key Americans married New Mexican women, or cohabited with them, including Charles Bent, perhaps the most important figure in Santa Fe Trail activity, and Kit Carson, the famous Indian scout. Romance figured in these cross-cultural arrangements, although self-serving motivations could have dominated. According to the Mexican Colonization Decree of 1823, marriage to a Mexican citizen spelled virtual naturalization. As David Weber observed, these were the kinds of connections to be expected among "marginal" border peoples whose loyalties are modified by emerging economic, social, and cultural interests.[220]

Rico elements underwent a cultural shift in this contact zone. Many learned English, spent leisure time in the United States, and consumed American household products.[221] High status families drifted toward identification with the United States by sending sons to American schools, especially to the Jesuit Saint Louis University. Certain young Nuevomexicanos, educated in American schools, would go on to play important political roles once New Mexico became an American territory; Miguel Antonio Otero, José Francisco Perea, and José Francisco Chávez counted among them.[222]

The cultural historian Douglas Comer points out that the U.S. "culture of modernity" infiltrated New Mexico in the preconquest days such that whole "new identities" formed. Governor José Antonio Chávez's 1830 report to the Mexican minister of interior referenced New Mexicans who valued commercial relations with Americans so much that they favored a North American takeover of their department.[223] Mexico City officials feared Nuevomexicanos captured by American political ideas such that they might not resist if Americans made a move to appropriate New Mexico and California. Governor Manuel Armijo warned Mexico's minister of war in 1840 that because of New Mexico's sour economic condition, rico members of the "American party" could not be counted on for financial assistance. Only the clergy "exhibited patriotism toward their country during this crucial period."[224]

One Nuevomexicano imaginary hailed political liberalism under U.S. influence. An editorial in *El Crepúsculo de la Libertad*, for example, stated: "The reign of brute force has been replaced by that of reason. . . . We can be sure that the Americans will not take our lands with bullets . . . their weapons are others. They are their industry, their ideas of liberty and independence. The stars of the capitol of the North will shine without a doubt even more brightly in New Mexico where the darkness is most dense due to the deplorable state in which the Mexican government has left it."[225] Editor and owner Antonio Barreiro clearly suggested a future of effective civic modernity for New Mexico under U.S. tutelage a decade before the actual American conquest.

Craver sees unions between enterprising Americans and prominent Mexican families in "collusion" on the eve of the American conquest to safeguard the economic and political positions of both. Donaciano Vigil ruminated in an 1843 letter to Governor Armijo about the inability of Mexico to achieve true liberal principles. Vigil looked kindly on Texas for having fought a war of independence with Mexico "to rid herself of an abominable tyranny." An 1845 Missouri newspaper reported that Governor Armijo had recently hosted a number of American traders and in his toasting of them "manifested in the strongest terms his wish for the peace and welfare of the two countries." If war were declared, "there would be no fighting by the people of New Mexico."[226]

Resistance and Contact

Consensus did not constitute the entire story of nativo-newcomer relations prior to the U.S. military invasion. Nuevomexicano acceptance of matters foreign in what they witnessed as the transformation of their land into an international contact zone was far from universal. Within the population as a whole, "ambivalent loyalties" sprang from the Mexicans' frontier encounter with incoming Americans and Europeans. Some Tejanos (Texans), accepting American nationalism as theirs and rejecting the centralist government in Mexico, joined Euroamericans who led the movement to have Texas secede from Mexico in 1834–36, while others opposed it in defense of

Mexican nationalism. If a "cooperative fusion" between Nuevomexicanos and Americans evolved at certain levels, a centrifugal development stemming from certain destructive activities of the American incursion led to Nuevomexicano discontent.[227]

American newcomers thus did not cut a uniform figure. A "different breed" of American, the Tejano, sparked nativo resentment to certain outsiders. Anglo-Texans were implicated in the problems that led up to the internal New Mexican revolt against Governor Albino Pérez.[228] Reports filtered in during 1840 that Tejanos were preparing to expand their independence movement by taking control of New Mexico. Agents traveled to Santa Fe to see about organizing a Texan county. Texas President Mirabeau Lamar, motivated in part by the profitable Santa Fe trade, attempted to convince New Mexicans to affix their land to Texas. Vicar Juan Felipe Ortiz, sensing the threat of this Anglo-Protestant power to his historic Catholic enclave and national pride, issued two circulars to his priests and parishioners, warning of the Protestant encroachment.[229] The American consul in Santa Fe took the brunt of hostility. Insults were hurled at him and foreign-born traders suspected of being Texas sympathizers, including Charles Bent, owner of Bent's Fort and one of the richest merchants on the Santa Fe Trail.[230]

The Texas Republic made its imperial move in 1841. Approximately four hundred Tejanos appeared in New Mexico with orders to seize the department, or at least the portion extending to the Río Grande, which the Texas Republic claimed as its national territory, and to establish a new government to join with Texas. Nuevomexicanos easily repulsed the invaders. The prisoners were marched out of the territory to Mexico City, a number of them dying on the way.[231] The Mexican government treated the incident as a foreign military invasion and the capture of the Texans as a great international achievement. Vicar Ortiz requested that his priests give a mass of thanksgiving in tribute to defeat of the Texans. Governor Armijo was lauded as a patriot and hero for having successfully defended the homeland with limited loss of Nuevomexicano lives. Other Nuevomexicanos to gain from their patriotic defense of the homeland were Manuel Chaves, Albino Chacón, and Sgt. Donaciano Vigíl, who got promoted to captain of the regular regiment.[232] Another Texan attempt at takeover came in 1843, again to be met with defeat. Initial skepticism toward Texans turned to a burning hatred as bands of outlaws raided New Mexican towns and Nuevomexicano trade vehicles. A notorious case involved don Antonio José Chávez, whose wagon train was attacked; he was murdered by a former Texas officer. The label *tejano* connoted the demonic. Nuevomexicanos once again unleashed hostility against the American consul and personal attacks against Texans on the plaza of Las Vegas.[233]

Many Euroamerican traders engaged in smuggling contraband articles. Armed, often drunk teamsters caused trouble at dances and public gatherings. According to an American visitor, "the Mexican has long been the dislike of the mountaineer, for over-bearing conduct." As the American consul in Santa Fe found, up to the 1840s a steady string of killings of American settlers by Mexicans occurred. Many went unprosecuted and unpunished.[234]

Ultimately significant, New Mexico's material progress and dependence on the American economy came at the cost of creating "a powerful clique of foreign-born entrepreneurs whose riches were only matched by growing political influence, and raising concerns about the frontier's wholesale Americanization." Americans who originally arrived in New Mexico on merchant business moved to the other big frontier opportunity: land speculation. Acquisition of new and existing land grants by foreigners grew to significance in the 1840s. In its high water mark the Taos area saw the transfer of eleven major land grants to outsiders in six years, enabled by the policy of Governor Armijo to give away large tracts to the *americanos*. The department assembly deplored the federal regime in the mid-1830s for its inability to prevent foreign merchants from taking the riches of its mineral deposits out of the country as contraband, much to the detriment of the entire country. Settler Americans designed stealthy schemes, conniving to have native prefects removed from office in the Taos and Río Arriba districts in favor of individuals of their choosing.[235]

Nativo priests spearheaded the collective opposition to this incipient settler colonialism. As one historian notes, "Catholicism emerged as a cornerstone of resistance." The stern Santa Fe Vicar Juan Felipe Ortiz, the charismatic Taos educator Father Antonio José Martínez, and the gregarious pastor of the Alburquerque parish, José Manuel Gallegos, objected to American destructiveness, sparing little in bringing cause against the stranger. What Angélico Chávez says about Padre Martínez applied to the others—that he was never "violently anti-American" as he was accused of being until his death. He had scores of Euromericans and Euro-immigrants as members of his parish and had presided over their marriages with native Mexican women. But he did oppose the "covetousness" of some Americans and others while standing as a "staunch Mexican patriot . . . watching out for the best interests of his native land."[236] The land issue flashed as a major concern. Martínez repeatedly warned the authorities of Americans who he said took advantage of local land holders, abused the administrative land grant system, and gained possession of alarmingly large tracts.[237] Martínez challenged the foreign-generated "land syndicate," as Chávez brands it, consisting of a powerful clique of foreign-born entrepreneurs and their Mexican governmental partners. He put his small press in the service of exposing the land grabbing of men like the Taos trader Charles Bent and the French Canadian Charles Beaubien.[238]

Father Gallegos, president of the departmental assembly toward the end of the Mexican period, independently denounced the American takeover of native lands. Gallegos signed a decree concerning foreigners and land grants, in which the assembly affirmed that public lands could not be granted to foreigners except under authority of the national government. Department secretary Juan Bautista Vigil y Alarid complained to the governor of Charles Bent, William Workmen, and William Dryden interfering with the collection of duties on the Santa Fe trade and trying "to dominate the inhabitants of Taos and control [their] activities."[239]

Another major issue of foreign intrusion concerned detrimental effects on Indians. In a testimony titled *Esposición* and forwarded to President Santa Anna, Father Martínez accused the American trading post managers on the Arkansas and Chato rivers out of Bent's Fort of recklessly providing alcohol and guns to both Indians and Mexicans. He charged that Americans, thanks to permissive Mexican local and federal policies, contributed to the "moral decay" of the "miserable barbarous nations" who stole and overhunted the buffalo, seriously depleting them for trade, with the Americans paying for animal skins with dry goods and liquor.[240] President Santa Anna gave the message "hearty approval" and suggested that the Department of New Mexico take into consideration its practical recommendations to curtail the American contact with the mobile Indians. The problem was also noted by Manuel Álvarez, American consul in Santa Fe, who issued a complaint to the Mexican minister of war in Mexico City and U.S. Secretary of State James Buchanan regarding the excessive contraband being traded at Bent's Fort.[241]

A religious complexity involved Father Martínez. Angélico Chávez finds Martínez telling Durango Bishop Zubiría in a letter that "sooner or later New Mexico would come under the government of the United States." He was calmly resigned to it, he noted, except for one thing. "This nation . . . tolerated all religions, but he himself was prepared to continue as a faithful servant of the Church and would resist the propagation of sects being introduced by force." The evidence for Martínez's conjecture came in the more than forty foreign families, perhaps Texans, who had settled in the Mora Valley just off the Great Plains backed by a contingent of armed guards. He speculated that if the New Mexico authorities tried to prevent those families from settling there permanently, the guards would come to their aid. He figured that they, too, were connected to attempts by outsiders to gain title to land grants.[242]

A rift among Nuevomexicanos emerged over the Americans. Martínez assailed Nuevomexicano officialdom, including the hombres de bien Governor Manuel Armijo, Lieutenant Governor Juan Bautista Vigil, Guadalupe Miranda, and the American consul, Manuel Álvarez, for conniving in "deals" with foreigners who had designs on the land. Martínez held meetings in 1843 at his Taos home with Nuevomexicano compatriots, including Father Gallegos, to discuss the loss of lands to outsiders. Governor Armijo considered this a conspiracy of secrecy against his administration and ordered Vicar Ortiz to have Martínez and Gallegos appear in Santa Fe for an accounting of themselves. The accused refused to comply.[243]

When don Mariano Martínez de Lejanza replaced Armijo, Padre Martínez's congratulatory note complained that Armijo had ruined the department. Martínez noted that the "same bad spirit of Armijo's party" in the departmental assembly had given up the Cimarron and Huerfano parcels to aliens who were already occupying them.[244] Governor Armijo, a self-made man of humble origins who as a young man had engaged in illicit sheep running to start his financial career, had become the most powerful and one of the richest of the native Mexicans with a diverse portfolio as merchant, rancher, and career politician, the closest New Mexico offered of the classic Mexican regional *caudillo*.[245] Economic modernization widened the traditional gap between rich and poor. Many of the rural folk became tied to the Santa Fe trade through production of market goods and trade with nomadic Indians, but pobladores who relied on sheep for their upkeep could not compete with ricos whose exploitation of the partido system only increased. Wealth in the form of cash and capital became more important to the local economy but was largely reserved for the upper-class elements.[246]

Capt. Donaciano Vigil nonetheless issued a modernist's complaint of fellow Mexicans who did not place faith in the markets and goods that American trade brought into New Mexico. Vigil's speech, delivered to the department assembly and which the author hoped to have circulated in the republic's capital, deplored the protectionist leanings being expressed, characterizing the challengers to American trading as "imbued with the doctrines of other centuries and of another type of government." Obstructionist policies hurt New Mexico, Vigil argued, by preventing the U.S.–New Mexican trade system from keeping the marauding Indians at bay. In the history of market changes, Vigil complained, anti-Americano politicians worked to curtail the American traders by imposing nationality requirements on the system of trade and removing progressive Nuevomexicanos like Governor Bartolomé Baca, who had exempted Americans from laws that restricted them from certain enterprises such as beaver trapping.[247]

The countering point of view remained firm. Vicar Ortiz described to Governor Armijo the "evils that unavoidably would befall us if we do not resist by all means the enemy of Mexico's territorial integrity." The enemy consisted of the administrators who made intermarriage with Mexican women too easy, Ortiz argued. Increased fees needed to be placed on the processing of marriage ceremonies and other requirements should be imposed. Foreign-born residents complained bitterly about the church obstacles. Governor Armijo appears in the form of a complicated politician. He consorted with important American traders who had made New Mexico home. When it came to defending the national religion, he proved the staunch patriot and moderado, rhetorically asking his fellow New Mexicans in the context of the Texas expedition, "Will you look on with indifference as a handful of foreign adventurers march all the way to our communities to take away our freedom and interest, to pollute our innocent traditions, and to do away with our true and loved Religion?"[248]

Mexican antipathy toward the American intruder reached fever pitch just before news of the coming American invasion. Frank Blair and George Bent, half-brother of the important trader Charles Bent, one day stumbled onto the Taos Plaza publically inebriated and disorderly. Reséndez describes what followed:

> Such public display of drunkenness galvanized the ire of a group of no less than thirty Nuevomexicanos, who promptly retaliated by beating the two celebrants and inflicting serious wounds on Blair. Revealingly, the crowd cheered on the assaulters, screaming, 'kill the *borrachos*' [drunkards]. The subsequent investigation showed that nuevomexicano authorities were within ear shot of the commotion but refused to intervene, preferring to leave the crowd to vent its ire. Moreover, incidents like this one demonstrate how the newfound availability and consumption of alcohol could generate a popular nationalist backlash and underscore Mexican officials' waning ability to regulate activities unleashed by the market revolution.[249]

The incident put an unvarnished Nuevomexicano resentment toward Americanos on display. The priests' critical discourse of American exploitation formed the tip of deep offense being taken at the Americans.

And thus were the key sociopolitical props set for New Mexico to receive the conquest and wholesale annexation by the United States.

CHAPTER TWO

Bloodless and Bloody Conquests, 1846–1847

Nationalists had been spoiling for continental expansion since the start of the nineteenth century. As a result James K. Polk ran for president in 1845 behind the Democratic Party's plank calling for possession of Texas, California, and Oregon and in the name of the moral superiority and special destiny of "Anglo-Saxon Americans." In New Mexico the Taos trader Charles Bent presciently conveyed to the American consul Manuel Álvarez, a native of Spain, that the Polk presidency would "cause difficulty" with Mexico.[1]

Polk looked to purchase New Mexico and California, which had worked as imperial strategy in the acquisitions of Louisiana and Florida. His administration gave covert encouragement to Americans in California to rebel against Mexico as those in Texas had.[2] Mexican president José Joaquín Herrera, not relishing war either, dug about for an agreement with the United States on the question of whither Texas.[3] Herrera would have Texas become independent rather than fall into U.S. hands. His countrymen condemned this attitude of sacrificing Texas as a violation of their *patria*'s honor. The American annexation of Texas in 1845 forced Herrera to war preparedness, although his build-up proved feeble.[4] Herrera stayed with negotiations in hopes of a peaceful settlement over Texas. The hue and cry from compatriots over this "treason" was worsened by the arrival in Mexico City of Polk's envoy extraordinary and minister plenipotentiary charged with settling the border matter. The New Mexico Assembly joined other northern departments in objecting to a treaty with the United States.[5] The aristocrat Gen. Mariano Paredes y Arrillaga proclaimed at San Luis Potosí in December a plan for returning the national government to tighter centralization. In their approach toward the capital, the Paredes detachment overpowered the president's political and military defenses, and Herrera resigned his post as chief of state.[6]

The international tension stung New Mexico. Joab Houghton—

originally from New York and a trader, civil engineer, and temporary American consul—impulsively led a group in an attempt to wrest control of the department, including its courts, in anticipation of war. Houghton's filibustering reflected the attitude of ownership American settlers had begun to assume over New Mexico.[7] Department officials, well aware that Polk had placed troops on the Texan border, thought themselves in control of the situation. The *asamblea* endorsed the plan of Potosí. Governor Manuel Armijo, assuming the proper role of an administration patriot, publicly heralded Paredes as one to "cause to repent and bite the dust those who with daring hand are trying to appropriate the larger part of the Mexican territory, those good-for-nothing enemies and cowards who, not respecting treaties like a civilized nation, are even making it apparent that they do not know how to respect any right of a people."[8]

Paredes too saw the futility of outright war with the United States, and it helped that his administration needed hard monetary currency. He thus engaged in quiet diplomacy with the United States for a possible sale of Mexican northern lands.[9] The talks floundered. Polk and Congress grew increasingly bellicose, and Mexico City authorities warned citizens of impending war. Governor Armijo in New Mexico put out the call for a patriotic defense of *la República*. Consul Álvarez warned Secretary of State James Buchanan of the determined opposition to American aggression surging through New Mexico, and as a result recommended a military force to protect American citizens, and suggested, seeing over-determination, the preparation of reparations to American merchants at war's end.[10]

It may be, as one essayist claims, that Polk was "no war hawk" and had no understanding of war or "how to make it," but he *was* prepared to war up should purchase of Mexican territories fall through. As American and Mexican troops moved along the disputed boundaries between the two countries, he alternated between offers of friendly agreement and threats of military force, carrying the "twin torches through a powder magazine" from March 4, 1845, to May 13, 1846.[11] U.S. senators balked on providing the funds to consummate Polk's desired purchase. The president scowled at Mexico's refusal to recognize both his minister and the claims of Americans for settling portions of Texas. He advised his cabinet and Missouri Senator Thomas Hart Benton on the possible need to declare war and asked that Congress be informed.[12]

Mexican soldiers amassed on the Texas border to enforce their country's claim of the more northerly Nueces River as the international border, not the Río Grande as the United States claimed. Mexican troops crossed the Río Grande and attacked General Zachary Taylor's forces, killing and capturing two companies of dragoons. Mexico had invaded the United States, Polk decried. He grossly argued that Mexico could only afford to indemnify American losses on the border by surrendering California.[13] Congress ratified his request for a war declaration on May 13. The United States launched the biggest enterprise the American people had ever embarked on, a multi-pronged military attack on a foreign country.[14]

The war from declaration to peace treaty lasted a quarter short of two years. In New Mexico the martialized contact zone came packed with dramas of confrontation and accommodation initiated on both sides of the national divide. The Nuevomexicano piece of the larger story of American invasion was etched in three distinct phases of occupation. The Bloodless Conquest and the Bloody Conquest are covered in this chapter. The Integrative Conquest is presented in chapter 3.

The Bloodless Conquest

Of the two direct expeditions the U.S. War Department launched to take California, the southern one involved the need to occupy New Mexico along the way. The march out from Missouri was entrusted to Col. Stephen Watts Kearny based on his prior service out West. From the start, the president's directive maintained a resolve to conquer, yet the planning and implementation of the operation reflected a project of continental liberalism.

Polk was made to understand that New Mexicans harbored a favor for Americans. To counter the rumor that the American army intended to beat them into submission, he envisioned a nonviolent capture of their territory and he ordered officers to respect and protect Mexican religion and church property. As he told a Protestant clergyman who objected to this latter policy based on the principle of church and state separation, Polk rejected a war of "ferocity & fanaticism."[15] The president received support for this position from advisors, who stressed how loosely connected New Mexico and California were to the Mexican government. Senator Benton, who originally disagreed with Polk's war mission, reinforced to the president that the northern sections were too distant from Mexico's center to generate hostility among Mexican citizens toward the American campaign of annexation. Hanging on with the liberal's diffusion sensibility, Benton assured Polk that the New Mexicans would readily appreciate the American benefits of peace, trade, and "full protection of all their rights of person, property, and religion."[16]

Benton introduced James W. Magoffin to Polk and U.S. Secretary of War William Marcy. Magoffin—a former U.S. consul at Saltillo, Chihuahua businessman, widower of a Mexican wife, and veteran Santa Fe–Chihuahua merchant—had intimate knowledge of northern Mexico. He offered ideas about the "means" of conducting a military march into New Mexico. Magoffin felt confident of a peaceful occupation, Santa Fe appearing too compromised by the merchant trade with the United States to offer resistance.[17] Marcy ordered Kearny to protect the trade between U.S. citizens and northern Mexico "as far as practicable under the changed condition of things between the two countries."[18]

Kearny, as Marcy ordered, would abolish "all arbitrary restrictions that may exist, so far as it may be done with safety." He would act in "wisdom and prudence" by continuing the employment of all the existing government officers "as are known to be friendly to the United States." Kearny was to have New Mexican officials "voluntarily" swear allegiance to his national flag and inform the people of a virtual replicative intent, "the wish and design of the United States to provide for them a free government, with the least possible delay, similar to that which exists in our Territories." The precedent lay in the 1803 acquisition of the Louisiana Territory and was reinforced by Mexico's status as a republic and New Mexico's own form of territorial administration. Polk's imperial democracy sought to extend the advanced principles of the United States to the downtrodden. Mexicans were "to be called on to exercise the rights of freemen in electing their own representatives to the Territorial legislature." Kearny received a clear inclusionary instruction. He was to "act in such a manner as best to conciliate the inhabitants and render them friendly to the United States."[19] He would assure them in particular of his respect for their religious institutions. The orders dictated that "a person of high character and good repute in the Roman Catholic church" attend the expedition along with some priests, a provision that was applied in the taking of Catholic Louisiana before it became a formal U.S. territory.[20]

Colonel Kearny (he was promoted to brigadier general during this campaign) organized a regiment of regular and volunteer troops at Fort Leavenworth, Kansas. The self-styled "Army of the West" consisted of 1,658 men, 1,300 of them Missouri Volunteers, two batteries of 6-pound artillery and four 12-pounder howitzers, three squadrons of dragoons, 107 Laclede Rangers, and two infantry companies.[21] The troop headed out on May 27, 1846. Polk's concern for Santa Fe merchants was invested in a caravan of American trading wagons that trailed the Army of the West. Mexican traders homeward bound with American wares came under its wing as well and were told that the U.S. government would compensate them for any losses due to war.[22] A Mexican official in Chihuahua heard this bit of news from Mexican merchants who did not side with the United States. He thought the American protections a "paradox," a liberal conquest vexing his notion of aggressive international war.[23]

The Polk war plan laid the foundation for the first bits of integrative working in the machinery of the New Mexico occupation. The young José Francisco Chávez, from the most prominent Nuevomexicano merchant family in the department, was returning from a New York academy in one of the civilian wagons. Kearny ascertained that Chávez was a classmate of two of his own sons. Chávez consented to the commander's request to serve as an interpreter along the Santa Fe mission.[24] Another conquest co-optation involved one José Gonzales, a Chihuahuan trader, who received a Spanish-language lesson from James Magoffin on the American principles of liberty and equality. Magoffin highlighted the advantages Mexicans were destined to see with a U.S. annexation. Gonzales reportedly reiterated them to his fellow citizens.[25] Magoffin's daughter Susan described in her trail journal the arrival of a striking middle-aged Mexican, "the curiosity of the crowd waiting to escort the remainder of the troops coming out with Capt. [Phillip St. George] Cooke." He was a "considerable oddity and apparently a great friend of the Americans—talked much of Gen. Kearny and some of his officers." He would, as noted, help the Mexicans rally "*los amigos de los Americanos*" to Kearny's entrance.[26]

Kearny laid the ground for his arrival in New Mexico by having known American traders advance ahead of his troop to gather intelligence, warn resident Americans of impending danger, and advise Mexicans to surrender for their own good.[27] Consul Álvarez tried to convince Governor Armijo and other Nuevomexicanos of the advisability of capitulation. It was preferable, Álvarez implored, to be part of a powerful republic than to remain in an unstable one.[28] Armijo's reflex, however, was to rise in honorable defense of the Mexican nation. The governor announced to his gathered troops on June 6 that "the giant, our Neighbor" had taken Texas and now desired that the upper Río Grande be the boundary of their "usurpation." Armijo showed knowledge of international diplomacy, notably Polk's dicey attempt to have his minister plenipotentiary fool Mexico into giving up its northern territories. In the name of the "supreme government," and calling himself their "comrade and best Friend," the governor rallied his forces to courage in the face of this evident forboding.[29]

Armijo sounded the alarm of the "undoubted enemy aggression" to an extraordinary session of the assembly. Delegates pledged all disposable measures for defense and summoned absent members so that the assembly could "decree measures in accordance with their prerogatives." All physically fit men were called into service and the people were ordered to drive their livestock into the mountains with word of an overwhelming enemy headed their way.[30] On Armijo's appeal, the commander of the military in Chihuahua pledged to send a 500-strong cavalry force and 500 infantrymen. The governor of Durango promised to start his militias from Chihuahua.[31] Vicar Juan Felipe Ortíz announced to parishioners on July 4 the disturbing news of the enemy approaching Bent's Fort, and he sounded the alarm of the very antithesis of Polk's objective of friendly conquest. It was "a reckless band of destructive adventurers who would pillage towns," Ortiz declared, "rob the people of their property, desecrate churches, and destroy the Catholic faith."[32]

Mexican law permitted government to extract loans from the wealthy to deal with emergencies.[33] The New Mexico assemblymen debated on July 13 and 16 an anticipated request from the governor for authority to force out loans for the defense of the department. The Pecos rancher and captain Donaciano Vigil doubted their authority to endorse the measure, as Armijo had not been handed emergency dictatorial powers. Armijo asked the assembly to remain in permanent session and to grant him extraordinary authority to take discretionary measures for mounting an army. Santa Fe citizens grew excited; business was suspended; and troops were quartered. Principal men debated at a com-

FIG. 3. *General Manuel Armijo*, ca. 1840, artist unknown. Armijo was governor of the New Mexico Department when Gen. Stephen Watts Kearny marched in to conquer Santa Fe. Courtesy Palace of the Governors Photo Archives, NMHM/DCA, negative #099938.

munity meeting the possible means of resistance. Popular opinion overruled Armijo's mention of surrender as a possible need. Two citizens were dispatched to join Armijo in organizing the defense force.[34]

At the August 8 assembly session, Armijo read the report of an alcalde in eastern New Mexico of five thousand U.S. troops bearing down and determined to take Santa Fe. The alcalde pleaded for military assistance to save the department. "Let us be *compadres* in arms," the governor appealed to the people, "and, with honest union, we shall lead to victory." His government was fully prepared to "sacrifice, if it be necessary, its life and interests in defense of the Nation and of its most beloved rights, as well as its nationality," the governor affirmed.[35] Assembly members bemoaned the miniscule time left to prepare for the inevitable. Assembly President Father Manuel Gallegos proposed that a committee draft a message to the enemy. Donaciano Vigil was a friend to many an American, but here he defied the threat to his sovereign, perhaps feeling that the existing mercantile trade, which he promoted, did just fine as an international enterprise. He urged the members to consider "exciting the communities to contribute voluntarily, according to their means, the assistance requested by the governor." Antonio Sena said the brief time remaining rendered formal diplomacy and renewed insurgency untenable. The governor's request for the assemblymen to tax themselves to pay the troops was seconded by Gallegos and Felipe Sena y Armijo. Vigil again questioned their right to do so.[36]

The only members present at next day's session—Gallegos, Felipe Sena, and Juan Perea—voted to support the governor. Gallegos decreed that the loan extractions would apply only to themselves. Armijo received word at one in the morning from the justice of the peace in Las Vegas of U.S. troops just outside the international border at the Río Colorado (Canadian River). An American officer and twelve soldiers had walked into the village with documents from Kearny announcing his mission to occupy Santa Fe. Armijo asked the assembly for a thousand pesos to organize a volunteer regiment in three days. He again requested the right to coerce loans. He acknowledged resistance to this appeal from his old local enemies even as the "considerable foreign force" approached. Vicar Ortiz secured a hundred pesos from the funds of the penitential confraternities. Some of his priests had already fled New Mexico. He pleaded for the rest to remain with their parishioners.[37]

Assemblymen debated the matter of how to meet the emergency with the concentration it deserved. They complimented the governor's patriotism, cited their own authority by the laws of the Organic Bases to direct Armijo to authorize loans from the department's notables, and called on citizens to volunteer resources "without exception of jurisdiction or privilege." Some lament was expressed for the late warning of the need to generate funds. The body would afterward charge the national treasury for reimbursements and additional costs incurred in defense of the patria.[38] Armijo placed the department under martial law and called on the people to prepare for a defense. Friendly relations and economic interests with foreigners failed to dampen the fear among the people at this haunting moment of Americans intending "to invade their soil and destroy their property and liberties," as Armijo proclaimed it.[39] Back on the trail, Kearny troops captured Armijo scouts. The spies on their release reported the size of the American force to Santa Fe officials at between two and five thousand soldiers.[40]

Secretary Marcy made the fateful decision of giving Kearny his head in organizing the appropriation of New Mexico. Rather than adopt a policy of "liberal imperialism"—brandishing a token nod to liberal values, only to usurp domination of New Mexico—Kearny interpreted Polk's orders quite literally on the basis of continental imperialism, authorizing him to undertake an effective integration of Nuevomexicanos into the American polity. At Bent's Fort in the last week of July, Kearny composed his proclamation of annexation. This document would serve as his trusty warrant for dealing with the Mexicans as he proceeded to overtake New Mexico.[41]

Kearny's annexation proclamation staked the American territorial claim all the way up the Río Grande to its northern New Mexico headwaters. It was the line that American Texans had marked out as the international border with Mexico. The practical difficulty, Capt. Phillip Cooke perceived, was that "it cuts the isolated [New Mexico] province in two!"[42] Historian Thomas Edrington claims to see Kearny's "subterfuge" designed for the eyes of Mexican leaders to enable establishment of a temporary civil government on securing the territory.[43] The proclamation warned of "a large military force" on its way *and* expressed a socially conjoint purpose, "seeking union with and ameliorating the conditions of its inhabitants." New Mexicans would

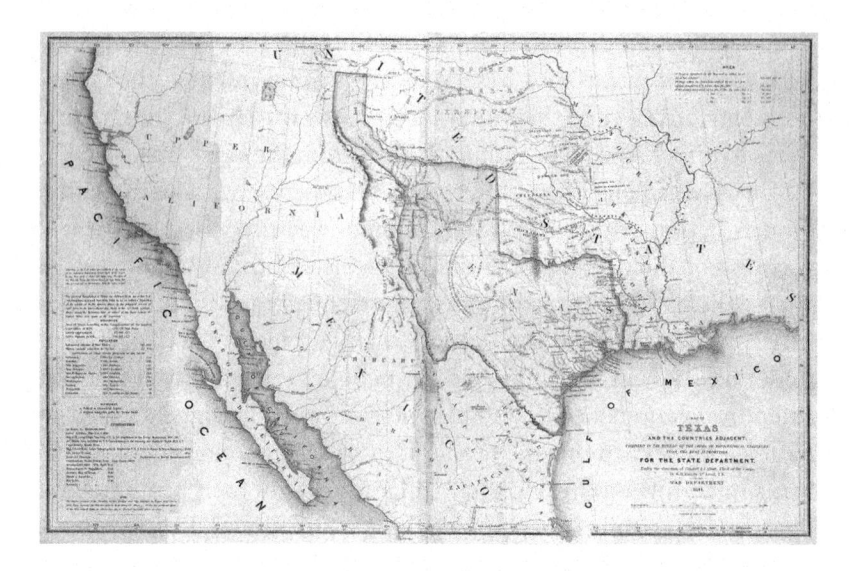

MAP 2. Map of Texas and the countries adjacent, 1844. It indicates the international boundary line up to the headwaters of the Río Grande used by General Stephen Watts Kearny in 1846 to justify the American occupation of New Mexico. Hand colored, 54 x 82 cm, prepared for the State Department under the direction of Col. J. J. Abert, Chief of the Corps, by Lt. William H. Emory, United States War Department. Source: Library of Congress Geography and Map Division, Washington DC, G4030 ct0010066.

be invited to "remain quietly at their homes, and to pursue their peaceful avocations." So long as they continued in such pursuits, the proclamation upheld, they would not be interfered with by the American army, "but will be respected and protected in their rights, both civil and religious." The gift of friendship and protection came wrapped in barbed wire. Those who took up arms or encouraged resistance would "be regarded as enemies, and will be treated accordingly." Kearny ordered the proclamation disseminated in long and short versions throughout the Río Arriba.[44]

Kearny had sent a Major Howard ahead to determine the disposition of Mexicans toward his intrusion. Howard reported finding the "plebian" classes inclined to favor his offer of peace. The "patricians who held the offices and ruled the country, were hostile and were making warlike preparations," Howard affirmed, adding that 2,300 men were armed for the defense of the capital, with more assembling at Taos. John Hughes, a member of Col. Alexander Doniphan's regiment, noted that it "produced quite a sensation in our camp. It was now expected that Col. Kearney's entrance into Santa Fe would be obstinately disputed."[45]

Kearny announced his impending arrival to Governor Armijo in a dispatch that iterated the terms of his occupation. The invading officer would reinforce the Texas-defined boundary and extend the U.S. Constitution's respect of home and hearth while protecting persons, religion, and property. "I come as a friend," he proffered, "and with the disposition, and intention, to consider all Mexicans and others as friends who will remain peaceably at their homes and attend to their own affairs." Kearny sharpened his verbal bayonet with mighty presumption, adding that he had come to "this part of the United States" with an overpowering military force and a larger one to follow. "I therefore, for the sake of humanity, call upon you to submit to fate," he offered, "and to meet me with the same feelings of Peace and Friendship which I now entertain for you and offer to you and to all those over whom you are Governor." Armijo should see it in his best interest to yield, it was urged. The people would appreciate it, but should he decide to fight, he would bear the responsibility for shed blood.[46] The letter was entrusted for delivery to Captain Cooke and a squad of dragoons. Joining Cooke were Magoffin, Magoffin sidekick and veteran Chihuahua–Río Abajo trader José Gonzales, and Henry Connelly, the Virginia-born, Kentucky-raised trained physician and stepfather of Kearny's trail man and translator José Francisco Chávez.[47] Researchers have yet to discover the precise exchange at this meeting. Armijo's response via Cooke informed Kearny that an emissary would meet the general, defiantly if need be, at the head of a force of six thousand defensive troops.[48]

Kearny had the veteran trader Eugene Leitensdorfer go to Taos, sixty miles to the west, under a flag of truce and a military escort to inform the people of his peaceful entry and ascertain the sentiments of the Pueblos about his coming. Kearny believed that the promise of protection to them and the "lower order of Mexicans" would make it difficult for Armijo to raise a defensive unit while making real the legitimacy of his intrusion.[49] Kearny released captured Mexican spies so that they could warn Armijo's compatriots of his intimidating force.[50]

As Kearny marched through Ratón Pass into Mexico proper, a random Mexican was ordered to Taos to hand the annexation proclamation along with personal letters to the alcalde and local priest. Kearny regaled captive spies with his anticipatory declaration of New Mexico as a part of the United States destined to be covered by American laws. The occupation rambled into New Mexico laced with modernization ideology, its condemnation of oppressive tradition. Replicating the very words of his liberally informed orders, Kearny affirmed that his laws would overrule the "arbitrary will of dictators" and defend the weak against the strong, the poor against the rich. Two Mexicans from the village of Mora declared their fealty to the Americans. Kearny held one as a possible spy and sent the other, along with two Pueblo Indians, off with the proclamation.[51] An American returned from Taos with the report that Mexicans were taking up arms and Pueblo Indians planned on joining them. A "Mr. Bent" (Charles or William) brought in several Mexicans who possessed Armijo's call to arms with its threat of death for citizens who failed to respond. A Kearny officer recorded that Armijo had organized men, guns, and other war implements. Three hundred of his dragoons were in Santa Fe, the report went, from "the lower country and three thousand more were daily expected up from below."[52]

A Mexican lieutenant and two sergeants delivered Armijo's reply to Kearny's annexation proclamation on August 14. Armijo, standing by his government's rejection of the Texas boundary, declared himself duty-bound to lead his people, who had arisen *en masse*. He offered to meet with Kearny at the settlement of Las Vegas at the western edge of the Great Plains for a "frank discussion" and warned of his preparation to fight if necessary. He too genuinely wished to avoid spilling blood but would not accept the responsibility if it occurred. Armijo would consider Kearny's sentiments of peace and friendship "in the spirit" offered once the justice of his contention was established, "and the differences resolved in conformity with the rights of man and to the honor of both nations." Connelly delivered Kearny's reply. The invader looked forward to the meeting "between friends" and reaffirmed his goal of establishing official dominion over New Mexico. He expected the governor to surrender and swear to uphold the laws and constitution already being established by the United States. Armijo would be permitted to remain a citizen of Mexico if he so choose. Connelly, with a vested interest in the conquest, urged his friend Armijo to accept Kearny's terms "safe from dangers and safe from the responsibilities of Government."[53]

Armijo received plenty of warning of an invading army, yet he had no representation at the point where Kearny crossed into Mexican national space and reached Las Vegas. The American general organized his troops pursuant to the U.S. Constitution. They would respect all residents, observe the rights of private property, and not take provisions without paying for them.[54] He prepared, then, to welcome personally the Mexican inhabitants to their membership in the United States.

Kearny delivered his first replicative message to a 150 assembled Nuevomexicanos from atop an adobe dwelling in the company of the local alcalde and two militia captains. "Mr. Alcalde, and people of New Mexico," he began. "I have come amongst you by the orders of my government, to take possession of your country, and extend over it the laws of the United States." The rationale behind the Texas boundary became clear. His country had considered this piece of Mexico "for some time a part of the territory of the United States," Kearny explained. "We come amongst you as friends," he assured again, "not as enemies; as protectors—not as conquerors. We come among you for your benefit—not for your injury." The liberal emissary absolved the people from allegiance to Armijo and Mexico and he arrogated the right to declare himself their governor, signifying New Mexico into an American federal territory. As such, he cleverly told the assembled ones he did not expect them to take up arms against their own people, his soldiers. Kearny expressed his sensitivity to the people's anxiety over the inability of their officials to thwart raiding bands. "My government will correct all this," he announced. "It will keep off the Indians, protect you in your persons and property." The benevolent conqueror pulled the American ace-in-the hole of religious tolerance. "I know you are all great Catholics," he stated, and "that some of your priests have told you all sorts of stories—that we should ill-treat your women, and brand them on the cheek as you do your mules on the hip. It is all false. My government respects your religion as much as the Protestant religion, and allows each man to worship his Creator as his heart tells him is best. Its laws protect the Catholic as well as the Protestant; the weak as well as the strong; the poor as well as the rich." He himself was not Catholic, he noted, but one-third of his army was. He respected "a good Catholic as much as a good Protestant."[55]

Kearny moved on to political incorporation, which he considered a virtual *fait accompli*. He would not disturb the local government, but officials should understand that U.S. laws required all men holding office to take the oath of national allegiance. "I now tell you," he added, brandishing the no-nonsense side of his word, "that those who remain peaceably at home attending their persons, and their religion . . . not a pepper, not an onion, shall be disturbed or taken by my troops, without pay, or by the consent of the owner. But listen! He who promises to be quiet, and is found in arms against me, I will hang!"[56]

Kearny held out fruits of his republic at the point of his bayonet again to a "great" crowd in the settlement of San Miguel from another roof top overlooking the plaza and with the aid of an interpreter. He strategically announced that the people should begin regarding themselves as citizens of the United States. This extraordinary offering fell outside Polk's plan but followed Kearny's replicatory intent, the legal commonplace that residents of American territories were citizens. Kearny's chief of ordnance, Lt. Alexander Dyer, the modernist's eyes wide open, looked upon "the miserable and degraded state in which the lower class (comprising indeed nearly the whole population)," and figured that the prospect of a liberal amelioration of their condition "would be hailed by them with delight."[57]

Yet Kearny threatened to "subvert" the town unless the people submitted. The journal entries of Kearny personnel relate shades of response from the locals to the foreign extension of friendship and ultimate threat.[58] Capt. Abraham Johnston recorded the Las Vegas alcalde telling Kearny prior to the occupation of his village that he was a Mexican "and had to obey his government, but that he was pleased to see the general's proclamations were so favorable to the people." As such he resisted the treachery of taking the oath of allegiance to American authority while still legally Mexican yet could yield to Kearny with dignity.[59] The extraction of consent here reflects what Michael Hechter calls a passive or negative form of legitimation in the absence of resistance outright.[60] The Missouri volunteer Pvt. Marcellus Edwards had a clear understanding of the meaning of legitimation. As he observed at Las Vegas, "If all compulsatory [sic] oaths are illegal, this oath of course is of no effect, for these poor creatures were evidently compelled to take it for fear of giving offense to our army."[61] Lt. W. H. Emory witnessed a discontented militia officer and alcalde taking a "bitter pill . . . with downcast eyes. The general

[Kearny] remarked to him, in hearing of all the people: 'Captain, look me in the face, while you repeat the oath of office.'"[62]

Captain Cooke beheld pressure and steaming resentment. "Whether from the priest's influence, the crowd, or his own peculiar firmness," he commented, "the alcalde positively refused to take the oath." Kearny had enlarged on their government's "perfect freedom of religion," mentioning that his chief of staff "was a Roman Catholic," yet persuasion failed. At last, Cooke observed, "the old man was forced to go through the form and semblance of swearing allegiance."[63] Johnston too saw the priest refusing to accompany Kearny on the roof, protesting that he was "a citizen of the world and he could not, if the general should point all his big guns at him, ascend the ladder to speak to the people. The general said he would not ask him to address the people but he wanted his company up there. He then consented to ascend the ladder."[64]

An anonymous officer wrote to the *St. Louis Republican* of a slightly more dramatic breaking down of resistance. The alcalde and priest had received Kearny politely enough, "but it was evident they did not relish an interview with him." The padre flatly stated he was "a Mexican, but should obey the laws that were placed over him for *the time*, but if the general should point all his cannon at his breast, he could not consent to go up [on the roof] and address the people." Kearny did not want him to speak, only to listen. The cleric ascended showing an unwillingness to take the oath to the United States, preferring to wait until the general had taken possession of New Mexico's capital. "The general told him," the anonymous officer reported, 'it was sufficient for him to know that he had possession of his village.' He then consented, and with the usual formalities." The alcalde would take an oath provided, he said, "I can be protected in my religion." Kearny had the alcalde swear to defend the United States "against all her enemies and opposers [sic], in the name of the Father, the son and Holy Ghost—Amen." Kearny left the alcalde in office, ordering the people to obey him and the existing laws until "any change can be made that will be for your benefit." He shook hands with the priest and invited the crowd to refreshments; "sundry hugs, jokes, and professions of friendship" followed. The conquering general held forth in projective comity, that the "better they became acquainted, the better friends they would be." Kearny invited the "evidently. . . ruling spirit of the village" to visit at Santa Fe. The witness concluded with a grand hope of cross-national consensus: "The visit to the priest, and the frank and friendly manner of the general had the desired effect, and I believe they parted the best of friends, and [I] have no doubt that the inhabitants of St. Miguel will soon be as good democrats as can be found in Missouri."[65]

Observers perceived a spectrum of response among the populace. Johnson detected a "faint shout" from among villagers at the closing of the ceremony when the alcalde and officers drew the sign of the cross.[66] Emory looked upon citizens who "grinned" when enjoined to obey the alcalde, "and exchanged looks of satisfaction, but seemed not to have the boldness to express what they evidently felt—that their burdens, if not relieved, were, at least, shifted to some ungalled part of the body."[67] An unnamed officer (probably Lt. George Rutledge Gibson) found clear approval among the farmers who saw Kearny disciplining the soldiers who had damaged their fields, appearing "delighted with this exemplification of equal justice." The officer called it "a thing not dreamed of in New Mexico under the rule of Armijo" (although it is not clear how he would have known it). In a micro-market legitimation, peasants approached the American troops to sell green corn, cheese, chickens, and other provisions. "The poorer natives were glad to trade with us and seemed to bear no malice for Kearny's conquest," a sergeant recorded. Edwards observed the sellers on burros, two on an animal, "perfectly friendly," demanding "a very high price," which "went very well with men who have been so long on half rations." Hughes noted that the traffickers had "drained most of the specie from the purses of the American soldiers."[68]

Cooke, among the more skeptical observers, typified the U.S. brand of missionary Anglo-Saxonism then sweeping like a sea wave over the western plains. He marveled at the "shock and awe," as he put it, of Kearny's enlightened bombardment of the great unwashed: "The great boon of American citizenship thus thrust through an interpreter, by the mailed hand," he put it in his own modernism, "upon eighty thousand mongrels who cannot read—who are almost heathens—the great mass reared in real slavery, called peonism, but still imbued by nature with enough patriotism to resent this outrage of being forced to swear an alien allegiance, by an officer who had just passed their frontier." Cooke could not help but think that "this people who have been taught more respect for a corporal than a judge, must still have been astonished at this first lesson in liberty." Later, however, he found from inquiries at various houses that the people "were evidently averse to our stopping, regarding us perhaps, in the light of a swarm of locusts" (an observation to realize its nonpeaceful confirmation later in the occupation).[69]

Kearny established a foothold on Mexican soil, finding in eastern New Mexico a propitious stage to rehearse the annexation of the department. His enforced consensus was rewarded by shades of legitimation, by turns cheery, sullen, resigned, and smolderingly resentful—but not violently resistant. As Kearny busied himself with the country folk, Governor Armijo set up a defense of several hundred regulars, militiamen, Pueblos, and artillery at Apache Canyon on the road to Santa Fe behind a blind of trees and trenches. Kearny heard of the positioning, although the alcalde of Pecos denied any such defensive measure. Kearny's scouts arrived to find no one there. The American phalanx passed through with no enemy in sight. The news rapidly spread that Armijo had disbanded his forces and fled south to Chihuahua.[70]

For all the bravado Armijo had mustered in defense of *la patria*, it is one of the head-scratchers of New Mexico history that he abandoned the commanding fortification at Apache Canyon.[71] Armijo himself later explained that disputes broke out among the leaders of the militia, while some of these auxiliaries turned against him in favor of the invading Americans. Many voices urged capitulation, Armijo declared, including clergymen and judicial authorities. He deemed his forces patently insufficient to the task and would not put them in danger of being slaughtered.[72] John Hughes, who was on the scene, had a slightly variant narrative based on "good authority," that Armijo and certain generals fought over the chief command "and that the common people being peaceably disposed toward the Americans, readily seized upon the dissension of their leaders as a pretext for abandoning the army." Taos Pueblo chiefs reportedly refused to join Armijo against such a power.[73] According to an 1880 report, leading citizens had started a militia, only to be informed by Armijo that he had enough regular troops and their services were not needed. When volunteers showed up anyway, Armijo found them armed with bows and arrows, slings and clubs, and hardly any firearms.[74]

Word of Mexicans quarreling at Apache Pass reached Kearny before he set out from San Miguel.[75] Armijo may have been a reluctant war chief all along. Recall that at a Santa Fe meeting he had raised the possibility of surrendering but had been shouted down.[76] He may have wanted to cover his bases to see what he had on his hands, if not quicken the blood of the assembly for combat. Lieutenant Emory heard of the people's suspicion of Armijo's unwillingness to fight and the impression that he felt forced into a military leadership under threat of death from countrymen. If Armijo was loathe to resist the invaders, his patriotic rally and call to arms might have reflected the rite of duty of a Mexican official or a performance under duress.[77]

Armijo may well have been compromised by the Santa Fe trade. Cooke thought Armijo's "avarice" saw opportunity in enhanced customs charges under U.S. rule. Armijo remained friendly with American merchants through the ordeal of impending occupation. Joab Houghton stated that Armijo had planned for the American takeover, agreeing to settle duty accounts on goods arriving before the American occupation and expecting to bill the United States $4,000.[78] Armijo and his partner, Albert Speyer, had a wagon train filled with arms, munitions, and goods worth $70,000 moving ahead of Kearny. The blockade that the war imposed on British and German competition made for high prices in domestic shipments. Conquest meant discontinued duties, important as Kearny had sent a squad ahead to hold and detain all trading caravans, putting a premium on the arrest of the Armijo-Speyer wagons. (The detachment failed to catch them, and the train arrived in Santa Fe ahead of time.)[79] Armijo appears torn between a commitment to the merchant network and official obligations to defend Mexico, between the centripetal pull of fatherland patriotism and centrifugal commitments to international partnership. Cooke found Armijo "in painful doubt and irresolution; halting between loyalty to his army commission, lately bestowed, and a desire to escape the dangers of war upon terms of personal advantage. Although perhaps much superior to those about him," Cooke commented, "he is unequal to the trying circumstances of his present situation. Even the patriotic spirit developed by his proclamation [of war preparedness] appears to embarrass as well as surprise him." As Cooke predicted, "Undoubtedly he must go on to direct this current, but to some weak and disgraceful conclusion."[80]

The unrevealed August 12 conversation with Cooke and Magoffin may have convinced the governor to refrain from resistance. Cooke later congratulated the merchant for his skill in reinforcing Armijo's disinclination to defense, "to which, I believe, according to your instructions, you gave important encouragement particularly in neutralizing the contrary influence of the young Colonel [Diego] Archuletta [sic]." One account has the Kearny interlocutors strenuously arguing that Archuleta's impulse to fight would be quieted by his desire for an extension of New Mexico's western boundary as a U.S. territorial possession. The prospect of this "*pronunciamiento* of Western New Mexico," they urged, would sway Archuleta to favor annexation as he would have all of New Mexico west of the Río Grande under the Texan international boundary. Historian Ralph Bieber sees Magoffin pushing the argument that "American rule would increase the price of real estate and make New Mexico prosperous."[81]

There is also the possibility of outright bribery. A major theme in the literature, inflamed by George W. Kendall's distorted description of the famed New Mexico governor, portrays Armijo as the proverbial crooked Mexican politician.[82] While the charge is commonly expressed, hard evidence goes lacking.[83] Historian Dwight Clarke has Magoffin explaining to Kearny "how he hoped to induce Governor Armijo and his officers by persuasion or bribery, or both, to submit peaceably to the occupation of their province." Clarke sees "strong circumstantial evidence that bribery was used," supported by "Armijo's previous record of venality."[84] Cooke did not mention bribery in connection to Apache Canyon. In a later letter on the subject of Magoffin's capture in Chihuahua, he acknowledged Magoffin's offer of a "large bribe" for the destruction of incriminating documents, seeming to justify its payment in light of "how narrowly you escaped with your life, in further efforts to serve our Government in Chihuahua."[85]

Senator Thomas Hart Benton charged after the war that a bribe took place and that Kearny was responsible for it. The claim is qualified by the fact that Benton's son-in-law was being court-martialed for disobeying Kearny in California. Historian Bernard Devoto observes that Polk's specific instructions to Magoffin were "a secret he kept even from his diary." While the learned trader likely described to the president the "miniature Santa Anna" that was Armijo, Devoto believes Benton's intimation that Magoffin "bought" Armijo "presumably for

$50,000 is almost certainly untrue." Magoffin at least would have convinced Armijo that it would be both safer and more profitable to let the conquest proceed unopposed.[86] Beyond Armijo himself, interpretation of the overall action confirms the frontier's market encroachment onto this parcel of Mexican sovereignty.

Mexican officers, including the hard-boiled Facundo Pino, reportedly offered to lead the Mexican regulars against the Americans at Apache Canyon. Armijo resolved to keep the soldiers for his own protection as he fled south into Mexico. In the darkest telling, Armijo turned the cannon on his compatriots. Citizens branded the governor a traitor, disloyal, and cowardly.[87] A Río Abajo *señora* indicted Armijo's manhood. The governor "had a good army to back him," she told a Kearny officer, "and could have driven you all back."[88] Susan Magoffin visited with a woman who spoke "in favor of the foreigners, and without hesitation says General Armijo is a *ladrón* [thief] and coward."[89] Captain Cooke met a "wealthy man" in Valencia named Otero (likely Antonio José), a "malcontent" who had "vented his spleen on Armijo and his conduct which he regarded as disgraceful," then "*professed* that he would have favored a voluntary annexation."[90] Significantly, 105 Nuevomexicanos sent a petition to Mexico City excoriating Armijo in the name of national dignity. They would have "put up a fight," they affirmed, had the governor not abandoned them at the crucial moment, subjecting them to a "state of conquest and slavery."[91] Some signers had been critics of the American presence in New Mexico. Col. Diego Archuleta attached a report to the president of Mexico detailing his efforts to resist the invaders. Others, like Donaciano Vigil, had been quite friendly with the Americans prior to the occupation yet signed the condemnation of Armijo.[92]

The Army of the West tramped out of Apache Canyon and arrived in Santa Fe on August 16 unimpeded. Kearny ordered his command to obey the Texan boundary and treat the people as U.S. citizens. The troops were subjected to his integrative and precisely liberal mission. "We are taking possession of a country and extending the laws of the United States over a population who [has] hitherto lived under widely different ones," he rolled out, "and humanity as well as policy requires that we should conciliate the inhabitants by kind and courteous treatment." The 54th and 55th articles of war were read to each company "that all may be made sensible of the responsibility imposed upon them. And it is hereby made the duty of each one to report at this office any violation of the spirit or purport of it that may come to his knowledge."[93]

Kearny trod uninterrupted to the door of the Palace of the Governors on August 18. On his departure from the defense of New Mexico, Armijo had appointed department secretary Juan Bautista Vigil y Alarid interim governor to take charge of representing the department (although he was not in the formal line of succession), persuading him to surrender to avoid certain disaster. On meeting the conquering general, Vigil y Alarid affirmed that Santa Fe was prepared to receive America.[94] Still, some residents fled. Cooke thought them panic-stricken at the sight of "such an imposing array of horsemen of a superior race, and, it appeared, over-estimated our numbers, which the reports of ignorance and fear had vastly magnified."[95] Edwards found the "illiterate portion of the population . . . expecting to be branded on the cheek with the letters 'U.S.,' such as are worn on the soldiers' sabre belts. Women could be seen in various parts with their hands covering their faces or sobbing aloud."[96] The same anonymous officer cited earlier said the people "appeared satisfied."[97] These emotions and others were undoubtedly manifest upon Kearny's mighty appearance.

Vigil y Alarid formally received Kearny. The general reiterated his assurances of protection and safety for the peaceable populace and the familiar extension of friendship. Over the yin of unyielding power and the yang of surface consensus, the anonymous officer described the scene: "In explaining his object in coming into the country, and the kindness he felt for the inhabitants, [General Kearny] was mild and courteous; but then (would add) 'I claim the whole of N[ew] M[exico] for the United States. I put my hand on it from this moment (bringing his hand firmly down on his thigh) and demand obedience to its laws."[98] Kearny would henceforth be governor of New Mexico. Soldiers hoisted the American flag. Thirteen howitzer salutes shot off and a bugle blew. "There," Kearny intoned, "my guns proclaim that the flag of the United States floats over this capital."[99]

Vigil y Alarid publicly swore obedience to "a great and powerful nation," to "the Republic that owes its tradition to the immortal Washington, whom all civilized nations admire and respect."[100] Sociologist Thomas Hall claims that the response represented economic

Fig. 4. *Capture of Santa Fe, 1846.* Brigadier General Stephen Watts Kearny capturing Santa Fe, New Mexico, 18 August 1846, during the Mexican-American War. Wood engraving, nineteenth century, artist unknown. The structure in the left background would have been a presidial *torreón* used for defensive purposes in Nuevomexicano fighting with Indians. The Granger Collection, New York.

Fig. 5. *S. W. Kearny, from an original daguerreotype. Engraved by Y. B. Welch, expressly for Graham's Magazine. Peter A. Juley & Sons, photographer.* Gen. Stephen Watts Kearny creatively enacted President James K. Polk's call for a liberal conquest of New Mexico. Image courtesy of the Bancroft Library, University of California, Berkeley.

motives among elite Nuevomexicanos.[101] The scholar of literature Genaro Padilla argues that Vigil y Alarid's proclamation "operated as an early example of multivoiced encodation, a rhetorical appeasement that made the occupation sufferable," articulating Nuevomexicano fidelity to a homeland "that would not be summarily dissolved by conquest, governmental reorganization, or dispossession at the material level."[102] Samuel Sisneros calls the statement submissive and ambivalent, expressing both nationalistic loyalties toward Mexico and resignation to the conquering force before the Nuevomexicanos.[103]

Politically it was the earliest instance of a Nuevomexicano translating the liberal ideology of the United States on behalf of occupied New Mexico. Vigil y Alarid ratified Kearny's presumptuous political idealism and assisted liberal diffusionism. "It is not for us to determine the boundaries of nations," he conceded. "The cabinets of Mexico and Washington will arrange these differences. It is for us to obey and respect the established authorities, no matter what may be our private opinions. . . . No one in this world can successfully resist the power of him who is stronger. In the name of the entire department I swear obedience to the Northern Republic and I tender my respect to its laws and authority."[104] The Santa Fe alcalde and local officials stepped up for the required oaths as those in the San Miguel ceremonies had done.[105] Kearny held out confidence that the common people basically understood the advantages of their new government. He sounded a distinction destined to find its discursive niche in the forced, modernist annexation of New Mexico. It was the "intelligent portion" that, he felt sure, was "much gratified."[106]

With more legitimation work ahead of him, Kearny disseminated his message of comradeship and raw power to the Santa Fe populace four days later. He conveyed a promise of protection and reinforced that he had taken New Mexico with a strong military force with another on the way, which "it would be but folly or madness for any dissatisfied or discontented persons to think of resisting." While the existing laws of New Mexico were needed for a while, a mission of political replication would introduce a "free government," as Kearny noted, "with the least possible delay, similar to those in the United States." The people would "be called on to exercise the rights of freemen in electing their own representatives to the Territorial legislature." Those in office would need to consider themselves "good citizens" willing to take the oath of allegiance to the United States as they no longer belonged to Mexico.[107]

On this last point Kearny made an important shift in policy, submitting a claim to the whole of New Mexico. "This overleaps the first announcement which seemed the assertion of the old Texan claim," Cooke noted.[108] Edrington argues that the general "had no further use for the Texan claim." Kearny made his intention crystal clear on August 22. He would "hold the department, with its original boundaries, (on both sides of the Del Norte [Río Grande]) as part of the United States, and under the name of 'the Territory of New Mexico.'" Again he absolved the people of allegiance to Mexico and declared the "wish and intention" of the U.S. government to provide New Mexico with a "free government."[109]

Kearny's occupation altered Santa Fe's social landscape with 3,500 American personnel. Commissaries, quartermasters, "and a tribe of clerks" affected an air of industry and progress.[110] The Army of the West engorged Santa Fe with disciplined sentinels, tent settlements, and marching drills. The American flag, "liberty's emblem," Hughes deemed it, "continued to stream bravely from the top of the tall staff... in the plaza." In a sign of liberal as well as constitutional consideration for the masses, the soldiers did not think it proper to dispossess the people of their homes in order to quarter themselves. The soldiers of the American army were said by a partisan to exhibit "a degree of moral firmness and a regard for the rights of property which is truly characteristic of the American people."[111]

Kearny's literate military men praised the liberality of Manifest Destiny and prided themselves as the agents of its extension to the remote corners of the continent. "Our success—we never doubt it!" rationalized Cooke. "And the very desperation of any alternative must ensure it—shall give us for boundary that world line of a mighty ocean's coast, looking across to the cradle land of humanity; and shall girdle the earth with civilization."[112] Edwards saw the occupation as stunningly prophetic. The sun on this day went down "having witnessed the dawning glory of New Mexico, and shone upon the Stars and Stripes that floated over its capital."[113] The patriotic narrative had the spread of America reigning with permanent reform. "There is evidently a large proportion of very ignorant people here," wrote the anonymous officer in Whig Party optimism, "and many of them seem to think, judging from their deportment, that they have no rights, and are bound to obey their superiors. When our laws and institutions are established here, the resources of the country will be developed, and these people will become prosperous and happy."[114]

Cooke looked to the imperial dismantling of a perceived medievalism. On one hand, the spacious residences of the few rich Mexicans, built around large courtyards, were "quite imposing," he recorded, "and each contains the key of their wealth, a store of necessaries for their dependent laborers." On the other, it would take time and effort for the Nuevomexicanos to become truly a part of U.S. destiny because of the "system of peonage" wherein the aristocrats kept the "poor peons always in debt, and this legally binds them and their families to endless service and dependence; and they can be cast off, without any provision in their old age. They have been informed that they shall soon have a voice in their own government. Doubtless this flagrant servitude will be gradually broken up; but when shall such people be capable of self-government! There will be a territorial government for thirty years—and the language will not change faster than the color of the citizens."[115] Not a bad bit of sociopolitical forecasting, this. In the meantime, the scene prompted another officer to remark that self-government rejected monarchy. What the Mexicans called the governor's palace, "we democrats must call. . . the governor's house."[116]

George Rutledge Gibson gauged the view of average New Mexicans for whom this high-toned perspective might not hit home, observing that while the people may have been "civil and well disposed, not being able to resist the force brought against them," they were therefore "shy and far from receiving us generally as deliverers." Nevertheless, he perceived the leading and principal men of the region regarding the Americans as liberators and assumed that those leaders "no doubt will influence the balance and bring [their more plebian compatriots] to the same state of mind."[117]

Kearny further replicated by seating himself as the governor of a presumptive American territory. He officiously reported to the Mexican general in Chihuahua that everything in New Mexico was "quiet and peaceable," expressing his "sincere" belief that the people understood the advantages to derive from a change of government "and are much gratified with it."[118] Kearny felt confirmed by the parade of spontaneous welcoming ceremonies that filed in to greet him. "The general sits in his room and is constantly receiving visits from the officers of ex-Governor Armijo and others, who fled on his approach," noted the anonymous officer. "Many of them come into his presence very much disquieted, but he has the happy faculty of calming all their fears, and he is winning laurels among them daily." Pueblos chiefs paid their respects and declared fealty to the United States, relating the legend in their tradition of a white man coming from the east to release them from the "bonds and shackles" of the Spanish conquerors. Kearny accepted an invitation from Santo Domingo Pueblo, where he was placed at center of a peace ritual, ironically involving a mock battle. As in other meet-and-greets, Kearny paid the obligatory visit to the local priest and addressed the people in a message of friendship translated into the Spanish and Pueblo languages. Jemez Pueblo found Kearny and those under him treating them well.[119]

Such demonstrations index widespread acceptance of conquest. Well-known Nuevomexicano figures offered congratulatory messages. The Perea extended family of Bernalillo and Corrales in the Río Abajo and major participants in the Santa Fe trade unabashedly welcomed the Americans, journeying to Santa Fe to form an acquaintance with their officers and negotiate an understanding of the primary motivations of the occupation. José Leandro Perea, the great don of Bernalillo County and uncle to José Francisco Chávez who had ridden into New Mexico with Kearny, ascertained that as a close family friend disclosed, "in the future, he owed his allegiance to the United States."[120] "Various deputations" arrived from Taos, asking for protection from aggressive *indios*.[121] Kearny's adjutant, Henry Turner, wrote of "many dignitaries" calling in late August, "much finer and more respectable looking men than we have yet seen in the country—less of the Indian tinge in their complexion."[122]

Kearny reciprocated the gestures of hospitality, inviting prominent New Mexicans to confer and visit. The Catholic clergy had been among the most vocal critics of American abuses in New Mexico prior to the American intrusion. At the moment, however, descriptions on the spot suggest rather captive conciliators. A special request went to Father Antonio José Martínez of Taos. The Church's importance commanded a military escort to the capital for Martínez and his brothers and other Taoseños for their swearing in as American citizens. On the surface "this looks like a forced invitation," historian

Angélico Chávez notes, but as an early biographer recalled from personal memory, Martínez took it "as a gesture of honor and highest esteem on Kearny's part," although Martínez's loyalty to the American invasion would appear to shift from time to time.[123] Vicar Ortiz had fled into the mountains, but with the assurance of peace returned to continue heading the provincial Church. Kearny attended mass and spoke to "get the shut" of the people; he and Ortiz were reported to have become "good friends," although here again, the vicar's attitude toward the incoming American institutions would undergo change.[124] Hughes took note of the priest of San Felipe and the curate of the Taos Valley arriving to "acknowledge the authority of the conqueror, receive his commands and ask protection for the churches and church property." Assured of protections, the clergymen returned to their "temples of worship" and homes "peaceably and favorably disposed toward the Americans, more subdued by kindness than by force of arms."[125] The priest from San Felipe would have been Padre José Manuel Gallegos whose reception is called "exuberant" by one historian and "tacit acceptance" by another. The other priests of the Río Abajo prepared to accept the new order.[126]

Kearny adorned the occasion with a celebratory ball. Four to five hundred civilians of both nationalities made for a highly sociable event. American and Mexican bunting graced the hall. In Cooke's description of what represented a rite of legitimation, it was "a political, or conciliatory affair, and we put the best face on it." It "went off harmoniously, and quite pleasantly," Cooke observed, "considering the extravagant variety in its make-up." The Americans "did not feel particular out here." Cooke found the music "execrable," but nothing transpired "to mar the harmony of the evening. Americans and Mexicans harmonious."[127] Gibson thought it "a new thing for plain republicans to revel in a palace, which, if not Montezuma's, is claimed by the aborigines as a portion of the dominions over which he swayed his scepter." Turner thought the event to have come off "remarkably well," for it included "a great crowd of males and females," and "Mexican musicians." One historian discerns an awkward friendly decorum in the "motley throng." An aspect of sociality involved "American army officers in gold-braided dress uniforms, dignified Spanish and Mexican dons in picturesque contrast, sturdy traders in ill-fitting 'store clothes,'" male and female gamblers, and Mexican men and women "studying with interest the handwork of the women of Missouri who had sewed and embroidered the company pennants of the First Missouri." The dances alternated between American, "Spanish," and Indian types, each "race" finding "interest in the steps and movements of the others." Kearny earned "unfading laurels for his affable and kind treatment of the people and the wise and statesmanlike policies which he pursues."[128]

As the ball appealed to a certain elite society, the untiring Kearny ingratiated his rule to the settlements in a three-week journey to the Río Abajo. The "gala procession," as Cooke called it, visited a string of villages so that, as John Hughes personally observed, the people "might see the conduct of [Kearny's] soldiers and have confidence in the efficiency of the protection he had promised. The civil behavior of the troops toward the inhabitants greatly conciliated those who were disaffected toward the American government."[129] At Algodones the soldiers were "sumptuously entertained" by the family of José Leandro Perea. José Leandro's cousin Juan, son of a former Mexican governor, feted the conquering entourage with a banquet down the road in Bernalillo. Guests numbered more than fifty.[130]

Kearny and company were welcomed into the home of former Governor Armijo on the outskirts of Alburquerque. Villagers sold the occupying troops melons, peaches, grapes, and other provisions.[131] Don José Chávez, father of José Francisco who had served as Kearny's interpreter during the march, feted the general. The local clergyman appeared to an American observer as "priest, fop, courtier, and poet curiously combined in one person," yet delivered an eloquent discourse after Mass, "eulogizing the grandeur, magnanimity, power, and justice of the United States." The Tomé folk put on their saint's day festival with games, skyrockets, pine fagots, and morning Mass. In this wholly revamped contact zone, young Mexican women and the American soldiers flirted, "signs supplying the place of conversation, as neither party could speak the language of the other."[132]

Next to the face of consensual co-mingling ran a current of *nativo* resignation to manifest power. Many chose to participate politically in the affairs of their native homeland, "even though they had not supported the U.S. invasion," a historian notes. "Those in this group perhaps acted reluctantly but according to the realities of the political situation." The influential northern New Mexico family of Pedro

Ignacio Gallegos consisted of tacit legitimizers. The prefect José Pablo Gallegos typified Mexicans "who continued their political commitment to New Mexico after the change in sovereignty as an effort to safeguard their personal interests as well as those of the Hispanic community."[133]

The incorporative process included solemn administrative duty. The war was far from decided, yet it was considered acceptable "under the law of nations," as the secretary of war would later declare, that a "power conquering a territory or country has a right to establish a civil government within the same as a means of securing the conquest."[134] Kearny thus acted with solemn officialdom to fix merchant license fees, abolish a stamp tax on legal documents, and make local appointments of alcaldes and prefects.[135] This too produced legitimation. As Hughes noted, Mexicans who fled the conquest returned to Santa Fe and gradually sustained the new government, "the administration of justice appearing to them to be conducted "upon safer and broader principles than had hitherto been known in New Mexico," and in which society seemed to be "reforming and reestablishing upon a new and republican basis."[136] But Kearny went considerably further with the initiative to apply the law of nations to distinctly impose American civil law. In Kearny's boldest replicative act, citizenship was bestowed on a foreign element within the structure of an American territory with rights and obligations appropriate to the American state. The whole territorial appropriation had its certification in the so-called Kearny Code of Law. Three Kearny staff members and an American resident trader borrowed portions from various state constitutions, a common practice in nineteenth-century America.[137] They defined a legal-administrative structure for New Mexico based on the Organic Law of the Missouri Territory.[138] As Hughes noted, New Mexico was now "styled 'the territory of New Mexico in the United States.'"[139]

Kearny usurped a right of Congress by pitching his book as New Mexico's Organic Law. Article 1 declared the Territory of New Mexico a U.S. possession with a political structure identical to the U.S. territorial model.[140] Article 2 established a two-term governor as executive with civil, military, and law enforcement duties. The posts of territorial secretary, U.S. marshal, district attorney, three Supreme Court judges, and county coroner would be filled by presidential appointment. Article 3 established the legislative powers in a general assembly to consist of a council and a house of representatives with enumerated representation for each county. It marked the first appearance of the republican construct "county" in New Mexico. U.S. policymakers have "almost universally" viewed elections as the "most important indicator of a pro-liberalization policy," which can be taken as the "central component of any 'pro democratic' policy."[141] Kearny counts as an early representative of such a "policymaker." The popular election found its place in the Code, with rules for determining eligible voters and qualifications of officials. A pointed presumption appeared in the scheduling of an election for assembly representatives. The governor was mandated to designate the polling places for the election to be held on the first Monday of August, 1847. New Mexico would be a part of the United States regardless of war's outcome, so it seemed. The first assembly was scheduled in Santa Fe on the same day and every two years thereafter. Article 4 defined judicial powers of superior and inferior tribunals and established the auditor and treasurer, both to be named by the legislature.

Mainstream America valued education for inculcating good citizenship and aiding economic development. Public education was fast becoming available to white Americans (and some blacks), making for one of the world's most literate societies. As the United States expanded across the continent many American anti-imperialists called for giving the schoolhouse preeminence over the military in the campaign to spread ideas of freedom and equal rights.[142] Kearny's Code ordained that the means of education in New Mexico "be forever encouraged." At least one school was to be established "in each village as soon as practicable, where the poor shall be educated free of all charges," a classic American image extended onto a Mexican socioscape.

The Code exuded a conscious, virtually didactic liberal light. Its Bill of Rights, modeled on the Declaration of Independence and the first ten amendments to the Constitution, vested political power in "the people" under the "great and essential principles of liberty and free government." The people's right to peaceful assembly had its protection "for their common good." The redress of grievance by petition "or remonstrance" was included, as was "a natural and indefensible right to worship Almighty God according to the dictates of [one's] own conscience" and their Christian church, with "none oppressed" and no religion restricting a right to elected office, "office of honor, trust or profit." The inviolate right of trial, the right to counsel in criminal cases, freedom of speech, and the responsibility to prevent its abuse found their places. Clergy and religious teachers were absolved from bearing arms, jury duty, road work and military duty.[143]

Kearny's set of laws exceeded in its liberal foundation what appeared in a Mexican department. A forty-two page leap of rationality introduced a mountain of rules for the running of the territory—attachments and prosecutorial regulations for circuit attorneys, clerks, constables, courts, judicial powers, crimes, punishments, Superior Court decisions, executions, fees, guardians, habeas corpus, water courses, stock markets, and much more.[144]

As a member of the asamblea, Donaciano Vigil had helped plan for the defense against Kearny's conquering army and joined in the patriotic condemnation of Governor Armijo's withdrawal from Apache Canyon. Signaling a change of heart, he reviewed the Code's legal formula for accuracy. He and Capt. David Waldo, a scholar of the Spanish language, had the laws printed in Spanish and English on Padre Martínez's hand press.[145] Kearny kept New Mexico under ultimate military control and proclaimed the rules and regulations of his Code in effect.[146] He proceeded to appoint his territorial administrators, first naming Francisco Ortiz and José García treasurer and collector respectively, although it does not appear that they actually served. Two resident Mexicans received high level appointment. Donaciano Vigil accepted the post of territorial secretary. Former delegate to the Mexican Congress and Río Abajo sheep magnate Antonio José Otero became chief of the superior court.[147] These two made up the de facto inaugural class of Nuevomexicano political integration into the American political system.[148]

Kearny's consensual occupation swayed the cultivated *hombres de bién* Vigil and Otero.[149] Both were conversant in English and connected to Americans by bonds of friendship and mercantile alliance. Their appointments in the conquest carried a dual purpose. On one hand, they adhered to Polk's injunction for friendly Mexicans to be involved in the transition to American rule. On the other, they fulfilled Kearny's need for general legitimation in the territory, suggested by his ever specifying their status as native. It was an early instance of the hegemonic amplification and appropriation of Mexican class structure when Kearny took note of Otero's coming from "a prominent and influential Spanish family."[150] The willingness of Vigil and Otero to participate in the administration of conquest of their homeland represented the collaborative pact among foreign agents, here within a liberal project and for the practical running of the new political order.

In another respect, however, the initial Mexican appointments fell short of nativo parity. Kearny had initially kept Juan Bautista Vigil y Alarid in place as civil governor in part to allay fears and make it seem like no major changes were being made in New Mexico's status quo. He would perhaps have kept him on, but Vigil y Alarid counted among the Mexicans who could not countenance the gringo appropriation of New Mexico, choosing to leave New Mexico.[151] Kearny reportedly offered the governorship to José Leandro Perea. Legend has the wealthy Bernalillo don declining as no formal transfer of New Mexico to the United States had taken place, although it is probable that Perea wanted no distractions from his lucrative business.[152] Kearny shortchanged Polk's wish for indirect rule by naming as governor the famous Taos trader and Bent's Fort proprietor Charles Bent. Kearny noted in announcing the appointment that Bent was married to a native of Taos, a relative of Donaciano Vigil. Kearny turned to American settlers and immigrants as well for two Supreme Court justices, solicitor general, and marshal. Kearny again noted that superior court judge Charles Beaubien, another Taos trader, "was married to a native wife." Joab Houghton became a Supreme Court justice though he lacked legal education and experience with the law. He was a close associate of Bent and Beaubien.[153]

Col. Mauricio Ugarte withdrew his Chihuahua troops from the lower Río Abajo on news of Kearny's settled occupation.[154] A soldier-occupier noted that in the short space of fifty days an army had "been marched nearly 900 miles, over a desert country, and conquered a province of 80,000 souls, without firing a gun—a success which may be attributed mainly to the skill and ability with which General Kearny has managed this arduous and delicate business."[155] Devoto notes that for the first time the Americans "had conquered a foreign capital. And they had done exactly what Mr. Polk had instructed them to do: they had taken New Mexico without firing a shot."[156] Polk, Gen. Winfield Scott, and the American press praised Kearny's "great feat."[157]

By mid-September Kearny had full confidence in the people's satisfaction and contentment with his political change. He prided himself in a message to Washington that they "apparently vied with each other to see who could show to us the greatest hospitality and kindness." Kearny could discern no movement toward organized resistance in all the territory.[158] At a dinner party local merchants gave in his honor, the general toasted the United States and Mexico. They were "now united, may no one ever think of parting [them]." Nuevomexicanos reportedly responded with "Viva, Viva."[159] Having secured New Mexico with "order, peace, and quietness," and pressed to make California by year's end, Kearny embarked on the next leg of his westward campaign. He marched a bulk of his army out on September 25, 1846, with the aim of replicating in California the consensus, "free" civil government conquest he had instituted for New Mexico. Col. Alexander Doniphan sallied southward with another detachment and orders to capture Chihuahua. Col. Sterling Price was left to hold the command of New Mexico.[160]

It later came out how much Kearny had exceeded his orders of occupation. He acted illegitimately in declaring Nuevomexicanos U.S. citizens and New Mexico an American territory. The U.S. Constitution held that possession alone could not bestow the basic rights of citizenship for native inhabitants. Several essential legalities were required, including assignation and ratification of an international treaty, subsequent legislative declaration of the annexed land as a federal territory, and congressional determination of the rights of citizenship for specified territorial inhabitants.[161] Kearny's colonial government "should have been of a character purely military," a historian noted, "with the right to perform only such civil duties as were necessary to the full enjoyment of the advantages resulting from the conquest, and to the due protection of the rights of all persons and the property of the inhabitants."[162]

Instead, a self-appointed messiah of republican virtue and self-designated instrument of liberal diffusion adopted the model of Andrew Jackson's free-wheeling, controversial, and less successful appointment as governor of the Florida Territory.[163] Kearny failed to observe the distinction between a temporary government of occupation, which had federal authority, and permanent annexation with legitimate citizenship. After Kearny left New Mexico, General Scott warned him not to declare California formally annexed, reminding him that permanent incorporation "must depend on the Government of the United States."[164]

Whig enemies of President Polk expressed alarm at occupied lands being declared U.S. territory. They called the Kearny Code excess and an abuse of Kearny's discretion, and they questioned the administration's authority to grant any civil power to Kearny. Whigs refuted the Democratic claim that Kearny possessed authority to "relieve Mexicans of their national allegiance, declare them citizens, and command from them oaths of allegiance to the United States." Politically, transforming the benighted race of Mexicans into voters appeared especially egregious. As one historian notes, "By imperial decree and no doubt at Polk's urging, Whigs argued General Kearny had swelled Democratic ranks by extending suffrage to another foreign-born Catholic group who, like the Irish, would not shed their unrepublican habits easily. Nor could a people so bereft of all experience with liberty be expected to resist the demagogic tactics of the Jacksonian Democrats."[165]

Polk surged to defend Kearny, emphasizing that the instructions given those military officers in charge of securing Mexican territories were required by the exigencies of occupation. A universal principle formed the cornerstone of Polk's method. The political terms of engagement facilitated "the amelioration of martial law, which modern civilization requires," he maintained, "and were due as well to the security of the conquest as to the inhabitants of the conquered territory." Polk was made to confront the fact that he had not approved Kearny's governmental decree nor his purporting to establish and organize a permanent territorial government of the United States over the territory "and to impart to its inhabitants political rights which, under the Constitution of the United States, can be enjoyed permanently only by citizens of the United States." The president refused to censure his occupation general, and he used liberal, inclusive, argument to back him. If Kearny had exceeded his legal bounds, it occurred as "the offspring of a patriotic desire to give to the inhabitants the privileges and immunities so cherished by the people of our own country, and which they believed calculated to improve their condition and promote their prosperity." As he continued, "Any such excess has resulted in no practical injury, but can and will be early corrected, in a manner to alienate as little as possible the good feelings of the inhabitants of the conquered territory."[166]

Secretary Marcy notified Kearny privately that his legal code went "beyond the line designated by the President, and proposed to confer upon the people of that Territory political rights under the Constitution of the United States." Polk did not approve the code, Kearny was reminded, "and only Congress could confer the rights of citizenship; therefore it should not have been carried into effect, even though the broad outlines of civil government for New Mexico had been authorized." In point of partisanship, the "extent and character of our possession in the territories conquered from the enemy should not be open to question or cavil."[167]

However, the deed was done in New Mexico. Colonel Price received no orders to rescind Kearny's declarations of political integration. The Kearny Code and Nuevomexicanos-as-U.S. citizens remained as living, ground-level realities.[168] The social intercourse of key Mexicans and Americans would continue to reinforce an understanding of New Mexico as attached to the United States, not to be dislodged even under conditions of violent resistance.

Bloody Conquest

Not all Mexicans were prepared to hop on Kearny's co-opting wagon. "Deeper and deadlier hatreds" lurked in the minds of many in the populace, observes Devoto.[169] As Lt. Dyer saw, "it began to be apparent that the people generally were dissatisfied with the change [in national government]." Lawrence Waldo, from an important trading family in the Río Arriba settlement of Mora, told his father that those who knew *la gente*—the people—recognized that the rulers had made a "general mistake in regard to their willingness to be subject to the rule of the United States." It was "satisfactorily ascertained" that "not one in ten is *agusto*"—happy. Waldo did not see "one in one hundred" content with the conquest on the eastern side of the mountains.[170] The British frontiersman George Ruxton found "over all New Mexico that the most bitter feeling and most determined hostility existed against the Americans, who certainly in Santa Fe and elsewhere have not been very anxious to conciliate the people."[171]

Embers of resentment were stoked by Kearny's top government appointments, awarded precisely to members of the resident American community who had previously offended Mexican sensibilities.[172] "Governor" Charles Bent, recall, had carried a running feud with Padre Martínez over land and the treatment of prairie Indians. Bent admitted to the American consul in Santa Fe to the horsewhipping that he and another American gave to Juan Bautista Vigil y Alarid in the latter's home over a dispute regarding illegal trafficking along the Santa Fe Trail. Bent was arrested and jailed but continued to bully Vigil y Alarid. The incident gained fame in the context of the Texan expedition to take possession of New Mexico.[173] Little wonder that, as a Missouri volunteer noted, Bent as governor produced "a good deal of dissatisfaction." Nuevomexicano nationalists recognized Bent's Fort as a conduit for Kearny's occupation. In this context Kearny snubbed some of New Mexico's leading families by delivering the new government into the hands of the Taos "American Party" and the merchants of Santa Fe.[174]

Rowdy members of the U.S. military degraded the liberal occupation. Ruxton observed that "by their bullying and overbearing demeanor" towards the Mexicans, soldiers had "in a great measure" been the cause of anti-American hatred. The American volunteer units generally formed unruly lots during the war, compared to professional soldiers. They resisted the disciplinary measures and austere treatment accorded regulars. The latter were "trained to obedience," as one contemporary writer described it; the former were "bred to freedom."[175] A regular officer characterized the volunteers in New Mexico free from Colonel Price's control in more reviled measure as a "well-drilled set of Goths and Vandals." Susan Magoffin viewed them as "ruffians" who could "soil the property of a friend much less an enemy." Another contemporary said the volunteers had "degenerated into a military mob."[176] Volunteers antagonized communities, ran roughshod over villages, and converted Santa Fe into "a roaring Wild West town, full of jubilation, offensiveness, and personal insult," drinking, robbing people, and stealing cattle and corn.[177] Rampaging volunteers evinced greater quantities of the American military's racist mentality, a felt confidence of prowess as soldiers "merged with the widely popular notion among Americans that they represented a racially superior stock," confirmed by victories on the march against Mexico.[178] A new breed of American wagon masters appeared. One group ran off with the cannon that Colonel Doniphan gave the people of Doña Ana for protection against Indians, deeming it "unfit for Mexicans."[179]

Significantly, Kearny's departure depleted the occupying military and security weakened the more with expeditionary forces sent out to Navajo country. The wellsprings of nativo bitterness swelled into an evident movement. Lieutenant Gibson heard one day in late October 1846 the rumor "industriously circulated" that "the Spaniards were to have attempted revolt" the night before "by cutting off the officers, producing confusion, and then seizing upon the artillery and magazine." Authorities paid little attention, Gibson noted, "notwithstanding it is countenanced by some men of influence who reside here." Gibson saw the best informed tending to lay the plot "at the doors of a few men who have been reaping a rich harvest from the soldiers, and who adopt this plan to retain a large force at this point." A proliferating nativo grapevine threatened populace and troops, serving to keep up a "hatred or contempt which should be kept down, now that they are our fellow citizens."[180]

Others were said to be responsible for the talk of a "rising of the people." Occupiers perceived the manipulating, ineffectual hand of clerical and "feudal" elites unable to accept that their star had fallen under the new order. Cooke attested to priests and "some of the millionaires" pushing "to attempt to regain their despotic sway and grinding oppression of the people." He was disappointed with the blind ones who refused to accept their good fortune: "[T]ake them all together I think the cowardly barbarians—too fortunate in having a decent government forced upon them—are selfish enough to refrain from any risk in the world." Dyer wrote home in a similar tone regarding the clergy and wealthy class having "motives of interest" in rebellion, and the "*tiers etats*, because degraded and ignorant as they were, they were wholly under the influence of the other two classes, and were unable to appreciate the advantages to be derived by them in the change [of government]." Dyer said that many began to predict an effort to be made "to wrest the government from us. . . . [W]e received certain intelligence that the plot was formed, and nearly ripe for execution, that in its ramifications it extended far and wide."[181] Colonel Price received on December 15 credible word of an attempt to excite the people.[182] Governor Bent reported to Secretary Buchanan that a Mexican "friendly" to their government told of a conspiracy among the Mexicans to force the expulsion of U.S. troops and civil authorities. Cooke found "many of the most influential persons in the northern part of the territory" engaged. Oral histories collected by Ralph Emerson Twitchell point to clandestine meetings at a house on the south side of the Santa Fe Plaza and in other places in the Santa Fe area.[183]

Evidence of core conspirators coming from those who complained of American excesses in the decade before the war is the inclusion of the clergymen Vicar Juan Felipe Ortiz, said to be a "leading spirit" of resistance, and Father Antonio José Martínez, though it contradicted the earlier report of his being fine with Kearny.[184] Some suggestion exists that Father José Manuel Gallegos was in on the planning.[185] Price's informant labeled Diego Archuleta and Tomás Ortiz instigators.[186] Twitchell's oral histories recalled the influential Pino brothers, Facundo and Manuel.[187] The research of amateur historian Amado Chávez added Manuel Chávez, Domingo C. de Baca, and Tomás Cabeza de Baca, who would have been among the wealthy elites mentioned by the Kearny officers. There were the brothers Miguel and Nicolás Pino (grandsons of New Mexico's first delegate to the Spanish Cortes, Pedro Bautista Pino), who had condemned Armijo's abandonment at Apache Canyon and later refused to take the required oath of allegiance to the United States.[188] Important to note, practically all of these hailed from the Río Arriba district, mostly in the Santa Fe, Taos, and Abiquiú regions. Kearny's tour of New Mexico communities to gain legitimacy for his occupation had neglected this area entirely. Technically, the important figure of Tomás Cabeza de Baca lived in the Río Abajo, but his Peña Blanca village sat closer to Santa Fe than the center of Río Abajo where rico families maintained their *estancias*. A host of other figures would surface in the resistance.

Historians consider Diego Archuleta a leading light of rebellion. Archuleta was both a colonel in the Mexican army and New Mexico lieutenant governor at the time of Kearny's occupation. His involvement in the Kearny march is linked to the August 12 visit that James Magoffin paid to Governor Armijo. Magoffin is supposed to have notified Archuleta that President Polk had authorized granting him the land that lay west of the Río Grande on the Texan international border in exchange for his cooperation in the occupation. Archuleta did not press a full stand at Apache Canyon based on this commitment, the narrative has it, believing that he would become governor of the non-occupied portion of New Mexico. Kearny subsequently negated the offer when he declared U.S. annexation of the entire department. Adding fuel to the betrayal, Archuleta received no appointment in the occupation government, possibly because the president's office reversed its previous plan to co-opt Archuleta, nor was it possible that he would receive what Paul Horgan calls a "lordship over all New Mexico lying across the Rio Grande."[189] In Clarke's reading, it was "developing events," not any individual, that had "double-crossed" Archuleta.[190] Twitchell flatly states that Archuleta "organized the first conspiracy for the over-throw of the government at Santa Fe."[191] At the least, the attribution was destined to become a legendary piece of New Mexico's political annexation, to be heard anon.

Tomás Ortiz, half-brother of the vicar and assembly *vocal* at war's start, is considered an important agent of resistance.[192] An American military report had him arranging "the organization of. . . several detachments and the plan of attack." One company would assemble in the church, another in a valley north of Santa Fe. "In the dead of night, at a signal from the bells of the church towers, the conspirators were to rush into the streets, seize the guns and massacre the whole body of troops," the intelligence had it. Select parties were to seize and capture Governor Bent and Colonel Price.[193] Susan Magoffin heard that because of "some sign of discovery," execution of the rebellion was deferred until the 25th of December.[194] One report has Gertrudis Barceló, the saloon owner having political capital, tipping off Donaciano Vigil in early December, who gave the information to Price.[195]

Price instituted martial law. Guards and field weaponry were stationed at the Santa Fe Plaza. Governor Bent begged the people in a circular to ignore the stirring animosity against the United States. Seven of what Bent called "secondary conspirators" were captured, including Manuel Chaves and Nicolás Pino, after which they shifted allegiances to the United States. Diego Archuleta and Manuel Pino fled and escaped civil and military search nets. Disheartened Americans heard about Archuleta's strong support among the people of his Río Arriba district.[196] The people in the area of San Miguel, where Kearny had made his initial entreaties of friendship, remained agitated. Lt. J. W. Abert reported that "the whole country seemed rife and ready to tear down the glorious stars and stripes; to tear down the nest of the eagle from the rugged mountains of the west." Abert issued a liberal's imperial caution to the rebels. The "noble bird looks down from his lofty position, and sees through the puerile attempts to dislodge him. Beware, beware of the eagle!"[197] Bent advised Secretary Buchanan of the need for the United States to maintain a military force there "for years to come."[198] He too sought to lay a liberal vestment over the conquest, advising the people in his circular not to throw away foolishly "the benefits of their new citizenship by supporting or participating in any future overthrow effort." The governor sought to douse a report of a Mexican army on its way from Chihuahua to liberate New Mexico. He urged all to turn a deaf ear to "false doctrines" and remain quiet, "attending to your domestic affairs, so that you may enjoy under the law all the blessings of peace."[199]

As 1846 drew to a close Bent suggested normalcy by hosting a gala event at the Governor's Palace. Abert witnessed "all the luxuries of an eastern table, and delightful champagne in greatest abundance." He honored one cultural heritage at the expense of another, noting that all present "concluded it was better to revel in the halls of the Armijos, than to revel in the halls of Montezuma, for the latter were poor uncivilized Indians, while the former may, perhaps, boast to be of the blood of the Hidalgos of Castile and Arragon [sic]."[200] Bent issued an official proclamation on January 5, 1847, to assure "citizens" of his commitment to their destiny. The conquest's liberal sermon resounded. He beseeched them to believe in the "free government" being bestowed on them and not to follow the "false and poisonous doctrines" of the "turbulent spirits," naming Tomás Ortiz and Diego Archuleta as key agitators.[201]

It availed nothing. Two handbills dated January 20, 1847, went out to the Mexican military commanders of the New Mexican Department under authorship of Juan Antonio García, the "Inspector of Arms," and signed by Pedro Vigil, Antonio María Trujillo, and Jesús Tafolla. They were, it was announced, appointed by the "Legitimate Commander for the Supreme Government of Mexico." War was declared "with the American." The call went out for the organization of companies, "together with all the inhabitants that are able to bear arms," with the plan of connecting with rebels in San Juan de Los Caballeros (San Juan Pueblo). They would cast off the "yoke bound on us by a foreign government." The uprising was arranged for January 22.[202]

The alarmed Governor Bent trouped to San Fernando de Taos, "imprudently" as Dyer notes, to recoup his Mexican wife and household items and to reassure the people, of a place known at least since 1837 for its insurrectionary proclivities, of his unswerving loyalty and intent to serve them.[203] Kearny had previously organized a company of volunteer infantry, appointing a "Mexican captain and an American first lieutenant."[204] The unit never got formed.

Bent received while at Taos a request from friends of two Pueblo Indians to release them from the local jailhouse. He responded that the matter was outside his authority until they were tried in court. A band forcibly released the prisoners in the early morning of January 19 and proceeded righteously to the Bent home. An official military report decried Bent "barbarously" murdered and scalped. Others of his entourage were killed with gunshots, arrows, and knives. Included were Sheriff Louis Stephen Lee; District Attorney James Leal; Narciso Beaubien, son of one of Kearny's appointed judges; and two Nuevomexicanos, Pablo Jaramillo, a Bent brother in-law, and the Taos Prefect Cornelio Vigil, an uncle of Mrs. Bent and Donaciano Vigil. Leal was reportedly scalped while alive. A circular went to the unnamed local priest (Antonio José Martínez), "stating that Mexicans and Indians of Taos had risen against the invaders of their country, and requesting that he join them."[205] Others identified as instigators were the 1837 revolutionary Pablo Montoya and Tomasito, a Taos Puebloan. Mrs. Bent and the wives of two other members of Bent's team were unharmed and managed to escape.[206]

"It appeared to be the object of the insurrectionists to put to death every American and every Mexican who had accepted office under the American government," Colonel Price feared.[207] Cooke commented more wryly that the incident, which came to be known as the Taos Revolt, represented an "uprising against our bloodless, but perhaps stern, change of rule." Dyer wrote that it was "so sudden and unexpected that we could not realize or believe it. Before morning the naked truth was before us." With the rumor of 1,500 to 2,000 rebels prepared to march on Santa Fe, the Mexicans there were "immediately disarmed and prohibited from leaving the city without permission from the Comdg. officer."[208]

The lenses of imperial democracy colored American interpretations of the assassinations. Captain Cooke saw the "murders" making no sense in the context of U.S. largesse except as irrational and antiliberal savagery. They proved that "the best traits of our nature at a low stage, combine with the forces of ignorance and confirmed customs and habits, to resent and resist an abrupt and forcible bestowal of the greatest boons—the comforts of civilization—Liberty itself!"[209]

FIG. 6. *Governor of New Mexico Charles Bent*, ca. 1846–47, artist unknown. Appointed civil governor by General Stephen W. Kearny upon occupation of Santa Fe, Bent was the key target among those assassinated in the Taos Revolt on January 19, 1847. Courtesy Palace of the Governors Photo Archives, NMHM/DCA, negative #007004.

Little acknowledgment was had of a natural act of national liberation against foreign usurpation or at least the memory of Americans who had provoked wrath by selling liquor to Indian marauders and had acquired land by suspicious means. Cornelio Vigil was a known American sympathizer, three of whose family members, connected by marriage to Americans, had profited from the acquisition of land grants.[210] Civilian Lewis Garrard, on the scene, considered the violence that of "designing men," "inflamed passions," and "perverted minds."[211]

The worst of fears gripped Americans. Susan Magoffin felt the intention of "nearly every one" of the Mexicans "to murder without distinction every American in the country if the least thing should turn in their favor."[212] Indeed, the assassinations triggered a major anticolonial rebellion, greatly expanding the Taos Revolt. Agit-prop letters and circulars implored the people to join in ousting the Americans. The burgeoning contingent of Taos rebels set out to take Santa Fe. Apaches from the Mora area enlisted.[213] At Arroyo Hondo, north of Taos, Simeon Turley, a longtime settler who ran a popular mill, and seven of his companions were set upon by five hundred Mexicans and Pueblos. Their belongings were ransacked and they were butchered after two days of siege.[214] Two Americans traders were cut down on the Río Colorado.[215]

Members of an American grazing party at Mora, forty miles southeast of Taos, were "cut to pieces," in the words of Capt. I. R. Hendly.[216] At least five Americans were killed in the ensuing three-hour battle, including the same Lawrence Waldo who had expressed alarm to his father over burning resentment among the people. Fifteen Mexicans were killed and fifteen taken prisoner. Rebels ran off with the horses of the area's American settlers.[217] The alcalde of Las Vegas, one of the first to swear allegiance to Kearny, and the whole community of Tecolote declared for the rebels. It appeared to Hendly that the whole population was "ripe for insurrection."[218] Two days later a detail of American troops in the vicinity fell to a surprise assault. Further skirmishing erupted in the Las Vegas area.[219]

Colonel Price fatefully appointed territorial secretary Donaciano Vigil provisional civil governor. Vigil in his first public statement after the revolt assailed in Spanish the "barbarous" assassinations and asked the people to calm down. The hombre de bien resonantly conjured the ghosts of the 1837 Revolt, warning of the intent of the rebels Pablo

Montoya and Manuel Cortez to wage war just as Montoya had fomented in the assassination of Governor Pérez, whose administration Vigil served. At that time this "mischievous fool [Montoya] took, as a motto for his perversity, the word 'canton,' and now it is 'the reunification of Taos!'" declaimed Vigil. "And can there be a single man of sense who would voluntarily join his ranks? I should think not. Why?" the acting governor challenged. "[T]o prevent the entry of American forces in the month of August, instead of glutting his insane passions and showing his martial valor by the brutal sacrifice of defenseless victims, and this at the very time when an arrangement between the two governments, with regard to boundaries, was expected? Whether this land must belong to the government of the United States or return to its native Mexico," the collaborator beheld, "is it not a gross absurdity to foment rancorous feelings toward people with whom we are either to compose one family, or to continue our commercial relations?"

"Unquestionably" it was, Vigil answered. He warned of the "respectable body of troops" on way to quell disorder and protect "honest and discreet men." Vigil invoked what would become the Nuevomexicano campaign of liberalism in order to legitimate the conquest. "Happiness" for the individual within state politics had become an integral piece in the Western discourse of modernity. Spain and Spanish America transformed the public ideal of happiness from a Catholic eternal afterlife to a secular one but pinned it to the weal of *el pueblo* (the people), or the social body.[220] Vigil implored his public accordingly. The people should hark the voice of reason for the sake of the "common happiness," he put it. Their collective preservation depended on their keeping quiet and engaged in private affairs. Vigil relied on the Kearny Code of Law as the foundation of Nuevomexicano life. He emphasized that he headed a transitory administration. Neither his qualifications nor the interim nature of his appointment, "according to the organic [Kearny] law in which I take the reins of government," could encourage him to continue "in so difficult and thorny a post, the duties of which are intended for individuals of greater enterprise and talents." Liberalism and the Kearny Code powered Vigil's understanding of Nuevomexicano national belonging. He promised in the name of the people and "in the utmost fervor of [his] heart," to devote himself exclusively to securing all the prosperity— another important liberal notion—"so much desired by your fellow-citizen and friend."[221]

Vigil became more insistent in another communiqué three days later, in which he poured out a liberal warning to those who would challenge the occupation regime. Carrying the brightly imperial title *¡Triúnfo de los Principios Contra la Torpeza!* (Triumph of principles over stupidity!), the proclamation warned of the full force of law bearing down on the perpetrating rebels while announcing that steps would be taken to "consolidate the union of all the residents of this beautiful country under the aegis of law and reason [*consolidar la unión de todos los habitantes de este hermoso país bajo la egida de la ley de la razón*]."[222]

Colonel Price armed teamsters and organized volunteers from Santa Fe and Alburquerque into a company of 340 men. Most were Americans, with a sprinkling of Nuevomexicanos. Facundo Pino, Nicolás Pino, and Manuel Chávez had participated in the planning of a Mexican attack on the American military force in Santa Fe, but the Bent assassination convinced them of the necessity to help put down the rebellion that did erupt. The civilian company headed by the French settler Ceran St. Vrain moved behind Price and his troops northward on January 23 with four twelve-pound Mountain Howitzers to stop insurgents before they could reach Santa Fe.[223]

In the first encounter in the canyon at Santa Cruz de la Cañada, Price faced a barrage of small-fire from above, the 1,500–2,000 rebels led by the Generals Jesús Tafoya, Pablo Chávez, and Pablo Montoya. Thirty-six insurgents were killed and forty-five taken prisoner, with two American soldiers killed and seven wounded. Superior American tactics and arms dislodged guerrillas, forcing them to retreat northward. Price brought up additional guns, ammunition, and cannon. More than 600 rebels positioned themselves in the first week of February on the rocks of a steep ravine on the Río Grande at Embudo. An intense skirmish left one American killed, another severely wounded, with twenty Mexicans killed and sixty wounded. Reinforcements joined the American force and they pushed the rebels back toward Taos.[224]

Another U.S. detachment of eighty squared off with Mexicans, Cheyennes, and Apaches at Mora. As the Americans prepared to attack armed residents, a party of Mexicans ran toward the village from the mountains. Hand-to-hand combat went door-to-door. Mexicans who were hunkered down in an old fort killed Captain Hendly. His successor and fresh troops used cannon and "completely level[ed]... the town." Rebels suffered twenty-five casualties and seventeen taken prisoner; one American was killed and two compatriots were wounded.[225]

The decisive battle began on February 3 at Taos. Mexicans and Indians had fortified themselves behind the adobe walls of the pueblo church 2.5 miles outside the major Mexican settlement of Fernando de Taos. At the appearance of the American forces, insurgents raised what Lt. Dyer called "a most unearthly yell." Americans assaulted the building with rifle shot and heavy artillery to little effect at first. With what Donaciano Vigil later conceded as "great bravery," insurgents held to a staunch defense.[226] The Americans applied superior arms and brutal cross-fire to storm the thick adobe church, throwing in artillery shells and barraging with a six-pound cannon. U.S. soldiers were ordered to storm the building. Smoked-out rebels took refuge in neighboring houses, only to be forced out of the area, when many were killed and the church left in a ruin. The next morning Dyer witnessed "old men with the women and children bearing before them their religious symbols and crying, kneeling and begging for mercy and protection." The Americans took seven soldiers killed and forty-five wounded. Of some 600–700 Mexican rebels, 154 were killed. The people of Taos Pueblo surrendered the next day as the American flag flew over their burnt-out church. Colonel Price demanded the head of Tomasito, but at his capture an American coldly shot him dead. Some 350 Mexicans and Indians and forty-seven Americans were killed. Among the leaders lost in the campaign were Pablo Chaves, Jesús Tafoya, and Pablo Montoya. Manuel Cortez escaped.[227]

With order restored, 1,300 Americans and a "vast concourse of Mexicans" attended the funeral pageant for the slain Governor Bent.[228] Victors deliberated the meaning of the resistance and questioned the concept of liberal conquest. Dyer feared that the annexation of the territory had been "both a moral and a political error," more so as the inferior land held no value "whatever." Edwards bitterly thought that the revolt nullified Polk's agreeable approach to taking foreign territory. The policy of kindness clearly did not work, he reflected. "We should not be protecting our enemies, though it is a scriptural command and one of General Kearny's." A "gentle" occupation defied not just liberal "reason," but "common sense," Edwards thought. Certain qualities of the enemy fell short of superior humanity. Far better that the American military act "more upon the principle of an 'eye for an eye and a tooth for a tooth' with such people as Mexicans." The alcalde would greet the American troops with "a great deal of cordiality," Edwards imagined, for the people in his area "had heard with pleasure of our treatment towards the New Mexicans, and were glad we had come to take possession of their country." Who would not, "when they received such kind treatment as we have showed toward the inhabitants of New Mexico?" Edwards took note of improvement in New Mexico's economy already. The place had not enjoyed "half the prosperity before that she has since the American army invaded her territory. She has had protection against the savage hordes that infest her border. We have bought articles of them at the highest [price], which they heretofore could not have disposed of. We have forced nothing from them unless necessity compelled us, and for which they have always received the most liberal compensation. And instead of war being made a curse upon the nation, it is made a blessing." As Edwards concluded, "Never half such kind treatment did they receive from their own armies." The insurrection was "the fruit of our kind treatment towards them."[229]

Governor Vigil interceded to do right by the occupation. His circular lamented the manner in which the rebellion rejected reason and liberality. Vigil infantilized the rebels not simply under moral American liberalism but in the frame of the civilized hombre de bien. "Just like a child who does not respect the law because of a lack of fatherly discipline and deserved castigation and who therefore creates a habit of life that does not fear the severe punishments of the law," he phrased it, "so can a whole people do so when they find themselves in the same circumstance [*Como cuando un padre de familia la descuida o mejor dicho se desentiende de los desmanes de sus hijos y los deja sin reprensiones merecidas, van creciendo en ellos la pretensión de amparse en sus escasos hasta el grado de crearse un hábito de que ya ni el temor de los castigos severos que imponen las leyes es bastante para separarlos de la carrera que se han trazado; así mismo sucede con un Pueblo entero cuando se haya en el mismo caso*]." The governing chief of New Mexico noted a previous series of crimes "from the history of [Taos'] civil existence," the 1837 Revolt. Taoseños struck after that rebellion, Vigil recalled, "with savagery and inhumanity as to cover us with mourning, filled with pain and sad memories [*con tan salvage en humanidad que nos ha cubierto de luto, colmado con dolor y de tristes recuerdos*]." Vigil charged Governor Armijo with failing to punish them severely enough so that they rioted in 1843, plundering granaries in the valley. The government of New Mexico at the time, which should have punished the intellectual engineers, actually approved of the crimes and kept them from becoming public knowledge. Later, Vigil went on, the disgruntled Taoseños, "encouraged by the impunity of this previous crime," plotted to kill the few Americans living in the Taos Valley, along with the "French married among them." Once again the "apathetic and criminal conduct" of the administrations encouraged these "popular commotions." Fortunately, they failed for lack of an adequate plan of surprise, Vigil pointed out. They then satisfied the savage cravings "in their breast" with avid pillaging of the commercial houses and the larger dwellings of the strangers among them.

Vigil held up Diego Archuleta, Pablo Montoya, Manuel Cortez, Jesús Tafoya, and Pablo Chávez as the December plotters of revolution, thinking that the American military should have responded more strongly than it did then. The American commander absolved the people of Taos Pueblo, he lamented, permitting the "coward" Archuleta to flee the territory before start of the revolution that he planned and counseled, and which produced the deaths of his co-conspirators Chávez and Tafoya. Cortez now hid in the mountains a fugitive, Vigil announced. But at last the "forces of government triumphed over the rebels at La Cañada, in Embudo and in Taos."

Vigil attested to his people as to where the decisive incidents took place: "[A]bout 200 rebels died in the forest and the Pueblo of Taos, the rest begged for their life and forgiveness and it was granted, leaving them at liberty to dedicate themselves to their work with the security and peace that they themselves had wanted to deprive us of [*murieron en el campo y Pueblo de Taos, cosa de doscientos rebeldes, los demás imploraron por la vida y el perdón y se les otorgó, dejandolos en libertad para que se dedique á sus industrias con la seguridad y paz que ellos mismos hos habían perturbado*]." Vigil would urge officials to redouble their efforts to preserve order. He implored the "good citizens" to contribute "with their influence, with their talents and with their patriotism to the same objective; and that they push the people to their industry, the only fount of riches." Then would they find deliverance under "the protection of a strong government and of the just laws that rule us." Vigil signed off with the wish that the people "be happy." It was the "most desired by your best friend [*lo que más desea Vuestro mejor amigo*]."[230]

The strong arm of the de facto government came down on the rebels. About fifty prisoners were detained by the military and civil authorities. Vigil, still technically a citizen of Mexico, steeped himself in the American state with the view of an hombre de bien. His appeal to Buchanan made on behalf of the "future peace and safety of the Territory" called for the captives to be dealt with according to the severest penalties of the laws of the United States "when proved guilty as perpetrators or participators in the late barbarous outrages."[231] Twenty-two Mexicans and five Indians found themselves bound over for trial in a civilian Taos court in April 1847, singularly or in groups of three or four. It was a "Trader's and Trapper's Court," a civilian witness called it. The three judges were Kearny's Supreme Court appointees: the French Canadian Charles Beaubien, a political enemy of Padre Martínez and whose son was killed in the battle of Taos; Joab Houghton, who had participated in the negotiations that led to Governor Armijo's Apache Canyon abdication; and Antonio José Otero, venerable hombre de bien and Donaciano Vigil's close friend. Fourteen of nineteen jury men were American, five Mexican. It symbolized Euroamerican dominance that the grand jury foreman, George Bent, was the brother of the slain governor. Most members of the petit jury were longtime trappers and veterans of the Army of the West. Even some Mexican jurors were trappers. In no case among the juries did Mexicans constitute a majority. Fragmentary data suggest their numbers ranging from one to four jurors.[232]

The wry commentary of the firsthand observer Lewis Garrard suggests the trial's odd combination of conquest, racial hegemony, ethno-legitimation, and institutional incorporation on foreign soil. "American judges sat on the bench," he noted, "New Mexicans and Americans filled the jury box, and an American soldiery guarded the halls. Verily a strange mixture of violence and justice, a strange middle ground between the martial and common law."[233] All the accused pleaded not guilty of "disregarding the duty of his allegiance to the government of the United States aforesaid, and wholly withdrawing the allegiance, duty and obedience which every true and faithful citizen of the said government should of right ought to bear toward the said government of the United States."[234] Volunteer privates from the occupying army legally represented the defendants. Garrard rendered them "poor things . . . as much frightened as the prisoners at the bar."

An American jury foreman, a mountain frontiersman whose primary motivation appeared to be revenge for his slain countrymen, reportedly bullied the jurors into rendering convictions and death sentences.[235] Fifteen of the seventeen Mexicans up for murder were found guilty, two not. One of the five indicted for high treason was convicted, one acquitted, and the cases of the other three dismissed. All five Indians were convicted of murder. The guilty were condemned to death by hanging.[236]

Antonio María Trujillo, found guilty of high treason, was Diego Archuleta's father-in-law and one of three rebels who called the Mexican military commanders to arms against the Americans. The sentence of execution bespoke sacrificial victims in service of overreach by the state system being replicated on Mexican soil. Trujillo was condemned for "seconding the acts of a band of the most traitorous murderers that ever blackened with the recital of their deeds the annals of history." The pronouncement hailed the fact that an "enlightened and liberal jury" had reached the verdict of guilty "of treason against the government under which you are a citizen."[237]

Trujillo's lawyer challenged the Kearny civil court jurisdiction and criticized the indictment on the ground that Trujillo was not a U.S. citizen, "nor bound to yield allegiance to that Government." Pressure was brought to bear on his behalf in New Mexico. The district attorney Francis Blair referred the matter to Washington for instruction.[238] Secretary Marcy's answer arrived too late for the executions, which took place within days of the trials, 150 yards from the jailhouse, with no opportunity for appeals, and in the absence of transcripts.[239] Garrard witnessed Trujillo contemptuously declaring his innocence, and the unjustness of his trial, and the "arbitrary conduct of his murderers" in subjecting him to the gallows. Garrard sympathized with Trujillo. "The atrocity of the act of hanging that man for treason is most damnable," he wrote. "Treason, indeed! What did the poor devil know about his new allegiance?"[240] Padre Martínez questioned before the former U.S. consul in Santa Fe the propriety of charging Mexican citizens with treason for resisting an occupying power in war time. Governor Donaciano Vigil felt that a fair trial was had yet asked the president to bestow a pardon for Trujillo, as he himself had done.[241]

The kangaroo court in Taos followed on Kearny's replication process, illegitimately conferring citizenship on a foreign people. Official

Washington had it this way. The trial and verdicts of treason were illegal because a state of war existed between the United States and Mexico. None of the rebels had declared allegiance to the United States. Most important, they could not have been considered citizens of the United States on Kearny's decree. Marcy's letter to Price declared that "the territory conquered by our arms does not become, by the mere act of conquest, a permanent part of the United States, and the inhabitants of such territory are not, to the full extent of the term, citizens of the United States." Marcy held the convictions for murder and other common crimes justified but not on the charge of treason. As he noted, it was beyond dispute that the inhabitants of a country conquered by an established temporary civil government were bound by its laws and could be tried and punished for offenses. It pertained to New Mexico's late insurrection, in which those found guilty of murder and instigating others to crime "were liable to be punished for these acts, either by the civil or military authority." It was not, however, "proper use of legal terms to say that their offenses were treason committed against the United States." Nor was it technically correct to say that they "owed" allegiance to the U.S. government. Marcy called the indictments of treason "error." The offenses were against the temporary civil government of New Mexico and the laws provided for it, "which that government had the right, and, indeed, was bound to be executed."[242] Polk backed this interpretation in July in response to a request from Congress for information on the trials, executions, and the treason charges, stating that the error had been pointed out to U.S. military commanders to prevent its recurrence.[243]

A later U.S. Supreme Court case rejected the military's claim of authority to require the inhabitants of occupied territory to show allegiance to the United States. Laura Gómez suggests that the legality of the 1847 court in New Mexico should have been litigated, although after the Trujillo trial and the executions, the grand juries composed of majority Mexicans refused to return any more indictments for treason. "In this respect," she argues, "the system worked as it was designed to, with lay jurors operating as a check on prosecutors and judges."[244] Gómez regards it as an element of resistance to Euroamerican dominance in the context of the American enforced colonization of New Mexico. It also signified more subtly another step in the driven integration of the Nuevomexicanos into the American civic system, ironically after a flagrant rejection of conquest. Nuevomexicano participation in American institutions would prove empowering. "Legitimation" appears here as a harbinger of empowerment and power-sharing. Holding the double-edged sword of co-optation and stakeholdership, Governor Vigil praised the diligence, fairness and justice of the territorial tribunals in the discharge of their duties in the Taos treason and murder trials.[245]

CHAPTER THREE

Integrative Conquest, 1847–1848

The air of insurgency hovered over New Mexico after the Taos Revolt trials. Poblador and indigene neighbors on the plains reportedly solicited the support of Mexico to expel the Americans and preserve their trading practices. Isolated attacks on the American military broke out from May to July 1847, the running off of horses mostly, although in one instance the killing of an officer and soldiers in a grazing party and the plundering of their field camp, resulting in the retaliatory capture of Mexican suspects, their trial, and the hanging of six.[1] Rumor had Diego Archuleta, former governor Manuel Armijo, and others amassing troops from the south in preparation for rebattlement.[2] The recently promoted Gen. Sterling Price, in charge of the New Mexico command, understood "New Mexicans" sustaining a "deadly hatred against the Americans." Price regretted as late as July 20 the reduction of his forces by the departure of companies whose terms expired. He worried about a Mexican battalion possibly heading north from Chihuahua to reclaim New Mexico.[3]

Price concentrated his troops in the Santa Fe area and imposed a nononsense martial law. He permitted Kearny's civil government to continue nonetheless. Interim governor Donaciano Vigil offered to resign from office to make way for new appointees. Price refused to accept the offer and Vigil remained as territorial secretary and acting governor.[4] Vigil fulfilled the call of routine duty: assisting a widow arrange the ambiguous estate of her deceased husband; drafting instructions for the sheriffs whom former governor Charles Bent had appointed; hearing complaints of a biased sheriff; creating the office of county auditor; and authorizing a local militia to address Comanche raids.[5]

Vigil proved *the* critical collaborator for the remainder of the American occupation. To him went the responsibility of calming the populace in the aftermath of civic violence. Vigil exhorted citizens not to heed Pablo Montoya, who somehow escaped prosecution for his part in the Taos Revolt and was now agitating the people to resist a certain tax. Vigil spiked the official communication channel with bright and mighty liberalism. To accept the Kearny laws was to possess "principles" and "reciprocal concord and confidence," he stressed, under the "aegis of the law and reason" and "security and protection of the law."[6] Vigil, an old promoter of friendly relations with Americans, condemned allegations of Nuevomexicanos fomenting a "mischievous hatred" toward members of the "Anglo" race, as he put it. He understood Father Antonio José Martínez to be spreading "rumors of threat" to the Americans. Vigil advised against such acrimony. Far better that "we combine ourselves [*más es necesario combinar*]" with the Americans, he conveyed to his friend and Supreme Court Judge Charles "Carlos" Beaubien.[7]

Technically, Vigil was charged with heading up the type of provisional wartime government the U.S. War Department defined as valid for an occupied foreign territory. However, he was given no reason not to fulfill Kearny's declaration of New Mexico as an American territory replete with an understanding of Nuevomexicanos as effective American citizens. This policy tended to promote a proleptic politics, quite as if New Mexico was already a subset of the United States. A caucus of five Nuevomexicanos pipe-dreamed a request to the American Congress to accept the application of the American consul Manuel Álvarez to be their delegate to the House of Representatives. The petitioners cited Álvarez's credentials of personal demeanor, compassion, and bilingualism to show how well equipped he was to represent Nuevomexicano interests.[8]

On firmer ground, Vigil's adherence to republican virtue and his modernist knowledge of American legal principles formed the ticket for institutionalizing an American political organization in New Mexico upon the existing Mexican version, like a cathedral atop an Andalusian mosque. Vigil reinforced to allies and friends the dawn of a new day of liberal openness in the homeland, conveying in Spanish the incessant tropes of enlightenment: "public affairs," "public business [*negocios públicos*]," and "public office [*oficio público*]." Thomas Jefferson had forged the political identity of the United States theoretically with the concept of the "natural rights republic," Locke's secular emphasis on the "art of governing men in society" based on transcendent morality. Vigil knew enough to remind a private correspondent

FIG. 7. *Donaciano Vigil, Governor of New Mexico 1847–48*, photograph ca. 1880–82 by Albright's Art Parlors. The liberal Vigil was the principal collaborator in the American conquest and annexation of New Mexico. Courtesy Palace of the Governors Photo Archives, NMHM/DCA, negative #011405.

of the necessity of "friendship among men in public action [*la amistad de los hombres en actos públicos*]" and he pointed out that he conducted himself in office according to "natural law and society [*la ley natural y la sociedad*]."[9]

Vigil invoked his venerable aristocratic racial identity to mark the distinction between modern liberalism and the mestizo legacy. Certain *nativos* failed to uphold the rule of law, he noted. The prefect in Bernalillo County betrayed the dignity of the prefecture by not upholding his oath. As Vigil framed it in a classic Hispanic political image, this kind of neglect was all too common in the fawning and flattery of public officials, "a damned condition of the sons of Montezuma and of the mixing of Spanish blood [*maldito condición de los hijos de Montezuma y de la mescla con sangre Española*]." Vigil regarded such faults as the effect of an inveterately "lying race [*raza embolicida*]." As he regretted, "Not without reason have we [in Mexico] been wracked in the war that is at the brink of conclusion [*No sin razón hemos sido (fregados) en la lucha que esta al (punto) de concluir*]." If Vigil thought the Nuevomexicanos too divided politically, he staked his allegiance clearly to his friends. "The friendship of men is person to person [*La amistad de los hombres es de persona a persona*]," he swore, and he, for one, would conduct his public services when he could "with friendship, as with his words [*cuando puedo con mi amistad, así mis palabras*]."[10]

Vigil questioned the capacity of locals to carry out the mechanics of republican government while abstractly seeking to protect the people's rights. The key instance was his forceful objection to military overbearance. Vigil complained to Missouri senator Thomas Hart Benton of the "two ills" the occupying army perpetrated on New Mexico. Officers interfered in the business of civil servants in violation of the Kearny Code, and the military command failed to have government workers paid, including himself. Vigil claimed, as any red-blooded citizen of an American territory would, the right to chafe at the colonial character of stiff martial oversight. The "honor and pleasure" of putting into effect the "republican investments" that the United States had made in New Mexico were being thwarted, he proleptically alleged, when instead they "should so much contribute to its attachment to the American Union [*que tanto deben contribuir a nuestra agregación a la unión Americana*]."[11] Vigil recalled as well Kearny's promise to stop the war relations with Indians, putting Secretary of State James Buchanan on notice regarding his lack of confidence in Price's ability to enforce Navajo pledges to return prisoners and curtail raiding on the settlements of the southern district. New Mexico needed the return of regular U.S. troops to replace the volunteer force, Vigil affirmed in the translated passage, if the "turbulent savages" were to be forced into a "lasting submission" for the good of the "native citizens."[12]

Vigil wrote to one of his *hombre de bien* compadres that Price had suspended him from office. Vigil considered it an *atentado* (assault), and he noted that the commanding officer was expecting to appoint another *de los hombres de mi tiempo* (from his generation), although Vigil doubted Price could find one whose opinions he could accept.[13] The suspension apparently did not become public; Vigil remained in office. Euroamericans flocked to support his challenge to the military yoke. What Lieutenant Dyer called a "large" and "very impressive" meeting "of citizens" took place at the Palace in October 1847, adopting resolutions of dissatisfaction at the course of the commanding officer. One citizen decried in the newly founded *Santa Fe Republican* that the citizens of a former political tyranny believed in their new "enlightened" country, not the "kind of half way civil and military rule" in place. Citizens did not know "which way to look for protection."[14]

Nuevomexicano colleagues appreciated Vigil as well. Father José Manuel Gallegos, the former member of the Mexican departmental assembly and possible participant in the pre–Taos Revolt movement, commended the governor for his positive commitment to the new political order, establishing, as he put it, "a line of communication with those in political power."[15] The former Mexican governor Francisco Sarracino, writing privately from Alburquerque in the Río Abajo, congratulated his friend; praised his philosophy, prudence, and dignity; and called him "the touchstone on which everyone is depending."[16] Vigil does not seem to have been entirely comfortable with his visibility—and for liberal reasons. "If we wish to shape public opinion," he wrote to a fellow hombre de bien, "it is necessary to appear without personal aspirations so as not to compromise our work." Vigil placed his political role above the fray. "As you already know me," he emphasized, "when it comes to the public business of my office, I am independent [*Como ya vd. me conoce que en los negocios públicos de mis oficios soy independiente*]."[17]

Vigil, in discharging the U.S.'s continental liberalism, carried out the letter of the Kearny Code as assuredly as its creator would have. The war with Mexico continued; indeed, to Lieutenant Dyer, hearing of the U.S. invasion of Mexico City, the prospects for peace appeared "gloomier than ever." Yet Vigil announced preparations for an American territorial legislature. His clarion call delivered in a proclamation to "Fellow Citizens" heralded the precedent of his countrymen exercising "without impediment the high privileges inherent in free citizens [*ejercer sin ninguna traba los altos privilegios inherentes a ciudadanos libres*]" by choosing the representatives for a house of representatives and a council. As a historian of the Mexican-American War notes, patriotism and the responsibilities of a citizen were merged in this century. As such, Vigil translated it for his political charges. "The most important measures of a republican country," he proclaimed, "are those of the suffrage or election, in which the People gather in mass to exercise their power, and to entrust the regime of their destinies to those persons who, by their talents, their patriotism and their Virtues, convene the popularity of their constituents [*Los actos más importantes en un país republicano, son los de Sufragio o elección, en que el Pueblo en masa se reúne para ejercer su poder, y para confiar el régimen de sus destinos a aquellas personas que por sus talentos, su patriotismo, y sus Virtudes, reúnen la popularidad de sus comitentes*]." His "sacred duty [*sagrado deber*]" decreed by statute in the Organic (Kearny) Laws was to announce the first Monday of August as the date for voters to convene in the territory's "electoral precincts [*precintos electorales*]." It was the first time for this political unit to appear in New Mexico, and for particular named settlements to be made "precincts." Vigil expressed his heart's joy in "contemplating that an era will begin of happiness and fortune and that our situation is advantageous for a thousand reasons depending on the grand manner and the speed of realizing the benefits in the success of the elections you will conduct [*mi corazón se regosija contemplando que va a comenzar una nueva era de felicidad y de ventura, y que vuestra situación os es ventajosa por mil títulos, dependiendo en gran manera el pronto goce de los Beneficios que el cambio de circunstnacias franquea, del acierto de las Elecciones que hagais*]." He recommended that voters have "only the view of the good of the country" (New Mexico) by giving preference "with total impartiality [*con toda imparcialidad*]" to men already distinguished by their talents, and for their honor, and reject entirely all those who, without merit, move only with a spirit of personal aspiration which has caused so many ills in the Societies where it has existed."[18]

Vigil transcended Mexico's restricted suffrage and answered the call of Mexican liberals for popular democracy. The document that announced Río Arriba County's seventeen new electoral precincts, naming the election judge for each precinct, puts in dramatic relief the broadening of New Mexico's democratic base.[19] Hombre de bien friends were at one with Vigil's heightened liberalism. Sarracino thanked the governor for his electioneering lessons to the local prefects, work appreciated for the "happiness and advance of these communities [*felicidad y adelante de estos Pueblos*]."[20] Vigil redeemed himself in the eyes of General Price, who rewarded his skills as a regional statesman by changing his interim status to regular governor.[21]

War flared in interior Mexico the second week of August 1847, just as a sufficient mass of Nuevomexicanos turned out to vote for members of a presumptive legislature, electing members for a house of representatives and a council.[22] How many actually voted is unknown. The performative act stood in any case on par with voting in an American territory—or a state, for that matter. Local political headmen, called *jefes* or *caudillos*, fulfilled mobilizing roles in the manner of the American precinct worker. Prefects, judges, alcaldes, economic *patrones*, and priests directed male citizens on how to vote and for whom.[23] Vigil received the report of a smooth electoral process in one precinct of Santa Fe County and of problems of interpersonal conflict among candidates and supporters in another.[24] Nuevomexicanos were elected to seven of nine seats on the council and eighteen of twenty-two in the House.[25] Vigil privately expressed the hope of progress ushering from the session in the form of public reforms in the branches of government, the courts, education, and in the regulation of social mores according to the advanced republican principles of the day. It concerned Vigil that certain men were elected to the council who did not "harmonize with republicanism and tolerance [*En el consejo hay algunos que no se harmonían con el republicanismo y tolerancia*]."[26] That is, the factionalism that fed Nuevomexicano collaboration with the Kearny occupation on one hand, and the Taos Revolt on the other, remained in Vigil's proleptic political field.

The socio-civic integration of Nuevomexicanos moved apace in the four-month interim to the legislative session. Social events sponsored by Euroamerican merchants promoted cross-cultural intercourse. The brief description in *El Republicano*, the *Santa Fe Republican*'s Spanish-language section, of a winter gala suggests the gathering of a single nationality, at least among Santa Fe elites. "The Spanish and the Anglo Sons of New Mexico and [a] Brother Jonatas," it described, "they all met like people from the same land and as fellow citizens of our great Republic. It was a great thing and the best part is that everyone enjoyed themselves."[27] The account could have reflected what Andrés Reséndez calls the "distinctive, self-confident, almost boastful expansionist edge" that Euroamericans of the frontier used to help "forge a national/ethnic imagination," whetting the appetites of potential readers more than reflecting the realities of life at the border.[28] Still, the dance seems clearly enough to have reinforced the forging of a trajectory of Euroamerican-Mexican social consensus in New Mexico.

Nuevomexicanos were structurally affected by the birth of a modern print culture during the American occupation. The First Amendment to the Constitution prohibiting infringements on the press made news print a resource for the protection and enhancement of democracy. Modern communications in pre-industrial frontiers of the nineteenth century required newspapers to connect across widely dispersed populations. The print revolution arrived in Texas in 1822. Newspapers tended to be crude affairs on the extended frontier, yet they fulfilled a need for inexpensive local news.[29] The ubiquitous American newspapers provided vital detail of the Mexican War on a daily basis for an avid readership in the states.[30]

In Santa Fe Gen. Oliver Hovey loaned his quartermaster's press for the publishing of the *Santa Fe Republican* (republican in the liberal, nonparty sense). Experienced newspapermen Edward T. Davies and George R. Gibson remained in New Mexico after mustering out of the Kearny volunteers. They cobbled together the first American paper in New Mexico. Hovey later told another journalist that at its peak, the *Republican* had seven hundred subscribers, remarkable for a scattered population, each paying five dollars a year.[31] As liberal theory holds, modern society's legitimate inclusion of ethnic out-groups depends on the differentiation of societal institutions from each other combined with elements of the ethnic culture that are compatible with the values, practices, and culture of the social system. Academic liberalism regards differentiation as a characteristic of societal centers. Jeffrey Alexander argues that it applies to internal colonial, colonial, and postcolonial societies since "they themselves have been so vitally affected by the modernization process." Rather than producing only an undifferentiated dominant-subordinate relationship leading inevitably to force, conflict, and secession, "the colonial situation is subject to the same kind of analytical differentiation and internal variation as any other relationship between core group and subordinate out-group."[32]

Republican editorial policy laid down a differentiating agenda. Its objective was to serve the communication needs of the public prior to governing authorities. This first Euroamerican press in New Mexico realized the necessity for the United States to incorporate Nuevomexicanos politically and civically. Davies and Gibson believed they could generate an American public through a Nuevomexicano readership. In the key device (to become the organizing staple for New Mexico's newspapers until appearance of exclusively Spanish-language journals in the 1880s), the *Republican* went out with Spanish-language pages following the English columns. Davies and Gibson themselves took responsibility for writing Spanish-language editorials and translating English-language sources into Spanish. Governor Donaciano Vigil personally enlisted ethnic compatriots Antonio M. Trujillo, Diego Aragón, Francisco Sarracino, and José Sena y Quintana, as well as Charles Beaubien, to solicit subscriptions.[33]

Gibson assumed responsibility for promoting what he himself called the "diffusion of our laws and institutions throughout the continent." In providing Spanish and English columns he sought to reach the "equally interested" among the "old [American] as well as the new [Nuevomexicano] citizens."[34] The paper's editorial stances reflected the aim of bringing Mexicans to America through a primitive civic pluralism. The Whig Party at the time defined public schooling as more than a means to economic advancement in terms of personal refinement and the individual's informed role in a republic.[35] Gibson called for a school to be founded in every Santa Fe neighborhood. Audacious in the traditional Mexican context, he recommended that women, those persons most "deficient" in "even the rudimentaries [sic] of education," be taught to read with the establishment of public and traveling libraries.[36]

A couple of Vigil's agents generated *Republican* subscriptions among Nuevomexicano readers. Father José Manuel Gallegos lamented that paisanos did not appreciate the value of the press.[37] Gibson, assisted by Vigil, persisted in setting down the building blocks of a modern space "in which such a thing as public opinion can be formed." As Jurgen Habermas emphasizes, "Citizens act as a public when they deal with matters of general interest without being subject to coercion."[38] Michael Warner emphasizes the new form of republican-informed communication that emerged by the end of the eighteenth century out of a prior stage of strict personalized communications in print, a more abstract *"Res Publica* of Letters," as it were.[39] The *Republican* aimed to make such a public accessible, and literate Nuevomexicanos jumped at the opportunity.

The Western world of the late eighteenth and early nineteenth centuries saw many political contributions signed with the use of pseudonyms. Warner establishes an important point regarding pseudonymity as a form of civic representation: that it represented the abstract importance of the citizen of the public sphere, "enabling the virtue of the citizen by the very fact that writing is not regarded as a form of personal presence" but as a voice on behalf of the common weal.[40] Nuevomexicanos submitted their commentary on matters of community import with the use of pen names in the context of pronounced martial law. *Don Simplicio* translates into Sir Simpleton (although it can be noted that Simplicio was also a participant in Galileo's seventeenth-century Italian dialogues over the Copernican and Ptolemaic visions of the world).[41] Another adopted *Inocencio* (Innocence). Inocencio was a known given name in New Mexico; it was also the name of a powerful and innovative twelfth-century pope.[42] *Un Labrador* (A farmer) requested use of the columns of *El Republicano* to advise his countrymen about the need to conserve water in yet another season of drought.[43] *Imparcial* (Impartial One) opined on the question of religious tolerance, provoking *El Cristiano de Estos Tiempos* (Christian of these times) and *El Amigo de los Pueblos* (Friend of the settlements/communities) to debate the character of the Roman Catholic tradition and how contemporary priests were conducting their clerical duties.[44] *Un Minero* (A miner) looked on Santa Fe's embryonic public "with pleasure" because, in Enlightenment intonation, "out of the comparison of opinion comes the truth."[45]

Nuevomexicanos took advantage of the free-speech right to knock the local oppressions of the occupying army. An anonymous stockman began to think the prospect of U.S. citizenship and enlightened nationality fool's gold. He learned on a business trip to the Río Abajo of the Illinois Volunteers (recently arrived on a mission to occupy Chihuahua) committing depredations en route to El Paso, pasturing their horses without permission on cultivated lands at Sandia Pueblo and San Fernando, stealing burros at Los Padillas, absconding with a household servant at Belen, insulting the alcalde at El Sabinal, stealing chickens, and whipping a respected *vecino*. "What protection do the *Nuevo Mejicanos*, considered as Americans since publication of the Laws by General Kearney, have?" the rancher interrogated in the *Republican*. "Certainly none," he auto responded, "not even the small consolation of a reprimand of the perpetrators of such atrocities [*Ciertamente que ninguna, por que ni siquiera se advierte el pequeño Consuelo de que los Gefes [sic] de Aquellos cuerpos de Voluntarios repriman tales desordenes*]."[46] A *Republican* editor agreed that American troops inflicted "many unjust and uncalled for acts of violence upon the citizens of the lower part of this Territory," stimulating "greater complaints about the manner in which they passed through the country." If anything of this sort had been done, the writer hoped it was "without the knowledge or sanction of the officers."[47]

Lay Euroamericans focused on the territory's civic questions, including the meaning of the occupation and the future of New Mexico as the United States steadily overcame Mexico. Many of their positions represented variations of what Thomas Jefferson set forth as the tradition of imperial democracy. Jefferson wrote in 1786 that the United States "must be viewed as the nest, from which all America, North and South, is to be peopled." The U.S. founder predicted the colonies of Spanish America remaining in the "decrepit hands" of the Spanish Empire until such time as "our population can be sufficiently advanced to gain it from them, piece by piece."[48] "Anglo-Saxonism" in the Americanization process drove its distinctive democratic imperialism on the idea of a superior racial stock.[49] The American press in Texas had been tapping roots stretching to England and their early colonial experience to classify human groups on the border "according to shifting racial categories that placed Caucasians at the top. The expansionist venture was thus conceived as an attempt to introduce a measure of civilization to a spectrum of inferior races."[50] A contributor to New Mexico's early public suggested a certain ascriptive determinism, if not circular reasoning, to ameliorate the unenlightened condition of the Mexicans. "New Laws will have to be framed," the imperious writer declared, "a New Government will be put in complete operation and its Anglo-Saxon institutions and spirit, which have given so much character to the [American] race, will begin to show themselves in this interior and remote region."[51]

Euroamericans who could have not cared less for the positive incorporation of Mexican natives sought to impose a hegemonic American imperialism. With every battlefield victory over the Mexicans, national American sentiment elevated the U.S. soldier to eminent representative of American patriotism.[52] A contributor to the New Mexico discourse proudly pointed to American troops swarming southern New Mexico. It was, he stated, a

> grateful sight to Americans who are so proud of a country possessing so many resources and so much wealth, and adds fuel to the flame of their patriotism which burns so brightly and has upon so many occasions shed a luster upon their history. How can any American help but feel proud of his country? How much better does he love it after witnessing the poverty, ignorance, and imbecility of another nation, and how much better satisfied is he with his own laws and institutions after an opportunity to compare them with others?[53]

Such material patriotism, as it might be deemed, made for an "essential prop to republicanism."[54] The correspondent went on to show a correspondingly redemptive liberal hubris: "No wonder that Americans who breathe such a free atmosphere should always look to their own country as the best, the freest, and most happy on the face of the earth." Reflecting the ideological distinctions within Euroamerican colonizers, *Republican* editor Gibson defended New Mexico and its people against any of his fellow countrymen who doubted their worth.[55]

On September 24 the *Republican* quoted the *St. Louis Republican*'s hope for Congress to inquire into the "present anomalous condition of the Government at, and of the People of New Mexico." A more "extraordinary state of things never was presented than now exists there," the paper noted. The key question concerned what power was given to the people to establish a government in New Mexico, "its propriety and legality under the Constitution—and the extent of protection which it has afforded to the people of the conquered territory." The *Santa Fe Republican* agreed that the people of New Mexico should have a government "of some kind which they can see and feel and understand, either military or civil." New Mexico had civil judges and administrators, but they served "at the pleasure of the military." The people had been "promised all the benefits of annexation and protection yet have enjoyed neither fully enough to experience the least." Would titles derived under the given condition be good? "Would the officers who have been acting receive the salaries provided for them? Will criminal offenses have to be tried in the States or by those courts?" The weekly wondered, quite pointedly, if the acts of the upcoming legislature would be recognized "and binding?"[56]

The actual territorial legislature that came together in Santa Fe proceeded authoritatively for twenty days. Governor Vigil labored to have the proceedings stand as an exercise in American government. "In assembling for the first time as a legislative body," his opening address began, "chosen by the free and unbiased vote of the people, one of my duties, as imposed upon me by the Constitution and laws under which we have lived for the past year [*por la Constitución y las Leyes que nos han regido desde el año pasado*], is to inform the general assembly of the condition of the country and to recommend what measures may be deemed necessary for the internal government of the Territory."[57] Vigil intermixed a ringing liberal sermon with practical recommendations. It became them all, he stressed, to exercise "the functions of a free government [*Es propio que al reunirnos así por la primera vez para ejercer las funciones de un Gobierno Libre*]." He spoke in terms of a practical and proven republican system having been introduced by the American invasion. He gave thanks "for the prosperity attending the general abundance of our agricultural productions and the usual health of the people." More especially did it become the body to be thankful, Vigil invoked, that, in the *Republican*'s translation, "whilst the two nations of which we compose a part are engaged in a bloody and unfortunate war [*una guerra desgraciada y sangrienta*], we are left to pursue the quiet occupations of life, and cultivate those pursuits which conduce only to our comfort [*egercer las vocaciones que solo conducen al bienestar*]."

Vigil had previously complained of some military oppressions, but to the elected legislators he cut a contrast between the Kearny laws and those in force "in our country—to appreciate the manner in which crimes have been punished, property protected, and contracts endorsed." He asked for appreciation of the "universal participation that every citizen enjoys in executing the laws throughout the country [*apreciar el modo en que los crímenes han sido castigados, la propiedad protejida, y los contratos entre particulares hechos efectivos, y de calificar la participación general que cada Ciudadano goza en la ejecución de las Leyes en todo el País*]." Vigil hoped he could soon announce the cessation of U.S.-Mexican hostilities. He shared in the Euroamerican perception of American victory in process. He desired the restoration of peace, for it would "certainly exercise an important influence upon our prosperity and happiness." Like a virtual member of the American Whig Party, which called for progress, Vigil anticipated freedom and prosperity, as they all lived in an "age of improvement in both government and society."[58]

Vigil did not neglect the liberal's faith in common education. Only one public school existed in New Mexico, he complained, crying out for increased learning opportunities for poor and rich alike. "If our government here is to be republican," he maintained, "if it is to be based upon democratic principles, and if the will of the majority is one day to be law [of] the land and [of] the government of the people, it is most important for this will to be properly exercised." However, in a moment of traditionalism, he seemed to imply an objection to the *Republican* editor's prior inclusion of consideration for the literacy of Mexican women. In his gendered language, "The people must be enlightened and instructed so that every man shall be able to read and inform himself of matters important to his country and his government." Vigil praised the great governmental "magistracy," a term radiating out of New York State's volatile political arena to mean the grand republican scheme of the United States.[59] He called on representatives to conduct their work "in that spirit of harmony and good feeling which is so well calculated to promote success." Vigil shared his confidence in the forthcoming legislation. It would redound to the good of the country and the people's happiness. He closed by pledging his cooperation to the delegate's endeavors to the best of his faculties.

"*Viva el Gobernador*," exclaimed *El Republicano*. The public was receiving the governor's message well, according to the weekly. The clear, explicit, and well-written document credited *el Señor Gobernador* with an address "as respectable as the messages of any of our governors in the states [*tan respectable como los mensages de cualesquiera* [sic] *de nuestros Gobernadores de los estados*]," the editorial declared in the spirit of national incorporation and in distinct Nuevomexicano idiom.[60]

The session proceeded with the solemn deliberateness of an American bicameral body replete with committees on the judiciary, education, elections, and other institutions. The twenty-five elected Nuevomexicanos in attendance can be said to represent the second cohort of American-integrated politicos after the initial set of Kearny conquest appointees. A "big impediment" arose in completing the business in a timely manner due to the need for translating everything from one language to the other, yet members plowed through a grand agenda.[61] Clerks translated the U.S. Constitution into Spanish in the hegemony of American protocol. House members elected former Kearny officer W. Z. Angney as president and James Giddings as secretary. The council selected Henry W. Henrie secretary. While Nuevomexicanos understood a legislative body, these Euroamerican settlers provided the leads for the American variety. A Nuevomexicano, Antonio Sandoval, took the top honor of council president. It was telling that the year before, he had been the lead signatory on the petition of protest to the Mexican government over Manuel Armijo's abdication to Kearny.[62] With their clear majority, Nuevomexicanos looked to have their people's interests met in particular.[63]

The proceedings stayed doggedly faithful to the rational bureaucratic course introduced by the Kearny Code and sanctioned by Vigil. The systematic rituals of introducing and debating bills, combined with the sheer volume of legislative business, appeared as innovations over the proceeding of a typical Mexican department assembly. A gamut of laws saw the light of day. Official positions were abolished, the duties of others spelled out. Levies were placed on incoming merchandise and restrictions were imposed on gambling halls. Prefects were granted the right to call local emergency militias. Popular elections were significantly firmed up for prefects and county offices. Judges would be subject to rules and codes for crimes and punishments. A law passed providing for the legal recovery of land (ejectment, in the terminology of the day), another for holding circuit courts, and one incorporating the Pueblo communities as political bodies. County sheriffs would henceforth take the census every four years. Allowance was provided for titles lost in the Taos Revolt to be claimed in circuit court. Legislators even passed a bill establishing a territorial university "for the promotion of literature and the arts and sciences." An incorporated board of curators with set duties would run the institution. No religious qualification or sect would be required of any curator, president, tutor, instructor, or officer, nor as a condition of admission for students. In a highly proleptic act, a committee would select a site and take charge of a campaign to fund the construction of public buildings.

It was a pragmatically necessary step for Valencia County representative Rafaél Armijo y Maestas to take charge of implementing the provision in the Kearny Code calling for a convention of elected delegates to deliberate and vote on the question of New Mexico's annexation by the United States (a move that drew considerable consternation in Texas).[64]

The laws were slated for review and the approval of General Price and Governor Vigil. Price perceived the assembly assuming too much sovereignty. He abolished by Special Order the offices of U.S. district attorney and marshal for New Mexico, reminding the assembly members that their government was "essentially military in character." Price emphasized that the president would consider the provision of laws "in some *few respects*" going beyond the line designated by his own authority. Only Congress could bestow the proposed political rights of the people of New Mexico under the Constitution of the United States he argued.[65] Price's distinctions failed to make an immediate difference. Neophyte American lawmakers took their functioning political system for granted, adjourning with a consciousness of their role in reinforcing the legitimacy of American democracy.

The mere fact of the legislature hit home among Nuevomexicanos. Father Antonio José Martínez and twenty-eight of his Taos County compatriots put out a major statement endorsing New Mexico's political progress. Martínez, it is important to recall, was the renowned Mexican patriot and inveterate critic of American excess in the Mexican period. Moreover, Governor Vigil and Euroamericans had branded the people of Taos as violent rabble-rousers, as shown, they claimed, in the 1837 Chimayo Revolt and the assassinations of Governor Bent and his retinue. It was in this context that Taos spokesmen soberly deliberated the nature of modern politics. The *Republican* editors translated their opening lines as follows:

> The object of all government in every well organized community is the public good, the conservation of civil rights generally and the protection of the individual governed [*Naturalmente se palpa que el blanco de los de gobernación en las sociedades bien organizadas es el bien público, la conservación de los derechos civiles en general, y la protección en lo particular de todos los individuous de la gobernación*]. The enacting of laws by wise legislators of exalted views tends solely to the benefit of the citizen under any government, be it monarchical or republican, or any of their many varieties. And why? In order that all may alike enjoy the common resources of the territory they inhabit, as well as the happiness of a people and as a body politic [*para darles mas a los arbitrios y medios de su subsistencia, pues el bien de los habitantes y la felicidad del cuerpo político que componen, es su fin*]."

The group echoed routine imperial democracy, contrasting progressive American and stagnant Mexican republics. Mexico, the Taoseños held, "originated from Spain and from thence came its political system. Its inhabitants originated from an amalgamation of the Spaniards with the indigenous who inhabited this new world discovered by Cortes [*derivado cuanto a su sistema político del Gobierno Español por medio de conquista, y sus habitantes que resultan de Aquellos y de las indígenas que habitan ese nuevo mundo, descubierto por Cortes*]." The American system "derived all from England, and in time, by the enterprises and wisdom of its people, and by their energy constituted a republican government which shines resplendent in the world by a system both political and religious, relevant and unexacting, it has cherished Christianity in its bosom, and under it religion is practiced with pride, piety and decorum [*mas el segundo, derivado de la Inglaterra y de su saber y de su poder, hechos en gobierno republicano que brilla y resplandece en el orbe por su sistema político y religioso que tolera lo conveniente, y con esto es protejido el cristianismo de su seno y llevado decorosamente*]." Mexico, "as no one could deny," the group noted, had gone "to a point of anarchy, profound political division, and great monetary debt."[66]

It rang like the typical Anglo-Saxon condemnation of Mexico as neither a "pristine Indian world" nor a "civilized nation" but a "disquieting hybrid, closer to savagery than civilization."[67] Martínez and his fellow signatories concluded with the old grievance of the Mexican government failing to protect New Mexicans from the "barbarous tribes" in spite of repeated pleas. The people had every natural right to resist the American invasion (as in the Taos Revolt), they expounded; however—reflecting a split among Taos inhabitants— nothing could forgive the murder of the civil governor Bent by "ignorant" assassins, even though it was done for "love of country." It was an important admission regarding the meaning of resistance to imperialism in this particular case. Given the "obstinate" war and the American promises of government and protection from tribal aggression, and if only their confiscated arms were returned, the citizens' caucus declared that it and fellow Nuevomexicanos would henceforth pledge to uphold social order.[68]

The proclamation appeared at this liminal moment as capitulation to the new political and civic order in the homeland of a highly oppositional community. Someone, perhaps a Euroamerican, signing off as *Un Conciudadano* (A fellow citizen) openly congratulated Martínez, the "perfectly eminent [one] to small and grand people," for acknowledging a liberal legislature and elections as protectors of the religious and personal rights of his people and for leaving aside "prejudices and superstitions" in "defense of tolerance and conscience."[69]

The work of the proleptic legislature sparked public debate. *Un Labrador* questioned in Spanish the House's defeat of a bill mandating the fencing of agricultural fields, as it would prove costly for poor farmers, and asked how land owners with fields trampled by loose animals could gain legal redress. *Un Labrador* predicted that the bill would pass sooner or later. It defied logic to *El Minero* that the council rejected mining regulation.[70] *Don Simplicio* called officials to account for the foolhardiness of establishing a university in the absence of a primary education system: the legislature "desired to race before it could walk [*un deseo de carrera antes de poder andar*]." *Simplicio* had his reasons for liking the passage of election laws for local officials, and he regretted the defeat of a couple of provisions that would have given protection to sheep owners.[71] Inocencio dove headlong into a long-winded critique of Simplicio's political thinking as short-sighted and incomplete, wondering about a lack of adequate literacy; or perhaps it reflected insufficient skills in the Spanish language.[72] The curmudgeonly liberal grumbled about the abrupt curtailment of the assembly as it prevented the representatives from fulfilling all the duties "the people" hoped for because they feared change and social reform. What little had been done, Inocencio judged, was "poorly coordinated."[73]

The resounding defeat of two measures—one to establish civil marriages by magistrate, the other to create public cemeteries, which would permit burial ceremonies for non-Catholics—drew various levels of rebuke. The liberal proposals grated on Mexican tradition. Non-Catholics had been forced to bury their dead on private property only, and the defeat of the reform measures sustained Mexican laws providing for Catholic marriages only and for only Catholic burials in the churchyard or chapel grounds.[74] Inocencio commented with precise knowledge of the norms regarding the relations between religion and government in the United States. Had the bills been well written in the "spirit of the U.S. Constitution [*conformes al espíritu y letra de la Constitución de los Estados Unidos*]," he surmised, they would have passed. Everyone recognized the importance of the marriage proposal, he continued, there being no reason for the Catholic Church not to sanction it, not least because the intervention of the government meant reining in the "misconduct of humanity [*extravios de la muy débil humanidad*]." Decades of foreign influx backed the argument. Inocencio emphasized that New Mexico was characterized by people of many Christian denominations. The American territory must conform in the legal protection of "this religious diversity [*esta diversidad de personas de diferentes religiones*]," as he put it. The U.S. Constitution did not protect any one religion exclusively, Inocencio lectured, nor did it exclude any, and it persecuted none. Nothing in the law threatened the importance of the Catholic clergy, it was assured. The assembly retained responsibility for the civil protection of individuals and for conferring on county prefects and alcaldes the authority to perform marriage ceremonies. A civil government maintained the responsibility of prescribing cemeteries not only to allow people of various religions to bury their loved ones with dignity but for the sake of decency and public health and, Inocencio concluded, "because it preserved the principle of 'a free people.'"[75]

Some American settlers, endeavoring to torque Nuevomexicano minds to their radical liberalism, spoke with far less moderation over the modern/pre-modern tension. A furious reaction to the marriage and cemetery failures in the pages of the *Republican* vented a vicious attack on the Mexican priesthood. The United States by this time had absorbed more than twenty years of immigration, mostly from northwestern Europe, most of it Catholic. Anti-Catholicism had intensified in response to Irish immigration. The Reverend Horace James, the leader of American theological liberalism no less, pointed to the "first dangers" in the United States, "barbarism," the influx of foreigners, and "Romanism next."[76] Euroamerican religious bigotry leaked onto the frontier's public discourse, the allegation of Mexican fanaticism, "not in the sense of blindly adhering to arbitrary religious precepts, but rather in the more ominous sense of primitiveness and irrationality."[77]

Euroamericans stated their reasons for going after New Mexico's Catholic Church beyond the threat of perceived religious anti-Americanism. Kearny's inflated American value of religious tolerance translated in the immediacy of the occupation into a pledge not to abolish Catholicism.[78] However, the U.S. principle of religious tolerance bore the mark of intolerance toward any particular religion or denomination seeking to dominate society and politics. It verged in New Mexico on a suspicion, if not outright paranoia, of Catholic politicking. Such perceptions were fed by Bishop Zubiría's mandate that priests fortify their church resources and infrastructure. Americans frowned on the Church in the northern Mexican provinces rivaling the civil administration "in influence, wealth, geographic reach, and hierarchical and centralizing impulses."[79] The stereotype of the Mexican tyrant priest in cahoots with the proverbial corrupt politician, would recur in New Mexico's tabloid discourse. Americans added a racially prejudiced view of the Mexican priests as personally profligate.

An anonymous letter to the *Republican* bundled in Spanish the themes of political ambition, low religious ethics, and the "presumptively rational voter." As Jeffrey Alexander reminds us, "Citizen voters make the crucial decision about the civil and uncivil qualities of candidates." Or at least it is assumed that they do. "Voters are imagined in terms of the discourse of liberty. If this is myth, it is a fiction upon which democratic truth depends." It is therefore that voters are projected "as rational, honest, independent, and capable of decisions that are wise. Like the candidates themselves, they are discursively constructed in terms of the binary discourse that sustains the civil sphere. Unlike the candidates, however, voters are primarily conceptualized in positive terms."[80] The assumption, it can be added, is that suffrage bestows them with the ability to perceive what is in their liberal interests.

The rhetoric of the contributor to the New Mexico discourse assumed Nuevomexicanos to have become rational voters instantly, or implied that they should get with it now. Nativos knew, the argument went, that they now had a right to exercise judgment of the elected delegates insofar as they "may have secured and enlarged your rights as citizens of a free government, or have left you to endure for a while longer the illiberal, intolerant and oppressive control of the government from which you have a right to consider yourselves separate." In the American nation "a whole people are not like a single individual—able to change views and adapt themselves in circumstances in a day or a year," it was maintained. "The institutions and the feelings of a people must be left to change gradually." In the shifting of national identities, nativos were counseled, as if they were rational voters in waiting, not then to "be disappointed that you have not obtained all you wished or expected from your representatives." The writer reminded his "fellow citizens" (Kearny's civic adoptees) of the "many oppressions" to which they had long submitted, "because you had neither a free Government nor a free legislature." Now with the suffrage they could impose their will on public officials, but democracy, the "object of all free governments," was a work in progress. The particular setback in the attainment of their liberties, in the pundit's portrayal, was the failed bill to establish public cemeteries "where all should alike be allowed to bury their dead with or without the ceremonial of the Catholic Church as their consciences or belief might dictate." That same bill would have allowed non-clerics to perform civil marriages. The writer made the liberal distinction between the rational voter and the corrupt politician, even though the politician might serve the cultural interests of the people. The refusal to allow the legalization of marriage by magistrates came from "that class, who, under the pretended sanction of heaven have imposed the most grievous burthens [sic] and exactions for the support of the most shameful and glaring vices. Who, claiming to be the teachers of divine origin, have in their lives, both private and public, placed before you examples of the most shocking human depravity."[81]

Un Conciudadano had earlier praised Father Martínez's acceptance of the new government. Not to be outdone in the art of condemning Mexican culture, he cast in Spanish prose the "vicious and depraved clergy" among the "lovers of the old corrupt office holders" who feared losing their power to oppress and exact from the people's funds to support their vices and who partook in the Taos uprising as "murderers and insurrectionists."[82] Another writer, a settler apparently, pointedly signing off his Spanish message as *El Azote de los Reveldes* (Whip to the rebels), explained that the bishop in Mexico City betrayed the liberal ideals that had animated the Mexican revolt against Spain by maintaining a stranglehold on the people, also imagined as rational entities, the local priests forcing them into debt servitude should they fail to meet imposed tithes. The Nuevomexicanos responsible for defeat of the cemetery and marriage proposals acted as the "handmaidens of the Gentlemen Curas [priests]," he sneered. El Azote named the three delegates who led the opposition to the bills. He hailed "All the people" to "see them! Territory, see how you erred in your present elections." El Azote presaged the order of pollution many Euroamerican liberals would commonly douse onto Mexican Catholicism. He chastised the voters for giving their power "to men who remain marked by their bad faith: who deprecate the ... duties that they should link with their communities ... to protect with your sweat the purses of their friends, the Gentlemen priests."[83]

Liberal free speech proved itself for lashing the foreigner to the mast of the red, white, and blue. Another settler suggested the power of the clergy to cloud the minds of the presumptively rational and liberal masses. "When our Lord and Savior Jesus Christ sent his Apostles to the world to preach peace and good will to all men," the commentator declared,

> he gave no recommendations to his servants to attempt the control of their fellow men in other than teaching them to practice those divine principles which make men better fit to meet his God when called to the bar of Divine Justice. The Priests of this country, on the contrary, preferring to be followers of the same Lord Jesus Christ, attempt the exercise of the most baneful domination over the minds of the people, and step aside from the exercise of their religious duties to use the influence which their superior informa-

tion gives them over their more ignorant countrymen, not for the benefit of the flock confided to their care, but for the purpose of self-aggrandizement.

Only when "the people" dared to "look into the motives which at the present crisis have caused the opposition of some of these men to a measure which tends to increase the civil and religious freedom of their own people," would they no longer countenance a priesthood of robbers and murderers of innocent civilians, the author allowed.

The liberal whip, confident of a successful annexation, could see the Western Diocese of the United States taking control of religious affairs in the territory. Were the "ecclesiastics of this country [to] overstep the links of their duties and privileges, they will doubtless be removed from a position which gives them the power of doing harm by the bishop of the diocese." The prescient forecast would have its fruition soon enough. The angel of religious social tolerance alight on his shoulder, the writer did not wish to be understood "in the most remote degree, as desiring any interference with the religious tenets of the people. We solely aim at freeing them from a bondage which enthralls alike their minds, their bodies and their souls, makes them the servants of a class of men, who neither preach nor practice the laws of God."[84] The writer no doubt felt the injunction consistent with the promise of religious acceptance afforded by the liberal conqueror Kearny. Coincidentally or not, the *Republican* published a New York dispatch on the election of Pope Pius IX, leader of democratic and modernizing reforms in Italy and in the Church.[85]

Public attention turned to the annexation convention decreed by the Kearny Code and ratified by the late legislature. The mechanism of a "convention," still new in the United States at the time, evolved to bring about unity to promote a civic or political goal.[86] Opinionators packed the *Republican* with another spate of emotion-charged commentary. *Conciudadano* exploited comparative history, modernization tenets, and the virtues of continental liberalism to win the Nuevomexicanos over to annexation. As he phrased it, "The country comprising the

> mis-called Republic of Mexico, from which you are now virtually freed, was colonized more than a century before that which now spreads its protection over you. But how wide the contrast. The

U.S. has upwards of 20,000,000 of inhabitants—Mexico less than 8,000,000. The people of the U.S. are united, happy and prosperous—Mexico weak, torn by unhappy internal dissensions and foreign war—her people oppressed, unenlightened and vicious. The commerce of the United States spreads its sails in every port of the world—in not a port of the world is a ship of Mexico known.

Was the contrast accounted for by the difference "in climate or soil, or productions? No," Conciudadano didacticized:

Mexico is as happy in climate and soil as any country of the known world. Why then is this contrast? History and the current story of the world tells you why. The infant colonies of the United States based their first institutions upon freedom of minds. The first settlers fled from tyranny over conscience, and invited the oppressed for conscience sake to come to them. And from the whole world the oppressed for conscience sake found peace and protection in the U.S., and living in harmony and peace, all creeds and all religions free have built upon a great and prosperous nation. Mexico, with bigotry and intolerance, shut her ports to the stranger, and oppressed him when with them, persecuted with cruel intolerance all who dared to differ from the one creed and drove them from the land. The result is before you. The destiny of which Republic do you choose?

Based on war intelligence that New Mexico, California, and Texas would be retained forever by the United States, Conciudadano asked the people to permit themselves "not to be misled or deceived. Accept the boon offered you—equal rights, civil and religious, to all; a membership in the model republic of the world."[87]

Patriotism for many Americans during the Mexican War stemmed from a providential messianism, what one historian calls "a common perception of America's uniqueness and of its peculiar 'genius.'" The guiding hand of Providence "united all Americans with God's plan for the world . . . the cause of liberty and democracy, the 'American idea,' was God's cause and, as so many Americans pointed out, it was the United States that was charged with bringing to fruition God's plan for all mankind."[88] An essayist tailored in the *Republican* America's providential cause in a contrast to the Frenchman, the Spaniard, the

Hollander, and the Portuguese. "[C]ramped with the fetters of monarchy," he proclaimed, they had been compelled to acknowledge the "irresistible superiority of the power" and "almost incomprehensible enterprise and activity of the Anglo-Saxon blood." Anglo-Saxonism, combined with republicanism and equal opportunity, would usher in a New Age to New Mexico, without the "slightest necessity for rapacity or lust of conquest in this, our irresistible progress." Americans moved "by the God of Nature" to a new chapter in human history, beyond the politics of conquest.[89] New Mexico in this view formed the cradle of a new era where might met right, where the power of imperialism found itself tempered by republican enlightenment.

Euroamericans pushed Nuevomexicanos rhetorically to cohere as American citizens in spite of their cultural diversity. As one pointed out, the discharge of the voter's duties did not end with the mere election of delegates to the convention. People would have to pressure their representatives during the convention to stand up for American annexation and oppose those who had, "as if by divine right," tyrannized them in the past, deceived them, and betrayed the object for which they were elected. Annexation as such was far from the point. The "march of the armies and the predominations [sic] of commanding generals" had decided that New Mexico belonged to the United States. The delegates were obligated to take the steps for acquiring "such a constitution as of right belongs to you, as the new inhabitants of a portion of the territory of the great northern Republican to hasten the time that the strict surveillance of armies and the necessary severity of military control not be required."[90]

A liberal imperialist compelled all Nuevomexicanos to realize how the American acquisition of New Mexico meant little materially to the United States, though some residents may have had a pecuniary interest in annexation. The "statesmen of the day" (President Polk and his team), in their "enlarged and philanthropic spirit," had taken "a deep interest in the subject." These high-minded members of American rule desired "that the people of this land should have the benefit of liberal institutions—that the 'area of freedom should be extended,' and that the Constitution of the United States should spread its broad shield of protection over this distant region."[91]

Republican editors took issue with Americans who did not believe the impoverished New Mexican landscape capable of economic flow-ering. New Mexico would be annexed willy-nilly, they pointed out; imperial economics, if little else, would serve as a vital connector to the Pacific, a link in the international trade system from China around Cape Horn to San Francisco. "If we would but throw away our petty prejudices," the wisdom counseled, "our own ideas of the greatness which a little brief power may give us in this land while depending on itself, and look to the magnitude of the question in a great national point of view, as beneficial to the country we inhabit, and also to the people whose laws and institutions we wish to adopt."[92]

Shortly after Governor Vigil ordered the election of delegates to the annexation convention, a Nuevomexicano posted under the *nom de plume* CEMAPA two forceful justifications for annexation. "CEMAPA," it seems, signified *se mapa* (he who maps out). CEMAPA announced that New Mexico was effectively cut off from Mexico by the branch of the Army of the West that succeeded in taking Chihuahua. The United States and Mexico were in negotiations to end the war. Only a dispute over the international boundaries stood in the way of a formal cessation of hostilities, he pointed out. A rejection of American annexation at the convention could dissuade the United States from wanting to keep New Mexico. This lead piece gave the familiar liberal's political rationale for urging that Nuevomexicanos go with the United States. The mass-based popular election provided for virtuous, independent, and patriotic persons to hold office in order to make good laws, CEMAPA emphasized— especially important under the regrettable circumstances in which all in New Mexico found itself.[93] CEMAPA composed in his second missive a uniquely comprehensive and revealingly nuanced economic, social, and political script. For this should its entire argument be noted.

CEMAPA raised the specter of Mexico retaining possession of New Mexico. Disaster would follow. Exorbitant customs taxes would be levied on merchants and would be illegally kept from garrisons, as they had been since 1830. The centralized Mexican government would appoint a non-nativo governor, giving him all power and leaving the unhappy troops poverty stricken, with little resort but to public robbery "to sustain their poor existence [*obligandolos por la miseria a cometer robos en público para sostener su triste existencia*]." Nuevomexicanos had gone down the road toward the United States so much that a whole re-nationalization would be necessary under the rule of Mexico. Paralyzed businesses would leave cash-poor farmers to "fall back on selling their grains to rich land owners with losses [*tendrían que volver a vender y con trabajo sus granos a los ricos, fanega por vara*]. Business interests would have to loan increasing sums of money to take care of urgent needs of the kind the government had guaranteed with grand [false] promises and which would be [not] fulfilled as they have been [*Tendríamos que prestar crecidas sumas para remediar necesidades urgentes que nos garantizarían como hacían con grandes promesas y que cumplirían como ya han hecho*]." Should these measures prove insufficient, businesses would be obligated to move. The confiscation would follow of equipment, horses [*bagaje, caballada*], personal services and the products of trade, "all for our own well-being and patriotism [*todo para nuestro propio bien y por patriotismo*]." Since not all deserving of these services could part with their funds so liberally, if it meant the impoverishment of their families, they would see the label of traitor pinned on them when they refused or be forced to pay "gifts" [*regalitos*] to avoid legal and other entanglements; no patriotism in any of that.

CEMAPA feared for those Nuevomexicanos who had become affiliated with the Americans (the potential price of a liberal consensus). Mexican officials would brand them as traitors for having worked in the American administration, for having become the friend of Americans, for selling them meat, preparing their mules and donkeys, putting them up in their houses, or helping them in some small way. And what would Mexico do with those who had served as representatives in the recent general assembly? What of the members of the annexation convention and those electing them? No family in the entire territory could escape persecution based on the pretext of guilt in such associations, having their money confiscated or personal vengeance exacted on them. "Returning the Mexican administration to New Mexico would bring so many disadvantages and such discontent it would finally produce some popular movement similar to the one in 1837 [*La vuelta de la Administración Mejicana al Territorio lo colmaría en tantas desavenencias a descontento que al fin producirá algún movimiento popular semejante al del año 1837*]," CEMAPA obsessed like a proper law and order hombre de bien. "Even should the Mexican General Government take steps to suppress some of the ills," he queried, "is it now possible to govern the people of New Mexico according to its accustomed arbitrariness and caprice? I do not think so." The Mexican administration would doubtless promise reforms, "like it always had according to the beautiful theories it has always pronounced and that in reality leaves us in the unfortunate position of lost Israelites in the Desert who only landed to breathe the waste of Egypt [*desgraciada posición de los Israelitas en el desierto que solo acertaba a suspirar por las perdidades de Egypto*]." If Nuevomexicanos rejected that prospect, "as any man of honor would in their country," CEMAPA put it, they could see "what to expect with the admission of New Mexico into the American Union [*veamos que podemos esperar de la admisión del N. Méjico a la Unión Americana*]."

CEMAPA spun a wondrous tapestry of political freedom for New Mexico under the American wing. Though a Mexican, he made a positive continental liberal comparison with the recent history of Louisiana and Florida, both created by the Spanish imperium, their French and Hispanic inhabitants now realizing amplified privileges. The United States guided those people with great care to understand and enjoy the benefits of a republican democratic system. In the brief time since their annexation, they were the "most happy of the world and among the richest and greatest supporters of the American Union."

CEMAPA emphasized development as if a member of the American Whig Party. The United States would serve as the instrument to stimulate prosperity. New Mexico already had the healthiest climate in the world, and now, with its growing reputation, would become an ideal destination. People would arrive from afar to enjoy its clean air and temperate summers, bathe in its many springs as they did in Saratoga. New Mexico's mines, not developed since the Pueblo Revolt of 1680, would become the richest with intelligent capitalist investment (a dream to reach fantasy proportion in decades to come). A practical disciple of Adam Smith's free market, CEMAPA highlighted the "spirit of enterprise" protected and guaranteed by the government, that would open up to the industrious, rich and poor alike. New Mexico's poor quality sheep, racked by sickness, would grow and improve once crossed with other strains such as the Merino. High quality wool from the best fields in the continental frontier would render New Mexico's sheep an article of export, CEMAPA envisioned. The production of abundant and high quality wool would establish manufacturing plants amid New Mexico's beautiful mountains. In a romantic allusion of the sort that would become common in the late nineteenth century, New Mexico's sheep lands were hailed as the equal to those of Spain. American troops, now stationed in New Mexico out of necessity, would, upon annexation, guarantee protection for thriving ranches.

Such were but a few of the advantages New Mexico would see by annexation to the United States, CEMAPA enthused. Signs of progress had already appeared since Kearny took possession in the price of farm articles, house rentals, craftsmen's salaries, and the comfort of people from all classes. The disciplined army of occupation was proving an irritant, to be sure, yet the contrast in the present circumspection and direction of good government to the "arbitrariness and egotism" of the past was impressive. An efficient, impartial court system was now in place, CEMAPA argued, responsive to public opinion and bereft of corruption.

CEMAPA noted that the annexation convention formed the preoccupation of "all the parties" [*todos los partidos*] of the territory. Each partido had procured the means to elect the candidates representing its opinion. The result of such efforts would constitute the opinion of the territory itself.[94] Donaciano Vigil likely wrote as CEMAPA. Carlos Beaubien privately told Vigil he "very much" liked the governor's (unnamed) essay calling for American annexation.[95] An anonymous commentator used the CEMAPA report to reason that annexation "made at our own request, and of our own free will is far more preferable than our allowing the supreme government to surrender this country by a compulsory treaty of peace."[96]

Clean elections were held in Taos County, Río Arriba County, and at the town of San Miguel del Bado. Seats in the Bernalillo County precincts of Chaves and Armijo went contested. The alcalde who was charged with resolving contests was also one of the candidates in the dispute. Vigil issued instructions on how to handle the delicate case.[97] The report from the southwestern districts of Valencia County had six gentlemen elected on the "annexation ticket," the first for candidates to be organized in such a fashion in New Mexico. Five were Spanish-surnamed. That two from Bernalillo County, both Nuevomexicano, were elected on the "anti-annexation" ticket, signified lack of total legitimation going to the American conquest.[98]

At the opening of the convention, General Price stated that by the "movement of armies and military occupation," New Mexico had "become permanently subject to the government of the United States." By their proceedings "conducted with the strictest propriety and decorum," Price reinforced, conventioneers could free themselves from the oppressive and anarchic Mexican government to secure the protection of a civil government "under a Constitution which guarantees to you the rights of *freemen*, which permits no exactions but such as are imposed by the representatives of your choice." On the other hand, the commander warned at the point of his bayonet against "seditious and indecorous language against the constituted military or civil authorities, calculated to inflame or excite the people against the government."[99]

The basis of Price's latter concern is suggested in the letter Carlos Beaubien wrote to Governor Vigil expressing the hope that "this time we have chosen men who will not be prevented [from voting for annexation] by the influence of the copper Christs [*Espero que por esta vez hemos conseguido hombres que no se dejaran prevención por la influencia de los cristos de cobre*]," referring to pendant representations of Christ on the cross, "tin Christs," as it were.[100] A correspondent going by *El Amigo de los Pueblos*, possibly a Euroamerican writing in Spanish, reported a disruption in the convention proceedings at the hands of agitators among the Nuevomexicano delegates. El Amigo described the offenders as former conspirators in the assassination of Governor Bent. They reportedly took a stand at the convention in opposition to annexation on the grounds that it would spell the people's loss of their religion.[101]

A certain religious-secular scrape indicates how seriously the clergy stood in opposition to the liberal groups, Father Martínez aside. It began when Vicar Juan Felipe Ortiz suspended Father Nicolás Valencia, a recent transplant from Mexico City. The more secular hombres de bien Antonio José Otero, Francisco Sarracino, and Manuel Baca vigorously protested Ortiz's action to Governor Vigil. They pointed out that Valencia and his loyal parishioners were "friends of our [annexation] party." Such was the real cause of the suspension, they claimed, and Ortiz simply aimed to nullify their influence in the territory. Noting that the suspension went against the principle of due process, they asked for Vigil's intervention to see that the case go before the appropriate district judge, and they offered to pay Valencia's legal expenses.

Vigil, exercising powers over civilian life more appropriate to Mexican law, suspended Ortiz and replaced him with another pastor; he also took the liberty of suspending a Nuevomexicano magistrate who was under the control of military authority.[102] The rift would have led Nuevomexicano traditionalists to fear for their home culture under American sovereignty.

In the results of the convention, a majority of delegates passed a resolution calling on Congress to formally annex New Mexico (as it had done with Texas in 1845) together with a request for a territorial form of government. Price signed off on the document, which went to Senators Benton and John M. Clayton of Delaware, with a request that they serve as representatives of the New Mexico people in Congress.[103]

El Republicano noted on March 18 the rumor circulating in the Mexican populace that a treaty of "Peace and amity had been entered into by the two governments." The reports had been so strong "that many are inclined to give them credence." The editor doubted it himself because the Americans had not heard it from the states.[104] However, American and Mexican envoys had signed the Treaty of Guadalupe Hidalgo on February 2, a week before the annexation convention met, bringing an end to the hostilities between the United States and Mexico. Congressional advocates of the treaty overcame Whig and some Democratic opposition. The U.S. Senate ratified the treaty on March 10, 1848. The story of the treaty's signing did not appear in *El Republicano* until May 3.[105] The Mexican Congress ratified the accord on May 19; Americans in New Mexico passed the news around in early June. The British chargé d'affaires in Mexico City recorded that the Mexican commissioners who negotiated the treaty were grateful that the New Mexicans had declared themselves in favor of U.S. annexation as it eased the worry they felt for abandoning the people of the surrendered territory.[106] The treaty was finalized on July 4, 1848.

The laws passed by the 1847 legislature were nullified because New Mexico was still a foreign entity at the time. The true importance of the 1847 session for the political incorporation of Nuevomexicanos was recognized in 1894. A Nuevomexicano weekly recalled the "first" legislative assembly of the Territory of New Mexico as "informally" convoked by the most notable men of the various districts of New Mexico. They decreed laws of little "relative" interest but "of great actual importance for being the first pass given by the sons of New Mexico under the new regime [*de gran importancia real por ser el primer paso dado por los hijos de Nuevo México bajo el nuevo régimen*]."[107]

In retrospect, Donaciano Vigil's role glows like a poster child for the liberal theory of modern political diffusion. Ralph Emerson Twitchell noted that he "must have been well informed as to American ideas, or else in one short year he had absorbed more than many of his race."[108] His idealistic and practical policies as governor opened the gate to an experience of participatory dignity for Nuevomexicanos under immovable American power. Vigil's command kept a volatile condition of ethnoracial dynamics under control in the wake of the Taos Revolt. Vigil modeled for Nuevomexicanos who intuited a value in being part of the United States and for claiming the equality enjoyed by Euroamerican male settlers. His conciliations exposed Nuevomexicanos to a vision of participatory democracy greater than they had known while part of Mexico. The spectacle of Nuevomexicano participation in a conquest government, egged by the diffusion of sophisticated republican mechanics, including voting democracy, made for the congealing of a new national identification.

For months after the Mexican-American War the only major change in New Mexico's political terrain involved the departure of the volunteer units.[109] Vigil remained in place as New Mexico's de facto governor. He continued to demonstrate how the relation of power-sharing with Euroamericans might look. A month and a half after passage of the Treaty of Guadalupe Hidalgo an *amigo* hombre de bien complimented Vigil: from the moment when he read Vigil's speech in the press, José Félix Benavides wrote from Alburquerque, "I recognized the liberal principles which adorned it. Then my heart felt a commendable enjoyment, seeing that it discovered that the hero and precursor had planted the sweet and significant honesty in the [home] land [*reconocí los principios liberales de que se halla adornado. Entonces sintió mi corazón un plausible gozo, viendo que se descubrió en el país que habitó el héroe y precursor de la dulce y appreciable honestidad*]." Benavides wished for a monument to Vigil one day so that "our successors in the coming centuries could sing the sweet song of hymns that your fine person merits [*un monumento para que en el se vea una efigue de su persona y para que nuestros sucesores en los siglos venideros[vean] con dulce canto los himnos que usted merece*]."[110]

All the while, however, the factional demarcation that had evidenced itself during the annexation convention and in the battle between the traditional priesthood and the liberal authorities remained. Vigil found himself in late 1848 continuing to dampen oppositional reflexes, this time in the person of Cura Francisco Leyva. Leyva mourned the dismemberment of New Mexico from Mexico caused by the Treaty of Guadalupe Hidalgo, and he questioned the sincerity of the American establishment. Vigil concurred about what happened to Mexico as a result of the war with the United States, as any of her citizens would. He followed up with the advice he had for all Nuevomexicanos: retire old hatreds so that the people could grow and prosper in the United States.[111] However, Leyva's attitude of mistrust toward American rule ran generally enough among Nuevomexicanos (and some Euroamericans) that, in tension with Vigil's accommodationism, it could well fuel a politics of factionalism as the annexation of New Mexico by the United States was being said and done.

2

Política in the Ante Bellum

One historian who studied the negotiations in the Treaty of Guadalupe Hidalgo finds the United States dictating the settlement "with an arrogance born of superior military, economic and industrial power."[1] The United States came away with more than 50 percent of what had been Mexico's land base. Article IX of the treaty somewhat balanced this lopsidedness by allowing annexed Mexicans remaining in New Mexico and California to have American citizenship if they wanted it. The provision in a sense ratified the instincts of General Stephen Watts Kearny and his liberal caretaking in the New Mexico theater of the U.S. occupation of Mexico.

Many Mexicans in what became the American Southwest did not want to be a part of the United States. The Mexican government established repatriation commissions for California and New Mexico to manage the movement of Mexicans south across the new international border and to arrange their settlement in designated lands in northern Mexico. Ramón Ortiz—a Santa Fe–born priest, Mexican nationalist who harbored anti-American sentiment, and critic of the Treaty of Guadalupe Hidalgo—became the chief commissioner for New Mexico. As a consul he supervised the relocation of those opting to move to points south of El Paso.[2]

Ortiz described Nuevomexicanos "enthusiastically" presenting themselves for enlistment in the program, and he anticipated repatriating thousands. Their primary reasons for getting out, he recorded, involved a fear of losing rights in the United States because of their race and a discouraging New Mexico economy resulting from war and harsh weather.[3] Ortiz found American authorities hampering his effort.[4] New Mexico remained under American military control after the war, with Colonel John M. Washington serving as commander of the New Mexico military department. Washington discouraged Mexicans from leaving because of the costs to government for transportation and disposition of their property and because the departure of too many people threatened to weaken community defenses against Indian attack. Ortiz offered Nuevomexicanos the counter inducement of land on the Mexican side.[5]

Donaciano Vigil, now New Mexico's secretary, had a detachment of Colonel Washington's troops deliver orders to Ortiz to suspend recruitment and immediately report to Santa Fe. Authorities charged Ortiz with disturbing the peace by agitating locals to reject the United States and making them uncooperative toward the new government. Washington, claiming to find unrest and rioting in the villages, officially recalled Ortiz's assignment. The repatriation campaign ended despite the complaints of Mexican authorities. Ortiz continued coordination of transportation and provisions for those electing for a permanent removal to Mexico.[6]

Ortiz's dismissal and Mexico's lack of financial support for repatriation agents may have reduced the number of repatriating *mexicanos*. Samuel Sisneros's meticulous search uncovered about four thousand individuals on the trek to Guadalupe, Aldama, and Chihuahua.[7] Historian José Angel Hernández finds the majority of repatriates coming from the "most impoverished classes."[8] Capt. George Archibald McCall observed in 1850 that a "few men of wealth, with their peons" went to Guadalupe, where the Mexican government held out inducements "to bring over to their side the rich and better class of people." Juan Bautista Vigil y Alarid, the New Mexican official who had received the conquering Kearny in Santa Fe, repatriated.[9] Certainly, Río Abajo patricians would have lost a great deal in wealth and power by pulling up stakes, aside from the motivation many had to stay because of identification with the United States. It is difficult to conceive of most rooted Nuevomexicanos risking land holdings sanctified by Spanish and Mexican land grants and their personal property to start again in another frontier outpost.

Those who remained in New Mexico retained the option of keeping their Mexican citizenship. Nuevomexicanos had until May 30, 1849, to register as continuing Mexican citizens. Colonel Washington had the responsibility of guaranteeing registration forms for those intending to remain as such. Vigil advised Nuevomexicanos from atop his liberal soapbox on the need to decide their citizenship. "I cannot believe that you will for a moment hesitate in making your selection," went the slanted instruction, "whether it be best to secure harmony and equal rights under the protection of a great, powerful, and sustainable nation, under whose government you will find peace, or return to the anarchy and oppression of the Mexican Republic [*Yo no puedo creer que V.V. se detengan un momento en hacer su elección, sea para quedan seguros bajo la protección de una grande, poderosa y sustentable nación, bajo cuyo Gobierno V.V. hallaran paz, armonía y iguales derechos o volver a la anarquía y opresión de la República Mexicana*]."[10] Some two thousand Nuevomexicanos stayed with their Mexican citizenship while choosing to live in New Mexico, nine hundred in the Santa Fe area. The larger majority of Nuevomexicanos became citizens of the United States by default or choice.[11]

What "citizenship" would come to mean substantively in the American context was an open question. It could have sprung into a total farce. History demonstrates that the granting of citizenship does not guarantee civil and democratic rights. "Through the precedents set by the Northwest Ordinance of 1787, the Louisiana Purchase Treaty of 1803, and the Wisconsin Organic Act of 1836," historian Joseph Sánchez notes, "inhabitants of territories were considered a dependent people and not entitled to full participation in the political life of the United States."[12] This is not to say that citizenship rights were closed off for territorial denizens. A complex mix of liberal and hegemonic citizenships shaped the political experience of Nuevomexicanos, what I am calling integrative colonialism, during the first three decades of their permanence in the United States.

The Statehood Spur to Republican Government

That the Treaty of Guadalupe Hidalgo made civic citizenship possible reflected what Evelyn Nakano Glenn calls "standing citizenship," an implied recognition of a full adult capable of exercising choice and assuming responsibilities.[13] Civic citizenship is supposed to open channels of participation for recruited or enlisted subjects in political, civic, and free-market arenas.[14] For annexed Nuevomexicano males to be integral participants in the politics of the new American territory, a grounded republican system of some kind would have to be provided. The U.S. Congress exercised firm control over American territories but fully expected that each would someday become a state. The goal of "statehood citizenship," if we can term it that, lit the fire of political activity and moved residents to build a functioning political system.

In calling the American territories of the nineteenth century "seedbeds of democracy," political historian Roy Nichols noted that the "device of creating and operating frontier communities or 'Territories' as a preparatory step toward their admission as states has been one of the most inspired inventions of the American political experience." The process of "constant experiment, adjustment, and rearrangement within the framework of democratic procedure" made for a "recurring opportunity for political freshening and renewal." The republic was kept flexible and vital by democratic behavior patterns generated in scattered communities, "not in Washington."[15] It was, in fact, what Kearny well understood in establishing an American territory on Mexican soil in 1846.

The political status of territories originated as an issue in the early question of the "western lands." Small, non-expanding states of the eighteenth century feared the imperial intentions of states bordering the frontier to stake claims over vast tracts to the Mississippi River and beyond. The tension stalled ratification of the *Articles of Confederation* until states on the edge of the frontier surrendered their claims to land situated along the Ohio River. As northwestern lands were ceded to the central government, Congress faced organizing them to avoid their unregulated settlement. Small-state objections to large-state aggrandizement steered the *Articles* to an important proviso: "To prevent the establishment of imperialism, the scheme of colonization must provide for ultimate statehood as a matter of right; otherwise the right of self-government which had been the chief issue of the Revolution would be denied the people who settled these western lands."[16]

The Resolve of 1780, under committee chairmanship of Thomas Jefferson, stipulated a compact between the Confederation and the states that any non-appropriated lands a state should cede to Washington be disposed for the common benefit of the United States and be "settled and formed into distinct republican States, which shall become members of the federal union, and shall have the same rights of sovereignty, freedom, and independence as the other states."[17] Historian C. Perry Patterson's emphasis on "trusteeship" suggests the significance of the 1780 compact for group incorporation attending continental annexation. The compact presented the basis for a trusteeship by Congress for the exclusive purpose of the ultimate attainment of statehood, setting forth a complete and "absolute negative on the permanent holding of territory by Congress by express language." No conceivable purpose appeared for which Congress could use acquired lands or unused lands within states. As Congress was not a whole governmental entity with its own ownership of territory, "any other scheme of things than a trusteeship would have been completely inconsistent with the character of the Union, would have been tantamount to a radical change in its character." It is "unthinkable," Patterson emphasizes, for Jefferson, the architect of U.S. state-building, to propose non-self-governing, permanent colonial status for non-state possessions.[18]

The expectation of statehood for lands coming into congressional possession went into the Ordinance of 1784, which provided for the disposal of appropriated lands to citizen settlers. Patterson calls the 1784 Ordinance a "monumental scheme of state-building, involving the future destiny of the Republic." Jeffersonian territorial principles were consummated in the Northwest Ordinance of 1787, ratified in Article 4 of the new U.S. Constitution and readopted by Congress in George Washington's administration in 1789. Significantly, Congress did not *create* states but *admitted* them. The obligation to develop a colony in the direction of the state model resided in the citizen-residents of the territory.[19]

To be taken as a serious contender for statehood, the territory had to demonstrate, beyond the demographic minimum of 60,000 population, evident internal political development. The indicators involved the election of a territorial legislature, fulfilling the positions of territorial administration, and setting up town councils with law enforcement capability. Territorial residents were at liberty to form a permanent constitution and state government if it were republican in form and consistent with the general interest of the confederation.[20] The governing principle of the territories became by the 1850s "a system for organizing the participation of the population in government rather than one for restraining it." Thirty-one states entered the Union after passing through trustee dependency.[21]

Representational Citizenship

The spur to statehood rendered mass suffrage and the popular election fundamental features of territorial governance. They followed from the "popular choice" dictum in mainstream liberalism, "the presentation to the public or electorate of alternatives concerning policies and leaders, and choices by the public or electorate among such alternatives, primarily in elections," and served as the "great practical fulcrum of American democracy in a large complex society."[22] The incorporated territory evolved by 1850 into what a political scientist designates "self-government." As the people chose officers, "the general structure of government differed from the ordinary structure of state government only in the appointment of governor, secretary, and judges at Washington." For the establishment of an incorporated territory Congress required an Organic Act, which would serve as its temporary constitution, another point Kearny recognized.[23]

Congressional enactments set the framework of government for incorporated territories. A legislature could be formed with a minimum of 5,000 free adult males. Voters elected members of a house of representatives who served for two years. The president appointed members of the council at first, but a second wave of territorial administration made the members of the council popularly elected. The legislature approved sub-administrative offices. The incorporated territory had a representative in Congress. Members of the territorial house and council initially elected the delegate. By the 1840s a territory-wide election by qualified voters determined who would fill the position. The delegate did not have an official vote in Congress, but his status steadily mounted. It acquired more of the typical influence and functions of a state representative, the delegate serving as "a disseminator of information, lobbyist, agent of territorial officers, of the territorial legislature, and of his constituency, self-constituted dispenser of patronage. The delegate interceded at various times in virtually every exercise of control over the territories, and generally no one challenged his right to intercede."[24]

The Statehood Revolution

In the underlying reason for having a republican democracy, citizens in the typical territory periodically engaged what a collective of Puerto

Rican scholars calls the Statehood Revolution; that is, campaigns to convince Congress to grant them statehood.[25] Citizens in a territory with at least 60,000 inhabitants became increasingly invested in the politics of their territory, and as they did, awareness of their essentially colonized status sharpened. As an editorial in a New Mexico weekly commented, "Territories are really to be pitied; they are like children under a bad stepmother."[26] Abiding resentment of colonialism among territorial citizens "brought life to a process of social mobilization geared towards their admission into the Union." The colony "slowly transform[ed] itself into 'a people,' or 'a community of shared meanings' with common interests and goals. Territorial citizens began to think themselves more as Illinoisians, Alaskans, Alabamians or New Mexicans instead of mere colonial subjects." Activism and enhanced internal political integration drove petitioners to U.S. loyalty, but once they became aware of "the clash between the American principles of justice, freedom and equality and the Federal colonial policy and of their identity as a unique people, the creation of the individual State became imminent."[27]

To gain statehood territorial citizens were impelled to draft a constitution in popular convention. Elected delegates defined the government for themselves as a distinct people. The creation and organization of a state "necessarily involved the overthrow of the colonial status and the formation of a new government, republican in form, and in response to the needs of the people. Consequently, to a lesser or a greater degree, depending on the will of the people and their desire to experiment, the statehood process tended to bring about a constitutional, political, social and economic revolution." The building of a state and the movement for its admission "constituted a reenactment of the American Revolution and a reaffirmation of the principles embodied in the Declaration of Independence." Self-determination in the Statehood Revolution represented a viable formula for decolonization and a means of delivering "to a community of American citizens, significant, constitutional, social, political and economic change" (much as Donaciano Vigil envisioned).[28]

In the process, politics became colored by a "growing anticolonialistic spirit."[29] The people, in case after case, came to recognize themselves as victims of a subject status, "first by being deprived far longer than necessary of any real representation in Congress; second, by being denied the right to elect the officers who governed them, that is, the governor, the territorial secretary, and three Supreme Court judges [all appointed by the president as a matter of patronage]; third by being subject to the humiliation of having to make their laws subject to the whims and pleasures of Congress; and fourth, by being cynically exploited as a source of political patronage." Objection turned on a want of confidence in government, "which led in turn to local lawlessness and demoralization." Feelings of hostility among the people stemmed from a sense of "degradation and wounded pride." Affected as they were by discontent, indignation, and humiliation, it was "only natural" for citizens to attempt to draw a historical parallel "between the territorial 'struggle for freedom' and the American Revolution," a connection "measured by the deep feelings of patriotic reverence Americans associated with the Revolution and its arguments."[30]

Some territories faced opposition to their statehood because of their racial and cultural compositions, as in Louisiana with French settlers, Utah and its Mormons, Hawaii and other territories presenting indigenous groups, and New Mexico being prominent for its Mexican population as well as indigenous folk. Yet as the Statehood Revolution maintains, the integration of different racial, social, ethnic, and religious groups into a common democratic nation was successfully accomplished "in spite of the inherent colonial and undemocratic nature of the American territorial system." Called "one of the wonders of American federalism," it occurred because as territorial peoples cohered around "yearning for self-government, the individuals began to share the same aspirations with their fellow citizens living in the States. Thus, together with the process of internal integration, a parallel process of national identification began to take shape." Ethnic leaders realized that cultural pluralism without real political power would not guarantee equality and ensure "their liberation from the bonds of colonialism." The political process offered an alternative, and so coalitions pushed for admission. If any ethnic group prided itself into self-determination, the creation of a state for its territory provided a viable solution with economic prosperity and "the political power to safeguard their particular interests and aspirations" (neglecting the first nations). The struggle against civic colonialism took form as a cultural reaffirmation of ethnicity and racial pluralism within the American social fabric.[31]

Rather than territories remaining a permanent periphery, the inevitable trend moved toward national integration via statehood. As historian Earl Pomeroy emphasizes, the end point of statehood could at times be obscured in the territories but was "never forgotten" in Congress.[32]

The Governed New Mexico Territory

In the case of New Mexico, the terms of the international treaty that effectively blocked Mexico from contemplating a press for claims of its lost northern lands set a permanency of expected American integration. The chronology in this book ends well before 1912, when New Mexico finally became a state.[33] The point is more that the underlying expectation of statehood some day animated a political process in the territory and it affected Nuevomexicanos in New Mexico's early territorial period, setting the stage for a "tutelage in democracy."[34] The Northwest Ordinance's trustee principle, that colonies or territories not be treated as property "to be held in a state of dependency or to be sold or given away," found its place in Article IX of the 1848 Treaty of Guadalupe Hidalgo.[35] Former citizens of Mexico, it held, "shall be incorporated into the Union of the United States, and be admitted at the proper time (to be judged of by the Congress of the United States) to the enjoyment of all the rights of citizens of the United States."

New Mexico remained under military rule until 1850, when its Organic Act made it an incorporated territory. The Organic Act of 1850 stipulated: "Every free white male inhabitant, above the age of twenty-one years, who shall have been a resident of said territory at the time of the passage of this act, shall be entitled to vote at the first election, and shall be eligible to any office within the said territory, but the qualifications of voters and of holding office at all subsequent elections, shall be such as prescribed by the legislative assembly."[36] The granting of honorary whiteness to Nuevomexicanos is sometimes considered a ploy to keep them placated in their colonial subjugation.[37] From another angle it represented the diffusion of race nationhood. The edict concluded with an integrative proviso: "That the right of suffrage, and of holding office, shall be exercised only by citizens of the United States including those recognized as citizens by the treaty with the Republic of Mexico."

The office of delegate to Congress linked New Mexico to Washington more firmly than the Mexican equivalent had connected to Mexico City. He, together with others who frequently traveled east, provided important information to constituencies regarding New Mexico's standing in Congress and national developments. Elections of the delegate and the legislature held every two years generated a relatively constant attention to politics among Nuevomexicanos. Scheduled election seasons encouraged territory-wide political networks. For an ethnic grouping participating in the replication of American governance, prestige attached to having a Nuevomexicano delegate.

Members of the Nuevomexicano rico class were overrepresented among New Mexico's successive delegates to Congress. Yet the rico monopoly of politics was not absolute and went contested, as we shall see. Michael Hechter argues that one should not assume, as classic liberal theory does, that political integration "trickles down" from elites to the masses in all cases of national development. The ability of the elite to influence rank-and-file elements varies in effectiveness.[38] As historian Mark Stegmaier notes, the citizenry of territorial New Mexico, "including peons," elected members to the council and lower house as well as electing the delegate to Congress.[39] The electoral system lessened Nuevomexicano cultural and social segmentation at least for the purpose of conducting politics.

American territorial politics heightened local integration. The county operated as the central territorial unit (as anticipated in the Kearny Code). The 1852 legislature added two counties to the seven laid out by the Kearny Code, and two more appeared in 1860. As historian David Holtby notes, county and local officials represented a distinct tier of Nuevomexicano politicians. "[L]likely numbering fewer than twelve hundred," they exercised power for four decades "in the villages, precincts, and counties as well as serving as delegates in both houses of the legislature."[40]

The Mexican *ayuntamiento* shifted seamlessly into the American town government. The probate judge (evolved from the prefect) ran the county until appearance of the board of county commissioners in 1876. He became the "virtual ruler in local politics, the key local jefe, having "complete power" over elections, articulating a broad electorate with higher-level politicos and territorial conventions.[41] Sheriffs, first appointed by the governor for two-year terms, were picked by popular vote by 1853. This official served under direction of the clerks of circuit and prefect court. The sheriff was the principal law enforcement officer in the county and ex-officio collector. Bonds between $1,000 and $50,000 were required for the shrievalty (jurisdiction of the sheriff) and for tax collector. Sheriffs served warrants; issued subpoenas and other writs; conserved the peace by suppressing assaults, arresting batterers, and holding criminals in custody; supervised the county jail; and summoned the *posse comitatus* (power of the county) consisting of able-bodied adult males.[42]

Prefects, justices of the peace (derived from the alcalde), and constables contributed to local power. They were elected after a short period in which the civil governor appointed them. "By tradition the prefect and alcalde had many powers," a historian writes. The first alcaldes and prefects "were those very men who had held office under the Mexican regime."[43] The arrival of the U.S. republican structure on preexisting positions promoted a sense of Nuevomexicano integration. Most nineteenth-century probate judges, prefects, and alcaldes (community mayors) were Nuevomexicanos.[44] The territory thickened the fabric of local government to look like a state.[45] Scientific bookkeeping expanded. A list of registrars for nine precincts in Santa Fe County in 1868 showed all to be Nuevomexicanos. Registrars made complete lists of all legal voters in precincts. The lists were reviewed and corrected at the polls three days before the election. The names of persons entitled to vote but unregistered were duly registered and persons wrongfully registered were stricken.[46] The county tax assessor came into being.[47] Precincts, continually created by the legislature, proved essential for the political incorporation of Nuevomexicano constituencies. From their ranks were drawn those individuals who would be elected to fill the positions of justice of the peace and constable.[48]

Public service salaries arrived more steadily than in Mexican days. Material rewards sped up acculturation. As Seymour Martin Lipset pointed out, the center's values and major symbols acquired legitimacy to the extent that they were associated with an economic "payoff."[49] County offices, including sheriff, probate judge, justice of the peace, coroner, and petit and grand jurors were remunerated from the generation of territorial taxes, called an essential provision in the center's integration of peripheries.[50] Territorial legislators while they were in session were paid three dollars a day out of yearly federal appropriations. Legislative clerks and executive office interpreters and translators were paid $500 per legislative session.[51] Competition for political office could turn fierce as election to office brought power, cash, and influence in deciding territorial laws, rules, and regulations. The question of who would gain the rewards of public service received intense public attention, the subject of high-stakes political contestation, and eventually, as we shall see, an issue among Nuevomexicanos regarding a party rival's true motivation for wanting to be a public servant.

The public sphere expanded beyond that of the occupation. Citizen mobilization appeared to an unprecedented degree.[52] New Mexicans expounded on community problems in spontaneously organized public meetings. Euroamericans in Alburquerque convened in 1859 to express their sympathies for a group of emigrants set upon by Indians as they attempted to travel to California. Resolutions called for military authorities to provide sufficient protection for American travelers. Regarding the meeting as a public event, the officers requested that the proceedings be published in both local and national newspapers.[53]

Nuevomexicanos took to the form and organized in their accustomed Mexican manner. A Taos County cooperative formed in 1864 to run the *camino del Cañon de Mora* (the Mora Canyon Road). An Alburquerque gathering, well attended and "animated with the greatest enthusiasm," addressed a labor issue with the object of seeking "from those in authority relief of our grievances consequent upon the involuntary labor on the Rio Grande which is demanded of us." Citizens in Mexico tended to formalize their spontaneous or celebratory mass meetings by electing formal officers.[54] In Taos the territorial legislator José de Jesús Luján, and in Alburquerque the Bernalillo County leader Ambrosio Armijo, called for a motion to elect a president, a vice president, and two secretaries. The president outlined the objective of the meeting; participants' remarks followed; and a committee was named to present resolutions. Participants in the Taos meeting were Nuevomexicanos, while in Alburquerque they made up nine of twelve officers.[55]

Nuevomexicanos appear as necessary players in the dramas of electoral hay-making. They turned out to vote, campaigned for office, stimulated the voters to the polls, lobbied for policy, and became aware of national issues. In greater scope, citizen mobilization in the nineteenth century meant grassroots organizing for one's community issues, learning the language of public debate, and communicating in public to a mass audience. Clearly, republican government is not a lame pastime. In the western community it entailed a "vigorous brand of democracy."[56] Nuevomexicano enthusiasm for American politics reflected in part the necessity to compete if they were to survive adequately in the new national environment. Still, a pragmatic attachment to politics morphed into unmitigated patriotism for the Stars and Stripes. The report of the Valencia County convention of 1871 described "patriotic speeches" given by Juan Salazar y Ximines, Manuel A. Otero, and don Bonifacio Chaves.[57]

Politics emerged so centrally that many who kept their Mexican citizenship got pulled into it. If civic citizenship means to include, it also sets boundaries of exclusion with consequences.[58] Studies of Manifest Destiny focus on the policy of excluding laboring classes, women, and racial minorities from full political and legal personhood as enjoyed by white male property owners.[59] Citizens of Mexico staying in New Mexico voluntarily denied themselves standing citizenship in the annexation process. Yet individuals from those ranks took the initiative to run for local and territorial office, gaining *destino* (public office); one example was Jesús María Baca y Salazar, who held multiple offices and took his bow earlier in this book (see the section To Illustrate, in the introduction).[60] Frowning Euroamerican liberals demanded compliance with the rule that only U.S. citizens serve in public office, often blowing it into an issue at election time, as we see later.

The territorial assembly decreed in the session of 1859–60 that Nuevomexicano males who stayed with Mexican citizenship could serve on juries if they qualified in other respects provided by law. Many petitioned to be granted U.S. citizenship. In 1851 the Nuevomexicano-majority territorial legislature requested assistance from Congress through special provision for them to be fully incorporated "into the community of the Citizens of the United States in this Territory." Congress demurred, and further attempts came in 1853, 1859, 1862, and 1866. The 1866 memorial described the petitioners as "the best citizens of the Territory and none are more patriotic and devoted to the Government of the U.S. of America as they have evinced by their services during the late [southern] rebellion."[61] Many Mexican petitioners eventually fulfilled the requirements set by federal law for naturalization.[62]

Party Citizenship

Two dominant political parties roared in head-to-head contention in the United States. Whigs and Democrats stood at the apex of the country's political passion and excitement. A distinct culture developed with "a system of habits, forms, and rhetorical modes" to assist in the contest for power.[63] It had taken some time for the two-party system in the United States to gel. Politics at the start involved disparate interest groups contending in a free-for-all that has been called "an indigenous, deeply rooted, conflicting pluralism."[64] Early American leaders mistrusted the proposition of an independent political organization for fear of the enfeeblement of public administration, agitation of petty jealousies, selfish men exploiting members for personal ends, and, as George Washington put it, "riot and insurrection." Britain's party anarchy and influential anti-party tracts led early leaders to idealize government as a consensual unity, society's parts working together harmoniously.[65]

Hard challenges in the developing state called in time for concentrated attention. A combination of factors led to the gestation of political parties. The materials and language for extra-constitutional organizations had existed since colonial times in the political clubs of Boston that put up nominees for local office on primitive "tickets." The legislative "caucus" of self-interested groups diffused through the New England states.[66] The pressures to coalesce into parties came as well from a soup of pressing needs, including platforms for groups to voice their issues; central regulation of the increasing demands of political, economic, and social interests; a way to address constitutional problems (e.g., regulation of federal branches); and a means for arranging the central government's relation to the debts of individual states.[67]

The American political party was a product of "human ingenuity and not simply a natural growth." Building it took the efforts of skilled political craftsmen, "including major leaders at the center and hundreds or thousands of lesser leaders in outlying localities." Architects knew they were devising coordinated means to their immediate ends but may not have been wholly aware of the fact that they were shaping a party.[68] Those who provided the materials for Alexander Hamilton to use in creating the Federalist Party did so out of a "politics of opposition." Public argumentation, town-square polemics, collective advocacy, and popular debate over matters of national and community import formed the necessary materials out of which to sculpt a party competition from scratch.[69] Factional differences laid the foundation for parties in the thirteen states, one historian points out, and "taught Americans to argue, polemicize, legislate, and on occasion to make compromises."[70]

Ambitious, powerful politicians poured their programs and republican ideologies into the party mold.[71] The Federalist Party emerged under Alexander Hamilton during Washington's presidency based on the interests of bankers, merchants, and industrial captains. Thomas Jefferson and James Madison opposed the Federalist movement in the politics of ratifying the Constitution, calling their group the Republican Party. A major face-off turned on Hamilton striving for economic reform linked to foreign policy and the Jefferson-Madison team prioritizing domestic matters. State-local combinations organized and endorsed candidates. A system of peaceful parties contending under a liberal constitution was recognized by 1801.[72]

The collapse of the Federalist-Republican contention in the 1820s inaugurated the Second Party Era. Martin Van Buren, called by a biographer a "genius for political organization," and the Albany Regency (Albany-concentrated politicians who controlled New York politics in 1822–38) redesigned politics. Envisioning society as social conflict, not harmony, they accepted the party not only as a necessary good but to square with liberalism. Parties enabled the people to participate in government in the name of democracy. They protected the state from selfish individuals by subordinating their will to the party's welfare. Parties could produce a "bond of national union," they proposed.[73] The Van Burenites constructed the engine to move a mass electorate. Their distinctive national nominating convention worked to include the rank and file in the selection of candidates, which improved on the systems of caucus and dominating figure. Party cohesion, platforms, and functional committees appeared.[74] A machinery to succeed in elections and provide services and patronage became the "life blood" of collective politics.[75] Andrew Jackson's 1828 presidential bid utilized such tools to make the Democratic Party the first truly mass-based party in history.[76]

The Democratic Party increased party participation with recruitment campaigns.[77] The requirement of property ownership for voting dropped off, and presidential electors were elected by citizens rather than legislators. Voting for president rose from 400,000 in 1812 to 2,400,000 in 1840.[78] Whigs coalesced around the intractable mistrust of bureaucratic party, fearing problems such as organizational shackles constraining individual choice. Whig "antipartyism" favored the election of individuals with integrity as well as "elevated views, cosmopolitans aware of the world beyond their constituencies and able to take a broad, detached view of public affairs."[79] Democrats meanwhile moved into perfecting organization. They instituted the "first commandment" of "regularity" in the Jacksonian era (roughly 1828–50), enforcing party discipline, loyalty to the organization, and devotion to procedure.[80]

Party identification primed popular political awareness.[81] Parties ignited grand, exciting electoral campaigns highlighting stump rallies, torchlight parades, picnics, songs, and slogans. They zealously courted grassroots support. Voters began to see themselves as Whigs or Democrats on a national basis. Party affiliation rationalized electoral choices in the states. Parties sought to balance the interests of farmers, manufacturers, mercantilists, immigrants, Catholics, and Protestants between 1836 and 1852.[82]

Mexico, by contrast, had been falling short of realizing a viable system of regular and consistent party opposition. The president of the republic was chosen by the various state legislatures or coups d'état. Irregular municipal elections were held in Mexico City starting in 1808. The municipal council distributed ballots amid a wide-ranging and volatile public debate discussing hundreds of political programs "ranging from bizarre tracts on social control to entire draft constitutions." The poor had room to act independently or in alliance with elite factions, and they tended to burst out in enthusiastic demonstrations, which elite politicians, including *hombres de bien*, called "mob rule." The major liberal and conservative factions had concerns about "an unfettered, anarchic urban underclass" with little interest in recruiting adherents from lower elements.[83] Party formation in the United States trended toward a mass-based, formal, ritualistic, and enduring organization.[84] In Mexico, the major national factions came to be organized by competing Freemasons. Scottish Masons directed the conservative elements to a considerable degree, while the Yorkish Masons (*Yorkinos*) tended to control leftists. One historian sees the Masonic organizations functioning as political parties throughout the early decades of Mexican independence. Yet another historian was not too far off in commenting that parties came and went in Mexico's volatile sectional turmoil, only to reemerge in various forms as the ideologies of liberalism and conservatism "fragmented into dozens of divergent sects."[85]

Government in the U.S. territories needed to have the collateral institution of party competition to fulfill its republican formula and conform to the macropolitical structure. The western expansionist Stephen L. Douglas started the ball rolling in his earnest efforts to take the essentials of the modern party organization of Van Buren and the New York Regency to Illinois and from there to the far western territories.[86] For the typical incorporated territory, political parties proved instrumental for petitioning Congress for statehood. Congress came to regard the party composition of the western territories as central for the heated debate over North and South sectionalism, which became a critical issue in the question of New Mexico statehood, as we shall see.

Historians of the Southwest, however, maintain that for the first three decades after its annexation by the United States, New Mexico exhibited no national political parties, implying a Mexican model of chaotic politics. The early territory was racked by localized factions, in their view, organized by clan and led by a strong man *patrón*. Herbert T. Hoover envisioned this in his 1966 dissertation.[87] Howard Roberts Lamar, the dean of southwestern territorial history, rendered it gospel. In his influential portrayal, New Mexico's early politics were dominated by "multitudinous factions" that hopelessly split the legislative assembly. They coalesced temporarily into two major "parties" only around the elections for delegate to Congress. "Nothing could be more incorrect," Lamar notes emphatically, "than to call the two groups [supporting the candidates] Democrats or Whigs. These names had meaning only to the Americans [not Mexicans] . . . and even then the labels were often misleading." When the Democrat Franklin Pierce was elected president of the United States in 1852, Lamar affirms, "many local Whigs conveniently took refuge under the rubric 'National Democrat.' Those in opposition, for want of a better name, were called 'states rights,' 'Douglas,' 'Buchanan,' or regular Democrats."[88]

Other scholars dutifully followed suit. Gary L. Roberts argued that New Mexico's isolation led to party connections having "little meaning in terms of national issues or ideology. Nuevomexicanos regarded themselves prior to 1870 as members of the 'Chaves Party' or the 'Gallegos Party' or the 'Perea Party' rather than as Democrats, Whigs or Republicans." Roberts sees New Mexico politics in the 1850s forming a "welter of local interests without a real party system." He adds, "Partisan advantage was the active ingredient" in these "interest politics," which ensured "a volatile system marked by intimidation and fraud."[89] Electoral shenanigans formed the essence of Nuevomexicano politics, in this view. That it was customary to accuse one's opponent of corruption thirty years after the conquest means to Lamar that "New Mexican local politics were still based more on family alliance, cultural ties, anti-Americanism, church faction, and crass economic interest than on any party principles. The [voting privilege] was taken so lightly that corruption characterized every election. The mere party labels Republican and Democrat became caricatures in this unique situation."[90]

Hubert H. Bancroft commented that charges of fraud were freely made during the territorial period, yet the evidence is too meager for an impartial determination of their merits.[91] The prevailing picture of New Mexico's chaotic factionalism with no valid connection to national parties before and after the Civil War is mistaken in any case. Researchers have been misled because the running dynamics of New Mexico politics are not obvious in much of the primary evidence without a comprehensive and meticulous pulling together of hundreds of stories and editorials from the territorial press, including important data appearing in the Spanish-language editions. Territorial citizens enacted a great deal of their politics in the columns of the weeklies. Stitching the accounts together produces a truer portrait of New Mexico's political structure than what has been presented to date.

The Democratic-Whig contention spun politics in the United States, and because of it, an imperative to organize a corresponding party duality befell New Mexico, just as it did the other territories. Researchers have failed to see the manner in which politicians of territorial New Mexico actually factionalized themselves. It took a strategic form. Serious and ongoing political competition congealed in rapid order into two major groupings. "Working the binaries" is how Jeffrey Alexander characterizes the fierce and vitriolic rhetoric utilized by campaign operatives in the Democratic and Republican parties to set their candidate off from the opposition in the bitter presidential election of 2008.[92] A general notion of "working the binaries" is the way to comprehend how New Mexicans organized their early territorial politics. Two dominant and permanent group associations (not multitudinous factions) appeared from the start of annexation and continued to operate within the parameters of the institutional and ongoing political development of the territory, with few people switching from one side to the other (see appendix 1 for a list of the individuals who remained stalwart members of the two principal parties in the period covered in this work).

New Mexico had already inherited the material for organizing a binary politics. The "American party," as it was called at the time, had roots in the Mexican period. Recall its usage to denote the Nuevomexicanos who cleaved to the incoming Americans and the political and economic institutions of the United States. That element went on to collaborate with General Kearny to help establish American dominion in New Mexico. Donaciano Vigil and Antonio José Otero had carried the torch of the American Party in alliance with U.S. occupiers. Attempting to cultivate acceptance of the occupation among the Nuevomexicanos, they assisted Kearny in forming a civil government and enjoining the call for annexation. The other faction soon came to be known as the "Mexican party." (Obviously the linguistic convention of the day, dating to colonial times, applied "party" to signify an interest group distinction). Miguel Chávez, Diego Archuleta, and Father José Antonio Martínez, all of them longtime critics of Americans, appeared as representative Mexican Partyites.

We shall see the original "American" and "Mexican" designations getting transformed into American political factions almost immediately upon the formal U.S. annexation of New Mexico. It is important to note that both had combinations of Euroamerican and Nuevomexicano memberships. Euroamericans tended to drive the American Party, although Nuevomexicanos had their moments of ascendancy in it. Euroamerican leadership in the Mexican Party grew increasingly significant over time. The American and Mexican parties started out with differing economic interests, as profiled later. Ideologically, however, they were split over the question of what policies should be applied in order to guide the majority Nuevomexicanos to effective and useful membership in the American nationality. Their positions on this issue are best left for the discussion of the territory's efforts to become a state. For now it suffices to emphasize how doggedly they worked the factional binary. They became *the* camps to construct rationales for taking sides on particular issues and in the struggle to accrue power within the conventional political system. The character of the American and Mexican parties as deeply competitive entities prototyped the political parties of the nation. Each espoused views, local and national, to defeat the other in the cycles of agenda-setting elections. A dual, to the point of Manichean factional competition served to decide who should fill territorial, county, and local offices. The parties competed for supremacy in the running of the territory, and they contended over policies for doing so. The Mexican and American parties so dominated the political arena that federal appointees arrived in New Mexico only to get drafted by or voluntarily joining one or the other.[93]

Mexican and American Party conflict approximated the U.S. pre-party "politics of opposition." In a distinctive feature, it formed the material for attempts at bringing home the parties regnant in the United States. What the sociologist Arthur Stinchcombe calls a "functional causal imagery" infiltrated the dividing political arena. In this imagery, the "*consequences* of some behavior or social arrangement are essential elements of the *causes* of that behavior. The commonest kind of functional explanation in everyday life," Stinchcombe affirms, "is that of motivation, of 'wanting.'"[94] Among the objects "wanted," the most compelling are those that define the validity of one's membership in the community. It has eluded researchers how strongly and consistently New Mexico politicians identified with the national parties, how badly they yearned to have these for their political system in New Mexico, how explicitly determined their efforts were to organize them, and in end how they eventually succeeded, following a distinct saga of struggle to gain them. The goal was inherent and necessary in a territory if was going to replicate the American political order and advance toward the greater goal of statehood.

The key question in the functional analysis of action and behavior regards the difficulties in achieving the end being envisioned. As we shall see, the primary difficulties for New Mexicans in achieving stable political parties concerned the difficulties of maintaining a national organization under frontier conditions and the extreme ambiguities that affected the national organizations in the so-called Second Party Period, dominated as it was by the grand sectional conflict in the United States. The establishment of an operative party machinery moved in fits and starts but did not deter the wanting of an actual organization. In the imagery, the social wanting of an object governs the labor for its acquisition. In this context, the American and Mexican parties each operated as a "shadow party" attempting to establish a national party for itself out of the competition with the other. Contrary to the Lamarian thesis of Nuevomexicano ignorance, former citizens of Mexico were quite modern in outlook, and they joined Euroamericans in the efforts to form U.S.-style parties. As activists sought to replicate the national political parties at elections for the delegate to Congress in particular, they formed a major structuring component of the electoral seasons starting with the one in 1853.

As will emerge, nationally oriented Euroamericans and Nuevomexicano elites crafted their reasons for associating with one or the other of the country's parties at the moment of a given election. Party identification represented an important credential for connecting with those who wielded power in Washington, part of the project of gaining sorely needed resources for the territory from Congress or to promote one's personal ambition. Regional issues gave cause to call for an American political party. As Nuevomexicanos assumed a broad civic identity, party principle became the standard for realizing competent public service. In the game of partisan organizations it became common for one's maladroit public service to be blamed on the influence of a party's alleged faulty policies, philosophy, or habitual corruption. The tendency to identify with a national political party at every election formed the key development for the final attainment of a permanent two-party system for New Mexico in 1871 and for firm consolidation of Nuevomexicano political integration.

Alexander argues that the party binary is cut deeply by operatives who pollute the opponent with vitriol and specious name calling. The normative response to mudslinging is disdain for the "dark side" of politics grating on liberal ideals.[95] Alexander calls it a necessary part of the "harshly agonistic" democracy. The politics of vitriol sharpen an adversarial system for the purpose of deciding who should govern and who merits rejection. Politics in a democracy is founded on a contest of winners and losers, over who gets what. Partisans appear in constant vigil out of a commitment to republican virtue and to defeat the dishonest, irrational, domineering or dictatorial opponent or party. Working the binaries by casting the opposition in harsh light polarizes political contention, making the choices starkly clear for the voter.[96]

The rhetoric of vitriol mortared the Mexican-American party boundary. Keynoters exaggerated, distorted, and sometimes lied in the interest of reinforcing their factional interests and in reaching for their political reward. It was far from symbolic only. Organic organizations with core and constant memberships squared their solidarity off against each other. Each declared hostility to the oppositional other for adopting positions antithetical or threatening to its ideals and interests. Mudslinging backed by variant rhetorics of liberalism formed the weapons of attack and parry. Each side claimed its national party to be the true representative of the abstract "people." Press propagandists threw themselves into partisan wranglings in races for delegate to Congress and territorial legislature. Creative and zealously crafted rationales drew the line between candidates.[97]

Loyalty provided the glue for forming and reinforcing the binaries, especially when identification with a national party occupied the agenda. As a political scientist noted, "Party identification matters because it influences perceptions of and participation in the political world."[98] Nineteenth-century New Mexico laid the groundwork for affective attachment to one's associates, leaders, and party label. Such attachment required the emotional reaction to an "enemy." When politicians betrayed their party's instantiated loyalty, they drew the condemnation appropriate to the norms of American binary partisanship.

New Mexico's dual-party dynamic, stoked by national party doings, produced classic American ambition for Nuevomexicanos. Ambition theory, pioneered by Joseph Schlesinger, sees American politics driven by ego-centered actors. Ambition-driven politicians work for their political ends by cooperating among themselves, forming party alignments and establishing party factions.[99] Political scientist John Aldrich focuses on "'office-seekers'—*those who seek and those who hold elective office*" (emphasis his). They desire the benefits of elective office and seek to turn politics into a lifelong profession. Principles, values, and policy concerns serve the ambition to obtain office. "Just as winning election is a means to other ends for politicians (whether career or policy ends), so too is the political party a means to these other ends." The ambitious politician is an institution, a sine qua non of political development and important for sustaining a political party.[100]

The complicated phase of factionalism in New Mexico following annexation, which Lamarians discounted, was less an anomalous vestige of Mexican chaos, more a developmental stage for the eventual establishment of the American two-party system. Rather than a wheel-spinning time of specious localism, it activated a predictable political conflict and carved out the arduous road to bone fide political parties for Nuevomexicanos and Euroamericans, which finally arrived in 1871. The organization of a binary party system framed disagreement over the proper administration of the territory in the legislature, which Lamar considered hopelessly rent by particularistic interests. Finally, it permitted the expression of conflicting interests and deflected the potential instability on the frontier, bringing such volatilities as political violence into a comprehensible institutional order.[101]

Print Citizenship

Philip Freneau and Benjamin Franklin Bache turned the *National Gazette* and the *Aurora* into Republican Party instruments in the 1790s. Journalism became an extension of the party.[102] New Mexico's weeklies were no different. "Until 1879 the press and the politicians were closely aligned," it has been noted, "with most of the journalists being opportunists who hoped to use their profession to attain political ends."[103] The point for the annexation of New Mexico concerns the part played by the press in constructing a binary politics. Territorial New Mexico expanded on the technology of the modern newspaper from its beginnings in the Kearny occupation. The press helped break down New Mexico's isolation and facilitated the diffusion of liberalism across the frontier by bringing the news regarding the latest organizational ideas and knowledge of recent events from Washington and the states.

The journals reveal New Mexico's political contentions in the first quarter of the territorial period motivating the active citizenry toward a party system for itself. Weeklies relayed the news of national political developments to the territorial public. The information guided the rhetorical competition at election time to various extents depending on the prominence of purely regional issues at a given electoral season. The lines of national partisanship revealed in the press carried into the legislative sessions and the contentious application of policies during the year. The editorial page promoted Nuevomexicano socialization toward Washington, illustrated when the *Santa Fe New Mexican* translated President Franklin Pierce's inaugural address into Spanish.[104] The letters to the editor column offered a megaphone for partisans to voice their candidate preferences, support or denounce office holders, and uphold or denigrate existing or proposed policies. The forum invited rhetorical debate with other weeklies, dailies, and oppositional campaign sheets. Much political copy was intended for consumption by Congress, eastern editors, the outside public, and presidential administrations.

Some 70 percent of Nuevomexicanos were illiterate until the twentieth century. As one historian notes, newspapers in Mexico "were embedded in a culture where public reading had long been established, making the ideas contained in the papers accessible to a much larger audience." New Mexico editors in conjunction with local Spanish-speaking leaders ensured the propagation of news and ideas in group, family, and open-reading settings.[105] Editors positioned in the middle of the political bull ring used their print instruments to establish political careers for themselves. It was taken for granted that they would maintain partisan communication with officials and national leaders and play decisive roles in who would be nominated for office.

The account of New Mexico's partisan process depends increasingly on the content of the territorial newspapers, supplemented by other materials. The weeklies enable us to follow the rhythms of the biennial electoral seasons, including county conventions, relations with the governor and legislature, and the rest of the infrastructure of partisanship. Considerable care, sensitivity, and judiciousness are required when relying on press accounts. On one hand, they offer a gold mine for capturing the essentially gritty nature of political finagling and for revealing the parts played by Nuevomexicanos in the shuffle. On the other, when a published press reveals an objective pattern or fact, or subjective expressions to interpret, and when it reflects strategic bias is always a question to bear in mind. The problems are compounded with reference to the Spanish-language editions. Not only did they participate in the partisan game playing; they did so in their contemporary regional dialect.

Double Colonialism

New Mexico citizens of the nineteenth century were subject to the domination of federal government as a whole. Euroamericans who settled in New Mexico from elsewhere were included as subjects of Washington colonialism, recognized in the theory of Statehood Revolution.[106] They all complained, for example, of the fact that residents of the territory, whether Nuevomexicano or Euroamerican, were neglected when it came to the appointment of federal officers to run New Mexico, the president favoring outsiders. (The Mexican and American parties each claimed to be the best for delivering this patronage to New Mexicans.).

At the same time that they endured administrative colonialism, Nuevomexicanos were placed in a veritable double colonialism by Euroamerican xenophobia, racism, and ethnocentric bias. As Richard Schermerhorn points out, racism is an inherent feature of annexation as a form of creating ethnic minorities, whether manifested mildly in terms of darker peoples as backward and less evolved or in the more absolute terms of racializing the Other as a completely different kind of human being.[107] The process of annexation gives rise to the phenomenon of "settler colonialism." Several versions of settler rule appear in the literature, from latent to blatant.[108] In one variant, settler colonialism denotes a foreign element dispatched to implement power in the colony, shaping itself cohesively and realizing or articulating "a clear conception of its group interests."[109]

A species of settler colonialism appeared in New Mexico as an aspect of liberal imperialism. A crucial source of the consensus-conflict duality stemmed from segmented Euroamericans. Far from a homogeneous lot, they diverged politically. A competitive political system split them irreconcilably on the public if not the economic stage, complicating the notion of ethnic power-sharing. Some Euroamericans truly recruited Nuevomexicanos into the American fold of liberal historicity. Others acquitted themselves as racially conscious settlers enshrining the "era of white supremacy" in various degrees of racialized ideas and actions.[110] Manifest Destiny was fraught with Anglo-Saxon ideology, ethnocentrism, forced acculturation, pioneer violence, and the racialization of the conquered, as classic studies show. As liberalism diffused to New Mexico, so did outright racism. It lurked, certainly, in the governance structure. Race conflict arose in the territorial legislature, where Nuevomexicanos clamored for the protection of their representational rights against opposition.

In annexation, colonial administrators, military personnel, and businessmen retained "preeminent authority to function as guardians and sustainers of the controlling value system." It reflected the dual demands of the conquering elite, their "privilege *and* responsibility" in the public life of the occupied territory.[111] Territorial governors in this light often opposed the policies Nuevomexicanos devised to serve the interests of the Mexican masses because they appeared prejudiced against whites even though they reflected a majority vote.

Annexation involves a state rapidly expanding its borders "empire fashion," so that it typically refracts the nationalistic fervor of the dominant state. As we have seen, American nationalists represented Manifest Destiny by projecting their civic nationality as exclusively necessary.[112] The typical settler colonialist arrived in New Mexico with a nationalistic chip on his shoulder. American control of the territory meant to many that Euroamerican culture should ascend and predominate. The colonialist sought to discipline Nuevomexicanos into accepting consensus integration, mutual acculturation, and cross-ethnic cooperation. American liberals were bound and determined to impose their liberal-democratic systems on the western landscape. As Michael Walzer observes, territorially concentrated ethnic groups are often suspected of hoping for a state of their own or for incorporation into a neighboring state where their ethnic relatives hold sovereign power.[113] Some Euroamerican settlers demanded that Mexicans demonstrate their unqualified loyalty to the United States. Military and civic officers laid the suspicion of American disloyalty on Nuevomexicanos who felt disgruntled over Euroamerican power. Patently liberal Euroamericans could succumb to the urge to whip Nuevomexicanos into line ideologically with liberal profundity should their public behavior appear to lag in the face of the forces of Americanization, a taste of which we have already seen in the American occupation. The line between the coercive and the consensual acculturation of Nuevomexicano masses in republican virtue could appear thin indeed.

A domineering white identity deemed the Nuevomexicanos incapable of possessing the requisites of true civic custom. Some, feeling them to be inherently corrupt, called for their political exclusion. Others placed intense cultural demands on Nuevomexicanos, not only challenging their Spanish language and Catholic religion but accusing them of immoral and loose habits. Even national leaders exercised their partisan prerogative for the purpose of accusing the Mexicans of cultural and racial backwardness, incapable of conducting virtuous republican principle. Nuevomexicano leaders negotiated a power-sharing arrangement yet contended with Euroamerican ploys and strategies to manipulate them or the populace for their particular interests within the party. When Nuevomexicanos controlled the agenda, and when their roles derived from Euroamerican conniving, are questions to keep in mind. Settler colonialism diversified. Racist and/or incompetent federal and military officers could exercise their will of prejudice with virtual impunity. The typical western outlaw and the stray hardened frontiersman posed their threats to Nuevomexicano peace of mind.

Another critical source of administrative colonialism clustered around hardships with origins that pre-dated American annexation. The violent relations between Nuevomexicano villages and the several indigene tribes that moved around in New Mexico and the greater Southwest took on political significance. Violence between Indians and Mexicans spiked in the early 1840s and passed into the American period.[114] Indeed, it worsened. Kearny had pledged a pacification program for the protection of Mexican ranchers. The appearance of American troops and settlers only intensified Indian mobilization. But the conquest of New Mexico "unleashed some two decades of furious fighting with various Indian groups, worse than all previous hostilities," due to the increasing invasions of Euroamericans unto the lands of the Navajo, Utes, and Apaches.[115] It thus took much longer than Kearny could have anticipated for peace to reign in the war-affected lands. A constant thorn in the side of normal life on the agrarian frontier up to the 1880s involved waves of Indian raiding of Nuevomexicano villages followed by retaliatory expeditions to recover stolen livestock and sometimes family members while taking captives as slaves and household servants. Important to recognize, the rancor Mexicans harbored for the tribes was mutual. Indians, particularly the Navajo, inflicted heavy losses in property and human life.[116] But Nuevomexicanos launched unprovoked attacks as well, providing the bands with additional reasons for considering the Mexicans eternal enemies.[117] Yet Nuevomexicanos constructed the inability of the United States to correct the problem as a colonizer's betrayal of the guarantee of civil rights.

Another problematic area involved imperial threats to preexisting culture and institutions. Classic liberalism saw annexed folks gladly surrendering their traditions upon exposure to superior Western ways. Assimilated elites notwithstanding, people would likely want to hang on to their longstanding habits, rituals, and community structures. Conquest annexation does not simply bring into its national space individuals from foreign places. Entire lifeways and native sociocultural structures are absorbed. An important issue concerns the fates of native institutions impacted by a replicative annexation. As George Steinmetz emphasizes, "All forms of colonialism involve a cultural, political, and psychological assault on the colonized."[118] Contact with Euroamerican culture did not inspire a smooth transition in which the indigenous were gently urged to leave their traditional cultures to better themselves in a new modern society. It reflected instead an experience of "trauma and strife, of interference and rupture with the past, as well as the boon of continuity, of successful adaptation and adjustment."[119]

Settler colonialism in territorial New Mexico produced clashes over the displacement or dismantling of Nuevomexicano institutions, a dramatic and telling instance of imperialistic domination. The colonial face of liberal annexation meant a fearsome assault on Nuevomexicano culture. The replication of U.S. society at the hands of the settler colonists debilitated much of the Nuevomexicano way of life. External systems replaced, demolished, or crowded out native institutions and customs.

The clash of civilizations cannot be reduced to a struggle between Euroamerican hegemony and an abstract or idealized Nuevomexicano national identity or regional culture. Traditional New Mexico had its own ideologies, power dynamics, and oppressions to contend with, some of these the legacy of a Mexican evolution. The attempt to develop a liberal political framework in the territory confronted certain decidedly non-liberal (or pre-liberal if not anti-liberal) expressions and structures that came into the American polity from Mexican society, particularly its systems of labor peonage and Indian slavery. The interactions between these older institutions and the "advanced" and "enlightened" political principles and republican values were complex, often with unpredictable results. Instead of fading away as classic liberal academics may have wanted, the old ways had a tenacity to survive even as they became political issues at both regional and national levels. In one sense, the attempt to dismantle these practices reflected a colonial assault on nativo culture, but it would be difficult to justify their retention from the perspective of any liberal or critical perspective.

Institutional Politics as Resistance

It would surprise many if a colonized folk did not resist, challenge, or direct outright combat against specific oppressions of colonialism affecting them. The social problems caused by forced annexation and the institutionalization of internal colonialism often inspired a politics of secession or irredentism among the conquered. Michael Hechter and others have argued that a core solidarity among the leadership of an internally colonized grouping, sparked in particular by a distinct sector, is necessary to mount a secessionist movement.[120] Modernization and neo-integration theories, acknowledging native resistance because of failures in the incorporative project, make a similar argument. Ethnopolitical identity is apt to appear because institutions remain affected by the legacy of a nation founded on the "core solidarity" of a dominant Anglo-Saxon center. Ethnoracial groups enter into civic participation on their construction of a unified community and differentiated identity.[121]

Nuevomexicanos were taken into the United States through a process of forced annexation, and so plenty of reason arose to confront collectively the settler and national prejudices that befell them. They might have formed themselves into widespread unity to take up a cause of radical national liberation. Apart from the fact that they would have faced a crushingly powerful reaction, a gripping partisanship dichotomized them into warring political camps. The adversarial nature of binary Americanism helped incorporate Nuevomexicanos yet established a cleavage among them that would never close. That its roots went deep into Mexico's political culture made the condition that much more concrete.

Among the two major parties that emerged in the territory, the Mexican Party most clearly invested in the politics of resistance to the forces of settler colonialism. The American Party was quite capable of challenging the more egregious forms of racism appearing on the scene from among their Euroamerican compatriots, as we shall see. However, as territorial politics developed, the American Party clarified its ethno-ideological favor for assimilation as Americans, stressing individualism, cultural Americanization, citizenship in the American state, and market enterprise founded on the classic liberal interpretation of the U.S. Constitution. American Partyites disdained explicit references to race in political affairs and promoted a holistic assimilation for Nuevomexicanos. The normative core of this mindset expected Nuevomexicanos someday to resemble the typical Anglo, English-dominant, educated citizen attuned to U.S. nationality. A sector of Nuevomexicanos would follow Donaciano Vigil's lead, finding the assimilation view of American belonging compatible with their collective identity.

The Mexican Party embodied the resistance reflexes of the Mexican period and the American occupation. Members recognized and legitimized the conquest of New Mexico but insisted on placing the interests and rights of the nativos front and center in the political arena and on protecting the Spanish-speaking populace from the destructions of Americanization, much as they did in the Mexican period. Euroamerican partisans of the Mexican Party provided important resources for the cause. Nuevomexicanos and their Euroamerican allies took on responsibility for dealing with settler and national racism. Whereas the American Party would come to the point of calling for an early instance of "color-blind" politics, the Mexican Party based its racial outlook in opposition to unreasonable cultural and racist demands of their Euroamerican conquerors. They inserted issues of colonial domination into their discursive and active political agendas. Mexican Party proto-pluralism contrasted sharply with the assimilation perspective associated with the American Party. Nuevomexicano resistance to Euroamerican racism was often expressed in a homeland cultural identity. As one historian perceives, cultural differences created an appeal among Nuevomexicano politicians for loyalty to their heritage, "which often sought to imply prejudice on the part of the opposition party." This appeal became a "popular symbol during the entire territorial era."[122]

New Mexico's integrative colonialism gave rise to a deeply competitive dynamic over the scarce resource of political spoils of the sort to encourage ethnic identity and mobilization. Political modernization in a culturally diverse region tends to open up the structure of political access to ethnic competition and produce ethnic political policies. Politicians are enabled to represent their ethnic constituency by the gains acquired in a competitive arena. Rather than shutting off access to societal resources, modernization presents the opportunity, or necessity, of protest. The poorest or most oppressed do not mobilize. It requires political resources, position, and education to leverage on behalf of a native clientele.[123] From a somewhat different angle, Chaim Gans argues for the contribution that national cultures can make toward the realization of political values "that are neither derived from nor directed at the protection of particular national cultures."[124] Liberal mechanisms, such as a claim to rights under a republican government, provide the means for an ethnic-based oppositional politics. Having the vote in situations of ethnic annexation makes a constitutional approach to addressing ethnic grievances logical.[125]

Mexican Partyites were most impacted by the boundaries that certain Euroamerican forces established to the disadvantage of Nuevomexicano interests, including Mexican cultural ones, and which tended to favor the competing American Party. The Mexican Party, armed with a homeland identity and the weapons of partisanship, was strategically positioned within the political structure to challenge policies and social disorganizations stemming from conquest. Resistance emerged with particular volatility when political and economic resources seemed to be taken from the rightful Nuevomexicano possession. The distinctive and significant aspect of colonial resistance in New Mexico involved its location within the development of the political, factional, and party field. Indeed, the very definition of the colonial dominator was often laid on the American Party enemy.

The two party factions took turns advocating statehood for New Mexico. It was, however, the Mexican Party that mostly generated petitions for statehood. The rationale tended to include opposition to race-colonialism. The Statehood Revolution thesis neglects the fact that resident groups were capable of contesting the statehood proposition, especially if it was proposed by a party opponent. The proposal arose in New Mexico amid the contestation between Mexican and American parties. The Mexican Party took the lead in developing a triple identity: that is, American nationality, general New Mexico peoplehood, and Nuevomexicano cultural pluralism. The reason is clear. Statehood assumed vital significance for Nuevomexicanos who entered the United States through military occupation and war. With a population majority, the republicanism of statehood portended Nuevomexicano self-determination itself. American Partyites had their reasons for contesting the attempt to petition for statehood, not least the proposition that the Mexicans and New Mexico themselves were not ready in their progress toward modernity to make it work.

The chapters in part 2 cover the process of instituting a political binary in territorial New Mexico from 1848 to the onset of the Civil War. The stories comprise a tangled web of political intrigue characteristic of Western democracies, complicated by the presence of a conquered ethnoracial element and the necessity of dealing with colonialism. The "hard grind of inclusion" and the exercise of power by Nuevomexicanos within limited structural circumstances are dramatized in contentions between American and Mexican parties, in the context of national party events and pressures, exhibited in spirited public debate, imprinted in manifestos, and founded on liberal convention and principle.[126]

CHAPTER FOUR

A Budding Binary, 1848–1852

President James Polk announced that the peace ratified by the Treaty of Guadalupe Hidalgo rendered the temporary military governments in the western territories "necessarily" ceased.[1] An anonymously authored editorial in the Spanish edition of the *Santa Fe Republican* understood Congress prepared to grant New Mexico a purely civil government. Visions of liberal plums danced in New Mexico heads. Schools for the education of the poor were in the offing. A "good society" was headed their way, equal to one of "any other place," particularly if Mexicans and Americans dedicated themselves to studying and doing what was necessary to plant the "most appropriate means" for developing their resources and promoting the people's well-being. A prepared citizenry awaited the power of the vote to select their representative in Congress. Statehood would naturally follow, and New Mexicans would see "the same [civic] spirit that prevails in all far eastern reaches."[2] Donaciano Vigil, who stayed on as the civil governor within the continued military regime, assured the people they would soon exercise their rights "in such a manner they would find New Mexico worthy as a member of the glorious Union, the world's republican model [*Puedo asegurarles que V.V. ejercerán sus derechos en una tal manera que harán a Nuevo Méjico digno de componer un número de la gloriosa Unión [,] del modelo republicano del mundo*]."[3]

A cloud of worry set in, however. Congress dawdled over what to do with the territories acquired from Mexico and failed to follow through on New Mexico's expectation of a prompt civil government. Local *cognoscenti* fretted over an imminent political vacuum, absurd under an expectant continental republicanism. Their territory had been operating its own government from the time Spain conquered Mexico, one recalled, and it functioned throughout its membership in the Republic of Mexico and on through the Kearny occupation. It meant a great deal to locals as a measure of citizen sentiment that the

1847 territorial legislature had endorsed Kearny's civil government, legal code, and official positions. Congress had not rescinded them; therefore they rightfully remained in force, went the self-interest logic.[4]

The worst came to pass. Secretary of War William Marcy announced continuation of a de facto military government "with the presumed consent of the governed" (as if they had a choice in the matter). Marcy guaranteed the protection of personal and property rights. The president assigned Congress the task of providing an "adequate" civil government to the unincorporated territory.[5] Congress failed to deliver in its next session. Nuevomexicano political incorporation into the United States thus began in the context of a problematic, duly nonliberal governance structure. Howard Roberts Lamar states: "Resistance and debate over military rule resulted in the birth of the first political parties in American New Mexico."[6] More precisely, the issue of military rule opened up alternative proposals, whether for statehood or territorial status, around which the mechanics of party contention hardened.

Working the Binary in an Army District, 1848–1850

Euroamerican merchants branded General Sterling Price's 6 percent duty on imported merchandise unequal and unconstitutional. Angry merchants and their supporters crowded into a demonstration and declared in a proclamation with eighty-two signatures a determination to use "all fair, legal and honorable means" to resist paying. Price refused to lift the levy because it was what defrayed the costs of a civil government. Moreover, Price explained, the measure had the president's approval.[7]

Tensions in the territory were tightened further as the Texas legislature resumed its claim to the vast country up to the Río Grande, taking in the most populous portion of New Mexico.[8] A Texan circuit judge set out for Santa Fe to establish his state's legal jurisdiction. A Spanish-language opinion piece called it a "most absurd and unjust" assault on New Mexico's merited sovereignty.[9] President Polk supported Texas imperialism, which had the immediate effect of maintaining military control over New Mexico. Mexicans abhorred Texan aggression, as did all who adhered to the civil government established by Kearny. A civilian government would deflect Texas territorial ambition, New Mexico citizens maintained. Missouri senator Thomas Hart

Benton advised New Mexicans to meet in convention, "provide for a cheap and simple government, and take care of [yourselves] until Congress could provide for [you]."[10] Governor Vigil issued a call for an election to be held on September 30 to appoint delegates to a convention that would craft such a government.[11]

The second popular election for a majority Nuevomexicano electorate was apportioned for the seven counties marked out by the Kearny Code, and which the 1847 territorial assembly ratified. Participants in a Santa Fe County mass meeting nominated Vigil a delegate together with the veteran merchant Joab Houghton and "Ricardo" [Richard] Weightman. The editors of *El Republicano* posted their names on the weekly's masthead. Weightman withdrew from the election on the ground that he had lived in the territory only eight months.[12] Valencia County Nuevomexicanos endorsed Vigil's "patriotic conduct." Convened *en masse* in Peralta, they represented an early instance of Nuevomexicano civil mobilization under American rule. Clearly aware of national issues, they denounced the Texas menace as "unjust, the unholy offspring of a few designing men—fabricated to defraud the Government and the people of this Territory of their just rights, on which every good citizen, both on this Territory and the State of Texas, should look with scorn and disdain." Four of five candidates nominated by Valencia's citizens were Nuevomexicanos. The crowd called for an incorporated territory for New Mexico.[13] A sense of integration among subregions of the territory appeared as the citizens of Bernalillo County in the Río Abajo held their "large and respectable" meeting in the villa of Alburquerque, placing faith in the ability of the American government to provide them with "justice, power and equality." They joined in the objection to Texas's geopolitical ambitions and agreed with Valencia County's preference for a territorial as opposed to a state government.[14]

Not all the territory's counties sent delegations to the convention. Moreover, discord at the proceedings' start caused a third of the delegates to withdraw. Indicating raw, lingering feelings from the conquest, two delegates who had retained their status as citizens of Mexico refused to take the oath of loyalty to the United States. The *Republican* offered the ironic comment that the oath would "bind them to carry out the true wishes and principles of American citizens."[15] The meeting proceeded with the restoration of order. Nuevomexicanos played clutch procedural roles. Vigil called the session to order while Padre Antonio José Martínez served as president. Others involved Santiago Archuleta, Gregorio Vigil, Manuel A. Otero, Ramón Luna, José Pley, Antonio Saenz and Juan Perea.[16]

The minutes indicate no disagreement at this moment on the question of what New Mexico should ask of Congress. The theory of Statehood Revolution tends to assume statehood to be the exclusive obsession of territorial citizens. At this juncture in New Mexico history a federal territory appeared progressive, the step out of a military regime onto the road of self-government—a Territorial Revolution, as it were. The convention's call for a territorial government, "purely civil in character," went into a revised Kearny Code. The president of the United States would fill defined offices and popular elections would select individuals to serve in Congress. The convention denounced the Texan aim of "dismembering" New Mexico and, significantly, rejected slavery. Eight of thirteen signatories were Spanish surnamed. Copies of the petition were mailed to Senators Benton and John Clayton (Delaware) for presentation to Congress.[17]

The memorial kicked up a debate in Washington. Congressmen took positions between statehood in order to stem the spread of slavery, on one end, and stricter military rule, on the other. A southern congressman called the no-slave provision "disrespectful" to the people of the cotton states. The petition died in committee, and the people of New Mexico were counseled to "live peaceably and quietly under the existing government" until their concerns could receive proper attention.[18] Congress disappointed New Mexicans by formalizing a military administration for them, which technically began in October 1848. Col. John M. Washington replaced Colonel Price as the supreme authority. Donaciano Vigil was demoted to territorial secretary in what remained of Kearny's government. Colonel Washington kept Price's duty on imported goods in force, stoking further civilian resentment.[19] The colonizing arrogance of racist American soldiers rankled Nuevomexicanos in the settlements.[20]

Just as a territorial government seemed like a good idea for New Mexico, a new president was elected and a move to propose statehood for New Mexico originated in Washington. Texas's territorial claim intensified the sectional dispute over whether slavery should be permitted on former Mexican lands, making New Mexico's official status a national concern. Senator Benton and President Zachary Taylor concluded that New Mexico must become a state to extinguish the Texas boundary claim and stem the spread of slavery. Their assumption was that New Mexico had the requisite organizational material to carry out a state government and so the normal Statehood Revolution need not be carried out. As Taylor argued, New Mexico did not have to go through the step of an incorporated territory, as Congress retained the power to make it a state instantaneously if it so desired.[21] It was a hard sell to make. Indications are that in the summer of 1849 Taylor appointed the former Georgia state congressman James S. Calhoun as the first Indian agent of New Mexico and assigned him the added task of promoting activity to build a cause for statehood. The *Republic* of Washington DC reported as much, and according to a near contemporary, Calhoun announced on arriving in Santa Fe that he "had secret instructions from the government at Washington to induce the people to form a state government."[22]

Calhoun would favor statehood while in New Mexico. How much actual politicking he conducted on its behalf is not clear. The evidence shows him engrossed in the important work of establishing New Mexico's first Indian agencies among the Pueblos and prairie tribes.[23] He may have dropped the word of Benton's and Taylor's wishes on denizens. What Lamar calls "Benton Democrats" and Missouri merchants wanting to keep Texas from controlling the Santa Fe–Missouri trade took an interest in statehood.[24] Nuevomexicano stakeholders coalesced around Manuel Álvarez, the Spanish immigrant and former Mexican consul who stepped forward as an advocate of *nativo* interests in the accomplished American reality.[25]

Facundo Pino of Santa Fe enlisted in the statehood "Álvarez party," as it was deemed. Recall Pino as a participant in the 1846 conspiracies against the Kearny occupation, stopping short of the Taos Revolt after the Bent assassinations and helping to put it down. Statehood held out the promise of "home rule" to the Nuevomexicano likes of Pino, which Texas particularly threatened.[26] The Álvarez party crystallized into the organized leadership for the statehood cause. Richard Weightman would prove an important member. Weightman was born in Washington DC, graduated from West Point, and served as a captain in Kearny's Missouri Volunteer unit. He returned to New Mexico a retired colonel in 1851. Other Euroamericans to associate

FIG. 8. *New Mexico Territorial Governor James Silas Calhoun*, ca. 1851–52, artist unknown. Calhoun was one of the early American members of the Mexican Party in territorial New Mexico. Courtesy Palace of the Governors Photo Archives, NMHM/DCA, negative #050460.

with what was shaping up as the Álvarez Mexican Party were Calhoun and Weightman's friend, lawyer Palmer Pillans.[27] Weightman later described the diverse composition of the pro-state team: "some of Mexican, and others of American blood; some [W]higs, and others [D]emocrats, some southern and others northern born." The group took cognizance of California and Utah's strong statehood movements. Weightman's manifesto published in the weekly paper called for throwing off the military's "slavish manacles" and deemed territorial status for New Mexico inadequate.[28]

Those who had pushed for territorial status were far from convinced of the desirability of statehood. The statehood stir prompted them into an interest group under the so-called Houghton party, named for Joab Houghton, the Kearny-appointed Superior Court judge and longtime partner of settler land owners Ceran St. Vrain and Charles Beaubien. Former Nuevomexicano collaborators with the American occupation clustered into what was becoming the longer-term American Party, most prominently Secretary Donaciano Vigil and presiding judge Antonio José Otero. Beyond the argument that an incorporated territory needed to precede a petition for statehood, the problem involved the fact that an abrupt shift to statehood would remove those who served in the existing governing and administrative offices. The Houghton party had a pro-territory manifesto of its own to disseminate, and it was signed by sixty-two circuit court judges, prefects, sheriffs, alcaldes, and civil-military officers who served by virtue of the military commander's patronage. Territorial propaganda feared for New Mexico's prevailing political and social stability. The prospect of a binary square-off appeared as territorialists denounced the "factious" statehood group.[29]

The Álvarez Mexican Party accused the Houghton party of self-interested corruption in supporting the military establishment. Weightman sought to oust Houghton from his judgeship on ethics charges, accusing him of profiting from links to the military.[30] The two sides rallied separately in Santa Fe. A request came out of one meeting (it is not clear whose) to have Colonel Washington order a convention so that delegates could form plans for a nonmilitary government. Maj. Benjamin Beall, standing in for the absent Washington, instructed county officials to designate sites for "mass meetings" to select delegates for a convention to deliberate the question of a civil government.[31]

The election, which took place on September 5, 1849, produced fierce local partisanship in localities. Weightman from the start defended nativo priests against their American and hombre de bien critics. An anonymous Nuevomexicano liberal in Valencia County raged in the *Santa Fe Republican* against Weightman's tactic of publicly criticizing Father Nicolás Valencia, who had joined the Houghton-Vigil-Otero party to challenge the resistant Nuevomexicano clergymen.[32]

The convention met in Santa Fe on September 24 sporting the complement of American-style committees. Once again the erudite Padre Martínez presided. Of nineteen delegates, thirteen were Nuevomexicanos.[33] That five worked for the military government and five others had formerly worked for it signals the Houghton party's edge over the Álvarez contingent and a presiding favor for a territory over statehood. In the election within the convention for New Mexico's presumptive congressional delegate, Weightman was beaten by the Houghton candidate Hugh N. Smith—a Missourian and court secretary who in 1847 served in the St. Vrain volunteer company to help put down the Taos Revolt.[34]

Conventioneers wrote a territorial constitution modeled on the one for the Minnesota Territory. The appointed positions would consist of a civil governor, secretary, supreme and circuit court judges, district attorney, and marshal. Qualified voters were to choose a delegate to the U.S. House of Representatives and members of a legislature. Apparently to avert suspicion of Mexican resistance to conquest, memorialists called for government servants "to renounce and abjure allegiance to every foreign prince, potentate, state or sovereignty, whatever."[35] Consistent with national law, the right of citizenship was upheld for all "free white male inhabitants residing within the limits of this territory, not already citizens of the United States, but who, on the 2d day of February, 1848, were residents within the territory of New Mexico."[36] The rights of those who wanted to remain citizens of Mexico but live in New Mexico were guaranteed. Delegates asked for protection against the overbearing Texans, including their threat to control the Santa Fe–St. Louis trade.[37]

A paradigmatic anti-colonial tract in the declaration extended the grievance of military rule that had begun during the war. "For the last three years," it set out, "we have suffered under the paralyzing effects of a government undefined and doubtful in its character, inefficient to protect the rights of the people, or to discharge the high and absolute duty of every government, the enforcement and regular administration of its own laws, in consequence of which, industry and enterprise are paralyzed, and discontent and confusion prevail throughout the land." The military failed utterly in protecting the people from the "barbarous tribes" that surrounded the settlements, it was emphasized. Neither the means nor a government plan existed for educating the "rising generation." Delegates cast New Mexico in terms that suggested an underdeveloped internal colony, instructing Smith to press Congress for resources for buildings, roads, land surveys, and access to saline lakes.[38]

The statehood group's minority report instructed Smith to argue for the need to include in every organic law made for the territory a provision "to secure the Catholic population in the full and free enjoyment of their religious rights and privileges," while prohibiting interference by military and civil tribunals in the rights and privileges of the Catholic Church. A guarantee to retain the old master-servant contract reflected a Mexican concern to preserve nativo institutions, though it contradicted philosophical liberalism.[39]

Free-Soilers and northern Whigs in Congress deemed Smith a legitimate representative of New Mexico's interests. Southerners maneuvered to defeat his report in the contentious House Committee on Elections. Moderates feared Texas reacting to the seating of Smith with a military occupation of Santa Fe. Southerners and Texans fiercely attacked Smith's program. A Texas congressman moved to suspend the rules and have the president explain if he had indeed sent an Indian agent to "incite the people of Santa Fe and vicinity to form a State," and whether or not he had sanctioned the New Mexico convention to prejudice Texas territorial claims. The motion was defeated, but legal questions arose as to Smith's authority to represent New Mexico. They included the fact that he was not elected by plebiscite (according to the terms of the Statehood Revolution), the claim that divisions over territory or statehood for New Mexico existed, and the specious argument that New Mexico was not acquired as a political unit but as part of "a large tract of country," and so "all political laws, all governmental organizations, ceased to have any legal existence."[40] The Texas legislature anted up its pressure with a "Joint Resolution to Protest the Election of Hugh N. Smith." "Fire-eating" Texans (militantly pro-slavery) proposed that armed forces be sent "'to suppress the existing rebellion in Santa Fe,' and to 'straighten those rascally traitors into a sense of duty.'"[41]

Congress would take no action on the appeal of the New Mexico convention. A demoralized Smith returned to New Mexico dedicated to statehood because it would defeat the westward spread of slavery. New Mexico, he counseled, needed to set its political house in order.[42] Smith's change of heart hardly disturbed the budding factional binary. In Santa Fe's expanding public sphere, statehood advocates called attention to the California and Utah efforts to form state governments, while territorialists argued that New Mexico could not afford the burden of taxation as a state. Territorialists downplayed the Texas threat. "Realistic moderates" in Congress, they contended, would guarantee a no slavery policy for New Mexico.[43]

President Taylor pressed his statehood aim, dispatching to Santa Fe a new emissary, Brevet Lt. Col. George A. McCall. The new secretary of war, George Crawford, reinforced to McCall the mission of aiding and abetting the home agitation for statehood.[44] Crawford showed a vague understanding of the citizen's initiative in the normal Statehood Revolution. As he stated, "it is not believed that the people of New Mexico are required to await the movements of the Federal Government, in relation to the plan of a government proper for the regulation of their own internal concerns." Crawford believed that the U.S. Constitution and the treaty with Mexico served as provenience to guarantee the admission of California and New Mexico into the Union subject to congressional judgment. It was the right of citizens in want of statehood "to appear before Congress and ask for admission into the Union."[45] New Mexico's state promoters welcomed McCall's mission with "unbounded enthusiasm," according to one historian.[46]

McCall reported finding Mexicans and Pueblos in New Mexico "greatly excited" about the prospect of statehood. He strategized to have Houghton allies work a coalition with the Álvarez-Weightman group. His strong suit, he thought, lay in the fact that New Mexico could only be taken off the military dime by the president's will to have statehood while Congress refused to approve a territorial government.[47] McCall failed in his plan to break the factional line. Houghtonites grabbed the statehood initiative from the hands of the Álvarez party.

Houghton had the president's statehood policy published in Spanish and English. Weightman circulated statehood manifestos of his own, geared specifically to Nuevomexicanos. Public meetings erupted tumultuously and with near violence. Col. John Munroe had replaced Colonel Washington as the military governor of New Mexico, and he found it necessary to mount troops to quell the bad blood spilling over.[48] On April 20, 1850, Houghtonites who gathered at the Santa Fe courthouse passed resolutions in favor of a state government and asked Colonel Munroe to call a convention. Munroe, citing the meetings and petitions of the "people's leaders," announced his duty to respect the laws not rescinded by Congress, meaning those in the Kearny Code. He called for an election to name delegates for a convention to draft a state constitution for presentation to Congress. President Fillmore assumed that Munroe adopted this course as a follow-up to Crawford's instructions.[49] Matters grew urgent as a Texas commission defied President Taylor by occupying El Paso en route to "take the rest of New Mexico." One of the commissioners was already present in Santa Fe to see about carrying out the extension of Texas jurisdiction to Santa Fe.[50]

The process of selecting delegates for the convention proved volatile. Wild rumors flew into the offices of the Indian agency of a mass rebellion afoot to cast off the American occupation of New Mexico. It may have been a campaign of rhetorical terror. One agent repeated the word of a Puebloan that the constable of Río Arriba County issued a request to the Mexicans to "meet at his house on the day of Election for Delegates to Convention—that he had some important facts to communicate." The informant understood him to tell of a large army coming from Old Mexico, "and he wished to know if the Mexicans here, would join them or the Americans."[51] The anecdote would have reflected popular resentment at Euroamerican dominance. In a more direct impact on the election, agent Calhoun complained to his superior in Washington that a dissident band, "to secure a result adverse to a State Organization," had illegally escorted Taos Indians to the polls and induced them to vote with the "factious purpose of thwarting the supposed policy of the Administration."[52]

Nineteen individuals from both factions met in convention. Álvarez-Weightman Nuevomexicanos included four priests—José Manuel Gallegos, Ramón Luna, José María Martínez, and José Manuel Gallegos—and José Pablo Gallegos (Father Gallegos's brother),

Diego Archuleta, and (likely) Juan Antonio Baca y Pino. The American Party predictably included Donaciano Vigil and Judge Manuel Otero, but also José Antonio Manzanares, Francisco Ortiz y Delgado, and Juan Perea. In addition to Otero and Vigil, several of the Euroamericans either worked for the existing government or were former employees, including Judge Houghton, former quartermaster Thomas S. J. Johnson and Attorney General Murray Tully. They were joined by other Houghtonites, including James Quinn, Vincent St. Vrain, Levi Keithly, Charles Overman, and Robert Carey. Revealing American Party dominance, Quinn was elected president and Vigil one of two secretaries.[53]

Participants had the same objective in mind ostensibly, yet differences of opinion, obstacles, and appeals for support of the Mexican population kept the binary line aflame. The Diego Archuleta incident proved telling. Recall Archuleta as the former Mexican colonel who helped with the Taos Revolt, though he was never arrested or indicted, and whose father-in-law was executed in the Revolt trials. Euroamericans objected to his election because of his revolutionary reputation. Archuleta chose not to sit as a delegate, attending only to support the Álvarez party. Euroamerican friends of slain Governor Bent threatened to withdraw. Archuleta left and nativo allies threatened to derail a quorum. Houghton, wanting to write a state constitution in conformity to how petitions for statehood usually proceeded, talked his associates into allowing Archuleta stay.[54]

The proposed state constitution called for the American three branches of government. A unanimous and unequivocal stand opposed slavery. Texas's imperial claims were defied with a stipulation that extended New Mexico's eastern border deep into Texas territory, according to the old Spanish-French maps. The military was subordinated to the civil state. Freedom of religion had its guarantee. However, an implied threat to the monopoly of the regional Church appeared in the provision subjecting public education to taxation and dropping any religious test for school attendance. Other old-order institutions were protected, including aspects of Mexican civil law not contrary to the U.S. Constitution. Citizens of Mexico would have the right to vote, significantly enough, as would the native Pueblos, but not the "uncivilized" Indians until they renounced allegiance to Mexico and supported the constitutions of the United States and the State of New

Mexico. An income tax would apply except for agriculturalists and "mechanical" (construction) workers.[55]

The slavery policy prompted what one historian calls a "tremendous debate" in Washington, bringing the country to the brink of fracture.[56] Nonetheless, the referendum for citizens to ratify or reject the constitution remained on New Mexico's public docket. Munroe instructed the prefects to organize precincts "convenient" for a June 20 election. The colonel instituted an unprecedented bureaucratic procedure for New Mexico. Prefects were to compose and send to the territorial secretary certificates of election for winners and extracts of returns of the constitutional referendum and elected offices. Munroe would permit the legislature to assemble should the people vote for the constitution. He reinforced his authority, though, that would stand in force regardless of referendum's outcome until Congress installed another government. The Álvarez-Weightman cohort called this illegal, a design to "intimidate the people."[57]

Each side met to nominate candidates for state offices. The Álvarez-Weightman party nominated the former occupation resister Tomás Cabeza de Baca for governor. Manuel Álvarez himself received the nod for lieutenant governor. The Houghton-American Party chose only Euroamerican settlers as candidates, including for governor, Henry Connelly, longtime settler recalled as a negotiator of the Kearny march into Santa Fe.[58] New Mexico saw its first real campaign hustings. As a leading political science historian remarks, to promote one's party rather than oneself when campaigning in the nineteenth century, a candidate for the House of Representatives was expected to stump his district thoroughly every two years. "Slogging by carriage from one small town to another, at each of which he would be expected to speak for hours before a few hundred of the voters in what was for them both entertainment and a civic duty, the candidates developed a largely set piece that served with minor changes for the duration." Invariably the stump speeches were "arraignments of the opposing party and encomiums for one's own."[59]

Just so did party representatives in New Mexico begin to beat their campaign path (for the hustings that came to be filled across desert and mountain; see the map in chapter 11). Weightman addressed Mexican and Pueblo audiences directly, pressing his policy of defending the Church, a counter to the anti-priest *hombres de bien*, and speaking as a friend of the people against the allegedly oppressive, corrupt, and incompetent military and what he himself labeled the "American party" dominance. Intimidation tactics on both sides produced near violence.[60] Houghton partisans sent 150 civil officials to reach the people. Álvarez and Weightman disseminated 1,500 to 2,000 handwritten ballots.[61]

Indian agents and some military officers described the Taos Valley contest assuming a violent, even "revolutionary" aspect. A first lieutenant portrayed a "dangerous situation" for American citizens there. He, like others invested in the bourgeois American Revolution and its development afterward, attributed the ruckus to the "lower class of Mexicans" who did not understand the "present political excitement in this country." The "intelligent citizens" feared "that outrages may be committed before it is over." Recalling Donaciano Vigil's opinion of the people in Taos, he said: "The revolutionary character of the inhabitants of that Valley is well known, and should be guarded against."[62] The captain of his troop assigned a company to preserve order in Taos during the approaching election. He had not the "slightest confidence in the honesty, patriotism or fidelity of the people of Taos Valley—on those three points I regard them as but slightly superior to the Apaches."[63] Theodore Wheaton, young lawyer and Indian agent, wrote an appeal to Capt. William Angeny for help in the election at Arroyo Hondo, where he understood one of Álvarez's "party" was to be arrested as a ploy to take him out of electioneering. In a mild mudslinging gesture, he called it "nothing but a dirty party trick which is of a piece with all their [Houghtonite] conduct at this election in this district." Wheaton requested an "American [Euroamerican] of our party at Mora on the day of the election to keep things straight," and two from Santa Fe for Taos, as he felt that the majority of voters would follow them.[64]

Calhoun described an alarming scene to his Washington boss. "The Pueblo Indians are excited," he reported, "the Mexicans are excited and a certain class of Americans are greatly excited. The most unimaginable incongruities have combined, and are divided into two parties, neither possessing the characteristics of a national party. It is a contest between those who have controlled, officially, since Genl. Kearny's organization of this territory, and a portion of the people who have not approved the civil administration of public affairs—because they thought it was arbitrary, partial and unjust in its operations, and all territorial legislation suppressed."

Calhoun sided with the people who had "never... been permitted a solitary voice in the selection of public functionaries." He too called the campaign "extremely violent," as reflected in the Pueblo Indians being "called upon by both parties" to vote for them. It contradicted the official position of the United States that the Pueblos were not American citizens, he noted.

Calhoun said the Pueblos were previously disposed to having nothing to do with the elections, of which he approved, but Colonel Munroe's election proclamation had the effect of "agitating and disturbing the minds of these Indians," rendering his own situation "exceedingly awkward and disagreeable." Calhoun enclosed in his report to the commander of Indian Affairs in Washington evidence of interference in the Indian communities. Munroe had put out a Spanish handbill dedicated "To the Pueblo Indians of New Mexico," conveying their right to vote in the election if they so wished and advising them that no official agent of government had authority to govern, direct, or in any other manner influence them in the "free and independent exercise of this right." Calhoun considered the overture, republican though it be, to leave the Pueblos subject to the influence of nonfederal officials. Pueblos were left feeling that they had been abandoned "by their Great Father," he conveyed, "the President of the United States." Calhoun thought it best to abstain from any overt effort to "counteract the apparent design" in the issuance of Munroe's proclamation.[65]

Calhoun further believed in the reports of insurrectionary designs against the old territorial organization on the part of Mexicans because Munroe moved troops from several of the Indian country outposts "to concentrate at interior points." He did not think there was "one man in this territory, who, in his wildest moments, ever dreamed of attempting to seize the reins of government by force.... There can be no contest between the people and the military power of this territory."[66]

Calhoun called the election itself a "hurried affair," in which "manageable voters" were "picked up at whatever place found."[67] The basics of a popular electoral process seem to have been observed, however. The territorial secretary's report showed a remarkable 8,410 filled ballots.[68] The voters, "with a voice, almost unanimous," Calhoun phrased it, endorsed the state constitution, 8,371 to 39. The remainder of the results were split. The American Party candidate Henry Connelly had strong support among Río Abajo ricos, into one of whose families he had married. Connelly handily beat Cabeza de Baca for governor, 4,604 to 2,706. Otherwise, the Álvarez Mexican Party swept the other top races. Álvarez came out on top for lieutenant governor, 4,586 to 3,465, and his faction gained a majority of New Mexico's "first" American legislature. Ironically, the original statehood party garnered the fruit of McCall's mobilizing efforts with the old territorial Houghton group.[69] Whereas Calhoun knew of a previous danger "of civil strife and bloodshed between antagonistical [sic] parties for political supremacy," in which he had reason to believe the Pueblo Indians were tampered with, "the overwhelming defeat of the supposed invincible party has established, so far as I am able to judge, perfect tranquility among the people, notwithstanding the great efforts made to provoke an outbreak."[70]

Connelly departed to Washington to meet with the president regarding New Mexico's political situation. The acting governorship thus passed to Lieutenant Governor Álvarez, making for a consistent tie with the majority of the legislature. First up on his agenda, Álvarez addressed the hurriedly convened legislative session of July 1. Calling the popular will his "sovereign guide," he proceeded to itemize the problems needing attention, including the lack of common schools and a military government that trampled on the people's civil rights by appointing prefects and alcaldes it could control. Revealing a Mexican Party leaning, Álvarez condemned anyone who sought to oppress the native clergy. The session proceeded on the basis of the Statehood Revolution, enacting laws, including the adoption of a state seal, setting regulations for elections of state officers, reforming the judiciary and criminal justice system, laying rules for the system of peonage to benefit both master and employee, and pleading for the right of the Pueblos to choose whether or not to participate in the new political order. Representatives hailed the right of the people to choose their public officers as democracy in action.[71] Lawmakers honored the American procedure of state legislatures selecting U.S. senators. After maneuvers by the weakened Houghton faction, delegates settled on the Mexican Party leader Richard Weightman and the compromise figure, military paymaster Maj. Francis A. Cunningham, to be New Mexico's U.S. senators.[72]

The legislature's memorial to Congress objected to the obstacle of the military establishment as an injustice laid on the Mexican people specifically. Since the Treaty of Guadalupe Hidalgo, the people of New Mexico had "groaned under a harsh law," it read, "forced upon them in time of war, when they were thought undeserving of confidence." A force had posed itself as "superior to the civil power." Its power was "other" than Congress's power, subjecting the people "to a jurisdiction foreign to the constitution, and unacknowledged by our laws." Taxation was imposed without the consent of the people, the manifesto continued, and the funds collected were "not appropriated for the public benefit, but are embezzled by officers irresponsible to the people." The push challenged the American Party as much as the military. The alcaldes appointed by the commander "assailed the right of the people freely to exercise their religion without restriction," it claimed, "and dictates to congregations what priests shall administer the sacraments of the church." Acting solons emphasized the fact that the president had encouraged them to set up a state government. They were therefore doing "nothing inconsistent with respect to the Government of the United States."[73]

In his own proleptic moment, Acting Governor Álvarez assumed control of a state government as if was a *fait accompli*. He sought to replace judges, Houghton included, with his associates, like the political lightning rod Diego Archuleta. Houghton followers flailed back. The "minority" (American Party) in the legislature charged the majority "with revolutionary and treasonable designs," Calhoun noted. In his Mexican Party view, Calhoun felt that this reaction could hardly be "dignified as a hallucination."[74] Colonel McCall, looking like an agent for the American Party, disparaged the nativo legislators in his report to Washington. They were, he said, "'like all Mexicans, easily turned [a]round in their opinions & feelings." McCall reinforced the faction-making dynamic, portraying Mexicans being "led by the nose, & used as tools by the leaders of the Weightman faction." McCall begrudged a home rule agency to the subordinated Mexicans but persisted in polluting their motivations. "[B]ecause of ignorance," he noted, "the native leaders had even begun "to talk of the day" of diminishing American influence and Nuevomexicanos rising as "masters and sovereign people in their own land."[75]

Colonel Munroe, looking with alarm on the course of political affairs, reminded Acting Governor Álvarez of the legal technicality in which military rule overrode popular sovereignty. The presumptive legislature's authority was inoperative until Congress deemed otherwise, the commander insisted. Privately, the colonel questioned the ability of Nuevomexicanos to conduct a competent administration.[76]

A lawyer probably composed Álvarez's sophisticated legal-political response. The militant statement defended the right of citizens to organize their government outside military jurisdiction, which itself, the statement pointed out, existed only by the consent of the governed as affirmed by the White House. Álvarez questioned Munroe's authority to impose his will against the principle of "states rights." Falling back again on the Statehood Revolution, the acting governor explained that as long as New Mexicans did not violate the U.S. Constitution, they had as much right as the people of New York or Virginia "to reform and remodel our old system, or to establish a new and different one." The statement recalled the Taylor administration's principle that the return of peace after the war superseded military authority. The precedent had been set in California, where the military commander ceded power to its citizen-legislature and went along with the call for local elections. On a presumption of the ultimate authority of republicanism, Álvarez held that the citizen government superseded Munroe's until the national Congress "shall undo it, or refuse to sanction it." As he posited, the right of the "vice-governor" to order the selection of U.S. senators for New Mexico represented the right of the states of the Union.[77]

Maj. Gen. Bennet Riley may have accommodated the statehood movement in California, but Munroe had stipulated in his election proclamation that the authority of all the officers of the election remained null until Congress admitted New Mexico as a state under a ratified constitution. Until then, the "present Government," with the officials authorized under the Kearny Code (who had originally opposed statehood), would remain in force.[78] Feeling little choice but to pull hard on his reins, the colonel charged the legislature with intentional subversion of his legally constituted authority and members with violating their duties as citizens of the United States.[79]

A furious Álvarez "dictated" what Lamar calls "a primer on civil rights to the autocratic commander" based on the people's sovereign right to form a government without consulting anyone. It was the people's duty "to do just that" in the absence of congressional legislation, and not even the president was enabled to delegate more powers than the people.[80] The "legislature" came out with its joint resolution condemning Munroe's attempt to "overawe" militarily the peaceable desires of the people and the newly created government offices. Members claimed to have the support of seven-eighths of New Mexico's population in claiming authority over the "abhorrent" military rule. They approved Álvarez's stand, declaring the people's "clear and sacred right to take any step to put in operation the state government." The right was "superior to, and entirely independent of, the military government hitherto existing in this Territory."[81]

Munroe refused to comply. Assisted by Secretary Vigil's Spanish-language circular, he ordered the county prefects under threat of a charge of treason to ignore the call for local elections and the legitimacy of anyone who might be elected. Álvarez gained a compromise of sorts. Munroe ordered the prefects to ignore or not hinder a local election, and Álvarez asked them not to assume that elected officials had authority to take office until November 1 or until duly commissioned to act as such by a territorial government.[82]

Munroe expressed the hope to Maj. Gen. R. Jones, adjutant general of the army, of the legislature agreeing to a reasonable delay on the prospect of New Mexico receiving a civil government. Munroe saw Mexicans as forming the central problem in the statehood politics. Opinions were prepared for them, he charged, "by those having no ties binding them to the Territory, except the possession and expectation of office, and, if any serious consequences arise from the adoption of their advice, will be found safely beyond its limits." The colonel portrayed cynical Euroamericans catering to Mexicans. The former "well" understood "the unstable elements of the Mexican character, the general ignorance of the people, their manifest dislike (although latent) to Americans, and the strong sympathies a large number entertain for Mexican institutions and its government, as opposed to that of the United States, yet, with this knowledge [pursuing] a course, understandingly, from which sooner or later disagreeable consequences will undoubtedly arise."[83] Munroe's opinion reduced itself to a fear of what an undeserving Nuevomexicano majority might do if it ruled the roost of a state government.

A hostile Congress greeted Weightman. Discrediting his senatorial credential, members said New Mexico had no authority to effect a state government and claimed the statehood agitation to be nothing more than the administration's doing.[84] Weightman waved the legislature's memorial as justification to be considered for statehood. To reject the written constitution, he argued, was to condemn "the new theories that *Native Americans only* [i.e., not annexed Mexicans] are entitled to rights and privileges, and that the colonial system of England can legally be engrafted on our free institutions" (emphasis his). New Mexico citizens were being placed in a state of "colonial dependencies," Weightman bewailed. To withhold statehood from New Mexico was nothing short of "a sarcasm" on the sympathy the United States extended to Hungary (struggling at the time for its national independence). Weightman slyly sought to betray Houghton's antislavery campaign, claiming that New Mexicans were neutral regarding slavery, although he pointed to the important work of the abolitionist W. G. Kephart, a Presbyterian minister and editor of the weekly *Santa Fe Republican*.[85]

New Mexico's state movement was thrown into doubt by the sudden death of President Taylor. His successor, Willard Fillmore, refrained from taking an active part in the Texas boundary dispute and left the territory/slavery controversies to Congress.[86] Meanwhile, Texas's imperial commission arrived in Santa Fe. Calhoun took note of New Mexico's contested condition:

> No. 1 . . . Texas has taken the initiatory in extending her jurisdiction over this territory, by ordering certain elections [within the State of Texas] on Monday next.
>
> No. 2. Governor Álvarez [issued a] proclamation ordering certain elections to be held on the second Monday in August next, under the recent State organization of this territory.
>
> No. 3. Governor Munroe [disseminated a] proclamation announcing his purpose to continue the military organization until he is otherwise instructed from Washington.

As Calhoun highlighted, Munroe spoke "in emphatic terms in relation to Governor Alvarez's proclamation, but not a word in allusion to the Texan order."[87]

The U.S. War Department feared a large body of troops trailing the Texas commission. The orders to Munroe specified how to handle the "delicate" situation and any violence that might ensue from the attempt to force a Texan civil government onto New Mexico.[88] However, these orders arrived after the Texans showed up. On reflection it seemed to Calhoun that the "conflicting efforts" had "not created the slightest excitement" among the people as opposed to the "immediate actors in this triangular love of order and good government, and the old and time honored incumbents of misrule, as they are called by those who are not in office."[89]

Yet did the Texas commission disseminate the proclamation from the governor of Texas announcing a general election. The citizens east of the Río Grande—involving the counties of Santa Fe, Taos, Santa Anna, Bernalillo, and San Miguel—were eligible to vote for a complement of state officers and new county officials. New precinct officers were slated for appointment.[90] On the day of this announcement Lieutenant Governor Álvarez issued a proclamation of his own, calling for the election of officers for all counties to be held on the second Monday of August, as decreed by the legislature "of the State of New Mexico."[91] Munroe ordered county prefects to keep from organizing the election, nor were they to "recognize those elections as giving the persons chosen, any right to assume the duties of the offices to which they may be elected, until the competent authority has so decided by giving the act the validity of its sanction."[92]

Calhoun recorded that "not a solitary effort" was made to proceed with the Texan election, "nor did it excite the talking qualities of our very inflammable fabricators of public sentiment." Neither was any attempt made to induce the people "to assemble at the polls" for the election regarding the proposed state. As Calhoun saw it, Munroe's silencing of the extensive talk of "insurrectionary designs," and his heavy-handed positioning of troops in Santa Fe to quell revolutionaries "so completely chilled the anxieties of those who had been honestly desirous of a state organization, it required a much earlier and more powerful effort . . . to animate and bring to life again, the really laudable design."

As the election fell through, Calhoun spoke to the one fact not to be questioned. Although bloody and fearful civil strife could still erupt, "it will never happen that the people of this territory will ever array themselves against the military authority of the Government of the United States, unless they are sustained by stronger arms than they possess. It is true, the people feel deeply mortified[.] I mean the reflecting portion of them who desired to assume what they supposed was a natural right, that of self government, that the very power which authorized them to confer together upon the subject [Statehood Revolution], is the very power that compels them to submit to the old order of affairs, and continue their submission and obedience to rulers they have long detested—a party that violently opposed a State organization until Governor Munroe *required* them to do otherwise—and they have now come to the conclusion, if their attempted State organization is now to be set aside, these old rulers are to be their masters under a territorial government, as they take it for granted, that Congress will adjust the Texan Claim.[93]

Calhoun did not realize, so it seems, that he was witnessing the binary formation in New Mexico that was destined to remain for the long term.

The Omnibus bill of Kentucky senator Henry Clay intended to grant statehood to California, territorial distinction to New Mexico and Utah, and set a halfway point on the Texas–New Mexico boundary dispute. The bill went down in defeat, but it set the terms of debate in the exceedingly complex issue of what Congress should do with its western territories. At the least, Washington saw some moderation in the expressions of extremist southern slave advocates, hardline supporters of statehood, anti-slavery northerners, and Texan imperialists. Maryland senator James A. Pearce introduced his Omnibus compromise measure. A round of debate and adjustments to that bill resonated in both chambers. Congress made California a state on September 9, 1850. Texas agreed to Pearce's border compromise, induced by a congressional indemnification of $10 million. With delicate sectional conflict teetering, Congress mandated the status of incorporated territory for both Utah and New Mexico.[94]

Secretary of War Charles Conrad extended to Colonel Munroe "the pleasure" of informing him that Congress had passed a law providing for the establishment of a territorial government for New Mexico. "I hastened to relieve you," Conrad conveyed, "from the embarrassment in which that misunderstanding [the statehood insubordination] has placed you." On the president's appointment of territorial officers, all controversy as to what was the proper government of New Mexico, "must be at an end, and the anomalous state of things which now exists there will be determined." Munroe was ordered to keep the civil and military departments of the government "entirely distinct." The secretary emphasized what Calhoun had observed. Things were tranquil in New Mexico, he noted, and while inhabitants had undertaken to establish a government for themselves without the authority of a previous act of Congress, nevertheless there was no reason to believe that, in so doing, "they intended to throw off their allegiance to the United States, and as the government they seek to establish is entirely consistent with the lawful authority and dominion of the United States in and over the Territory and its inhabitants, the President does not consider himself called upon to suppress it by military force." Should it become necessary to suppress rebellion or resist actual hostilities against the United States, an event Crawford could hardly apprehend, "or unless the inhabitants or a portion of them should demand from you that protection which is guaranteed to them by the 9th Article of the Treaty of Guadalupe Hidalgo," he affirmed, "you are directed to abstain from all further interference in the civil or political affairs of that country."[95]

The territory-state dispute in New Mexico, on top of functional local governments (appointed by the military), served the purpose of demonstrating New Mexico's worthiness for a republican government, much like preliminary political activity set the stage for a territory to become a state. Statehood advocates feared that territorial status would sustain what they regarded as an autocratic party, the interests of which stemmed from association with the military establishment. The momentum of binary partisanship grew strong enough to stream into the politics of an incorporated territory.

Republican Democracy in the Opening Years of the New Mexico Territory

Weightman remained in Washington to lobby for territorial appointments. He failed to deliver the coveted post of territorial secretary to Manuel Álvarez. The line on Álvarez had him a Democrat in Whig's clothing. Secretary of State Daniel Webster did not care for the outspoken Spaniard. Alburquerque monsignor Father José Manuel Gallegos commiserated with Álvarez. Webster nominated one William

Allen for secretary. Allen had never visited New Mexico. Webster, insensitive to the territory's embryonic politics, felt that its "chaos" called for outside influence. Allen lasted a few months on the frontier. His abrupt resignation left an important position in the territory inopportunely vacant.[96]

Weightman did triumph in getting his friend and ally James Calhoun appointed New Mexico's governor. It was doubly ironic. Calhoun had supported the movement for statehood, not incorporated territory, yet had been in alignment with the president's office. In this regard, a key credential was the fact that he was a "staunch if not rabid" Whig and a friend of the former Whig President Taylor. Calhoun had provided distinguished military service in the Mexican War, and he proved himself a worthy administrator in setting up New Mexico's Indian agency. For all that, the appointment of someone as governor from one of the two clear factions in the territory could only serve to intensify partisanship.

Calhoun's gubernatorial inauguration took place on March 3, 1851. As historian Lawrence Murphy emphasizes, the American territorial system was established with the idea that those appointed by the president would "direct a developing area's political affairs until its maturity had been recognized by admission as a state." The federal positions of governor, secretary, and others "could also instruct residents of the territory in the operation of the American governmental system."[97] Calhoun set out to build the apparatus of a civil government for a neophyte territory. He invited Nuevomexicanos to help commence New Mexico's "career in self government." Calhoun organized the first census of the territory and ordered the apportionment for thirteen legislative councilmen and twenty-six representatives.[98] With the excitement of New Mexico's first republican election as an incorporated territory, a fresh ideological cover, nonpartisan in character, arose so as to organize a process for generating credible candidates. President Fillmore appointed Whigs other than Calhoun, some "ardent" in their party loyalty, to New Mexico's various federal positions. John Greiner (famous for his singing of William Henry Harrison's presidential campaign song "Tippecanoe and Tyler Too"), replaced Calhoun as territorial Indian agent. James S. Watts took one of the Supreme Court associate justice assignments.[99] Col. John Munroe was the first of the Whig military commanders assigned to the

New Mexico Territory.[100] District Judge Hugh N. Smith and Attorney General Merrill Ashurst, an Alabama lawyer who came to New Mexico in 1851, counted as members. Those prominent Whigs who came to New Mexico without an administrative appointment included James L. Collins, Henry Connelly, and the Missouri-bred businessman Preston Beck Jr.[101]

With such a presence, Whigs might have rallied to create a party organization for New Mexico. However, Whigs in general lacked the requisite skills and party discipline to cohere, being "less predisposed to organize." By the 1850s, national Whigs identified as a weakly organized party, clutching to the ideological mistrust of the proposition of a bureaucratic organization, addressing the volatility of faction by avowing opposition to the self-serving, conspiratorial party. Encountering the boisterous and caustic anti-Mason movement, Whigs, opposing the selfish narrow-mindedness of a permanent party's interests, feared "intrigue" and conniving party men, preferring a conglomeration of conscientious and virtuous men devoted to the common weal.[102] The concept continued in attenuated form up to the 1850s.[103] The New York editor Horace Greeley exaggerated only slightly when he observed that the Democrats were, "'strictly speaking,' the only political party in the country; the Whigs were simply a group of concerned citizens."[104]

One commentator recalled that Whigs in New Mexico refused to draw party lines, stood as "sticklers for no party action," and postured to select men "ostensibly according to their qualifications."[105] What was described by promoters as a "large and respectable" bilingual meeting turned out at the Santa Fe courthouse for the purpose of forwarding county nominations for the territorial council and house. Participants rightly called the first legislature "of paramount importance" for the foundation on which the structure of the territory's government was to be built. They pledged Whiggishly to support persons deemed "best fitted in ability and worthiness without regard to party politics." Attendees, seeing no democracy in party activism, resolved that in selecting candidates, "the whole people have a right to be heard, and their feelings and interests consulted." They would not, they challenged, "tamely submit to caucus nominations and dictations made or emanating from private meetings, or from any source whatever, at which the whole people have no right to be heard."[106]

As the only gathering to occur prior to the election, the meeting seems to have reflected the suspension of combat between the two main factions in Santa Fe. A committee of seven, most from the American Party—Merrill Ashurst, James L. Collins, Donaciano Vigil, William Angney, James J. Webb, E. J. Vaughn, and José Durán—recommended a combination of candidates. The Mexican practice of conjoining church and government streamed in, such that three clergymen—the Vicar Juan Felipe Ortiz, the Presbyter Jesús Luján and Cura José Francisco Leyva—were tabbed to run for the council. For the House, other friends of Richard Weightman—Palmer J. Pillans, Tomás Ortiz, and Cándido Ortiz—came up. On unanimous adoption of the report, speeches rhetorically denounced "private caucuses and authoritative dictation," while proclaiming "the right of the people to be heard and their feelings and interests consulted in a public manner."[107]

Not much is known of the campaign. Tickets do not seem to have contended. With no system of voter registration in place, election day saw some illegal voting by nonresident soldiers, transient teamsters, and underage youth. The candidates selected by the Whiggish Santa Fe meeting who won council seats were Vicar Ortiz and Cura Leyva. They were joined by other Mexican Partyites, Padre Antonio José Martínez of Taos and Tomás Cabeza de Baca, who had lost for governor in 1849 to Henry Connelly and was not among the Whig candidates, an indication of his popularity or common power. Ortiz became council president. For the House, Pillans from the Santa Fe meeting got elected. Other friends of the Mexican Party included Spruce M. Baird, Hilario Gonzales, and Miguel Sena y Romero. Because of the timing of New Mexico's admission as a territory, the first federally sanctioned territorial legislature convened on the odd date of June 3, 1851.[108]

Calhoun's address to the assembly set the pattern for the territorial governor's opening messages, stressing the need for legislators to call on Congress for the resources to develop the territory by way of such institutions as public schools for all economic classes, men and women, Indians and whites; calling for a secure and humanitarian prison system; and securing implements for farm improvement. The assembly was asked to pass a voter registration law and stringent penalties for voting fraud, "whether by the voters or [poll] managers." The governor added a concern for the rights and protection of the Mexicans, telling as a partisan marker, whom he described as "among the best citizens, patriotic and devoted to the interests of the territory," and the Pueblos, said not to be "aliens" and deserving of treatment with equanimity. Race was another matter. The southern Calhoun recommended the barring of Negroes from New Mexico, considering them a nuisance, criminals and "degraders of society" wherever they went.[109]

Assemblymen failed to act on Calhoun's voter recommendations. They passed acts to articulate the new government with the Kearny Code, especially regarding certain legal and judicial provisions.[110] It would prove symbolically significant in the context of a tendency toward partisanship that the majority in the legislature, twelve of thirteen in the council, and nineteen of twenty-six in the House, followed up on Calhoun's concern for the rights of Mexicans, passing a bill of rights for the people and a law declaring the assembly officially bilingual. Solons went further. They petitioned Congress for translators and interpreters for members who could "speak and write, one portion in Spanish, and the other in English."[111] (In practice, the proceedings were conducted almost wholly in Spanish. Euroamerican settlers who did not learn Spanish would be at a clear disadvantage, as one of the territory's appointed governors painfully discovered. By learning Spanish, Euroamericans were enabled to establish relations, alliances, and collaborations of many sorts with Nuevomexicanos.)[112]

The scheduled date of the election for delegate to Congress, the first week of September, left little time after the June legislature for campaign mounting. Still, certain citizens had seen enough of the administration. The attempt at building a bipartisan process broke down precipitously. The looming election for delegate spurred aggravated participants to take a stand. Calhoun reported to Washington of "enemies" circulating articles filled with the "most inflammatory" messages and "abounding in falsehoods." The governor felt gratified at having the support of the majority in the assembly.[113]

As it developed, individuals who had worked for a territorial government and opposed statehood smarted over who had been placed in the territorial executive. In addition, the Whig-like pre-election meeting backfired on those of the old territorial party as they witnessed the majority of legislators congealing into Mexican Party form and allying themselves with the governor. A brash abandonment of no-party sentiment hit the scene in the time-honored American method of attacking the proverbial "irresponsible or vicious fellow citizen," or the "petti-fogger," thought to be working as a usurper of power to corrupt the political system or society.[114] A circular entitled "To the People of New Mexico" began innocently enough with the claim that the authors had expected at first to "sustain" the new governor; that is, until he showed a "mal-administration and abuse of power."[115] They could not for this reason support his "dominant party." Fifteen Euroamericans and thirteen Mexicans signed on. The appearance of Joab Houghton, coming off his leadership in the territorial movement, signaled party-ism at play. Others, like Houghton, were destined for careers as venerable American Partyites. First and foremost, James Collins was a Kentuckian who came to the territory in the 1820s as a merchant trader, settling in Santa Fe permanently early in 1850.[116] Collins would go on to leverage his ownership and editorship of the *Santa Fe Weekly Gazette* into the anchor of the American Party until his death. To stand with Collins in the long run were Merrill Ashurst, Joab Houghton, and Ceran St. Vrain. Nuevomexicano members to remain in the party included the Kearny-appointed judge Antonio José Otero, Donaciano Vigil, the Whig House member Serafín Ramírez, Río Abajo sheep rancher Mariano Yrisarri, and the Santa Fe figures Antonio Sandoval and Tomás Ortiz. Surprisingly, former Kearny enemy Diego Archuleta, the object of American Party scorn during the military reign, signed on. Archuleta, we shall see, would be among the few who would tie his allegiance to New Mexico's parties based largely on the situationally defined interests of his bailiwick.

In the circular the dissidents saluted the liberal flag, standing, as they claimed, on a "platform of principles." An eloquent shift to party distinction followed. "We unfurl our banner, confident that upon it, is inscribed Justice and the Rights of the people. Beneath this banner and by our principles, we are willing to stand or fall. Let us submit to your consideration the principles of our political party," they told the citizenry. A flash of Whiggery worked the binary, antagonists holding that their opposition was "not factious" but founded, rather, "in justice and forced upon us by the abuse and usurpation of power."[117]

A bevy of charges next assailed the governor. Calhoun's "sole aim" had been "to build up a political party that would secure the election of a certain [unnamed] individual" as delegate to Congress, one accusation went. The "whole power and influence of his office" had been "prostituted from what was its proper end and aim to the securing of this object." The ever-consolidating binary had Calhoun removing and appointing local officials without just cause, "solely with an eye to the person who could bring the most political strength to sustain his political friend in the approaching election for Delegate to Congress." The "very best and most trustworthy" of the people's officers had been removed "to make place for political partisans," the group fulminated, among them the prefects of Río Arriba and San Miguel counties and the alcalde of Galisteo in Santa Fe County.

The party of critics alleged in their circular that Calhoun interfered with the judiciary by requesting the resignation of two circuit judges because they were political opponents of "his Excellency's candidate for Congress, and because some two or three individuals who had important suits pending, desired their resignation." The individuals in question belonged to a family "of great influence" whose support the governor wanted. Calhoun allegedly told the third circuit judge that his official acts were null and of no effect. The whole judiciary was thus swept from under the citizens "only to gratify caprice, revenge or ambition." Calhoun allegedly tampered with the provision in the Organic Law that said persons resident in the territory at the time of its passage "should be entitled to vote in your elections." In mandating that to be eligible to vote citizens show proof of residence in the county, not just the territory, Calhoun allegedly "altered" the territory's effective constitution. As his duties were defined in the Organic Law, the governor "must not presume to blur or blot one article upon its page."

An important matter concerned Pueblo Indians. The governor allegedly calculated to disfranchise them of their rights "if they had them, either as citizens or residents of the Territory." To the governor's claim that Pueblos were not citizens, the sheet retorted, "We say to our Pueblo friends, that whatever rights were guaranteed to them when they became residents of this Territory under the Mexican Government, are still secured to them."

> It was not the purpose or intention of the Government of the United States to take from them one jot or tittle of their rights [the statement held forth]; that our Government holds the rights of all living under the broad fold of its banner as sacred; that her treaties

are inviolable, and that if our Pueblo friends had rights, either as citizens or as owners of the soil under the Mexican Government, that right is still secured to them, that it is not the intention of the Government of the United States, nor has the legislature and Governor of the Territory, if they desired so to do, the power to make slaves (dependents) of them, or to remove them quickly to another location against their will.

This statement, it can be adduced, confirmed what Calhoun had complained about when he was Indian agent, the filibustering of Pueblos into the election.

There was finally the matter of Negroes. The Calhoun enemies interpreted his recommendation to ban them from the territory as "calculated to raise a strong and influential party in the Congress against us," presuming to say that "the entire society where free Negroes are tolerated is degraded." The question of slavery had been "a vexed and dangerous one in the States for a number of years," critics told fellow citizens, "the cause why the civil and political rights due to you for the last four years [were] withheld from you, and now, when that question has been settled and taken away from the Legislature, your Governor is exciting a discussion that must result in injury to you."

Five planks composed the platform of the unnamed party. Three tied into the Calhoun grievance, calling for "separate and distinct" governmental departments to prevent the governor's interference with the judiciary and legislature, modification of the absolute veto power that the Organic Law bestowed on the governor, and "people's" elections to determine the county and district officers. An administrative demand called for an equal and just system of taxation to support an economical administration. Signaling the group's identity from the military period, the document opposed a state government "at this time, on account of the heavy burden of Taxation."

A contextual thicket lay behind the charges. Regarding the accusation that Calhoun built his own party and was denying citizens the right to vote, the governor had postponed the roll-out for electing local and county officials through his rule that voters needed to prove residence in a county as part of the requirements for voting for local office. He thus retained the discretion of filling these positions. Calhoun would likely have replaced local officials appointed by the military with Nuevomexicanos of his party. He built a "political machine of sorts," Lamar observes.[118]

The charge in the circular relating to taxation came out of the fact that the legislature had refused to pass a tax law at its session, leaving the territorial treasury "bare," as one critic noted. The legislators had not assigned any tax because "the people would not submit to it." Nothing in Calhoun's extensive correspondence with the Department of Indian Affairs indicates conflict with the circuit judges. For Calhoun's side of the story, a district court clerk by the name of Caleb Sherman swore in a letter to the new chief justice of the territory, Grafton Baker, that the leaders of a faction "hostile to his Excellency" had appeared "extremely anxious" to have the two new circuit judges identified with it. Judges reportedly reacted "in the most emphatic manner" to the attempt to politicize them such that the judiciary "could not participate in any partisan political matters, whatever." The party wanted the judges in its pocket, Sherman suggested, because the first legislative assembly, "composed mostly of Mexicans" had hailed with "unfeigned delight, the arrival of the Judges as an omen of a better state of things; they having the utmost confidence in the civil Government of the Territory, and of the United States; looking upon the Judges and the Executive with great veneration, being themselves, a law abiding people, and appearing very anxious to conform to the customs and laws of the United States." The "extreme anxiety" of the faction to secure the influence of the judges, hoping for the aid of the military as well, stemmed from a desire to "raise up a party in opposition to the Executive; and thereby render the Governor unpopular, if possible, with, the Mexican people, with whom [he] was . . . very popular." Calhoun was, in Sherman's estimation,

> justly entitled to their confidence for the extreme care he [had] taken of their interests, & his manifest desire to make them feel that they were American citizens, and entitled to all the rights and privileges of citizens of the United States, and to make them forget that they are a conquered people, by appointing many of the eminent & prominent and influential ones to such offices as he thought them capable of fulfilling properly. And that appears to be the head and front of his offending with this faction.

It was a clear rendering of the Mexican Party perspective. The "eminent," "prominent," and "influential" appointees replaced the local officials aligned with the dissidents.

If the statement seems to glorify Calhoun, the version sent to Washington was certified "as to its facts" by Calhoun, the territory's U.S. marshal, and the territorial district attorney. It counts that it conformed to Baker's own view. Even more telling of the developing line of partisanship, the specific charge Sherman heard against the governor was that he "endeavored to conciliate the Mexican portion of our people and pays less attention to the Americans than to them."[119]

The accusation that Calhoun was out to deprive the Pueblos of their rights "as citizens" can be seen as an honest difference concerning the citizenship status of the Pueblos. Calhoun believed that rights should be extended to them but that they should otherwise be left alone to their own institutions.[120] However, as Calhoun reported to Washington, the faction that was "defeated in the previous territorial election" (under Colonel Munroe) had been putting into circulation among the Pueblos "reports to the effect, they were to be driven from their Pueblos [by the administration], and their lands and property taken from them."[121] The American Party interpreted this from Calhoun's ambiguous section on the Pueblos in his legislative message. Calhoun saw a distorted campaign of "sowing the seeds of discord and treason" extending to the Comanches, who were reportedly told by "infamous individuals" that all Americans were gathering in a plan to wipe them out. The governor boasted of having the confidence and friendship of the leaders of all nineteen Pueblos. They sent delegations to him expressing their wish to be left alone and not interfered with for political purposes. He likewise claimed the confidence of the Comanches to whom he had provided provisions. As he put it, "I think the last effort of a desperate faction, has strengthened me in their estimation, and increased their confidence in the American Government."[122]

Calhoun's race consciousness poses an enigma for the history of Manifest Destiny. His racism was of a selective kind. He viewed blacks as the lowest pit of humanity, but when he reported to the commander of Indian Affairs that the Indians in the territory were "not the worst people in this Territory," he meant to say that the members of his enemy faction were the worst.[123] While he looked down on the Mexicans who plied their provocative trade with the Plains Indians, others who encroached on Pueblo lands, and some of the "wicked" priests who worked their prejudices on the people, he admired and sympathized with the Nuevomexicano people who were subjected to a conquering regime and who were now American citizens after all.[124]

Calhoun may have felt constrained from issuing a public response to his organized critics. Members of the territorial legislature convened a major protest meeting (*manifestación*) for the purpose.[125] Only two members, S. M. Baird and Theodore Wheaton, were not Mexican, and the latter was not only House speaker but Calhoun's former colleague in the Indian agency. Four clergymen stood out among the major players. Antonio José Martínez's signature appeared first, the others—Juan Felipe Ortiz, José Francisco Leyva, and José Manuel Gallegos—rounding out the element that Donaciano Vigil and his hombre de bien compadres condemned as "vile clergy" and betrayers of freedom.[126] Others included Vicente Martínez, Hilario Gonzales (a Weightman ally), Tomás Cabeza de Baca, Miguel Sena y Quintana, and Gallegos's brother, José Pablo.

Their manifesto to fellow citizens, written in sophisticated Spanish, it is stressed, opened with a ritual of Mexican yet republican humility, noting they would never forget that "the communities [*los pueblos*]" of the territory "had placed their will and confidence in the limited sphere of our modest understandings [*han depositado su voluntad y su confianza en la esfera limitada de nuestros pequeños conocimientos*]." A spiritual allusion, mixed into the liberalism, noted that New Mexico's "prosperous or unfavorable" fortune "was given by the wise creator of societies [*la suerte próspera o desfavorable del país, esta señalada por el sabio autor de las sociedades*]," and "secondarily should it be enshrined by the march traveled by our first constitutional legislature [*y secundariamente debe ser sistemada por la marcha con que camine nuestra primera Legislatura*]." The freshly American patented politicians pledged themselves to demanding the satisfaction of the people's desires, improving their condition, advocating for their equal rights, and assuring that the property of the most humble person be guaranteed with "the same preeminence and prerogatives of the most opulent [*con las mismas preeminencias y prerogativas que las del opulento*]," implying the wealthy members of the American Party who had profited from their loyalty to the military establishment.

It was well known, the legislators noted, that the law should be universal to promote and protect all social classes, "to banish the despotic spirit from society" as it was "regularly engendered by injustice and particularistic tendencies [*por la arbitrariedad y por tendencias meramente particulares*]." These mexicanos could sling the binary mud with the best of them, it was becoming clear. Uniform laws for the people of New Mexico would make up the "fundamental base of the social edifice, without the exclusive object of a destructive aggrandizement of specific persons, and without the mask of miserable views, or the infamy of protecting parties [*como base fundamental del edificio social, sin tener por objeto esclusivo, el engrandecimiento destructor de determinadas personas, y sin la máscara de miras mesquinas e infames de protejer partidos*]." They could also praise the highest ideals of government. Impartiality, experience, and knowledge based on the clear necessities of the territory would stand for this body as the "cardinal" principles for the discharge "of such difficult and important work," though the mission "surpassed the limited knowledge" of its members.

Florid rhetoric keyed into the opposition. Nothing presented as much difficulty as "bringing together the sympathies and intelligence of a political community [*reunir las simpatías e inteligencias de una comunidad política*]," they noted, when it found itself attacked by the "slander of some men well known for the color of their operations [*cuando se halla atacada por la maledicencias de algunos hombres, bien conocidos por los colores de sus operaciones*]." Such men, rather than guide the innocent citizens to the path of progress, maliciously preyed on ignorance to misinform "with ridiculous and imaginary stories, characterized by superstition, with the aim of taking them to the edge of the Ocean of scorn, or better said, to the descent of their fatal ruin [*con cuentos ridículos e imaginarios caracterisados de superstición, a fin de precipitarlos más alla del Oceano del desprecio, o por mejor decir, al descenso de su ruina fatal*]." The objective of such miscreants in perturbing the "equilibrium and repose of public tranquility" was to sow the "abominable seed of suspicion" against those the people had chosen as their representatives. The malcontents would come under the approbation not only of the general Congress, but of "the people." The statement did not name the offending party, but cited the "semi civil behavior" of those associated with the prior military administration, which had neglected and made a mockery of the "sacred interests" of the people. "Sad to have to record it for the pages of history, in the century of light! [*¡Triste caso, que recordar para las páginas de la historia en el siglo de las luces!*]," the modernist legislators decried. It was all the more so as the same preoccupations of the former military ran current "and the means and subterfuges able to procure a victory more dreamed-of than obtained, cannot take their authors to the apogee they lost [*y los medios y subterfugios de que se valen, para procurar una victoria sonada que conseguida, realizaría a sus autores al apogeo que perdieron*]."

Some choice praise followed for the "Liberality of the Supreme Government" and the Organic Law that created the legislature. The caucus members declared themselves able to constitute a territorial form of government. In a defense of Calhoun without naming him, they pointed to the Organic Law as the authority that denied Indians the right to vote, demonstrated in the instructions the federal government gave to the superintendent of the Pueblo Indians. Here lay proof that neither the territorial governor nor the legislature, but rather the "Sovereign Congress of the Union," excluded the Pueblos from citizenship. Yet, the humanitarian officials patronizingly declared that to take legitimate pity on the "poor" Indians was the responsible thing to do to access the best rational means available to assist them in proceeding "with intelligence and liberty, [and to desist] from subjecting them to violence, fraudulent betrayal, and seductive voices" of the opposing party. At the same time, the legislature voiced general objection to anyone invading Pueblo lands, a concern maintained by Calhoun. Those lands and other properties were inviolable by their just titles and should therefore never be touched unless the Indians voluntarily transferred their rights by contract. Should the Indians one day in the distant future compose their communities under the conditions of equality with the other citizens, the legislature should petition the central government that they come to enjoy the rights of citizenship they had under the Mexican government, so long as the authorities declared them qualified. The lawmakers said that the unjust alarm caused by the "despicable, mysterious and contemptible interference [*interrumpida por miras misteriosas y rastreras, que baticinan los profetas que las inducen*]" conveniently neglected to recognize that the governor's message to the assembly session did not have the character of law. They declared the need to respect the integrity of the legislative chambers, free as they were to agree or disagree with the governor's message.

The spokesmen warned the citizens of the "repugnant," "damaging," and "sinister" imputations made against the legislature by the "enemies of truth [*no menos repugnante y nocividas son las imputaciones siniestras que hacen a la Legislatura, los enemigos de la verdad*]," claiming that they had surrendered the power of their voluntary will to the governor. The offenders, without consulting the will of the people, besmirched every branch in the administration of justice, the indictment continued, which belonged to the different counties of the territory. Such "inanities" would be belied one day not distant, the politicians exclaimed. The representatives desired that the "People, and only the People," be the ones to name their authorities as provided by the law. They declared their intention to derive "sentiments truly republican." Conforming to the people's desires, they pledged to do everything possible "in just testimony" to their intentions. Impartiality should "crown the grand product of our work [*que la imparcialidad coronará la grande obra de nuestros trabajos*]."

The manifesto cast the boundary of contention for the election of delegate to Congress in bold relief, even though the protesting legislators failed to mention the charge that the governor manipulated politics to advance the candidate of his choice. Three hats were thrown in the ring. The moderate merchant and independent lawyer William Messervy proved a minor candidate and may have entered to split the vote of the Mexican Party. Richard Weightman, Calhoun's friend, whom the governor had hired as an Indian subagent, self-nominated.[127] Weightman would have been the man the American Party meant as Calhoun's favorite. Unfortunately, the New Mexico territorial records do not contain the individuals whom Calhoun appointed to county positions prior to the election. However, the American Party may have feared the network that Weightman formed from among them and others, and which he perceived as giving him an electoral advantage. Capt. A. W. Reynolds, the third candidate, was the assistant military quartermaster; research has shown that he was the richest man in New Mexico due to his fraudulent accessing of military funds. Previously he had turned the military's printing press over to the territorial party, which used it to publish the *Weekly Gazette*.[128] Reynolds was a signatory to the anti-Calhoun proclamation. Calhoun implied that he was the key "traitor" fomenting dissension among the Pueblos. As Reynolds intently canvassed the territory on behalf of his candidacy, Calhoun suggested that his base be called the "Reynolds party."[129] Reynolds dubbed himself in the title of a handbill *Amigo de los Pobres* (Friend of the Poor) underneath a cross to appeal to the Catholic majority of the electorate. But would it be sufficient to counter the labeling of himself and his backers as rich outsiders? Reynolds's campaign material took from the charges the American Party proclamation had posted. He accused Calhoun and Weightman of removing prefects, alcaldes, and judges to make room for their friends and of threatening to steal the lands of the Pueblos and enslave them.[130]

As the campaign waged on, volatile race relations continued to be noticed. "There is a *great* and *deep* gulf between the Americans and Mexicans yet," wrote the Indian agent John Greiner in a private letter, "and the love they bear each other has by no means waxed warm. There is hardly an American here that stirs abroad [Greiner continued] without being armed to the teeth, and under his pillow, pistols and Bowie-knives may always be found."[131] District judge and longtime resident of the Taos Valley Charles Beaubien, claiming to "understand the native Mexican well," observed sufficient indications "to convince me that a rebellion against the constituted United States authorities is in contemplation among the Lower class of the inhabitants of the country of Taos." Every effort had been made "to excite the mass," Beaubien explained, "by which I mean the Vagabond and unoccupied part of the population against the Americans. From information I have had from reliable sources, secret meetings have been held under various pretences [sic] for the purpose of organizing an insurrection, its object the extermination of the Americans and the Robbery of their Property. Every report false or true in regard to the Proceedings of the existing Government and citizens of the United States has been put in circulation to unite the People here." The source of the excitement was hard to discover, Beaubien relayed, "but such sinister excitement is afoot." Should an insurrection be raised, he observed, it would result in the massacre of the isolated Americans and foreigners in that part of the territory [shades of the 1847 Taos Revolt], "that the retributive justice [to] follow would be the extermination of the Insurgents. But this, it appears to me, should be an event much to be deplored & that it should, by timely and prudent measures, be avoided." Based on Beaubien's report, Colonel Munroe, in consultation with Governor Calhoun, reinforced the Taos post with two artillery companies.[132] The major commanding the Taos post perceived that the excited rumors of insurrection originated through "political feeling" and that the placement of additional artillery in his station would "operate unfavorably" on his own "character" with the people.[133]

It was in this context that two interrelated incidences of violence marred the race for delegate to Congress. A soldier who joined a band of drunken Reynolds men in bullying voters and polling officials was shot and killed in Los Ranchos de Alburquerque. Judge Houghton sent William Skinner to investigate. Skinner was a participant in the 1849 territorial convention, an American Party member of the legislature, and a signatory on the anti-Calhoun manifesto. He brandished a pistol at Juan Cristóval Armijo, brother of the Alburquerque prefect, with whom Skinner had previously quarreled. Armijo shot him dead. The *Weekly Gazette* propaganda charged native insurrection enabled by Governor Calhoun's "corrupt" policies favoring Mexicans. Calhoun let the judicial process run its course rather than dispatch a company of armed militia to enforce law and order, as demanded by his political enemies.

The grand jury failed to indict Armijo. American Partyites hued and cried to President Fillmore and Secretary of State Daniel Webster. *Gazette* owner James Collins described the governor to President Fillmore as so indebted to the "natives" that "he must protect them or fall." Collins predicted a "sanguinary civil war" were Calhoun be permitted to continue as governor. The Nuevomexicano majority of legislators defended Calhoun, Collins lamented, with the false claim that "the people" of New Mexico approved of his acts.[134]

Weightman came out ahead in the results of the election by 742 votes out of more than 7,788 cast. Reynolds filed formally to contest the election, initiating what would become a common practice in New Mexico's races for congressional delegate. Reynolds, in setting out his case, accused Governor Calhoun of rigging the election schedule and ballots and Weightman of waging a campaign of intimidation and violence. Weightman reported to the U.S. House of Representatives as a Democrat. The distinction made a difference in context of the Whig-dominated American Party. On the House floor Weightman issued a passionate defense of the legality of his win. It was not Governor Calhoun but the U.S. military that had unlawfully tampered with the election (presumably in support of Reynolds), Weightman inveighed. Weightman had previously exploited the editor of the *Weekly Gazette*, W. Kephart, before Congress for his anti-slavery efforts; he now charged the editor with lending the weekly to prop up the Reynolds candidacy. According to Weightman, Kephart, as manager of the sole printing press in the territory, made it impossible for the governor to have the election proclamation printed in a timely fashion, forcing the "state party" to write out 15,000–20,000 hand-written ballots. Weightman accused Reynolds partisans of cynically claiming to represent the Spanish-speaking majority fairly. He quoted from a memorial allegedly signed by Reynolds, Houghton, and other *Amigos de los Pobres* to President Fillmore, which stated in ethnoracial vitriol, "We are fully convinced that there is no hope for the improvement of our Territory unless Americans rule it, that the spirit of Mexican rule must be corrupt, ignorant, and disgraceful in a Territory of the United States, and that . . . under such rule there can be no sufficient guarantees for the secure enjoyment of property, or even of life." Weightman affirmed to the House speaker that the only way 538 American settlers could control the 61,547 native Mexicans was to repeal or disregard the law that had established a territorial government for New Mexico, and that had acknowledged the right of the people to elect their own officials, and to control them instead "by the *reestablishment of the military government*" (emphasis his).[135]

Congress confirmed Weightman in the delegate's seat. He proceeded on a tireless mission of making Congress see that in New Mexico, as one of the world's "colonial dependencies," the appeal for statehood did not differ from the popular sovereignty movements that resulted in statehood for other territories. He sought to dissolve Washington's perennially prejudiced view of Nuevomexicanos. Taking the ethnic ideological tendency of the fresh Mexican Party to the fore, he highlighted in an address to Congress the "spirit of moderation, forbearance, and conservatism exhibited by the people of New Mexico since the Treaty of Guadalupe Hidalgo," which was "deserving of the commendation of every good citizen of this Republic, and might be imitated with advantage by other portions of the country but little blessed with those virtues."[136]

One historian has Weightman cynically "corralling" Nuevomexicanos for personal agendas and to subordinate them.[137] Another more accurately calls Weightman the "champion of the newly made citizens of the United States."[138] The Spanish-language letter Weightman sent to Representative Hilario Gonzales and Miguel E. Pino reads as a sincere effort to counter the "lies" about native New Mexicans circulating in Washington DC. He referred to the American "misperceptions" of the recent political killings and their constant misrepresentations "that all the New Mexicans are ignorant, vicious and totally unfit for self-government and unworthy of freedom." Weightman included the "slander" toward "our friend, Governor Calhoun and myself for being capable only of administering to the atrocious passions of a corrupt and brutal people." Critics attacked Calhoun and himself, Weightman pointed out, for endeavoring to represent faithfully "the rights and interests of the people of New Mexico, instead of turning traitors and playing the role of ungrateful beings." Defamers dishonored the calling of the native priests by casting them as "worse than brutes." He continued: "To us, these slanders are so enormous that it is almost impossible to believe that there are men so depraved as to invent them." Weightman related how the opposition—naming Houghton, Collins, Tully, and Quinn—had gone to Washington to support Reynolds's appeal of the election. They presented "false complaints" to the president with "old lies" published in the *Gazette*, touching on the character of the New Mexico population. He feared their prejudicing the president against the "old" inhabitants of New Mexico as not deserving admission to the exercise of their full rights, "nor to govern themselves as citizens of this country; and further, that in order to protect the lives of the Americans, who are living among such a mob, it was necessary to re-establish the military government." Weightman claimed a triumph against Reynolds's contest because his account of the election was "based upon truth."[139]

The faction that Calhoun called the "American combination" returned to attacking his administration.[140] *Gazette* editor Kephart, assisted by Houghton and former quartermaster and anti-Calhoun man Thomas Johnson, put their pens to the task of fomenting the binary. Kephart, a member of the American and Foreign Anti-Slavery Society, accused the southerner Calhoun and the Texan Weightman of supporting slavery in New Mexico. In an English-Spanish broadside partly titled the "Political Evils of Slavery," he maligned Calhoun as "the overseer's whip from Georgia . . . a southern missionary [sent] to see whether there is a possibility of introducing slavery into this Territory." Kephart accused Calhoun of encouraging Mexicans to hold Indian slaves. He questioned Weightman's priest friends for claiming to be men of the Church while mucking about in politics. Kephart's sheet attracted the attention of eastern anti-slavery newspapers.[141]

Weightman affirmed in a speech before the U.S. House that he did not consider southern slavery viable in New Mexico. He denounced the "reckless and unscrupulous" Calhoun critics. The delegate praised the governor for wanting to bring the Mexicans to the American nation. As he emphasized, Calhoun pursued a course "calculated to make the Mexicans—who have been separated from their government by no act of theirs, and who now owe allegiance to the government of the United States—feel that they are at least a part of this government; that they have rights here that ought to be protected; and that the government to which they belong was created by the people, and ought to be administered for their benefit." Weightman used his time in Congress defending the right of Mexicans to worship as they would, citing the provisions in the Hidalgo Treaty and the U.S. Constitution that protected it no less than the elective franchise.[142]

The ethnoracial distinction between "Mexican" and "American" parties intersected with the structural statehood-versus-territory issue to initiate a party binary at the dawn of New Mexico's time as an American possession. The bipolarized loyalties it generated would go on to inform the experience of New Mexicans attempting to bring about a national political party for themselves.

CHAPTER FIVE

Mexican Democratic Party, 1853–1854

On March 10, 1851, Marcelino Vigil, a *vecino* of Don Fernandez in Taos County, forwarded a letter of protest to Col. John Munroe, charging that a soldier of H Company stationed at Cantonment Burgwin outside of town had broken into his home while he was away and attempted to rape his wife. When she fended off the soldier's advances, he offered her eight dollars "as the price of prostitution." The soldier fled upon hearing neighbors who were approaching the Vigil home. Vigil grieved sorely, for it was not the only outrage visited on his family by American soldiers. In a tumult at a local fandango, several of them stabbed and killed his son. Other families in the area suffered abuse from the troops at the temporary army encampment. His plea, translated by the captain of Company H, who delivered the complaint, conveyed that "if you let it run on [like] this, it will not be long before the choice of the inhabitants shall ask for a remedy and that remedy shall be the removal of these men who are the terror of the Plaza."[1]

Vigil left it to Munroe to determine the appropriate justice to mete out as a result of the offenses the soldiers had been committing against the Taoseños. It is doubtful that he or they received redress of any sort, and soon Munroe was being replaced as commander of the Ninth Military Department (New Mexico) by Col. E. V. Sumner. Such incidents continued to fuel the animosity and resentment Nuevomexicanos had been feeling toward American misrule. In June the captain who took Vigil's complaint reported on the "excitement got up at Taos," although he attributed it to the Mexicans who first heard reports of "revolution" from the "Americans." His own character and standing with the community were being compromised, and he feared for what might happen if he were to move a section of artillery amid the people of Taos when he had already told them that he could handle any "excitement" with what he had.[2]

Colonel Sumner noted to Governor James Calhoun that there was "some ill will towards us on the part of the Mexicans." Sumner admitted it was "perfectly natural with a conquered people," but, he said, "I think in this case, it has been considerably aggravated by our distrust of them." Calhoun vouched for the "angry condition" but he refused to believe it reflected a "contest of the races." He too claimed political agitation behind bad feelings, although it does not seem that Munroe reported the outrages of his troops up in Taos to the governor. Calhoun referred to the "evil-disposed persons hoping now to accomplish their fiendish purposes of Revolution which they have been attempting for more than twelve months past." Freshly memorable in the territory was the death of William Skinner, sent to investigate after a soldier involved in voter intimidation was shot dead, and then himself also killed. Calhoun lamented his lack of arms to fight against the "infamous Combination that has been so long & so stealthily at work to bathe this Territory in blood." He felt Colonel Sumner to be on course, perhaps, to prevent "for a time the dreadful horrors of a civil war."[3]

Various intelligences led Calhoun to believe that a "rebellious feeling" coursed among the Nuevomexicanos. Certain elements awaited a favorable opportunity to attempt carrying their "treasonable purposes into effect," he reported to Sumner. He perceived that "the better informed portion" of the Mexican population was not encouraging revolt but feared some who, "writhing under disappointments of cupidity and political ambition," did not admonish "their more benighted countrymen of what is for their true interest." Calhoun thought the more imminent danger to be the surrounding "savages" who were "being excited against us by [Euroamerican] emissaries and traitorous persons."[4]

Sumner told one of his officers there was nothing to fear so long as the Mexicans were treated "justly and properly." He offered as proof that several of the "principal and most influential" of them had sent large merchant trains to the United States and prepared others for California, "intending to leave their families and property here." Sumner's reported causes of rumor-mongering appear somewhat inconsistent. He stated, on one hand, that most stories of rebellion originated with "some unprincipled Americans, or if they do not create them, they distort and exaggerate them for the purpose of keeping up this excitement," so as to have increased government expenditures for the territory. The problem, he thought, was that the reports sometimes had a tendency to "verify themselves, by creating distrust, and serving to alienate the different classes from each other." Sumner reserved for himself the right to request the authority to put a "vigorous execution" against any difficulty. On the other hand, he told someone else there were "several desperadoes" who were "conspicuous in the revolution of 1847," together with "a few desperate, unprincipled gamblers and speculators," who had "everything to gain and nothing to lose by fomenting commotions." These men would be closely watched, the colonel assured.[5] One of Sumner's framings thus reflected Euroamerican agitation, and the other showed Nuevomexicanos declining the American peace structure.

As Calhoun completed his first year as governor, he came down with catarrh and jaundice so seriously that he announced the need for a recovery away from New Mexico. His imminent departure portended a vacuum in the executive office because the territorial secretary, who would have filled in as acting governor, had resigned and no one had yet been appointed to replace him. Colonel Sumner thought himself the man to take over as interim governor. The chief reason, he told Secretary of the Interior Alexander Stuart, concerned a territory that was "ripe for a revolution to overturn the Govt. here." The malcontents expressed an intention "of putting in a Gov. of their own upon the departure of Gov. Calhoun," Sumner averred. Time would tell what would come of it.[6] Sumner affirmed to an officer in the Department of Defense that there was "strong reason to believe that efforts are being made by some unprincipled men to subvert our government in this territory." He did not, however, see them forcing the people to break out in rebellion, "especially when they see we are ready for them. There is not a man among them of the least intelligence who does not know that we could have troops enough here in sixty days to grind them all into dust."[7]

Calhoun died while en route home to recuperate. Nuevomexicanos in the legislative assembly—newly minted participants in American civics, whom Sumner likely included among the rebellious *nativos*—joined in the privilege of mourning the passing of their "beloved Governor." His death, they grieved in a joint resolution, "was caused by his extreme application to all the difficult and urgent duties of his office." A partisan note appeared at this somber moment. Members praised the governor as an official who "felt the deepest interest of this territory," and they wished the "eulogy of the people over which he presided will be heard much louder than the prattling voices of his enemies."[8]

The fear of rebellion remained after Calhoun's death. A young officer reported to his superior in Washington that the "people themselves [were] almost in a state of civil revolution." It was "a very serious & alarming state of affairs," he feared. Still no territorial secretary was available to serve as acting governor. Adding to the stress, the military complained of the lack of resources to manage restless Indians.[9] Sumner stood by his will to take over the civil government.[10] However, the return of a military officer to civil power did not sit well generally. In Washington, congressional delegate Richard Weightman recommended Spruce M. Baird to the president to succeed Calhoun. Baird was a Texan and affiliate of the Mexican Party who had assisted Calhoun with Indian work. *Gazette* editor W. G. Kephart condemned the recommendation as another attempt to introduce slavery into New Mexico.[11] President Millard Fillmore appointed the popular Missouri physician and Whig politician William Carr Lane New Mexico's governor. Lane on his arrival visited the counties and found New Mexico in a deplorable state. The course his partisanship would take became evident when he called the legislature a "unique construction" passing defective laws.[12] Most troubling to Lane, however, would be Mexican Party solidarity in the session of 1852–53.

While Euroamerican officials feared uncalled-for Mexican insurrection, Mexican Party legislators viewed their people as under civil siege. Calhoun had phrased their assessment well: the people were "not properly cared for."[13] One complaint centered on the lack of adequate military defense against raiding tribes.[14] Matters were worsened by a lack of authority to form community militias.[15] The judiciary posed another set of problems. The Second Legislative Assembly's memorial to Congress cited judges who did not understand the language of the territory, requesting the appointment of residents who would more diligently dedicate themselves to the duties pertaining specifically to New Mexico.[16]

Lane deplored the discontent, and he let the legislators know it. In his opening address to the session he said he understood how Mexican leaders could feel betrayed by their "high expectations of advantage from annexation." He sensed how the "laws and legal usages" introduced by the United States could be, "in many particulars, unsuited to the present condition of the people of New Mexico," and he knew the grievances "might perchance cause some disturbances of the peace in some particular places."[17] Yet he feared the consequences of nativo resistance mostly because he failed to understand it as a yearning for home rule. It was his "confident opinion" that the great mass of the people "were, and would continue to be, faithful to their allegiance to the United States, under all trials; and that the idea of a revolution was a chimera of heated imaginations only."

Lane would have quelled Mexican disgruntlement by encouraging nativos to accept their American incorporation peaceably. He inaugurated the myth of the pure, friendly American conquest of New Mexico in a history lesson in a certain Whiggish effect. Whigs in general, in their anti-party, anti-faction, and humane frame of reference, emphasized "social harmony, not conflict." Society for them was held together by "shared moral codes." John Quincy Adams, a converted Whig, elevated such a value to philosophical principle.[18] Lane wanted all in New Mexico to view recent change through such a lens. He called the territory "not so much a conquered Province, as a community that had voluntarily annexed itself to the United States." The newcomer presumptuously reminded the legislators that they had "surrendered to the invading force without a gun being fired on either side, while the force was insufficient for conquest, [as] annexation [had] been acceptable to you." This partialized memory took the slice of collaboration as the singular Nuevomexicano response to the American conquest, to the neglect of the violent resistance it also generated. Painting malcontents as betrayers of the consensus legacy permitted him to underscore the necessity of a "harmonious co-operation between the natives of the country and strangers, in all matters affecting the public welfare." A "common destiny, for good or evil," awaited all alike, he affirmed, "whether the parent stock be Castilian or Anglo-Saxon." The governor projected a certain cultural pluralism, benevolently advising Mexicans not to change any of their "beneficial or praise-worthy customs," not to forget their "parent stock, and the proud recollections that cluster around Castilian history," nor to "disuse their beautiful language," not to lay aside their "dignified manners, and punctilious attention to the proprieties of social life," nor to forgo the "profound deference that is now paid to parents by their children."

FIG. 9. *New Mexico Territorial Governor William Carr Lane*, ca. 1852, artist unknown. Lane used Whig ideology to help promote the Spanish heritage and conjoin it with the American Party. Courtesy Palace of the Governors Photo Archives, NMHM/DCA, negative #009999.

The disquisition sounded suspiciously like a Mexican Party tune, in which case the governor would paint himself into an ideological corner. Whigs did not especially care for ethnic enclaves. They resented "Irish bullies," for example. Their elite nativism demanded that immigrants assimilate into the core American nation as rapidly as possible.[19] Lane recovered and readily pivoted toward a situational Anglo-conformity. He called for the Nuevomexicanos to learn the English language and adopt the customs that in the United States were deemed "suitable and proper for this country. Let the people of New Mexico obey the obvious dictate of common sense," he urged, no doubt mindful of Thomas Paine's popular phrase to enhance American freedom, however racialized its framing needed to be in the present context.[20] "[E]mbark *upon* the Anglo-Saxon wave which is now rolling from East to West, across the Continent, and ultimately prosper, instead of attempting to resist it and perish. These, Gentlemen," he concluded in swearing his cordial cooperation, "are the alternatives which are now before the people of New Mexico."[21]

This latter allusion better matched American Party thinking, and so the *Gazette* followed up. Kephart's continental liberalism had the United States affording a "fair opportunity of testing the capabilities of the descendants of the Spanish race, under free institutions, the maintenance of which depends upon the morality and intelligence of the people."[22] This Whiggish view of heritage, despite Kephart's Democratic Party membership, flattered the nativos on their presumed Castilian high culture, adapted from *rico* identity, intended to deflect the racialized stereotypes of the Nuevomexicanos while counseling them to assimilate into American ways and nationality.

Mexican Party hands ignored the admonition to harmonize. On the contrary, they launched an offensive against the American Party in the territorial legislature. Santa Fe's Facundo Pino assumed Mexican Party leadership in the House of Representatives, joined by another Santa Fean, the Weightman friend Cándido Ortiz, and Santa Ana County's Tomás Cabeza de Baca, San Miguel County's Jesús Sena y Romero, and the Valencia County priest Rafael Chávez. Mexican identification was moderate in the council yet vigorously represented by Vicar Ortiz, who was reelected president. The American Party *Gazette* failed to describe Mexican Party grievances objectively or comprehensively, but enough comes through its slanted coverage to reveal the issues in the House, at least. A key battle erupted over Miguel Antonio Otero, the younger brother of Kearny Supreme Court Judge Antonio José Otero. Miguel Antonio had recently served as Lane's private secretary. Educated in St. Louis and New York in the late Mexican period, he exuded core American whiteness. His racial ideas aligned with those of the Deep South. The rumor that he might be a candidate for the next election of delegate to Congress made for American Party notoriety and rendered him a target of Mexican Party recrimination.[23]

Representative Rafael Gutierres challenged Otero's legitimacy to the Valencia County seat on the argument that its occupant failed to meet the minimum age. Speaker Pino supported the measure, and a sufficient number of votes were mobilized to eject Otero. Otero supporters charged retaliation by the Pino faction because Otero had caused the firing of a House clerk for larceny. Otero cited as evidence that Gutierres had not advanced his challenge until after the clerk's expulsion. Otero called himself an "independent" who would not turn himself into a subservient "tool" of the "selfish [Mexican] party." According to the *Gazette*, Weightman "partners" had "immolated Otero because he would not vote for a thief." The paper did not disprove Gutierres's documented claim of Otero's ineligibility and did not pause to ask how Otero could have mustered a majority vote to fire the clerk against the faction that dominated the session if the bias against him was so strong among Mexican partisans. The expulsion of Otero held.[24]

Two other issues hit on ethno-factional sensitivities. A bill submitted by a Euroamerican to tax residents to pay the costs of a territorial government generated discussion concerning the culturally equitable imposition of taxes. An incredulous *Gazette* editor stated that Representative Cándido Ortiz "strangled" the bill "by moving to insert a section exempting all *Mexicans* from taxation!" Kephart massaged the devil's binary. He pointed to the "deficiency" of Ortiz's brains, the "inveteracy [*sic*] of his prejudices," and his inability to reconcile with principles of justice, there appearing "only the light of the impertinent insult of a puppy whose greatest security lies where he least suspects it—in his own littleness and meanness." Ortiz, the editorial maintained, had "paid a very sorry compliment to his own countrymen."[25]

The *Gazette* acknowledged a part of the Mexican Party's complaint. Disbursed tax funds did not always benefit the people, but Kephart thought it "exceedingly unkind" to accuse government officers of dishonesty. The Mexican people needed to know that every officer dealing with public funds was under bond, Kephart reminded. He hoped "our Mexican friends" did not doubt "there is such a thing as honesty, even among Americans." The exceptions, Kephart stated, were the officials of the opposing party. He cited Elias P. West, the late territorial district attorney, whose appointment owed to Weightman's influence. Weightman himself was called "not particular about either honesty or qualifications, provided he got men who would prostitute their influence to set him forward on his slimy road to distinction." Kephart wagged his finger regarding the need of public taxes to support a liberal government's contingent expenses. They needed to read Lord [Henry] Brougham's sketch of English taxation, Kephart admonished, publishing it so that they could realize their good fortune under the American system of taxation.[26]

Kephart warned of a dangerous cabal in the House "doing more to bring ruin upon their own countrymen, as well as the American residents of the territory than all other causes combined."[27] As he argued, the policy of conspiracy would in the end be more disastrous to the Mexicans. The editor lay trust in the presumptively rational and even wise voter. Facundo Pino and Cándido Ortiz would thus be held to account come the election. Any other members seeking the "gratification of an embittered and narrow-minded prejudice" would be left to their constituents "for disposal."

But Mexican Party warriors were only warming up. The next brainstorm carried a critical sign of resistance to settler domination. Assemblymen proposed to exclude all *americanos* and anyone not Mexican from participating in any territorial public office. No ban on foreign settlement in the territory seems to have been contemplated, but the desire for nativo rule hit home.[28] Sponsors may have proposed to test liberal majoritarianism to see if the governor would sign the measure. No governor coming in from the outside would, of course, or if one did, Congress would reject it outright. If the proposed measure strove to raise American Party hackles and feed the factional binary, it succeeded. Kephart's liberal indignation flogged this expression of un-Americanism. The Mexicans in the House were out "to trample underfoot all the rules of legislative decorum," he huffed, "the principles of law and justice, the Constitution and Organic Law, under which, and by virtue of which they held their seats as members of a Legislative body." Great ruin would befall the Mexicans should they "preserve" and "sanction" a move to drive out Americans and foreigners. Attacking the business interests would spell misfortune for the poverty-stricken masses, Kephart drove home. No one could ruin the "Americans," for "whenever these find that their rights and privileges cannot be respected here they have a remedy in their hands . . . withdraw their capital and business to the States, and leave the territory to a lingering death." They might ask for redress to the main government "and they will not appeal in vain."

"Do you suppose the Government of the U. States would give up the Territory into your hands," Kephart harped, "and tamely submit to see her own native-born citizens outraged and insulted, and their rights trampled underfoot? Never!" It was not the policy of the United States to yield "tamely" what it had acquired, Kephart fumed, though it appeared to be the "secret desire" of the "cowardly" traitors, too cowardly to attempt such a thing "by means that would endanger their own precious necks, seeking by insidious means to effect what they *dare* not attempt openly." The "sword and bayonet" would return as the consequence of any such assault to "oppress and annoy American citizens"; the laws would be made "in *Washington*" instead of Santa Fe; military guardhouses would take the place of "rickety adobe jails." New Mexico was destined to remain a part of the United States, Kephart reasoned. Why not submit to its Constitution and laws, rather than to a "silly prejudice of races" fanning "prejudice and discord amongst the people"? Kephart sought to educate Nuevomexicanos on how to be the rational voters by repudiating their own leadership. "Reject their counsels of evil," he barked, "and when another election comes 'round, teach them a lesson at the ballot-box that shall enlighten their eyes for all future time."[29]

Kephart's editorials developed the American Party perspective, here by pressing the recalcitrant Mexicans to open their eyes to American nationality. "No people can be prosperous without a unity of feeling, aim, and purpose," he counseled. A grander view would come in "being true to themselves." The notion of "being true to one's self" derived from the Epicurean philosophy of virtue as natural (not religious-transcendental) right. Worked over by Locke, Spinoza, and Shaftesbury, Epicurean virtue fed into the radical deist inclinations and writings of

American founders, among the anti-British guerrillas Ethan Allen and Thomas Young at first, followed by the cultured statesmen Jefferson, Ben Franklin, and Washington (in his inaugural address). Americanism by the 1850s was seen to tap into a virtuous human nature, converting it into a virtuous government. As Matthew Stewart interprets the logic of the American assumption, virtuous people were the "consequence, not the cause, of virtuous government."[30] In Kephart's application, the Mexicans should "sustain for themselves such a character at *home* as shall give them respectability and consideration *abroad*" (emphasis his). The editor eschewed the policy of an exclusive American imperialism in favor of a virtuous liberalism. As an American by birth, by education, and in "all his feelings," he would "gladly" see "the *free* principles [of] our republican government in full operation, not only in New Mexico but throughout the world." Kephart as universalist argued that the United States should "not have others excluded from a free participation in all the privileges and benefits of that government, within our own limits who wish to embrace them and have merit to entitle them to such enjoyment." He nonetheless beheld the people of New Mexico in need of federal government assistance in the provision of schools, including manual labor institutions, to develop their minds, bodies, and the "habits of industry."[31]

Euroamerican settlers once again filled the public space with commentary and debate over the character and potential fate of Nuevomexicanos under the American flag. Kephart may have held out faith in the mass of Mexicans thinking and acting for themselves, but an anonymous pundit thought them not any more "enlightened, liberal-minded, and intelligent" than those who had controlled the last legislature.[32] A modernist distinction pitted shrewd Mexican demagogues, believed by Euroamerican authorities to be racializing agitators, against the popular classes, who, lacking the capacity for self-government, gave the former free rein. Not to degrade them, nor was there any shame in it, observed the pundit, but they were the equal of France, "and all but England among the European nations, who constantly reverted to the crouching at the feet of vain, petty, usurping tyrants, in spite of their occasional spasms of commitment to 'Truth, Friendship, and Fidelity.'" The great portion of Americans did not understand the "science" of self-government either, but at least their exercise of it constituted an experiment in freedom, the critic held forth. For centuries Mexicans had been accustomed to the rule of "petty despots" and forms of government containing "scarcely a single element of true republicanism." Expecting them to understand fully at once and "without any previous instruction in, or practice of, those principles" was as absurd "as to suppose that an acorn could spring from the ground in a single night a towering oak, or that a child should spring from the arms of his nurse a full grown man." A common grassroots assumption in the United States was that behind power lay the tendency of men to hold dominion over others, control human life, and compel obedience.[33] The writer heeded the need of liberty to protect the people from the unprincipled demagogues who were "always ready to pander to any popular prejudice, or take advantage of any popular feeling, to advance their own ambitious schemes."

A problem for consensus liberals arrived from the United States in clearly racialized cast. Colonel Sumner's disdain for Mexicans went deep. In a private communication to the secretary of war he explained why he refused the Mexicans who requested reinforcements in their conflicts with the Indians, their lack of "manliness to defend themselves," and their "cupidity," which made them desire troops among them to acquire "government money."[34] Sumner touched off a firestorm after portraying Nuevomexicanos to Secretary of War Charles Conrad as "thoroughly debased and totally incapable of self-government [with] no latent quality about them that can ever make them respectable." Sumner, confounding Governor Lane's upbeat Hispanophilia, decried the Mexicans' more evident Indian than Spanish blood. In "some respects," he wrote in a pointed disparagement, given the stratified racial order, they were "below the Pueblo Indians, for they are not as honest or as industrious." Sumner acknowledged the Mexicans as a "conquered people," harboring therefore a "natural dislike toward us," but so long as they were kept supplied with money, they had nothing to do "but revel in their vices" and be content to stifle their Mexican patriotism. "It requires but very little to subsist them," he persisted, "and, thereafter a small pittance enables them to pass their time in idleness and vice; but that little they must have, and there is now no way they can get it."[35]

Somehow, perhaps through a leak from Conrad's office, the *Gazette* published Sumner's opinion. It forced assimilationist Americans to pull Nuevomexicanos into their nation. American Partyites James

Collins, Joab Houghton, Charles Spencer, Francis J. Thomas, Hugh Smith, and Joseph Nangle came together as an indignation meeting to oppose any suggestion of excluding the Mexicans from the American government. The difficult commander had given deep offense, they informed the president. To recall him would be "hailed with universal joy by the inhabitants of New Mexico."[36] An anonymous Nuevomexicano decried Sumner's "indiscriminate slander," declaring it the duty "of every honest man, to defend himself and his race, from such assaults."[37]

That prominent American Party men exercised their social control over Sumner's transgression reflected a normative core of inclusionary liberalism. In the weekly columns, an anonymous Euroamerican excused Sumner's prejudice as born of a short sojourn in the territory and defended the political and mental capacity of the Mexican people. More important, he praised the "honesty" of the Mexican men and the "chastity of [the] women standing quite the equal of Utah's Latter Day Saints of Jesus Christ upon the Earth." The writer extended his graciousness to the poorest of peons, seeing something exceptional about this breed of primitive people. The Mexicans were "susceptible of improvement," he wrote, a quality not so marked as would be the case "with a community from any nation similarly isolated from the world." They demonstrated a "quickness of comprehension," a "feeling of emulation, and a desire to excel," which was "alone stimulated by constant observance of something superior, which is desirable to imitate or to surpass." The opinionator confirmed the effect of continental liberalism. Already he could observe a common acculturation as in the native farmer discarding his "rude" stick to scratch his fields for the "American Plow," the folk trading in their crude buckskin and coarse cloth for finer clothes from the United States "after the fashion of other countries."[38]

Another Euroamerican reported that he had been observing the "mental oscillations" of the Mexican neighbors "with the greatest anxiety." They often entertained hostile feelings toward the Americans, but happily, attitudes were "giving place to a more generous, liberal, and a kindlier feeling to the Americans." It benefited the teachable Mexicans. By overrunning the territory with schools, the children of the "natives of this land," so "deplorably" ignorant in all branches of knowledge, would be "snatched from the gloomy abyss of ignorance which hems them in on all sides." They were to be guided toward "an inclination to plunge deeper into the pleasures of study, and would become as learned and refined as those other nations." In such a manner would the differences between the races "be reconciled."[39]

Congress put the pleasant gesture of overrunning the benighted territory with schoolhouses on hold for the rest of the century practically. In the immediacy of the moment, its factional imperative grew ready to consider a U.S. political party.

A Democratic Party for New Mexico?

The Whig Party in the United States came to suffer from exhaustion and dissension, in part because Whig leaders could not unite around the battles over the New Mexico–Texas boundary and the question of whether slavery should be permitted out West.[40] As the Whig Party declined, the Democratic Party grew in popularity in spite of its own internal stresses. Democrat Franklin Pierce took the presidency in 1852 by winning all but three of thirty-one states in the Union. In New Mexico, army captain William Angeny, the former commander of American infantry who put down the Taos uprising of 1847, and other American Party travelers reportedly talked of establishing a Democratic Party for the territory.[41]

The American territory offered fertile ground for one with political ambition. James Collins, the owner of the *Santa Fe Gazette*, was a Whig, but according to historian Loomis Ganaway, he perceived opportunity for a federal appointment after the Pierce administration scolded New Mexicans to stop filing endless complaints to its offices about one another, which apparently curbed criticisms of Collins.[42] Collins himself later described his shift away from the Whigs as a matter of principle. He had held the *Gazette* to a policy of party neutrality, he averred, because his acting editor Kephart was a Democrat. He did not believe that "the advocacy to political rule in favor of either party could result in benefit to the Territory at that time." Collins spent eight months in Washington in 1851–52 in part to do some lobbying in the congressional session. He claimed to have observed at that time many changes taking place in the political creeds of both parties and that "the Democratic party ... emphatically [appeared] the party of progress." The Democrats seemed "best suited "to the genius of our people and government," Collins perceived. Democratic principles had been drawing "many patriotic recruits from the ranks of my former political friends, and especially did I become convinced that if anything was done for this Territory, it must emanate from the Democratic [P]arty." Collins corresponded with friends in Washington and Missouri on the subject. He broached it with his editor Kephart on returning to Santa Fe in October 1852. They agreed that the *Gazette* should advocate Democratic principles and the organization of a Democratic party, "as soon as such an organization was approved by the Democrats of the Territory."[43]

Collins took the editorial reins of his paper and proceeded to convert the weekly into an unabashed Democratic tool. He kept readers abreast of Democratic electoral victories in the states, alerting citizens to national and international developments. Collins did not leave the American Party behind. He did, however, alter its ideological footing with his shift to the Democrats. The American Party had stood decidedly against slavery in the state constitutional conventions of 1848 and 1850. Collins abruptly repudiated abolitionism and proceeded to drive his paper's mast full steam in the direction of the "doughface" President Pierce, a northern Democrat who defended southern slavery.[44] For this, the northern Democrat Kephart would have to go as the managing editor of the *Gazette*.

One's identity is constructed according to who one is not, as much as who one is. Forging an effective identity on the negative requires an overbearing, if not exaggerated, accentuation of the other. Democratic Party hopefuls needed a clear partisan enemy to bestir themselves organizationally. Options abounded. The Whigs stood first and foremost. The *Gazette* now complained that New Mexico had been "singularly unfortunate" in that only Whig administrations had governed affairs in Washington since the Democrat Polk left office in 1849. Whig neglect stemmed from incompetent and dishonest appointees, the paper contended. Collins debated the terms of continental liberalism. The Whigs forgot the responsibility to promote republicanism in all of America's territorial possessions, he claimed.[45] Collins argued that a Democratic administration would not withhold that "parental attention and liberality, which so many States have needed and received during their territorial, or infant, state." It was one of those twists of logic to become more common with the development of the partisan binary in the territory for Collins to call Pierce's support for southern slavery an instance of constitutional fidelity.[46]

New Mexico Democrats identified two other nearly inextricable bugbears—congressional delegate Richard Weightman and the Mexican Party. Weightman was a long-standing Democrat whose political views coincided with those of the wing that sought the civic and political incorporation of immigrants, as consecrated in the Declaration of Independence, and which this wing applied, partly with its own newspaper, in support of incorporated Texan Mexicans against the xenophobic assaults of the Know-Nothing Party in the 1852–56 elections and politics of Bexar County.[47] From the start of his political career in New Mexico Weightman had supported Mexican Party members, and for this Collins called him a "disturber of the peace of the Territory . . . slanderously laboring to create division and dissension between the Mexican and American races, a crime against which there should be a heavy statuary penalty." The editor condemned Weightman's speeches in Congress, which he described as "matter intended alone, hypocritically, to ingratiate himself with the Mexican people, and to advance his own personal ambition." Collins tried using the delegate's Texas background to advantage, instructing his "Mexican fellow-citizens" to judge Weightman's trustworthiness when, as an imperial agent, he worked to sacrifice New Mexico to Texan schemes.[48] That Nuevomexicanos were willing to have Weightman as a leader Collins claimed not to understand. Were Mexicans "so ignorant that they cannot see the extent of the injury his treachery would inflict upon them?" he queried indignantly. Did Weightman suppose "that he has them so entirely in his power that they will not complain of his shameful and unworthy conduct?" Collins projected the majority Mexican citizens able to act like rational voters. They would show Weightman, he emphasized, that they knew "how to appreciate such treachery, at the next September election."[49]

Historian Robert Larson finds little proof in the charge of Weightman as an unscrupulous opportunist.[50] Collins's overheated partisanship met the need of aspirants to have an iconic object as a basis to found a U.S. political party. Other American Partyites were prepared to move. According to a retrospective essay published in the *Gazette* four years later, Francis J. Thomas, a lieutenant under Colonel Sumner's command, and one Henry C. "Spectacle" Johnson called in the first week of June 1853 a meeting in Santa Fe to get a Democratic Party going in the territory. Thomas and Johnson were reputedly "sound Democrats." These recent transplants pitched into the diffusion of the idea of the American political party westward. They called several meetings at the homes of individuals, including Collins. In the "principal ground" taken, "unless the Mexicans would unite in forming the party the action of the Americans would be of no avail." The concern reflected twin considerations—the desire to integrate the Mexicans into a party structure and the fact that there were not enough Euroamerican settlers to run a mass-based party. Nuevomexicanos were invited but, with few exceptions, refused to attend. Those who did "seemed to take no interest in the matter." In late June a flyer asked Democrats to hold county conventions for the election of delegates to a central nominating convention. Democrats named a committee so that it could call a convention planning meeting, emphasizing that it should "especially . . . invite the Mexicans to attend . . . and to participate in the organization of the party."[51]

The throng of two hundred who gathered in Santa Fe that last week in June testifies to the awareness of, interest in, and wish for a national political party in the territory. The *Gazette* described the crowd as "enthusiastic," including both "Whigs and Democrats" and "Mexicans and Americans." The proceedings failed to congeal, however. Trouble arose amid confusion over whether the majority vote in officer elections was either for or against the nominees. Dissidents prevented Thomas from reading a report on the committee's actions and the meeting's rationale. A motion to adjourn was voted down. "Here was a sad fix," the memorist noted, "and the movers of the meeting seemed sorely troubled; they could neither move back or forward." The majority finally "took compassion" by adjourning. The breakdown was not for lack of Democratic "feelings," according to the observer (perhaps Collins), but from fear of a domineering faction, bent on elevating particular individuals who had "no claims to the confidence of the voters of the Territory, nor the Democratic party." Dissident elements charged that by railroading the convention, organizers arrogated to themselves the exclusion of Democrats who did not want to formally nominate Democratic congressional candidates. A challenge to the party credentials of some was lodged, among them the former Whig Collins.[52]

Thomas afterward composed a petition, signed by a dozen others, protesting the obstructionist "mob force" that had sabotaged an intended open meeting *"with the preconcerted intention* of preventing *any* citizen from expressing his views on public matters." "Blackguards" had stopped the people from "exercising the very right for which our fathers risked and pledged their lives," the petition charged. Thomas upheld, in the name of his "personal sovereignty," the people's "sacred honor, the right to be heard on any subject of a public nature in which I may be personally interested."[53]

The retrospective hinted at the identity of the culprits as Mexican Party members.[54] The reasons for disagreement with the meeting's organizers from that side would have appeared in *El Amigo del País,* the weekly that Weightman and friends established with his printing press to counter the editorial policies of the *Gazette.* No issues have survived.[55]

In the vacuum following the June–July organizing debacle, the Mexican Party seized the moment. Delegations from Bernalillo, Río Arriba, Santa Ana, Santa Fe, San Miguel, and Taos counties convened on August 5, 1853, in Algodones, on the Río Grande north of Alburquerque, midway between Río Arriba and Río Abajo district center points. The agenda formed around the goal of creating the Democratic Party of New Mexico and nominating someone to run for the U.S. Congress under its banner. Thirty-seven individuals were official delegates to the convention. Facundo Pino, the Santa Fe die-hard Mexican Party speaker of the territorial House of Representatives, was elected president. José Gutierrez, another charter Mexican Party member, held the post of secretary. Diego Archuleta, *el antiguo revolucionario* (the old revolutionary), as Donaciano Vigil had called him, appeared, his reputation as Kearny foe still fresh in New Mexico's collective memory. So did Juan Cristóval Armijo, the man who had killed William Skinner months before, and Father José Manuel Gallegos from San Felipe de Neri Parish in Alburquerque. Somewhat surprisingly, a Río Abajo *rico,* Bernalillo County rancher and merchant José Leandro Perea, whom General Kearny had purportedly wanted to make his occupation governor, attended. The Euroamerican minority included S. M. Baird, John Mink, Elias Clark, Charles Spencer, Caleb Sherman, Crohan Ker, and James Quinn.[56]

That Euroamericans played important roles in the proceedings is evident from the minutes. Nuevomexicanos appear as competent conventioneers nonetheless. Official county delegations reported to a Credentials Committee. Delegates passed Gallegos's call for a committee of six to prepare parliamentary rules. The small contingent of Euroamericans provided key lessons in the art of party formation, mobilization, and organizational maintenance. They demonstrated convention procedure to Nuevomexicanos through motions that included the naming of a committee to prepare the convention's platform.[57] The minutes show Spruce M. Baird quite active in the proceedings. He was already a Democrat but not aligned with the American Party.[58] A friend and ally of congressional delegate Weightman, Baird served as a federal Indian agent and had worked alongside former Governor James Calhoun. Baird arrived in Santa Fe in 1848 as a representative of the commission pressing Texas's claim to New Mexico's territory east of the Río Grande and had hoped to serve as a county judge in the new Texas jurisdiction. Pino had organized a mass meeting in 1848 in opposition to Texas expansion. That he and Baird appeared together at the convention raised American Party eyebrows. As historian Larson notes, such seemingly strange alliances were not uncommon: "Many early adventurers coming to New Mexico stayed in the territory as permanent residents to befriend former enemies."[59]

The Algodones Democratic Convention submitted its preamble and resolutions, signed by twenty-eight Nuevomexicano and four Euroamerican delegates, to the *Gazette*, which published them in Spanish only. Nuevomexicanos were being brought further into American political historicity and in their own language. The opening "whereas" noted that in all republican forms of government it was necessary that a free people "work in unity and in concert with the promotion of the best interests of the people." It was in conformity with the use of the Democratic Party, since the administration of "Tomás Gefferson, the grand apostle of liberty [*el grande apóstol de la libertad*] in order to produce the most good for the most number of persons [*de modo a producir el mayor bien para el mayor número de personas*]," that the Algodones Democrats declared the organization of a permanent Democratic Party.[60]

The convention tilted decidedly toward the national Democratic Party. The Van Buren legacy had established the norm of political parties distinguishing among themselves on the basis of "principles."[61]

The Algodones group affirmed their recognition and approval of the party's fundamental principles. It was because, as members affirmed, "we believe these principles are the most conducive to the happiness and well-being, and for the common and general interests of the people, assuring equal rights and equal privileges, and extending equal protection to all, renouncing all distinctions not founded on their merits [*creemos que estos principios son más conducentes a la felicidad y bienestar, y para los intereses communes y generales del pueblo, asegurando iguales derechos e iguales privilejios, y extendiendo igual protección a todos, renunciando toda distinción que no sea fundada en el mérito*]." It is quite significant to note for this early date in New Mexico's territorial history that the convention resolved to adopt the principles enunciated in the platform of the Baltimore Democratic National Convention held on June 1, 1852, as they conformed to those of "*Gefferson y Jackson.*"

The Algodones Democrats constructed their party identity around an implied distinction from the American Party while conforming to the Jeffersonian principle of local control (as opposed to the Whig preference for federal centralization) and serving a native-son, home-rule aspiration. With Colonel Sumner's disparagements easily remembered, Resolution 5 recognized the "capacity of the people [*la capacidad del pueblo*]" of New Mexico to govern themselves. A number of citizens, "of talent and integrity on the land [*de talento é integridad en el terreno*]" were said to have the requisite "understanding [*comprensión*]" to fulfill the appointed positions successfully in the territorial government.

Mexican Party Democrats would not support for Congress any individual not known as a Democrat and not "recognized as such in name and principle [*que no sea conocido por Demócrata y reconocido por tal en nombre y principios*]." Nor would they vote for anyone in future elections for any position "of honor, confidence or benefit [*honor, confianza o provecho*]" who was not known as a Democrat, "good and loyal [*bueno y leal*]." They would reject any who did not submit their candidacy "to the action and determination of Democratic friends in convention and who are not capable [*que no quiera someter sus pretensiones a la acción y determinación, y que no sea capaz*]."

To sustain the party binary, the Algodones conventioneers reproached New Mexico's rotten factionalism, "the unfortunate and unnecessary contention [*desaprovamos el carácter de la desgraciada y no necesaria contención que hasta ahora se ha sostenido en este Territorio*]." The platform called for the "immediate abandonment of the parties that created it for personal reasons [*partidos que se crearon sobre resultados personales*]"—disregarding the fact that the binary factionalism before them provided the material for building an American party contention. The convention opposed, in Mexican Party form, "all intent, no matter from where it comes, that tries to create party distinctions based on the difference of the races [*desaprovamos todo intento, no importa de donde venga, que procure criar distinciones de partido basadas sobre la diferencia de razas*]." It also defensively rejected any suggestion of local nativo "anti-American" sedition. The distinctly Mexican Party platform denounced the term "American" as an ethnic distinction on par with "Native Americanism" of the Know-Nothing variety, for it was, as they noted, "feared in horror by all the true Democrats [*lo cual es temido en horror por todos los verdaderos demócratas*]." The program appeared in its own way consonant with the reigning "age of egalitarianism," in the context of Manifest Destiny.[62]

The convention's nominations for delegate to Congress suggest Euroamerican settlers committing to a Nuevomexicano candidate. Weightman could doubtless have arranged another run at the position for himself, yet neither his nor any other English surname appears in nomination. Token support favored don José E. Ortiz of Taos. The ultimate rally went to territorial senator José Manuel Gallegos of Alburquerque. Taos County voted for its native son Ortiz in the balloting. The other counties came in solidly for Gallegos. Fulfilling the nomination *voz viva*, the delegates blessed Gallegos as the one to run as New Mexico's first Nuevomexicano and first Democratic Party candidate for Congress.[63]

Why would Gallegos attract such strong support? Certainly he was an experienced politician, having regularly served in the New Mexico Department assembly followed by his getting elected to the American territorial legislature. The strategic association concerned his membership in the religious wing of what historian Angélico Chávez calls the Algodones "Mexican Democratic Party."[64]

In the general sweep of liberalism, modernist sensibilities were offended by the sight of native clergymen in the Mexican borderlands.

FIG. 10. *José M. Gallegos*, 1872, photograph by Frederick Gutekunst. Gallegos was the first Nuevomexicano and Latino American elected to Congress, going on to become one of the most consistently powerful politicians in territorial New Mexico. Courtesy Palace of the Governors Photo Archives, NMHM/DCA, negative #009882.

As we saw, Mexican progressivism grew to disdain the clerical establishment of New Mexico. The *hombres de bien* Donaciano Vigil and Antonio José Otero suppressed pastors who did not exercise the profession on their standards. As acting governor, Vigil, with the support of the military command, suspended Vicar Juan Felipe Ortiz for approving priests who charged parishioners for services. In his trademark liberal orientation, Vigil admonished Ortiz for going against "the public will." Bishop José Antonio Laureano de Zubiría retained Ortiz as New Mexico's vicar.[65] Judge Otero backed the alcaldes appointed by Col. John Washington who took control of two parishes in the Río Abajo, replacing priests with independent, recently arrived ones. Nuevomexicano supporters of the native clergy submitted protests to the civil authorities in Santa Fe and feared violence over being forced to accept politically appointed priests. Alcaldes detained parishioners on the day before a local election. The religious conflict fed into the political binary of the territory. Richard Weightman vigorously defended the traditional church, but the charge that the rights of the church itself, guaranteed by the U.S. Constitution, were being infringed upon, fell on deaf ears.[66]

The anti-clerical party received a powerful boost for its contention with the regional priesthood by the jurisdictional change that the Vatican approved. American Party members who controlled New Mexico's 1849 territorial council, seeing a "crying need" for a new church structure in Santa Fe, requested a pre-diocesan vicariate specifically for the new American territory. Based on its "urgent recommendations," the Vatican created the Vicariate Apostolic of New Mexico under the Seventh Provincial Council of the Church headquartered in Baltimore. In 1851 Jean Baptiste Lamy, a Frenchman who had been in the United States since 1839, received the appointment of vicar apostolic of Santa Fe. The vicariate became the Diocese of Santa Fe in 1853 with Lamy as New Mexico's first-ever bishop.[67]

Article IX of the Treaty of Guadalupe Hidalgo stipulated that the Mexicans in the new American possessions would be secured in the free exercise of their religion "without restriction." What this tenet of denominational freedom might mean for the particular changes wrought by annexation could not have been presaged. While it did not violate the treaty's guarantee specifically, what did occur amounted to a modern imperial Christianity invading the ground of a traditional regional church.

The Mexican church in New Mexico had long operated in ecclesiastical independence from the Durango diocese. The sixteenth-century Council of Trent defined bishops as the "center of gravity of the Church."[68] The question in frontiers around the world concerned a bishop's ability to effect control of far-flung parishes. Long distances, weak communications, and poor transportation kept the Durango diocese from administering New Mexico clerics. Bishop Zubiría had visited New Mexico but thrice in his long career as the bishop of Durango. He came away alarmed each time over its religious affairs and the accreted Catholic customs of the mountain folk, the penitential cofradías in particular.[69] Since 1832 Vicar Juan Felipe Ortiz had grown accustomed to acting "with almost complete autonomy," reinforced by his upper-class background. It suited the individual pastors for him to maintain a low level of supervision over the individual parishes.[70]

Lamy inherited a bishop's authority to demand obedience from the faithful as freshly mandated by the 1852 First Plenary Council of the American Catholic Church.[71] Based in part on the Vatican Propaganda Fide's view of the United States as "mission territory," Lamy defined his mission as bringing the Nuevomexicano church into a religious annexation, reorganizing, consolidating, and reforming it altogether. The task extended as well from the spread of the gospel at the hands of bishops charged with "get[ting] the job done."[72] Lamy subscribed to the medieval Christology of the nineteenth-century Church, emphasizing Christ's "divine, perfect and supra-human attributes, faculties and powers," which theologians expected to communicate to the world in a strict "one-way street ... with the communication of cultural traits between a colonizing power and its colonials."[73]

Lamy's first modernizing project in New Mexico was to erect a rising cathedral out of brick and mortar materials in preference to New Mexico's traditional adobe constructions, and the second was to educate the provincials by establishing a parochial school worthy of the name. He and his vicar general, Father J. Projectus Machebeuf, reported in letters to France on the need to correct the neglect of the sacraments in the New Mexico outpost. He attributed the "grossest immorality among the people" to the lack of Catholic teaching, especially for girls. Lamy's imported nuns started the School at Loretto as a spreader of civilization. Nuevomexicano priests had nothing to do with the school. Its establishment stripped fom them the role they had traditionally possessed as the principal educators of New Mexico youth, a blow to their community significance.[74] Church development also meant shoring up the cadre of priests. Missionary bishops were instructed to build communities of native clergy. Lamy at first encouraged Padre Martínez's work with young New Mexicans to enter the priesthood, but it proved insufficient.[75] Lamy yearned for "some young priests zealous and devout."[76] Lamy recruited European clergy based on his relatively easy access to the Catholic Bishop's Plenary Council in Baltimore. By the mid-1850s French, Polish, and Spanish priests virtually equaled the number of Nuevomexicano clergy. The outsiders were unfamiliar with the culture of the region. The strict orders from Santa Fe had them institute a relationship with the village communities that differed from what Mexican priests exercised.[77]

Lamy's missionary project would result in the actual removal of practically all the native Mexican priests from their clerical posts, bringing a distinct era of public service by Mexican priests to an end. The story is controversial. The classic view propagated by Paul Horgan portrays a virtuous bishop suffering unjustified resistance from corrupt priests resentful of his right to lead in spreading the gospel.[78] Angélico Chávez and Thomas Chávez, examining archdiocesan records, see the priests oppressed by the prejudice of Lamy's vicar general first and then by Lamy himself. Ray John de Aragón finds an unavoidable and "unfortunate cultural clash," the product of a transition to a new era for New Mexico.[79]

Local priests did not realize Lamy's intent to extend and replicate the modern church that he helped develop in nine years' service in the dioceses of Ohio and Kentucky. Like Vicar Ortiz, nativo priests would have known little of the strict hierarchical structure in the American church.[80] The bureaucratic church demanded not only uniform doctrine, ritual, and behavior but external disciplines "binding the parishes into proper dioceses, the dioceses into the unified American Church, and the American Church into the universal Church."[81]

Lamy and Machebeuf superimposed on their formal mission the moral rigidity of Jansenism, what one researcher calls an "underground river of Calvinism within the French Catholic Church." Jansenism promoted an obsession with the proper comportment of the "revered position of the priest." Its application was most often "quite puritanical."[82] The French clergy of the Restoration (1815–48), espe-

FIG. 11. *View of Santa Fe Plaza and cathedral before installation of clock*, 1866, photographed by Nicholas Brown and showing Lamy's completed cathedral. Courtesy Palace of the Governors Photo Archives, NMHM/DCA, negative #038025.

cially the seminary professors and their students, "were largely out of touch with the socioeconomic realities of their actual world." They tended to drift into an "unworldly and next-worldly eschatology" and a Catholicism that "suffered from a sentimentalization of piety . . . and a world-view that emphasized the strange inverse power of poverty, simplicity and humility—the weapons of traditional rural innocence."[83] The Nuevomexicano priests in their rural innocence had escaped the strictures and rituals of piety laid down by European norms of observance. They had become quite secular, practically as one with parishioners in their enjoyment of the local recreational pleasures. As a scandalized Nuevomexicano noted in 1848, these did not exclude the dance hall, the gambling den, and the open maintenance of a nuclear family.[84]

Lamy and Machebeuf looked aghast at the padres who rarely if ever

FIG. 12. *Archbishop Jean Baptiste Lamy and St. Francis Cathedral as originally planned.* This brick and mortar vision reflects Lamy's modernist approach in establishing his diocese in New Mexico's capital. Courtesy Palace of the Governors Photo Archives, NMHM/DCA, negative #010005.

FIG. 13. *Santa Fe, July 20, 1866*, by Thomas Worthington Whittredge. The stone and adobe construction of St. Francis Cathedral is at far left, and other American-style buildings are set among traditional Mexican adobes. Yale University Art Gallery. Gift of the Estate of William W. Farnam, BA 1866, MA 1869, to the Peabody Museum of Natural History.

preached, violating thereby the disciplinary decree handed down by the Council of Trent, which entrusted priests with the care of souls to deliver sermons regularly at Mass and on holy days, based on scriptures, divine law, and other themes. Faithful attendance at Sunday Mass had hardly received enforcement in New Mexico, against the grain of the strict, pietistic French doctrine.[85] One historian has the new prelates under the spell of the Black Legend, believed widely in northern Europe, that stereotyped "a brutal, sanguinary, and sadistic Spain, torturing and killing wherever she went—in tacit contrast, no doubt, to the lily-white colonialists from France, England, and the Netherlands."[86] Angélico Chávez finds the new clergy having been impacted by a jaundiced view of Nuevomexicano priests while on the road to New Mexico. In Galveston another French bishop, Jean-Marie Odin, "began filling their heads with all kinds of evil things concerning the native people and clergy of New Mexico," Chávez finds. Odin never visited New Mexico, yet he related scurrilous stories about its occupants and their priests that American travelers and merchants had circulated for more than a decade. Lamy and Machebeuf heard the same "gossip" from Euroamericans in Santa Fe, who had long maligned the native clergy. The two expressed in letters grave suspicions of careless, lazy, and sexually active pastors before getting to know the individual New Mexico priests.[87] Angélico Chávez and Thomas Chávez perceive Machebeuf acting with a pure "hatred" of them. Lamy went along with Machebeuf's recommendations on dealing with them from dependence on his vicar general's stronger, "sex-obsessed" personality.[88]

Relations among co-religionists began amicably enough. Excited about Lamy's arrival and the prospect of a resident bishop for New Mexico, Vicar Ortiz organized a grand welcoming procession, Mass, and stately dinner.[89] That Lamy had the support of Nuevomexicanos was shown early on when many of them backed him in his effort to take back a church that the military had been controlling.[90] However, Ortiz never received orders from Durango that he should bow

FIG. 14. *Tomás Cabeza de Baca*, photo taken between 1860 and 1889. Cabeza de Baca became a bitter enemy of Archbishop Jean Baptiste Lamy and lifelong leader of the Mexican Party in territorial New Mexico. Box 1, Donald S. Dreesen Collection of Pictures of Prominent New Mexicans, #987-012, Center for Southwest Research and Special Collections, University of New Mexico.

to Lamy's authority. Until he did, he would refuse Lamy's claim to ecclesiastical supervision.[91] Matters with the Nuevomexicano clergy rapidly deteriorated once Lamy departed to Durango to settle his Episcopal jurisdiction with Bishop Zubiría, whereupon the work of managing the vicariate fell to Vicar General Machebeuf. Machebeuf took to bringing the far-flung churches of New Mexico under his management with intense energy. He rode the circuit not simply to introduce himself but to advance district consolidation and demonstrate the new expectations for the pulpit. His determination was reinforced by what he came to view as the need to educate the religiously ignorant and loose-living people.[92] Machebeuf is described by historians who have conducted primary research as traipsing the New Mexico trails with the air of superiority characteristic of the people from the Auvergne region of southern France such that his conflict with the native priests began to look like a "Franco-Hispano contest."[93]

By the time the Algodones Democratic Convention, Machebeuf had suspended Cura Francisco Leyva, the pastor in San Miguel on the Pecos River whom Donaciano Vigil had sought to quiet in 1848 over fears for the fate of Nuevomexicanos under the American regime, on allegations of drunkenness and womanizing. Padre Antonio José Martínez convinced Lamy to reinstate Leyva, but the incident built up the image of the padres as corrupt and decadent. A priest's behavior became an obsessive theme for the diocesan officials. Father Ramón Salazar of Santa Clara was suspended on the charge of being a drunkard and living with a married woman. Machebeuf served his organizational consolidation by appropriating the resources of Salazar's parish.[94]

In Mexico in this epcoh it was not uncommon for priests to have relations with women. The Catholics on the Ohio River saw a priest but three or four times a year. In New Mexico "the church had been established for centuries and *mexicano* communities were used to having a resident pastor. Secular priest or Franciscan friar, he became an organic member of village life. Local cultural values, with their emphasis on community and family, saw permanency in the priesthood as more important than minor personal failings. Machebeuf's "sporadic if well-intentioned visits" could not compensate for the loss of their resident pastors through suspension.[95]

Chávez and Chávez see Machebeuf conducting a "rampage" on the native priests. The vicar put two others under suspension, José de Jesús Luján at Albuquerque, and Antonio de Jesús Salazar, on the usual charges of drink and sex. Machebeuf again appropriated church funds. Luján challenged Machebeuf's authority to serve as a vicar general. Machebeuf, in an act of spiritual annexation to the culture of the great Catholic Church, proclaimed that any priest determined to remain faithful to his calling must place himself under the protection of Mary, recognized as "Queen of the Clergy."[96]

Another issue for Lamy concerned the political careers of nativo priests. That they continued with these in the American territory, as if still in Mexico, did not sit well with the modern Church. The bishop clung to the American principle of the separation of religion from government. Vicar Ortiz appeared dismayingly as a leader in the legislative assembly and a county probate judge. The famous Padre Antonio José Martinez served as president of the council before Lamy's presence. If separation of church and state signaled modernity, Lamy led the charge, ordering the Nuevomexicano priests to refrain from the politician's profession.[97]

Father José Manuel Gallegos committed all these sins and then some. Historians characterize the renowned Río Abajo padre and Mexican Democratic Party candidate for Congress as a "worldly man beyond the canonical sense of 'secular' priest (one living in the 'World'), distinct from one with vows living a monastic life." Gallegos may have lacked "a true sacerdotal vocation." His motive for entering the priesthood "could have been prompted by the considerable influence which this could contribute to a political career during the Mexican regime of his youth."[98] Gallegos's seemingly weak religious avocation rent the cloak of piety that Lamy and Machebeuf took as proper for a priest. Their assessment was exacerbated by Gallegos's mercantile business. That he kept his store open on Sundays shocked modern Church sensibility. It was common knowledge that a woman lived with Gallegos and served as his partner behind the store counter.[99] Based partly on complaints from Alburquerque parishioners, Lamy forwarded written warnings to Gallegos regarding his business, adding a protest about his gambling.[100]

Matters intensified when Gallegos made a merchant's trip to Durango and had failed to acquire diocesan permission for the venture. Lamy ordered Machebeuf to remove Father José de Jesús Luján, whom Gallegos had left in charge, and to occupy the parish, from which he could supervise the Río Abajo district. Lamy authorized Machebeuf to issue a writ suspending Gallegos from his priestly duties. Machebeuf excoriated Gallegos from the pulpit, stereotyping Mexican priests in Gallegos's image, portraying them as "typically Mexican in their (political and pecuniary) ambitions along with their love of worldly pleasures and, above all, their (sexual) scandals."[101]

The simmering dispute between Lamy's office and nativo priests boiled over at the end of 1852 in the bishop's Christmas Pastoral letter, which imposed a set of admonitions on Catholics within the diocese.[102] Lamy ordered the proclamation read at Sunday Mass and had it published in the *Weekly Gazette*. Five new rules were defined for strengthening Catholic devotion. Parishioners were to contribute materially to their parishes or be seen as outside the faith. They should avoid divorce, dance, and gambling.[103] The other orders clipped the wings of the priests. Lamy was astonished at what he considered the exorbitant fees they charged for the marriage, burial, and baptismal sacraments.[104] He centralized the church's finances in his office. A standard tithe system was ordered, the proceeds to go to Santa Fe rather than to individual priests. Lamy thus deprived nativo clergy of their traditional form of sustenance by banning individualized charges to the faithful. Clergy would henceforth prearrange pomp and patronal ceremonies according to the wherewithal of the lay celebrants and could not demand payment for them. Finally, priests were to offer Mass at least once a month for settlements of three families or more.[105]

Historian Father Thomas Steele noted that Nuevomexicanos violently resisted Mexico City's administrative centralization in 1837, but here they lacked the power to stop the centralizing Christmas edict and Lamy's other innovations.[106] Not that the will to object went lacking. As Horgan puts it, "The dutiful, clear, firm pastoral message was like a hot coal touched to a fuse, and the explosion was immediate." Fathers Jesús Baca and Antonio Otero immediately resigned over the pastoral orders and protested over their loss of parishes.[107]

Padre Martínez and several Río Arriba priests mailed letters of protest to Lamy seven months prior to the Algodones convention, lodging hard objection to Machebeuf. In Lamy's absence, they charged, the vicar general unlawfully assumed the bishop's Episcopal authority by confiscating parish funds. Machebeuf's sermons had only the intent of extracting tithes, it was alleged, with threats to withhold the sacraments from those who did not pay fully. The suspension of priests on publicly made allegations without due process and the usurping of church obventions violated Canon law, Martínez emphasized. The pastors defended their colleague Gallegos. It had been impossible for him to get permission to take his business trip, they explained, because the only church authority that could grant or deny it, Lamy himself, was gone at the time. Machebeuf was accused of celebrating Mass in certain private homes, a rite reserved only for bishops. He hated the New Mexico priests, they sensed. Most damning, it was alleged that Machebeuf broke the seal of the confessional by revealing on the altar the contents of certain parishioners' confessions. Martínez requested of Lamy what Machebeuf had denied the New Mexico priests: a formal proceeding to hear the charges against him. In proposing an ecclesiastical trial, the learned Martínez volunteered to act as prosecutor before the ultimate judge, Lamy. In longer correspondence, Martínez sought to disabuse the bishop of any false notions fed to him about the relation of the native priests to the 1847 Taos Revolt.[108]

Fathers Ortiz and Martínez sent a dispatch to the pope signed by a score of native Nuevomexicanos detailing charges against Lamy and his staff, chiefly the treatment of Gallegos. Gallegos too wrote to Pope Pius IX, condemning Lamy and Machebeuf for suspending priests sans observance of Canon law.[109] Important laymen got into the act. Tomás Cabeza de Baca—the Peña Blanca alcalde, former liberation conspirator against the Kearny invasion, member of the territorial assembly, and candidate for governor in 1849—joined Ambrosio Armijo in support of the complaints. Cabeza de Baca and the parishioners of Cochiti–Santo Domingo coordinated efforts with Gallegos to challenge Lamy's authority. Again the serious charge of publicly revealing confession was laid at Machebeuf's feet. The Armijo appeal demanded the return of Gallegos to his parish.[110]

Lamy responded to the resistance with a combination of resolve, leniency, and caution. He stiffened the sacramental fee requirements beyond those of the 1852 Christmas Pastoral. He reinstated most of the suspended priests (some of whom had repented). Gallegos was excluded, however, and the bishop told Armijo that his rehabilitation would be difficult.[111] Lamy reinforced the seriousness of the accusation that Machebeuf had revealed confession, as it could lead to a summons from Rome and possible defrocking. Rather than put his vicar general through a court hearing as Martínez proposed, Lamy demanded proof positive of the charge. Machebeuf admitted only to revealing information he had heard from sources other than the confessional.[112] Machebeuf wrote Martínez protesting his innocence.[113] In February 1853, six months before the Algodones convention, Baca replied to Lamy's demand for proof. He offered himself and three other instances as cases in point. He added other charges that went against the interests of parishioners. Lamy, viewing some Nuevomexicanos as outside the church pale and dispensable, ruled Cabeza de Baca's allegations not constituting "judicial" proofs. Cabeza de Baca was admonished to refrain from criticizing the bishop's office. He persisted in his demand that the current priest—his brother—be kept in Peña Blanca, and he asked for Machebeuf's removal for the sake of the people's religion. Lamy did not comply, and the priests continued in open opposition to him. Four signed a letter of objection at Easter, four months prior to the Mexican Democratic Convention, deeming any of Lamy's administrative acts "null."[114]

Father Gallegos returned from his six-month business sojourn to discover he had been suspended from the priesthood and deprived of his church. Ambrosio Armijo fired off another letter of protest to Lamy and organized 950 heads of family to forward letters of appeal for the return of Gallegos. They argued that Gallegos had acted within parish bounds by leaving Father Luján in charge. Armijo continued to levy specific allegations against Machebeuf, including the fact that he had named himself head of San Felipe Parish, yet, in being mostly absent, had left the people without spiritual care. When he did appear, he preached only the demand for tithes and revealed things he had heard in confession. The petitioners did not appreciate Machebeuf defaming Gallegos. They begged for "his Lordship to [give] their pastor back and to suspend Vicar Machebeuf instead!"[115] Lamy maintained that Gallegos had disobeyed orders in going to Durango. On the charges against Machebeuf, he would await proofs before taking action. He otherwise demanded that the petitioners submit themselves to ecclesiastical authority or face serious difficulties.[116]

Gallegos continued to defy the diocese with his open store, and he acted to take back his parish. In late spring 1853, three months before Algodones, he took up residence in the rectory in Machebeuf's absence. He planned to use the pulpit to challenge his suspension. Gallegos followers blocked Machebeuf from entering the church on Sunday. As Gallegos occupied the pulpit, Machebeuf, armed with a new copy of Gallegos's suspension, forced himself to the altar to refute all charges being made against him. Gallegos left the church, and Machebeuf proceeded to celebrate Mass. Gallegos organized his lay forces, most of them from Cabeza de Baca's county. Mobbing Machebeuf's residence, they demanded that he vacate the parish on a threat of "other measures" to be taken if he did not. Machebeuf resumed control of the San Felipe de Neri Parish with the support of certain Alburquerqueans.[117]

Gallegos gave up hope of ever being allowed to return to a practicing priesthood as he would never apologize to the House of Lamy for any allegation of misbehavior. As he phrased it, the bishop had deprived him of his living "to make way for imported French priests of his own selection."[118] The confrontation positioned Gallegos for Mexican Party leadership.

The New Mexico Democratic Convention, meanwhile, ordered the formation of a Central Democratic Party Committee and decided on Peña Blanca, upriver from Algodones, for its next territorial convention. Whether this was coincidental or intentional, Peña Blanca formed the bailiwick of Lamy's arch enemy, Tomás Cabeza de Baca.[119]

On Baird's motion, a committee of county delegates was named to meet with the governor and introduce to him the convention's platform, proceedings, and nomination.[120] That governor was David Meriwether, who arrived in Santa Fe to begin his term in the same week as the Algodones convention. Meriwether, appointed by President Pierce, knew New Mexico from previous experience. As a former army officer, he had been imprisoned in 1819 in the Palace of the Governors in Santa Fe on charges of being an American spy working the Spanish borderlands. He later became a member of the Kentucky General Assembly and was appointed U.S. senator from that state. Meriwether found to his surprise when he arrived in Santa Fe in 1853 "a great deal of hostile feeling existing between a portion of the American population and a part of the Mexicans." In his inaugural address as New Mexico governor, he offered the Epicurean counsel that if "we stayed true to ourselves, the day is not far distant when

New Mexico may claim her position as an equal in the glorious sisterhood of States composing the American Union."[121]

As a proven Democrat Meriwether had no reason not to validate the formalized Algodones Democratic Party and its nomination of Gallegos for delegate to Congress. He recalled Gallegos in his memoir as a "shrewd, intelligent man" who asked him about the principles of the Democratic Party. Gallegos confessed to knowing nothing about them. Meriwether explained the Democratic preference for the "strict construction" of the U.S. Constitution and the Whig Party's "more latitudinous construction." The Democrats would allow slave holders and those opposed to slavery to emigrate to the federal territories with their property, he explained to the Mexican politico, "and leave each territory to settle the question of slavery when it becomes a state." A majority of the Whig Party and a minority of the Democratic Party were in favor of excluding slavery from the territories "until they were admitted as states into the Union." The governor believed Gallegos to have understood well the differences in policy between the two national parties.[122]

Baird and Weightman campaigned for Gallegos on the national party standard of using a newspaper to broadcast its propaganda, deploying *El Amigo del País* in service of the Democratic Party. Significant for the party's identity, they added the subtitle *y la Voz del Pueblo* (and voice of the people). Facundo Pino served as the paper's Santa Fe agent, while Miguel E. Pino, technically a citizen of Mexico, managed the campaign sheet to reinforce the Mexican Party link.[123]

Santa Fe members of the American Party, who had moved a Democratic Party for New Mexico in the first place, were caught off guard by the Algodones convention, the nomination of Gallegos, and Meriwether's sanctioning of them. Eighteen Euroamerican settlers, calling themselves "true" Democrats, issued their "utter repudiation" of the Algodones "pseudo-convention." Less than two-thirds of the territory's counties were represented at Algodones, they chortled. Critics claimed that most of the delegates were "in reality, under the control, directly or indirectly" of Delegate Weightman. The Santa Fe County delegation in particular was "not deputed" by a majority of the county's Democrats, they continued. It was, rather, "foisted by a discontented and ambitious few, who utterly refused to assimilate with, or admit to even the privilege of debate in their meetings," a reference to the failed June meeting. The dissidents would use "honorable means" to defeat the election of the nominee of the "so-called [D]emocratic convention."[124]

The *Gazette* took the fracas from there. Long, colorful, and emotional broadsides served as both shaper and barometer of American Party opinion. Editor Collins boosted the "intelligent portion of Democrats" who "would have nothing to do with this silly" Algodones meeting. Disregarding his recent past as a Whig, he challenged the party credentials of the convention's Mexicans and their settler comrades for they appeared "unconscious of their democracy" before the election of Pierce. Collins hammered the idea of Gallegos lacking independence from the "self-serving agents" Baird, Weightman, and Pino. He inaccurately portrayed the convention as the work of a small faction aiming to send Baird, "the worst Indian Agent of New Mexico," or "some other man equally unworthy and unfit," to Congress. The "Baird faction" had not secured the nomination for its man, it was further denounced, but found and nominated "an individual fully as unfit for so exalted an office." The apoplectic editor cited the "deplorable fact" in New Mexico of "a feeling of dislike and distrust between the Mexicans and American races," but with the liberal disclaimer: "We esteem all good men alike, whether Mexican or American, irrespective of nationality." He claimed to oppose Father Gallegos for the same reason he had opposed Weightman, "and not because he is a Mexican born citizen." Collins hailed the majority Nuevomexicano populace, claiming that if two men were equally fit for the office, "one American and the other Mexican, we would prefer the Mexican, and would give him every aid in our power"[125] (if he were properly assimilated, it would become clear).

Collins packed the passions of religion into the campaign. If "a few obscure men who possessed the audacity to style themselves the 'true democracy' of New Mexico had determined to nominate a priest," he proclaimed, they could at least have "had the decency to select a good one in place of a bad one." Collins piled on old, exaggerated legends that had circulated for over a decade about New Mexico's corrupt priesthood. That the convention chose a priest suspended for the "grossness of his immorality" showed its disrespect to the bishop and the church, he put forth.[126] The separation of church and state, which Collins called "the genius and spirit of American institutions," would serve the Democratic Party and the people. The delegates ought to have known, Collins steamed, that there was "no connection in the United States between religion and politics. It is not possible for a clergyman of good character to get into the Congress of the United States; but if Padre Gallegos be elected, we think it will be the first instance in which a disgraced clergyman has ever been elevated to so important a position."[127]

Collins sermonized like an actual Whig who would object to the right of certain southern European foreigners to engage in American elections.[128] He would have cast Gallegos outside the constricted cultural or linguistic citizenship of the United States.[129] He cast doubt on Gallegos's eligibility to sit in Congress on the basis of length of citizenship (he understood the minimum to be seven years) and his inability to speak English. Gallegos, unlike the rico youth of the Río Abajo, was not educated in the United States prior to the conquest. Collins introduced what would become a long-term issue with regard to Gallegos's political career. As he put it here, Gallegos's lack of English would prevent him from "even the poor privilege of speaking non-sense" in Washington. Collins accused Gallegos of abusing the confidence of his constituents while in the territorial legislature by staying away from Santa Fe in favor of a "trafficking expedition to Durango in search of soap and *rebosos* [shawls]" to sell in New Mexico. Collins estimated Gallegos incapable of modernizing New Mexico and disabled from bringing home the railroad and other industries. He would leave the federally colonized New Mexicans "as we now are, perhaps the most miserable and unfortunate people on the wide dominions of the United States."[130]

The mudslinging did much to firm up the oppositional binary of a young territorial politics. The *Gazette* allowed "Some Friends of Mr. Gallegos," calling themselves "legally constituted delegates" of the Democratic convention, to publish a response to the "odious article" of insults thrown against their candidate. In the tradition of Mexican humility last seen in the opening of the anti-Calhoun tract two years before, they would not defend themselves against their own unfitness as public servants as imputed by Collins, but could not let the attack on Gallegos go unchallenged. Their leader "had always been one of the first men of the territory [*uno de los primeros hombres en el territorio*]"; he was "one of the most enthusiastic of citizens [*uno de lo mas entusiastas ciudadanos]*"; they themselves had "confidence in his full eligibility to serve in the national Congress [*nosotros tenemos la confianza de su eligibilidad para Delegado al Congresio nacional*]." Gallegos "eschewed pecuniary interest in favor of the happiness of their province." The partisans astutely observed that Gallegos had always lived the "views," if not the principles, of a "loyal Democrat [*las miras de un fiel Demócrata*]." He traveled to help provision communities in need, often to his own detriment. Collins erred "enormously," they affirmed, in calling Gallegos's intellect limited. He acquired "deep knowledge" in the sciences (training at the Durango seminary). But he also learned by the "pain of experience," and he knew more than anyone of the "sad position" of their province. If Congress found him ineligible based on time as an American citizen, why rush to express anxieties over his candidacy? The impromptu caucus did not wish to recall the actions of the bishop, but "as he made an offensive imputation against Mr. Gallegos, we cannot tolerate such an outrage so scandalous as it is little founded in right reason [*pero como se hace una imputación falta al señor Gallegos no nos es dado tolerar un ultrage tan escandaloso, como poco fundado en la recta razón*]." Bishop Lamy's hatred of New Mexico's native clergy led to the suspension of Gallegos, these Democratic novitiates emphasized, who nonetheless remained loyal to his ministry. Besides, who decided that a priest could not be a statesman? Who were "the people complaining of a priest in Congress? (*¿Quién es ese pueblo que se queja?*]" An educated priest like Gallegos was "always a political man and consummate Democrat [*Un Sacerdote instruido como el señor Gallegos es Siempre un hombre político y un consumado Demócrata*]," they noted in clear Mexican vocality. The group transposed the Mexican nationalistic stamp *Dios y Libertad* to their present liberal context. If, as their enemies charged, the people were but some jealous individuals, then "To God is the happiness of the territory owed, and to God also the liberal bases of the Democracy! [*Si el pueblo son unos cuantos envidiosos, ¡A Dios felicidad del Territorio, y a Dios también bases liberales de la Democracia!*]," a rich invocation not heard among Euroamericans in the public square at the time. They condemned Collins for seeking to hinder the united will of the people. They too relied on the rational voter to participate in the public forum, stating that election day would prove their point. The group had no patience for Mexican traitors, the few "corroborators of inequity, though of Mexican origin, trying to cast as evil that class of society that only labors for the future happiness of their territory [*corrobadores de la iniquidad, que siendo de origen Mejicanos procuran poner en mal aquella clase de la sociedad que solamente trabaja por la futura felicidad de su Territorio*]."[131]

The charge that Lamy had unjustly suspended Gallegos reignited Collins into another rash of liberal colonialism. The American Party editor was the first of several Catholic Irish-American journalists to make a home in nineteenth-century New Mexico. He developed an immediate affinity with Lamy and the bishop's project of reforming the Mexican church in New Mexico.[132] Collins defended Lamy's parochial primary school in Santa Fe at a time when Anglo settlers pressed for establishing secular style public schools.[133] He linked religious reform to the question of Nuevomexicano capacity for political independence, assuming the responsible settler-colonial's authority to discipline liberally recalcitrant Nuevomexicanos. The editor claimed longtime friendship with the people; he intended to evince it by "a candid and honest exposure of their faults, when in our opinion it can be productive of good." Nothing surprised him more than "intelligent Mexicans of this territory willing to sustain and uphold an immoral and probate priesthood." In Collins's American nationalism, the support of Gallegos represented the "greatest curse with which not only New Mexico, but the whole Republic of Mexico has had to contend." Assuming the voice of Lamy, he rehashed the old charge of religious exploitation, the priests living in "all the luxury of a life of wealth, obtained by grinding the poor."[134] Not only would a victory for Gallegos mean "a victory of vice over virtue," but "a victory of ignorance over reason," Collins claimed. Gallegos supporters were "trying the hopeless experiment of making a good politician out of an immoral Priest."[135]

Collins went on to accuse the Gallegos "Anti-Church party" of having seized the Algodones convention, itself formed by men he said had no legitimate claim on the Democratic Party. Collins stripped the Euroamericans of blame for the Algodones convention. It was Gallegos himself who conceived the "unholy idea of revenge" on the bishop, he proclaimed. Collins proved incapable of acknowledging Gallegos as an organic candidate of the conquered Mexicans. He struck out at the "audacity" of priests asking the people to vote for him. "[S]till more strange," the editor noted, "there are men amongst us who have the boldness to defend his conduct and to recommend him as worthy to receive the suffrages of the people for a seat in Congress."[136]

Gallegos probably saw the wisdom of refraining from a direct campaign against Lamy, although former vicar general and bitter Lamy opponent Juan Felipe Ortiz chimed in occasional support of his religious colleague.[137] Lamy denied any electioneering, but according to one historian who has examined his correspondence, he recommended to the clerics he trusted "that they work and influence the people to obtain the success of his favorites."[138] Angélico Chávez finds that Lamy's conversations with "intimate friends . . . no doubt reveal where their sympathies lay, and in this can carry the weight of active participation."[139]

Collins's unmitigated attacks had the primary purpose of agitating the base of the American Party to action. Activists on this side of the party binary came to realize the importance of nominating a culturally relevant candidate for Congress. Somewhat mysteriously, they eyed Ambrosio Armijo. Armijo had recently gone to the front in the community attempt to depose Vicar Machebeuf. Yet his appeal to the American Party lay in being a "native of New Mexico" and therefore "well-acquainted" with the "wants of the territory, and the habits and customs of her people." More important were Armijo's established American Party credentials. His family had sided with the Americans during the U.S. military occupation of New Mexico, and he was a successful Bernalillo County merchant and probate judge. Bernalillo County supporters flattered Armijo by assuring him of Mexican confidence in him and of his invincibility against Gallegos. They forecast that worthy candidates would yield to such an able, honest, and respected man as he. Armijo declined the courtship, citing family interests and the impatience of his nominators, who would not wait for the opinion of certain advisors he wanted to consult, although he could have had reservations about siding with Lamy in a political campaign. He recommended former governor William Lane as the candidate in his stead.[140]

American Party leaders turned to the political resources available on the national stage. As their enemy, the Mexican Party, had appropriated the Democratic Party label, American Partyites launched a People's Independent Party. The first People's Party, committed to "revolutionary republicanism," had arisen among dissident elites in the New York City election of 1823; it expanded to the legislative election; triumphed in the general election of 1824; and indirectly put John Quincy Adams in the White House over the Albany Regency's Martin Van Buren.[141] The party dissolved in late 1825, but the notion of a "People's Party" remained throughout the country as a self-labeling recourse for situational dissidence.[142]

Significantly, Nuevomexicanos formed the large majority of the "highly attended and respectable" People's Convention.[143] Together with Euroamerican settlers who served as both campaign drivers and teachers of party building, the Mexican showing assured a viable partisanship. These Nuevomexicanos too responded to the accoutrements of an American political party. Murray T. Tully (spelled Tuley in the Spanish reports), a former attorney general and staunch opponent of Facundo Pino in the territorial house, was elected president. Anastasio Barela and Santiago Gonzales served as vice presidents, Nestor Montoya and Miguel Antonio Lovato as secretaries. The proposal from the floor to establish a territorial party passed handily. Tully expressly appealed to the Mexican audience, proclaiming the fundamental principles of a people's initiative based on the "equality of rights of all men without distinction and the sovereignty of the people." A rules committee having a Mexican majority designated a day for the precincts to hold nominating conventions for local offices and territorial legislative positions, and it was given the charge of appointing a chairman for each precinct.

A nominating committee of twenty-one (rank and file Nuevomexicanos) would have preferred a Spanish-surnamed nominee for Congress, but none appeared suitable. The venerable Donaciano Vigíl had been the nativo American Party icon. The *Gazette* saw his previous election to the territorial house as a token of the fact that "the old prejudices and bickerings of faction fanned and kept alive by such designing men as Weightman" had "given place to a better judgment and sounder policy."[144] However, the saintly liberal kept true to his disavowal of advantage or personal notoriety in spite of his critical leadership in New Mexico's transition from Mexico to the United States.[145] Chairman Antonio Sandoval, a leader against former governor Calhoun, reported the recommendation of former governor "Guillermo" (William) Carr Lane. Amid "many Vivas of acclamation," the choice received unanimous adoption. Lane spoke to the territory's needs "enthusiastically." The erstwhile Whig Serafín Ramírez y Casanoba read Lane's speech in Spanish, again to cheers. The recommended candidates for territorial council, House, and sheriff of the Bernalillo–Santa Ana district were unanimously approved. Indicative of party building *à la Americaine*, one committee prepared an official statement of principles while another arranged correspondence, announcements, publicity, and other organizational details. Tully and Ramírez rallied the convention to its climax.[146]

The *Gazette* published Lane's speech in Spanish only, on the assumption, presumably, of Euroamericans easily accessing it. Lane was not with the individuals who fomented the original idea of a Democratic Party for the territory. His address consequently kicked off the people's liberalism in decidedly Whiggish form. New Mexico had always found itself in the unfortunate condition of an abandoned stepchild of Spain, Lane portrayed it, then Mexico, and now of the United States. Obtaining just rights and elevating its dignity were therefore to be accomplished by embarking on a strategically planned institutional development. He would make use of all "honorable means" as delegate in Congress to obtain resources for the development of the territory and to establish security for the livestock industry against Indian raiders.[147]

Lane returned to the theme of social consensus, which he pioneered in his first message to the legislature while governor, without, however, reconjuring New Mexico's Spanish heritage. He proclaimed that for "harmonious cooperation among the different races of this territory," no one who asserted hostile national feelings deserved respect or confidence. "Turn your back with indignation and scorn to all who attempt to excite national antipathies," he ordered, "and may the citizens of the territory, natives or adopted, solidly unify, as members of the same grand and glorious political family, and participate equally in the well-being of the family of the province." Lane further prayed the people in assimilationist evangelism to reserve a civic pride in the "Divine Providence" that had made them citizens of the United States. They would follow in the steps of the residents of Louisiana, Florida, Texas, California, and Oregon, who saw rapid wealth and power in their territories, he foresaw. In their elections, he said in decided meritocratic throttle, it was not asked, "'Where were you born?'

The only inquiry that was made was, 'is he right for the position?'" The politicians who eschewed liberalism were "indiscrete" *caudillos* (Latin American bosses) preventing the people from thinking for themselves. Reject them, Lane pleaded, and "then we shall travel well and our *patria* will prosper."[148]

Collins at the *Gazette* took Lane's implicit meaning to project Gallegos's candidacy as a ploy to foment national prejudice. The "sad truth," the American Party militant wrote, was that "the Mexicans hate the Americans and many Americans hate the Mexicans," but "this unnatural and fatal antipathy is not indulged by the better and more intelligent classes." Collins too adopted a Whiggish elitism familiar to him. He called on all "to work harmoniously together in the same direction. If the different races of men in New Mexico will but consent, as becomes intelligent beings, to lay aside their bitter prejudices, and consult the dictates of reason and common sense, they will soon perceive that their happiness and prosperity will be augmented, and that their country will blossom like the rose."[149] Tapping into the Whig preoccupation with the wholesome "social system," Collins called for the "united efforts of "a few good men" to diminish sensibly "the crying evil of which we are speaking, and introduce a state of social intercourse, such as becomes a respectable and well ordered community."[150] Collins feared racialized voting booths; votes going against Lane because he was an "American-born citizen"; and that if Gallegos were elected, it would be only "because he is a Mexican born citizen; and not because he possesses one single qualification for the office to which he aspires."[151]

In the campaign Senator Benton condemned Lane for having switched to the Whig Party while in Missouri. Benton thus strengthened the territorial process of building a party system and gave New Mexico Democrats some national recognition and credibility by urging the electorate to vote for Gallegos.[152]

Weightman, Baird, and chief clerk of the territorial house David Whiting (former governor Calhoun's son-in-law) set up a campaign weekly called *Campaña Demócrata*. No copies of that campaign sheet survive. Collins called *Campaña Demócrata*'s commentary a "mass of cunning falsehood and baseness." Yet his responses in the *Gazette* reveal that its editors shrewdly criticized Collins, on the one hand, for endorsing Armijo, and, on the other, for criticizing Gallegos for not being an American citizen long enough to qualify for the office of delegate. Collins yielded the point that Congress would have to determine Armijo's eligibility as well. Reflecting a particular air of sympathy for the South starting to blow into the territory's politics, *Campaña Demócrata* discredited the *Gazette* by calling it an "abolition sheet." Collins took pains to deny the epithet. The previous *Gazette* editor Kephart had articulated an abolitionist policy, but Collins boasted of having emphatically repudiated it on taking control of the paper. *Campaña Demócrata* recognized national conflicts, imputing that Collins and company had belonged to the American nativist party the Know-Nothings. Collins found this allegation galling even if it was commonly hurled onto Whigs. He scoffed at *Campaña Demócrata*'s claim that Gallegos would deliver a "glorious future" for New Mexico.[153]

An important Mexican Democratic Party rally took place in Santa Fe. Gallegos expounded on the principles of the Democratic Party. Governor Meriwether recalled that he had done so "with cleverness," his speech making "a very favorable impression upon the audience."[154] The governor abstained from participating in the proceedings, but those who had wanted him to eschew a Mexican Party association interpreted his attendance as an official endorsement of the Mexican Democratic Party. The stump crowd spilled out into the street. The *Gazette*'s wildly biased account four years later portrayed "an infuriated mob of those disaffected Mexicans . . . parading the streets of our city on a Sunday night led by a drunken fiddler crying 'death to all Americans.'"[155] The *Gazette*, incredibly, had Meriwether and recently appointed district judge J. J. Deavenport heading the "mob." Meriwether and Deavenport were hanged in effigy on the Santa Fe Plaza the next day, so starkly was the dual partisanship becoming. Collins paid a visit to the governor to warn him of talk of his assassination should he attend another Democratic meeting. Meriwether recalled different reasons for the symbolic hanging—for one, his dismissal of a Whig attorney general for corruption, and for another, the excitement Gallegos's speech provoked among the people of Santa Fe, which "greatly exasperated" the Whigs. Mexican Democratic Party leaders expressed gratitude for Meriwether's support of their organization.[156]

In spite of the *Gazette*'s attempt to engender a reputation for Gallegos as incompetent for the post of delegate to Congress, the Democratic Party effectively moved the electorate. Lane at first thought things going his way while on tour of the northern district. As the campaign wore on he wrote to his wife that it appeared the Mexicans were "determined to elect one of their own race—God bless them." He was the most acceptable of the "Americans," he was told, but "they must try a Mexican." Lane never really embraced or became close to nativos. He betrayed his role as a culturally patronizing liberal, adding the comment to his wife, "If you knew how very little the very best informed know, you would be amazed at their conceitedness."[157]

The task of vote counting fell to Governor Meriwether and the new territorial secretary William Messervy. The former favored Gallegos, the latter backed Lane. The Lane camp tried holding up the governor's awarding of the election certificate to Gallegos because a probate judge had thrown out 200–300 votes at a Pueblo village that had gone for Lane. Messervy, in with the American Party's claim that the Pueblos were citizens, claimed that all votes were bound to be counted. Meriwether handed the certificate to Gallegos based on the count that showed him with the majority by at least 300, the Indian count included. Lane announced his intent to contest the election on allegations that Mexicans who were not U.S. citizens had voted for Gallegos and based on irregularities in the ballot counting.[158] Coming to the support of Lane, Collins charged the "Gallegos Anti-Church party" with having "perpetrated the most stupendous frauds."[159] The "christening" of "Padre Gallegos" as a Democrat at Algodones was "a mere cover and device to enable him and his friends to succeed more effectually in the contest they were about to wage against the Americans."[160]

Collins further alleged that Lane was deprived of a thousand votes. False ballots allowed people to vote in more than one precinct, he claimed. Citizens of Mexico had voted for Gallegos out of "national antipathy." Collins called the citizens of Mexico "influential gentlemen" who had induced underage youth to vote. "Would it not be more praiseworthy in them to set a better example before their young countrymen, by teaching them to abstain from such depravity?" Whether the charge was true or not, Collins moved himself to a racialized essentialism: "Until they do this there must always remain a reproach upon the Mexican character."[161]

Gallegos arrived in Washington in December 1853. He was introduced through Meriwether's letters to the national Democratic Party leadership.[162] The House of Representatives formally recognized the

Democratic Party in New Mexico. Gallegos was affiliated with the "Old Line Democrats," the main faction in the Democratic Party distinct from the officially designated Independent Democrats and Whigs.[163]

The *Gazette* published Gallegos's letter to the governor. The new editor, William Watts Hart Davis, who also served as New Mexico's new U.S. attorney and Meriwether's private secretary, recommended that "all Mexicans" read it. Gallegos recounted the success of Meriwether's introductions. The president and cabinet ministers received him "with consideration and appreciation," and he was recognized by "many friends" in the House with whom he had corresponded. Gallegos urbanely praised the eastern states' progress in "the arts and sciences." He was impressed by how "providence" had blessed the country with particular political "gifts." He cited as an example a sense of mutual agreement on the country's fundamental values and ways of conducting party politics. In commenting that New Mexico would benefit from such habits and characteristics, Gallegos represented the greater impulse among nonassimilated Nuevomexicanos to learn from and adapt U.S. political practice. Mindful of the factional volatility at home and identifying himself with the American nation, he claimed to observe a "contrast" in the moral conduct and politics "that guard our compatriots in these parts compared to what some Americans observe in our territory, and I'm surprised to note an extraordinary difference, as between darkness and light. I hope that with time we can come to the enjoyment of a peaceful and intelligent society [*He observado el contraste de la conducta moral y política que guardan nuestros compatriotas en estos mundos respecto a la que observan algunos americanos en nuestro Territorio, y con sorpresa distingo una extraordinaria diferencia tal como de las tinieblas a la luz; ojalá que con el tiempo recibimos los goces que brinde una soeciedad pacífica é inteligente*]."[164]

The House Committee on Elections found the votes at Taos and Laguna pueblos rightfully and legally rejected by the probate judge. The Indians at those pueblos retained their autonomous tribal, community, and governing characteristics, the Committee established. Lane's camp never submitted proof that citizens of Mexico were allowed to vote in any precinct. Even if all contested votes had been excluded, Gallegos would have retained a majority. On the charge of "gross fraud" in the vote count, the committee recognized the status of a conquered territory struggling on behalf of its political integration. A "very great irregularity" had occurred in the returns, it affirmed, but no more than might be expected "under all the circumstances." The government there had been "but recently organized; the people are not accustomed to the precision and accuracy of our election forms; they do not understand our language or our system of laws." Allowance could "very properly be made for the want of strict compliance, in every minute particular, with the complex requirements of the territorial election forms." The final tally had Gallegos's majority at more than six hundred. The concurring House awarded Gallegos New Mexico's delegate seat in Congress.[165]

Gallegos serves as a significant symbol for the cause of ethnic political integration in the nineteenth century. He was the first Nuevomexicano and American Latino to serve as a representative in the U.S. Congress. His request for an interpreter was denied, and his lack of English proved a handicap in the Capitol corridors. Nevertheless, it was a reproach to those with racial prejudices who considered the Nuevomexicanos incapable of meeting American political standards that he used prepared statements to deliver benefits to his homeland. He accomplished as much as any early New Mexico delegate to Congress could hope for.[166] Motivated by a love of his native land and a desire to serve his people, Gallegos was called a "man of ability" by a Washington insider.[167]

Collins quit as editor of the *Gazette* after the election, though he continued to own it, and removed to the Washington DC area. In his adieu column he returned to Epicurean ethics, specifically the theme of happiness and its pursuit, which was consecrated in the Declaration of Independence as the foundational virtue in the world.[168] He told the Mexicans that if they expected to see their people happy and the territory prosperous, "they must be true to themselves." He assumed that they naturally desired assimilation. Lay your "national prejudices" aside, he requested in spirit of classic American assimilation, and "act as becomes American citizens; give a hearty and honest support to the government." They should also regard "all those who attempt a factious opposition to it as enemies to yourselves and the Territory; determine to respect yourselves and you will secure the respect of the Government of the United States."[169]

The solidity of a Democratic Party for New Mexico appeared beyond the race for congressional delegate. The majorities in both legislative chambers were elected as members of the Algodones convention. Davis at the *Gazette* accordingly saw the election results as something of which the Democrats could be proud, the "overthrow" of the "Whig clique."[170]

CHAPTER SIX

American Democratic Party, 1854–1859

In July 1854 W. W. H. Davis, the new editor of the *Santa Fe Weekly Gazette* and the New Mexico territorial secretary, contemplated the next general election. It was more than a year away, yet Davis alerted New Mexico citizens of the necessity of having an organized Democratic Party "as in any part of the Union." He noted the indispensability of political parties "in a country where the people rule themselves, and make their own laws." Taking "the people" to be rational in choosing their party, he mentioned the "common opinion" that the "masses" in New Mexico were "in feelings" essentially Democratic because the party's doctrines kept "with our republican institutions" and was "best adapted to promote the prosperity, and secure the political rights of the country." Davis exhorted the counties to assemble in convention to begin nominating "good and reliable men" and to take special care that the best qualified Democrat be selected for delegate to Congress.[1]

Davis fretted as the Algodones Democratic Party structure slipped after the 1853 election. The appointed central committee did not hold to develop a permanent organization for the territory. *El Amigo del País* closed down for want of subscribers.[2] The key backer, Richard Weightman, shot and killed a prominent merchant in a bar over a story in *El Amigo del País* that the victim claimed defamed him. Weightman was acquitted, but he left New Mexico for good.[3]

Mexican Democratic Party members remained in the territorial assembly at least, but Davis himself ran into trouble when he opposed certain laws of theirs that he said were hostile to American institutions. He entangled himself in a messy patronage battle with *El Amigo del País* over the legislative contract for printing session documents. Davis questioned whether Facundo Pino, David Whiting, and Baird knew what it meant to be a Democrat.[4] Yet Davis worked for a Democratic administration and governor. When he spoke of developing the territory's Democratic Party, he meant that it should stay out of the hands of the American Party. Davis sustained territorial partisanship by demonizing the American Party as a nest of mad Whigs or Whigs in disguise. The Whig presence seemed real enough. In the legislative assembly of 1853–54, Bernalillo County Representative José Serafín Ramírez y Casanoba castigated Algodones Democrats for their devotion to "false parties of personal views" and "private interests." Ramírez called for a Whiggish harmony among his colleagues that would "tend to the common good."[5]

The Algodones Democratic Convention decreed Peña Blanca as the place for its 1855 convention. The preparatory county conventions that Davis called for would have met, as would those of the opposing party. Unfortunately, the press coverage of the 1855 canvass is unavailable.[6] Important traces of the campaign appear in reports after the election. Davis himself served as president of the established Democratic nominating convention, and José Manuel Gallegos was renominated for delegate to Congress.[7] As for the opponents, Miguel Antonio Otero's moment arrived. After the Algodones Democrats denied Otero his seat in the territorial legislature, Governor William Lane appointed him New Mexico attorney general. In 1855 the American Party nominated him to run against Gallegos. To Euroamerican assimilationists, the polished, well-appointed "gentleman native" glistened as the ideal Nuevomexicano leader.[8] Otero claimed membership in the Democratic Party.[9] One report notes the Otero campaign challenging Gallegos's Democratic credential.[10] Not known is whether Otero ran as an alternative Democrat or as a People's Party candidate. Anyway, this race for delegate would be the first among a majority of elections for that office in the next three decades to pit a Nuevomexicano against a Nuevomexicano.

Religion remained in political balance. A certain Father Benigno Cárdenas advised the people in a letter to the *Gazette* from London, of all places, not to vote for Gallegos. According to Cárdenas, it would deny the bishop's progressive reforms and efforts to relieve the people from the "oppressive" exactions "levied solely to maintain a corrupt and profligate Clergy."[11]

Late press reports indicate a heated contest for delegate. Otero's camp perceived Gallegos people intending to steal votes. A band of Otero supporters accosted the clerk of Río Arriba County, the former Weightman partner Elias T. Clark, as he horsebacked to submit his

FIG. 15. *Miguel Antonio Otero I*. Otero was the second Nuevomexicano and Latino American to be elected to Congress. A lifelong American Party member, he became one of three Nuevomexicanos to build political machines in territorial New Mexico. Courtesy Palace of the Governors Photo Archives, NMHM/DCA, negative #152218.

county's poll books to the territorial secretary. The hijackers confiscated Clark's books, sure that they recorded a majority for Gallegos, and they believed that the Valencia County probate judge, a friend of Gallegos, had not counted the votes for Otero, nor submitted the poll book with its proof of a large majority for Otero. The Otero posse claimed the citizen's right to know of the disposition of the books and to hold the Río Arriba records until the Valencia County results came in. When apprehended by the sheriff, they surrendered the Río Arriba books but only after the Valencia County records arrived.[12] Davis accused the Oteroites of perpetrating a fraud on the voters. An Otero lawyer called Davis corrupt if he, as territorial secretary, would issue Gallegos a certificate of election without the whole poll count.[13]

Information on stump and election-day dynamics goes lacking, but it is known that Gallegos took the election by an extremely close 99 votes out of 13,729 cast. Gallegos ran very strong in the counties of the Río Arriba and got whipped in the Río Abajo district where the Otero family shared in the dominance of the rico families. Governor David Meriwether and Secretary Davis, both Democrats, certified the election on September 18, 1855.[14]

Partisan juices flowed from Otero's intent to contest the election. Taos district judge Perry E. Brocchus rose to the support of the American Party. The remarks Brocchus made at a dinner to honor his impending trip to the states to be with his ailing wife illustrate the importance of the public keynoter for American settlers to consolidate politically on the frontier. His proud assault on Governor Meriwether and the Mexican Democratic Party fed pieces of political interpretation to the consumptive needs of the American Party base.

Brocchus started in on Elias Clark, the Mexican Democratic Party man whom Otero henchmen had accosted on election day. Brocchus had earlier fired Clark as his clerk on charges of dereliction of duty. Brocchus noted in his speech that Meriwether had just hired Clark to work for the New Mexico Supreme Court. The judge read from the angry letter he had fired off to Meriwether for not having been consulted on the hiring of Clark. Brocchus felt it reflected on his own professional integrity that the governor did not respond to his letter. Clark later claimed Brocchus never told him why he had been fired, implying that it was because of his party affiliation.

Brocchus blasted Meriwether for associating with the Mexican

Democratic Party, and he enlarged his assignment of the "reckless" administration with an imperial modernizer's view of backward Mexicans. It was "peculiarly proper" for federal officers to be "delicately scrupulous" in the discharge of their official obligations, given this territory's population, Brocchus charged, "ignorant" as it was of the American language, with minds "yet to be enlightened as to the principles of our government, and whose affections are yet to be won by a consciousness of the beauty, the majesty, and the value of our political institutions." Brocchus inadvertently confirmed Mexican resistance to American overseers. "With an eye of suspicious jealousy," he had it, "these people strictly mark our official misdeeds, when committed, and although they may remain silent, they nevertheless keep those marks indelibly recorded against us and the government of which we are the representatives and agents." It was a "natural consequence of the state of things existing on this theatre of our duty." The oppositional attitude in this foreign theater could only be counteracted and suppressed, Brocchus proposed, "by the most scrupulous and unwearying fidelity on the part of those who are clothed with official authority." Brocchus questioned how far the "mind" of the governor had been "imbued" with corruption while seeking to maintain the laws and promote the public welfare.

On the issue of party identifications, Brocchus revealed the hegemony of the Democratic Party by wanting to refute those who "whispered in the dark" that he was a Whig in disguise. "If the author [of the rumor] had manliness to avow himself," Brocchus swore, "I would brand him as an unmitigated liar." The only reason for anyone to suspect the "soundness" of his Democracy was that he had never been "a brawling member of what a few officious persons have chosen to set up as the great [D]emocratic [P]arty of New Mexico." It was because he obeyed a sense of "propriety and justice" that Brocchus had withheld his sympathies for Gallegos in the last campaign. If this be the test of his Democracy, he feared not the "shame of the verdict."

Brocchus kept to the American Party concern for the proper assimilation of Mexicans, and for this, Miguel A. Otero appeared the finest specimen. In him Brocchus had a local with the "very highest character," one who revered New Mexico as "an enlightened and efficient representative of her interests," a "native" who had passed several years in the United States, had become "liberally educated" by "one of the most eminent lawyers of the West," one who had acquired "an intelligent view" of American political institutions "and the character of the American people," who spoke English "with strict propriety and graceful fluency," being "in all respects a gentleman" and a Democrat besides who knew what democracy meant. The tawdry example of Otero's opponent carried less value for Americanization. Gallegos went to Washington as delegate "with his lips sealed and his ears stopped: for he can neither speak, or comprehend when spoken the language of the body in whose deliberations he goes to participate." What Gallegos might accomplish came from the sympathy of congressmen who were charged with obligations from their constituents "to leave but little room for the dispensation of charities to helpless delegates." By sending an enlightened Mexican, Brocchus intoned, "who speaks well our language and perfectly his own, a channel of intelligence would be opened between our Mexican fellow citizens and the government and people of the United States, through which their minds would rapidly become enlightened in reference to the great and liberal principles which characterize the national institutions of their new sovereign. Such considerations should have influenced the mind of every man who had in view the welfare of this territory."

Brocchus adopted James Collins's model of the liberal colonizer: speak kindly of native Mexicans, but express firmness with them when necessary for their own good. He pledged his heart to New Mexico and her prosperity, her "moral and intellectual elevation—with the brightness of her future. She is part of my country," he avowed in the vein of the Statehood Revolution, "and a large majority of her people are my fellow citizens." He cleaved to the "great mass of the native people," but it pained him to have to disown the many who claimed and exercised the rights and privileges of citizenship "yet did not legitimately possess them." It saddened him to see the men who had remained citizens of Mexico yet filled the offices of sheriff, alcalde, prefect, and territorial legislator. Brocchus saw some of them keeping allegiance to their former sovereign out of affection for their native institutions and others refusing U.S. citizenship "in a spirit of bitter hostility to Americans and American institutions." In their bosoms "still rankles that sentiment of bitterness while for purposes of profit and self-aggrandizement, they become zealous actors on the theatre of your elections and voracious seekers after the emoluments and honors of office."

The judge stipulated the Democratic Party's naturalization policy. "God forbid," he commenced, "that there should arise in my bosom a sentiment of hostility to that high and holy purpose of the wise and illustrious sages of the revolution.

No: let them come. From the land of poverty, let them come to this land of plenty. From the lands of famine, let them fly to our fertile fields. From the clime of oppression's might, let them fly to this of freedom's glorious day. Here let them worship God according to the dictates of their conscience and peacefully enjoy the rights which that God has given them. Here let them acquire and enjoy the high privileges and immunities that appertain to an American citizen; but let that acquirement and that enjoyment only follow a strict conformity to the naturalization laws of the United States.

Brocchus did not extend this integrative generosity to the citizens of Mexico in New Mexico. Echoing the American norm of Donaciano Vigil he wondered by "what unmitigated force" should naturalization laws be automatically applied to those who "when the fruit was tendered, spurned it—when the prize was offered, trampled it beneath their feet. With how much more scrupulous rectitude should we bind to the requirements of law the men who by their own free will and affirmative act, declared that they would not be citizens of the United States?"

Brocchus's firm American nationalism shamed the men who had sworn fealty to Mexico only to make themselves "de facto citizens" by the "usurpation and wrongful exercise of the right of suffrage, the right of holding office, and the prerogatives characteristic of citizenship" in violation of the Treaty of Guadalupe Hidalgo, the 1850 Organic Law, and an 1853 ruling of the New Mexico Supreme Court (*Quintana v. Thompkins*) stipulating that the New Mexicans who retained Mexican citizenship were aliens and prohibited from voting and holding public office. Brocchus condemned Meriwether's twice commissioning as the alcalde of Santa Fe County the very individual who had lost in that decision of the Supreme Court. It was "an unlawful usurpation of privilege," adding to his "seeming contempt of the will and the laws of the people of New Mexico." The governor faithlessly disregarded the authority of the country's highest judicial tribunal, Brocchus charged on, "whose province and whose duty is to give interpretation to all laws in regard to which questions of construction may arise, and whose interpretation, when duly given, becomes the supreme law of the territory." He feared for the future of New Mexico's liberty under this nullification of the law by federal officers. Soon, he hoped in a proud operatic finale—"may there burst upon the shades of mental darkness which overspread this land, a flood of light as brilliant as the beams with which kind heaven illumes its deepest vallies and crowns its highest peaks! And that we all may gather here again to greet the coming of that light is the fervent aspiration of this heart, whose full emotions leave me nothing more to utter, than the plaintive word, farewell!"[15]

The *Gazette*'s publicizing of the speech elevated Brocchus to heroic American Party proportion, but the editor of a Texas newspaper saw his performative attack on the governor as opposition to the Democratic Party itself.[16] Meriwether asked Secretary Davis to investigate the charges Brocchus levied against Clark. Davis, a Meriwether partisan, found them without warrant. In response to the issue of Mexicans participating in government, Davis advised that he considered *Quintana v. Thompkins* to have been overturned by a subsequent district court ruling. The governor's willingness to work with Nuevomexicanos who had remained citizens of Mexico was therefore lawful and proper, Davis concluded. He grimaced at the "odium" of a judge turning a dinner party into a political meeting, Brocchus's "treachery" to the Democratic Party being "well understood."[17]

The majority of the territorial council and house (led by the Mexican Party men Tomás Cabeza de Baca, House Speaker Facundo Pino, Miguel Pino, and Cándido Ortiz) put out a public declaration of support for the governor. The joint resolution, signed by Acting Governor Davis, petitioned the president for the removal of Brocchus as a judge on allegations that he did not live in the district of his court, causing the people to suffer injustice and inconvenience and seriously retarding the administration of justice. They complained as well of the delay in the business of the Supreme Court to be caused by Brocchus's departure to the United States.[18]

The binaried discourse widened with two anti-legislature protests. American Party Euroamericans in Santa Fe deplored the "pain and indignation" being cast on Brocchus, one of the territory's worthy citizens, as he was called, "alike upright in the walks of social life, [and] an ornament to the bench of which he is a member." The gathering deemed it unfair that the judge was not allowed to respond to the charges. The assembly's right to interfere with executive appointments was questioned, and confidence expressed that President Franklin Pierce would rebuke its action for risking the "ultimate disorganization" of the territorial government.[19]

That Brocchus had Mexican friends in Taos County was made clear by the self-described "great convergence of the principal citizens" in the plaza of Los Luceros. The gathering looked on the assembly's anti-Brocchus memorial with "great indignation." The members' "odious procedures [*procederes odiosos*]" made the "malicious and false" charge of Brocchus not living in the county. The offenders "crowned their stupidity," it was charged, by "foolishly demonstrating their perfect corruption in sending to the president of the United States a memorial falsely claiming that the Hon. Judge of this district had failed in the discharge of his high duties [*para coronar su estupidez, nuestros Legisladores han demostrado neciamente su perfecta corrupción en dirigir al Presidente de los Estados Unidos un memorial pretendiendo falsamente que el Hon. Juez de este Distrito había faltado en su alto empleo al fiel desempeño*]." Taoseños took offense at the "great undemocratic [*demasiado indemocrático*]" lack of representational republicanism in the failure of the assemblymen to consult with the residents of the county on the validity of the calumnies against a man "eminently qualified for the position that he now occupies, as much for his private virtues as his dignity, open-handedness and legality with which he has discharged his duties while living among us."

One speaker saw the legislative memorial having been instigated by some "schemer" who desired Brocchus's post. Another noted that many of the legislators took part in the "ill-fated" memorial out of ignorance, not necessarily bad faith. Anger was vented on all but one of the Taos County delegation, the rest having all been party to the memorial. The ten-member Committee on Resolutions called on them to resign from the assembly. The unanimously adopted resolutions went to the president of the United States.[20] Nuevomexicanos were picking up on the finessing of American partisanship, and it was for this reason that they refrained from universal condemnation of the xenophobic suggestions in the Brocchus speech; such restraint was remarkable in Taos County, known for its rabble-rousing pride (Revolt of 1837) and tradition of opposing foreigners (assassination of Governor Charles Bent). That Brocchus presided over a well-functioning court may have been an important factor. It is highly significant from the standpoint of a developing partisanship that the Taos meeting was chaired by don Diego Archuleta. The Río Arriba warhorse who entered the United States as Mexican Partyite surprisingly joined the attack on former governor James Calhoun, switching then to participate in the Algodones Democratic convention.

The importance of Brocchus for Archuleta was that the judge stood as an enemy of his own enemy. Archuleta at the time served as an Indian subagent for the Abiquiú district, an appointment made possible by the endorsement of the Mexican Party leader Delegate Richard Weightman. Concurrently, New Mexico governors served as the superintendent of Indian affairs. Territorial Indian policy was one of the most important of their responsibilities.[21] Congress and the president gave Meriwether special approval and resources to negotiate treaties with tribes at moments of war in his jurisdiction and to grant rights of occupancy to their lands. The policy failed, however, to curb Jicarilla and Ute raiding and the killing of settled Mexicans and Pueblos in the Taos region. The policy caused the withdrawal of troops and the return of violence when chiefs broke the treaty. Archuleta led Río Arriba citizens and some in the Río Abajo to oppose Meriwether's practice of signing treaties without consulting them.[22] The position aligned with the American Party's critique of Meriwether's treaty signing, particularly with the Apaches. As James Collins argued, the governor should have known better, given the tribe's history of destroying white men's "estates" throughout the northern reaches of Mexico with their unending ravages.[23]

Brocchus returned to Santa Fe in May to a triumphant welcome at the Exchange Hotel. The main speaker said his praise of the judge was guided "by no party or political considerations" but rather by "the warm, devoted, disinterested and affectionate regard for a friend, just returned to our midst." Brocchus thanked those who had "lifted" their voices in his defense when "malevolence and falsehood" had "assailed" him.[24]

New Mexico partisanship spiked higher when the legislative assembly moved on Bishop Lamy. Mexican Democratic Partyites and Acting Governor Davis mailed a condemnation of Lamy to the Pope, pointing to his abuse of power, his intervention in elections, and his crusade to oust nativo priests. Because Lamy favored Protestants over Catholics, the petition further charged, his holiness should replace the bishop with former New Mexico vicar Juan Felipe Ortiz. Included in the packet were copies of the charges the padres had previously leveled against Vicar Machebeuf, descriptions of three community defenses of them, and Lamy's Christmas circular. Delegate Gallegos was not mentioned as a sender, perhaps because his brother was at the time in the assembly. Nevertheless, Gallegos compiled the documents, inserted a cover letter, and mailed them to the Vatican from Washington.[25]

Angélico Chávez concludes that Gallegos orchestrated the mail-in and authored the letter. Lamy understood that the legislators' petition had been "under the sponsorship" of Juan Felipe Ortiz and Gallegos. Gallegos, for his part, conveyed that it was his constituents who demanded that he transmit the information to Rome, and he voiced objection to Lamy's removal of the Mexican priests, relegating them to poverty and leaving the people without spiritual sustenance. Machebeuf was forced to the Vatican for a formal defense of the charge that he had violated the confessional. Parallel to Brocchus's view of Mexicans as ignorant of American political practice, Lamy denounced to the Propaganda Fide in Rome and his superior in Cincinnati the scandalous behavior of the Mexican people, not just the clerics. He characterized their elected representatives as Catholics in name only and brayed about the "crassly ignorant and unlettered politicians who were under the dire influence of the more wicked native clergy—especially ex vicar Ortiz before whom they trembled!" He charged the "corrupt" priests with rebellion following the Christmas Pastoral. Machebeuf reiterated these charges at the Vatican and cited delegate Gallegos's "scandalous" image, the reason Lamy had suspended him.[26]

Otero filed his notice of intent to contest the election. Lawyers for each candidate took testimony to establish their cases from a four-score of individuals in November and December.[27] Otero lawyers alleged in the U.S. House Committee on Elections over a thousand ineligible citizens of Mexico voting for Gallegos; unsworn poll judges in Doña Ana and Río Arriba counties; judges including a certain priest conspiring to deny Otero his rightful share of votes; confiscated poll books containing registered votes for Otero; violation of the secret ballot; and judges illegally receiving votes after sundown.[28] The committee agreed that serious fraud had been committed and concluded that Otero had won by 290 votes. It recommended to the general House that he be declared New Mexico's delegate to Congress.[29]

Gallegos argued in his appeal that the fraud committed by Otero partisans was greater than that in support of the incumbent and that even if the votes of Mexican citizens and of the precincts where fraud allegedly took place on his behalf were discarded, Gallegos would still have the majority of legal votes. Still, Gallegos held, it was not proved that citizens of Mexico had voted. Witnesses may have testified that they registered individuals reputed to have declared their Mexican citizenship in 1849, but it was not demonstrated that they were the ones with the same names who voted in the election. The Gallegos team made the point that witnesses said they had not seen Mexican citizens voting. It held that any declarations of Mexican citizenship were invalid because Congress had not officially recognized them, nor was it proven that the appropriate military commander had ratified them. Gallegos claimed a majority of 149, discounting 578 illegal Otero votes.[30]

The House allowed the unusual procedure of each candidate having his personal statement read on the floor. The ensuing face-off featured two iconic figures coming from a segmented regional heritage with contrasting cultural profiles and identities, practically encoded now in party partisanship, and each claiming to be the true representative of Nuevomexicanos.[31] The theorist of nationalism Anthony Smith observes that native elements coming under the influence of an expansionist nationalism in the nineteenth century assumed one of three types: the pure assimilationist (merging into the dominant cultural strain); the traditionalist (denying the value and power of the scientific state, choosing to remain within the authority of the ethnic past); and the dual legitimist (neophytes accepting the scientific state but remaining traditional in defense of the native culture from intrusive modern institutions).[32]

Georgia Representative A. H. Stephens agreed to read Gallegos's statement, which cast the Mexican Party candidate in the role of dual legitimist. The preamble submitted a poignant appeal of ethnoracial colonialism. Gallegos expressed his "painful disappointment" at the "sneers and jests" with which certain House members had treated the representation of his case by counsel because of his inability to make a "formal discourse" in English "such as would be becoming the dignity" of the House. He acknowledged the respect, kindness, justice, and moderation given him in Washington but linked the language issue to his "extraordinary and anomalous" position. He and his conquered people had "peculiar demands" upon American justice and magnanimity. The Nuevomexicanos were "in their origin, alien to your institutions," as Gallegos told it, "your laws, your customs, your glorious history, and even strangers to your language."

Gallegos staked a claim on his homeland's cultural authenticity in relation to the "native" folk in the "very soil" of New Mexico. "I am," he said, "and have ever been one of that very people. They have chosen me as their representative, and I am not ashamed of whatsoever is common to them and to me. As I am their true representative under the laws, so I claim to be their true type in all that has been the subject of sarcasm and ridicule in the debates which have followed the report of the Committee of Elections, and I receive it all as the representative of my people." That Gallegos had an organic place in the heart of New Mexico meant that the insults flung at him pierced Nuevomexicanos as well.

Gallegos framed an inevitable cultural crisis among Nuevomexicanos. House members themselves would have made "quite as sorry a figure" as he in a like situation. Yet he would not "moot" any question as to the power of the United States to incorporate New Mexico. Gallegos denied any possibility of irredentist rebellion even on the forced annexation of his people. Though "a foreign territory, with all its inhabitants," he emphasized, the New Mexican soil was "American, and the people American. These things were practically settled long ago." Gallegos affirmed, based on the pragmatic legitimation of U.S. power and on the United States as culturally diverse, that no language issue obtained in his candidacy. Refracting nativo class and regional distinctions through the Treaty of Guadalupe Hidalgo, he pointed out that it did not require the people to elect someone "from the limited number of inexperienced youths who have been educated out of their native Territory, so as to be more familiar with the language and the condition and wants of others than of those whom they aspire to represent." Besides, the making of speeches was "not the chief or vital function" of a congressional delegate.

Gallegos spoke to the threat being made to his cultural integrity through force of a religious imperialism. A "foreign Bishop" had deprived him and all the other New Mexico *sacerdotes* of their living, he decried, "to make way for imported French priests of his own selection." They were the first to meddle in the canvass "not to support, but to crush me," Gallegos put it, and for this the New Mexico legislature had to make its appeal to the pope. Gallegos regretted having to bring it up, realizing the "sordid" account would not sit well in the House. As the rumors were forced on him, he was "compelled to notice them."[33]

Otero in response acquitted himself as close to Smith's pure assimilation type as one could. He diametrically contradicted Gallegos on what New Mexico was all about and what it needed. On the social and cultural significance of the election, Otero's modernist comparison between New Mexico and the United States assumed that assimilation was equal, if not superior, in value to the retention of any aspect of Mexican tradition. Gallegos's cultural authenticity was not proven by a lack of English proficiency, Otero challenged. If the former priest found himself in an "extraordinary and anomalous" situation, it showed his disqualification for the post he aspired to fill. American Party reasoning tended to deny that the vaunted American political system suffered from ethnocentrism. Otero defended Congress from any suggestion of race prejudice. He had never heard any sarcasm or ridicule directed to Gallegos. Otero expressed certainty that no such indignity had been "offered to the people of New Mexico." He would not allow Gallegos to impute any "personal deficiencies or errors" as representing the people of the territory. Otero turned Gallegos's claim to real Mexican culture on its head. His "people" would not knowingly send a representative to Washington so that he could "boast of his incapacity and claim a seat on the "very ground of being unable to fill it." A responsible Spanish-speaking representative would have consulted a Washington grammar school. Not to speak in a "boastful spirit," or because he and other young men of the territory had availed themselves of American advantages, but it was his to point out how all could see in "how different a light" he viewed the duties of his position "from that which seems to strike the mind of the sitting delegate." Gallegos should have been able to defend his people against any jests, sneers, or ridicule, had they occurred. That he could not repel the insults was his "greatest possible misfortune," Otero had it.

Otero ironically othered Gallegos into race traitor, ridiculing his appeal for House magnanimity with the elitist's lash. To the House speaker Otero queried, "When, sir, in the history of the race [of] which [Gallegos] claims to be a *type*, did Castilian blood ever congeal in the presence of power, and so far degrade itself as to seek to crawl into favor?" Otero positioned himself far from such conquered self-degradation, the equal American appealing in the name of "fraternal justice." If New Mexico had no rights, "she seeks not to be your pensioner," he worded it. If Congress's favor was to be obtained "at the sacrifice of dignity and equality, she will disdain to purchase it at such a price.... *These*," Otero pounded, "shall never be surrendered through my agency, so help me God!"

Otero came to the defense of his young assimilated generation whom Gallegos sought to diminish. There had for years been two parties in the territory, he contextualized, "one calling itself the Mexican party, and indulging great hostility against the institutions of these States; the other denominated the American party, which looked to annexation "as the only security from the perpetual discords and civil wars of Mexico." The latter description was accurate enough; the former binaried New Mexico's ethnopolitical differences. The contestant drew a straight line from his distinction here to the days of war between the United States and Mexico. He proudly claimed attachment to American institutions. "Though a native of New Mexico, and of unmixed Spanish descent," he swore (in hark to fellow American Partyite, former governor William Lane),

> I received my education in this country; and I am happy to entertain the thought that I am the first native citizen of that acquired Territory who has come to the Congress of our adopted fatherland and address it in the language of its laws and its Constitution. And I am proud to know that my own people at home do not consider me the less qualified, on that account, to represent them in this body, whatever may be the opinion of the sitting Delegate.

Otero rejected the "libel," "calumny," and "villainous accusation" that he was a demagogue for not understanding his own people and not being at one with them culturally.

Otero keyed up religiously, in the mold of *hombre de bien* from whom he descended, with an affront on the "corrupt priests." Any "honest man who is acquainted with the facts," he maintained, knew the priests to exert influence to secure the election of his competitor. Bishop Lamy, the truer representative of the people's religion, tried to restrain the Mexican priests from "the scandal of an active and zealous participation in the canvass." The "hypocritical" Padre Ortiz, "while professing obedience to the wish of his superior, utterly disregarded the instruction." He was "a zealous partisan of the sitting Delegate, and made use of all the influence of his position to aid him in the election." Otero noted the "influential and respectable citizens" of Gallegos's own county who drew a petition requesting that the priests be forbidden from using the Church "for so corrupt a purpose" as electioneering. Lamy, the victim of unjust charges, was "eminently" worthy of respect for his "piety, intelligence, and public spirit." Otero told of the bishop finding the New Mexico church "sunk into the most deplorable condition of immorality." Echoing common American disparagement, Otero said they were "notoriously addicted to the grossest vices," the "disgrace of every gambling-house and drinking saloon, and the open frequenters of the brothels." The good bishop, "seeing how the holy office had been prostituted and the Church disgraced," proceeded to remove the delinquent priests, and substitute others. Such was the "'head and front' of his offending." Lamy had for the first time "since the days of the pious padres who first settled in the territory" established schools on a firm foundation. It was unsurprising that the "corrupt and degraded priests," the "worst enemies of the people, should find fault with the measures of reform adopted by the new dignitary."

On the terms of his contest, Otero held Meriwether and Davis complicit in arbitrarily refusing to accept the abstracts of probate judges in certain precincts that had majority votes for him, in not reporting them in the election transcript, and in altering votes in other precincts. Gallegos failed to prove his case, Otero argued, that ballots or tickets had been fraudulently changed. Otero accused citizens of Mexico of voting for Gallegos in Santa Fe and Río Arriba counties. The match of individuals who had renounced U.S. citizenship and voted against him constituted *prima facie* evidence of illegal voting, the brief stated. Speaking as *hombre de bien* collaborator, Otero tagged those who retained Mexican citizenship as the ones who fomented the 1847 revolt against the United States, not out of an understandable loyalty to their nationality but out of their disdain for American institutions. "Having deliberately and voluntarily made their election under the Treaty [of Guadalupe Hidalgo] and having chosen to retain the character of Mexicans," Otero noted (as if Judge Brocchus had contributed to the brief), "they have no right to participate in the elections, until they shall have been regularly naturalized according to law." New Mexico had previously petitioned Congress for an act to benefit the inhabitants who had disfranchised themselves according to the treaty, Otero noted. "If they have repented of their choice, there is no alternative but to come in at the door provided by the laws. They cannot break through, or climb over, the barriers established by the Constitution and laws of the country." Discounting the illegal Mexican votes would give him a majority of over a thousand, Otero calculated. Because Davis delivered the decision of the district court ruling that had gone against *Quintana v. Thompkins* and for Gallegos's case, Otero argued that a district court decision could not overrule a decision of the territorial Supreme Court on the political participation rights of the citizens of Mexico.[34]

Apparently because Gallegos forces retained ownership of New Mexico's Democratic Party, which had been recognized by Democrats in the United States, Otero gingerly kept from mixing the intrigues of party into his argument. His contest had nothing to do with any "party platform" and sought no aid from "party sources." It rested on the merit of truth, justice, "and upon that sentiment which will respect the sovereign will of New Mexico, whose son I am; for I am native there, and to the manor born." In an implied slight of Governor Meriwether's administration, Otero said he went to Congress "not as a successful adventurer from the restless waters of political speculation; I come because my people sent me." Regardless of the House's final decision, he would hold his Americanism sacred. "I will never cease to believe and promulgate the sentiments I have always entertained," Otero proclaimed, "that the brightest and happiest day that ever dawned upon New Mexico was that on which she was annexed to this Union."

With eloquence to rival Brocchus's oratory, Otero concluded by touching on New Mexico's Statehood Revolution. "And I here, as I have there," he put it, congratulate

[New Mexico] most heartily upon the happy event; and hope that she, wheeling in the line of her adopted sister Territories, and following in the train of this bright constellation of States shall, by strict observance of the Constitution—by a proper devotion to the principles of liberty—by keeping step to the music of the Union, present, in the future of America, no mean glory or cause her sister States to blush, either for her want of fidelity to the bond of Union, or the patriotism and virtue that make you one and indissoluble.

Angélico Chávez has the House "naturally elated by Otero's oration, coming from a genuine 'Spaniard' of New Mexico who corroborated what they themselves had heard or read about those horrible priests both in Mexico and New Mexico," implying that perhaps Otero's locution may have figured more prominently than the facts of the case.[35] In any case, the House overwhelmingly passed the resolutions of the Committee on Elections. The twenty-six-year-old Otero was immediately sworn in as the delegate from the New Mexico Territory.[36]

The glow of Otero's triumph radiated out ecclesiastically. The Propaganda Fide found Machebeuf innocent of violating the seal of confession, agreeing that it had been the bishop's Christmas Pastoral that had provoked the "ignorant and vicious" Mexican priests to unwarranted resistance. Gallegos was deemed a corrupt priest, to the detriment of his poor flock.[37] Bishop Lamy thanked his Rome colleague for the verdict of innocence, complimenting him with a copy of Otero's contest speech. "Providence has seen to it," he told the newly appointed cardinal, "that a young man of the world has come to the defense of church discipline, has pointed out the scandals of which he himself is a witness."[38]

Otero's ascendance was an important one for the party that championed assimilation and Americanism for incorporated Nuevomexicanos. The majority of the territorial assembly remained Mexican Democratic. The next territorial election would iron matters out more uniformly.

The National Democracy in the Election of 1857

W. W. H. Davis surrendered the editorship of the *Weekly Gazette* back to James Collins in February 1856. Davis advised the territory's Democrats in his adieu to keep up their organization and "never lose sight of the good old principles upon which your political faith is based."[39] Davis did not mean to counsel members of the American Party, clearly enough. For over three years the latter had seethed at the Mexican Party's hold on the Democratic Party identity and the blessings given to it by Meriwether and Davis, not to mention its control of the legislature. Collins, in returning to the weekly helm, swore allegiance to the Democratic Party but in support of what he proclaimed a "legitimate" organization.[40] Portentously, Davis also warned official Democrats to watch for "every combination" that might arise in opposition to the party, "whether they are known as progressives or by any other new fangled name."[41]

Nuevomexicanos and Euroamericans took note of the Democratic national convention scheduled for Cincinnati on June 2–6, 1856 where a "new fangled" name would indeed surge.[42] The politics of that event helped pitch the sectional dispute into a constitutional crisis. Party doctrine charged abolitionists, northern Congressmen, and what it stamped the "Black Republican Party" (the new Republican Party held its first nominating convention earlier in 1856) with threatening the unity of the United States in its attack on the institution of slavery. Each state and territory, the dominant Democratic line stressed, held the right to determine policies and laws regarding its domestic matters, slavery included (as Governor Meriwether had informed José Manuel Gallegos). State rights were not an essential liberal concept but could be interpreted to mean the people's democratic sovereignty, as former vice president John C. Calhoun emphasized.[43] Conventioneers were urged to consolidate their platform beyond the radical state rights position of Stephen A. Douglas, regarded as giving too much flexibility to states, and especially the territories soon to become states, on the slavery question. They fixed on "national unity" as the overarching theme coupled with a limited central government with regard to slavery, commerce, banking, and international relations. The party core accepted that the South would never give up slavery. To them the North's obsession with abolition therefore constituted a politics of "sectionality," seeking to "embroil the States and incite to treason and armed resistance to law in the territories; and whose avowed purposes if consummated, must end in civil war and disunion."[44]

Delegates did not renominate Pierce and, in a storm of party reorganization, came to call theirs the "National Democratic Party" founded on a "national platform." A Kentucky delegate waved the banner of the National Democracy, affirming that the organization was built by the "heroes in the land who had disdained the senseless mummuries of the Know Nothing order and the treasonable doctrine of the Black Republican Party." The convention, steering between the Scylla of anti-Catholic hysteria and the Charybdis of traitorous abolitionism, and standing blind to the racism of slavery, at least adopted Douglas's plank of bringing European immigrants under the party tent.[45]

In the September presidential election, the National Democratic candidate James Buchanan beat John C. Fremont, of the anti-slavery Republican Party, and the Know-Nothing candidate, former Whig president Millard Fillmore. Buchanan narrowly lost to Fremont in the North but won handily over Fillmore in the South, where Fremont fared badly. The "National" label in the Democratic Party carried symbolic weight. James Collins was greatly impacted by the National Democracy. In the *Santa Fe Weekly Gazette* he growled in his post–presidential election piece at the "treason" stalking abroad in the land, "even in the Senate of the United States," against which the Democratic Party was "the only national party, and upon that party depends the salvation of the Union."[46]

Identification with the National Democracy began to sweep across New Mexico in the fall of 1856, appearing in county conventions, local rallies, the territorial legislature, and opinion pieces in the *Gazette*, the self-proclaimed organ of the movement.[47] In "point of numbers and enthusiasm," the Santa Fe County Democratic mass meeting had "never been exceeded," the *Gazette* reported. In Fernandez de Taos, where residents had rallied behind Judge Brocchus, "a great number of Democratic citizens" met at the house of don Felipe Sena.[48] Collins led the charge against the dominant Mexican Democratic Party in the assembly. Facundo Pino was singled out and accused of running a session that did nothing to advance the welfare of the territory, clogging it with elections laws calculated to the advantage of his party. Collins acknowledged Pino's fitness to be a responsible legislator but worked the binary nonetheless. "[I]t seems impossible for him to rise above the contemptible position of a political juggler," the editor signaled. "It is strange that a man will prostitute his talents to purposes so unworthy." Collins maintained confidence in the voters to act like true Democrats so as to replace Pino "with [some]one more efficient, or more honest."⁴⁹ The National Democratic appeal went out to Mexicans in a load of Spanish-only reporting in the *Gazette*. Early gatherings in Santa Fe, Taos, and Río Arriba counties—the places won by José Manuel Gallegos in 1855—gathered behind President-elect "Santiago" Buchanan to preserve the Constitution and the Union and organize under the new Democratic Party.⁵⁰

New Mexico's National Democratic movement, led by the American shadow-party, translated the planks of the Cincinnati platform into the issues facing its "much abused and neglected territory."⁵¹ The principle of state rights, as it developed from the Kansas-Nebraska Act and the 1850 Compromise, appealed to those seeking self-government in the territories. In a variant on the Statehood Revolution, the Santa Fe County Convention recognized each territory with the right, when the number of residents justified it, "to form a constitution with or without domestic slavery and be admitted to the Union in perfectly equal terms with those of the other States of the Union." Ironically, the convention rode the wave of "national unity" while keeping Stephen A. Douglas's opposition to the southern domination of the Cincinnati convention. Rather than state rights, Douglas, who was narrowly defeated for the Democratic presidential nomination, stayed close to the *Dred Scott v. Sandford* decision and the individual's right to choose whether or not to adopt slavery apart from any legislative body's intervention into a citizen's property rights. This notion of "squatter" or "popular" sovereignty squared with the mind of Delegate Miguel Antonio Otero.⁵²

Santa Fe National Democrats offered up territorial rights as self-determination, affirming as an "essential" principle that the territory's official posts, "from the highest to the lowest should be occupied by citizens and permanent residents of the Territory." The "principle" suited Mexican natives and Euroamerican settlers alike. The former maintained their historical homeland ties, while the latter's attachment to New Mexico reflected the Statehood Revolution's dual identity, the regional territory and the national state. The convention generalized to those "brothers in other parts of the planet that are now struggling to establish the principles of free government on which are founded this Union."⁵³

The National Democratic opposition to the Know-Nothing Party suited New Mexico's cultural and religious diversity. A Santa Fe resolution drew a parallel between foreign immigrants and annexed peoples. No party could consider itself national or even constitutional, "or in accord with American principles," if it was founded on "religious opinions and accidental place of birth." Liberal Santa Feans upheld the "base" of the Union, "its prosperity, extension and preeminent example of its free government... built on a complete liberty on matters of religion and without respect to persons on account of class or place of birth."[54]

It was important for the surging Nationals, involving settlers and Nuevomexicanos, to put claims on Democratic "principles" and "doctrines" more than to spell them out. Copying the trend in the Mexican Democratic Party, rising Nuevomexicano leaders did the job of familiarizing the village folk with American political ways, four of seven speech makers at the Santa Fe conclave being Mexican.[55] The partisan imperative drove the application of principles and doctrines to flay the Mexican Democratic Party. To codify the charge of corruption, the virtues of public service, personal honesty, and "the people as sovereigns" were called principles of Jeffersonian Democracy. Speeches, proclamations, and resolutions called for unity to rid New Mexico of "knavery and betrayal," "lies and false promises," and "the demagogues and corrupt party influences" that had "for the last four years controlled the affairs of this territory." Elect "public servants," audiences were told in prose of popular sovereignty and republicanism, and recognize "in the people the right to select their offices and the doctrine that the officers are not the masters but the servants of the people."[56] The Nationals transposed the charge of sectionality from Cincinnati to their situation. In accusing the Mexican Democrats of divisiveness, an early National resolution pledged (in a logic of color blindness) not to recognize "distinctions of race." The anti-American proclivities of the Mexican Party would receive their due with extension of the party's "true" principles of unity throughout New Mexico, the assertion went.[57]

The National Democracy, following the agenda set by Diego Archuleta, addressed the Indian wars, condemning in particular Governor Meriwether's peace strategy, which, it claimed, failed to stop the thieving "rapaciousness" of the Utes. Mexican Democratic Party legislators were lampooned for not concentrating on the Indian menace, which, Nationals said, kept them from engaging in a "manly and patriotic devotion to the true interests of the country."[58] The word *manly*, it can be noted, was consecrated for general civic use by the Declaration of Independence as the "firmness" with which the colonial legislatures had been opposing King George. Secretary Davis was skewered for covering up the governor's Indian policy when he was *Gazette* editor and for feuding with the revered Indian fighter Kit Carson.[59] Meriwether, it was said, left the Mexican Democrats holding the bag as he departed New Mexico to plan for his impending dismissal as governor under a new president. National Democrats called him a deserter, taking a salary while leaving three offices, including the acting governorship, in the hands of Davis. It was a greedy monopoly, the Nationals proclaimed, that went against "old" Democratic Party principles.[60] The *Gazette* reminded readers of how Judge J. J. Deavenport and Meriwether had been hanged in effigy in 1854.[61]

The hat switcher Diego Archuleta was elected president of the Río Arriba National nominating convention. A flock of Nuevomexicanos followed Archuleta into the barn of the National Democratic Party. It was a remarkable transformation for the former Mexican revolutionary. Archuleta recited the whole Santa Fe convention platform, which he had helped author. Sounding much like the old Donaciano Vigil, he didactically emphasized that to obtain a republican government and the common well-being, it was necessary that "all the people should always take an active part in the public issues [*que todo el pueblo debe Siempre tomar una parte activa en los Asuntos públicos*]." On his steadfast issue with Meriwether, the convention resolved that it was of the utmost importance for the "inhabitants" of New Mexico to effect the "subjugation and complete submission of the barbarous Indians, be it by arms or whatever other means, such that there results a permanent security against their deplorable and repeated depredations [*Que la subyugación y la completa sumisión de los indios bárbaros sea a fuerzas de armas o de cualquier otro modo, de manera que resulte una permanente seguridad contra sus deplorable y repetidas depredaciones es asunto de primer importancia para los habitantes de Nuevo Méjico*]."[62] Finally, local Nationals endorsed the renomination of Otero. Taos and Río Arriba counties instructed their delegates to vote for him at the territorial convention. Otero was praised for delivering appropriations, for his popularity, and for his "friendly intimacy" with president-elect Buchanan.[63]

The *Gazette* published Otero's post-contest proclamation. The delegate refuted rumors that he had failed to get certain bills passed that would have benefited New Mexico. In a criticism to become common against sitting delegates, Otero claimed to have found that his predecessor had done "literally nothing" for the people who elected him and had left town without presenting him with the documents needed to follow up on New Mexico projects, "a most reprehensible disregard." Otero again harped on Gallegos's language inadequacy while deeming himself "humble." Though young, he considered himself the best bet for accomplishing what was needed of a delegate, including seeing that the people received protection from tribes the settled people defined as marauding. It no doubt sat well in the public mind for this powerful personality to promise several important measures for lands to construct roads from the Mississippi Valley to the Pacific. He called on New Mexicans to unite so as to secure their prosperity and progress "as a people." Otero reinforced the party binary, calling on "patriotic hearts" to relieve the territory of misrepresentation, falsehood, and calumny. American Party compatriots tended to eschew the suggestion of an immediate Statehood Revolution. Otero held that his "highest pride" would be to see New Mexico "in the future shine amongst the brightest stars in the galaxy of States."[64]

It was unbecoming in the United States generally for a man to push his ambition for office. Should Otero choose to run, Collins stated, "the people" needed to read his address and understand his claims, for it was the National party that should bring him out.[65] A rumor had Otero wanting to run but waiting to obey the will of his party's nominating convention. Collins reproduced a letter from Otero that congratulated the *Gazette* for its forthright stand on behalf of the Democratic National Party, on which depended "the safety" of American institutions. Otero lauded president-elect Buchanan, compared to whom there was "no better patriot in this wide spreading country."[66]

The New Mexico National Democracy held its territorial convention in Alburquerque on March 8–9, 1857. The *Gazette* hailed it as the best organized convention ever in the territory. If true, that signaled a steady process of political development. Sixty-eight delegates, twice as large as the Algodones convention, from seven of the territory's nine counties presented credentials. The agenda followed the Cincinnati platform in unity with the Democracy "of the whole country" and to support Buchanan. Participants identified as National Democrats opposed to the "old" Democracy. Planks of the substantial platform were previously defined by the county conventions and meetings. Miguel A. Otero was renominated for delegate to the 35th U.S. Congress. Collins, the Santa Fe County Convention president, was recommended to the president for New Mexico's next governor.[67]

The convention included the original sector of U.S. collaborators in the Kearny occupation, among them Donaciano Vigíl and Kearny judge Antonio José Otero (Miguel's older brother).[68] Illustrating the capacity of a binary system to recruit former outsiders to a central polity, Nuevomexicanos constituted fifty-seven (84 percent) of the delegates. Diego Archuleta was elected president. Mentoring his people to recognize the importance of having a party, he watched with "renewed satisfaction" the dominance of the National Democratic faith in his "hitherto neglected territory." Twenty-three of the delegates, most of them Nuevomexicanos, had participated in the 1853 Algodones convention. Of the thirty-seven Algodones delegates, only nine remained loyal to the Mexican Democratic Party. Businessman José Leandro Perea had attended the Mexican Democratic Party convention in Algodones; he now aligned himself with the Nationals.[69]

The *Gazette* explained it by claiming that the "native Mexicans," composing the territory almost entirely, spurned the Mexican Party's rejection of American institutions and had come to bestow their legitimacy on American incorporation. Delegates were said to be men "born and reared under the foreign governments of Spain or Mexico, and speaking a language different from that of the American Government and people." That they cleaved "with the tenacity of patriots to the land of which they are now citizens, and whose protection they enjoy," showed alike "their loyalty to this Union and their faith in the Democratic cause—the only two essentials to the bona fide National Democrats." The editor shared his comfort in seeing their territorial party "likewise a part and parcel of that great phalanx of the National Democracy" headed by Buchanan, the "model statesman."[70] Collins propagated the notion of "native" status complementing national and regional identities. He urged Nuevomexicanos to adopt an Otero-style dualism. By casting their suffrage for Otero, "a son of your own soil," the voters would declare their "adhesion alike to the country of your nativity and of your adoption, and vindicate your just and rightful claim to citizenship of the United States."[71] Collins noted that the New Mexico population was composed of "two distinct races" but argued that their interests were the same. "They are all American citizens, and should labor unitedly [sic] to promote their common good." Otero's opponent labored under "national prejudices by trying to create an American or Mexican party, with hostile interests, a wretch for whom we have no sympathy."[72]

The extent of local conventions and rallies for the Mexican Democratic Party in the early campaign is unclear. No reports of them appear in the *Gazette*, although there is an indirect reference to limited organizing activity.[73] Also missing are descriptions of the Mexican Democratic Party territorial convention, in part because of skips in the *Gazette* record, although one was held in Peña Blanca, it seems. It would have been in late March or early April. Published on April 18 was the party's campaign weekly, *El Demócrata/The Democrat*, a successor to Weightman's *El Amigo del País* and *Campaña Demócrata*. One issue of *El Demócrata* survives, appearing in October after the election.[74] This issue is significant for revealing key aspects of the political thought and agenda on this side of the partisan divide. What transpired at the convention and afterward in terms of platform, ideology, and canvass strategy can be teased out and interpreted from the *Gazette*'s mostly hostile reports of them.

Territorial assemblyman Miguel E. Pino, Territorial Secretary W. W. H. Davis, District Judge Spruce Baird, and District Judge J. J. Deavenport led the charge, but many others participated.[75] These men were either veterans of the Mexican Democratic Party or members or outside supporters of the Meriwether administration. Miguel E. Pino, like his brother Facundo, had been in on the 1846 planning of rebellion against the Kearny occupation but did not conspire in the Bent assassination or take part in the Taos Revolt. He now stood out as a stalwart Mexican Party leader.[76] The party had material support in a contract from the governor's office to have *El Demócrata* serve as the public printer. Others were veteran Mexican Partyites: Santa Fe County Sheriff Jesús María Baca y Salazar, the entrenched Lamy enemy Tomás Cabeza de Baca, and former vicar Juan Felipe Ortiz. Pino edited and managed *El Demócrata*; Davis, Cabeza de Baca, and Baird helped out.[77]

The Pino-Davis-Baird combine reinforced a collective identity to oppose the Cincinnati shift in nomenclature and program and to deny support for the Buchanan presidency.[78] As one observer put it, the "old Democrats... never bowed the knee to 'Baal.'"[79] The epigram at the head of *El Demócrata*'s editorial column said it all: the established (Mexican) Democratic Party was *"Firme en Sus Principios Sin Cambiar de Nombre"* (Firm in its principles without changing its name). These militants settled on the Independent Democratic Party as the formal name for themselves. The Independent Democrat Party, dating to the 1830s, was recognized as an official partisan body standing in opposition to the dominant Democratic organization and its policies. Here it reflected the dissident Democrats who had not gone along with the dominant Democracy's doughface program since 1854. New Mexico's Independent Democrats called the National Democracy *el partido proscriptivo*.[80] The correct rendering in Spanish is *proscrito*. The important essay was likely composed by a settler member of the Mexican Party, Davis perhaps, judging from the apparent transliterations from English. In any case, it spoke to the question of proscription, indicating abuse by dictators of a party's right to keep its members loyal.[81]

Democratic partisans in the nineteenth century sometimes characterized Whig opponents, particularly rich Whigs, as devils or regarded their attempts to establish a government of morality as the work of the devil.[82] Moreover, historian Marc Simmons notes how the Río Grande cultural corridor has always comprised the "devil's domain." He cites one form of demonology in which individuals "deliberately sold their souls to the Devil in exchange for power and wealth. They were spoken of in traditional Hispanic New Mexico as being in a compact with the devil (*pacto con el Diablo*)."[83] The Independents appropriated the idiom of the devil's apparition in the remote New Mexico villages by tagging the National Party as *Democracia con cola* (Democracy with a tail). They themselves were the unadulterated *Descolados* (Bobtailed Democrats, as the English-language source translated it). A Douglasite populism, battling the proscriptive National Democracy, appeared on the masthead of *El Demócrata* in the form of *El Pueblo es Soberano y Capaz de Gobernarse Por Si Mismo* (The People are sovereign and capable of governing themselves). Proscription and subservience had a clear class dimension. *El Demócrata* referred to the leaders of the National Democracy as "the aristocracy [*aristocracia*]." Miguel

Otero stood out in this regard due to his job as an agent for the well-to-do land speculators arriving in New Mexico daily. Independents accused the Nationals of disdaining the Mexicans as too poor "to sustain a party composed of the people." Independent propaganda painted the Nationals looking down on the commoners as "wholly incapable of self-government" and themselves as rich, and "money was power." Years later a commentator suggested a difference in resource distribution in the campaign of 1855, observing that a certain "Rich Man's party" had expended a considerable quantity of hard cash, merchandise, credit, and dry goods. The Independent's populist reasoning argued that the opponents contested the very meaning of liberalism. The elitism of the National Democracy "trampled on Liberty, Equality and Fraternity," the very foundations of the "old school" Democratic Party, or the conservative Democracy (*la Democracia reservada*).[84]

The charge of proscription associated the National Democracy with the Know-Nothing doctrine of opposition to professed Roman Catholicism and the exclusion of the foreign-born from offices of trust and governmental emolument. Stephen Douglas opposed the Know-Nothing Party. New Mexico Independents draped the National Democracy in the robes of the older Native American Party, calling them Know-Nothings "in disguise." The links in New Mexico were to Bishop Lamy's subordination of the nativo priests and National Democrats impugning politicians who were citizens of Mexico, especially Miguel E. Pino. The Know-Nothings said immigrant Catholics were threats to the U.S. Constitution by their allegiance to the pope. New Mexico's Independents mimed the association, portraying Miguel Otero, "Santiago" Collins, Bishop Lamy, Hugh N. Smith, and the other "American" (settler) Nationals as wrongly accusing the Mexicans and their native priests of being anti-American subversives, "thieves, assassins and barbarians." Independents lambasted what they considered Miguel Otero's racialized descriptions of Nuevomexicano priests put before Congress in his contest of election against José Manuel Gallegos.[85]

Nationals in New Mexico conceded that Know-Nothing elements may have been in the ranks of their movement but protested that they did not equate with each other. Miguel Otero was himself a practicing Catholic, the *Gazette* noted, as were his entire family and New Mexico friends.[86] The *Descolado* Independents, however, argued that it was the people's Catholicism that was under attack. They clearly hit the mark concerning the demonization of Miguel E. Pino. The Nationals alleged that Pino's continued Mexican citizenship reflected anti-Americanism, proved, as they argued, because he had been among the instigators of the 1847 revolt and had helped engineer the retention of Mexican citizenship among the people in 1848–49, sowing therein "the seeds of discord throughout the Territory." Pino, it was charged, opposed the very party that represented "American sentiment."[87] However, Pino appears by the mid-1850s to have been playing by American political rules. The *Gazette* ignored the very reports that appeared in its own pages of Pino fulfilling the responsibilities of probate judge and administering the oath of office to members of the new board of education of Santa Fe, which included a pledge to uphold the Constitution. Pino served as a captain in the battalion of volunteers, a military appointment that required allegiance to the United States.[88]

Pino's role on the Fourth of July drives home the point. The celebration in this election year was unprecedentedly grand. In the making of a civil society, Freemasons, Odd Fellows, and the Literary Club walked in the procession to the courthouse next to public officers, the governor, judges, a military brass band, the commanding general and his staff, the 8th Company Infantry, and "citizens and strangers." Juan Tapia and A. P. Wilbar read the Declaration of Independence in Spanish. José Manuel Gallegos delivered a Spanish oration, called by a nominal enemy "in fine taste and [doing] credit to his patriotism." The *Gazette* noted the enthusiasm with which the Mexicans celebrated the great day, giving "additional evidence of a genuine love for the country in which they are now with their native American brethren the common fellow citizens." The "manifest heart" felt by these "adopted citizens should inspire, as indeed we have no doubt it does," Collins said, "the native American breast with an increased affection for the native New Mexican people who have but recently come into the enjoyment of the equal blessings vouchsafed to all by the protection of the American flag." Among the toasts at dinner in the Exchange Hotel, one went to "The Ladies," symbolic inclusion into the American cultural, if not civic nation. At one end of the table Col. John B. Grayson presided; at the other don Miguel Pino himself held forth.[89] The National Democrats polluted Pino artificially to reinforce party boundaries. In truth, his political vantage point was that of the dual legitimist. Opponents could not accept his politics as a pluralist-informed figure keyed into the interests of his nativo people in the American system, or else their exercised partisanship held him as easy game for ascribing anti-Americanism.

In the campaign, the Independent Descolados were far from kind to those who had gone to the enemy. The former anti-occupation revolutionary Manuel Chávez called the defections an ironic benefit, for the turncoats were "snakes, swollen with the poison of their species, want[ing] to destroy our rights and subject us to servitude, delivering us to the hands of tigers so that, with their ferocious claws, they will annihilate the unhappy community of the Territory."[90]

Significantly, W. W. H. Davis served as president of the Independent Peña Blanca Convention.[91] Nationals speculated that José Manuel Gallegos, District Judge Spruce Baird, or District Attorney and former House speaker and former Kearny volunteer Theodore Wheaton would receive the nomination for delegate to Congress. Collins had deemed Gallegos an ineffective delegate, but he reasoned that the Independents would not consent to run an "American" if there was any chance of electing him "or any other Mexican." Neither Baird nor Wheaton, Collins essayed, "would be so green as to allow themselves to be used for the mere purpose of trying to keep up a party organization that is now fast decaying and that must soon be repudiated by the people in all parts of the Territory." The people seemed to have "settled upon the propriety of filling the office of delegate at least for the present with a Mexican citizen."[92]

The nomination did not go to Gallegos, surprisingly, but to the Texan and Río Abajo Judge Spruce Baird. The reason is not entirely clear. The calculation based on the results of the prior contested election may have meant it was considered difficult for Gallegos to run against Otero, and no other Mexican candidate appeared viable. Baird had solid credentials as a Mexican Democratic Party member. He had lived in New Mexico since 1851 and participated in the 1853 Algodones convention. He had lawyered for Weightman, provided important support to Gallegos in 1855, and counseled Gallegos in the Otero contest. One Independent informant told the *Gazette* that his party had gone with Baird in order to ease the ire of the "American" settlers and prevent them from fighting so hard against their candidate as would be the case with Gallegos.[93] The *Gazette* regretted that the judge would allow himself to be used for the purpose of trying to float a "sinking organization."[94] The weekly reported later that five persons treacherously met prior to the convention to "cheat" Gallegos out of the nomination and force him to run for a position in the assembly.[95]

David Miller, an Alabamian who arrived in Santa Fe in 1854 to become the Spanish translator for the newly formed surveyor general office, took editorial control of the *Gazette* in May after Otero secured an appointment for James Collins as New Mexico's superintendent of Indian Affairs, an office no longer under the thumb of the governor.[96] Miller took to the National Party line with gusto. He meant it as a disparagement of the Independent Democrats to call Gallegos the "legitimate chief of his own party."[97] Indeed, Nuevomexicanos disgruntled over the rejection of Gallegos defected to the National Democracy. One felt that a Gallegos win that year would have vindicated the "injustice" dealt him in the Otero contest. Another stated that the people deserved the right finally to decide which nativo they preferred to be their territorial leader.[98] Baird reportedly boasted of the support from the "Gallegos party." Running for a seat in the House, Gallegos appeared on the same ticket as Baird in Santa Fe County.[99]

The Nationals had a field day with the contradiction of a party committed to Mexicans nominating as its highest candidate an outside settler and, moreover, one who had come on a mission of "outrage, insult, and oppression" to deliver New Mexico to Texas.[100] The critique wound into charging that the nomination reflected Know-Nothingism. The nomination of Baird was said to go against the principles of the Constitution "for it produces nothing more than bad feelings against the Anglo Saxon and Spanish races that comprise the population of our Territory—sentiments of repugnant caste in the mind of all men who desire peace and prosperity of their fellow citizens."[101] Nationals chided Baird for making his organization out to be the Democratic Party. They called him *el Chino Tejano* (the Chinese Texan), referring to his facial features.[102]

Descolado Independents had Nationals not liking Baird because he did not submit to "Santiago" Collins, David Miller, Hugh N. Smith, "other Whigs," and "the major part of the Americans of Santa Fe." They turned the tables on Otero by calling *him* a race traitor. Mexican born though he was, he had strayed from being a tried-and-true nativo, it was suggested. That he was educated in the United States meant he was "an [ethnic] American in principle." Baird evinced more

Mexicanness, the Independent line had it. Baird indelicately offered as proof of Otero's "American sentiment" the fact that he had married an American woman, one from the South, no less. The *Gazette* called the slap antipathy to American institutions, claiming that it sought to instill a feeling of war with "the whole aim and purpose of the U.S. government towards the inhabitants of New Mexico." Independents questioned the credentials of those claiming membership as Democrats who had been devoted Whigs. Miller argued that at the time "there was no division of parties here upon the old political issues." The Whigs were here as American citizens, Miller apologetically pointed out, laboring to reconcile the tensions in the first Democratic Party movement, "warmly attached to the genius of our institutions." They saw "a formidable political organization risen here when leaders and controllers among the Mexicans were in open opposition to the American government." As loyal citizens, "they united with the liberal Mexicans who from the very introduction of American laws, had asserted their attachment to them—with a view to counteract the evils of the enemies of their government. It was patriotic, it was honorable."[103]

Campaign activity intensified from the spring conventions to the September election, although the evidence relates mostly to the Nationals. Political fever hit Santa Fe County. The enthusiastic rally hosted by don Felipe Sena endorsed the platform of the Alburquerque National Convention and the candidacy of Miguel Otero. The resolutions of the veteran American Party man Felipe Delgado condemned W. W. H. Davis for dereliction as territorial secretary.[104] The formal Santa Fe County nominating convention sustained a bi-ethnic leadership. Merrill Ashurst served as president, Luis Griego and José María Martínez as vice presidents, and A. P. Wilbar and Jesús María Sena y Baca as secretaries. Nominees were mostly Nuevo Mexicano: Nasario Gonzales (territorial senator); Ashurst, Joaquín Perea, Francisco Ortiz, and Teodoro Gonzales (the House); Antonio Matías Ortiz (probate judge); and Jesús María Sena y Baca (sheriff).[105]

The "united" Nationals in Taos County met at the home of don Ramón Durán. Don Celedonio Valdez and Carlos Beaubien were elected co-presidents and Frederick Muller and Aniceto Valdez secretaries. Nationally women were excluded from the electorate but had begun to utilize such instruments as the petition to voice their political opinions and social concerns. Yet many men objected that they had no business in politics.[106] The sexist norm carried the day in territorial New Mexico. At the least, the Taos Committee on Nominations included *señorita* Gertrudis Mora. It was a unique reference to a woman in a nineteenth-century political proceeding. Out of ten nominees for the offices of probate judge, sheriff, the council, and the House, only one was a Euroamerican.[107] In Alburquerque all officers of the Bernalillo County Convention were Mexican, a greater portion of its nominees than in either Santa Fe or Taos.[108]

The National convention at the Plaza de la Capilla in Río Arriba County carried out "frank deliberations" on the merits of the proposed county and local candidates. That none had run for office before was deemed a credit to their belief in the people's sovereignty; they were not driven by ego or personal aspiration, as was found among traditional Democrats. All twenty-eight candidates for county office were Spanish-surnamed. The two candidates for probate judge, Antonio María Pacheco and Pedro García, leaders in the large pro-Brocchus meeting in Taos, received an equal number of votes. In the recount deliberation, each was asked whom he would name as his clerk. Pacheco held that it was not appropriate to designate one beforehand. García received the nomination for stating in explicit partisanship that he would replace the Independent Democrat Elias Clark. The anonymous correspondent noted that only four Untailed Democrats in the county pushed for Baird. One had served as a delegate to the Peña Blanca Convention; another was loyal to Manuel Chávez and the "Pinos of Santa Fe."[109] The Prussian immigrant Charles P. Clever organized an ad hoc meeting to counter the "false" claims of the Descolados.[110] The existence of a Santa Fe County National Democratic Central Committee suggests a functioning organization. Nuevomexicanos comprised seventeen of twenty-three members.[111]

Miguel E. Pino figured prominently at the nominating convention conducted by the Central Committee of the Santa Fe County Independent Democracy. All Democrats were invited. However, the *Gazette* projected it as a modest affair, "a mass meeting" more than a convention, to benefit the City of Santa Fe more than the county. The partisan report deemed the National Democracy's nominating process more exciting, meant to signal a genuine democratic representation of the people.[112] Four to five hundred citizens reportedly attended the Bernalillo County Independent Convention in Alburquerque. An intriguing scrap suggests that the gathering was visited by near violence. The governor's private secretary reported Miguel Otero and friends attempting to break it up for some unexplained reason. A "committee of twelve" warned Otero off. Gallegos ostensibly stated it was with "utmost difficulty" that "the people" were deterred from physically beating Otero.[113]

An unprecedented wave of popular opinion appeared in Spanish and English letters to the editor. Obscure individuals came out of nowhere, often under cover of the pseudonym, as many had done in the days of the Kearny occupation. *Uno con Cola* (A tailed one) humbly noted it was his first public statement, hoping that his arguments against the Santa Fe County sheriff concerning Delegate Otero's land policies were worthy of publication.[114] Diego Archuleta's friend Francisco Repito Gonzales challenged his county's "false" representatives for supporting "the famous Democrat, 'our uncle Meriwether.'"[115]

Mexicans refreshed the party binary between the *Gazette* and *El Demócrata*. *Un Demócrata sin Cola* (A Democrat sans tail) called Repito's role at the Albuquerque National convention "swinish." Gonzales speculated in response that the writer was the "only mortal enemy" he ever had, Padre Antonio José Martínez, and if not he, one of his "foot-licking pimps and minions [*Habra sido alguno de sus chuchos alcahuetes*]." Gonzales called Un Demócrata sin Cola's use of a fake name to defame him "impudence," challenging him to come out "honorably with signed names in the public newspapers." To Martínez directly Gonzales rehashed the "revolution" of 1847 via a recitation of a Martínez letter to Manuel Cortez with its plan to lead a militia "in defense of the gilded eagle of the Republic of Mexico [*en defensa de la Águila dorada de la República de Méjico*]." It pained Gonzales to go after Father Martínez, who had given him his education and taught him to become "such a friend of the revolutions," and to "love madames and for that reason I do love them [*aprendí muy bien á querer a las madamas, y por tal razón las amo*]." It was when he came to disagree with the need for revolution and began seeing what made for the common good in civic politics that Martínez degraded him in public, starting in 1853, Gonzales charged. Gonzales sighed that he was tired of "living in this world." He wanted to accompany his opponent in the eternal life, walking a bit behind him "to the glory of Lucifer [*caminé adel-*

antito de mi para la Gloria de Lucifer]," making themselves "intimate friends in the foreign land." The Lamy partisan accused Martínez of being a "schismatic heretic and enemy of the Catholic Apostolic and Roman religion."[116] In another partisan scrape, *Un Demócrata Nacional* took Un Demócrata sin Cola to task over the reasons Diego Archuleta decided to abandon the Independents.[117] *El Espectador* [The spectator] and *Preguntón* [One who questions] clashed pens.[118] Another contributor warned citizens of the Independents that they were "vile ones" who sold their opinions for material favors.[119]

Debate turned the weekly editor into a target. Charles Clever took aim at Miguel Pino and the "Texas Democrats" for publishing the "spittle" of W. W. H. Davis in *El Demócrata*. Clever responded to the accusation that he was speculating in land certificates to the detriment of Mexicans. It was Pino himself, he stated, who had conspired to persuade former Mexican soldiers to sell their claims to a "certain merchant" with whom he had a partnership. Clever said Pino's anger flowed because Clever had refused to participate in the scheme. Clever pointed to "unscrupulous birds" in Santa Fe who knew no other form of argument than insult slinging. He refuted the claim of the Untailed Democrats that Otero had spoken in Congress during his 1855 contest against his "paisanos," quoting the Otero passage regarding the "Castilian blood" that would not degrade itself by asking Congress for special favors. Someone read Otero's contest statement at a political meeting Clever chaired in Alburquerque. Clever reported that Otero's words were received by those in attendance "with a grand enthusiasm." Gallegos was in attendance at the event, but Clever refused him the opportunity to speak, stating that he should have responded at the appropriate time in Congress. Davis accused Clever of abusing Gallegos. Clever said he had instructed Gallegos that he could refute the basis of the Otero claims once Clever had concluded his speech but Gallegos did not do so. Gallegos should have known the gathering did not convene to hear his arguments, Clever noted. "The fact that Otero defended his paisanos," Clever went on, "and that Gallegos failed to do it remains established and neither *el Demócrata* nor the Untailed can make the people of New Mexico believe differently."[120]

Spanish political verse had its inauguration. One J. L. penned a dedication to the Nationals' highest candidate and the Otero family name:

El Sol con sus rayos baña	The sun bathes with its rays
Desde lo alto del imperio,	From the heights of the imperium,
A Nuestra fiel democracia,	On our faithful Democracy
A Nuestro ilustre partido	On our illustrious party
A Miguel Antonio Otero;	On Miguel Antonio Otero;
A este joven tan querido	On this young man so dear
A quien se ha dignado el cielo	Whom the heavens have blessed
Colmarle de beneficios;	Showering him with beneficence;
Proclamamos sin recelo	We proclaim without hesitation
Y sin cobardía a mi juicio	And without cowardice in my judgment
Viva MIGUEL, viva ANTONIO	Long live MIGUEL, long live ANTONIO
Y viva también OTERO.	And long live OTERO as well

The rest hails the party best advantaged to take the unfortunate territory to its happiness, condemns the "terrible" administration of Santa Fe County that submerged liberty, and calls for the September election of Otero to remove all of New Mexico's "perverse" officials.[121]

Tomás Cabeza de Baca, of the opposition, encased some classic liberal thought in a traditional Hispanic *cuando* in dedication to the old Democracy:

Ya el tiempo se está acercando,	The time is rapidly approaching
de la decisión final;	of the final decision;
El Iris arco triunfal	The triumphant rainbow
la Democracia reinando,	the Democracy reigning,
libre el pueblo está nombrando	the people in freedom are appointing
hombres contra el despotismo	men against the despotism[;]
ya se acabe el servilismo	servility is already at end
y ya consentirnos cuando.	but to accept it[,] when.

It goes on to liken the Nationals to cats who convened secret meetings and politically threatened the people with a "fierce rabidness." The Independent struggle on behalf of Baird is praised. Because the *cuando* ended by wondering "when would he win?," an anonymous critic said that Cabeza de Baca "with his ounce of brains [*onza de sesos*]" did not actually believe in the arguments in favor of *el Chino Tejano*.[122]

The war of the weeklies expanded. The wrangling of the *Gazette* with *El Demócrata* over the true Democratic Party shows how effectively national developments had penetrated the territorial public. As some of the leaders of the decimated Whig Party had gone to Cincinnati to help forge the National Democracy, *El Demócrata* questioned the genuineness of the National wing, its purpose appearing as recast of the old Whig party. New Mexico Nationals denied it.[123]

The precise quality of *El Demócrata*'s argument is unknown, but if the soaring response by David Miller sought to match its rhetoric, it would have been formidable indeed. Miller accused *El Demócrata* of betraying a "remarkable obliviousness or ignorance" of the "political revolutions" that had marked the recent history of parties. The need to prefix the Democratic Party with "National" arose for the first time, Miller lectured, because new parties had abandoned the principle of national unity. Miller embroidered the line out of Cincinnati. "There was no North in open array against the South," he wrote. "There were no party platforms exclusively for the North and claiming the right to despoil the South of her property and her constitutional guarantees. A spirit of broad and comprehensive nationality gave vitality to both. With either party the Union would have been safe."

Miller not only contested the Independent Descolados but adjusted the locals to the national scene. *El Demócrata*'s "unfair" misstatement of political history was an "attempt to wrench from the National Democracy its just honors and rewards," Miller argued. He equated former Whigs in New Mexico with those on the national stage who had become "the most ardent and influential friends" of President Buchanan and who "exhibited a lively interest in every effort to spread liberal principles among this people" of New Mexico. Nor were Whig converts the majority in the National Democracy, Miller observed. He challenged the authority of the "ostensible editor" of *El Demócrata* (Pino)—who, himself "not a citizen of the United States, knows nothing about Democracy or [W]higgery, and can neither speak nor read the English language"—to read anyone out of the Democratic Party. Mexicans in the National Democracy were valorized as friends of American progress and liberal movements. Miller heralded the family of Miguel Otero for extending "a lavish hospitality to the American troops and federal officers" in the Kearny days. Otero's brother accepted a judgeship in the first territorial government, facing down the "threatened decapitation from the very faction with which Messrs. Davis and Deavenport are connected in this contest!"[124]

Another front to last was the personal rumble between editors. *Gazette* owner James Collins and W. W. H. Davis were initially partners in running the *Gazette* until Davis dissolved this by switching its position to the Mexican Democratic Party. Davis questioned Collins's personal character in relation to Collins's application to be federal Indian Affairs superintendent. The *Gazette* called *El Demócrata* a "dirty little paper," an "incendiary little sheet" that had permitted Davis to launch a campaign of personal vilification and defamation, blackening Collins's reputation in Washington. The *Gazette* did not want a personal war, Miller advised, but was being "provoked to an eye for an eye and a tooth for a tooth." The name-calling targets included Deavenport and, on the other side, the recently hired assistant *Gazette* editor S. M. Yost. Threats of fisticuffs and lawsuits abounded.[125]

If it seemed off kilter for a Mexican Party to nominate a Euroamerican settler for the territory's highest office, an even more glaring contradiction struck the Nationals when the public became aware of Davis's book *El Gringo, or New Mexico and Her People*. Under the screaming headline, "Read this, New Mexicans!," the *Gazette* translated portions of *El Gringo* into Spanish, capitalizing numerous phrases as in:

> This manifests a TERRIBLE IGNORANCE AMONG THE PEOPLE, and is sufficient to QUESTION THE PROPRIETY of conceding them the power to MAKE THEIR OWN LAWS. The politics of Spain and Mexico has always been to have the people IN IGNORANCE and as it touched on NEW MEXICO the system has been executed COMPLETELY.... To say the least, these [legislative] proceedings were very unfortunate and can be used as evidence that the PEOPLE OF NEW MEXICO IS NOT CAPABLE OF GOVERNING THEMSELVES....
>
> They have inherited a part of the cruelty, fanaticism and superstition that has marked the character of the Spanish since the first centuries. These characteristics appear to be CONSTITUTIONAL AND NATURAL IN THE RACE, and *the most generous and illumi-*

nated sentiments that characterize the present century appear not to have penetrated the veil that covers the human heart, the sentiments most noble in our nature.... [T]he rule of feminine purity is found deplorably low, and the vicious ones overpower by much the virtuous ones.... It is the custom among the married men to maintain a wife and a concubine at the same time and very frequently the wife also has a male friend.

On and on it went for paragraphs with the Black Legend disparagements.[126]

El Espectador pointed in debate with Preguntón to the irony of these words coming from the president of the Independent Territorial Nominating Convention, adding that Davis insulted them both, though they worked for opposing parties.[127] The *Gazette* said not only was the book an injustice but it caused great injury in appearing throughout the United States.[128] Miller accused Davis of duping his allies. "We have too high an estimation of the character of the members of [the Peña Blanca] convention," he wrote self-interestedly, "to believe that had all this been known, W. W. H. Davis could have been appointed the President over the members of that body." With what impudence, Miller queried, did Davis apply to the president for the governorship of New Mexico, seeking continued residence "among the people he had defamed."[129]

El Demócrata lamely blamed the critics for publishing "garbled extracts" from *El Gringo*. The *Gazette* shot back that what it quoted had been taken "without variation, jot or tittle from the original," and it invited anyone to peruse the copy in its office to see for themselves that the president of the Peña Blanca convention stood "guilty before this people of all the exaggerations, slanders and untruths contained and published in *El Gringo*."[130] In a racial tit-for-tat, *El Demócrata* reproduced a letter from the *New York Daily Times* containing derogations of Nuevomexicanos, reputedly signed by the American Partyite Sydney Hubble. Hubble accused Davis of planting the story.[131]

How, the question becomes, did Davis's low esteem of Nuevomexicanos jibe with the author's membership in the Mexican Party? Davis's politics might have reflected a cynical allegiance to Governor Meriwether, although his devotion to Gallegos in the contest with Otero appears genuine. Perhaps Davis recognized that the popular reading market demanded jaundiced views of primitive, foreign others.

The integrative colonialism in the mind of Davis comes into focus in an earlier essay in which he expressed, on one hand, objection to moral and intellectual issues arising among the Mexicans and, on the other, the belief that citizen policies in New Mexico should rightfully focus on the needs of the majority population. His low view of Nuevomexicano lifeways was not absolute. Rather, he saw them as backward or less evolved, not fundamentally flawed. Thus, while supporting the Mexican Party Independents, he held a "deep interest in the improvement of our New Mexican brethren." He would "gladly" see the Mexicans "the equals of the most favored population of the Union; but the mission of intellectual and moral culture belongs more especially to themselves, and they must seize the bull of ignorance and vice by the horns, and not wait for outside aid, because 'whoever will be free himself must strike the blow.'" Davis urged Nuevomexicanos to the necessity of educating their children and of "checking the vice of various kinds which now stalks over the Territory like an army of terror demons sapping everything in the shape of morals." A change was needed for "this people" to take their "proper position in the country," opening a path "onward and upward in the great race of human progress."[132] This reasoning of a flexible mental and moral capacity was contradicted by *El Gringo*, which called the Nuevomexicano shortcomings "constitutional and natural in the race."

There was another angle, however. In letters to his hometown newspaper, Davis expressed utmost disdain for ricos. Those who attached themselves "to the customs of the old Spanish aristocracy," he described, embraced a system "that may be properly called the twin brother of our ancient English feudal system, and which customs they will do anything in their power to perpetuate." Davis sneered at Miguel Otero in particular for "harping" on his "pure Castilian blood," which the "thinking people" may come to consider either "some mistake" or "no better than other blood."[133] His greater hope for reform of the common Mexican than the affected upper class helps explain his affiliation with the Mexican Democrats and his rejection of the effete American Party National leaders personified by Miguel Antonio Otero. At the same time, Davis clearly differentiated between the rights of citizens, particularly the majority, and the constitution of their culture. Indeed, his musings reinforce the suggestion that he authored the major editorial in the surviving issue of *El Demócrata* with its undoubted class struggle.

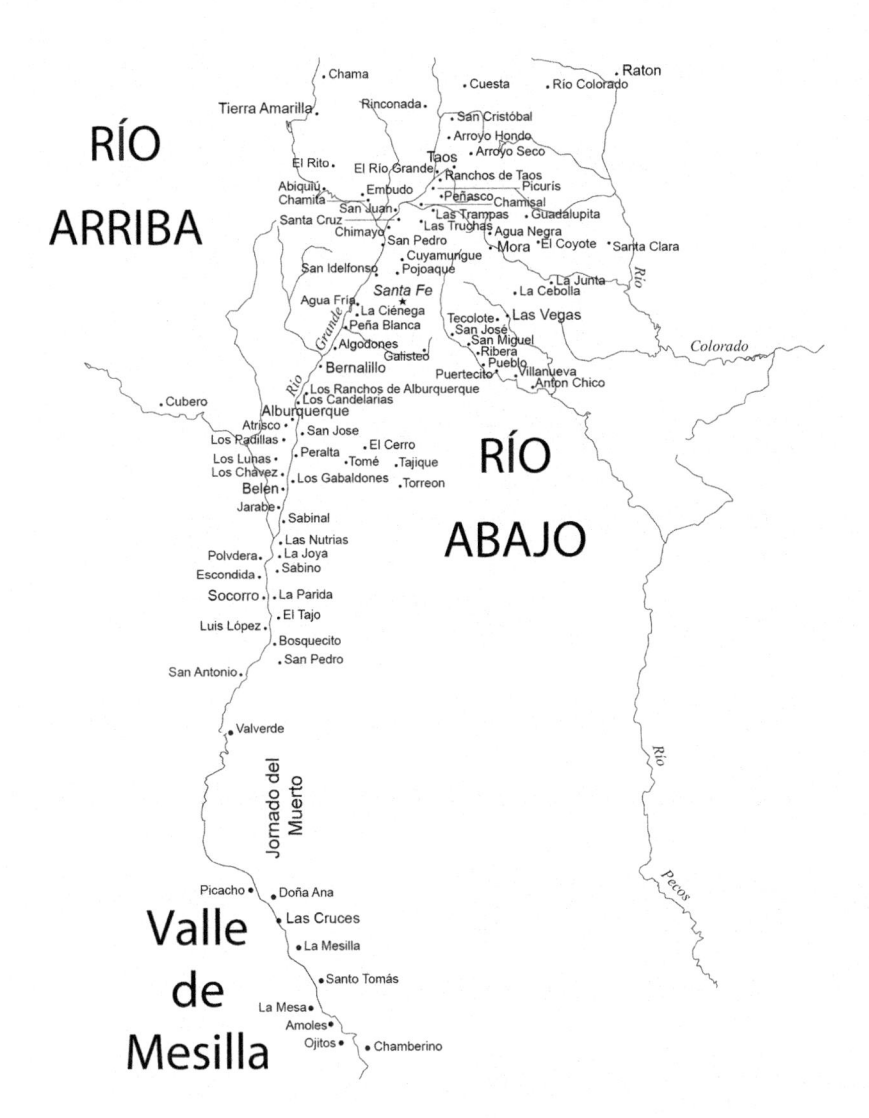

MAP 3. Precinct stops along the nineteenth-century campaign trail in the elections for delegate to Congress. Adapted from Giovanni Banfi/Map of New Mexico/Thinkstock (with the assistance of Mark Montoya).

Press reports depicted candidates and entourages taking to the stump all through the territory. Coverage of the hustings kept villagers connected to political doings and posted on the issues. The trail of 1857 lit the campaign to excitement. Some of the electricity sparked from the star quality crowds accorded Miguel Otero. "Throughout the entire trip to the Río Arriba," a citizen correspondent reported, "Mr. Otero has been received by the people with open arms. The roads have been lined with the people who wished to see the man who has in the national council of the country boldly and manfully battled for the interests of the territory, and who, now that he has returned among his constituents has the frankness to go forth like an honest statesman and explain his position before the people."[134]

Controlling for the partisan enthusiasm here, the generation of a conventional political public seems clear. A Euroamerican vecino in the Mora Valley reported on the "warm and enthusiastic reception" given to "the lion, Miguel Antonio Otero." The welcoming event bore the hallmarks of the contemporary American rally:

> A procession of some seventy mounted men headed by Don José Pley, started from the town of Mora to the Agua Negra [River] to escort Mr. Otero into town. On their arrival they found him delivering an address to the inhabitants of the place after the conclusion of which the procession repaired to the house of Don José Pley in Mora.
>
> On their approach the citizens welcomed his arrival with a salute of musketry which was kept up without intermission for an hour— the musicians playing at the head of the procession as it moved along. Never was there witnessed in this or any other valley in the Territory so universal a disposition manifested to give to the Delegation such a warm and hospitable reception as was given Mr. Otero here.

Otero's assimilated persona apparently presented no problem for the Spanish-speaking masses or their local campaign handlers, who would have beheld modernity incarnate. Otero held special attraction: "The inhabitants at this little valley are proud to find one of their own countrymen so eminently fitted by talent and education to represent them."[135] Of course, Otero's brilliance would have bounced brightly off the figure of his Texan opponent.

Rallies spread from the far north down to Socorro in the Río Abajo and on to Mesilla in the far south, below the Río Abajo on the border with Mexico.[136] The trail took in debates, one at Santa Clara between Baird and the Otero supporters C. P. Clever and Merrill Ashurst.[137] Another at the plaza of Don Fernandez de Taos involved Otero and Baird before a *concurrencia* (great audience) of "some thousands of spectators."[138] The old-Catholic/new-Catholic rivalry ratcheted up. Lamy continued to believe Gallegos a threat and an embarrassment to his religious authority (problems reinforced by a land dispute with Gallegos, who had moved from Alburquerque to Santa Fe). Lamy ordered his cadre of priests to stay out of the campaign.[139] He was not obeyed, and so the campaign assumed the character of a religious battleground. Lamy came to take "a very active part" in the counties of San Miguel, Taos, Río Arriba, Santa Ana, Santa Fe, and Bernalillo. One witness commented on the great influence he exerted on the people.[140]

A number of new federal officers, owing no allegiance to Governor Meriwether, openly worked for Otero. The surveyor general William Pelham wrote letters on behalf of the rico *hijo del país*. An eyewitness suggested how Otero's friendship to their landed interests played to the crowd. "Nothing could be better calculated to work upon these [Mexican] people than this mode of argument," he noted. "Many have very large claims pending before this officer, and it is not to be supposed that they would do anything that was calculated to injure their cases."[141]

The *Gazette* reported high turnout rallies, said to reflect the people's refusal, behind the National Democracy, to submit to the "dictation of political demagogues."[142] The eloquence of the Otero team triumphed in the settlements, while Baird was hurt by his ties to Davis, "the calumniator of New Mexico," and by his "intimate relationship" with the Meriwether administration. Baird's portrayal of Otero as a "know nothing enemy of the Catholic religion" did not resonate, Miller reported, and the people were "well satisfied that Mr. Baird is not the patriotic man or friend of the poor as *El Demócrata* portrays him."[143] Of course, *El Gringo* was "everywhere being read by the people ... causing them to rise up en masse in condemnation of the candidate of that [Independent] convention," making them "determined to rebuke in an unmistakable manner the slander of this people and of this country [by the man] who, as its President, is the embodiment of that convention and the great friend of its candidate, Judge Baird."[144]

National Democrats debated Baird in the *Gazette*, focusing on his promise given at the northern precincts of Taos County to procure millions of dollars for the promotion of public education in New Mexico, said to be a scheme to favor his political friends.[145] The Nationals were called only too eager to accept the last-minute bravado of the Bobtailed betting that their man Baird would take every county with large majorities.[146] Yet the Nationals expressed fear of fraud at the polls. A citizen recommended that major precincts appoint special committees to keep watch over the official taking of the votes, counseling: "As long as honor and good faith dominate we will not fall to the darkness of doubt of the winner in this election [and] of the glorious cause of the National Democracy."[147]

An organizational effort to whip up the electorate reaped dividends for the Nationals. The final count pegged the total number of votes cast at over 15,000, some 2,000 more than in 1855. Otero won by a margin of over 3,500, about 60 percent of the total. In the far north a major reversal from the 1855 results occurred. Whereas Otero had lost that region back then, he now took all its counties, some by substantial margins. Otero cleaned up in his home Valencia County and adjacent Socorro. Baird fared well in the far southern county of Doña Ana with its decided Texas influence, although the low turnout qualified the result, as it did in Santa Ana, which Baird also won.[148] According to the post-hoc guesstimate of David Miller, nine-tenths of the voters "not Mexican born" voted against Baird.[149] Adding to the crush, José Manuel Gallegos lost his bid for a seat in the territorial house.[150] Moreover, the National Democrats captured the assembly. Victorious Donaciano Vigil came out of political seclusion to become the council's president pro tempore.[151]

The story of the election was told in several factors: the inspired American Party machine built around an excited national movement, manned by settlers and nativos alike, working to agitate voter sentiment; the defections of Mexican Democrats; Diego Archuleta stoking the unpopularity of the Meriwether administration; the explosion set off by *El Gringo;* the *Gazette*'s monumental booming of a sophisticated incumbent; the inability of Baird to present himself as a people's candidate; and the late start of *El Demócrata*.

A jubilant Miller saw the liberal American sentiment "fast spreading among the people." The masses were becoming enlightened "as to their duty and their true interests," he crowed. "Anti-Americanism and anti democracy were rapidly declining."[152] The results were a "bold and decisive declaration of the confidence of the sovereign people in the honesty, fidelity, and capacity of the Hon. Mr. Otero," representing "explicit and tangible condemnation and repudiation of the Meriwether, Davis and Deavenport administration." It was a "pertinent rebuke to the traducers of the native inhabitants of the Territory."[153] Nationals saw proof positive of their party as the only organization entitled to Nuevomexicano support, at least from those who professed to be loyal citizens of the United States. The invitation went out to "every honest man" who was misled to the opposition by "designing men" to unite with the true Democrats in the aim of developing the resources of the territory and establishing more fully "our claim to the fostering care of the U.S. government."[154] Miller reiterated his gratitude at the "rapid decline" of the anti-American sentiments of the Baird-led party. The "good work" of the National Democracy would eradicate "every feeling hostile to the American" and bring about the day when New Mexicans would become a "homogeneous people animated by a common ambition to carry out the spirit of our republican laws and institutions."[155]

The Nationals in the legislative assembly grabbed the spoils of their victory. In a symbolic show, the chambers jointly repealed the memorial of the previous session that had asked the president to fire Judge Perry Brocchus.[156] A Spanish-language editorial caricatured Bobtailed Independents in the territorial legislature "in the vale of tears without hope of rest [en el 'valle de lágrimas' sin esperanza de descansar]," having vigorously tried in the assembly to take advantage of the victory of others by kissing the hand of their contraries so as to gain some employment the legislature had at its disposal.[157] The rank and file in northern New Mexico moved to build the National Democracy. One local called for an all-out mobilization to elect a National in the Taos special election to fill the seat of a representative who resigned.[158]

Nationals taunted Independents. A certain Q.S.M.B. reported in Spanish about a meeting held in the village La Cañada in which the Bobtailed prefect Antonio Royval and House member Pedro Aragón warned the people against supporting the assembly memorial volunteering New Mexicans for a regiment to help put down the Mormon rebellion. Not only did they object to the low salaries volunteers got; they questioned whether Nuevomexicanos should march against the *Mormoros*, a "very brave nation [*una nación valiente*]," so powerful and numerous that all the U.S. forces were "insufficient to defeat them." The Mormons were "GIANTS, not people like us," warned Royval and Aragón, "each one of them having had their fifty or hundred women when we barely could maintain one, and one Mormon was well equipped to eat a poor *mexicano* for breakfast, the same as we eat a small chicken."

Q.S.M.B. saw ethnic identity as the key issue. "Where are the noble sentiments that have always characterized the Castilian race?" he queried, in the vein of Delegate Otero. "There is no doubt that men capable of talking like these cannot be other than fools and without shame, but thanks to God there are few of this class in Río Arriba." The writer boosted American acculturation favored by the National Democratic leadership, linking a Spanish heritage to worthy membership in the American republic. As he put it, "We know that we belong to a glorious and powerful nation, and we are not yet so destitute of all sentiment of honor to suggest that we be treated as cowards. Say whatever of the meeting of the Cañaderos; only put our patriotism to the test, and if ever volunteers are called, then we will see who are the ones to present themselves first for service."[159]

Royval and Aragón admired the Mormons as an example of resistance to Washington domination. The National Democrats, out for blood, unseated Aragón and two other Río Arriba representatives, replacing them with Nationals on charges that citizens of Mexico had voted for them and claiming other fraudulent acts at the polls. A correspondent to the *Gazette*, going by *Un Chimayó* (one from the village of Chimayó), noted the "strange situation" that Aragón and the other contested ones were themselves not U.S. citizens. Un Chimayó laid down a forceful lesson on the importance of guarding the "sacred rights of the people" and the "purity of the electoral urn." Aragón reportedly left the council chamber making a "very furious speech," departing the public and political stage only on being convinced that neither "giants nor hidalgos [landed gentry] of his color" remained in the chamber. The writer expected him to recognize that from then on the National Democracy stood as the guardian of the people's rights and would put the sword to anyone who would disturb their enjoyment of those rights.[160]

Power consolidation spun around the new Democratic Party identity. A company of men led by Joab Houghton purchased the *Gazette* for the express purpose of having "an organ of the National Democracy." As envisioned by Samuel Yost, the new operating editor, following the tenets of the Nationals would spell the "true and genuine prosperity of the Territory." To keep the partisanship running, Yost swore an "uncompromising hostility" to Bobtail Democracy, not only because of differences in principles but so that the National Party could maintain core strength and not itself dissolve into factionalism.[161] The editor expected a windfall of increased subscriptions. He soon boasted of at least twenty-six salesmen across all counties. Some of the paper's American Party agents had just played major roles in the campaign, including Diego Archuleta, Donaciano Vigil, Antonio José Otero, Juan Cristóbal Armijo, Vincent St. Vrain, and José Pley.[162]

The *Gazette* spared no effort after the election in poking the territorial solons to do their part to promote the party. The integrity of the National movement, the strengthening of the bonds among the members, and the maintenance of the organization required them to watch "with ceaseless vigilance every movement that may tend in the least to distraction or dissension." The "wily foe" would appeal "affectingly to the sympathies and charity of many members of our party," but "let each one bear in mind that every step towards compromise or conciliation is tantamount to an acknowledgment of his own wrong, and a virtual endorsement of the political character and principles of the enemy."[163] The Nationals were reinforced by federal appointees who arrived soon after the election. The new governor, Abraham Rencher from North Carolina, bore the "enviable reputation as a man and a statesman" who had received an endorsement from congressional delegate Otero and a U.S. senator closely aligned with Buchanan. Another southerner, Alexander M. Jackson, took over as territorial secretary.[164]

Another for Otero: The Election of 1859

Independent Descolados wished the results of the election had reflected the "will of the people" and a triumph of "liberal sentiments." Instead, the people had "disposed in another Democratic manner": they would submit "humbly" until the next election, when once again they would rise to the contest and continue the fight "until victory under the Democratic flag."[165] If the Independent Democratic Party was to rise from the ashes, it would have to make some important leadership adjustments. Away for six months prior to the election and facing dismissal under a new president, Governor David Meriwether resigned effective September 30, 1856, never to return to New Mexico. Chief Justice J. J. Deavenport departed in anticipation of his removal, none too soon for the tastes of the Nationals.[166] Territorial Secretary W. W. H. Davis left New Mexico in October.[167] "Let him go!" the *Gazette* rejoiced at the news of his resignation. "With his book of stupidities and calumnies, called *El Gringo*, and with his acts as secretary of this territory, he has killed himself before this people completely and remains without any hope of resuscitation." On Davis's "very deep sepulcre" the weekly would inscribe "Here lie the remains of W.W. / Who never again will trouble you, trouble you!"[168] The impacts of *El Gringo* and its author were laid to rest, but only for the moment. Both would rise from the grave in the late 1880s to taunt New Mexico politics once again.[169]

Spruce Baird resigned as Indian agent but stayed on in Santa Fe.[170] He later tried smearing the National Democratic Party of New Mexico before audiences abroad. In a letter to a Texas newspaper, which he asked New Mexico papers to print, he accused the leadership of the Nationals of being wholly "old Whigs." He insinuated as well that many of them were Know-Nothing partisans. The attributions would have gone completely against the core Democratic Party of the United States, he insinuated. David Miller challenged what he deemed Baird's misstatements, audacious given the mass of defections that had occurred from his Algodones convention in the previous election and against himself. Miller justified the move of Whigs into the Democracy of New Mexico as a result of their "cherished" party falling apart. As Miller put it, however, "I know of none, not one, who has ever been an abolitionist or a know nothing either there or here [United States or New Mexico]."[171]

The National tide rolled through 1858. The Bobtailed defections of the 1857 election glowed in the collective memory of the Mexican villages.[172] The precinct and county conventions for the local and territorial legislative season that began in July 1858 relied on a continuation of the intra–Democratic Party feud. Reflecting a determination for a permanent political party, the local meetings in Santa Fe and Taos were mandated by the respective National Democratic county central committees.[173] An anonymous Nuevomexicano correspondent highlighted *el hombría de bien* of the Santa Fe County candidates under the wing of Delegate Otero while assailing the Mexican Democrats who had conducted their studies in the seminary of Durango like those *presumidos* (pretenders) whose common sense was replaced by cheap Latin words.[174]

While the evidence is sparse, the Bobtailed Independents seem to have hounded the National office holders.[175] However, in the results of the 1858 races for the territorial house, the Nationals captured twenty of twenty-six seats. Traditional Mexican Partyites, among them Facundo Pino, Cándido Ortiz, and the various priests, were rejected. Nothing by way of Mexican Party–American Party conflict appears in the assembly proceedings.[176] The victors continued asking Washington to appoint resident citizens to New Mexico's federal posts, to little avail.[177]

The available descriptions of the 1859 canvass for delegate to Congress in the *Gazette* and other sources are sketchy. Enough of the campaign's contour comes through. Accounts after the nominating conventions suggest a reinvigoration of local National Democratic activity. Informal meetings, precinct conventions, and county conventions endorsed the principles of the National Democratic Party, President Buchanan, and Otero for delegate.[178] The Bobtailed Democrats would have conducted parallel events, more modest in scale as the Nationals outspent them in effective campaigning.[179] An early report has Miguel Otero preferring not to run for reelection but assuring he would submit to the will of the people in their desire that he continue or not as their congressional delegate. So great was the National Democratic confidence of an overwhelming victory that the *Gazette* predicted the Bobtailed opposition, lacking anything "to give" or "tangible inducements for presentation," might not have a candidate to put forth. Otero predictably received the unanimous nomination of the Nationals at their Territorial Nominating Convention in Alburquerque.[180]

Spruce Baird was one of the few in the slate of American settler members to remain in the Independent Democracy. He was elected to serve as chair of the territorial convention. The Descolados turned once again to José M. Gallegos to serve as their standard bearer. While nothing is known of the deliberations that went into this decision, the serious defeat of 1857 signified that, given the premium of a nativo candidate and delegate in Congress, a Mexican was needed to challenge Otero, and Gallegos appeared the possible one.[181] It appears that the Gallegos nomination inspired some local leaders who had defected to the Nationals in 1857 to return to the Independent fold for this election.[182]

Another hard-fought campaign ensued. *Gazette* editor Yost followed the prior strategy of addressing the Independent candidate as "Padre" Gallegos while banging on the theme of the priest suspended from his clerical vocation for dereliction of duty. Yost argued that Gallegos had no record to run on as compared to what Otero accomplished in Washington, including strengthening trade with Missouri. Otero was applauded for defending the "Americans and Mexicans" who had been "offended" by "certain persons," *El Gringo* haunting the proceedings.[183]

Gallegos is said to have spent considerable personal money on the campaign. Another legend has John S. Watts, former member of the territorial Supreme Court and a Mexican Party settler, insulting the Otero family as he stumped for Gallegos, leading to a "bloodless duel" with Otero. Also, Bishop Lamy applied his influence to defeat Gallegos.[184] The Bobtailed campaign appears without a campaign weekly, *El Demócrata* shutting down after the 1857 election. The Descolados put on a spirited stump nonetheless. Facundo Pino keynoted the Gallegos candidacy on tour through the territory.[185] Pino accused the National Democratic Party of serving the special interests of the rich. He hit hard on the assimilated Otero, especially his predominant use of English. An anonymous citizen said he pitied "poor Facundo" for insulting the American people and the "young" rising generation, "the scions of the Chávezes, Armijos, Pereas, Oteros, Senas," and the other young men with the vision to study the "beautiful language" of Shakespeare, Milton, Pope, Walter Scott, and Byron, the language in which the Declaration of Independence was written, "the greatest document ever recorded in history." Pino did not realize, the writer exclaimed, that the English language [a key instrument of democratic imperialism], was "bound to conquer" New Mexico as it had New Zealand, Australia, the West Indies, and other places around the world fortunate to have received its benefits.[186] Descolados called for greater assistance to its people in a debate over the socioeconomic condition of New Mexico. To the Nationals the people of New Mexico were not as "degraded as some imagine."[187]

National Democratic confidence turned in no small part on the diligent local organizing of both settler and Mexican partisans.[188] While the regional breakdown is impossible to tell from the poor quality of the report, a strong victory for Otero is evident.[189] In addition, the majority of the territorial legislature came from the Otero Democratic Party.[190]

The South-leaning National Democracy reinforced its power in New Mexico. Due in great part to Delegate Otero, the political and civic incorporation of Nuevomexicanos would be dealt as integration into the orbit of the slave-holding section. Nuevomexicanos were becoming part of the American political system through some of the classic mechanisms of liberal integration, yet Otero nudged them toward the southern weltanschauung. Following on the 1857 *Dred Scott* decision, in which the Supreme Court denied free Negroes and slaves citizenship and voting rights, Otero, with the assistance of Rencher and Jackson (the latter known as a "virulent secessionist") pressed the territorial assembly to pass an act "for the protection of Slave Property." A special committee of legislators of the Ninth Territorial Legislature, assisted by Jackson, confirmed the growing southern influence over Nuevomexicano politicians by introducing a resolution declaring that *Dred Scott* had demonstrated to New Mexico the necessity of a "slave code" to protect slave property and the desire to induce slave holders to immigrate to the territory. The National Democratic legislature swallowed Otero's line that it would facilitate statehood. Taos representative Pedro Valdez led the passing of a series of laws providing protection for owners of Negro slaves to keep their chattel in the territory and imposing political restrictions on freedmen. The number of slave owners was quite small, most of them military officers who came from the South and people with slaves passing through.[191]

The measures adhered to Stephen A. Douglas's state rights philosophy. Otero had long agreed with Douglas and the results of the Kansas-Nebraska Act. An attempt to establish a slave territory would likely have failed, although pro-northern political activists would state that New Mexico's slave code was the work of "some Southern politicians" meant to lay the path for bringing southern slavery into New Mexico.[192] The measures passed the Nuevomexicano legislature overwhelmingly. It was a remarkable reversal of the 1848 and 1850 constitutional conventions that rejected slavery at the helm of the same faction that now sponsored it. It was thought for one thing that it might protect New Mexico's long-existing institution of Indian slavery. It also suited another law that reinforced debt peonage. It is thus possible to see Nuevomexicanos, in supporting the slave code, acting to head off a colonial assault on two of their cherished institutions, although a critical perspective would have to concede the normative point to the classic liberal call for the undermining of oppressive tradition.

In any case, Rencher set the possibility back by vetoing a bill that would specifically have brought Indian slavery under the terms of a slave code. Rencher argued that acquired Indians were not technically slaves and could be considered only captives or peons. He admonished the assembly for not recognizing its lack of authority to "create or abolish slavery," for it could only be regulated where it existed.[193]

Since 1853 New Mexicans had struggled to have an organized political party. The contention over ownership of the Democratic Party reflected a rapidly developing will of factional citizenship. It was an essential step for New Mexico's political development and for the political incorporation of Nuevomexicanos. The National Democracy that had left the Independent Democrats in the dust earned the right to confidence about establishing a regular party organization. However, the wings of national political change were at that time beating at break-neck speed, soon to complicate what a political party system meant for both the United States and New Mexico.

3

Party Modalities in the Time of Civil War

A new Republican Party came into being in 1854 at Ripon, Wisconsin. The agitation over the Kansas-Nebraska Act split the Whig Party such as to force its demise. The modern Republican Party came out of anti-slavery remnants of the Whig, Independent Democratic, Free Soil, and American Parties in large part to combat the Kansas-Nebraska Act, which proposed to extend slavery to the western territories. The first national Republican nominating convention took place in 1855, and the party quickly developed across the northern states.

Perhaps it was the growing abolitionist cause in the country that led the speaker of the territorial house, Missouri transplant Levi Keithly, to submit a bill in the session of 1859–60 to repeal New Mexico's Slavery Act. Keithly, it is important to note, was a charter member of the American Party at a time when it opposed slavery. Democrats, however, beat back the measure with blackguard ferocity. Name-calling abuse caused Keithly to step down from the house speakership and to resign his house seat.[1]

In the background, however, the national Democratic Party had been careening in dissension. Independent Democrats precipitated a major crisis in opposing the slavery provision in the U.S. Senate's organization of the Nebraska Territory. Stephen A. Douglas's northern faction challenged both President Buchanan and the National Democracy over their support of the Nebraska Act and attempts to extend slavery legally to the Kansas Territory.[2] What one New Mexico editorialist called the "derangement" of the American economy since 1857 divided Democratic leaders further over national finance policies. Reports of a crisis-ridden Democratic Party filed into New Mexico.[3]

The tremors in the Democratic Party presaged the Civil War. That cataclysmic event would result in even more drastic changes in party dynamics. As the war disrupted party lines, leaders found themselves pinning their factions to advantage in the context of swirling positions over it and the question of slavery. Emergent collateral issues, momentary collapses of party lines, and shifting alliances were the order of the day. Organizers qualified the policies of their parties, symbolized by the series of nicknames they adopted for their organizations at presidential nominating conventions. Dependent New Mexico was positioned to catch the rumbling fallout of both the war itself and the party realignments on high. The contagion of political ambiguity affected the experience of partisan building in New Mexico, as organizers strived to keep up with national trends.

Individual Republican operatives loped into New Mexico, and as they made their partisan leanings clear, they adjusted to the content of the binary imperative. Their work would begin a prolonged process of establishing a Republican Party for New Mexico while conditions within the territory made for some deep reasons for keeping the party binary alive. Remarkably, through it all, the same established bodies in the territory, designated as Mexican and American proto-parties, kept the structure of political competition going through the war.

CHAPTER SEVEN

Low Tide in the Partisan Divide, 1861

The fractious 1860 Democratic National Convention in Charleston, South Carolina, adjourned without a slate of candidates. It reassembled in Baltimore, where Stephen Douglas battled opponents and won the presidential nomination. Southern Democrats pulled out as a result and reconvened in Richmond, Virginia, where they proceeded to nominate the pro-slavery incumbent vice president, Kentuckian John Breckinridge, for president.[1] The nomination of Abraham Lincoln by the Republicans implied a real threat of its own to slavery. The editor of the *Santa Fe Weekly Gazette*, the Virginia newcomer John T. Russell, swooned into the doughface camp that James Collins, Miguel Antonio Otero, and other members of the National Democracy initiated for New Mexico, assuming a commonality of interest between New Mexico and the South. In his initial editorials Russell worried over the irreparable wounds of division being inflicted on the Democratic Party by the "negro worshipping abolitionists." He perceived the election of Lincoln spelling "a dire calamity to the country," sure to bring upon it "evils that will not be easily remedied."[2]

Lincoln won the presidency with 40 percent of the popular vote, mainly from free states, as New Mexicans could read for themselves.[3] In a publicized letter to Collins, Otero called Lincoln an "awful manifestation on the part of the Northern people," seeming to "disregard the equal rights which the Southern people claim in the common Territory belonging to the United States." Otero noted that many anticipated slave states would secede before Lincoln's inauguration. "And for what?" he scoffed. "For the accursed negro." Horace Greeley, the militant abolitionist editor of the *New York Tribune* and a Lincolnite, accused Otero of rankly favoring secession, of even attempting to mobilize New Mexicans to declare themselves in favor of secession. Otero opposed secession, actually. If the South had not taken part in the election, he would not fault secession as an option, but, he reasoned, "as she entered into the contests with her candidates, I think it would be, to say the least, imprudent to secede because she failed to win the fight." Otero made very clear he was "very far from being a Republican either in principle or feeling," and he would fight that party "to the bitter end." Still, he believed it unnecessary to dissolve the Union "merely because that party happens to elect a President."[4] True to his National Democratic affiliation, Otero blamed the sectional crisis on congressional abolitionists manifesting their "wonted fanaticism" and showing a "disposition to carry on their anti-slavery war to the bitter end."[5]

The Crittenden Compromise, named for Kentucky senator John J. Crittenden, was the most important of the proposals circulating in Congress meant to head off southern state secession. Its proposed constitutional amendment would allow slavery below the line of the Missouri Compromise, which did not include the upper slave states but extended to the Pacific shore.[6] President-elect Lincoln opposed the proposal. Otero agreed with Crittenden. He considered his fellow New Mexicans ready to accept membership in the extended slave area.[7] As various amendments to the Crittenden proposal made the congressional rounds in an attempt to gain the loyalty of slave states bordering the North, the reviewing House committee recommended statehood for New Mexico "with or without slavery." This proposal, brought forward by Unionist Know-Nothing Henry Winter Davis of Maryland, was meant to placate the South since the territory had passed a slave code. However, in the rancor and politicking that it touched off, slave states expressed fear that it would close off the issue of whether slavery could be taken to the new states of the West.[8]

Historian Mark Stegmaier has Otero urging Davis to submit the statehood measure. At that very time, the New Mexico legislature introduced a bill calling for the election of delegates to a convention for the purpose of forming a state constitution. The constitution would be ratified or rejected in the regular election the following October. What role Otero played in generating this initiative is not clear. Easterners interpreted the bill's appearance in the session as an endorsement of the Davis statehood bill. The proceedings of the previous legislature indicate that a letter from Otero to the territorial council was read, although the proceedings failed to reveal its contents. It can be noted in any case that the legislature was dominated by Otero Democrats, and one of its members, Sydney Hubbell of the Bernalillo–Santa Ana district, introduced the bill in the council. The pro-Otero *Weekly Gazette* endorsed it. Moreover, Russell used the mainstream sovereignty justification of the Statehood Revolution to justify his support, adding the assuredness of security for settlements under Indian attack. However, Russell denied that the proposal had any connections "with the fortunes of any party, nor should it be viewed as a party question." The people would have plenty of room for exercising party interests once statehood was gained, the editor pointed out. There were opponents to the proposal who raised the specter of high taxes if New Mexico became a state and doubted that New Mexicans could maintain a state political system. While the council passed the measure, it died in the New Mexico house when time ran out.[9]

The call for statehood with an allowance for slavery remained in the U.S. Senate. As it did, free-state congressmen took to throwing stones at Nuevomexicanos. Otero had spent his political career attempting to lead the Nuevomexicano folk to the ideological cover of one the most illiberal institutions ever harbored by the United States. He now found himself the proverbial Don Quixote, swinging in attempts to slay one prejudiced Republican windmill after another. His direct challenge to John Sherman of Ohio, chairman of the Ways and Means Committee, for having degraded New Mexico's peons in a speech, did not end well. Stegmaier suggests that it left Otero humiliated in the House chamber.[10]

Otero ensnared himself in op-ed spats with Wisconsin Representative Cadwallader Washburn and the powerful Republican Radical, Pennsylvania representative Thaddeus Stevens. Washburn intimated that Otero's interest in statehood was an anticipated senatorship. Stevens complained that the people of New Mexico had entered the United States as a free territory, only to be taken toward slavery by Washington fiat. The people there did not ask for admission as a state, Stevens pointed out, an implicit reference to the need for a citizen-driven Statehood Revolution. Rather, they demonstrated their incapacity for self-government, "by the infamous slave code, which establishes the most cruel kind of black and white slavery." Otero strained on the House floor to explain that citizens in New Mexico were capable of self-government. In his self-serving speculation, it was not out of the question that the territory might have become a slave state; after all, it was possible that Texas might have succeeded in acquiring the land up to the Río Grande. That the United States paid Texas for giving up its claim to New Mexico confirmed the validity of the assertion, Otero felt.[11]

Otero got sucked into a squabble with the unyielding Greeley. Greeley deemed New Mexico unworthy of statehood because it would come in with slavery even if its geography made wholesale slavery impractical. Had the territory come in as a state in 1850, it would have been free of slavery, Greeley figured, but Democratic administrations purposely assigned "Zealous Slavery Propagandists" as federal officers and military commanders. Kansas "Border Ruffians," and the "scum of rascaldom" run out of San Francisco, imported southern prejudices to New Mexico, Greeley claimed. The editor opposed slavery as a gross violation of a liberal society but showed that American abolitionism did not preclude racism.[12] As the historian James Bilotta states, "The same racist ideas promulgated by some Southerners were used quite effectively by some Northerners to attack."[13] Greeley's xenophobic variant characterized the Mexican masses of New Mexico as "a hybrid race of Spanish and Indian origin ... ignorant and degraded, demoralized, and priest-ridden." His Radicalism condemned Nuevomexicano institutions as socially and morally backward. The "debasing Mexican system of peonage" appeared as a "modified slavery," he declared. Politically, a "few able and unscrupulous" men controlled everything. The masses were their "blind, facile tools," in the lens of the liberal modernist. Greeley ignorantly claimed that there was no press "of any account; no Public Opinion." For Greeley, the Republican Party guaranteed civilization and liberty, and as he noted, New Mexico had no Republican Party. President Lincoln would rectify the evils New Mexico harbored, Greeley foretold.[14]

Otero replied to Greeley's "defamatory and malevolent" message in a letter to the *Constitution* of Washington DC, later putting it and Greeley's piece in a pamphlet for widespread dissemination.[15] Otero assailed Greeley's misrepresentations, calumnies, and "frenzied animosity" to New Mexico and its population as the work of a "sectional enemy." He charged Greeley with trying to poison New Mexico in the minds of the members of the Republican Party with "unscrupulous exaggerations, most of them utterly malicious and basely false." In answer to Greeley's claim that New Mexico would have come in a free state in 1850, Otero countered by pointing out that President Taylor would not have fostered anti-slavery sentiments in New Mexico, for he was "a Southern man, of Southern interests, Southern education and Southern sympathies." Otero misrepresented New Mexico's recent political history in saying that anyone asking in 1850 about Nuevomexicano opinion of slavery would not have found it "in the slightest degree repugnant to the state of opinion and feeling existing upon the subject at the present day." In fact, the American Party itself had originally opposed slavery before the dominance of Otero, and Collins and others had redirected its policy to a friendly footing with the South.

Otero challenged Greeley's assertion that federal appointments to New Mexico, most of which he had taken the initiative to propose, were based on the sectional opinions of those appointed "either by the appointing power or myself." Otero thought it minor that a half dozen army officers had taken slaves with them to the territory for domestic convenience and with no intent of propagating the institution of slavery. The imputation of military officers being instruments of pro-slavery propaganda Otero called "nothing more or less than the miserable subterfuge of a pressed demagogue." Otero over-generalized in saying "New Mexicans" viewed slavery with a sense of justice due to the South, although it held true that none were "deranged by a religious fanaticism, not perverted by an erroneous sectional education; not maddened by an inordinate and unholy lust for political power." Otero adjusted the significance of New Mexico's slave code to a liberal fold. It meant nothing more than to respect the right of U.S. citizens to bring into the common domain "every lawful species of property, and there enjoy the same as fully and uninterruptedly as they were accustomed to do in the State from which they respectively come."

Otero confronted Greeley's racism with a bit of race baiting: the disdain commonly held in both North and South for what Bilotta calls the "dreaded prospect of miscegenation."[16] "It may be," the New Mexico delegate put it, "that Mr. Greeley finds some ground for the charge of atrocity in the 23d section of the code, which forbids the amalgamation of white persons and negroes, declares marriages between such persons void, and punishes with a severe penalty any white person who may procure or attempt to procure marriage with a negro." It is intriguing to consider whether Otero had Thaddeus Stevens, who had a rumored relationship with a black woman, in the back of his mind when he indicted Greeley for regarding it "rather atrocious and inhumane for any law to impose a restraint upon the exercise of a taste which the ultra members of his party occasionally evince to indulge in the luxury of that sort of conjugal association."

Otero responded to Greeley's modernist attack on New Mexico by placing Nuevomexicano tradition on par with that of the United States so that it should not be destroyed. New Mexican peonage, he claimed, was "merely a system of apprenticeship or temporary voluntary servitude." Otero's soft peonage saw nothing debasing in the ancient system of labor exploitation as it represented nothing more than a contract among free and equal individuals. A person's social and political status was not affected by entering into the condition of a peon. "His right of suffrage and all other civil rights remain unimpaired," the delegate affirmed. His services did not entail his family. "It is simply a voluntary engagement to render personal service at a stated hire for a valuable consideration," Otero declared. "It is an obligation entered into with the entire will of the obligator, which may be satisfied and discharged by him, at any moment, upon the payment of the debt on which the obligation was founded." Moreover, "if the slanderer of the people whom I have the humble honor to represent means to insinuate that the existence of this system of voluntary servitude has exercised an agency in producing that pro-slavery sentiment in New Mexico which has been manifested by the enactment of a slave code, I denounce such insinuation as an unwarrantable assumption." Conveniently omitted in Otero's proto-ethnic nationalism was any mention of Indian slavery as a justification for New Mexico's pro-Southern disposition.

Otero countered Greeley's other criteria for regarding Mexicans outside the ring of civilization in order to demonstrate their rightful membership in the American nation. As he asserted, "every mind" familiar with New Mexico history could "refute and rebuke" the claim of regional hybridity. Otero expanded on the theme of *Hispanidad* as he had hailed it before Congress during his 1855 contest against José Manuel Gallegos for election as delegate. "Ever since the conquest and colonization of the valley of the Rio del Norte under the prowess of Don Juan de Oñate in the latter part of the seventeenth century," Otero began, "the Spaniards and the aborigines or Indians, have been separated and distinct from each other, and have so remained up to this day." He elaborated further.

> The conquest of New Mexico by the Spaniards reduced the aborigines, or Indians, to a state of abject but sullen and reluctant slavery. In that relation they continued—socially separate and distinct races—until a servile insurrection of the aborigines drove the Spaniards from the land. At the close of the seventeenth century the country was reconquered by the Spaniards; and from that time to the present day the Indians within the settlements have occupied pueblos or towns exclusively set apart for them, and they have scrupulously refrained from intercourse with the Spanish population, excepting so far as became necessary for the ordinary transaction of business. They have their own exclusive and peculiar government, their own places of worship, their amusements; their social intercourse is exclusively amongst themselves; they never intermarry with the Spanish people, and are to all intents and purposes separate and distinct from them ... although the Spanish blood has sometimes manifested itself on the aboriginal race, and the Indian blood less frequently on the Spanish race, those instances are of rare occurrence—so rare as to render the sweeping allegation that the mass of the people of New Mexico are a hybrid race of a Spanish and Indian origin grossly defamatory and shamefully mendacious.

Otero's mission of making Nuevomexicanos as legitimately white as the Anglo population rested on selective memory. He distanced his folk from the settled Pueblos but would have been hard pressed to deny the significant mixing between Mexican families and captives from the plains tribes and *genízaro* settlements, even if a strain of white physiognomy appeared in the people as well.[17]

Otero conceded the pre-modern condition of education among Nuevomexicanos (even if they were white) but denied that it devalued their intelligence and morality. It was true that his people were not as enlightened as those in the "more favored portion of the earth," he noted, but it was their "misfortune and not their fault." Otero shifted ethnological gears. It was not the part of "magnanimity or justice," he put it, to taunt them with a deficiency in mental culture, "for which they are not responsible, much less so to attempt by such an imputation to retard their advancement in the path of political, intellectual, and material progress. If their minds are not highly illuminated by that kind of intelligence, which books and scholastic cultivation alone can impart, I am able to assert, without fear of contradiction, that there is not to be found anywhere on the face of the earth a people possessing greater mental aptitude or a more finely organized moral structure." Nuevomexicanos might not have been "abundantly blessed with schools and school-teachers," and yet, Otero assured, there could not be found anywhere "a community of people who under the same disadvantage exhibit less of the inferiorities of the human mind and heart or manifest more of the higher attributes of our nature."

It is notable how this characterization of Nuevomexicano uniformity contrasts with the older *hombre de bien* view of a differentiated populace based on such blunt distinctions as localized tendencies to engage in mob behavior and resist the American presence. Of course, some thirteen years had passed since the end of the Mexican-American War, enough time to begin allowing for the flattening of the populace and declare a universal element of civic patriotism residing in the Nuevomexicano bosom. As Otero emphasized, there were none who more faithfully obeyed the laws of the land or rendered "more cheerful obedience to the legally constituted authorities, none more devoted to their country, her honor, and her cause." What naturally followed was the theme of a blessed American conquest, implanted by Otero's American Party colleague William Carr Lane back in 1852. "Only" a few years ago, Nuevomexicanos were "reluctantly brought by the hand of conquest," Otero began, "beneath the folds of your national flag, as it was thrown to the breach, on which just before, had floated their own national ensign. They have had the intelligence to discern and the wisdom to appreciate the blessing of the benign system of government of the United States and now they proudly call the American flag their own." With the "high commendations to the favor and affection of their conquerors," it was pure insult, Otero pushed it, for the "unscrupulous demagogue" and "miserable reviler" Greeley to "retard their progress and suppress their patriotic development by calling them ignorant, degraded, demoralized, and priest ridden." Otero came out of the discursive skirmish wondering why the United States even wanted to take possession of New Mexico, and he changed his mind regarding statehood. Not until Congress afforded its people the resources to cover the costs of administering a state should statehood be granted them, he came to conclude.[18]

Abolitionists defeated the Crittenden Compromise quite as Otero's quarrels with Washington figures subsided, and Congress quickly defeated an alternative attempt to integrate New Mexico as a state.[19] Southern states were a decided minority in Congress, and so, facing a strong anti-slavery North, seven of them seceded. The Confederate States of America was established before Lincoln took office, as Otero mentioned might happen.[20] Some in the Río Abajo and Río Arriba districts of New Mexico preferred neutrality. New Mexicans should be left alone, they said, without interference from abolitionists or separatists.[21] Otero next would have annexed his Nuevomexicano people to an imagined confederation of Pacific states to side with neither North nor South. This brainstorm was just as treasonous to U.S. integrity as southern secession. Spruce Baird agreed that New Mexico should avoid direct involvement in the sectional dispute but disagreed that a "similarity of resources" with the Pacific necessarily produced "a sameness of interest."[22]

Sympathy for the Confederacy had always run high in the far southern Mesilla Valley next door to Mexico and Texas settlements. The Mexican Constitution assigned this section to the Department of Chihuahua. The Treaty of Guadalupe Hidalgo transferred it to New Mexico, but Santa Fe had trouble bringing it into effective administration. Deprived of such necessities as courts and law enforcement, residents had previously contemplated seceding from New Mexico. Two days after Lincoln took office, Mesilla folk declared affiliation with the Confederacy, supported by Americans in Tucson who had commercial ties with Texas merchants.[23]

When the critical moment came, the popular will of Nuevomexicanos defied Otero and banked its national integration on the North. On March 27, 1861, the people in Las Vegas, San Miguel County, conducted a mass meeting to voice opposition to the Mesilla declaration. "The meeting was organized by calling to the chair don Juan M. Baca," read the official report, "and on motion, Faustín Baca y Ulivarri was chosen vice president, and Severo Baca and A. Morrison, secretaries." Valentín Vásquez joined two other Euroamerican speech makers. Participants perceived in the nation's crisis a threat to the liberal basis of American government. The preamble to the resolutions expressed "with deep regret the present distracted state of our country, whose rapid march in civilization and progress is unparalleled, whose banner has ever been the protection of the oppressed, and the rallying standard of the most free people on the face of the earth." It is impossible to tell whether these words, which were publicized in English only, originated in Spanish. That the whole gathering knew what it was declaring cannot be denied. As participants noted, the "most violent passions [were] raging in the public mind of some sections of our country and are now threatening the very existence of the Union, and with it the hope of the world, who are looking to our Union to solve the problems of man's capacity for self government." The group confirmed Otero's position in one major respect. Every patriot's heart, they proclaimed, "should throb in devotion to his country, as the only true home of the free, and every patriot's hand should be ready to do so, to suffer and sacrifice all and everything consistent with honor and propriety for the perpetuity of our Glorious Union, which until now, has been the home of the oppressed of all nations." The unanimously approved resolutions guaranteed that the citizens of San Miguel County cherished "the fondest devotion to the Union." San Miguel County nativos affirmed that no cause in the existing state of affairs justified dissolution of the ties that bound them to the federal government. Anyone, they declared in an implied disaffiliation from their original Mexican Republic, would search "in vain the annals of history, ancient, modern and contemporary for an account of any Government which affords to its citizens so much liberty and protection and prosperity, as the least favored section of our country enjoys."

It all amounted to a significant step toward inclusion in the North's version of the United States. Yet the neutrality doctrine did not recede completely. While they urged good citizens everywhere "to give cheerful obedience to a constitutionally selected chief executive," the citizens recommended "mutual forbearance" to their countrymen, North and South, in granting the right of any section of the territory to secede peacefully from the Union. Rather than fight their "brothers" in any cause of abolition, they would "bid them Godspeed, and let them go, while we prefer to remain."[24]

Such a position stood at odds with the president. As sectional hostilities intensified, Lincoln declared secession a betrayal of the nation.

After the secession of four more southern states, armies were raised on both sides. Confederate forces fired on South Carolina's disputed Fort Sumter in mid-April. Lincoln dispatched 75,000 troops to recapture the fort. The ensuing battle ignited the American Civil War.[25]

The New Mexico secretary and several military officers resigned to join the Confederacy.[26] The suspicion remained that the former National Democrats would deliver the territory's lot to that quarter as well.[27] However, the outpouring of support for the Union forced the hand of Governor Abraham Rencher.[28] Rencher, himself from the South, proudly conveyed to Secretary of State William H. Seward that the people were law-abiding and loyal to the Union, as shown in "all the popular meetings" where they expressed "great attachment" and an "earnest desire" that it be preserved."[29] Associate Chief Justice Kirby Benedict, a Connecticut native, at first notified President Lincoln that the "entire Mexican and Spanish population" remained "calm and quiet while the convulsions have been so rapid in the states," and later informed U.S. Attorney General Edward Bates, "I have abundant evidence in my possession that the New Mexican population (seven-eighths of the people) have little sympathy for the disorderly and revolutionary movement to which some have given so much prominence."[30] Exaggerating the predominant situation, the old-timer Henry Connelly commented to the president that there "was not a disloyal native in the territory."[31]

New Mexico served as the westernmost theater of the Civil War. A Texas regiment marched in from the south in July 1861, capturing Fort Fillmore below Las Cruces. Lt. Col. John Baylor took possession of what he declared the Territory of Arizona for the Confederate States of America. Baylor cited the social and political condition of Arizona as "being little short of general anarchy and the people being literally destitute of law, order and protection." He named a temporary military government for Arizona and established the settlement of Mesilla as its seat. Baylor declared all civil and military offices under the laws of the United States invalidated until the Confederate Congress provided otherwise. Baylor appointed a probate judge and other minor officials in various precincts. One Mexican received the honor.[32] Governor Rencher activated several hundred militiamen and ordered them to report to the territory's adjutant general, Charles P. Clever. Prefects in Mora, Santa Fe, Sana Ana, Bernalillo, Valencia, and Socorro counties were each ordered to organize a company of one hundred men. The larger counties of San Miguel, Taos, and Río Arriba were instructed to order two companies each. A company of U.S. dragoons and thirty mounted New Mexico volunteers, commanded by Capt. James "Santiago" Hubbell of Los Padillas, met a hundred mounted Texans within the area Colonel Baylor claimed as the Territory of Arizona. The Union forces drove the Confederates to retreat with few killed and wounded. People in central (Río Abajo) and northern (Río Arriba) New Mexico braced themselves for a probable Texan thrust. *Pobladores* (settlers) had been focused on the Apache and Navajo menaces, emboldened by the withdrawal of federal troops. Rencher wondered if they would take an active part in the sectional bloodletting.[33]

The outbreak of war failed to disrupt routine politics. The new president had his territorial appointments to make, for one thing. Once again New Mexicans insisted on the necessity of having their own residents serve as the territory's federal officers. Lincoln proved the first president to accommodate the desire. He did so under the influence of John S. Watts, a former Indiana lawyer and Whig in the Indiana House, who had been appointed a federal justice for New Mexico in 1851 by President Fillmore. Watts stayed in the territory to practice law after resigning as justice in 1854. He was a leading Unionist by 1861, gaining the confidence of Lincoln and Secretary of State Seward. Watts counseled Lincoln that putting nonresidents in territorial office would encourage the election of Democratic delegates to Congress and the assembly. The judge suggested a first phase of appointments going to New Mexicans, followed by another reserved for Republicans.[34] The plan conformed to Lincoln's policy of instilling citizen loyalty by having northern states bordering the South form cross-party coalitions. Lincoln noticed secession activity in the far southern portion of New Mexico, lack of Republican Party structure, and the Spanish-speaking majority. In adopting Watts's recommendation, he departed from the patronage custom of appointing territorial officers as a reward to individuals in return for service to the party or his political interests.[35]

Lincoln replaced Rencher as governor with Henry B. Connelly. Connelly was a nominal Democrat, but Watts beamed him to the president as "the most able, influential and popular man in New Mexico."[36] Born in Virginia and raised in Kentucky, Connelly enlisted in the commercial trade from Missouri and New Orleans to interior Mexico. He lived in the City of Chihuahua for twenty years before moving to Santa Fe, becoming a prosperous merchant, regularly journeying to Missouri, New Orleans, and the interior of Mexico. He married the widow of don Mariano Chávez, a former Mexican governor of New Mexico, enhancing his credibility and regional identity among Nuevomexicanos. As we have seen, he played an instrumental role in negotiation of the surrender of New Mexico to General Kearny and was elected governor in the mooted pre-territorial elections (chapters 2, 4). Connelly served several terms as an American Party member of the New Mexico territorial council, where he worked with minimal partisanship.[37] He took office as New Mexico governor on September 4, 1861. Representing the territory's desire for "self-government," the adopted nativo was treated to a rousing reception. All the vehicles were filled, horses mounted in great numbers, Home Guards on parade, "all ready and eager" to meet their new governor. The procession wound through Agua Fría Street and on to the Governor's Palace.[38]

Connelly emblazoned in his inaugural address that New Mexico had gone from neutrality in the war to an unshakable volunteer for the northern cause. The territory's first position excluded "any deep feeling of sectional interest in the feud" that endangered the integrity of the Union, he claimed. New to the "federal garden, distant and isolated from the contact of any of the States, and having no sectional sympathies," New Mexico felt at liberty "to pursue the dictates of duty and patriotism in an adherence to the Constitution and laws of that Government alone to which she has sworn allegiance under whose banner of stars and stripes she has sought protection from her enemies and from whose vast resources she has ever drawn the succor due to her minority. To that Constitution and to that banner she will adhere until they cease to exist, or are lost in the vortex of Revolution." Connelly reversed the legacy of Miguel A. Otero with this liberal interpretation, calling on the assembly to repeal the slave act that had caused so much consternation in the states. He went on to order the organization of several militia forces five days after his inauguration.[39]

Lincoln heeded Watts further in appointing another American Partyite, Sydney A. Hubbell, an associate justice on New Mexico's Supreme Court, replacing Miguel A. Otero's brother-in-law. Hubbell, of Bernalillo County, was another long-standing Euroamerican settler-merchant, a member of the territorial council at the time. The *New York Times* praised the appointment of one who had "the full

FIG. 16. *New Mexico Territorial Governor Henry Connelly*, 1861–66, photographer unknown. Called New Mexico's "Civil War Governor," Connelly helped transition the territory from Mexican to American nationality and committed himself to public service to the territory until his death. Courtesy Palace of the Governors Photo Archives, NMHM/DCA, negative #009846.

confidence of the bar and the public in devotion to his country's service."[40] The next appointment of a New Mexican proved controversial. Delegate Miguel Otero had built a significant political machine in New Mexico up to 1860, but the sea-change events of 1861 rendered his incumbency problematic. The electorate might not accept his commitment to the Democratic Party that had supported the South, while Lincoln's presidency caused Otero to lose influence in Washington. Watts's lightning thought was to give him the post of territorial secretary. He would, Watts figured, assure the success of the Lincoln administration in the territory. Otero's nativo status made him symbolically important for the electorate. Connected to New Mexico's leading families, he would guide Nuevomexicanos to stand for the Union "and freedom" while heading off dissent. It would also keep him from deciding to run for delegate, which would severely split New Mexico's electorate. Persuaded, Lincoln appointed Otero the territorial secretary of New Mexico.[41]

It proved a mistake. As Otero hastened home from Washington to begin his term, his appointment raised hackles back East. Greeley saw his chance to nail the "traitor," whom he insultingly called the "half-breed Hidalgo." As Greeley smirked, "There has been no more pliant tool of the Slavery Extentionists than this same Otero."[42] The *Tribune* editor urged New Mexicans to elect Republicans as legislators and delegates. After a short duration gaining power, they would drive the "horde of infidels" from the capital, he calculated, "and you, as well as your fellow citizens of the States whose rights are menaced will be left in peace and prosperity." Republicans in Congress pointed to Otero's pro-slavery record, recent public attacks on their party over New Mexico's slave code, and his warning to New Mexico Republicans of his "hostility to the death."[43]

"Rejection of a Traitor's Nomination," is how the headline in Greeley's *Tribune* read following the Senate's return of Otero's nomination. The *Santa Fe Weekly Gazette* objected on the other hand: the cause of the Union," editor Russell had it, "for which Greeley professes to have great concern has not a more devoted friend or a more ardent advocate in New Mexico than is the Hon. M. A. Otero."[44]

The political career of Miguel Antonio Otero appeared with considerable complexity in the story of Nuevomexicano political incorporation. He accomplished a great deal to keep New Mexico and Nuevomexicanos plugged into the American political system. His struggle to have assimilation be the capital mode of integration into the American civic body followed a standard liberal course based on his biography, and it appealed to many a Nuevomexicano. Technically he advanced Nuevomexicano power-sharing; however, from a pure liberal standpoint of universal humanity, it filtered almost anomalously through the bent of his southern connection. His influence would remain in New Mexico, and he would attempt a political comeback in 1880 in another run for delegate to Congress. For all intents and purposes, however his career as a politician ended in 1861.[45]

Virtual Unity: The Election of 1861

Gazette editor John Russell, looking forward in early 1860 to the fall 1861 election, commented on the need for a convention to reorganize the National Democratic Party. Russell's American Party colleagues disagreed.[46] One question concerned which faction of the party New Mexicans should claim. The split between the followers of Stephen Douglas and John Breckinridge, not to mention the anti-disunion Constitutional Union Party that brought together Know-Nothing and former Whig elements, denied a dominant Democratic line for New Mexicans to adopt. The June 1861 death of Stephen Douglas symbolized the weakening of New Mexico's ties to the Democratic Party. Importantly, the Democrats of the North were overshadowed by the Republican Party's quick, albeit unsteady, ascendance on the election of Lincoln and the fact that after Fort Sumter, the South had no representation in Congress. Republican power appeared in the special session that the president opened the first week of July to construct the policies for best conducting the war.[47] The political historian Michael Les Benedict seems to exaggerate the condition of party collapse in saying, "Despite the efforts of Martin Van Buren and the other leaders of the second-party system, race emerged as the dominant issue in national party politics by the late 1850s, destroying two-party competition in the process. The rise to power of the Republican Party during these years in many ways represented the antithesis of Van Buren's vision of party politics."[48] It is true that no explicit Democratic Party convention was held in the election season of 1861, but party division survived on the national level largely in a mode of rearticulation.

Of course, New Mexicans committed their future to the fortunes of the North and so the pressure was on for them to demonstrate loyalty, not to the Republican Party, to be sure, but to preservation of the Union. Russell came to common sense. In January 1861 Mexican Partyites in the territorial assembly floated the idea of statehood for New Mexico. The issue of statehood had tended to divide the political territory into warring camps. Russell foresaw an acrimonious debate. He therefore queried, "For the time being, would it not be acting the part of wisdom to disregard party questions—to let them rest; whilst we are engaged in the determination of other matters that are to have so momentous a bearing upon our future weal?" New Mexico should put its statehood desires on hold, Russell suggested. "This is not an occasion for petty divisions among the people," he put it. "Enlarged and enlightened views should predominate now, and after the noble work of erecting ourselves into the high position of a sovereign State shall have been accomplished, we will find ample time and numerous occasions for the settlement of all minor differences of opinion."[49]

The war compressed the electoral season into two months. A contingent from the former National Democratic Party, composing the American shadow-party, held a hard-pressed meeting on July 2 to begin advancing a "suitable candidate" for the position of congressional delegate. John Watts had previously associated with the Mexican Democratic Party alongside Richard Weightman, Spruce Baird, and José Manuel Gallegos.[50] The impromptu convention focused on the selfsame Watts, even though it was headed by American Party Nationals such as Miguel A. Otero, James Collins, John Russell, territorial senator Merrill Ashurst, Judge Joab Houghton, Governor Connelly, and the pioneer Santa Fe-to-Chihuahua merchant Felipe Delgado, whose family had counted among those to welcome the American incorporation of New Mexico.[51] Watts's record in guiding Lincoln's hand to appoint resident New Mexicans for the territory's federal offices, American Party ones at that, garnered fame and admiration for the former judge and territorial attorney general. As the preamble of the convention stated, "the lion" Watts was selected "for the active and efficient services he, as a private citizen, has rendered the Territory, and [the] hope he will continue, as such, to act in our behalf."

The convention avoided both Republican and Democratic reference points and adopted the Independent Party as its organization label. Watts's acceptance remarks made clear that this option did not signify the 1859 Miguel Pino–Spruce Baird Independent Democratic Party. "My friends throughout the Territory are at liberty to use my name as an Independent candidate," he said, "without regard to parties as they have heretofore existed in New Mexico." The convention called on citizens who approved of the Watts recommendation to organize "without delay" to have county meetings to promote "to the extent of their power" the election of Watts, and to do so by corresponding with the recently appointed Independent Party Central Committee.[52]

Russell in the newfound role of nonparty man praised Watts's personal credentials, his public and private business acumen, and his uncanny ability to collect claims as attorney general for "an almost incalculable amount of money." These qualities favorably trumped all prejudices not only personal and political but with regard to the accustomed desirability of a candidate belonging to the same ethnicity as the electorate, "those of nativity." Watts appeared for New Mexico's future greatness as "*the* man for the times."[53] The *Gazette* seemed to reverse its adherence to party to justify the selection of a man "without distinction of party." Those who blindly adhered to party were advised to consider the people's selection of different individuals for delegate on the basis of their "peculiar fitness for the position," Russell stressed. It was his independence as a private citizen that would give Watts success in obtaining the needed favors from Washington for the territory. But when it appeared to Russell that "the ascendancy of political parties" was "so uncertain," it suggested to him that perhaps Lincoln might not be around for too long as the administration was liable to be changed every four years.[54]

The provision in New Mexico's Organic Law that made the month of March the end of a congressional delegate's term left the territory without a sitting delegate for the middle part of every year. With such a short time to the election, the Independents must have thought no one else would run for delegate. Watts went to Washington with a petition, signed "extensively" by citizens, asking Congress to recognize him as New Mexico's interim representative. The presumptuous gesture received an ill welcome.[55] To grant the request would have violated the requirement in the Organic Law, and the standard policy of territorial governance, of an election to determine a territory's delegate.

The year 1861 saw the weakest link in the territory's chain of binary politics, yet not all in the territory considered Watts as the great holder of the "qualities and culture of mind" to make a desirable delegate.[56] The developing political system would not allow a total deflation of partisan competition. A separate nominating convention was called for July 22. Who called it is not known; perhaps a group who believed the New Mexico delegate should be a nativo. The men of the 1859 Bobtail Democrats would have been the natural organizers if party opposition still carried momentum. An initial report said territorial councilman Tomás Cabeza de Baca, the Peña Blanca veteran Mexican Party man, was to be tabbed as a candidate for delegate to Congress.[57] Baca's record as a Mexican Party firebrand, hard-core Lamy enemy, late supporter of José Manuel Gallegos, and opponent of Miguel Antonio Otero made him the logical choice to go against the core American Partyites who nominated Watts.

Baca, though flattered by the honor bestowed by his friends, both "personal and political," declined the overture. Chief Justice Kirby Benedict announced in a speech that it was important for Watts to know that Baca was "surprised and alarmed" to learn from intimate and confidential friends that "almost every decided secessionist in these parts of the Territory desiring the destruction of the Union and the success of the rebellion, were in his favor for Delegate." Some had "mixed largely in party politics" and were prominent. Don Tomás saw that "suspicions as to his fidelity to the Government would crowd themselves into the canvass," Benedict avowed, "and that he would seem to occupy a position contrary to his principles, sympathies and wishes, and that he must go under a cloud to Washington [should he be elected], and be crippled in his power to do good for his people and Territory."[58]

In addition to the need Cabeza de Baca felt to have his patriotism go unquestioned in the context of the war, he reportedly said he did not want to oppose his friend Watts. Watts was worthy and capable of representing the people of New Mexico in Congress "with energy and ability," Cabeza de Baca stated in a public announcement. Everyone should give their suffrage to Watts, he recommended.[59] The *Gazette* had previously disdained Cabeza de Baca for his Mexican Party activities. It now postured as the beacon of inclusion. Cabeza de Baca would have been the sure favorite in the race, the paper pointed out, and so his "momentous sacrifice" commended him for "preferment in the future, for a generous people will not forget actions of this nature when they come from good and true men."[60]

The July 22 convention surprisingly nominated the Río Arriba County luminary Diego Archuleta as its candidate for delegate to Congress, the same Archuleta who had entered history as a resistance fighter against the Kearny occupation in 1846–47. He began his American political career as a Mexican Party chief, member of the Mexican Democratic Party, only to switch to the American shadow-party as a result of his opposition to Governor James Calhoun, then Governor David Meriwether. Archuleta now seemed to swing back again. He opposed those who had been his most recent partners in the National Democracy. The paucity of press reports for these weeks makes it difficult to glean whether Archuleta was motivated by the National Democratic Party's favor for the South. Certain press scraps hint at unnamed secessionists in the Río Arriba taking political cover under his wing.[61]

A personal consideration suggests itself. Archuleta and James Collins began to feud. Collins as the superintendent of Indian Affairs was Archuleta's supervisor in the New Mexico Indian agency. He suspended Archuleta for refusing to accept an assignment to the Mescalero Agency. Collins, joined by miners in the San Juan area, protested the order that Archuleta be reinstated as agent at Abiquiú, not least for his alleged anti-Americanism.[62] Collins and Archuleta had been exchanging public charges of incompetency and neglect of duty in each other's Indian work.[63] Archuleta's power-sharing candidacy could well have been driven by this situation. Abandoning its opening conciliation and reverting to mudslinging, the *Gazette* noted "small minded men" advancing Archuleta, filled with "party feelings of private vindictiveness."[64]

Archuleta was thwarted by leaders from the Independent Democratic Party who jumped on the Watts wagon. Former delegate to Congress José Manuel Gallegos was elected president of a nine-precinct Santa Fe County convention to nominate candidates for the assembly and county offices. These Santa Feans resolved to sustain the Watts candidacy and deprecated "without distinction of party" the southern endeavor to "overthrow the glorious edifice which the immortal Washington and other founders of the Republic erected." It is surprising, as historian Gerald Theisen writes, that Gallegos and Miguel Antonio Otero "buried all their rivalries and sympathies and united in support of Judge Watts."[65] And it was not only Gallegos; Facundo

Pino and Miguel E. Pino, the erstwhile Bobtailed enemies of Collins, Russell, and Ashurst, came on board. If indeed there were pro-Confederate elements in support of Archuleta, or ranchers wanting to defend Indian slavery, they may have wanted to make sure that the Nuevomexicanos not be marginalized in politics for following a weak candidate.[66]

Judge Benedict consented to speak at the county convention even though, he said, it violated his personal ban on mixing his role as a jurist with an open political proceeding. Benedict expounded on the present moment with no precedent in government annals when a portion of the country had sought to overthrow and "rend to fragments, the fairest, most just, and heretofore most prosperous government ever achieved by man—great and good men and consecrated to freedom, justice, greatness and power." Benedict called for unity to halt the Texan invaders. This line transposed to the idea that New Mexico should have, as a matter of "first importance," a delegate who could "meet and be equal to the requirements of the times." Benedict praised Watts's ability to unite people without uttering a word against the public or private character of Diego Archuleta. The judge looked forward to a "more propitious" time when Watts could be the recipient of people's votes. Benedict represented a major assumption of New Mexico politics. If the practical responsibility of a monolingual Spanish speaker was to learn English while working in Washington, the responsibility of the monolingual English speaker was to learn Spanish when working with the people of New Mexico. Watts had sufficient Spanish to attend to the people's interests, Benedict added. Following the *Gazette* script, Benedict tipped his hat to don Tomás Cabeza de Baca, whose election for Congress would have seemed sure, as "a native of high character and universal popularity with the people."[67] Watts appeared at the head of the convention's ticket on which appeared Gallegos and Pino for the assembly.[68]

Gazette editor Russell worked the unbalanced binary, questioning Archuleta's "mental capacity" and disparaging Archuleta in much the same way former delegate Gallegos was earlier polluted. Russell's assimilation perspective, inherited from the American Party, refused to value the cultural inheritance of the conquered Mexicans. The editor branded Archuleta "utterly disqualified" for discharging the duties of delegate because of his inability to speak the English language. Miming

Judge Brocchus's eloquent condemnation, Russell waxed of Archuleta: "Ears would he have, but could not hear. His tongue would be as useless to him as if he were a mute." The binary workout deemed Archuleta "wholly inexperienced" in public affairs. He had never occupied positions that could familiarize him to them, as opposed to Watts's ability to collect funds for victims of Indian "depredations." By the same token, Watts's acquaintance with the "practical workings" of the different governmental departments was said to enable him to bring other benefits to New Mexico, such as funds to finish building the territorial capitol and to start public roads.[69]

No Archuleta-based convention to nominate candidates for local office took place either in Santa Fe County or elsewhere. The sole ticket that appeared at the polls was headed by Watts. The uncertainty of a state of war caused 4,500 fewer votes (9,212) to be cast than in 1857.[70] That Archuleta had support was reflected in the available tallies showing him winning by good majorities in the counties of Mora, his own Río Arriba, and Santa Ana; that is, in areas of intense Indian conflict.[71] Watts swept in as New Mexico's delegate to the Thirty-seventh Congress with 66 percent of the vote and a majority of 2,978 (6,095 to 3,117).[72]

The veteran Mexican Partyites Tomás Cabeza de Baca, Facundo Pino, and José Manuel Gallegos won seats in the legislature.[73] The 1861–62 session, which convened as efforts were being made to organize militias for the coming battle with invading Texas Confederates, reinforced the loyalty of the territory to the Union in a joint memorial recommending to President Lincoln that Kirby Benedict be retained as chief justice of the territorial Supreme Court. President Franklin Pierce had first appointed Benedict, the former associate of Stephen Douglas in Illinois, in 1858. President James Buchanan reappointed him and recommended to Lincoln that he be kept on the New Mexico bench. Benedict knew Lincoln personally through work in the Illinois Douglas debates and shared legal cases.[74] Benedict was a War Democrat, a Democrat of the North who brooked no southern separatism. In this spirit he fed the binary political picture in a private warning to Lincoln of the southern or neutral spirit in the editorial policies of the *Santa Fe Weekly Gazette*, even whispering of Governor Henry Connelly having Indian slaves.[75] He emphasized in a white lie that as a judicial officer he strived to keep away from the "parties or factions that sometimes rage amid this people."[76] Legislators considered Benedict supportive of their initiatives. Their memorial, reflecting a consensus between the Nuevomexicano legislature and the high judicial bench, lauded the judge for his constant and decided opposition to the rebellion and his effective service to the people, "the poor as well as the rich."[77] Congressional delegate John Watts tossed in his support for the reappointment. Lincoln retained the chief justice, and Nuevomexicano legislators sustained a loyal figurehead.[78]

The territory committed itself to the Union, but a contradiction glared in Miguel Otero's three-year-old Slave Act. Governor Connelly, in repentance as a Lincoln appointee, took a major step toward abolition by asking the legislature to repeal the law. Nuevomexicano members of the legislature complied by a large majority. The governor rejoiced over the fact that New Mexico had "condemned, and put slavery from among our laws." The deliberate turn away from the Otero regime could not have been more blunt. The new narrative branded slavery "not congenial with our [New Mexico] history."[79]

The mood of unity among New Mexico politicians, borne of stunning crisis, would prove unique in the history of territorial New Mexico. Something about Diego Archuleta's decision to challenge Watts could be seen as a weather vane for the coming torrent of oppositional dynamics.

CHAPTER EIGHT

Republican Toehold and the Partisan Normal, 1861–1863

Evelyn Nakano Glenn calls service in the armed forces "allegiance citizenship."[1] The military often serves as an effective means of social integration, especially if signing up means local purposes are served and compensation forms part of the bargain.[2] As noted in chapter 1, Nuevomexicanos inherited a military tradition dating to Spanish colonial days. If Donaciano Vigil and Diego Archuleta and their fellow military officers indicate anything, service in the regular armed forces signified their allegiance citizenship under the Mexican Republic.

A civilian militia had formed an important branch of community service as well. As it helped repel Texas attempts at annexing New Mexico, it would have implied allegiance citizenship. However, militias were employed mostly to address conflict with Indians. Commoners were more likely to see their participation in that regard more basically as defense of family, home, and property. American governors and legislatures periodically called out militias. Governor James S. Calhoun ordered the formation of a volunteer corps in 1851, providing an incentive of officer commissions to the commanders of local companies.[3] He followed with the mandatory enlistment of all men into companies by regional district.[4] In a precedent for New Mexico, each county company would elect its officer corps based on a ballot provided by the brigadier general and with the use of poll books, judges, and clerks. Democracy of a sort resided in the normal organization of American militias. Kearny ordered militia suffrage at Leavenworth for his Missouri companies. Nominations were made for field officers; candidates made speeches and issued promises to protect the interests of the unit and safeguard against fraud. The election of replacement officers occurred in the camps of the army's occupation of Santa Fe and during the Indian expedition at Zuñi. The formation of the Mormon Battalion at Santa Fe called for privates to elect a captain, first lieutenant, and second lieutenant, subject to approval by a regular captain.⁵ Territorial regulations for organizing volunteer militias in Indian campaigns required the election of commanders, including those commissioned to lead forces of 200 to 225 men. The results and correct roll of the unit were to be certified by a justice of the peace or probate judge.⁶

It is difficult to tell whether or not militia democracy enhanced enlistments and allegiance citizenship. In any case, loyalty stands as a cardinal principle of military doctrine, and American governors made the wars with the Indians a matter of loyalty to country. Recruits and conscripts were obligated to swear allegiance to the Constitution of the United States, and "be true and faithful to the Territory of New Mexico."⁷ An 1854 editorial described the unwillingness of men in one county to turn out as stipulated by law. It was tantamount to treason at a time of war, the weekly stated, calling for severe punishment. The positive example was provided by territorial legislator José Antonio Manzanares and vecino Pablo Gallegos, who organized and equipped the required two hundred militiamen in Río Arriba County. José María Chávez was elected the unit's brigadier general. Other officers were elected and deployed to head companies, and they fought with military acumen in a campaign against the Jicarilla Apaches.⁸ Additional incentive was provided in 1859: officers were allowed to receive a double share of property seized from Indians, while owners of stolen property were to pay a third of its value to get it back. It may have helped generate an 1860 planning convention in Santa Fe for the defense against the Navajo. Don José Leandro Perea presided. José Manuel Gallegos, Miguel E. Pino, and Felipe Delgado participated in developing a territory-wide strategy and system of communication.⁹

The Civil War posed a wholly new reason for mounting militias, yet it should have generated allegiance attachment to the North among all New Mexico citizens. In October 1861, with the threat of another Confederate invasion imminent, Col. Stephen Canby, the commander of the New Mexico Army Department, asked Governor Connelly for 1,200 militiamen. Connelly's call appealed to the "patriotic sentiment of the militiamen" and warned that disloyalty and lying would be prosecuted as crimes. Connelly warned the legislature of the serious threat Texas posed to New Mexico. He praised New Mexico's "patriotic citizens" for having defended themselves before against Texas aggression. They would have to oust the hated Texans who yet again attempted to capture their cherished territory.[10]

Politically experienced Nuevomexicanos robustly mobilized their allegiance citizenship. The legislature granted the governor extraordinary defense powers. Members issued a clarion call to "Drive off the audacious invader." They transplanted their ethno-regional identity onto the national and liberal cause and spoke on behalf of all resident citizens. "This people will never consent to [the Texan's] rule, his military, his slave despotism," they declared. "Let every Mexican in the Territory rally to the brave in the field; your fathers, sons, and brothers."[11]

Command central issued distinct procedures for organizing militia companies. As historian Jerry Thompson notes, "Many of the ranking officers were selected because of their political clout in the territory and because they had served in the Territorial Militia since it was first organized." They, in coordination with prefects and Euroamerican civilians, quickly formed divisions, regiments, and brigades. Nuevomexicanos commanded two of three militia divisions. Gen. José Leandro Perea headed the third, consisting of Santa Ana, Bernalillo, Valencia, Socorro, and Doña Ana counties. Brig. Gen. Diego Archuleta, former anti-American revolutionary, commanded the second, involving troops from Río Arriba, Mora, and San Miguel. José S. Perea also served as a brigadier general, and José Pablo Gallegos was a major general in charge of a regiment. Nuevomexicano captains, many of them alcaldes and prefects, did the yeoman work of mustering companies as ordered in Río Arriba, Bernalillo, Santa Ana, San Miguel, Santa Fe, Valencia, Socorro, Doña Ana, and Mora counties.[12]

Among the public figures on record for the Union, many were standing political foes among themselves. Mexican Partyites Facundo Pino, José M. Gallegos, Manuel Chávez, Rafael Chacón, and Manuel Pino marshaled shoulder to shoulder with American Party men Donaciano Vigil, Miguel Antonio Otero, José A. Martínez, and Francisco Perea. Younger Nuevomexicano volunteers destined to become political figures included José D. Sena, Trinidad Vigil, Trinidad Romero, Pedro Sánchez, and Francisco P. Abreu.[13] José Francisco Chávez, Pantaleón Archuleta, and Antonio Abeytia were sworn into Río Arriba County's regiment, the First New Mexico Volunteers under Kit Carson. Lt. Col. Miguel E. Pino, still a citizen of Mexico and a Mexican Party veteran who was labeled a seditionist by the American Party, headed the infantry of the Second New Mexico Volunteers. Capt. Nicolás Quintana and Capt. Jesús Baca y Sena "labored zealously" and succeeded "excellently" in recruiting volunteers.[14]

The picture for the rank and file appears mixed. Some observers reported enthusiastic responses. Dewitt Peters, an army surgeon in the New Mexico battlefields, remarked on how the "inhabitants of New Mexico promptly responded to [the] call [for volunteers], by flocking to the places designated for them to organize.... The willingness which the Mexicans exhibited on this occasion to volunteer, does them great credit [Peters felt], and clearly proves the fact that they do not always lack in courage, but that they are prompt to defend their homes when properly disciplined and aided with the means necessary to do so."[15] Another eyewitness wrote that in battle New Mexican soldiers showed "their patriotism and courage. They were ever among the foremost in the fight, and were noted for their good order and discipline; and I am justified in saying that a desire to serve the country sent them into the field."[16]

Examining New Mexico militia records from the Civil War, Thompson reports considerable resistance, demoralization, and desertion among conscripts. Adjutant General Clever found individuals putting up obstacles to recruitment, "inciting the citizens to resistance." Forced conscription and coercion became necessary in many cases "through the assistance and aid of the civil authorities." General Perea raised his forces in Bernalillo County according to the "administration of the Mexican government, that is to say they were raised by force." Draft resistance occurred on the eastern slopes of the Sangre de Cristo Mountains. Many buck privates were *peones* who mustered up only on orders of their village *patrones*. Thompson calls the elections of officers in such cases a "sham."[17] A Euroamerican officer referred to the arrival in the field of a certain sergeant. "Herrera Grandee is here," the officer's report said half facetiously, "and is a man who has a great deal of influence and control over his people. When he goes [to do battle] all desire to go."[18]

If many commoners were reluctant to commit their allegiance citizenship to the war, a number of factors would have been responsible. Lack of salary was one. The War Department determined that it was not responsible for expenses. However, the strapped territorial government did not have the funds to pay for war service as promised, nor to provide for food and uniforms. As many as fourteen hundred men were never paid, Thompson finds. Militia men at Alburquerque mutinied and refused to obey orders on complaint of not being paid, stating that their families were hungry. A riot broke out in January 1862 at Fort Union, near Las Vegas, among men who did not receive payment and clothing. Nuevomexicanos went home "bitter and angry, with pronounced anti-American, anti-government propensities," according to Thompson.[19] Nuevomexicanos were subject as well to a strong arm of racism wielded by Euroamerican army regulars. Mexicans found their loyalty questioned even as they fought in the war. Colonel Canby himself made his disdain for rag-tag Mexican units evident.[20] A strict segregation was observed between the militias and regular army units. The biographer of Rafael Chacón, a Nuevomexicano Civil War hero who suffered the "supercilious contempt" of Euroamerican military men, affirms that "there can be no conjecture about the incidence of prejudice [on the part of Euroamerican military men]; there is far too much documentation supporting it."[21] Such treatment slowed integration of Nuevomexicanos into American allegience.

No sooner than the New Mexico militia got going, Socorro County saw a pitched battle with invading Texas Confederates at the settlement of Valverde. The *Weekly Gazette* and a new weekly, the *Santa Fe Republican*, went into suspension while mail deliveries stopped. Governor Connelly felt confident of conquering the Texans. In spite of many desertions, the Nuevomexicano militia—units led by Col. Miguel E. Pino, Lt. Col. José María Baca y Salazar, and Capts. Antonio Sena, José E. Durán, and José de Merced Sánchez—played critical roles at the Battle of Valverde, leading assaults and negotiating with Rebels over terms of a possible surrender.[22] The larger Confederate force, led by Brig. Gen. Henry H. Sibley, routed the New Mexico Volunteers and Union forces at Valverde.[23] Sibley set out northward and was soon raising the Confederate flag in Alburquerque. After forcing another capitulation of Nuevomexicano militia at Cubero in the desert west of Alburquerque, where Capt. Francisco Aragón had problems keeping his company from deserting, the Confederates marched out to occupy Santa Fe. On March 10, 1862, Sibley preemptively proclaimed a Confederate territorial government for New Mexico. He announced the requirement of the people to swear allegiance to the South or lose their property. Governor Connelly moved the territory's executive offices to Las Vegas, seventy miles east of Santa Fe (close to where Kearny had made his first conquering appearance in New Mexico). The Rebels never ruled, as they were forced to move out in order to capture Fort Union. Connelly returned to Santa Fe. The U.S. flag went up in a patriotic ceremony on the plaza.[24]

The decisive battle for New Mexico took place on March 26–28 at Glorieta Pass southeast of Santa Fe. Colonel Canby asked the governor of Colorado for reinforcements. The First Colorado Infantry force-marched four hundred miles from Denver to join the First New Mexico Volunteers. The Nuevomexicano Lt. Col. Manuel Chaves, a former anti-Kearny rebel, and infantryman Anastasio Durán distinguished themselves in battle, as did *Gazette* owner Col. James Collins.[25] Federal forces defeated the Confederacy at Glorieta. They prevented the southern capture of Fort Union and held back the Confederate control of the entire southwestern section and its mineral deposits. New Mexicans, relieved of combat, conducted a special Fourth of July celebration. Citizens assembled before the portal of the Governor's Palace, alongside military units, Masons, and Odd Fellows. The Nuevomexicanos Antonio Sandoval, Facundo Pino, and José María Baca y Salazar joined Connelly, Territorial Adjutant and Attorney General Charles Clever, former territorial secretary J. H. Holmes, and Judge Joab Houghton on stage, where José Manuel Gallegos delivered the keynote address, extolling George Washington for having renounced forever all particular interest in favor of a program to assure liberty for all the American people and assuring that the visions of Washington and Andrew Jackson had not died as a result of the war. These men, who would array themselves in opposing camps during the upcoming election, honored the national holiday "in a manner that showed that the patriotic fire blazes in their bosoms with undiminished ardor." Taos Nuevomexicanos conducted a full-blown Fourth of July as well.[26]

Politicians now faced the task of formulating their positions regarding the war itself. The stripes on the Democratic tiger would not so easily fade even with the figure head of Miguel Antonio Otero. Nettlesome Copperheads on the national stage condemned Lincoln's conduct in the expanding and increasingly bloody conflict. Peace Democrats, as the Copperheads were also called, favored an immediate treaty to end hostilities with the South while restoring the country to status quo ante. In their notion of "preserving" the Union, they believed that the cotton states should be permitted to keep their slaves. *Gazette* editor John Russell sided with the North in support of a government that had proved "the best in existence" and was now engaged in a life and death struggle. And yet, he and other Copperhead Democrats in New Mexico abhorred "abolition patriotism."[27]

Russell made his Copperhead stance clear in an editorial fulmination on the Radical Republican and *New York Tribune* editor Horace Greeley. Greeley had just criticized Lincoln's address to the 1862 congressional special session for failing to hold slavery responsible as a cause of the war, demanding that the president prosecute the war as a "crusade against slavery." Radical Republicans, who emerged out of the moral and religious reform movements of the 1820s, attacked Lincoln for resisting the spreading northern call for slaves fleeing their southern bondage to be accepted as equal citizens.[28] Sniping at Greeley, Russell argued that Lincoln was too moderate; even that he should establish peace with a restoration of the Union "as it was." Russell picked up the sword taken from the hand of his former top territorial leader, Miguel Antonio Otero, condemning Greeley for belonging to the "Abolition party." That faction betrayed American liberalism, Russell expounded, composed as it was of men who were "arch traitors to the governmental institutions which in a few brief years made the United States a model of greatness and power that had never been attained by any nation before."[29]

Lincoln's Emancipation Proclamation, which came out in January 1863, brightened the hope of abolitionists by "strik[ing] at the heart of the rebellion," as one historian puts it. For this very reason it enraged Peace and Conservative Democrats and other anti-abolitionists.[30] Russell, steaming in hostility to the administration, reprinted national Copperhead articles from the *National Intelligencer*, famous for chastising "abolition fanaticism," and the *New York Journal of Commerce*, owned by Edward G. Roddy, an intensely partisan Democrat who regarded black people as an inferior race and Abraham Lincoln as a despot with low intelligence.[31]

Russell would have had Santa Fe's field of discourse to himself had it not been for the arrival of certain individuals from back East. An incremental trend set in, shaping the territory's party binary toward more than one national party. Lincoln served as the fount for the diffusion of Republican flashpoints by making New Mexico's federal appointments on the basis of demonstrated loyalty to the Republican Party, not least as a means of dealing with the *Gazette*'s constant harping on his administration. Lincoln made the New Yorker James H. Holmes New Mexico's territorial secretary. Holmes had been in New Mexico for three years. He came to Lincoln's attention at the recommendation of two Republican senators. Soon after taking office in early 1862, Holmes established the *Republican* in Santa Fe as a weekly "to represent in New Mexico the Party whose name it bears." The paper would "labor loyally to sustain the Federal Arm against the infamous efforts of traitors," and would at the same time "advocate and endeavor to live by the doctrines of the great Party now in power—the Republican Party, whose fundamental principles are based on the Declaration of Independence and of the Constitution."[32] Fresh Republican settlers invested in Holmes's paper. Joseph G. Knapp, a Wisconsin native, was a Lincoln-appointed associate judge for New Mexico recommended for secretary by a Wisconsin Republican senator. Holmes and Knapp used the paper to assault the *Gazette*, nominal Democrats in New Mexico, and men their critics called their "accomplices" during trips East. Governor Connelly and Judge Kirby Benedict came in for it, not least because Knapp desired to replace Benedict.[33] Sam Watrous, a rancher and merchant at La Junta de los Ríos on the Santa Fe Trail in northeastern New Mexico, contributed to a rooting Republican presence, sending abolition arguments to the *Republican* and stateside newspapers. His freight wagon partner, William Tipton, joined Holmes to expose Russell's "disloyalty."[34]

Holmes seriously denounced the military command in New Mexico. He criticized what he considered deficient design in Fort Union's building structure and published a confidential report that criticized the fort's poor physical condition. He also proclaimed it well known that "in New Mexico military rule is more severe than in any other loyal part of the United States." Holmes, deeming the citizens of New Mexico no threat to the Union, condemned Colonel Canby for suspending *habeas corpus*, restricting civilian travel, and arbitrarily arresting anyone on weak suspicion of treason. Canby, influenced by reports that the Confederacy might return for another assault on the territory, had Holmes and his publisher, Putnam O'Brien, arrested for publicizing Union troop movements, even though they had appeared in a San Francisco newspaper, which Canby called useful to the enemy. Holmes saw partisan motivations behind Canby's action, the idea being to "Dry up that abolition sheet," the "only National Union paper in New Mexico." Found guilty, Holmes was given a suspended sentence and had his property confiscated for government losses. O'Brien gave notice from Lawrence, Kansas, that he would reorganize the *Republican* with a new editor, although it never happened.[35] The *Gazette* gleefully concluded that the paper's end came after Holmes failed to "make some capital among the abolitionists by exciting their sympathy and in that way busy up his fortunes which he and every person else knew to be in a sinking condition."[36]

Smelling blood, Democrats raised the question of Holmes's federal position. Watts complained to Lincoln that Holmes had left the territory at a time when the Texans were poised to conquer New Mexico so that he could "slander the Governor, the Superintendent of Indian Affairs [Collins], myself and other friends of your administration because we are not rabid abolitionists," almost as if to pressure the president to a Copperhead position.[37] The *Gazette* charged Holmes with conflict of interest for founding a partisan newspaper in his capacity as territorial secretary and awarding printing contracts to its inexperienced publisher, only to have the monies revert to himself for the print work. Russell filed an injunction on behalf of the printer he said merited the contract. Holmes and his wife, a feminist activist, were well connected, and U.S. congressmen told Lincoln the attacks on Holmes were motivated by those with questionable loyalties to the Union and who wanted to keep New Mexico Democratic and Holmes from establishing a Republican press and party. Removing Holmes, they argued, would prove disastrous to the "best interests" of New Mexico. The Holmes controversy generated national recognition of New Mexico Republicans. However, serious accusations against Holmes accumulated, including once running a brothel near a military reservation, securing public monies as territorial secretary for relatives and friends, and issuing public drafts as payment for public service, including to territorial legislators, without sufficient funds to cover them. Watts's influence prevailed, and Lincoln fired Holmes.[38]

The party pieces continued to fall into place, however. Holmes's replacement was William Frederick Milton Arny, who hailed from Illinois and was an acquaintance of Lincoln. A reform activist, Arny was inspired by Alexander Campbell, the zealous social reform founder of the Disciples of Christ. Arny went to the bloody political theater of Kansas as a Free-Soiler. He received praise for his programs to relieve families victimized by drought and grasshopper plagues. His support of Lincoln turned him into a staunch Republican. In 1861 Lincoln named him to succeed Kit Carson as the agent for the Utes and Jicarilla Apaches. Lincoln put Arny into service as New Mexico's secretary in 1862. Arny had been in office a month when Governor Connelly left for the United States to have an illness treated. Arny, as second in command in the territorial government, became acting governor.[39]

The Organic Law granted the acting governor full authority to execute and perform the powers and duties of the governor's office.[40] Arny built a gang-busting reform agenda during his term as acting governor. He started by going after those known to have aided Confederate invaders, exercising confiscation powers, ordering marshals to punish collaborators in Mesilla and Alburquerque and urging the U.S. attorney to prosecute them vigorously and confiscate their property. Arny revealed his affiliation with Republican Radicalism in his executive address to the territorial assembly, where he chastised New Mexicans who perpetuated Indian slavery in their homes and ranches after the legislature outlawed the slavery code and the U.S. Congress banned slavery in Washington DC and the territories. Arny sympathized with destitute Indian slaves and citizens facing the cost of their upkeep when freed. The acting governor recommended a memorial to Congress for assistance. Based on the Republican emphasis on free labor for economic and moral progress, Arny branded the practice of indentured servitude—affecting hundreds of Nuevomexicanos in positions of perpetual bondage—as an abuse of the assembly's 1851 reform of debt peonage. Arny called for a law to compel masters to collect their servants' debts such as not to continue their exploitation, alluding to it as a "disguised form of slavery" based on an earlier court case that had ruled in favor of a peon against her master.[41]

Territorial house members, headed by speaker and former congressional delegate José Manuel Gallegos, were not prepared for Arny at first. An issue arose in what were called the "erroneous, absurd and ill-sounding ideas" of his opening address. Mexicans saw the necessity of clarifying the cultural bubble into which the upstart secretary had stepped. Arny's historical interpretation offended. His field service as an Indian agent led him to state that "from the year 1505 up to the present time the people of New Mexico and the neighboring tribes of Indians have been mutually plundering each other." It was phrasing to grate on the reigning Nuevomexicano narrative, which portrayed the settled people as peaceable victims of savage terrorism. The legislators were further slighted because Arny neglected to praise the people's patriotic defense of the Union on their own soil. They decreed officiously that every member of the assembly and the people of the territory should "arrive at a full knowledge of the subjects and ideas" contained in the message. A thousand copies of their memo were ordered printed in English and another thousand in Spanish to be inserted as a preamble to the governor's published message. Things worsened on the rumor that, on receiving the resolutions, Arny threatened their authors with some kind of political action.[42]

Arny denied threatening anyone. He explained in a follow-up speech in the House of Representatives that the clerk had misunderstood what he said. It would cause him "great worry," he assured the assemblymen, should the required harmony between his office and the legislature be disturbed.[43] The *Gazette* set aside Arny's Republican credential in a special moment of sympathy. Arny had been racially ambushed, Russell declared. The house resolutions were cast as unprecedented and insulting in their official fixation on the mode, as opposed to the substance, of the executive's "carefully prepared" and "responsible" message. Russell answered the legislators' demand for a detailed narrative of the Texas invasion. Such a history would be "a truly interesting work," he stated, "and we have no doubt will be read with great avidity by our people when it shall have been written." However, Russell noted, "a true and complete history of the events occurring in our territory growing out of the armed invasion by a rebel force from the State of Texas would look in the most supreme degree ridiculous in a Governor's Message. The writer of histories and the writer of messages are two distinct personages and occupy very different positions before the world." As Russell advised, the solons might well appoint a commission to write the history of the invasion and accept Arny's forbearance, good sense, and courtesy toward them.[44]

The gap between executive and legislative branches widened when Arny vetoed the House's contract for the printing of public documents by Samuel Ellison, a Kentucky native who went to New Mexico in 1848 as an attorney and became an all-purpose clerk. Arny called for "some person" who would execute the contract not only with economy and in a workmanlike manner but about whose loyalty to the Union there would be "no doubt." Ellison was a Democrat. The *Gazette* might have been expected to question Arny. Instead, it chastised the assemblymen for devising a convoluted, time-consuming, and costly process for deciding who should receive the contract. Congress complicated matters by annulling the procedure for territories to choose printing contractors. Speaker Gallegos objected to Arny's impingement on the territory's sovereignty. The *Gazette* called Gallegos's remarks "incendiary," with "no light attacks" on Washington, calculated to instill a "spirit of discontent with the Government into the minds of those who heard him."[45] The unity around Watts broke down. Yet the initial oppositions involving legislators, Arny, and the *Gazette* were headed toward colorful reversal.

Arny seems to have had someone in mind for the printing contract all along. Holmes's defunct *Republican* found new life under another name in the winter of 1862–63. Arny created a position, or at least a title, of territorial superintendent of schools, and hired Charles Leib, a physician fresh from Cincinnati, to fill it. Leib, another tried and true Republican, had worked the 1860 election in Illinois for Lincoln in a divide-and-conquer strategy to defeat the Democratic Party by forming an alliance between Republicans and proponents of the anti-slavery Lecomptian Constitution. The work steered the dissension in the Democratic ranks to convert Douglas Republicans to Lincoln. Leib was also an experienced newspaperman, having run a Republican sheet in Chicago. Taking control of the facilities of the *Republican*, he changed its name to the *Santa Fe New Mexican*. Arny raised American Party suspicions by giving Leib the official printing.[46] Russell changed his tune on Arny when Leib began taking pot shots at his Democratic positions and critical stance on Lincoln. Justice Benedict soon joined Leib in the writing of abolitionist editorials under the pseudonyms "Friend" and "Patriot."[47] American Partyites (former National Democrats) characterized Arny and friends as bent on building an "abolition party in New Mexico."[48]

Pressure on American Party Democrats intensified with a campaign that started up against James Collins, the superintendent of the New Mexico Indian agency. Republican Sam Watrous publicly attacked the superintendent for failing to remove or reduce tribal raiding in northeastern New Mexico where Watrous had his ranch.[49] According to historian Lawrence Murphy, Arny coveted Collins's post for himself. The acting governor influenced the legislature to conduct an investigation on the extent to which Collins's policies as Indian Affairs superintendent could be held responsible for the rise in Indian depredations.[50] The significance of an attack on Collins lay beyond his federal appointment. He was still owner and publisher of the *Gazette*, anchor of the American Party, and former Miguel Otero crewman. The whole field of territorial partisanship was in for it. The territorial legislature undertook an evaluation of Collins's performance as agency superintendent. Diego Archuleta, still feuding with Collins, sat in the house. The charges against Collins included administrative ineptness, possible fraud, and letting undefended settlements fall to Navajo, Apache, and Ute attacks.[51]

Leib and Arny tried getting Collins fired based on the evidence of the Copperhead editorials appearing in the *Gazette*.[52] Leib urged Lincoln to appoint Arny Indian superintendent. The U.S. Territorial House Committee on Indian Affairs investigated the controversy and consented to the request of Collins's lawyers, the veteran American Party pals Richard Tompkins and Merrill Ashurst, to swear witnesses to testify. Arny retaliated by calling into question Collins's loyalty to the Lincoln administration and the Union. He "angrily" vetoed legislation allowing the committee to administer judicial oaths and subpoena anyone living outside the capital. The assembly moved to squelch the committee hearings. It condemned Collins and proposed that a "more suitable, capable, and honest person" be hired to replace him. Delegate Watts, and a new military commander in New Mexico, Gen. James H. Carleton, vigorously defended Collins, challenging the charges of ineptness and corruption against him. Watts's influence failed this time, and Lincoln removed Collins. The president did not, however, put Arny in his place. The appointment went instead to the physician Michael Steck, a Pennsylvanian who had served off and on during the previous ten years as agent to the Mescalero Apaches. The Republican Steck had lobbied U.S. Commissioner of Indian Affairs William Dole for the post.[53]

Lincoln's reappointment of Arny as territorial secretary in February 1863 extended his term as acting governor. Arny welcomed Steck into his growing circle of Republican associates, which included Leib, Knapp, John Greiner—another Free-Soiler, whom Arny appointed as administrator of the territorial depository of public funds—and Greiner's son Theodore.[54] Collins returned to editing the *Gazette* three weeks before election day.

Improvements in the Stanhope hand press and its cheaper price than the Albion press made it easier to establish newspapers on the frontier.[55] Hezekiah S. Johnson started the Alburquerque *Río Abajo Weekly Press* in January 1863.[56] Pennsylvanian Johnson was a lawyer who came to New Mexico in 1849 following his brother, a territorial federal appointee. He began working as an apprentice printer for the *Gazette* in 1853 and edited the paper for a short time in 1859. Delegate Otero appointed him Alburquerque postmaster in 1860.[57] Johnson started his paper declaring a rejection of "partisan views." He noted the time in New Mexico when he preferred, "by great odds," the "Old Line Whig or Democratic party to the Republican." However, he affirmed his respect for lawfully chosen government officers without regard to the party of the one who appointed them so long as they refrained from abusing the people among whom they had come to live.[58]

The comment of historian Aurora Hunt that the rivalry between the *New Mexican* and the *Gazette* resulted in "many charges and countercharges" involved three weeklies.[59] The expansion in public communication with an important political resource in the Río Abajo marked an advance in the territory's political development, not least because it magnified partisanship. The struggle for control of the territory anted up in the press pages. The *Gazette* spearheaded the group that continued from the 1861 Independent Party. The Arny Republican group had the *New Mexican* at its back (until late in the canvass) and would move to the side of the traditional Mexican Party. Hezekiah Johnson's *Weekly Press* expressed open hostility to the Copperhead *Gazette*. Johnson started as a War Democrat, faithful to those of his native Pennsylvania who supported slavery up to war's outbreak. They had since became proud to earn the "abolitionist epithet," even as they damned Lincoln as the "patrical and wort incumbent."[60] Johnson stamped the *Gazette* as a traitor to the Union and trashed its editorials for having given the invading General Sibley hope for capturing the hearts and minds of New Mexicans.[61] Johnson needled the men of the *Gazette* with anti-Copperhead articles from around the country.[62] The habit of putting out harsh, insulting attacks picked up again, epitomized by the hurling of the liberal demon label "demagogue" from one editor to the other.

José Manuel Gallegos floated the idea of a petition for statehood, around which Arny Republicans developed a political agenda. The national Republican Party supported the Statehood Revolution for territories to encourage the country's economic development. The Union Congress urged new states to be formed of the territories "as speedily as possible."[63] Proponents saw statehood for New Mexico leading to the end of the Indian wars. They advised the people not to be bullied by the "eternal cry of taxes" that "demagogues" habitually raised every time the issue came up. The actual taxes under statehood would be a "trifle" in comparison to the protection to be purchased, pro-staters argued.[64] Leib backed Gallegos by claiming that the people overwhelmingly wanted statehood. He stated that they had been ready for it but were always "stabbed in the back by public functionaries and political sharks" with hands dipped in the public treasury. The comments put Leib at the partisan front against the American Party. Confidence about the prospects for statehood led him to say that no one could hope to get elected delegate to Congress without supporting it.[65]

Hezekiah Johnson started out in favor of statehood for New Mexico on the classic civic-colonial principle of citizens being deprived of voice in the appointment of federal officers, resulting in outsiders who, subjected the New Mexican "vassals" to "tutelage and domination."[66] However, Johnson grew independent of both parties, shown when he declared: "Some leaders of both the '*democratas coludos*' [Tailed Democrats] and '*democratas sin cola*' [Bobtailed Democrats] vied with each other in misleading the people on the subject of a State Government." Johnson said he and his friends had protested "frequently but in vain." Johnson rhetorically relied on the abstract "people." As he stated, the officials were "deaf to our appeals, and as they have 'sown the wind' of popular delusion, so shall they 'reap the whirlwind' of the disabused popular mind."[67]

Opposition to statehood came out of a whole new political segment. The political integration of Nuevomexicanos, and Euroamericans for that matter, living within the New Mexico Territory's officially designated borders would not be complete until the far southern communities lying along the border with the Mexican Republic, well below the Río Abajo district, could be brought under Santa Fe's governmental reach. Historically, those lands had belonged to the Mexican Department of Chihuahua outside New Mexico proper. Then, because of errors in the map utilized by the framers of the Treaty of Guadalupe Hidalgo, the national provenance of the Mesilla, Doña Ana, and Las Cruces settlements fell into dispute.[68] Their stability as territorial townships was disrupted by Euroamericans who invaded the lands of Mexican inhabitants with impunity.[69] The New Mexico legislature did not create Doña Ana County until 1852, and the permanent location of the three principal sites was not settled until 1854 with ratification of the Gadsden Treaty, which settled the Mexico-U.S. border dispute. The attachment of Doña Ana County to the territorial structure was slow in coming. Supreme Court justices held court for the southern district in Socorro, forcing citizens to travel two hundred miles over a treacherous and dangerous road to address their legal needs.[70] Structural integration was delayed further by the favor Euroamericans and Mexicans there had given the Confederacy.

Arny complied with the request of the legislature to secure the border region by appointing probate judges and sheriffs for Doña Ana and Arizona, as no elections for them had been held. The acting governor acknowledged in an official proclamation the lack of self-government there, even of the territorial variety, other than the "six shooter and the knife, the instruments resorted to for the redress of real or fancied wrongs, and for the enforcement of real or pretended rights." Lawlessness stemmed from forbidding distances, Arny pointed out, three hundred miles to the Santa Fe seat of government, including a stretch with no water for a hundred miles, and intervening country "infested by the most savage and cruel tribes of Indians" subjecting the "loyal white population" to "savage murders." Such conditions had permitted the rebel invasion to begin with, Arny noted. He promised protection for the discoverers of the mines of gold and other minerals at the headwaters of the Gila River and the Río Prieto in the Organ Mountains, an issue to grow in territorial politics.[71]

Doña Ana County residents deemed the effort insufficient. Probate Judge Nepomuceno Ancheta chaired an anti-state mass meeting, which Arny attended. One of its resolutions called statehood a prejudice, "present and prospective," to the interests and welfare of the county citizens. Such a connection to New Mexico would be a "forced alliance, contrary to geographical position and to the laws of climate and of commerce; an alliance between people of diverse interests and between Territories of diametrically opposite resources." The Doña Aneños would, "to the best of their abilities," support the U.S. Constitution (reversing their loyalties from prior to outbreak of the war) but would move to establish their own federal territory to be called Montezuma. Such a liberal, economical, and accessible government would restore them to prosperity and happiness and lead to the development of the county's "manifold resources." The gathering thanked Arny for his supportive speech and interest in the welfare of the hitherto neglected section. Knapp was acknowledged for being the first judge to reside in the county. Arny was elected to serve as the county's delegate to present its memorial to the U.S. Congress calling for the organization of the Territory of Montezuma and the reasons for its opposition to "any connection with New Mexico, either as a State or a Territory."[72]

Arny had no choice but to leave southern New Mexico off the statehood call. Leib pressed on with the movement, circulating a petition in the spring of 1863 asking the governor to call a statehood convention. Ten reasons were given why the lands, minerals, and industries of New Mexico would prove money makers for common schools, roads, bridges, effective government, and military posts.[73] As statehood proponents waited for the governor to act on the petition, the election season dawned.

After more than a decade of the western territories sitting in the front row of Congress's deliberations, the Civil War relegated them to the far back of the chamber. Delegate Watts industriously worked to bring needed resources to the neglected territory with little success.[74] It was later suggested that Watts's measure for a loan program disenchanted James Collins. Collins, still reputed as the "party manager" of his faction, reportedly "deemed it advisable to look about for a new candidate."[75] Watts announced as his term wound down that he would not run for reelection.[76] The field lay open for fresh and renewable candidacies. Electoral energies quickened in early January 1863 by the sounding of three names as contenders for delegate to Congress. Each had a newspaper ready to display his virtues and slay the prospects of any others.

House Speaker José M. Gallegos leaked his intention to run.[77] A Gallegos candidacy appeared viable among culturally conservative Nuevomexicanos and those who cottoned to his defense of the rights of Mexicans. His record as house speaker for the previous three sessions and his strategic connections became his candidacy. There was in addition his special qualification of recent heroism. As the Texans approached Santa Fe, most of the territory's officials fled to Las Vegas. Gallegos and Facundo Pino stayed to defend their capital. Texas Confederates placed them under arrest for their known territorial leadership. While in jail, Gallegos provided intelligence to Col. Manuel Chávez on enemy movements.[78]

Sheer ambition seems to have figured in the contest. Gallegos resonates with the gravitas of ambition in American politics, stamped with a regional identity. Gallegos was not even a neophyte Republican, yet the *New Mexican* under Leib moved to support him because his ambition set him against the Copperhead American Party. Gallegos, moreover, represented to the Radical Republican mindset the plight of a racial minority in need of civil rights and social succor. To Hezekiah Johnson, the alliance smacked of the "hydra-headed monster."[79] In the stream of factional formation in the territory, Arny and company inherited the legacy of Euroamericans in the Mexican Party, the tradition of Weightman, Calhoun, and Meriwether. It was symbolically significant that Leib reversed the usual order of the language sections in New Mexico weeklies, placing the Spanish articles ahead of the English-language material.

The *Weekly Press* settled on Joab Houghton, the Kearny judge, American Party founder, former district court judge, and current territorial land commissioner. Hezekiah Johnson knew Houghton dating to frontier trading and hunting days in the Taos area. The lone-wolf Johnson, in putting up Houghton, intended to "shatter the phalanx of demagogues we recognized under a many colored garb." One set of miscreant's robes in Johnson's mind was worn by the (Mexican) "party hacks" who had controlled the legislature "since the organization of this Territory"; another by the newcomers wanting to lay the foundation for a Republican Party; and a third by the Copperhead *Gazette* "clique." Johnson hailed Houghton as the "Independent" candidate for delegate. Houghton did not authorize Johnson's nomination but went along, removing him from association with Collins's American Party.[80]

Johnson's aging candidate held a dim candle next to the young José Francisco Perea. Perea was born in Los Padillas, south of Alburquerque, to one of the powerful families of the Río Abajo who had welcomed the American capture of New Mexico. He received private tutoring in Bernalillo County and Santa Fe in the 1830s and attended the Jesuit College in St. Louis and, during the Kearny occupation, New York City's Bank Street Academy. One of his best friends while living in St. Louis was the son of the editor of the St. Louis *Republican*. Perea traveled along the eastern seaboard in company with his uncle, Henry Connelly, meeting President Taylor in one adventure. The U.S. conquest of New Mexico opened up huge markets throughout the West and, out of military installations, for the ranches and stores of Nuevomexicano ricos and entrepreneurs. In what can be called "material citizenship," they earned great profits and became a distinct class in the American frontier economy. Perea participated in the trade caravans of his merchant uncles to Mexico and California. He engaged in stock raising and commercial pursuits from 1850 on, carrying merchandise by mule train from St. Louis and Independence to Mexico. He was elected to the territorial council in 1858 and received an officer commission in the Civil War, commanding a battalion at Glorieta Pass and fighting in Navajo campaigns.[81]

Perea announced his candidacy on January 3. He had been drafted in a wholly reactive move. James Collins took a particular interest in him, although the party line had friends of the *Gazette* approaching Perea so as to have an "even start" with Gallegos "and to watch and circumvent, if possible, his movements." Perea's appeal to the American Party was his appearance as a practical twin of Miguel Antonio Otero. The difference was Perea's lack of Otero ambition and drive for political office. Perea expressed little enthusiasm for the nomination, claiming he would have stepped aside for someone with more experience. Yet the public relations balloon with his name on it flew well over the Río Abajo District counties, where friends numbered "their majority" over anyone "by hundreds." It worried American Partyites who endorsed him, including Otero, that after Perea announced his candidacy, business interests took him away from New Mexico for several months.[82]

The Mexican shadow-party lost one of its charter members in the last week of January 1862 when president of the territorial council, don Facundo Pino, passed away at the age of forty. Hezekiah Johnson momentarily suspended his usual enmity toward the assembly "demagogue" to praise Pino's love of American institutions, which, Johnson said, he held "with an ardor equaled only by that of one born and bred under them."[83]

No preexisting faction made an early public call for a territorial nominating convention. The Mexican shadow-party came to life when house member Diego Archuleta (Río Arriba County) and Councilman Pedro Sánchez (Taos County) called assemblymen to a special meeting in the first week of February. The confabulation over which they presided came out with the announcement of a territorial nominating convention for the first Monday of June. Delegates from the counties would decide on the candidate they felt best qualified to nominate for delegate to Congress. Organizers opted for a "People's Convention." A bit of partisanship found its way into the resolution that heartily approved the course of the *Santa Fe New Mexican* and cordially recommended the weekly to the support of "our people."[84]

On March 14 the *New Mexican* published a letter from Faustín Baca y Ulivarri, esteemed San Miguel County rancher and major in the New Mexico Volunteers who led the Las Vegas meeting the year before in commitment to the North, putting up the name of José Manuel Gallegos for Congress. The *New Mexican* went on record in favor of the recommendation. The public announcement of the People's Convention went out in mid-April.[85]

Meanwhile, as the petition to the governor for an election of delegates to hold a statehood convention seemed to be going nowhere, the *New Mexican* proposed that the People's Convention be the forum for writing a state constitution. "We care not who opposes it, we are for a State organization now," the paper affirmed, "and think the June convention is the very body that should consider the question, because it will be a convention of the people, and as framing a constitution will be for the best interests of New Mexico, in our view, they should not hesitate to do so." Editor Leib hoped to see the "whole people" united in favor of statehood without regard to party.[86] There is no indication of the People's Convention organizers deciding to inject the *New Mexican*'s recommendation into its convention agenda even though it was consistent with the Mexican Party's general desire for Nuevomexicano home rule. Yet critics would project the convention and the statehood movement as conjoined from the start.

The People's Convention announcement blew the whistle for the second quarter of the season's partisan games. Russell at the *Gazette* smelled a scheme led by the "political intriguer" Arny to establish a "partizan Republican State" and a Republican Party in the territory using "political trickery learned in Kansas." It was the sort of thing, Russell mused, committed by government officials from the United States who had "merely a transitory interest" in the territory.[87]

An important reaction accused Gallegos of manipulating the majority in the legislature to pass the proposals for a nominating convention and influencing the *New Mexican* to support his run at Congress.[88] Advertisements for the convention suggested a more open nominating event. Russell, however, threw all manner of garbage on the "June Bug Convention," as he derisively labeled the event. It was not, nor was it intended to be, a convention of the people, he insisted; rather was it launched by the Gallegos tool Archuleta for the purpose of nominating a candidate for delegate "who would suit the faction to which these men belong." Russell posted the ad "Francisco Perea, Union Candidate for Delegate," on the *Gazette* editorial page.[89]

Hezekiah Johnson called the legislative assembly's adoption of the *New Mexican*'s candidate, Gallegos, "unjust and absurd." Why, he rhetorically wondered, did the members not procure passage of similar resolutions recommending the people "to purchase the necessaries of life exclusively from one dealer?"[90] Johnson lashed out at the "wire pullers of the summer party" while singing the virtues of public service in the American tradition. He tore into the alleged practice in New Mexico of serving the "gratification of personal likes and dislikes of leaders," the "exclusive" aggrandizement of party leaders, and the "gratification of base passions" as endorsed by the other two papers.[91] Johnson implied that only his political corner could offer any semblance of liberal and republican material to the people of New Mexico. Gadfly Johnson streamlined the factional divide by abandoning the Arny-Leib-Gallegos statehood project. Mesilla's popular opposition to statehood figured in his decision, as did the cold shoulder given to it by the hard-luck citizens in his Río Abajo backyard, who would not be able to handle any increase in taxes. The clincher involved the plan to have the People's Convention write the state constitution. In effect, Johnson sensed that it violated the Statehood Revolution's requirement of a democratic election to determine the delegates to a constitution-forming effort. Johnson disdained "Johnny Newcomers" seeking to elevate their fortunes with senatorships, painting Leib as a key culprit. A year hence would be time enough to elect delegates to a state constitutional convention, Johnson figured. As he concluded, "Best we not go off at 'half-cock.'"[92]

An anonymous citizen agreed that those proposing a change in New Mexico's government were strangers from the "Eastern States and Europeans," few of whom intended to make New Mexico their home. This writer volunteered that other outsiders who had been in the territory "many long years" did not want statehood, and they had gone through "the trials and hardships incident to founding settlements in the heart of our Continent, with its bravest Savages all around them." They had "full knowledge of the wants of the people," felt a "true interest in their welfare," and would be ready "when the time shall come and they (*los del país*) are prepared for a change, to be the first to grasp every opportunity to carry out the views of the masses." When the "cruel" war ended, "hardy Yeomanry from the Eastern States" would settle in the "beautiful valleys, bringing wealth, education and industry to New Mexico." The land would flourish "with great fields of golden wheat and wavy corn, and gold will circulate as in former times."[93] Leib, meanwhile, grieved over Nuevomexicanos who he said opposed statehood because they believed that their own people were not capable of self-government.[94]

Hezekiah Johnson apologized to his personal friends for not going with his Río Abajo neighbor Perea for delegate. He relieved the majority of the people of embarrassment by exercising his inalienable rights as a citizen and editor. Johnson continued to lay faith in Houghton's characteristics as a gentleman; his long residence in the territory; his intimate acquaintance with the people, their language, "genius and necessities"; his active part in the people's public affairs; and his unremitting promotion of their interests and welfare.[95] Houghton himself did not put out a statement regarding his candidacy.

A viable Houghton candidacy would have tripped up New Mexico's binary factionalism. Johnson thought so even as Leib at the *New Mexican* sneered in Spanish at his choice coming from a "ONE MAN [Gallegos] convention." Johnson haughtily responded: "In politics, as in other matters, we speak and act as we see proper; we are no person's Man Friday, and sneeze for ourself [*sic*] when we take snuff, if we find it convenient. The editor of the [*New Mexican*] is so infatuated with his pet idea of a convention (which he thinks the orthodox mode of doing political business) that he considers all men political heretics who will not submit to its rule." Johnson said he did not propose Houghton for the purpose of "pleasing Dr. Leib or the clique which concocted the [June Bug] convention." The clique did not purport to belong to "any existing National or Territorial party." It was well known, rather, that the Republicans expected to "come in for the lion's share of the spoils."[96] Not an expression of the people's will, Johnson argued, this People's Convention was a "caucus," a "mass meeting," a "partisan affair," or a "transaction of party or faction." Leib had called the organizers of the People's Convention "bold, intelligent, able men," but Johnson caricatured them as puppets doing the dirty work of Gallegos, who had rigged it for himself, in spite of his assurance to others that they could emerge as the convention's candidate. Houghton was therefore not obliged to ask anybody's permission to run for delegate; he would "stand a good chance in a 'free fight.'"[97]

A circular sent out by "Many Friends" invited "all citizens" to the Santa Fe County People's Convention. The *Gazette* and the *Press* cynically predicted a closed meeting. Interestingly, a feel of openness prevailed. A motley assortment made up the "goodly crowd." Mexican Partyites—Secretary Arny (no longer acting governor with the return of Connelly), Leib, Miguel E. Pino, and Gallegos—attended. Civil War officers enjoyed a special status in the territory, and their war records gave them a certain political cachet, a kind of "veterans citizenship," as it might be called.[98] This election saw the rise of what can be termed the 1.5 generation of conquest Nuevomexicanos who were teenagers at the time of the American annexation. Among them, the articulate Capt. Nicolás Quintana had recently given the keynote address at the Fourth of July celebration (where he lauded the heroes of American independence and Nuevomexicano adhesion to "our adopted *patria* along with the indissoluble links that have come to us").[99] Quintana was not yet known in association with either of New Mexico's main factions. At the People's Convention he nominated the Mexican Party man Miguel E. Pino for president of the proceeding. He in turn was nominated secretary. Capt. Jesús M. Sena y Baca debuted in a public role. The senior American Partyite Felipe Delgado, a Civil War vet himself, made an appearance along with several Euroamerican settlers, including former *Gazette* editor David Miller. Houghton showed, perhaps to see about some traction for his candidacy. José Manuel Gallegos explained the object of the meeting. Nine Santa Fe delegates of mixed political association were named to the territorial nominating convention—Miller, Quintana, Delgado, Nicolás Pino, Miguel F. Pino, James Johnson (brother of Hezekiah), José M. Baca y Salazar, Simón Delgado (brother of Felipe), and Albino Roibal.[100]

Six of nine counties sent delegates to the territorial People's Convention (Arny and Greiner serving as proxies for Doña Ana). Significantly, the body deferred Mora County's request for a ruling on the statehood question. The *New Mexican* had earlier said that no candidate could get elected delegate without affirming support for statehood, but the growing objections to the proposal and the media that demonized it seem to have ruined the proposal. The convention deemed that the proper time for considering statehood would be after the election, when the process could be conducted "in a legal [Statehood Revolution] manner." The delegates were "purposeful in their vagueness," one historian notes. The tactic of saying little as possible was meant to appeal to the "widest possible spectrum of support."[101]

Justice Benedict attended. The *Gazette* would later claim that he went to garner support for a candidacy of his own for delegate but that Gallegos stood in the way of his mustering more than "a corporal's guard of friends before the convention."[102] Leib submitted the Gallegos name in nomination. No one else received a nod. Gallegos received the nomination "with great unanimity," the *Gazette* reported. Russell may not have been far off in calling the proceeding a "conspiracy" with a program to force the nomination of Gallegos. The editor characterized the Gallegos choice "pretty much as Louis Napoleon was elected President of the French: all had a fair opportunity to vote for him, none could vote for any person else."[103] The convention concluded by inviting Gallegos into the hall of the house to address the delegates.[104]

Just as the People's Convention disbanded, word spread of Francisco Perea's presence in the plaza. A spontaneous Perea rally robbed the People's Party of a heady climax. The celebration for Perea continued to the next evening, when he was "complimented" with a serenade outside his room at La Fonda Hotel. It was a sign of the growing political importance of the military command, that the Fifth Infantry Band performed for Perea amid a gathering assembly. The crowd moved to the Exchange Hotel with hurrahs for Perea. The *Gazette* promised that the great confidence reposed in Perea would "not be betrayed." If elected he would be the "representative of all the people without distinction of races or tongues"; no consideration "of a personal nature" would mar his official conduct. Perea denied the rumor that he was "Colonel Collins's candidate." He called himself a non-politician, much less a public speaker. Yet he affirmed articulately that none could exceed his devotion to New Mexico. Perea pointed "with pride" to the position his ancestors had assumed in New Mexico "for generations back."

American Party hands dominated the Perea rally. Merrill Ashurst and Charles Clever obliged the call for speakers. Their "felicitous and eloquent" remarks were "frequently applauded," the *Gazette* reported. Significantly, Captains Quintana and Sena y Baca peeled off Gallegos's People's Party, migrating then to the Perea camp. Supreme Court Chief Justice Benedict abandoned the People's folks, saying it was for their failure to declare political and policy principles. Celebrants, trailing the band and looking like the typical crowd of an American political party, marched to the residences of well-known figures. The band played "Hail Columbia," "Yankee Doodle," and other national airs at Benedict's place. It led everyone to the Palace of the Governors, where Governor Connelly received its serenade and the praise of speakers. James Collins was not home, but friends complimented him with interesting tidbits of his long, eventful, and "useful life." Benedict regaled Sena y Baca at the latter's residence. Others to receive a serenade were don Felipe Delgado and don Albino Roibal, both defectors from the June Bug Convention. The political party ended at three in the morning.[105]

Nicolás Quintana put out a public statement in which he condemned the Santa Fe delegation at the People's Convention for exercising control over the proceedings to benefit Gallegos. Quintana broadcasted the lament of a liberal American patriot and combat veteran onto the collective ear of a Nuevomexicano audience. The convention should have manifested its patriotism in its resolutions, Quintana declared, "penetrating the heart of our compatriots [*penetrando en el corazón de nuestros compatriotas*]." The present circumstances called for it. They were of "bitter and dangerous crises" in which the integrity of the Union was caught, . . . a time when we should interest ourselves

FIG. 17. *José Francisco Perea, New Mexico delegate to United States Congress, 1863–65*, photographer unknown. Perea was one of two Río Abajo ricos to be elected a delegate to Congress as a stalwart American Party member up to 1871. Courtesy Palace of the Governors Photo Archives, NMHM/DCA, negative #105371.

FIG. 18. *Plaza looking west, Santa Fe, New Mexico*, 1866, photographer unknown. The plaza was where innumerable political rallies were organized in the capital, including that for José Francisco Perea in 1863. Courtesy Palace of the Governors Photo Archives, NMHM/DCA, negative #011256.

by our nationality; when we should lament the loss of so many lives, which are being sacrificed daily in the cause of our sacred country; when we should think of the martyrs who fell defending our flag; when we should sympathize with so many orphans and widows who are left to cry their misfortune and misery; when we should demonstrate to our government our adhesion and loyalty.

> la crisis amarga y peligrosa en que esta empeñada la integridad de la Unión, y cuando debemos interesarnos por nuestra nacionalidad; cuando debemos lamentar la pérdida de tantas vidas, que son sacrificadas diariamente en la causa santa de la patria; cuando debemos pensar en los mártires que sumben defendiendo nuestra bandera; cuando debemos simpatizar con tanto huerfano y viudas que quedan llorando su desgracia y su miseria; cuando debemos manifestar a nuestro gobierno nuestra adhesión y fidelidad.

Quintana saw Gallegos's dictatorial politics threatening the integration of Nuevomexicanos into American civics. It was why he fled the convention, he claimed. The Civil War hero assimilated the Enlightenment view of clique politics going against the grain of liberalism. He did not want to be accused of being anti-American (*no quiero que se me acuse de anti-americano*) by staying with the convention. The captain sympathized with his government, "with our army or with the conservation of our nationality and our Union [*con nuestro ejército o con la conservación de nuestra nacionalidad y nuestra Unión*]." New Mexico was fortunate for being "an integral part of a grand nation [*parte integrante de una gran nación*]," Quintana affirmed pluralistically. "We thus conserve its institutions [*Conservamos pues sus instituciones*]." These institutions merited the highest grade of veneration and respect (*el más alto grado de veneración y de respeto*). Men learned to govern themselves from them, he intoned. They elevated the people and instructed them on how to judge those who directed the pubic business. Under free institutions, "each man has the right to form an opinion [*cada hombre tiene el derecho de formar una opinión*]." Though it produced conflict, dissension, and differences, free thought was the only means of reaching the truth and realizing the public good, Quintana observed, and it all went missing in the People's Convention.[106]

The *Gazette* and the *Press* went on to launch double-barrel attacks on Gallegos, even as they flung dirt at each other. Hezekiah Johnson blasted Gallegos for having done nothing for New Mexico while in Congress. Those who called the former delegate a "talented" statesman" in the columns of the *New Mexican* were of "inferior caliber." Gallegos did not speak English; Perea did.[107] Russell took the impromptu June Bug Convention to task for failing to devise a platform of principles. He showered invective onto the *New Mexican*, raunchily calling it "the half-organ of the little Padre." How its editor could have allowed a nominating body pass without a statement regarding the "mighty struggle" going on in the country was "more than passing strange," Russell noted, particularly as Leib could "see nothing loyal" in the *Gazette*.[108] In light of the People's weak party representation, Johnson believed that without a platform, Gallegos could only be a "political acrobat or Flying Dutchman."[109]

The People's Convention and the Gallegos camp quieted down on statehood, yet Russell and Johnson ripped into the proposal to the bitter end. It was a "scheme" lurking *sub rosa*, in one account. Russell portrayed the People's "caucus" as fraudulently engineering the nomination of Gallegos and intending to wait until the election of the entire "Gallegos party" of candidates for the assembly to spring a state constitution on the people out of the legislature. With the taxes to come with statehood, Gallegos would enrich himself even further than he had already, the harangue went on.[110] Perhaps accurately, Johnson had Arny and his "little coterie of small-potato demagogues" using statehood to sustain the Republican Party. He said the Arny group "deceived" itself in thinking the Union and general government served thereby.[111]

Russell went so far as to accuse Gallegos of using fraud to secure a certificate of election over Governor William Lane back in 1853 and said he tried again in Otero's contest but was found out. Gallegos realized that the exposure of these "rascalities" would not vault him to the delegate's seat, Russell prattled, so he settled into being a "county demagogue." The fraudulent strategy landed Gallegos in the territorial house, where he passed "barbaric" legislation.[112] Gallegos was framed into a mercenary on the charge that he had not contributed to a charity drive for the destitute people of Socorro County.[113] Another tale, repeated over again, had Gallegos introducing a bill to permit him, as executor, to "plunder" the estate of the deceased Antonio Sandoval. That failing, he allegedly worked out a deal with a probate judge to enable his "villainy" by receiving $45,000 of a $350,000 estate. Nicolás Quintana, his fame growing as a Perea advocate, authored a verse that reviled "El Padrecillo" (the little priest) for ignoring the needs of fellow Mexicans while swindling "sweet women" (Sandoval's widow).[114] However, Capt. James "Santiago" Hubbell of the Independent Company of Mounted Men made an important point. If any information regarding administrators taking unlawful fees from the Sandoval estate existed, the responsibility existed to prosecute rather than publish calumnies in the paper.[115] No one did.

The image of Gallegos as a crotchety old goat originated in reference to the Santa Fe meeting to choose delegates for the People's Convention. In the legend, Gallegos launched a "Bombastes

Furioso" attack on Quintana and Sena y Baca because they did not name him convention chairman. Not explained was how serving as chair would have advanced Gallegos if he was supposed to have rigged the nomination from the start. In any case, the *Gazette* had the neophytes Quintana and Sena y Baca replying to Gallegos's fury "in a most felicitous manner," and to the approval of all present.[116]

Johnson pitted the aging Gallegos up against the youth of Quintana and Sena y Baca. Quintana had "taken the affairs of Young New Mexico under his especial care," went the line, while Gallegos forgot that under American institutions "all free white males of over twenty-one years of age are as much entitled to enjoy their opinions and to participate equally in public assemblies as older men are." They were not to be characterized as "'MALCRIADOS' [ill-bred, misbehaved] because of differing opinions with the latter." Were Gallegos, Arny, and other "aspiring" politicians "wise," they would judge "that the people are not to be humbugged any longer either by fogyism or insipid newspaper articles or communications; and that SESOS [brains], not PESOS, will rule in New Mexico."[117] Russell urged young, educated men to run for office against legislators selected "without regard to their qualifications or fitness for the place."[118]

No attack on Gallegos earned its salt without reference to his morals. The Episcopal missionary Hezekiah Johnson had a special calling to wring out Gallegos's religious record even though the former priest had left his canonical duties far behind. Gallegos was "knocked out of the ring by the Bishop on account of his grossly immoral life editor Johnson put it. "Instead of repenting of his sins and leading a new life, Mr. Gallegos became a demagogue and endeavored to attain honors as a layman; but habit holding him as in a vice. . . . the people have not been so successful as when in a sacerdotal sphere, [he] became divested of the immunity of the long gown."[119] Critics felt they had plain reason to howl in ugly reaction at the idea of Gallegos and a woman out in public. "By this time, it was no secret in the territory," Gerald Theisen writes, "that the ex-priest was involved in a serious romantic liaison with Señora Candelaria Montoya, a Corrales widow." Russell pontificated as to how the "little padre" had left on a pilgrimage to the county of Mora and did not take "his Candelarita with him, like he did when he went to Rio Arriba." Russell projected the people censuring Gallegos for his "effrontery in attempting to introduce her among respectable families," cautioning him not to try the "experiment" again.[120]

Johnson's more wickedly pious castigation said Gallegos "may, before he 'shuffles off the mortal coil,' start a new religious denomination. Cande laraus Gallegois-ites, or Chimayoses [from the notoriously rebellious village of Chimayó], and one hundred or one hundred-and-fifty years hence, the Padre may be canonized as the patron saint thereof on account of his miraculous election to Congress in 1863." Johnson had a lascivious time with Leib's claim that Gallegos had a deep love for his people. Several "inquisitive individuals have asked us for which branch—male or female—of the human family of New Mexico Mr. Gallegos has most love," he cut in. Johnson recalled some twelve years before "hearing women say that Mr. Gallegos was *'el mejor confesor para las mujeres'* [the best confessor for the women]; from which fact, the inquisitive may draw their own inferences."[121]

Leib pointed out that every time Gallegos came before the people as a candidate he was "most vilely abused and misrepresented by his opponents.'" Johnson answered by denouncing Gallegos, the "eminent disciple of Galen, consummate archangel and profound jurist."[122] Leib argued that the "private and clerical character" of Gallegos was not the business of politics. As horrified Russell countered, Gallegos might have been a horse thief or a murderer, yet Leib "would not have anything to do with his private character." He might have been a gentleman "possessed of all the virtues and addicted to none of the vices, yet the editor of the New Mexican would have nothing to do with his private character." Only one whose moral sensibilities had become "so blunted by contact with immorality" could take that stance. Sermonizing in liberal tenor, Johnson had Leib incapacitated from rightly performing the duties of a citizen "in a republic where the officers of the government are elected by the people, or from one who is so ignorant as not to know that republics have flourished whilst their rulers were virtuous and have fallen when their rulers became corrupt." As Russell took the case, "A bad man in private life cannot be a good man in public life."[123]

The journalists lit the fires of race. Russell and Johnson harangued with the stereotype of Gallegos as a hater of *los gringos*.[124] Leib defended Gallegos, Mexican Party style, in Spanish. Nuevomexicanos had a "just political cause" in expressing their bitter sentiments against the "gringo strangers." Too many Americans arrived as "scoundrels," Leib noted. Gallegos represented the "just" and "manly" cause of standing up to them.[125] Gallegos reflected as much in his statement before Congress in the contest that he lost to Miguel Otero in 1855. It appeared this electoral season in what Miguel E. Pino, Gallegos's Mexican Party brother, was overheard telling Euroamerican *caballeros*, to wit, "'¡O! *Ustedes son todos Americanos, pueden hacer conmigo lo que quieren: aquí, esto es el poder de Ustedes, pero no me espantan*'" (Oh! You are Americans; you can do with me what you will; it is in your power to do so, but you do not frighten me).[126]

Johnson and Russell both wore liberal blinders regarding the extent of Euroamerican ethnoracial power. A few months before Johnson's paper had reported on an army soldier given a dishonorable discharge who, it was known, had "expressed great contempt for the natives of this Territory."[127] Yet Johnson used some essentialist baiting to put the burden for race problems on Nuevomexicanos. He jabbed at Leib for his "low catering to the passions" of the "native race," whose "indiscriminate hatred of a race on account of individual wrong" was but a "prominent trait of Indian character." Claiming greater authority to speak of "existing prejudices" from more time in the region, Johnson did not think "calling names, or working upon the passions for partisan ends" could remove them. He trotted out the assimilationist's favorite cultural dichotomy. The "gentleman natives" (like Perea) would never respect Gallegos and the other racist demagogues stooping to "water the seeds of prejudice." Unable or unwilling to acknowledge the generally subordinate position of Nuevomexicanos, Johnson deemed it "natural" that there be discrimination between Americans and Mexicans, and "no sensible man would expect otherwise." Even then, Leib had allegedly taken the "wrong course" in doing away with these prejudices among the one race or the other. "We have observed with pain," Johnson philosophized on the presumption of basic equality among the races, "that instead of blending together and doing away with prejudices of race, as citizens of a common government should do, they keep aloof from each other as much as possible, and these prejudices increase with the increase in population." Johnson recounted a legend to illustrate Gallegos's alleged racism. When a certain legislator proposed a memorial to William Skinner, killed by a Nuevomexicano in a political fight in 1851, Gallegos objected to a resolution for a *"gringo perro"* (gringo dog).

Johnson had other tales of race to tell. As a priest and in the legislature, he charged, Gallegos had failed to preach "the Gospel of Peace and Concord." Instead he "excited the fanatic prejudice of the natives against the Americans as heretics and off-scourings of the earth." Johnson referred to an old man he met who considered Gallegos a "saint" and thought the Americans heretics and thieves. "When we recollect that this man was under Mr. Gallegos's pastoral care and instruction," Johnson commented, "we may correctly infer that his prejudices were cultivated by Mr. Gallegos." The origins of race problems in New Mexico were clear to Johnson, who said "upon the celebration of the Treaty of Guadalupe Hidalgo, had Mr. Gallegos and other clergymen then in this Territory done their duty towards God and their fellow men, there would now exist little or no prejudice of race." What should be admired most, Johnson wondered—Leib's "effrontery in making against his own countrymen or his low estimate of Spanish magnanimity and Christianity?"

Johnson held up heroic Euroamerican colonizers as a point in contrast. In his fourteen years of residence in the territory, he claimed, "a great many Americans" had employed natives, "paid them good wages and abundance of food for their services; and as a general rule, they would rather do a native a benefit than an injury." Euroamericans led "the natives" along the liberal road by the hand, endeavoring to "instruct" them "in their rights as citizens of the United States without regard to rank or condition. Euroamericans had "infused into" Mexicans "by example a portion of their own energy, enterprise, public spirit and indomitable courage, and at Valverde, Apache *Cañon* and on innumerable Indian battle fields have poured out their blood like water in defense of New Mexico." Yet would an American like Leib "justify and prescribe the measure of hatred that should be had by the natives of New Mexico towards their fellow citizens from the States. For shame!, say all just and grateful New Mexicans," Johnson binaried on. "For shame, say all, except demagogues and toadies."[128]

Johnson claimed not to regard all Euroamericans as saints for having availed themselves of the license "attendant upon a small quantity of moral public sentiment in a community." Leib recognized his principal patronage coming from "Americans, Germans, Irish, Scotch," Johnson affirmed, "to all of whom the natives apply the generic term 'Gringo,' and whom they consider Americans." Johnson's integrative colonialism asked if "the stranger" should withdraw from the territory. "[A]ny person who has witnessed [New Mexico's] advancement since the acquisition by the United States can readily conjecture what would be the result." Similar to W. W. H. Davis, Johnson had the "masses of the natives . . . not what would be considered intelligent in the States." Unlike Davis, who detested the upper class, Johnson saw the "few educated and observant men among them" acknowledging and regretting the lack of literacy in the masses, and "no 'Gringo' reproaches them therefore." Johnson saw the lack of intelligence as deriving from a want of the rudiments of education, the fault of Gallegos and his co-priests "who managed the Territory before the acquisition," the "co-demagogues who have largely participated in the management of its affairs since the acquisition." Johnson faulted Nuevomexicano "prejudice" for New Mexico's lack of schools. The "native demagogues" in the legislature incited a fear of taxes to reject a law for the establishment of territorial public schools.

American institutions would fix racism, Johnson reflected. "The cause of Dr. Leib's Quixotic enterprise against the 'strangers,'" he averred, "appears to be that some native individuals have aroused his sympathies by informing him of their private grievances." It was fodder for controversy, but "the complainant who seeks redress in that manner in preference to the substantial remedy of a court must have a very weak cause, or none whatever." The courts were available to natives who suffered wrong "either in person, property, or reputation, at the hands of a 'Gringo,'" Johnson persisted. As 99 percent of the justices of the peace and jurors were natives, "the 'Gringo' will not be to blame if a native plaintiff does not obtain judgment in a just cause. But as the *New Mexican* has brought suit at the bar of public opinion, it is now his duty to state names of plaintiffs and defendants, circumstances, &c., in order that extenuating circumstances may be alleged in defense."[129]

A Nuevomexicano going by *La Verdad* (The truth) opposed Gallegos based on some of these charges, but at the least the writer had the respect and civility to credit the "patriotism" Gallegos had displayed during the Texan occupation of Santa Fe.[130] The partisan *Gazette* and *Press* would never grant the concession. Still, such lengths of condemnation came out of a fear of Gallegos's strength among Mexican voters and the felt need to keep the partisan binary blistering.

The platform Perea circulated in a public proclamation said nothing regarding his opponent Gallegos. One plank portended much regarding future politics of tribal Americans. Perea adopted the call, originated by Colonel Canby and picked up by General Carleton, for the final defeat of the Navajo. Perea rationalized that it would be "acting the part of wisdom in our behalf and the part of philanthropy on behalf of the savages for us to place them upon reservations, judiciously selected, where they may be compelled to earn their subsistence by the labor of their own hands, and have the opportunity given them to cultivate the habits and enjoy the blessings of civilization and Christianity." Perea invoked a passage from a Lincoln address to emphasize the need to defend the mining districts against Indian violence, attaching his homeland to the issue. As delegate he would secure appropriations "to put these pests out of our way and reinstate our people in their rightful control over the destinies and prosperity of the beloved country for which our gallant forefathers endured and suffered so much, redeeming it from savage hands and reducing it to the civilizing influences of our pure Christianity."

Perea expressed opposition to statehood in line with his American Party friends. His rhetorical flourish covering much like that of Miguel A. Otero's, Perea said:

> We do not belong to that restive class of people who always yearn for something new and who are never satisfied with things as they find them, though they may be ever so good. We and our ancestors have inhabited New Mexico for hundreds of years. We know the Territory, its wants and its people better than some of those who have recently set themselves up as our teachers in this respect and the new State question is one that we will dispose of in our own way whenever it may be forced upon us.

The statehood idea did not originate in "the people," Perea declared (as if it could have); rather, it came from "men ambitious of place and power and regardless of the interests of these who would have to bear the burden of the government, whilst these men, secure in their well-paying offices, would live at ease and on the fat of the land."

Perea held that the political integration of the Nuevomexicanos in Doña Ana was best facilitated by letting them have their own territorial government, much like the South was thought by many in his party to have the right to secede. Those in the north may have had in common with them a "community of language and religion," but shared material interests went lacking. The two areas were separated "by a lateral boundary that almost forbids our being united under the same local government." The people in the middle and northern parts of the territory never had reason to object seriously to the Doña Ana desire for secession. "Practically their connection with New Mexico has been of no advantage to us," Perea argued. They had professed "to maintain a separate existence," had levied and collected taxes for themselves, while their officers refused to enforce tax laws enacted by the assembly. As delegate, he would "interpose no objection to their petition" to have their own territory.

Perea rode high on Copperhead shoulders. He prefaced his position on the war by emphasizing that the day had passed for discussing its causes. The issue would later involve questions of political philosophy of more importance than statesmen in the past could decide, he assured. The political problems pronounced by the fathers of the country were yet to be solved. The solution would depend on the manner in which the war would terminate. It was the duty then of all citizens to occupy themselves with the "stern realities" confronting them, to do all in their power "to maintain the integrity of the government." With its "benign influences spreading equal and exact, justice from the farthest north to the farthest south and from the rising to the setting of the sun on this continent should be the last, best early hope of every American citizen." New Mexico had a deep interest in keeping the government in common with the people in other parts of the country, Perea instructed the Nuevomexicanos. "Since we have been part of it, we have felt all the benefits that can be bestowed by a government upon a people and have had none of the inconveniences incidental to the conduct of a government to encounter. We would therefore be recreant to every duty were we now to refuse support and assistance to that government in the day of its sore trial and when it is struggling for existence itself." Should the people favor him with a seat in Congress, Perea would use the whole of his influence in favor of bringing back the Union as it was and the "enforcement of the constitution as it is."[131]

The proclamation may not have reflected a rico's desire to continue with peonage and Indian slaves. To the opposition, it bore the "earmarks of the *Gazette* men." The *Gazette* did not deny it exactly. "No person would ever suspect the *New Mexican* man of producing as clever a document as is the letter of Col. Perea," Russell put it.[132] When the *New Mexican* accused the Perea campaign of trying to catch Copperhead votes, Russell quipped, "If we may judge from the kind of bait used, the *New Mexican* fishes for Mullethead votes. It certainly cannot catch any other sort. Mullets delight in the soft."[133] Similarly, Hezekiah Johnson heard from a "devilish" friend that "blockheads" would be in support of the padre Gallegos.[134]

Nuevomexicano Mexican Partyites sneered at an elitist, Otero-style regime in the Perea candidacy. Diego Archuleta and Pedro Sánchez, who had called the People's Convention, represented the counties of the north in resistance to the pending return of the hegemony of the proverbial Río Abajo rico.[135] Archuleta wrote to don Juan Ignacio Cruz about those Nuevomexicanos who never lent a hand to their paisanos, nor respected the people of the territory. They now proclaimed Perea as their delegate, "without any other qualification . . . than being a rico and that he reads a few books in English and some few adulators among our paisanos sustain him." Archuleta doubted not that Gallegos would best him. Then they would show the world "that we are not as some malevolent ones have wanted to represent us." Ever true to his far northern district, Archuleta lamented the loss of the Conejos region. When the Colorado Territory was formed in 1861, its politicians included within its boundaries the strip of land called the Conejos to make its southern border a straight line and augment its population for statehood. The Nuevomexicanos who had settled that area in the 1850s petitioned Congress to reinstate the Conejos to their New Mexico. Congress ruled in favor of keeping it in Colorado, influenced by the Colorado delegate, who with the most "earnest tenacity" would not agree to relinquish it. Archuleta conveyed that with Perea willing to let the southern portion of the territory go, tomorrow would they take Taos away "until they leave us like the [defunct Indian] Pueblo of Pecos."[136]

The *Weekly Press* prepared to launch its media campaign for Joab Houghton together with Hezekiah Johnson's run for sheriff of Bernalillo County. Houghton's candidacy signaled a major departure of a popular leader from the Santa Fe–based American Party. Coming now it might split that vote to Gallegos's advantage. Houghton asked Johnson to meet with Perea to effect an agreement for the withdrawal of one of them. Houghton would leave the decision "absolutely" with them. Johnson found Perea "obtusely bent" on running. Perea personally asked Johnson to withdraw Houghton's name. Houghton thanked the voters who desired his election and declared as his principal reason for dropping out "the imperative duty of all citizens who wish to save the Territory from disgrace to do all in their power to prevent the election of José Manuel Gallegos."[137] Johnson too made clear that his newfound support of Perea was governed by a desire to defeat Gallegos. He carefully steered away from the party spearheaded by the *Gazette*, however. Johnson squirrelly called Perea the true "Independent Candidate" for delegate, as he had Houghton.[138] Russell welcomed Houghton's decision, declaring Gallegos's defeat a "moral certainty."[139]

Another calamity befell Gallegos. General Carleton hired Charles Leib away from the *New Mexican* to serve as a surgeon for Fort Union. Gallegos could not sustain the *New Mexican*, nor did Arny have the resources.[140] Charles Clever, the adjutant of the territorial militia and attorney general, purchased the weekly. Clever, born in Cologne, Prussia, had come to the United States in 1848, settled in Santa Fe in 1850, and launched a merchandising business. Under the influence of Houghton he secured a place in Collins's American Party.[141] Clever took the helm at the *New Mexican* five weeks prior to the election with the sole intent of defeating Gallegos. He changed the Spanish edition to the more Latinate *El Novo-Mejicano* for the brief time that he would own it, and proceeded to launch reams of Spanish-language attacks on Gallegos. Judge Kirby Benedict, who may have lost out to Gallegos at the People's Convention, authored condemnations of the former priest in the Russell-Johnson style of rancor and with much of their substance. He assailed Gallegos lieutenants Miguel E. Pino and Diego Archuleta especially on alleged anti-gringo attitudes.[142] Gallegos would later call Benedict his "most active and virulent opponent" in this canvass.[143]

If the Union Democratic, or Copperhead, Party did not convene a territorial convention, the Santa Fe meeting to nominate county candidates served the purpose. Houghton, Russell, Quintana, and Clever dominated the proceedings. The "finest spirit" reportedly prevailed in the nearly filled courthouse. Russell chaired the Resolutions Committee, an assignment for which he likely volunteered, proclamations sounding much like his distinct propaganda. Important for party identity, the territory's prewar Democratic Party was brought out of hiding and adjusted with the title the National Union Democracy of the County of Santa Fe. The party deemed it proper, given the condition of federal politics, to "reannounce" faith in Jefferson's fundamental principles of government. A clear Copperhead resolution appeared. "Abolitionists in the North and Fire Eaters in the South," it stated, were "equally instrumental in bringing the present disasters upon the country." "Conservative counsels" needed to prevail to head off the ruin of the country. The "spirit of compromise, which marked the policy of the fathers of the Republic in its infancy, shall assume its proper position and dictate terms of reconciliation and re-union."

The convention rebuked the "pretentious demagogues" who had advanced the "unwise and impolitic" statehood proposal. Indicating Carleton's rising influence, a policy was declared in favor of a reservation system to relieve New Mexico of the "sufferings from marauding tribes." The obligatory call for the president to appoint citizens of New Mexico to the territory's federal posts appeared. Finally, the convention deprecated and denounced the effort being made "to create jealousies and animosities among the citizens of the Territory by appeals to prejudices of races." The delegates would cultivate "harmony of feeling among all classes of citizens regardless of birth or race." The resolutions were unanimously adopted.[144]

The convention sponsored open-ended nominations. Anyone could "bring his friend" and "have his claims fairly and openly considered," the *Gazette* affirmed, not like the People's managers who dictated the nomination of Gallegos.[145] Clever and Quintana roused participants with their speeches. They and Captain Sena y Baca were nominated for the territorial House. Other nominees who had rejected the People's Convention were Probate Judge Felipe Delgado and council member Jesús María Baca y Salazar. Delegates pledged to effect the election of Perea and with "might and main to accomplish the utter defeat of Padre Gallegos."[146]

Johnson and Russell both supported Perea for delegate. Yet Johnson reacted to the resolutions, touching off a sparring match with Russell on national issues. Johnson, failing to stomach the "repugnant" Copperhead Democracy, fingered Russell as the author of the faction's christening. He called it the latest of the party names that New Mexico had always been "very prolific" in inventing. The convention had not heeded the advice to forget the question of who was to blame for the war, so Johnson characterized Thomas Jefferson and George Washington as abolitionists. They therefore logically came "categorically under the censure of Mr. Russell and the meeting which adopted the Resolution." Russell retorted that if Washington and Jefferson were abolitionists as Horace Greeley and Wendell Phillips were, "we certainly have no desire to discuss the opinion or attempt to change it," no doubt on the ground that both founders owned slaves.[147]

Johnson questioned Russell's search for conservative counsels for compromise between Union and South. He recalled that the secessionists had deemed the day of compromise done. Johnson said Russell's compromise implied continuance of the principle that a slave was to be considered three-fifths of a person when representation and direct taxes were apportioned, and property "to all intents and purposes in other cases." Though not a fan of the president, Johnson pointed out that Lincoln had after all been elected, and so he was under "solemn obligation to 'Support, Protect, and Defend the Constitution of the United States' with hundreds of thousands of brave men" to put down the rebellion. The rebels must lay down their arms, Johnson held. "To do so is our conservative counsel, and the Union Army is rapidly enforcing it." Russell, however, declared: "The saving conservative counsels, which we wish to prevail are those which would crush out the hatred and bitterness of feeling which prevail in both sections and which stand in the way of reconciliation between the sections. How that is to be accomplished will have to be decided by wiser heads than ours," he concluded. "Our prayer is that it may be accomplished."[148]

Russell denied responsibility for his party's resolutions. He emphasized that the report came from a committee appointed to draft them, and the resolutions were unanimously adopted by the convention. But as Johnson called him out personally, he would answer on the dual causes of the war. Russell cited the role of southern fire-eaters for "a pretty fair share of the responsibility for the disasters and the manner of doing it." As for northern abolitionism, he quoted extensively from the "representative" abolition newspaper, Greeley's *New York Tribune*, including an anonymous verse of 1859 titled "The American Flag," which called for destruction of that "flaunting Liszt" with its "bloody scars." Should it keep "a man in chains, / Deep sink it in the waves! / For it bears a fellow man / To groan with fellow slaves." Russell saw the poem's "blasphemy" reflecting the abolitionist's hatred of the U.S. government and its constitution, and the *Tribune* denouncing both in "'a covenant with death and a league with hell.'"[149]

Johnson insisted that the author of the convention's resolutions and the editor of the *Gazette* were the same person, implying that Russell was trying to turn Perea into his Copperhead puppet. He said Russell beat the hobby horse of the causes of the Civil War with information on which he himself was well posted. As Russell offered a prayer for "righteous" compromise, Johnson held he should "learn that the prayers of the righteous can do a great deal for the United States, darkeys and other representable [*sic*] chattels. Furthermore, that however lovely Truth and Justice may be in the *abstract*, they should no more be discarded by editors in practice than etiquette, and are just as essential to their happiness as to that of others."[150]

Russell insisted equally on claiming that the resolutions came out of the people's representatives in a convention procedure. "[W]e do know, beyond doubt that the resolutions were read in English and then in Spanish and then each one was read separately and voted upon separately," he wrote. "Before any vote was taken the President distinctly asked if any person wishes to make remarks upon the resolution. If this did not allow the high standing gentleman time to say something, we think he was quite a slow motioned gentleman, or a gentle man that inveigles the *Press*."[151]

The rhetorical combat served to bring home major contentions swirling around the country regarding the war, providing thereby the terms for firming up party division in the territory. Yet, in spite of his beef with Russell, Johnson endorsed the Santa Fe County ticket because not a "particle of fogyism" (Gallegos) was on it and because of the quality of the candidates selected. He asked the county organizations to select equally qualified candidates for their tickets.[152] He himself authored the resolutions of the Bernalillo County nominating convention calling for the defeat of Gallegos for his statehood stand and the support of Perea for his fidelity to the Union.[153]

The hustings resembled the bitter Gallegos-Otero bouts of yore with Euroamerican Republicans nowhere to be seen. Both candidates stumped hard from mid-July to late August. Perea men worked Taos, San Miguel, and Rio Arriba counties. Perea kept locals connected by negotiating "some views respecting subjects of public interest belonging to the well-being of the territory."[154] The participant-observer reports to the *Gazette*, though biased for Perea, suggest the excitement of the village rally. The courthouse in Taos was said to be "jam full of the independent voters" and in support of Perea. The local opponents were "rotten wire workers for the Padre [Gallegos]" who saw that "they must do something to break down the force of this meeting, so they commenced their dirty work by nominating one of their own *stamp* to preside." Don Pedro Sánchez, the People's co-organizer, along with the other Gallegos men, Santiago Valdez and Pedro Valdez, allegedly attempted to interfere with the proceedings. In the observer's skewed account, they were orally lashed by John Leroux. Another meeting for Perea convened in the Taos Plaza, where the statehood proposition was beat down. "The feeling here is violent and warm and came near breaking out in personal conflicts," said the correspondent. "None, however, occurred."[155]

Perea appeared in another Taos event where "a band of political guerrillas representing the pretensions of the little Padre Gallegos" supposedly took control of the courthouse as the crowd assembled. Perea men confronted the intruders before withdrawing to the plaza for a "large and enthusiastic meeting of the friends of Col. Francisco Perea." Euroamericans outnumbered Nuevomexicanos as officers and speakers. Ceran St. Vrain, Alfred Bent, Dr. William Foos, John Leroux, Ferdinand Maxwell, and Robert Cary accompanied Col. José María Valdez of Mora, don José Benito Martinez, and Julián Espinosa. Perea was received "with the most deafening cheers, indeed with every demonstration of popular favor and confidence." Maxwell recalled in his remarks how he had "allowed himself unwillingly to become a member" of the "late Gallegos convention in Santa Fe," the one that exposed "clearly and forcibly and to the heart's content of all present the sly intrigues and unholy purposes of the little *Cura* [priest] and his satellites."[156]

Another report had Gallegos workers foiling a Perea meeting in the town of Mora. St. Vrain was invited to preside, being one of the oldest and "most respected American residents of this territory." As the meeting began, someone, "prompted" by ill will toward St. Vrain, "moved to depose the Colonel [St. Vrain] and substitute some person else as chairman! The motion was sustained by some of Gallegos's disorderly friends who were present at the meeting, and the Colonel, not wishing the disturbance to proceed any further, withdrew." Another larger rally for Perea was held two days later with St. Vrain presiding. As there was "scarcely an [Euro] American in New Mexico" who did not respect St. Vrain, "the Gallegosites will find they have 'bar[k]ed up the wrong tree' by offering an indignity to an old residenter [sic] who has never been guilty of an ungentlemanly or ungenerous act towards a political opponent."[157]

In Bernalillo County in the Río Abajo, Gallegos agents produced advanced tickets on which Hezekiah Johnson and Perea supporter Thomas Gutierres appeared as candidates for the legislature. Perea asked Johnson and Gutierres to publish a flier saying they did not want the votes of Gallegos backers. Johnson refused, calling it an insult to the voters, but told Perea he could reconvene the county convention so that it might expunge their names from his ticket, as he did not think it proper for himself to do it alone. Perea men asked Johnson and Gutierres to run as candidates for the territorial council on their ticket to replace the old Whig Serafín Ramírez, who stood accused of "treachery." They agreed only if the officers of the convention gave other members of the party the opportunity to apply.[158]

Gallegos never responded in print to the character assassinations heaped on him by the three weeklies. An observer said he did complain in meetings.[159] His speeches in Río Arriba and Taos counties belabored the papers for their dirty pool editorials. Gallegos invited Perea to accompany him in debate throughout the territory. Perea declined with no reason given.[160] In one local imputation, Perea's only qualification was that he was the "son of a rich man and family." Moreover, if he got elected, there would be "no end to young men running for Congress upon the sole claim that their fathers are wealthy," merit and talent to be overlooked. Recall, however, that Miguel A. Otero seemed not to have suffered on the stump for his rico lineage. Over at the *New Mexican* Clever conceded there had been no time to hold a full convention to consider others, yet Perea had the "elements of fairness and truth," able to make him Washington friends. It counted that he was "liberal towards Americans, and devoted to the American institutional government."[161]

In Santa Fe the People's Convention defectors Nicolás Quintana and Jesús María Baca y Sena, as well as *New Mexican* owner Charles Clever, spoke before enthusiastic crowds on behalf of Perea and against Gallegos.[162] Gallegos had his friends out, although none of the weeklies would have cared to give an accurate description of his events. Miguel Pino headed the Gallegos campaign in Santa Fe County at the same time that he ran for justice of the peace.[163] Don Faustín Baca y Ulivarri, who submitted the first public nomination of the former priest for delegate, pledged to deliver the vote of San Miguel County for Gallegos. The *New Mexican* sniffed that Gallegos promised Baca the position of Indian Affairs for New Mexico upon his victory.[164]

The *Gazette* betrayed its earlier confidence, cautioning a week before the election for Perea friends to be on the alert "and not repose too much on the consciousness of an easy victory." While the elements of victory lay in their hands, "they must make use of the elements in order that they may be available."[165]

Table 3. Majority vote by county, delegate for Congress, 1863

	Perea	Gallegos	Whole Number
Santa Fe		47	1,333
Taos	77		1,837
Río Arriba		648	1,602
Mora		18	1,252
San Miguel		291	2,391
Santa Ana		20	426
Bernalillo	796		1,360
Valencia	333		1,355
Socorro	940		1,298
Doña Ana		316	808
Totals	2,146	1,340	13,662

Adapted from "Official Vote for 1863," *Gazette*, September 9, 1865; cf. Waldrip, "New Mexico," 85.

On election day 13,662 turned out to vote, 4,450 more than in 1861. Perea won by a mere 806. Voters reflected their poblador identity in the counties of the Río Arriba by going for Gallegos. Diego Archuleta delivered Río Arriba County by a substantial majority. Those in the other counties were smaller. Pino delivered extremely divided Santa Fe County in spite of two weeklies in the town opposing his candidate. Whether isolated Doña Ana would even participate was a question. It did, going for Gallegos, likely due to Arny's influence. As expected, Perea's strength came from the counties of the Río Abajo district, where almost a third of the territory's votes were cast. The Perea machine came out in force in the Río Abajo, overcoming the majority support of the territorial assembly for Gallegos.

The *Gazette* refused to extend a gentleman's congratulation to Gallegos for a good run. It brightened the partisan boundary by harrumphing that the results would make the people joyful. Their public honor remained "untarnished and . . . they will be represented in the Congress of the United States by an honest man and gentleman," the weekly boasted, "instead of the rogue and demagogue whom some selfish leaders attempted to foist upon them."[166]

Reports of fraud soon abounded. Gallegos "ruffians" were accused of taking control of several polling places. Irregularities occurred in the Embudo precinct of Río Arriba County, where poll books were allegedly stolen and destroyed. Stolen Perea tickets were allegedly replaced by Gallegos tickets, called by the *Gazette* "one of the most shameless efforts to defraud the people out of their votes that was ever known." Gallegos operatives were later arrested on that one.[167] The *Gazette* accused Miguel Pino of rigging the precincts of Santa Fe by appointing his men to serve as judges. The weekly named co-conspirators who allegedly insisted that certain private houses serve as voting sites, instead of public buildings, and who were themselves candidates for office on the Gallegos ticket.[168]

Socorro County had the most volatile time of it. Votes were not counted and certified within the six-day limit. Someone set on fire the house containing the unexamined votes. William H. Allison, a close friend of Perea, reported much later that a Gallegos partisan had ordered the house torched, knowing that without the Socorro count, his man would be elected. County judges and secretaries of election in each precinct retained duplicates, and Governor Connelly ordered a reconstruction of the votes based on these.[169] Another problem arose from the fact that it was the territorial secretary's job to count the vote, but Arny was in New York. He had appointed Theodore Greiner acting secretary, and Greiner inherited the job of tallying the vote. Greiner, deeming the Socorro County vote invalid, prematurely announced Gallegos the winner—"damnable conduct," the *Gazette* charged. Greiner broke the law if he thought he could perform functions rightly belonging to the governor, Russell charged.[170]

In another long editorial Russell sustained the partisan imperative well after the election. He argued that the attempts at fraud, including other cases of vote substitution at Abiquiú and the early closing of the polls at Taos, showed a premeditated scheme connected to Gallegos. Again the refrain rang of Gallegos as a "most intense" hater of Americans "and everything American . . . not even excepting the government which has conferred so many of its blessings upon New Mexico," an accusation difficult to accept for one who so assiduously coveted the post of delegate to Congress. Russell recycled the time-worn stereotypes of Gallegos: a chief instigator of the Taos Revolt when Governor Bent and other Americans were so "brutally massacred"; a priest "officiating at the Holy Altar . . . [staining] his hands with the best blood of the land by encouraging that massacre with letters written to his associates in murder and treasons, from the sanctuary of the church"; using "all the powers of his mind" to inculcate among his fellow citizens "a hatred of our institutions, and propagating in them a spirit of jealousy and opposition which naturally ripens into animosity between the races"; and so on. The Archuletas, Pinos, and the rest of Gallegos's allies were condemned "as the leaders of the anti-American sentiment, their enmity deep seated, their prejudice knowing no limits," nor did they "scruple in the choice of the means they adopt to carry with them what portion of the Mexican population they can." These resisters did not trouble themselves to become acquainted with American laws and institutions, "knowing some aspects in the abstract but nothing of their practical workings"; for these reasons they stifled the vote of the people "by resorting to the violence and fraud which have so recently covered them with disgrace and ignominy." They did not know in their "superlative ignorance" of the process in place to establish the vote of Socorro County after the poll books were burned. A "mere handful" of Euroamericans gave Gallegos and his sympathizers any countenance. Russell wondered why. It was a question they had to answer "to their own consciences. It is beyond our comprehension to understand the link that bound them together."[171] He made no mention of the desire to lay a foundation for a future Republican Party.

The dispute came close to defining the binary factions along racial lines. Gallegos certainly understood the election contest and a great deal more about the American electoral process. He contested the result because Governor Connelly exceeded his authority in authorizing the Socorro County count in Arny's absence, and Connelly refused to recognize Arny's appointment of Theodore Greiner in his place as territorial secretary. If any fraud took place in Socorro, it was not designed for him, argued Gallegos. Indeed, all the county races there went contested. However, his contest encountered obstacles. The territorial attorney general, who handled the investigation of the irregularities in Socorro County, was the same Charles Clever who had purchased the *New Mexican* to bring Gallegos down. Clever, one historian says, acted more as the lawyer of Perea than of the territory. Arny and other Republicans supported the contest. The territorial secretary obtained approval from the assembly to conduct territorial business in Washington, including carrying Gallegos's contest to Congress. Governor Connelly, however, who was Perea's uncle by marriage, argued that a secretary's business should be conducted within the territory, not in the nation's capital. If Arny persisted in going, Connelly would ask for his removal. Perea, seeing Arny as the perpetrator of a plot to unseat him, asked Lincoln to fire him. The president assured Arny he would not be "hasty" in considering Perea's complaint. Arny departed for Washington in early February 1864. While there, he was distracted by the need to refute Perea's charges of tampering and lying, which included rounding up known Republican associates to testify as to his good character and devotion to the party.

Arny's attempts to seat Gallegos went to early April 1864. Gallegos's petition to the U.S. House of Representatives cited the difficulty he would have in generating testimony in front of Judge Benedict, who had actively opposed him. Arny requested time to examine witnesses. However, one allegation was that James Collins, of all people, represented in Washington that Gallegos was a Democrat, apparently to imply Rebel sympathies. The House Committee denied Gallegos's request for more time. The full body agreed with its recommendation to end the contest and validate the lawful election of Perea by a thousand-vote majority.[172]

The (American Party) National Union Democrats had once again pulled out the stops to prevail in the election for delegate to Congress. During the campaign for assembly seats the *Gazette* had returned to isolating the Mexican Party that had generally controlled the sessions. "Men of the Gallegos stamp have no business in the legislative halls," Russell charged. "Another class of men must be selected if we would preserve a good reputation and avoid becoming the bye word of the country."[173] The results produced a split in the legislature. The Gallegos slate, which included Theodore Greiner, won Santa Fe County. Diego Archuleta came out president pro tem. In Bernalillo County the Perea ticket won every office except sheriff. Hezekiah Johnson won his race. Donaciano Vigil returned to the council.[174]

Clever sold the *New Mexican* two months after the election. He boasted that the purpose for which he had purchased it, the defeat of José Manuel Gallegos, had been accomplished. The paper's shop foreman William H. Manderfield took control of the paper. Clever wished him luck. The paper, he said, was "untrammeled by the position or history of the recent election in this Territory. It is free to move as its will, judgment, sense of justice and right shall dictate and direct." Should delegate Perea fail in doing right by New Mexico, "his failure should be examined and regarded with candor," Clever advised, "and when condemned, should be condemned with fairness and proper consideration."[175] The *New Mexican*'s politics formed a blank slate at this moment—but not for long.

CHAPTER NINE

Bosque Redondo and the Rise of José Francisco Chávez, 1863–1865

"Dear Frank," began the private letter.[1] "Frank" was José Francisco Perea, New Mexico's delegate to Congress, and he was being addressed by his first cousin, José Francisco Chávez.[2] Chávez addressed Perea in the conversational style of the typical middle-class American, of the sort that young "native gentlemen" of the Río Abajo—offspring of New Mexico's *hombres de bién*—had cultivated since before the American conquest of their ancestral Nuevo México. Chávez spoke English so well, a press appreciation had it, "that no one from his accent would suspect him to be Spanish born."[3]

José Francisco Chávez came from the generation of elite Nuevomexicano families who had collaborated with the Kearny conquest. He was born in 1833 in Perea's very birthplace of Los Padillas south of Alburquerque in the Río Abajo. Three of his ancestors were Mexican-era governors, including his father Mariano (1833–34).[4] Chávez began his education in Chihuahua. In 1843 a covered wagon caravan transported him, Miguel A. Otero, two cousins, and other young aristocratic *nativos* over the Santa Fe Trail to St. Louis so that they could enroll in a Jesuit College. Chávez attended an academy at Fishkill on the Hudson and, planning on a medical career, enrolled in New York's College of Physicians and Surgeons. He became a classmate of General Kearny's sons; recall him as an interpreter on Kearny's march into New Mexico. He abandoned a career in medicine after the Mexican War and made his permanent home in the village of Los Lunas, downriver from his birthplace, where he took over the family's business of marketing sheep far and wide. Chávez was elected to the territorial House of Representatives in 1859. He served meritoriously as a major of the New Mexico Volunteers at the Battle of Valverde.[5]

Chávez sent his fateful letter to Perea, which would be made public for partisan purposes, while he was a lieutenant colonel in the First New Mexico Infantry and engaged in holding off Navajo and Apache raids. He had supported his cousin for delegate in the election of 1863.[6] It was while he was on assignment to see about livestock stolen from ranches in San Miguel County that he heard of Perea's plan to run for reelection.[7] "I have just returned from a trip to [Fort] Union where I have been to recover some sheep belonging to Doña Gertruditas," Chávez mentioned, "and it struck me that I could not do better than to write to you and post you up a little in matters and things in general." Chávez had been having "a great many" opportunities to speak with Nuevomexicanos in San Miguel County and from them he needed to clue Perea in on something important. "I can assure you certainly that the whole of that county," he clarified, "with the exception of [the mercantile company] Moore & Kitchen, and what little influence they can bring to bear, is opposed to the colonization of the Navajo Indians on the Pecos River."

Chávez here alluded to the Indian reservation project of Brig. Gen. James H. Carleton, the commander of the New Mexico Military Department. It was Carleton's determination to finally conquer the Navajos and have them permanently settled at a place called Bosque Redondo on the Pecos River. As Chávez cautioned, Bosque Redondo would hurt his cousin's chance for reelection. "Above all things you should not compromise yourself to the measure," he warned. "It is not, nor has it at any time been any of your doing, and by *all means* you should keep your skirts clear." San Miguel polled the largest number of votes of any county. Keeping "aloof" of the Carleton boondoggle would insure Perea a large majority of the territorial vote. Already certain parties were "trying to create an influence" to remove the Bosque Redondo reservation, "and they will succeed in that county." Chávez assured Perea of his "honorable" intention in bringing it all up, done "with the desire" of furthering Perea's interests.[8]

The problem was that Delegate Perea had long mortgaged his political ranch to Carleton and Bosque Redondo. Not only did Bosque Redondo seem like the immediate means of bringing about the coveted pacification of the Navajo and Apache bands; but to abandon the general meant throwing his party base overboard, a sure sabotaging of his candidacy.[9] Perea would later claim that he could not effect a change in Carleton's reservation policy if he tried.[10]

Chávez may have been giving Perea a last-ditch chance to shake off Bosque Redondo with his letter. The remarkable story in the election of 1865 is that Chávez went on to challenge his cousin, producing a particularly bruising contest even by the territory's established standards. The Bosque Redondo issue, arising late in the Civil War, drove New Mexico's binary cleavage to Grand Canyon depth while making for new Nuevomexicano leaders. National party developments helped to reshape New Mexico's central factions even as organizational identities at that level bent themselves to events in the Civil War.

The Politics of Bosque Redondo

Several publications tell the saga of Carleton's New Mexico experience.[11] Briefly, the stern, proud, and stubborn New Englander marched into Santa Fe at the head of the 1,500 strong California Volunteers to drive the Texan Confederates out of New Mexico. That job was done when Carleton arrived, and so he turned to hunting down the Navajos and Apaches to their final surrender, and if not, their extermination. Following public meetings of indignation over Indian raids, the well-mounted *mexicano* militia joined in scouring the Navajo country in western New Mexico, taking captives and livestock and driving Navajo warriors into the deep recesses of their rugged country. The Navajo dealt not only with citizen foes. From the north above the San Juan basin, Utes descended on vulnerable Navajo *rancherias* (for the location of the Navajo home lands and Bosque Redondo, see map 1, chapter 1). The Navajo called it the Fearing Time. José Francisco Chávez served in this campaign, Carleton having him command forts in the Navajo country.[12]

Carleton's predecessor, Col. Stephen Canby, envisioned a reservation for the Navajos in the middle of the tribe's historical lands on the Río Chiquito west of Zuñi Pueblo on the New Mexico–Arizona border. Carleton considered this frontier too bereft of water and lumber for a large reservation and military fort. He had business motivations as well. Carleton did not want any war mongering near the areas of potential mining and the road projects to Arizona. He himself took advantage of investments in such activity.[13] Carleton became acquainted with Bosque Redondo in 1851 while on duty under Col. E. V. Sumner. The location was an ancient rendezvous site for Plains tribes clear over on the eastern side of the territory across the central Río Grande Valley from Navajo land, some sixty miles below the village of Antón Chico on the Pecos River. Carleton built Fort Sumner

FIG. 19. *Brevet Brigadier General J. H. Carleton, Santa Fe, New Mexico,* 1866, photographer unknown. Carleton's Bosque Redondo Indian reservation project became inextricably caught in the partisan politics of the New Mexico Territory. Courtesy Palace of the Governors Photo Archives, NMHM/DCA, negative #022938.

FIG. 20. *Bosque Redondo era Indian captives at Fort Sumner, New Mexico*, ca. 1864–68, photographer unknown. Courtesy Palace of the Governors Photo Archives, NMHM/DCA, negative #038205.

at Bosque Redondo at first to guard against Confederates, should they return; to head off Comanche raiding from the eastern plains; and for the temporary housing of Mescalero Apaches until they could be returned to their country in the southwestern territory. With Confederates nowhere in sight, the Bosque Redondo grasslands appeared ideal for a permanent reservation. Carleton marked out forty square miles for the purpose and established Fort Sumner at the site. He aimed to use the reservation for teaching Navajos and Apaches how to farm, converting them into horticulturalists like the peaceable Pueblos. Carleton received approval for the reservation from Secretary of War Henry Stanton and Secretary of the Interior J. P. Usher, although reports of Carleton officers suggested it might not work so distant from Navajo country.[14]

Carleton's aggressive campaign raised hopes initially among settlers for peace at last. Superintendent of Indian Affairs James Collins helped organize the transport of Apaches and Navajos to Bosque Redondo and would stay committed to Carleton to the bitter end. It mattered that Collins became Indian agent based on Carleton's nomination. Acting governor William Arny, in his message to the 1862–63 assembly, praised the endeavor for affording long-sought protection for citizens.[15] Governor Henry Connelly proclaimed the Navajos at peace after the legendary Christopher "Kit" Carson managed the force-walk of five thousand Navajo men, women, and children to Bosque Redondo.[16] Delegate Perea worked to acquire congressional appropriations for the project. The *Sana Fe Weekly Gazette*, owned by Collins and edited by John Russell, billed it as important for Perea's record.[17] The *New Mexican* praised Carleton for bringing order to southern New Mexico, calling the mass assault on the Navajo "fairly well managed."[18]

Soon, the *Río Abajo Weekly Press* noted that like previous commanding generals in New Mexico, Carleton was passing through an "ordeal of detraction."[19] Reaction filed in from various points. Like many a commander during the Civil War, Carleton ruled over his district unconditionally.[20] His martial law proved unpopular with many. New Mexico Supreme Court Justice Joseph Knapp, for example, after getting arrested twice for not carrying an identifying passport, as Carleton ordered for civilians to distinguish them from Confederate spies, protested that his presidential commission was sufficient for him to travel in discharge of his duties.[21] As the winter territorial court went into suspension, Knapp found in the columns of the *New Mexican* an outlet for lobbing verbal missives on the general's "despotic" rule.[22] Knapp fed his editorials to the national press.[23] Hezekiah Johnson at the *Río Abajo Weekly Press* supported the beleaguered jurist.[24]

Carleton's popularity rapidly deteriorated. Discharged California Volunteers in the Mesilla Valley publically condemned Carleton for "gross dereliction of duty, frauds, unwarranted delays, marches and countermarches without any progress," and military nullification of civil law. The veterans confidently predicted that facts would produce "the awful sentence of history, [and] forever shroud the name of James H. Carleton in the darkest obloquy and disgrace." They disseminated their pamphlet throughout New Mexico, Arizona, California and the East. A shocked Carleton was reportedly "grievously offended."[25]

A clear binary of opinion formed around the figure of Carleton with supporters seeking to balance out the criticism. The men associated with the *Gazette* had transcendent reasons for standing by the general. Former editor John Russell had a cozy contract to print military material, and Carleton hired him to work in the military headquarters as a Spanish translator and interpreter, while James Collins and family profited from military contracts.[26] Collins, no longer Indian

Superintendent and now running the *Gazette*, publicly called Knapp a "libelous mischief maker" out to subvert civil and military government. Other American Party members R. H. Tomkins, Merrill Ashurst, Samuel Ellison, and Joab Houghton sided with Carleton, attacking Knapp in editorials and depositions to Washington.[27]

A Santa Fe public meeting condemned the calumnies being hurled at the general, brought on by unfounded "private disappointment."[28] An Alburquerque gathering denounced the national attacks that suggested a "tyrant and oppressor." Carleton, participants affirmed, had "manifested himself as a true friend of the people of this territory and [was] a strenuous defender of their liberties."[29] In Lemitar, Socorro County, Nuevomexicanos and Euroamericans called the general's plan "wise," the "most effective and feasible . . . that could be adopted" for dealing with the Apaches and Navajo.[30] A Doña Ana County crowd regretted the "exceedingly false and malicious" newspaper stories and citizens opposing the commander. Nine of fifteen leaders here had Spanish surnames. The curate of Mesilla, José de Jesús Baca spoke in "forcible terms" for Carleton who, he said, found a "deplorable state" in the territory and gave his labors "to bring it into the good condition in which we now find it."[31] Doña Ana County was split, however. An "impromptu" Mesilla gathering lent its "expression of feeling" to Knapp.[32]

Indeed, a veritable boulder of invective moved on Carleton inexorably.[33] Alarms of race prejudice sounded. Carleton was said to favor Euroamerican over Nuevomexicano contractors.[34] The sharp rise in the price of goods was attributed to an oversupply of stuffs to the reservation, which unfairly impacted poor families.[35] Carleton was described as egotistically taking credit for the conquest of the Navajo when, it was noted, Nuevomexicano volunteers had conducted the bulk of expeditions.[36] The enforcement of martial law on innocent civilians fell most heavily on Nuevomexicanos, it was averred, people being hauled to jail on minor or nonexistent charges, elders being made to suffer the "wanton abuse of power" in their locales.[37] Quite damaging, the *New Mexican* publicized a copy of Carleton's diary from his New Mexico service in 1853, which he sent to the Smithsonian Institution, containing descriptions of Nuevomexicanos in Casa Colorada (Valencia County) not unlike those in W. W. H. Davis's *El Gringo*: their "dirty little villages"; living without a "solitary indication of industry, thrift or cleanliness"; their "indolence, squalid poverty, filth, and utter ignorance of everything beyond their corn-fields and acequias."[38]

Center stage in the controversy was occupied by the Bosque Redondo reservation. The new Indian superintendent for New Mexico, Dr. Michael Steck, engaged in a turf battle over which of the federal offices should have ultimate oversight of Indian affairs.[39] While agreeing on the necessity of compelling the Navajo to reservation, and thinking Bosque Redondo good for Apaches, Steck reported to U.S. Commissioner of Indian Affairs William Dole that the Navajo were being ill-served.[40]

One citizen told of insufficient security at the facility allowing internees to escape.[41] When José Francisco Chávez warned in his letter to Delegate Perea of parties "trying to create an influence" in Bosque Redondo's backyard, he partly meant Miguel Romero y Baca, the San Miguel County probate judge. Romero sent an open letter to the *New Mexican* claiming to represent the sentiments of the sheep and cattle owners, who had for decades treated the range around Bosque Redondo as common pasture, and who were now complaining of losses due to Navajos and Apaches leaving the reservation. Eleven persons were killed and seventy horses and mules were stolen at Chaperito, southeast of Las Vegas on the edge of the Great Plains, Romero reported. Two-thirds of the brooding sheep in San Miguel and Mora counties were lost to the curtailment of pasturage along the Pecos River. Romero foresaw larger losses coming with the increase of Navajo placements at Bosque Redondo. A massive increase in military presence would be needed to contain them, Romero foresaw. Calling in the chip of a right to the American racial nation, he rhetorically queried, "Is it just that the Indian shall be preferred to the peaceful white citizen? No sir, this cannot be so." Put the Navajo on their ancient lands, Romero demanded, with its abundance of land and wood. Mexican communities would then be preserved. Romero, acting on standards of the concerned American citizen, forwarded his comments to Congress.[42]

Partisans positioned themselves for and against the Romero tract. Hezekiah Johnson, thinking of the importance of the territory's sheep industry, found Romero's letter "precise," "to the point," and "worthy of profound consideration," though he doubted Romero's power to have his sound arguments take "proper effect" on authorities.[43] The *Gazette* asked in counterpoint for proof that it had been the Bosque Redondo Navajos who committed raids in San Miguel County. Collins found the *New Mexican*'s figures on animal losses due to Indians unsatisfactory. He preferred to rely on the military forecast of "many more years of peace and prosperity" among the Navajo.[44]

A set of players from San Miguel County orchestrated an attack on Romero's claims. The Nuevomexicano Lorenzo Labadí, Carleton's agent for the Mescaleros at Bosque Redondo, accused Judge Romero in Spanish of condemning the Navajos and Apaches without noting their "good customs [*buenas costumbres*]." Labadí chastised complainers for knowing nothing about the business of managing Bosque Redondo. He empathized with inhabitants who suffered at the hands of "criminal" Indians but assured victims that the culprits did not come from Bosque Redondo. Romero, as official of the law, should have known better than to "discredit the Indians of good faith who had asked for peace, and the government had placed them here [the reservation] to be educated on making a civilized life [*desacreditar los Indios que, de buena fé, han pedido la paz, y el Gobierno los ha puesto aquí para enseñarlos hacer una vida civilizada*]." Labadí recited Carleton's narrative of no other lands in New Mexico comparing with Bosque Redondo for agriculture, comprising an immense space for use by all. He laid on citizens the obligation to make the reservation a success for the happiness of their children.[45]

The familiar accusation of Santa Fe conspiracy took its place. A Carleton defender calling himself Observer stated that Romero fell victim to the "settled determination" of a "certain clique," mastered by "malice and jealousy," willfully to misconstrue, misinterpret, and unfairly criticize Carleton's "every act." Observer claimed good reason for believing Romero the non-author of his protest, for no one in San Miguel County had complained about Bosque Redondo until the Santa Fe clique induced them to think its Indians had committed the recent raids. Opponents falsely manufactured public sentiment to have the legislature request the removal of the Bosque Redondo internees to Arizona in the "extreme" desire to defeat Carleton, Observer claimed, whether or not it advanced the interests of Indians and the people. The authority of Kit Carson appeared important for the Carleton defense. Who was to be believed regarding marauding Indians, Observer asked—the legendary Indian fighter or a mere probate judge? The people of the county saw the "brilliance" of Bosque Redondo as the proper policy for dealing with warring tribes "who have more than one century murdered and pillaged the people of the country."[46]

Twenty San Miguel County denizens formed the signal detractors of Judge Romero. Their comprehensive protest was composed in Spanish, although its grammatical construction strongly suggests an English-dominant author. A host of arguments countered Romero. One said the judge produced "movement and surprise" in the county and territory with the aim of joining other Carleton critics having suspect motives. It was bogus, they charged, to claim that the reservation's location displaced stock from needed pastures. Vast grazing lands were available in New Mexico without anyone needing to come near Fort Sumner. Troops kept Bosque Redondo captives too well guarded for them pose a danger to livestock, the manifesto argued. Everyone's faith needed to lie in governmental means to "liberate" the people from the danger and losses of Indian depredation. Colonel Carson gave his personal assurance of protection for settlements, the people needed to note. Romero misled the people about escaped Apaches raiding and killing at Chaperito; recent outrages were committed by Indians from the mountains southwest of the Pecos River, neither captured nor subjugated by the military. Carson revealed that much of the livestock stolen by other Apaches had been retrieved by a troop of Navajos on the reservation and returned to the owners, the narrative continued. A fierce battle followed, and Navajos lost ten warriors, with five wounded. "Their voluntary pursuit of the Apaches to bring back the stolen sheep merits all our commendation," the group held, "and is conclusive evidence that they maintain friendly feelings for the Mexicans, as well as the Americans." Beyond security for the people, the Bosque Redondo facility brought a market for ranchers, farmers, and store owners.[47]

This last assertion was basic for the interests of these challengers to Romero. Romero in his public response to them pointed out that they were government contractors, sutlers at Fort Union and Fort Sumner, "fortune-seeking speculators," businessmen with moneyed interests in Bosque Redondo.[48] Fourteen of the twenty signees were English-surnamed. Three owned Moore & Kitchen, the mercantile outfit that Chávez mentioned to Perea. Their profits derived from the most lucrative patronage machine in the territory, Carleton's military installations. One supporter unwittingly confirmed it when he described the businessmen as having "more interest in the well-being of San Miguel

County and the territory at large than the editor [of the *New Mexican*] and his associates [could] ever hope to acquire."[49]

San Miguel and Mora County farmers faced a difficult season with erratic weather, a grasshopper infestation, and a bud worm epidemic.[50] As Romero saw it, the produce going to the Bosque soldiers and Indians was worth more as provision for the people of the county. Some Nuevomexicanos profited from freight to the military, Romero conceded, but for most, the rate-busting prices paid by the government led to losses. Citizens may have been grateful for the defenses performed at Fort Sumner, but they could not consent to keeping Indians permanently on lands they themselves needed for survival. Romero responded to Observer's argument that Bosque Redondo and its companion Fort Sumner afforded a major market for area ranchers by pointing out that supplies going to and from the United States were blockaded by the Indians of the eastern plains. Besides, Romero objected, how could Observer propose to Mexican wagon train owners that they haul provisions to the Indians when Carleton's policies violated their rights as loyal citizens? Romero stood by the veracity of ranchers claiming that their animals were stolen by obvious Bosque Redondo internees. Observer spread falsehoods, Romero charged. Should the legislature seek the removal of Indians, it would be because "Sr. Observador" suggested the idea to them. Romero had his own conspiracy to claim, accusing a complicit government of placing Indians adjacent to civilized settlements with the intent of forcing mexicanos out. Romero confirmed Laura Gómez's point about the territory's race-stratified social system. The "white man" (Nuevomexicano) had always been "and will be superior to the Indian, he affirmed.[51]

Two supporting affidavits signed by eighty-nine Nuevomexicanos accompanied Romero's letter, testifying to losses at the hands of Apache Bosque Redondo escapees, along with inventories. A message of support from an anonymous citizen billing himself San Miguel was included as well.[52] The *New Mexican* promoted the public binary by backing Romero. Thomas S. Tucker, a Pennsylvanian, New Mexico Volunteer and William Manderfield's partner at the paper, cited the government contractors and freighters for being induced to public commentary by their private interests.[53] The *Gazette*, on the other hand, supported the contractors, calling the *New Mexican* the "mouthpiece of Arny, Steck, & Co."[54] The *Gazette* praised the contractors as

FIG. 21. *Sutler's Store at the base of the Gallinas or Turkey Mountains, Fort Union, New Mexico,* ca. 1866, United States Army Signal Corps. The sutlers who contracted with General Carleton politically mobilized in defense of the Bosque Redondo Reservation. Courtesy Palace of the Governors Photo Archives, NMHM/DCA, negative #014544.

the "most prominent citizens and most enterprising businessmen" of San Miguel County, who provided a "most conclusive reply" to Romero's "feeler" for political capital.[55]

Carleton publicly justified Bosque Redondo as a responsible federal agency. He contributed what would become a lasting line for his side in the controversy: that critics actually rebelled against the government itself. In self-delusion or fabrication, the general claimed in a Spanish-language statement that the Indians had no reason to abscond for they were among the "happiest people," working industriously and "ardently" to be self-supporting. He too accused Euroamerican politicos in Santa Fe of misleading the people. They were "strangers," he said, with no "permanent interest" in the territory, not even sheep to lose, who had not lost a friend or relative at the "bloody hands" of the Navajo, who cared not if New Mexico grow prosperous and powerful. A personally offended *New Mexican* editor pointed out that the general himself was a stranger with peculiar interests in New Mexico, and he betrayed nativos in calling them anti-American simply for voicing opinion on Indian management. The editor resented the imputation that being new to the territory meant losing the right as Americans to state opinions. The general would find his ends rejected by nativo and non-native citizens alike, the editor predicted.[56]

What went largely lacking in the debate was true compassion for Navajos and Apaches. Euroamericans and Mexicans shared in the same Western xenophobia and race determinism when it came to indigenous peoples. In one essentialist example, an editorial in the *New Mexican*, in challenging the claim that the internees had no reason to flee, remarked that the "Almighty made them Indians, and Indians the present generation will remain; and from the many causes that might give them a pretext, real or imaginary, for leaving the reservation, if it should be in ten, fifteen or twenty years, they will still leave there Indians, and be governed by their horrid superstitions and thirst for plunder and human blood." It annoyed the writer that Carleton would coddle Indians at the expense of the rights of the "white man." A mite of empathy spoke to the "poor wretches" in the winter made to "carry the root of the mesquite on their backs from eight to ten miles, and cedar or pinewood from fifteen to twenty miles, to cook their food."[57]

Michael Steck evinced low intensity humanitarianism. He referred to "wild savages" while recounting the alarming fatalities suffered as Navajos were forced on the trek to Bosque Redondo. Only the poorest of the tribe were under capture; the majority, including the richer and more powerful ones, remained free, probably never to be caught. In reports to Washington Steck depicted internees as disease-ridden with diphtheria, small pox, pneumonia, malnutrition, and Euroamerican-induced syphilis, their receiving reduced rations, and many escaping to take their chances in the wild.[58]

Carleton defended himself to Commissioner Dole, claiming that his enemies calculated to mislead for political effect. It was "a pity" that anyone should undertake a "studied" effort to undo all that had been done with New Mexico Indians, he held. Steck followed up with a report on Mescalero dissatisfaction at being placed next to the "inveterate" Navajo enemy. Mescaleros would desert out of fear that the numerically superior Navajos would "annihilate" them. The Navajos themselves wanted to be returned to their own country, Steck remonstrated, where they could live in former houses with orchards and fields and without government assistance. Being forced to Bosque Redondo, they naturally would return home stealthily, return to raiding, "and thus keep up a state of insecurity for a generation to come."[59] Dole believed in Steck and recommended to Secretary Usher that Bosque Redondo be shut down. The War Department prevailed, however. Even after Steck visited Bosque Redondo and reported on wretched conditions, Carleton stifled his work with Indian Affairs. Fort Sumner at Bosque Redondo remained open. Carleton knew the rate of escapes yet persisted in having Delegate Perea support him.[60] Perea called on Secretary of State William Seward and President Lincoln to fire Steck, Arny, and Greiner and replace them with individuals who would support the general. Arny saved their jobs in a visit to Washington to place their arguments before DC authorities.[61]

Bosque Redondo suffered the first of three summers of failed crops and chaotic Navajo-Apache fighting. Critics delighted in calling it "Fair Carletonia," the "paradise of the Pecos River."[62] American Party politicians who had enjoyed widespread popularity got publicly castigated, Governor Connelly for mouthing Carleton's boast that the Navajo were subdued while raids continued and Indians could not be provided with fair rations.[63] John Watts got it for working behind closed Washington doors in Carleton's interests.[64] Perea was denigrated for being a "tool," a "flunky," under the "influence, control and manipulation" of Carleton, Watts, and Collins.[65]

Lincoln Matters

The 1864 presidential election came into focus through the haze of the storm over Bosque Redondo. Lincoln's popularity grew among Republicans, not least for his shrewd manipulation of the press, having them publish his letters, which compellingly explained his war policies. The *New Mexican* pitched in as a showcase.[66] Radical Republicans nonetheless pressured the moderate Lincoln on his "peace and reconciliation" plan for Reconstruction. It rankled that the Emancipation Proclamation applied to slave states only. Lincoln's veto of Radical bills for constitutional amendments to prohibit slavery and guarantee legal race equality deepened the divisions within the Republican Party.[67]

The quickly formed Radical Democracy nominated John C. Frémont for president. Frémont was the Republican Party's first presidential standard bearer in 1856. The flamboyant general had angered

Lincoln by declaring slavery outlawed in the West on his own authority. He resigned his officer's commission to challenge Lincoln.[68] Hezekiah Johnson called Frémont's military career less than stellar, his political voice inarticulate, his personal style "scandalous to American sentiment," and his expenditure of public monies questionable. Johnson faulted Frémont's faction and Democrats for wanting war without the "sacrifice of lives" and the expenditure of great sums of money.[69] The *New Mexican* cast aside Frémont's "total lack of principle," which had "taken from him the little strength and influence he never possessed."[70]

Lincoln Republicans scheduled their national convention for June 7–8. Citizens in the territories could not vote for president, yet Republicans extended invitations to have them send representatives to Baltimore.[71] In Santa Fe a call went out in April for the "Unconditional Union Men of New Mexico" to meet so as to select their local delegates to an Alburquerque convention, which would choose their representatives to Baltimore. Out of the blue, county Unionists were instructed to send delegates in numbers equal to their county's representation in the legislative assembly.[72]

The politics of "unconditional unionism" had been surging during the war in states lying at the boundary between the North and South (so-called border states). The label's usage varied. Most unconditional unionists fought the secessionist Democrats in their midst. Some supported the moderate unionists who put conditions on preservation of the Union, such as not giving civil rights to freed slaves. Some were coterminous with Radical Republicans, like those in Missouri, who formed state parties, took control of state government, and challenged Lincoln over how to deal with slavery and the conduct of the war, some opposing the president's renomination.[73] Important for New Mexico, many Democrats counted as Unconditionals. Tennessee Senator Andrew Johnson, for example, was the one congressman from a secessionist state to stay with the Union, a Lincoln loyalist.[74] Unconditional unionists contributed to victories over Democrats in local and state elections in 1863 and early 1864 to Lincoln's advantage.[75]

Talk of a permanent political party gained ground in New Mexico. Hezekiah Johnson exaggerated the momentousness of the "loyal Republicans" and Democrats coming together as an Unconditional Union Party. He perceived the obliteration of old party distinctions.

New ones meant preservation of the Union, Johnson analyzed, overthrowing its enemies and "perpetuating Liberty," and such an organization needed to come out of the Alburquerque convention.[76] Instead, with the Democratic Party still hitched to the South, each of New Mexico's extant factions competed to be the organizational representative of the president's ideals.

Johnson seems not to have known who sent the anonymous call for the Alburquerque event. The invitation to the Republican Convention would have gone to Delegate Perea, who sent it down to Governor Connelly. John Watts obviously joined them. Connelly, Perea, and Watts were Union Democrats without a viable national party on which to adhere. They took to controlling the selection of territorial delegates to Alburquerque so as to jump on the Lincoln wagon.[77] An Unconditional identity proved opportune for staying with Lincoln without associating with the Republican Party. It counted pragmatically that Lincoln appointed Connelly New Mexico governor, a wise move indeed. There was also what at least one observer witnessed, a developing friendship and confidence between Perea and Lincoln.[78] Hezekiah had called for "Unionists" in each county to decide on delegates in caucuses to prevent their being chosen by "officious persons" seeking to advance their "selfish desires."[79] It did not go that way, apparently. Reports of the meeting to select New Mexico representatives to Baltimore reveal the dominance of the Connelly-Perea-Watts (and even Carleton) alliance. An anonymous citizen complained of special invitations being sent to certain caciques in the counties, and as if in an *estufa* (a Pueblo underground chamber for holding secret meetings), they were the ones to finger the county's representatives.[80]

Of the three chosen for Baltimore, two were the Connelly men Perea and Watts. (The third, Joshua R. Jones, was a lawyer who had resided in New Mexico less than three years.)[81] Three counties were represented and six individuals showed. Bernalillo County delegates walked out "in disgust." Johnson claimed it was the only county to send representatives chosen democratically. One "delegate" told him that Governor Connelly authenticated him as a representative. Johnson accused Connelly of undercutting any attempt to form an organization of Unconditional Union Men and of converting participants "to his own use." Johnson mistakenly said no instructions were given to support anyone for president at Baltimore. As the gathering failed to develop a platform, he despaired as to what to call the group. The governor's scheming, he feared, would force a delay in the formation of a "permanent party."[82]

The *Gazette* disputed much of this but confirmed Connelly's heavy-handed role. The paper under John Russell was dastardly anti-Lincoln. With Collins in charge, a presidential election in the making, and war winding down, the weekly proudly marched behind the Lincoln drumbeat. Collins hailed Connelly's astuteness in seeing the need to preempt the Bernalillo County delegation because of its support for the staunch abolitionist and Radical Salmon Chase for president.[83] When the object of the Bernalillo "political schemers" appeared, Collins had it, "the friends of Col. Perea put themselves to work" and succeeded in selecting enough delegates to Alburquerque to make sure the territory went for Lincoln, not Chase, "who was then the favorite of those who intended to manage the convention to suit their own purposes." Bernalillo County withdrew, in the Collins line, knowing it was in the minority. Sans guile or guilt, Collins called the Pereaites the "respectable administration party," the one to prevent the territory from being turned over "to the interest of the Chase faction."[84] The *New Mexican* objected to the suggestion of anyone going for Chase (although the Bernalillo County caucus at the convention may have pushed him).[85] The *New Mexican* and the *New Mexico Press* (formerly the *Río Abajo Weekly Press*) blasted Collins for finding religion in Lincoln, publicizing private letters that revealed his Copperhead views and reminding readers that Lincoln had dismissed him and Russell as Indian agents.[86]

Collins justified the *Gazette*'s Copperhead legacy by marking a difference between an abolition party and an administration party. When he had warned about a calamitous Lincoln presidency, abolitionists waged a "most vindictive warfare" on the president and his wartime policy, he explained. The *Gazette* and thousands of fellow citizens opposed Lincoln's election because they thought him to be an abolitionist "in the usual acceptation of that term." Collins quoted from national heavyweights who had become friends of the president as anti-slavery men, including Andrew Johnson, who said that abolitionists were as much "disunionists" as secessionists, and he contrasted them with the anti-slavery disunionist Wendell Phillips to show what hard abolitionists had hoped and planned for, "the elevation of the black man." Collins clarified that he opposed Lincoln back then because he thought him like Phillips rather than Johnson. He realized his mistake in the president's inaugural address, which indicated no intent to interfere with the institution of slavery, having neither the legal right nor the inclination to do so. Lincoln pledged the protection of property, peace, and security to all sections, a relieved Collins beheld. The *Gazette* "wiped away all the objections" it held of Lincoln and "became a friend of his administration," giving assistance to suppress the rebellion.

An anonymous friend of New Mexico reporting from the Baltimore Convention described Delegate Perea, his heart "burning with enthusiasm for the deliverance of his native land from the thralldom of usurpation and oppression," bearing aloft the star-spangled banner, "over which streamed a pure white pennant bearing in large letters the motto, 'New Mexico—the Union and the Monroe Doctrine forever.'" Perea attracted "great attention," the witness said, and elicited loud applause.[87] Republicans resolved to call its organization the National Union Party to draw support from War Democrats who hated Copperheads but would not vote for a Republican. Warming the hearts of New Mexico Unconditionals, Democrat Andrew Johnson drew the nomination for vice president on the ticket with Lincoln.

The *Gazette* editor (and Perea if he was consistent) must have winced at the convention's wholly abolitionist resolutions. Slavery was the cause, "the strength," of the rebellion," it declared. As slavery must be "always and everywhere hostile to the principles of republican government, justice and the national safety require[d] its utter and complete extermination from the soil of the republic." The party would uphold and maintain the acts and proclamations "whereby the government in its own defense has aimed a death blow at this gigantic evil." Delegates favored an amendment to the Constitution to be made by the people in conformity with its provisions to terminate and "forever prohibit the existence of slavery within the limits of the jurisdiction of the United States." A no-compromise-with-rebels position appeared, no peace except "such as shall be based upon an unconditional surrender of their hostility and a return to their just allegiance to the Constitution and laws of the United States." Lincoln adopted the abolitionist charge as his own, symbolized by his hiring of black Union soldiers.[88]

No one of import in New Mexico openly declared for the Democratic Party. Maj. Gen. George B. McClellan became its candidate for president, the man Lincoln removed as general-in-chief of the northern army for his indecisive command in battle and insubordination. McClellan declared himself a Democrat and announced his intent to oppose Lincoln for the presidency. He favored prosecution of the war but not abolition. Peace Democrat George H. Pendleton was nominated for vice president in a spirit of compromise. His faction forced out a Copperhead platform calling for an immediate halt to the war, a negotiated settlement, and the preservation of slavery. In opposing the platform of his own organization, McClellan carried a handicap if ever there was one.

Frémont, assessing the Democratic Party platform as "union with slavery" and feeling that the Civil War must be won to preserve the Union, offered to withdraw from the race if Lincoln fired the U.S. postmaster general. Lincoln agreed, for Frémont ran strongly. The *New Mexican* saw Frémont's action as intended to "secure the triumph of the ideas represented by the Radical Democracy."[89] Lincoln's chances were not clear, given recent Confederate battle victories, but Frémont's withdrawal greatly reduced McClellan's chances. Atlanta fell to northern forces shortly before election day. The *New Mexican* declared the election of "Old Abe" not in doubt.[90] Markedly different from 1860, Lincoln won the popular vote by 400,000 (55 percent), including three-fourths of the military and an overwhelming majority of the Electoral College. An exultant *New Mexican* saw him implementing the people's instruction to drive the secessionists to utter defeat. "Lincoln is to be President again for four years from the 4th of March next," it observed. "We shall anticipate much from him and his administration in favor of New Mexico."[91]

Dragging the General into the Campaign

New Mexico's two informal parties backed the president but held the line of demarcation between themselves for the 1865 election for delegate to Congress. The *New Mexican* jumped to make Carleton and Bosque Redondo key in the campaign. First was to ripen Carleton into a Lincoln anathema. He was an "original Democrat," it was claimed, a friend of the chief Copperhead, Clement Vallandigham; an "enthusiastic partisan" of McClellan; and an enemy of the administration.[92] *New Mexican* agitprop charged that only one of Carleton's vast corpus of contractors was a Republican; all his officers were McClellan men; the general dispensed of a Lincoln soldier "quicker than a Turkish scimitar could do it, his remains packed off to Fort Union as so much useless rubbish, a frightful example to warn others, from following in his footsteps." Carleton arrested Knapp allegedly because Knapp was an abolitionist. Carleton's rag, the *Gazette*, spoke contemptuously of "Arny, Steck & Co." due to their Republican affiliation. Demonizing for party, Carleton was crowned the "political general," manipulating politicians to wheedle a legislative recommendation for his promotion. The general reportedly urged New Mexicans to apply for a state government so that he could be a U.S. senator. He allegedly told Perea he had "set the wires" to secure his election and whispered to José Manuel Gallegos of his "deep regret" over Gallegos's defeat in 1863. Carleton made a fool of Governor Connelly, it was charged, convincing him that the Indians had been subdued. He arrogantly talked the bishop's vicar into giving a mass for his army, only to spurn the Church, congregants, and governor by not attending.[93]

Carleton's "most brilliant feature," management of the Navajo, rose to electoral meaning. "For two hundred years has there been an hereditary feud between this most powerful tribe of Indians and the people of New Mexico," the *New Mexican* offered:

> In defiance of this strong and deadly hostility, these savages, the scourge and terror of New Mexico for two centuries, have been brought from their own country in the territory of Arizona, by only the mere will of this one man and placed upon the rich pasture lands of the Pecos by the thousands—a stench in the nostrils of the people. Whether this insane policy is to be attributed to the brain of an unscrupulous and designing politician or the visions of a depraved ambition, it is difficult to determine.

Carleton took the Navajo hundreds of miles to an inhospitable place at a cost of millions to gain "much party capital" for the McClellan candidacy, the paper partisaned away, an effort to accuse Lincoln of the extravagances of its public spending. Editors shook their heads in shame: "It was a sorry day for our Territory when this man Carleton first set foot within her borders."[94]

Perea formally announced for reelection as delegate in mid-January 1865, as friends had urged another run, he said.[95] Collins tried fading

Carleton out of the campaign. He pitched Perea as having grown in stature and popularity while in office, seeing "a large majority of the mass of the people in his favor," and having proven himself an efficient public servant. His "good common sense and his knowledge of human nature" qualified him to discharge the duties of delegate, the campaign maintained, as well as "if not better than some of those amongst us who made more pretensions than he."[96] Someone writing from Washington linked Perea to Carleton. The delegate had been busy "with great promptitude and zeal," the letter said, repelling the "malignant" assaults being made on the general in the press and within the War Department. Perea's "tireless and indomitable" defense of that officer emanated from a sense of duty to a "gallant and faithful officer." It was worthy of praise "instead of censure and denunciation."[97]

Steck publicized Carleton's letter to him that regretted the loss of cordiality and cooperation between the two. The *New Mexican* saw Carleton threatening Steck and proclaimed that the general should be the one to go, as Steck retained public confidence.[98] On March 18, 1865, Dole notified the exhausted and pessimistic Steck of his dismissal as New Mexico's Indian superintendent. A Nuevomexicano replaced Steck. Felipe Delgado was a Santa Fe merchant, the territorial treasurer, an American Party man, and a firm Perea supporter.[99] Lincoln, meanwhile, removed Knapp. Knapp claimed that Watts demanded his removal because the judge would not be useful in Watts's efforts to gain ownership of a New Mexico land grant. A public meeting in Mesilla hailed Knapp as "no ordinary man," possessing "many of the elements of true greatness," the victim of a great many lies about his character.[100] The pressure on Carleton mounted. A congressional joint special committee, headed by Wisconsin senator James Doolittle, began investigating the treatment of Indians by civil and military authorities. In New Mexico it planned on interviews with religious, business, and political leaders about Bosque Redondo. A "bright omen, a ray of hope," the *New Mexican* hailed it.[101]

The "Administration Party's" Candidate

José Francisco Chávez was born a scion of traditional privilege but whose reputation carried the stuff of the Mexican Party. According to legend, Chávez's father saw in the American invasion "heretics . . . going to over-run all this country." He instructed his son: "Go and learn their language and come back prepared to defend your people."[102] Apocryphal though the tale be, it adorned the fact that Chávez matured into an advocate of Nuevomexicano rights. An 1863 appreciation pointed out that the Río Abajo native distinguished himself while a member of the legislature "by his efforts to obtain the passage of laws to ameliorate the condition of the laboring classes, the poor and unfortunate," doing so "free from all hostility about races and desir[ing] above all things the progress of his native land and her people."[103]

Chávez witnessed heretical violations of enlightenment liberalism during the Civil War committed by Euroamerican servicemen who disdained the "greaser soldier" and unjustifiably labeled the Mexican officers and soldiers "cowards, ready to run at the first fire."[104] Chávez recalled years later "how the volunteers and militia were relegated to the 'low watery bottom,' and how [Nuevomexicano] men were 'subject to rheumatic pains and other diseases caused by the unhealthy, stagnant' environs, while the regulars were housed within the far healthier confines of the fort." The key obstacle lay with Col. Stephen Canby, New Mexico's commanding officer at the time, who disdained the Mexican soldiery, blaming them for the losses at the Battle of Valverde.[105] Stationed at Fort Union in 1862, Chávez filed an official complaint on behalf of Nuevomexicanos for being "slighted in every respect" by the "American" soldiers and officers. Mexicans complained about not being paid for months. Canby dressed him down for the impudence of such a report. Not only had the volunteers not been slighted; they had "never been so well fed, clothed and quartered as at present," Canby charged, "and never will be again after they have left the Service of the U. States." Canby observed that if officers entered the service "with the expectation of carrying with them the luxuries, or even the comforts of the home, it is an idea of which they cannot too soon divest themselves." Canby as colonial overseer turned the table of prejudice on Nuevomexicanos, revealing that he was not promoting his own officers, even though they deserved it, because it would incite "the prejudice of the Mexican population towards the Americans." The policy delayed the promotion of "American" officers and harmed the organization of their regiments, Canby claimed, all because of the "character of the [Mexican] people we have to deal with." Canby ignored the complaint of the men being disrespected under his command.[106]

When Canby conveyed to the War Department that Mexicans had

"no affection" for the institutions of the United States, he conflated institutions and occupiers. As he put it, "they have strong but hitherto restrained hatred for the Americans as a race, but they are not wanting persons, who, from the commencement of these troubles, have secretly and industriously endeavored to keep alive all elements of discontent and fan them into flames." Canby confirmed the Mexican grievance of race prejudice in the military when he addressed compensation. As he noted, the "long deferred payment of the volunteers has given much plausibility and coloring to their representations as to have produced a marked and pernicious influence upon these ignorant and impulsive people."[107]

Chávez's service under Carleton appears problematic. The Chávez record showed strong service in the Indian campaigns, which included mediating the surrender of Navajo peace chiefs for deliverance to Bosque Redondo; almost getting killed in a skirmish, the arrow whizzing by his head; and having built a wilderness road for miners and officials into the newly formed Arizona Territory.[108] Yet Chávez noted in his warning to Perea regarding Bosque Redondo that his officer's commission was due to expire and hinted that all might not be good with the general. He added, "PS: Carleton is absent at the Hot Springs near Taos; until he returns it is uncertain whether I remain in the service or not."[109]

Chávez mustered out of the military two months later. The *New Mexican* regretted the loss to government service of "one of New Mexico's favorite native sons." He liked military life, and no officer had done his duty more faithfully "and at the same time been so persecuted by General Carleton by every means in his power," the story said. Carleton allegedly exerted "his known activity to see how he could harass Col. Chávez, and if possible humiliate and crush his spirit. He would put and keep him upon service and drudgery to try to degrade him in the eyes of officers and soldiers and among the New Mexican people." Were it not for this, Chávez would have stayed in the service, went the report. Now, at least, he would not "further risk Gen. Carleton's power to oppress, persecute and humiliate him among his friends and countrymen."[110] No specifics were given in the editorial. Correspondence between the officers reveal Carleton denying Chávez's requests for leave and hint at Chávez resenting orders to report from post to post seemingly at random.[111]

Chávez's first political act as a restored civilian came during the

1864–65 legislature. Members had mutually exclusive resolutions on the table. One was a petition, signed by 1,974 citizens in San Miguel County, asking the legislature to have the Department of Indian Affairs effect the removal of Navajos and Apaches from Bosque Redondo to another reservation "more appropriate for them."[112] The other expressed appreciation of Carleton's Indian work. It is surprising in view of the previous election for delegate to Congress that the latter was moved by veteran Mexican Partyite and former delegate José Manuel Gallegos. Gallegos, it turns out, never left the merchant's profession that had given him so much trouble in the eyes of Bishop Lamy in the 1850s. He and his brother profited from the Carleton patronage system, holding a contract to supply foodstuffs to the Bureau of Indian Affairs and deliver sheep to Bosque Redondo.[113] Gallegos now walked through the partisan gate onto the field of the *Gazette,* which had so ripped into him in the election of 1863.

The legislature was equally divided on the propositions with one member on the fence. Carleton lobbyists appealed to the Nuevomexicano representatives at evening meetings and private conferences to give the general his due.[114] José Francisco Chávez reportedly labored at a night caucus "with zeal" against the hyping of Carleton and indeed had been "foremost among the first" of the Carleton opponents. The *Gazette* had Chávez violating House privileges and decorum by taking a seat beside one of the House members to assist him in defeating Carleton.[115]

In another contradiction of the prior political binary, Council President Diego Archuleta sided with Carleton. The consistency in this position lay in supporting a hard Indian-fighting commander, although Carleton co-opted Archuleta materially by having him hired as an agent for the Indians of Río Arriba County. Archuleta and House Speaker Pedro Valdez had planned to have a committee of their choosing visit Bosque Redondo, as Carleton knew. The measure failed, but they felt they had enough information to compose a legislative resolution expressing gratitude for Carleton's energy in prosecuting the "successful" war against "our savage enemies." According to the *New Mexican,* the logjam was broken by votes bought by Carleton forces. Speaker Valdez called for a *viva voce* while a member was speaking and reportedly declared a majority for Carleton. Interestingly, the final version of the resolution referred to the "provisional" reservation at

Bosque Redondo, perhaps reflecting a compromise after all.[116] In the upshot of the incident for the territorial binary, it was during this legislative debate that the leaders of the Carleton opposition "learned to have so great faith in Mr. Chavez," the *Gazette* regretted. "This is where and how he proved himself worthy of their confidence."[117]

Letters soon appeared in the *New Mexican* from someone in the Río Abajo signing off *Ranchero*. The Ranchero communiqués had some special qualities. They demonstrated an intimate knowledge of specific Indian battles and unprecedentedly referred to particular Navajo chiefs with their native names rather than their Spanish given names. They dared question the battlefield wisdom of Col. Kit Carson, referring to an encounter where he was badly beaten by the Navajo.[118] The *Gazette* claimed that Chávez wrote in as Ranchero, for only he had the audacity to "demean" the vaunted Carson for being "unfit to command the Navajo campaign." Ranchero neither admitted nor denied being Chávez, and he clarified that he did not blame Carson for particular defeats so much as Carleton for not strengthening the troops in battle. The *Gazette* alluded to the difference between Chávez and Carson over the way to wage the Navajo campaign successfully, Chávez's leadership not faring well in the account of one battle.[119]

Because the nominal Democrats Connelly, Perea, and Watts had adopted an Unconditional Union identity, opponents might well have organized a Republican Party. The risk was not worth it. The national party had decided to call itself temporarily the National Union Party. Tellingly, the national organization was yet to be sold on New Mexico. Congress passed a statehood enabling act in 1864 for the Colorado, Nebraska, and Nevada territories to deliver their Republican majorities to Lincoln. New Mexico, with its strong Democratic legacy, was deliberately excluded.[120]

Unused linguistic devices lay about to possibly symbolize a pro-Lincoln stand. As the Ranchero letters circulated, a "large number" of the legislative assembly and "many of the most prominent citizens of Santa Fe" met to appoint a central committee for an "Administration Party." Organizers foiled the bulldozing American Party by billing theirs as a "people's" initiative. Administration leaders in the counties were asked to select delegates for a general convention to be held in Santa Fe on April 15 to nominate an Administration Party candidate for delegate to Congress, specifically "in opposition to the Hon.

Francisco Perea." Santa Fe Probate Judge Miguel E. Pino, one of the longest-lasting Mexican Party chiefs, served as Central Committee chair. House member Vicente García was on board, along with Santa Fe County Councilman and Treasurer Anastacio Sandoval (another conquest generationer), and Santa Fe representative Theodore Greiner (signifying the endorsement of territorial secretary Arny).[121]

The *New Mexican* hailed the "glorious event" of the announcement, a "brilliant presaging" of a "new order of things." A party with an "incontrovertible fealty to the federal union" appeared certain, as did "adoption of the principles that govern the present administration in its efforts to conquer the most stupendous rebellion that has threatened to destroy the existence of the best government under the sun." The weekly disdained to respect the opposition's adopted name, claiming it was the Democratic Party that had nominated Francisco Perea, and it was still not a real political organization, the reason why the territory had not sustained an influence in Congress. All "patriotic men" who repudiated the bad management of the territory's business and desired the rapid development of New Mexico's "great" mineral and pastoral resources were urged to respond to the new call.[122]

The *Gazette* blew right past the fact that most of the Administration Party initiators were Nuevomexicanos. The real power behind the scenes, it charged, consisted of federal officers who had lived in the territory from two to twelve years and not yet removed, meaning at least Arny, Greiner, and Benedict. Collins accused the *New Mexican* of falsifying the party situation. Why, he asked, had these "newcomers" not thought of organizing an Administration Party by now in order to lend a helping hand to the administration and defend it against its enemies? At this late day when the president was about to be inaugurated, Collins linked their motivation to the small share of public patronage falling to New Mexico. "It looks to us," Collins chided, as if "they should be ashamed to come out now and plead for that which they have wholly neglected to advocate during the trying four years through which the administration has just passed, and during which time they have been the recipients of its favors." Working the binary with his favorite straw man, Collins insisted that the opposition had acted to put its influence against the administration to favor the nomination and election of Salmon Chase.[123]

The *New Mexican* corrected the *Gazette* on who had appointed the Central Committee of the Administration Party and scheduled the convention. Tucker emphasized that the Administration Party intended to nominate someone "emphatically" as a *"people's candidate"* [sic], not the choice of a clique of "demagogues and office seekers." Collins's charge of too little, too late did not count as it was never too late to do good, Tucker had it, "though the *Gazette* should so sedulously oppose us in so doing." Had the organization of an Administration Party been left to *Gazette* friends, it would never have had an existence. Francisco Perea did not run as a leader of any administration party when he was nominated for delegate to Congress, Tucker correctly pointed out. It seemed "very strange, even suspicious that the *Gazette* should embrace the first opportunity, if it belongs to the Administration Party, to assail in the bitterest terms the call of an Administration Convention." The Copperhead and anti-Lincoln notices that were the *Gazette*'s stock-in-trade were regarded prima facie evidence of Perea opposing the president. Not impressed with Unconditionals at the Republican Convention, the *New Mexican* said it was not evident that the opposition had changed. It was too late now for it to "attempt to steal the laurels."[124]

The *Gazette* indignantly threw out the names of "leaders" in its "party" who had gone into service at war's outbreak and had actively organized volunteers and militias, "who went into the field and remained there battling with the foe until they were expelled from our limits." Included were Col. James Collins, Governor Connelly, the deceased Gen. O. P. Hovey, Col. Ceran St. Vrain, Col. Kit Carson, John S. Watts, Gen. Charles Clever, "the Oteros and Pereas of Río Abajo," Maj. Jesús Baca y Salazar, Col. Francisco Abreu, Maj. James Pfeiffer, Capt. A. M. Vigil, Capt. Jesús Sena y Baca, Capt. Nicolás Quintana, Maj. A. Morrison, Col. José M. Valdez, Capt. Bonifacio Romero, "the Tapias," Maj. Luis Baca, "and a score of other men, good and true."[125]

The *New Mexican* tore into the *Gazette*'s accusation that Administration Party leaders were motivated only by the desire for federal patronage. "Can anyone believe their eyes when they read this?" Tucker queried incredulously. Members of Collins's immediate and extended family had received a great number of government jobs, he noted. The *New Mexican* asked, "What family has three fourths of the offices in the Territory and are mad because they have not the other fourth? If the editor had said nothing about offices, we should say nothing;

he would have displayed more discretion, because it is not forgotten *why, how* and the *reason*, the Government kindly relieved him of his duties as Superintendent of Indian Affairs," implying malfeasance of some kind.[126]

Collins argued in a long-winded screed that his side had sustained the administration, realistically meaning that Connelly, Watts, and Perea had not bucked Lincoln. Collins continued to accord value to his side getting organized first. "The Gazette and its friends may be slow about forming political organizations," he put it, "but we showed pretty clearly, two weeks ago [at the Unconditional Union Convention], that they were nearly one year ahead of the new-born [A]dministration party men." Collins twisted the party line with the rather incredible claim that his critics in office had not sustained the administration that had "fed and pampered them" and were, rather, for Chase, aided by Missouri abolitionists "hostile to the administration."[127]

Known Mexican Party men filled the top leadership of the Administration Party General Convention. Joining Central Committee Chair Miguel E. Pino was Tomás Cabeza de Baca, of old anti-Lamy and anti-Miguel Otero fame, as president. Eight of the now ten counties sent delegates. Placed front and center were a pledge to the principles and institutions of the "high government" and "sincere wishes for its prosperity and success." Delegates "heartily" approved the "wise measures of his Excellency, Abraham Lincoln, as the supreme magistrate of the nation in his efforts to crush the most gigantic rebellion the world has ever witnessed." They stood by the National Union affirmation that slavery should not exist under a civilized government "and much less under the form of a republican government." The proposed constitutional amendment outlawing slavery was "heavily approved." Nuevomexicanos received specific attention. All honor went to the "brave natives . . . and their companions in arms in their struggles with the Navajo Indians, the deadly foes to our people and interests, for their perseverance and endurance in that campaign."[128]

Carleton did not receive mention in the resolutions, not while the Doolittle Committee investigated Bosque Redondo. One indirect jab demanded justice for territorial troops—that they "ought to be commanded by officers appointed from our people, and that the native citizens of this territory are entitled to the same rights, privileges and liberties as any other citizens from other parts in the United States who may establish themselves among us." That allusion sprang from the bad experiences particular delegates had been made to endure in the military. Col. Miguel E. Pino had led a company of the Second New Mexico Volunteers under Canby to stage a work stoppage at Camp Connelly because his troops had not been paid. Orders came down to suppress all participants "either directly or indirectly, and reduce them to the most absolute subordination to law and discipline." Thirty volunteers bolted to the mountains. Pino and Lt. Col. Manuel Chávez, a former Kearny foe, were absolved of the acts of their regiments, although Canby bolstered security troops to keep tabs on any "seditious" activity among the volunteers.[129] Rafael Chacón, representing Bernalillo County, had been a captain and veteran of the Ute campaigns since annexation, serving with Chávez at Fort Wingate.[130] Recall him as having suffered the outright prejudice from Euroamerican soldiers and officers and not receiving the promotions due him, yet remaining patriotic and dedicated to the Union in the war.[131]

The convention condemned the frequent abuses committed under martial law. The Santa Fe County delegation likely submitted this resolution. José D. Sena was the sheriff of Santa Fe County and a former major in the volunteers. At thirty-one years of age, he was a 1.5 generationer, educated at Alexandria, Virginia, an officer in the Civil War, praised for speaking English "quite well," called "energetic and ambitious and anxious to do all his duties." Sheriff Sena felt the resolute power of Carleton's military officers. In a notorious incident, a provost sergeant and his men beat up a private citizen at a local fandango, getting away with it because of the military's impunity. According to the *New Mexican*, the responsibilities of the sheriff were "usurped, and his powers trampled out of sight, under the pretense that [Carleton's] Provost Sergeants and their assistants have been substituted in the place of civil officers of the land."[132]

The *New Mexican* later reported on a conspiracy hatched among the "claquers of Carleton," planned by Supreme Court Justice Sidney Hubbell, a Perea brother-in-law, to plant secret delegates in the convention. Captain and U.S. Marshal Abraham Cutler submitted a surprising amendment to the resolutions calling for approval of Carleton and Bosque Redondo. Antonio Ortíz y Salazar, the Santa Fe clerk of probate and principal secretary of the council, moved that Cutler's amendment be rejected as inappropriate to the convention's policy of not praising or attacking anyone. Ortíz's motion passed unanimously. The mischief maker Cutler withdrew in a huff. He would later explain that his county citizens favored the reservation, so he conscientiously sought to represent their interests.

Antonio Ortíz y Salazar's nomination of José Francisco Chávez as the convention's candidate for delegate passed unanimously. Chávez's virtues were said to include "sympathies with the afflicted and destitute." Chávez's speech was greeted enthusiastically. The candidate and other speakers, including Sena, emphasized the need of a reservation for the Indians that was well managed and reflected the people's sentiments.[133] The *New Mexican* hailed Chávez as a native conqueror ever identified with the territory's interests; a front rank debater whose "industry, his aptitude for the investigation and discussion of public questions, and his sterling honesty [were] conceded by all, opponents as well as political friends"; one of the first young men to respond to the need for the defense of the country "against the machinations of traitors and the hoss [horseman] of rebellion"; "a young man with a thorough liberal education, and of affable and courteous manners"; and in political principles, "an ardent advocate of the Administration and its measures."[134]

Chávez's instant popularity was reflected in what the *New Mexican* noted as the score of Spanish and English letters it received in praise of him.[135] Citizens acknowledged the Administration Convention as well. A Socorro writer held up its platform as "all that could be desired by men who regard the perpetuity of the Federal Union as paramount to every other political consideration."[136] A Belén resident called the Perea backers Collins and Watts the "trucking parasites of Carleton."[137] A Doña Aneño said no Perea men lived in the southern district "outside of Carleton's monied influence." The Carleton "strikers" were already at work for Perea and did not hesitate to say that his election was assured, "if the General's patronage can accomplish it." They would find that "the people are not to be bought by misapplied government funds, and that Chávez will triumph over all such sordid attempts to control the popular will."[138]

The *Gazette* had little choice but to bet on a trend of great favor toward Carleton and his reservation. Collins found it incredible that the Administration Party or anyone else would oppose Carleton, given the economic boom attending Bosque Redondo in an impoverished land and the reduction of Indian raids. He thought it immoral for the *New Mexican* mouthpiece to fill its columns with articles to bring the reservation "into disrepute before the people." Collins slammed Hezekiah Johnson for endorsing Chávez and criticizing Cutler. The design of the "getters up" of the Administration platform, Collins held, was to practice a fraud upon the voters in regard to the all-important reservation question."[139]

Sorrowful Interlude

It took two weeks for the news of President Lincoln's assassination to reach New Mexico, but it devastated the territory, and the tragedy served to clutch the people to the Union all the more.[140] The weeklies left an ethnographic snapshot of community grief. In Santa Fe, "not a public house on the Plaza, not a public office in the city was without its emblems of mourning for the loss of the Nation's President. Private houses were profusely hung with crepe and the whole city presented a funereal appearance."[141] Heavy black drapery hung on the quarters of military officers and soldiers. The Palace of the Governors, the houses of civil officers, and those of citizens on and contiguous to the plaza "displayed from their fronts the dark emblems of death. . . . There was scarce any sound save every half an hour the deep roar of cannon from Fort Marcy, which together with the intervening stillness, and the dark drapery on every house, betokened too plainly that some awful and terrible calamity had befallen our nation."[142]

Liberal hearts rose to inspired and poignant expressions of citizen allegiance. That the people's president should fall by the assassin's hand was "never among the things anticipated as probable," a *Gazette* writer noted. "The simplicity of our system of Government, the facility with which changes of President can be affected under the Constitution, and the direct responsibility to which the President is held to the people, are such safeguards against an undue abuse of the executive power, that as one thought it would ever come to pass that such a thing as encompassing the death of the Executive officer would be entertained by the most reckless adventurer to be found within the broad limits of the Republic."[143] Thomas Tucker, it appears, evoked Antiquity:

Erostratos is said to have set fire to the temple of Diana in order to perpetuate his fame. Empedocles to have leaped into a burning volcano for a similar purpose; but the dark fiend in human shape, who, at one blow, struck off the great head of the American Republic will have greater notoriety than either of them. He will go down to posterity the cursed of the accursed with his name enshrouded in the darkest infamy and disgrace, and unborn millions of freemen as long as time shall last, will remember him and read of him as the meanest of his race.[144]

Nuevomexicanos joined the grieving nation with their deep sympathy. Political enemies shared their reverences in the capital. American Partyite Jesús María Sena y Baca called the meeting to order. Governor Connelly presided in front of the Palace of the Governors. Don Felipe Delgado served as secretary and don Miguel Pino and don Anastacio Sandoval as vice presidents. Chief Justice Benedict headed the committee, which included Pablo Delgado, to author resolutions of condolence. Nine resolutions read by Capt. Nicolás Quintana were unanimously adopted. Citizens were asked to wear a badge of mourning on the left arm for thirty days. Santa Fe Sheriff José D. Sena, among others, addressed the gathering in Spanish. Col. Oscar M. Brown, commander of the Santa Fe post, spoke for the military men present, including General Carleton. Benedict spoke as a friend of the fallen leader. Quintana damned "in the strongest terms" the "wickedness" of the killing. Miguel Pino assured the people that the "wise measures" of the late president would be adhered to by his successor.[145]

Redolent reveries flowed through the vales of the territory. In the Río Abajo the Valencia County probate judge issued the call for a public eulogy at Peralta in the Hall of Miguel Antonio Otero. Citizens of adjacent Bernalillo County accepted the invitation to attend. Soldiers stationed at Los Pinos filed in. Sheriff Dionicio Chávez called the ceremony to order. Vicente Otero nominated the Hon. Juan Salazar y Jimenes for president. Juan José Sánchez, José María Aragón, Lieut. Nelson Thomasson, José Vigil, and José Felipe Chávez filled the vice president seats. Lt. Thomas W. Smith and Vicente Otero acted as secretaries. A committee of nine, including one of the original Kearny appointees, Judge Antonio José Otero, and the Administration Party chief José Francisco Chávez, drafted resolutions. The gathering observed "in light of God" who "in His inscrutable government of the universe" had permitted "the revered Chief Magistrate of this Nation to be removed from his exalted position by the hand of a dastardly assassin. . . . The people had lost a Father, the ship of state its guiding hand, Liberty its boldest champion, Republics their ablest defender, and the world a glorious example." While those gathered "blushed" with shame "to know that a man could be found so debased as to conceive so foul an outrage as the murder of our loved President, we trust that the names of all concerned in the damnable act will be blotted from the memory of the universe; and that we know of no punishment sufficiently severe for those who planned, connived at, executed, or in any wise sanctioned so horrid an offense." It was the hope and belief that President Johnson would "emulate the conduct of his illustrious predecessor and lead us safely through our present troubles." He had the community's "undivided and heartfelt support as far as lies in our power." José Francisco Chávez went first among the speakers to eulogize the head of state.[146]

Residents of Taos in the Río Arriba gathered around their plaza. Col. Kit Carson chaired. John Schock, Jesús Santistevan, and Julius Friedman served as secretaries. John T. Price, don Inocencio Martínez, Fredrick Muller, and don Gabriel Lucero drafted resolutions "suitable to the melancholy occasion." They noted that "in the treasonable assassination of President Lincoln, the bloodiest records of history furnish no example of crime so diabolical in its conception, or so infamous, brutal and inhuman in its execution." Not only had the feelings of all loyal citizens been shocked and outraged beyond expression, "and the popular heart lacerated with grief, but the Nation has sustained an irreparable loss, and Liberty her staunchest friend and ablest champion." After four years of fraternal strife "unnatural as sanguinary, and when the dawn of peace is about to dispel the clouds of civil war, and beams of prosperity promise once again to bless a bleeding and distracted land, it was to be fondly hoped that he who had guided the Ship of State triumphantly through the terrible storm, might long have lived to behold the glorious spectacle of a restored Union, and enjoy the merited homage of a grateful people." General Carleton was asked to forward the resolutions to the family of the slain magistrate and President Andrew Johnson on behalf of the united New Mexican community.[147]

A Cockfight across the Binary

In spite of the deep collective mourning for the fallen president, politics pressed for attention—indeed, it could be seen to honor Lincoln. His passing favored neither Unconditional nor Administration parties in New Mexico.

Perea forces kept the development of New Mexico politics moving by appointing an Unconditional Party Central Committee. Diego Archuleta came out president. The former opponent of John Watts for delegate in 1861 sat in Watt's establishment tent along with his in-party rival, James Collins.[148] Archuleta touched off a rhetorical cannon ball in defense of the Carleton fortress. The document forms an important source for the story of Nuevomexicano political integration. It sparked a fascinating verbal duel with his counterpart in the Administration Party, Central Committee Chairman Miguel E. Pino, with others chiming in. Stitched into a fearsome dialogue were a debate over public issues, a personal spat between erstwhile friends who together had challenged the Kearny invasion, a quarrel over the value of loyalty to principle, and an argument over the proper way for Mexican leaders to serve their people in the U.S. government and whose Euroamerican pals were really the other's political puppeteer.

Archuleta's gauntlet proclamation, delivered in nativo idiom, took aim at the opposition for making Chávez an "idol" only because of his opposition to Carleton. Archuleta challenged his Administration Party counterpart Miguel E. Pino to have greater respect for Carleton's reduction of Nuevomexicano captives, deaths, and stolen sheep. Perhaps he would if he had to fight the Indians at Santa Fe's "doors," as so many Nuevomexicanos in the outlying settlements were forced to do at theirs. Archuleta accused Pino, the "politically bitten" Santa Fe probate judge, of being the author of anonymous assaults on the *Gazette,* revealed by their peculiar word usage. Archuleta championed the Union Party–Carleton line. Chávez should understand that his "American" [Euroamerican] supporters had no property in New Mexico, had nothing to lose, came with their government employees, did their time, then retired, not caring that the Indian "devil demon" ravage the people; yet they falsely accused Carleton of bribing legislators. Archuleta denounced the "great politics" of the Administration Party for instigating an argument between Carleton—who, with the "permission of the people," wanted to subdue the Navajo—and Indian superintendent Steck—who would let the Navajo roam free.

Archuleta spotlighted the "new Apostles" of the Administration Party. "[C]on el respeto que nos tiene, nos quiere dar a comer gato por liebre [with their brand of respect, they wish to pull the wool over our eyes]," forgetting that the people were "more than satisfied" with Carleton's project, and "impurely" and "grossly" accusing the general of corruption and illegalities. All should remember the vulgar adage: "que aunque la mona se vista de seda, mona se queda (though the monkey dress in silk, monkey it remains]." Such was the "party of adulation" kowtowing to Chávez. The Administration organization was far from a "people's" party, Archuleta charged. Invoking the apostle Matthew, he accused Chávez of using it to siphon off the support of Carleton's enemies while falsely calling Carleton "despotic": "¿Por qué, pues, vea la pajita en el ojo de tu hermano, y no ves la viga en tu ojo? [Why, then, do you point to the straw in your brother's eye and not see the pole in your own?]."

Archuleta defended his Central Committee colleague José Manuel Gallegos for the "abuses" he felt Gallegos to have sustained at the Administration Convention. The memorial to Carleton that Gallegos introduced in the legislature was justly merited, Archuleta explained. No other commanding officer had subjugated the Navajo with the promise of peace, Archuleta advanced. On the binary, Archuleta called Arny the *caudillo principal* of the Administration Convention, dredging up the story of the "monomaniacal" secretary having said in Missouri that his whole endeavor while in New Mexico was to "keep the Greasers and Indians loyal to the Union." Archuleta seemed less concerned with the racial insult and more with the Administration Party casting Nuevomexicanos as "disloyal rebels to the American government." Archuleta accused Arny of stealing a thousand dollars from the territorial treasury.

Archuleta afforded a human interest angle. "It appears up to now there are two candidates for delegate to the general Congress," he noted. "One is don Francisco Perea y Chávez, the other is don Francisco Chávez y Perea. The two have lent their services to the government in the recent war, they were educated in the United States, are from the same family, and they both comprehend the Spanish word. Properly are they *sinónimo*." Archuleta understood that their grandfather, "an honored man . . . of good fortune," was anxious for his progeny to reconcile.[149]

The honor of his party, let alone his manhood, compelled Pino to respond. He did so in English, perhaps because Archuleta had criticized his Spanish constructions. "This gentleman, Archuleta," he opened, "with his usual audacity, to secure position and bread, again sells himself to the highest bidder" (Archuleta's job as Indian agent under Carleton). It was Archuleta and his clique who cared not for the people, Pino retorted, their sole concern being to secure the patronage of the government for themselves. Archuleta misconstrued the territorial legislature, Pino claimed. Pino explained that in spite of the tricks to whip up support for Carleton (the Cutler incident), the majority of legislators tried hard not to get caught in the Steck-Carleton feud, but believed it improper to take the Navajos from their home country and locate them near the settlements at Bosque Redondo, and proper to ask Congress for the authority to find an appropriate location. At no time, Pino claimed, was anyone opposed to a reservation, the only hope for safety and peace, but Archuleta's "pretended defenders of the people" prattled that their opponents did not favor reservations only to make political hay. Because of the Archuleta-Collins treachery, Pino wrote, "it was thought best to rid ourselves of them entirely, "call a convention of the true friends of the Government from every county in the Territory for the object of establishing a party that would be acceptable to the people, and reflect their sentiments upon the national politics of the day, and to nominate an acceptable candidate for delegate to Congress and adopt a platform upon which our friends could unite." Archuleta and Collins, Pino continued, had "so often treated their party and party friends as Judas treated his master."

Pino defended partisan friend Arny against the charge of defrauding the territory, pointing out that Archuleta was in the legislature when the secretary applied for the monies and had shared in approving the request. As for what Arny had written concerning the people of New Mexico, he was responsible to the people for his own acts, yet compared to Carleton's Casa Colorada letter, Arny's record appeared "bright." Pino negated Archuleta's "wailings" over his compadre Gallegos. He pointed out that two years before, both Gallegos and Archuleta had received the "most villainous abuse from the same parties for whom they were now herding [sheep]." Gallegos willingly surrendered his mantle of Mexican leader for a contract. Archuleta should not go "into spasms," Pino advised, over the Administration candidate for delegate. Chávez needed none of his praises and cared nothing about his censures. The assertion that Chávez was pre-selected for the nomination was "utterly false." The attack on the Administration Party would "recoil" on Archuleta, for its members were "honorable and honest men, well known for their probity and honor." Pino pointed at Archuleta: "no bombastic threats or promises from your pen can change public opinion with regard to the [delegates at the Administration] convention or their acts."[150]

Archuleta came back rebuking Pino for avoiding the fact that the Administration Party viewed Mexicans as disloyal to the United States (in calling for civil rights) while lying about having the only men in the territory "with affection" for the government. Archuleta regretted having to use "rude" words, but Pino needed to understand that "*no quiere la puerca el maíz, no mas la masca y lo deja* [the sow does not want the corn to eat, only to chew and spit out]"; that is, the Administration Party was insincere in its promises to the people. Echoing the Baroque Spanish balladeer Luis de Góngora y Argote, Archuleta blamed Pino for taunting his formerly "adored" José Manuel Gallegos: "*Acabandose el amor y comenzando los agravios* [Love dies, and the insults commence]." He indicted Pino for not responding to the charge that Steck, in secret agreement with those who called themselves the Administration Party, plotted to proclaim the Indians not well placed at Bosque Redondo. "I knew more through my years than any wisdom," Archuleta put it, "that in this was a *gata encerrada* [a cat entrapped]," meaning that Steck and company had worked to ensnare Pino, Chávez, and others for their interest in unjustly attacking Carleton. Archuleta claimed to see how the government made it possible for federal officials to develop their power bases. Archuleta did not blame Pino; perhaps he was innocent, the true criminal being the one who authored the plan. "Well, after God," the people owed themselves to their parents, "yet if they have spent some hundreds of dollars to obtain a small education" (as Pino apparently had), "it should not be to leave us betrayed by political speculators."

Archuleta upped the ante on political patronage by linking it to corruption, string pulling, and lack of loyalty to Nuevomexicanos. Pino need not have been so alarmed at the accusation of Arny stealing territorial funds, he advised. He only had to ask his friend Anastacio Sandoval about the arm twisting it took to get the assembly's approval for Arny's contract. That the governor signed the award proved nothing. Connelly was capable of making mistakes. Besides, he was a "supremely nice" man, desiring only "harmony among all"—anything to avoid difficulties between the legislative and executive branches. Archuleta personalized deeper. After Pino dutifully followed instructions from on high—informing Gallegos not to reveal that Chávez's candidacy had been arranged back in October—Gallegos supposedly confided to Archuleta, "Little Miguel 'is making his own,' wanting to play us as don Tomás [Cabeza de] Baca did when he was a candidate for delegate." That is, Baca allegedly removed himself from the 1861 election because his opponent, Watts, promised "his little compadre" a colonelship if he withdrew. Archuleta accused Pino of feathering his nest by currying his boss's favors. It was known that the Unconditional chairman would not accept the *pastel* (cake, or "pie" in the American form) of federal jobs if not at two or three slices at a time.

Even so, Archuleta pointed out, Pino accused *him* of having had too much pastel. "Well, I do love it, but I never wanted it against my people," Archuleta explained, "because then would I gain nothing: *"en la pasa perdía en la uva* [in the raisin would I lose what is in the grape]." Pino had no children, Archuleta observed. It was for this reason that he could judge a man capable of sacrificing his (ethnic) children for "vile interests." Archuleta took pride in his own eight children; and he considered them "included among the people"; that is, he loved the Mexican people as part of his family. Archuleta regretted being provoked to such a personal level. However, "If you were a loyal son of New Mexico," he lectured Pino, you would be indignant to see a newspaper, the one you associate with [the *New Mexican*], accuse the majority of your people of corruption, saying that their [elected] representatives accepted some hundreds of dollars to obtain praises for Gen. Carleton. Don't you see this as an insult to your people, saying his chosen ones are so miserable that they should wait for his gifts? The conclusion is that the whole people of New Mexico are miserable and corrupt." It was an interpretation of the betrayal of republican representative government and the Carleton patronage machine from a self-interested partisan standpoint. Archuleta classified Pino as one who would say, "*que me cuido la casa agena y olvido la mía*

[I take care of another's (racial) house while neglecting my own]." The issue of whom to vote for delegate was one thing, Archuleta affirmed; hurling insults at his people was quite another.

Archuleta recalled Pino (as a Mexican Partyite) having formerly preached more than anyone against the ricos of the Río Abajo because they wanted to "enthrone" themselves over the territory so that their families owned the position of delegate to Congress. Now he lay at the feet of one of them, Chávez. He mocked Pino by congratulating him in his new position as committee chair, "and so much more because you already speak English." Archuleta's only regret was that "*a el que hambre tiene, en comer piensa* [the hungry man thinks only of eating]"; that is, Pino would sacrifice his principles in a desperate desire for jobs. Archuleta said he felt satisfied in receiving less of the political pastel that caused so much envy. He flagged the rumor that Pino was prematurely relieved of his colonelship in the volunteers and assured that, "in good faith," he would, if he could, "freely" restore the position torn from him, the poor one.

Archuleta credited Pino's reputation as one who used to honor his paisanos, "because they are of my own race." Implying the days of their shared Mexican Party solidarity, Archuleta enjoined Pino that they should both seek to destroy the "destiny of fatalism," or the "punishment," that Providence had laid on "our Mexican race" dating at least to the fifty-five years of his own life. They were American citizens now, and Nuevomexicanos had received "all the protection of the government that we belong to." General Carleton's work, which was "obvious to all," tied into American protections, Archuleta proposed, yet some preferred to sell out to the Carleton enemy, the *New Mexican*, betraying the people with the charge that the general caused their ills. Tugging on the partisan cable, Archuleta accused the Administration Party of purposely impeding New Mexico's progress. Pino and friends needed to see the interest of the community in avoiding those who would seek to betray with "sophisms and lies."[151]

Pino pecked back by calling Archuleta an "infamous imposter, traitor and coward, saturated [*engolfado*, conveying in Spanish now]" in his "new position of Agent of Indians." It was false, "and patently false," Pino affirmed, that he had portrayed Nuevomexicanos bereft of loyalty. As Archuleta raised the subject, Pino would, "like a ring on the [Pope's castigating] finger," remind him of the common saying, "*pescado por la boca muere* [the fish dies by the mouth]." Pino saw in Archuleta's perorations a politics of private interest because, "for such a gentleman, politics is nothing but a branch of speculation." Archuleta nonetheless deserved forgiveness for his eight children, Pino patronized. Pino acknowledged that his commission as a volunteer officer was cut short, but he was honorably discharged, and for Archuleta's information, the same happened to two Euroamerican colonels when their regiment was disbanded. "Mr. Archuleta" could not compete with these "Honorable gentleman," for they had engaged the enemy while the "Patriot Archuleta" played political games, "his services so distinguished that up to now no one has made any appreciation of them." Pino ironically accused Archuleta of engaging in the game of personal insult, referring to the money formerly invested for Pino's "small" education. Pino parried by pointing to the donation the "honored Padre" (Gallegos) had made to the education of Archuleta's son, unfortunately so badly employed that it would have been better to let him remain in ignorance as the development of his understanding had not served other than to "discredit our race."

Pino called Archuleta a "false calumniator" for accusing him of only desiring federal pastel, and in claiming that Pino defiled ricos. On the latter charge, Pino claimed he would never attack any person without just cause, although he admitted that perhaps his memory failed him and he might now be having a lapse of memory in addressing his "friend," don Diego.

Pino could hardly let Archuleta's accusation that he was a disloyal son to New Mexico go unchallenged. Yet, Pino noted, Archuleta had admitted the error of his ways, "being a man of principles . . . with 55 years weighing on your back, and with eight children in your sacred loins." Pino claimed his disloyalty had not been proved. Instead, he told his counterpart, "engulfed in your grand talent, and I mean no disrespect to that, you have only pretended to abuse me in an insolent manner." For those who may not know what "class of man" Archuleta was, Pino pointed to Archuleta's hypocritical loyalty to Nuevomexicanos with an account of how he had not remained true to his original (Mexican) party. The territorial legislature of two years before had condemned the *Gazette*'s racially insulting commentary against its Mexican members, pointing to John Russell, who had descended from somewhere else "to our political circles, calumniating very particularly the reputation of the legislative assembly." Archuleta signed that resolution, but now the *Gazette* was his favorite paper and it supported him. There was also Collins's 1851 editorial telling President Fillmore there was no hope for the improvement of New Mexico unless it be governed by "Americans," since the Mexican "spirit" of government was "corrupt, ignorant and embarrassing in a territory of the United States." Pino pointed out that Collins for many years received the good will of the "people of this country, their hospitality and benevolence," only to be repaid with his insolence. Would don Diego perpetuate the memory of such men out of convenience, as if they were "liberators of the people," or would he cast them to their deserved oblivion? The matter would be left to the people to decide on election day.[152]

Each spokesman accused the other and his Nuevomexicano colleagues of being the tools of Euroamerican schemers in his party. But Archuleta in his opening statement accused rank and file delegates to the Chávez nominating convention of being under the thumb of more powerful Nuevomexicanos. These men would consign their party, "by my *Señor Jesu Cristo*, to the hells," Archuleta swore, never to see its "resurrection . . . according to the Gospels." Archuleta singled out Maj. Rafael Chacón as a *"sujeto de bellas cualidades* [a fellow of fine qualities]" but of "little influence." Chacón responded in mock obeisance of Archuleta's "ascension" to the position of party chairman, his becoming a "true son of God," empowered to reprimand his neighbors, being, in truth, a religious hypocrite and "sacrilegious assaulter, using the words of the Gospel merely to advance his personal interests [*palabras del Evangelio que un sacrílego atentador se atreve á proferir con el único fin de adelantar sus propios intereses*]." Chacón countered Archuleta's condemnation of the Chávez party, prophesying its being crowned "with the triumph of its resurrection" in the election, leaving Chairman Archuleta out for eternity. Chacón identified with the younger men of the territory who had been cast to oblivion by the older politicians but who were now taking possession of the true interests of the "Nuevo Mejicano People." His own political choices were determined by what he, in his "enthusiasm and patriotism," learned about sacrificing his own existence, "at the height of privation," by responding, in his "sole and absolute discretion," to the War Department's call for volunteers to fight for the "true interests of the natal land" equating traditional New Mexico and American territory per the Statehood Revolution). Archuleta and his compadres, Chacón concluded, were the "usurpers" of New Mexico, "giants" destined to fall.[153]

Archuleta had also accused one Leandro Sánchez of being the *criado político* (political servant) of Tomás Cabeza de Baca. Cabeza de Baca, Archuleta wrote, appointed at his "sole and arbitrary discretion" the delegates to the Administration Convention from Río Arriba and Taos counties. Sánchez condemned the assertion as a "solemn lie" told by one with self-interest uppermost in mind in the form of "little" jobs to make money, without the least consideration or respect of families living "under the tightest of chains." Had he been the criado of anyone, Sánchez put it, it would have been of the self-same Archuleta, for he was born and raised as Archuleta's longtime neighbor, and his parents could afford only a humble education for him. Perhaps Archuleta bossed delegates to conventions, Sánchez noted; he himself took pride in being nominated a delegate at a "respectable [liberal] meeting" held in the seat of Mora County, on a motion by the Hon. José María Valdes, approved by "close to a hundred persons, all very respectable." Sanchéz accepted the call with no expectation of remuneration; rather, for the opportunity to serve "with such dignified gentlemen."

Sánchez buffed the binary by rolling out a knave's biography of Archuleta. It consisted of Archuleta's youth under the tutorship of the deceased Vicario Juan Felipe Ortiz; his decision to become educated at the Seminario de Durango; returning with the philosophy of Cupid to take up residence at the house of the well-to-do Señora Collantes, until her money ran out; falling on the mercy of his parents, whose resources he wasted; revealing his restlessness in 1845 in a conspiracy to make money, only to be arrested by Gen. Manuel Armijo; moving to Alburquerque to make certain claims "against the house of the Armijos"; made by the deceased probate judge Francisco Sarracino to leave the county within twenty-four hours under penalty of two hundred lashes; appealing to Governor Bent, only to be kicked out of his office; organizing a conspiracy that resulted in the unfortunate death of Bent, "don Cornelio Vigil, don Pablo Jaramillo, a son of don Carlos Beaubien and others"; baptized *el antiguo revolucionario* by don Donaciano Vigil; abandoning New Mexico after the Taos Revolt and leaving his compadres in the "most high and worrisome compromise"; given amnesty by the Treaty of Guadalupe Hidalgo; and presenting himself from the moment the U.S. territory was organized as one of New Mexico's "biggest champions." Sánchez invoked the value of party loyalty in the new American domain. *El Tejano Chino* allegedly caricatured Archuleta in a speech as a pinto pig whose constant moving in circles made it impossible to know who his friends were, "showing the colors that suited the group he was with at any given moment."[154]

On the Trail

With the war winding down, the qualifier "Unconditional" no longer made electoral sense. A stripped-down Union Party called under Archuleta's signature for a general convention. Organizers announced their dedication to assisting President Johnson's program of national reconstruction and linked it to their policy on Indian affairs. They reiterated the notion of opponents attacking Carleton to thwart the placing of the warring Indians on reservations for the sole reason of personal ambition.[155] The Taos County Union Convention conformed, instructing delegates to the territorial convention to reject José Francisco Chávez and his "anti-reservation platform."[156]

An anonymous critic saw a shadow-party in the Unionists, a "secret conclave of the most essential men in the National Democratic Party of New Mexico" who "must control the grand Democratic Party in its convention to be held in Santa Fe on the 15th of June." The writer's ditty had the governor addressing the convention "in terms most eloquent and sublime":

> You can scarce expect one of my age
> To speak in public on the stage,
> Nor wonder if I fall below
> Demosthenese or Cicero;
> But while I stand before you all–
> I can't sit down before I call
> Dear Collins to the chair
> He's Union now, since Lee's no war.

Jefferson Davis, the "most renowned president," would be captured "from beneath his dar mother's dress."[157]

Diego Archuleta called the Union General Convention to order.

The would-be saboteur of the Administration Convention, Abraham Cutler, served as one secretary, former *Gazette* editor John Russell the other. Pablo Gallegos, brother of former delegate José Manuel, was elected president. The Santa Fe delegation boasted a number of the old American Partyites, including Merrill Ashurst. A tellingly distinct number of merchants who did business with Bosque Redondo stood by. Charles W. Kitchen, of Kitchen & Moore, was a San Miguel County delegate. Carleton's command had its endorsement. The policy of placing warring Indians on permanent reservations was endorsed as the only means of protecting the people. The "government" received thanks for its "generous manner" of sustaining the general against the "unjust" accusations of his personal enemies and for the "triumphant manner in which the war was closed by the surrender of the Armies of Lee and Johnson to those of our gallant Generals, Grant and Sherman."

Swiping at the Administration platform, the convention resolved to deprecate and denounce "all efforts . . . made to create jealousies and animosities among the citizens of the territory by appeals to prejudices of races." Delegates pledged, American Party style, to muster their power to "cultivate harmony of feelings among all classes of citizens" regardless of race. Indian Superintendent Felipe Delgado was praised for his independent and consistent support of the administration of President Lincoln. Francisco Perea's nomination for delegate passed unanimously. Ashurst called on county friends to effect an "immediate organization" for the purpose of using "all honorable means" to secure Perea's election. Delegates authorized another term for the Union Central Committee.[158]

Perea was in Washington at the time.[159] He later expressed gratitude for his nomination, reinforced his support for Bosque Redondo, and condemned the Administration platform for making a "distinction of races." He disclosed how he had been governed since attaining manhood by the rejection of such distinctions. The "cultivation" of any other sentiment was "in the highest degree censurable and should be rebuked by all lovers of peace in the Territory." Should appeal to the different races arise in the territory's politics, it would "excite those passions which can only be excited by appeals of this character" and would soon create "a most deplorable state of feeling which would eventually result in the extermination or disfranchisement of the weaker party." Typical of the American Party, Perea hailed his patronage policies as race neutral—"Americans" selected for federal appointment in some instances and Mexicans in others, in all cases from the territory's citizenry.

Perea recited the script of Union Party policy script: "Whilst I am at all times ready to welcome strangers to New Mexico who desire to become good industrious citizens, and help to develop our country I am unalterably opposed to the introduction from abroad of broken down politicians as the occupants of our best offices. They use those offices for their own aggrandizement, without having regard for the interests of those to whom they are strangers, and whom they forsake as soon as their offices are taken from them." Perea meant Holmes, Arny, Steck, Greiner, Knapp, and Benedict, the *New Mexican* noted, all Lincoln appointees and supporters of the Mexican Party.

On a personal note, Perea mentioned that "Mr. Chávez is my friend and relative. Our families have always been connected by the most endearing ties of consanguinity and it would grieve me sorely if the present canvass should disturb those relations which have existed through long years." Circumstance left him with one course. It was during his absence and after he announced himself as candidate for reelection that his cousin allowed himself to be placed in the field "as a candidate of a party which in its call for a convention avowed its object to be to nominate a candidate in opposition to Perea." That party turned into the "violent" assailants of the public policies Perea and his friends advocated. Perea communicated in full partisan distortion, fingering the class of politicians who had "seduced" Chávez so he could represent their opinions, "which are odious to the people because they militate against the general welfare." Had Chávez made a bid for delegate under his own Union Party, Perea said he would have yielded. In truth, it was the rule of partisanship that kept Perea from conceding or recognizing the philosophical difference between the policies of assimilation in the American Party and the race-critical approach of the Mexican Party. As he conveyed, his cousin allowed himself to "pass into the hands of my enemies, the enemies of my political friends, and, as I hold, the enemies of the Territory." Perea felt he had little choice but to accept the nomination as tendered by the Union Party.[160] Significantly, Perea made no mention of the Copperhead policies that his main backer, Collins at the *Gazette*, had been promulgating.

According to the *New Mexican*, only three counties with bona fide delegations attended the Perea Union Convention. Standing prominent were men who happened to be in Santa Fe on business, not acting with any party authority but taking it upon themselves to represent San Miguel County. Two had large contracts pending with Carleton's command. They would work for their own interests even though "aware of the gross injustice they were doing to the citizens of the county they pretended to represent." The commanding general would hear of it if they did not go along with his preference. If they failed to support Perea, Carleton, "for the sake and better preservation of his faction, would have punished the refractory gentlemen by throwing impediments in the way of the fulfillment of their contracts." The paper portrayed the military's economic leadership forming itself into a political unit. The commander in this view loaned himself, his power, and his patronage to be used by its faction, "until everything is concentrated in the hands of a few and the Territory has passed under the influence of a set of men who would sacrifice its prosperity to advance their own private ends."[161]

The *New Mexican* called out Perea for having the nerve to label his opponents seditious when the *Gazette* published pro-southern editorials to sow discord in the territory.[162] The *New Mexican* had a field day with the *Gazette* story of a "pleasant interview" with José Manuel Gallegos, who had visited Bosque Redondo and found bountiful crops growing out of "excellent soil," an abundance of water for irrigation the year round, plenty of firewood, the "peaceful" Indians making every effort to persuade their "refractory" brethren to remain and, when that was found impossible, giving "early information of the departure of the disaffected." The *Gazette* disingenuously called Gallegos "one more reliable witness who can have no motive for making misrepresentations and has no interest in endeavoring to lead his countrymen astray in regard to a matter in which all have so vital interest."[163] "Truly a change had 'come over the spirit" of the paper's dream, the *New Mexican* declared, "since no longer ago than eighteen months they charged [Gallegos, in the previous election for delegate] with cheating, lying, arson, etc."[164]

Gallegos was later elected president of the Union Party Convention of Santa Fe County, at which he sought to vindicate himself against the charge of party inconsistency. He avoided mention of contracts with Bosque Redondo, resting his argument on the fact that everyone was originally in favor of Carleton's Indian policy. Administration Party chief Miguel Pino was a most enthusiastic speaker in favor, he pointed out. When support for Carleton chilled, Gallegos said he could not go along with those who wanted to pass resolutions against him, the governor, and Bosque Redondo in "diametrical opposition" to the general welfare of the people. Gallegos pointed out that Chávez had never been a political friend of his "and had no claims upon him whatever for support, looking at the question in a party light." The *Gazette* called Chávez one of Gallegos's "most unrelenting partisan opponents" two years before, who had done all he could to defeat Gallegos for delegate. It acknowledged that Perea, Chávez's cousin after all, was Gallegos's opponent in that race. Claiming to speak for Gallegos nonetheless, the weekly said that in the present election, the former priest recognized in Perea "an honorable and upright man and an able and efficient Delegate who exerted himself to promote the interests of the Territory and as such he was entitled to his respect and support and he would do all he could to have him returned to Congress." Chávez would have had a "fine career" in the army "and could have gone on to great things, but abandoned it and is now seeking a career somewhere else and is losing both."[165]

The *Gazette* launched a vitriolic attack on territorial secretary William Arny after Delegate Perea failed to have Arny fired on the charge of using federal funds to subsidize a partisan newspaper, and it recommended Watts as a replacement.[166] The *Gazette*'s tirade turned unrelenting. The *New Mexican* caricatured the *Carletonian Gazette* having "Arny on the brain." The *New Mexican* claimed that a "near half dozen" in the *Gazette* clique wanted Arny's job for the power of being in charge of public printing.[167] Arny, who loathed the sludge of the press brawl, came out to answer some of the "abuse" being heaped on him by Collins, Perea, and Watts. He turned the table on the Union Party habit of castigating transitory officials, calling Watts one of a "host of strangers" who knew nothing of New Mexico and cared little, a "transient" living more than half his time in Washington, his family living in the United States, leaving him with no official residence in the territory, making him ineligible to vote in the territory.[168]

Hezekiah Johnson had supported Perea in 1863 after Joab Houghton withdrew from the race but dumped him this time. When Collins called him a turncoat, the inflamed and consistently independent Johnson detailed Perea's "treachery" to the *Gazette*'s "ass-toot writer." Johnson did not like how Perea had violated the rule of party loyalty when he ordered voters in precincts outside Bernalillo County not to vote for certain candidates in a local election who had helped him win in '63 so that more of his power could be distributed to bigger Bernalillo County. The *Gazette* failed to acknowledge the point and had Johnson putting himself "up for sale" to "Arny, Knapp & Co." in a printing contract, which Johnson denied.[169] Johnson reminded Collins that he and his Bernalillo County delegation had rejected the Copperhead platform under Perea in 1863, coming to regard Perea not as a statesman or respected head of a party organization but as the "tail-piece of a faction."[170] Johnson felt that the issues of Bosque Redondo and Carleton only added credit to his arguments against Perea.[171] Johnson turned hostile to Governor Connelly, whom he called the "uncle" of the "Perea party."[172] Yet Johnson remained no friend of Arny's.[173]

As for Chávez, the *Gazette* was disabled from flinging the order of pollution on that "native gentleman" that it had on the "fallen" priest Gallegos. The tarnishing turned instead on Chávez's "private squabbles" and the "abuse of prominent gentlemen in the Territory."[174] Collins ignored the legitimate issues being raised about Bosque Redondo as real jobs were at stake. It suited quickened partisanship to cast a pall of shame over Chávez for opposing Carleton on personal grounds.[175] That the Administration Convention neglected to endorse the principle of the Indian reservation permitted Collins to claim that it refused to recognize the necessity of change or modification in the system that allowed the Indians to rob, pillage, and murder citizens "and desolate our country without restraint." Straining to smear Chávez on the hustings, the paper accused him of telling different audiences different things—criticizing Carleton and Bosque Redondo from Doña Ana north to Bernalillo County, moderating in Santa Fe, and becoming positive in Taos and Río Arriba, even agreeing with the resolutions passed in Mora "directly approving" Bosque Redondo. Pulling too hard on the partisan distinction, Collins held that even in San Miguel County, Chávez "discovered" that his statements of last September were "without foundation."[176]

Late developments damaged Perea. The *Gazette* accused Chávez supporters of exaggerating or lying about Indian raiding. More compelling were the constant reports of Navajo and Apache hits on ranching settlements resulting in stolen animals, wounded herders, and loss of human lives. Indians appeared to be winning. The entire lower country of the Río Abajo and Doña Ana was said to be "entirely at the mercy of Indians." Citizens filed graphic accounts of prominent ranchers being wounded. Eyewitnesses testified to perpetrators being Bosque Redondo escapees. Lending credence to the reports, the assaulters were said to be well armed with breech-loading rifles that could only have come from Fort Sumner.[177] That Governor Connelly raised militia units signaled serious trouble—trouble that Carleton's command failed to resolve. Those who were most active in raising volunteers tended to be on the side of the general and Perea, including Gen. Charles Clever, Col. Jesús Baca y Salazar, Capt. Nicolás Quintana, and Capt. Jesús Baca y Sena.[178] According to a Peralta citizen, a Nuevomexicano captain was prohibited from pursuing a particular band because they had escaped from Bosque Redondo.[179] Carleton's new campaign against Comanches to the northeast appeared politically disquieting when troops were needed to contain the Navajo.[180]

The image of Carleton the faulty authority figure expanded. When the general received orders to lift martial law because of war's end, the *New Mexican* blared that he had been "brought down a peg" by his commander, who told him the president had not declared the territory in rebellion and the United States had not conquered it. The southern invader had been expelled "and the country upon his expulsion returned to its normal condition of peace."[181] Citizens reported Carleton men intimidating naysayers of Bosque Redondo as "lying" enemies of the general.[182]

The *New Mexican* sustained an effective assault on the record of Delegate Perea, adding a critique of former delegate Watts. In "gross and palpable neglect," went one charge, they failed to obtain monetary relief for civilian victims of Indian depredations, as a Minnesota congressman had done for his constituents, though the damages New Mexicans suffered were far worse and of longer duration.[183] The *Gazette* emphasized the efforts of Perea and Watts to have the Committee on Indians include New Mexico in the bill, meeting with the objection that there had been no treaties in force with Indians, leaving the government non-liable for damages.[184]

The northern region of Conejos returned as a public issue. In January 1865 Perea delivered an appeal to the chairman of the House Committee on Territories in support of the plea by Conejeños for the return of their lands to New Mexico from Colorado. Perea offered a cultural basis for the justice of rescinding the rupture. "The population of Los Conejos, numbering about three thousand, are almost entirely Mexicans," he emphasized. "They are foreign in language as they are in nativity from the great body of the people of Colorado." They could not understand Colorado laws published in English only, nor the legislative discussions and deliberations, nor could they participate in public discussions over the issues affecting them, an "anomalous and extraordinary condition of those people." They were "entire strangers" to Colorado's system of jurisprudence based on civil law rather than their accustomed common law.

Perea recognized the civic norm of a foreign element needing to assimilate to American standards but said that in the case of Conejeños, its enforcement was "ungenerous and unjust." If they had come in on their own, "for purposes of protection or other benefits, it would be proper that they should conform in language and other usages, political and juridical, to the customs of the country with which they had formed a voluntary association." It was far from the case. "Those people were brought under that sovereignty and authority of this government not by their own volition but by the fortune of war . . . and [the] conquest of New Mexico by the United States." Had they been consulted, "they would greatly have preferred remaining under the authority and protection of their native sovereign," Perea affirmed. This interpretation departed from the usual American Party interpretation of Nuevomexicanos voluntarily submitting to the American conquest. As Perea maintained, they "formed a patriotic fondness" for the U.S. government and became "earnest and true" in their commitment to their new sovereign, though the change was not "a matter of their own choice." Because their country was acquired as the fruit of war waged by the United States, they were, by "every consideration of justice and humanity," entitled to the enjoyment of their "native language and their system of law and domestic usages" as long as these did not conflict with the principles of the general government. In light of their history—their struggle against the incessant "aggressions of the aborigines"; their generations of tilling the land; their affection for the mountains that surrounded them; their "harmonious, fraternal" peoplehood, "bound together by the ties of ancestry, a common language a common system of law and a common religion"—it would be "ungenerous for this Government to rend them asunder." New Mexico as a whole deserved the restoration of her people, Perea insisted. The "treasure" that the Conejos represented gave New Mexico a right to be heard in the cause. With its "well organized Christianity," the region had "long been a part of her soil."[185]

The arresting critique of American race-colonialism should have warmed the hearts of Mexican Partyites, but the *New Mexican*'s election-driven partisanship would have none of it. Instead, it charged Perea with "criminally" waiting until the short session of Congress, when the most important of its affairs were to be addressed, "to make a *feeble* effort in the form of a lame letter." An able and intelligent delegate would have embraced the first opportunity to protest earnestly "in the sacred name of violated rights."[186] Collins pointed out that Perea had petitioned the first session of Congress to have the Conejos returned. Should Congress fail to have the region reannexed to its rightful owner, it would not be for lack of negligence on the delegate's part.[187] The House Committee on Territories ran out of time, and Perea's bid to rescue the Conejos for New Mexico fell through. (The *Gazette*'s confidence that it would pass in the next session was confidence beyond hope.)[188] On the question of land, Secretary Arny trashed Watts for trading "some of the best portion of the Territory away" while using his sinecure to obtain some claims of land for himself, on which, "strange to say," military posts were established.[189]

The *New Mexican* criticized Perea over the issue of much needed land surveying. All other territories enjoyed liberal appropriations for surveying, but Perea followed previous delegates who failed to obtain it for their constituency though they numbered one hundred thousand souls and suffered from "almost endless litigation caused by want of titles."[190] A defensive Collins said he could not believe the *New Mexican* did not know that Congress had supplied "liberal appropriations" for the surveying of land in the previous three years, as it did for other territories. Collins accused the *New Mexican* of "carefully and studiously" concealing everything Perea had done for the territory. While the *New Mexican* spoke of the "deplorable condition of New Mexico," Collins said its condition was the best since the United States took possession of it. His imagination painted good times in the territory and implied that the benefits resulted from Carleton's efforts. The people no longer feared the "large robberies" and "numerous murders" previously committed by the Indians; stock owners no longer feared sending their herds to good pasture; the frontiers were rapidly becoming populated; new ranches occupied the ground "formerly roamed over and desolated by the savages." Prosperity sprang up in all the branches of business (implying the work of Carleton's contractors) "and the whole extent of New Mexico smiles in peace and security." Perea did not bring it about by individual exertion, Collins claimed, but it was the consequence of a policy that he had "manfully sustained and zealously assisted in carrying into effect."[191]

Collins's Polyanna view of conditions in New Mexico did not keep Samuel B. Watrous from hurting Perea. The prominent rancher and merchant in northern San Miguel County was instrumental in the removal of James Collins as New Mexico's superintendent of Indian Affairs. Watrous tried while in Washington in 1864 to persuade Perea to have Congress remove the Utes and Jicarilla Apaches from the Cimarron Indian agency near his ranch. Watrous's own recent incursion onto traditional Indian ground probably provoked Indian discontent. But in any case Watrous publicly charged Perea with refusing his request for troops along the Santa Fe Trail to protect settlers and travelers from Plains tribes, accusing the delegate of claiming that nothing could be done.[192] Watrous returned to New Mexico embittered with Perea, Watts, Carleton, Russell, and Collins. His weekly correspondence to the *New Mexican* in the month before the election exposed private correspondences, analyzed pro-southern and slavery histories, questioned past Indian policy while defending Steck and Arny, and called for Chávez's election.[193]

Charges of race prejudice worked to the advantage of Chávez. The Union Party, put up by the American shadow-party, continued to reject the enlightened appeal to the rights of minorities, calling the Administration Party plank that affirmed the rights, privileges, and liberties of native military officers itself an appeal to prejudice.[194] But it could hardly contend with such reports as that of Carleton elements appealing to "German Irishmen and all others born beyond New Mexico but who reside here . . . to combine as a race" against Chávez. It is impossible to confirm the report's veracity, but the Chávez word-masters drew a righteous defense of group rights. The *New Mexican* praised the "sentiments and opinions" in the Administration Party's civil rights resolution. "Where is the man ready to propose the contrary opinions," it queried, "prepared to claim that the native citizens of this Territory are not entitled to the same rights, privileges and liberties as any other citizens from other parts of the United States who may establish themselves among us?" These were distinctions the Union-American Party would not respect. As the *New Mexican* hailed, the Treaty of Hidalgo guaranteed the native citizens their rights, followed by the Organic Act and the laws "founded on the clearest justice." The Administration men felt sorry to see "any party, however desperate may be their situation and hopes, maintaining war upon a candidate and his friends, because he and they have insisted upon the justice of those principles." Chávez was "one son of this country able and willing to stand up for these principles and his countrymen," "boldly" advocating the "equality of all citizens here, before the laws, in 'rights, privileges and liberties.'" Eschewing race-blind liberalism, the *New Mexican* pointed to the problem of those "Americans" who, "if they have a difficulty with a Mexican citizen, do not hesitate in trying to arouse the feeling of races among his countrymen, against the Mexican. [T]hese practices are not fair, nor right, and if persisted in must lead to bad consequences."[195]

Both candidates met large and enthusiastic crowds on the campaign trail, where *bailes* (dances) and festivities abounded. Diego Archuleta accompanied Francisco Perea to Taos County, where they visited the central plaza of the county and the villages of Peñasco, Don Fernando, Red River, Río Seco, El Rancho, Río Colorado, El Sello, and Arroyo Hondo. The extensive outreach loosened voters from the clutches of local bosses. In another sign of increasing citizen mobilization, a quantity of local keynoters hailed their candidates and condemned the evil opponent on the stump and in local and county conventions.[196] Liberalism resounded. The San Miguel County Administration Party Convention resolved in favor of "all free men," their rights, "*natural y inagenable* [inalienable]." All persons were assured of their right to talk freely "over whatever matter or which-

FIG. 22. *José Francisco Chaves [sic], Member of the U.S. House of Representatives from New Mexico Territory's At-large district*, photograph by Matthew Brady. Library of Congress Prints and Photographs Division, Washington DC.

ever party he believed in" as long as there was no abuse of anyone or reference to "personalities."¹⁹⁷ Craftily representing the humbler elements in favor of Chávez, a writer going by A Peón, self-described as "one of the saddest members of society [*uno de lo mas tristes miembros de la sociedad*]," begged permission to register in bad grammar his resentment at the money the family of James Collins earned in governmental jobs, their buying votes and falsely accusing Chávez of deprecating the vote of the poor ones when his leadership helped them cast off the servitude of the vile traitors to their land and realize their liberty "in equality and so have justice [*promover la libertad y no para establecer la servidumbre que todo lo que desais es la igualdad y así tendréis justicia*]."¹⁹⁸

The onslaught from the Chávez mobilization landed on "the whole pack of army contractors, sutlers and speculators and the adjuncts of the Military Dynasty," businessmen whose fortunes would be lost on a Navajo reservation on the Río Chiquito near Arizona.¹⁹⁹ The very contractors for their part pulled out their partisan stops. Chávez would have noticed the sign sutlers put up on behalf of "JAMES H. CARLETON, THE BRIGHTEST STAR IN THE CONSTELLATION OF AMERICAN GENERALS."²⁰⁰ Mora County Nuevomexicanos were not as receptive to Chávez as those in neighboring San Miguel. They were polite enough, but Moreños clearly supported Perea. While both San Miguel and Mora counties extended to the eastern plains, Mora sat mainly on mountainous ground where farming was more important than ranching, as in San Miguel. Farmers in Mora County kept their economic fortunes primary. Their support for Carleton followed on the commerce established with Fort Union and government contracts for citizens. Mora County was the leading grain producer in the territory. Its farms along the valley to La Cueva and Buena Vista reaped abundant harvests in grains, vegetables, fruits, and other products. The largest portion of merchants at Mora were German, a contemporary noted, although French and Irish people immigrated to the Mora Valley "and along with local mexicanos, many had established thriving mercantile stores and farms. Mora farmers and merchants alike were welling the products and merchandise to Fort Union and other forts in New Mexico." It counted that the Indian hazard was minimal in the settlements within the Mora Valley.²⁰¹

Table 4. Official returns for delegate to Congress, 1863 and 1865

Counties	Perea, 1863	Gallegos, 1863	Perea, 1865	Chavez, 1865
Bernalillo	1,078	282	634	751
Santa Fe	643	690	618	654
Santa Ana	203	223	116	308
Socorro	1,116	176	413	745
Taos	957	882	874	995
Río Arriba	477	1,125	1,209	626
Mora	617	633	1,072	488
Valencia	844	511	362	1,111
San Miguel	1,050	1,341	782	1,761
Dona Ana	246	562	100	1,072
Totals	7,231	6,425	6,180	8,511
			For Perea	6,180
			Majority Chavez	2,331

Sources: "Official Returns of the Election," *New Mexican*, September 29, 1865, 2; "Territorial Election," *Gazette*, September 30, 1865; Steve C. Martinez, "Political Life," 31–32.

The "Greenbacks and WHISKY flowed freely" on election day, "and all sorts of tricks were resorted to in order that [Chávez] might be politically prostrated," the *New Mexican* decried. It would be surprising if the same currencies did not flow out of the weekly's own camp. Still, it was Manderfield and Tucker's turn to exult: "Rejoice ye people of New Mexico!"[202]

As table 4 discloses, José Francisco Chávez's election to the thirty-ninth and fortieth Congresses was delivered by a majority of more than 2,000 votes out of 14,767 cast (a thousand more than in 1863). Chávez won all counties except Río Arriba, which Archuleta delivered to Perea, and Mora, with its stake in the military economy. As Chávez had predicted to his cousin a year previously, more than two-thirds of the vote in San Miguel County went against Perea. At the celebration in Las Vegas, *vivas* sounded for *todos los hombres libres* (all free men), *nuestros derechos* (our rights), and in a new liberal expression, *la igualdad* (equality).

The Administration Party garnered majorities for local and territorial races in all counties save two. In the town of Santa Fe the important offices of sheriff and prefect went that way. The Santa Fe County government was set to be ruled by the Administration Party, headed by the new probate judge Antonio Ortiz y Salazar, who nominated Chávez for delegate to Congress. A majority of the territorial legislature backed Chávez, four-fifths in the estimate of the *New Mexican*. Chief of the Administration Central Committee Miguel E. Pino was elected to the council in spite of the *Gazette*'s efforts to paint him as an "enemy of the poor people."[203]

The Chávez win put a chink in Carleton's political armor. The *New Mexican* noted that Chávez had opposed the commanding general in a "bold, decided and defiant manner."[204] Chávez himself in his appreciation to fellow citizens appeared most sensitive to the accusation that he was racist, as strongly implied by his own cousin, Perea. The rational voters themselves did not hold to such views, he presumed. He thus thanked those who, "notwithstanding there were the utmost efforts made to prejudice, defame and stamp me as anti-American, have generally given the lie to so unfounded an accusation by giving me a majority of their suffrages throughout the Territory." He highlighted "this great principle—that the citizens of the United States, in all parts of the Territory thereof possess equal privileges and rights under our constitution and laws; and any attempt to lessen them, or to draw a line of distinction between citizens is unjust, illiberal and contrary to the spirit and purity of our institutions."[205]

Secretary Arny publicly noted how the *Gazette* organ of the Union Party dedicated five columns of attack on him on various counts. Arny thanked the paper for granting him so much importance. He recalled the letter Collins had written to a friend stating that Arny had no chance of building an abolition party in New Mexico. The secretary pointed out that the honorable Administration Party was built in opposition to the "Union Democratic Party." The "Watts-Perea Party" fired government employees who voted for Chávez, Arny charged. "Go on, gentlemen, with your 'rat killing,'" he allowed. "[A] few more columns like last week's issues will make our party a permanent institution in New Mexico," he offered, instinctively perceiving the American political binary reproducing itself.[206]

4

Political Agonism
under Reconstruction

José Francisco Chávez strategized with a clear-eyed mission to capture the seat of delegate to Congress from New Mexico. His substantial majority in 1865 counted not only for the issues but in relation to a formidable figure. As one Spanish-language voice hailed, the support for him erupted as an "explosion," his "well acquired fame" backed by his image as a "pure and noble defender of American liberalism."[1]

Persona could hardly quiet the territory's rousing partisanship, however. Followers of Francisco Perea believed he had made an effective delegate and were convinced that Chávez's sole reason for challenging him was to satisfy a personal beef with Gen. James Carleton, in whom they believed as a deliverer of goods and security to the people of the territory.[2]

Bitter contention pulsed through Chávez's first congressional term as a result, and so forcefully that three chapters are needed to do it justice. In the first, Chávez's party struggles to establish dominion over the territory on a number of major issues, including those of ethnoracial colonialism, while opponents fight it tooth and nail. In the second, an incredulous vision grips the backers of Chávez in his quest to get reelected delegate to Congress. In the temple of liberal enlightenment, that particular partisanship took a culturally and politically compelling but most unholy form. The third story involves Chávez's desperate attempt to keep his congressional seat after the 1867 election and its volatile effects on territorial politics.

CHAPTER TEN

Party Definitions of the Colonizer, 1865–1867

Issues and controversies plucked the chords of New Mexico's partisanship as José Francisco Chávez assumed the office of delegate to Congress. The controversy over the Bosque Redondo reservation continued and, from the angle of Chávez's Administration Party, demanded resolution. The Statehood Revolution, always a potential, craved attention. The appointment of new federal officers usually caused ruffles in executive-legislative relations, and 1866 proved no exception. Contention in the governing structure ramped up around a certain awareness among members of the Mexican Party of the stranger arriving in the homeland from eastern points to subjugate the Nuevomexicano people socially, economically, and politically. This whole line of heat fired up the 1867 processes of nominating the two candidates for delegate to Congress.

Taking Out the General

Popular resentment of Gen. James H. Carleton led to a Doña Ana County grand jury presentment for his importing corn for soldiers at a rate twice the price he would have paid for New Mexico corn.[1] A citizen accused Carleton of committing a number of offenses, including ordering the return of Indian slaves and *peónes* to their masters rather than freeing them, as required by law, and illegally supplying a private speculating and mining firm from Mesilla with seven thousand pounds of bread stuffs from his commissary. Chávez was asked to call such irregularities to the attention of Congress.[2]

Carleton's Indian management was damned by constant reports of raids. Bosque Redondo Navajos were blamed for much of the violence after Carleton claimed to have "safely sheltered" them.[3] Apache movements in the south were said to be another indication of the impunity with which Indians committed their "hellish atrocities and [went] unpunished under Carleton's regime."[4] *New Mexican* editor

Thomas Tucker accused the *Gazette* of using its unending attacks on the legislature to draw attention away from Carleton's "maladministration."[5] The *New Mexican* called for Carleton's dismissal. He could be sent "to some point where his greatness can develop itself, and not waste itself and run to seed, as it is destined to be should he remain unappreciated in New Mexico."[6]

The legislature voted in favor of Carleton's firing—nine votes to two in the council and sixteen to six in the house. After Governor Connelly vetoed the resolution, the majority of the assembly memorialized the president and Secretary of War Edwin Stanton with the charge that for more than three years the "general commanding" had failed "entirely in reducing the Indians to subordination or in giving peace and security to the people of this country" and had, moreover, "acquired credit and military position which he does not deserve." Carleton allegedly insulted Mexicans when he accused them of fomenting murders and thefts on settlements, "thereby vilely calumniating our people." In the "terrible calamity" of Bosque Redondo, only sutlers and speculators profited, claimed the Nuevomexicano officials as they humbly prayed that the government immediately replace Carleton with a more able officer.[7]

The *New Mexican* held that the legislative memorial expressed but the "voice and wish of the people," shown by the fact that the principal issue in the late election for delegate to Congress was Carleton's "usurpation and mismanagement" of Indian affairs, as confirmed by the defeat of his candidate Perea for delegate by more than two thousand votes. The paper pinned on the general new charges of financial, political, and moral corruption, throwing former delegate John Watts in for good measure and threatening to reveal other offenders.[8]

A minority in the territorial house opposed the proclamation of the majority. Its report expressed appreciation of Carleton's four years of concentrated military action, which it said had curtailed Navajo and Apache fighting.[9] Disgusted with the "false misrepresentations" made by "that ignorant majority for the purpose of venting their own private spleen against gentlemen with whom they have grievances," the *Gazette* noted the nugatory character of the anti-Carleton proclamation. The legislature had shot for a joint resolution but failed, said the paper, knowing that Governor Connelly would veto the attempt at character assassination.[10] The territorial binary vibrated. Nuevomexicanos in Mora County, which had gone for Perea, condemned by resolution the majority of legislators as men "controlled and directed by persons who have sinister motives, demagogues without principle, of doubtful patriotism and friends only of their own personal interests, who labor without ceasing to aggrandize themselves out of public offices."[11] The *Gazette* cited the gathering to alert readers of the "powerful indignation" rising against the "old imbecile" editor [Manderfield, probably] who was "exerting his feebleness through the columns of the *New Mexican* to justify the unprecedented, unjustifiable and unparliamentary, not to say disgraceful, conduct of the majority, or Chávez party, of the legislature."[12]

Un Ciudadano Libre (A free citizen) saw how the Mora gathering reflected the skewed regional economics of Bosque Redondo. As he recorded, the "loyal champions of the Carletonian cause" loved their country "very much," though "'the dog danced for the money,'" and interest was "more powerful than love [*'Amo a mi país mucho,' dicen los fieles campeones de la causa Carletoniana, pero 'por el dinero baila el perro'; y el interés más poderoso que el amor*]." The highest bidder owned the people's patriotism, Un Ciudadano Libre observed. It was with "traitorous hearts [*traidores corazones*]" that the Moreños "paid homage to the fiercest enemy of our land and its progress, to assure the prospect of some contractors [*le rinden homenajes públicamente al más feroz enemigo de nuestro país y su progreso, para asegurar el prospecto de algunos contratos*]." True to his moniker, Un Ciudadano Libre posed the issue of the liberal integration of Nuevomexicanos. The Mora demonstration was a "pretty way to demonstrate to the world that we appreciate our liberty, that we understand the institutions of our government, and that we know how to maintain and respect our rights, and that we are at the same time capable of governing ourselves [*Bonito modo de demostrar al mundo que apresiamos nuestra libertad que comprendemos las instituciones de nuestro Gobierno, y que sabes mantener y hacer respectar nuestros derechos, y que somos al mismo tiempo capazes de gobernarnos por sí mismos*]." The goal of the general government was to take its citizens to the "most elevated sphere of civilization and progress [*la esfera más elevado de la civilización y el progreso*]." Military agents, meanwhile, sought to degrade the people, to reduce and relegate them "to the disregard of the civilized world, like some weak miserables and underlings." Thanks to God, prayed

Un Ciudadano Libre, "an ant does not a summer make [*Pero gracias a Dios que una hormiga no hace verano*]." The people who appreciated liberty and respected their rights did not mind if Carleton "got pricked in the butt with his own bayonets" [*que Carleton le pique las nalgas con sus bayonetas*].[13]

In Valencia County the villages of Cebolleta, El Rito, and Cubero, located nearest the Navajo country and claiming to have more interest in the policy pursued by the military than the people of the interior, asked the secretary of war to keep Carleton in New Mexico. An Alburquerque meeting led by the veteran American Partyite Ambrosio Armijo praised Carleton's actions and the confidence the national government reposed in him, unanimously advising the legislature to "attend to legitimate subjects of legislation and not meddle with matters of a nature not pertinent to their trust."[14]

Carleton reminded the president of the fact the two previous legislatures had endorsed him, and he requested a court with a judge advocate to summon New Mexico legislators and other critics to answer under oath for their false and injurious charges.[15] The president's office assured Carleton it would not act on the New Mexico legislature's memorial that requested his removal.[16] But following the Doolittle Commission's visit, Gen. John Pope, commander of the Missouri Military Department, was appointed special agent to collect additional intelligence through interviews with private individuals, the governor, assembly leaders, and Carleton himself. Pope found unanimous endorsement of a reservation system but sharp differences of opinion regarding Bosque Redondo.[17] Carleton asked for the Indian Department to take over management of the reservation so that he could pursue bands that harassed ranches and travelers (due to the depletion of game at the hands of American frontiersmen). Congress was unwilling to appropriate monies for the support of Indians.[18] Massachusetts senator Charles Sumner called for an investigation into charges that Carleton approved his officers placing captured Indian children under their personal peonage.[19] California senator John Conness condemned on the floor of the Senate the administration of military affairs in New Mexico as "a shameful disgrace for many years." Conness recalled the fruitless years of effort he had made at reforming the system.[20] It mattered that Sumner, a leading Radical Republican, reserved special interest in the rights of the Freedmen, and

Conness, a Douglas Democrat, became close to President Lincoln politically and personally.

Chávez had his opportunity to lay the people's case against Carleton in Congress's hearings to consider withholding appropriations for management of the Navajos. On March 2, he pleaded before the House for continued funding and in the process presented a major critique of the actual military command in New Mexico. Colonel Canby, he began, had succeeded largely in bringing control over the Navajos. Broken treaties with consequent losses of stock and lives were ever present risks. Yet the sheep industry prospered in the aftermath of U.S. annexation. A treaty with the Navajo was fairly respected for seven years. Disaster was unleashed in 1858 when a Major Brooks, commanding Fort Defiance, ordered his guard to fire on Navajo stock that had been grazing at a hay camp. Navajos claimed the camp and surrounding land as exclusively theirs, Chávez explained, and their law called for "an eye for an eye and a tooth for a tooth." Navajo chief Cayetano, in the narrative, "proceeded to the Fort and knowing that a black boy at the post was the property of the commanding officer [Brooks], he deliberately drew an arrow and shot him dead on the spot." The ensuing war, Chávez portrayed, could have been prevented with skillful diplomacy on Brooks's part, instead turned unrelenting.

For a former citizen of Mexico, Chávez rode fast on the back of power accorded an American elected to Congress. He held federal Indian agents blameless in the Indian travesty, as the military failed to listen to their better counsel. The delegate cited Coyotero Apaches who in 1864 were thwarted by Carleton from visiting with trusted agent Dr. Michael Steck; Carleton forbade Steck from meeting with them. Offended Coyoteros refused to talk to the two officers Carleton sent in place of their friend. Chávez had Carleton unjustifiably inflicting a scorched earth policy on Navajos and compelling them to his Bosque Redondo reserve. The general demanded a pledge of surrender, submission, and compliance from warriors but proved incapable of providing promised feeding, care, and protection for their people. Chávez condemned Carleton as a false representative of the "great and powerful" and "humane" U.S. government, recognized as such by "every American and Mexican citizen and by every Indian that came in contact with him." Chávez contributed material for those in Congress who claimed that the Bosque Redondo enterprise cost too much and for those who said they were deceived by Carleton's promise to make Indians self-supporting. As he pointed out, the estimates should have been made before establishment of the reservation. Fault lay with those who had appointed "incompetent or dishonest officers" to discharge their "wishes."

Chávez blamed Carleton for Congress's lack of support for the Navajo. His impassioned protest against racialized colonialism called for Nuevomexicanos to stop being made to suffer for the general's irresponsibility. The people had done nothing to make Congress forget its treaty stipulations, he pointed out, yet they failed to receive their just protections. Congressmen may have considered New Mexico so poor that it would never repay their outlay. "Sir," Chávez addressed the House speaker in terms similar to Perea's in relation to the plea for the return of the Conejos, "supposing that this were true, did you do not force them to come into your government? They were living very happily under their own, and if you fail to make a good bargain are you going to play the child?" Chávez hoped not. As he asked, "What would you have done without the mines of California and Nevada during the late [Civil] War . . . [w]here you have procured your gold? Yet California and Nevada are only a small portion of the cession of the magnificent territory which Mexico made to you in 1848." He referred also to the five regiments of "gallant volunteers" that New Mexico furnished in defense of their "adopted mother" in the Civil War. Nuevomexicanos had a "love and affection" for the American government, Chávez noted. Did congressmen propose to forget their "solemn obligations by turning them over to the tender mercies of savages, goaded to desperation by the mismanagement of your authorized and recognized agents and by your failure to comply with your most solemn promises? God forbid that such a course should be pursued and that such counsels should prevail," Chávez concluded.[21]

Congress increased the Navajo appropriation.[22] Chávez pressed on with letters to Secretary of the Interior Orville Browning and Indian Commissioner Nathanial Taylor reiterating the charge of Carleton's "alleged mismanagement" at Bosque Redondo, pointing out that Carleton "came very near" to defeating the bill for Indian appropriations throughout the country in urging that the Navajo be relocated to other territories.[23] Shortly thereafter Gen. William T. Sherman and Samuel F. Tappan, a Christian crusader, of the Peace Commission that Congress established to work out treaties with the numerous Plains Indians in the West and northern Plains, met with the Navajo at Fort Sumner next to the Bosque Redondo reservation to negotiate their return to the lands of their ancestors.[24] The "proud and haughty General Carleton" relinquished his command of the District of New Mexico. The Department of the Interior conveyed authority over Bosque Redondo to the Bureau of Indian Affairs. Carleton left his command feeling proud of what he had accomplished.[25]

Final word of Carleton's removal arrived in New Mexico later in the fall.[26] The *New Mexican*, Arny, Benedict, and Watrous rejoiced at his repudiation. Not to let the partisanship go slack, the *Gazette* lauded the Bosque Redondo reservation and predicted that history would vindicate Carleton.[27] The War Department reassigned Carleton to his old regiment on the Gulf of Mexico.[28] Granted a leave from duty, he remained in Santa Fe to see about developing his mining investments and received an extension on the time off, which lasted until December 1868.[29] He thus remained among friends and against his partisan enemies. On June 1, 1868, the Navajo chief Manuelito and the other Navajo leaders signed the "last treaty between their tribe and the Americans." As Jennifer Nez Denetdale observes, "Even though the Navajos would be allowed to claim only a portion of the land they had once inhabited, they were still joyful. Seventeen days later, more than eight thousand began the journey home."[30]

Fixing on the Settler Colonial

The *New Mexican* held great expectations for the 1865–66 territorial assembly, dominated as it was by its Administration Party allies, followers of the powerful José Francisco Chávez. President Miguel E. Pino controlled the council absolutely. At a caucus held at his home to name the session's officers, the posts of house speaker and the lion's share of clerks and other session employees were assured for his party; representatives from counties that went against Chávez would miss out on the spoils. Members of the minority did not take well to their exclusion, particularly those from Taos County, one of the largest districts with four members in the house. Taos councilman Pascual Martínez made an effort in the caucus to give his county a voice in the selection of legislative officers. This emerging partisan moment was reinforced by the *Gazette*, which accused Pino of falsely prejudicing the representatives of the National Union party, labeling them incapable officers and accusing them of always being under the influence of whiskey. The *Gazette* labeled the Taos critics of Pino "independent men who so manfully cut themselves loose from the [assembly] clique and did their duty to their county and to their Territory."[31] They were indeed becoming a force to reckon with.

The strength of Pino's majority accomplished much, beginning with adoption of a Republican Reconstruction plank. The spread of egalitarian ideas throughout the western states was causing a transition in the relations between masters and servants.[32] The abolitionist Secretary William Arny encouraged the assembly to break with recent history by repealing the last of the "offensive and noxious" slave laws Miguel A. Otero and party had foisted on the territory, their standing in direct conflict with the laws of Congress. The legislature did not exactly expunge peonage; the system was reformed by granting the worker a greater voluntary warrant in his contract. Servant and master were obligated to respect each other's rights under penalty of law.[33] Provisions for enforcing the servitude law remained weak, and so peonage itself remained customary in sections of New Mexico.[34] Governor Connelly and James Collins explained to the public that the institution had existed in New Mexico for over two hundred years and could not be abruptly ended without bringing injury to both masters and servants. Peónes needed to file a legal brief against masters to break their financial bondage, they advised. At the start of 1866 the *New Mexican* affirmed with pride that progressive Administration Party legislators were starting to eradicate debt bondage.[35]

The partisan energies were recharged with a change in the *Gazette*. José Francisco Perea managed to have James Collins appointed director of the territorial federal depository before leaving the delegate's office. John T. Russell took ownership and editorial duties of the *Gazette*. Russell proved his mettle in a previous stint as *Gazette* editor, supporting Perea's run for delegate. Here he stepped into the role of dissident enraged at the government that had swung back to the Mexican Party orientation. Territorial legislators provided the close range targets for his invective, racialized at that.

The *Gazette* printed a letter that Judge Benedict had sent to Indian Affairs Commissioner William Dole regarding two Nuevomexicanos who had taken oaths of office and made bond to be commissioned as

Indian agents. Benedict vouchsafed their community standing but thought it prudent to note that they and four other agents could not keep their accounts or report back in the English language. Clerks or friends would be required to translate the paperwork. Benedict warned the commissioner that much depended on the "good faith" of the assistants "who may be trusted in a confidential relation with the officers in this portion of the Indian affairs." Russell interpreted the request, appropriate though it seems to have been, to mean that Benedict believed those who did not understand English were "not competent to discharge the duties of an Indian Agent." The judge would find not one in fifty persons "to the manor born fit for positions of public trust and profit," Russell wrote. Russell had Benedict boasting of having "furnished brains for the Mexican people" and making "such strong professions of paternal feeling and love for the dear people whose confidence he has hoped to secure whilst he was thus giving them a stab in the back through the Indian Department in Washington City."[36]

Majority members of the assembly denounced in a resolution to President Andrew Johnson the "vile calumniators" of Benedict and the Mexican people. They declared the *Gazette* men "positive enemies of our interests and of the Present Administration."[37] The *Gazette* dismissed their effort as a "legislative mendacity," its sponsors "unconscionable liars" to whom Russell accepted the title of enemy. He claimed to have the sympathy of the Democratic president, swearing that he and his cabinet could have no respect for those who had fomented the memorial. All but one in that majority did not know what it published, he lampooned, for they did not understand the English language, "and yet they, ignorant as they are, intend to sit in judgment upon us and tell their lies to the administration. Poor, pitiful, low bred souls," he sneered. "Do you think that the Administration—that is, those who are entrusted with the conduct of the Government of the great United States—will be gulled by the malicious lies of such creatures as you, who are but little above the savage who eats the vermin that he picks from his filthy body?"[38]

Mexican Party Nuevomexicanos obliged Russell's double-barreled provocation. Their flushed indignation may have failed to offer an explicit defense of the indigenes against the editor's scurrilous allusion, but they did not fuel it at least. Indeed, one characterized the editor's body itself as the one tormented with insects.[39] An anonymous Nuevomexicano legislator defined Russell's chief sin as one of attempting to ruin his people's republicanism (for the full Spanish text, see appendix 2). The representative and his colleagues were elected by "the people," he laid out, in order to secure and defend their rights. The "scamp" and "bandit" Russell attacked them for this reason and also for the benefit of the governor who paid the editor for his favoritism. Since the annexation of New Mexico, the solon affirmed, close to three thousand Americans had emigrated to reside within "our borders" from other parts of the Union, some with their families. A majority of them sympathized "in all respects" with the Nuevomexicano people. "Notwithstanding their ignorance" of the people's customs, they arrived with the aim of establishing themselves to help in the advancement of "our country" and not to consider themselves superior "to us." In return they received the patriotism and help of Mexicans. Others harbored prejudices against "our race." The images promulgated by Russell (adding those of *New Mexico Press* editor Hezekiah Johnson), were prime examples, said the legislator, of insulting attacks on the people. They humiliated Nuevomexicanos "in all manner and in the most low and miserable terms, making us appear as the most ridiculous, if not immoral, corrupt, and ignorant people that has resided on the land." "Santiago" L. Collins was placed among the "bedbugs" of prejudice in New Mexico.

The statement went on to characterize Russell's presence as having "fouled the land." The editor was not even acceptable in his home state of Virginia, the writer claimed. He would never respect the humble, simple, and generous Mexican people, who extended their hospitality to all emigrants wanting to reside among them, whose good and benign heart did not admit of any false preoccupations against any person. Would they permit Russell, the "resuscitated flea," continue his abuses and taunts? Would they patiently tolerate the "invader of our rights" using the power of their liberties against them, placing a cloud over their eyes to make them believe he was one of their loyal defenders? Would the people submit to the mandates and orders of the *Gazette*, the "vile instrument of miserable egoistic agitators?" If the people supported their representatives so that legislators would defend their rights, the elected official affirmed, they would express their gratitude. They did not desire to be the representatives of slaves or of a people who patiently received the outrages made against them at every pass.[40]

In the spirit of a homeland's resistance to colonialism, another complainant called Russell a *vagabundo pelado* (wayfaring ruffian), enemy of the New Mexican soil, scorpion in disguise, who, with "diabolical sentiments," insulted the people with his rag of a paper, principally because the legislature did not fund him (for the full text in Spanish, see appendix 3).[41] Council President Miguel E. Pino pulled in a once usable label for his party, calling on the people not to patronize "certain tailed men" who made themselves known by the way in which they treated Mexicans in order to have their booty. Pino defended the members of the legislature as knowing their sphere. Nothing was done out of the wisdom of man, Pino philosophized, but according to the will of the Most High (*por voluntad del Altísimo*).[42] A self-denominated elder likened Russell to the "perfidious Hamman [*pérfido Amán*]" in the Book of Esther, who would have exterminated the Jews of Persia if he could have. Russell would do likewise to Nuevomexicanos, slowly, on every occasion he could find to dishonor and disgrace them. Just as Hamman had the support of King Ahasuerus, so was the defiler Russell backed by the governor, who assumed that in the "provinces of his rule [*provincias de su mando*]" the people were not capable of governing themselves or of deriving profit for themselves. The writer recalled the "taunting furies" and "dishonest perversities of hell [*furias dicterios desacatos, deshonestidades y todas las perversidades del infierno*]" that the *Gazette* had hurled at don José Manuel Gallegos when he ran for Congress, which discredited Nuevomexicanos by extension, subjecting them to all the "cultivated Powers [*Potencias cultas*]" in the land so that they passed judgment on the people. It was not necessary to learn English to see it, the Spanish speaker declared.[43]

The unfazed Russell accused Pino of stirring the pot in his official position to advance personal ambition. Pino denied it.[44] After Carleton, Russell helped Pino allies get the icon of the racist and exploitative colonizer, an agent of oppression, into the political system, in due time to affect other Euroamerican settlers.

Statehood Revolution Sabotaged

Governor Connelly asked the legislature to deliberate a request of Congress to make New Mexico one of the "sovereign states" of the

Union. Connelly offered a historical lesson. Its independence was undercut by the three parent governments of Spain, Mexico, and the United States. Statehood, conceived much like its own nation state, would strengthen New Mexico and protect it from further reductions to its land base beyond its recent losses of the Arizona section and the Conejos region to Colorado, especially as many citizens in the southern portion continued to lobby for their own territory. New Mexico was in a "retarded condition" compared to its neighbor territories, Connelly put the modernization argument. Arizona, with its mineral resources, seemed to develop faster than New Mexico and, along with Colorado and Nebraska, could well beat New Mexico to statehood. Progress would come in road construction, increased land cultivation, and the end of Indian wars, benefits to override the costs of taxes.[45]

Connelly seems to have acted independently, interestingly enough, for the American Party position of the year before had rejected a move for statehood, and here, Pino's Administration Party legislature responded positively to the governor. Connelly was authorized, as he requested, to announce the holding of a convention on the last Monday of April for the purpose of framing a state constitution for submission to the people for a vote of approval or rejection, and if approved, that it be presented to Congress. The election of delegates to the convention, to be organized by the judges of probate in the counties, was scheduled for the first Monday of March 1866, the election on the constitution for the fourth Monday of June.[46] The Pino-dominated legislature advocated on behalf of statehood as it had in 1864–65. The preamble to its congressional memorial asking for approval of the constitution-writing plan stressed Nuevomexicanos fully capable of self-government. Members claimed that Congress waited to hear of the people's wish to form a republican government. Delegate Chávez submitted the memorial to the House Committee on Territories.[47]

True to his party, Secretary Arny supported the statehood effort by citing the Massachusetts Radical Republican senator Benjamin Wade and credited himself for repeal of the "odious" Free Slavery Act and for defining a "voluntary" peonage system to replace the coercive form. As no color qualification for voting existed in New Mexico, Arny emphasized, it would be a "Free State, in the full sense of that term." Arny received a ninety-day leave from the legislature to join Chávez in Washington, ostensibly to encourage investment in mining with an implied intent to lobby for statehood. In February legislative members and other officials rallied to express their enthusiasm for the movement.[48] The *New Mexican* reported on statehood as an Administration Party initiative. It praised the Administration (Mexican Party) legislators for their labor on behalf of statehood "that must forever cover their names in glory."[49]

The *Gazette* approached the Statehood Revolution circumspectly at first. Russell suggested that it would be better to let the proposal stand as the primary issue to distinguish candidates in the next election for delegate to Congress.[50] Russell grew hostile as the legislature pressed the issue. It had been "so suddenly and so unceremoniously sprung upon the people," he feared, that everyone had little choice but to submit. There was no appeal process in place, "no power in the hands of the people to prevent the election of delegates, the assemblage of the convention and the formation of the constitution."[51] The more Russell pondered, the ornerier his resistance grew. The only reason the assembly ordered a constitution, he opined, was that delegate Chávez informed them that they were "all on their own," for he was incapable of having his friends appointed to particular positions, citing as an example Tomás Cabeza de Baca, who had made clear his desire to be governor.[52] The timing of the convention was all wrong, Russell nitpicked, with delegates having to leave at the busiest time and needing to remain the whole time the convention was in session without compensation. He advised folks in the counties to stand aloof from the effort, "neither put candidates in the field nor vote for those who are brought out." In square partisan stance, Russell affirmed, "If the opposition party should proffer to make up mongrel tickets, we would counsel that the proposition be declined." Leave it in the hands of those who had originated it, Russell counseled.[53]

The *Gazette* reported a finding that the people in the territory were giving statehood a cool reception. Only those who expected a reward of office pushed for it. "There are some ambitious persons here in Santa Fe who cannot, by their own exertions make a respectable living," Russell assayed, "and who wish to mount the people and ride upon them into office and emolument, who would gladly see a State government formed," citing "Pino, Benedict &c, &c," as "specimen bricks" of pro-statehood. Tax increases under statehood for a poor citizenry had been a consistent American Party complaint from the beginning, and

Russell repeated it here. The people did not see why they should "consent to be taxed and oppressed in order that such men may live in idle [ease] and luxury, whilst they are toiling and earning their bread in the sweat of their brows." Russell predicted the statehood proposition going down regardless of the content of the constitution.[54]

The *New Mexican* thought the opposite. It argued that no "good citizen" could possibly object to a well-written constitution. There were two classes of men standing opposed to statehood, the weekly explained. The members of one had lived "perhaps for twenty years in the territory, accumulated fortunes and have done well [implying American Party vets with their monopoly on the spoils of territorial government], and now they imagine that any change would be ruinous to their future desires of property." Next to those who opposed progress, and feared for the destruction of their beloved resources, were the less honest set of "hungry demagogues" who thought that by agitating against statehood they could raise themselves above their "merited place in oblivion" to a level of respectability. This group was a type dangerous to any community, for its members never acted from pure motives, "their designs" always "dark and ulterior," their "guiding star ... self-aggrandizement, instead of the welfare of the whole people though it carry with it destruction to all others." Yet, as the writer allowed, everyone had a right to an opinion. For those who thought a constitution undesirable, they could oppose it. "The [presumed rational] people are to decide, and to their will we will have to submit."[55]

Counties conducted nomination meetings for the convention election. The one in Santa Fe, according to the *New Mexican*, was dominated by the Pino-Chávez Administration Party but was attended by the Union Partyites José Manuel Gallegos and R. H. Thomkins.[56] Indicating popular differences, "tickets" were formed in Bernalillo, Valencia, and Doña Ana counties. The *New Mexican* beamed that the civic field put up "some of the best, ablest and most influential men [as candidates] in those counties; men who would stand high" at the convention, "in whom people have confidence, and who wield a powerful influence and will reflect credit on whatever measure they undertake."[57] Two of five Bernalillo County candidates were Nuevomexicano, a sign of the growing presence of Euroamericans there.[58] Socorro and Doña Ana counties, on the other hand, saw only one Euroamerican among the six nominees.[59]

In San Miguel County, the statehood slate lost by a sizeable majority of the 730 votes cast. The official report showed that all twelve of those elected and all twelve of those defeated were Nuevomexicanos. A current of liberal principle ran through the process, perhaps because of its growing partisanship. Probate judge Rafael Romero reported that those who self-nominated were rejected because they would "convert themselves into usurpers of the public right." As "the people" were the ones having the right to deliberate in common in all the issues before them, Romero advised, "this doctrine would be followed in the County ... from then on."[60]

The *New Mexican* still saw the statehood proposal winning out. Tucker expressed faith in the "intelligent" native population accepting the constitution "so framed." Not to forget the recent jagged past, the weekly said that the opposition emanated from the "friends of the late rebellion." Significantly, the *New Mexican* expressed the ongoing objection to race-colonial settlers, calling for a provision allowing the people to "escape from the rule of strangers, who, be they ever so patriotic and intelligent, are ignorant of our language and people and are not identified with the interests of our territory." The weekly named the territorial adjutant general Charles Clever as an example, someone who held office for more than four years, during which time thousands of dollars had been appropriated for surveys of lands in the territory, yet remained unused while not an acre was surveyed. The paper lashed out at former delegates Watts and Perea for not making the surveyor general perform his constituted duty.[61]

The *Gazette* thought the *New Mexican* contradicting itself, first stating that the opponents of statehood were the "cowards" who had lived in New Mexico a great number of years, then calling the anti-statehood advocates secession sympathizers. In classic assimilation posture, Russell accused its opponent of venturing to draw lines between the "natives and the American citizens," a "dodge" that would "not win" as the Mexican population did not seem to be so largely in favor of a state government at this time. Russell heard large numbers of persons, "of all classes," seriously objecting to the movement. The reasons would be known, he assured, not only by the Mexicans but by Americans before the vote on the constitution, save in Valencia County, implying the sway of delegate Chávez in his home district.[62]

Chávez, for his part, had every confidence of the convention devising a strong constitutional framework. He disseminated a long Spanish-language call for the people to ratify it before it actually got written, didactically tallying minuses and pluses.[63] The costs of maintaining a state government would be more than offset by the "stream of prosperity and riches to spring from the power of influence and the independence in which the contemplated change would advance the people of New Mexico [*la corriente de la prosperidad y riquezas que diminará del poder del influjo y de la independencia en que el cambio contemplado trata de avanzar el pueblo de Nuevo Méjico*]," he argued. Chávez saw the popular will invested with the power to moderate and limit the salaries of public officials. The legislature's laws would not be subject to revision and abrogation by an authority "most high." The people would have the right to elect their own representatives and remove at their pleasure any officials who were "disloyal, instead of being obligated to send your grievances to [Washington], where they are treated with negligence and indifference, and frequently depreciated" [*cuando fueran infieles, en lugar de estar obligados de mandar vuestras quejas á esta ciudad, en donde se atienden con negligencia é indiferencia, y frecuentemente menospreciadas*]. Sounding in the key of liberal anti-colonialism, Chávez emphasized that the "most sacred and beloved right [*el derecho más sagrado y más caro*]" of freemen was to "make their own laws and elect their own governors [*hacer sus Propias leyes y elijir sus propios gobernadores*]."

Chávez jabbed like a loyal Mexican Partyite at the Euroamerican outsiders, governors, and judges who exercised dictatorial authority over the people but who did not deserve their posts and had no special interest in the territory's well-being. He blamed past presidents for sending too few who were "capable, honorable and loyal." Under statehood, Chávez guaranteed, the laws would be the people's laws, "subject to be changed, emended and abrogated only by our own will." While New Mexicans had the right to elect their delegate to Congress, in no way was he a "true legislative representative," being completely "impotent and devalued," even though New Mexico had a population larger than one or two existing states in the Union.

Statehood would settle the Indian wars, Chávez pressed it. The tribes had roamed practically without interruption and there had not been any security "for any part of life and property, except in the settlements, and even there, the people have not been free of their bloody invasions and predations."⁶⁴ The delegate envisioned a grand future for New Mexico's bucolic but threatened beauty, reminiscent of CEMAPA fifteen years before when New Mexicans debated whether to ask for American annexation. "Your beautiful and fertile valleys," he wrote, "cultivated and fomented by the hand of industry, would produce measures of riches and infinite prosperity, instead of what has remained stripped and fruitless, and our stock and herds have been robbed before the fury of the savage like the leaves of the bosques [forests] snatched by the winds of the storm [*Vuestros valles hermosos y fértiles, cultivados y fomentados por la mano de la industria, producirían riquezas medidas, y prosperidad infinita, muestras que al contrario han permanecido despojado é infrutuosos, y vuestros rebaños y manadas han sido arrojados delante la furia del salvaje como las ojas de los bosques son arrebatadas por el soplo de la tempestad*]." The government turned a deaf ear to the people's shouts for more troops. Self-interest perhaps in mind, Chávez highlighted the benefits of having U.S. senators and congressmen. The states of Minnesota, Oregon, and Kansas had suffered equally from neglect, Indian problems, and injustice while they were territories, he argued, "until they came out of obscurity to the light of the robustness, leaving behind the imbecilities of a territorial government, as they appropriated the healthy and powerful attributes of a state." To follow their example, New Mexico's "beautiful forests [would] blossom with the fruits of industry, its hills reveal their hidden riches, and the whole land shine with the happiness of prosperity, and the peace of the hand of justice will extend to the people who have been despoiled of their possessions by the disordered Indian."

"When New Mexico presents a constitution with the title of its Independence and sovereignty," Chávez bore on, "ratified and sealed by the voice of its people, the doors of the Union will open widely, and it will be cordially received into the family of states. It will be a very important occasion. . . . a festive day, in which its troubles and tribulations will be consigned to the tomb of the past and its future will be illuminated by the rainbow of promise." Only the coward would raise the shout of "taxation" to impede the march to that future. Chávez closed by calling on the people to unite without concern for personal relations or past parties in the work of "patriotism and duty" to their common country.

A who's who from both sides of New Mexico's partisan line participated in the statehood convention. Judge Sydney Hubbell called it to order, his nominal Mexican Party opponent, Miguel E. Pino, serving as president pro tem. Kirby Benedict made a number of nominations. Delegates from nine of ten counties presented credentials, Santa Fe represented by Anastacio Sandoval, R. H. Thomkins, José Manuel Gallegos, Kirby Benedict, Miguel Pino, and Simón Delgado. The proceedings of the second day involved an ambiguously reported series of exchanges over the credentials of delegates and whether or not a quorum existed. The Committee on Credentials confirmed the eligibility of the thirty-one members who reported, and no other delegates presented certificates. Noting a quorum, Hubbell asked for the convention to proceed to a permanent organization. The motion was disputed. The minutes report a "long discussion" involving Gallegos, Thomkins, Benedict, and R. H. Stapleton of Socorro County. The Credentials Committee accepted the certificates submitted late by Gregorio Otero of Valencia County and Francisco Sandoval of Santa Ana, and on Hubbell's motion the convention voted to accept Otero and Sandoval as delegates.

As the proceedings reconvened after a break, Hubble reported the lack of a quorum and "no prospect to obtain a majority of delegates from the several counties." With a handful in attendance, he moved adjournment. The minutes mention "some remarks" made regarding the "prejudicial conduct towards the community" by "some persons whose efforts" had been exerted "to embarrass the progress and advancement of this people." Miguel Pino and the other acting officers were thanked for their "good disposition" in assisting the convention to comply with the intent of the law under which they had met. The convention disbanded *sine die*—without a plan to reconvene.[65]

It is hard to know what happened, although the defeat marked a blow to the Chávez-Pino force. In his allusion, historian Robert Larson says one observer reported scorn having been heaped on the statehood leaders.[66] It would suggest a key number of delegates attending with the aim of laying the movement in its grave. In a later communication to the *Gazette,* a Nuevomexicano indicated a strong reaction to Chávez's call for the people to support statehood and younger people in the Administration Party skeptical of the pie-in-the-sky prospects of statehood, expressing especially the concern for a poor population exposed to exorbitant taxes for the material and institutional upkeep of statehood.[67]

The *Gazette* claimed to have in its possession a letter Chávez wrote to Diego Archuleta, chairman of the opposing Union Party Executive Committee, expressing support for statehood. (Archuleta may have provided the letter to Russell.) Chávez supposedly said that the "strongest argument which my opponents use is that I am anti-American, besides others which they

> have not been able to maintain, but every person believes the first because it is only necessary to state that I am an Anti-American, and it is believed. . . . One of the chief projects of these men is, if they cannot rule New Mexico, to divide her and in this way destroy our political existence and self-regard forever. It ought to incite us to unity of action for the purpose of combating the suicidal policy of these adventurers. This is not written for the purpose of exerting an influence over you, but for the sole purpose of putting you on your guard against your friends, in whom you have so much confidence. We ought, as sons of New Mexico and descendants of a noble race, to unite ourselves and make common cause against the policy of our common enemy.

Chávez expressed the Mexican Party's objection to race colonialism, the belief that New Mexico was being run by outsiders removing the rights of Nuevomexicanos. His position defined Nuevomexicanos as the majority interest group that should have democratic control over the territory within a pluralistically informed advocacy for statehood.

Russell interpreted the letter to demonstrate both Chávez and the *New Mexican* using the statehood cause to drive "Americans" out of the Territory, oppressing them "by a system of legislation that would make it almost an impossibility for them to remain." The editor hoped that the people of New Mexico would not join Chávez and his organ, the *New Mexican*, "in their efforts to stir up a war of races in this part of the country. We hope they will repudiate and spurn the diabolical proposition and leave these impostors to work out their own salvation." Russell asked according to a core American Party line for the people to "conduct themselves as citizens of the United States and not as 'Sons of New Mexico and descendants of a noble race' in the sense that Mr. Chávez and his supporters would have them understand it."[68] It was an argument that Russell could well have used in the private effort to defeat the statehood movement.

FIG. 23. *Governor of New Mexico Robert B. Mitchell, 1866–69*, ca. 1869, copy photograph by William R. Walton. An American Partyite, Mitchell became one of the bitterest enemies of the Mexican Party in all of territorial New Mexico. Courtesy Palace of the Governors Photo Archives, NMHM/DCA, negative #010294.

Extraordinary Executive-Legislative Imbroglios

In the credible report out of Washington in February 1866, President Andrew Johnson was set to dismiss Governor Henry Connelly, Chief Justice Kirby Benedict, and Territorial Secretary William Arny. It did not surprise the *New Mexican*. The government had been endeavoring to record those who heralded their lives and fortunes in defense of the union, it noted. They had demands; it would be "ingratitude" to refuse them.[69] *New Mexican* editors William Manderfield and Thomas Tucker had been opposing much of Connelly's gubernatorial program, but they regarded the governor as eminently qualified based on his superior knowledge of the Spanish language and intimate ties to Nuevomexicanos. He had endeavored to discharge his duties "with an eye single" to their advancement and to the best of his abilities.[70]

As historian Gary Roberts notes, "No one understood the fragile nature of the Republican hold on New Mexico better than Arny, and when rumors reached New Mexico that changes were contemplated in the territorial offices, even he confessed that it would be advantageous [for building the Party] 'to ignore all applications from persons in New Mexico and appoint well known and reliable Republicans who have never been here.'" The new appointees for New Mexico were understood as "warm and personal friends of the president."[71] The problem, of course, was that President Andrew Johnson was no Republican at all.

Connelly introduced his successor on a stage in the plaza on July 16, 1866. Robert B. Mitchell, born in Ohio, received his political indoctrination in Kansas, was severely wounded as a lieutenant in the war with Mexico, rose to major general in the Civil War, and was cited for outstanding bravery. He had most recently fought tribes in Nebraska and Wyoming. Connelly noted Mitchell's brilliant record as a statesman, patriot, and soldier. Mitchell forecast in his remarks a bright future for New Mexico with increased immigration. He referenced New Mexico's well-known needs, such as a worthy educational system, and he (prophetically) mentioned the "sealed treasures of uncoined gold and silver" waiting to be recovered.[72] Connelly suffered a precipitous illness soon after stepping down as governor and passed away on August 12 at age sixty-six. Bishop Lamy presided in the cathedral over the funeral for the stepfather of delegate Chávez. Connelly had played a pivotal role in the conquest of New Mexico. He occupied a prominent place in the shift of the Mexican department to an American territory, and he led with decided firmness as New Mexico's "Civil War Governor." As one of the "adopted natives," he engaged New Mexico's binary politics, serving as an American Party traveler with tempered partisanship and as an agent for promoting the inclusion of Nuevomexicanos in American historicity.[73]

The *New Mexican* saw signs of independence in Mitchell's initial conduct in the governor's office, appearing with "wisdom," seeking to "unite the people" by promoting all their interests while putting down the "strife, jealousies and bickerings" that had "hung like an incubus over us, retarding our prosperity and caus[ing] us to appear ridiculous abroad."[74] The weekly felt consoled by the other fresh federal appointees for they had not "emanated" from the friends of its traditional partisan enemy in the territory, the "clique" that had so long "sucked government pap to support a precarious existence."[75]

Mitchell settled in, only to catch the investor's extractive fever in the desert, the fancy that New Mexico's mineral lodes dwarfed all others in the West. There they lay, it seemed, waiting for the hand of the crafty entrepreneur.[76] The governor inspected the traces of gold, silver, platinum, copper, iron and zinc in company of Gen. James H. Carleton and Charles Clever, a portentous duo indeed with respect to the partisan imperative waiting to crank up again. His temperature running high, Mitchell left New Mexico four months after the start of his term in company with Carleton to see about attracting investors for their mining interests.[77] It soon enough became clear that Mitchell held no interest in building a Republican Party in New Mexico. The politics resulting from his absence—accentuated by Mitchell's imperious bearing, akin to Carleton's unyielding arrogance—would go on to gash New Mexico's political structure and cough up the challenger to José Francisco Chávez's seat in Congress.[78]

The *New Mexican* now found itself scoffing at Mitchell offering "gingerbread titles" to mines he barely knew. Distressing too, the governor packed off ostensibly to exert influence in Congress when New Mexico already had an "able," "worthy," and "competent" delegate to conduct its work. Personal considerations motivated the gratuitous trip, it was charged: not only Mitchell's hope of profit from mining speculation but his effort to politic for an increase in his salary. It was understood that Mitchell planned on stopping in Kansas

FIG. 24. *Don Trinidad Alarid*, ca. 1890, photographer unknown. Alarid became one of the younger Nuevomexicanos to enlist in the Mexican Party in the 1860s. Courtesy Palace of the Governors Photo Archives, NMHM/DCA, negative #006988.

to work for the reelection of one of its U.S. senators, a Democrat at that. Most critical, the people wanted to see the governor tending "to his *legitimate duties*" as presider of New Mexico's legislative session, which he would miss, rather than going off on a "political pilgrimage in behalf of his alter ego Carleton, and his party." The *New Mexican*, picking up on a new national coinage, stated that the Mitchell-military "ring" hid the "shameful desertion of his Excellency" when he was most needed in the territory.[79]

Miguel Pino's legislature groused at a governor abandoning his first assembly session. At least the Administration majority had the consolation of a friend in the territorial secretary.[80] Arny was slated for replacement, but in one of those situations rife with entanglement, the new appointee was delayed in getting to New Mexico. Arny, toting the unanimous support of the council, successfully requested Congress to allow him to continue as secretary until expiration of his term in February.[81] Thus would he step in as acting governor in Mitchell's absence.

Arny took to the governorship with the charged energy he had adopted in the same assignment in 1862, advancing in his address to the assembly a forceful plan for the development of the territory. But National Unionists balked at what they called their old enemy's self-appointment insofar as his replacement had been named by the president. The main opposition to Arny blew from five-sixths of Taos County's legislative delegation, headed by Councilman Pascual Martínez, whom Miguel Pino had nixed out of any legislative committees. The Taoseños lodged a formal request for attorney general Charles Clever to render a legal opinion as to the validity of Arny's assumption of the role of territorial secretary. Clever, the Union Partyite, determined in his brief that Arny, the Administration Partyite, assumed the authority of acting secretary illegally. Arny's acts were null and void as both acting governor and secretary, Clever found, for they worked against the rights and interests of the people.[82] The *Gazette* described Arny as lacking the personal qualifications to discharge the duties of governor. The *New Mexican* said the disparagement stemmed from the fact that Arny had recently canceled the *Gazette*'s printing contract. The *New Mexican*, which had the contract, flew into a raging support of Arny as acting governor, praising his "able" and "faithful" discharge of all his official duties.[83] Arny appealed Clever's decision to the council, which, after what the *New Mexican* called a "full investigation," voted to recognize the acting governor.[84]

Former congressional delegate Francisco Perea joined the dissenting Taos delegation—including, in addition to Pascual Martínez, House members Buenaventura Lovato, José Antonio Martínez y Medina, Pedro García, and Santos Muñiz—in an effort to remove Arny as acting territorial secretary and acting governor based on Clever's finding. In putting Arny's authority as secretary on the table, the protestors blocked legislative business.[85] The *New Mexican* called it sedition, malice, and improper influence.[86] But in the evolving round of partisanship, Taos County became severely split. The Chavista Rafael Chacón decried the "obstructionism" of his fellow Taos County colleagues and called the *Gazette*'s attack on the majority legislature anti-Mexican bias. Russell scolded the "whipper-snapper" Chacón for laying his "dirty hands" on the paper and condemned him for having, "peon-like, gone to the service of Pino & Co." Russell swore to help elect to public office "gentlemen and Christians."[87]

Chacón may have lain behind the mass meeting in Taos County that disavowed Pascual Martínez's caucus. Its resolutions emphasized the "rightful" business of their assemblymen to legislate on subjects of relevance to the "necessities and requirements of the people," not to oppose the constitutional authorities of the general government. The "erroneous counsels" of Francisco Perea should not have been followed, they further declared. In not recognizing the territorial executive, they negated their own power as representatives, for without a governor, the legislative body could not exist. The governor was an essential member of the legislature, the assemblage pointed out, shown in the absolute power to approve or veto the bills passed by the assembly. Their own representatives failed in their duty by refusing to "unite with the legislative Council to hear the message of the governor," failing to give attention to his "many and useful" recommendations, "thereby failing to comply by the duties for which they were sent and occupying themselves only in applauding a seditious clique headed by F. Perea."[88] An anonymous Nuevomexicano took the voters of Perea to be non-rational for associating with the "party" famous for "trampling" on the interests of New Mexico and the Organic Law, sending up individuals not interested in the problems afflicting paisanos.[89]

The anti-Arny, anti-Pino Taos legislators responded by calling themselves independent fighters of the resolution's "despotic authors," who attempted to act as an "omnipotent power," dispensing with truth and making attributions that betrayed the "intelligent people of Taos." Their own acts in Santa Fe were impartial, they affirmed, carried out with due respect to the honor and solemnity of the legislative mandate, and with the "free mission of the people of Taos" in mind in order to work "with honor and conscience for the rights and wishes of their constituents," not as instruments to do the will of "any ambitious persons of Santa Fe, or from any other places." They asked the Taoseños to grant them justice and to refrain from managing their political deliberations based on the despots rather than their "free rights."[90]

Arny submitted airtight confirmation of the validity of his acting secretary role. The U.S. secretary of the treasury placed $20,000 to his credit for disbursement in territorial expenses. The allotment was presented to the U.S. House, together with provision in the Organic Act that required the territorial secretary to assume the responsibilities of a governor in the case of death, removal, resignation, or other "necessary absence" from the territory until another governor could be duly appointed to fill the vacancy. The Republican Congress decreed that as the appointed secretary had not yet arrived, and it was rumored that he was lobbying for a federal appointment in one of the states, the position of acting secretary legitimately fell to Arny. The *New Mexican* published the coincidental proceedings of a U.S. senatorial committee in which two members severely criticized territorial officials who absented themselves from official duty, a "very great abuse," one called it. The other called the appointment of such men as would leave their posts for months on end "a plague upon the people of the territories of the United States," and recommended that selection for such positions be made "with more care." Midway through the session, the procedural obstacle in the territorial house was removed and the assembly proceeded with its work.[91]

The majority immediately approved Arny's request for two militia regiments to confront increasing Indian conflict.[92] It also adopted Arny's measure to outlaw indentured labor in New Mexico to conform with the Thirteenth Amendment to the U.S. Constitution, outlawing both servitude and absolute slavery. In passing the anti-peonage and anti-Indian slavery bills, Nuevomexicano members participated in the colonial, albeit progressive, proto-Republican dismantling of two of their people's traditional practices.[93] In politicizing these issues, the *Gazette* expanded on the terms of partisanship. Russell answered Senator Sumner's attack on Connelly, Carleton, and Democrats for allowing peonage and Indian slavery with the claim that they had been the ones to "set the seal" in 1861 of "official disapprobation upon a custom which they found in full force in New Mexico upon their installation to power, and they used all means at their command to prevent any further traffic in captive Indians." According to Russell, the personal enemies of Carleton could not cite a single instance in which he had "done injustice to a peon, an *Indian slave*, or any person in an humble position in life." Then came the irony out of José Francisco Chávez's family: "[H]is mother, with whom he stays while at home in this territory, has, beyond a shadow of a doubt, the most numerous lot of Mexican peons and Indian slaves of any one family in New Mexico." As such, Arny stood as a "propagandist of peonage and Indian servitude."[94]

The *New Mexican* claimed to have proof of Carleton using troops to return a runaway peon to a Nuevomexicano rancher who furnished provisions to Bosque Redondo. "This looks like the general setting his seal of official approbation upon such a custom, rather than disapprobation." It pointed out that Chávez's mother was the wife of Governor Connelly, and if the governor had "'set the seal of his official disapprobation upon peonage in 1861,' why did he not liberate those same slaves, peons and Indians that are now placed to the credit of Col. Chávez? In this we see a shameless attempt to misrepresent Col. Chávez at the expense of a good man who has gone to his grave and was one of the best friends of the [*Gazette*] editor." The *Gazette* was challenged to come up with any evidence that Chávez had been a propagandist for peonage as there was "no rule that makes a man responsible for what his relatives may do." On one hand, the editors argued, *Gazette* partisans called Chávez the head of the "pro-peons and pro-Indian slavery party in New Mexico"; on the other, they charged that he was the "head of the vile radical abolition party of New Mexico." Finally in the *New Mexican*'s rhetorical arsenal, nowhere in Arny's proclamation of 1866 was there a sanctioning of slavery or peonage. Arny's anti-slavery views dated too far back to be impeached by "such a clique" as supported by the *Gazette*. "He drew up the law abolishing involuntary servitude in New Mexico. He has always worked against the peon law, and did so in 1865 and 1866."[95]

Congress passed "An Act to Abolish and Forever Prohibit the System of Peonage in the Territory of New Mexico and Elsewhere" on March 2, 1867. It provided severe penalties for violations, declaring null and void all laws, resolutions, orders, regulations, usages, or customs that purported to tolerate or permit peonage in New Mexico, while prohibiting the voluntary or involuntary service or labor of any persons as peons in liquidation of any debt or obligation. On April 14 Governor Mitchell followed up with a proclamation freeing New Mexico's peónes.[96] It would take some time for it to take effect and so the issue would return as a political football.

A huge controversy to dog Arny's reign stemmed from the need of the territorial government to appoint the territory's administrative officials for the following year. The Organic Act required that the appointment of offices be confirmed by both the council and the governor. Typically, the governor submitted his nominees for council confirmation. Pino's council set out to address terms due to expire the first week of February in Mitchell's absence. The extant holders of positions were almost all Connelly-appointed members of the National Union Party. Most prominent was Clever himself, who occupied two territorial posts: attorney general and adjutant general of the militia. Epifanio Vigil was the auditor of public accounts. Jesús María Alarid served as territorial librarian. Only Simón Delgado, territorial treasurer, claimed the Administration Party.

Arny would later say that Mitchell informed him before his departure of his wish to have the sitting officers retained. The only change he admitted was a concession to Arny's request to have his old partner, Theodore Greiner, appointed district attorney of the second judicial district. Otherwise, Arny claimed, he promised Mitchell nothing. He found Pino's council in no mood to confirm any of Mitchell's incumbents save one. The council's slate of nominees consisted of Chávez backers. Among them Stephen B. Elkins, a recently arrived lawyer, identified with the Republican Party, had given speeches in favor of the Administration Party of Santa Fe County, and opposed General Carleton's usurpation of the authority of the territorial courts under martial law. The council advanced Elkins as a replacement for Charles Clever, the very attorney general who had denied Arny's right to assume the role of acting secretary. Also nominated were Anastacio Sandoval, hard-core Chávez fellow, to replace Epifanio Vigil as auditor; James M. Taylor as district attorney of the third district; and Trinidad Alarid as territorial librarian in place of Jesús María Alarid (no relation). Confirmed, too, was Arny's recommendation of Greiner. Of Mitchell's appointees, only Simón Delgado, actually a Mexican Party hand, was supported to stay on.[97]

Between the council's nominees and Mitchell's order to retain his officers, Arny found himself in a tight spot. The council appears to have been bound and determined to prevent the reappointment of Mitchell's team, and partisan affiliation seems to have tipped the scale for Arny's decision making. As Arny reported to the legislature, he thought about declining the council nominations but was swayed by legislators' sense of urgency. In the liberal's rationale, he was not willing to take from the hands of the council the power vested by the people and the law. Arny dared not admit his partisan ties to the council members, the hell to pay if he did not go along. He approved all the council's recommendations save Taylor, who declined the nomination.[98]

The assembly also complied with Arny's request to review the position of adjutant general of the New Mexico militia. That position was empowered with representing the unpaid claims of militiamen, totaling a million dollars, as payment had yet to be made as required by law. Second, and most important, the council ended the term of the incumbent, the self-same Charles Clever whom it had just cut as territorial attorney general. Arny was asked to forward a name to fill that position. He nominated the known Republican John Gwyn to replace Clever. The council endorsed Gwyn, seven to three. Gwyn began discharging the duties of adjutant general, including management of militia claims.[99]

Mitchell returned to the territory on February 26. He immediately acted in conformity with Clever's opinion that invalidated Arny's authority as acting governor, and he declared illegal all measures passed by the legislature and signed by the acting governor. Holding that Arny had acted in bad faith and "betrayed" him on the territorial appointments, Mitchell removed Attorney General Elkins and Adjutant General Gwyn and refused to sign the vouchers that Gwyn drew for payment of militia claims.[100] Mitchell reinstated Clever as both attorney general and adjutant general.[101] The governor fired the Arny appointee Anastacio Sandoval and put Epifanio Vigil back in place as auditor, and he reinstated Jesús María Alarid in place of the Arny-appointed territorial librarian Trinidad Alarid.[102]

The *New Mexican* called Mitchell's action a high-handed usurpation of power in "plain" violation of the Organic Act and "in higher disregard of the voices of the legislative Council, the representatives of the people."[103] Spanish language letters to the *New Mexican* portrayed the governor taking out his "claws [*saca las uñas*]," declaring war against the people [*guerra contra el pueblo*]," and "turning the bitter enemy loose on the people [*se ha entregado al enemigo acérrimo del pueblo*]." Clever's European provenance was held suspect, with Mitchell said to be seeking to pay off "the foreign faction," meaning Jewish merchants, as would soon become evident.[104] A citizen going by *Centinela* (Sentinel) fumed over the insults and disrespect "at every step committed by the imported federal officials that the government sends to this territory, . . . tyrants and despotic in all their forms [*Viendo que los insultos y desprecio que á cada paso cometen los importados oficiales Federales . . . que pasan a tiranos y despóticos en todo sus formas*]." Centinela condemned Mitchell for coming out to "our people not to improve our condition, which is the object for which he was sent, rather to make a commerce of our country, our people, and our rights [*con el fin no de mejorar nuestra condición que es el objeto para que fue mandado, sino de hacer un comercio de nuestro país, nuestro pueblo, nuestros derechos*]." Mitchell allegedly ditched New Mexico's legislature to sell mining claims, leaving the territory in the "swarm of its difficulties" to "that corrupt faction that in all times has tried to subjugate us to nothingness [*dejando . . . al pueblo de Nuevo Méjico sumerjido en un enjambre de dificultades que ya él dejaba bien consertadas con esa facción corrompida que en todos tiempos ha tratado de someternos a la nada*]."[105]

A piece in *El Nuevo-Mejicano* titled *Ultraje Brutal* (Brutal assault) praised Arny for interceding when Jesús María Alarid, Governor Mitchell's "illegally" reappointed librarian, attempted to take possession of the territorial library by breaking down its doors.[106] A Nuevomexicano accused Santa Fe County Sheriff José D. Sena of being the secret author of *Ultraje Brutal*, a vain attempt to put the "corrupt" Arny on a pedestal.[107] Alarid himself called the author of the piece an "adulator [of Arny] and true wretch" who did not understand a basic principle—that when Governor Mitchell returned to his seat as the executive, he retained the authority to either confirm or not the actions and decisions of the interim governor, choosing not to authorize his appointments, plain and simple. The author had suggested that Mitchell appointed Alarid only because of his poor and destitute condition. Alarid said he had not applied for the position; rather, Mitchell confided in him and he was glad to accept. If the author had any doubts, Alarid declared, he was welcome to come to Alarid's house to see from his own kitchen table how well he ate. Alarid said he would feed the author better than Arny could pay him; it would not surprise him if the critic's trade was "big talker [*hablador*]."[108]

Mitchell's appointees refused to relinquish their posts. Elkins requested a district court ruling on the legality of it. Since Clever did not give adequate justification for his ruling to the court, Elkins argued, he must not have wanted the position. Moreover, the new chief justice of the territory and presiding judge of the first judicial court, Judge John T. Slough, declared Elkins's appointment by Arny legal against the prosecuting arguments of Merrill Ashurst. Elkins defended council members. If through their representatives they "did not feel bound by yours and Governor Arny's plans as to their rights," he challenged Mitchell, "and thought proper, under the law to do as they desired, [was] not some respect due to their solemn acts and opinions when they are so vitally interested?" In this republican take, Elkins had the appointing power invested equally in the council as in the executive, "and generally entitled to more consideration." Elkins asked if Arny's alleged "bad faith" afforded a good reason for violating his own rights, guaranteed under the law "by the will and solemn sanction of the people."[109]

Gwyn too appealed his dismissal on republican grounds, in the name of "the public" that was directly affected by the claims of the voluntary regiments, whose payment Clever had never fulfilled as adjutant general. The people's representatives passed a law for the adjustment of their accounts, Gwyn held, and appointed an officer "of their own choosing." Gwyn fired at Mitchell: "instead of approving of their action in your absence and lending them your hearty cooperation . . . it seems you now attempt to thwart their wishes," and he challenged Clever as a legitimate holder of the adjutant general position. Clever rendered himself "so odious to the people," Gwyn pressed on, in opposing the assembly and the people generally (at the Taos mass meeting) "that nothing could have induced the legislative council to confirm his nomination."[110]

Mitchell had stated in his letter of dismissal to Sandoval that he promised Epifanio Vigil he would reappoint him clerk of public accounts, not only because he was a gentleman and professionally courteous but because he was "poor" and "entirely dependent on his own efforts to make a life," and that he intended to make all his appointments to "favor the poor over the rich when they have equal qualifications." Sandoval said this "vein of philanthropy [*rasgo de filantropía*]" and the "good feelings in favor of the proletariat against the powerful [*sus Buenos sentimientos en favor del proletario y en contra del poderoso*]" would have honored the governor but was contradicted by his having hired the well-to-do Clever. Sandoval called Mitchell's removal of him illegal and arbitrary, and it offended his "outraged honor [*honor ultrajado*]." Should the governor ignore his reasons for staying on the job, Sandoval might have to appeal to the public for an impartial judgment.[111]

Mitchell did not mention his advocating for the poor to any of the other officials he recalled. Gwyn, learning of the governor's principle, asked why Mitchell removed him and Elkins and consolidated their offices in the person of Clever, "thereby giving him $6000 out of the territorial treasury and he being a rich man?" Gwyn accused Mitchell of aiming to usurp the territorial offices and force someone on the people as an act of pure politics. It was known, he said, that Clever aspired to be the delegate to Congress and that the governor would promote it by arming him with appointments. In Clever's haste to build up a party, Gwyn charged, Mitchell should not aid him "at the people's expense." Gwyn acted as adjutant general, adjusting claims for unpaid militia accounts and compensation for property lost in the war.[112]

Arny's challenge to Clever's original opinion had requested U.S. Attorney General Henry Stanberry and Congress to render a decision on his assuming the acting secretary and acting governor positions. A congressional joint resolution adopted Stanberry's opinion and confirmed Arny's authority to serve as both in Mitchell's absence. The laws passed by the assembly and signed by Arny had "the same force and effect as though the same had been approved and signed by the governor duly appointed," it was decreed.[113] On Elkins's official confirmation in Washington to serve as district attorney for the territory, the *New Mexican* praised him for his "genial courtesy, perseverance and energetic fidelity" to the people, observing presciently, "A future is before him of brilliant promise."[114] But the ruling did not prevent the absurd situation of two sets of territorial officers in play, those nominated by the council and confirmed by Arny, and those reinstated by Mitchell.[115] It could not have happened in a state.

The *Gazette* saw an underlying significance to the face-value terms of the congressional decision. In Russell's gnarly thought process, Congress actually "condemned" Arny's declaration of being only the *acting* secretary. In this logic, future litigation would find that as acting secretary, the "pretender" could not serve as acting governor, invalidating his acts in that role. It took an act of Congress to validate the laws illegally passed by the assembly, Russell noted. Arny falsified the record in saying he followed the wishes of the people by signing off on the nominations of their elected officials. Whereas the Legislative Council continued from the 1865 election, all members of the House of Representatives had just been elected, "fresh from the people." The nominations never went to the House for approval, and it would not have approved them for their election meant the "repudiation" of the council. Rather than the wishes of the people, Arny had consulted with the wishes of partisan leaders, Russell had it, "giving men offices who were inimical to Gov. Mitchell and who would do all they could to embarrass his administration." More credible was Russell's point regarding the dismissal of Clever, whose term had supposedly expired. The attorney general's term did not expire until late February; Governor Mitchell could well have returned prior to that date. In "hot haste" had Arny intended to undermine the executive's authority.[116]

The *New Mexican* pointed out that Congress's joint resolution declared Arny de facto territorial secretary and acting governor up to February 18, when his term of office expired by commission. The *Gazette* assaults on the "faithful, honest and efficient public servant" were "brutal and unseemly," and its editor was a "miserable cur," Tucker put it, "vain-making and snarling at the Moon." Mitchell inexcusably deserted New Mexico at a time of need without a purpose to serve the welfare of the people nor the development of the territory's resources, and for allying himself with partisans, "voluntarily yield[ing] his potent influence and illustrious name" into the control of a party ever alert to make war on the general good." Arny's letter to the editor affirmed Congress's endorsement of his presidential appointment, showing "the estimate" placed upon Governor Mitchell's misrepresentations of him. Mitchell's censure for leaving his post of duty, Arny agreed, "should make him cautious how he now takes partisan action in New Mexico, especially as he has no legal authority to remove officers who had been confirmed by the legislative council."[117]

In the seemingly endless round of debate, Russell rued how the world was given to slander and abuse, "no less true now than in the days of Shakespeare," quite as if it did not apply to himself. His halo askew, he noted how "some minds seem to be so constituted as to be unable to speak a good word, think a good thought or do a kind action to their neighbor." That the *New Mexican* would think Governor Mitchell, with his "high reputation as a gallant soldier and brave and skillful commander," absent only in order to promote his personal interest and aggrandizement reflected nothing but "slander and vituperation." Russell, without giving justification for the timing of Mitchell's departure from the territory, slammed the *New Mexican* for its "brief and dishonorable existence," plundering the public funds with the assistance of Secretary Arny and "for its worthless and disgraced attempts at doing the public printing."[118]

In the next pass in the blunt political game, Clever resigned as adjutant general of the militia and Mitchell shocked the world by naming in his place John T. Russell, the very Administration Party–hating editor of the *Gazette*.[119] Gwyn warned the public of Russell's "spurious circulars" that announced resolution of the militia claims sent to Clever, those "laboring under the delusive idea that they are the Adjutant General of the militia of New Mexico."[120] The *New Mexican* said Russell, who knew nothing of the duties of the office, was "forced upon the people," resulting in a waste of the $3,000 salary, an "unjust and illegal, insult to New Mexico."[121]

Mitchell defied the Organic Act, the law of the legislature, and Congress, Arny charged, and he warned against Russell's "bogus warrants." Mitchell, Clever, and Russell had delayed the militia payments a year, he claimed. A dismayed Arny stated that he had not wanted "controversy" with those men, had never expected to have "any pecuniary interest in the claims," and was "perfectly willing to have the interested people vindicated at the polls for their rights which have been delayed by this unwarrantable interference." The U.S. government sustained him, he noted. It would in time notify the governor that he had "transcended the duties of his official position by attempting to undo what was my right to do when he left me to act as governor in his absence and which official act was unanimously authorized by the Legislature, confirmed by the Council and unanimously approved by Congress."[122] Mitchell had appointed Russell after the legislative session ended, escaping the need for council approval. Russell continued to play adjutant general into the early fall of 1867 at least. The *New Mexican* accused the "usurper" of defying the law by levying a fee on citizens for processing claims. It advised the militia vets not to pay, even if the payment of their warrants be delayed, for Clever, the adjutant general for five years, had made no effort to clear their claims.[123] Meanwhile, the field of partisan battle opened up to bring in delegate to Congress José Francisco Chávez.

Questions of Patronage

A Doolittle investigator looking into the management of Indian affairs in New Mexico during the command of General Carleton had recommended the dismissal of Felipe Delgado as the superintendent of territorial Indian affairs because he did not know how to read or write English. Delgado also made a problem in response to President Johnson's edict to have Indian slavery in New Mexico abolished, calling the negative characterization of the institution "exaggerated." Delgado transposed Miguel Antonio Otero's former attempt to defend peonage before Congress, in the process harmonizing with Jefferson Davis's line that "African Servitude" was "the mildest and most humane of all institutions to which the name 'slavery' has ever been applied." As he described it to Commissioner Dole, Mexicans purchased Indians out of "Christian piety" to educate them in the ways of civilization. That they could go free at the age of twenty-one if they wished was "favorable, humane and satisfactory" to the Indians. When they wanted to marry, he added, "their guardians do not object but rather treat them as their adopted children and give them aid at the time of marriage. When the guardians die they usually leave something to the captives."[124] Delgado objected to tampering with homeland culture, but his apologist's rationale grated on even moderate forms of Reconstruction.

FIG. 25. *Taoseños*, 1881, photograph by Bennett & Brown. The specific occasion for the convening of this group portrait is unknown. Felipe Delgado is identified seated in the first row, third from the right, and Diego Archuleta is the second person to his right. Courtesy Palace of the Governors Photo Archives, NMHM/DCA, negative #013144.

Delgado was in effect a charter member of the American Party, an unrepentant Otero Democrat and unabashed supporter of Francisco Perea. Collins protested Delgado's firing to Dole. Donning the robes of advocacy for the fair inclusion of Nuevomexicanos in federal office, he argued, "We have a population in New Mexico of some ninety thousand souls, more than nine tenths of whom are Mexicans and it seems to be improper to exclude them entirely from any participation in the federal appointments for that Territory." Articulating a stand against race-colonialism for a change, Collins allowed that few Mexicans spoke English, yet called it no fault of theirs, for they had been "forced into our government by the fortune of war." They were citizens of the United States and it was necessary to recognize their willingness to take up arms in defense of the government during the late war. Were they to be "prescribed" in the way of excluding them from federal appointment, it would be "a poor recompense for their fidelity and loyalty," Collins waged on.

Should the Bureau of Indian Affairs find no Mexican fit for the position of superintendent, Collins, falling back on his accustomed role as broker for government patronage, pointed to New Mexico's

"American residents" who knew Indians and were qualified "in every way" to discharge all the duties of the office in a manner more satisfactory than those strangers who were "ignorant of the Spanish language, through which all the business with the Indians has to be done." Collins, the apostle of partisanship in New Mexico, pointed out that divided though they might be politically, New Mexicans were no longer willing to accept strangers as their appointed officials. As he explained, New Mexico had been organized sixteen years before, and since then many enterprising and worthy citizens had encountered the hardships and perils "incident to emigrating to that far off region, and have taken their all with them, and it is certainly fair and right that they should have, all else being equal—a share of the public patronage." Collins was in Washington when he wrote the letter, in company of other "citizens of New Mexico." He requested a meeting with the commissioner before the nomination for Indian superintendent went to Congress.[125]

The *Gazette* subsequently reported that the blame for the removal of Delgado lay at the door of Delegate Chávez, that he had disparaged Delgado's abilities and personal character. Chávez's stern answer, in Spanish, related an interesting tale. As he walked into President Johnson's office as summoned, he was surprised to see Collins, Watts, one H. B. Denman, and W. W. Mills there. Chávez denied as "entirely false" the charge that he had insulted the capacity and honesty of Delgado and claimed to have told the president he had not been responsible for his removal. Indeed, he considered Delgado's honesty and integrity beyond reproach, for he was a man with a "fine" lineage. Yet Chávez made clear his opposition to retaining Delgado. He affirmed, "I want my friends and political enemies to know, that in political business, I walk with my political friends whatever our luck may be, good or bad." Clearly, loyalty to party had become entrenched among Nuevomexicanos. Chávez considered don Felipe one of his best personal friends, but the Santa Fean opposed him in the election and he retained every right to do so. For that Chávez saw little or no hope for him continuing as Indian superintendent.[126]

The Johnson administration upheld Delgado's dismissal but that did not end the episode. The *New Mexican* condemned the "knot" of unscrupulous and unprincipled "demagogues and tricksters" led by the *Gazette* doing all it could to disparage Chávez's name before the president and in the halls of Congress. It was an effort to sabotage his good work for the territory, and for which his friends were justly proud, the *New Mexican* had it. Chávez's "bold, manly and independent course" had met with the "warmest of good will, and his refusal to strike bands with the corrupt and desperate faction who seek to again rise into power is the surest proof that the confidence reposed in him and our people is fully merited." Chávez would fight the whole "power party" that had dominated for ten years, the weekly promised, "and who had formed combinations that were difficult to overcome; who were numerous and unscrupulous, and would use any means to regain power wrested from them by an indignant and outraged people."[127]

Russell sniped back by claiming to have the "credible" report of Watts, Collins, and the others benignly offering their assistance to Chávez in the task of asking Congress for needed New Mexico legislation. This "offer" seems to have included the very odd, and perhaps not so benign request Governor Mitchell put in to have Congress accept former delegate John Watts as either a New Mexico delegate during its summer special session when New Mexico would not have a seated delegate, or if the rules of the House prevented Watts from acting as a paid delegate, Mitchell requested that he be permitted to sit as special agent to procure legislation as might be necessary for the interest and welfare of the territory.[128] Watts showed up in the halls of Congress apparently with credentials under the "great seal of the territory," appointing him New Mexico's delegate. The *New Mexican* had blasted this latest "fantastic caper" of the governor, one reflecting his "Cervantian" lack of common sense.[129] Indeed, the attempt received a sharp rebuke from Congress, Ohio Republican Robert Schenck calling it an "unprecedented, unauthorized and illegal act on the part of the Governor of that territory." Massachusetts Republican Henry Dawes asked that it be sent to the House Election Committee for investigation to "prevent such attempts in the future." The Committee tabled the request.[130]

In any case, Russell felt justified in arguing that it was not attributable to the efforts of Mitchell, Watts, and Collins that Chávez had not succeeded in accomplishing anything for the citizens of New Mexico—rather it was due to his "utter incompetency." Russell slighted the sitting delegate with the claim that Chávez thought the distribution of federal offices to be the "chief occupation of a delegate, only to be rebuffed by administration functionaries who wanted their political friends to occupy the official positions in the territory." Failure was "inherent in the man," Russell binaried, for nature "never endowed him with those qualities of mind which fit men to occupy high positions in the land with credit to themselves and with profit to those whom they represent. He did not even comprehend the magnitude of the duties he was expected to perform," the rant continued, "and his place, consequently, might as well have been vacant, except insofar as drawing the per diem and mileage was concerned."[131]

The *New Mexican* described Russell's article as "teeming with falsehoods" meant to deprecate Chávez's ability and civic service. Chávez had done his duty in Washington, the weekly pointed out, "and performed it well," giving by way of illustration that he had improved mail facilities, provided for the surveying of the lands along the streams and main *acequias* (irrigation ditches), submitted bills to erect a penitentiary, given the probate court authorization to decide civil cases, and reduced the veto power of the governor.[132]

Russell inflated the refrain of personal impotence. Better men did not whine, Russell maintained, "about what others would not *let them do*. They assert their manhood, they stand forth in their dignity and they manifest their works by what they do in spite of opposition." Such men did not "come down to that point of humiliation which makes them confess their incapacity and utter worthlessness, as a public servant." The *Gazette* saw no ground for Chávez's men to claim interference with the discharge of the delegate's legitimate duties. "To not a single man who did this, can they point," it argued. The only point of such blaming was to relieve Chávez "from the very embarrassing position in which he finds himself placed before his constituents. It is a weak subterfuge which will beguile nobody, gotten up by a man who well understands the utter indefensibility of the cause he espouses, and who hopes to derive some personal advantage from his attempts to have [a second term as delegate] foisted upon this people."[133] The *New Mexican* saw the *Gazette* seeking to taunt Chávez with the claim that he had "lustily" cried out with the "silly palaver" that "somebody would not let him do anything."[134]

A Euroamerican replaced Delgado. He was the brother of Senator Daniel S. Norton of Ohio, well known to Chávez and someone whom

Chávez seems to have recommended for governor of New Mexico.[135] Chávez enemies had another bomb to toss at Chávez. He took out a Nuevomexicano and replaced him with an "American," hypocritically posing as a native son and champion of the Mexican people while succeeding "in having all his own countrymen removed from office and their places filled with Americans."[136] Francisco Perea in his two years as delegate had a net gain of Nuevomexicano appointees, it was noted, yet Chávez had specifically gone to Congress requesting removal of all the appointments Perea effected.[137]

Appearances seemed to validate the picture. When a vacancy arose in the office of U.S. assessor, Chávez did not nominate a *nativo*. The appointment went to William Breeden, a confirmed Republican and Arny's personal friend. Breeden's nomination easily passed muster in the Radical Republican Congress, especially as it meant removing a Euroamerican member of the Johnson-supporting party.[138] The selection of Breeden indicated Chávez's concern to see a more activist Republican Party presence in New Mexico. The *Gazette*, however, questioned on ethnic grounds the appointment of an "American" over a Mexican. The *New Mexican*, sensitive to divided interests between party and Nuevomexicano representation, replied that Chávez did not appoint the new assessor, "and if he did, some two years residence in the territory ought to have given Breeden the right to claim citizenship over such crude importations as Mitchell, [Judge John] Slough, [U.S. Marshal] Hugh Pratt and [T. H.] Thomson," all Constitutional Party members. Russell was described as a "jaundiced party flunky," a "good old partisan bigot," attempting to thrust an "apple of discord" into the circle of Chavez's friends by pretending the appointment of an "American" was a personal insult to his "countrymen." Tucker turned the tables on the American Party, claiming that in raising the question, the *Gazette* was endeavoring to foster a "caste spirit" from the "very Copperhead principle that hissed encouragement in the North during the rebellion in the less degraded Rattlesnake of secession." Breeden was a "consistent and unflinching enemy of treason.... If the editor of the *Gazette* is not a countryman of Frank Chávez, then he is not an American."[139]

Another vacancy occurred in the important office of territorial secretary. The *New Mexican* regretted President Johnson's final decision to remove Arny after five years of service to the territory. At least the post went to another Republican, the former Union general and Nebraskan H. H. Heath. Chávez, who considered Heath a "gentleman of undoubted capacity and sterling integrity," clearly wanted him for the position for partisan reasons. The delegate "openly" and correctly predicted that Heath would prove to be "an invaluable asset to New Mexico Republicans." The *New Mexican* noted that the editors of the *Gazette* had done what they could to prevent the appointee known for his "radicalism." Arny stayed in the region, helping to sustain the presence of active Republicans in his new capacity as agent for the Utes.[140]

The Heath and Breeden appointments revealed Chávez's national party leanings at the sacrifice of his image as defender of nativo rights, even if what one political insider reported was true: that he had protested the replacement of two Nuevomexicano Indian field agents by Euroamericans.[141] Chávez claimed that the point of the American Party attack on him was a precise plan to thwart him from "placing the natives of the territory in the inferior [lower-level] positions which they could fill with advantage to the Government and benefit to themselves."[142] In any case, the demonization of Chávez would only grow in resonance, principally by the constant pounding of his messages from his enemies, Nuevomexicanos included.

National Effects in the Off-Year Elections of 1866

Taking a step back in this whole chronology, New Mexico geared up at the start of 1866 for the upcoming election of all seats in the territorial house. Parallel elections were on throughout the country. President Johnson's active program of Amnesty and Reconstruction sought to restore the southern states fully into the Union with a minimum of disruption in southern institutions except slavery. Secession had set off the Civil War and so Johnson's policy, combined with the recent southern "black codes," infuriated Radical Republicans. Radicals refused to recognize southerners elected to Congress under Johnson's plan until they endorsed the Fourteenth Amendment prohibiting states from denying any citizens of their fundamental rights, or enacting discriminatory laws, to include freed blacks. Johnson himself opposed the Fourteenth Amendment, and he further provoked Radicals by emasculating the powers of the military commanders charged with enforcing the Reconstruction Act in the South. Johnson deemed it unconstitutional to prevent states from full membership in the Union and he vetoed the Freedmen's Bureau. He anticipated the fall House elections by working to build a wide base of support for his policies. He did not have the total support of the Democratic Party and needed moderate and conservative Republicans. He therefore sought to form a new party with himself at its center.[143]

The *Gazette* published the opinion of the *National Republic* that if Johnson's policy succeeded in defeating the Radicals, it would "not only likely be universally acceptable, but sure to rout and ruin Radical expectations [for] they regard it as a matter of life and death that the coming Congress shall not be carried in its favor."[144]

Johnson's new National Union Party scheduled its convention for August 14–16 in Philadelphia. In addition to at least two delegates from each congressional district in the states, two from the District of Columbia, and four at large from each state, it requested two from each territory.[145] On July 21 the Conservative Party of New Mexico held a hasty meeting to nominate delegates to the Philadelphia Convention. The names reveal the exclusive participation of American Party Euroamericans: Merrill Ashurst, chairman; George P. Beall and Ben C. Cutler, secretaries; Charles Clever, W. T. Strachan, Thomas Roberts, James L. Johnson, James Hunter, W. W. Griffin, and James Collins, committee on resolutions. As the call for the meeting went out late, Nuevomexicanos in all counties would have been reprised. Members approved the Philadelphia Convention, sustaining with the "warmest approbation" its "principles of political policy." They endorsed the president's program of Reconstruction, committing the party's energies to "uphold and strengthen" Johnson in his "patriotic exertions to restore the Union with its former prosperity and greatness and to preserve the Constitution in its purity by protecting it from all unnecessary innovations." Governor Mitchell stood squarely in the American Party and behind President Johnson. His assigned responsibility was to name delegates to represent New Mexico in Philadelphia. A committee of three, including Charles Clever, was appointed to "wait on his Excellency."[146]

Mitchell appointed a two-person delegation to represent New Mexico at what critics called the "Southern Loyalist Convention."[147] The *Gazette* showcased the convention's proceedings and President Johnson's address. The convention chairman, a War Democrat, laid into Congress for "capriciously" springing the Fourteenth Amendment as a requirement for the southern states to come into the Union even after they had agreed to the abolition of slavery and repudiated the debts contracted to overthrow the government. The exaction of new conditions was unjust, he avowed, "a violation of the good faith of the Government, subversive of the fundamental principles of our political system, and dangerous to the public prosperity and peace." The speaker saw the amendment failing to garner three-fourths of the states, as required for confirmation. The convention highlighted Johnson's stand on the Fourteenth Amendment, denounced any suggestion of "impeaching motives," and considered the "scheme of exclusion adopted by Congress to be the offspring of views warped by prejudice and passion."[148]

Russell put the *Gazette* to the service of the National Union Party. His Copperhead position intact, he deemed any further punishment for the South unjust and a betrayal of the cause for republican government and its free institutions. He lauded the Philadelphia Convention as the "embodiment of the patriotic and wise principles which were entertained by and which controlled the fathers of the Republic." The people of the United States had proved themselves equal to the task of dealing with the difficulties of the previous five years, Russell noted, but the work was not yet complete. Radicalism would overthrow the American system of government with "baneful results to the nation as would have been the triumph of the rebellion." The action of the "prudent men and experienced counselors" who met in Philadelphia and who proposed to bring the southern states into equal participation with the rest of the Union, and thereby restore the Union to its "glorious whole," would derive the remedies needed to counter the evils visited upon the American people. For this did the Santa Fe convention nominate candidates, Russell assured them.[149] Governor Mitchell joined in signing a letter to Johnson endorsing Johnson's Reconstruction, expressing alarm over Radicals out to destroy American government and institutions. The veteran American Partyites who signed included Sidney Hubbell, Joab Houghton, Charles Clever, and Depository Director James Collins.[150]

President Johnson and his entourage prepared for an unprecedented speaking tour across the states to win popular support for his policies, the infamous "swing around the circle." New Mexico's National Union Party convened to nominate its candidates for the House from Santa

Fe County. Nuevomexicanos who had supported Francisco Perea for delegate included Capt. Jesús María Baca y Sena, Antonio Sena, and Santiago Armijo, joining Charles Wesche, Charles Conklin, Merrill Ashurst, David Miller, and John Russell. The group called Johnson's restoration and reconstruction policy "humane, wise, just and constitutional." Opposition was declared to the "despotism and centralization of Radicalism, with as much zeal and determination as we were opposed to secession and disintegration." Chávez's party continued to be linked to the Statehood Revolution, members affirming unequivocal and unalterable opposition to state government until the territory's mineral resources were developed and it had attained sufficient strength, population, and wealth to lessen the feeling of "the great burden of taxation which it must necessarily impose on us." The policy of establishing Indian reservations "as far distant as possible from the settlements" appeared. Ashurst, Felipe Sena, and Juan Cristóval Romero were unanimously nominated for the territorial house.[151]

Nationally, the Republican Party did not try to counter President Johnson's special national convention with a convention of its own. Nor did José Francisco Chávez's Union Administration Party hold a territorial convention in New Mexico. County organizations, especially Santa Fe and San Miguel, organized to nominate candidates for the house.[152]

President Johnson's bellicose performance rendered his swing around the circle a disaster and public relations debacle. Moderate Republicans pulled out of the National Union Party, which became the shell of the Democratic Party. The tour lost at least a million northern voters. As the returns of the election came in, the *New Mexican* reported that the next Congress would be "as radical, if not more so, than the last."[153] More accurately, Johnson's opponents had overwhelming majorities, bad for a president struggling for veto-proof power.[154]

The results in New Mexico mirrored the national trend. The Chávez affiliated Administration Party largely swept the election and retained its power in the legislature. That its local jefes, supported by the likes of Arny, Breeden, and Heath, led the charge at the polls was indicated in Santa Fe County, where pro-Johnson National Union Party candidates lost their majority, the stolid and highly successful Merrill Ashurst going down in flames. Santa Ana, San Miguel, Valencia, and Socorro counties proved disasters for them as well. Only in Mora and

Río Arriba counties did the majority of its ticket win (although interestingly, former delegate to Congress Francisco Perea was reelected to the house from Bernalillo County). The *New Mexican* trumpeted its satisfaction in announcing to friends and public that the election resulted in the "complete and utter overthrow of the opposition, and the election of the Union Administration ticket by a very handsome majority," notwithstanding the strenuous efforts of opponents who "left nothing undone" to aid in the selection of their candidates.[155]

1867 Convention Season

The House elections done, an anonymous Spanish language correspondent sounded a Mexican Party alarm in a piece with the headline *¡¡¡HORRIBLE ATENTADO!!!* (Horrible assault; for the full Spanish-language text, see appendix 4). The "Nuevomexicano people" needed to know of a plot among some recent arrivals to their homeland to strip them deliberately of their rights and privileges guaranteed by the Treaty of Guadalupe Hidalgo. These were "horrible and criminal attacks," the warning sounded, by certain unnamed individuals who had already slandered the "native citizens" of the territory and considered Mexicans as no better for advancing progress than the "barbarous Indians," who deserved greater respect as they at least believed in a "Great Spirit" and punished bad deeds and lies, whereas the Mexicans, while having faith in a supreme being, did not believe in punishment for sinners because of their belief in the Divine Authority of the Church, whose job was to pardon the sinner. The defamers, it was proclaimed, advanced the stereotype of Mexicans as not to be believed when under oath and therefore best disqualified as jurors and prohibited from giving court depositions.

The town crier depicted without naming the offending outsiders who aimed to strip Nuevomexicanos of the "sacred right of suffrage" and believing Mexican officials unsuited to serve in office because of their "ignorant coarseness" and inability to follow the instructions of the U.S. government. The "illustrious emigrants" had been writing a petition or memorial for the president of the United States to divest them of their rights and privileges mistakenly given them, it was charged. They would request that the governor and Supreme Court be combined to run the government; that the legislature, now represented by members "among our own people," be abolished; that government have the power to name the territorial and county officials from the probate judge to the constable; and that the right to be judged by jurors be abolished and substituted by a body of lawyers who would pronounce their decisions in all the cases pending before the court. The horrible punishment being prepared for Nuevomexicanos was motivated by the malice and perfidy of men who had recently settled in the bosom of their land but who thought of themselves as having more rights than the other inhabitants. Nuevomexicanos needed to fight back. The author could not believe that they would let such an outrage pass in silence without uniting to liberate themselves of the danger that threatened their rights and privileges. If not, the future would pass mournfully, the opprobrium over them to remain indelible forever.[156]

The *Gazette* editor maintained that the manifesto came from the camp of the "noble delegate" J. F. Chávez, its object being to put into "odium" the federal officials and the "entire American population" before the Mexican population. No "intelligent person" in the territory would "conscientiously" believe that there was any desire on the part of the newly appointed officials to disfranchise a "single Mexican," he proclaimed, much less that they desired to do away with trial by jury or deprive anyone of the privilege of giving testimony in the courts. Every "American" knew it would be "utterly impossible" to accomplish this anyway. "Such measures would be wholly at war with the spirit of our institutions and could not be made applicable to the Territory of New Mexico without being made applicable to all the people of all the Territories." It would be "ridiculous in the extreme" for anyone to send a petition to the president for these purposes. The president had no more power over the matter than had "our excellent Governor, and would give no more attention to the petition of the kind than it would the latter." The "whole invention" was "so preposterous that it would not be worthy of attention," Russell scoffed, "were it not for the fact that the dishonest persons who are making use of it understand the disposition of the great mass of the people among whom they work their politics."

Russell said promulgators of anti-Americanism could maintain themselves only by "rid[ing] in on the prejudices of races" and the credulity of the people. If they could engender a feeling of hatred and animosity in the minds of the Mexicans against the Americans, and the American officials in the Territory then they will have things, in a small way, just as they want them. They will get the votes of a large majority of the people, hold all the petty offices throughout the Territory, elect an American hater, like Mr. J. Francisco Chávez, as Delegate to Congress and bring the Territory into disrepute before the people of the country and have a Delegate to the Congress of the United States who will be without influence, spurned and avoided by those who should be his associates and well wishers.

The *Gazette* claimed to make no threats "for or against any person," merely to place before the people "the political state as it now is in New Mexico and ask them to avoid the scheme that is prepared for them by their professed friends, but really their worst enemies."[157]

Russell sent a long letter to the Radical Senator Sumner touching on many political items and seeking to bust Arny, Heath, the *New Mexican*, and Chávez as the most hypocritical of Radicals. "While they run most beautifully with the Hare they take most excellent care to hold with the Hound," Russell put it. "While they appear most excellent radicals to you in Washington City, they are the mainstay to peonage and Indian Slavery in New Mexico." He repeated the slur of Chávez's mother owning more peons and Indian slaves than anyone in New Mexico. He disparaged Arny as a "Janus-faced Radical," demonstrated when, as acting governor, he called on citizens to organize expeditions into Indian country to protect themselves, even though Governor Connelly had put a stop to such iniquitous things. "We here all knew what that meant," Russell conveyed. "The more so did we know it, when we considered it was made at a time when there was not a hostile tribe of Indians within the limits of the Territory [echoing the Carleton propaganda]. It meant nothing more or less than a license to steal women and children and reduce them to slavery." As the militias found no warring bands in Navajo country, they headed to the ever peaceful Moqui villages in Arizona. "Quaker Indians," the Moquis were pacific even when facing warlike tribes, Russell portrayed. The party attacked the villages, killing four men and carrying home twelve women and children to make slaves of them. This kind of "diabolism" was what Arny's law was meant to accomplish, given its popularity "among the native population." Russell accused Arny of cooperating with the "pro peon and pro Indian slavery party of New Mexico whose Representative is Mr. Chávez. Radicalism should be made of sterner stuff than this," Russell commented in feigned respect for his national enemy.[158]

Both territorial parties began to prepare in late January for the September election for delegate to Congress. Guided in part by the U.S. presidential scene, the American shadow-party went guided by President Johnson's fight against what he called "anti-American Radicals." Johnson remained opposed to the Fourteenth Amendment in the name of restoring the integrity of the southern states in Congress and in the country, claiming adherence to the "letter and spirit" of the Constitution.[159] The friends of the Constitutional Union Party of New Mexico (previously the Conservative Party) convened on January 19 in the office of the *Gazette* to plan the call for their territorial nominating convention. Former delegate José Manuel Gallegos served as president, and former delegate and Chávez cousin Francisco Perea was crowned honorary chief. A central committee included Gallegos, Russell, Nicolás Quintana, and Felipe Delgado. The special committee to suggest a suitable time and place for holding the territorial convention and decide on the appropriate number of county delegates featured Diego Archuleta and Taos Representative Pascual Martínez, leader of the dissident House members, with four more Nuevomexicanos serving. Counties were to send three delegates for every member they had in the legislative assembly to the territorial convention set for March 20 in Santa Fe. Perea headed the committee to put out the public announcement of the convention.[160]

Their aim of standing up to the chief powers of their opponents, the Nuevomexicanos Chávez and the "Pino Clique," signified the eclipse of the centrality of the Euroamericans Arny and Benedict since their removal from territorial appointments.[161] Chávez was called "the most signal failure of a man that has ever been sent to Washington City as a representative of any constituency in the broad expanse of the United States," with the claim that he had operated to the "great damage of the people of New Mexico." The people needed an overthrow of the Pino crowd to "get up in its stead men who have experience in and knowledge of, public affairs and who will look after the general well-being, instead of engaging their time in the prosecution of petty personal malice with which the people at large have no interest."[162]

The *Gazette* expanded the call further, accusing Chávez of failing to secure a number of measures, including confirmation of private land claims for the people of New Mexico; payments to the New Mexico militia for the Texas invasion; geological and mineralogical surveys; new bridges across the Rio Grande; return of the Conejos from Colorado; road improvements; relief for "that portion of the people of New Mexico who elected to retain the character of Mexican citizens from their disabilities by declaring them citizens of the United States upon their now taking the oath of allegiance"; and a free school in each county.[163]

That the Constitutional Union Party backed President Johnson allowed Chávez's supporters to adopt the National Union Party as their identity, a symbolic link to Lincoln's legacy. A week after the Constitutionals held their planning meeting, friends of the National Union Party met at the house of don Anastacio Sandoval. The mainstay Mexican Party leadership appeared: Miguel E. Pino, W. F. M. Arny, Rafael Chacón, Simón Delgado (brother of Felipe), Vicente García, Samuel Ellison, "Miguel" Steck, and José D. Sena as well as staunch county leaders, especially in San Miguel. New characters Stephen Elkins and John Gwyn appeared, two of the territorial officers acting governor Arny had appointed at the behest of the Pino-led council. *New Mexican* editor William Manderfield stood out next to the mercurial Kirby Benedict. The party sported a central committee and an ad hoc committee of correspondence. Communication of party principles and policies went through the seventy-six-member body, all but two of them Nuevomexicanos, the largest numbers from San Miguel (13), Santa Fe (11) and Bernalillo (8).

The first item appearing in resolution seemed to take from the screed of a few months earlier that warned Nuevomexicanos of the "horrible" plot by recent Euroamerican arrivals to strip them of their constitutionally guaranteed rights and privileges. Delegates reinforced the need to protect the rights and immunities of all the citizens of the territory, the same as those of the United States, "without regard to nationality, condition or circumstance." Those who fomented questions of nationality were to be looked on with "contempt and indignation." Fear for the future was expressed, a coming flood of the "most uncompromising enemies of our people and interests, whose selfishness, like Judas Iscariot, makes them hold themselves open to the highest bidder" (paralleling President Johnson condemning Radicals as "traitors and betrayers equal to Judas"). A clue as to whom might be meant came in the provision that thanked Delegate Chávez for the courage and manliness with which he had "encountered the many difficulties thrown in his way by the enemies of New Mexico who thronged to Washington for the purpose of embarrassing him and gratifying their ambition and private interests." Chávez's course as New Mexico's representative had its endorsement, affirming the "respect and gratitude of every person" having the territory's interests at heart.[164]

The Central Committee's Spanish-language directive to counties for delegates to the territorial nominating convention intended to send citizens to the front against their colonial subjection by holding conventions in their respective "plazas and villas" to "liberate their land, their liberty, their lives and those of their wives and children." The refrains of rights and liberties soared against the cabal that had for years attempted "with all its might to unrecognize them before the general government and to establish among us a division by means of a denigrating and embarrassing question of race." The likes of the *Gazette* editor were the "true enemies" of the country, the resolution stressed, the "retrogrades" of progress, the "usurpers of our rights and the assassins of our interests." The enemy needed to be looked at "in the face" and should not be allowed to trample on the people's rights and privileges. While emphasizing the colonial victimization of Nuevomexicanos, the Committee instructed people to remember "that we are all Americans and that under the Constitution and laws that are the foundation of our Republic and government, all are equal.... Show our children [how] to sustain the Constitution and the laws.... We appeal to your good judgment and healthy sentiments; we appeal also to the love that you have of liberty, to our pride as a nation and to the sentiments that characterize every patriotic man."[165]

On the side of their opponents, a plea went out from the counties of Mora and Taos for the Constitutional Union Party's convention to nominate as candidate to Congress someone from the Río Arriba district. An anonymous Nuevomexicano calling himself Mora said it was time for citizens to use their "liberty" and demonstrate their rights through the vote to press their delegates of the north for such a nomination. It did not matter whether the nominee be an "American" or a "son of the land." Mora rejected references to that "pernicious, so hateful, question of race," the work of demagogues and those who worked to disunite the people by an overbearing commitment to political parties. Rather than open a breach with the Río Abajo, the goal was to realize justice for the north, which had plenty of men with requisite qualifications. The other requirement was for the candidate to follow the politics of President Johnson and work to open the market for industrial work for citizens.[166]

A recommendation came in from Taos for Ferdinand Maxwell, brother of Lucien Maxwell, an American who had settled in New Mexico prior to the Kearny occupation, becoming one the largest land owners in the United States through a Mexican land grant. Ferdinand had lived in the territory nine years. His nomination was said to align with most of the men of Taos County not "blinded by party prejudice and vindictiveness." The people of northern New Mexico had always "in good faith" supported men as delegates who came from the Río Abajo "without a murmur." Justice called for those friends to reciprocate as they had "always had the delegate from that part of the Territory." Maxwell spoke Spanish "sufficiently to be understood," and was a "gentleman of strict habits and high integrity" who had held in the territory and the United States "high and important positions."[167] An anonymous Nuevomexicano agreed that Maxwell had better qualifications than the current delegate, predicting that Taos County would nominate him.[168] The *Gazette* declared itself ready to endorse someone from the Río Arriba. It had its preference, though, as to who would receive its "best aid" at the proper time.[169]

Former delegate José Manuel Gallegos presided over the Constitutional Union Convention. The *New Mexican* observed that what it called the "Carleton-Mitchell Convention" was a "disharmonious assembly."[170] The *Gazette* conceded that "discordant elements" had recently "grown up in the party," though the gathering was one of the largest and was composed of "the most intelligent members that ever convened in this city for such a purpose." One tension turned on Francisco Perea, from the Río Abajo, and don Vicente Romero, a *ranchero* in Mora County. Each had "numerous and warm friends in the convention." The *New Mexican* suggested that Perea was promised territorial secretary at the removal of Arny, but when his supporters, including Governor Mitchell, failed to accomplish it, Perea was promised the nomination of delegate to Congress. Whether this can be trusted or not, it is likely that the issue between Perea and Romero turned on the choice of one from the Río Arriba or the Río Abajo. A deadlock caused Perea and Romero to withdraw their bids (Maxwell not figuring), leaving the members "unembarrassed" in their subsequent action in the selection of a candidate. The nomination ultimately and unanimously went to the Prussian immigrant, Attorney General Charles P. Clever, though he was absent from the convention but may have been finagling for the nomination all along. The *Gazette* did not publish the proceedings of its party as it usually did, perhaps a tactic to avoid mention of the tensions in the ranks. Clever coyly said he preferred to pursue his profession quietly but could not ignore the wishes of his friends. He would render "whatever sacrifice may be demanded" of him. He conceived it his duty to place himself at the disposal of his friends in his "adopted country."[171]

Clever was in some ways the logical challenge to Chávez. Few had recently defied the (Mexican) Union Party with action against it as clear as his, most recently in his defense of Governor Mitchell's appointments of the year before.[172] The crowd at his rally in the portal of the Palace in Santa Fe invited José Francisco Perea to speak, and he responded with remarks in favor of their nominee. The big guns of the traditional American Party appeared. James Collins was named president, and speakers included Ashurst, Gallegos, Archuleta, and J. M. Alarid. Governor Mitchell made a cameo appearance. The torchlight procession through the streets of the territorial capital, headed by bright banners and the city band, stopped at intervals to serenade principal party friends at their houses. Should the rank and file in the other counties do as well, the *Gazette* beheld, Clever would win by the largest majority ever.[173]

If the (Chávez) National Union Party decried enemy outsiders, the Constitutional Party projected homegrown corruption. Mariano Larragoiti—a young and politically rising figure in Río Arriba County whose father was an immigrant from Spain—warned modernistically of the "party of the don."[174] Miguel E. Pino and company came off the despots enforcing their will over the members of the legislature, sending them home from the session saddened and dejected. In the caricature, solons were unable to serve their constituents with dignity and independence because the cacique Pino turned them into the blind shields of the horseman Don Quixote of la Mancha (Chávez) while forcing them to obey the "little governor, Arny [*obedecer al gobernadorcillo*]." Should they refuse, salaries would be denied, Larragoiti charged, and because many got themselves elected only to receive their three dollars a day, they did as commanded. Larragoiti inveighed against Pino's monopolizing the official positions of both chambers, recommending his relatives for being "good partisans." Pino did not have friends to be loyal to, only "instruments and serviles" whom he rewarded with little jobs. Larragoiti implied Euroamericans together with Chávez being the hidden heads of the enemy party making Pino do their bidding.

Larragoiti's depiction could well have isomorphed lingering *patronismo*, peonage, and pre-republican politics. At any rate, he rode underling legislators just as hard as he did the bosses. They were, he said, "in love with themselves"; they did not own their own opinions, others filling their heads with political ideas, just as they were prepared to receive the orders of their commanding boss, whoever he was. The name of the Hon. Francisco Chávez was already being bandied about for delegate without anyone consulting them, yet they would be bribed because that was how things were done under the cacique who managed the strings so that the doll could dance. It struck Larragoiti strange that Unionists did not want to unite with the people of the Río Arriba as called for by the correspondent, Mora, and endorsed by legislators independent of Pino, preferring the *Ricos del Río Abajo*, who because of the "excellence of that title" felt they could always impose their preferences. Larragoiti saw a problem in San Miguel County's inability to join Mora because of its subjection to the disposition of others at the point of the branding iron, members of the council among them. He mocked San Miguel County's vaunted liberalism. "They say that principles govern them and they have none [*dicen que los principios los gobiernan, y no tienen ningunas*]." In the end their party was the party of the don, of the master, "and their principles are the employment that they aspire to, though they are not capable of fulfilling the offices nor can they sign their names on a sheet of paper, worthy representatives, they were, of Sancho Panza who, by being governor of the *Insula Barataria* [fictional isle awarded by a noblemen to Sancho Panza as a prank in Cervantes' Don Quixote, barato meaning cheap] served and obeyed, in all, his masters, silly monkeys [*que por ser gobernador de la Insula Barataria sirvió y obedeció en todo a su amo que era monos mentecatos*]." Larragoiti closed in classic Hispanic humility, begging the indulgence of the public for having brought his communiqué to light, expressive of his sentiments in terms that, if not in a sublime or literary style, at least came from a frank and sincere heart. The impartial citizens, who knew the past acts of the persons alluded to, would judge his words.[175]

Larragoiti made special reference to the politicians of San Miguel County because, in the aftermath of the Bosque Redondo conflagration, relations among the men of the public square had deteriorated into a turf war. The supporters of Chávez—including the increasingly influential Juan José Herrera, Celso Baca, and the brothers Romero, Trinidad and Eugenio—extended an invitation to those of the opposition for a special meeting to end the difficulties. Viewing clean republican competition as the vehicle for fixing matters, they authorized committees from each party to form in all of the precincts "without advantage nor for the first nor for the second." A meeting of representatives of each party was planned to provide for civil debate over the September election and issues of local concern.[176]

The wholly Spanish-speaking planning meeting of the National Union Party rebroadcast to the grassroots the propaganda lines the *New Mexican* had been setting forth. Governor Mitchell's record—leaving the territory on taking office, not opening the legislative session, and abusing his power by removing the officials who had been legally named and confirmed by the council—were all pounded into collective consciousness. All citizens who had "honorable sentiments and appreciated [r]epublican institutions" were commanded to condemn his violation of territorial laws. The governor was motivated by "private animosities and personal interest," it was explained. The "insignificant charlatan" editor of the *Gazette* wrote infamous descriptions of the people of San Miguel County, it was pointed out, "despicable" in their attempts to prevent them from enjoying the right of suffrage. They would support the candidate for delegate to Congress to be chosen at their convention and would "equally oppose" other nominations for the office.[177]

The National Union Party's territorial nominating convention of April 1 ratified the planning committee's critique of the partisan enemy. That it convened at the home of José D. Sena signified the rapidly rising star of the Santa Fe County sheriff. In noting that the fifty-two credentialed delegates exhibited a more "complete unanimity of thought and action" than at any previous territorial convention, the *New Mexican* implied a tighter party than the Constitutional's but was likely accurate, as it was done in less than a day. Some new faces came to light. San Miguel County's Severo Baca was elected president; Salvador Armijo of Bernalillo County and Pedro Sánchez of Taos vice presidents; and John W. Dunn and Clemente P. Ortiz, both of Santa Fe County, as secretaries. While their opponents associated Chávez and his chiefs with Radicalism, the Convention hailed the end of slavery and involuntary servitude without referencing the Reconstruction battle consuming Washington DC. More pointed was the aim of skewering those in New Mexico who disparaged the Chávez family on the issue of Indian slaves and Mexican peons and Chávez's party on the false accusation of racially hating "Americans."

Usurping and helpful colonizers were distinguished. On one hand, a resolve was to treat "with the ultimate disrespect and contempt" the official conduct and acts of those federal officials who followed the official conduct of Robert B. Mitchell, "our current governor, who, instead of maintaining and enforcing the laws, has been and is an obstacle to the loyal administration . . . and that we consider [Mitchell] a plague sent to the people of the Territory." Still, the commitment to liberal ideals was not forgotten. Delegates also upheld their duty to "treat with major consideration and respect" federal officials who were mandated to administer territorial laws "when such officials use all their efforts to comply with the duties as such functionaries, with the fidelity, honesty and energy necessary to maintain the integrity of the law." The notion of helpful settlers extended to the private sector. The fever of hopeful wealth in the desert had become hegemonic and the National Union Party would not leave itself out. It pined for the eastern capitalist who would desire to assist in the development of the territory's "vast" mineral resources and establish the branches of industry and utility conducive to its future progress and "aggrandizement." Honest efforts were pledged by members themselves to develop those resources, advance New Mexico's wool interests and pastures, and have the congressional delegate work for construction of railroads and telegraph.

The convention went on to express Mexican Party satisfaction with the energy and "manly firmness" with which Chávez had repulsed the attacks on, and misrepresentations of, Nuevomexicanos by persons resident in the territory. With "intrepid valor" had he denied the "lies of vile columns" from persons "sent here with the aim of opposing the loyal discharge of their duties and retarding the development and progress of our country," it was claimed. Miguel Pino's nomination of Chávez for delegate to the Fortieth Congress of the United States received unanimous ratification. U.S. Assessor William Breeden counted among those called to deliver remarks, a sign of his growing prominence.[178]

Sheriff José D. Sena rose to second the nomination of Chávez and reinforce the stands of party leaders on the issues. For the first time that can be discovered, a weekly published an entire Spanish-language speech from a nominating convention. Sena's four columns' worth of text suggest a firebranding performance at a highly emotional moment. Sena spoke to Nuevomexicanos directly. The fight with the enemy had most to do with "the interests of our people [*los intereses de nuestro pueblo*]," as Sena posed it. The tone of the Sena address might suggest the author of the radical anti-colonial manifesto of the previous fall. In detailing the offenses of the Mitchell gang point by point, he cast Clever and Mitchell as chiefs in the "faction of demagogues," the "vile usurpers, of our accomplishments ever since political parties were known in New Mexico." Sena accused these two "despots" who had succeeded Carleton as the dictator of New Mexico of working to establish a preoccupation "and a certain distinction among ourselves as conquered citizens and they as original citizens of the American government [*debemos tener presente el cual ha sido la conducta de estos viles usurpadores de nuestros hechos desde que partidos políticos fueron conocidos en Nuevo Méjico. Ellos han procurado establecer una preocupación, y una cierta distinción entre nosotros como ciudadanos conquistados, y ellos como ciudadanos originarios del Gobierno Americano*]."

Militant as it resounded, Sena's declaration against offensive colonizers followed liberal precept. The despots had planted the seeds of discord to usurp not only the nationality Nuevomexicanos had chosen for themselves on becoming part of the United States but the "rights, privileges and immunities that, by the Constitution and the laws, had been guaranteed to us by the government." The offenders repeatedly stated that the Mexicans were not capable of governing themselves, calling them before the general government in Washington "the most immoral, corrupt and degraded people in the world," failing thus to deserve the territory's federally appointed positions. Sena reinforced Chávez by isolating the "gang of pirates" who had gone to Washington on Mitchell's behalf to subvert the work of the active, energetic, and honorable delegate, to create a bias against him in the federal departments so that they could sell mining claims on behalf of the governor's favorites, "peddling appointments for his satellites." Sena stood up for Mexican Party legislators, describing the governor "violently" removing the territory's officials who were duly appointed by the council and acting governor to satisfy the ambitions of his friends. Such had been the conduct "among the chiefs of the opposition during the last twenty years that we have lived under the American government," he invoked. For Sena the cliquism found in a liberal forum reflected the most odious type of tyranny, a "handful of individuals" seeking to "execute the most brutal and abominable despotism over a population of close to a hundred thousand residents."

Sena, building further on the theme of New Mexico as an innocent victim of foreign intrusion, assailed an enemy who promoted the industries "for the sake of their pillage," leaving the "humble and honest worker to sweat and work, not for his own benefit but to satisfy the lugubrious capacity of these invasive tyrants." Providence determined them living "under a system of despotism and anarchy without equal in the history of the world," Sena portrayed. However, those men would not succeed in realizing their initial desires. Sena held out confidence in the people "rising in defense of reason, equality and justice" and their beating back the "resonating, ignominious shout of viva Clever [*El pueblo se amotinará en defensa de la razón, la igualdad, y la justicia y procurará al hacer resonar el ignominoso grito de viva Clever*]."

In deprecating the foreigner arriving to exploit New Mexico, the sheriff accused the men behind "Carlos" Clever of using money to corrupt the will of the people. He then pushed the partisan envelope to a wholly novel plane. As he providentially put it, "only a frenzy, only a complete blindness and delirium" could have directed these "political conspirators" to "commit the crime of elevating over all of us [in the territory] the most vile renegade of the descendants of Israel [*Solo el frenesí, solo una completa sieguedad y delirio ha podido diri-*

jir á esos conspiradores políticos á cometer el crímen de elevar sobre todos nosotros al más vil renegado de los descendientes de Israel]."[179]

These allusions appeared in the middle of the address and not as a rousing climax; it is unclear if Sena meant to strike a "dramatizing communication" for his party soldiery to adopt, thus binding them more closely for the coming battle.[180] It proved incendiary nonetheless.

CHAPTER ELEVEN

Política Judaica e Literaria

Northern European law in the nineteenth century recognized the right of Jews to be free of exploitation, bondage, regulation, and ghettoization and awarded them civil rights and equal citizenship. The liberal demand was that they assimilate as individuals. As they remained clustered among themselves, being religiously reclusive or evincing nationhood, legal emancipation did not always head off old conservative feelings turning into modern anti-Semitism.[1] Spain did not end its Inquisition, established as a tribunal in 1480, until 1834. Mexico terminated its waning Inquisition in 1820 on breaking from Spain. Modernizing liberals in Mexico City politicked for religious tolerance and for suppression of the non-Catholic exclusion clause in the Mexican Constitution, and they sympathized with Jews as victims of clerical prejudice. A small Jewish community emerged in Mexico City, many of its members advancing liberalism. But Jews and Protestants could not become citizens until 1843 and then only if they converted to Catholicism. The important Mexican nationalist Carlos María de Bustamante wrote in an 1847 essay (partly in response to the American invasion of Mexico) that Mexicans had "cried for the loss of the Sacred Christ, just as the Jews could have wept for the Savior in the sepulcher." Such a faith, Bustamante lamented in Latin, "would not be found in Israel [*Non inveni tantam fidem in Israel*]." The "noble" and "ultimately pious" Mexicans merited the beautiful and daunting reputation of having suffered the redemptive pain of "this idolatrous people," Bustamante heralded.[2] If Bustamante reflected opinion in the city, a tendency to express anti-Semitism remained in Mexico's provinces as well. In 1859 the children of practicing Jews were expelled from rural public schools.[3]

The few Jews in the United States migrated to commercial and manufacturing centers, forming ethnic communities prior to the Civil War and circulating in and through proximate economic and civic environs.⁴ Official decrees and social toleration enabled their integration, yet as one historian notes, an image persisted of the Jew "as Satan's ally, as the Antichrist, as the murderer, as the betrayer, as Shylock and Fagin."⁵ General Ulysses S. Grant generated anti-Semitism during the Civil War. The former Know-Nothing general condemned "unprincipled traders" who engaged in clandestine activity with the South in contraband cotton, and he reserved a pique for Jews among them as privileged and able to "travel anywhere." Grant's notorious Order No. 11 required district post commanders to expel Jews "as a class" from his military district, which cut across Tennessee, Mississippi, and Kentucky.⁶ Congressmen and newspapers objected, Jewish leaders breathed down Lincoln's neck, and the president ordered Grant to rescind the blanket order.⁷ Economic discrimination and incidents of violence against Jews and their property marred life in some localities, and anti-Semitism spurted from the pens of journalists and the mouths of politicians.⁸

Then we may reflect on the phenomenon of the surrogate Jew, collective action applying anti-Semitic stereotypes onto a non-Jewish group. Claudio Lomnitz studied opponents of the Mexican dictator General Porfirio Díaz at the turn of the twentieth century. They vented their hatred of the technocrats and economists who advised him, the so-called *científicos*, by hurling anti-Semitic epithets, derived from the Dreyfus Affair, at them even though no Jews counted among the científicos.⁹

Charles Clever immigrated to the United States from Prussia. He moved to Santa Fe in 1850 and found refuge clerking in the stores of Santa Fe's German-Jewish merchants. Clever developed professionally by establishing partnerships with Jewish businessmen, and he prominently evinced universal liberalism, as in the major speech he addressed at the 1862 Fourth of July commemoration.¹⁰ Clever's Jewishness has been "less than established," finds the historian of New Mexico's Jews.¹¹ Definitively, Father Juan de J. Trujillo, from the Santa Cruz parish north of Santa Fe, declared that he knew Clever to be Catholic, as Trujillo publicly swore "in obedience to truth and justice, before God and the people of New Mexico [*diré ante Dios y ante el pueblo de Nuevo Méjico, que conozco al dicho Clever, desde su juventud, por espacio de 18 años y he reconocido que es Católico*]," adding that "in his conversations, I found him able to assist at Mass, and he manifested to me his moral and religious sentiments [*en sus conversaciones le encontré capaz hasta para ayudar á misa, y me manifestó sus sentimientos morales y religiosos*]."[12] José D. Sena called Clever a "renegade" of Israel, perhaps meaning a convert to Catholicism. In any case, Father Trujillo spoke up precisely because the charge that Clever was a Jew, and therefore not fit to be New Mexico's delegate in Congress, had been blowing like a gale on the sea of the 1867 canvass for New Mexico's congressional delegate.

To Out a "Jew" on the Frontier

Charles Clever was rendered vulnerable to a Jewish configuration primarily because he was an effectively ambitious outsider. His facial features, not exactly Anglo or Nordic, likely contributed, and he spoke with a Germanic accent.[13] The attributions were framed in a three-part symbology: grubby fortune hunter, Svengali-type instrument, and the Jewish *gemeinschaft*.

Grubbing Wanderer

A load of anti-Semitic representations began landing on the person of Clever soon after the National Union Territorial Convention. It derived considerably from the fact that the well-educated immigrant did well in a frontier economy and along a path of public mobility in particular. He was appointed acting sheriff of Santa Fe County in 1852 and U.S. marshal in 1857. He joined the New Mexico bar in 1861 after becoming a naturalized citizen, "probably looking for politics as a career," a researcher notes. Clever's financial capacity was indicated in 1863 when he single-handedly purchased the *Santa Fe New Mexican*. Governor Henry Connelly appointed him to two important territorial offices at the same time, attorney general and adjutant general of the New Mexico Volunteers, recalled as helping to fuel the fight between the territorial legislature and Governor Robert Mitchell during the 1865–66 session. Clever also partnered with Gen. James H. Carleton and Mitchell in mining ventures.[14]

The *New Mexican*, which seems to have been under editorship of former Supreme Court justice Kirby Benedict, carefully avoided the Jew label while meaning it. From an obscurity "unsuited to his chivalric aspirations," it held, Clever reached to the halls that had resounded with the "eloquence of Webster, Clay and Calhoun." Should the "odor-

FIG. 26. *Augustine De Marle* (left) *and Charles P. Clever*, 1860, photographer unknown. The original title of the photograph mistakenly calls both Marle and Clever delegates to Congress from the New Mexico Territory. Marle had served as a clerk to the New Mexico Supreme Court. Clever came under anti-Semitic attack in 1867 in his run for delegate to Congress. Courtesy Palace of the Governors Photo Archives, NMHM/DCA, negative #007131.

ous breeze which has wafted him from the dunghill, still lingering in his sails, [be] moored at the portals of the national capital... [would] he sigh, like Alexander [the Great], that inscrutable fate has set a limit to his greatness? Would he not seek to overcome that obstacle in the Constitution which prohibits a foreigner from becoming president of the United States? In a republic," the piece belabored, "the ambitious climber always treads upon the rights of the people." It was the reason Clever had to be removed from his "snug offices" as attorney general and adjutant general.[15]

The *New Mexican* stated in another scurrilous bit that Clever did as delegate what he had done "as attorney general, adjutant general, etc., i.e., line his pockets and neglect his duties." Embellishing the notion of Jewish greed, the piece said Clever's friends were concealing the fact of his "hoarded gains... safely stowed away in the vaults of a European banker until the hour of its proper appreciation in this country when he will retire to their enjoyment beneath the flag of Prussia, who claims him as her faithful subject." Clearly, the jingoism ran, Clever could not lay a claim on "Americans" for their support based on his "nativity, religion, or accent."[16]

Spanish-language texts penned by Nuevomexicanos tapped with remarkable explicitness into the modalities of anti-Semitism that had circulated globally. Karl Marx fed a particular imaginary in 1844, money as the "zealous God of Israel, besides which no other god may stand... [t]he bill of exchange [being] the Jew's real God."[17] In a letter to the editors of the *New Mexican,* José Durán from Peñasco in Taos County accused Clever of daring to challenge the honorable Chávez because the delegate had not brought him "gold and silver to fill his pockets [*por que no te trujo* (sic) *el oro y la plata para renchir tu volcíos* (sic)]." Durán claimed to be unsurprised at Clever being one to conduct the "profession of the Jews," for he had been following that path and some of it understandably "stuck to him [*pero este no estrañó para mi porque esa es la profesión de los judíos, y tu siguiendo esta misma senda algo se te habra pegado.*]"[18]

"José Durán" was the nom de guerre of J.A.M. y Medina, whose byline appears at the end of the letter; that is, José Antonio Martínez y Medina, a rancher and Mexican Party leader in Taos County. Martínez has his character Durán issuing his message from scripture. In Spanish, John 6:61 in the non–King James version reads: "Jesus knew beforehand whereof the apostles complained [*Jesús sabía de antemano de lo que se estaban quejando*]." Durán calls Clever the "apostle of his new sect" and "false apostle of his immaculate general," meaning Carleton, "sustaining the ideas of the bitter enemies of this country [*sosteniendo ideas de los más asérrimos enemigos de este país*]," meaning New Mexico. John 6:62–63 follows with: "Are they disturbed by this lesson?... Will they be disturbed when they see the Son of man return to the place from which he came? [*¿Les molesta esta enseñanza?... ¿Les va a molestar cuando vean que el Hijo del hombre vuelve al lugar de donde vino?*]."[19] Chávez is Durán's proverbial Hijo, Son of New Mexico. Durán goes on to declare: "In justice he wanders, preaching to the Territory the doctrine that he set out to spread in union with his friends [*Con la justicia anda andando, predicando al Territorio la doctrina que esparcio en unión de sus amigos*]." Durán conveys his politico-spiritual conversion. He had originally sided with the forces of the *Gazette,* but, he declares, "I will repent. Pardon me, pardon me for the love of justice that is finding Chávez the man of valor [*Pero me arrepentiré, perdón perdón por amor, que la justicia la haye Chávez hombre de valor*]." Durán exclaims in closing, "Viva Chávez, viva his party; they are what I respect [*Viva Chavez, viva su partido; es lo que respeto yo*]."

Nuevomexicano politicians had been imbibing from the fountain of rational liberalism since being made to engage the American political system. However, the Durán contribution to the public discourse bespoke another *letrado* legacy. Hispanic Romanticism, Spain's Baroque Golden Age of literature, the legends of antiquity, Old and New Testaments, and even English-European literature gilded what fanned into a robust outbreak of verbal anti-Semitism in 1867. It is clear that from family inheritance these politicians had access to the works of the classics, including such religious texts as *Salomón Coronado* (*Solomon Crowned*) and other Old Testament texts, and others likely arrived in the American trade wagons.[20] Distinct political imaginaries came out of such sources. Marx fomented the stereotype of usury forming the "object of the Jew's worship in this world."[21] *Socorroeño* (One from the county or town of Socorro in the Río Abajo) submitted a biting allegory: Morocco is the place, Shakespeare the inspiration, a biblical Roman-style court the scene, usury at issue, and Jewish liberal hypocrisy a dominant theme. Moors punished the sin of usury by cutting off an amount of flesh from the usurer corresponding to the amount of money being claimed—"no better method for keeping him from getting fat," Socorroeño's fable begins.

In the story a Jew comes forward with a charge of usury against a Christian. He informs the judge of his proofs, testimonies of his neighbors, Samuel Levi and Jonas (Jona, the prophet of wickedness). The judge asks the Jew if he has some Muslim testimony. The Jew admits not; his were Jews but "good men and creditable in all." The judge asks for some Christian testimony and the Jew has none. The Christian states that he loaned the Jew money in his urgent need "without any interest and now the Jew, refusing to pay me back, accuses me of usury." The Christian has no proof, and the judge says it is possible he is right, but his accuser has evidence and he does not. The law orders his condemnation. The Jew claims obedience to the law "because there should be equality for all." The Jew as accuser must execute the sentence with a knife and a weight. As he prepares for the operation, the judge asks the Jew if he insists on observing the law. The Jew insists, for "the law is the law and for nothing would I not observe it." As the Jew begins to cut an ounce of flesh from the Christian, the judge warns him that exactly an ounce must be cut. If too much, the Christian must die; if too little, the remainder of the ounce will be cut from his own body. The Jew trembles in terror. He asks if he may withdraw the accusation. The judge affirms he can by paying the Christian his credit and becoming his slave. The Jew submits, confessing that he lied. The Christian pardons him "because God is Just." Secretly though the Jew acted, "justice always triumphs," the Christian intones. Socorroeño pointed out that one of the candidates running for New Mexico's delegate would have to submit his falsehoods like the allegorical Jew: "It will not be the last time," he prophesied.[22]

Catholic propagators historically exploited the Passion in an ancient prejudice against Jews as figures who killed Christ.[23] The Spanish Renaissance left the idealization of the pastoral folk as carriers of wisdom. A self-identified "herder of sheep" had Clever prepared to betray one of the people's sacred rights. A rico in the Río Abajo told the herder of Clever selling Jesus out for thirty coins like Judas Iscariot, wanting the people's vote only for the money it would bring him.[24] A fictive epistolary paralleled the drama in *Fuenteovejuna,* a tragicomedy by the Baroque playwright Félix Lope de Vega Carpio depicting the abuse of neighbors in Fuenteovejuna by the local military commander and his assassination by villagers during the battle for the Spanish crown. In the New Mexico epistolary, a man in Taos County complains to his sister of the despotic rule the residents in the villages of Guadalupita and Coyote are suffering at the hands of men who have muscled in to take control of the common pastures, a Nuevomexicano in particular. The twist comes when the sister admonishes the people that whatever they do, they should not vote for Clever, who rather than come to their assistance would sell them out for thirty coins, the well-known "Judaic price" for betraying "*el Señor JesuCristo [sic]*."[25]

One calling himself A Voter posited Clever as a Jew aiming to do away with the religion of New Mexico. Clever had criticized the Mesilla priest Padre José de Jesús Baca for shifting his loyalty from Carleton to Chávez. A Voter had Clever, wanting to "suppress the free will of New Mexico," starting the fire of the campaign like a "German scoundrel [*bergante alemán*]." In attacking Father Baca, A Voter stated, Clever "perhaps thought he had given a mortal blow to the Holy Catholic Church [*habrá creido quisa que ha dado un golpe mortal á la Santa Iglesia Católica*]." When the time came to count votes on the day of the election, he would find "to his grief" that he was not "as successful as his progenitors in their order for the execution of Jesus Christ [*el hayará para su mayor congoja que le es tan ventajoso como á sus projenitores la orden para le ejecución de Jesu-cristo*]."[26] An ex-militia volunteer conjured the wandering Jew, exclaiming, "No and no to a deserter of Israel, who abandoned his natal country." He raised the notion of Jews wandering to speculate on disasters: Nuevomexicanos were satisfied, the writer stated, that "Clever and Co." were "only out to enrich themselves at our cost."[27] Clever took New Mexico as his Israel to betray in a place where "the saints whipped themselves [penitente brotherhood] and sold themselves out (in alto voice) to the highest bidder."[28] As it has been generalized, "Real tensions and difficulties were particularly exacerbated by the fact that the traditional notions about the Jewish character were melded with the disagreeable aspects of the new conditions."[29]

The Jew Leading Political Schemers

Clever inevitably joined the American Party in partnerships with the likes of Joab Houghton, a key investor in Jewish mercantile establishments, and Miguel Antonio Otero, who as delegate to Congress made him a federal marshal.[30] He was in with American Party Democrats who fomented the idea of forming a Democratic Party in 1853.[31] A writer going by Un Ranchero challenged the *Gazette*'s praise of the Union Party Territorial Convention by denouncing conspiratorial bosses for "managing the Mexican race" with "lies, with money and other similar things." Finding Francisco Perea useless for this purpose anymore, the enemy patrones turned to the "pursuit of a Jew in his place."[32]

Shakespeare's figure appeared in a Spanish-language condemnation of Chávez enemies wanting to submerge the people beneath the ground "of the errant speculator . . . that swarm of Shylocks, or Bloodsuckers [*ese emjambre de "Shylocks" ó Sangijuelas*], willing to take the last pound of flesh from the Christian's body, if with it they could gain their capital, selling it for ten cents." Such were their liberal ideas "of the fluorescent and progressive 19th century, very fecund and empowering: ideas of an infinite health, and arguments very much founded in reason and justice."[33] Similarly, the *New York Dispatch* had written of Williams Street and Exchange Place with its "'descendants of Shylock,' and all you would hear would be 'Up to shixty-five, up to sheventy-one! Mine God, it vill go up to von hundred!'" There was as little truth in this as in any other blanket stereotype, as the historian who found the item points out: "The New York Jewish editors dared their secular colleagues to walk to the gold curb and count Jews, so certain were they that a very small proportion of Jews could be found there."[34]

Nuevomexicano ink wells poured out the ancient technique of the fictional dialogue. Several *diálogos* focused on the Clever-Jewish association in *el Nuevo-Mejicano*. The caricatures portrayed a dismal, dreary politics, melancholia, pessimism, or abjection, deriving from stories and character portrayals in Hispanic moralizing Baroque literature and drama.[35] One type of dialogue appeared in satirical conversation between old friends, tragicomic, caustic, and morose. Many modern writers evoked the figure of the "oracle" (prophet) from classical antiquity, the biblical priest or priestess, and religious traditions around the world. In 1647 Baltasar Gracián y Morales came out with *Oráculo manual, y arte de prudencia* (The oracle's manual of the art of prudence). Gracián supplied maxims of conduct for the refined

Spanish courtier to become a public oracle, a man of prognostication, based on the essential quality of prudence. The Baroque philosopher advised that to be a social prophet, the learned individual must surround himself with sagacious men. The oracle's brilliance would sound when he "spoke in a public assembly with the wit of many; or rather, you hear as many Sages speaking by his mouth, as have before instructed him."[36] In 1845 the Spanish playwright José Zorrilla published his poetic drama *Traidor, Inconfeso y Mártir* (Traitor, Unconfessed One and Martyr) as tragic dialogue.[37] Gracián's oracle and Zorrilla's *Traidor* encased in a mood of anxiety resonated in a farcical dialogue penned by a Chavista, which mocks Clever's Constitutional Party, the latest incarnation of the American shadow-party. The dialogue involves two members of the Constitutional Party who discuss in a hidden place how it was that their leaders could possibly have settled on a Jew to be their candidate for delegate to Congress (for the full Spanish text, see appendix 5).[38]

In the skit *Traidor* is meant as a traitor to New Mexico and Nuevomexicanos, for he is one of the "spurious," or false, sons of la Casa Blanca (the White House), which happens to be the name of the Río Abajo settlement where General James Carleton has his personal headquarters. Carleton is not named in the story, but it is clear that he is meant to be the oracle of the Constitutional Party. *Chulito* (cutie) is the lap dog or favored one of the party rulers and an insider at the Royal Palace, signifying the Palace of the Governors, where Robert Mitchell, though not named, holds court as the Union Party governor. Chulito is liked by party chiefs for his ability to deliver the vote in his locality, but as Traidor knows, he is among those party loyalists who are angry that his party leaders forced the nomination of a Jew to be its delegate to Congress. Chulito admits that for years it had been known "by my angry fist" that he detested that "degenerate race." Conjuring the wayfaring Jew conceived for centuries as condemned to "eternal homeless wandering," Chulito thought no person of a "free opinion" could ever support the "errant Jew whose sentence of expulsion [from *his* homeland] was predicted by God"; moreover, Clever appeared an ungrateful betrayer of New Mexico, and the disappointment was made worse in that the "ancient oracle of the famous White House" usually held in his "tender hands" the interests of Nuevomexicanos. Why, then, would he favor the Jew, Clever?[39]

Traidor must keep Chulito from defecting to the Chávez side in the election. He tries by giving an account of how Clever's nomination came about. But first Traidor has Chulito promise to keep their confidence because there were "lobos," if not "coyotes" (gangster speculators), on the road to eat them up over the nomination, and not all assumed friends could be trusted. Traidor notes in hushed tone how the defeat of their man Perea in 1865 produced such a "scary" crisis for their party, leaving it hesitant, indecisive, and pensive. Their lamentable condition could be remedied only by the strength of "greenbacks." Prior to the nominating convention, the Grand Oracle (Carleton, in the garb of both courtier and Old Testament priest) requested a secret *concilio* of the true friends of the White House and the Royal Palace (Gracián's sagacious men encircling the oracle). It was far from a liberal gesture, Traidor admits, but the concilio at least accepted parliamentary rules for its deliberations. The Grand Oracle reminds the members of their sad political condition, telling them that a committee had submitted to him the persons likely to be considered for nomination at the (Constitutional) convention. They were Francisco Perea; Antonio José Otero, the former Kearny Judge; Vicente Romero, Mora County probate judge, rancher, and Bosque Redondo contractor; and Clever. As the Grand Oracle stresses to the wise committeemen, money is the key factor to consider in deciding who should be their champion.

When Perea's name lands on the table, a "profound silence" comes over the concilio. A member, trembling with fear, his teeth chattering and he a bit drunk, fears saying anything against this powerful man, but he mourns the deep loss they all suffered at Perea's defeat. Worse, Perea spent his fortune and credit trying to get reelected. The concilio would have to pay for his campaign, the worst recommendation possible. As for Otero, he would make a fine delegate, one of the wise concilio members notes. However, once nominated he would stay at home to await the results, could not be counted on to stump plaza to plaza, and would not spend money to herd the voters into line as they themselves had been taught; he had never done it, so he could not be managed. If elected, he would benefit *his* people only, turning party soldiers like themselves into "brute lobos," their mouths left open in hopes of some scraps thrown their way; nor could they demand appointments. It was unclear whether Otero wanted the position anyway, and so no castles in the air should go up around him. The concilio rejects him.

Mention of the powerful Vicente Romero causes eyes to well up. Lips are stilled until one, trembling for fear of a possible Judas in the group out to betray confidence, stands to speak. Their party was left hanging in the last election, he notes, for its tendency to commit shenanigans at the polls were too well known as in Romero's Mora County. Romero was a respectable person who might carry the (Constitutional Party) nominating convention, but someone, probably themselves, would have to pay for his campaign to raise him to a level of respectability. His name is removed from consideration.

The concilio president (meaning the unnamed James Collins) explains why the members should not hesitate in adopting Clever as their candidate, as the Oracle wants. In all frankness, he says, the time is not good to risk going with a true friend. He blurts out that Clever pretended to be an errant Jew. They knew it was not so, but Clever put it up to signal his money bags as a desperate remedy for their desperate political problems. They must remove their masks of pride and admit that if they do not go along with Clever's idea, they will admit of their coming defeat, "not before the people but before ourselves." On reflection they see that his bad qualities are a minor problem. Fear grips their faces, but they come to see Clever's ambition as equal to the task of standing up to their competitors (in the National Party). Throwing it out as bait, they might catch a newspaper to boost the campaign, the strategizing goes. Best of all, the enormous weight of campaign costs would come off their shoulders to be placed on Clever. Tying him down (shades of Gulliver), they would make him "vomit the Greenbacks," which this "meat-eating Lobo" had accumulated—the coyote, as he was better known, who in sheep's clothing had "sucked the blood of the imbecile people," harvesting the sympathies of the descendants of the people of Israel (German Jews), who since coming to New Mexico had done nothing but hoard their "coveted metal." Placing the "idol" Clever before the people, they, though miserable, could present themselves smilingly as "Liberals" for their longtime campaign.

All depended on the concilio's dear friends to express hope and confidence to the public and doubtful friends as Traidor was doing with Chulito. The people's opinions might differ, but their own (conspiratorial and cynical) agreement would be kept secret. Concilio members as party leaders would support the candidates who fell into line behind Clever. The president would vouch for Clever's victory in print, as the people did not understand that "by their Solomon (that is, Carleton, the wise, and wealthy King of the Israelis) would they see their champion (Clever)." It was ridiculous and almost unnecessary for the president to mention to the convened advisors their eventual need to deal with the swarm of politicians who would daily present themselves to dip into Clever's pockets, if they wanted to keep the comers loyal to their principles. The president calls such a development a victory for their candidate. By September they would pluck Clever for the appointed jobs to be filled. Those kinds of positions for which Clever had been made a "compulsory heir" (by his longtime political patrons) would pass into their hands, serving them well for two years more at least. Perhaps things would change in two years. They would need to see which road was best for them at that time. For now, anything they could hope for must come from the (government) trough.

The president regrets that their opponents will not "remove their finger from the line" (in accusation) regarding Clever handing out public positions left and right, and he had to admit that Chávez had them "perplexed and dejected" because of this. No matter how much they lied about Chávez, their writings would remain as nothing because of the adage saying, "the lie prevails until the truth arrives." Concilio members knew they were "known shrubs" (well recognized for their cupidity) on the political landscape. Though they talked with the mouth of an angel, the people would not accept their sophism, yet they must try (with their finest rhetoric). The president closes his case and asks for everyone's concurrence. Concilio members express their respect and courtesy by mounting a caravan to their elderly consultant, the Grand Oracle. Their moribund (Oracle) hero confirms the president's recommendation. The question is called for *viva voz* vote. It is unanimous to connive for the nomination of C. P. Clever at the convention, the one in whom they will repose their faith for delegate to Congress. Compelled to keep their proceedings confidential, each signs a card titled "Secret Council held in the famous white house of the three powers [i.e., Carleton, Mitchell, Collins] in the sad circumstances in the year of our Lord 1867." Traidor is named secretary, ordered to conserve the testimonials in the most secure place for "perpetual memory."

Traidor respects Chulito so much as an agent of the (governor's) Royal Palace that he decides to break his vow of silence about the secret concilio. Did Chulito agree, Traidor wants to know, that their elderly leader deserved the title Prophet now that he knows how the Clever nomination came about? Chulito comes around. Impressed by the wise secret council, of which he had known nothing, he agrees that the ancient consultant deserves the title of wise Prophet in predicting that Clever would come out his party's nominee, for the process went just as the pre-convention concilio had planned, while the Prophet stayed aloof. He congratulates Traidor for his new power-role in the party, and he looks forward to the showers of money and jobs soon to fall from Clever's candidacy "until our champion and his race go back to the way they were before." Traidor explains the next step: to accuse their political enemies of being the ambitious anti-Americans and of corruptly defrauding the people of their rights, while treating Clever as the "guardian angel who was, from the hand of God, chosen as our future champion, the man in whom the people could pin their hopes." Chulito pledges his part to confuse the ignorant people into "contemplation and delirium over our newfound champion and his race," while leaving the opposition most degraded. "Enough, my fine Chulito," Traidor concludes. "Until another time, take your cash and go to comfort the grief-stricken doubters; so much pleasure it gives me to see you so happy; go, have a drink and shout !Viva C. P. Clever!."

The Jewish Community

Classical allusions and fanciful stories seem today like strange currency for a political campaign, but at the time they were not especially unusual and served as acceptable ways of responding to some undeniably awkward developments. They combined well with other forms of oppositional assault. In the key meaning of socio-psychological displacement, aggression manifestly directed to one target is meant to injure another object. Some of New Mexico's 1867 anti-Semitism transcended Clever for the purpose of outing an important sector that lay quietly behind the public discourse. Resentments that could not have been expressed in routine campaigns found their outlet.

German-Jewish merchants built a modern mercantilist system in territorial New Mexico on top of the markets Nuevomexicano sheep magnates developed, extending merchant contracts to the east.[40] The minute group, less than 1 percent of the population, succeeded remarkably. Individuals in the network achieved well beyond their fractional representation. "There can be little doubt that New Mexico's economic climate agreed with them," Henry Tobias observes. Of course, with neighbors as customers and suppliers, it was for them to adjust to the realities of the settled Nuevomexicanos and the "givens of American practices and laws." The year 1860 initiated what Tobias calls the "Golden Age of the German-Jewish Merchants" in New Mexico. Diversified mercantile activity spelled expanded fortunes and a greater share of merchant business, and considerably broke down New Mexico's Gellnerian economic segmentation.[41] The German-Jewish community became a "ubiquitous lot."[42] Its position in New Mexico was enhanced by an association with General Carleton and providing goods to the sutlers of Fort Union and Bosque Redondo.[43]

An anonymous Chávez partisan flagged German Jews in scriptural prose. As it was put, Clever's "Israeli meditations" were "pre-ordained" for one seeking to represent "his people that for so many years has not had any representation [in politics] whatever." Should he lose the election, [the Jewish merchants] "Friedman, Staab and whoever else from Israel" would hire Clever back as their clerk.[44] This politicization of the growing Jewish influence represented the part played by Jews in rural areas as an "economically strong but politically vulnerable 'pariah' ethnic minority," performing commercial and entrepreneurial functions that were "conspicuous, remunerative, important, but socially disparaged," particularly by a "politically dominant yet economically unskilled agricultural majority."[45] Chávez's campaign made a token rendering of the German Jews into a political pariah. The idea of Santa Fe as a "little Jerusalem" had been expressed a few years before.[46] An anonymous Spanish writer, taking from Revelations, pointed at the "cursed sons of Israel . . . with their doctrines wanting to convert New Mexico into the new Jerusalem," transposed from a Christian symbolism actually, suggesting a final glorious salvation in the newly inhabited land.[47]

Two reports referred to the hustings in Alburquerque in which a group of Jews were said to have rallied in support of Clever. Sources indicate that Clever showed up at the pro-Chávez event and was invited to speak before the crowd of three hundred. The story from the organizers patronizingly caricatured the *Judillitos* (little Jews) having "so great a time" foot-stomping in order to drown out Clever's remarks. As Chávez took the podium, the group attempted to get the people to leave his rally, without success.[48] The Jews then held a rally at the home of a Euroamerican, and in the evening the Judillito called "Four Eyes" and an associate gathered the people with flute and drum. Some fifteen of them carried lanterns on a march through the streets to the plaza. Speeches were delivered before the flag pole. Chávez was invited to join in debate, but he excused himself stating that he had sufficiently covered the key questions earlier in the day. An Alburquerque correspondent sarcastically reported that "*La Judaica*" resolved that Chávez was the cause of the Civil War, flooding rivers, and a wind storm blowing for two days straight.[49]

The Avenging Prodigal Son

The liberal basis of the Mexican party supported the collective rights of Mexicans and called for progressive legislation. A sense of liberal pluralism informed these politics, but it was centered on a populace struggling in their homeland. The Mexican shadow-party, working under the National Union Party this election, employed anti-Semitic theatrics in rhetorical confrontation with the colonial dominance of Clever's (American) Constitutional Party. The campaign answered in practical terms to the disparagements and insults that had been accumulating against the Nuevomexicano "people" and José Francisco Chávez particularly.

It seems Chávez did not associate himself with anti-Semitism. He could have fueled the fire anonymously. Certainly, he does not appear to have been seeking to curtail or halt it.[50] The advantage for him involved a counter narrative. Political culture in interior Mexico had already constructed the image of the "virtuous caudillo," set against the "vicious elites," in discourses of messianism. The virtuous caudillo appeared in 1867 New Mexico in the form of the noble native son rico, defender of *la patria chica* against the Jewish interlopers. If Clever arrived as an "adventurer from Israel" to make his fortune, "abandoning the standard of his nationality," as one Nuevomexicano put it in Spanish, the virtuous José Francisco was "born in New Mexico, is Nuevo Mejicano, known by all his fellow citizens," and had never been a "deserter to his own country in order to find nations to represent [*Chávez nació en Nuevo Méjico, es Nuevo Mejicano, conocido por todos sus Conciudadanos . . . y nunca há sido desertor de su país para irse á buscar naciones para representar*]."[51] *Cubereño* (one from Cubero on the edge of Navajo country) drew the stark distinction. Chávez was "born in our land," had always been "*un hombre de bien and caballero*," as no one could deny. Clever came to New Mexico in contrast to be a general in the militia for money, a prosecutor for money, and an attorney for money. All his jobs "in this country" were for money, "filling his pockets" with the coin that rightfully belonged to the people of the territory.[52]

Primeriso (first-timer), speaking for Nuevomexicano youth, struck the messianic note in shaming those who relied on someone foreign to their community, who did not care about its interests, willing to sacrifice the people for his aggrandizement, when their happiness lay in the person of a young and energetic native son, one prepared to support the cause of the people, ready to protect their families and properties, as he had done for two years, more than any other delegate, including casting off an oppressive military commander, acquiring appropriations to manage Indians, and halting Coyotero Apache raids. To go with the foreigner Clever was to believe shamefacedly that there were no competent Nuevomexicanos. By sending the *nativo* Chávez to Congress, the people would know they had someone much better than the Carleton-Mitchell "gang" and would prove that New Mexico had *criollitos* (young creole ones) who were "able and expert . . . over any foreigner living on our land"[53]

Another hailed Chávez for being "born here; here are his generations, his interests, his family, all, finally, that are necessary to rest our confidence in him." Other Euroamerican politicians were castigated for being outsiders, and Clever received the weight of that attribution. Standing on a liberal anti-colonialism, Chávez's homeland attachment signified American loyalty. He did not abandon the Union in the War, it was said, based on the rumor that Clever did not engage in combat.[54] The occasional Euroamerican joined in the praise of the native hero. Fidelio asked, "[W]ho, among all the citizens of this territory will so insult common sense as to affirm Gen. Clever, a foreigner, cares more and will do more for the Mexican people then Col. Chávez who, by birth and by every consideration that could make him so, is their countryman?" Native status made Chávez more the American than the immigrant to the United States. It had been "the misfortune and disgrace to the United States, no less than the territory of New Mexico, that patriotism and loyalty have been sought among the European importations that darken our seaports, ignoring almost entirely the merits of native born citizens, and their better claim to public confidence." Make Clever delegate, the warning went, to ensure injustice to "New Mexican talent and loyalty."[55]

The Push-Back . . . and Forth

Clever reportedly announced at a stop on the speaker's trail to those who spread the idea he was a Jew that *"they lied from the top of their heads to the soles of their boots"* (emphasis in the original).[56] No other public denial by him appears, though he might have published others anonymously by referring to himself in the third person. A spate of refutations on his behalf did appear. Opposing verbal warriors answered them back, sometimes in still higher anti-Semitic pitch.

Some called the anti-Semitism with pure cynicism. *Un Alburquerqueño Libre* (A free Alburquerquean) accused the "charlatan" reporter of the Alburquerque rally of lying in describing the Jews as fools. The people were not so ignorant as to believe that a group of "little Jews" would stay in such a meeting, it was claimed. Chávez was the true Judas for doing nothing for his homeland. Returning him to Congress would reflect stubborn confirmation of his "Judas-feeling" that the people of New Mexico were incapable of knowing their own wellbeing, the Cleverite wrote, not seeing that he had been repudiated on the issue of his federal appointments.[57]

A citizen accused Chávez men of "working his politics" through deception and secrecy and well knew it. The critic said they called Clever a Jew, "coyote," German, and foreigner but trembled in shouting "Jew." So loyal were they to their own religion that they recognized "coyote" as their own type of politician and knew very well that Clever was neither Jew nor coyote. "German he is," the writer said, "and he should be proud of it, as Chávez should be when he thinks of the aristocracy of his upbringing." As for his "foreignness," Clever's citizenship was unquestioned, "and now only those who do not want to confess the truth, propagate the idea that behind it all, the major, unworthy, falsehood is that he was truly a herder."[58]

Clever supporters denounced the anti-Semitism on fair liberal grounds. One saw the anti-Jewish attack going against material modernization. That the Santa Fe Plaza had recently undergone an aspect of progress, with newly planted trees and beautiful green shrubs, was via the philanthropy of the merchants from the "Jewish race," those the enemy "abhorred."[59] Others likened the fear of Jews to an apparition from the mists of the pre-Enlightenment. It was because Chávez had done nothing for New Mexico, a Nuevomexicano charged, that he proclaimed Santa Fe the land of Israel. "Miserable ideas!" declaimed *Yanos Veremos* (We shall see). "Ideas of two or three centuries ago, ideas of superstition, ideas of ignorance, miserable defense, defense without reason [*¡Miserables ideas! Ideas de dos ó tres siglos pasado, ideas de superstición, ideas de ignorancia, defensa miserable, defensa sin razón!*]."[60] Another said the most humble workers and laborers recognized "with horror" that in Chávez and Pino, "the darkness" of the Inquisition would return to reign in New Mexico.[61] A Euroamerican addressed Chávez in Spanish:

> I am a Roman Catholic, so are you, so is *Mr. Clever*. If then he is a Jew, so are you and so am I. But don't you think that a party has arrived at a very low ebb, when it can profess no better arguments against an opponent than that he belongs to a particular profession of faith. Have we not yet arrived at that state of progression in the world's history, when we can allow the possession of honesty, intelligence and ability to those who, by education or early impressions, may differ from us on some points of dogma?[62]

The *Gazette* saw in the appeal to religious prejudice a move to curry the vote of the clergy.[63] Whether for this or another reason, Nuevomexicano priests in Doña Ana, Taos, and Mora counties worked for Chávez, while the priest in Valencia County, at least, went against him.[64] The favorable ones may have fed anonymous anti-Semitism into the discourse.

Some linked Americanism and human universalism. One José de Jesús García countered el Cubereño's paisano identity, declaring himself an "Americano." He figured Cubereño to be one too; that is, not a citizen of Mexico. If Clever was a descendant of Adam and Eve, "well, according to history," there was no other "origin for the human race [*el señor C. P. Clever, naturalmente, es descendiente de Adán y Eva, pues según la historia, no hay otra origen de la raza humana*]." García did not like favoring a candidate based on who had given him birth, for being a "caballero," or as *hombre de bien* "and who knows what else." Cubereño was badly mistaken to have citizens taking such as reasons to support their "idol [*en favor de su ídolo*]." He may as well have told them who his own parents were to win their votes. Cubereño had accused Clever of taking public appointments to make money only, but any worthy worker was entitled to his salary. If Cubereño did not believe it, García had a field of corn for him; he needed a worker, and "I believe that you think only men like yourself can censure a man who asks for work [*vengase para esta plaza, que aquí tengo un pedaso de maíz, busco un trabajador, que creo lo que V. cree, pues solamente hombres como V. pueden censurar que un hombre pida por trabajo*]." García challenged Cubereño to see him voting "in favor of the one you hate." "Do you hear me?" García barked. "Listen well! Viva Clever! [*¿Me oye? Escuche bien, ¡Viva Clever!*]."[65]

A contributor charged José D. Sena with the sin of wanting to "distinguish more races in the world."[66] The *Gazette* accused in true American Party style the Chávez campaign of turning on "a question of races," of depicting New Mexico as composed of "an American element and a Mexican element—and ask which shall prevail," when all were Americans, the real issue having to do with the "wants, the necessities, and the best interests of New Mexico."[67]

In a couple of give-and-take letters, an advocate of American liberalism attacked the anti-Semitic voices and was promptly challenged by a Chavista. A Nuevomexicano first criticized an abject meeting held at the home of Miguel E. Pino in which Chávez expressed himself "with a tenderness truly worthy of compassion, and in his argument, if that's what you want to call it," tried to get his friends to pardon him for his acts in the Congress yet could not point to anything he had done. Suggesting a displacement to have something to crow about, the Chávez men had the "egoism" to mistreat the foreigner only for his luck of being born in another place, presenting a "repugnant question, shouting against the Jew, Jew [*esa cuestión repugnante, que horroriza, gritando contra el Judío, Judío*]." Oddly, this commentator believed Clever to be a German Jew. That he came to make himself into an American citizen meant he was entitled to the same privileges and rights as any other native of the country, a credit to him for it was evident that many foreigners did not want to be legal citizens of the United States, Pino being the one implied. Clever's immigrant status made New Mexico look like the United States, the writer held. To understand the issue better, he wrote, it needed to be recalled that two-thirds of the population of the states and territories were foreigners, "arrivals from Europe, and they made themselves into legal citizens, protected by the laws with equal rights, with equal privileges [*más de dos terceras partes de la población de nuestros Estados y Territorios son extranjeros viendos de la Europa, y hechos allí ciudadanos legales y protegidos por las leyes con iguales derechos, con iguales privilegios que aquellos que nacieron allí*]."[68]

Hasta Otra Vista (Until we meet again) accused this Cleverite of falsely describing the Pino rally (for the full Spanish text, see appendix 6).[69] Referring to the claim that Chávez had done nothing while in Congress, Hasta Otra Vista sarcastically noted that the act of knocking down another was the "most precious jewel" of the era, product of the "most brilliant passions," associated mostly with the "cursed son of Israel and with his doctrines wanting to convert New Mexico into the new Jerusalem." Chávez appeared to be being forced into battle with those who had conspired to trip him up in Washington. Chávez's intrepid and "manly" disposition defied the "vile, black and miserable representations" made of him and the people. It proved that he demanded appreciation and respect for the American government and Nuevomexicano adhesion and *amor* for its "magnanimous and liberal institutions." Chávez came from the bosom of his people, pure, clean, without compromise, and uncorrupted. He found himself among "poisonous serpents and ravenous tigers" (as in *Romans*, where Bishop Ignatius is sacrificed for his love of the Christian God by "being torn apart by wild animals in the public arena").[70]

As for "Carlos" P. Clever, according to Otra Vista, the "innocent" people who worked with the sweat of their brow needed to beware of the "speculator" out to make them the victim of his "rapaciousness." If compatriots elected Clever—"the father of the poor, the vindicator of the impossible, the protector of the bandaged wounds, the consoler of the afflicted, the protector of the necessities of the poor, the liberator of the oppressed, the immaculate protector of the impeded, and so many other virtuous titles"—they could be sure that "with his power without rival," he would "move the treasury of the United States to Santa Fe, or the new Palestine more appropriately." On his return he would fatten his pockets (*engruesar sus bolcillas*); take control of public positions "bequeathed to him by his deceased Grandpa Henry Connelly, confirmed, sealed and submitted by the 'scrupulous' R. B. Mitchell, administrator of the territorial receipts"; and favor friends who sold musical instruments, guns, and liquor "with their spirited desire to inform the people of their rights, but who no doubt were the lovers of progress, the trains, the telegraphs, the developers of mines, in order to fill their pockets." Hasta Otra Vista denied that Colonel Chávez made promises of patronage to supporters, nor did they expect any in return for their allegiance. They knew Carleton of the "white house" with his "fingernails extending far" to appoint his satellites to federal positions. The "miserable Santiago Collins" would do anything to get pastel for his descendants. With "embarrassing lowness," he and friends had gone to Washington and "on their knees" begged the president for jobs," yet they accused Chávez of doing nothing as delegate. "This is the Americanism that they enjoy," the author proclaimed, "their adhesion to the government and its institutions." While the treasury held money, the government could not have happier friends than Collins, Mitchell, Clever, and company, whom they put up as the "most prominent pillars of the people," who by means of military contracts wanted to satisfy the "mistaken and adventurous sons of Faran" (the mountains surrounding the Jews in Exodus]) They were the ones who went to the people's hovels claiming to be the most patriotic and most interested in the well-being of New Mexico "as its own children, as of those who had never known any other than the New Mexican land."

The "horrifying shouts against the Jew" raised a "repugnant question," Hasta Otra Vista insisted, but it did not compare to the horror of the "faction of speculators" prostrating the people, the "whip and the plague of New Mexico, who, after usurping our posts, devastated our homeland, claimed to be more American than us, grabbing the reins to govern us." That gang knew Clever was born in Prussia but failed to say that, as a mere buck soldier, he deserted the ranks of his native government and that he, "unmasked, traveled the oceans to come search for a people sufficiently savage to elevate him to the position of delegate." Yet the people of New Mexico had not their own government. "Go forth, People of New Mexico," it was sarcastically invoked. "Elect the General, Clever, and you will see how he will not vacillate in deserting our interests by right and proper seal, just as he deserted the ranks of his government to come search for his elevation and aggrandizement among you."

William Zeckendorf was one of two Jews to chime in. Zeckendorf was a Union officer in the Civil War, one of two brothers with businesses in Alburquerque as well as Santa Fe.[71] He noted that he did not profess the Jewish religious observances but was a "Jew by birth" and so had to address the "low, mean, contemptible conduct of the leaders of the Chávez party," bringing the election "to a point of religion." Zeckendorf inverted the betrayer. Should the Chávez men succeed in their "miserable designs to deceive the people," the liberal put forth, they would elect the man "who is no more fit to be our delegate than the traitor Arnold was to be president of the United States at the time when the father of this great country, George Washington, was elected to that position." A man so ignorant "as to raise the question of religion in a political contest under our present government, and in the nineteenth century, is a contemptible defamer of the glorious constitution of the United States, a malignant enemy of civilization, a putrid obstruction on the march of progress, and a venomous friend of the sacred rights of every human being."

Zeckendorf asked the "true and good citizens" if the Jews of the territory had ever, "by their conduct," deserved opprobrium. "There may be bad men amongst them," he asserted, "but show me the religion or creed, that does not contain bad men; and if you do I will never assert again that I am a Jew and forever renounce my forefathers of whom I think I have reason to be proud." If the Jews killed Christ in former times, only the "malicious, ignorant fanatics" would blame the present generation. "Has not the race of Israel suffered enough?" he posed. "Does not the precious blood of thousands of martyrs of that creed satiate the voracious scoundrels who are trying to incite the demoniacal spirit of revenge in the minds of the low and vulgar? Does true Christianity teach this? No, it does not." The Jews did what thousands since the Pilgrims had done, "left their beloved homes and emigrated to the United States to enjoy the benign protection of our free and glorious institutions, and there is as proof that they behaved as well as those of any other creed or religion."

Zeckendorf laid responsibility for the false Jewish issue squarely on Chávez. The Jews would show in this election, he vowed, "that their rights are as sacred to them as they are to Chávez or any other man."

He denied that the Jews supported Clever on the belief he was Jewish, "and if he was a Jew I do not think that would make him a worse man. Clever and Chávez are both Catholics; in this they are equal. No religion should be discussed in a political contest—but only the merits of the men." Chávez's inferior qualifications and friendship with "vile demagogues" made him unacceptable to Jews, Catholics, and Protestants. Clever always showed respect for the rights of every citizen and was not the candidate of "a sect, creed, or clique, but of a poor people whose interests have been prejudiced by the incompetency of our late incubus." The citizens in favor of progress, civilization, and prosperity, no matter their religion, would "combine to vote for him and vindicate the noble constitution of our beloved country."[72]

Another writer, signing off as *Un Americano de Nacimiento y no Judío* (American by birth and not a Jew), took Zeckendorf to the shed in a Spanish Renaissance diatribe that could have appeared only behind the cloak of a non-English language. Zeckendorf had applied his "intellectual talent" and "brilliant passages" to argue that the election had turned on religion but he did not understand religion itself, the argument went. "Religion is understood to be a rule of morality established by Jesus Christ, and everything else is called sophism or infidelity, sustained by some without any authority [*Religión se entiende ser una regla de moralidad establecida por Jesucristo, y todo lo que no es así se llama sofisma ó infedilidad que sostienen (ciertamente) sin autoridad ninguna*]." The various sects were founded on the law of Jesus Christ. Zeckendorf should know that the Jewish religious principles, "if as such he wants to call them," were "not recognized by natural law nor by municipal law or by the law of revelation [*que los principios religiosos (si así les desea llamar) de su religión no son reconocidos por la ley de la naturaleza, ni por la ley municipal ó por la ley de la revelación*]." While Zeckendorf was one Jew to accept that his people killed Jesus, neither he nor his fellow travelers ever forgot the "Israeli principles." If it were true that the three laws did not recognize his religion, Zeckendorf was "too wrapped up in the ignorance and stupidity" of mixing religions to help his political champion and needed to "select a more appropriate plan [*si es que ninguna de las tres leyes reconoce á la religión mencionada, entonces señor autor esta V. demasiado enrollado en la ignorancia y estupidez de su mente, con querer mezclar religiones para auxiliar a su campeón en la política, escoja V. un plan más Propio*]."

Un Americano had Zeckendorf being ashamed of his origins in claiming that no man of reason would blame him and his present generation in the death of Jesus Christ. The hypocrite Zeckendorf wanted to betray the Catholic people, judged Un Americano. He both converted from being a Jew and begged repentance for the fact that his ancestors had nailed Jesus Christ "foot and hand [*de pies y manos*]." But if in the election there were those working against Jews, Un Americano claimed not to know it. If there were, Zeckendorf was not included because of his conversion. As such, his "sorrowful tears of regret" caused by his ancestors having crucified "the Creator" was filled with "bitters and vinegar [*llora lágrimas pesarosos á causa de que sus antecesores hallan crucificado á nuestro criador, manda hiel y vinaigre en su hecho*]." Independent voters must reflect on Zeckendorf's politics, Un Americano warned the independent readers. If Chávez must defend himself against one of Zeckendorf's countrymen, though he be equal to the traitor Arnold, Clever's fault was to deny his heritage while Chávez stood before them a native son, "a free citizen and able." Zeckendorf needed to remove his predatory lobo hide, Un Americano remonstrated, and reveal his claws, as it served nothing to hide them. "You defend your political party as you execute your feigned attack on the shop-keeper, until you squeeze him out of his last coin." If he now believed in the "New Testament of Our Jesus Christ," he was a hypocrite, like those of his "breed." Un Americano dogged away with his essentialist anti-Semitism. "Do you want to crucify a Jesus Christ every day? Wasn't one enough? [*¿Que deseas crucificar un Jesucristo todos los días? ¿No te acabalaste con uno?*]," he prosecuted. Did he repudiate the *marrano* (crypto-Jew of the Inquisition), "like your grandfathers and great grandfathers? If so, what religion is found to be in question? Yours is nothing and as we have said, Jesus Christ is at the foot of all religious sects."[73]

Another opponent of anti-Semitism placed New Mexico on a cosmopolitan footing. A man had the right to leave his natal country to emigrate to wherever he wanted, the anonymous writer held, and to "put himself under the claim of the flag he choose[s], and no government should refuse to take him into its bosom, nor distance him from its protection." The history of all the nations in ancient and modern times presented innumerable examples of foreigners occupying "eminent posts." Europe sat at the center of civilization; its nations did not discriminate against foreigners but took advantage of the honest and energetic ones. The people of New Mexico should know that not being born in the country was not a crime. The injustice to Clever was a detriment to free enterprise. The United States nourished three million individuals who were not "American natives," and New Mexico had a "great number" of foreigners who did not aspire to high position, the liberal affirmed. Why should they be dishonored with epithets, be called enemies, when their interests were the same as those of the natives?[74]

The charge against Chávez of anti-Americanism floated on the stream of the American Party's contention with the Mexican Party. Fidelio called the insinuation that Chávez would want to expel Americans "trumped up, false and absurd."[75] Chávez critics saw the issue going deeper than a hatred of "men belonging to the race of people denominated Americans" to a hostility toward American institutions and the government. The *Gazette* trotted out its old charge of Mexicans who had never reconciled to the change of government, charging for partisan effect that Chávez had secretly addressed them for their votes. Russell feared for how Washington would look on a territory sending a delegate with enmity toward the government.[76]

The *New Mexican* challenged the prejudice against Chávez's homeland identity by reminding that Clever was a foreigner and so it was he, or his party, who needed to prove that he had been, or was now, a friend to Americans or American institutions. The weekly claimed to know of "innumerable" instances of Clever's open and bitter hostility to Americans "merely because they were Americans." The weekly racialized John Gwyn, on whom Clever allegedly dealt a "cowardly, base and malicious" attack during the last legislative session. "Burning with rage and mortification at the idea of losing one of his offices, more especially as an American was to fill it," Clever was said to have drawn up a series of "most unjust, unfounded and malevolent resolutions, and induced one of his henchmen to present them in the House of Representatives." As Clever bid for "American votes," the *New Mexican* bid those Americans to "remember how low and contemptible he descended to injure an honest man whose only crime consisted in the fact that he was of American birth and parentage and his speech was free from foreign accent."[77]

Cleverites countered with a vengeful attack on Chávez's prodigal son status. Chávezites were the actual "renegade Americans," one put it. They were pretended defenders of nativos, though their hero had not accomplished a thing for their people. "Outrageous hypocrisy!" he cried.[78] To another, Chávez's native son pretension was betrayed by Mitchell's making more appointments to the "sons of our people," yet Clever was condemned for being a foreigner by those who said they would work for the incumbent only because he was being challenged by a Jew.[79] In a mock interrogation by the people, Chávez admits that James Collins is an intelligent *americano* who worked for the territory's progress, had a greater interest in the people, brought needed resources with important government contacts, while admitting he cared nothing for the people, yet believed they would vote for him because he was a *mexicano* and spoke to them in their language.[80]

Un Escuelero (A schoolboy) said he learned a hard lesson as a child when he paid too much for the whistle he bought at the store. When he heard that Chávez was a native son and for that reason the people should support him, though they lose their future, he thought they paid too much for their little whistle.[81] One critic calling himself *Un Hijo del País* (A native son),[82] scolded Chávez because so many of his critics were themselves of the "infinity of citizens that you call children of the land, of those, according to your hypocritical arguments, who have the Mexican blood running through their veins, of those whose sympathies and suffrages you come to look for, and to whom you go saying 'I am the defender of the [New Mexican] country,'" and yet violated nativo honor in standing by Arny, who had called them greasers and accused them of being unable to govern themselves, who declared the Nuevomexicanos little more civilized than the barbarous Indians. "It was not like two years before when the people did not know you," the critic continued. "Now we do, and we will tell you, do not use chickens to take us to the coyote."[83]

Russell, dusting off his assimilation jacket, noted that Chávez may not have evinced the "odor of the dunghill lingering around him," as the *New Mexican* had described Clever, but his odor stunk "of something much worse in the nostrils of a republican people—that is, pride of birth, unsustained by mental capacity—ambition without brains, and a tongue that rivals that of a simpleton in chattering nonsense." "How refreshing it is for us to know that we have in New Mexico such aristocrats who have never been in the dunghill," it editorialized, "and who have no offensive odor in the sails which bear them onward and upward to the accomplishment of their high aspirations." The *New Mexican* betrayed the American value of individual advancement, Russell charged. "We have never before heard that because a man was born poor he should, in the United States, be therefore forever deprived of the right to hold office, high or low. On the contrary, we have always understood that in this country honors were alike open to the rich and poor, and that this principle was regarded as a stimulant to the poor to emulate the rich in all the pursuits of life." The people would not turn their noses in disgust "of the man of humble origin," Russell affirmed, "who will relieve them from the consequences which have followed the incumbency of the high-born Delegate who vacated his office on the 4th of March last."[84]

Another critic got quite personal. The National Unionists boasted of their nativo Chávez "from a grand family," yet he chose for a wife a "foreigner" who did not belong to New Mexico; he bought land in Canada and, word had it, considered Canada his place of residence.[85] *Amigo del Pueblo* preferred that nativos be understood as having been adopted by the United States rather than conquered. Not for this would he deny that he was *mexicano*. "Naturally," he averred, "I am excited to sympathize with my race and blood," but more important was the oath taken by the Nuevomexicanos to support the "flag of stars." The native son obsession made them repugnant before the government and the "face of the world," as did the attacks on officials being sent by the president and Congress. To make themselves properly adopted children and walk the road to true public benefit, the "dear people" must "open their eyes" and forget their preoccupation with distinctions of race.[86]

As another Ranchero opined, Chávez's native son preoccupation was what sparked discord between nativos and foreigners who, "with so much work, had become their *vecinos*." This Ranchero's liberal antidote required the "fraternal sympathy" of all residents of a community, called happiness itself, the only "aura" that could crown the people with the blessings of heaven, what "union" itself meant. The "people" had cherished it until the recent conflicts had produced misery. To get back, the focus on class, status, and race should be abandoned, Ranchero pleaded, for the people were citizens of the same "majestic government," as proved by the contentment enjoyed by some of the neighboring territories. Though beginning in misery and poverty, they had become popular states. Those that remained territories were not submerged in New Mexico's dejection but thrived because the settlers from different nations lived in cordial friendship. No ill will came from one being German, another Jewish, one white, the other black. Nor had they sustained a party to attack the stranger. They received the blessing that "we the Nuevomexicanos desire." To imitate them, the author preached, New Mexicans must unanimously support the candidate they knew would protect their interests, eschew personal causes, and appreciate the gratitude of his constituents. The wisdom of this energetic man would not allow him to have his hands tied, nor be silenced, nor blame others for his weaknesses, as Colonel Chávez had done. The delegates who had trekked from their homes to Santa Fe to nominate Clever with the aim of ending the disharmony deserved their due recognition, as Un Ranchero wished it in all the "tenderness and respect" in his heart.[87]

So long as the Río Abajo ricos had collaborated with, legitimated, and facilitated the American annexation of New Mexico, helping to support the American Party, its Euroamerican leaders heralded and supported them as the "intelligent" portion of the Nuevomexicano mass. Their enemy Chávez complicated matters by running against his rico cousin. With Perea out, the Clever keynoters turned Chávez's aristocratic class into a principal point of objection. In Ranchero's (rather wild) propaganda, the ricos of the Río Abajo had gotten one of their "nephews," Francisco Perea, elected in 1863, and decided that it was now José Francisco's turn in spite of Perea's merits, especially as Chávez had thrown his money away on business ventures in California. Such was the patriotism observed by this particular segment, the Cleverite harrumphed.[88]

The cry against the oppression of aristocracy was commonly heard in the United States, although it symbolized various issues.[89] Here the American concern interwove with old Mexican class conflict. One commentator, writing as the common man, chastised in Spanish "the Oligarchs" who sought to rule New Mexico with an iron fist, who scapegoated emigrants, and who wanted expulsion of the Jews. Inverting the peculating enemy, the writer said it was the ricos, not the Jews, who used "that powerful agent," money, to win San Miguel County, loaning it to the people with the interest to be paid in cattle or sheep. They formed the oligarchy that detested the people's opinion.[90] In calling Chávez "grandee," much as W. W. H. Davis had pricked the puffed-up pretensions of Miguel Antonio Otero, a Clever Nuevomexicano snubbed the National Union leader as the "*hidalgo coronel, Hon. don J. Francisco Chavez, M.C.*"[91]

Parallel to the 1850s assault on the nativo priesthood, this whole critique condemned the upper-class families who came from a long tradition for not keeping up with modern times. One correspondent, Pepe, noted that for twenty years New Mexico had been part of the most civilized and advanced nation in the world, with its republican government, laws, and customs, yet it found itself playing the "saddest role in the American Union." At the time the United States took the territory, *ricachos* (the filthy rich) kept the people as slaves with no remorse or scruple. They manipulated the "class of unhappy ones," kept their eyes closed, yet feared the day when the lowly ones would seize the law of equality, as was now happening, though their oppressors derided them for it. Pepe saw rich Mexicans taking advantage of a liberal government, neglecting the "mendicant classes" 264 days of the year—the rich stole from them, humiliated them, prosecuted them, and offered them up to meat-eating wolf-officers. As election day, their favorite, approached, they praised the parental lineage of the poor, halted their machinations, became good boys, good husbands, solid parents, loyal friends, useful citizens, upholders of Christian piety and works of compassion; they dressed the naked, fed the hungry, gave drink to the thirsty, tended to the sick, consoled the afflicted, offered counsel to the bereft, and provided a saddle to those with a horse and a horse to those with a saddle—so long as the poor voted for their privileges. After the election they forgot their promises, betrayed half the people who had voted for them, and persecuted the other half for not having walked with their caprice and sophism. The partisan counseled citizens to aspire to a more flattering future, not fall for the misanthropes and defamers. "If you want liberty, guaranteed progress," he advised, "vote for C. P. Clever . . . so that, with satisfaction, pride and dignity, we say, 'Death to the tyrannical power that has oppressed us.'"[92]

Another critic went after the *aristocracia* in stylish slang. Chávez's agenda did not favor what was needed to meet the development needs of the territory, he stated, but rather, the Chavistas "worked their hatred of the foreigner so inveterately that, in the young people's refrain, as the hawk gobbles the chicken, so the colonial Spaniard exploits the creole [*el odio al no nacido en el país y tan inveterado que, como refrán, dicen los achavados que, gabilán con poyo, gachipa con crieyo*]." As the wit sarcastically explained, it was valid when this "fortunate" land was a Spanish colony, "referring to the despotism with which we were treated by the conquistadors [*aludiendo al despotismo con que eramos tratados, por los conquistadores*]." Even now under the shade of liberty, the oligarchs continued to abuse through their fondness for public office, which they considered their patrimony in those counties where their probate judges exercised "omnipotent" power. These judges distributed the offices at their discretion, yet the aristocrats feared that the bone given to them by the honesty of the people might escape their hands. By their own petulance did they manage community affairs, the affront had it.[93]

Another contributor going by *Un Navajoe* depicted Chávez supported by the *aristocratas* and C. P. Clever by the *demócratas*. Money resided in the former, power in the latter, Un Navajoe noted. The people were advised to reserve the inalienable right to elect their representatives and public functionaries and dismiss officials who worked out badly so as to avoid the consequences of their "invalidity and bad faith." It was important to cast off forever the "abuses and sophisms" with which the poor people had been dragged down by powerful persons having a "plundering fortune." Chávez abandoned the people's cause, Un Navajoe claimed, in going to Washington obsessed with General Carleton. Shame on the many who said in *el Nuevo Mexicano* that Clever could not represent the people as a descendant of those who crucified *a nuestro señor Jesucristo*. "Barbarism!" he shouted ironically given the pen name he had chosen for himself. If Jesus Christ was crucified it was by His own people. But it happened more than 1,800 years ago, Un Navajoe pointed out, and Clever was barely thirty years old. How could he be found complicit? No signs existed to show Clever denying the rights of man. He would represent the people well; God had reposed in him the qualities of honor, rare ingenuity, happiness without baseness, seriousness without presumption, and friendship for the poor. Un Navajoe invited the hundreds of poor people liberated from slavery and servility endured for centuries under the "hard arm and cruel yoke" [*bajo el duro brazo y cruel yugo*] of those in support of Chávez, to give their suffrage on the day of battle to Clever so as not to return to their "primitive slavery [*para no volver a su primitiva esclavitud*]."[94]

An English-speaking Cleverite posited conspiratorial ricos. Rich Mexicans could secure a victory for Chávez "without any great exertion" if they wished. They depended on greenbacks to give the election to Chávez (reversing the Oracle farce that gave the greenback advantage to Clever), "incompetent and unworthy" as the people knew him to be. The money flowed from Bernalillo County; the purse strings were unloosed; the cash went out to buy an election "for a man who has lost the confidence of the people." Those voters who could not be bought into the service of the "iniquitous cause" would be controlled by intimidation. "We hear of force being used in all parts of the country by the Chávezites to intimidate the friends of Gen'l. Clever," he wrote. "We have but one thing to do . . . meet the enemy in any shape he may present himself. This is a free country in which no special privileges are granted to any."[95]

Clever's Ranchero applied the Romantic form to alter the image of aristocrats haunched over the election like vultures for the pickings. In the parody, New Mexico, *la madre patria*, scolds Chávez, *el mal hijo* (the bad son), for having forsaken her, abusing her name by abandoning her rights and privileges purely for his personal interests. *La madre* warns the errant son; only a couple of uncles supported him with their capital (implicating the support Chávez had from his mother's brother, prosperous Bernalillo County merchant and former Kearny backer José Leandro Perea). Most of his rico kin demurred because they saw his disobedience and ingratitude sending her to her tomb, for recruiting men who were not naturalized, removing his Nuevomexicano brothers from their public positions, and not obtaining work for his hopeless but qualified godsons. If he did not recognize the hand of Divine Providence hovering over him, he was more obstinate than the disobedient angel Lucifer who wanted to usurp the power of the Divine Eternal God. But his motherland, although offended by his crime, would never stop being his mother. *La madre patria* advises him to forget the destiny that would forever make him hated, abandon the anger he harbored against Carleton, let go of the false prophets whose dreams had captured him in the hope of triumphing without having anything to support him other than their own private luck. He needed to heed the sovereign power of the government opposing his Indian politics. Otherwise, he could never win the respect of the human power that weighed on him.[96]

José D. Sena for his part did not shy from an upper-class identity. An anonymous Nuevomexicano called him a "charlatan" and "brute" for having made Clever out as a Jew. Needy as most Nuevomexicanos were, the critic wrote, Sena would be doing well were he to have the very "ability, talent and moral conduct" possessed by that "so-called renegade of Israel." Sena's response condemned the "plebian" Clever, whose dialect and style revealed a commoner pretending to be a professional leader. Sena's critic, a delegate to the Union Nominating Convention, stated that it was the larger figure of Kirby Benedict, for whom Sena acted the lackey, who had actually written Sena's speech for the Chávez nomination. Reminiscent of the Chulito-Traidor dialogue, Sena called his nemesis the *chulito* (lap dog) of the Constitutional Convention, a "miserable slave and minion" of *his* "favorites" Clever and Mitchell. Sena dared his critic to unmask himself, not hide like a coward behind a fictitious name, so that the people would know whether he was Nuevomexicano or "foreigner." The sheriff lunged at the American Party's pretense to consensus race relations—"the villain calls all men brother." Sena, declaring himself independent, affirmed that he wrote his own speech, expressed his own "principles," and would not change for anyone. Clever held no virtue, he charged. The people of New Mexico knew him "from the foot to the elbow," and they would not "venerate" the "practitioner" of the gospel doctrines of Israel, the founder of "the reserve of Jerusalem" in New Mexico.[97]

Joseph Hersch, another Jewish respondent, was one of the more successful Santa Fe merchants with interests throughout the territory and a strong record of supplying military posts.[98] Hersch had heard that Chávez mentioned him at the famous Alburquerque rally "in gross terms and calumniating my reputation and private character, injuring me with the most vile words that do not square with the imagination of a man of fine education," expressing only his "financial power." He thought Chávez to have been a better man than that, "clothed with the high dignity of delegate of a territory," a man of "consolidated principles," a better man than to take advantage of the absence of another to insult him publicly. Hersch said he was surprised to think of Chávez expressing "infamous insults" against someone who had not attacked him. The cheeky Hersch proclaimed that as a foreigner, he was "better established and better viewed by the people of New Mexico" than Chávez. Hersch became of greater benefit to the people than Chávez because of his experience of "public calamity, of hunger, of misery and of prostration" and said he had wiped the tears of many unhappy ones who "without my help would have perished." Thank God that Chávez had mistaken his own well-established reputation: "The people know me and esteem me," Hersch declared. "I know how to farm this place and I do not believe that your peat bogs could destroy my work." He had lived in Santa Fe many years, had acquired things by industry and "constant work." "What I own has not been stolen, is not obtained if not by my sweat and work," he proudly declared. "And am I to blame for your being born rich only to squander your patrimony in droves? Am I to blame that a great majority of the people are against you, that they know your work has been nothing more than a farce, tales and entanglements?" See things with better judgment, Hersch implored. His sole object in writing was to vindicate himself in view of the "atrocities and unjust calumnies with which you have treated me before the public."[99]

Más Diálogos

Clever penmen proved just as creative as Chávez scribes. Lope de Vega established a new comedic theater for Spain in the late sixteenth century, infused with realism, social description, and political commentary with ironic dialogue and slapstick characters. The theatrical performances of those times took place in the open such as squares or corrals, called in Madrid the "corrals of comedies." The tradition transposed to New Mexico, where a home-grown theatrical comedy flourished as entertainment. As one American had some years before observed, 1,500 persons in Tomé sat on the ground to hear a "comedy or some kind of theatrical exhibition which was being performed by several ladies and gentlemen on a stage erected in a large piazza fronting the square."[100] The print culture of the American territory gathered up the theme of comedic theater. A good many parodies lampooned Chávez and his squad of supporters. It proved a means to carry forth with the campaign, pound the issues home, respond tit-for-tat to opponents' claims, and generally smear their community standing. Practically all the *diálogos* were written anonymously. Out of their exercised imaginations the corrupt ward politician, the incompetent party chief, the unscrupulous and designing power behind the scene, the chump citizen, the virtuous people, and other ready-made typecasts took their bows in colorful costume.

One picaresque Baroque dialogue involves two lowly members of the Chávez organization engaged in a fatalistic conversation over their party's unsavory character, its illiberal qualities revealed to the world. In the parody, *Servil* (Obsequious one) and *Adulón* (Adulator, flatterer) represent Mexicans under manipulation of Chávez power mongers. In the liberal vernacular of nineteenth-century Spain, the *adulador* was a servile political hack equated with the *infames sacristanes de amen* (infamous sextons of the amen or clergyman's Word: affirmers or yes-men).[101] Servil conducts a friendly interrogation of Adulón. "Tell me, brother, are you Anti-American?" Adulón responds, "Yes, by the grace of Chávez, the Publican." Adulón tells Servíl he follows Chávez for his incompetency, "as you well know." Adulón cannot point to anything Chávez did as delegate. It was ruining his faction but he supports Chávez because his *amo* [master] has ordered it. Servil wants to know if Adulón is under some unfortunate foreign influence. Adulón admits his bridled misery. Servil cries out: What role do the "spurious" native sons play? Nothing less than a fugitive culprit (*reo prófugo*), admits Adulón. Why throw so much garbage at Clever, Servil wants to know. Because we cannot move on our own, Adulón concedes—"they drive us." Was his faction not shamed? No, because it suits us, the despondent Adulón responds. What, Servil asks, could the people assume from this? Nothing more than to treat you as adulator and me as servile, Adulón notes. And how, Servil wants to know, should they themselves respond? "[C]onfess our fragility and say amen," Adulón concludes in resignation.[102]

The construction of the adulator and the portrayal of servility signified as a challenge to anti-democratic political organization (or "despotism," as embodied in American liberal vernacular) and Mexico's traditional *patronismo*. The master-peón relationship was neatly translatable into the imaginary of liberal freedom for the individual.

Another tragi-comedy inverted the partisanship of the Traidor-Chulito dialogue by featuring two members of the National Union Party discoursing on the hijinks of its leaders. The narrator hides in the bushes like a Shakespearean spy to overhear the compadres converse in a mood of gloom and desperation. One figure, apparently a local politico, exhibits a "soaring, arrogant, majesty. His precipitous manner, impetuous character and violent habit" earn him the title "the Despotism" (a term of monarchical villainy in the Declaration of Independence). The other, who plays the part of a worrywart, asks, "Good God, compadre, what do you think of this election?" The Despotism responds, "Like what, compadre? That we will win?" The startled Worrywart responds, "Don't say that, compadre. Are you not seeing that all the sons of the people of Israel are against us?" The Despotism: "And what of it? We too have Americans, though I cannot see them and though they do not know us, but they are helping us in our causes, the few we have, but better that we not have on our side those of that race who crucified our *Señor* Jesus Christ." "Don't say that, compadre," exclaims Worrywart (harboring the conscience of the party), "because for me, I believe that they are the privileged ones of the Lord, although they had him crucified as you say. But now, if we touch on points of religion, I would say that God made man when he was on the cross, pardoned those who crucified him, it seems to me, having seen the following words: 'Deus Israel Benedicto pupoil sui [God of Israel blessed the orphans themselves].'" The Despotism queries: "And these are the ones here [in New Mexico], compadre?" Worrywart: "Yes, compadre, these are the Jews." Worrywart hopes his party does not open the "race question," for it will doom their chances in the election because "everybody wants to be an American." He fixes on the perils of supporting one county candidate, a bully whom the people do not like. The Despotism suggests they must be quiet about that, for the party owes much to him and he must be sustained.

The compadres agree that Clever is the better candidate, though they must hush, for as the adage went, "The fish by the mouth dies." Be strong, the Despotism advises. They had no choice. Though Clever be German, "we will say, 'he is Jew, Jew, and pure Jew (the two).' Yes, yes, that he is Jew, Jew, Jew, Jew, etc., etc., etc., and more, we will say that the Americans, Mexicans, Irish, French, Italians, Germans who defend the cause of Clever are Jews." The worried one asks: And us? What will we say we are? Anti-Americans, *compadrito*, the Despotism declares. "But," Worrywart fears, "have we not denied that we retained the character of being a Mexican citizen?" The Despotism: "Yes, compadre, but when will it happen [that we return to Mexico]? You know that one cannot have a [government] appointment there, and so what can we do?" The worrier admits it is so. "But tell me, compadre, do you know English?" "*Hay compadrito*," says Despotism. "If I knew English, another *gallo* [rooster boss] would sing to me; then I would be a Jew, even a heretic, and I would not sustain these principles nor the politics you now observe, because a federal job is better than all territorial jobs together." The Despotism continues:

> But now it's impossible to hope that those federal jobs fall into my hands, and the reason is that, although I saw the Americans come into our territory, I saw that there were treaties that were called 'Guadalupe Hidalgo.' I thought I was dreaming and you know very well that I spent many years providing for myself until finally the need of a job made me say that I was American . . . now it grieves me not knowing English.
>
> [Worrywart:] What do you mean it grieves you?
>
> [Despotism:] Yes, *compadre*, don't you see that the appointments . . . Oh God! If we lose the administration this year, then we are definitely lost.

When the hidden witness reveals himself, the compadres fall to their knees in shock, fleeing to avoid his condemnation. The narrator, being a Jew, is left astonished. Reminded of the voice of his "first Pilate," he shouts, "*¡Ecco Homo!* / Behold Man. Crucify yourselves, traitors."[103]

Miguel E. Pino, not a U.S. citizen and who in the previous election had debated with Diego Archuleta over the danger of addiction to government pap, perceived himself caricatured as the Despotism and was not amused. The dialogue in the "filthy newspaper" defamed him before the "whole people," he protested. Pino challenged the writer, or writers, to remove their masks, open their names to the light, so that the people could judge whether his own accounting of them was just. To the insinuation that he needed to have a government position or "die of hunger, or ask for charity," he emphasized in a fine liberal hail that the positions he had held in his career had been entrusted to him "by the will of the people." He challenged the writer to prove he had been dishonest in any way to obtain work, or forced anyone to vote for him, as those of the corrupt clique were accustomed to doing by "bribery, fraud or intimidation." Pino omitted mention of the dialogue's Jewish imputations.[104]

At least eight other dialogues appeared during the campaign. Among these are three conversations between Pancho and Chepe, prototypical *pobladores*—ordinary hardscrabble rancheros—one from the Río Arriba, the other of the Río Abajo—*cuando se topan,* as they bump into each other on country roads. The one that chronicles a conversation regarding the nomination of a Jew for delegate and Chávez's allegedly corrupt National Union Party is anchored by allusions from Revelations. That dialogue sparked a counter narrative from a pro-Chávez writer who claimed to have overheard the same conversation, filling in some things said to have been left out by the pro-Clever writer.[105] The second ramified into a four-way debate among contending Chávez and Clever partisans.[106]

Another figurative dialogue in the *Gazette* involved Pancho and Juan. Unfortunately, that edition goes missing. A reaction to it in *el Nuevo-Mejicano* included a remarkable, if cynical, tale of a speech that Charles Clever, the "grand prophet," gave on the porch of the Palace of the Governors. A white dove descends "like the snow" [Matthew 28:19, the baptism of Christ, when the Holy Spirit descends on him like a dove] to contemplate the wisdom of this "second Solomon."[107] Two other dialogues between Pancho and Juan, including interpretive allusions to Revelations, brought together European history and images from the folklore of Hispanic New Mexico.[108] Juan and Pedro get into three dialogues (one of them lost) that caricature Chávez lieutenants and ricos in various counties, Chávez's record as a delegate, his backward-looking vision, and slapstick local campaign meetings.[109] Another conversational fable involves a Chávez county leader, appearing like a sultan, who cannot believe, and is aghast at, the news from a visitor that the people in Río Arriba County are not falling for the lie that Clever is a Jew.[110]

An arresting comedy involves the Chávez Central Committee meeting in convention to create a number of committees in order to secure the campaign. The *comisión de bobos* (committee of dunderheads) is charged with attacking in public meetings any and all aspirants for public employment who are not on their side. The "committee of frauds and abuses," consisting of the county administrators, will determine in whom to confide for the secret support of their candidate. The "committee of promises" will consist of all the same people, their candidate, "and of the (so-called) ricos."[11] Yet another piece detailed the convention farce further, suggesting that the president of the committee of promises was none other than Chávez himself.[112]

Sheriff under Attack

Anti-Semitism and its indictment served campaign purposes, but the question of Clever's religion did not exhaust the media jousting of 1867. The unprecedented spike in Spanish-language political expression, much of it literary, augmented the citizen involvement of Nuevomexicanos in the developing print medium.[113] A sage styling himself *El Trueno* (Thunder clap) in Doña Ana County noted that the spoken word no longer counted as it once did. The written word had become triumphant "in space and time," for the voice could not be heard more than a short distance and "in more than some brief instances."[114] A great many letters to the editor, pointed debates among individuals, poetic devices, and more satirical dialogues enlivened the political stage as never before. The duel between the *New Mexican/el Nuevomexicano* and the *Gazette/Gaceta* fueled much, but intra-ethnic feuds and personal grudges sprouted as well. Their argumentations were generously beaded with notions of modern liberalism. In this sense, the sheer amount of public creativity, if not always the content itself, served to expand a Nuevomexicano *res pública,* thereby advancing their modern development, as it were.

Cleverites zeroed in on Jose D. Sena, the one who had launched the anti-Semitic attack on Clever. Un Ranchero charged him with abusing his power by misusing public monies when the territorial capitol went into disrepair and making the poor men in jail bargain for an early release by agreeing to build his house. It was the practice, Ranchero pointed out, of constructing sitting rooms for the rich (*edificar ricos' salones*). Sena, the "Chávez aristocrat," was accused of falsely attacking worthy public officials in San Miguel County.[115] Sena publicly denied the charges. He suggested that Un Ranchero was Governor Mitchell's territorial librarian, Jesús Ma. H. Alarid. He challenged Alarid to prove his "corrupt" charges and claimed that he personally paid for the labor in the construction of his home, compensating convicted criminals out of charity. Sena defied Un Ranchero to expose himself with his real name or else be regarded as a "rogue, shamed, and a coward [*bajo el nombre de 'Ranchero' solo te considero como un bribón, un sinverguenza y un cobarde*]."[116]

Alarid denied being Un Ranchero but anted matters up. He accused Sena, as captain of Company C of the New Mexico Volunteers, of exploiting soldiers to work on his house.[117] Un Ranchero did not doubt Sena paying for labor but said a superior officer had stopped him from using volunteers for his private benefit. Un Ranchero accused Sena and cronies of directing public funds for public works without consulting the people and of hiring friends. He explained that his pseudonym was meant to tame Sena, who tended to break out passionately but with a loose bridle. In the small pueblos "malicious" people talked of his exploiting those who were under him. Un Ranchero asked the sheriff to answer "from his own mouth."[118]

Sena jested at Alarid's "big discovery" of soldiers making adobes for him. He claimed that in 1862 eight soldiers of Company C, under his command at Fort Marcy, volunteered to make him a thousand adobe bricks for a "just compensation." Sena paid them, under the "bright sun," from his own money, and by the agreement of their superior officer. Alarid should file a legal case if he could prove that the troops were made to work against their will. Sena affirmed that he was currently building on his home; he had the adobes ready; anyone who needed political points could inspect the work and ask the laborers what they got, or if he had them working under pretext of his being sheriff, or how he obtained the money, although he demanded a face-to-face report in respect of his honor. Should they wish to publish anything for the "intelligence of the people," his accusers, including the *Gazette*, were authorized to publish anything thought useful to obtain political capital. He said he did not depend on votes and cared not who knew what he did. If they attacked him for votes, "until the end of the centuries," so be it.[119]

Sena became the object of derision following the appearance of an anti-Clever piece submitted by someone styling himself a little-educated wood cutter from Tesuque. Claiming to take up his pen for the first time "respecting politics," Wood Cutter, as we can designate him, reacted to a *Gazette* editorial he felt would put "all free men" under a political yoke. He did not desire a government position, as he was able to meet the necessities of life honestly and live peacefully, nor was he out to adulate anyone. A "dandy," sporting the "manners of urbanity,"

FIG. 27. *Major José D. Sena, Albuquerque, New Mexico*, ca.1880, photograph by Albright's Art Parlors. Sena rose rapidly in the ranks of what would become the Republican Party of the New Mexico Territory. Courtesy Palace of the Governors Photo Archives, NMHM/DCA, negative #105536.

gave Wood Cutter an issue of the *Gazette* so he could see the editorial praise of Clever's program. The people rejected the pro-Clever literature, Wood Cutter submitted, as "swishy spittle." Obviously written by a "gang of bluffers," the author said, the offending article sounded like "Lies or Comedy [*Embuste o Comedia*]" to promote Clever, Mitchell, and Collins, "discharging ire against Mr. Chávez" with calumnies. The comedians lied in saying that Clever shamed Chávez in debate at Alburquerque and Santa Fe. Wood Cutter claimed to have been present and witnessed the weak arguments of the scared and shamefaced Clever men. Not believing the people of New Mexico capable of governing themselves, they let "tongues of a snake" loose with sarcasm and grossness under cover of the *Gazette*. Their comedies were incredibly meant to persuade men who were already known to vote for them. It only demonstrated their "embarrassing and sad political history," in which they had previously defamed some who were now their favorites (José Manuel Gallegos). Both parties would reject them. Considering them as traitors to both, the people would not believe their impudence and comedies, Wood Cutter noted.[120]

Quien tu Sabes (You know who) accused Sena of being the wood cutter and did so by laying enormous stock in scientific reason and citizen happiness. "The light of Reason is an admirable thing under the heavens," he wrote, "a healthy guide to the road of happiness." Quien called the recent rise of reason the best guide to truth in the western world, "loyal," a "celestial voice" not subject to opinion or caprice. Error-free Reason was a "divine voice," he gushed, an "echo of the eternal truth that sounds in the concave of our brain and where the spirit passes, and as such cannot betray us." Superior to all human force, Reason defeated "loose passions" and condemned "with liberty and frankness" those who disrespected its voice with vulgar, ignorant, or sophistic preoccupations. José D. Sena—the "Poor one!"—denied Reason's "excellent virtue," charged Quien tu Sabes (the lancer's assault on the Romantic windmill). Why did the "imbecile" want to hide the light of Reason? Did he not see that the most recondite among his friends could not destroy it? He knew it yet he lied constantly, Quien rolled on. But the light was revealing his disposition. If he continued to falsify the grand force that guided the people, he would not return as sheriff. By taking the name of a "poor and rustic worker," turning it into a "vile instrument" to hurl insults, Sena betrayed the people to conceal Chávez's phoniness. Did he actually think he could trample Reason by negating Clever's abilities? "No, false one," Quien exclaimed. The people were persuaded by them. Reason was enlightening them. They knew it, and knowledge distinguished them from animals. The windmills of Don Quijote Chávez turned to air. He presented himself to the poor territory in a manner so low and vile as no man with even soft [dumb] brains would have. Sena would see his shotgun insults driving him crazy. Under "wood cutter" or whatever name, Quien affirmed, the people knew him even if he was covered in thick chile sauce.

Quien tu Sabes knew Sena to be the wood cutter because he himself had been the "dandy" political comedian who had handed Sena the *Gazette*. Quien tu Sabes wrought havoc on the wood cutter's comedy-of-lies routine. It was a barbarity, an imbecility, for the sheriff to consider himself a tragic comedian as he could not distinguish black from white. That he found it necessary to sway the people back to his direction was an admission of his errors. "You see, José, how powerful Reason is," Quien challenged, "see how it does not hide?" Sena did not know what historical comedy was, as in the case of Raousett (Count Gastón Raousett-Boulbón made an ill-fated attempt in 1854 to take control of Guaymas and the State of Sonora to rebel against the Mexican government; he was captured and executed by firing squad). The comedies of the great writers like Spanish playwright José Zorrilla and Calderón de la Barca attracted actors who "had the good grace" to play their characters. The "very bloody war" in Spain would soon draw the attention of talented writers dedicated to poetry. They would render a "comedy (drama)" regarding its successes, which would "adhere to history." Actors would represent the proverbial "General Grande repulsing the enemy with immense valor and other heroes whose names are immortal to us." Sena would see someone composing a comedy of the acts of bloody war in Valverde and Cañoncito, Nuevo Mejico, actors at the ready. Quien's heart skipped at the prospect of seeing the brave General Canby on stage, "a cigar in mouth, filled with calm and giving orders (even you will remember your times when you were eating the ham [of the military] which you now hurl [at your enemies]." Sena would weaken at the sight of the heroism of Joseph Cummings directing the artillery with valor and "Santiago" L. Collins spurning the enemy with heroism until taken prisoner. Sena would see some comedy in the current Mexican civil war, the actors playing Juarez, the Archduque Maximiliano, etc. He should not confuse comedy to call history a lie.

Quien tu Sabes conceded how comedies could serve lies, as in the wood cutter's account of Chávez's record in the *Congressional Globe*. But if Sena considered himself playing a part in New Mexico's comedic politics as his profession, he should better declare himself a fan of New Mexico. If Quien acted politically, it was because he saw the foreigner that Sena loathed (Clever) needing him, and because he knew the theater would not denigrate him for it. Quien did not have the good fortune of being taken under a sponsor's wing to be educated in the United States. Former delegate José Manuel Gallegos had done that for Sena, and the sheriff repaid his former *patrón* by calling him a political enemy. "I realized I needed to know more than what my teachers taught me here," Quien stated, "and so I went into the [political] theater. There I would act as one of the personages at various levels such as king, duke, prince, etc." Quien claimed the grammar of the true Spanish language. Not only did he become an aficionado of the political state, not only did he learn proper behavior but also to be a director, setting the scene. Drawing on the *Divine Comedy*, Quien concocted a play, *The County Sheriff*. In the first scene a grand ball is to the right. The sheriff and his jailers dance the night away. A jail is on the left. As sheriff and jailers enjoy themselves at the ball, a prisoner, convicted of killing his wife, escapes. No one shouts for the guards to stop him. In the second scene the sheriff sits in the gloomy "pumpkin" (soft-walled, ramshackle) jail with his jailers, a veil in his hand, puzzled about how the prisoner got out. In the last scene, the scowling sheriff sleeps, and "he who sleeps does not see." "How did I do as a comic?," Quien smilingly queries. He concludes by noting that Sena had forgotten to add another insult to his accuser. More than a dandy, Quien admitted himself to be a musician, his real profession.[121]

Four other long Spanish-language attacks were launched on Sena, one with no byline, one by *Adios,* and two by *Zurriago,* the latter being the name of a liberal, rabble-rousing newspaper in early nineteenth-century Madrid.[122] All opened as patronizing endearments to "Josesito" (Dear little Joe) and relied on biting lines of poetic lyricism. Adios ridiculed Sena's "addiction" to the "pickpocket," former Supreme Court judge Kirby Benedict; Adios called it a shame that a man who had dedicated "glorious" service to the United States had turned into such a liar to gain votes from poor, ignorant, men and supported a man who, if reelected delegate, would only seek the removal of Mitchell, Indian Superintendent James Collins, and other federal officials he did not like while battling Carleton to no good end. Citizens elevated Clever, Adios stated, because they saw in him the ideal person to relieve the people of the "sad situation" in which Chávez had left them, to lift the unfortunate territory to the sphere it deserved with its hidden riches and the patriotism of its children, who deserved justice.[123]

If anything, the lyrical storm may have enhanced Sena's status in the National Union Party. At the Party's convention in Santa Fe, held at the home of Anastasio Sandoval, he was called "one of nature's true noblemen." Rising, Sena noted that he had been honored with the suffrages of fellow citizens for sheriff three times. He knew of others more deserving and better qualified and thus advised the convention to nominate one of them. The partisan report had supporters submitting his name and unanimously nominating him "amidst enthusiasm and vociferous applause." The veteran Euroamerican Unionists William Arny and Kirby Benedict, and the surreptitious Republican, William Breeden, cheered on.[124]

On the Campaign Trail

The opposing Santa Fe Constitutional Union (American) Party Convention sported the usual suspects: Merrill Ashurst, James Collins, Felipe Delgado, Vicente Romero, and former delegate José Manuel Gallegos. Chávez was condemned for abusing the governor and "lying" that Mitchell would give the certificate of election to Clever, whether elected or not.[125] A grand demonstration greeted Clever. The people assembled at an early hour in the plaza and in the portals on the street leading out to Alburquerque. With the announcement that the general and his escorts from Algodones were approaching from Agua Fría, a crowd lined the east side of the river with torches and "handsomely devised transparencies [film posters] without number." Clever's carriage crossed the stream and neared the crowd. The air "was made to resound and the hills to echo with the loud and long *vivas* of the enthusiastic friends who had spontaneously gathered to welcome to our city the people's favorite candidate for delegate." Music and the "prevalence of an uncontrollable enthusiasm among the masses" escorted Clever. The assemblage concluded with an "explosion of fireworks and the shooting of rockets from the four sides of the Plaza."[126]

The *New Mexican* aimed to spoil the Constitutional Party's party by printing the bitter and vindictive denunciations of Gallegos that Clever had made in 1863 when he was the owner of the weekly, including regarding the padre's alleged mistress.[127] It failed in this undermining effort, and the territory's electric binary led to every county putting up tickets for each party.[128] Each side predicted lopsided victories for its congressional candidate and his slate, which actually indicated a close race. The tactic of expressing confidence thus sought to persuade undecided or independent voters to go with a sure winner.[129]

Citizens in the southern Mexican-border section no longer spoke of seceding from New Mexico. William L. Rynerson, a Kentuckian who after mustering out of Carleton's California Column stayed in Mesilla to become an influential businessman, served as chair of the pro-Chávez nominating convention alongside the venerable don Nepumoceno Ancheta. Rynerson led a rousing vote of confidence for Chávez. When the presiding officer, a Clever man, refused to recognize a motion to have the convention praise Chávez, Rynerson moved for the three hundred Chávez men to withdraw from the hall and hold an "unadulterated Chávez meeting in the street, which was responded to with a huzza, and a rush for the door." The Clever spies quieted, the convention resumed in the hall. A Rynerson-headed committee nominated Chávez supporters for local office. The committee, consisting of nine Nuevomexicanos and four Euroamericans, nominated Rynerson for the Legislative Council.[130]

The boisterous Chávez rally at the Mesilla precinct sounded the National Union Party issues, boring into Governor Mitchell for naming Watts an agent in Congress, "giving evidence of the worst statesman and diplomat, and the worst *politicastro guisachero* [supreme corrupt politician (colloq.)] New Mexico ever had." Thanks went to Chávez for removing "that incubus" Carleton and for putting in "an officer and a gentleman," whose only business was that for which he is commissioned and who allowed the parties to manage their own affairs "without let or hindrance."[131] An eyewitness reported that Father José de Jesús, called a "violent partisan" of Chávez, "used personal and political influence" to secure his election, "paraded the streets on

Sundays, and made stump speeches in every precinct in Doña Ana County but two or four."[132]

Great fun was had at the expense of opponents. The Doña Ana County Convention for the Chávez ballot resolved to give Clever, Carleton, Ashurst, and Mitchell "three groans" as their representatives paraded through the various precincts.[133] Clever, who could afford it, established the *Mesilla Times* as a campaign sheet. A Las Cruces Nuevomexicano reported on the "blowhard" signing off as an "uncompromising Clever gringo" offering a $1,000 bet that Clever would carry the county.[134] In the mining town of Pinos Altos, a Chávez person reported that "Bob Mitchell and Junior Carleton" would not help Clever "*much* in the 'diggings' by legging for him.'" The "American influence" guaranteed Chávez's supremacy.[135] Not to be outdone, the *Gazette* received the "good cheer" of Doña Ana County "spread[ing] her sails for Clever." Socorro County was said to be disgusted by the Chávez clique in the last legislature. Clever friends were reportedly doing well in Valencia County, "Mr. Chavez's native county." Santa Ana County had grown tired of the Baca-Pino rule in Santa Fe, it was said, and was eager to be relieved of it.[136]

Following the call of the Constitutional Party Central Committee, voters assembled in "mass convention" at the Alburquerque courthouse. Conquest generation figures presided. Mariano Yrizarri, Donaciano Vigil's old friend, served as president; the former Whig Serafín Ramírez got elected secretary; and Ambrosio Armijo, once considered a potential candidate for delegate, appeared on the Committee on Resolutions. Former delegate Francisco Perea spoke for Clever and condemned his cousin Chávez for betraying his native son status, forcing "[Republican] persons [as appointees] who were entire strangers to us, to our customs and to our wants."[137]

The speaker's trail went from the Río Abajo and Santa Fe up to the settlements along the Río Grande into the Río Arriba section, cutting east to Mora County, doubling south to San Miguel County. Speeches at the large Clever receptions in the precincts of Socorro County were given in Spanish and English. Clever's demonstration in Socorro highlighted the ruined condition of the territory, its political causes, and the appropriate remedy, interrupted by *vivas*.[138] Felipe Chávez of Belén, another José Francisco cousin, a rico of the Río Abajo who did not switch out of the American Party, hosted the Clever rally at his home.

Clever on rico turf adopted a gracious tone with no nods to the anti-Semitic outburst, referring instead to one of its sons, José Francisco, *con dignidad y decoro*, emphasizing that his rival was simply the wrong man for delegate, demonstrated by his misbegotten management of his office in Washington. The *Gazette* correspondent noted the antipathy in those parts to the election of foreigners but affirmed that Clever dispelled them with "wise and judicious" words.[139]

Both top candidates visited Cubero in Navajo and Laguna Pueblo country, reflecting the continuing importance of the partisanship over Indian policy. The Spanish-language report from A Laborer had Clever giving a "profound and heroic speech," causing all to shout "*!Viva! ¡Clever! ¡Viva Clever! ¡Viva Clever! Y muera el adobe de Chávez y el reñoso de Arny* [and death to the blockhead Chávez and the filthy Arny]."[140] The Chávez rally at the house of don Magadaleno Calderón was called to order by Gregorio Otero at nine in the morning. President Pablo Pino reported that such a crowd of "mature people" had never been seen in that plaza, "even for the local issues."[141] The Clever camp boasted of another "grand, spontaneous" demonstration on the Santa Fe Plaza. Jesús Ma. Alarid, Nicolás Quintana, and Albino Roibal spoke.[142] The *New Mexican* panned away: "On last Sunday evening our music loving citizens were aroused at hearing in the Plaza the enlivening strains of a brass band, and, upon seeking to elucidate the origin of this harmony outburst, we were astonished at the holding for stalwart *hombres* zigzagging their devious way through the principal streets, holding aloft an equal number of greasy transparencies and embellished with mottos expressive of something perhaps known to the constructor thereof. One legend, however, we succeeded in deciphering: 'Clever, *el amigo Del Progreso*.'" Paralleling the farce in which the Grand Oracle demands a rich candidate for delegate, the weekly had Clever furnishing the "necessary amount of greenbacks to pay for the band, transparencies, their holders, and the steering candles." The parade moved through the Plaza, "followed by a number of small boys who volunteered their services upon the location regardless of pay, but with the implied stipulation that they should applaud at the most improper intervals in the mongrel harangue delivered by the oft-quoted friend of progress."[143]

The first debate between Clever and Chávez was well attended on the plaza. The *Gazette* carried Clever's progressive business program calling for the material development of the territory. It shorted Chávez's best shot, claiming that all he had was three New Mexican citizens named as incorporators in a railroad charter and making a speech in favor of an appropriation for the management of the Navajo, but only after it had already passed the Council on way to the House. Oddly, the *New Mexican* failed to give a detailed report. "All went off well and quietly," it stated. "Clever lost his temper towards the close of the meeting. Chávez's speech made the Cleverites squirm like h . . . , they not liking to be flayed alive."[144]

Both parties hit the trail to the Río Arriba at roughly the same time. The hefty entourage of eminences accompanying Clever included José Manuel Gallegos, Diego Archuleta, Nicolás Quintana, and the Jewish merchants Manuel Spiegelberg and Louis Felsenthal.[145] Correspondents depicted the visits in long and oft-debated reports as hot and emotionally contested affairs. In Río Arriba County, Clever's route took in Truchas, Chimayó, Santa Cruz de la Cañada, Chamita, Abiquiú, El Rito, and Tierra Amarilla. An anonymous fellow traveler described old men, women, and friends greeting the worthy candidate with jubilation. A wonder it was that "such an industrious class of society" should be so highly interested in such a change in politics, as if Providence had made it obvious that the state of things required mighty efforts to cast off the *ex delegado* Chávez, as if God himself had descended to impart to them the "spirit of the Nuevo Mejicano people," fed up as they were with the "yoke of the demagogue, the staunch enemy of progress."[146]

Chávez lost Río Arriba County in 1865 by six hundred votes, and so he spent fifteen days at its precincts.[147] Two critics in San Juan, a Nuevomexicano and a Euroamerican, co-authored a parody of Chávez before a large audience "in the manner of an errant comet (of the kind worried folks believe will announce war or peace)." As the curious sought to get a glimpse of such a one, they engaged him on the problem of the river flooding their district. His county "shield," don Francisco Salazar (a clerk of the legislature), took him on a tour of the pueblo before he could promise to do anything about it. It was decided at a meeting at the home of don Juan García to invite Clever's friends for a discussion. Salazar flew out the door shouting that Chávez would be speaking to the people in an hour. Chávez would take the floor first, according to the rules, with a Clever friend to respond, and Chávez concluding. Don Mariano Larragoiti argued for the right to speak as inviolate, and if Chávez could give an accounting of his record, any citizen could respond. The meeting should not end until every citizen who wanted to do so could express himself.

The remainder of the account is a sendup in quasi-comedic form. Chávez takes the floor and gives the same speech he had made in Santa Fe and other places, filled with excuses. As he finishes, the people respond with *"vivas* for Clever and death to Chávez." Francisco Salazar stands behind like a pantomime figure in his disproportionate praises of his hero, looking like an obsequious legislative clerk. Don Diego Archuleta gives an "eloquent and sensitive" retort to Chávez. Chávez speaks for fifteen minutes but does not answer to anything that Archuleta raised. Chávez appears tired in his misadventure. Agustín Sisneros, a peón of Salazar, tries ordering people about. Chávez, sporting a toga in his *bogue* [buggy], hits the road noisily while the people shout after him that as delegate he had neglected to fix the roads. "Little Agustín" trails the buggy on a horse, moping, the good patriot "suffering the weary scene."[148]

The 100 percent Nuevomexicano Río Arriba County Nominating Convention, held at the home of don Juan B. López, nominated the "peon" Agustín Sisneros as its candidate for the Legislative Council and heard campaign remarks from Francisco Salazar. Participants would combat all of their ticket's political enemies and, "under their word of honor," support their candidates as men of energy, ability and honesty.[149]

None surpassed Taos County for partisan intensity. It was imperative for Diego Archuleta to press the campaign as the county had not gone for Perea in '65. He asked Chávez friends to schedule a debate between the two chief candidates. Citizens from every precinct attended at the courthouse in the county seat of Don Fernandez. Inocencio Martínez, nephew of legendary Padre José Antonio Martínez, testified that he had gone for Chávez in 1865 only to realize his ineptitude as delegate. The meeting moved to the Plaza of San Francisco del Rancho, where the pro-Clever correspondent claimed that the people were generally against the "rancid" Chávez emphasis on "nativo," for Clever proved himself a true representative of New Mexico after fifteen years' residence, broke no laws, and discharged his duties "honestly" in his various appointments.[150] It counted, according to Archuleta, that Clever came from the other side of the oceans yet intended to ask a Nuevomexicana to marry him.[151]

An anonymous Chávez correspondent, claiming many years of experience in politics, disputed the claim of Clever debaters winning the day. For one, Chávez supporters composed the majority of the audience and the applause given to the Clever representatives was "very weak," and don Pedro Sánchez "outgeneraled" the *paid orators* sent up to "enlighten" Taos. "They must import better stock if they wish to carry this county at the coming election," the reporter proposed. The applause for Chávez was "terrific and sounded like a death knell to the ears" of the Clever writer and his few friends. The correspondent looked for Taos to roll up a good majority for Chávez and the whole county ticket. "Mark this," he finished off.[152]

Mitchell and Carleton joined Clever through the far-flung precincts of Taos County. Local reinforcements included Archuleta, Larragoiti, Daniel Vigil, Gabriel Lucero, Santiago Martínez, and an impressive new young man, Antonio Joseph, a 1.5 generation figure destined to make a major mark on territorial politics as a Democrat. Kirby Benedict, William Arny, and Francisco Salazar joined Chávez part way. Both teams followed the same grind, starting in the southern mountain regions of Las Trampas, Chamisál, Peñasco, Picurís (to visit voting-eligible citizens living within Pueblo Grant); proceeding to the far northern settlements of Arroyo Hondo, La Cuesta, and El Río Colorado; U-turning to the villages of Arroyo Seco, Ranchos de Taos, and El Río Grande, and winding up in the county seat of Fernandez de Taos (present-day Taos municipality).

A fury of field reports depicted campaign excitement, some fantastically partisan. Groups went out to escort candidates into town, more than a hundred on horses and in carriages reported at El Río Grande. Entourages arrived to rallies at the home of a prominent individual—Juan B. Laroux at Arroyo Seco, don Pedro Sánchez at Picurís, don Jesús Lucero at Arroyo Hondo, don Juan Antonio Baca at Arroyo Seco, don Felipe Archuleta in Río Colorado, don Vicente Martínez and Antonio Joseph in Fernandez. Formal speeches sounded on the plazas. Rallies were announced after mass on Sunday. Women and children joined men in a fiesta atmosphere with music and banners. Meetings in someone's home—for example, don Ventura Lovato at Fernandez—featured debates among local leaders, of locals with chief candidates, or Chávez toe-to-toe with Clever, lasting for hours. Primary speakers had an hour followed by three responders.[153]

Citizens feared not to take on the main candidates. A young Mexican "of good education and lover of the truth and justice" confronted Chávez in Chamisal with "solid arguments, not sophisms or calumnies," as would professional politicians. "Oh," the author dreamed, "what luck New Mexico would have if all the people behaved this way." Chávez answered convincingly, apparently, and offered to return to continue the debate. The young man showed up the next day at Miguel Griego's in Peñasco. Chávez, "loyal to his word," continued the discussion. The young man did not positively declare in favor of Chávez; but at least he abandoned the intention of attacking him, making "the pretenders" Archuleta and Larragoiti anxious.[154]

The *Gazette* assured that Clever had Taos County in his back pocket, but the spirit infused in the campaign could not "with safety be allowed to die out" until election day.[155] *El Nuevo-Mejicano* gave convincing accounts of Chávez enthusiastically received at all stops. He encouraged the people of El Rancho with the promise of having *la merced* (Spanish land grant) *del Río Grande* confirmed and returned to heirs, removing it from the hands of the "speculator" Carleton, who bought it for the purpose of conveying it to a third party.[156] Clever partisans tagged the Chávez leaders as *sismáticos* (schismatics)—a recall of the religious wars in which the Mexican Party bucked Bishop Lamy—because they included two priests in the county. Father Tafolla and Father Luján were condemned as Chávez *pilguanojos* (mistresses, lovers, or whores to the rico dandy, colloq.). A Taoseño charged two of the correspondents who wrote pro-Chávez letters of being sismático and pilguanojo bosses of Taos County.[157]

Diego Archuleta preceded Chávez at each precinct. The pro-Chávez correspondent, *Un Curioso Espectador* (A curious spectator), described Archuleta as the "precursor" who had been taken to the plaza del Río Colorado "in the dark of the night by virtue of a white dove [*llevado allí en las tinieblas de la noche por virtud de [una] paloma blanca*]" to herald the coming of his candidate Clever. The writer rendered real life events as spoofed theater to convey that Chávez reigned supreme in the local debates. Archuleta reportedly found the going rough at Arroyo Seco. He conceded that he was now an "old and haggard man [*ya estaba viejo y abatido*]" and that he would leave it to younger people to carry on with his party. Juan Laroux stepped up to defend Clever "with proper energy and skill [*con la energía y habilidad que las son propias*]," only to hear the hoots and howls of the audience, forcing the two Cleverites to flee on horseback. Archuleta then showed up "very proudly" at don Juan Antonio Baca's home in Arroyo Hondo. The people gathered to hear Chávez. When Archuleta, "old and depressed," realized that the delegate would take a half hour to respond, he "cowardly and boldly" decided not to speak, claiming that someone else wanted very much to talk. Laroux spoke for Clever once again. The precursor Archuleta twice tried to exit to avoid the battle he had started, giving some cock-eyed story. The people shouted that he had no respect for them or for common decency. Laroux quieted his friends so as to hear Chávez's truths, but the precursor, instead of preaching penitence, shouted for "obstinacy, obstinacy, tenacity, and disorder [*y gritaba obstinación, obstinación, tenacidad, y desorden*]." Chávez refuted Laroux's charges to the audience's satisfaction. Archuleta and his horsemen fled to Fernandez. Archuleta reportedly pulled a similar stunt at El Río Grande. This time the people demand that he speak for a half hour. Archuleta defends his role in the Taos Revolt of 1847, confessing it was true he had "made the revolution [*confesando que era verdad que el había hecho la revolución de 47*]," calling it an honorable thing to do at the time. When it became evident that he might be found out, he fled to Chihuahua until after the trials of the rebels. If it had been up to him, he reportedly declared, New Mexico would never have belonged to the government of the United States.[158]

The village of Fernandez saw a big blow-up, according to Un Curioso Espectador. The people converged at the courthouse after mass to hear Chávez, but the overflow crowd was moved to the *plazuela* (large patio) at the home of don Santiago Martínez. Un Curioso painted Cleveritos perpetrating a comedy of horrors. As the crowd moves to the new site, the Clever lout, Esteban García, following the "*dicho que en agua revuelta ganancia de bribones* [rascals take advantage of confusion]," and thinking that no one has seen him, dodges into the home of vecino Rafael Tenorio, wounding him with a deadly weapon, a crime for which he would need to be prosecuted at the first opportunity. Precursor Archuleta bops "citizen Juan Romero" on the head from behind. The "venerable elder" Juan Rafael Pacheco throws Archuleta back five or six feet, causing him to fall. Archuleta flees amid pandemonium. Chávez continues to account for his policies while his enemies are left defeated. Many in the crowd shout *"Viva la Cubeta* [Long live the keg]," as a Clever dope fills himself with *aguardiente* on Antonio Joseph's porch.[159]

Un Testigo de Vista (An eyewitness) challenged the Chavista's absurdity, especially the idea of Diego Archuleta fearing a debate with Don Quijote Chávez and leaving it to others. Un Testigo had Chávez being the one suddenly to accuse Archuleta, in a discussion of Capt. Santiago Martínez's role at the battle of Valverde, of having been the author of the revolt at Taos. The *anciano* Juan de Herrera shouts "Liar" from the audience. If Chávez wanted to know the real author of the despicable act in Taos, the elder said, it was one José María Martínez. Archuleta was in Chihuahua at the time, Un Testigo stated. Un Testigo has Chávez men booting the respectable Herrera out of the meeting on the pretext that he was intruding in a private discussion. To the imputation of Archuleta and Esteban García acting violently with no cause, Un Testigo said Un Curioso failed to mention that the men under assault were paid by the Chávez camp to insult Archuleta and García. Un Testigo accused Chávez pilguanojos of instigating the din at El Rancho when Chávez could not respond to Archuleta's charges regarding his neglect of duties as a delegate. Luckily, Un Testigo pointed out, it did not work, and the people requested that the young Larragoiti, who had given Chávez such a fright with his strong arguments at Red River, should challenge Chávez. In this version, the ridicule that Chávez sustained at the hands of a young man proved a greater defeat than that dealt by Archuleta. Such were the truths the unworthy Un Curioso Espectador needed to see. And if he wanted to make capital out of his lies and enlist the Archduke of the Río Abajo (José Leandro Perea), seeing if he could get from him cows, sheep, and loads of provisions, he was mistaken. The Archduke told his nephew and supporters to go to hell as they never left him alone, "and I say, *secuando secundo asecundo* [I know second rate when I see it; in hybrid Spanish/Latin]."[160]

A four-way exchange involved the writers *Un Tauseño, La Verdad, Fernandeño,* and *Un Testigo de Vista*. Both Un Tauseño and La Verdad claimed that Chávez was afraid to face the people in Fernandez, hiding out at the homes of the Martínez brothers, Santiago and Vicente, or using them as his shields. La Verdad called Chávez a "wild mustang," refusing to sit with the people for conversation on topics of interest to them.¹⁶¹ Fernandeño contested the notion of Chávez as an untamed, unresponsive official. He contended that Un Tauseño's lying signed letters were written in the offices of the *Gazette*. Moreover, Chávez no more relied on his political friends in the county than Clever did on his, and Fernandeño said he had seen Chávez huddling with groups of citizens. Fernandeño had Clever supporters mistaken in having the "Gabrieles of Fernandez" (ranchers Lucero and Valdez) side by side with the "Duranes" (José and Luis) of Peñasco. The latter two were "sublimated" Mexicans who had retained their character as citizens of Mexico. Fernandeño claimed Clever had come through Taos County on his way to Denver when the Valverde battle broke out, making himself hated for talking nonsense to justify his flight. Fernandeño said Clever was hated for having Carleton at his back and also Collins, Hubbell, the author of *El Gringo* (Davis), and many others pretending to represent the government but regarding the sons of New Mexico as no better than the barbarous Indians. Clever would be lucky to receive forty votes in Taos, and the same in Mora, because the hated Clever caudillos pocketed public money. The great reception given Chávez in Mora proved the favor he earned against the Jew, as Fernandeño drew it.¹⁶²

Un Testigo charged that nothing in *el Nuevo-Mejicano* could be believed. In fact, the Gabrieles were clearly in the Clever camp, he countered. The major problem was that La Verdad, a good herder, put himself under the wing of the schismatics, lured into the family of corrupt pilguanojos, not only in Taos but with men like Tomás Cabeza de Baca "and his brother, the priest."¹⁶³

Reflecting Chávez's lack of support in Mora County, the *New Mexican* reported little from there. County attorney Pedro Valdéz and probate judge Vicente Romero supported Clever and Carleton. A reporter going by the tongue-in-cheek pseudonym of *Un Espectador Imparcial* (Impartial spectator) penned a highly comic, Cervantesque, virtually ridiculous account of Chávez's visit. On arrival, Chávez locks himself in a room for three days, although he is attended to by his friends in the county and from San Miguel County and Taos "*hasta en sus necesidades naturales* [even in his bodily needs]." Chávez is made depressed by scares in the encounters with the people and friends of Clever in Río Arriba and Taos. Chávez extends an invitation to Vicente Romero for a joint public meeting but fails to show. The friends of Clever send a committee to remind him of the event, repeating it several times before Chávez arrives accompanied by a gang of forty men sporting clubs and pistols to instill fear and intimidate peaceful citizens. Bursting onto the scene, the gang rambunctiously appoints a president, vice presidents, and secretaries. Clever friends treat the clownish scene with dignity, magnanimous hearts, and noble breasts. Chávez speaks for two hours without saying anything real. His men, including a pretentious priest, fumble and bumble an attempt to control the meeting. They are unable to keep Chávez from being rebuked by sensible, spirited, and locally respected men regarding his preoccupations with race and the good General Carleton while defaming his corrupt county supporters. Chavistas make a mess of their appearance in the community, taking their "idol" out into the middle of the street, and "*al sordo con de un violín y guitarra* [to the deaf with a violin and guitar]" playing to a clutch of boys who follow along, not caring a whit about him.[164]

Territorial House member Trinidad López, noting it was not his career to be a public writer, was prompted by the outrages in *el Nuevo-Mejicano*, the "organ of Benedicto [Kirby Benedict]" to state the "naked truth" of why Chávez would not gain more than one vote in Mora County. Chávezites sowed discord and insanity, he said. Their five candidates qualified as the "hookers of our society," save one honest hard worker. Hopefully Mora citizens would give them the kind of reception they deserved, and the same to Colonel Chávez, all birds in the same haystack. Similar to Un Espectador Imparcial, López portrayed the hurry-up-and-wait organizing of the Chávez public meeting, poking special fun with a four-line verse at president pro tem, "*el Indito R[afael] Chacón*." Chávez speaks until he loses his breath, his intent being to leave no time for response, a tactic aided by Chacón's meaningless resolutions. The people tire of these games. They leave the Chávez men to bray as loudly as they can, and the latter suppose they have defeated Clever's friends. But their "gross rant" leads many of their disgusted and deceived friends to abandon them. Confused and embarrassed, Chávez flees until reaching Sapello. López boldly names the county's prominent supporters of Chávez—Father Luján and his "cook," Anastacio Trujillo, who like Sancho Panza aspired to be "governor of Mora"; Santiaguito (little Santiago) Abreu, sheriff aspirant; Jesús María Pacheco, whom Chávez recruited in Los Rincones;

Juan José Gallegos, lawyer, justice of the peace, and legislator, pining to be probate judge—sad figures all, moving against General Clever.[165]

The few supporters of Chávez in Mora complained that the big providers, backed by the sheriff, "our eternal enemies," would not sell them wheat seed. They affirmed that the local enthusiasm for the "dignified son of New Mexico," led by Maj. Rafael Chacón, was strong, and Clever would not get more than five votes there.[166] Trinidad López appears to have shut them down in the public discourse by responding that Julián Romero, the leader, engaged in black market activities. López was not aware of anyone else willing to vote for Chávez, though some, like Jesús Pacheco, would out of fear because of prior commitments. López took note of the evil and perverse men—hired with Chávez money, food, and liquor—to insult and assail the main men of the county who favored Clever. The local priest violated his profession with the profanity of harangues rather than remain within "our holy mother church." His ilk demanded that the foreigner not comment on their customs. López dedicated some verse to him:

Antes que tú te maduras	Before you grew up
El condado estaba en paz;	The county lay in peace;
Sembraste tu la zaína	You sowed the treachery
Ministro de Satanás	Minister of Satan
Tenemos un cruel azote	We have a cruel scourge
Se llama 'Cura Luján'	His name is 'Father Luján'
Las Virtudes se le van	The Virtues have left him
Los vicios lo traen al trote.	The vices drive him at a trot.

López concludes: "In the belief that he who is slain suffers when the noose is tightened, I do not doubt that each [confraternity] brother will light his candle, that is how it should be so that they die at first light [*Creyendo que el que esta matado se padea cuando le aprietan el cincho, no dudo que cada cofrado prendera su vela, así lo deben de hacer para que mueran con la luz*]."[167]

An ethnological missive blew in from Q. Esperanza. This writer gave a similar description of the chaotic Chávez meeting, naming as villains don Francisco Salazar and Father Luján, who led the celebratory procession for their leader. In the "curious triumph" of Chávez,

Q. Esperanza was reminded of *el Buey Gordo,* the Fat Ox ceremony celebrated in Europe. On the last day of the Mardi Gras carnival, the Tuesday before Ash Wednesday, the men and principally youth gather to quit their pleasures, delights, and joys before going into the penitential Lenten season. They select the prettiest, fattest ox in the neighboring haciendas, adorn it with flowers and robes, lay a rare, precious and beautiful mantilla on its back, itself adorned with flowers of different colors and laced with gold and silver. The beast is paraded about the streets to music. Two well-adorned maidens startle the pacific animal with ribbons. The boys come behind shouting, with all the might of their lungs, *"¡Viva el carnaval! ¡¡¡Aquí esta el Buey gordo!!!"* The most burlesque dances rend the plaza. The downtrodden animal goes to slaughter in late afternoon. The poor folk are given a place to celebrate. The people feast in a raucous banquet of joy and libation well into the night. The triumph of the ox ends as its bones are burned in castles of fire on the highest hills. Colonel Chávez, though his hide was not good enough to patch the shoes of the people, nor his head smart enough to represent them, played the Fat Ox of the campaign. On election day he would be the most depressed, spellbound, and humiliated ox, casting his eye over the vanity of the triumphs of this world, the falseness of his promises, his hopes forever lost. His shame (switching metaphors): the coyote made prisoner by a chicken.[168]

The campaign heat burned on the day of the election. Disturbances broke out at sites in more than half the counties, with several outbursts in some of them. A row with clubbing and shooting erupted in Las Truchas, Río Arriba County. It was decided to close the poll booth at a private house early because the first count did not match the ballots reported in the poll book. A wholly Nuevomexicano crowd demanded to take possession of the ballot box from the judge's attempts to secure it for official counting away from the excited crowd. One judge was almost assassinated. The ballot box got lost in the melee. The open-tent station at La Junta, Mora County, two miles from the residence of any voters, saw attempts at ballot stuffing, quarrels, drawn pistols, and certain "Americans," known as the "Kansas boys," mule whips in hand, intimidating the poll watcher to "swear their votes in," one of them knocking down a voter who declared himself for Chávez. In Santa Fe soldiers and U.S. marshals reportedly intimidated the judges and men to vote for Chávez, a near riot stirring after judges rejected twenty-three voters, and the judges being forced under duress to count the votes they considered illegal. A challenger at Santa Clara, Mora County, claimed to have seen poll books and the ballot box taken into a house where the votes were counted secretly. He was threatened by drunken bullies and a member of the household for objecting. Ruckuses broke out in Bernalillo County. Judges at Barelas quarreled over the ballot count, causing a rowdy crowd to gather outside the house where the votes were counted. Clever men were reportedly pushed away from the window at the Bernalillo precinct where the ballots were submitted. The Alameda precinct saw verbal accosts and threatening language used by Chávez men, some drunk. Drunks in the Tierra Amarilla precinct disrupted the poll with boisterous questioning of voters. Tomás Cabeza de Baca reportedly forced voters with physical threats at Peña Blanca, Santa Ana County, to vote for his candidate.[169]

Three thousand more votes were cast for delegate than in 1865. Most of the spike in the 14,767 total came from two volunteer regiments that mustered out after being ineligible to vote in 1863 and 1865. Holding this constant, the vote increase was 1,300, in line with the trend of steady rises in turnout in the territory.[170]

Chávez said he felt "easy" about a handy victory.[171] However, dispute immediately arose at the office of Secretary Heath between Clever and Chávez agents over the admissibility of certain votes. Initial returns in the confusion had Clever ahead by 549 votes. According to this return, Chávez took San Miguel County overwhelmingly, as expected, and Taos solidly, getting whipped in the known enemy lands of Mora and Río Arriba counties. Key majorities seemed to have come in for Clever from Doña Ana and Socorro counties. At the same time, however, Chávez tickets garnered majorities for seats in both assembly chambers.[172]

If the fantastical dramatics of Clever's Jewishness served to pull the Mexican Party together as such a phenomenon was meant to do, it equally mobilized the opposition.[173] The *Gazette* reported that the news of a Clever victory spread over Santa Fe "like wildfire." Enthusiastic crowds formed and a band played, "accompanied by a large numbers of citizens, cheering and hurrahing in the most lively manner." A throng at the Governor's Palace congratulated Clever. "General good feeling prevailed . . . and the people looked as if they thought a better day had dawned upon New Mexico. The day of redemption is at hand," the *Gazette* enthused, "if the people only continue to prove true to themselves." The bells of liberal hyperbole—rung by classist and ethnic pride—pealed once again. Russell basked in enlightened futurism. The "first step" had been taken, he rejoiced, "in the grand forward movement that is destined to sweep away the cob webs which have accumulated on New Mexico through the centuries of ignorance and oppression, and bring to light the natural beauties and intrinsic worth of our Territory." The Chávez "stand-still, anti-progressive element" would no longer hold New Mexico back "to grovel amid the darkness of the sixteenth century." The people were where they should have been long ago had they displayed "the nerve at elections which they have manifested this year and broke down the dynasty of rich men who ruled them with a rod of iron—oppressed them with poverty—kept them shut up in the night of ignorance and used them as peons out of whose labor to increase their own wealth and establish their political powers."[174]

Clever barely won, if the numbers were correct, yet in the American style of winner-take-all, Russell had the "enterprising merchant, the well-to-do farmer and the recently enfranchised peon" recognizing him as the man "who would be their friend in all the ways that a representative could be the friend of a constituency." Chávez friends put up "a Mexican candidate," as Russell put it, not on merit but "as a man for whom his countrymen would vote regardless of his incapacity—as a candidate belonging to the family of ricos (rich men) of the Territory who would as they had done before, lavish their money to secure his election by purchasing up voters—as a candidate who would favor the rich families, to which he belongs, and do all in his power to perpetuate the iniquitous system of peonage out of which they had amassed their wealth through long years of oppression."[175]

In a final diálogo of the campaign, Cleverites Pancho and Juan celebrate the restoration of ethnic consensus. Juan lashes out at the manufactured Jewish accusations against foreign adventurers and at the native son anti-Americanism of the "stupid charlatan" Chávez. Pancho affirms that the people would have nothing to do with the enmity against the stranger who brought progress to the territory, waged by men who themselves were not citizens of the United States and refused to become naturalized citizens, yet enjoyed public positions and "liked" to serve as jurors. Juan identifies the members of the enemy cabal, including Euroamericans Benedict (*don uñas largas*) and Arny (*el Reñoso*). He beholds "the people" rejecting the capricious native sons, *el Archiduque* José Leandro Perea, *don Chato* Salvador Armijo, "all of the magnates of San Miguel and Valencia counties, and the sismáticos of Taos." Pedro congratulates Juan for learning so much about the people rejecting any question of race while sustaining the "dignity of a free people" and identifying with "equality as a right in a republican government." Juan notes that Chávez fanatics reprimanded him as an "ingrate" for having deserted the candidate who was "our paisano, our nativo friend of New Mexico in whose veins ran our own blood."[176]

The *Gazette* perceived the end of its opposing organization. "Thanks to a kind Providence and the good sense of a majority of our people," Russell intoned, "that party is dead and cannot be resurrected."[177] But the election occurred in the midst of a trend of swelling partisanship in the territory. The prognostication could not have been more off base.

CHAPTER TWELVE

A Contest for the Ages, 1867–1868

The *Santa Fe Gazette* proclaimed Charles Clever the elected delegate to Congress immediately after the election of 1867. However, José Francisco Chávez heard so many reports of Clever followers committing fraud at the polls that he expected Territorial Secretary H. H. Heath to investigate them immediately, adjust the total count of the vote, and declare Chávez the official winner. Heath agreed that egregious cheating occurred, and he scanned precincts where frauds were alleged to have taken place. However, he balked at doing all Chávez wanted of him. It was a "critical blunder," historian Gary Roberts states. Governor Robert Mitchell stepped into the breach and certified Clever the winner.[1]

Mitchell in this action violated the 1851 amendment to the Organic Law that gave to the territorial secretary the responsibility of counting the votes (in the governor's presence) and issuing the certificate of election. Heath's report to Congress two weeks after the election had Clever winning by an "apparent majority" of ninety-seven and Chávez ahead once illegal votes in four counties were thrown out. On a calculation of fraud in certain precincts, Heath described Chávez "fairly elected by 1,292."[2] Chávez thought this sufficient for Congress to award him the delegate's seat. Heath complicated matters, however, by including in his packet to Congress the certificate that Mitchell signed. Chávez whisked himself off to Washington to clarify matters to Radical Republicans and the president's cabinet.[3]

The *Gazette* set out to flog Heath incessantly. It called him an "unscrupulous and unworthy demagogue" for declaring Chávez legally elected. As editor John Russell put it, Heath's "crime" sought to "thwart the voice of the people."[4] Russell thought it incredible that Heath should find 440 improper votes for Clever and not one improperly cast for Chávez. Congress would quickly award the delegate's seat to Clever, the editor foresaw.[5] Clever and his cronies fled to Washington as well, just to be sure. Chávez found himself countering what he called their "base, false and vile lies," including the rumor that he was not a Radical but a Johnson man. Chávez impressed onto his friends the imperative of his getting the prima facie appointment to put the burden of a contest onto Clever. The *Gazette*'s abuse of him was "annoying," he felt, but he idealistically considered that the attacks "upon honest men only recoils upon themselves, for they always tend to bring out the history of the *Gazette* clique." Chávez maintained confidence in the talent, "accompanied by the honesty of purpose," in Congress, and in the number of Radicals sure to support him and whom he came to know while working in the nation's capital. Still, as he observed, "the fight" was on.[6]

Heath was left with a load of important work to realize Chávez's election. The Nuevomexicano delegate's Man Friday would have to convince key Washington leaders— against the protestations of the *Gazette*—of the large-scale frauds committed by Clever people. He would need to link the governor to frauds on behalf of Clever, and he ought to organize the territorial legislature to support Chávez.[7] Heath got busy on the tall order. Lengthy letters to U.S. House Speaker Schuyler Colfax discounted the Mitchell-signed certificate of election by enumerating the precinct counts that showed the actual majorities for Chávez; Heath explained that he reported a Clever majority under duress of Mitchell's pressure. The fact that the majority of those who ran for the territorial legislature came from Chávez's party, composing two-thirds of the council, was an important indicator of voter preferences. Heath sent House Committee on Territories Chairman Henry Dawes a voluminous account of the frauds. Conceding that he was a personal and political friend of Chávez, he nevertheless vouchsafed his reading of the returns, claiming they represented "justice and outrage" among the people of New Mexico.[8]

Chávez's strategy played to the Republican dominance in Congress. The effect put in bold relief the otherwise weak Republican-Democratic references in New Mexico. Heath's report to Dawes cited irregularities and frauds committed by "the Democrats at the Polls" against "Col. Chávez, the Republican candidate, and by which the Democrats succeeded in obtaining an apparent majority for their candidate of 97." The "foul fraud" on the voters, Heath put it, was "perpetrated thus, and I regret to add, to all appearances, with the aid and connivance of Federal office holders here who cling to Democratic faith, and with true Democratic instinct, prowl for success in all modes known to Democrats alone." The (abstract) people of New Mexico were "from the very nature of [the] circumstance Republican," he assured, "zealous of their rights, yet confiding toward their public functionaries."[9]

Heath was allowed to use the columns of the *New Mexican* to sustain the Republican perspective. The *Gazette* did not exaggerate much when it noted that the secretary had taken over its editorial management.[10] Heath's propaganda binge cast the *Gazette* as still and always a disloyal Copperhead organ and anathema to Republican sensibility. Heath called Russell a "rebel editor" during the War and James Collins an unrepentant, traitorous Confederate Copperhead.[11] In cataloguing the "abhorrent frauds" of Cleverites, Heath hitched the contention between settler-colonial and *hijo del país* to the contest of election.[12] In the "dens of vicious men" on the Canadian River, Heath had it in a quasi-anti-Semitic allusion, the plan was hatched for a poll official to defraud the honest voters of their rights "and to elevate a foreign adventurer [Clever], who keeps the pelf which he has wrung out of the people of New Mexico during fifteen years back, in a foreign land, over a true and gallant son of New Mexican soil, and who has fought for the integrity of his country and the maintenance of our glorious union."[13]

Heath, in referring to the dead-heat tie in Santa Fe County, commended the fidelity and energy of Chávez followers for contending against the "most active and unscrupulous odds." The governor, Heath charged, under the "pretense" of keeping the peace, deployed armed U.S. deputy marshals to "overawe the timid voters." Reinforcing the Semitic theme, he said that the "whole body of European merchants" were, "as if in the final struggle of desperation for the candidate of their blood and language," to have "exerted every possible means in their power," including "carrying men to the polls to vote the Clever ticket." The Chávez party meanwhile formed the picture of rectitude, utilizing no labor "to deceive the uninformed or to "overawe the timid with threats. Governed by principle and sentiment," Heath capped it, "they came calmly but resolutely to the polls, voted and exercised their influence."[14]

The *Gazette* suggested an equality of fraud.[15] It was "very probable" that "sharp practices" had been indulged in on both sides in some localities, accompaniments, it said, of elections all over the United States, concluding that "as a rule," neither party had much the advantage over the other "in the practice which had better not be indulged in by either."[16] In a weak argument, it attributed the startling rise in voters in Río Arriba and Mora counties this election to in-migration from the states.[17]

Territorial Council President Miguel E. Pino died shortly before the day of the election. Pino left his leading oppositional positionality in the persons of Anastacio Sandoval, his successor in the council, and House Speaker Francisco P. Abreu. Sandoval and Abreu enabled Heath's work. The collaboration opened with Heath's intervention in the Doña Ana County returns, in which he informed council candidate William Rynerson of the "probability" that the probate judge would refuse to grant Rynerson and the two legally elected representatives from that county their certificates of election. Heath charged the judge with illegally counting the ballots to get himself and other parties elected to office, persons "whom the people had rejected." Claiming that "the people" ought not to be cheated of their rights, Heath, backed by the legislature's approval, handed the election certificates to Rynerson and the house candidates, Ignacio Orrantia and Pablo Melendres. The legislature dismissed the appeal lodged by Rynerson's opponent. Heath impressed on Rynerson, Orrantia, and Melendres of the necessity to claim their seats for which they were legally elected "on our ticket."[18]

Chávez delivered bad news. The House Elections Committee would not recommend him for the prima facie delegate seat. The stumbling block proved to be Heath's report on the official form that Clever had an "apparent majority" of ninety-seven votes. To favor Chávez would set a precedent making all candidates with a losing count in future elections eligible for the seat simply by claiming fraud. As Chávez conveyed to Heath, their friends regretted that the secretary had not taken the responsibility of issuing him a "clean" certificate at the outset "without explanations" (had this been done, it would likely have put Heath under dire threat). The committee would accept a new certificate based on documented frauds if Heath furnished them within sixty days of the notice of contest. Chávez instructed Kirby Benedict to take some testimony "so that I may not be barred on account of [Heath's] negligence."[19] Heath failed to get sufficient testimony from the field to Washington on time. Congress, Mitchell's signed certificate waving in its face, handed the prima facie appointment to Clever. The *Gazette* cheered Congress for giving Heath a "most emphatic rejection" of his "impudent assumption." It had "kicked this imposter, together with his certificate [for Chávez] out of the House."[20]

What an anonymous correspondent called in Spanish a "grand demonstration"—attended by "all manner of people, the elderly, children, gentlewomen"—took place in the Taos Valley to celebrate the seating of "our champion delegate [Clever]." The "grief stricken Chavistas," the "fanatic Chavistas, or better said, those who desired federal jobs and had anticipated the untailing" of Clever whom they now cursed and condemned, were said to have shown up, "so grave was their remorse." The consolation for these "good Catholics," the correspondent said, lay in what Christian doctrine promised, that the grief-stricken would rule the heavens. Now that the people had triumphed, they should treat "these friends of perdition as lost children." A dance followed the political rally. The writer saw the territory embarked on a new era, Taos County giving "proof-patent" of its support for the territory's progress. Riding symbolically on the wings of Clever's wealth, it was noted, and under the direction of its capable delegate, the people would have the good fortune of seeing New Mexico "the richest of all the territories belonging to the United States." "*Que viva Clever y nuestra prosperidad,*" the writer celebrated.[21]

Don Vicente Romero in Carleton-friendly Mora County convened a mass meeting in resentment of the "false rumors" that election frauds had been committed at its precincts. Nuevomexicano leaders congratulated Clever in Spanish for the "happy triumph" of occupying his seat in the Fortieth U.S. Congress. Among them were Federico Benítez, Severiano Martínez, Felipe Romero, Pedro Sánchez, Pedro Valdez, and Col. José Ma. Valdez (the last described by a contemporary as having "none of the narrow and vindictive feelings of those who have striven to foment the prejudices of races").[22] Heath "and his satellite, J. F. Chávez" were slighted for fighting the people of Mora County with their "false, malicious and contemptible" accusations. The only illegal votes in the county were cast by the friends of the "Hon." Kirby Benedict, the resolution charged. The crowd had changed "from a sad and melancholy aspect caused by the false rumors of demagogy, to praising to Heaven the glorious news of the true leader of New Mexico, the Hon. C. P. Clever representing our sacred and free rights as our delegate to the Congress of the Union."[23]

A Nuevomexicano baptized Clever honorary native son for his uninterrupted residence of twenty years "among us," for his familiarity with "our customs," his identification with "our common interests," and his knowledge of the "needs of our land." Peeling off the label of exploiter of the natives, Clever was deemed "a man of honor, "who embraced noble sentiments in his heart," had "fine manners and an attractive and sympathetic temperament, gaining numerous friends from all over." His status among the people was proved by his election over Chávez, *el hijo del país*—"who had in his favor many powerful weapons, for example, the question of race; the influence of money; the intervention of seven probate judges [in counties won by Chávez] who, dressed in the robes of legal authority, took the liberty of taking control of elections, named persons of no scruple to judge the election—[and] the efforts of Secretary Heath, well known by everyone." General Clever had triumphed in spite of them, the citizen noted, only to face a second challenge, [the election contest] in which he was vindicated.[24]

Heath rued in his communication with Chávez his being placed in a "very unenviable light before the [House Elections] committee and the country." He stressed that he never claimed to have issued a certificate of election. Pushing back, he accused Chávez of an error in calling it such before congressional eyes that could see it was not a certificate. He could not have given Chávez a "clean" certificate without "stultifying" himself, for the law required the secretary to issue a certificate to the person receiving the highest number of votes. It was not up to the secretary, as canvasser, to "traverse the legality or illegality of any vote polled," he argued. Heath said he meant his document as advisory to the committee and that it would more than balance out the apparent majority of ninety-seven for Clever. "We agreed," Heath recalled, that it was "just as near" a certificate as could be given, "*without being one*: and that, if Congress, upon all the testimony you could adduce upon the prima facie case chose to regard it as a Certificate, which we hoped it would, all so well." His protest of Mitchell's certificate carried him "very far" on his prerogative, he believed, especially as Clever had not applied to him for a certificate.[25]

Heath informed Chávez and Assistant Secretary of State F. N. Seward of the gauntlet of public and private abuse he was made to pass through at the hands of enemies who had been pleased to "dignify" his statement as a certificate despite his denials. His enemies forwarded complaints about him to the State Department. Heath tied the slanders, vituperations, and "malignities" to what he characterized as the primary feature of politics in New Mexico, different from any other place he had seen. As he grieved:

> [P]arty policy & party action have been based solely upon *personal* grounds—political personalism. Such was the character of the last canvass for Delegate in this Territory—in which I took no part. Only when the law made it my duty to act as a canvasser of the votes cast was I brought in contact with these political personalisms, & unfortunately, the view which I took of law & duty have been so divergent & antagonistical to the opinions of one of the parties in this Territory, that no hostility, and no abuse, have been too gross to heap upon me.

Essentially the system of federal appointments to territories put Heath into the crunch of a storming imperative toward binary partisanship, which he chose not to acknowledge here but of which he was aware, perhaps in light of the anti-Semitism of the election. He did not want Chávez's failure to secure the prima facie seat to be laid on the idea of his certificate as ambiguous.[26]

Regardless, Chávez was forced to be the one filing a formal contest. Heath pointed out the need to raise funds for taking testimony, though where or how, "*quien sabe.*" But, he told Chávez, "it must, and it will be done. That you are lawfully entitled to your seat is certain. That you will ultimately obtain it, I feel assured & the great thing I regret in the whole matter, so far as the Committee is concerned, is that it should have stood upon *precedent*, when the rights of a whole people [citizens of New Mexico] were to be set aside and destroyed because of the precedent." While Chávez friends in New Mexico were "staunch and unwavering friends" of Congress, it was crucial, he concluded in full knowledge of recent party dynamics, "that the Clever Copperhead party here is the uncompromising foe to Congress. We do not, therefore, despair of justice, in the end."[27]

The Chávez contest stretched on, not to be resolved for more than a year. Along the way it was absorbed by other head-knocking politics in New Mexico's binary structure. First up, an episode of fired-up politics was already starting to burst at the seams in part because of Heath's efforts to create political conditions favorable to Chávez's contest and as another Euroamerican official found himself being cast into the role of the dangerous settler colonial.

Partisanship and Homicide in Santa Fe

Governor Mitchell opened the 1867–68 legislature calling for "personal motive" to be banished from politics in a united effort of "all parties to procure for the masses lasting benefits of congressional legislation." No man needed the advice more than Mitchell himself, the *New Mexican* snidely commented. Still, were he to strike out in this direction no one would "more heartily rejoice" than the editors.[28] And yet a most severe bout of personal politics was about to break around John P. Slough, the judge who replaced Kirby Benedict as the chief justice of the territorial Supreme Court.

In the loose wording of the *Organic Law*, territorial legislators were to give their oath of loyalty at the start of every session to the governor, the secretary "or some judge or justice of the peace."[29] New Mexico custom tended to favor the chief justice with the honor, and Slough had done it the year before. This time the legislature invited Secretary Heath to administer the oaths. Heath might have suggested the idea himself.[30] That the Mexican Party legislature would agree stemmed from its working alliance with José Francisco Chávez and the fact that Slough was associated with the opposing party. The Organic Law required that the governor and secretary be commissioned with the authority to take the oaths, but Heath had not been so empowered. Rather than turn to Slough, the legislature asked Santa Fe County probate judge Antonio Ortiz to perform the swearing in. Slough took it as a calculated slight. Historian Roberts calls Heath's role "misconduct." The *Gazette* said the enterprise represented another one of Heath's "monstrous usurpations."[31]

By way of background, Slough had arrived in New Mexico only to be shocked at the way Nuevomexicanos interwove politics and partisanship into the judicial system and local courts.[32] A sensitive colonial overseer might have thought to dispense avuncular guidance regarding American jurisprudence to the new Americans. Slough bent himself to ripping the judiciary from the clutches of politics, corruption, and the refusal to adhere to judicial impartiality. Roberts, taking the judge's view, had Slough tearing into the "sacred cow" of locals using the court system for biased, personal, and political purposes—a carryover, he claimed, from Mexican days. But it is possible to see Slough abusing Nuevomexicano jurors in various authoritarian ways, as his critics would soon charge. Additionally, Roberts himself shows Slough to have been no political innocent. A Democrat who had served in the Ohio legislature, he rapidly climbed the Democratic ladder there and later in Kansas. His conduct on the New Mexico bench leagued him with the party of Clever. In the summer of 1866 Indian Agent William Arny sought to stain Slough's reputation, telling Secretary Seward that the judge had participated in advancing a memorial in support of President Johnson's efforts to *"stay the threatening tide of* RADICALISM*."*[33] Arny sabotaged in the 1866 legislature Slough's attempt to assume leadership of a project to build a monument in honor of New Mexico's Union dead, charging that the justice had egotistically and inappropriately inserted himself into it. The measure was amended so as to remove the chief justice from the oversight committee. His ire aroused, Slough took to the streets denouncing to anyone in hearing distance those who had worked against him "in language unbecoming a judge or a gentleman."[34]

That factor—a belligerent, argumentative, vulgar, and violent aspect, for which he had been known back east and during his time in the military, and for which he had been physically threatened—would play a providential part in Slough's immediate destiny. Before the session started, Slough exhibited this brutish side, accosting Mitchell on the plaza because the governor pardoned a Nuevomexicano who had been convicted in his court for murder. The Organic Law gave the authority to the governor for such a pardon. Slough raged at what he considered the undermining of his judicial authority. He sent a letter of resignation to Washington, only to retrieve it from the mail before it left town. The *New Mexican* reproached Slough for this "shameful" act of public aggression and private impetuosity. It argued that the judge should have stuck to his resignation and should not "further tax the confidence of men by showing that, although he could be brash, yet that he had no nerve to stand up to the position he had taken."[35]

Such was the setting out of which Slough blew up over the oath-taking business. The day of that snub he verbally accosted Arny on a

Santa Fe street, accusing Arny of plotting against him, denouncing him as a liar, a "dirty dog," and a "damned dirty son of a bitch." Arny declared that no gentleman would take to such language in public. The incensed Slough threatened to beat him up. A paranoid Slough borrowed a derringer in case "conspirators" moved against him. The *New Mexican* called Slough's attack on Arny "most brutal and cowardly," "disgusting and unmanly," pointing out that the "non-combatant" Arny did not cause the change in the oath-taking matter.[36]

Arny took out a warrant on Slough on charges of assault and battery. A crowd flowed over the court before justice of the peace Abrán Ortiz. The American Partyites Governor Mitchell and Attorney General Merrill Ashurst testified against Arny's reputation. Slough interrupted the proceeding, challenging Ortiz to admit that he himself had bound over some weeks since to answer to charges of perjury and malfeasance. Slough tore up his papers and stormed out. The *New Mexican* felt Ortiz should have had Slough arrested for his "outrage upon law, and the dignity of the courts of law." Slough publicly apologized but accused Heath and Arny of instigating the swearing-in insult. He was ordered to appear in the next term of court.[37]

Speakers at a mass meeting held in Santa Fe in support of Slough condemned Heath and Arny. The Mexican Party legislature countered with a glowing tribute to Heath and criticized the chief justice for violating the law against the use of profane and blasphemous language in public. In the swiftly moving current, Heath prepared a set of resolutions for the legislature to condemn Slough's behavior. He asked the new Taos Councilman Jesús María Pacheco to introduce them. Pacheco refused, handing them to William Rynerson, staunch Chávez man from Doña Ana County whom Heath had insured would serve in the council in a disputed election. Owing the secretary one and agreeing with the criticism of Slough's ill-behavior for a judge, Rynerson introduced the resolutions in the council on December 7, 1867.

Eleven charges were preferred against the chief justice. Some gave special focus to the Nuevomexicanos who came in contact with his court: imprisoning jurors who failed to render verdicts "in accordance with his own expressed views and wishes"; imposing fines on jurors amounting to their entire pay "because they refused to follow his instructions"; intimidating juries such as to instill fear, witnessed by members of the bar; bringing "political antipathies" to the bench;

and acting the bully more than the judge under the direct influence of "ardent spirits." Extra-judicial charges included assaulting officers and employees of the military service without provocation in "vulgar and blasphemous terms"; denouncing the governor and other territorial officials on the streets of Santa Fe "in the coarsest and most violent terms"; attacking a "venerable" federal officer (Indian Agent Arny) "in a most outrageous and unmanly way"; violating his arrest for assault and battery by abruptly leaving the examining court; being under bond to answer for the offense of assault and battery "much to the discredit of the dignity of the bench of this territory, and to the mortification of the people of New Mexico." The resolutions finished in a call for Slough's removal from the bench. Slough submitted letters of support from attorneys and court officials attesting to his fairness as a judge. The Legislative Council passed the resolutions on a vote of ten to two, Pacheco himself voting for sending them on to the House.[38]

Slough called Rynerson a thief and suggested he wear a collar with the tag reading "I am Heath's dog." The next day Rynerson hunted Slough down for a retraction. When Slough refused, Rynerson shot him at close distance. The judge died hours later. Rynerson surrendered to Sheriff José D. Sena amid talk of his lynching and gestures of a riot. At a mass meeting organized in Santa Fe to lament the "regrettable" and "unexpected" demise of the judge, the leaders and most prominent participants came from the camp of delegate-elect Clever.[39] Resolutions of bereavement from the meeting of the Santa Fe Bar Association that Merrill Ashurst organized praised Slough's professionalism, his "magnanimity of character," and his "liberal and obliging disposition as a man."[40]

The partisan binary sustained the incessant squabble of the *Gazette* and the *New Mexican*. The former laid responsibility for the tragedy on the pro-Chávez cabal, while the *New Mexican* shook its head over the *Gazette*'s "intemperate" language in the face of such "melancholy" scenes caused by Slough's personality.[41] Federal Depository Superintendent James Collins irresponsibly wrote to the U.S. attorney general that a conspiracy had caused the murder so as to forward Kirby Benedict's name as a replacement for Slough as chief justice. At least Collins advised that someone unrelated to either of New Mexico's factions replace Slough lest he be tainted by political affiliation. Governor Mitchell suggested someone he knew from outside the territory for the post. Delegate Clever added his praises of Slough, "an honest, fearless, and upright judge who introduced many wise and salutary reforms in the administration of justice in the territory." Heath on the other hand advised the U.S. assistant attorney general that the killing resulted from a "personal difficulty" between Rynerson and Slough, weighing Slough's belligerence heavier than the politics.[42]

The *Gazette* published a private letter from Manuel Romero, of Sapello in San Miguel County, to his House representative, Aniceto Salazar. Romero counted Slough among the territory's vicious colonizers. While one should not be happy over the misfortune of others, Romero conveyed, the news from Salazar of the death of the chief justice "did not leave me sad, because an enemy of our party has come to his end, one of high rank, which is a great triumph for us, and a great loss for them, and as they say, 'the less of a bad thing the better.'" While at it, Romero hurled a leftover flame from the late election, calling for the cleaning out of the "nest of Jewry" in the territory. "War!!! War!!! War!!! War!!!" on them, he exclaimed. Romero hoped for a good outcome in Chávez's contest. The militia commander and Clever supporter Jesús María Baca y Salazar and his henchmen should not be allowed to walk the streets of the territorial capital laughing at Chávez's defeat, Romero ruled. "For this," he affirmed, "there would be Providence."[43]

Baca y Salazar himself had gained possession of the letter and sent it to the *Gazette* to show the stuff of which the "magnates of the Royal party" of "the rico," Chávez, were made.[44] Party dispositions flew wildly. The *Gazette* pointed to the "pleasure" in the Chávez party at the death of the chief justice and their "demand" for "more victims." San Miguel County, "through this Romero," Russell put it, demanded "the blood of Don Jesús María Baca y Salazar." Russell wondered at what other victims in every county were targeted by the "secrets of the conclave." Romero "must have a war of extermination against the Jews," the editor portrayed it. "And why? Because they, as a general thing, opposed the sending of a worthless and wholly inefficient man as a Delegate to Congress a second time." The men that the Chávez partisan would exterminate were the "most enterprising and progressive people, and leave far in the shade such men as Chávez and his anti progressive adherents," Russell elaborated. Reverting to the election campaign, he affirmed that they "differed widely from this man Romero whose views and recommendations would be a disgrace and stigma to the sixteenth century and are a shame upon the enlightenment of the age in which we live." As Russell culminated, "Shame! Romero, shame! Shame, Chávez, shame!"[45]

Representative Aniceto Salazar confirmed that Romero had sent him the letter, and he denounced Mora representative Fernando Nolan for stealing it from his room in Santa Fe and handing it to Baca y Salazar.[46] Aniceto argued that Baca y Salazar tried to cast a shadow not only on Romero but on the party that had supported Chávez. He implored his Nuevomexicano audience to know that Romero's views were those "of a man and not of a party." As Aniceto wisely put it, the impartial reader who knew the history of politics in the territory would recognize the impossibility of determining which crimes of partisanship were worse between the two major parties. Moreover, "noble men, the men of great heart, of just sentiment and honest" never concerned themselves with insignificant questions in order to win over the foreigner, nor yet to brag of their good works, much less submit themselves to calumniating three parts of a free people (Nuevomexicanos) by the expressed opinion of one man. Rather than primp, Baca needed to remember that more than anyone else he was a "true [party] magnate," out of principle at that. Baca and all who held his beliefs would find the party of Chávez composed of men "so honest, so capable, so worthy of the confidence of the public, so interested in the progress of the country and so affectionate of the stranger that they love them and his country." As Aniceto wished to make clear, Chávez's party eschewed "men of intrigue, disobedient men, and men who were so low-down as not to respect country and honor.[47] Aniceto made no recommendation along these lines with regard to Romero.

At center stage, the hapless Heath was propped up for American Party bombardment. A spontaneous Santa Fe meeting unloaded on him as the cause of the Slough murder when he authored the resolutions to remove the judge. In a fit of either paranoia or cynical partisanship, the resolutions, implying a connection to Manuel Romero, accused Heath of seeking to pursue the assassination "or murder of other citizens."[48] Heath and Rynerson received death threats. Redirecting an anti-colonial line thrown at Clever in the late election, Heath was called one of the "vagabonds of civilization" who had gone to New Mexico to gain the favor of decent men.[49]

Heath told Chávez he was being pursued by "the assassins of the other party whom you well know..., so that I am forced to go armed day and night; and at night my friends never allow me to go even from my office, unattended. Such is the posture of affairs here at this time.... Indeed I have been also threatened with mob violence."[50] A Missouri newspaper said Heath had been the "real cause and instigator" of Slough's death and threatened to expose the "base murderer of reputation," this "base murderer of truth," that he be "made known to the world," sure to have a "surfeit of compensation whereof at our hands."[51] A letter to the *Dubuque Herald* said Heath would surely be killed if he stayed in Santa Fe. His association with the assassin of Slough was characteristic of the man, the letter declared, apparently in Spanish, "and perhaps no more proper instrument of vengeance" could be found "than the bandits of New Mexico." Heath himself saw secret assassins to be the supporters of Mitchell. Heath's effigy was hung in Mora and Las Vegas. In the latter a visitor from outside the territory described the figure pleading for mercy for having been forced to sign the certificate of election for Rynerson, by Chávez presumably.[52]

To Washington officials Clever attributed New Mexico's "present disorganized and dangerous state of feeling solely to the reckless and lawless proceedings of the secretary." Unless Heath was "speedily" removed, Clever agued, it would be impossible to foretell the consequences. Clever recounted to Secretary Seward, in addition to the circumstances of Slough's death, Heath's attempt to award a certificate of election to Chávez, the swearing-in controversy, and his giving a territorial council seat to Rynerson.[53]

Río Arriba County organized mass meetings both for and against Heath.[54] The legislature supported the former and called the Heath opposition the result "solely" of antagonism to the manner in which the secretary had performed his official duties, but which it found "both proper, and in accordance with right and justice." Singling out his role in the aftermath of the election, solons called Heath "eminently worthy of the confidence of this body, and of the entire people of New Mexico." Their resolutions were transmitted to the president, secretary of state, the president of the U.S. Senate, the speaker of the House of Representatives, chairman of the Senate Committee on Territories, chairman of the Committee on Territories in the House, and José Francisco Chávez.[55]

A citizen billing himself as S implied that Council President Anastacio Sandoval had helped pressure Taos Councilman Jesús M. Pacheco into introducing the legislative resolutions that criticized Slough. Though young, Pacheco would not be frightened into compliance (*no le puede hacer coco*), S made plain, and though Sandoval's toadies and liars had criticized Pacheco in Taos, the people would not have it, for it was well known that he had discharged his duties with more dignity than what could have been hoped for given his limited experience, and the people approved of his public conduct. Pacheco had enemies, it was admitted; there were more bad people than good in the world, and probity was always persecuted. "*Vivan* the honorable men," impartial and concerned for his land, S concluded, "and death to the adulators and liars who betray the public" (Sandoval doing Heath's bidding).[56]

The subject of adulators occupied a unique *diálogo* driven by the nightmarish politics and inspired, it seems, by the filth-ridden third circle of Dante's inferno, Gluttony (for the full Spanish text, see appendix 7). A woman, Bárbara, nicknamed "Bab," engages don Bartolo. A despondent Bartolo relates the dream he had the night before, after "emphatic" prayers with his family, in which he bathed in a lake with crystalline water. At the entrance to the lake the inscription on a marble slab says, "Corrupted ones, enter and purify yourselves, but all who sacrifice their homes by some vile interest will be spit out of these waters unpurified." A shivering Bartolo is thrown out of the crystalline water onto the bank of a putrid pond in which a lion, a bear, and a pig bathe in sludge next to a sign that says, "This is the asylum of the adulators." A little dove with an olive branch in its beak and seventy-eight pigeons fly above, a sign on their extended wings reading, "We gave the victory to who deserved it." The dove sings:

> I do not fear the roar of the Lion
> because already fortunate, I have triumphed
> I care not of the Bear's venom
> Sing, coo-coo-coo, 99, which we have won.

The pigeons sing:

> Stop there, little dove with that
> See that the pig is walking off
> He abandoned his most unworthy Office
> Coo-coo-coo, his destiny will be for the worse.

Look, Bab exclaims, how your face is turning!

That it was an apocalyptic dream Bartolo did not doubt. "Do you know what an apocalypse is?" he asks Bab. "A revelation," because, he says, he also dreamed that when the dove passed, many people walked out of the putrid hole with long faces. A fortune teller told him that the crystalline lake contained justice and truth, and "no one like yourself could bathe in it because justice knew who to hate and you well knew that the party of Chávez was corrupt and that is why it spit you out, because you seek your own ruin." Bab offers her interpretation. The cesspool represented the putridness of the Chávez circle. The lion was Chávez, the bear Heath, the pig Arny. The sign meant that only fawning and servile men could serve their stupidities for they had caused the death of one of the best men to have stepped onto their soil. Who knew how many crimes they had committed, having Bartolo and his colleagues (with the exception of nine legislators) as their vile instruments, ready to assassinate. The dove represented Clever and his wise intentions. The olive branch signified the defense of Clever and his triumph. As the dreadful dream is told, Bartolo faints from fright. A stunned and astonished Bab, filled with horror, exclaims, "The same apocalypse as Pancho's!" (from a prior diálogo).[57]

At Rynerson's indictment Judge Joab Houghton ruled that proof of guilt was not evident but the "presumption" was great, setting off another round of editorial crossfiring between the *New Mexican* and the *Gazette*. The *New Mexican* argued that Rynerson acted as any man would in the face of Slough's belligerence, condemning Houghton for a tendency to a premature conviction.[58] The *Gazette* slammed the *New Mexican* for exculpating Rynerson in the name of the "small knot" of politicians who hated the late chief justice, and fearing the day when a "Judge in New Mexico shall fail to do his duty for fear of having visited upon his head the vituperation of a newspaper and particularly of such a newspaper as is now under the editorial management of H. H. Heath in this city, the *New Mexican*."[59]

Executive-Legislature Redux

While the Slough case filed into the courts and spilled onto society, a majority in the legislature was provoked once again to buck the governor. Mitchell's choices for auditor, territorial librarian, and adjutant general were the same controversial individuals from the impassioned 1866–67 session. The Legislative Council's opposition was part retaliation for Mitchell's refusal to recognize the appointments of Acting Governor Arny and his previous fight with the council. They were provoked by the fact that Mitchell's nominees were all Clever men and also because the governor had submitted the names after the deadline stipulated by the Organic Act. Anastacio Sandoval (auditor), Trinidad Alarid (librarian), and John Gwyn (adjutant general) resisted as well, each entering into the record his account of the appointment and unceremonious removal by Mitchell. Gwyn in particular emphasized the claims of volunteer veterans remaining unprocessed.[60]

Mitchell again galled the Mexican Party by renominating *Gazette* editor John Russell adjutant general. The *New Mexican* argued that it allowed the "unrepentantly" disloyal Copperhead to usurp federal salaries as he also served as the Spanish-language interpreter for the district military commander. The weekly sided with the legislature for vindicating the law "as well as its own dignity" by challenging the Russell appointment. It framed the governor as one who granted authority to his partisan friends in terms of an insider-outsider problem: "We shall now soon see who is the power in New Mexico, the governor, who is a comparative stranger among the people or the representatives of the people in their annual assemblage." The representatives would remain "as they are, in the ascendant," given the governor's limited powers, the editor predicted.[61]

Here the *New Mexican* hit on the important issue of the relative powers of the territorial governor and legislature. The federal legislation that formed the basis for territorial organic laws established a strong governor's office with powers that went beyond those of the assembly. Since 1836 when Congress established its "absolute" control of the territories, the governor had represented the U.S. government itself.[62] Russell's position that the governor's office had "as much, and more, dignity and power" than did a legislator was technically correct, although he bent it to his partisan interests. As he emphasized, the governor was the supreme authority in the legislature, seeing that the laws were faithfully executed. He was entitled to "far more consideration than the two houses who can in reality do nothing, who are powerless, without his co-operation." If the legislators arrogated to themselves the right to ignore his acts, the governor would be justified "in asserting the dignity of his office to the fullest extent and teach the Legislature a lesson that would be highly beneficial to itself and to those who may follow them in a similar capacity." As the issue touched on the ethnic division of powers in the territory, Russell heated up to his southern proclivity for racialization. The legislators exhibited their "ill-breeding," as he described it. These representatives lacked the dignity usually pertaining to legislative bodies, and so the governor would be "perfectly justifiable in leaving them to the full enjoyment of their ignorance and the occupation of the position in which they have allowed themselves to be placed by selfish and evil advisers." On the fact that the legislators had accepted the reports of the Arny appointees and ignored their replacements, Russell saw the gauntlet thrown down to the governor, "and there is nothing left for him to do but maintain his dignity and rights under the law, or submit to the indignities which these men attempt to place upon him." Russell saw its "large majority" and the U.S. government supporting Mitchell's rights above the attempts to trample them. "[L]et us see who will be the victor," the editor laid down.[63]

The *New Mexican* called Russell, who had been holding the office of adjutant general eight months, a "mendicant" about to lose his alms. He allegedly "exhibited about as much logic as an aged specimen of the canine race would over the prospect of losing a well fatted bone." The writer, Thomas Tucker or Heath, challenged Russell's opinion of the "unintelligent" legislators, observing that there was not one who was not the equal of the *Gazette* editor in "sound sense and judgment, and in every other respect infinitely his superior." If the legislature could do nothing without the cooperation of the governor, the reverse was also true, it was noted. No more "dignity and power" resided in the office of governor than in the legislature or "of a legislator." As one historian notes, Americans often complained that the powers of the territorial governor were "too great."[64] The *New Mexican* tackled the problem from the angle of republican representation, adding a general struggle against dictatorial centralization. The executive was thus "the servant of the people." The people were above him because they were the "source of power." That the governor was sent to execute the laws by the "supreme of authority" invested him with no special power, the argument went, for his business was "to execute the laws of the people." Russell was called either "the supple tool of power, or, the fit object alone to be a slave," the governor standing with him "as a sort of God among mortals, who, like Jove, in his estimation, is supposed to shake the universe."

The *New Mexican* contested Russell's position that the legislature existed only to ratify the governor's acts. If accepted, it would mean a "new doctrine in a representative government," Tucker argued. The *Gazette* editor's threatening call for the governor to "assert the dignity of his office" failed the test of political wholesomeness, it was argued. Would the governor "disperse the legislature, as we are informed he has himself already threatened to do?" Would the *Gazette* invoke force on the part of the governor to maintain his rights and dignity by the use of illegal acts? Where did the force and the power lie? "And when these are found, if found they can be," the critique followed, "we should like to see the law, under which they can be exercised by the governor." Should the "measure of strength" between the governor and the legislature go to the extent of the application of force, the "people of eight counties of this territory [who had voted for Chávez], whose representatives are a majority of the legislature will not be slow in vindicating the dignity of the people and the right of the legislature; then we shall 'see who will be the victor.'"[65]

Nothing symbolized the power of the governor more than the authority he retained to exercise absolute veto over legislation passed by the assembly. But the unqualified veto did not exist in all territories.[66] In New Mexico the legislature defied the governor by deliberating a memorial, drafted by Heath, asking Congress to reduce the governor's absolute veto officially, as the Colorado Territory had recently done. With its realistic promise of increased power for Nuevomexicanos, the measure passed unanimously, including votes of members from the counties that went for Clever. In the ironic but officially reflexive procedure, the memorial went to the governor for approval. Mitchell rejected it, of course, citing his duty to dampen the territory's "overexcited public sentiments" and the need to subdue the "excited personal" bills emanating from the legislature. Perhaps in the future it would be "convenient" to amend the terms of the governor's veto, he noted; to do it now would mean the "destruction of the well-being of the territory."[67]

New Mexico's Organic Act did not include a procedure for the legislature to override a governor's veto. As a result, all but four of the legislators fired off a set of resolutions in rebuke of the governor's "direct insult." One resolution accused Mitchell, in rejecting their memorial, of continuing to commit his "arbitrary acts" against the people of the territory.[68] The *Gazette* offered the culturally catty suggestion that if the legislators wished to adopt a memorial curtailing the veto provision, it should also resolve that "no person shall be eligible to a seat in either house of the legislative assembly who cannot read the Organic Act & payroll in legible hand." The *New Mexican* reminded Russell that he was insulting his own friends in the legislature, if there were any left, with this "foul witticism."[69]

The *New Mexican* lashed out at the "will of One Man" and countered Mitchell's rationale for not approving the memorial with the point that "there was never greater tranquility existing among the people." The weekly asserted that the governor would deny thirty-nine representatives who understood the wants of their constituents "as well as his Excellency!" As the writer queried, who gave the governor the right to question the acts of the representative body "known as" the legislature of New Mexico? The governor's action violated the republic's electoral principle, the finding continued. The *New Mexican* added the officially *"sacred right of petition,"* which had been *"invaded in the most ruthless uncalled for, and anti-republican manner"* (emphasis in original). Yet the rights and interests of the people were safely in the hands of the legislature, it was assured, and no executive power could "swerve them from their proud position." The governor would learn that no "executive on earth" could maintain his assumed position. No monarch could refuse to recognize the right of people directly, or through their representatives, to "petition the throne."[70]

According to a Nuevomexicano citizen, *Progresista* (Progressive), two members of the council had debated during the session as to whether the legislature's resolutions and memorials required the approval of the governor for them to be forwarded to Congress. Committee on Projects Chair Jesús María Pacheco argued that such documents were indeed of no effect without the governor's signature. San Miguel County Councilman Celso Baca cited what Progresista called the "Constitution" (the Organic Act) to argue that the legislature did not have to depend on the governor to establish rules with regard to its own memorials. Progresista, siding with Pacheco, mocked Baca's "expounding with such formality and airs of triumph like a professor with the book in his hands citing laws and pronouncing sentences although going off on tangents as always," as if the council could itself amend the Organic Act, casting aside the governor's approval by the simple application of its majority vote.[71] As the *New Mexican* noted "with pleasure," Republican Nebraska senator Thomas Tipton was heading a movement to secure an amendment to the Organic Act to qualify the governor's veto.[72]

The populist press in the states called Mitchell's cancellation of the legislature's bid for greater power an act of "undemocratic despotism."[73] An anonymous member of the legislature took pleasure in this greater awareness, a sign, he noted, of Congress and the people of the United States noticing the lamentable conditions existing among the people of New Mexico, a willingness "to recognize us as brothers and to raise their voices to help support our rights of equality."[74]

The legislature ordered a joint committee to consider the governor's rejection of the veto bill and his general policies. The committee, in resolutions having the lead signature of Representative William Henry Henrie and authored by Heath, condemned Mitchell's entire record of alleged malfeasance, including his becoming the partisan immediately on his arrival in the territory and leaving for Washington before the legislature of 1866–67 "in disregard of his duties and of the interests of the people of New Mexico," remaining absent from his post during the entire session. The whole fiasco of the territorial appointments and their cancellation by the council was rehashed, with the odd technical point made that a territorial governor had the right to appoint anyone qualified to office but lacked the power to remove appointees. Mitchell was accused of election fraud, illegally establishing new precincts, and usurping the right to "appoint" a delegate to Congress, done "during the pendency of a canvass in this Territory for Delegate." He violated the law stipulating that such duties devolved to the territorial secretary, which had existed "nearly the fifth part of a century, having been approved by Congress and which is in full force and effect." Finally, Mitchell refused to approve the legislature's memorial to Congress asking for an amendment to the Organic Act regarding the governor's veto, a veto that legislators felt trampled on the right guaranteed to the people of New Mexico through their legislature "for the relief of their grievances, a right sacredly guaranteed to American citizens by the Constitution of the United States." The amendment would have placed the "free people" of New Mexico on an equal footing with other territories, restraining the governor from the exercise of power "to overthrow the entire legislation of the Country, notwithstanding that the laws might be passed by a unanimous vote of the Legislative Assembly."

The committee deemed Mitchell's official course "so gross and illegal in many of its parts as to render him an object almost of aversion to the masses of our people instead of their true friend." The time had arrived "when his power to do good among our people has entirely passed, when the occupation of the executive chair, can but be considered by us, as an imposition upon our people, who are ignorant of having committed any crime where they should be so punished." The members respectfully urged the early if not immediate removal of Mitchell. Secretary Heath was directed to remit a copy to the president of the United States, the U.S. secretary of state, the chairman of the House Committee on Territories, and the presiding officer of each chamber of Congress. The U.S. House referred it to its Committee on the Judiciary.[75]

While the *New Mexican* sent the committee's report for national distribution, the *Gazette* accused the "irresponsible" legislature of devoting its time to personal and partisan politics while disregarding the duties pertaining to legislation.[76] Russell upheld Mitchell for discharging his official duties in a manner "entirely satisfactory" to the mass of the people, like visiting the counties to become acquainted with the people and their wants and resources; calling on the legislature to establish public education, which the legislative houses neglected (it called for a tax on property owners); encouraging enterprise for internal improvement; advocating laws to renew the territory's "sluggish system of agriculture"; encouraging the erection and working of "manufactories in our midst"; and inspiring the confidence of capitalists to "come hither and participate in the expense and profits of developing our mineral resources." Russell again questioned the legislators' (that is, the Nuevomexicanos') capacity to discharge their duties as public servants.[77]

A mass meeting at Santa Fe's Library Hall, attended by "hundreds," rallied for Mitchell. Reflecting an intact dual-party structure, it sported a clear American Party cast: José Manuel Gallegos calling it to order, Merrill Ashurst serving as president, and Nicolás Quintana sitting as one of three Nuevomexicano secretaries. Five other Nuevomexicanos served on the Resolutions Committee alongside the Jewish merchants Manuel Spiegelberg and F. Gold. Secretary Heath was condemned for usurping the authority of the probate judges in giving false certificates of election for the assembly. The legislature was accused of failing to honor the proper certificate of election given to one candidate by his probate judge even though his seat was not contested; also for passing memorials and resolutions for strictly partisan purposes to injure individuals who disagreed with them politically, and wasting time in partial resolutions to attack or praise federal officers "for the selfish ends of the two or three outsiders who ruled them. The American Party took its turn to claim insider authority. "By order of said outsiders," it proclaimed, the legislators had passed resolutions against the private and public conduct of "our late lamented Chief Justice John P. Slough, who was finally killed by Wm. L. Rynerson, one of said majority and who was admitted into their body contrary to law on a bogus certificate from the Secretary of the Territory." The resolutions, forwarded to President Johnson, asked for the removal of Heath. At adjournment, the crowd, carrying torch lights and sounding music, marched around the plaza to serenade the governor.[78]

The *Gazette* saw great significance in the mass meeting, a general revolt against the legislature's "vindictive and false" resolutions, which found "no sympathy among the people, who now look more earnestly for something, some measures of legislation, or for some public spirited and progressive officers, that will effect the elevation and tend to increase the wealth of our Territory, rather than for a silly legislative and personal warfare upon individuals." Russell returned to framing the territory's political problems as a pre-Enlightenment and premodern dilemma. The legislature's "kind of conduct" may have been tolerated by the people "during the old rule, before the abolition of peonage; before we thought of having railroads and telegraphs; before we concluded that our mineral resources must be developed into a source of wealth; before the spirit of the Yankee Nation came over us and opened our eyes to what we were and what, under other auspices, we might be." But now the people demanded to see something more in the acts of their legislators "than the change of the boundaries of precincts and resolutions for and against federal officers." This would not be the last of the people's reproof of the legislature, Russell affirmed, for the "feeling of resentment" was not confined to Santa Fe, existing in "every county." The voice of the people would be "heard and heeded." Though far from being the first, this would be the last session of a legislature in New Mexico "that will make for itself so ridiculous a record and reflect upon the constituents of its members a disgrace that will bring to their faces the blush of shame."[79]

The *New Mexican*, on the other hand, called the Santa Fe meeting a "junta of Copperheads, speaking professedly from the rear room of a doggery for the people of New Mexico to stigmatize a loyal territorial officer who had made himself obnoxious to them by his fidelity and loyalty to the people," and the paper called the Alburquerque meeting "scandalous," meant to "whitewash an unworthy" governor "and to denounce faithful citizens and faithful public servants in New Mexico." The piece, perhaps written by Heath himself, underlined the character "and standing of the leaders of the Copperheads" in the territory, although it regarded the resolutions as composing "a tissue of falsehood, toadyism, and black guardism from the beginning to end," disgraceful "even to the Copperhead party of New Mexico, which is low in the scale of morality and decency." Governor Mitchell would surely feel pride in the party "whose literature runs to lies and falsifications; traductions and slander alone. Considering all the political affinities, it is not to be wondered that he, in his speech to his sans culottes, said that he appreciated 1000 times more their resolutions than any endorsement of him could be passed by the most dignified and respectable legislature that ever convened in New Mexico." "God save this or any other country ruled by such influence as govern the *pinchecuantos* [lousy bunch]—Copperheads—of New Mexico today! The stench of that meeting hangs like the atmosphere of a slaughtering bull pen over the city," the editorial concluded. "Indeed the Sabbath was profaned and the sin smells to heaven yet."[80]

Alburquerque sponsored its own pro-Mitchell event at the home of the businessman Morris Miller. The meeting had been announced in Bernalillo, Santa Ana, Valencia, Doña Ana, and Socorro counties, with copies sent to Santa Fe, Las Vegas, Mora, Taos, and Fort Union. The proceedings, conducted under the stars and stripes flying over the portal, took a nonpartisan tack, claiming "no political sentiment or belief." However, the partisan reality shone when the president, one Manuel Armijo, announced that he had solicited the presence of known Chávez followers, assuring respect for their "right to express their feelings." Other Nuevomexicanos besides Armijo served as leaders alongside Euroamericans. One Francisco Armijo sought to illuminate the uncomplimentary legislators, aiming particularly at his own Bernalillo County Representative William Henry Henrie, who had presided over the investigation into election frauds. The resolutions gave "cordial assent and approval" to the proceedings of the Santa Fe mass meeting and its sentiments. Full confidence was given to the "ability, integrity, and honesty" of Governor Mitchell. The Organic Act, in putting power in the hands of the governor, was endorsed. The legislators, "whenever they praise or censure anyone, act outside of their official capacity, and do that for which they were not elected," it was pronounced in modernist style.[81]

The binary held firmly across the territory, and so popular opposition to Mitchell found its representation in a well-attended public affair conducted entirely in Spanish by Nuevomexicanos in Los Rincones, a valley in Taos County containing four precincts. Rumor had previously circulated that the Mitchell crowd intended to bribe members of the legislature as a means of overcoming the minor status of its men. Chávez discounted this, not believing they had the funds to pull it off.[82] Perhaps the president of the meeting, Maj. José Antonio Martínez y Medina, had other information, for he issued objection to the bribes of the "partisan Clique of Clever." Loud vivas went up for the prospect of New Mexico under the influence of its "legitimate supporters" of Colonel Chávez, people whose principles were based on equality and the encouragement of Progress and the arts "and did not make us slaves of the officials who come here to trample our laws and subjugate us with the conviction of a few adulators." Secretary Heath was the "loyal servant" of the territory's government, the possessor of the "sympathies" of the people of New Mexico. A protest condemned the "repugnant indignation" in Mora that had hung Heath in effigy, the perpetrators of which may have considered themselves "sovereign magnates and philanthropic men" but whose acts "without scruple against honest men discredited them to the world."

The gathering further deemed the legislature worthy of the confidence of the majority of the territory's people. Mitchell was to it a "dictator and a usurping tyrant," having carried on "with the scandalous and capricious management of the executive since his arrival to this territory." All agreed with the "loyal" legislature's call for removing the governor. Challenging Russell's vision of the people moving against the legislature, the Rinconeños asked "all citizens of free spirit spread through all the places in which we live" to recognize "with indignation those malignant men who cooperated, induced and helped to commit" the election frauds, meant to rob the "sacred suffrage of our people, to aggrandize that degraded clique that has so defamed the character of our people." Together with the *Gazette*, the "repugnant and detestable" clique was said to discredit New Mexico, scandalizing the moral character of its people, censuring the legislators only because they did not "walk in their [party] dominion." The crowd acclaimed the *New Mexican* as the one paper prepared to "approve and sincerely recognize and appreciate the cause of the people of New Mexico."[83]

Back at the capital, the legislature, enabled by Heath's counsel, did its own scrutiny of the voting record in the election for delegate to Congress. Seeing "palpable grounds" of certain frauds at the polls, a Joint Committee was given the ostensible task of conducting an investigation of the allegations. The committee acknowledged in its final report that it did not have time to send for individuals to interview; it "investigated" the case via the official records of the secretary and the members who had "concluded in their own minds upon many points from facts within their individual knowledge." According to its report, the evidence showed that enough fraud was committed that someone with a minority of the votes cast received the certificate of election. It repeated points that Heath had sent to Dawes, including the very table, with the counties re-ordered, showing Chávez with a legal majority of 1,292 votes. It also cited the Doña Ana case involving Rynerson and one of the two Chávez candidates for the House. Both chambers, "in the most formal and solemn manner," set the "seal of condemnation" on what they called the illegal transactions of the Doña Ana County probate judge of admitting to their seats Rynerson in the council and Señor Ignacio Orrantia his seat in the house, both of whom were legally elected by almost the same majority received by Chávez over Clever in Doña Ana. The committee put in its "high approbation" of the "candid and honest, as well as the legal and just course" pursued by Secretary Heath in the canvass, though at the hands of "opposition" he suffered "threats of violence, vituperation, and slander." The assembly as a whole passed the committee's resolution proclaiming

Chávez having received a large majority of the legal votes cast at the general election, deeming him the legally elected delegate.[84]

The report stimulated further public commentary. A Euroamerican verse mocked Mitchell for having certified Clever:

> Bobby, or Booby (or both connected)
> Sat down one day
> to find a way
> to get his man elected;
> but when he had wrought,
> and when he had thought,
> no plan could be detected.

The bit of amateur verse claimed it was necessary to cast Chávez off to perdition through the theft of votes, for should he win, Mitchell would lose his governor's post.[85]

Mitchell waited until the last minute to forward his set of appointments for the following year. The council approved his three nominees for major generals of the militia, including Diego Archuleta. It confirmed four of his six brigadier general nominations. The two not approved, Santiago Valdez and Antonio Roival, were long-standing burrs in the hide of the Chávez party but less powerful and venerable than Archuleta. The council rejected the Mitchell friends Merrill Ashurst for attorney general, John Russell for adjutant general, Epifanio Vigil as auditor, and J. M. Alarid as librarian. It did, however, confirm Felipe Delgado as territorial treasurer (as Anastacio Sandoval had resigned). After the legislature adjourned Mitchell defiantly commissioned all of the nominees the council had rejected, interpreting his veto power, still technically in effect, as granting him the authority to do so. The *Gazette* editorialized, "Had he paid attention to the factious course of that [council] caucus, for it was nothing more than a party caucus [as opposed to an expression of 'the people'], he would have had around him a lot of officials with whom he could have no intercourse and who would have done all in their power to embarrass his administration and to molest and annoy him as did the Legislature which has just adjourned." Mitchell's independent course produced the appointment of such officers as were agreeable to himself, "and who would discharge their public duties with honesty and fidelity."[86]

The *Gazette* said the legislature had been represented by a "combination of impudence, prejudice and dishonesty," disgracing the territory with "puerile and factious proceedings." The paper, "[w]ere it not impossible to do so," would have thrown the "mantle of oblivion over their disgraceful conduct [to] hide all their shameful acts from public view. But their masters, those who took advantage of their ignorance and bigoted prejudices have made this impossible." The editor anticipated citizens being more careful in the selection of candidates, electing men of character and ability who understood their duties, "and understanding them, will discharge them in a manner that will ensure their works to redound to the benefit of New Mexico."[87]

In diametric opposition, the *New Mexican* congratulated the body of men "more deeply imbued with a desire to do so much good to the people than was this last one," filled with the "best talent of the territory, Mexican and American." It noted the passage of a general incorporation law and a voter registry law as examples of important accomplishment in spite of a "radical executive" in their way. That much was left undone was due to the governor's "partisan malevolence and limited knowledge of the wants of the people."[88]

In the meantime, the Chávez contest remained in abeyance and would as New Mexico underwent still another round of political change.

5
Arriving

New Mexico inherited the possibility of a fully organized party system practically from the beginning of its official shotgun marriage with the United States. The "wanting" of an actual political party evidenced itself in the various attempts to grasp what was being laid out by the national organizations by way of identity nomenclatures, and it was generally assumed that a successful acquisition of party structure, as modeled in high places, would strengthen the belonging of citizens to the family of American civics.

Although New Mexico's political binary had held for nearly twenty years, the "planning" for establishing a party came in spurts at election time. The organizing of a stable party was thwarted by rapid-fire changes in party configuration on the national stage. The need to attend to deeply rutted regional issues also contributed to the delay. Yet the primary material of a binary opposition was firmly in place, and indeed the competition between the two key factions kept the fire of desire for a real party burning as the critical means for dealing with the issues they quarreled over, or cared about on their own, and for the struggle to keep the members of each in ascendance. The arrival of new political elements who made no bones about their party affiliations triggered both hope and fears of a Republican Party getting formed. As we have seen, a particularly momentous change in a national party during an election season could well catalyze a New Mexico shadow-party. It happened again in 1867, but this time it would clear the path for constructing an official two-party contention for good.

CHAPTER THIRTEEN

Republican Party Debut, 1867–1868

On November 5, 1867, the editors of the Santa Fe *New Mexican* proudly pointed to the message posted on its masthead, "the name of *The Great Soldier of the Union*—General ULYSSES S. GRANT—for the Presidency, in 1868!"[1]

National politics since Lincoln's death and the end of civil war had been turning on Reconstruction and the battle between Democratic president Andrew Johnson and a Republican-dominated Congress. The complicated scenario involved Radical Republicans, Moderate Republicans, Conservative Republicans, Southern Republicans, Moderate Democrats, Conservative Democrats (Copperheads), and Southern Democrats. Radicals who promoted racial equality as social morality and federal policy waged combat on the president and Democrats who opposed the Fourteenth Amendment, which would give citizenship and civil rights to freed slaves. Johnson sought to stem, modify, or veto components of the congressional Reconstruction Acts that under Radical leadership would have kept the South under military rule; made southern states rewrite their constitutions to take out racialized sections; force-purchased homesteads of former Confederates who had held slaves to pay for Civil War costs; and restricted the president's attempts to reincorporate the South immediately into Congress with a minimum of sanctions.

The issue of the loyalty of the president's officers figured in. Secretary of War Edwin M. Stanton joined Radical Republicans in criticizing Johnson's stand of readmitting formerly seceded states without guarantees of civil rights for freed slaves. Stanton's confidence in standing up to his boss relied on the Tenure of Office Act, which provided that all federal officers whose appointment required Senate confirmation could not be removed without the consent of the Senate. Should the Senate not concur with the dismissal, the official had to be reinstated. Republicans sustained the act over Johnson's veto. Johnson defied the override and suspended Stanton after the congressional session broke up.[2] Johnson picked Ulysses S. Grant to serve as the interim secretary even though the commanding general of the Union Army had expressed support for the Fourteenth Amendment and provisions of the Republican Reconstruction Act and opposed Johnson's removal of General Philip Sheridan on differences in administering Reconstruction. Stanton, backed by Radicals, refused to resign. In what proved a shrewd move, Grant accepted the interim secretary of war position.[3]

Radical chiefs held Grant's militancy on Reconstruction suspect, as reflected in his prior congressional testimony recommending against impeaching Johnson and his positive report on Johnson's Reconstruction policies. Radicals favored Ohio senator Benjamin F. Wade and Supreme Court Chief Justice Salmon Chase as candidates for the presidency, tending to disregard Grant. Looked at differently, northern popular sentiment regarded Grant the soldier-savior who had defeated the rebellion and thus the one for the Republican Party to support for president. The fall state elections rendered the situation critical for Republicans. Voters in most of the northern states gave Democrats power or reduced Republican majorities at the same time that they rebuked the Radical program. They may have favored equal political rights for blacks in the South but were unwilling to grant rights in their own northern districts. Democrats saw in these outcomes hope for their national prospects. The results served among Republicans to yank the media bullhorn from the hands of Radicals and hand it to more moderate elements. Moderate and agnostic Republicans, jolted by Democratic gains, turned to Grant as the man to save the Union. He, they believed, would reconcile hardliners on both sides of the Reconstruction controversy, restore civil law, and bring order and peace to the country while keeping the party ascendant in the North.

A craze for Grant coursed through the editorials of major newspapers in the states, including the *New York Times*, called by one historian "the leading moderate Republican journal." Grant clubs sprouted widely. Moderate Republican politicians at various levels and local pundits added to the surge. A strong push came out of the meeting at New York's Cooper Union. Feeling "sickened" with politics and politicians, "and anxious alone for the prosperity of the perpetuity of the union," participants grabbed at the business of nominating Grant for president.[4] Grant ignored Democratic entreaties to change parties. Radicals like *New York Tribune* editor Andrew Greeley and Congressman Thaddeus Stevens criticized Grant for not supporting the impeachment of Johnson and for refusing to endorse the federal confiscation of southern lands. Other Radicals drifted to the Civil War hero, feeding off the general's criticisms of Johnson, Grant's favor of black suffrage, and his support for congressional Reconstruction.[5]

If any doubts existed as early as the second week of December 1867 as to who would be the Republican Party's candidate for president, they were dispelled by the overwhelming informal vote for Grant by the Council of the Republican National Committee. The leading *New York Herald* projected the selection of Grant by acclamation at the Republican nominating convention.[6] The *New Mexican* closely followed the Grant trend. The "grand Republican meeting" at the Cooper Institute, the weekly said, was the "largest, most harmonious and enthusiastic political gathering" ever held in New York City, endorsing the "illustrious hero, who is as true to the cause of equal rights and impartial justice as to the demands of patriotism."[7] The weekly reproduced a Grant-for-president rhyme from the *Herald*.[8] The paper cited the "redolent" voices in the country calling out to Grant, including that of House Speaker Schuyler Colfax.[9]

New Mexican editors William Mansfield and Thomas Tucker spilled their laudations. The war had made Grant "the choice of the people everywhere," they observed. New Mexico would have no electoral college vote, yet its residents, "as American citizens, devoted to the great principles of liberty and free government," had "a right to a voice among the people, and that voice is, for every solid reason, for General U. S. Grant for President in 1868." Enjoining the Republican appropriation of the iconic Thomas Jefferson, the *New Mexican* changed its motto to embrace "a sentiment upon which our whole superstructure as a Republican government rests," to wit, "We hold these truths to be self evident: that all men are created equal."[10] The weekly found material to make Grant out the Radical.[11] By extension, it moved the New Mexico binary toward a Radical stamp, weighted in sharp contrast to New Mexico's Copperhead legacy. In a piece most likely penned by Tucker, the paper knocked the Democratic Party as the "special champion of slavery," extending the rebellion with its refusal to accept equality, aided by its Copperheads, and standing by rebels who had "lost all their rights under the government by the rebellion and deserved hanging for their treason."[12]

The *New Mexican* drew cross-national parallels in the name of the movement. Grant and reelected Mexican president Benito Juárez were both "Republican heroes," it observed.[13] More centrally, the paper began to brand territorial politics in dominant party terms. José Francisco Chávez stood tall for Republican central casting. The *New Mexican* confirmed the fears of the *Santa Fe Weekly Gazette* that Chávez was "the radical candidate for delegate to Congress." In the forging refrain, Chávez was the "unswerving patriot and the faithful exponent of the Republican sentiments of the loyal masses of the people of New Mexico."[14]

The majority in the territorial legislature was of the "Republican (Chaves) party," ran the new narrative, the house having "twenty-one loyal Republicans and five Copperheads." The council showed "nine loyal Republicans and four Copperheads."[15] The *New Mexican* described Republicans organizing the territorial legislature with their own officers, rebuffing the "importunities and bribes of the Copperheads." As the weekly exclaimed, "The Republican party in New Mexico is in ascendant. *Viva Nuevo Mejico*."[16] Legislators confirmed the generalization by designating the new unit being carved out in southwestern New Mexico "Grant County" in honor of the man credited with winning the Civil War for the union.[17] Chávez, talking to a Missouri newspaper on his way to Washington about his opponent's fraud in the previous election, confirmed the "Radical Triumph in the recent territorial election making the Legislature strongly Republican."[18]

The *New Mexican* exploited the rumor that Charles Clever intended to obtain the aid of Secretary of the Interior Carl Shurz and Union general Franz Sigel to secure his seat in Congress. He would find these "Radical gentlemen" looking into his record before committing "so suicidal a step, as aiding a Copperhead of Clever's stripe to a seat in Congress to which he is not elected." Whether true or not, it suited the budding Republican consciousness to report that Clever said in a speech, "If I were President Johnson I would drive the Radicals in Congress out of their halls at the point of the bayonet a la Cromwell."[19]

A private person revised the history of party dynamics by refuting the claim of the *Gazette* and the *Southern Arizonian* that the real issue in the New Mexico's late election had to do with General Carleton. It centered, he said, on "[former president James] Buchanan Copperheadism led on the part of Clever by stump-tail Russell, against Radical Unionism."[20] *Una Voz del Pueblo* (A voice of the people), writing in Spanish from Las Vegas, said the people knew the efforts of the "colossal hero" Grant had "not gone toward any other than to make us see that we are free and that we should acquire this right by our fidelity, our submission and our adhesion to the sane principles of Republicanism, contrary to the odious and repugnant ideas of despotism and nobility! [¡contrarias á las odiosas y repugnantes ideas del despotismo y la nobleza!]." Una Voz gave extra emphasis to the idea: "We have for ourselves the self-evident truth: that all men are created equal [Tenemos para nosotros estas verdades como evidencia por si mismas: que todos los hombres fueron criados iguales]," and he acclaimed the "illustrious patrician [el ilustre patricio]" Thomas Jefferson, the "new Moses [cual un nuevo Moisés]" Abraham Lincoln, and Juarez, the Goliath-slaying David (quién cual Davíd señalado por el Eterno para ser el vencedor de Goliat) while censuring the "dictator Andrew Johnson" and his "few pirates" in New Mexico.[21]

The essential American Party–Clever side panned the whole pretension to authentic Republicanism, particularly among Nuevomexicanos, just as it did when the Mexican Democratic Party surged in 1853. One *Vox Populi* understood Heath to have boasted in Washington about his "loyal, radical legislature!" As Vox opined, "You can shout Congress with your farce, which is calculated to have effect outside of this country and which only holds good during the contest between Chávez and Clever; but *here* we know these *would be Radicals!* How beautifully calculated," he assayed.

> It shows you are a general and know tactics; but don't you blush a little when you see your new radicals? Look at them. What are your Legislature men? Who are your Sandovals, Garcías, Torres, Sánchez, Valdez, Pinos, Martínez etc. etc? What are they, Mr. Nothing, but pro-peonage men, such as are called in the states, Pro-Slavery men, Secessionists, Copperheads, etc. You and your no account sheet the *New Mexican* must be very green if you think that such great and enlightened men as compose our national [C]ongress will believe such nonsense, which you could better tell to your old washwoman.

Vox had Heath wishing such were Republicans. "It is laughable to us to see these *would be radicals* walking in the street," he wrote, "to us—who know them, know their past history and know that they don't know more of what they have signed, as do we know to dance on a rope."

Vox Populi called for mass meetings in every city, town, and village of the territory to condemn Heath and ask the president for a commission to inquire into his conduct in the counting of the votes in the delegate election. He further advised that "our most prominent men" file a petition to Congress to investigate "fairly" the "foul play of Chávez, who was *fairly and squarely defeated* in this Territory, not upon any issue of 'Radicalism,' as we can prove by all the Nos. of the now radical 'New Mexicans' published *before* the Election; but upon his own issue of '*Anti-Progress.*'" If Chavez was a Radical, Voz had it, "then was [leading Copperhead Clement] *Vallandigham* one too and that a strong one; but Mr. Chávez is nothing more nor less than a Pro Slavery man and as such he tried to galu votes [force out like a gangster]."[22]

Such partisan protestations notwithstanding, a real Republican movement appeared afoot. With Chávez's Republican associations in Congress, an appropriate alignment in the legislature, and the winds of Grant-for-President blowing, the time grew ripe for an organization. Years later William Breeden remembered that he had called a "few well-known" Republicans to a meeting to form a Republican organization. In his letters to Washington, H. H. Heath took credit for bringing the Republicans into "tangible cohesion." Both were instigators, clearly, although contemporary sources tend to show Heath conducting more of the work of party organizing.[23] In any case, a Spanish-language circular announced the scheduling of a meeting of the Union Republican Association in order to discuss "Important Business." Ironically, given liberal sensibilities today, the message came from José D. Sena, billed as the association secretary.[24]

The December 31 event formally organized the Union Republican Association (URA) of New Mexico. The URA pledged to support and disseminate Republican principles and encourage "true loyalty" and the perpetuation of the Union "as established by the fathers of the Republic and preserved by a successful war against the late rebellion." It gave priority to the progress, well-being, and improvement of the territory, "embracing the development of our minds, subjugation of our savage enemies, the construction of railroads and telegraph lines, the encouragement of agricultural and pastoral interests, and the establishment of schools and institutions of learning for the education and improvement of our territory." The promise was to foster "by all legitimate means" emigration to the territory to settle New

FIG. 28. *William Breeden*. Along with H. H. Heath, Breeden was a key originator of what became the permanent Republican Party of New Mexico. Courtesy Palace of the Governors Photo Archives, NMHM/DCA, negative #007019.

Mexico's vacant lands for enterprise. On the usual good-cop/bad-cop colonizer distinction, the URA pledged opposition, "by all lawful means," to such men (presumed settler colonists) who, by their "schemes and conduct" cared nothing for New Mexico, "who without hesitation or scruple sacrifice her interests for their own aggrandizement and who willingly resort to flattery, falsehood and bribery for the accomplishment of their own selfish purposes." The organization would support those public officers who were in "concord and sympathy" with these principles.[25]

The URA cleaved to the national Republican Party. It pledged to fuse the "loyal" sentiments among the people of New Mexico with the "loyal men of the country in making the results of the late war successful in the maintenance of Liberty, Equality, and Union." Only under a Republican Party government could New Mexico enjoy the benefits of freedom and liberty, it maintained. It was "earnestly" hoped that General Grant be elected president, "and so far as our feeble voices and efforts can aid in securing that result they will be freely given." The URA rejoiced at slavery's downfall, and rejected the Copperhead party that opposed freedom and hated liberty. Members adopted what had been the Mexican Party's support for New Mexico's statehood. Their energies would go to the "noble task of aiding in making New Mexico one of the brightest stars in our national constellation." "*Viva la Libertad*," the platform hailed, "*Viva la República Americana; Viva Nuevo México!*"[26]

The URA launched an unprecedented organization. A president, three vice presidents, two secretaries, a financial secretary, a treasurer, a sergeant at arms and an assistant sergeant at arms were to be chosen semiannually by membership vote. An executive committee, consisting of seven members and a secretary to be chosen by members, would take charge of the general supervision of business, the secretaries to keep a careful and complete record of all organizational proceedings. Any citizen of the territory or the United States, "of good character and standing" who sympathized with the association's purposes, sentiments, and principles could join on recommendation of a member and a majority vote of the members. An admission fee of ten cents to meetings and monthly dues of twenty-five cents were set, "provided that by a majority vote such admission fee and monthly dues may be remitted." Importantly, the mandate went out for the organization of local branches, based on the recommendation of one member for each branch. A rational system of branches would communicate memberships, attendance, and self-established dues to the secretary. A quorum of one-fifth of the membership permitted the holding of monthly meetings. A member could be expelled by two-thirds of the vote of the members present at any meeting and after due notice and a fair hearing.[27]

Six of the nine initial officers were Nuevomexicano, all supporters of J. F. Chávez and veterans of the original Mexican Party. Nuevomexicano charter members of the URA included vice presidents Anastacio Sandoval (the Legislative Council president), Pablo Delgado, and Vicente García; one of the secretaries, José D. Sena; the sergeant at arms, Trinidad Alarid (one of the Arny appointed officials in 1867); and assistant sergeant at arms José Ortíz.[28] Indicating the lead roles of the Euroamericans, former Democrat Kirby Benedict was chosen president, and six of eight on the Central Committee were English-surnamed, all of them Chávez allies, including chairman Heath, William Arny, William Breeden, R. H. Tompkins, John E. Wheelock (secretary) and *New Mexican* editor Thomas S. Tucker.[29] A Nuevomexicano majority held among county representatives on the Central Committee. Only Santa Fe had more than one county representative. House speaker Francisco Abreu was chosen as the at-large representative, joining the officers Sandoval, Sena, Ortiz, Heath, and Benedict. Members were urged to establish a branch in each of their county precincts and take responsibility for maintaining correspondence between their offices and the branches and from there to the territorial organization.[30]

The URA in its first official act expressed regret, from the "recesses" of its heart, that Congress had awarded Clever the seat as delegate, the association affirming José F. Chávez as the one legally elected by a majority of the "actual votes" at the September election. The *New Mexican* had earlier published a letter sent from a Chávez supporter to the *New York Tribune* claiming that Clever was trying to pass himself off as a Republican and even a Radical to fool congressmen into supporting his case to retain the delegate's seat in the face of Chávez's contest. It was with "ineffable disdain" that the URA learned that Clever, "the pretended delegate from New Mexico," had endeavored, "and in part succeeded, in imposing on the loyal members of Congress as a

Republican; that we know him now, as in the past, as a Democratic Copperhead, and we repudiate him and his pretended Republicanism, as unworthy of the confidence of the Republican members of Congress, let his pretensions in Washington, politically, be what they may."

The URA hailed Chávez's qualifications for office as the equal of Grant's, heroically—"as a soldier in the war of rebellion," proving him "faithful and brave." Clever, by contrast, had remained at home "in safety" when the Confederates occupied the territory, to be transported out of the scene of combat "for safekeeping." The URA was sure Chávez would occupy his rightful seat in Congress when the evidence of the frauds perpetrated by the Copperheads, at the "instigation" of Charles P. Clever, could be procured as required by law. The people of New Mexico were congratulated for their loyal support of the Republican legislature, showing that the "public heart of New Mexico beat in unison with the Union." That eight of ten counties had returned "solid" Republican individuals to both houses of the legislature proved "in itself, the falsity of the pretended majority under which Charles P. Clever wrongfully, and against the wishes of the people of New Mexico, temporarily holds his seat in Congress." The *New Mexican* was declared the "true exponent of the loyal Republican sentiments of the people of New Mexico," worthy of the support of the "people of this territory."[31]

Heath pinpointed thirty-two of thirty-nine legislative members joining the URA.[32] This was close to the thirty-one Republicans reported as returned to the legislature, compared to eight who ran on the Clever ticket.[33] On the legislature's adjournment after an "arduous service" of sixty days, the *New Mexican* did not fail to note that its majority was "largely Republican—all but unanimous."[34] Heath felt justified telling a Washington correspondent that the "*Republican party heretofore organized, has been transformed from a nebulous mass into a consolidated party.*"[35] Much still needed to be done to spread the gospel. Queried later in a congressional investigation on the Chávez contest, Antonio Guadalupe, a former member of the territorial legislature from Las Truchas in Río Arriba County, acknowledged that he did not know the difference between Democrat and Radical. Rather, he said, "I belong to the Chaves party. I did belong to the Clever party, but now belong to the Chaves party."[36] The work of party inculcation advanced itself nonetheless. A mass meeting held in late February in

San Marcial, Socorro County, at the house of José Tafoya and consisting of an overwhelmingly Nuevomexicano cast, defended the legislature, Secretary Heath, former acting governor Arny, and District Attorney Stephen Elkins while dressing down Governor Mitchell and the *Gazette*, the "Copperheads who are the enemies of progress."[37]

Heath took to establishing a New Mexico chapter of the Grand Old Army (GAR), an organization of Civil War veterans associated with Radical Republicans. Chávez in Washington garnered the GAR's support for his election contest. Heath had at least ten veterans prepared to join, the minimum required to apply for a charter, and he was named department commander. His application emphasized the importance of a chapter for the territory's Republican cause.[38]

Cleverites acted to stem the Republican wave. In a fictional letter, Pancho, dredged out of the Semitic *diálogos*, corresponds with his compadre, Don Chepe, about the suddenly appearing, ambiguous party being foisted on them (for the full Spanish text, see appendix 8) and which indicated the changes in party linguistics coming down. Pancho has just been elected to the legislature for the first time, and he marvels at the things going on at the capital. "¡*Compadre de mi vida!*" he exclaims. For so many years, we called our party *Democrat*; we even fought to be Democrats, and for the last two years, it had no other name than the *party of Chávez*, with principles of anti-Americanism and pro slavery (well, we had always been in favor of the law of peons)." Now were they baptized with another name, "which is Radical, which I had never heard mentioned, nor do I know what it means. What is certain is that all of our party tries to be

> radicals and sometimes I'm tempted to submit a resolution that would have all of our party wear on our heads a big R as an emblem to distinguish our party from the Copperheads, as we call them.
>
> ¡*Compadre de mi corazón!* We have the majority of both houses, which is frightening for being subject to the disposition of the Secretary of the three H's [H. H. Heath], the big granddaddy [Benedict], and the little governor [Arny]. The Secretary of the three H's is very loved by our party for the fraud he committed to see if he could gain our faith that Chávez had received the majority in the election for delegate; the granddaddy because of the help of his *Nuevo Mejicano* in discharging our fury against the enemy; and the little

governor for conspiring in the oaths against Judge Slough. These three characters manage us like puppeteers and we are so obedient to their orders, it gives them pleasure.

¡Compadre de mis entrañas! [heart strings]. As long as we are controlled by foreign will, there is little hope we can do good things. For sure, we will pass resolutions fulminating anathemas and false calumnies against those ordered by their majesty, the Triumvirate, giving fame to who does not have it, and take it from who deserve it.

Pancho advises Chepe, when he writes back, to put on the envelope: "'To the Hon. Pancho,' because that is what we are called, 'honorables,' and no one will dare to criticize us because we will shout them down [*por que oirá nuestras bocas*]."[39]

In another dialogue between the proverbial Pancho and Pedro, Pedro speaks of the Apocalypse, signaled by Heath as he preached in a speech, like Fray Gerundio in the desert (Fray Gerundio de las Campazas, a character in an eighteenth-century Spanish novel, mocked for speaking in Baroque), about the need to establish valid Radical principles and political parties in New Mexico and take part in issues where the people had no rights. As Pedro offers, these arguments appeared prejudicial to the people of New Mexico and to their position of a dependent territory still under government patronage. Rather than stirring up partisan bad blood and exhorting their friends to engage on principles they did not understand, Heath and Breeden needed to assess objectively the "brutal acts [*los actos brutales*]" produced by partisan views, letting crimes go unpunished and punishing frivolous offenses. They needed to work to lower the high (property) taxes the citizens suffered, Pedro says, work together to support the efforts of their delegate in Congress to provide effective protection to the people in all branches, and protect the people from the incursions of the barbarous Indians who were still raiding horribly. If they did so, then the people could hope that no one would have a bad opinion of their party or call it a clique. But as Heath and Breeden and their friends were not peaceable, "Now was it certain, the Apocalypse was here [*Ahora es cierto que la Apocalípsis se ha cumplido*]."[40]

The Grand Army of the Republic came in for bashing, being seen as in league with the "preposterous full fledged Radical party," neither of which was thought of in New Mexico "during the canvass or before the election."[41] A Nuevomexicano going by PS spotlighted the political war Chávez unleashed on Clever through a contest, declaring that the "clique of the [G]rand [A]rmy" would set about persecuting the Jews just as they had Judge Slough and just as Manuel Romero went after Commander Dn. Jesús Ma. Baca y Salazar.[42] Gaspar Ortiz y Alarid, the don of Los Cerrillos, said much the same but with extreme bitterness. "I am a witness," he began,

> to the fact that I owe to Judge Slough that my interests were left untouched in this territory. I am witness to the fact that he protected equally the properties and lives of others who now are his ingrates. I am witness to the fact that he repulsed the enemy and liberated the Territory of its terrible cruelty [*Yo soy un Testigo que, al Juez Slough debo el conservar intactos mis intereses en este Territorio. Yo soy Testigo que el protegió igualmente las propiedades y vidas de otros que ahora los son ingratos. Yo soy Testigo que él repulsó al enemigo y libró al Territorio de su saña terrible.*]

For these reasons and "because that party had closed its eyes and covered its ears to all Justice," [*por que ese partido ha cerrado los ojos y tapadese los oídos a toda Justicia*], Ortiz swore, "today I too close forever all sympathy and alliance with the ridiculous supposition and fiction of a 'Grand Army' when the chieftains are involving our poor people in the most ridiculous political principles ever known. Ridiculous! Ridiculous! Ridiculous! [*hoy yo también cierro para Siempre toda simpatía y alianza con la ridícula supueste y ficticia 'Gran armada' cuando sus caudillos estan envolviendo á nuestro pobre pueblo en principios políticos que aún las hemos conocido. ¡Ridículo! ¡Ridículo! ¡Ridículo!*]"[43]

Russell noted in the principles of the URA the vigor with which they anathematized Copperheads and slavery, "neither of which institutions ever existed in the Territory to any dangerous or alarming extent." It was no little distortion of recent history, yet Russell returned to posting what he wished to project as the key contradiction of this Republican Association: not "one word" said in its statements about the peonage existing as "extensively and as banefully in New Mexico as did African slavery in South Carolina before its abolition"—as such, an "institution of the Chávez party and the Chávez party is the peon party of New Mexico." Russell panned the *New Mexican*, as the "organ of the party," for not publishing Governor Mitchell's order requiring the civil officers of the territory to enforce the anti-peonage law, their enmity to Governor Mitchell "unmeasured." Moreover, the editor continued, the people behind the URA were "not measured" in their abuse of Clever, an early advocate of the abolition of peonage. "They conciliate the friends of peonage in New Mexico," Russell pounded, "whilst they would have it believed outside of New Mexico that their radicalism is of that rigid class which knows no sympathy with the oppressions of slavery in any of its forms. No expression escapes them that would offend the ear of the owner of peones."[44]

Russell reiterated the notion of the Chávez party as really Copperhead. The New Mexico URA had absorbed the "few true Copperheads left in the territory" (apparently wanting to admit that he no longer harbored Copperhead ideology). Russell parodied Chávez needing two parties, one for territorial consumption, the peonage party, and another for use in the states and Congress, "composed of the gentlemen who did what our Legislature, composed of a Chávez majority, never would do, that is, abolished and forever prohibited peonage in our midst." As Russell spun the story, Radicals in Congress did not take the bait. In the New Mexico peonage party there was no "mixture of honest [R]adicalism," no mixture of "honest [R]epublicanism," none of the "progressive element" for a respectable political opponent, none of the "spirit, enterprise and intelligence that lead on to greatness, wealth and power," nothing "to aid in bringing us up to the level of the civilization of the era in which we live," nothing to commend "to any people under the sun, and particularly to a people as those who live in the United States of America."

Russell predicted that the "so-called" Republican Association would "lag and flounder and exhaust itself until it becomes nothing in the great and growing elements which surround and overshadow it." Assuming Heath the party's chief representative, Russell said he would be the first to lose out for he had not character and individuality enough "to make himself a self-preserving element in the general decay that is progressing around him." Still reluctant to claim the Democratic Party by name, perhaps because Clever had tried to pan himself off as a Republican while in Washington, Russell stood by Clever's party of "school houses, telegraphs, railroads, manufactories and active enterprising industry in all its branches." This party did not have "a hankering after the furisms [sic] nor is it surrounded with the odor of peonage and the oppressions of that intolerable and most oppressive system of servitude," Russell explained. "Here is the difference between the two parties in New Mexico and it is a difference that cannot escape public observation."[45]

Delegate Clever, whose New Mexico career would not have disposed him to the institutions, pushed the issue in Congress by submitting an "Act to Abolish and Forever Prohibit the System of Peonage and Indian Slavery in the Territory of New Mexico, and other parts of the United States." It was virtually identical to the federal law passed in 1867 with strengthened enforcement provisions. The *Gazette* first learned that it was before the House Judiciary Committee from the *New Mexican*. It accordingly picked another fight, fallaciously noting that the *New Mexican* had not indicated whether it was in favor of passage. "We are in favor of the passage of this act," Russell affirmed, "and will be in favor of its strict enforcement after it shall have been passed. Can the *New Mexican* get its courage up to offend the magnates of the Chávez party by saying this? We venture not."[46]

Actually, the Republicans in New Mexico had publicly described J. F. Chávez as one of the true friends of the "late peons of New Mexico, who look to him as their emancipator."[47] The *New Mexican* responded that the *Gazette* may have had doubts as to its position on the question, but "our Republican friends have none." In a piece likely by Tucker, the *New Mexican* asked when the *Gazette* considered it convenient to convert to the policy of abolishing peonage when not long before, as a Copperhead paper, it had supported the institution. "And how many of its friends still hold these peons yet, in violation of law?"[48]

An important and revealing argument followed over what constituted peonage in New Mexico and who supported it. *Un Observador Imparcial*, writing from Mora, detected a ploy on Clever's part, arguing that the abolition law was intended to serve the cause of retaining Clever's seat in Congress against the expressed and manifest will of the people, who had legally voted for Chávez. It was well known "here and among all the people of the United States that neither the system of peonage nor Indian slavery, nor African, exists in New Mexico," Un Observador claimed, "nor in any other part of the union" (for the full Spanish-language text, see appendix 9). It was thus "ridiculous, unnecessary and absurd" to have requested additional legislation for New Mexico over an issue that did not exist, "if not in the capricious mind of Clever." The people of New Mexico obeyed the constitutional amendments destroying all classes of human subservience and the corresponding one of their own legislature. In submitting additional legislation regarding "dead and buried material," Clever appeared to be throwing his bait out to Congress.

Un Observador challenged anyone to express doubt that "our people" had always been against slavery [in the southern connotation]. He revealed key members of the local Clever brokers in the counties of the Río Arriba. Perhaps, suggested Un Observador, Clever received instructions from his friends to carry out his legislation—Juan María Baca of Las Vegas, José Benito Martines of Taos, Pablo Gallegos of Abiquiú, Gerónimo Jaramillo of El Rito, and Estanlisado Montoya of Socorro. Just because these gentlemen had been known as loyal citizens to the government, obedient to the Constitution and the laws, the argument had it, did not mean they did not have human beings enslaved in their houses in some aspect, such that when Clever went about looking for votes in their counties he would not have seen them. Perhaps it was for them that Clever asked for the additional legislation. Perhaps Clever took with him the additional instructions of Antonio Roival so as to make legal the four hundred votes that were tacked on to the count in Tierra Amarilla in the election, calling them the votes of peones and captives, not to mention the additional votes that the secret meeting invented in the precinct of Santa Clara.

Un Observador advanced his case with a history lesson on Indian slavery. When New Mexico was conquered by Spain, he averred, it became necessary to form companies to quiet the "savages" and have them submit under the yoke of law and religion. After Independence, the Mexicans continued the custom, more so in relation to the Navajos, "the desolate tribe of New Mexico." When New Mexico became part of the U.S. government, volunteer companies were authorized "when the necessity of a proper defense demanded it." Since then captives had been brought among the people of New Mexico and many paisanos were taken into captivity. However, those taken in by the Nuevomexicanos were "never considered as slaves," Un Observador claimed, "rather as adopted children." They remained with their "adoptive parents," providing their services until they married. The captives were put "in total liberty under the same circumstances of the legitimate children of the whites." Many captives had married Mexican women and "many children of the whites" had married with captives. When they left to build their families or their adoptive parents died, they all generally received some help or inheritance in land, houses, money, and other goods according to the possessions of the household. Many of the captives knew how to read and write, the account continued. They had their own families. Many served the government in the late rebellion and in the campaigns against the same Navajos.

The only exceptions, in this interpretation, were captives who continued to "love their people," departing to their homelands or reservations. Some who remained were recaptured by the reservation Navajos, according to Un Observador, noting that in recent days, Navajos had come to his county and taken back practically all the ones who resided there, including those belonging to Pedro Mares. As he understood it, Navajos had gone to the counties reclaiming all the captive children, leaving behind the emancipated adults or those who preferred "sacred liberty" to being with the "barbarous ones." Such were the truths with respect to the captives and peonage, regarding which, Un Observador believed, no sensible man considered it necessary that Clever should bother Congress with additional legislation against New Mexico's interests; he closed with a declaration that he would "always be for the Constitution and laws."[49]

It is well to note here the official reports by an Indian commissioner and a military officer showing destitute "Navajo peons" remaining under control of masters. One estimate was that there were "1000 persons in a condition of slavery and peonage." While it was said there was considerable ill treatment, one officer claimed that the ones he talked to in the Santa Fe area did not want to be released to their new reservation, even though it lay in their traditional lands.[50]

The *Gazette* did not address Un Observador's social history directly, but Russell had Nuevomexicanos to expose as well, Republican ones that is. The Legislative Council would not become the New Mexico Senate until 1912, but "councils" were generally precursors to "senates" in the American territories, and so Russell seems to have considered it more effective in this argument to say: "A few days since, one of the [R]adical Senators from Taos County, Juan Benito Valdez, was brought before the U.S. Commissioners for the first District of New Mexico on a charge of holding slaves contrary to the laws of the United States." Valdez owned ten Indians, Russell said, the same as before Congress passed the law abolishing peonage and Indian slavery. "The Commissioner liberated the slaves," Russell noted, "and held Senator Valdez over in bail for his appearance at the July term of the U.S. Court in this city." Valdez was "one of the most influential Chávez partisans in Taos County," the editor stated, "and during the session of the legislature last winter was accounted one of the most reliable of all the [R]adicals who composed the majority in the Senate [Council]."

Russell argued that an investigation of the domestic relations of almost all the other Chávez "or [R]adical Senators" would find a similar "state of facts," referencing the "two Bacas of San Miguel, Sandoval of Santa Fe, Sandoval of Santa Ana, Romero of Bernalillo," and a "senator" from Valencia whose name he could not remember. Further demonstrating the "true status of the party," Russell pointed to the "influential and controlling element" in the Chávez-Radical party in the lower counties of the territory (Chávez's blood relations). Possessed of the wealth of that section and being numerous, they were "no mean political element," able to carry the territory for their own relatives as political candidates, having peones and slaves "almost without exception." Russell called slavery and peonage "policy elements" of the New Mexico Radical Party. For those setting themselves up as its leaders, to oppose these institutions would be to "shear themselves of this, their main strength in the southern counties." Rather than "emasculate" themselves, they said nothing regarding the enforcement of abolishing the systems. Mirroring Un Observador Imparcial, Russell said that the men alluded to in his article were "good citizens and respectable gentlemen" but "bad material out of which to manufacture a [R]adical or any other party that would keep up with the progress of the age and shake from its skirts the debris of past centuries. Of such is the Chávez or [R]adical party of New Mexico."[51]

The *New Mexican*'s riposte to the *Gazette*'s attempts to undermine the start of a Republican organization referenced social conditions. Before Congress and the territorial legislature legally abolished peonage and Indian slavery, Tucker explained, those species of servitude permeated every class of society. "It existed among all parties and there are as many such persons now held or remaining with their former masters of the Clever party as of the Chávez party," he argued. The *Gazette* may have paraded certain persons belonging to the Chávez party who still had persons once held as peons but forgot the names of some of the prominent men in its own party, "like the Roivals and Archuletas, and Garcías and Jaramillos of Rio Arriba, and others whose houses are still filled with them, whom we might name." The *Gazette* knew that the Republican Party in New Mexico was not the "peon and slavery party," the *New Mexican* stated, though it persisted in the accusation. Chávez sat as New Mexico's delegate when Congress passed the anti-peonage act, Tucker emphasized, while the *Gazette* and friends were then and had always been pro-slavery. The *Gazette* turned out articles on the subject of peonage for "foreign" consumption, to advance Clever's cause in the contest of his seat in Congress to which he had no "just right." The proof of frauds in the election, lodged in Washington, would show how much his election depended on peonage, the Chávezite argued. If the *Gazette* wanted that record published, it had only to "continue its perverse misrepresentations."[52]

Russell, hardly intimidated, claimed it had finally induced the *New Mexican* to tip its hand on peonage and slavery. He found Tucker speaking for New Mexico's "Radical Party," apologizing and excusing the systems since passage of the laws abolishing them. When the *New Mexican* said that because peonage had permeated every class of society, the argument went, "it must stay permeated now, when there is an attempt being made to establish a different kind of civilization." Thinking to have found a point of attack, Russell claimed that the *New Mexican* omitted to say whether the "Radical Chávez" party was or was not in favor of enforcing the laws of Congress, indicated by the fact that the *New Mexican* did not publish Governor Mitchell's proclamation requiring the civil authorities of the territory to enforce them. "Indeed, it was known that the wealthy and influential relatives and political supporters of Chávez in the southern counties made "the promulgation of that proclamation a cause of complaint against Gov. Mitchell—saying that the law was no more than any other law of Congress and there was no necessity for him to disturb them in their possessions by calling particular attention to it in the manner he did." While Chávez labored to capitalize from this against Clever, "the permeating process did not go on in that case." It did not work. Clever's friends had "inscribed on their transparencies in a torch-light procession in the streets of Santa Fe, 'NO MAS PEONES,' 'NO MORE PEONAGE.'" With these principles and "others in openness with the spirit of progress by which we were surrounded in the outside," Clever "went forth to fight the battle and was triumphantly sustained by the voters of the Territory."[53] The whole argument, with its tricky and slanted social and political interpretations, did its part to keep the territory's partisan binary on the march.

Mitchell manipulated his contacts in Washington to undercut Heath's plan to take a leave of absence, finagling it so that he himself could take leave.[54] With Mitchell off on a sixty-day sojourn, Heath became the acting governor of New Mexico, another of those opportunities for an underling enemy of the executive to take over administering the territorial government.[55] The governor's office provided a platform for advancing the Republican Party. Heath composed a position paper upholding the 1867 congressional and territorial abolition acts for New Mexico. Slavery and involuntary servitude were "antagonistical to Republicanism," his partisan proclamation affirmed. The system of slavery "known as peonage" was "alike at variance with the principles of a Republican Government and repugnant to the moral, social and political advancement of the victims of the system of slavery." Heath constructed his resolution according to the "true Republican spirit of the age," which had inspired the territorial legislature to abolish involuntary servitude. Heath attached the entire congressional act, including its call for enforcement. It noted, without reference to party, that "either through ignorance of the laws or in willful violation thereof," some people continued to hold peons in violation of laws, which was "incompatible with good citizenship, and an infraction of the rights and liberties of such peons so held." Holding any person as a peon in possession, "or hindering any such peon, of liberty and free will, to go wherever or whenever he or she may will in the territory of New Mexico, [was] under pains and penalties fixed by law." Heath earnestly requested all civil officers in the territory to aid the executive in "utterly" destroying the system of peonage, asking that all true and loyal citizens give such information to the proper officers of the law and the military as would lead to the discovery and punishment of anyone continuing to hold "their fellow man in the bondage of peonage—which is no less a crime against mankind than God, the maker of us all."[56]

The *Gazette*, rather than spin a volatile partisanship by arguing that Heath wanted to preempt Clever's bill, offered the milder criticism of his taking so much time in promulgating the proclamation and for issuing it only in English. "Few if any who read the English language hold Peons," Russell noted, while "few who hold Peons, and therefore infract the law, read English." The proclamation would fall "far short of the practical effect it should have." Russell surmised that the document was not meant to liberate peons but to "cover the former laches of the so-called Radical party in New Mexico" on the subject. Their opposition to peonage and slavery placed them in a weak position should they "directly or indirectly attack an interest in which the most influential parties of their adherents were largely involved." Yet, given the "great end" to be attained, if the *New Mexican* and its party would "henceforth labor in the cause and do what is in its power to have the laws enforced and the Peons and slaves released in fact as well as in name, there will be no inclination on the part of any lover of genuine liberty to cavil at their past delinquencies."[57]

The *New Mexican* assured that Heath's statement "had no earthly relation to politics." The delay in getting it out was caused by Governor Mitchell's departure and the ambiguity as to when he would return. When it became evident that Mitchell would not return by the end of summer, Tucker emphasized, "Gov. Heath promptly and properly issued the proclamation in question. And for the information of the *Gazette* we will say that the proclamation is to be published in Spanish, and will be subject to wide circulation in that language." In a rare moment of friendliness, the *New Mexican* congratulated its neighbor on the tone of its article.[58]

A difference in the ongoing debate is that grand juries began indicting violators of the prohibition of slave and peon ownership. Many prosecutions occurred in Taos County, as distinct from the Río Abajo where, as the opponents of J. F. Chávez liked to point out, the rico lot of families ranched. Hundreds of interested persons reportedly appeared in court. Another report, however, had the grand juries in Taos and Río Arriba counties failing to find a single indictment against some two to three hundred people who were summoned to answer to charges of holding Navajo captives and others in bondage.[59] The *New Mexican* implied why. There were "few subjects upon which there is greater misunderstanding and ignorance, than this one question of what is termed 'Navajo captives,'" it said. "And this very misunderstanding, particularly on the part of Congress, causes this territory, and our people great injustice." The writer, developing Un Observador's sociology, emphasized how most of the Navajos—men, men, women and children—either scattered over the territory or captured by whatever means, "passed into the families of our citizens." The editor, or citizen contributor, described what we now would call New Mexico's version of *mestizaje*, the coming together of European and Indian strains and the admixture of *indio* bloodlines and cultures among themselves (definitive in the peopling of Mexico and Latin America). It applied within his racialized framing. As he had it, the Navajos were "savage and barbarous" while the captives, having lived among "civilized people," learned the language "of the country" and "become Christianized"—all being Catholics. Their "habits" had become those of the civilized race "among whom they dwell." It was claimed that not one in fifty desired to leave their civilized life "for a renewal of their barbarous and uncivilized life with the tribes." How many of them were caught in suspension between the two worlds was not addressed. The argument was that they preferred life "among our people to one among their own." Captives may have been regarded "in the light of peons, perhaps of slaves," it was claimed, but "as soon as Congress and the legislature of this territory passed laws abolishing peonage and every other class of slavery in the territories, these people became free, and there are few, if any of them, who do not know that they are, and have been, since passage of those laws, at liberty to go when, and wheresoever they may have pleased."

The claim that Navajo captives were free to hire out to any person whom they pleased to serve was no doubt exaggerated, but once again, the humane interpretation of bondage found its advocate, only this time posed as the result of Republican liberation. As the argument prevailed, "most" of them preferred to remain in the homes "where they have so long been domesticated, and where they possess the advantages of not only religion, but of civilized life. These they cannot possess if returned to their nation." This condition was not one of bondage nor involuntary servitude, the editor argued; rather, it was "in fact, an abandonment, voluntarily, of a savage, barbarous life for one of civilization and religion." It thus became "a serious question of humanity whether those Navajos who now voluntarily live amongst our people [the assumption here being of Nuevomexicano and Euroamerican social convergence], and in the manner named, shall be forced back of upon savage life against their will, and only because their tribe desired their return, or whether, by their voluntary action they shall remain as they are, the objects of care by the church, and civil protection by the territory."[60]

Other issues in 1868 came under party inflections. Hezekiah Johnson returned to journalism, establishing the *Semi-Weekly Review* in Alburquerque. Johnson billed his twice-weekly paper "free and Independent on all Subjects" but he clearly backed the national Republican Party.[61] At home, he considered the New Mexican Republican platform "not repugnant" to the principles of the national Republican Party, nor conflicting with his own views on territorial affairs, yet he stood aloof from the organization, unsure, along with other Republicans who had problems with the Chávez campaign of 1867, of the integrity of those who had given rise to the Republican Association. Johnson pricked the *New Mexican* on its presumed Republican credentials.[62] He thought Heath not a real Republican based on his prewar pedigree as a Confederate. He sought to marginalize the acting governor, accusing him of purposely delaying the publication of the new voter registration law to "accomplish a coup d'état for his party at the next election, through the non-registration of Mr. Clever's friends." Johnson asked his Republican friends, "black, white, blue, red, and of intermediate colors—to procure, surreptitiously if need be, a copy of this registration law, and have it published in the Republican newspapers of this territory, and thereby frustrate this monstrous scheme."[63]

J. F. Chávez remained in Washington, coordinating Heath, Arny, Breeden, Elkins, and Benedict to advance his contest, convinced like never before of Clever party illegalities in the election. "If I fail," he observed with a sense of heavy responsibility, "a large portion of our party will be fearful that fraud used against us will always win." Favoring Radicals exclusively, he disdained the Conservative Republicans, agreeing with many in Washington that there was more honesty in being a Democrat than in being a Conservative Republican.[64]

Mitchell received a thirty-day extension of his leave, which postponed Heath's departure from Santa Fe for three months at least. Heath told Chávez of Mitchell's "low trick," especially outrageous after the governor had taken six months off the year before.[65] Hoping to thwart Mitchell in Washington, Heath sent 260 copies of the legislature's memorial calling for his removal for distribution in Congress and planned to send affidavits of the fraud testimonies.[66] Heath had time finally to take testimony from precincts in which voting fraud was to have taken place, which included cross allegations of Mexican citizens having voted. It was difficult work, expensive, and fraught with the risk of conflict of interest.[67] Late February brought the disappointing news of Clever given ninety extra days to compose his response to the contest. Heath wished Congress had looked at the existing testimony.[68] He advised Chávez to return to New Mexico to serve as a "tower of strength" to his friends. Both Benedict and Elkins were unavailable as attorneys for the contest. Heath feared that he himself would have to fill in.[69]

Heath refused to take compensation for working on the contest. He strategized with Chávez, Perry Brocchus (now a member of the Mexican Party legacy), Elkins, William Henrie, and Benedict and monitored the movements of Clever's lawyers, Merrill Ashurst especially. An awkward situation arose as other team members were unable to take testimony. It was something of a liability for Heath. He contemplated the propriety of being in the governor's office and acting as a private lawyer, overcoming the concern by likening himself to Elkins, who was both a district attorney and representing Chávez in the contest (reflecting the territory's sketchy political and administrative development).[70]

Heath continued to service the Republican Party. When a copy of the Wisconsin legislature's letter arrived asking U.S. senators and representatives to adhere to the policy of the "loyal people of the Republic as adopted by Congress," Heath wrote to the Wisconsin governor that Mitchell favored President Johnson, while he himself supported Congress and its policy of rehabilitating the rebel states. As he put it, "Congress, thus far, has nobly, faithfully, patriotically, assumed the great task imposed upon it by the loyal millions who saved the country from destruction." Wisconsin had proved true to the "high principles of a true Republicanism, Heath observed, "which she exhibited whilst the flames of rebellion lighted up the land." New Mexico had no voice in the national councils, "by which her Republican, patriotic voice [could] be essentially heard," yet "within her bosom dwells an ever living spirit of loyalty; which continually breathes pure devotion to the union and Republican principles."[71]

Behind florid declarations, Heath desired to be New Mexico's governor. Reading the tea leaves of the impending end of a Johnson administration and the removal of Mitchell as governor, he considered himself the perfect replacement, as it would have received the support of the majority in the legislature. His political compadres may have thought otherwise. Heath was disappointed to hear that Arny had informed Chávez and their Republican friends in Washington that Heath had declined being a candidate. It was a misunderstanding, he told Chávez, based on his tactic of keeping his interest in the position in the background since he authored the legislature's resolutions calling for Mitchell's ouster. Heath emphasized the partisan significance of his being governor. It would "lay the Collins-Mitchell party out like a corpse, whilst our party would rise like an eagle." Heath could not afford to be "over sloughed" for the gubernatorial appointment, "particularly by my party," given all that had transpired politically in the previous eight months. "I should have but one recourse in such an event," he stated. "Humiliated & politically disgraced, I should be inevitably forced out of the territory." He trusted Chávez and their Republican allies not to sympathize with Arny's report, as it would do "a great injustice & woefully misinterpret . . . what I consider to be a very plain statement of my position."[72]

Heath subsequently wrote to one Charles Moss, who showed interest in the New Mexico governorship. Heath informed Moss that this ambition interfered with "a programme long since laid out, and one which I am sure would disappoint, if consummated, the wishes of the Republican party of New Mexico." His friendly feeling toward the correspondent notwithstanding, Heath would be frank. The leaders and "masses of the party," he emphasized, desired and expected his appointment as governor and "Col. Chávez has been anxious for this and is so now." It is not clear that this was true, but Heath reinforced his proven credentials in the trenches: "If you knew what I had passed through here," he wrote, "in the incipient efforts to establish a Republican *party*, where only a Republican element heretofore existed, how, in pursuit of my principles, my life has been endangered months at a time here, you would be for me too."

Heath revealed the rest of the plan among New Mexico Republicans for regime-change. Oddly for a Mexican Party legacy, only one Nuevomexicano was included, although it was José D. Sena, proposed for collector of internal revenue. Most of the others were also dedicated to Chávez: David Miller, the *New Mexican*'s Spanish-language translator, for head of the pension office; Perry Brocchus for chief justice; *New Mexican* co-owner/editor Thomas Tucker for registrar; and W. H. Manderfield, the other proprietor of the *New Mexican*, for U.S. marshal. The post of public depository and receiver would go to "some friend of [Kansas] Sen. [Samuel C.] Pomeroy." Also odd, the plan included Hezekiah Johnson, of the *Semi-Weekly Review*, for an associate justice position. It would indicate some backdoor conversations having been conducted since Johnson had previously criticized Heath and stood apart from personnel in the Republican organization. In the part that would "please" Heath's correspondent, Moss would be appointed the other associate justice. Other positions with no names attached were to be left in abeyance, "and others of our friends [already] in, to remain in their present positions."[73]

That this plotting may well have come out of some collective thinking is indicated by the fact that Chávez highly desired Brocchus (the former American Party propagandist for Miguel A. Otero), for the position of Supreme Court chief justice, vacated by Slough's death.[74] A problem arose from the fact that Brocchus had presided over the trial of William Rynerson for the killing of Slough, and it appears that his instructions to the jury, which emphasized the need to consider the possibility that Slough had brought about his own downfall by insulting another man's honor, led to a quick not-guilty verdict (the Nuevomexicano jury out but ten minutes).[75] Rynerson may thus have survived his legal problems and remained in good standing in the Republican ranks. Brocchus's reputation remained suspect, however.[76]

Brocchus was a clear arm of Chávez.[77] Clever, who presented credentials in Congress as a Democrat, nixed the possibility of his becoming the chief justice by nominating for delegate to Congress former delegate John S. Watts.[78] It was a setback to Chávez, who thought he had pull in Congress.[79] Heath and the *New Mexican* suspected Congress would not confirm Watts, not least because President Johnson submitted the nomination after his impeachment proceedings began.[80] Heath wrote to U.S. senators in hopes of persuading them to vote against Watts, attacking him as the "offensively active partisan" Copperhead. Heath claimed to speak for the sentiment of the "entire Republican party" in the territory, "and especially of the members of the loyal organization at the head of which I have the honor to be."[81]

They had done all possible to strengthen the "loyal element" of the territory "by consolidating the loyal Republican element" with "Republican associations, Republican committees, etc. etc."[82] He warned "loyal Senators" against any pretension of Watts to be a Republican in order to win the nomination, quoting "quasi-treasonous" remarks he supposedly made at a dinner at the start of the war.[83]

The *Gazette* lodged hard charges against Brocchus's work in the Rynerson trial, accusing him of taking a bribe for protecting Rynerson from conviction and associating this alleged corruption with Heath's "treachery."[84] The *Review*, for its part, noted that Brocchus was really a "Democrat or 'conservative'" (or at least a former Democrat, as we saw in chapter 6). Hezekiah Johnson of the *Review* tapped New Mexico's partisan potential. As he put it, the opposition to him by the "organ of the disguised [D]emocracy of this territory," was therefore demoralizing because "the separation of discordant elements" into Republican and Democratic lines was "essential to harmony and political morality." Because the parties of the territory had been run "solely" on behalf of "officials, office seekers, contractors, and the government employees having axes to grind," as Johnson thought the case to be, the formation of "genuine Republican and Democratic parties would reverse the positions of individuals of the grindstone, and secure a just disposition of 'loaves and fishes.'"[85]

The Clever-Mitchell strategy sought to spoil Heath's credibility in Washington. A petition signed by reportedly two-thirds of the citizens of New Mexico accused Heath of engineering the legislative resolutions against Judge Slough and was presented to President Johnson. Quite damaging, Mitchell and friends in Washington exposed a document, the infamous "Offutt letter," in which Heath had purportedly asked Jefferson Davis in 1861 for a commission to serve as an officer in the Confederate Army. A startled Chávez said he could not believe "such a thing," yet he thought enemies might use it successfully to remove Heath as secretary. Chávez promised to do his best to prevent the confirmation of his successor.[86] The *Review* charged that attachment to the Confederacy was precisely why President Johnson appointed Heath territorial secretary.[87]

Heath assured Chávez that the charge was the "wildest forgery and calumny ever heaped upon a man," although he would admit that he was once a Democrat, not of the "ultra-southern school," never thinking that the sections would go to war. When they did, Heath went with the Union. He accused Chávez of not doing enough to defend his reputation in Congress. Chávez called it unfair, laying the blame for a lack of support of Heath on a split Republican Party that "could not hold together."[88] The *Gazette* chortled at the record of the GAR post commander, the "high chief of the Union Republican Association" coming home to roost. A demand for a change of leadership "in the Radical camp" was probable, Russell guessed. Who would be the "fortunate man," Russell wondered. His recommendation was Hezekiah Johnson. "On his record as a [R]adical there will be found no blot," Russell commented. "In his zeal for the success of Grant and Colfax, he is not equaled even by him who is about to be deposed. And he has a newspaper which he edits in a manner more acceptable to the party than is the now recognized [*New Mexican*] organ, which will in all probability go by the board when it loses its head and support by the deposition we contemplate." The opinion was left "for the consideration of those interested," but it seemed that Russell's aim was to jam a wedge into the Republican ranks.[89]

Watts's confirmation sailed through and the *New Mexican* accepted it, on the principle that judges were supposed to be nonpartisan. If Watts assumed the bench "desirous only of a fair and just performance of his judicial functions; without friends to reward or enemies to punish," the weekly assured, he had not only the undivided support of the bar of the territory but also that of many who had been antagonistic to him. "The business of the court is going forward under the new Chief Justice vigorously," the editors observed.[90]

Clever also tried to get URA co-founder William Breeden removed as New Mexico's territorial assessor based on Breeden's embroilment in a legal dispute involving the pension of a Nuevomexicana, which the *Gazette* prosecuted editorially with the assistance of its owner James Collins. Breeden was acquitted in the first trial. Nevertheless, Clever asked for a successor to replace him. That effort failed. Both the legal and political pursuit of Breeden would go on for a year, his friends calling it a political persecution.[91]

J. F. Chávez's desire to get on with his contest ran into another road block.[92] Key moderate Republicans, offended by the president's summary dismissal of military officers in violation of the Tenure of Office Act, joined Radicals to force the impeachment of Johnson. The partisan trial in the Senate, based on eleven charges, began on March 30. Impeachment further cemented New Mexico's Republican firmament. Heath impressed on Republican leaders in Washington his support for the president's removal to save the Union from "Andy Johnsonism," sharing the editorials he had previously authored in the *New Mexican* on the "great question," and linking them to the needs of the Republican Party in New Mexico and the desired success of the Chávez contest.[93] The *New Mexican* foresaw a "speedy settlement" of the case and "a full conviction of the president and his ejection from office."[94]

In long, detailed, analytical essays the *Review* stood militantly for impeachment. Against the doomsday projections in forcing a president out of office, Hezekiah Johnson reassured that "Republican institutions are equal to any exigency, and that the people of this country are capable of government." He would have had the Conservative Republicans and Democrats in the Senate let Johnson go for his defiance of the Constitution. The country would be spared "the scandal of a strict party vote by the minority."[95] As for outreach to the Nuevomexicano citizenry, the *Review* was the first paper in the territory to hire a Nuevomexicano as a Spanish-language editor. Blas Mata, an Alburquerque native, noted the many persons who expressed their opinions of the results of the proceeding according to their sympathies in favor of or against the accused, and without "calmness and judgment that should be hoped for in rational men and without disrespect to the accused and the high tribunal that tries him [*y sin la calmesa y juicio que se debe esperar de hombres racionales, y sin desprecio al acusado y al tribunal alto que le juzga, y aun denuncian algunos a la Cámara de Representantes por haberle puesto acusación contra el Presidente*]."[96] Russell viewed impeachment in predictable partisan form. It was, he editorialized, an effort to tear down the Constitution rather than build it up. "Instead of rescuing us from the perils of disintegration in which the termination of the war left us," he believed, Republicans were "rushing us upon still greater and more imminent peril. States are kept in a condition of disorganization." Congress had proved unequal to the task of providing substitutes for the civil institutions, "which it declared annulled by operation of the rebellion." Yet Russell found Johnson powerless since close of the war. The president was being punished "for offending against the policy of that party and not for any violence done, or attempted to be done, by him to the Constitution." The *New Mexican* called this unadulterated Copperheadism but was relieved to see the *Gazette* showing its Democratic Party hand at last. After having gotten "so badly beat in the rebellion, and its pet idea of a southern Confederacy exploded under the solid persuasions of Grant and his Union Armies," the *Gazette* had become a friend of President Johnson.[97]

The debate on the articles of impeachment began in the Senate at the close of the trial portion of the proceedings. Thirty-six votes were required to convict the president. Radicals twisted the arms of moderates and those Radicals who might defect. The Senate voted on one of the articles on May 16. Reflecting his national contacts, New Mexico District Attorney Stephen Elkins personally witnessed the scene of extreme suspense and anticipation in the Senate chamber. The president survived by a single vote.[98] Ten articles remained. Conviction on any one would be sufficient to oust the president. Amid self-flagellation on the wisdom of voting first on the most complicated article, Radicals requested a postponement of the proceedings so that they could go to Chicago for the presidential nominating convention of the still qualified National Union Republican Convention, where they hoped to scrape together the one vote they needed to impeach.[99]

The New Mexico Republican Central Executive Committee called a territorial "mass Republican convention" to appoint delegates to the Republican National Convention.[100] It does not appear that any such meeting took place. J. F. Chávez would not have attended, heeding the advice of his Washington supports to keep tabs on Clever in the Capitol.[101] Both the *Gazette* and the *Review* commented cynically, the former ridiculing Radicals and Republicans of the territory "who desired to keep up with the spirit of the times," but would not follow leaders "who pander to Mexican fogyism of the sixteenth century, the peon system &c." The *Review* held that the leaders, "being notorious political weathercocks—a batch of Vicars of Bray, in fact—[were] waiting to see more clearly the probable result of the next presidential election in order to christen their bantling accordingly, and thereby get office."[102]

The *New Mexican* feared Grant not having the support of Radicals to be the Republican Party's standard-bearer, many preferring U.S. Supreme Court Chief Justice Salmon Chase.[103] Grant went unopposed at the Convention on the first ballot. His nomination was affected by the Democratic Party's hold on electoral votes in many large northern states. The former Democrat Grant called himself thoroughly Republican. After some dissension, the Radical speaker of the House, Schuyler Colfax, with whom Heath had been communicating in reference to the Chávez contest, received nomination as the vice president. The convention's platform extolled Lincoln "as the grand champion of the party, but said nothing about Johnson's efforts to implement the great liberator's policies." Indeed, it read like a bill of charges for impeachment. Many Republicans were "disgusted" with the Radical plank that demanded Congress's guarantee of equal suffrage to all loyal men in the South while the question of suffrage in the loyal states "properly" belonged to the people of those states, meaning many northern states would deny blacks the vote. Another plank congratulated the country on the assured success of the reconstruction policy of Congress. It noted the adoption in a majority of states lately in rebellion "of constitutions securing equal civil and political rights to all, and regarded as the duty of the government to sustain these institutions and to prevent the people of such states from being remitted to a state of anarchy." Statements such as these, a historian notes, were meant to "salve wounds" for the purpose of gaining as much support as possible on the ten remaining articles of impeachment.[104]

The swift nomination of Grant vindicated New Mexico's Republican movement.[105] The URA Executive Committee called a ratification meeting. Anastacio Sandoval and Pablo Delgado took their seats as president and vice president respectively. J. F. Chávez's brother, José Bonifacio Chávez, served as a secretary. Heath, Arny, and Breeden spoke. The caucus unanimously adopted resolutions "as the expression of the loyal [U]nion men of New Mexico." They were read in English by William Breeden and translated by José D. Sena. It was deemed proper that the "voice of the Republicans of New Mexico" be heard "in endorsement of the platform adopted, and in approval of the nominations made" at Chicago. Reflecting a liberal colonialism at work, the meeting resolved that "as a territorial people we are sensible of our weakness, our want of the influence and of sovereignty, yet we love our whole country, we desire the perpetuity of our government and are devoted to our Republican institutions and the great principles upon which they are based." Their "feeble voice and efforts" were pledged "to the support of the glorious Grant, the conqueror of rebellion, and to his distinguished associate Schuyler Colfax, the fearless champion of justice, freedom and human rights." Congress's Reconstruction program was sustained.

Most of the Chicago resolutions received endorsement. As the Democratic Party had been successfully patronizing and capturing the millions of unskilled workers from Europe, especially German and Irish, Union Republicans included two immigration resolutions, one of which entitled naturalized citizens to protection in all their rights of citizenship "as if though they were native born." The other hailed foreign immigration for contributing so much to the nation, calling for the fostering of asylum for those from the "oppressed of all nations." The URA meeting did not mention them specifically, perhaps because they contradicted the thrust of opposition to Charles Clever in the election. It did resolve to constitute its executive committee as a Board of Emigration to maintain correspondence with the Emigration Society of Washington "and for other like purposes," to get in league with a craze in Washington and the states encouraging foreign immigration to the United States. The proceedings were submitted for publication to the *St. Louis Democrat, Washington Chronicle*, and *New York Tribune* as well as the *New Mexican*.[106]

New Mexican editorials enhanced the Republican motif in the territory. Seasonal hyperbole hailed the Chicago convention as "the most remarkable in the history of conventions. Such unanimity of sentiment never before exhibited itself.... The platform is a model of precision, principle and sentiment."[107] The *Gazette* cackled that the few present at the ratification meeting were, "we are told, about equally divided—Grant and anti-Grant." The *New Mexican* exploited the remark to "presume that the existence of the two parties in New Mexico—Republican and Democrat—will be no longer disputed by the friends of Mr. Clever. Their organ admits it at last."[108] The *Review* seems not to have acknowledged the URA rally. It did post Grant and Colfax at the head of the editorial page. As Hezekiah Johnson put it, "because they are the nominees of the party we belong to, we hope for their election."[109]

Privately, Francisco Chávez continued to regret differences in the Republican Party. Although they were "greatly in the majority" in the United States, many were "unreliable men and notwithstanding the example set them by the Democrats who always vote in solid phalanx for their men and measures, are utterly incapable of supporting and sustaining their party. I have never seen such a damned set of fools for partisans in my life," he spewed. Chávez no doubt felt that a united Radical body would spell a speedy decision in favor of his contest. But he also bemoaned the impact of internal factionalism for the party's national prospects. "It would not surprise me at all if Grant were defeated. The Republican party—the rank and file are disgusted with their leaders, and I don't wonder."[110] Confirming Chávez, Radicals desperately scrutinized the backgrounds of dissident senators in hopes of blackmailing them into voting for the impeachment of Johnson. As the day for voting on the first ten articles approached, Radicals feared they did not have sufficient support for conviction. Suspense returned as new voting began. The writing splashed onto the wall when the vote for acquittal came on the article in question. A motion for the Senate to adjourn as a Court of Impeachment *sine die* passed. Andrew Johnson emerged from the travail still president.[111] Historians would conjecture as to what forces had led to the outcome. In the analytical conclusion of one, "Historians should view the trial of impeachment for what it was: not as an attempt by a violent majority to remove an innocent president for partisan purposes but as one of the great legal cases of history, in which American politicians demonstrated the strength of the nation's democratic institutions by attempting to do what no one could justifiably expect them to do—to give a political officer a full and fair trial in a time of political crisis."[112] Even so, hardline Radicals sought to destroy the careers of colleagues who had turned against them. President Johnson went on to serve out the remainder of the term, continuing Lincoln's plan for restoring the Union.

The National Democratic Convention opened in New York City on the Fourth of July. Clarifying the party binary in New Mexico, Governor Mitchell, along with Capt. George W. Cook, represented New Mexico.[113] A motion to give territories representation on the Permanent Organization and Credentials committees would have made for unprecedented participation of New Mexicans in the forum of a major national party. The measure lost 184–106.[114]

President Johnson felt entitled to consideration for the Democratic presidential nomination, but his name was far too blemished. Well before the convention, several individuals gunned for the nomination or received support for it. Nine candidates went up on the opening ballot. Johnson came in second. The balloting took up three more days. With no one gaining the necessary two-thirds majority, new names were thrown in. Horatio Seymour, the former governor of New York and chair of the convention, emphatically declined his nomination. Seymour was nominated again, with such stirring praise that the assembly burst into raucous cheers and called for his nomination by acclamation. He could hardly resist. The nod for vice president went to Gen. Francis Blair, a defector from Lincoln's Republican Party, Johnson supporter, opponent of all of Congress's reconstruction acts, and advocate of leaving southern whites alone to organize their own governments.[115]

Pro-rebel and racist lobbyists seeking to block Negro suffrage and immigration planks agitated the convention. As one proclaimed, "'the accursed Memory of Abraham Lincoln will never be forgotten while the English language is read or written. . . . Generations yet unborn will shudder, and ask in astonishment why such a monster was permitted to live a month in the Presidential chair.'"[116] Bold rebel symbolism appeared. Backing the readmission of seven southern states to Congress, many delegates appeared in gray, especially after Johnson had issued amnesty pardons to Confederate officers and politicians not under indictment for treason.[117] The platform took on what one historian calls the "character" of Johnson's veto messages on the Tenure of Office Act, the Freedman's Bureau Act, and the Reconstruction Acts. The Freedman's Bureau was called a political instrumentality "designed to secure Negro supremacy." In defiance of Radicals, calls were made for the immediate restoration of all states in the Union, restoration of civil government to the American people, amnesty for all political offenses, and the regulation of the elective franchise in the states "by their citizens." The platform included a call for equal rights and protections for naturalized and native born citizens "at home and abroad."[118]

The *Santa Fe Gazette* posted in favor of Seymour and Blair. The abuses of the party in power needed the application of the "hand of reform," Russell declared, and it was through the accession of the Democratic Party to power that the United States would return to its former glory, earning the admiration of the world.[119] The *Review* and the *New Mexican* aimed their rhetorical cannons at the Democrats. The former quoted from one of Blair's private letters arguing that the

Democratic nominees would be amenable to the "sympathizers with the late rebellion and non-combatant rebels."[120] The latter rebuffed Blair's suggestion at the Democratic Convention that it might require war to defeat the Republican Party in the presidential campaign, a counter to Grant's signature call for peace.[121]

As the presidential campaigns lifted off, the *New Mexican* converted to a daily. The editors marked the start of a new era for New Mexico through the aid of the electric telegraph, and saw New Mexico taking its place "beside the other states of the world in the march of enterprise and intelligence." The politics of the daily would remain unchanged. "We shall not fail to yield a hearty and unwavering support to that great Republican Party and Principle which have first as a leader," it proclaimed, "and secondly as a true exponent, ULYSSES S. Grant as a candidate for the Presidency." The paper would not be entirely political but devoted to the "development of the country and the interests of the people generally."[122]

Because of the peculiar scheduling of elections for the territories, in 1868 New Mexico would go to the polls on the first Monday of September in order to fill all seats in its house of representatives, while the presidential election would be held on the third of November. On the election season altogether, the *Gazette* called for its political friends to make a "little exertion" to effect an organization, or "let [the election] go by default." No name was suggested for the lingering American shadow-party.[123] Hezekiah Johnson noted that a couple of pro-Clever visitors in town were both in favor of "drawing party lines, and walking them as straightly as circumstances will permit."[124]

In contrast the *New Mexican* reveled in its party certainty. It recalled that its side never failed to carry by large majorities both branches of the legislature at general elections. It was in the off-years, when the interest in voting waned, that the opposition might win one or the other chamber. Republicans must heed the importance of securing a majority in September, the editor noted, for there were measures of great importance that the legislature would have on its docket.[125] "Republicans (Chavez men)" in the counties were reminded that in the last legislature both houses were composed "of the very best of men," a "more sensible and earnest minded body of men," for it was to such men "that we must naturally look for practical and intelligent legislation." With the council in the hands of the Republicans, it was only necessary in considering members of the house for friends to "Select good and true men; set aside all doubtful ones."[126]

Cleverites continued to imply that Nuevomexicanos had no business pretending to be Republicans. In a previous dialogue described earlier in this chapter, Pancho marvels to Chepe at the new Republican shroud over the legislature, admitting that he had no clue what it meant. In the most recent dialogue, Pancho had not learned much, remaining in his "natural state" since going to the legislature (for the full Spanish text, see appendix 10). Though he had been empowered to embark on the "glorious and difficult career of lawyer in the courts of the Río Abajo," he made the most destructive racket in court, scaring everyone in the legal profession with his bombast. Pancho, retaining his modesty, confessed to a lack of ability "from his own mouth." Pancho still did not know if he was a Radical or Democrat. He was for impeachment yet sympathized with the rebels and had fled to the mountains so as not to fight the Texans who invaded the territory. Pancho had given proof that he was not anti-American, standing in harmony with the two acting governors (Arny and Heath), one of whom had said the greasers and Indians were equally thieves, the other having abrogated the law of elections that Pancho himself had made for his government. In his run for reelection Pancho once made party noises, sure he would win and admitting that while the people remained in the darkness of ignorance and stupidity, the caprice of the party would keep proper men from getting elected to the legislature or to administer the laws, and for that would he continue to occupy his seat.[127]

As the New Mexico campaign came to life, the hard work of Heath and J. F. Chávez to influence the chairmen of the territorial committees in the House (James Ashley of Ohio) and the Senate (Richard Yates of Illinois) and Speaker Colfax paid off when Congress approved the petition of the New Mexico legislature (authored by Heath) to limit the governor's absolute veto. Any measure vetoed by the governor could now be overridden by two-thirds of the legislators. The practical effect would give Nuevomexicanos greater control over territorial affairs. It did not hurt in the lobbying that Heath characterized the people of New Mexico to the Radicals "in all respects Republican in sentiment, national in spirit and imbued with the principle of true progress."[128]

Back at the electioneering, critics straightforwardly accused territorial Republicans of betraying the Republican emphasis on economic and social development, a carry-over of the charges filed in response to the recent anti-Semitism. The *New Mexican* denied that its politics represented the "anti-enterprise party—the non-improvement party," expecting Santa Fe to prosper with the coming of the railroad, rejoicing with all businessmen. The motto of the new daily would be "'onward and upward.'"[129] *Tecolote* (Owl) took J. Francisco Chávez to task in Spanish as an obstructionist to the aim of promoting New Mexico's development.[130] *Un Mejicano* blamed the dominant party within the county, from the legislators down to the justices of the peace, and the "thicket" of sheriffs, for the territory's lack of prosperity. The "torments" of the Republican Party forced the *hijos de Nuevo Méjico* into voting for unqualified men of "indelicate" character (*poco delicado*), men with no scruples. Soon the people would remove such figures who sold themselves "body and soul" to the odious orders from above, Un Mejicano claimed, replacing them with honest, educated, and virtuous alternatives.[131] The complaint reflected incipient party solidification in localities. If anything, the Chávez-led party appeared to be growing in strength. In the report out of Alburquerque, the "better portion of the Clever party" had gotten "tired of their party leaders," declaring an intent to vote with the Chávez party this year.[132]

Most county nominating conventions took place in mid- to late August, less than a month prior to election day. The early ones generally held to the Chávez party–Clever party tags or did not name themselves party-wise.[133] However, two nominating conventions in Santa Fe County planted the banners of the Republican and Democratic parties.

What was announced as the convention "of the Republican Party" went first on August 23. Chávez followers presided. José D. Sena called it to order; Antonio Ortiz y Salazar was elected president; Breeden and Matías Dominguez became secretaries; and Anastacio Sandoval headed the committee to select candidates for the house "to be supported by the Republican party at the coming election." After R. M. Stephens (Santa Fe), Juan García (Santa Fe), and Benito Romero (Pojoaque) were nominated, Sena got down to the business of the party preamble and resolutions. "Whereas it is important that the Republican [P]arty in New Mexico should maintain its integrity for the good of the people," he affirmed, "and Whereas it is the opinion of the convention that the great interests of New Mexico lie in a pure Republican administration of the government, both national and Territorial:

> therefore / Resolved, that the Republicans of Santa Fe county adhere to the principles of the National Republican party of the United States as presented in the Platform adopted at the National Republican Convention held in Chicago on the 20th of May last. / Resolved that, although without a vote for the National Republican ticket in the coming presidential election, yet we have a voice; and we earnestly raise this in favor of Grant and Colfax, candidates for President and Vice President of the United States, and hope for their election.

The convention thanked the Republican Party for passing the law abridging the governor's veto, which Governor Mitchell had been using "solely in the interest of our political opponents and abused by him to the great detriment of their interests, the will and wishes of the people of New Mexico." Reinforcing organization, a Republican County Central Committee was formed consisting of Heath, Sena, Benedict, Sandoval, and Pablo Delgado.[134] In lock step, explicit Republican nominating conventions were organized in Santa Ana and Valencia counties at least.[135]

The opposition matched the binary assumptions, if not needs, of Republicans, coming out unequivocally for the "Conservative Democracy." The Central Committee of the Democracy of Santa Fe County announced the convention. Veteran American Party shadow-figures did the honors. Nicolás Quintana called the assembly to order. José Manuel Gallegos got elected president. Gaspar Ortiz y Alarid became one vice president, the turncoat T. H. Tompkins, the other.[136] Jesús María Alarid served as one of two secretaries. Felipe Delgado made it onto the Committee on Resolutions. The president's opening address made the convention's identity clear. "We are assembled here today not as partisans of Clever, not as partisans of Chávez," Gallegos affirmed, "but as National Democrats to reiterate our adherence to the great principles of the party that has put forth as its candidates for the presidency and vice presidency, Horatio Seymour and Francis P. Blair (Cheers)."

Gallegos forcefully pushed the official organization he was originally elected to in 1853. Theirs was not a sectional but a national party, he emphasized. Under Democratic administrations the country had prospered, he explained, but "for well nigh eight years the Radicals have had control of the government and yet we have not all the states represented in that government; our people are ground down by oppressive and excessive taxation, and if such a state of affairs continue[s] to exist[,] national bankruptcy will be our inevitable lot." Pouring his partisan energies into the conservative Democratic attack on Radicalism, Gallegos blamed the Republicans for opening up the territory to Negroes.[137]

The platform of the Democracy of the County of Santa Fe (of which the *New Mexican* later claimed Quintana was the "father") echoed the racialized parent organization. While it had "no hatred towards the colored race," it declared, and was "willing to protect them from every

> assault upon their natural rights, we are unalterably opposed to Negro suffrage and Negro equality, it's logical issue. / That we believe 7/8 of the population of New Mexico is Democratic in sensibility and sentiments, and will in due time give utterance in a manner not to be misunderstood, that they are in favor of "white men's government." / That any encouragement given to the black Republican party in New Mexico will greatly injure our territory, because when the Negroes have more rights here than elsewhere, they will rush to this country en masse and soon throw us into such anarchy and troubles, as now illustrated to us by scenes in the south. / [Under Democratic Party rule] the Negro was happy and well taken care of, while now he is forced by the Radicals to be our equal and superior which doctrine must finally lead to the extermination of the colored race.

Ironically, given the history of the Democratic thrust in New Mexico, which had started with such an impassioned contestation between Gallegos and Miguel A. Otero, these Democrats reinvigorated the latter's association with the cause of the southerners, declaring it "in the spirit of humanity to recognize their claims as men, as citizens and kindred." In their version of liberal integration, they declared for the immediate restoration of all the states "to their rights in the union under the Constitution of civil government and the American people."

The convention parroted national party policy further, yearning for the days when the Democratic Party promoted the country's union and opposed the current disunion, when the executive was powerful, the supreme court "respected and honored." On the great question of the economy plaguing the Republicans in the aftermath of the Civil War, delegates followed the Philadelphia economic platform, including the abolition of the freedmen's bureau. They condemned the Republicans for having "taxed the poor and enriched the bondholder," ordering gold for the rich and paper for the poor. The only "remedy" to better the country's condition, the resolutions proclaimed, was a "victory of democracy." The "heartiest sympathies" were extended "to our Democratic brothers throughout the United States and hope it will not be long before New Mexico will also be able to give strong support to a revived [D]emocracy!"

Resolutions were adopted "amid tremendous applause." Quintana advocated for the "great principles of the Democracy." With the suppression of the rebellion, Quintana reinforced the party duty "to harmonize with our fellow countrymen in the southern states," noting that they had already been severely punished and that they should be restored to all the rights pertaining to American citizens. Though New Mexico had no vote in the electoral college, Quintana affirmed, "nevertheless we are awake to the great questions which agitate the public mind." Tompkins in his address said he had voted for Chávez in the previous election, but now the issue was "Democracy against Radicalism." National questions had "absorbed" local ones, he emphasized, and the Democratic Party fought "for truth and right."[138] New Mexico's binary politics wuld remain vital.

Río Arriba County Democrats held their "Democratic Conservative Party Convention" at San Juan de los Caballeros. On motion of Antonio Roival, Diego Archuleta served as president. Mariano Larragoiti, former Carleton agent, was one of the party's nominees for the House of Representatives.[139]

Hezekiah Johnson toyed with the "Santa Fe clique's" new party. It was called "Conservative Democratic" in Santa Fe and "Democratic Conservative" in Río Arriba, he observed. In Santa Fe the "principal man" signed himself "Central Committee," while in Río Arriba, the "big chief" was Diego Archuleta, "fair and square." Johnson implored the Gazette to "let the people know what the name of its party will be next year; and also whether niggers are included in its declaration of 'equality' and the 'greatest good to the greatest number.'" As the organ of the new party, the Gazette had in its Spanish columns only "a pathetico-jubilant appeal for people in general to participate with that party." In now wanting those who had lain in obscurity, Hezekiah Johnson perceived "that it and its followers have been political hypocrites, through motives of gain, till such time as they found that throwing off their mask would make them lose nothing, and might be profitable to them."[140]

His racist reference to blacks notwithstanding, Johnson challenged the Democratic planks on the Negro as "decidedly rich, and some of them behind the times." What did it mean by the "natural rights" of the Negro?" he queried. "Jurists defined them for "all men" as life, liberty, and the pursuit of happiness, yet the "unsophisticated" could infer that the Santa Fe concept of the Negro's natural rights were "Life and *Slavery* and its consequences to the white man and the black man." Johnson saw the declaration of Negro inequality as the "logical issue of Negro suffrage, beyond the bare right of voting," as "absurd as it would be to say, because an illiterate man's vote counts the same as the learned man's, the illiterate man is the equal of the learned man in every respect." He went on: "Most Negroes are aware of the fact they are legal voters in every territory of the United States, and in several of the Eastern states, yet we do not hear of their rushing there in masses." Democratic newspapers asserted that on the abolition of slavery the Negroes would overrun the northern states and reduce the price of labor to such a low point, that

> white laborers would starve, yet although four years have elapsed since Mr. Lincoln's Emancipation Proclamation, this Democratic prediction has not a shadow of realization. Although a Republican—yes, a "Black republican," if the [D]emocracy please so to style us—anarchy and troubles are as repugnant to us as to a Democrat of the best regulated intellects; we would like the democracy to explain how the immigration of Negroes to this territory will cause anarchy and troubles; or, is it to be inferred from the phrase, 'as are now illustrated to us by scenes in the South,' that the Santa Fe democracy contemplate organizing Ku Klux Klan's, and to adopt [KKK founder] Albert Pike's recommendation to the southern young men to take an oath to kill every northern white man who comes here to settle? Have they the backbone to try it on?

They may have, Johnson stated, "if Seymour be elected."[141]

A registration law passed in a rare moment of unity between the assembly and the governor, modernized voting procedures. County probate judges would now name a registry board of three in each precinct, one of whom would belong to the political party opposed to that of the prefect. It would meet thirty days before the election to take its first cut at identifying the legal voters of the precinct, organized into five subdistricts. Voters could then see their names listed or not. The board reviewed the list three days before the election. Improper names were to be stricken. Missing names could be inserted at that time. It was the responsibility of the citizen to assure that he was properly registered at least three days prior to the election or lose the vote. The official list was given to the judges of election on or before election day. Only those appearing on the list were allowed to vote.[142]

The numbers came in erratically, yet Republicans clearly carried seven of eleven counties. Not surprisingly, Mora, Río Arriba, and Socorro counties went Democratic. Republicans took seventeen of twenty-six house seats. The *New Mexican* observed that at least one of the adverse party declared his independence "of the party that claims him." Nor could the *Gazette* take much comfort from its success in Valencia and Socorro counties, Tucker pointed out, "where it is undeniable that the Democratic ticket was only carried through the unnecessary failure of our own friends to do their duty in the canvass."[143]

Oddly, Republicans lost in Chávez's home Valencia County. The party "ought not" to have surrendered it, the *New Mexican* observed. *Un Enfermo* (A sick one) scolded fellow partyites for falling asleep and abandoning the political leaders of the county. The good people very well knew who buttered their bread politically, El Enfermo asserted, but, indicating a general condition of citizen liberation from political bondage to local jefes, disapproved of the Republican promoters who did not pay sufficient attention to the "honorable peasants" and others who fixed themselves on gaining the best advantage for the agreeable advancement of their particular businesses and honest sustenance of their obligations or families. They tended to want everything from the political promoters, putting their faith in those who appeared compatible with the honor of their government and the progressive advancement of the general welfare of the people without being subjugated or abused. Did his friends forget to tell the voters that "our political banner flows purely according to the salvation of our Republican institutions and to the honor of our grand and glorious Union? Let us recognize this more carefully, for its importance was great [¿Que no se consideran, amigos míos, que nuestra bandera política se encamina puramente a la salvaguardia de nuestras instituciones Republicanas y al honor y engrandezimiento del Gobierno de nuestra gran y gloriosa Unión? Veamos esto con más Cuidado que su importancia es grande]." Un Enfermo noted that Republicans lost neighboring Socorro County because they had nominated the wrong individuals, resulting in the withdrawal of a discontented important county chief, don Nestor Gonzales.[144]

The key county of Santa Fe assured the election for Republicans. "Our party did its darn here," the *New Mexican* observed. Whereas a year before the "Clever [D]emocracy made a tie against us," the weekly announced, "we swept it this year by near two hundred majority!"[145] Using a popular term of derision, the *Review* observed that the "*pinchecuate*" (fucking brotherhood) Democracy did not carry Santa Fe because of the "New York platform adopted by them, and the elaborate one they made under their own cloak, did not afford standing room for the people they expected to help them." Quite likely, Hezekiah Johnson observed, "it was foolish to expect Republicans to vote for candidates nominated on the New York platform and the insulting and proscriptive manifesto adopted by the convention which nominated them."[146] Johnson observed that defectors from the Santa Fe Democracy were migrating "down this way," and were "now thinking of cooperating with us in organizing the [Republican] party. They say that the candidate for delegate who will get their votes next year must show that he has a clear Republican record; that they want no more Modern Democrats."[147]

Democrats placed blame for their defeat on the new voter registry. Those selecting boards in the precincts were heavily partisan probate judges, Un Mejicano argued, who interpreted the laws and manipulated the lists to favor their candidates. Constituents manipulated the process by inventing voters with impunity and to the advantage of the dominant party in the county. The Republican legislature that created the law intended it this way, Un Mejicano charged in clear partisan form, ultimately with an eye to the election of the next delegate to Congress. Considering the way it worked, there was little if any hope for the coming legislature to repeal the law, he observed. If by chance they did, those responsible would be "forever praised" by the people.[148]

The *New Mexican* called all this sour grapes and understandable, as the precincts where Democratic partisans had committed their "great frauds" in the prior election were this year "unmasked" in their treachery. The weekly gave the example of the Tierra Amarilla precinct, which had registered 450 votes for Clever when this year the registry recorded 190 legal voters. Similarly in La Junta, the partisan stimulus generated 652 votes for Clever when "under the lens of the registry law," but 280 voters were documented.[149]

With the territorial council unchanged, Republicans looked forward to the next legislative session, the "now dominant party" to have a majority of two-thirds in both houses.[150] As the *New Mexican* interpreted, "For the first time since the war, the issue [in the New Mexico election] was made strictly upon the question of national politics, both conventions having strongly endorsed the respective platforms of the Republican and Democratic parties as framed at Chicago and New York." The candidates in New Mexico "stood upon the same platforms that Grant and Seymour are running upon."[151]

Hezekiah Johnson relished his role of party pooper at first, holding that it did not make much difference "for any present useful purpose" which political party predominated in the legislature, "as we expect to have the same botched legislation as we have heretofore had, until we have a State Government."[152] Later, with the national election a month away, Johnson changed his tune. The people were "rapidly coming into line on the platforms of national parties," he beheld. "Yes, reader," it was a notorious fact that National party lines—

> Republican and Democratic—are drawn in New Mexico. We rejoice thereat, because it is a condition of partisan affairs which we have several years longed for, and henceforward the selection of persons for political offices will be on account of their political principles, and ability to carry out those principles, and not on account of mere personal preference, as has hitherto been the case in this Territory. To those who desire the advancement of the interests of the Territory—which will ever keep step with the intellectual progress of the people—there could be nothing more unsatisfactory than the heated personal election contests heretofore in vogue, because the defamation of the character and abilities of candidates, by those opposed to them, was not calculated to enlighten the people as to

the principles of our system of Government, but rather to degrade it in their estimation.

People objected to the organization of national parties in the territory because they believed that "the natives" did not understand their principles, Johnson sought to explain with a bit of social blindness. "And to the argument that they *can* learn them," he observed, "objectors respond that they can never be made to understand them!" These objectors, Johnson gladly reported, were not Republicans. "Indeed," he continued, "we hear from Republicans on all hands expressions of the utmost confidence in the favorable reception of our principles by natives of this Territory; and those of them with whom we have conversed on the subject base this confidence on the fact that the natives take to controversial reasoning with alacrity." Johnson said the people of the territory would not be any less open to the conviction of the Republican principles, which he intended to publish in Spanish, "than those of other parts of the country."[153]

In November, then, Ulysses S. Grant won the presidency with 53 percent of the national vote. The electoral colleges of key northern states went for Grant, and he garnered the votes of newly enfranchised blacks in the South.[154] The result fortified New Mexico's Republican solidarity. A throng of two thousand participated in Santa Fe's "Grand Jubilee" celebration. Four thousand witnessed the procession around the plaza to the Palace of the Governors, where the Republicans of Santa Fe and the surrounding country "covered themselves with glory . . . by the magnificence of their demonstration over the late victory of the Republican Party." Bonfires lit the skyline; banners proclaimed "trite but beautiful" sayings for Grant and "Equal liberty to all"; an eighteen-piece military band pealed, and the Grant and Colfax Glee Club added patriotic songs. "The ladies, heaven bless them," the *New Mexican* was pleased to note, "without regard to party or nationality, crowded the balconies and windows, and even the stand, and by their bright eyes and smiles added to the *celat* of the hour."

Secretary H. H. Heath, Santa Fe County Sheriff José D. Sena, and Union Republican Association Central Committee member William Breeden delivered halleluiahs. Heath's speech was published at the behest of rally officers including President Anastacio Sandoval. The "Great Republican Party under Grant, over the Democratic Party under Seymour," and the "sacredness of the Union cause, as developed by the Republican Party" were extolled. In Heath's inspired eloquence, "Hereafter, the clank of no chain that once manacled the slave is to be heard in the marts of men."[155] Sandoval, Vicente García, and Trinidad Alarid represented Nuevomexicano integration, sitting alongside familiar Euroamerican Republicans Michael Steck, Thomas Tucker, and Breeden.[156]

Alburquerque conducted ethnically segregated tributes. Euroamericans placed the United States flag on the courthouse immediately above the hall door. It was "brilliantly illuminated by bonfires on the roof and in the streets," and it waved "gloriously over the scene, while a *feu de joie* was kept up with guns and pistols."[157] Nuevomexicanos dominated the more formal occasion. Tomás Gutierrez acted as president. Nestor Montoya was a vice president. Teófilo Chávez served as secretary. Salvador Armijo, José Armijo y Ortiz, Manuel García, Román Gutierrez, Nestor Jaramillo, Lorenzo Montaño, and Román Ortega formed the majority of the Committee on Resolutions, with Hezekiah Johnson in attendance. Seven resolutions tendered gratitude for the platform of the Republican Party and the "triumph of Unionism over Secessionism, of Lawful Government over Anarchy and of National Honor over Repudiation," and the "march of Peace and Progress." In an aspect of a convention, members requested the president to choose residents of New Mexico to recommend for federal appointments. Candidates should belong to the "organization of the Republican party" and be "well informed" on the resources of the territory, with "that understanding of the genius of its people which is acquired only by long experience." Active members of the Republican Party, otherwise duly qualified for office, should be preferred over "No-Party" men and Democrats who were No Party men "for the sake of office."[158]

A Republican illustrated how thoroughly Democratic sentiment was demolished in New Mexico. He claimed in a letter to the *Missouri Democrat* that only three of a dozen federal officials in New Mexico voted Republican in the September election for territorial house members. Certain officials "loudly advocated the election of Seymour and Blair while praising the "New York revolutionary repudiation platform." Included were Governor Robert Mitchell, Depository Director James Collins (noted as a Whig under Fillmore, holding office as a Democrat under Pierce and Buchanan, as a Unionist under Lincoln, "and securing his present office as a conservative under Johnson"), various Indian agents, and others. It was now difficult to find a Democrat here "of any prominence," the Republican noted, "and only two Federal officers would admit that they were supporters of Seymour and Blair."[159]

The Democratic sector was clearly weakened, but enough Democratic oxygen remained to keep the idea of a party afloat. However, it turned out that as politics arose after the election, members were still not ready to raise the banner of an explicit Democratic Party title replete with a permanent operating organization. A quite practical reason lay behind the reluctance.

CHAPTER FOURTEEN

Steady Republicans, Hazy Democrats, 1869

Republicans kept their party corral well marked during the 1868–69 territorial legislature. The session was organized at the home of Anastacio Sandoval as a "purely Republican operation," and members were composed "of many of the best and staunchest Republicans anywhere to be found, several of whom are Americans" (seven, in fact). Members spoke at the Republican Association meeting, said to have 240 participants. In one action, a new county was named after the assassinated Lincoln and another for Vice President Shuyler Colfax. The Republican majority was enhanced by the switch of at least two members to their side. Party memberships well understood, a spirit of shared power prevailed, two from the opposing party obtaining officer appointments, including speaker of the house.[1]

The assembly's effort to see Robert Mitchell fired as territorial governor had fallen through. Not much hope appeared that his relations with the assembly would go well, for similar efforts had failed dismally in the previous two sessions. Mitchell annoyed Nuevomexicanos this particular year by failing to provide a Spanish-language copy of his opening message, forcing them to make a special request for it.[2] Mitchell alluded to Reconstruction and the financial management of the country as the two major matters that had divided the Democratic and Republican parties. Hezekiah Johnson, *Republican Review* editor and freshly elected justice of the peace, docked Mitchell for not acknowledging the Democratic Party's support of the rebellion, which, he emphasized, had fomented the political problems of the day. Johnson noted that Mitchell served as a delegate to the National Democratic Convention, "which nominated Seymour and Blair." He should have known that the "platform which he then helped to place before the country made *vital* issues other than those two questions." A "general reader" would have known "that the Republican platform, adopted several weeks before, offered more issues than these questions."[3]

Mitchell noted the obligation of New Mexicans to express confidence in the new president and he asked the legislature to attend to the important business of having New Mexico represented at Grant's inauguration. The gesture followed from the fact that a governor's appointment and retention depended on the largesse of whatever party held Washington power. The *New Mexican* did not allow him the right to blur the territory's partisan distinction; it offered the reminder that after returning from the "Copperhead convention in New York," he infused into his party "what little hope it possessed that Seymour would be elected—*he* was certain of Seymour's success. Now that he feels the sand sliding from beneath his official feet, he has confidence in the great Republican soldier—Grant. Mitchell's confidence in Grant comes too late," the paper pronounced.[4]

For the first time a Nuevomexicano-dominated assembly had the power of the two-thirds veto override and was not afraid to exercise it. It straight away overturned the election of the Doña Ana County probate judge on the basis of fraud as documented in the proceedings of the Chávez contest, installing instead a candidate of its party. "Well done," commented the *New Mexican*. "The People of New Mexico are in power."[5] The alleged offender, probate judge candidate John Lemon, was supported by Mitchell. After the veto override a public meeting thanked the legislature for its action.[6]

The legislature also forced the assignment of the district judges to each of the three districts over the governor's veto. The Clever backer Chief Justice John Watts found himself cast to the remote third district along the Mexico border, and Judge Perry Brocchus of the Chávez brain trust was given the coveted first (Santa Fe) district. Brocchus did not affiliate with the Republican Party, but the judicial bill fit into Chávez's power scheme. Mitchell complained that it was for the purpose of "humiliating or to degrade one of the Judges of the Supreme Court, and to gratify the ambition of another." As the *New Mexican* argued, it was "obligatory" under the provisions of the Organic Law to bring some order to the assignments, for as it was, judges could hold court "anywhere in the territory." Rubbing salt into the wound, the killer of Judge Slough, Councilman William Rynerson, delivered the resolution rebuking the governor's justification for the veto "as discreditable to its author as it is distasteful to this body."[7]

Audits showing the territorial budget deficit headed in a worsening direction formed another reason to oppose the executive. The issue of the territory's indebtedness of over $17,000 was noted as important prior to the session, and Governor Mitchell called on the legislature to adopt a system of equal taxation to redeem the territory's credit. Instead of what it called Mitchell's "wild system of taxation of the people," the *New Mexican* called for a process of revenue generation by collecting on debts due from defaulting sheriffs and other officials, who, the paper said, overran the period of indemnity "to the great detriment of the people."[8] In a command address to the assembly, former secretary and former acting governor William Arny blamed the governor's "enormous extravagance and wastefulness" for the territory's bankruptcy.[9] Rather than exact a tax measure, the legislature declared null and void all the territorial warrants that had been drawn in favor of the governor's slate of territorial appointees, including the adjutant general John Russell, attorney general Merrill Ashurst, territorial auditor Epifanio Vigil, and territorial librarian J. M. Alarid. For any payment made by them, the treasurer was instructed to file suit for recovery.[10]

Another blow to the Mitchell side of the political equation occurred as Secretary H. H. Heath escaped the ax of dismissal that delegate Clever had tried to drop on his federal appointment. The *Weekly Gazette* tried polluting him as before. The *Semi-Weekly Review* said it was because of Heath's refusal to grant the *Gazette* a territorial printing contract. The assembly rattled off resolutions affirming its commitment to the clear Republican Heath and citing the resolutions of support it had generated the year before. "It must be gratifying to you to be so fully and cordially endorsed by the representatives of the people after the violent attack of the *Gazette* clique," Chávez wrote to Heath after receiving the resolution from assemblymen Raphael Chávez and Antonio Ortiz y Salazar.[11]

The anti-Republican forces registered in literary opposition to the legislature such as to hint at a Democratic Party perspective. In a Pancho-Chepe diálogo, Republicans are caricatured as carpetbaggers, for example.[12] In another contribution, what the author calls an "anecdote," a leader of the alleged secret Republican Union Society waves off a beggar, feeling insulted because he was supplicated in the name of Jesus. The next day the mendicant is puzzled to receive the same treatment from the Republican for begging in the name of Mary.

The plot is a play on the holy names. In the story line, it is a dissident Republican by the name of Jesús María who dares to buck the secret Republican "speculators," the reason for the Republican aggravation. The allusion is to Jesús María Pacheco, who began his political career in association with the Republicans but left them after the Slough episode. Territorial Republican committeeman William Arny and Heath are named as secret Republican conspirators.[13] Another missive from *Un Mejicano* totally disparaged the legislature when its session opened, accusing it of bad and corrupt legislation, disrespecting the sacred laws, and creating personal, combative havoc with members not of their party, to the point of fisticuffs.[14]

Nonetheless, with a greater balance of power in the legislative chambers of the Palace of the Governors, contention between the assembly and Mitchell emerged much less heated than before. The unrelentingly partisan *Gazette* complained of legislators who sold themselves "in the market for a less price than Judas sold the Savior," but solons and the governor got along on several points.[15] In late January John Russell resigned as the territorial adjutant general. In one area of governing cooperation, a unanimous Legislative Council cheerily confirmed Mitchell's replacement nominee, Capt. George W. Cook—evidence, the *New Mexican* confirmed, "of the desire of that body to act, so far as possible, with the Executive, where the interests of the Territory are concerned." Besides this and in addition to his promise as a "good and efficient" operative, Cook was a legal officer, as his predecessor was not.[16] Other compromises involved the appointment of Anastacio Sandoval as territorial auditor in exchange for Mitchell's priority for other appointments and an agreement to sell some real estate belonging to the county.[17]

Mitchell preempted Heath's third application for leave after the session. Heath complained to the secretary of state, but Mitchell traipsed to Washington to see about his professional future given the inauguration of a new president, an inauguration that the governor himself attended, along with José F. Chávez and Kirby Benedict.[18]

On December 18, 1868, the Union Republican Association of New Mexico named its officials for the new semester. Antonio Ortiz y Salazar was elected president; Anastacio Sandoval and Vicente García (with R. M. Stephens), vice presidents; José D. Sena (with Eben Everett), secretary; José Ortiz, sergeant at arms; and Rafael Rodriguez, assistant sergeant at arms. On the Executive Committee Pablo Delgado, Ambrosio Ortiz and an important new recruit, the former Cleverite and venerable Santa Fean Felipe Delgado, joined William Breeden, S. B. Wheelock, J. L. Barbe, and Edward Miller.[19] They were now set to deal with the upcoming election for delegate to Congress.

Beating the Electoral Drum

Hezekiah Johnson was now on record wholeheartedly supporting the Republican Association.[20] Johnson treated with contempt self-styled "conservatives" in Santa Fe who appeared to be hiding from their Democratic stripes as planted in their last convention platform. Johnson saw the Republican Party of New Mexico as destined to have "a thoroughgoing Republican candidate for delegate" in 1869 and to "make no compromise with Democrats, let them up here under whatever name they may."[21] Johnson pushed his *Semi-Weekly Review* to the Republican front, coming out for José Francisco Chávez as the Republican nominee for delegate to Congress. Johnson claimed to understand Chávez as the "unanimous" choice of members of the "Republican party" in Santa Fe, San Miguel, Taos, and Río Arriba counties, while the Republicans of the Río Abajo were "almost unanimous for him." Chávez had proved himself true to Republican principles, Johnson heralded, and as the Republicans would "shortly have complete control of all the political branches of the government, no sane man would imagine for an instant that he will sacrifice his own political prospects, and render himself forever infamous, by betraying his friends for the benefit of the [Clever] Clique."[22]

Johnson provoked a spat with the *New Mexican* with this initiative. It came out in discourse around the measure introduced in the legislature to change the date of the election for delegate from fall to spring. The *New Mexican* supported the proposal because it would mean more time for the delegate to work for New Mexico's interest in Washington. Johnson editorialized that it was inimical to the interests of the young Republican organization. He accused the Santa Fe weekly of going for the change as a means of propping up some weak aspirant for the delegate's seat who would be nominated by a legislative caucus rather than a Republican nominating convention.[23]

Johnson's brashness strained the credulity of the *New Mexican*. Thomas Tucker, *New Mexican* editor and Republican Association treasurer, regarded his paper as truer to the wishes of a Republican territorial nominating convention:

> We beg to remind our not very amiable contemporary that in discussing the merits of the proposed change in the delegate election law, we have been governed by no other sentiment than that which looks to the good of the Republican party of New Mexico and of the Territory. . . . Indeed, we are at a loss to know who the *Review* refers to, when it speaks of our preferences. We have not indicated them yet, and in this we think we have been more respectful to the party than the *Review*, which has undertaken to forestall the action of the convention by a premature expression of its wishes.

Tucker reminded Johnson that his paper had supported Chávez when the editor of the *Review* "was not only opposing that gentleman, but *abusing* him withal [in his assault on Heath's Confederate past]; and we think we understand our duty to the party, should he be re-nominated for Congress." The *New Mexican*'s past services to Chávez rendered it "entirely unnecessary for us to make any ado about our future course. Can the *Review*, which has apparently installed itself as Col. Chávez' sole champion, say as much? / We have no candidate, and therefore our position is not speculative." The editor, riding on the principle of a democratic republicanism, would await the decision of the delegate convention.[24]

Johnson objected to the imputation that by coming forward for Chávez he meant to forestall a nominating convention and depreciate the rights of others. The *Review* was one of the Republican Party's "units," he declared, one of the "thousands" of such units in the territory. He thus had as much right as any other "*unit* to express an opinion on all questions, whether of *men*, or *measures*, in which the party is interested." For Republicans in the territory not to agree with this proposition meant their lack of agreement with their brethren in the states "on the matter of equal rights, which is one of the fundamental principles of Republicanism and the sooner they inform themselves of the premises the better." Johnson again read a "scheme" in the *New Mexican*'s position based on a fear of Chávez's popularity in the Río Abajo and among its most influential men. Regarding the *New Mexican*'s "self-glorification" over having supported Chávez, Johnson acknowledged opposing him in 1865 but denied abusing him. At the time, the Republican Party was not organized, Johnson argued. The point now was that Chávez was the strongest candidate the party could nominate, although Johnson assured his "antiquarian contemporary" that he would support the nominee of a Republican territorial convention though he not be Chávez, claiming that the *New Mexican* did not know him well enough to see that he would conform to the party's usage through the control of the *Review* columns.[25]

The *Gazette* suggested, quite understandably, that Johnson's sharp turn from a "no-party" man to the Republican Party was meant for the consideration of some "government pap," although it was unsure in what "proportion." Johnson did not exactly deny the charge of trying to gain some patronage, which may help explain his surging to the front of the party's election activity.[26] Recall, in this regard, the inclusion of his name in the Republican plan for offices as evidenced in Heath's correspondence. Indeed, President Grant appointed Johnson as an associate justice of New Mexico's Supreme Court a few months after he had come out for Chávez. Johnson's Albuquerque neighbors, friends, and fellow citizens converged in a celebration with bonfire, music, and discharge of arms. The primary speaker, R. M. Stephens, hailed the appointment as meaning that after so many years of judicial instability, the citizens of the Río Abajo would have a stable and steady court docket at the hands of a justice who lived among them. Johnson, for his part, acknowledged the "frequent and sustained" efforts of his friends who had solicited this "promotion" to the bench since the first term of Lincoln. The *New Mexican* congratulated Johnson, calling him "our friend and fellow editor," expressing confidence that he would "preside over the courts of his district with strict impartiality, and give general satisfaction to those subject to his judicial decisions," and probably feeling relief at the removal of Johnson's annoying pretense of competing to be the leading Republican journalist in the territory.[27]

The Republican Association announced January 31, 1869, as the day of its territorial convention to nominate a candidate for delegate to the Forty-first Congress. As the Executive Committee noted, "No party convention has ever had more interest in the well-being of the people than this loyal Republican party convention of this territory because the well-being as a people in the future depends largely on the results that come from its actions."[28] The Bernalillo and Santa Fe

County Republican conventions called in advance for the nomination of Chávez for delegate, the former not only on account of his abilities and "fidelity to the interests of his constituents" but as "some compensation for his trouble and expense" in contesting the fraudulent election on which Charles Clever obtained the seat in the Fortieth Congress.[29] It was said in Santa Fe that the nomination was "unsatisfactory to but very few of the Republican Party, and is hailed with joy by every member of it whose sense of justice is not warped by personal ambition and whose desire of the times of the party is not misguided by individual preferences and antipathies."[30]

The important Republican Territorial Nominating Convention was called to order by Territorial Secretary Heath. The original Mexican shadow-partier Tomás Cabeza de Baca served as president. José D. Sena shared the secretary pro tem slot with William Breeden. Eighty-two percent (43 out of 52) of the delegates were Nuevomexicano. San Miguel County's Celso Baca shared in the leadership. The convention resolved anti-colonialistically that "as a territorial people we are sensible to our weakness, our want of sovereignty and of influence; yet out of love for our whole country, we desire the perpetuity of our [U.S.] government, and are devoted to our Republican institutions, and the great principles upon which they are based." The principles of the Chicago National Union Republican Convention were endorsed as expressions of political faith. Members rejoiced at Grant and Colfax. Only a Republican government could increase the people's intelligence, it was affirmed, "enhance their fortunes, sustain their freedom, defend their rights, and maintain their liberties." So as not to be misunderstood, the party repeated the development platform constructed for the previous legislators' election, including schools and universities for youthful minds, Indian subjugation, railroads and telegraph construction, and encouragement of agricultural-pastoral pursuits. The convention would foster "by all legitimate means" emigration to the territory to settle vacant lands, for prompting enterprise among the people (remaining blind to the negative impact such a demographic might portend for the nativos in terms of proportional power over the territory).

Santa Fe County submitted the nomination of José Francisco Chávez for delegate to Congress, and Heath moved his nomination by acclamation. Surely as a test of loyalty, Breeden moved that each delegate's name be called. The nomination was unanimous. Chávez had the "full faith and confidence" of the convention; he was the "true and unswerving Republican, worthy the support of all true Republicans." All "lovers of New Mexico" and all who had New Mexico's best interest at heart were invited to cooperate in his triumphant election.

Endorsed too was Breeden's resolution of "ineffable disdain" of Charles Clever, "the pretended delegate from New Mexico," endeavoring and in part succeeding "in imposing upon the loyal members of Congress as a Republican." Reflecting the American shadow-party's historical supremacy as far as Washington connections were concerned and the legacy of attachment to the South, the convention, following Breeden's lead, demanded that the Republicans control federal appointments following years of injustice in which corrupt demagogues were appointed to monopolize and control the government. "The majority of the people of New Mexico are Republicans," it maintained, "and the party is well organized here, and should be permitted to control the patronage of the government as a matter of justice, and as a measure of importance with a view to the future of New Mexico." After speeches by Heath, Breeden, and Sena, three cheers rang out for the Republican Party and Chávez.[31]

Russell, of course, denounced the "solemn farce" of the convention, Chávez's nomination said to be secured by no more than a legislative caucus, "small-fry politicians who forget nothing and have not capacity to learn anything." He described Heath "& co.," who had launched into "slang and abuse" of Governor Mitchell and Chief Justice Watts, as "about to retire from public, for the public good, under Gen'l Grant's administration." Soon, Russell forewarned, a candidate would be brought forward in sympathy with the people "who will represent their interests in all respects and who will be endowed with natural and acquired capacities to look after their welfare in the national capital. Around him they can rally with an enthusiasm worthy a good cause and a good candidate."[32] Russell accused Republicans of false Radicalism, not being truly concerned with the freedmen, and carrying on with peonage and Indian slavery in spite of the 1867 legislation that had outlawed them (actually, both were diminishing).[33]

Republicans no doubt hoped for the rise of an explicit Democratic Party. Beyond the desire for a system for dividing the political loaves and fishes more systematically, as Johnson had stated it, the establishment of a bone fide Democratic Party would hurt Clever's defense against the Chávez contest in a Republican Congress. It was a major obstacle to the realization of an accreted Democratic Party. According to the *Review*, a meeting headed by Diego Archuleta proposed a Conservative Republican Association of New Mexico. Territorial Councilman R. M. Stephens, calling himself an "undisguised" Democrat, reportedly would have no part in it. However, his recommendation that the name Democratic be substituted for Republican as their group title was unceremoniously rejected. In going back on their previous platform, the group was showing their weakness, Hezekiah Johnson noted.[34]

Russell at the *Gazette* would later deny that any suggestion of a Conservative Republican Party was contemplated by the Clever forces, and indeed it never formed.[35] What the *Review* called the "anti-Republicans" appeared organizationally crippled compared to the Republican appearance of unity.[36] Rather than raise the Democratic banner, Clever hatched the idea of Archuleta arranging passage of Stephens's bill for an April election, and once that was accomplished, Clever would go before a quick territorial nominating convention as "the People's [A]dministration candidate."[37] The *New Mexican* published a copy of Clever's telegram to Archuleta to the latter effect, Clever to be nominated as a "candidate of our people, supporting Grant's administration." According to José Manuel Gallegos, who was the new superintendent of Indian affairs for the territory now that Clever sat in the delegate's seat, Clever provided a definite course of action: "Our party is the people's party, endorsing and sustaining Grant's administration. We must be united—dissensions are detrimental to the interests of New Mexico."[38]

The *New Mexican* said it had never seen "a more precious piece of impertinence," its sole "upshot" to aid Clever against Chávez's contest. It would have meant a repudiation of Governor Mitchell, who had gone prominently to the New York Seymour-Blair convention, as well as of both Archuleta and Gallegos, who in 1867 had moved to Seymour and Blair and attacked the party they now sought to endorse, only to have "genuine Republicans turned out of office and disguised Copperheads and their political associates appointed."[39] More seriously still, assuming he would have supported it, Mitchell was not informed of Clever's plan in time, and so he vetoed the spring election measure. The Republican majority in the legislature, aware now of Clever's connivance, did not undertake to override the governor.[40]

The final nail in Clever's political coffin came shortly. On February 9—following two months of hearing the evidence, in which Clever's team threw at Chávez every pernicious name in the book—the bipartisan House Committee on Elections unanimously sustained Chávez's contest.[41] Chávez immediately telegraphed the news to the *New Mexican*, which published it the next day. The committee found the contestant's charge of fraud having prejudiced his votes in eight precincts greater than the irregularities committed on behalf of Chávez. The final count put Chávez ahead by a majority of 389.[42] Congress voted, 150 to 9, to assign to Chávez the delegate's seat for the Fortieth Congress from the Territory of New Mexico. He assumed it on February 20, ten days before Congress adjourned, eighteen months after the volatile election in question had taken place, and following one whole session in which Clever served as New Mexico's delegate to Congress![43]

National newspapers legitimated the decision. The *National Intelligencer* pointed to the "mockery of justice" in the time it took for the House to decide on election contests. The prima facie delegate usually sat out the congressional term, it was said, "even if he is wrongfully in place." The rule had been "grossly deviated from, for the purpose of ousting Democrats, and of keeping Radicals in place," although for the most part the cases were rarely decided until close to the end of the Congress to which the contestants were elected. The paper did not agree with Chávez's politics but understood that his case was disposed of "purely on its merits, undisturbed by any undue considerations, and without regard to political principles of the parties to the contest." It must have counted that Chávez was "a high-toned gentleman, sincere and honest in his opinions, conservative and temperate in his views of public policy, and worthy of the position to which dilatory justice has at last admitted him."[44]

"Tardy Justice" read the title in the editorial of the *Washington Sunday Herald*. Clever was elected "as a Democrat," it was noted, but had "studiously sought to win favor from a Republican Congress by conceding and often denying his party affiliations. Not content with this, he and his friends have not only denied the party standing of his opponent, but have sought to represent him as a rebel sympathizer, notwithstanding his service as the lieutenant colonel of a Union regiment." The "*quasi* Republican, *quasi* Democratic" Clever employed delaying tactics and made an "adroit effort" to call Heath disloyal, "as if the loyalty or the disloyalty of that gentleman had the slightest bearing on the question which candidate had received the largest legal vote." As the paper concluded, "the persistent pluck which has led Col. Chaves to prosecute his right to the seat has commanded universal respect, and added largely to the friends secured him by his uniform courtesy and fair dealing."[45]

The *Washington Chronicle* noted that as Chávez was a "native" of New Mexico, "our Mexican fellow citizens of the territory have naturally felt a deep interest in the contest." Over-generalizing the political views of the "natives," the editorial said they were afraid that "the circumstances of his nativity had stood as an obstacle in the way of his success," particularly as the election was characterized by "the most gross and flagrant frauds." The result, "achieved upon the law and the substantial merits of the case," would "happily avert such misconceptions," promote the confidence of "our Mexican fellow citizens in the impartial justice of the government," and "stimulate the patriotism ... already so handsomely manifested in their brave and successful resistance to the encroachments of the late rebellion upon the territory, in which Col. Chávez himself bore a patriotic and gallant part as an officer of the volunteer union troops in repelling the invading Texans."[46]

Interestingly, Chávez made the same point in an open letter of gratitude to the citizens of New Mexico concerning his friends "of Mexican nativity" who entertained apprehensions that the fact of his being "one of their race would be an obstacle in my way." As he reported, "the sequel has happily dispelled that illusion, and will give to them a confident assurance that impartial justice will always await their demands in the House of Representatives and the government of the United States."[47]

It is well to note that Clever did not advance the argument that his candidacy was prejudiced by false attributions of his being Jewish. The privacy of the voting booth assumed the right of the voter to register for a candidate for any reason whatever. The violation of Clever's personal civil rights would have been differentiated from the process of legally conducting the election. The legal understanding of personal rights at that time did not recognize the more amplified anti-discrimination or libel laws of a later time. The *Gazette* at first suggested that the decision was done out of charity to Chávez, later observing that his Republican affiliation was more important than the merits of the case.[48] Since Chávez men controlled all but three of the counties, Russell rationalized, his henchmen distorted the record of voting at the polls; moreover, he claimed, a dishonest man was imported to serve as the judge receiving testimony.[49]

Celebration dominated New Mexico's collective response to Chávez's re-ascendance. The *Weekly Review* noted the "sense of pleasure throughout the territory. People here about are expressing their joy with harp, violin, and guitar, song, dance and loud prolonged vivas!"[50] The heady spirit of a Republican Party soared. "¡*Arriba, Republicanos, arriba!*," the Bernalillo County Republican Central Committee shouted.[51] "Certainly nothing could have given us more pleasure, nor rendered the Republicans of this Territory more joyful," the *New Mexican* declared.[52]

"Col. Chávez and his friends and the Republican party in this territory, which elected him," the *New Mexican* declared in further jubilation, "stand vindicated before the world, whilst Clever, his partisans and party stand out before mankind disrobed, and presenting themselves in all the deformity that diabolical frauds, perjury, riotings and wrongs of every name and nature that could be perpetrated in an election can invest them with."[53] Propagandists of the binary exulted in seeing Copperheads, the Democracy, Mitchell, and Clever depressed, disgraced, and totally, utterly demoralized.[54] Reiterating the many charges of fraud and then some, the *New Mexican* queried to what end the Copperheads and their "tools" could resort to such infamy? "Why, simply that Clever might sit ignominiously in Congress for a few months and draw a few thousands from the public treasury?" The inquiry allowed: "What a grand achievement for so many partizans! What a noble result! For this little thing men have forfeited honor, manhood and dignity; some have even risked their soul's salvation. Now witness the grand result: Clever is whipped out of Congress like a disgraced spaniel he is, and his friends must share in his disgrace. Well, let them; they deserve no better fate; they made up their issue— they are beaten; now let them, one and all, share Clever's defeated fortunes." Justice had been "leaden heeled," the weekly concluded, but in the end it had served Chávez and the Republican Party of New Mexico, "and we are satisfied."

The victory had particular resonance for Nuevomexicanos. In the words of a *grito* from the community:

Long live happy Nuevomexicanos
Chávez triumphed in the federation
A vote of grace was given to the Republicans
by the members of the [House] committee

Vivan alegres Nuevo-Mejicanos,
Chaves triunfó en la federación,
Voto de gracia, dan Republicanos.
Aquellos miembros de la comisión.[55]

Another mocked saddened Democrats:

Our cause is lost
our party fallen
and our boss has been
defeated in the certificate

Vuestra causa está perdida
De caído vuestro partido
Y vuestro caudillo ha sido
Derrotado en la partida.[56]

Resplendent viva parties held by Chavistas and Republicanos adorned Albuquerque and Fernandez de Taos.[57]

The resolution of the Chávez contest stimulated a wave of Republican sentiment in the midst of another election season. Citizens expressed their pride in being Republican—"*¡Soy Republicano ahora, sí, que bueno es eso!*" (I am Republican now, yes, how good that is). They relished the combat with Democrats, like José Manuel Gallegos, "*admiradores de Seymour y Blair.*"[58] A verse from a self-described humble Mexican praised "*Querido Francisco Chávez, Amable republicano, Verdadero Mejicano*" (Dear Francisco Chávez, kind Republican, true Mexican).[59] In Bernalillo County, Manuel García, president of the County Republican Committee, called a self-designated Republican nominating convention to deal with the special election required by the resignation of the probate judge.[60] Nestor Montoya (a name to become a staple in the Republican Party across two generations) became the Republican candidate. Both the *Review* and the *New Mexican* stamped his opponent, the venerable Ambrosio Armijo with the epithet Democrat. Montoya's win in a hard contest was called a glorious triumph of Republican principles.[61]

In Taos, the county Republican Party held a formal meeting in the central site of Don Fernando, run almost entirely by Nuevomexicanos. The respected merchant Juan Santistevan announced the gathering's main purpose, to celebrate Chávez's victory in Congress against his opponent Clever and to take into consideration the party's nomination of him as the Republican candidate in the September election. It was a sign of how far the national Republican agenda had infiltrated this Spanish-speaking corner that the Taoseños resolved it to be their "cordial desire" to see their "master Union reestablished under constitutional principles, that we once again unite in harmony as one people, made equal by bonds and sentiments of fraternity, identical with our interests, so that our glorious republic in the grand march of progress of the nation take a place of pride, that it always remain the guide of liberty." Upheld were the "organic bases" of the Republican Party founded on "solid principles, to perpetuate the American Union and assure the fidelity of the great American people, disseminated from the Atlantic Ocean to the Pacific, and crowned with the laurels of loyalty and fidelity to the perpetual Union of the United States."

The Taoseños did not neglect the Radical belief in the equality of all "men," with no distinctions of race or religion, as a "natural right." Inter-mixing a Mexican political trait with modern liberal doctrine, they declared dedication always to sustain "this inviolable equality of the human race that Christianity and civilization clearly showed, that all men had equal rights and privileges before the law, and should enjoy them as the fortune of the splendid blood of the American soil, to establish them in New Mexico, when the fathers of the Independence fought to tear the hard chains of European despotism."

Faith was vested in the president, the "grand soldier of the century," to give an administration of peace, economy and impartiality, protecting everyone, such that the United States return to raise itself to the "apogee of its happiness." Yet did the effects of the Romantic constructions in the late election remain. The convocation recognized that their party respected true Democrats, "men free to hold their opinions," but rejected those who came "imitating *Judas Iscariote*, pretending to be Republicans to feed their ambition for public positions, supporting Gen. Grant after his election after they had defamed him." The invitation went out to all honest men, "of sane intention," whose views promoted the well-being of the territory and the perpetuity of the American Union. Speeches followed by Santiago Valdez, Pedro Sanches, and House Representative Juan Francisco Montoya. William G. Blackwood gave a history of the political parties in New Mexico, alluding to the evil cause of Clever's party, and the just cause of the Chávez party. This being the first time Blackwood associated himself with a party in New Mexico, he revealed that his "impartial experience" was finding the Republican Party the best for the well-being of New Mexico.[62]

Taos Republican energies culminated in a special election for the precinct of Peñasco's justice of the peace and constable. Two recognized Republicans were nominated, the Chávezite Rafael Chacón and Juan de Reyes Martín, and two explicitly called Democrats, Miguel Griego and Esquipula Fresquis (a peculiarly New Mexican surname?). Griego reportedly said he would not accept a single vote of a Democrat. He opposed the principles of the Democratic Party, he announced, shocking the Democrats who thought he was their candidate. According to the correspondent filing the report, the voting went smoothly, resulting in the election of the two Republicans. The triumph in a precinct that had always gone Democratic prompted the raising of a flag inscribed "*Progreso Unionista Republicano.*" Don José de la Cruz Leyba, a former Democrat, and a band guided a parade. Passing Chacón's home, the crowd burst out in vivas for the Republican Congress, the president, his cabinet, Colfax, and Chávez. An *americano* bumped into the procession and he joined in, throwing his hat in the air with vivas in English for the Republican Party. The band played; everyone got drunk with enjoyment, harmony, and liquor; the crowd launched into a dance at the home of don José A. M. y Medina; *señoritas* danced, no less happy than everyone else.[63]

The defiant *Gazette* had no regrets, for there was always a future. "If there be any virtue in the people," Russell surmised, the whole thing will be rebuked at the coming election . . . the day of retribution is not far distant and we are confident that the indignation of the people will be dealt out in no measured terms."[64] Spanish-speaking citizens on his side posted calls for the people to open their eyes and elect a better caliber of men to the legislature so as to make good laws and recognize that those who composed the tiny minority were "loyal and worthy of public confidence."[65] In Taos County a famous member of that minority, Jesús María Pacheco, taunted in an opinion piece his county's Radicals, their alleged self-serving machinations at home and in Santa Fe. Outraged Republicans sparked three indignation meetings to demolish Pacheco's charges.[66] Other critics kept the indictments of the "Radical party" coming in letters, essays, and literary forms. They accused it of being anti-American in the conduct of its criminal justice courts.[67] It was putting on the airs of an anti-American oligarchy.[68] Chávez was called a sell-out to the railroad interests of Colorado that wanted to keep New Mexico out of its track circuit (the reasons to become more clearly evident).[69] The *Gazette* piled attacks onto the Republican legislature, accusing it of wanting to create a slush fund for itself with the sale of county property.[70] This prompted the *New Mexican* to defend the members, highlighting the corruption of the "Watts-Collins-Gazette clique, like their protégé, Clever."[71]

It was an impressive mobilization, yet no party name appeared in the early election season to signify the organizational challenge to Chávez. An initial spurt focused on Clever as the basis for a rally. Russell recommended that he be renominated for being one of the most "successful," "industrious and attentive" delegates New Mexico ever had.[72] Rank and file Nuevomexicanos followed suit. One open letter signed by sixteen individuals commended him for countering a racist screed back East that defamed their people.[73] However, the *Gazette* came to see how the contest drove Clever out of the electoral field.[74] The *New Mexican* described him on "a wide sea all alone, no party to belong to, no party to sustain him."[75] The rico Felipe Chávez of Belen in Valencia County and Antonio José Otero, the Kearny Supreme Court justice, received mention as possible challengers to Chávez.[76]

Republicans nominated Chávez for delegate in January, but their opponents would not hold their territorial nominating convention until July. The latter met on a regular basis up to then but did not explicitly adopt the Democratic Party or even a People's Party title, as Clever had proposed. Not all of the faction's veterans participated; among those absent, quite critically, was José Manuel Gallegos, whose work as an appointed superintendent of Indian affairs may have kept him too busy.[77] The *Weekly Review*, where the new editor in place of Hezekiah Johnson was John Symington, kept the paper tied to the Republican

Party and delighted in referring to its opponents as the "Elements" and the "Party of the Elements," based on a report in the *Gazette* that referred to the elements of its political faction.[78] One Republican pundit writing in Spanish smeared them as "conservative Democrats."[79]

With mounting pressure to hold a nominating convention, the collective morale of the anti-Republicans was shaken by the murder of its American Party pioneer, James Collins, in a robbery by unknown assailants. A tributary poem to Collins appeared, the author calling himself a Nuevomexicano friend of his.[80] The death of Collins was followed closely by the passing of the other founding American Party stalwart, Merrill Ashurst.[81] Both had conducted two decades' worth of work on behalf of the political development of New Mexico, proving important agents for realizing the territory's binary process with certain results for Nuevomexicano political incorporation on what history determined as the unfulfilled basis of sectional distinction.

Two names finally surfaced in early and mid-July, one each from the Río Arriba and the Río Abajo. Vicente Romero was the powerful probate judge of Mora County. A successful farmer, merchant, and miller, Romero was no high-class rico, for he had risen from what one observer described as having "but few of the 'worlds goods'" to become independently prosperous. Romero's qualification for membership in the American Party stemmed from contracts he had with General Carleton's military industry. He had been a friend of Judge Slough and had helped lead his county's opposition to H. H. Heath.[82] The *Gazette*'s endorsement of Romero emphasized the fact that he was a native of the territory, "well and favorably known throughout its limits for his intelligence, enterprise, culture and capacity for the discharge to the progressives in New Mexico and has at all times been ready with his means and his personal assistance to advance our material welfare whenever opportunity has presented itself." A bouquet praised Romero for having withdrawn his name for delegate to Congress at the 1867 Union Party Nominating Convention "for the purpose of securing that harmony of action which was necessary to ensure the success of the ticket."[83]

According to *Rincón* (one from the village of the same name), the nomination of Romero was received throughout Taos County with great satisfaction "by all the friends of progress." Rincón's effusive recommendation claimed that a more energetic, "public spirited and honorable citizen" did not exist in the territory. Romero was furthermore "highly esteemed," a "most worthy gentleman polished in his manners, and a practical and fine speaker." The nominee had devoted a great portion of his time, "and no small amount of means, to the prudent advancement and general benefit of the people in the County of his residence." He was "emphatically a self-made man; and so much refinement in such is not often to be encountered. Our interests could not be confided to better or safer hands," Rincón assured. The two major factions in the territory had been competing over which one was the best for advancing the people's well-being. Much of the contention turned on the Manichean binary of virtuous liberals versus "vile" creatures. Rincón carried on with the distinction. Romero possessed "indomitable energy," it was said, the kind of man needed "in our present neglected and unprotected condition, and I am certain his nomination would be hailed rejoicing by a large majority of the people of our unhappy territory, who are anxious to wrest from the hands of the enemies to progress, the management public affairs, which they have so shamefully abused." The commentator called for a convention at the earliest possible date for the nomination of Romero, "and the organization of the campaign, for we are losing very valuable time."[84]

José Antonio Otero, the old conquest generation veteran who had served as one of Kearny's Supreme Court justices and had been spoofed in the anti-Semitic farce of the Grand Oracle, served as the potential candidate from the Río Abajo. Otero consented to have his name brought before the nominating convention. He was hailed as "precisely the right man for the right place in the right time," who would undoubtedly be the choice "without division of sentiment." Otero was choice Río Abajo rico. The *Gazette* did not fault him for it, as it did José Francisco Chávez in the race against Clever. After retiring from the bench, Otero resumed his vocation of ranchero and merchant "and never for a day lost the esteem of his neighbors." As a member of the council, elected frequently from Valencia County, as longtime probate judge and private citizen, "he was always honored by his peers for his sound wisdom, unimpeachable impartiality and humane and charitable qualities of heart."[85] It was the turn now of those from the Río Abajo to rally around a homeson to challenge Chávez. One adherent emphasized Otero's "clean" and "unblemished" record since New Mexico was made a territory, "one of the oldest and most beloved inhabitants . . . native and to the Manor born." He would be the one to oppose Chávez's "ruinous policy" that led to the murder of citizens "with impunity" (Slough), to people's flocks being driven off without regret (since Carleton's descent), and to the pampering of Indians living with cash donations on imaginary reservations.[86]

At what was called in lower case letters the "convention of the people"—presided over by José Manuel Gallegos and Diego Archuleta and with only seven of eleven counties represented—both Romero and Otero were nominated. Jesús Ma. Pacheco of Taos did the honors on behalf of Gallegos. Archuleta was advanced by the old Bernalillo County rico Felipe Perea. Romero won in the meager count, twenty-nine to nineteen. Romero accepted, overcoming his prior reservation about the nomination. The convention platform stood opposed to Chávez for representing "incompetent, dishonest or time-serving representatives" (Republicans in the legislature) and for advocating statehood for New Mexico. It called as usual for the advancement of the material development of the territory and increases in federal troops to help combat the "savage enemies." Whereas some Clever supporters had tended to excuse peonage and Indian slavery as fine institutions, this group recognized their abolition as "wise and humane" and called for the victims to be placed as "independent and dignified laborers, a class of citizens that contributed largely to the wealth of all countries." In a related circumstance, the national Democratic Party at this moment of decision failed to provide participants with a model inspiration on which to stake a party identification. As a result, the convention invited "all lovers of their country, without distinction of party," to unite in the support of the convention's nominee. As the *Gazette* explained, the convention developed its platform "eschewing entirely party politics."[87]

Whereas the *Gazette* had praised Otero's sophistication, it now stressed Romero's humble origins, born "without the advantages of those who dissented from a wealthy parentage," making his way through "life's battles." It was an obvious contrast to Chávez's privileged background, said to produce "stagnation and inactivity of business in all its branches." Romero's charity to those less fortunate received attention. "No man, woman or child in distress ever appealed to him for assistance in vain," Russell noted. As he followed up, "At times when in the dispensations of Providence the counties of Rio Arriba, Taos, and San Miguel were deprived of their usual harvests, and large numbers of their people reduced to the greatest straits to obtain the means of holding soul and body together, Mr. Romero's granaries were thrown open to their relief, and, according to our information, none who were unable to pay him after the stringency passed off, were ever reminded him of the obligation they were under the him." Those in the know could recognize the implied credit going to General Carleton. Russell added, "All these people will now remember [Romero] when they can do him a favor at the ballot box, and will undoubtedly be the steadfast friends of his election to the most honorable position within their gift."[88]

Romero emphasized in his letter accepting the compliment of the nomination that he had not coveted the office and its responsibilities but would support the principles of the convention point for point. He specified without concern for its possible colonial consequences support for the arrival of "industrious and intelligent persons" to advance the territory's progress. True to his faction's ambiguous state of identity this time around, he decried the divisive effect of "party" for the private and public raising of "sectional questions," a point he could afford to make, coming from the northern part of the territory that had not received equal billing in candidacies for delegate to Congress.[89] The *Gazette* felt that the letter showed Romero a man of the people, so unlike the professional politician who held the seat. Chávez's conniving "class of men" only resorted to keeping themselves in power "and thereby enrich themselves from the money of the public treasury." In a distinction thought to carry significance, Romero would have "distant capitalists" invest in the territory.[90]

The *Weekly Review* suspected in the convention's no-party politics a trap to get the territory's federal officers, presumably Radicals, to oppose Chávez. Symington said its effectiveness remained to be seen, although it would not prevent an overwhelming majority of votes going for Chávez. The editor figured that the anti-Republicans would have captured some of Chávez's "warmest supporters" had they adopted an "out and out Democratic platform." There were many men who had hitherto voted for him, he said, and would continue to do so "until there shall be a regular Democratic nominee."[91] Symington saw the need for formal parties, otherwise territorial voters would think that political oppositions were based on personal squabbles, which was the way Washington viewed New Mexico. It was precisely to meet this objection that the Republican standard was raised in the territory, he argued, so that those who believed in the party's principles could "rally beneath its patriotic folds." Symington perceived the challenge being posed to those who opposed the Republican candidate to reorganize a Democratic Party, but none "dared pick it up." Instead, as he put it, a convention "without the name, that gave no names to the party it endeavored to establish, has put in nomination . . . candidates in opposition to the regular Republican nominee; and that is all!" The heads of the national government could not be blamed for thinking that the territory's elections reflected mere personalism, "but it was not the fault of Chávez or the Republican Party of New Mexico."[92]

The *Review* predicted that in going with Romero against Otero, the no-party convention would sacrifice a large number of votes from the Río Abajo. The answer provided by *Zurriago* stated that the anti-Chávez men would have "gloried" in an Otero candidacy but that the delegates to the convention understood that his frail health might impede his ability to conduct the duties of delegate that "his heart and love of country demanded." He asked his fellow citizens from the Río Abajo to unite behind Romero. Why would they not, he wondered. Their candidates who had come from that section had received the "cordial and effective" assistance of those in the north. Now that one of theirs from the north had been nominated, Zurriago asked those of the south to "destroy the ruinous politics of the opponent and elect a man who with honesty should represent us." Chávez had been the instrument of the demagogues with "accumulating lying promises" and had "trampled on everything, *¡Patria, amigos y deber!* [Fatherland, friends and duty!]." The "free people" of the territory, "as an intelligent people, as a people possessed of a love for [their] *país* [New Mexico as much as the United States] and [their] fellow citizens, as a people who desire the advance of [themselves], should reject with dignity the fabulous voices that try to put in play anything to obtain their unjust ends."[93]

In 1855 the two candidates for delegate had struck contrasting cultural profiles. The Mexican Partyite in that contest, José Manuel Gallegos, appeared the medieval rustic with social peccadilloes. Miguel

Antonio Otero, his sophisticated opponent, conveyed urbanity, an acculturated American Party dandy. A parallel theme sounded in 1869 but with the party associations reversed. Mexican Party heir Chávez was described as a "talented, well-educated gentleman, with an untarnished reputation in private life."[94] The American Party leader, Romero, came off the overweight, virtually illiterate, and rough-edged ranchero with few of Chávez's acculturated refinements in spite of his backers' adulating characterizations of him. Romero himself fed the portrait. In a message to the citizens of the territory, he admitted that it was "very hard and arduous" for him to address them "because I am not one of those men who has received a great education and who are posted in all classes of scientific matters." He admitted that he was "of New Mexican descent who has never been out of this my country; here I was born, here I was raised, here I hope to live until the supreme being calls me to judgment." Significantly reflecting his personal isolation, Romero called the political parties that "agitated" the United States an "incomprehensible mystery," with which he would never mix himself.

Republican propaganda snidely suggested that someone else had written the "manifesto" because Romero was not educated enough to do it himself. Romero was said to have confessed to being an "ignoramus and corrigible dolt," his not having "as much book learning as the generality of Alburquerque schoolboys of 14 years of age." The *Weekly Review*'s flourish said that in a government like the United States, where power is derived from the people,

> and whose executive and legislative powers are composed of men whose official actions are regulated by the popular will, it is the pride and duty of citizens to inform themselves, to the extent of their capacity, of our system of Government, and of the various matters of government policy, the adoption or rejection of which is influenced by their action at the ballot box; and these are the matters which Romero, aspirant to a seat in the Congress of the United States, emphatically declares are to him, and always will be, 'an incomprehensible mystery. Therefore, fellow citizens, I am best qualified to represent you!!!' That's decidedly cool.

Chávez, by contrast, was a scholar, who studied medicine, which provided a profession, calculated to make him a practical thinker, speaks and writes fluently and correctly the language used in the legislative, executive and judicial transactions of the United States, and is in every respect qualified to creditably representing Congress the constituency of any district of the United States. Saying thus much affords us the greater pleasure, for the reason that Chávez is a native of this territory to whom all, without distinction of race, owe the highest appreciation and respect, as well on the account of the education which adorns his intellect as for the judgment and impartiality with which he makes it serviceable."[95]

Norberto Saavedra, the new Spanish-language editor of the *Weekly Review*, ironically bashed Romero's limited English, wondering how the candidate could be expected to carry on "in the glare of Washington" speaking "before the wise and illustrated Congress." No such problem existed with the "extraordinarily" talented Chávez, Saavedra assured, who had more influence in Washington than any other delegate who had represented New Mexico.[96]

Jesús Ma. Pacheco addressed the issue of Romero's language and education in a speech at a Mora meeting, exclaiming from Smith's "traditionalist" perspective: "It was not good English nor scientific wisdom that had procured fortune for the territory, rather, the work of experimental and mature men, as in the time of Hon. J. M. Gallegos, who obtained better advantage for the homeland than any other of his standing [*No son ni los buenos 'ingleses,' ni los sabios científicos los que han procurado la suerte del territorio, si no los hombres experimentados y de madurez, como nos sucedió en el tiempo del Hon. J. M. Gallegos, quien ha dado y procurado más ventajas al paso que ninguno otro de su mismo rango*]." Such was the sort of man the convention of the people now offered to the people of New Mexico, he clarified, "without trying to advance scholastic titles [*títulos escolásticos*], nor an accomplished linguist, but a self-made man and who had experience in all the vicissitudes of the human life." Reflecting the changing binary field, Pacheco railed against a new "foreign" element the Chávistas had brought into the territory, who cared nothing for the people of the territory, and against the legislature, of which he was a recent member, selling public lands for their own uses and increasing the per diem for themselves. Here Pacheco implied not only Breeden and Heath, but a recently arrived group of business types beginning to have a major influence on Nuevomexicano politics and fortune, as we shall see. Pacheco promised an all-out dedication to getting Romero elected, and he hoped for help from the people "unanimously without party distinction [*sin distinción de partidos*]."[97]

As the compressed campaign intensified, Chavistas made the pointed argument that only a valid Republican, nominated by a regular Republican Party, upholding the doctrines of the national organization, could hope to gain the legal and appropriation advantages New Mexico required in a Republican Congress. Sending a delegate who was not in harmony with the administration was fruitless, they argued. "It may not be right, it is true," the *Weekly Review* observed, "that party has much to do in getting any good measure adopted. All parties are alike in this, and we must take things as we find them, and not as they ought to be. It is more frequent that a member of Congress asks how a measure will affect his party than how it will affect the people." Without Chávez in Congress as the standard bearer of the Republican Party of New Mexico, the effect would be "obvious to everyone. He can then appeal to the majority on party grounds and secure a hearing at once." The delegate had no voting influence, "and what he gets for his people is due to begging. It is therefore necessary that we should send our delegate armed with all possible advantages. There is no organized political party in New Mexico except the Republican Party. You cannot call a party that which is 'no party.'" As the convention that had nominated Romero refused, "or at least failed, to attach itself to any party" he was not therefore the "candidate of any party." He was a "set-up man" for a clique, "merely to oppose Col. Chávez" as a "purely personal" contest. It made sense for true Democrats who advocated for party principles to help elect Chávez.[98]

As an indication of a fuller Republican spread, some in New Mexico apparently did not adhere to Radicalism, and some felt they were not within the inner sanctum to receive patronage for supporting Chávez. They would be voting for Romero or not voting at all. For them the *Weekly Review* attempted loyalty enforcement as any operative party would, belittling them as "political sneaks," defining them as "an administration man" who could not "swallow the platform of the party." The political sneak sacrificed party principle, doctrine, and the welfare of the people for "purely selfish motives," Symington philosophized. He was seldom found in the "old Democratic Party," for its members always called for the devil and "swallow[ed] the platform, even if some of the planks are a little rotten." But there was no regular organized Democratic Party in New Mexico "because the sneaks pulled the wool over the eyes of most of the leaders of the Democratic [P]arty in this territory," while the rank and file "refuse to be hoodwinked."[99]

No sooner had the *Review* queried the whereabouts of the two hundred "hard shell" Democrats who "vauntingly swore" the previous winter in Santa Fe that they would fight under none other than the old, "time-honored, Democratic flag," than the important Santa Fe County Nominating Convention, run by Nuevomexicanos, declared itself the "People's Party of the County of Santa Fe."[100] One wonders whether James Collins, Merrill Ashurst, and Henry Connelly would have encouraged an explicit Democratic Party identification. In any case, this people's party swore to defeat the new Republican Pino-Ortiz show running the county and allegedly using county funds and levying taxes on merchants for their own retention, and, in a healthy move, it called for a system of open bids for county contract work. It "heartily endorsed" Vicente Romero and the platform of the convention that nominated him.[101]

At virtually the same time, the Santa Fe County Republican Party held its nominating convention. Participants reinforced "national Republicans," as they put it, adhered to the "time-honored principles of Republicanism and to the organized Republican Party of the Union," to the Chicago national Republican platform, and the principles adopted by the territorial Republican convention that nominated Chávez. Confidence and trust were devoted to the patriotism and justice of President Grant. Only true Republicans would receive the convention's support for elected county offices, while the pledge was issued to renew "warfare" on the "old enemy, the Democratic party, which, whilst it has become too weak in this territory to bear the burden of odium that attaches to its name, nevertheless, [noted in order to bestir the electorate] still retains all its prurient and malignant hatred of Republicans and Republicanism unchanged." A hearty welcome went to William A. Pile, "a true and reliable, energetic and competent patriot and Republican," who had just arrived to replace Robert Mitchell as New Mexico's governor. The steely José D. Sena was renominated for sheriff and Trinidad Alarid for treasurer.[102]

The three weeks from the Santa Fe County People's Convention to election day were stuffed with English and Spanish editorial and citizen propaganda, local conventions, and public meetings but hardly a stump on either side. The Chávez organs opined confidently. The *Weekly Review* recalled the Clever party frauds of 1867, including those that the contest testimony suggested were committed by the then Mora County Probate Judge Vicente Romero, "the chosen standard bearer of the honesty party."[103]

The *Gazette*, throwing a wet blanket over the proceedings, said the convention demonstrated Republicans seeing the writing of a Romero victory on the wall. Russell accused Republicans of preparing to "over slough the will of the people" as they allegedly did when Secretary Heath awarded Chávez a certificate of election and stacked the polls with their corrupt men as precinct judges. An indomitable will, ordered by certain federal appointees, would have its candidate go to Washington no matter how large the majority by which the voters had elected its opponent.[104] Russell pressed on with some of the wearisome old charges against Chávez and his party, including his alleged "antipathy to all classes of Americans"; his fake Republicanism meant only to draw favor with the administration; and his anti-American "great liking" for peons and Indian slaves, the prerogative of his rico class. The Santa Fe probate judge would not "manipulate" the Clever party out of its majority, Russell guaranteed, as he did in the last election.[105]

Veritás attacked the "black Republicans or Radicals" as a foreign imposition, representing the "enemies of the homeland" with their politics "pernicious to the interests and advancement of a free people." The pundit unloaded on William Breeden. Breeden allegedly called Nuevomexicanos *cabezas cobriza* (Copperheads); he stole the money of a Nuevomexicana pensioner; and failed to take up a "single arm" in defense of the country when it faced its greatest peril. Returning the style of attack hurled previously at Clever, Veritás pleaded, "Until when, people of New Mexico, will you allow yourselves to be guided by the lies of people like Wm. Breeden who has no other principles than money and who, for this metal, will sell New Mexico as Judas did with his master?"[106]

In the zigzag debate, *Un Espectador* (A spectator) admired the organizational strength of the Republicans as the thing to value, "Republicanism so well raised in this land," which only an "imbecile" could not recognize properly. "You could well be Democrats," Un Espectador challenged Chávez's opponents, but if so, they should "present the principles of that [D]emocracy to the public suffrage." Without the arms of principles for their supporters to help them, the people could only consider their politics those "of caprice or superfluous and dangerous ideas."[107]

The entire legislature was up for contention this election. In the nature of the partisan imperative, the Romero party fixed on the Republican-dominated legislature as a special enemy flank. The issue of taxes and what the *Gazette* called the "disgraceful condition" of the territorial finances loomed large. If taxes were to be levied, the *Gazette* proposed, safeguards for honest collection needed to be instituted. As it was, "loose sheriffs," acting as collectors, tended to encourage corruption, leading to a reduction of the revenue that properly should go into the treasury. Laws were needed to make the collectors "strictly responsible to the territory for the monies that they may collect from the taxpayers and from fines posed by the courts for the public benefit," as Russell defined it.[108]

The newfangled term "fusion," landing from the political discourse of the states, was used to characterize the combination ticket of Republicans and People's candidates in Valencia County. The *Weekly Review* warned of the trap into which its friends fell "We do not believe that the Democrats will stick to the bargain that secured the fusion," Symington wrote, "which was that the county should go in a body for Chaves."[109] The news of another fusion ticket in Socorro County to support Chávez elicited no comment from the editor. It formed because it was believed that Romero would draw few if any votes in that county, and it was a way of getting some People's and dissident Republicans elected.[110] Much the same was said about Valencia County, where in Cebolleta don Román Baca and Padre Rafaél Chávez came out strongly for Chávez.[111]

The tickets for county offices went heavily contested. In Santa Fe County, the *Gazette* accused the Republican county officers of the previous six years of "corruption most foul." The dynasty needed to be broken for reform to take place, Russell stressed. No one knew what became of the money that went into the county fund. Transparency in the collection and expenditure of incoming funds was sorely missing, according to the editor. There should have been a surplus in the county treasury, but no one knew for sure, nor was there even a "lame apology" given for the officials' inability to report on the county finances. The idealistically rendered remedy was to be found in the election of the candidates on the People's ticket, all of them pledged to reforming the abuses of which so much complaint was made.[112]

Almost defensively, the *Weekly Review* could not urge too strongly on the Republican Party of Bernalillo County the necessity of nominating "good men," "strong men in influence," especially for territorial council and representatives, as questions would arise in the legislature that would require "able men to sustain the interests of the Río Abajo." The "live men" that the party nominated were established in the county Republican circles: William Henry Henrie for probate judge, Nestor Montoya for sheriff, and Harry Whiting for treasurer.[113] In the changing population of Grant County, all nominees for territorial and county office were Euroamericans, including William Rynerson for council.[114] Nuevomexicanos organized People's tickets in the various precincts where the justice of the peace became a hotly contested position.[115]

At 6,572, the turnout of voters was 8,195 fewer than in the general election of 1867. As the *Review* maintained, the "immense" confidence of the Chávez men meant no efforts were made in most of the precincts of Bernalillo County. As Symington generalized,

> The people of New Mexico, with few exceptions, expect to be personally solicited for their votes, and we doubt if half the voters of this County was spoken to about the election this year. No public meetings were held except the nominating conventions, and no effort was made to arouse enthusiasm; so the people, thinking that their votes were not needed, did not go to the polls in their full strength. The apathy of the Democrats induced like feelings on the part of many Republicans.[116]

The *New Mexican* offered a different explanation to the effect that the opposition slackened its efforts based on Chávez's obvious strength throughout the territory.[117]

Chávez took 64 percent (4,228) of the territorial vote. As expected, San Miguel and Valencia counties went hugely for him, with a majority of more than 1,800 in the former and 1,100 in the latter; Bernalillo came in strongly (over 800), with Santa Fe, Doña Ana and Grant registering handily for him. A severely ruptured Taos County gave Chávez a bare majority of 160. Romero won his own Mora County by a whopping 1,409 majority and took Río Arriba County by 562 and Colfax by 373, while a virtual tie occurred in Lincoln County.[118] The *New Mexican* called Chávez's victory a "noble triumph for the Republicans of the territory" over the frauds committed by the opposition in 1867.[119]

The *Weekly Review* questioned the significant tally for Romero in his home county of Mora with its thick record of frauds in 1867, gladly reporting that there was "no necessity of ferreting out the frauds of the Romeroites this year."[120] The *Gazette* thought much the same regarding the unexpected majority of 200 for Chávez in Santa Fe County, attributing it to the futility of the amended voter registration process. While the law was good, in New Mexico its execution was vested in "political knaves whose reputations can only be preserved by a perpetuation of their lease on the public office in the prevention of exposure that would follow a change." At the end of two more years of misrule and abuse of power," the weekly proclaimed, "the voters of Santa Fe County may be ready for the reform that is now demanded."[121] People's correspondents reported irregularities in the counties of Río Arriba, Socorro, and Valencia, although not to the extent that they would have affected the outcome in the race for delegate.[122]

The combination ticket worked in Socorro County. While voters went for Chávez, the elected councilman and probate judge were Republicans and the balance were "Democrats or no party men" (six of the seven being Nuevomexicanos). The *Review* commented that Chávez would have preferred to lose the county "than to have had his friends beat." Those friends who voted for the Romero ticket to gain votes for Chávez could have the consolation of knowing that they were not thanked for their efforts, for Chávez was the "very soul of honor; and if his friends fall, he is willing to fall with them." It was known because Chávez had sent his brother to Socorro to break up the combination. They were not successful, "although they warned the persons interested as to what the result would be. We hope to hear no more 'bargain and sale' transactions by any member of the Republican Party," Symington expressed.[123]

The People's Party suffered heavy losses in the big county races. Republicans practically swept Santa Fe County. Even the popular José

Manuel Gallegos lost for treasurer. In Bernalillo County, "scarcely any opposition," and certainly "no organized opposition," went up against Republican nominees for county offices. Republicans took eleven of fourteen precincts in justice of the peace races, all Nuevomexicanos.[124]

The organization of the Republican Party, set against the lack of it in the People's Party, best accounts for the results. Yet Russell could only express incredulity at the lopsided figures, noting according to his partisan wont that no political principles were involved in New Mexico elections. The key lay in the fact of the "one family of the Río Abajo" that assumed to furnish the "only fit material for candidates for delegate to Congress." As Russell saw it, this clan, "through its accumulated wealth and extensive relationship," exercised "potent influence," especially in the counties of Valencia, Socorro, and Santa Ana (which saw unbelievable majorities for Chávez), "and controls their votes to suit its own purposes." It made little difference to the rico family whether their candidate was competent or incompetent, as in the present case, Russell argued. They spent money lavishly to secure the vote, influencing the outcome in a way that the candidate could never do "through his own merits." Russell looked forward to the day when the family's crafty dominance would no longer control the political destinies of the territory for their own interests. The people desired it, he affirmed, for the day was not far distant when they would act independently of the influences that "now so closely hamper the majority."[125] In this whole kibosh, the editor neglected to mention that he had previously gone with two others from rico clans, Miguel Antonio Otero and Francisco Perea, and so the question would have been whether they had purchased their victories as well if the problems of domination and corruption were so congenital in that whole class.

Precursor de la Justicia (Precursor to justice) tended to agree with Russell, stating in Spanish that "the peonage of D. José Leandro and his rich collaborators triumphed over the vote of free men." The writer called on the men of Santa Fe and the northern and eastern counties, as well as the "peons" of the Río Abajo to "step on" the "philanthropic" family dynasties that confounded their interests. Precursor observed the importance of youth among opponents, "the most aggressive in the territory." Education had elevated them (an implicit nod to Bishop Lamy's parochial school in Santa Fe). The partisanship here considered the possibility of an attraction welling among the rising men of the territory to the Republican excitement in the country. As it was, Precursor said he himself would gladly have identified with "an Otero, a Perea, a Chávez, an Armijo, with an Yrizarri, with a Luna, etc. etc.," were it not for the politics of bossism involved. "If peonage does not dominate in the elections, we are free," he observed, "and so free, we shall enter into the field of leadership [en la lid]."[126]

The true fault resulting in Romero's defeat, the *New Mexican* argued, was the fruitless attempt of the Democracy to recruit Republicans to vote against Chávez. Chávez proved too strong in his party "to enable them to secure the required aid in the schematic plan, and, finally, the demoralization became so great in the ranks of our opponents, that when they held their convention they could secure no man of respectable talent or position to assume their candidacy for [C]ongress."[127]

Harry R. Whiting, the old Mexican Partyite who replaced Symington at the helm of the *Weekly Review* (when the latter went into medical practice) pointedly noted that Chávez had taken all counties but one where the "American [Euroamerican] influence" dominated. As such, his enemies could not endeavor to "poison the ears" of members of Congress by saying that Chávez was "a bitter enemy of all Americans." Chávez now had his opportunity to advance all the improvements desired "in a civilized community," and if the rule-or-ruin opposition threw no stumbling blocks in his way, he would undoubtedly succeed. The editor challenged the opposition on the charge that the people of New Mexico "were ignorant, knew nothing of politics, and could be easily deceived." The enemy had tried "all sorts of dodges," Whiting stated. "Romero was, to some, a no-party man, to others a Republican of the darkest dye, in Colfax County he was a sure-enough Democrat. But the people were not so ignorant nor could they be deceived. The Republicans saw through the shams, and stuck to their party, and many Democrats, disgusted with the trickery, voted for the Republican nominee. Hereafter, we expect and desire an opposition here based on national party principles," Whiting concluded.[128]

An anonymous Nuevomexicano, writing in Spanish and noting Russell's "melancholia," reversed the charges. It was actually the *Gazette* that represented the *politicastros* who always showed their "debility, attributing their defeat to whatever and all cause but the legitimate one." There were indeed "national politics" involved in the election, the opinion went. The "disposition to cry over the power" of the family of the Río Abajo was misplaced and "absurd," as shown by the fact that two from the same family went bitterly against each other in 1865 and again in 1867, when the family was divided between its favorite son and Clever. The People's Party lost because of the demoralized state of the Democratic Party and its inability to organize prior to its belated nominating convention with the assistance of non-Radical Republicans. When they finally met in convention, they could not "assure themselves of a man of talent or respectability to demonstrate his ability as a candidate for Congress." Though it was sure to be denied, the Republican element appeared "frightfully strong to the [D]emocracy of today. . . . We had the votes; this is the real reason which the *Gazette* should honestly have announced, as the great cause of the Democratic defeat and on which this press and its friends are so without hope." The pundit called the *Gazette* and the "old Democratic party of New Mexico . . . dead politically."[129]

It is understandable why the citizen made this prognostication. However, it proved to be wrong. Democrats took a step backward in their organizational imperative in the election of 1869. The election season of 1871 would find them more than making it up, and from an unexpected quarter with surprising results.

CHAPTER FIFTEEN

Realized Political Parties, 1869–1871

Republican strength hung prominently over New Mexico after the 1869 election. José Francisco Chávez was elected by a Republican Party "*per se,*" went the boast. A proven Republican held the governor's office. William A. Pile was a former Union major general in the Civil War, recruiter of blacks for the Union Army, and former Radical in the Missouri House of Representatives.[1] A Republican majority prevailed in the territorial legislature. Its members appreciated Pile's first message to the assembly. Harmony produced important legislation in the session of 1869–70, a property tax law in particular. The Grand Army of the Republic rambled on.[2]

A Republican press surged in the territory. The *New Mexican* carried on in Santa Fe as the official Republican organ, but William McGuiness replaced the *Río Abajo Weekly Review* in Albuquerque with the *Republican Review/La Revista Republicana*. Moreover, an important crossover occurred in the *Weekly Gazette*. Declining health forced owner-editor John Russell to leave New Mexico shortly after the election.[3] For some fifteen years he had sustained and shaped the territory's binary partisanship as a swashbuckling constitutionalist. No Democrat stepped in to take his paper. A Republican, A. P. Sullivan, the new territorial collector of internal revenue and a native of Michigan, bought Russell out. The departed James Collins surely turned in his grave. The operations of his *Gazette*, after some eighteen years as a propaganda machine for the American-Democratic Party would serve his old arch enemy. Sullivan changed the name of the paper to the *Weekly Post/El Correo*, and he hit town with a gang-busting Radicalism, calling for the rights, liberties, and privileges of the people, "irrespective of race, color, or creed," to be maintained and unequivocally supported by the Fifteenth Amendment.[4]

No less than six Republican papers appeared elsewhere for various durations. In the booming mining area of Colfax County on the

Colorado border, two Republican journals sprouted in Elizabethtown (the *Telegraph* and the *Argus*) and one in Cimarron (the *News*). Las Cruces briefly hosted the *Río Grande Gazette*. The *Acorn/Belota* appeared in Las Vegas.[5]

New Mexico Republicans began looking like their national counterparts. What that meant lay far from a rose-tinted unity among themselves. Any hope for President Grant to bring the Republican Party together was dashed within weeks of his inauguration. Grant was drawing fire from within his party by the time Chávez received his certificate of election in September 1869. The president clashed with Congress over repeal of the Tenure of Office Act. Grant's potential to be president had appeared on the back of Andrew Johnson's resistance to the act. Radical Senator Charles Sumner led the U.S. House and Senate to defeat Grant's attempt at repealing it. Grant retaliated by refusing to remove Johnson's appointments, depriving congressmen of their pet patronage. Dissension ran through a series of administration scandals, including a Wall Street fiasco that led the Republican Congress to scrutinize Grant after he single-handedly caused an investment panic and held off Democratic attempts to nail him.[6]

New Mexico Republicans could do no better, although their internal cracking reflected no simple mime of national issues. Some political scientists argue that a state-level party experiences factionalism when it faces little competition from a rival party. Others argue that intra-party factionalism is provoked by aspirants challenging established leaders to secure influence, power, or a nomination.[7] Both conditions helped shape the Republican contour in New Mexico. In due time, New Mexico Democrats would find in their national party the inspiration to coalesce organizationally.

A Fresh Republican Face

Proper protocol, if not common courtesy, should have guided a Republican newcomer with leadership instincts to ingratiate himself with Santa Fe's Republican establishment. The old guard would have welcomed A. P. Sullivan, or so it later said.[8] It hardly got the chance. The *Post* kicked off "very independently," as its editor boasted.[9] He focused on some personal differences existing between certain members of the Republican Party in New Mexico, the result being "an effort to maintain two 'wings' hostile to each other, and each one claiming to be *the*

Republicans." Sullivan denied the rumor that his paper was being used to represent the interests of one faction. He declared himself independent of "all cliques," an advocate of principles and not serving "private ambition or the gratification of private spleen."[10] Sullivan implied a "certain ring of demagogues," misrepresenting and maligning others, hanging about Delegate Chávez, another sitting in opposition to him.[11]

Sullivan shied from naming names at first. In the background lay an important addition of personnel to Republican command. A crop of aggressive Euroamericans had for a year been setting up in the territory. Lawyers mostly, they included W. W. Griffin, S. B. Wheelock, James L. Johnson, and most centrally Stephen B. Elkins and Thomas Catron. Elkins and Catron were both from Missouri and longtime friends, even though the former fought with the North and the other with the Confederacy. Elkins was already a Republican, while Catron became one upon arriving in New Mexico. Together they took the path of high-stake capitalists and financiers who were beginning to exercise disproportionate power in the national Republican Party.[12]

In New Mexico such Gilded Age Republicans had just established the territory's first bank, in alliance with Nuevomexicano elites José Leandro Perea (Chávez's uncle), Manuel A. Otero, and Francisco Manzanares.[13] These businessmen played something of a waiting game as New Mexico's land came under survey in anticipation of the railroad, which portended lucrative investment possibilities.[14] Their circle of mutual support increasingly included J. F. Chávez. Catron was "earnestly recommended by the leading Republicans" for district attorney, the *New Mexican* revealed. While the weekly usually deemed anyone who served the rebel cause an enemy of the Union, it authenticated the Republican credentials of Catron alongside Elkins.[15]

Sullivan denied the rumor of his including Chávez in a clique and still did he lay a threat on the delegate. "In reference to the recent election," Sullivan delivered, "I claim that you [Chávez] were the Republican candidate and your success was a triumph of Republican principles. Hence, I, through the *Post*, will support and defend you in your every act consistent with the principles on which you were elected. But," Sullivan flexed with the political muscle of a nineteenth century newspaper, "if ever you should prove false to those principles, I will lash you as vigorously and mercilessly, as though you were but a Ward Constable or even a dog."[16] This order of invective belied the promise Sullivan published in introducing himself to New Mexico of utilizing "respectful and dignified" language, to refrain from "vile epithets, and black-guardism upon our opponents."[17] He betrayed it again in relation to another Republican quarter, the territorial assembly. Members were to him "unprincipled, dishonest old drones," who, rather than support a "proper" tax to develop the territory, preferred a "rotten system of taxation" to protect and exempt their accumulated wealth.[18] Sullivan blamed ricos who, he said, "killed every public measure intended for the dissemination of education," preferring to see the people in "poverty and ignorance... the cause of the prevalent immorality" of idleness.[19]

Establishment Republicans moved swiftly and succeeded in getting Sullivan removed from his federal post. It was, the *New Mexican* editorialized, a "very just thing." A most serious offense concerned lack of party loyalty. In four months he had "totally disgraced" the government and the Republican Party in the territory, it was charged. Sullivan allegedly threw himself to the Copperheads, including his predecessor in the collector's office, which he staffed with Democrats only, leaving it as it was before. The *Post*'s policies had the effect, if not the intent, of dividing the Republicans, the *New Mexican* indicted, leading readers to infer "that the millennial day for New Mexico was at hand; that her apostle, her reformer and her saintly friend had made his advent.... All that was old and time-honored, everything that existed, even to the Republican Party that had, under its specific organization, won two hard, severely contested battles with the Democracy—all these were to be swept away in a moment in this new light." In moving in to "disjoint and divide" the Party, critics held, Sullivan aimed someday to "elect a conservative, mongrel ticket, with all its mongrel adjuncts." Even his Spanish translator was a Copperhead "of long and good political standing," the bill of charges included.

Sullivan sinned against the Republican press. The *New Mexican* had him acting as if there had never been a "decent" newspaper in the territory. His paper would be "the very inner Temple of Simon-pure Republicanism." There would be "no personality, no slang... nothing but the pure and simple truth, independently, though decently told, through the columns of this sanctified '*Post*.'" Sullivan instead made "a low and scurrilous, false attack" on Chávez, it was charged. He acted as if no Republican party existed in the territory, and "he was to erect one. There were no Republicans in New Mexico—he was going to create some!" Sullivan was binaried thoroughly. His editorial attack on the Republican Irish Club of Pennsylvania was said to have been carried out in terms "more befitting the vulgar habitué of a brothel, than those dictated by one who had ever possessed the first scintillation of a gentleman."

Sullivan was damned for criticizing the president. He reportedly "fulminated the most atrocious doctrines" against Grant's order for the military to establish peace treaties with tribes, advising "wholesale slaughter of them, without discrimination, wherever to be found by any person; and evidently with the intent of arousing hostilities between whites and the Indians within this territory, which, if carried out, as advised, would 'ere this have drenched the territory with the blood of both whites and Indians." There was also Sullivan's alleged acceptance of a note to purchase a printing plant from whiskey distillers, reflecting a "most unpardonable ignorance" on the proper relations of a federal officer with the government and the people. Sullivan's personal character came in for it. Rather than pursue "anything like a course of moderation," he exercised the "power to abuse." The *New Mexican* advised the public to deny him the respect of an editor who had a "hypocritical pretense" to be a Republican.[20]

Sullivan denied everything and affirmed that he had done his duty "fearlessly" as both collector and editor. "We are too young, too strong, and too much of a Republican to surrender our manhood for our independence and for an office," he claimed. He had "too much respect for ourselves and our party to associate with, or be governed by a ring of demagogues, composed of drunkards, debauchees, and convicted felons." He said "before ever seeing New Mexico" he had defended the right to advocate Republican votes, "to protect ourselves against a mob of cowardly traitors, with our revolver in hand." Misrepresentations made in Washington effected his removal as collector, Sullivan argued. When the interior secretary and the president learned the facts, they would not "consent to be guided" by them.[21] Sullivan accused a few men calling themselves Republicans of receiving him by recommending for one of his clerkships a man who had been prosecuted for "swindling a widow," a swipe at William Breeden and his legal dispute over a widow's estate, adding as a reason for not hiring Breeden his alleged dishonorable discharge from the military. Sullivan said H. H. Heath had recommended Breeden. Heath's notoriety made Sullivan suspicious of anyone he would recommend. He hired a Democrat because no one else would accept the low paying position with its travel costs. He was an "upright, honest man . . . a loyal man," who never participated in politics, the editor explained.

Sullivan furnished affidavits to show that his interest in the *Post* was under no pecuniary obligation to a whiskey distiller. While he did not reveal the endorsers of his note, he averred that he had no hesitation in publicizing his business affairs and exposing the falsehoods of the "cowardly scoundrels" who had published the charges against him. He had urged people to "shoot down every Indian who was caught on a marauding expedition" but called for the kind treatment of "peaceable Indians." Sullivan denied advising the slaughter of Indians but said there was "no humanity" in sacrificing "useful citizens to the base and brutal passions of those Indians who were not peaceable. . . . Neither is it sustained by the laws of God or man." Sullivan had neither time nor disposition to answer the charge that his weekly was not Republican. He responded for the benefit of those outside the territory unaware of the rationales of the "professed Republicans" in New Mexico. No one else wrote, advised, or suggested copy for the *Post*; he hired shop men for their mechanical skill, not their politics; his competent translator had never written a line for the *Post* other than a translation of what appeared in its English columns.

Sullivan accused Heath of authoring the attack on him. He rehashed the story of Heath attempting to gain position in the Confederacy. Sullivan would not "condescend to notice" other authors. "They live a life in utter violation of the laws of civilization and Christianity," he ascribed. "Their appearance at any public meeting, or any decent society has yet to be made in Santa Fe. From the whiskey shop and the gambling table to the dens of their concubines is their routine in society. Poor wretches, they deserve pity," he wrapped up.[22]

A nonplussed territorial legislature and the National Republican Association came to the side of the *New Mexican*. "A Republican legislature very well understands the difference between a spurious, pepper-and-salt Republican journal," the *New Mexican* testified, "and its old and tried friend of years gone by."[23] The association decreed the *New Mexican* its official paper, describing it as worthy of the confidence and patronage of New Mexico Republicans, for it had "manfully fought the battles of the Republican Party against its enemies, through every crisis, and ha[d] boldly enunciated the true principles of our party, without fear or reward, and further, that it is the only recognized exponent of the Republican Party in New Mexico, that no other paper, professing Republicanism in New Mexico has any other object in view, save to divide and distract the party, and restore the Territory to the hands of the opposition." The *New Mexican* noted the honor of this message coming from "the *Party* of this Territory," which was "not a *local*, but a *territorial* Association." The "most prominent Republicans, both American and Mexican, in the Territory" belonged to it. More than three-fourths of the members of the three last legislatures did too, the "ramifications" extending to "every corner of the Territory."[24]

Sullivan kept the *Post* working on behalf of the Republican Party undeterred and as he saw fit. The option of defying Republican honchos from within the party was thus inaugurated.

Intra-Party Strife in the Statehood Revolution

The big political story in 1870 involved an effort to make New Mexico a state of the Union, in which Nuevomexicanos stood at the forefront. Legislators talked at start of the 1869–70 session of calling a convention to draft a state constitution for submission to Congress. José Leandro Perea, J. F. Chávez's uncle and a major political patron, expressed in a letter to José Manuel Gallegos the hope for such a convention, urging Gallegos to drum up support among the people in the north. Statehood would fend off the territory's "miseries" and meet its necessities, Perea reinforced, which reflected his new partnership with Gilded Age Republicans. The "responsible" tax law just passed by the legislature would make Congress see how ready New Mexico was for statehood, Perea argued. The time was ripe, for their people were already "breathing the air of the nineteenth century, epoch of equal rights for all creatures of God, age of the telegraph, a time of railroads and of prosperity for the future generations," old Donaciano Vigil incarnated. The scheduled census would help by showing New Mexico's population at 125,000. Other territories were becoming states and moving beyond territorial representation, Perea pointed out. True, citizens back east thought Nuevomexicanos "ignorant, miserable... unable to govern ourselves." Shown the truth, those "miserable enemies" would support justice for "our people." Perea and Gallegos belonged to opposing parties. The former asked the latter to forget "all spirit of party and of race" so as to receive "in a day not too distant, the blessings of heaven."[25]

Two days after Perea dated his letter, a special legislative committee drafted a state constitution for the consideration of voters. "Thoroughly republican in form," as the *New Mexican* hailed, it stood on a bill of rights, a prohibition on slavery, and a declaration of loyalty to the Constitution.[26] The Fifteenth Amendment, removing race or color as a qualification to vote or hold office, was endorsed, and the standard division of powers among executive, legislative and judiciary branches was observed. Limits were placed on the legislature's ability to issue loans, pass exorbitant taxes, and create or foster monopolies.[27] The committee proposed the first Monday of October for voters to endorse or reject the constitution. If approved, they would elect the state's first legislative, state, and federal officers. The legislature passed the constitution and the call for an election, and Governor Pile signed both. The constitution was printed in Spanish and English in mid-March and sent to probate judges for distribution. The *New Mexican* encouraged all who believed in statehood to study it carefully.[28]

Concurrently, Delegate Chávez, remaining consistent on this score, introduced into Congress an enabling bill to authorize the people of the territory to hold a convention to form a state constitution. Some of its principles were covered in the territorial legislature's constitution. Chávez relayed his optimism to New Mexico concerning the bill's chances of passing in the U.S. House.[29] The bill appeared at odds with the territorial legislature's action, however. Chávez's measure was altered to provide for the submission of the legislature's constitution to the people for confirmation rather than have them construct a new one. The legislature's statehood committee called for a June convention in Peña Blanca to familiarize delegates with the constitution and prepare them to canvass their respective counties to convince the electorate to vote for the measure in October.[30]

Republicans got to the business of pushing for statehood. The *New Mexican* called arguments against it "trifles light as air," propagated as the mere "utterings of the sore heads" and a "few disappointed politicians who feel that they are not properly appreciated, who have lost positions gained by election frauds, or have failed to get some place desired." The old complaint of high taxes was "rel-

FIG. 29. *Don José Leandro Perea*, ca. 1860, ink wash drawing, artist unknown. A wealthy, modernist Bernalillo merchant and an uncle of José Francisco Chávez and José Francisco Perea, Perea was a significant behind-the-scenes patron of electoral politics in territorial New Mexico who never ran for office. Courtesy Palace of the Governors Photo Archives, NMHM/DCA, negative #050560.

ative and conditional," it was said, for they would purchase great wealth and population, railroad construction, land for schools, colleges, and internal improvements. The time had come to "hail the heroes" of statehood "with music and song, with acclaim and shouts of triumph."[31]

Touchy questions involved the relations between the two main population groups. A fear arose of statehood giving Nuevomexicanos the opportunity to impose "the same oppressions and wrongs" that had been and were being inflicted on the people of Mexico. A Euroamerican state advocate answered that New Mexico would be prevented from becoming like a Mexican state by the American republic's "personal liberty," a spirit to "foster the interest and protect the rights of the whole people." To this writer, republican government wielded the power to mold public virtue in anyone. Objectors to statehood were asked to show a single instance of the people not "animated by their connection with the union as a state—a single example of the admission of a state that has not been followed by prosperity, increase in wealth, population and power."[32]

A commentator going by State denied that statehood would allow Mexicans to exercise tyranny over Euroamericans. On the contrary, he affirmed, Mexicans exercised good will. Experience showed nativos not "half as proscriptive as those calling themselves Americans," State observed. Mexicans used their freely given votes to elect "Americans. How would it be if the 'boot was on the other leg?' Would Americans be as liberal to Mexicans? Yet what reasons have those calling themselves Americans given to the Mexicans to gain their confidence?" New Mexicans had done more in aiding "and sustaining Americans here than the circumstances required or than the Americans deserved." The fear of a "few rich Mexicans" ruling the new state did not hold. "Ever since I have known New Mexico this same charge has been made of a few men ruling the territory," State observed. "Is it more so here than anywhere else?" State denied the canard of Nuevomexicanos incapable of full citizenship. Nativos attended "well to their own business," made money "in all legitimate modes practicable here." They did themselves credit in the positions entrusted to them, compared favorably with others, and were "proverbially honest." "Brilliant talents" were not found in New Mexico, State admitted, yet "talents of that kind never aided France, or any other country in sustaining itself as a Republic.

What is necessary is but love of liberty and an affirmed determination to have and keep it," something the "natives of New Mexico possessed in as high a degree as any other people in the world."[33]

Public virtue aside, a particular objection to statehood turned on the proverbial American view of Nuevomexicano indolence. *Jornada,* a Euroamerican, queried as to why the people of New Mexico remained dormant, "waited for capital and enterprise to come from abroad to develop her vast mineral resources and garner the harvest for aliens to the territory." It was a question not easily answered. "If there are any who can solve the problem we would be glad to have them 'speak out in meeting,' and enlighten us on the subject." New Mexico had been part of "Uncle Sam's domain" for twenty years and its "great mineral wealth" known for more than a hundred years, Jornada observed. The critic beheld the placers near Santa Fe, which "were once prolific sources of wealth, but through the want of enterprise in our people they have virtually lost sight of the buried treasures in the hills of Galisteo." So many riches in their midst, yet "our people stand listlessly by, with their hands in their pockets, and see strangers come in and snatch the lion's share from their very fingers. The remark is often made, that if men and capital from neighboring states and territories did not develop our mines, they would remain unworked for years to come."[34]

G. W. O. from La Junta made a modernist comparison based on what the Anglo-Saxon race had established in New England and what a "band of hardy Spanish adventurers from the South" created in the "rich valleys" of New Mexico. "Almost simultaneous with the conquest in the New World the prestige of Spain began to decline," the tale went, "her colonies shared her fate, and for a period of two hundred years her people have made no progress in the arts and sciences of the world; the same implement that Cain used six thousand years ago, was adopted by the Mexican race in their agricultural pursuit upon American soil and yet to this day, a forked stick and a team of cattle make ready the soil for the reception of the seed." Living "in the old time style, taught them by their forefathers," none of the energy and enterprise that characterized the "present generation of Anglo Saxons" appeared in Mexico. The New World colony gave birth to "that spirit of freedom that rebelled and threw off the English yoke, and laid the foundation for a Republic, under liberal laws and institutions." Colonists turned to agriculture, manufactures, the arts and sciences, "and the grand result is manifest to all." The spirit of enterprise rode westward on the "star of Empire, spanning the continent with railroad and telegraphs, [driving] the Buffalo from its native haunts, [climbing] the Rocky Mountains to the northward of us, and are looking down upon unprogressive New Mexico, hesitating whether they shall come among us or not, lest they become contaminated with that torpidity that seems to paralyze enterprise."

"With but little increase of population in the territorial form of government, but dismembered from the dead trunk of the government of old Mexico, and grafted into the live trunk of the American Republic," G. W. O. figured, "we must seek a change of affairs or be forever doomed to our present lethargic chains of unprogressive thralldom." On a stimulus notion of improvement, the writer had statehood compelling "giant strides of civilization and progress." New Mexico needed to get ready for a coming mass emigration. "Our fellow citizens, the Mexican population, cannot do a better thing for themselves and their posterity than to vote in solid phalanx for the new state movement," G. W. O. emphasized. There were "numerous men, as of the Mexican class of people, of good abilities and fair education, who have seen much of the world, and who feel and appreciate that a change of some kind is necessary." They would prove important "in the coming contest for a state government."[35]

The Albuquerque Republican legislator Benjamin Stevens charitably pointed out that the Mexicans were conquered. Not only did they not speak English; they were unaccustomed to a "liberal mode of government" due to their exploitation by the Mexican government. In the United States they misconstrued the "liberality" of Congress, believing that it meant a duty to provide for all their wants, maintenance, and support. They therefore "took little care for themselves." Only recently were efforts made to lead the people from this "delusion." Yet with limited funds, leaders looked on New Mexico "as we look upon an indolent relative of a wealthy family, who chooses rather to live on the charity of his kinsman than to labor for his own support, when he is well able to maintain himself." Mexicans had the duty to vindicate their character, "remove this cloud from our atmosphere, and show, not only to the states of the union, to all the world, that we are willing and ready to support ourselves." Currently, Stevens argued, "scarcely a son of New Mexico was in office, save those elected by the people." So far as they had been permitted, "they have done as well as the people of any other territory," shown by the laws they passed comparing well with those of any state. The claim of Mexicans not fit for statehood came from Americans "with bad grace." If Mexicans, after twenty-five years of intimate association with Americans, were not sufficiently educated in the festivals "of our government, it speaks ill of American character influence," Stevens argued. He had no intention of exciting "one class against another," and did not believe such a feeling "ever existed to any great extent in this territory," offering as proof the Americans elected "by the votes of Mexicans."[36]

Advocates contended with outside anti-Mexican prejudices. The *Post* noted that since the beginning of the statehood discussion, it had been "almost impossible to pick up an exchange from the states which does not oppose our admission on the ground that people of this territory are ignorant. Few of them are just enough to give our case an impartial hearing, or take more than a surface view of our condition."[37] The *New York Tribune* said New Mexico should not become a state until it showed it had shed its tradition of peonage "in law and in fact." The *New Mexican* took umbrage at the presumption of New Mexicans disobeying the law as unjust to the officers who had been sent by the Republican administration. Peonage in New Mexico did not exist, Thomas Tucker claimed. The old system of slavery bequeathed to New Mexico by Mexico was "totally abolished, both in law and in fact." The territory's Republican administration was "strongly opposed to any form of slavery," and "if a single case of peonage—involuntary servitude—might be discovered, they would be prompt to enforce the law against it." The recently framed state constitution prohibited peonage and slavery, and so Tucker hoped the New York paper would extend "its powerful influence" for New Mexico statehood.[38]

Sullivan countered eastern biases with some anti race-colonialism of his own. The American acquisition of New Mexico was made with the full knowledge of her condition, he observed, "and that of her people. They were a conquered people, brought up under foreign institutions and speaking a foreign language. They were immediately required to obey the laws and support the institutions of our country. We required them to become American citizens, but never educated them in the duties of American citizenship. The people of New

Mexico are denounced for being ignorant[;] well they are denied the means of becoming otherwise." The Mexicans were not so ignorant "as to be unable to discriminate right from wrong during the late rebellion," Sullivan continued. "They spilt both their blood and their treasure for the national defense, and they had paid their share of the national taxes without a murmur."

Sullivan, backed by Radical race-liberalism, inveighed like an old Mexican Partyite. He said the great mass of the people of New Mexico were "not near so dishonest, inhuman and vicious as a heartless, soulless mob of all kinds of vultures who lived in our namesake's [*Chicago Post*] moral city." Assuming a colonial subjection, Sullivan had "No people. . . ever so much belied" as the people of New Mexico:

> They are generous, kindhearted, hospitable to strangers, and strictly obedient to the laws. Probably no people in the union, of the same in number, scattered over the same extent of the territory, and so debarred of all the privileges of the age, would make so good at showing, and have so small criminal history. Nearly all of the vices that do prevail were brought by Americans who were outcasts from society and came here to escape its vengeance. They were perceived as Americans, treated kindly and met with open doors and opened virtues. They found care in their sickness, home in their banishment, and plenty in place of poverty.

In turn, "many, too many" of the new arrivals robbed and ruled New Mexican families, "and after a sufficient time had elapsed to make it safe, returned to the states." They misrepresented those whom they had wronged and "gave our high-toned contemporaries food for future abuse of New Mexico." Nuevomexicanos blamed Congress for the ignorance and lack of public schools prevailing in New Mexico, but the newspapers that abused the people, misrepresented them, and censured them were not blameless for opposing statehood. "Let New Mexico for once have her hands untied," Sullivan begged. With the right to control their own affairs, New Mexicans would guarantee "that a change for the better would soon be seen."[39]

Sullivan's invitation to American historicity appeared fine to Nuevomexicanos. La Sociedad Progresiva de Las Vegas lauded him for standing up to the "atrocious accusations" of the *Chicago Post*. The organization honored Sullivan's "heroism, frankness . . . virtuous determination... [and] benevolence." He had "solemnly toasted" a people who had assumed "without complaint" the laws imposed on them and who were quick to shed their blood "when the hostile enemies assaulted our government." The "noble and generous spirit" of the editor would "live immortally" in the sentiments of Sociedad members. New Mexico's "capable people" needed to embrace Sullivan's sentiments, la Sociedad invited. Sullivan was asked to republish his essay from time to time.[40]

Republican statehooders decided to hold a more immediate planning meeting. A cordial invitation went out to Democrats with stress placed on the need for nonpartisanship, just as Leandro Perea had posed to José Manuel Gallegos in starting the movement. The rational choice of Republicans to join with Democrats stemmed from the fact that many Republicans opposed statehood, while many Democrats favored it "warmly."[41]

To loyal Republicans who had been feasting on combative polarization with Democrats, the bipartisanship in the statehood movement smelled bad in principle and practically. As *Amigo* put it, "It is believed here that the State movement has come to its death at the hands of its professed friends. Does anyone expect that the present Congress will admit a new state that is not thoroughly Republican in politics? If such there be, then there is a degree of credulousness existing beyond my comprehension." The real purpose of the Peña Blanca convention, it was feared, was to give Democrats some of the major offices of the new state. "Democrats were horrid things six months ago in New Mexico to the very persons who agreed in Santa Fe to call the convention of both parties to nominate State officers," Amigo observed. "Let New Mexico knock at the doors of Congress for admission as a State with any other than a clean Republican ticket and a clean Republican record," Amigo stressed, "and she will be rejected just as sure as the existence of the great national Republican party." To maintain its good name the party must reject the "both-party" convention, call another, "and nominate a full ticket of known Republicans."[42]

The defensive *New Mexican* clarified the meeting as not meant for a "general fusion" of the two parties, "much less to give up any distinctive feature or principle of progressive Republicanism." Prominent citizens "of all parties" would consult on the best interests of the people and make arrangements for a thorough canvass of the state question, the paper stressed. The distribution of offices was a "minor consideration" to be arranged "satisfactorily without difficulty." According to the weekly, the public welfare and material prosperity of the people were "of far more importance than the distribution of a few offices." Even if New Mexico assigned all federal positions to Democrats, Republicans in Washington would not reject statehood. The key requirement was a Republican constitution without slavery, without which the proposal would be up for partisan assessment in Congress. Amigo erred, Tucker concluded, in forgetting the importance of education under statehood. Squabbling over offices "for one or two years" was important only insofar as "competent and faithful men" would be needed. "Then," he concluded, "the other great interests are the matters upon which the canvass should turn."[43]

The Republican leadership may have regarded its party as powerful enough to afford a bit of bipartisan magnanimity. But the suggestion sounded like a stunning concession within a momentum of institutionalizing party duality. Sullivan, stepping in to keep some semblance of binary polarity alive, seized on the "swindle" of Republican interests in allowing Democrats to cooperate in the state movement and be given state offices instead of "competent and faithful" Republicans. He squinted at the "cowardly" *New Mexican* selling out to the Democracy. The *New Mexican* pointed out that the "pert young man" who edited the *Post,* and was assumed to be the leader and advisor of the Republican party, was at the meeting where the Peña Blanca convention was planned; he had sat beside the most prominent Democrat, Diego Archuleta; "they both made speeches and the said editor voted for the resolution calling the convention, and tendered his personal services and the services of his paper to aid in the canvass, as proposed at that meeting." He had no right to complain about "retaining Democrats in office." Tucker admitted not being at the meeting that proposed the Peña Blanca convention but had faith in the "good Republicans" who proposed it, those "far more competent than the editor of the *Post* to promote the interest of preserving the purity of the Republican party." They would assure a solid Republican delegation in Congress and a Republican state administration and would "not stoop to wrangle about the minor offices." The suggestion of the *New Mexican* going over to the Democracy was "unworthy of even contempt."[44]

The February 26 meeting was large and "earnest," if the *New Mexican* reported faithfully. Grand speeches proved citizen determination to have statehood. It was also impressively bipartisan. A bulk of Republicans (Kirby Benedict, Stephen Elkins, R. M. Stephens, Anastacio Sandoval, Thomas Catron, Tomás Cabeza de Baca, William Manderfield, Thomas Tucker, A. P. Sullivan, J. L. Johnson, Lehman Spiegelberg, José Leandro Perea, Ira M. Bond, Antonio Ortiz y Salazar, Vicente García, and Governor Pile) joined in "unity and harmony" with a chunk of Democrats (Diego Archuleta, Adolph Guttmann, Jesús María Pacheco, A. Seligman, C. P. Clever, Gaspar Ortiz y Alarid, Fernando Delgado, and Francisco Baca y Sena).[45] Republican José D. Sena called the proceedings to order, and Democrat José Manuel Gallegos served as president. Gallegos reinforced the cross-party slant. It had been his good fortune to have presided at many public meetings, he noted, "but never have I seen together so much of the talent, the respectability and wealth of our territory represented as on this occasion, an occasion which is fraught with so much interest to us. This is not a party meeting. All are in favor of a change and any change in our local condition will be a change for the better when it is worked in harmony." Seven speakers played up the statehood cause.[46]

Action items stayed consistently nonpartisan. Remarkably, a preamble chastised both the *Post* and the *New Mexican*, the first for its opinion that the Republican Party in New Mexico was capable and had sufficient power to proclaim a state government "without the necessity that the Democrats cooperate in the measure"; the other for saying that the Peña Blanca convention would guarantee only Republicans for top state officials, relegating bipartisanship to the "positions of little importance." Just as Amigo and Sullivan feared, Santiago Baca's resolution provided that the major state positions be "divided equally" among Republicans and Democrats, each party to decide its representatives to fill assigned positions so long as individuals were qualified according to the constitution. Cooperation was requested of the Santa Fe editors, for the measures conformed to the desires of the people, "who are interested in the future growth, progress and advance of the territory of New Mexico."[47]

The scheme would have broken the back of the territory's partisan imperative. *New Mexican* editors did not see the resolution as introduced. The idea of Democrats and Republicans sharing the federal and top state offices put them in shock. Calling the decision "hasty," they "unqualifiedly" dissented against going into any movement on a bargain over the division of offices. Nor was it necessary for unity. They knew some who had dissented but said nothing "as they were not willing to disturb the harmony in the meeting." The paper had José D. Sena swear in a letter to the editor that Governor Pile himself had recommended against the equal sharing of political offices under statehood after Sullivan had accused the governor of doing nothing to stop the resolution, and it assured that Elkins, Judge Ortiz, and others would back this up.[48]

The *Post* and *New Mexican* quarreled quite as if they represented opposing parties over whether the fusion resolutions were adopted in haste and without discussion.[49] Amigo rejected a fusion of parties that were "diametrically opposed to each other in principles, for the sake of office." A fusion for a Fourth of July celebration, "or for a *baile* at Knapp's [hall]," would be all right," but national politics should have nothing to do with the state movement, Amigo averred. "Democrats and Republicans can unite harmoniously for a state, or against it," Amigo posed, "without compromising opposed Republicanism and Democracy," who could no more fuse than "oil and water."[50] The third press voice, *Republican Review*, opposed any fusion "or Alliance inconsistent with the integrity of the Republican Party of this Territory." William McGuiness of the *Republican Review* moved away from what he defined as a movement propagated by persons interested only in themselves.[51]

The bipartisan statehood executive committee next thought it best to shift the planning convention from Peña Blanca to Santa Fe. It asked all who favored adoption of the constitution to hold local conventions to select "prominent and influential citizens" as delegates to the June convention "without distinction of political creed."[52] These plans changed because the U.S. House Committee on Territories agreed to sponsor Chávez's enabling act. Chávez associates (Arny especially), and sympathetic newspapers (including the *New York Tribune*, which reversed its position on the issue), and the chair of the Committee on Territories considered the chances of passage strong to certain.[53] The executive committee decided to put the June convention and October referendum on hold until Congress's final action, particularly as the act called for a November election of delegates to a convention to frame a state constitution.[54]

It proved fatal to the statehood proposition. The Senate frustrated Chávez's efforts by refusing to accept the bill, recommitting it to the House Committee on Territories. The measure was at the same time changed to recommend the organization of the territory of New Mexico into the State of Lincoln. No one in New Mexico understood why. It appears to have been a ploy to assure a thoroughly Republican state if there were to be one.[55]

The *Post* saw the death of the bill for this session or its indefinite postponement, blaming the fusionists' badly written constitution. The dissenting *New Mexican* called it very much alive, evidenced by the fact that it was read twice and ordered printed. Because Congress viewed it favorably, its passage before adjournment "was now reasonably certain," Tucker held, especially with Chávez's extensive work on it. No need to fret over changing "New Mexico" to "Lincoln"; it was probably unimportant what name the state should bear, "and if we must lose the name our territory now bears, it is a noble name that is proposed for us—that of our great and good martyr president."[56] Sullivan saw the bill sinking at the hands of the "lobbying and shystering course peculiar to some congressmen." In addition to the "illiterate and disgraceful pamphlet which was printed by the *New Mexican* and circulated as a Constitution," the enabling bill became unpopular, he claimed, "because of the treachery, imbecility and incompetence of the *New Mexican*, and of the so-called Republicans who agreed to divide offices equally between little parties." New Mexico must adopt "an intelligent" Republican constitution and put up a Radical Republican ticket "on a radical Republican platform," the maverick hailed.[57]

The press argument continued for considerable additional column inches. Sullivan claimed to know better what statehood was all about and boasted of his part in exposing *New Mexican* "treachery." Tucker hit on the "young Hibernian" for his impertinence.[58] Sullivan proved more adept at reading the political cards in Washington DC. The statehood issue barely lingered into 1871 as a fissured Republican Party entered the election season.

Opening the Electoral Gates

The statehood controversy kept the Republican Territorial Central Committee from carrying out an early election campaign.[59] Its call for an April 29 territorial convention to nominate a candidate for delegate to Congress came out the first week of March. The *New Mexican* explained that the call came from "a majority of the old Central Committee after full and careful consultation with the leading Republicans in different parts of the territory."[60] Some wondered why no names appeared as committeemen. McGuinness remained optimistic. "We have never yet seen the Republican committee composed of men who were ashamed to sign their names to calls for party conventions," he said, "but notwithstanding the informality of the style of the call, we believe it should be responded [to] by the 'Administration party of New Mexico.'"[61] Republicans considered their chances excellent, based on the fact that Democrats put forth no tickets in the 1870 council and house elections.[62]

Out of the blue the recharged national Democratic Party provided the spark for an imposing territorial initiative. The legal questions engendered by Reconstruction were well nigh settled by this time. As one historian puts it, "Even the former Copperheads . . . saw that the party could not continue to fight the Civil War."[63] What did rise on the national horizon was the Democratic Party's "New Departure." The phrase came out of Clement Vallandigham's resolutions for local Democratic organizations in Ohio. The Copperhead codger led the party to accept the outcome of the war, endorse the three civil rights amendments to the Constitution, and focus on the new problems in America, all on the basis of state rights.[64] In New Mexico the fusion politics over statehood undercut the potential of a New Departure in Santa Fe and the northern counties. Not so in the far southern section of the territory. Its autonomous and pro-southern leanings provided fertile ground for a Democratic renewal. The Mesilla Valley would prove its integration into the territory's political apparatus with a vengeance.

Nehemiah V. Bennett launched the Las Cruces *Borderer* on March 16, 1871, and immediately took New Mexico's partisan imperative by storm.[65] Bennett felt the "incoming tidal wave" of the Democratic Party. Were territorial Democrats interested?

> Is there anything more necessary to be said to those who have remained steadfast and true to the principles our fathers cherished—who have inflexibly kept the faith while many around us were

falling under the galling fire of ridicule, contempt, and insult, while others basely deserted us for places of power and profit in the ranks of the enemy, than the simple announcement that a live Democratic paper has made its appearance in New Mexico? We believe not—the fiery furnace has tried us—the scum has been cast off and we rise Phoenix-like in our power to rule the destinies of this nation.

A territorial Democratic movement would have to depend on the *Borderer*, Bennett warned. "Alone in the territory," he announced, "we boldly unfurl our flag to the breeze, confidently trusting that the gallant sons of [D]emocracy will rush to its support."[66]

At double the column-space of the typical territorial paper, the *Borderer* roared with dramatic copy and powerful policy making. Unrepentantly Democratic, the paper promoted state rights and the right of southern states to organize their own society against congressional carpetbagging.[67] Bennett aimed squarely at the president and disseminated national attacks on Grant's annexationist designs on the future Dominican Republic, his alleged corrupt patronage policies, and the administration's "peace-first" Indian policy, which, extending to New Mexico, he called the bane of the "sons of murdered sires."[68]

Deputy U.S. Marshal Ignacio Orrantia, the former lieutenant governor of the 1861 rump Arizona territory, aided Bennett's outreach to the Spanish-speaking community, volunteering to generate subscriptions to cover the extra expense of putting out a Spanish edition.[69] "With such backers we shall not fail," Bennett assured.[70] Twenty-five to thirty "Mexican subscribers" came from La Mesa, Chamberino, and Amoles, though they traveled some distance to the post office for the paper.[71] In far off Taos, the future Democratic star, Anthony Joseph ordered the *Borderer* to foster his county's "glorious Democracy," said to be "making gigantic strides towards a complete organization all over our county."[72] Two other Democratic papers cropped up, the *Moreno Lantern* in Elizabethtown and the *Mail/El Correo* in Las Vegas.[73]

Crystallizing a Democratic identity at this moment required a contextualized othering of the Republican enemy. Seven years after Civil War's end, the *Borderer*'s Spanish edition, *el Fronterizo*, unloaded a cargo of pro-southern propaganda based on the Democratic Party's assault on the "decadent imperial" President Grant. The Republican Party was "reaching its end," though it refused to see this; the narrative cast the opposition "seeking to reconstruct the southern states" several times with the strong hand of the military and "the lowest [carpetbag] missionaries." Republicans supported Negroes only to continue with the government of the party that unleashed the "meddlers" in their midst, while blacks really wished "to be governed by honest and intelligent white men of the South." The "power usurped by the president, which Mr. Sumner calls the prerogative of the King," would suspend habeas corpus "and the South should be trampled once again by this gang of meddlers, to see if they submit themselves to the will of the president." The nod to Sumner signaled Nuevomexicano Democrats keying into splintered Republicans. The follow-up came in the vernacular: "Like the lobos that cannot satisfy their appetites, they are not satisfied with the body of Uncle Sam, now they are eating each other."[74]

Dissension inside the Republican Party afforded Democratic opening. "When the malevolent ones get angry, honest men obtain their rights, and thousands upon thousands of men who do not aspire for positions are now wanting to leave the party that they now despise." *El Fronterizo* fingered Grant's peace policy for wanting to give the vote to the Indian. These "good Indians" were maintained by the cost of government "and why should they not vote for the hand that feeds them?" Yet the "noise of death in the throat of the Republican Party" could be heard from the last elections, congressional proceedings," and the blows of dissident Republicans. "Those of the Republican Party should give their souls to God because they are already close to death [*Los del partido republicano deben de encomendar sus almas á Dios, porque ya esta cerca su muerte*]."[75]

An anonymously authored parody tapped the theme of division in the New Mexico Republican Party. In "*Los Republicanos disputando entre si mismos la candidatura para Delegado al Congreso este año de 1871*" (The Republicans arguing among themselves the candidacy for delegate to congress this year of 1871; see appendix 11 for the full Spanish text), a squabble involves José D. Sena, Santiago Valdez, S. B. Elkins, Leandro Perea, Demetrio Perea, J. F. Chávez, his brother Bonifacio, and Francisco Abreu.[76] As one refrain goes:

> José (with arrogance)
> "I am Republican
> I want to go to Congress"
> (Santiago rushes in to say)
> "I am one too
> and right for it;
> I have the qualifications–
> to recommend me,
> Well, don't you recall
> that the republican
> should be black?"

Another has:

> Elkins (smiling)
> "Quit your fighting
> And don't get agitated
> That in the end and finally
> Will you play coyote;
> I am one of the many,
> who to Congress
> Want to go,
> but I prefer
> when it be a state,
> and if possible
> also delegate.
> I am a lawyer
> Who earns money,
> and in the Territory
> many [militia] bonds do I have,
> that I bought cheaply
> and will sell expensive.'"

Bennett mischievously stirred the Republican pot. "Who calls that Territorial Republican Convention to be held at Santa Fe next month?" he facetiously demanded. "This is a serious question, and ought to be answered. The *Post* don't know, and can't tell its inquiring readers, and the *New Mexican* won't tell. . . . Sullivan says it is the first Republican committee he has ever seen who were ashamed to tell their names.

Make them come out, Sullivan, for there are one or two Republicans left down here [Doña Ana County] who want to know who they are."[77]

Democrats flexed and Republicans did more damage to themselves. José F. Chávez indicated his intent to again run for delegate to Congress; he should have retained authority to organize the Republican campaign.[78] Instead, he appeared to be losing control of his party.

Chávez, thinking the removal of Territorial Secretary H. H. Heath unjust, nominated him for U.S. marshal. Santa Fe members of the New Mexico bar told Senator Lyman Trumbull, chair of the Senate Judiciary Committee, that Heath was "unfit" for the position. The *Elizabethtown Argus* and Sullivan's *Post* published Chávez's letter to Trumbull excoriating the bar for this. Chávez denounced Democrats, like Joab Houghton and Charles Clever, but Republicans also. Kirby Benedict was called "utterly demoralized from a too free use of ardent spirits." Elkins was designated a late comer to Republicanism who (in a specious statement) left Missouri to avoid the draft, and Thomas Catron was characterized as "a lieutenant of artillery in the Confederate Army." These were the men whose statements had "more weight than mine," Chávez purportedly complained to Trumbull, "who am the accredited Representative, by a vote of over two thousand majority." Chávez testified as to Heath's personal character and exemplary behavior and recommended his friend in the name of the "best interest" of his constituents.[79]

When someone else got the marshal's appointment, the *Borderer* commented that Chávez had "hung a millstone about his neck" and it would "sink him in the political waters of forgetfulness." It was none of his fight, Bennett noted, nor did he wish to take up the gloves that Chávez had thrown down to the "legal lights of Santa Fe"; yet he could not see the men whom Chávez labeled liars and rebels supporting his candidacy. Bennett saw the word of the bar members outweighing the influence of Chávez in spite of his position in the Republican Party, his boast of a majority of two thousand in the last election, and his military prestige.[80]

An early endorsement from the *New Mexican* might have bolstered a Chávez candidacy. Instead, the daily fell back on liberal purity as it did in 1869. True to the reaction it made to the *Post*'s endorsement of Chávez, it held out faith in the "people's choice" to determine how delegates to the nominating convention should vote and suggested they should seek out the "ablest and most active Republican in the territory."[81] It was a strategy to head off the contagion of dissension. As the editor noted, "party distinctions and caucus packing" had been producing their "illegitimate result in many parts of the union." It was of the utmost importance to have party unity going into the convention by an enthusiastic support of "strict adherence" to the party's principles, "the fullest canvass of the qualifications of the various candidates, and a fair and untrammeled expression of the preferences of the party." Favoring democratic participation over a pragmatic need to direct a campaign, the daily warned against "thimble rigging" in selecting delegates to control the convention. The individual claims of any candidate were of small account compared to party success, the policy went. Everyone in the party had a "perfect right to urge the claims of their favorite candidate in every fair way, but no undue or improper means should be employed by anyone to influence or control the choice of the convention." An earnest canvass and sure victory would come from "free conference" and the "expression of opinion" in selecting a "true Republican," the "unbiased choice of a majority of the party."[82]

Making matters harrowing, the *New Mexican* noted that only one county organization had put out the call for a meeting to select delegates to the territorial convention. Did friends not realize the stakes? Organization only would strengthen New Mexico's influence in Washington. A slate of issues waited for conveyance to Congress, including the status of the Spanish and Mexican land grants, to "enable the people to settle upon and cultivate with the assurance that they can acquire a good title." And, the editors avowed, danger lurked at this time in the history of the party, "when wranglings and dissensions are occurring in high places, and we have been weakened and defeated in several states hitherto Republican by these dissensions and the selection of weak candidates." Solution lay in the principle of the "fairly expressed will of the party, whether it accords with our personal views or not," to select the "very best men to represent their respective counties in the convention." Delegates should not be in "any ring [a snipe at Gilded Age Republicans?] formed to nominate any particular candidate or to defeat any other candidate, but who have only one desire, one aim—the good of the country, the success of the party—and who have intelligence and judgment to give this desire and aim proper direction." The delegate to Congress needed to be "a man of ability; a man of far-seeking and wise statesmanship," a man "of the highest integrity and honor."[83]

Had there really been such a thing as popular will, no Republican would have thrown his hat in the ring. Aspirants came out of the woodwork. The Santa Fe doctor Henry Hilgert announced at the urging of friends, according to norm. In visiting Washington, Hilgert found department heads and congressmen honoring him with attention to his account of New Mexico's natural resources and measures to develop them. Hilgert, juggling democracy and devotion to organization, would go as delegate of the "whole people without the feelings of a partisan" and show that he was, "from the bottom of [his] heart," a "Republican indivisible."[84]

Hilgert's self-nomination dissipated, while another surged. José D. Sena's entrance shook the Republican field. The Santa Fe County sheriff had been giving Chávez his unstinting support to the point of delivering a fiery anti-Semitic speech against Clever in 1867. Chávez had him on a short list for a federal appointment.[85] Sena now exercised the right, opened up by A. P. Sullivan, to buck the Republican chiefdom. He might run as a Republican independent, it was rumored, should the territorial nominating convention select Chávez.[86]

The alarm of "a certain gentleman of Santa Fe" threatening to run as an independent if not nominated by Republicans prompted McGuiness to put Chávez up as the choice of the *Republican Review*. It was "better," he thought "to do deal with the d[evi]l we know than the one we could not." McGuiness feared Sena weakening Republican ranks. Party unity paramount, McGuiness thought the "unanimously expressed opinion" of the Republican Party of Bernalillo County meant that Chávez would be the more acceptable candidate. Should the convention, in its "collective wisdom," find a better candidate, and "by a fair majority" decide on him, the *Review* would bow to their decision and "act with the party."[87] McGuiness shuddered at the sort of elections devastating the Republican parties of Missouri and New Hampshire. "Our opponents would be only too glad to see a split in the party," he noted.[88]

Except for Río Arriba, where Republican delegates were uncommitted, counties instructed their delegations for one or another potential nominee for delegate to Congress.[89] Bernalillo, Socorro, and Valencia stayed with their Río Abajo native Chávez.[90] Grave dissatisfaction with him arose elsewhere. San Miguel County threw out a second big surprise. Chávez founded his career on San Miguel County's dissatisfaction with the Bosque Redondo reservation. A departure appeared in the report of Francisco P. Abreu declining to have himself nominated, pointing to Sena as the one he "earnestly" desired.[91] An anti-Chávez wing took control of a San Miguel convention. In the instruction to delegates, no man was to be supported whose character and past record did not give assurance that he would "guard well the interests of his constituents," who would "scorn to sacrifice any public benefit to gratify private piques and jealousies," and who disregarded the paramount interests of the territory to punish his personal enemies and "reward his political tools" (Heath implied).[92]

It was a serious matter for Chávez to appear betraying his reputation as a champion of special Nuevomexicano rights. The San Miguel Convention demanded to know "of those who are responsible, why New Mexico is not represented, as she has a right to be, by *bona fide* citizens in the naval and military schools of the government—and why strangers who have no claims upon our people or Territory occupy places in those institutions which should be held by our sons." Damning evidence involved the approval given by the inspector general of the War Department to Chávez's recommendation of one Julius Hayden Pardee to the U.S. Military Academy. Pardee, as the *Post* explained (and West Point records attest), was from Syracuse, New York, and had never lived in New Mexico. Chávez nominated him to the academy in 1867 likely as a quid pro quo to a congressman.[93]

Moreover, none of New Mexico's twelve U.S. officers were nativo after years of demand for home residents to be appointed. "[B]elieving we have citizens who are competent and worthy to fill the various federal offices in this Territory it is due them that they should have those places," San Miguel delegates affirmed, "but while we consent to be represented in the National Congress by weak and incompetent men (a standard by which the character of the people is judged), we should not complain that strangers who have no knowledge of the country, language and people, are appointed to all offices of trust and honor."[94] The subtext involved Gilded Age Republicans. Chávez had criticized Elkins and Catron in the Heath affair, but he assured in a letter to Kirby Benedict, who publicly challenged Chávez on the derogations of him, that the published letter was not a correct or a true copy of his. He did use what he called "some very strong language" against the bar members for seeking to undermine his authority in Congress without coming to him first with their objections to Heath. If they had approached him, Chávez would have presented their concerns to the president and the Senate for their consideration in the recommendation. His explanation did not satisfy Benedict, while Elkins and Catron stayed true to Chávez.[95] If Sena believed Chávez to be "actively and earnestly" working for his appointment to a federal office as reported, the Gilded Age appointees stood as a barrier to his political ambition.[96] The San Miguel Convention instructed its delegates to the territorial convention to support Sena for delegate.[97]

An ad hoc San Miguel committee sent don Manuel Gonzales on a visit to the Republican convention in neighboring Mora County to suggest a joint movement for urging before the territorial convention the nomination for delegate of a person worthy of public confidence, in whose hands the most vital interests of the two counties not be, as in the past, "trampled and scorned." The Mora convention official report had Jesús María Pacheco demonstrating, in "forceful and convincing" terms, the benefits to come from a friendly and judicious alliance with San Miguel compatriots.[98]

A fight for control of the Santa Fe County Republican Convention took place a week later. A key issue turned on who should determine the delegates to the territorial convention. Elkins, representing the old guard, called the event to order. On his nomination, Antonio Ortiz y Salazar was made temporary chair. Elkins men were named officers of the permanent organization, including Deputy Land Surveyor W. W. Griffin, chair; Ortiz y Salazar and Thomas Tucker, vice presidents; and Trinidad Alarid and L. D. Fuller, secretaries. *Post* editor A. P. Sullivan headed the resistance. He called for a committee of five to nominate delegates to the convention. Griffin appointed a mixed committee of William Manderfield and Elkins representing the dominant faction, Sullivan and José Ortiz for the dissidents, and the independent Santa Fe County Probate Judge Antonio Ortiz. After they disagreed on committee recommendations, Judge Ortiz finally sided with the dissident duo.

The committee's majority report failed to receive a second on the floor. Griffin ordered a reading of the minority report, which was signed

FIG. 30. *Kirby Benedict*, undated, photographer unknown. A longtime justice of the territorial Supreme Court and frequent supporter of the Mexican Party, Benedict began as a Democrat but switched to the Republican Party. Courtesy Palace of the Governors Photo Archives, NMHM/DCA, negative #006997.

by Elkins and Manderfield. It was seconded and adopted by a distinct majority. Old guard Republicans were elected delegates to the territorial convention, including Manderfield, Anastasio Sandoval, Eben Everett, Breeden, Nicolás Pino, and R. M. Stevens. The *New Mexican* claimed that Sullivan wanted to foist on the convention as delegates citizens known as "influential, sound *Democrats*," offering as proof that one had been a candidate for probate judge on the Democratic ticket at the last election. Tucker welcomed the minority report's selection of prominent citizens "whose loyalty to the Republican Party is too well-known to be assailed." Sullivan was denounced as a "Puritan of dissension" attempting to further his scheme to break up the Republican Party. Elkins was defended as one who had supported the nominees of the Republic Party since its organization in New Mexico.[99]

Sullivan accused Elkins and Griffin of ramming their will through the convention, beginning with Elkins's dictating its organization and the selection of its permanent officers without input from county committees. He labeled Griffin a "Seymour and Blair Democrat" and new convert to the Republican Party. Sullivan said his majority report from the committee on delegate selections was actually seconded by three non–committee members, including Probate Clerk Trinidad Alarid, yet Griffin unilaterally disregarded the motion to adopt it, putting up the minority report for adoption, "and declared it adopted." Griffin's decision was appealed, but he reportedly refused to listen or "entertain it." According to Sullivan, a motion to adjourn was voted down "by the decisive majority," yet Griffin adjourned the convention, leaving the hall immediately with his friends without ruling on the appeal.[100]

The political historian and theorist Michael Les Benedict suggests that mid-nineteenth-century intra-party factional competition provided an opportunity for active partisans to influence policy and harness issues with a broad public appeal.[101] Sullivan charged that the rights of the "large number of Mexican people" present were violated—ironic this, in view of the Mexican Party roots of the established Republican Party, as none of the motions were translated as requested, their being left with "imperfect explanations which they got from friends in the haste and excitement with which business was rushed through." According to Sullivan, the secretaries stated that they would not and could not conscientiously sign the credentials of the delegates declared to be elected by the president of the convention. Those remaining included the probate judge, county clerk, and other "active, earnest Republican Mexicans who felt they had been insulted, outraged and deprived of their rights, [who] decided that they would ask the County [Executive] Committee to disregard the action of the minority... and to issue a call for another meeting of the convention."[102] A Nuevomexicano correspondent for the *New Mexican* disputed this account. Sullivan was the insulting party, he claimed. He was a *pendejo* (fool) if he thought the Mexicans did not understand his game.[103] That a block of Nuevomexicanos were unhappy with the convention would become clear.

Sullivan disputed the charge that he nominated Democrats as delegates. He correctly pointed out that some of the names on the list were Republicans, including Nicolás Pino, Anastacio Sandoval, Lehman Spiegelberg, and Antonio Ortiz y Salazar. Gaspar Ortiz was the one said to have run for probate judge on the Democratic ticket, yet, Sullivan charged, the *New Mexican* neglected to state that Manderfield and Elkins agreed to report him as a delegate provided that the majority of delegates compromise with them on their preferences. Sullivan pointed out that Ortiz had been a delegate from Santa Fe with Manderfield at the previous territorial convention, and it was said that his acquisition by the Republican Party was a "valuable and bona fide one." Ramón Sena and Gaspar Ortiz were the only ones who could possibly be alluded to as Democrats, Sullivan pointed out. Of Sena he knew nothing. Gaspar Ortiz was acceptable as a Republican to the *New Mexican* when it could control him "or further its ends by acknowledging him as a partisan," Sullivan asserted. All the "Americans" in the majority report had voted a straight Republican ticket, Sullivan believed, including Spiegelberg.

The name of J. F. Chávez did not come up, though Sullivan reasonably enough implied his nomination was the unstated goal of the Elkins faction. The time had come when "abuse" was of "no avail," he pronounced, "when crying 'Democrat' at every Republican who happens to oppose ... [the powers that be] fastening upon the territory an imbecile who can neither aid the interests of his territory or his party," and the abuse would not silence the majority "who were swindled out of their rights on last Monday."[104]

The *Post* published a call for what the *New Mexican* called, in the changing Republican idiom, a "bolter's convention."[105] None but Republicans would participate, Sullivan assured, "and none others are wanted at it." The *Post* and Santa Fe County Executive Committee coordinated in their refusal to submit to the "insolent treatment" of the majority at the Santa Fe convention and of "the Mexican people in particular." Many could not get into the rump convention. Pablo Delgado was made vice president. Anastacio Sandoval, chairman of the Santa Fe County Republican Committee and longtime supporter of Chávez, explained the meeting as necessary to protect the county Republicans "in the right to a fair expression of their will," as Griffin allegedly refused at the first convention to hear motions save those made by the ring "with which he was connected, and refused to allow time enough to permit the motions of members . . . to be interpreted for the benefit of our Spanish speaking portion of the population."

José D. Sena made a star appearance. He expressed a desire to see the harmony and strength of the Republican Party maintained while announcing that he was a candidate for the nomination of the Republican Territorial Convention for delegate to Congress. Should he not get it, he would support the nominee of his party. He wished only to "maintain his rights and those of the people." Should Chávez, Arny, or anyone else receive the nomination "honorably," so be it, but he was not willing silently to "permit the voters of his County to be swindled out of their rights." Sena appealed for Republicans to "give a hearty and honest" support to the principles and nominees of the party that had "saved" the country, they needing to "trust in the justice of their claims" and neither do nor say anything that would tend to disturb the party's harmony. Embodying the grievance of exclusion and out to defend his friends who had been "grossly wronged" by the Santa Fe convention, Sena advised them to submit their case to the territorial convention. Should he be nominated for delegate, he would endeavor to advocate faithfully and represent the interests of New Mexico, the *Post* recorded; "he would try to elevate the position of the people socially, pecuniarily [sic] and otherwise." Sena was frequently interrupted by applause, and he concluded his speech "amidst manifestations of greatest enthusiasm." It is not clear if Sena received the instruction of the rump convention for delegate to Congress. Alternative county delegates to the territorial convention were named, including Sullivan, Spiegelberg, Gaspar Ortiz, Nicolás Pino, Anastasio Sandoval, and Pablo Delgado.[106]

The *New Mexican* conceded that the caucus was composed "entirely" of those who were dissatisfied with the action of the regular Republican convention. It called Sullivan hypocritical for claiming that a Democrat had presided over the regular convention yet participated in it.[107] Sullivan claimed in response that he objected to Griffin's appointment and moved as an amendment that Judge Antonio Ortiz be elected instead. "Both of the editors of the New Mexican and every person who was at the convention knows that the editor of the *Post* did show dissatisfaction with the election of Mr. Griffin," Sullivan exclaimed. "The election of Mr. Griffin was submitted to for the sake of harmony but his acts, in defiance of the rights of the members of the Convention, and the Mexican people in particular, were not, and will not be submitted to."[108] The *New Mexican* conceded nothing. All who took part in, encouraged, or supported the bolt movement, it warned officiously, "should they at any time hereafter be candidates for office, their treachery to the Republican Party will be remembered against them, and they will fail to command the vote of a party whose convention's nominations they now bolt." The Missouri bolters were held up as the object lesson to those who turned "traitors."[109]

The *New Mexican* predicted that Sullivan would bolt the territorial convention if his candidate did not receive the nomination for delegate, as in Santa Fe. A bolter delegate reportedly said that if Sena failed to get the regular nomination, the sheriff would "certainly" run as an independent.[110] Sullivan called the assertion he would bolt an "inexcusable and unwarranted falsehood" and reiterated his intent to abide by the convention's decision regarding Santa Fe County's delegation and its choice of candidate for Congress. He would not support Sena "for any purpose or under any pretext" unless Sena gave assurance of obeying the convention. He conceded the possibility of Chávez nominated on the first ballot "and it is also quite possible that the delegates will show their affection for him by keeping him at home. If he is nominated we will support him; in the meantime, however, we emphatically oppose his nomination, and we earnestly protest against forcing upon the Republican Party the responsibility of Mr. Chávez's official record." Sullivan appealed to delegates to nominate someone who could give strength to the party and do good for the territory.[111]

Reports from the counties suggested a rough and tumble offing to be had at the territorial convention. The Taos delegation was "strictly" instructed not to propose nor accept "nor in any manner endorse" the nomination of Sena, although it gave no instruction for anyone else.[112] Nuevomexicano Republicans in Lincoln County rejected Chávez. In their homeland sentiment, they denounced the Indian agents in positions that the delegate had reserved for "strangers," called a "great loss to the constituents of the territory." They instructed for Arny because of his experience, his "incessant efforts" on behalf of the "abandoned" territory, his "true Republicanism," and his "energetic character." Somewhat oddly, then, it was decided that as the distance to Santa Fe was too great to send their delegates to the territorial convention, the split party members of Manderfield, Tucker, Sullivan, and Spiegelberg would represent them as voting proxies.[113]

Sullivan let fly a tirade on Chávez on the morning of the Republican Territorial Nominating Convention. The incumbent was said to have proven himself incapable of commanding the respect or attention of the departments in Washington or his colleagues in Congress; he had failed to get aid to protect lives and property against Indian raids; failed to get public buildings completed; failed to secure appointments for citizens of the territory; failed to have the revenue tax paid by New Mexicans returned for public works; placed at West Point a nonresident of New Mexico instead of "the son of one of our citizens"; and vilified the character of the leading members of the Santa Fe bar to gratify private spleen and secure the political success of the "most unworthy person [Heath] whose nomination the president finally withdrew."[114] Sullivan hailed Sena for having been an "energetic, industrious and successful official." He did "hard and faithful work in the organization of the Republican Party and New Mexico." Arny had, "even when without official position or prestige, done many good things," endeavored to advance education, secured legislation for railroads, worked to increase appropriations for Indian expenditures, and developed legislation to protect the people against Indian outrages and to form reservations.[115]

Republican Central Committee Chair Antonio Ortiz y Salazar called his party's territorial convention to order. Betraying the usual consensus in the selection of a temporary chair, Elkins nominated Salvador Armijo, and Sullivan countered with Anastasio Sandoval. Armijo won on the vote of the uncontested delegates, thirty-six to twenty-one. The power of the regulars was further demonstrated by the appointment of Thomas Catron as chair of the Committee on Permanent Organizations and Tomás Cabeza de Baca, still battling politically, as permanent president. At least two dissidents were named vice presidents. Regulars dominated the Credentials Committee with Elkins, Manderfield, Mariano Otero, Tomás Salazar, and William Breeden. The committee called for seating the regular delegation from Santa Fe County. Sullivan moved to replace it with the rump delegation. Elkins succeeded, thirty-eight to twenty-two, in tabling the motion. All members of San Miguel County appeared "irregular," the committee noted, and ten of the twelve were represented by substitutes, including Sullivan for one. While their entitlement to act seemed "very doubtful," the committee recommended, assuming good faith on the part of substitutes, that they be allowed to participate in the convention except Sullivan. Sullivan did serve as the proxy for Doña Ana's whole delegation.[116]

Regulars proved the majority on the Committee on Resolutions, chaired by Breeden. The dissident Antonio Ortiz y Salazar attempted to protect his faction with a motion to have the vote for the nomination of delegate be by ballot and another to form a committee composed of representatives of the supporters of each nominee, each member to receive the votes of his candidate and announce it to the convention. Both were defeated. Elkins's substitute motion for a *viva voce* on nominations was approved.

Resolutions upheld the principles of the great Republican Party of the United States and expressed commitment to President Grant's reelection. While Grant's reservation policy and "humane treatment" for all "peaceable Indians" were endorsed, the party favored "a vigorous war against the hostile bands" that refused to go onto reservations. The obligatory nod to material progress called for the government to grant lands "in liberal quantities" for railroads through New Mexico. The encouragement of immigration to the territory was included as well as the establishment of schools. In the necessary anti-colonial provision, the request went for the claims of the territorial citizens to be respected for federal appointment.

An addendum was proposed to have the convention call on the administration to "heed and respect the representations" of Delegate Chávez based on his record on the appointment and removal of the territory's federal officers. Because New Mexico had proved to be a "truly" Republican territory, it was entitled to the "confidence and sympathy of our Republican brethren everywhere," the measure stated, and "her delegate" was "better qualified to select proper persons for appointment to the federal officers here and to decide questions of local interest, than strangers." The intent seems to have been to neutralize criticism of Gilded Age members. Elkins moved adoption of the resolutions. Sullivan, supported by a number of delegates, moved to strike the expressions of support for Chávez. Elkins succeeded in having the motion tabled indefinitely. The platform, including the addendum, was adopted, sixty-four to four.

One resolution asked all Republicans "and all true friends of New Mexico" to unite and aid in electing the convention's nomination for delegate to Congress. Elkins submitted Chávez in nomination. Sullivan put forth Sena. Arny withdrew before the vote. Chávez took it, sixty-seven to forty-four, on the one and only ballot. Chávez's nomination was declared unanimous on Arny's motion. Sena rose to express acceptance of the convention's will and affirm his commitment to the chosen one. As a corps left to summon Chávez, the convention named a new Territorial Republican Central Committee. Party President Arny was instructed to organize county committees. Ten Nuevomexicanos were elected for the sixteen-member Central Committee. In an afterthought, Elkins successfully submitted a motion for the party to express favor for the admission of New Mexico into the Union as a state, with instructions to the delegate-elect to give his utmost effort to secure passage of an enabling act as soon as practicable. Chávez entered the Convention, heartily endorsed its resolutions and pledged to work the Republican cause for the interests of the people of New Mexico.[117]

The *Republican Review* agreed with the convention's program, including the nomination of Chávez, but demurred on statehood. McGuiness and a couple of correspondents feared Republicans not doing well if the Democratic Party adopted an anti-state plank.[118] The *Post* and the *Argus*, erstwhile supporters of Sena, hoisted the name of Chávez.[119] A relieved *New Mexican* congratulated them for their "submission to the will of the majority." The editors were glad to find groundless the claim of the "boomers of dissension" that Sena would run as an independent. Chávez, the daily announced, behind a Republican Party "undivided and indivisible," would win by a larger majority than he had ever gotten.[120]

To support the effort at organizing counties, the *New Mexican* emphasized the importance of a "thorough organization" of the territory with local Republican central committees. An important motivator was held out in the alleged "manifest determination" of the Grant administration to secure lands Nuevomexicano citizens had occupied for many years "by grants or otherwise from the Mexican Republic." The next session of Congress appeared ready to act on their confirmation, the daily emphasized. It was assured that the next delegate and the "indefatigable" chairman of the Central Committee, encouraged and sustained by the precincts and counties, would do much for the neglected territory.[121]

The Democracy and an Independent Ramp It Up

The very day of the Republican Territorial Nominating Convention, "reliable" Democrats from much of the territory assembled to form an ad hoc central committee and set the ball in motion until a territorial convention named a permanent one. Democrats were urged to organize county and precinct clubs and have their officers connect with the committee. "We are fully convinced that New Mexico is overwhelmingly Democratic," the *Borderer* chimed, "and all that is necessary to demonstrate this fact is a thorough organization of our forces." Most participants were Euroamerican, including N. V. Bennett, his brother Joseph, and William Rencher, son of the former New Mexico governor Abraham Rencher. Donaciano Vigil, the key collaborator in the Kearny conquest, added to the excitement of a reignited party. Other Nuevomexicanos from the American shadow-party to enlist were Felipe Delgado, Nicolás Quintana, Diego Archuleta, Vicente Romero, Fernando Nolan, Antonio Roival, and Ambrosio Armijo.[122] The Democratic territorial nominating convention was set for June 24 in Santa Fe.[123]

The *Borderer*, which was named the official organ of the party, declared the banner of the Territorial Democratic Party unfurled. Yet did it affirm that devotion to Democratic principles would avail nothing "unless our forces are thoroughly organized and known." Democrats should accept no middle ground, Bennett warned, no bargaining with any corrupt politician "who offers his influence for a bonus." Members from the multitudes needed to "organize—organize in every County and precinct so that you know the position of every man. It is time to go to work," he rallied out, "don't fail."[124] In Santa Fe the old *Democrat* campaign-sheet came to life to cover the northern section. Rencher stepped in as general editor and Nicolás Quintana took charge of the Spanish section. The *Democrat* claimed the policies and views of the Democratic Central Committee insofar as it could not "speak for the Democratic party at large." It would provide active aid for success in the election, especially to stimulate "systematic organization" for the party.[125] Bennett welcomed this other "engine" to "force strong blows upon the heads of our political opponents."[126] The *New Mexican* gave the *Democrat* a fraternal welcome into the ranks of journalism, although good-naturedly remarking that "with its creed and political doctrines we have no sympathy," and promising, "We shall endeavor fearlessly and mercilessly to expose the fallacy of its theories, and to denounce the purpose of its existence."[127]

The Democratic grassroots moved noticeably. The Doña Ana County Democratic Club greeted New Mexico Democrats with, "We are on our high horse and he wants to prance." Its first mass meeting formed the occasion when the people of the county "should once more assert their manhood and independence." A "magnificent procession of carriages, wagons and buggies, accompanied by a crowd of gentlemen on horseback," paraded the streets of Mesilla "to the music of a splendid brass band." A "glorious spectacle" greeted them at Las Cruces, putting folks "in mind of olden times," meaning before the Civil War. The meeting, conducted in both Spanish and English, elected N. V. Bennett its president. Three Nuevomexicanos were among eight representatives of five precincts. The group declared, "We gently laid the Republican Party of Doña Ana County in his grave; and pray God Almighty to have mercy on its soul."[128] The rhetorical device of death to the opponent would gain its real traction in Doña Ana County this electoral season.

Two Nuevomexicanos submitted public notes of gratitude in Spanish for the honor of being selected officers of the Democratic Club and for being members of "such a deserving party." José Ma. Pino, from Cimarron, beheld the Democracy moving "by the true light of justice and equality."[129] The Mesilla meeting filled José M. DeCámara of Chamberino with "jubilation of joyous ideas and of a loyal hope that it [would] enlarge the heart of general humanity." The Chamberino adhesion to the party spelled opposition to the Republican administration, DeCámara avowed, "for prejudicing the public interest." It meant the county's aspiration of a "true liberal and progressive government" (with no mention of how this squared with Democratic prejudice against blacks).[130] At the county convention Pablo Melendres was nominated for probate judge. The value of party loyalty held fast. A Republican onlooker noted that Melendres had been elected as a Republican two years before. He would be defeated "for his treachery." Joseph Bennett, brother of the *Borderer* editor, was nominated for the council.[131] The Doña Ana delegation would go to the territorial convention uninstructed. A hundred Democratic voters had a "most glorious time" at the "grand baile" at DeCámara's domicile.[132]

Bernalillo County Democrats put on a rousing convention. The rico cousins José Francisco Perea and José Francisco Chávez never reconciled as their grandfather once wished, at least politically. Perea presided and was made a delegate to the territorial convention. Participants merged into the expanding Democratic organization of New Mexico. The audience was exposed to the Democratic assault on Chávez, the Republican leadership, Grant, and Republican policies. Delegates to the territorial convention would go "untrammeled" in the vote for the delegate candidate.[133] Colfax County Democrats endorsed the nomination of the former Republican and Santa Fe district judge and chair of the Democratic Central Committee, R. H. Tomkins.[134] Sheriff Andrés Montoya called the Socorro County Democratic convention to order. Chair pro tem R. H. Stapleton declared the time over when the "pernicious feeling" of "prejudices in favor of some men [claimed] the votes of the people of New Mexico, to give them offices, as if it were theirs by divine right." President Pedro Baca said that he had "always, since the transfer of New Mexico to the United States [been] a Democrat." He would stand by the party "so long as he had strength to do so." Charles Clever appeared to clarify the Democratic creed. The *Borderer* said it was a subject "always sufficient to make eloquent any man of ordinary talent, but in Clever's language, became sublime." Jesús María Chávez noted New Mexico's prosperity "previous to its falling into the hands of the so-called Republican party." No instruction was given regarding the party's nomination of delegate to Congress.[135]

Perea received the honor of presiding over the Democratic Territorial Nominating Convention in Santa Fe. N. Bennett later claimed that many Democratic leaders had doubted that the time was right for their party to make a successful fight against Republicans, recommending therefore that it not advance any name for delegate. Bennett made clear the conviction of his Doña Ana Democrats, "strong in favor of a contest."[136] As it turned out, the convention received only one nomination for delegate. The honor of making it went to Doña Ana County, where the neo-Democratic movement got its start. Bennett proposed that the convention nominate by acclamation . . . José Manuel Gallegos! Bennett beheld Gallegos's intellect standing well above any opponent the enemy could bring on. The former delegate's integrity and honor flew beyond the shadow of suspicion, as Bennett hailed. At this moment of nostalgia for the golden age of Democratic Party dominance, the general appeal of Gallegos concerned his pedigree as New Mexico's first Democratic delegate. As Bennett said, his Democracy brought them all "back to the happy days of old, when office and preferment sought the candidate." It was a historically ironic coupling, as the original Democratic Party that had sent Gallegos to Congress was established by the Mexican Party, which had evolved into the Republican Party. Cheers rent the air, the proceedings reported, "and it was long before the convention could be restored to order." Amid their "wildest enthusiasm," each of the delegates gave his vote in favor of the nomination.[137]

This would be a fifth congressional run for Gallegos. He later explained that he came out of his "repose and tranquility" in response to his friends' supplications. It seems more than rhetoric. The *New Mexican* stated that Gallegos's nomination was agreed upon long before the convention. Bennett confirmed that Gallegos surfaced "by our [Nuevomexicano] citizens when they expressed to us their preference for his nomination." Bennett appears to have treated it as a valid pre-election poll. He said Elkins paid Diego Archuleta to dissuade Gallegos from running. A "deputation" of Democrats, which included Bennett, filed out to interview Gallegos to determine his intention regarding the plan to nominate him. They found him staying true to his party and "doubting his [Archuleta-led] friends."[138]

Gallegos eloquently presented himself "to the face" of Nuevomexicanos. His reflections in Spanish were of the wizened politico, beacon of liberal principle, humble man of God, and mortal in the winter of life (see appendix 12 for the full Spanish text). He sought suffrages not in his name, he made clear, but for the "respectable mass of the people" who named and instructed the members of the Democratic convention to make him their candidate. By the "sovereign will of a grand mass of the... people," he sensed an "imperative duty" to manifest his political sentiments, which were "far from any personal hostility, far from my views of personal aggrandizement [the businessman's contrition], and far from betraying the just rights of yourselves as free people." He esteemed the rights entitled under the "sacred letter" of the general Constitution, by the "wise" Treaty of Guadalupe Hidalgo and especially the local laws of the territory. Similar to what he told Congress in 1855 during Miguel Antonio Otero's contest, Gallegos stressed his knowledge of the people's character, their "necessities in all respects," and the "vital sentiment that palpitates patriotically in [their] generous hearts." These "essential attributes" had compelled him to consecrate his sacred duty in his last years by offering his small services to "the people of my birth." He would "happily descend one day not too distant to the tomb of eternal rest, in the long night of the centuries, with the sweet pleasure of having satisfied their clear desires."

Gallegos festooned the Nuevomexicanos in the colors of partisanship, liberalism, and tradition. "The day selected by law," he proclaimed, "in which the people freely exercised their sovereignty, will resolve emphatically the problem that today agitates the flames of attention of all the classes of our territory, without distinction of sex or condition; and then the wise providence that rules and governs the destinies of mortals will bless forever the work of their prodigal sons." Gallegos placed his liberalism in the frame of his original spiritual vocation:

> We all are equal in birth, all equal in the final fortune of death and also equal in the free guarantee of our rights. The divine sun, traversing over our heads, produces our fruit and admirably nourishes the land of the globe that formed us, which the divine creator provides for our use and sustenance; the flora and animals of all kinds are freely illuminated and fed by the resplendent star. We, as superior, rational, entities are illuminated by the magnificent star of the divine being, to proceed as independent and free men in the exercise of our spiritual and temporal actions. This has been and is the Christian doctrine that showed us our Señor Jesucristo, author of the militant and triumphant church that he built on the land for our benefit and the beings of the centuries.

Gallegos's divinely inspired partisanship asked voters to recognize the fruit of his work "with impartial justice and ask: What has my friend and competitor Mr. José Francisco Chávez done for our benefit?" To vote him in again would mean a continuance of the suffering, bad consequences, and poverty that "we have been mourning for six years."[139]

Republicans looked to charge at the New Departure's jugular, its association with the "great [recently] departed" Vallandigham.[140] One of them pinned the Democrats on the board of his party's hegemony. "To a Democratic Congress Gallegos would be a fit representative," one observed, "but his election would be an insult to the present administration and present Congress." Evoking past assaults on the Spanish-speaking candidate, it was said that Gallegos contradicted what it took to be a delegate, for he was "anti-American in language, habit and dress."[141] Sullivan joked at Gallegos's two prior failures. "The old gentleman is so used to defeat," he chuckled, "that it was probably best to select him."[142] A contributor said it was but a short time since that "his present fuglemen were defaming his personal and political character in the most outrageous manner."[143] Democratic contradictions stood out. As Rencher authored the resolution deprecating federal officers as "men who are strangers to our people," Sullivan fictionalized the obituary of his father, "that he was born in New Mexico, lived here 500 years before he was appointed, was of pure distilled blood, and one familiar with and to our people."[144]

Suddenly José D. Sena jumped onto the public stage announcing in the *Democrat* his candidacy for delegate to Congress. The *Denver News* condemned Sena's "unexpected course" for rendering the results of the campaign doubtful for Republicans.[145] The *New Mexican*'s correspondent in Washington was incredulous. It must have been a "Democratic fib," he exclaimed, regarding it as impossible that Sena "could so stultify himself after Chávez had worked so hard in his support, and I know but for the slanders against the Mexicans by the enemies of Chávez that he would have succeeded [in getting him a federal post]. Those same enemies of Chávez are now the men who are egging Sena on."[146] Tucker anguished over Sena going before the Republican convention as a candidate, receiving a large vote, being fairly defeated on the first ballot, rising in a speech of "considerable length" delivered in Spanish and translated by himself, swearing adherence to Republican principles and the decision of the convention. He received the respect due to a defeated candidate "who bows to the will of the majority, and patiently bides his time. And now this man at the instigation of the Democrats, nominates himself, adopts his own platform and pleads his own cause as an independent Republican candidate for delegate."[147]

Critics failed to mention a certain event in the time between the two territorial nominating conventions: the naming of A. P. Sullivan of all people as postmaster of Santa Fe.[148] The *Borderer* charged Chávez with first offering the position to the son of Tomás Cabeza de Baca. That he did not follow through was part of a pattern of the delegate promising to use his influence to secure appointments for Nuevomexicanos and Euroamericans, Bennett charged, including *New Mexican* editor Manderfield, only to see their hopes dashed by the appointment of outsiders.[149] Chávez could well have engineered the postmaster appointment, perhaps as reward for the *Post* abandoning endorsement of Sena. It can be noted that Sena's platform called on "every good patriot" to condemn "every man or gang of men who, by means of lies, adulation or bribery, sacrificed the interests of the people to obtain government appointments for themselves or their favorites." Sena asked honest citizens who had in their hearts the true interests of New Mexico to exercise their "indignation, malediction, detestation and hatred" against "every clique or newspaper that brazenly and unashamedly corrupted the people, using their vote to ratify their ambition, effect their cowardly vengeance and inflate their favorites in prejudice to the interests of the people of New Mexico." He would oppose "every man or class of men" who, "without scruple, sacrifice the interests of the people in order to acquire and effect their personal aggrandizement and pecuniary engrossment."

Sena grieved on the basis of Mexican Party tradition. He called on the central government to sanction and recognize the Spanish and Mexican communal land grants. Sena also sounded like a quite modern progressive, calling, in the newly insurgent Republican trend in the country against high-finance Republicans, for the abolition of Republican monopolies. Much of the rest of the platform replicated the calls for socioeconomic development that had become standard party planks. One provision had an eminently Radical pedigree: "dissemination and fomenting of liberty, equality of rights, privileges and immunities accordingly guaranteed by the Constitution to each and every American citizen." Sena's call for the intellectual and spiritual development of both sexes transposed Diego Archuleta's bill in the truncated legislative session giving women the right to vote and hold office, following the Wyoming Territory's action.[150]

Sena amplified the meaning of his candidacy in a speech in which he reportedly attacked New Mexico's Republican establishment. Sena criticized, "in bitter words, the conduct of the Republican convention. He is opposed to carpetbaggers and the doings of any clique," a clear enough allusion to Gilded Age Republicans. Sena went after "ring rulers," charging that the "poorer classes" were the "greatest sufferers," those who "had to pay the largest proportion of the public debt." In a personal rationale, Sena was said to entertain the hope of being elected, "but if he could not be, he at least prayed that his tutor Gallegos would be." Gallegos had taken the young Sena under his wing when he was delegate, sponsoring Sena's higher education in the United States. The shape of this election thus involved a close connection between Democratic and Independent campaigns, a near fusion to keep Chávez from getting elected. Keeping up with linguistic trends back east, the *New Mexican* reported on the mass meeting held by the "unterrified" Democracy on the Santa Fe Plaza. Gallegos spoke, followed by Sena, whose address lasted nearly three hours.[151]

The *Borderer* mocked flummoxed Republicans. As it portrayed the crisis, some "prominent citizens" were overcome with a paralysis "so alarming that the priest was sent for and the office of extreme unction was performed for the whole party" (the theme of party death again). A Democratic traveler caricatured President Grant sending a carpetbag emissary to New Mexico with a message to the Radicals— "Let us have peace."[152]

Issues

Going into the final third of the campaign, the *New Mexican* said the New Departure's only legacy, hating the Negro, was not sufficient to carry it to victory in the presidential election.[153] The *Borderer* warned voters to beware the "Radical Party," founded on hostility to the Constitution, its policies leading to "Negro senators, Negro representatives in Congress; in federal appointments of trust and honor to Negroes, and must inevitably end in equality of social relations, and amalgamation of the races."[154]

New Mexicans were brought up to speed on current affairs. Arny imported free labor awareness, which rose in Republican ranks after the Civil War. He assailed New Mexico Democrats for opposing the tariff as it protected capital and labor, important for ranchers seeing increases in wool production. Democrats, he argued, were interested only in ground rents and the desire to lower the salary of the worker at the "old Democratic" price of ten cents a day by relying on cheap European labor. Chávez was for protection of workers and the elevation of labor to change the "desert and the forest into cultivated fields." Gallegos would reduce the worker to poverty and put the country "in the hands of a few monopolists," who were growing, "while the poor each day will be more poor."[155]

The railroads came into focus. A political historian states: "An ambitious effort to extend railroad facilities was central to the Republican program in nearly every state.... They would permit farmers to exchange subsistence farming for cash crops; they would increase land values; they would end intellectual and cultural isolation."[156] The *Democrat* argued that the "extravagant" Republican policy of awarding two hundred million acres of open land to the national companies for the transcontinental railroad worked to the detriment of states and territorial residents. The *New Mexican* countered that Congress's total allotment to the railroads was the "wisest policy," of the greatest benefit to the territory. It shook its head at the policy of the Democratic Party in New Mexico being in "opposition to railroads!"[157]

The *Borderer* went populist on taxes. In one fable Bennett visits with the family of an old but Republican friend who complains about not being able to pay his taxes and the bank having sold the cow. He had no right to grumble, says the editor, "if you put men in office and know just what they will do when you cast your vote." By end of the visit, the host is made aware of exorbitant taxes paid for his family's clothes, dinner ware, salt and pepper, rice, wool dress, etc. Merchants were not to blame; "they have to pay these taxes ... so they must charge it to you." Little of the tax went to the treasury, most "into the pockets of the manufacturers of the East, whose industries are protected by Congress so that they charge more for their goods "and we have to pay them.... Does Congress pass any laws to protect the industry of the poor man?" How could any poor man vote Republican? "Well my friend I must go," says the editor." I'll take my hat if you please. I paid a tax of seventy percent on that hat."[158]

Euroamerican and Nuevomexicano Democrats savaged Chávez. An issue of cultural competency and authenticity was turned against him, ironically from the old American Party. *Democrat* editor Nicolás Quintana chastised Chávez for not speaking Spanish to his constituents, accusing him of not caring for his own race. The *Republican Review* responded incredulously. McGuiness recalled that in 1865 when Chávez ran against Perea it was charged that *he* was anti-American, "and that therefore all Americans (so called) should vote against him. Perhaps the editor of the Spanish side of the New Mexico Democrat can tell ... about this new departure."[159] A Euroamerican said Quintana was the one motivated by a hatred of Americans and American institutions. The virtue of assimilation was implied in the quite prescient warning that it would be the better policy for him "and all other anti-[A]mericans to refrain from the avowal of their sentiments of hatred through the newspapers; for in less than five years, the Territory will be traversed by railroads north and south and east and west, and Americans will have a controlling influence, numerically and otherwise in our politics. These facts may be very repugnant to him and men of his sentiments but time will verify them."[160]

The West Point issue haunted Chávez with the claim of his "bartering away the rights of the people." Republicans responded by pointing out that a congressional investigation found no wrongdoing. The *New Mexican* and *el Correo* uncovered the fact that Gallegos had done the same when he was the delegate in 1854–55 for the relative of a U.S. senator from Alabama who championed Gallegos during Miguel Otero's contest.[161] The charge of Chávez failing to do anything for New Mexico as delegate was backed by alleged failures—not having New Mexico included in legislation for territories to construct and complete public buildings, for example, or to acquire public lands for the railroad, or in the so-called "ditch bill" for irrigation improvements. Chávez's association with Gilded Age Republicans would not quit, his being the tool of "a ring of Santa Fe's speculators" who "governed and patrolled" the people.[162]

Chávez defenders tried balancing these charges by blaming the ill-informed efforts of former delegates James Watts and Francisco Perea for Congress's neglect of New Mexico. They cited Chávez's concerted efforts to amend the general territorial appropriations bill, only to face the argument that New Mexico was due to receive more money than other territories. Democrats were called obstructionists to the bills calling for railroad grants, except those that benefited the South, and congressional Democrats largely blocked useful appropriations for New Mexico, including the ditch bill, as they were opposed to "all classes of improvements" against the "Republican policy of the improvements and land grants."[163]

Regular Republicans emphasized as a positive the fact of Chávez's dedication to statehood for New Mexico. Also, even the military department was a friend, "ready to sustain him and the Territory—a great point gained," particularly in light of the prejudice the military tended to have toward the territory with its "ignorant and clannish" people.[164] Absent throughout the discourse of the weeks before the election was a focused debate on the qualifications of José D. Sena.

Political Death in Mesilla

Elections for all seats in both chambers of the territorial legislature became necessary in 1871 because Congress decided to fund sessions only once every two years starting with 1869–70. With no provision to continue council seats for an 1870 session, the slate of legislative office holders was wiped clean.[165] A groundswell of Republican and Democratic Party activity was stoked in the counties, filled with ad hoc meetings, conventions, rallies, and violence.

Counties saw superheated races. In Río Arriba the "very partisan subalterns" of the Democratic administration did not omit any measure to conduct "the war against their contraries," as a Republican put it.[166] H. H. Heath (who returned to Santa Fe to work in the U.S. assessor's office) became so incensed at the invective hurled at him by the *Post* that he broke a cane on Sullivan's person and fired shots at him. Heath missed the fleeing Sullivan. Sullivan fired shots at Heath sitting on his porch, and Heath returned fire with a carbine. Neither was hit; both were arrested. The press called the feud a "public scandal and nuisance."[167] It reflected a public emotionality about to realize its tragic crescendo.

This time, no place surpassed Doña Ana County, where the territory's New Departure originated, for factional storming. The Republican and Democratic "procession" became the rage. Typically organized in the larger settlements of Mesilla and Las Cruces, parades of partisans lumbered out to smaller communities along the Mesilla Valley. Festive affairs, these gatherings mobilized citizens, recruited voters, and rallied the party. They also provoked rancor all too real. Jeers and name calling from opponents standing along the plaza, streets, and roads greeted celebrants. In one report three hundred Republicans mounted horses and wagons bedecked with flags for a pass through La Mesa, San Tomás, Chamberino, and Amoles, only to be met, according to a Republican, with a collection of Democrats who had "been gotten up at the saloon on the principal corner of the plaza, and as the procession passed it was greeted with all sorts of insults. Only the determined and premeditated forbearance of the Republicans prevented a serious riot or 'row.'"[168] In another, Democrats on a wagon train on the way to the village of Doña Ana interrupted five hundred Republicans gathered on the plaza to hear leaders' speeches. A Republican portrayed Democrats in a failed event, their returning to Mesilla with empty barrels, "their lips sweating" with thirst, one of their drunken county candidates falling off his mule to the side of the road.[169]

A Democrat openly boasted of his party's provocations. Democrats planned to stalk Republicans in Las Cruces. When Radicals could not be found, a band of Democrats searched them out, finding only William Rynerson and the stumping Heath. Democrats marched to La Mesa and saw a "grand turnout." The next morning, the Democrat suggested to Rynerson and other Radical leaders that the two parties meet to discuss political questions. Rynerson thought it better to keep them apart. Republicans refused to hold demonstrations if Democrats were present. A Democratic woman described them as "like a turtle; while the Democrats were about, they hauled in their feet and head and hid; when we left they poked their head out again and looked about to see if the coast was clear." At La Unión, Democrats, escorted by retinues from Santo Tomás, La Mesa, and Chamberino, waited for the arrival of the enemy. As Republicans drew onto the Plaza, Democrats demanded a debate, but the Republicans "put up their mules and suddenly left town, without saying a word of goodbye to anybody." At Las Cruces, the Democrats again met with Republican refusal to engage.[170]

Bennett at the *Borderer* expressed disapproval of threatening gestures. "This mode of cheering, death to the Democrats, or death to the radicals," he warned, "is an incentive of the most bitter feeling, and we most sincerely want to see it discontinued." He heard from "radical gentlemen of the highest standing . . . that the [R]ads ought to have fired into the crowd of Democrats and wrote them down like dogs," which came "with very bad taste as long as his own party keep up the same custom."[171] If anything, *Borderer* columns fanned the flames of street aggression.

El Fronterizo had it from "various gentlemen" that one Rafael Bermudes had told a "Radical Party" boss and past failed candidate for justice of the peace that "if there were any more disorders among the parties in this County the radicals would go to Las Cruces and burn the home and store of Mr. [Henry] Lesinsk[y], because he belonged to the Democratic party." Republicans supposedly paid a "poor brute named Henry Henrie to go from precinct to precinct defaming the good character of men who belong to the Democratic Party." It was charged that Democrats traveling from Picacho to Las Cruces were insulted "to the point that some Radicals threatened them with arms to shoot over the Democrats" but were detained by their families. The culprits were "cowards," the paper said, who did not have the "valor to do such a thing." The act was characteristic of Radicalism itself, the editor held, the "unnatural, and insolent principles" expressed in all Radical meetings. The Radicals knew they could not win the election, though many in the Radical Party opposed this "mode of work."[172]

Republicans called the article false and ascribed the trouble to an incident of rallying Democrats returning to Las Cruces from Picacho, headed for Lesinsky's store, which the Democrats used for headquarters. Cheers for the Democracy and the band's music were drowned out in the main street with "vivas" from the sidewalk for the Republican Party. A large Democratic crowd gathered at Lesinsky's, some consuming alcohol. However, they were outnumbered by Republicans, who shouted, "[V]iva la libertad y el partido Republicano." Democrats struck a fighting mood, the "liberal proposition to whip the whole Republican Party one at a time. . . made by a little one of their number." An "unoffending" Republican was "knocked over the head with a pistol and severely hurt." Republicans ran home to gather arms, "determined to defend themselves against any further ruffianism by the Democracy." Leading Republicans appealed to the people to refrain from any violence, "which had the desired effect and no further trouble occurred." As the writer noted, "the Republican party is not a party of violence but of peace and good order. It is characteristic of the [D]emocracy bully, [to] brow beat, and flourish pistols at every opportunity. The candidate for sheriff on the Democratic ticket in this county is now under two or three indictments for assault with pistol, etc. The Republicans are determined that this thing of knocking men down and abusing them, and displaying pistols on every occasion by a few Democrats 'shall stop at all hazards.'"[173] While the account has a Republican slant, a physical encounter certainly occurred.

The *Borderer*, meanwhile, persisted with provocative copy. It published a letter to "the people" from Doña Ana probate judge Pablo Melendres saying the Republican probate clerk Ygnacio Orrantia had suggested to Melendres that he take off his Democratic coat, become a Republican, and if he did, would receive the position of customs handler with a $125 a month in gold or silver. To finalize the plan, they could visit that evening with William Rynerson, Padre Jesús Baca, and John Lemon. If this were carried out, and Melendres declared his strategy as one of "killing" the Democratic Party before the election, he would become "one of the greatest political men of this County," the "great man of the Republican Party." Melendres had Orrantia guaranteeing the Republicans winning the election, "whether they gained it by votes or the use of bullets, clubs, rocks or blows, and that he should feel very sorry to have to do it against me as I was his friend and he liked me." Orrantia asked Melendres for the right to run for probate judge to control the registrars of election and thus show those Democrats "that they are still children in politics, and we will send them [away] forever." Melendres swore to hold nothing confidential in politics; nothing could make him "the traitor to my party and its principles."[174]

The *Borderer* announced a crusade against an alleged Radical plot to curtail freedom of speech and free political action in the territory, which would strike "at the very root of political and civil liberty." The people of New Mexico and Doña Ana were implored to "awaken to the true condition" of threats to "country, our God and liberty." "Could it be possible," the paper asked, "that honest and honorable men of the Republican party will longer consent to be fed and controlled by such men? Are they anxious to see their [D]emocratic neighbors and friends shot down in cold blood?" Most county Republicans were honest and honorable, Bennett affirmed, were willing to see majority rule, and would deprecate the "outrages threatened by their leaders."

Would they adhere to a party "controlled" for violent purposes, "or like honest men and law-abiding citizens, leave a party the leaders of which threaten to water this fair valley with the blood of its own citizens"? Republicans would not again approach the judge of the county with their corrupt offers. Melendres did "as we might have expected he would. But in these days of corruption and fraud he has endeared himself to his fellow citizens by the knowledge that the vile advances of corrupt politicians have only been met by his just indignation. . . . *Be careful and go slow,*" the weekly counseled.[175]

What the *Borderer* called the "sequel" to the Radical office holder's threat to carry the election by pistols and clubs occurred as a party of men visited the field camp of the brother of the Democratic candidate for sheriff, Mariano Barela. Intruders called out for the candidate and fired a volley into the wagon in which he slept; his life was saved by a harness. The same night Ylario Moreno of La Mesa, son of the Democratic candidate for the legislature, on his way with his wife to a Democratic baile was shot at, "the ball barely missing him, passing over his shoulder." Radical leaders were called on to rebuke "this thing."[176]

The *Borderer* ridiculed H. H. Heath, who at the time stumped for Chávez, and the two chief Euroamerican Republicans in Doña Ana County, William Rynerson and John Lemon.[177] The smearing of Lemon was particularly egregious. Lemon, a Mesilla merchant and former Democratic probate judge, ran as a Republican candidate for probate judge.[178] A theme in the *Borderer*'s attack concerned Lemon's alleged corruption in elections when he was a Democrat. Lemon reportedly confessed at a Republican "love feast" at Mesilla to rejecting enough legal votes for Perfecto Armijo in the race for sheriff in 1867 to bring him down. Armijo and Lemon were now on the same ticket, and so Lemon reportedly sermonized on forgiveness, craving the pardon of his fellow candidate. "Pardon was granted," the farce poked, amid embraces and kisses. "[B]rotherly feelings established, don Juan said if he practiced the same anymore it would be on Democratic candidates."[179]

The *Borderer* quoted Radical Congressman S. Newton Pettis, who named Lemon among those who had committed "extraordinary, not to say outrageous and criminal" frauds in Doña Ana County in "absolutely" rejecting 393 votes that had been cast for Chávez in 1867 "without objection or challenge, with nothing to commend such action save boldfaced impudence and brazen insolence, and all in order to falsify the records of the County." Pettis said that "the evil which men do lives after them, and nothing is more foolish than injustice. The bad faith of these ballot box stuffers and election return manipulators, repeaters and rejecters, come back to pester and plague them and theirs." In some fateful words, Pettis said that Lemon and associates would die. Their infamy was on record, "and will live after them, reaching down through the tide of time to the third and fourth generation, and will stick to the ribs of posterity, and, like a chronic infirmity, will be felt at every change of the weather."[180]

The *Borderer* belittled Lemon in comic relief of the Doña Ana County Republican Convention. Chávez lets loose a monkey, representing Heath.[181] The animal attacks Lemon, mistaking him for a Democrat, making him "blush like a maiden," with "a bland smile that somebody said belonged to the heathen Chinese." The monkey scratches "Don Juan" and pulls his hair; "how we pity poor Don Juan," claims the narrator.

> The little thing is about to get him under the table, and make a finish of Don Juan, when a delegate calls out, stop you fool, he is one of us. The little thing seems frightened by the strange voice, tries to flutter his wings again, but can't rise—rolls his onion eyes around and calls to one of his amused spectators in pretty fair English—"I say, Applejack I didn't say anything agin' Don Juan Lemon did I Applejack?" / The amusement is terrific—Don Juan crawls up on the *bench* and blows his nose.[182]

The mocking of Lemon included a justice of the peace publicly accusing him of attempted bribery, willing to forgive a $52 debt if the J.P. worked for his campaign.[183] Lemon was also accused of taunting California Volunteers. Critics reportedly said "some hard things of the men who grow rich by the war, but never fought; and who now claim that they are the only *loil* [sic] ones of the land."[184]

On August 20 both Democrats and Republicans set out in procession from Mesilla, the first to Doña Ana, the second to Las Cruces. A Democratic reporter called his party's affair the "largest political demonstration that the citizens of New Mexico ever witnessed," six hundred strong, two hundred horsemen, "with the banners and music, followed by an immediate concourse in carriages and wagons." As he described it, "Both parties had worked hard to show their forces on this occasion.... The ladies of Mesilla and Cruces showered bouquets upon the Democrats, and circled with slips of patriotic poetry. Strangers from abroad... confessed themselves struck with wonder and astonishment." The partisan correspondent figured that the Democratic organizing had taught the Radicals a salutary lesson, "that it won't do to undertake to carry out their threats of gaining this election by the use of pistols and clubs.... Everything passed off pleasantly." In "good humor," the Democrats rejoiced at the *Borderer*'s suggestion against "offensive cheering," which had been abolished by both parties.[185]

Republicans and Democrats both planned to hold rallies on August 27 in Mesilla. Troops from Fort Selden were called in for security. At a meeting to defuse things, leaders of the two parties agreed to schedule their events at different places. The Democratic rally on the plaza and the Republican assembly at the home of John Lemon passed without incident, and the troops filed back to Fort Selden. Members of each party, reputedly on cheap whiskey and beer, decided to parade around the plaza. The contingents marched toward each other from opposite directions along the narrow Calle Parián, the Gamboa Band accompanying the Democrats, a brass band leading Republicans. As they met in front of the Griggs-Reynolds Building, Democrats taunted Republicans with "Marching through Georgia," a favorite Republican tune, with Spanish lyrics about defeating the enemy at the election and driving them back to Mexico.[186]

Neither County Sheriff Fabián Gonzales, a Republican, nor the constable was able or willing to establish crowd control.[187] I. N. Kelly, a printer in the shop of the *Borderer* and a Democrat, confronted John Lemon with an angry political argument.[188] In the background Apolonio Barela, U.S. marshal and Republican candidate for the territorial house, fired a pistol in the air, perhaps inadvertently. The startled Kelly struck Lemon on the head with an axe handle. Lemon hit the ground, his skull cracked open. One Felicito Arroyo y Lueras instantly felled Kelly dead with a gunshot. Arroyo in turn was shot through the heart. With a crowd of families pouring out of San Albino Church onto the plaza, panic turned into mayhem with shots fired indiscriminately.[189] An eyewitness reported, "It is no exaggeration to say that the plaza has been literally drenched with blood.... From five o'clock this afternoon until six, our plaza resounded with pistol shots, groans, yells and execrations." In one estimate, more than five hundred shots were fired. The Selden cavalry returned to establish peace and order.[190]

In addition to Lemon, aged thirty-nine, eight others died and forty to fifty were wounded. Six of those killed were Nuevomexicanos.[191] A grand jury convened to consider charges; however, no indictments were ever returned.[192] The *New Mexican* blamed the bloodletting on the "outrageous, unprovoked attack" on Lemon by Kelly, hinting at the fault of the *Borderer*. In Lemon, the *New Mexican* lamented the loss of one of Doña Ana County's "best and ablest citizens... universally esteemed and respected."[193] It pinned blame on the fact that the third judicial district, which included La Mesilla, had had no resident judge for four years. Government neglect had led to a general state of disorder, "some of the vilest scoundrels that ever infested a civilized community [having] enjoyed... immunity."[194] The *Borderer* hardly commented on the incident.

The *Chicago Post* blamed the riot on the want of public schools and the "custom of making Sunday *the* day of holding conventions, having processions, etc." The *Santa Fe Post* tended to agree. "So long as thousands of children are permitted to go uneducated, and the Territory remains without any means of education for them," it editorialized, "and while the custom of shocking all Christianity by the desecration of Sunday prevails, New Mexico can hardly expect kind comment or just treatment. Where these evils exist they are supposed to have their accompaniments and like the Quaker's cry, 'bad dog,' are sufficient to justify all other manner of attacks. It is to be hoped the future will remove these evils."[195]

A Spanish-language correspondent decried the unjust commentary in the eastern press for its damage to the people of the territory, observing that no one deprecated the violence as much as public opinion in New Mexico. The intent of the attacks was to keep people from investing in New Mexico, the writer theorized, thereby removing from New Mexicans the things that were necessary for their well-being. In no other part of the country, it was maintained, was there less danger of men being assaulted or their rights violated, nor could they receive any greater cordial welcome, protection, and generous treatment than in New Mexico.[196]

The *Borderer* pointed out a contradiction. While the big newspapers belittled New Mexico, "a half dozen revolting murders daily grace their social columns," and riots frequently "washed their pavements with blood." Even within their "enlightening and civilizing influence, they relieve their supercharged souls of holy horror by pointing to the astonished world for the wonderful fact that human passion exhibits its unhappy consequences on an isolated frontier."[197]

Indeed, a number of political riots had been occurring in the East, many of them reported in New Mexico. Hibernians broke up New York City's Orangeman parade, leading to the killing of about 150 persons and many wounded.[198] In Philadelphia the Republican Invincible Club accosted the Keystone Democratic Club as the latter marched past the headquarters of the Invincibles. Across from the mayor's office, fifteen to twenty persons were injured, including policemen and the president of the Keystone Club. Democratic toughs broke up an Irish American Republican meeting, speakers being beaten with clubs and shots being fired.[199] Shortly after the New Mexico election, Republican factions went at each other at a Radical convention in Syracuse, New York, where a number of participants were killed and injured.[200]

The Mesilla riot thus reflected the country's imperfect political culture, and for New Mexicans a devil's national integration.[201] The violence stemmed, moreover, from the fact that this was the first year of distilled Republican and Democratic identities in New Mexico. In this sense the Mesilla riot fit squarely into the context of Nuevomexicano political development. At a rally for Chávez in Doña Ana, a Nuevomexicano proclaimed he was "ready to die as John Lemon did for the Republican Party."[202]

Results

A week of campaigning remained, and neither party missed a beat to the end. Gallegos and Chávez both paid last minute visits to the communities of Doña Ana County, to the usual cheers and jeers of what appeared a routine canvass without threats, interference, or disruption.[203] The *New Mexican* labored to project a binary race, holding that the histories of the two parties were "embodied in the history of the country, and everyone who has ordinary common sense and can read the current literature of the day knows the difference between Democratic and Republican parties."[204] The two-party emphasis was necessary precisely because of a three-horse race for delegate. Republicans needed precinct managers to see all Republican voters registered. "If a full vote is cast throughout the territory," the *New Mexican* admonished, "the Republican candidate will be elected by over 2000 majority; but notwithstanding this large preponderance of Republican votes, the failure of the few in each election precinct to turn out on election date would defeat our ticket."[205]

It was in some ways ironic, given campaign histrionics, that the turnout was at such low ebb—at 13,489, below that of 1863.[206] While election day was free of the "bloody Sunday of the previous week," voters were turned off by the violent tone of the campaign.[207] Many Republicans seem to have stayed home out of frustration over the in-fighting of their party. As Sullivan noted, the lack of interest by Republicans was caused "by an unsatisfactory candidate and the dissensions caused by a bolt."[208]

Table 5. Official vote for delegate to Congress, New Mexico Territory, 1871

County	Gallegos	Chávez	Sena
Bernalillo	709	743	0
Colfax	329	207	0
Doña Ana	763	478	0
Grant	173	103	2
Mora	1,241	367	202
Río Arriba	975	544	160
San Miguel	842	256	1,438
Santa Fe	747	110	619
Socorro	729	475	0
Taos	471	752	20
Valencia	358	951	21

Adapted from "Official Vote for Delegate," *New Mexican*, September 19, 1871, 1; "Official Vote of the Territory for Delegate," *Post*, September 23, 1871, 2.

That Kirby Benedict appeared as a guest at the Democratic torchlight victory rally in Santa Fe bespoke how badly Chávez had hurt himself among friends.[209] The totals tell the story: Gallegos 7,670, Chávez 5,285, Sena 2,534. Republican dissidents in San Miguel County succeeded handsomely. The largest county in the territory and the one that had gone so avidly for Chávez since 1865, it was the only one in which Sena came out on top, casting Chávez to a distant third. Sena came out ahead of Chávez (behind Gallegos) in Santa Fe and Mora counties. Though Chávez fared badly in San Miguel County, the *New Mexican* pointed to the county and local election figures showing Republicans largely in the majority there. Had they cast their votes for Chávez, "as they ought to have done after participating in the convention which nominated him, the result would have been very different." As it concluded, "The split in the party created by the appearance of Sena as an independent candidate is the sole cause of our defeat in this territory, as the returns clearly show."[210] If voters who cast ballots for Sena had voted for Chávez, the Republican majority would not have been less than a thousand.[211]

More accurately, Chávez would have won but with a smaller majority than the *New Mexican* projected.[212] Effective Democratic organizing gave Gallegos seven of eleven counties in which Sena hardly registered. Doña Ana County, which gave birth to the neo-Democratic Party, went for Gallegos heavily and gave Sena nothing. Socorro County voted solidly for Gallegos. Río Arriba County went so substantially for Gallegos that Sena's absence would not have helped Chávez there. Taos was the only northern county to vote for Chávez, doing so handily. Chávez held on in two of the three Río Abajo counties. Even so, his majority in his Valencia home county was only half the expected thousand. He barely won Bernalillo County. The *New Mexican* noted that had Santa Ana's Republicans voted proportional to their numbers, they and Valencia would have offset Gallegos majorities in Santa Fe and Colfax counties.[213]

A new Democratic choir rang out the post-election hymns of liberalism. The "glorious" results represented the corrective of a republican form of government, the *Borderer* registered. "The people" had become tired "of the little serfdom under which they existed." Bennett saw the Republican wire pullers downed. Democrats had to "wrench from a set of political demagogues the power they had so long abused; to drive a clique of political tricksters from office who have only used position for the advance of personal and private interests." Bennett congratulated his Doña Ana County for leading the way.[214] Pablo Melendres was elected probate judge as no Republican substitute was named for the deceased John Lemon. Democrats swept the other county offices.[215] Bennett recognized the win as an upset. "Had the Santa Fe *Post* and others been listened to in the selection of a candidate, it is doubtful if the Democracy of the territory could have been brought to a nomination."[216]

Implying the likes of Elkins and Catron, McGuiness acknowledged the pain of having to support the choice of the new Republican leaders. As for the opposition, he asked, "[H]ow is it with the *Borderer*? Has that paper no objection to . . . a platform dictated by the North Carolina rebel [Rencher]? We presume it does not object to such leaders and political guardians, wherein we are proud to differ from the *Borderer*. In the next contest we trust the *Borderer* will have all the counselors in the territory of the class alluded to. We will gladly spare and triumphantly prosper without them."[217]

Sullivan noted that his paper had done all in its power to prevent the renomination of Chávez, "hearing, as we did, that such a nomination meant Republican defeat." Still, he had supported Chávez as a duty to the party, "and for the sake of our party and principles we did all in our power to prevent a result which people elsewhere might construe into a Democratic victory." It was consistent with the postmastership Sullivan received, and which appears to have driven José D. Sena to run. He claimed that New Mexico Republicanism was as "reliable and strong as ever" though it had met with this reverse because of the "imbecile management" of the Republican Central Committee.[218]

The *New Mexican*, though saddened at the results, continued in pride with its connection to the "great" national Republican Party. It felt satisfied that by "no indiscreet or treacherous act or word of ours has this misfortune befallen our party." There were others who pretended to be Republicans who could not "truthfully say this of themselves," Tucker had it. Nothing was spared in disparaging the "renegade Republican" Sena and a certain portion of the electorate.[219]

What Republicans found impossible to admit was that Sena represented a respectable champion of Nuevomexicano rights. Republican organization in this election effectively broke from special attention to the Mexican Party tradition. In a whole new wording of the territory's political problems, McGuinness argued that "capital" had too much influence in New Mexico, implying Gilded Age power starting to overtake the Republican Party in the territory. The party needed "purification from sycophantic office seekers," the editor noted. It was the duty of "sensible" Republicans to learn from the defeat "and prepare for a victorious next encounter." That would be in two years, and it would need all that time "to scrape off those *huaraches* [Mexican sandals] which have impeded us in the past."[220]

Another set of fires lit up the territory's political landscape, some dealing with relations of legislature and governor, others with the dissension among the Republicans over the selection of delegates to the party's national nominating convention. As they subsided, the *New Mexican* paused to comment on a new fad of condemning partisan spirit as the "special bane of a republican form of government." Given the evils in the system, it noted, average citizens who did not have the time to devote to politics needed to trust in others. There were many cogs in the political machine "which only the expert understands," it was claimed in defense of representative government, and the world turned on the principle of delegation. Parties were "both fast nearing the great assize [the 1872 presidential election] when they must submit to be tested by this balance sheet rule." The administration would be tested on its performance, while the Democratic Party must submit the sheet "of its most important responsibility." Both "must abide by the crucial test of the conduct of the men placed in power." Accordingly, a great deal could be said for the advantages of "having party lines sharply drawn."[221]

Conclusions

The election of 1871 inaugurated a new political era for New Mexico, generating both centripetal and centrifugal results for Nuevomexicanos. Fully organized Republican and Democratic parties went at each other for the rest of its term as a federal territory and beyond. Powerful parties of integration by then, they anchored Nuevomexicanos within the American political system for good. Candidates for delegate to Congress ran as clearly identified and competitive Republicans and Democrats. In 1873 Delegate Gallegos angered New Mexico Democrats by calling himself a friend of the administration of the Republican President Grant, to which he tendered his "most cordial sympathy." It was a serious gaffe across the line of party loyalty indelibly drawn in the territory. The *Borderer* led a Democratic abandonment of Gallegos, and he was soundly beaten for reelection by the Gilded Age Republican Stephen Elkins.[1] Elkins rose as a Republican of national repute. His win, engineered by his business partner José Leandro Perea, an uncle of José Francisco Chávez, initiated a decade of Republican control of the congressional post.[2] Elkins won reelection against the challenge of Pedro Valdez, whose Democratic credential stemmed from a staunch and long-standing opposition to Republicans in San Miguel County.[3] Reflecting the growing strength of the Republican Party, the Nuevomexicano-dominated Republican convention endorsed Elkins for reelection based on his having obtained appropriations for territorial public services and for his eloquent speech in Congress "calling attention to the rights of our people which had gone obstinately unrecognized." For what it was worth, Elkins's conduct and official action in the discharge of legislative duties as a Republican delegate were cited as exemplary for a leader of Nuevomexicanos.[4]

The next three elections for delegate were won by other Republicans. A Nuevomexicano was elected delegate to Congress in every election up to 1884. Valdez was defeated in 1877 by Trinidad Romero, another San Miguel County politician. In 1878 (when the territorial elections were changed to even-numbered years to coincide with presidential elections) Bernalillo County probate judge Mariano S. Otero, a nephew of Miguel A. Otero, beat out the San Miguel County Democrat Benito Baca. In 1880 Tranquilino Luna, heir to a rico clan in Valencia County, defeated Miguel Antonio Otero I, who came out of political retirement to take another shot at the delegate seat to boost the territory's Democratic fortunes in Washington.

This dominance of Republican delegates to Congress tracked along the consecutive presidential elections of Republicans since 1860. In 1884 New Mexico went with the national tide of electing Democrat Grover Cleveland president. The Democrat Francisco A. Manzanares, Río Arriba County merchant and political compadre of Diego Archuleta, beat out Luna for congressional delegate. Beginning with Manzanares a Democrat held the delegate position in New Mexico for twelve consecutive years in spite of the White House returning to the Republican Party in 1889. Rather than renominate Manzanares in 1886, Democrats went with Antonio Joseph. Described by one historian as "a smiling, urbane merchant and land speculator from Taos," Joseph won that race and the next four as well. Born in Taos in 1846 to a Portuguese immigrant family who had settled in New Mexico in 1840, Joseph was a 1.5 generation Euroamerican settler (a pre-adult during the American conquest), whose *nativo* followers identified with him as an ethnic brother.[5]

Party leaderships dedicated efforts to coordinate more fully a territory-wide organization.[6] The making of operative Republican and Democratic organizations proceeded apace after 1871. Republicans recognized the importance of organizing precincts, the "first and most important step taken in every election where the views of the people ought to be read as clearly as at the polls."[7] The legislature created precincts in rapid succession as new counties appeared.[8] Most members of precinct organizations in the homeland districts continued to be Nuevomexicanos by far.[9] The Republican Party steadily spread over counties. The Republican Central Committee developed local leaderships by responding to community needs and desires.[10] Republican-Democratic Party contention stamped the territorial legislature permanently. After leaving the position of delegate to Congress, José Francisco Chávez went on to become a Republican legend. Elected to the council in 1875, he was reelected for fifteen consecutive sessions and was elected council president eight times, up to his death in 1904. In 1895 a Spanish-language biography said Chávez enjoyed "high estimation, not only among the people of the community in which he has lived many years, but also of his party throughout the territory. In the council," it continued, "his colleagues secure his wise advice on parliamentary points and other matters without regard to party affiliation."[11] Chávez was called by one political veteran "without exception, the best presiding officer in the territory of New Mexico." Chávez applied his *jefe*'s power to uphold an unfailing commitment to the Republican Party.[12]

The train of Republican presidencies spelled a host of Republican governors for New Mexico. Gubernatorial custom, if not policy, instituted a type of affirmative action, reserving second-tier territorial appointments for Nuevomexicanos. A trend of Republican (later Democratic) administrations staffing the territorial government with Nuevomexicanos began in 1872 when Governor Marsh Giddings replaced Auditor Anastacio Sandoval and Treasurer Pablo Delgado, both of Mexican Party affiliation, with Antonio Ortiz y Salazar and Trinidad Alarid, of American Party lineage.[13]

The Democratic Party steadily developed out from Santa Fe after 1871. Executive committees coordinated every electoral campaign. County and territorial nominating conventions were held for each election. Nuevomexicanos involved themselves in the expansion of the binary structure. Epifanio Vigil served on the Democratic Territorial Executive Committee in 1876 and as translator and publisher of the Democratic weekly, the *New Mexico Union/Unión de Nuevo Méjico*.[14]

The Democratic Party gained its electoral edge in battles with the Gilded Age lawyers and entrepreneurs who increasingly dominated the Republican Party after José Francisco Chávez's ignominious defeat for congressional delegate in 1871. Democrats effectively hung the sobriquet "Santa Fe Ring" (*la Rueda*) around the faction's neck.[15] In the mid- to late 1880s the Democratic Party developed organizationally under Delegate Antonio Joseph and Governor William

T. Thornton. Thornton acted to repress Republicans. He reportedly forced the "politico-owners" of the *New Mexican*, William Manderfield and Thomas Tucker, to sell the paper by locking them out of territorial printing contracts.[16]

The electoral base expanded. Voter turnout on election day reached 55,880 in 1908, (even as the parties weakened in mobilizing voters in the states around the turn of the century, resulting in dramatically declining turnouts).[17] The territorial press was augmented concomitantly. From a handful in 1871, fifteen newspapers appeared in 1879, seven of them relatively stable and destined for long life. The total number in 1903 was sixty-nine, five of them dailies. In the partisan breakdown, four of the dailies were Republican and one was nonpartisan. Twenty-four weeklies were Republican and nineteen Democratic.[18] The *New Mexican* remained the primary Republican organ, somewhat in competition with the *Las Vegas Optic* and the *Albuquerque Journal*. The *Borderer* in Las Cruces, the spark of the revitalized Democratic Party in 1871, remained the primary Democratic organ only to 1875. The *New Mexican Review* and the *Sun* in Santa Fe took over, after which the center of gravity for a Democratic press shifted to Albuquerque.

Whereas a Spanish section appeared standard in the typical Euroamerican-run newspaper prior to the 1870s, a major development for the continued integration of Nuevomexicanos was the rise of the wholly Spanish-language newspaper with Nuevomexicano editors (with some immigrants from Mexico and Spain). The intriguing *El Clarín Mejicano* (The Mexican bugle) appears to have been the first effort, published briefly in 1873. Its name alone sounds the call to political arms for Nuevomexicanos. Unfortunately the editor and publisher are unknown and only one issue survived.[19] Fifteen Spanish-language papers appeared a decade and a half later, and the number was thirty-five in the 1890s (although it appears to have dipped by 1903). This important output was spurred by the increase in Spanish literacy among an emerging middle and professional class in the second generation of Nuevomexicanos, whose members were mostly educated in the Catholic schools of Santa Fe.[20] The papers' names reflected the cultural base of their readership: *El Tiempo, El Labrador, El Eco del Norte, El Sol de Mayo, El Hispano Americano, El Boletín Popular, La Luz, El Farol, El Nuevo Mundo, El Defensor del Pueblo, La Ban-*

dera Americana.[21] These new generation Spanish weeklies advocated on behalf of Nuevomexicanos' rights in the tradition of the old style Mexican Party.

These journals were almost all partisan affairs until the end of the Spanish-language press in the 1930s. Politics led to the founding of two of the best Spanish-language papers, *La Voz del Pueblo*, an unflinching Democratic journal, and *El Independiente,* the equally combative Republican weekly. Both papers ended up in Las Vegas at the turn of the twentieth century, *El Independiente* taken there by the Union's People Party. The able editors of both were intense political activists. Félix Martínez, Ezequiel C. de Baca, and Antonio Lucero pushed a wing of the Democratic Party, which resulted in part in C. de Baca getting elected governor of New Mexico and Lucero lieutenant governor.[22]

After Antonio Joseph's remarkable ten-year stint as congressional delegate as a Democrat, the Republican Party, matching Republican successes in presidential elections, came to dominate politics in the territory. After 1897 Republicans were all but one of the delegates to Congress up to statehood. By the turn of the twentieth century, the dynasty of Miguel Antonio Otero II, son of the former delegate to Congress, served as New Mexico's appointed governor for nine years. His administration increased Republican Party membership and coordinated local and central machineries while fashioning "a tightly disciplined unit out of its major wings." In the first decade of the century, Hoover writes, "the final touches had been given to the party's machinery.... Management of policy by a single individual now became a thing of the past, for here a leadership emanated from the central executive committees." In addition to dominating the territorial legislature, Republicans won the majority of county offices at every election. Republican leaders generally stuck together with the prospect of statehood growing in the territory. The "primary integrative force" of the party, Hoover writes, arose "when talk of a constitutional convention occurred.... The obvious reason was to dominate the proceedings of the constitutional convention."[23]

The majority of Nuevomexicano voters, especially in the Río Abajo and Río Arriba sections, evolved into diehard Republicans. As counties developed politically, Nuevomexicanos, especially the large sheep ranchers of the Río Abajo and some sections of the Río

Arriba, such as San Miguel, assumed the position of county party chairmen. Such figures, eminently bilingual, were tied on one hand to the territorial party leadership, largely in the medium of English, and on the other, to the Spanish-speaking electorate. They came to constitute a distinct political class. While some were scions of the rico element, the developing party opened up to non-rico, small-rancher, and labor elements. Their power was coterminous with the county as the principal administrative unit in the territory, making them particularly important for delivering votes and local patronage. They were responsible for doubly modernizing the Republican Party after 1900, linking precincts to central committees. Secundino Romero, editor of *El Independiente*, became an institution unto himself as chairman of the San Miguel County Republican Central Committee. Other county legends going into the new century included Solomon Luna, Celso Baca, E. A. Miera, Palemón Ortiz, Malaquías Martínez, Francisco Hubbell, Marcelino Ortiz, Jesús Romero, Eduardo Otero, Epigmenio Miera, Juan Ortiz y Pino, and Alejandro Sandoval.[24]

Another type of Nuevomexicano leader tended to be associated with the Democratic Party. Political scientist Maurilio Vigil describes individuals "who emerged from obscurity... [and] became professionals—lawyers, teachers, newspapermen. These professions were used as springboards for their political career." Octaviano Larrazolo, who ran for delegate to Congress in 1900, 1906, and 1909, was a lawyer whose main interest was politics. Ezequiel C. de Baca and Antonio Lucero entered politics as teachers and, along with Nestor Montoya, journalists.[25]

If, as liberals maintained, party competition fostered the political integration of marginal groups by providing them with ideological and factional options, the principle applied to intra-party fissures, especially in light of a party grown rigid and exclusionary. In the so-called Third Party system after the Civil War, internal strife defined both Republican and Democratic parties. That condition swept into New Mexico. Nuevomexicanos took full advantage, often innovating the terms of dissidence to suit their particular situations.

The conflict among Radical, conservative, and liberal Republicans that arose during the Grant administration set Republicans to distinguish "regular," corporatist, "old guard" factions and "reformers," "Mugwumps," "independents," and "progressives." The "bolt" from the Chávez establishment that Sena staged in 1871 became a common tactic among dissident Republicans, particularly as a capitalistic circle led by the Gilded Age lawyer Thomas Catron surged to dominate the party. A Republican bolt tended to spell "fusion" with Democrats at elections. Already in 1872, Liberal Republicans bolted from Ulysses S. Grant's attempt at reelection, charging old guard corruption and men using the party to profit in personal interests. They ended up favoring Horace Greeley, who had gone to the side of the Democrats against monopoly finance Republicans. Accordingly, a Democratic-Liberal, Greeley-Brown party came into being in New Mexico, three of its five-member central committee being Nuevomexicanos.[26]

Grant won the election by appeasing southern and racist northern whites on a platform of no special protection for blacks.[27] A decade later the *New Mexican* observed that the Republican Party had at times "offended certain elements and interests which combined with the Democratic Party," threatening its "overthrow."[28] Two years later it was defection in the Republican Party of the idealistic Mugwumps that helped shift the election in favor of the Democrat Grover Cleveland over Republican James Blaine, who was accused of high-stakes corruption.[29] Antonio Joseph won the seat of delegate to Congress in New Mexico in that election, largely on a split among Republicans in which former delegate José Francisco Chávez bolted the rulers of the Republican Party, putting up a third candidate, his old friend William Rynerson, recalled as the killer of Judge John Slough. Chávez, seeing that Rynerson would not win, switched his support to the Democrat Joseph, who won.[30]

Nuevomexicano county jefes at the turn of the twentieth century, armed with the assistance of the *New Mexican*, aligned themselves with the "regular" Territorial Republican Central Committee, considering themselves the carriers of true party principle. They faced bolts from progressives and independents within their own county races. Party regulars accused progressives of damaging party unity and being the real traitors to the organization. The politics were ruthless. José Francisco Chávez was assassinated in 1904 as he sat down for dinner at the home of a friend. No one was ever convicted for the crime, but the political context was unmistakable. Chávez had just been reelected to the territorial council, and as the press reported, his "entire ticket" carried the county "against an Independent Republican ticket. Much bitterness resulted from the contest."[31]

Democrats underwent internal fracture as well. New Mexico Democrats rallied on behalf of a new day, but the reform bug bit them as it did in the rest of the country. In the election season of 1876 delegates to the Bernalillo County Democratic Convention passed a good government resolution, declaring: "Reform is the cry of the whole people, and for this reason we bind ourselves to put forward the best men for public office."[32] The distinction between southern conservatism and Jeffersonian democracy was sustained well into the twentieth century. A major sectional gap developed between liberal Democratic districts in northern New Mexico and Democrats in the growing southeastern quadrant of the territory, where unreconstructed Democrats streamed in from Texas and other southern points.

In 1896 Harvey Ferguson ran for delegate to Congress as a staunch Democratic reformer. His win over Catron was prominently due to the support from an important Nuevomexicano Democratic group in Las Vegas. Articles in *La Voz del Pueblo* heralded progressive ideals, supplemented by guest editorials from Octaviano Larrazolo, who represented the struggle for equality of opportunity and civil rights for Nuevomexicanos particularly. The active conflict between these Democrats in Santa Fe and Las Vegas was made particularly evident when the charismatic Larrazolo twice ran for delegate to Congress only to go down to defeat in part because Little Texas Democrats did not support him on racial grounds. Larrazolo resigned from the Democratic Party in protest, joining Republicans just as New Mexico was winning the struggle for statehood in 1910–12. That move would eventuate in Larrazolo getting elected governor of the State of New Mexico in 1918.[33]

Thus far, this pattern of political integration at the turn of the twentieth century was founded on the reign of power-sharing in the frontier period, when Nuevomexicanos realized a fighting chance for attaining political place and power in the shadow of their conquest by forced annexation. Nuevomexicano actors simultaneously integrated themselves and gave as good as they got based on what they defined as in their own interests and those of their nativo folk, and which proved necessary for New Mexico to set down a functional political system for posterity. It is the primary message in the foregoing chapters, set against the backdrop of the United States establishing gross inequalities among other colonized minorities. The opportunity for Nuevomexicanos to establish an effective political legacy was afforded by a continental form of liberalism; by the historicity, that is, of American self-integration. Pure liberalism thought itself capable of positively incorporating foreign elements. That it would or could, in any given circumstance of the nineteenth century, arose as a critically low probability. Nineteenth-century New Mexico offered experimental ground for the implementation of classic and American principles, ideologies, and mechanisms of Enlightenment liberalism.

That said, however, could it be that the liberal framework works best when a single ethnoracial grouping predominates among the populace? For it was after the railroad started to transform New Mexican society demographically that the heavy hammer of colonialism came down on the majority Nuevomexicanos. As noted at the outset of this work, race distinction has always had a way of undermining the realization of true sociopolitical inclusion in the United States. While Nuevomexicanos continued to control politics within their respective counties, their share of power at the territorial level in the industrial era was profoundly weakened by a more classic form of imperialist invasion.

The story involved a common theme in the U.S. annexation of the northern portion of Mexico, for what this watershed introduced into New Mexico involved dramatic increases among the set of Euroamericans. To illustrate, the average rate of increase in the censuses between 1860 and 1900, when Nuevomexicanos constituted 85 percent of the territory's population, was 27.4 percent. Between 1900 and 1910 New Mexico's overall population increased by 67.6 percent, from 195,310 to 327,301. Moreover, a core segment of the American in-migration settled in the southeastern corner of the state, where they predominated among the electorate and came to rule a major faction of the Democratic Party.[34]

Table 6. Delegates to Congress from the Territory of New Mexico, 1884–1912

Election Year	Winners	Losers
1884	*Antonio Joseph	L. B. Prince and William Rynerson
1886	Antonio Joseph	J. W. Dwyer
1888	Antonio Joseph	+Mariano.S. Otero
1890	Antonio Joseph	Mariano.S. Otero
1892	Antonio Joseph	Thomas B. Catron
1894	Thomas B. Catron	Antonio Joseph
1896	Harvey B. Fergusson	Thomas B. Catron
1898	+Pedro Perea	Harvey B. Fergusson
1900	Bernard S. Rodey	#Octaviano Larrazolo
1902	Bernard S. Rodey	Harvey B. Fergusson
1904	William H. Andrews	George P. Money and Bernard Rodey
1906	William H. Andrews	#Octaviano Larrazolo
1908	William H. Andrews	#Octaviano Larrazolo

+ Nuevomexicano. * Born in New Mexico in Mexican period to Portuguese immigrant parents. # Mexican immigrant who came to New Mexico in the late territorial period.

These changes spelled dire political consequences for Nuevomexicanos. The Euroamerican share of power in New Mexico in the railroad period grew exponentially and out of proportion to their minority numbers. Quite centrally, Nuevomexicanos lost control of the office of delegate to Congress. As we saw, from 1853 to 1882 a Nuevomexicano filled thirteen of seventeen terms as congressional delegate. However, as table 6 shows, from 1884 to 1908 a Nuevomexicano served in one out of thirteen terms. Four Nuevomexicano delegate candidates ran unsuccessfully during this period. Of six actual delegates during that time, only one, the aristocrat Pedro Perea, was a Nuevomexicano. In the rest of the field of candidates who ran but lost, one of ten was a hereditary nativo. Octaviano Larrazolo was born in Mexico. The Nuevomexicano folk adopted him as a native son. If he is considered as such, that would mean two Nuevomexicanos against thirteen Euroamericans who could muster a campaign for delegate to Congress, a most dramatic recast of the pattern in the first thirty-four years of the territorial period, when Nuevomexicanos dominated the position of delegate to Congress. The increasing representation of Euroamericans in the territorial assembly signaled their growing power as well. A shocker came in the 1888–89 session when only five elected members were Nuevomexicano. Nuevomexicanos regained their accustomed majority of the 1890–91 council—but narrowly. They then constituted but half of the session in 1892–93. After that Nuevomexicanos became the minority in the territorial Legislative Council in every session until the last one in 1909. The low point came in 1907, when their representation dropped to three members. In the larger House of Representatives, Nuevomexicanos held onto bare majorities until the tail end of New Mexico's territorial period, when Euroamericans gained the majority in the council sessions of 1907 and 1909.[35]

The erosion in Nuevomexicano power extended to the Republican and Democratic Party organizations. Euroamericans went on after the 1870s to dominate top leadership roles and central committees. William Breeden led the charge in the Republican Party, solidifying the Euroamerican-dominated Republican Central Committee as its chairman until 1886.[36] The Gilded Age lawyer Thomas Catron took on the job in the late 1870s and 1880s of fostering Republican organizations in precincts and linking them to their county committees and the territorial Central Committee. Catron, who taught himself Spanish, understood the need for recruiting the Spanish-speaking electorate if the Republican Party was to gain the effective ascendancy that its Euroamerican leaders aimed for in the territory, but Catron held little interest in specifically recruiting Nuevomexicanos to lead the party.[37] The Democratic Party came under the leadership of a series of Euroamericans as well: Edmund F. Dunne in the 1870s, C. H. Gildersleeve after Dunne, followed by Jacob Crist, a bitter Catron enemy, in the 1890s.[38]

The political reality of the ethnic distribution of power sprung quite vividly in 1910, when Euroamericans held the clear majority of the popularly elected seats (sixty-five of one hundred) in the Constitutional Convention, which drafted the organic constitution for New Mexico to become a state, the final Statehood Revolution, which it did in 1912.[39] The central question at that point became whether Nuevomexicanos would be able to participate in the new state political system after all, much less as they had in the initial annexation period.[40]

Euroamerican colonialism extended materially. As anthropologist Eric Wolf emphasized, the dynamic of cultural capitalism penetrating indigenous peasant communities and disrupting traditional agrarian economies throughout the world produced "trauma and strife, of interference and rupture with the past." The spread of North Atlantic capitalism involved "an unequal encounter between the societies which first incubated it and societies which were engulfed by it in the course of its spread. The contact between the capitalist center, the metropolis, and the pre-capitalist or non-capitalist periphery [was] a large-scale cultural encounter, not merely an economic one." Capitalism "cut through the integument of custom, severing people from their accustomed social matrix in order to transform them into economic actors, independent of prior social commitments to kin and neighbors."[41]

Recall how both political parties in pre-railroad New Mexico envisioned great benefits to accrue for Nuevomexicanos once eastern capitalists arrived to provide vital economic development. It never happened. The frenzy for mining never received its immediate reward, and New Mexico provided no other natural resource base on which to offer large-scale, well-paid labor. Instead, the entrepreneurship that did materialize with the coming of the railroad produced a new fever, this time in land speculation. Its major consequence was to tear up the community integument of Nuevomexicano pobladores. An accelerated capitalist penetration undermined the viability of the communal Spanish and Mexican land grants, the *mercedes*, described in chapter 1. It was a problem that Padre Antonio José Martínez had seen coming in the 1830s.[42] Recall that in the 1871 election season, members of both political parties called on Congress to resolve the issue of the land grants for the good of the Nuevomexicano citizenry and the territory as individual outsiders had been acquiring individual tracts by hook or crook. What the railroad wrought involved a virtual movement of Gilded Age activists—most of them Republicans, grouped by their enemies as the "Santa Fe Ring"—whose land acquisitions ended up usurping the legitimacy of the common titles. Thomas Catron, one of the key figures in the effort to firm up the Republican Party in the 1870s, headed the venture. Ironically, Catron used the Republican

Party and manipulated the territorial legislature to serve his interest in acquiring as many of the Nuevomexicano land grants as possible.[43]

Catron eventually obtained an interest in some seventy-five land grants, becoming the largest land holder in the United States. Nearly every governor of the New Mexico Territory from the late 1870s to 1885 engaged in dicey land speculation, and key Nuevomexicanos were complicit. Some surveyors general themselves participated; three of the nine men to hold the office are now considered "blatant" land grabbers who acquired grant holdings while in office. By 1900 speculators used cattle ranching, mining companies, and railroad investments to capitalize acquired land grants. "With this network working against their interests," notes land grant historian Malcolm Ebright, "it was no wonder that Hispanic land grant settlers, unfamiliar with Anglo laws and language and often not aware of court proceedings involving their land grants had little chance of protecting their property."[44]

A modernizing judicial system contributed to the dispossession of the mercedes. The era of surveyor general lasted just over forty years. By 1886, New Mexico had seen 205 land grant claims filed, 13 rejected outright, and 141 approved. Of the latter, Congress formally approved 46, leaving 95 in limbo, and 51 were not acted on at all. The majority of titles were thus left in an unsettled state. The machinations of speculators in acquiring land grants took place largely away from the ken of heirs, many of whom were treated as squatters on land that rightly belonged to them or who were victims to conspiracies that excluded them from the petitioner groups. Often, because they were allowed to graze on the land, years passed before the unsuspecting villagers realized they had been bilked of the title to their land. Even when grants were confirmed to the appropriate Nuevomexicano heirs, the commons were often greatly reduced, and restrictions were placed on people's ability to graze and utilize the resources on the grant.[45]

With a backlog of 116 land grants, and other claims waiting to be filed, Congress created a new system to adjudicate the land grants in New Mexico, Colorado, and Arizona. The Court of Private Land Claims was formally organized, five judges presiding, at Denver on July 1, 1891. Regular sessions were to be held in Denver, Santa Fe, and Tucson, but as the great majority of cases were New Mexican, the bulk of hearings took place in Santa Fe.[46]

The Court of Private Land Claims heard 282 claims lying wholly or in part in New Mexico and involving 34,653,340 acres. Whereas claimants to the surveyor general were aided by certain presumptions that eased the burden of proof (such as the presumption of the validity of a community grant based on the existence of a settlement on the grant in 1846), the adversarial procedure decided as the standard for the Court of Private Land Claims laid a burden to prove the existence of the grant. While the court was sensitive to the old claims of fraud and wrongdoing, and recognized what were considered the excessive confirmations made by the surveyors general to non-Nuevomexicanos, it applied a harsher, more technical, cautious, and restrictive adjudication. Moreover, in contradiction of Spanish and Mexican law, the court judged as invalid all grants that were issued by officials who were not governors, such as alcaldes, ayuntamientos, prefects, lieutenant governors, and deputations. The court also applied harsh criteria for accepting supporting documents.[47]

United States v. Sandoval et al. (1897) proved momentous. The Court of Private Land Claims had awarded all the commons claimed by Nuevomexicano petitioners of the San Miguel del Bado Grant, which is situated along the Pecos River in northeastern New Mexico. In the appeal to the U.S. Supreme Court, federal lawyers adopted Surveyor General Julian's position that it was Mexico, and not the local community, that fundamentally possessed the commons. The Supreme Court concurred, holding that the Treaty of Guadalupe Hidalgo transferred ownership of the grants from Mexico to the U.S. government. As a result of *Sandoval*, the court tended to reject or significantly whittle down subsequent claims for commons. Contemporary experts consider the *Sandoval* interpretation, moving community lands to the public domain, a violation of international law. It is called the "single most important land grant decision resulting in the greatest loss of [commons]," for it enabled the United States to acquire a vast territory now comprising most of the Carson and Santa Fe national forests. In the one saving grace, the Supreme Court did not apply *Sandoval* retroactively, those commons confirmed before 1897 remaining in force.[48]

Another consequential departure came in *Hays v. United States*, in 1898, when the U.S. Supreme Court removed the presumption of authority of a granting official. After that decision, concerning the Embudo Grant in north-central New Mexico, the claimant had the burden of proving that the officials granting land or making copies of land grant documents—rather than the government that had actual physical custody of documents—had the authority to do so. Claimants still carried the general burden of proof but were left without the benefit of a key presumption that had previously eased that burden. The whole climate of the court favored the U.S. government. Federal lawyers employed witnesses who were knowledgeable with land grant archives and Spanish and Mexican law. Nuevomexicano claimants, lacking money and American know-how, were deprived of equivalent expertise and were often poorly represented by lawyers with unknown credentials and reputation.[49]

As the dust of the Court of Private Land Claims settled, thirteen years after it kicked up, 82 grants were confirmed, representing less than 2,051,526 acres, or 6 percent of the total acreage claimed. Rejected claims involved 33,439,493 acres. Of the 282 claims, 43 were filed by non-Nuevomexicano claimants, and 11 of these were at least partially confirmed. Seventy-three cases, including 58 from the New Mexico district, were appealed to the U.S. Supreme Court. In one calculation, if the Court had complied with the obligation assumed by the United States under the Treaty of Guadalupe Hidalgo, 8 to 9 million more acres of land would have been confirmed. As one researcher sums it up, "Modern scholars have found many of the court of Private Land Claims decisions to be unfair when tested by standards of fairness contained in international law and in the Treaty of Guadalupe Hidalgo."[50]

In the two adjudication experiences, the surveyor general and Court of Private Land Claims, 155 grants were confirmed, and patents were issued for 142. Altogether 24 percent of land grant petitions were confirmed, many of those brought forward by representatives of the commercial interests in the territory, who had acquired the grant rights from their Nuevomexicano owners by various devices.[51]

The memory of comprehensive land losses combined with the precious retention of some Nuevomexicano mercedes lay at the heart in the values of *querencia* that open this book. In this regard, Wolf noted how peasants generally warred against the modern capitalist penetration into their worlds. Likewise, Euroamerican encroachment on Nuevomexicano commons sparked a quality of resistance in the late nineteenth century to do the participants in the 1847 Taos Revolt proud. Early episodes occurred on the Maxwell Grant in northeastern New Mexico. By 1871 mass protests against the intervention of mining interests on the grant broke out. Pobladores joined up with squatters and American miners for self-protection. Shooting incidents that began in 1873 escalated up to 1875. The sheriff had difficulty enforcing order in what became a highly complex set of interests in contention. Periodic outbreaks, resulting in what one historian calls "an extraordinary amount of violence and an impressive number of murders," continued on the Maxwell until the 1890s, when the grant was finally broken up among several private interests.[52] Other regions of the territory saw violent ethnic conflict over land disputes. The oft-studied Lincoln County wars, involving well-known territorial legends such as Billy the Kid, began when Texans moved onto the old Mexican settlements throughout southern New Mexico.[53] Heirs of the dispossessed Tierra Amarilla Land Grant launched a movement of resistance in the 1870s that would last for several decades and that included lawsuits, clandestine fence attacks, and confrontations with law enforcement.[54]

Nineteenth-century confrontation culminated in the brief but highly significant outburst of armed resistance called *Las Gorras Blancas* (The white caps) in San Miguel County. Originating as an ad hoc local organization, Las Gorras Blancas turned their resentment in 1889 to Euroamericans and some Nuevomexicanos who fenced off disputed commons. Donning white sheets that covered rider and horse, armed bands of Hispanos rode at night, killing livestock, knocking down fences, and tearing out railroad tracks. The movement posed a considerable threat to the order that the territorial administration sought to maintain. It also produced celebrated court cases. The organization won political support and influence in San Miguel and nearby counties. But the leadership, affected by the rapid economic development of the region, conflated the matter of preserving an entire traditional culture, including its distinct land tenure system, with the more modern industrial aims of the general Populist Movement, such as just wages and the right to bargain with employers. Las Gorras Blancas faded as a potentially insurgent movement in the 1890s after the jailing of many of its leaders.[55] The folk in particular communities continued to ignore the fences meant to keep them from taking advantage of their accustomed usufruct rights, surreptitiously grazing livestock on the land they once owned. Their running personal battles with foreign owners over control and use of the commons did not cease but brought a minimum of return of the commons.[56]

In the long run, a fundamental outcome of forced annexation was conversion of the majority of colonized Nuevomexicanos into a sociological minority under the U.S. system of racial stratification. The loss of land began a process of twentieth-century impoverishment for an emerging Nuevomexicano proletariat in the long Rio Grande Valley from northern New Mexico to Doña Ana County. The industrial cash economy imported by the railroad eroded the sheep and mercantile system, disrupting traditional communities and social relations. As one historian observes, in the old Río Arriba area where the people had been employed by the region's ricos, "many started in the late 1800s to seek seasonal wage labor. First, they became members of railroad construction gangs and sawmill crews that cut railroad ties and poles used in trestles and mining props. Others turned to seasonal farm labor in the San Luis Valley, where Euroamericans had established specialty crop farms."[57]

As the greater Southwest rapidly and extensively developed, wage labor became the sine qua non of worker survival. In the meantime, the economically unstable valleys of historic northern New Mexico went undeveloped. Subsistence-oriented farmers, largely uneducated and bereft of their common ranges, could not adapt their small-acreage enterprises to a commercial, profit-based, system of cattle ranching being extensively developed in the Southwest. The transfer of public lands to the state further reduced the amount of land that could be used for free grazing, as did the federal land subsidization of huge grants of public lands to railroad construction and the establishment of the national forests. As one study concludes, "It was of the greatest significance that these developments in the Middle Valley's history started at a time when the [Nuevomexicano] population, because of its own expansion, was depending more and more upon the range resources of the valley." Nor were the resources available for the industrial development of the region, and, of course, it was Euroamericans who came to monopolize the professional, business, and political life of the cities. The majority of Nuevomexicanos became an impoverished regional populace as a result, eventually dependent on welfare, and their homeland site became one of the poorest regions in the country. Not even the large stock holders from the nativo upper class could compete with the large Texas-style ranching operations. They too were left bereft of their holdings.[58] As

George I. Sánchez famously put it, poor Nuevomexicanos became a "forgotten people."[59]

Could Nuevomexicano politicians have staved off the baneful impacts of corporate land dealings at fin de siècle had they not lost their former territorial power? Not likely. Even old Mexican Party hands, like the Lincolnite Republican William Arny, were swept into the frenzy of land speculation. Moreover, the land grants became a federal issue and the higher courts the final arbiter.[60] In addition, the hard attachment to party would have had to subside. As Carolyn Zeleny pointed out, "party pride and loyalty [among Nuevomexicanos] substituted for ethnic-group pride and loyalty." The issues of political strife tended to be reduced to party-political conflict. "Party politics... successfully submerged [direct] inter-ethnic conflict during most of the history of political relationships in New Mexico," Zeleny noted.[61] As conquered subjects Nuevomexicanos were hampered from an enduring solidarity by ideological and cultural divisions among elites and various subregional entities but most importantly by the agonistic quality of conventional politics. Even had it been possible to transcend these difficulties, the costs of ethnic unity are typically heavy, researchers point out, hard to sell in principle and harder to pull off in practical terms, given the lack of immediate and concrete benefits for adherents, especially for groups that are small in a large country.[62]

These longer-term consequences of American incorporation might be taken to mean that the conquest generation of Nuevomexicanos and their 1.5 generation offspring were led into the American polity through an experience of hegemonic colonialism, their being lured into participating in American politics via liberal tenets to render them vulnerable to dispossession. But is that any way to honor their legacy? What can be concluded about the fascinating nineteenth-century Nuevomexicano conquest generation is that its members fulfilled the range of role possibilities their historical circumstance opened up to them, and they constructed the foundation for permanent republican politics in New Mexico. Looking back on the arc, Nuevomexicano political integration was facilitated, indeed honored by the power-house careers of José Manuel Gallegos, Miguel Antonio Otero, and José Francisco Chávez. They figured in the clear balance of power between the two contending parties. Ambitious politicians gained status, office, coin, and power on the backs of their party. The constancy of cadre workers on each side reinforces the point—Miguel E. Pino, Facundo Pino, and Tomás Cabeza de Baca in the Mexican Party, for example, and Felipe Delgado, Vicente Romero, and Nicolás Quintana in the American Party, as well as their necessary Euroamerican allies.

It was no mean achievement, even if a great deal of it derived from Euroamerican initiative in institution building and in spite of the fact that republican politics often produces some mystifying, less than liberal manifestations. New Mexico communities ritualized their collective recognition of the generation's special experiences of adjustment, adaptation, and initiative. The individuals who had engaged the conquest and national transition firsthand in the 1840s were eclipsed one by one into misty memory as the century moved on. Among the principal players Manuel Armijo died in 1854, Manuel Álvarez in 1856, Vicar Juan Felipe Ortíz in 1858, Facundo Pino in 1863, Juan Bautista Vigil y Alarid in 1866 and José Serafín Ramírez in 1869. Passing in the 1870s were Antonio José Otero (1870) and José Manuel Gallegos (1875). Nicolás Pino died in 1896, while José Francisco Chávez lived into the first decade of the twentieth century.[63]

The preeminent among them were honored at their passing with public memorials, speeches at overflowing funerals, official proclamations, public meetings, and editorial tributes. Political enemies took time-outs from the agonism to pay tribute to charter members of their political class, and by extension to themselves.[64] Donaciano Vigil died in 1877 at 6:45 in the morning at the age of seventy-five. The governor called for a public commemoration in his honor for later that day at the legislative chamber. Ralph Emerson Twitchell's account captured the solemnity of the scene: "The old citizens, the civil and military officers, the merchants, the native and eastern population, everybody turned out on short notice." It was by far the largest and "most distinguished gathering ever witnessed in New Mexico." Resolutions hailed the "distinguished and worthy citizen" who had served the territory for more than fifty years. It was with sorrow that the people parted with the deceased, "distinguished for his administrative ability, his perfect integrity, just in the exercise of his prerogatives, when governor of the Territory [during the Kearny occupation]; respected by all[,] beloved for his kindness of heart."[65]

Miguel E. Pino died at the age of forty-five in the middle of the intense campaign of 1867 and as he chaired the Republican Executive Committee. Nuevomexicanos in Santa Fe, Albuquerque, Fernandez de Taos, and Las Vegas held memorials and wrote resolutions of condolence. As a patriot of Mexico, the young Pino had figured in the rebellion against the Kearny occupation of New Mexico. Annexation secured, he became a tough, unwavering, member of the Mexican Party. He never became an American citizen and proved a brave combatant in the New Mexico Volunteers in the Civil War. In the campaign of 1867, he led the attack on Charles Clever in the 1865–66 legislature, going on to champion the reelection of José Francisco Chávez, hosting a major post-nomination rally for the incumbent at his residence and earning the honor of the *Gazette*'s sobriquet "head man of the clique."[66]

The *Gazette* put its antipathy to Pino to rest at his death, rendering the most sensitive portrait of the worthy opponent. "The spirit of Don Miguel," it began, was fitted to life's hardest and most dangerous storms. It was quick, high, bold and defiant. In public life it was ambitious and aspiring, and ever ready to contend against animosities, however violent or unjust they were. He knew the disadvantages under which his countrymen had been born and circumstances had placed them, and was ever keenly alive to wrongs and oppression, whenever inflicted upon the poorest of his native countrymen, by any one born and educated under . . . favorable circumstances." It was natural to Pino's "proud and lofty nature," the *Gazette* concluded, "and a high merit in his character."[67]

Diego Archuleta died of heart failure in 1884 at age seventy. An active player of the entire annexation experience of New Mexico, he was remembered as a "bitter" opponent of the 1846 American occupation of New Mexico and as "an intense patriot" of the United States.[68] The Río Arriba and Taos County don served forty-five consecutive years in public service for two national sovereigns. He was a member of the territorial assembly when he died. Having taken ill while on the floor of the house, he rallied himself from bed to register his vote on an important bill. As a Santa Fe newspaper recorded, "he was still very weak and returned to his room immediately after casting his vote. The utmost care and attention was shown him, and every treatment known to medical skill was brought to bear . . . but despite all efforts he continued to sink and grow worse until death came to his relief at an early hour . . . when came the beautiful and peaceful close of an honored and busy official life." The resolution of the Legislative Council mourned the loss of "an able, valued and honorable citizen and public servant, his family a kind and generous protector, and the legislative assembly its wisest and most experienced member." Archuleta's remains lay in state in the territorial house before their removal to the Church of Our Lady of Guadalupe and returned once again to the legislative chamber until the funeral. All government and territorial official circles were represented at the burial. The Twenty-second U.S. Infantry band and the band of the Holy Trinity Society played. The procession to the cemetery—led by military escort, members of the legislature, the county commission, and secret and patriotic societies—was estimated at 2,500 people.[69]

In such partings and tributes lies the legacy of a remarkable extended political family, worthy of solemn keeping as history's *querencia*.

Appendixes

Appendix 1

Affiliations

American Party Stalwarts	**Mexican Party Stalwarts**
Ambrosio Armijo	Francisco Abreu
Juan Cristóbal Armijo	Manuel Álvarez
Merrill Ashurst	Nepumoceno Ancheta
Nehemiah V. Bennett	William Arny
James H. Carleton	Celso Baca
Charles P. Clever	Tomás Cabeza de Baca
James Collins	Spruce Baird
Henry Connelly	Kirby Benedict
Felipe Delgado	James C. Calhoun
Joab Houghton	Rafael Chacón
Sydney Hubbell	José Francisco Chávez
Bishop Jean B. Lamy	Simón Delgado
Pascual Martínez	H. H. Heath
Robert B. Mitchell	William Manderfield
Ignacio Orrantia	José Antonio y Medina
Antonio José Otero	Cándido Ortiz
Miguel Antonio Otero	Juan Felipe Ortiz
Jesús María Pacheco	Facundo Pino
José Francisco Perea	Miguel E. Pino
José Pley	William Rynerson
Nicolás Quintana	Miguel Romero y Baca
Serafín Ramírez y Casanoba	Anastacio Sandoval

Vicente Romero
John T. Russell
Antonio Sandovál
Pedro Sánchez
Francisco Sarracino
Felipe Sena
Donaciano Vigil

José D. Sena
A. P. Sullivan
Thomas Tucker
Faustín Baca y Ulivarri
José María Valdez
Santiago Valdez
Richard Weightman

Swing Politicians
Diego Archuleta
Perry Brocchus
José Manuel Gallegos
Hezekiah Johnson
John Lemon
Pablo Melendrez
Jesús María Pacheco
José Leandro Perea
R. H. Tomkins
John S. Watts

Certain regional colloquialisms are retained in the following reproductions of Spanish-language political tracts and literary editorials. Some grammar has been adjusted from their originals according to standard Spanish-language use, and certain spellings are corrected while retaining the heart of the authors' intent.

Appendix 2

¡¡Cuidado!! ¡¡Cuidado!! ¡¡De El Alarcán Colorado!!

El alacrán es un animal muy semejante al escorpión, con la sola diferencia que este es el animal [más] feroz y peligroso... de los animales ponsoñosos que se conocen. Su cuerpo es amarillento y delgado y la cabeza Colorada con dos cuernitos y en la parte superior. De la cola tiene un aguijón por donde suelta la ponsoña cuando quiere picar. Por la descripción arriba hecha fácilmente podra cualesquiera cuidarse del epidémico Russell, editor de la *Gazeta* de Santa Fé (con otras Palabras del azote... de Nuevo Méjico). Pues en su número de la semana pasada encontrarán un largo y espacioso artículo de descrédito degradación y abusos al pueblo Nuevo Mejicano comparandole solamente "un poco más adelante que el Indio salvaje que se come los piojos que se quite de su sucio Cuerpo." Si tal es la pintura que se haré de nuestro cuerpo legislativo, cuyos miembros que lo componen, se supone que han sido escojidos de la más capaz de sus Condados, ¿cuál será el grado de degradación y desprecio en que semejante Charlatón, como el referido Russell, da esa pintura y exponer al pueblo de Nuevo Méjico y no (obstante) por muchos años ha trabajado por su adelanto y se considera amigo de Nuevo México y de su pueblo?

¡La Verdad del pueblo de Nuevo Méjico!, que al pasar en silencio semejantes abusos es nada menos que dar lugar á que el bandido Russell y sus favoresedores se queden orgullosos y se saben en Maltratar á nuestro pueblo y sus representantes cuando les place.

Ahora, ¿quienes son los Representantes? Un número de hombres escojido por el pueblo el primer lunes de Septiembre de cada año. ¿Para qué son escojidos estos hombres? ¡Para representar y defender nuestros derechos! ¿A quien representan? Al pueblo, que les ha elegido. ¿Quién les ha conferido el poder que tienen como Legisladores? El pueblo. Luego, ¿sobre quién vienen los ataques calumnias y bajesas el tal Russell ha producido en su infernal papel de la semana pasada? Fácil á responder: sobre el pueblo. Además, el poder legislativo se compone de una Cámara de Representantes, un Consejo Legislativo y un Ejecutivo. Pues ahora permítanme preguntar al señor Russell de que pabiene [sic] la excepción que él hace de dos ó tres miembros juntamente con su Excelencia. ¿Será acaso porque le tienen pagado ó por favoritismo, ó sea probalemente porque a su Excelencia y á una minoría de débiles les puede manejar á su antojo? Indublemente ésta es la razón. Pues, si no es ésta la razón, no harían tan declaradas y patentes excepciones. Ahora, digamos, señor Russell, ¿si el señor Russell Enrique Connelly es superior en algo á alungo de los miembros que constituyen una gran mayoría en ambas cámaras, ó si esos miembros á quien V. desea excepcionar sobrepasan á los demás en educación, talento ó capacidad, ó si mismo es en algo más competente que algunos á quién V. se empeña en descreditar con su ponsoñosa lengua por medias de su indigno papelacho, el cual no debería ser leído por ningún Mejicano que tiene respeto personal y que no desea someterse á que usted le dé con una mano el pan y con la otra se [lo quita]? Ni tampoco debería ser leído por ningún Americano honesto cuya buena intención halla sido emigrar á este país con el fin de establecerse entre nosotros para ayudarnos en el progreso ó adelanto del nuestro país: y no para considerarse superior a nosotros tan luego como ha recibido nuestro patrocinio apoyo.

Desde que fuimos anexados a los Estados Unidos han emigrado y residen dentro de nuestros límites en número de cosa de tres mil Americanos de otras partes de la Unión. Muchos de los cuales han venido aquí con sus familias una grandísima mayoría de los mismos simpatizan en todos respectos con nuestro pueblo (no obstante su ignorancia), y á la verdad que no se advierte que exista otra preocupación en contra de nuestra raza que aquella divulgada de cuando en cuando por los mentecatos Russell y Johnson que mientras á su concepto de ellos se ocupan en defender al pueblo de Nuevo Méjico y sus intereses, le están atacando, insultando y sobajando de todos modos y en los terminos más bajos y miserables, haciendole aparecer no solamente ridículo sino como el pueblo más inmoral, corrompido, ignorante que reside sobre la tierra. Pues, tal es la pintura que la *Gazeta* y sus achichinchos han hecho del pueblo Nuevo Mejicano, por una serie de prolongados años.

Ahora, pueblo de Nuevo Méjico, cuyos representantes somos nosotros, permítanos preguntar á todos y cada uno de nuestros constituyentes: ¿Creen Vds. que el que ataca vuestros derechos los defiende? Claro que no. ¿Que el que usurpa nuestros privilegios los respeta? Por supuesto no. ¿Que aquél que os pinta y degrade de todos modos tiene algunos simpatías por vosotros? No, y mil veces no.

Pues, si todas estas cosas se oponen y chocan unas con otras, como podeis creer que [el] bribón de Russell, un bandido cuya presencia pestifera, no pudo ser ya soportado en la Virginia, y que anojado fura [sic] aquel estado por sus villanos procederes, cayó aqui repentinamente de carrero y poniendose de acuerdo con el miserable Santiago L. Collins. Comensaron desde luego sus escarnios, escendalos [sic], vituperios, censuras y abusos en contra del pueblo. No ignorante como ellos lo pintan, pero humilde, sencillo generoso, cuya hospitalidad es extremada para todo el que emigra y quiere residir entre nosotros cuyo buen y benigno corazón, no admite preocupación alguna contra ninguna persona; cuyas bondades se estienden con igualdad así á todo estrangero honesto y desprocupado. Permitiréis, pues, por un momento que el piojo resucitado de Russell continue sus abusos y escarnios en contra de nosotros. ¿Tolerareis con paciencia que el invasor de vuestros derechos, el usar poder de vuestras libertades? Quiere tirar una nube sobre vuestros ojos y hacernos creer que [él es] el vuestro fiel Defensor. ¿Consentiréis que los Representantes que vosotros habéis electo para defender vuestros derechos y representar vuestras necesidades se sometan á los mandatos y órdenes de la *Gazeta,* que sean hechos el instrumento vil y miserable de una pacota de egoistas ajiotistas cuya ambición no puede suciar un corazón negro?

Si tal es el carácter y conducta que nuestros conciudadanos aguardan de nosotros, y si con tales fines nos han conferido su poder y confiado sus intereses, nosotros les damos las más expresivas gracias, suplicandoles nombren otros en nuestros lugares, porque nosotros no deseamos ser los Representantes de esclavos ó de un pueblo que reciba con paciencia los ultrajes que a cada paso se le hacen.

Anónimo, *El Nuevo-Mejicano* (Santa Fe), 5 de Enero de 1866

Appendix 3

Refutando las Calumnias Hechas a los Legisladores de N.M.

El 23 de Diciembre de 1865 apareció en las sucias columnas de la *Gazeta* un editorial compuesta de disparatadas injurias, dicteras y falsas imputaciones contra los Legisladores quienes representan todo el Territorio de Nuevo Méjico.

Tirando una Ojeada hacia la conducta que por muchos años ha observado el editor de tal papelacho facilmente se persuadirán los lectores del mérito supuesto que algunos enemigos del país le atribuyen á ese aborto vomitado del infierno en cuya cabeza arden aún las llamas infernales y cuyos diabólicos sentimientos rasgue con osadia mano pintando un sombrío contra el pueblo Nuevo Mejicano á quien le ha patrosinado, á un pueblo hospitalario y bondadoso que no abrigando pasiones rencorosas é inobles, mira con despreciador desdén a los abusos cometidos por un pelado vagamundo que se ha engrandecido aprovechandose y abusando de la bondad del mismo pueblo que ya lo había de haber quemado y tirado al viento sufetidas [*sic*] cenizas. Pues, los motivos que el ha dado no merece otra cosa, si no hacerle desaparecer de ante una comunidad honesta y civilizada. Cuando dice en su editorial que están un poco adelante de los Indios quienes se comen los piojos de sus cuerpos sucios, sin duda su bajo educación y el tormento que á el le han dado tales insectos le trajeron á la mente tamaña ocurrencia y no dudo que el se haya aumentado de ellos en su viaje de los Estados Unidos á esta capital. Pues el semblante amarillento con pecas negras del tal caballero andante no demuestra otra cosa. Los jofenes Nuevo Mejicanos que han ido al Congreso de los Estados Unidos como nuestros delegados bastante justifican y prueban que lo que falsamente se le imputa á Nuevo Méjico no merece crédito ante los hombres, sensatos y pensadores. Pues bien se sabe que el de la *Gazeta de Santa Fe* únicamente ha proferido tales calumnias agraviado porque no ha recibido una parte de los fondos legislativos, y lo prueba, que guarda silencio hasta que fué considerado por la asamblea legislativa del Territorio de cuyos miembros el vil Russell no es digno de descalsar á ninguno.

Permitid mis lectores que dedique un recuerdo al editor de L. G., ó mejor dicho de la iniquidad. Guarda hombre escandaloso y deshonesto ese veneno que oculta tu negro corazón y trata de esparcir sembrando la discordia ante un pueblo culto y civilizado ante un pueblo apreciador de la virtud y que ya no se deja engañar con las sofismas que le presenta, una alma manchada como la tuya. Abra tu cara de alacrán mientras puede trazar un fiel retrato de tu desfigurado rostro, con tu cabeza colorada, y transmitirlo á las generaciones venideras para que conozcan la casta de hombre que desprecia a los Nuevo Mejicanos. Tus propios hijos te maldecirán y les será afrentoso haber nacido de un padre tan corrompido, y si no preciados de tu proceder y continuas insultando á unos caballeros cuyos honoríficos puestos enviados ellos mismos, no te daran otra contestación que la que merece un perro rabioso que corre ladra, y muerde hasta que muere.

Dispensen, mis lectores, si acaso he sido demasiado prolijo en narrar mi comunicado en un lenguage que no debía de expresarme si no fuera compelido á contestar las afrentas falsedades que han sido proferidas contra nuestros Legisladores.

LA VERITÉ

El Nuevo-Mejicano (Santa Fe), 5 de Enero de 1866

Appendix 4

¡¡¡HORRIBLE ATENTADO!!!

¡ESCUCHAD PUEBLO NUEVO MEJICANO!

Tenemos que informar, con gran sentimiento, al pueblo de este Territorio, los atentados horrible y criminales que algunos individuous que recientemente han venido á residir entre nosotros y que Unidos á algunos otros miserables . . . siempre han calumniado á nuestro pueblo. Se están esforzando á llevar á efecto lo cual están haciendo y tramando de un modo muy secreto, á fin de que el plan no llegue á vidos del pueblo, que en tal vez temen haga un vigoroso esfuerzo para libertarse de tan infame traición, pero parece que la Providencia, que nunca permite que sufra el inocente, ha permitido que algo haya salido á luz á fin de que estemos alerta para rechazar tan improvisto ataque.

En cierta conferencia privada, en la cual los infames autores del movimiento á que nos referimos, aludían á los derechos y garantías que el pueblo de Nuevo Méjico disfruta bajo el Gobierno de los Estados Unidos, los cuales le fueron concedidos y asegurados solemnemente por el Tratado de Guadalupe Hidalgo y después nuevamente sancionaos por el Congreso de los Estados Unidos al admitirnos como miembros de la gran familia Americana con iguales derechos á los demás ciudadanos de la Unión; en esta Conferencia, pues, estos individuos, que apenas han puesto el pie en el Territorio y ya están al tanto de las costumbres tan chocantes para ellos de este pueblo, quien ellos comparan al nivel del bárbaro en su presente condición de progreso, y cuyo carácter ponen todavía aun más abajo que el del mismo Indio bárbaro á quien contemplan que puede tener más respeto á su juramento y ser un Testigo más competente que un ciudadano nativo del Territorio por cuanto al primero sabe y cree con más fe que el segundo que hay un Gran Espíritu que castiga á todo el que obra mal ó no dice la verdad, mientras que creencia del segundo (el ciudadano Nuevo Mejicano) creyendo en su Ser Supremo, no cree que hay castigos para el que obra mal en este mundo porque su creencia le enseña que hay una autoridad Divina (la Iglesia) en la tierra para perdonar los pecados, y que por lo mismo no pueden ser creido bajo juramento. Esto le descalifica para servir como jurado en una Corte, o para dar disposición en causa alguna y cuyo derechos en juicio de estos individuos debe ser quitado al pueblo de Nuevo Méjico.

Siendo el pueblo bajo la Constitución de los Estados Unidos y bajo todas las formas de Gobierno Republicano, el soberano y en quien reside todo el poder, cuyo poder es el de eligir sus propios gobernantes para decretar leyes y para que estas sean ejecutadadas. El pueblo de Nuevo Méjico, en la opinión de estos Caballeros, debe ser despojado del derechos sagrado de sufragio por ser inaptos para juzgar respecto á la capacidad de sus gobernantes, los cuales, aunque son escojidos según su opinión, de aquella clase mas semi-ilustrada de entre nuestro pueblo son unos toscos ignorantes que nada saben respecto á las instrucciones del Gobierno de los Estados Unidos, á inaptos por lo mismo para ocupar tales puestos.

Plenamente convencidos estos ilustres emigrados y sus secuaces que el Gobierno magnánimo á que pertenecemos cometió un error al conferirnos tales privilegios, abiertamente han declarado que han puesto ya en práctica lo que deseaban, habiendo elevado una petición o Memorial al Presidente de los Estados Unidos á fin de que seamos despojado de estos privilegios, y que el Gobernador del Territorio y los jueces de la Corte Suprema sean constituido en un cuerpo Legislativo para dictar nuestras leyes, y que nuestra Legislatura, que ahora esta representada por miembros de entre nuestro propio pueblo sea abolida; que el Gobernador del Territorio sea además revestido con el poder de nombrar los oficiales del Territorio desde el juez de Pruebas hasta el Soto-Alguacil; que el derechos de ser juzgados por jurados sea abolido, y que sea sustituido por un cuerpo de abogados que pronunciarán sus dictamenes en todas las causas pendiente en las Cortes.

Tal es el ¡pueblo de Nuevo Méjico! el suplicio horrendo que os preparan la malicia y la perfidia de hombres á quienes habeis acojido en vuestro seno y les habeis dado pruebas bastante claras de vuestra ciega obediencia á ley y de todos aquellas nobles cualidades que constituyen á un pueblo digno de ser participen de todos los goceres de ciudadanos Ameicanos, y que solamente pueden ser negados por hombres enteramente preocupados contra vosotros sin otro motivo que no haberos dejando ser el instrumento de vuestra propia infamia, hombres que han venido á residir en nuestro propio suelo con el fin de hacer un gran papel á costa vuestra, á retardar el progreso de nuestro propio país, al cual ellos pretenden tener más derecho que vosotros que habéis nacido en este suelo.

¿Preguntaremos ahora al pueblo Nuevo Mejicano si bajo tales circunstancias todavía inmutable, dividido solamente por sostener caprichos, y no se unirán para rechazar y desvanecer tan viles calumnias, con las cuales están amagadas sus libertades y manchado su honor? No podemos creer que el pueblo Nuevo Mejicano deje pasar en silencio tal ultraje sin unirse para libertarse del peligro que les amenaza, y si por desgracia permanecen inertes, nuestro porvenir será funebre, y el oprobio siempre quedará indelible sobre este pueblo.

Anónimo, *El Nuevo-Mejicano* (Santa Fe), 15 de Septiembre de 1866

Appendix 5
Traidor y Chulito

De una conferencia o diálogo ocurrido entre uno de los hijos espurios de la conocida Casa Blanca, a quien le bautizaremos con el nombre de "Traidor," con el confidente o privado del Real Palacio, a quien lo ... contaremos con el nombre del—"Chulito," durante su concilio secreto, que dió principio por el primero en los siguientes terminos.

¡Traidor! Bien venido seas mi querido "Chulito." Cuanto tiempo á que deseaba tener una entrevista contigo, en un lugar aparte como el presente, pero las razones de no hacerme sospechoso de nuestros y ancianos amigos, ¿me entiendes "chulito?." Me habían privado de este placer y ahora que nos presenta un lugar tan propio, no deseo perder el tiempo, porque hay lobos en el camino, por no decir "coyotes."¿ me entiendes "chulito?." Y así es que espero me manifiestes con la franqueza de un fiel amigo. ¿Que te aparecido sobre la nominación de nuestro nuevo campeón, C. P. Clever? Entendido que te hago la promesa de hacerte revelaciones que no te han de haber pasado, ni por las narises, con lo cual te acabarás de convencer que las predilecciónes de nuestro anciano oráculo de la famosa Casa Blanca, son dignos de mérito, porque desde que nos tumbaron las "Jinetas" [el partido Chavista]; ¿me entiendes "chulito?;" este viejo varonil á tenido que quebrantarse los cascos, y ya verá como el tiempo no se a perdido, y con esto solo espero tu respuesta.

¡Chulito! El metal de tu voz, las cómicas palabras de cortesía y franqueza con que te diriges a quien siempre esta a tus plantas, amable "Traidor." Me revelan claramente que la cuestión del día sobre la nominación de nuestro Nuevo campeón, es un misterio que solo nuestro diestro y hábil anciano puede resolver. Pero, yo, por mi parte, para satisfacer tu deseo, te diré que años hace que he dado á conocer al mundo por medio de mi puño, lo que detesto á esta raza degenerada, y es mí firme convicción que ninguna persona que tenga libre su opinión pueda soportar á este Judio errante, el cual por el mismo Dios esta pronosticada su sentencia: pero no por esto, mi Señor, entiendas que yo abandoné la causa porque me apago aquel dicho muy vulgar que dice que "en desagradecido hasta traidor no para," mas cuando veo que nuestro anciano consultor tiene la causa en sus manos, y que desde el primero del Real Palacio hasta el más humilde de nuestros favoresedores con unas manos corderas. Es cuanto te puedo decir para que quedas proceder con toda libertad.

¡Traidor! Cuanto placer me causa mi fino chulito, "palmadas al hombre," que un hombre como tú, deje a un lado toda hipocrecía, y hago un reconocimiento que no deja que dudar, sino que se conoce que dimana del corazón. Si encontraramos una docena que lo incitaran, sería nada lo que se ha escrito de las doce pares de Francisco [Chávez], á que tendría que ver el mundo. Pero son pocos los que lo puedan imitar, porque aunque es cierto que tenemos amigos, pero hay amigos de amigos, y así es que dejando esto a un lado, voy a cumplir con mi promesa, y por ellos intimirá si nuestro anciano consultor es el hombre del siglo diez y nueve. La derrota esponatosa que sufrimos dos años—era con nuestro buen amigo Perea—nos dejó vacilantes y pernativos. Pero con la esperanza de que con el tiempo y a fuerza de "greenbacks," podriamos remediarlo, como que todavía contabamos con brazo fuerte las "Jinetas;" ¿me entiendes "chulito?;" *para que mencionara al heroe*, pero cuando éstas han dado por tierras, ¿cuál será nuestra posición? ¡Triste y lamentable! Porque á la vez en que recide este poder, es un hombre de hueso maduro que nada quiere saber de nuestros negocios políticos, se predecía y así sucedió. ¿Que hacer en tan críticas circunstancias? Aquí fue donde nuestro anciano, el Oráculo, tuvo que quebrarse cascos y dar su decisión, que en concilio que compondría los verdaderos amigos de la Casa Blanca, el Real Palacio y nuestro heroe, aunque [nunca] sería tenido para de liberal, sin . . . de amigos dudosos, porque como deja dicho . . . hay amigos "de amigos," el cual se reunió y . . . adelantar para el fin que fue convocado, habiendose procurado á organizar el concilio, cual organizado y aceptadas las reglas parlamentarias para su dirección; nuestro hábil anciano tomó 15 palabras é hizo un discurso de nuestra actual situación que los que lo componían parecieron una Santa María Magdalena, pues los . . . y suspiros, habían hecho enternersarse al más duro de corazón; á continuación según moción una comisión fue nombrada con el fin de someter á la cosideración del concilio los nombres de las personas que fingaren propias para . . . entre ellas escoger el candidato que debía ser nuestro campeón, cuya comisión haciendo cumplido con su cometido informe, que como ya había sido esparcido en todo el Territorio el llamamiento de la convención, y esta estaba tan próxima tenían que apegaran á recomendar á aquella persona de que pareciera más propio y demás proveían concilio, habiendo oído mencionado los siguientes señores: Francisco Perea, Antonio José Otero, Vicente Romero y C. P. Clever cuyo informe fue adoptado, habiendose prosedido á considerar los nombres de las personas recomendadas para la comisión en la orden en que fueron mencionadas. De consiguiente Perea se puso á la consideración del concilio, la discusión fue anunciada, el más profundo silencio se observó en los miembros, un... despaboridas [sic] manifestaba su aflicción. Uno de ellos tomó la palabra, trémulo y tembloroso, y habló que el hombre era digno de la posición, que el había sacrificado su fortuna y su crédito y á la ves, cosa muy poco podía contar, que lo tendrían presente para pagarle sus servicios de alguna manera, pero que las circunstancias hace mayor dejarlo á un lado y considerar el nombre de la persona que se le seguía. Pues si hablamos con franqueza respetable, miembros del concilio, nuestro principal aliento es el dinero y nuestro amigo, con muy poco puede contar, rechinido de dientes y briagues, fue todo lo solo se observó, cuando la cuestión hecha por el trémulo y temblaroso; quedandolo bajo la consideración del concilio el nombre de Otero, el cual habiendo sido anunciado y puesta la discusión á la consideración del concilio. Después de unirse y reunirse [los] respectables miembros, uno de ellos se dirijió al presidente con la más afable cortesía, y en seguida, á lo demás miembros del concilio, y, como quien quiere y no puede, al fin pronunció su discurso con estas ó semejantes palabras:

"Caballeros y y amigos, según yo entiendo, la persona bajo nuestra consideración, no solo es digna de ocupar la posición de delegado, pero, cualesquiera otra que fuere de mayor importancia, y entiendo que no me equivoco al dicerles que este [es] el hombre con que podríamos derrotar el partido opositor. Pero estaré muy engañado si al conseguir el triúnfo, no sea nuestra propia derrota, por la razones que paso a demostrar. Una ves nombrado como nuestro candidato, el permanecería en su casa á esperar el resultado. Este no es el hombre a quién vosotros puedamos manejar. El no embertirá [sic] un solo centavo de su fortuna en cartar voluntades. Á el no lo veremos andar de plaza en plaza, grangiando á nuestros amigos y llevandoles bolsa para que se marchan, como los tenemos enseñados; y en fin, si el saliera electo, iría al Congreso y procuraría todo el bien de su pueblo, y nosotros nos quedaríamos como lobos habrientes, abriendo la boca aunque con la esperanza de que algo nos dará, pero no porque lo puedamos exigír á que lo haya como estamos acostumbrados y mal impuestos, y entonces como él no haría lo que dejó, manifestado el resultado de su elección estaba en nuestras manos. Pero ustedes saben, mis amables compañeros y amigos, que nuestros trabajos siempre han sido con dinero; pues sin dinero nada contamos, y este por desgracia á desasparecido nuestras bolsas, pues con la esperanza de doblarlo, lo hemos gastado pero nuestra suerte ha sido adversa, y así es mí opinión, que por lo menos, nuestro campeón sea uno [que] distribuya de ese tan codiciado papel que le nombran 'Greenbacks,' que si en la elección, no conseguiremos con que hacer la vida mientras otra viene; . . . estoy plenamente persuadido que el caballero á que me refiero no aspira á tal posición, y así no hay para que pensar en él, porque es tanto como hacer castillo en el viento. Por lo tanto propongo que prosedamos á considerar el de la persona que nos sigue en razón de no creer propio en las actuales circunstances, el del Señor Otero."

Cuyo proposición fue adoptada, y de consiguiene fue anunciado que el nombre del Señor Romero que daba á la consideración del concilio. La cuestión fue anunciada, pero ninguno de los miembros movía sus labios. Aquí parecía decisorio. Las lámparas opacas descrían la melancólica de aquel cuerpo, cuando uno de los miembros, medio soñoliento y limpiandose las lagrimares—pues las muchas lagañas lo impedían obrar después de un sin numero de briagues—con que cortejo al presidente y concilio salieron de su boca estas palabras:

"Compañeros y amigos del concilio: Por más de media hora ha sido anunciado por el señor presidente que esta bajo nuestra consideración el nombre propuesto, y en esto, el profundo silencio que se á observado, que al fin me he resuelto á tomar la palabra, temeroso de no ir a quedar petrificado, así es que yo pregunto, ¿Somos ó no somos los que componen este concilio, amigos verdaderos, ó hay algún Judas entre vosotros? Yo responderé. Entiendo que no bajo esta confianza, voy á exponer mí opinión; hablando categoricamente poca ó ninguna esperanza, mejor dicho, debemos tener de que el candidato que se levanta por nuestra parte obtenga la Victoria. Ya somos matas conocidas, y según yo entiendo, y como [ha] sido explicado ya al personage por quién sea resuelto que tengamos que trabajar á decir copetón y no Sopilote, para poderlo desenplumar nuestras bolsas. Por más que nos quieramos dar tono, necesitan de renchirse si queremos tener amigos, porque no todos son amigos, y en cierto modo hacen bien, porque hacían como nosotros todo lo queremos para si, por más que lo quieramos negar. Es bueno que tengamos conque gratificar á nuestros corre-chepios [sic], como lo hemos hecho siempre, y sino lo hicieremos, tendriamos que perderlos. Por tales razones, muevo que sea borrado de la lista el Señor Romero. Pues, aunque es cierto que es una persona respectable, y según los informes, será el que hara más . . . en nuestra convención, pero no por esto faltara de Jugarle una sanganada y la caminara conforme á nuestros deseos. Pues, como luego dicen, á caballo viejo no tu tu, y que procedamos á consideran el nombre del Señor Clever que es el último recomendado por la comisión."

Dicha proporción habiendo sido sostenida, el Presidente la sometió á la consideración del concilio y fué aprobada, quendando por lo tanto para ser resuelto por el concilio el nombre del Señor Clever, como fue anunciado, y la discusión propuesta, "en este momento, mi afable" Chulito, "hubiera . . . haberte visto presente en aquel recinto." Un alboroto horrendo se observó en el concilio. Los ojos de los miembros desortigados se hechaban unas miradas que causaba terror. "Las viejas fué [sic] ordenado de dar más luz," cuando nuestro anciano consultor, haciendo ver de la palabra y fijando su mirada penetrante en todos y cada uno de los miembros, y con un temblor asombroso, comensó, diciendo, "á parece si no me equivoco, que este, tan respectable concilio esta peparado á buscar la persona que ha de ser nuestro futuro campeón tal como ya sea iniciado. Pues, si es así, como yo entiendo, creo que no habrá uno que vacile en poner duda por un solamente que C. P. Clever, la persona ahora bajo nuestro consideración, es el hombre que nos conviene, hablando con la franqueza con que debemos hacerlo. No es el tiempo para aventurar á uno de verdaderos amigos, y aunque este permitaremos que me espete en estos terminos. Judío errante pretende serlo, pero ustedes, mis amables compañeros, saben muy bien lo contrario. Pues, cuando se le borrara de la memoria que es amigo afuera de muñecas de lo cual es testigo, el Báculo que portó como luego dicen, para desesperados males desesperados remedios. De consiguiente, debemos considerar el asunto en su primitivo sea quitármenos la máscara de orgullo y confesemos nuestra derrota, no ante el pueblo, pero sí, ante nosotros y buscaremos con toda la calma que requiere el caso de los males el menos, y si así obramos, disciplamos á enforzar nuestros trabajos por la persona mencionada. Yo bien veo en el semblante de Vds. lo duro que será trabajar por un hombre en tanto el orgullo que ostenta que piensa tenemos á su árbitro. Pero nosotros que conocemos su ambición, no lo debemos perder de vista, y esta es la ocasión propia para manifestarlo que el es el hombre que puede dar por tierra con nuestros competidores. Tiremos pues, el anzuelo y si logramos pescar la presa, el peso enorme que pesa sobre nuestros delicados hombros recairá sobre el. Y una ves amarrado, le haremos vomitar los 'Greenbacks' que por tantos años á estado atorados [en] este Lobo carnicero, 'por no decir coyote, que es el nombre que generalmente es conocido,' que con piel de un manso cordero le ha chupado la sangre á este pueblo imbécil. Por otra parte nos [oiremos] todas las simpatías de los descendientes del pueblo de Israel, los que desde su aparición en este país, no han hecho otra cosa que atesoran ese tan codicioso metal. Pues, cuando vean á su Ídolo, C. P. Clever, puesto en tal posición, este será un móvil, paso que aunque miserables, se presenten risueño, y Liberales para soportar la carga que por tantos años hemos tenido que llevar y para que todo esto, se cumpla. Todo depende de vosotros amigos y fieles compañeros. Esperamos por todo el Territorio y ante el público y nuestros amigos dudosos. Demos muestras de desavenencia en nuestras opiniones. Reservemos nuestros acuerdos secretos para entre nosotros mismos y no perdamos un momento en llevar al cabo nuestra decisión trabajamos á los escojidos, por no decir o maldecir y yo respondo de la victoria, 'no se entienda por su Salomón, esto que digan al campeón.' Pues esta hasta ridículo es el mencionarlo, pero á por cierto el [desagradamos] de su enjambre de politicastros que día á día se presenta a nuestras puertas para saber el bolsillo si queremos tenerlos fieles á nuestros principios.' Esto es lo que llamo yo una victoria,' que por lo que es el campeón bajo nuestra consideración.' Nosotros mismos antes de Setiembre ya lo tendremos desemplumado,' porque los destinos que a la vez ocupa y de los cuales se ha hecho herrero forsoso, pasaron á nuestras manos y con esto y lo demás que se vaya presentando bien, podremos pasar dos años más, que tal vez la cosa cambiara y entonces veremos cual es el camino que nos conviene porque por á hora nada podemos esperar que no sea por 'artegia.' Pues, yo veo á las clases que nuestros opositores políticos no quitan el dedo del renglón y Chávez, ese Chávez que hoy nos tiene tan preplejos y abatidos, será su futuro candidato, y por más que nosotros mentamos y, y tratemos de desprestigiarlo, nuestros escritos quedarán en nada, porque hay un adagio que dice, 'que la mentira prevalerá mientras la verdad llega.' Y así es como ya somos matas conocidas. Aunque hablaremos por boca de angel sofisma, no tendra por ahora ningún mérito ante el pueblo; por lo tanto someto á la consideración del concilio las razones manifestadas, esperando la concurrencia de todos y cada uno, es mí proposición."

En tomar todos los miembros, manifestaron sus respectos de cortesía con una caravana á nuestro anciano consultor y tomando la palabra nuestro heroe moribundo, dijo "[endoso] en todas sus partes la proposición hecha por nuestro anciano consultor. Ofresco soportarla y pido sea llamada la cuestión llamandose la lista para que cada un miembro dé su voto a viva voz." No habriamos otra persona que manifestase deseos de explicarse; la cuestión fue llamada. Todos los miembros del concilio respondieron cuando sus nombres fueron llamados, siendo el resultado que todos fueron con . . . que C. P. Clever, sería la persona en quién debía resultar el nombre de nuestro campeón para delegado al Congreso en la futura elección. Habiendose acordado de la manera que debía ser distribuidos los trabajos para que ni por un momento hubiere quién pudiera saber de lo ocurrido en nuestro concilio para cuyo efecto, según morían Juramentado á todos los que lo componían de reservar para si todo lo practicado, siendo solos sabedores de los que ponen la famosa Casa Blanca, el Real Palacio y nuestro heroe. Pues, al efecto los procedimientos fueron firmados por todos y cada uno y empesados en tres cubiertas, manifestando los tres poderes con el siguiente membrete: "Concilio Secreto" tenido en la famosa Casa Blanca de los tres poderes en asiaga circunstancias en el año del Sor. 1867; el cual fuí yo ordenado, como secretario, de conservarlo en el lugar más seguro de aquel establecimiento para perpetua memoria. Esto es lo que deseaba [y] participarté. Ahora tu dirás, mí querido "Chulito," si nuestro anciano consultor es carta que cuenta. Tal vez lo difuso de narración. Te habré factidiado, pero yo por no dejarte nada secreto, me pareció propio hacere una mineriosa explicación de todo, aunque con el peligro de quebrar mí Juramento. Pero en la confianza que tu perteneces al Real Palacio, esto me hizo no bailar, que por lo que respecta á los demás posos que se dieron en nuestra convención y todo lo ocurrido en ella. Tu estas al tanto, y por lo mismo puedes inferir si nuestro anciano mas bien merece el nombre de "Profeta." Pues, á salido un pie á la letra, tal como por él fue dicho y á la vez ya no me queda otra cosa que decirte. Mas adelante mí nueva posición, pues, he recibido el nombramiento de ayuda . . . . [sic] de cámara del Real Palacio, cumplicéndose con esto lo que nuestro anciano dijo, nosotros mismos lo desplumaremos.

¡"Chulito"!: Santos Cielos! Mi amigo, y señor y respectable "Traidor." Te confieso que yo me considero por uno de esos que olfatean lejos, pero en tan sabio concilio secreto, no me había pasado no por la nariz, y ahora que estoy al tanto del, con fin que nuestro viejo anciano, me rece el renombre de Profeta y te puedo asegurar que en todo lo practicado en nuestra convención jusgaba yo á este, nuestro gran señor tibio e independiente. Por eso bien dicen los negocios de palasino siempre anda desprecio y con esto no hay otra cosa que amolar las tigeras asegurar el botín y el campeón que damos. Te felicito por tu nueva posición y que sigan cayendo las plumas hasta que nuestro campeón y su raza queden como antes eran.

¡Traidor! Nuestra conferencia ha sido mucho más larga que lo que yo la esperaba. Tal vez sera de provecho, pero como ahora somos de una misma casa, á cada paso se nos presentara oportunidad de hablar. Por ahora, lo que nos conviene es acusar á nuestros enemigos políticos de ambiciosos, anti-americanos y defraudadores de los derechos del pueblo corrompidos, etc. etc., y ensalzar á C. P. Clever, como el angel . . . que por la mano de Dios á sido escogido para nuestro futuro campeón y que este solo es el hombre en quien el pueblo puede cifrar sus esperanzas.

¡Chulito! Esto queda por mi cuenta. Yo lo haré de una manera que dejaremos pensativos á los ignorantes y embelosado á nuestra campeón y su raza; la Victoria será cantada á cada paso y á nuestros opositores, los disminuirvemé al grado mas degradante. Pues con esto no aventura uno mas que [sic] lo que Barbero la Navaja.

¡Traidor! Basta mi fino Chulito. Hasta otra vez toma tu cheque y vete Consuelo de afligiados. Cuanto placer me causa verte tan alegre. Anda a tomar un drink y grita ¡viva C. P. Clever!

Anónimo, *El Nuevo-Mejicano* (Santa Fe), 8 de Junio de 1867

Appendix 6

EL QUE DICE LO QUIERE, OYE LO QUE NO QUIERE

En el número 46 de la Gazeta de Santa Fé, aparese un editorial ridiculizando la junta tenida por el partido Nacional Unionista, el Domingo 21 de Abril de 1867, fechado Abril 15 de 1867 y llevando por título, "La nada es nada' [acusando a José Francisco Chávez que no hizo nada en la oficina de delegado al Congreso].

Nuestros lectores no podran menos que sorprenderse al ver que siete días antes que la junta que el editor se propone á ridiculizar fuese tenida ya él había penetrado lo que el señor Chávez y otros señores que hicieron uso de la palabra habían dicho, de modo que al ver tan semejante aborto no podemos menos que creer que el editor [de] la gazeta ó el autor de tal editorial, quien quiera que sea, no puede menos que haber estado briago, ó en un parasismo que no sabía en su juicio; ó tal vez los efectos de la luna le hisieron dar á luz á su hijo antes del parto, pues no se debe olvidar que la junta fue el 21 y el editorial fue escrito Santa Fé, Abril 15 de 1867.

Ahora en cuanto al nombre con que vanitizó á su sietemesino, "La nada es nada," lo contestaremos diciendole que el abatimiento es la alhaja mas digna de aprecio de la epoca presente, la que generalmente se encuentra adornada de los mas brillantes colores y de las cualidades mas recomendables, y la única por la cual las clases y el pueblo se pueden poner en paralelo con los maldesidos hijos de Israel y con sus mersenarios que siguen su ejemplo y predican sus falsas doctrinas queriendo convertir á Nuevo Mejico en una Nuevo Jerusalén.

Mucho les [acuse] que el señor Chávez haya manifestado al pueblo que si nada hizo, fué porque durante su epoca emisarios mandados de aquí mismo por esa clica corrompida que por una serie prolongada de 20 años no ha evitado medio para escandalizar, degradar y malrepresentar al pueblo de Nuevo Méjico ante el gobierno, ante los ojos y oídos de la preponderante república Americana y ante el mundo entero, se ocupaban en entorpecer sus trabajos, y no evitaban medios por bajos que fuesen para impedir al señor Chávez de dar paso alguno por el progreso Adelanto y el engrandecimiento de Nuevo Méjico.

Eso es nada menos que confesar su debilidad . . . [¿ s]e le podra tapar al pueblo el sol con la mano y podrá todo hombre honesto llegar á la absurda y erronea convicción que un hombre que ha tenido que pelear por los derechos, la moralidad y el honor del pueblo de Nuevo Méjico encontra de un enjambre de miserables ambiosiosos y cobardes, que maliciosamente é intencionablemente se han confabulado en su contra y en contra del pueblo; y que habiendo dado con ellos por tierra y triunfado varonilmente en la batalla: se halla culpable de confesar su debilidad?

Todo lo contrario, esto le hace mucho honor y le hace merecedor del sufragio de un pueblo que ama la virtud y detesta la corrupción; pues el tener la intrepidez y disposición varonil para desmentir los viles negros y miserables representaciones que se han hecho y se hacen del pueblo de Nuevo Méjico, es una prueba nada equivocal de que él ha tratado de exigir que el pueblo Nuevo Mejicano se a visto y considerado con el aprecio y dignidad que merece, por la siega obediencia y respeto que le ha sabido rendir y le rinde al gobierno y á sus leyes, y por la adhesión y amor con que se [devota] a sus magnánimas y liberales instituciones.

"Blanco salí y blanco volví." Confesión de parte reveló de toda prueba. El señor Chávez salió de entre su pueblo puro, limpio sin compromisos, y sin ninguna corrupción, y despues de haberse encontrado roleado de venenosas serpientes, y de tigres deboradores le es muy honroso haber vuelto al seno del pueblo que le elijió con la misma pureza que el supo conservar. Su carácter y el del pueblo ileso, puro y sin mancha y que la corrupción y desenfrenó de sus enemigos[. N]o fueron capaz de corromper ni el uno ni el otro; vea, pues, aquí una gran verdad confesada por el sonámbulo autor del artículo de la Gazeta; dice el adagio "el pescado por la boca muere," pues ellos no pueden ser tan negados de la justicia y no pueden menos que confesar que Chávez ha vuelto á su pueblo sin corrupción con un carácter sólido y firme como el que observaba cuando el pueblo que le elijió le conferió sus intereses, y cuando un hombre se presenta ante su pueblo con una honradez tan sin igual todo compatriota apreciador de méritos tan distinguidos y virtudes tan altamente recomendables de uno pueden menos que premiar con sus sufragios libres a quien les ha sabido defender en el caos de su mas profunda y tenebrosa situación.

Sí[,] pueblo de Nuevo Méjico[,] es necesario que vds. nombren a un hombre que les renumere los perjuicios y la ruina que les ha causado Chávez con no consentir que el especulador se sebe en el sudor de vuestro rostro y que vuestro trabajo sea la víctima de la rapiña y vuestra inocencia la causa de vuestra opresión. Si, compatriotas, nombres á Carlos P. Clever, el padre de los pobres, el vencedor de imposibles, el amparo de las vindas, el consuelo de los aflijidos, el protector de las necesidades de los oprimidos, el refujio de los malvados, el libertador de los oprimidos, el redactor de los cautivos, el inmaculado protector de los impedidos, el insigne milagroso abogado de las partulrentas, y en fin el padre de los misericordias etc. No se equivoquen, compatriotas, [que] él es el hombre que os puede hacer felizes pues; un ser humano, ó semidivino que esta adornado de tantos facultades, no puede menos que promover vuestro futuro bienestar; porque á su voz se abrirán las aguas, cesarán los vientos, y todos los astros y elementos le mostrarán obediencia y respeto; pues al ver aparecer en el Congreso de los Estados Unidos a un delegado cargado de epitafios como los que lleva sobre sus espaldas todos se quedarán estupefactos y no se atreverán á contestar ni á contradecir a quien todo lo puede; su voz allí será imperiosa y su poder no tendrá rival. El no hay duda que, cambiara la tesorería de los Estados Unidos á Santa Fé, ó la nueva Palestina, más propiamente, y á su regreso hara de los millones de dinero que consiga la distribución que hizo el payaso de la herencia que lo dejaron sus padres y después de hacer minuciosas y escrupudosamente las partes correspondientes. Todos vendrán á parar en los destinos Territoriales de procurador general, ayudante general, los que le fueron legados por su difunto Abuelo Henrique Connelly y confirmados sellados y entregados por el escrupulosos R. B. Mitchell, administrador de los vienes [sic] Territoriales, de todo lo cual no siendo el ambicioso egoista, ni demagoga. No ha hecho dimición porque vale mas pájaro en mano que . . . volando y porque cosa de cinco mil pesos anuales que esta extrallendo [sic] de la tesorería son un alimento muy favorable para sufragar los gastos de música, alumbrados cohetes y licor con cuyo espíritu desean hacer conocer al pueblo sus derechos; pero no hay duda que estos son los hombres recomendables, los amigos del pueblo los amantes de progreso, los ferrocarriles, los, telégrafos los desarrolladores de minas, trasfiriendolas [sic] á otro para engruesar [sic] sus bolsillos.

No es muy extraño que se supusieran que el pueblo debería haber visto con desprecio las predicaciones de los señores Pino, Sena, y demás, lo mismo que todo lo que se les pueda presentar por su odioso órgano el Nuevo Mejicano, pues siempre la verdad debe ser tratada con desprecio, mientras la intriga, la traición, la mentira, y el vilipendio, con que Clever, Weshe, Quintana, Alarid, etc. así como también todo lo que producen por su ponsoñoso órgano la Gazeta de Santa Fé, esa culebra, chirionera [sic] que ha sido el azote de Nuevo Méjico, de ser tratado con toda atención, consideración y respeto y debe ser seguido por el pueblo como un misterio de fé, pero es necesario que recuerden que no es el primer coyote que se visite con piel de cordero para destruir el más abudante rebaño. "Estamos en un caso de degradación," pero para no ser ellos los únicos degradados; por eso traten de corrumper al pueblo, de embriagarlo, de embiserlo, y de sacrificarlo para llenar sus bolcillos y ponerse al nivel de aquellos a quienes tanto odian y que les causan tanta melancolía y desvelos aunque por años así lo han procurado.

"No podemos colejir, ni nuestras alcansan á concebir á que aspiran con que mandar a Chávez para Delegado." ¿Será que pretenden que los hago á más gobernador, a otro juez & &? A nada de esto esta comprometido el coronel Chávez y los que le sostienen; no lo sostienen con esperanzas de empleos; pues están muy bien satisfechos que la casa blanca tiene unos descendencia muy numerosa y esta cubierta de satélites para ocupar todos los destinos federales de este Territorio, y Gracias a Dios que los amigos de Chávez ni sus nombres no han sido todavía mencionados para ningún destino, mientras el miserable Santiago Collins tan luego como no tiene torta así como otros de sus descendientes y ascendientes, con vergonzosa bajeza se van a Washington y no dudamos que rodillas impetran del presidente destinos sin los cuales como confiesan con su propia boca "la nada es nada." Este es [el] Americanismo que disfrutan; esta es la adhesión que le tienen al gobierno y a sus instituciones; pues mientras que haiga dinero en la tesorería del gobierno, no puede tener amigos mas fieles que Collins, Clever, Mitchell y compañía, quienes se han convertido hoy como los más salidos pilares del pueblo ebrio y los que por medio de contratos del militar quieren saciar la ambición de esos errontes y aventureros, hijos de Faran, de que arrojados á los soborbios [sic] de Nuevo Méjico por las olas del mar rajo; hay quieren ser más Americanos, más patriotas y estar más interesados en el bienestar de Nuevo Méjico que sus mismos hijos y que aquellos que jamás han conocido otro suelo que el suelo Nuevo Mejicano.

"Esta cuestión repugnante que horroriza gritando contra el judío."

Ah, Cuanto les horroriza que nos abatamos a esa facción de especuladores que han sido la [mina], el azote y la plaga de Nuevo Méjico, a esos que se han usurpado nuestros puestos, que han desolado nuestro país, y que en la actualidad tratan de ser más americanos que nosotros y de tomar las riendas para gobernarnos. Pues nosotros no nos admiramos que ellos se hayan convertido en traidores peores, y que antes que el gallo cante hayan negado a un pueblo. "Sabe que su delegado es nacido en Prucia," pero no dice que era soldado razo, que se desertó de las filas de su gobierno y que enmascarado pasó los mares para venir buscar un pueblo que fuese suficiente salvaje para elevarlo a la posición de delegado; de consiguiente deseamos que se nos compare con él, pues todavía nosotros no hemos desertado las filas de nuestro gobierno.

Si se va a ver la historia, se encontraran muchos de estos americanos clarificados, adornados de recuerdos muy vergonzosos.

Adelante, Pueblo de Nuevo Méjico. Elíjelo al General Clever y verías como no vasila en desertar nuestros intereses por el sello propio, como desertó las filas de su gobierno para venir a buscar su elevación y engrandesimiento entre vosotros.

HASTA OTRA VISTA

El Nuevo-Mejicano (Santa Fé), 4 de Mayo de 1867

Appendix 7

Diálogo Entre Bartolo y Bárbara

Bar. Buenos días, mi querida, Bab.

Bab. Se les de Dios, Don Bartolo.

¡Qué esto... ¡Dios mío! ¿Por que vienes Vd. tan macilento? ¡Jesús!....

Br. ¿Cómo no me he de asustar? ¡Qué horror!

Bar. Válgame Dios, Bárbara. Barbarita, ¿por que estas tan horrorizada ahora que me viste? Acaso....

Bab. ¡Jesús! Qué cara! Lárguese, Don Bartolo, ó Diablo, por que me muero tan solo....

Bar. ¿Pues que fisonomía descubres en mi ahora? Acaso... (Será verdad).

Bab. ¿Cómo que descubro? Que le estoy viendo la cara tan larga, tan pánfila.¡Jesús! Desterrado de mi sea todo espíritu maligno, lárguese Don Bartolo. ¡Qué horror! ¿Qué dice de acaso? ¿Acaso tiene pacto con el Diablo?

Bar. Bab, lo que digo es que si acaso mi sueño sería un apocalipsis.

Bab. Pues, deme un vaso de agua, Don Bartolo, y cuénteme su sueño. Por que vd. tiene pacto con el Diablo, yo no lo...

Bar. Siéntate aquí, Bab y oirás mi sueño que a la verdad es un... un....

Bab. Prosigue, Bartolo, por que no me ha quedado sangre en el cuerpo. ¡Jesús que cara!

Bar. Así és. Anoche luego que soñé, me puse a resar en alta voz con mi familia para que me oyeran los que por la calle pasaban. Como me había confesado por no dar en que decir, no vine a verte, como muy....

Bab. No empieses con excusas: empiesa.

Bar. Pues verás mi querida Bab, que luego que acabé de rezar (ya te dije que en voz alta) con el pesar que no podía verte, me acosté, y habiendome quedado dormido comencé á sonar que me estaba bañando en una laguna que tenía sus aguas muy cristalinas y que en la entrada estaban grabadas en un mármol estas palabras, "Corrompidos, entren y, puríﬁquensen; pero todo aquel que por un vil interés sacriﬁque su hogar será escupido por estas aguas, y no será puriﬁcado." Cuando estaba leyendo la inscripción, sentí en mi interior un temblor, y que la laguna me había escupido, cuando me fuí viendo en un poso que tenía sus aguas fétidas y corrompidas en el cual se estaban bañando un león, un oso y un marrano, lleno de lodo los cuales tenían este letrero.

"Éste es el asilo de los adulones."

Cuando sentí un viento fuerte encima de mi cabeza, hice la vista para arriba y observé que era causado por una palomilla que volara con un ramo de Olivas en el piquito y 78 pichoncitos que le seguían, y [que iban] volando llevavan las [ilegible] tendidas y les ví un letrero en la ala derecha que decía, "Dimos el triúnfo al que la merecía." Y la palomita puso por rededor de la Laguna cantando este verso.

"Y a la rugido del León no le temo
Por que ya venturoso he triunfado
No me importa del Oso el veneno
Curru cu-cu-cu, 99, que hemos ganado.
Los Pichoncitos cantaban
Párate, palomita en esa encino
Mira que el marrano está en camino
Abandonó su Agencia, él muy indigno
Curru-cu-cu que peor la su destino.

Bab. ¡Mira, Bartolo, como se te esta poniendo la cara!

Bar. No hay duda, Bab, que mi sueño fué un apocalipsis. ¿Sabes lo que es apocalipsis? Una revelación, por que también soñe que del poso habían salido cuando pasó la paloma mucha gente, y yo entre ella, con las caras muy largas, y vi un agrimensor muerto de la risa midiéndosela, y que tenía un letrero que decía [ilegible] y media.

Bab. ¡Mira Bartolo, como se te esta poniendo la cara¡

Bar: [Ilegible] también que luego que [ilegible] ó adivina y me había [ilegible] de mi sueño que [ilegible]. La Laguna esta [larga oración ilegible] . . . por la Justicia busando [intelligible] Cuando lo estabas bañando [palabra ilegible] la laguna signifía que tu [palabra ilegible] ese partido pero un vil interés te había fracasado y tú solo buscas tu ruina.

El poso corrompido significa el partido de Chávez. El León que viste es Chávez. El Oso es Heath, y el Marrano es Arny. El Letrero, bien sabes lo que es; solo el hombre adulón y servíl puede ayudarles en sus torpesas, por que ellos han causado hasta la muerte de uno de los mejores hombres que ha pisado nuestro Territorio y quién sabe cuantos crímenes cometerán, teniendole así y a tus colegas con la excepción de 99 por su vil instrumento, por que ya mero los hacen asesinar a . . . .

Bab. ¡Mira como se te esta poniendo la cara!

La Paloma era el mismo Clever, sus [buenas] intenciones. La Rama de Olivas significa la defensa de Clever y su triunfo. El verso que cantó significa que se sentará en el Congreso como Delegado de N.M. y [ilegible] que Chávez, Heath, y Arny se pongan a entorpecería. El hará lo posible por nuestro Territorio y el arco iris brillará con la aurora de la felicidad, que El Hon. C. P. Clever llevará por [ilegible] "el progreso," de las artes y ciencias hasta poner al Nuevo Méjico en tráficos calesales con el poderoso gobierno de la Unión

Los 78 Piconcillos que llevaban aquel letrero significaban 78 votos que Clever tendrá en el Congreso, las que verán una mayoría y juzgan a cada uno conforme sus obras, es decir conocemos el talento en el hombre y no al hombre en el talento.

El [ilegible] que cantaron significa que Arny se pondrá en [ilegible] para el Congreso. Aver si puede entorpecer de alguna manera, pero recuerdas haber visto al marrano lleno de lodo; esto quiere significar que Arny estará impedido por una lepra que Dios le mandará hasta que conozca su error.

El gentío que salió del poso con las caras largas, es bien sabido que eres tú y tus amigos, y que así se les ha de poner cuando tengan la funesta noticia de que Clever ha tomado su [puesto].

Bab. Mira como se te está poniendo la cara. ¡Que horror!

Bar. Ya no puedo, Barbarita mía, proseguir. Es muy largo mi sueño porque te diré que después que la [adame] anunció mi [oración], me hechó en clase de argumento una aprehensión, que mañana te la diré. Ahora no me puedo acordar bien, que uno dijo de imbécil, mayoría, Gobernador, abusos . . . . hay Bab. Préstame un espejo para verme.

Bab se levanta, le trae un espejo, luego Bartolo se ve. Se espanta con su caricatura, cae desmayado y Bab se queda asombrada, estupefacta y llena de horror exclama . . .

"¡¡Lo mismísimo que el apocalipsis de Pancho!! . . . .
X.X.X.

Gaceta Seminaria de Santa Fé, 4 de Enero de 1868

Appendix 8

Correspondencia entre los Compadres, Don Pancho y Don Chepe.

El primero, estando en la legislatura, escribe al segundo a la siguiente

CARTA CONFIDENCIAL.

A Don Chepe,

Querido Compadre: No piense que por que ahora me hayo ocupando el alto y distinguido empleo de miembro de la Legislatura me haya hecho otro, no; siempre soy el mismo—*el mismo gato* por mejor decir—con la diferencia que soy un *representante* de mi pueblo y legislador que aparentó al mismo *Minos de la Antigua Grecia,* aunque en realidad sea un ... pues yo y todos conocemos mis tamaños.

¡Compadre de mi alma! Como ésta es la primera vez que yo ando en estas danzas, he extrañado mucho el modo y manejo como se conducen los negocios políticos en la orbita congresional; de tal suerte que desde que llegué aquí me han querido hacer loco los que conocen la gamuza. Pero mucho más al instalar la sesión con las impertinencias de un ejército de aplicantes que se aproximó a buscar empleos en la Legislatura, como en otras ocasiones.

Esos aplicantes, compadre, sí que me dejaron aturdido. Mala es la comparación como cuando los tábanos se le apoderan a un buey en el verano y lo hacen rabiar; así me sucedió con los aplicantes, ni me dejaba un momento de descanso siquiera para comer. Regularmente vienen mas aplicantes que miembros por que cada uno de estos trae el suyo, y otros vienen de por si atenidos a sus propios méritos, y las plazas con catorce no más, que son: ocho para escribir; dos para mandaderos, a quienes les dicen Sargentos; dos para hacer saber nada que les llamen interpretes y sin saber su propio idioma; y dos para porteros que son los que alla en casa llaman *ceniceros*. Estos y los sargentos son los que tienen más competidores porque son los que todos *nosotros* podemos desempeñar y se ganan los mismos tres pesos. Los escribanos principales a más de sus tres pesos diarios tienen *manos puercas,* lo que hace ser uno de los mejores empleos, y por eso mi tocayo, Francisquito, quitó se ha adquerenciado tanto con la Secretaría Principal, con la cual se le pagan sus servicios por que es cabeza de partido en uno de los precintos de su condado.

Los aplicantes para pretender un empleo en la legislatura alegan todos los mismos méritos y privilegios; es lo que se tema en consideración aunque no tengan las cualidades necesarias. Los méritos son ser de el mismo partido y tener algún influjo en sus precintos para ganar muchos votos en las elecciones; los privilegios y preferencias se concede a los que han prestado mejores servicios en la última elección ó a los que estan dudosos y hay sospechas de que quieren cambiar; a esos les cumplen todos sus antojos por no perder su voto en la legislatura y pueden conseguir un empleo hasta para su madre. Aquellos que no caben y no se quieren perder les pagan unos pesos para que retiren su pretención para lo cual hacen contribuciones entre los cabecillas que dirijen la barca del partido, y de este modo todo camina a las mil maravillas.

¡Compadre de mi vida! Nuestro partido que por tantos años lo llamabamos *Demócrata* que hasta nos peleabamos por ser Demócratas, y que por los últimos dos años pasados ya no tenía otro nombre que el *partido de Chávez*, y otros principios que *Antiamericanismo y pro esclavistas* (pues siempre hemos sido en favor de la ley de peónes); ahora lo han bautizado aquí con otro nombre que se llama *Radical* el cual nunca lo había yo oído mentar, ni sé lo que significa. Lo cierto es que todos los de nuestro partido se jactan de ser radicales, y á veces uno da tentación de meter una resolución en la legislatura que disponga que todos los de nuestro partido llevan en la cabeza una B. grande como divisa, para distinguish del partido de Vds., los *Cabezas de Cobre*, como les decimos.

¡Compadre de mi corazón! Tenemos una mayoría en las dos cámaras que mete miedo, la cual esta sujeta á la disposición del Secretario de las tres H. H. H., a tata grande, y al gobernadorcillo. El Secretario de las tres H. H. H. es muy querido por las de nuestro partido por los fraudes que hizo, por ver si pedimos dar fé a Chávez la mayoría para delegado; el tata grande, porque nos ayuda con su "Nuevo Mejicano" para descargar nuestra furia contra el enemigo y el gobernadorcillo por ser ofender en algunas . . . jurados. Los tres sujetos que . . . . de mencionarle con los que nos manejan como el titirero a los muñecos y nosotros obedientes á sus órdenes que da gusto.

¡Compadre de mis entrañas! Según estamos llevados por la voluntad agena hay poca esperanza que hagamos cosa Buena. Lo que sí, pasaremos resoluciones, fulminaremos anatemas y falsas calumnias contra los que nos mande su magestad el Triunvirato arriba mencionado. Es decir que nuestra tarea ha de ser dar fama a quien no la tenga y quitarla a quien la merece.

Concluyo con decirle que cuando haya de escribirme, ponga en el sobre, "al Hon. Pancho," porque así nos dicen a nosotros, "honorable," y nadie se atreva a criticar porque oirá nuestras bocas.

Quedo de V. afectísimo, Compadre.

PANCHO

Gaceta Semanaria de Santa Fé, 25 de Enero de 1868

Appendix 9

CLEVER *denunciando a Nuevo Méjico*

Señores Editores del Nuevo Méjico—

Aunque después de la elección del señor Chávez en 1865, no he tomado parte con ningún de los partidos políticos del Territorio, sin embargo, con la mira de observar con calma la contienda en asuntos públicos con imparcialidad para concebir una opinión fundada en hechos, más bien que en [lecturas], me he constituido en observar los movimientos y operaciones de ambos partidos, y espero que Vds. darán un lugarcito en sus columnas a esta comunicación, que es uno de los resultados de mis observaciones. Pues, es cosa establecida en Nuevo Méjico que su perdiódico aboga el desarrollo intelectual y material de este país, especialmente en cuanto concierne a lo gobernativo, mueveme hacer este comunicado, el haber visto la resolución, que Clever, delegado aparente hasta hora, hizo al Congreso, pidiendo legislación adicional para desarraigar el sistema de peonaje, y la esclavitud de los indios cautivos en Nuevo Méjico. ¿A que fin se propuso con esto Clever? Es la pregunta que se hacen los ciudadanos unos con otros en sus gobernaciones. La respuesta mas clara y conclusiva es esta, para el conocimiento de todos que esto lo hizo Clever, para aver si de esto modo puede retener el asiento que aparentemente ocupa en el Congreso contra la espresa y manifiesta voluntad de este pueblo, mal representandolo para gozar el destino. Pues, es bien sabido aquí, y en todo el pueblo de los Estados Unidos, que ni el sistema de peonage, ni esclavitud India, ni Africana no existe en Nuevo Méjico, ni en ninguna otra parte de la Unión, por lo cual fue ridículo, innecesario y absurdo, haber pedido legislación adicional para Nuevo Méjico, sobre un asunto, que realmente no existe, si no en la mente encaprichada de Clever.

El pueblo de Nuevo Méjico en general se ha sometido a las enmendaciones de la constitución general, y a las leyes que tienden á destruir toda clase de servidumbre humana, su legislatura abrogó todas las leyes relativas a esa materia, anteriormente decretadas; el Congreso mismo lo hizo, antes que Clever pusiera sus pies en Washington. Entonces pues, no se palpa que fue inecesaria que Clever molestara en pedir al Congreso legislación adicional sobre esta materia muerta y sepultada. Parece lo hizo más bien para tirar su anzuelo en el Congreso, como lo tiró en Nuevo Méjico, cuando decía "lo que soy, lo debo a Nuevo Méjico."

Aquí esta parte de la ley a que me refiero pedida por Clever.

"Un acto para abrogar, y para siempre prohibir el sistema de peonaje y esclavitud India en el Territorio de Nuevo Méjico, y otras partes de los Estados Unidos. Decretese por el Consejo y Cámara de Representantes de los Estados Unidos de América en Congreso reunidos.

Sección 1a. Que el tener a cualesquiera persona, en trabajo o servicio, bajo las sistemas conocidos como peonage [y] esclavitud India, es por este declarado ilegal, y el mismo es por este abrogado, y para siempre prohibido en el Territorio de Nuevo Méjico, o en cualesquiera otro Territorio, o Estado de los Estados Unidos, hasta hora establecido, manteniendo y esforzando o en virtud del cual sea intentado de aquí en adelante, para establecer, mantener en esforzar, directo o indirectamente el servicio o trabajo voluntario, o involuntario, de cualesquiera persona como peónes en en liquidación de alguna deuda ú obligación, y también cualesquier Indio tenido en servicio como cautivo por cualesquier persona, que le ponga a trabajar, excepto según prohibido por la ley bajo el Departamento militar para su civilización, sea y por este es declarado nulo y de ningún valor; y cualesquiera persona o personas que tengan, o detengan, o retengan, o que sean causa a ser tenidos y retenidos, o en cualesquiera manera ayuden en la detención o retención de cualesquiera persona o personas, a la condición de peonage o esclavitud India, sobre convicción, seran castigados con una multa no menos que mil pesos, ni más de cinco mil pesos o con prisión no menos que uno, ni más que, cinco años ambos a las o dirección de la corte."

Ved sus obras, y por sus hechos lo conoceréis y jusgaréis; ¡Pueblo de Nuevo México! Entonces, que cuando aclamo y pregunto al buen Pueblo de Nuevo Méjico, solo me dirijo a aquellos hombres sensatos, cuyas miras tienden a favorecer el interés público; ¿y no a aquellos sin reflexionar y adulones, que todo su interés es personal siguiendo promesas y la botella? ¿Ha por ventura, pretendiendo este enviar un Delegado aparente para que le fuera a mal representar a usandolo de Esclavitud? ¿Acaso sembrar la semilla de la desconfianza y de la discordia ante el Congreso y preocuparle contra el buen pueblo de este Territorio? ¿Este es procurarle su bien estar? No y mil veces no. ¿Quiero [decir] por malicioso bruto y adulón, que sea que el pueblo de

Nuevo Méjico ha sido leal, rumiso, obediente al gobierno de los Estados Unidos en el tiempo de la paz y de la Guerra? El que lo dude y no lo crea, que levante el dedo.

El delegado aparente hasta ahora, no es realmente el delegado verdadero de Nuevo Méjico según todos los informes que he procurado adquirir, y esta ocasión que su hecho contra este pueblo en Washington lo hace merecedor del ignominioso título de chismoso y enredista supuesto que se ha ocupado en pedir legislación sobre cosas que ya estan legisladas; [por] tiempo ha puesto sentimienos... este pueblo, [que] siempre han sido contra la esclavitud, y Clever en el hecho de haber pedido legislación adicional sobre el asunto indicado no ha hecho otra cosa, sino a cesar indirectamente al pueblo de Nuevo Méjico, considerandole de desleal y de desobediente a la Constitución y a las leyes general del Gobierno? ¿Acaso llevaría instrucciones para hacerlo de este modo de sus amigos Juan María Baca de Las Vegas; José Benito Martines de Taos; Pablo Gallegos de Abiquiú; Gerónimo Jaramillo del Rito; Estanislado Montoya de Socorro y la autorización para hacer tal autorización? ¿Crea que no porque estos señores han sido conocidos como ciudadanos leales al gobierno, obedientes a la Constitución, y a las leyes en prueba de cuya obediencia ningún ser humano puede encontrarse esclaviado en sus casos bajo ningún aspecto a no ser que Clever, cuando andaba buscando votos, viera alguno en sus casas y tal vez para ellos sería pedida la legislación adicional? ¡Oh! Se me había olvidado; tal vez llevaría instrucciones adicionales de Antonio Roibal, quien le diría que los cuatrocientos votos de la Tierra Amarilla que fueron adicionados la noche que se juntaron a contar los votos eran peones y cautivos y que era necesario para hacerlos legales la legislación adicional por parte del Congreso al mismo tiempo. El delegado aparente consideraría en su sabiduría necesario también a la legislación adicional para legislar los votos adicionados en la junta de Santa Clara.

Cuando Nuevo Méjico fue conquistado por la España se hicieron necesarias las compañías voluntarias para reprimir la barbarie de los salvajes, y someterlos al yugo de la ley, y de la religión. Los Mejicanos despues de la Independencia siguieron esta costumbre establecida, mas particularmente, sobre los Nabajoes, tribu desolante de Nuevo Méjico; subsecuentemente desde que Nuevo Méjico pertenció al Gobierno de los Estados Unidos, las campañas voluntarias fueron seguidas y autorizadas, cuando la necesidad de la propia defensa lo exigía, y desde aquellos tiempos al presente, cuativos han sido traídos entre el pueblo de Nuevo Méjico como también han sido llevados en cautiverio muchos de nuestros paisanos; pero los traídos aquí jamás han sido considerados como esclavos, sino como hijos adoptivos, y así han permanecido con sus padres adoptantes durante su minoridad, o hasta que se han casado; de este modo poniendose en completa libertad, bajo las mismas circunstancias de los hijos legítimos de los blancos. Muchos cautivos se han casado con mejicanos, y muchos hijos de blancos se han casado con cautivas, y todos generalmente reciben alguna herencia de sus padres adoptantes, cuando estos mueren, o que aquellos se apartan con sus familias. En terrenos, casas, dineros y otros bienes conforme las proporciones de los adoptantes, muchos saben leer y escribir, y tienen sus familias—muchos de ellos sirvieron al gobierno en la última rebelión, y en las campañas contra los mismos Navajoes. Esto a mi modo de ver, es lo que ha sucedido con los cautivos de los Indios en Nuevo Méjico con la sola excepción de aquellos que han tenido amor por su gente y se han estado yendo para su tierra, o a la Reservación; citaré que en estos últimos días vinieron Navajoes a este condado y se llevaron todos los que había, incluyendo una que tenía don Pedro Mares. Por consiguiente, los Navajoes, estoy informado, que se han paseado en los diferentes condados del Territorio y han ido recogiendo a todos los cautivos menores de edad, y se los han llevado, dejando solo aquellos que estan emancipados, como dichos arriba, o que no se han querido ir con ellos; y es así se han quedado en uso de sagrada libertad, y porque ellos no piensan mas en ir con los bárbaros.

Tal es la verdadera, esta en que, en contra de Nuevo Méjico respecto a Indios cautivos y peonage; por lo que creo que ningún hombre en Nuevo Méjico consideré necesario que Clever moleste al Congreso en pedir legislación adicional sobre los asuntos arriba dichos.

Asegurandoles, Señores Editores, que mi afección y respeto siempre será por la Constitución y las leyes y así quedo de Vds. su obediente servidor.

UN OBSERVADOR IMPARCIAL
Mora, N.M., Marzo 25 de 1868
El Nuevo-Mejicano (Santa Fe), 14 de Abril de 1868

Appendix 10

He Aquí a Pancho

Sucede muchas veces que algunos objetos se nos presentan a la vista, y que estos objetos nos traen a la memoria otras cosas, de las cuales se siguen otras, muchas cosas más. Hace unos cuatro días que fuimos llamados para componer un camino y en el camino había muchos hombres trabajando bajo las ordenes de un inspector; en esto que andábamos entretenidos, pala en mano y pico en tierra, oímos rebuznar a un burro en ademán de cometer un asalto sobre el cuerpo de una burra que tenía adelante de él, pero ella no lo daba la cara y en voz bajo parecía que murmuraba, y el burro y la burra [ilegible].

Uno de los trbajadores del camino hizo la observación que aquellos burros eran los de Pancho. Otro notó que ya Pancho *no suena ni truena*. Un tercero dijo que Pancho desde que lo tumbó el burro (desde que fue a la legislatura) *se ha hecho otro.* Yo dije entonces, digo ahora, y diré todo el tiempo que Pancho es el mismo de siempre en *natural y figura:* Sin embargo que ha cambiado en algo en cuanto a su natural, desde que tuvo la *bondad* de representar a sus conciudadanos; y para que sepan todos aquellos y aquellas que gustan saber vidas agenas en que ha cambiado Pancho de natural, les diré: que desde la época que se retiró de hacer legal a esta fecha, ha emprendido la gloriosa y difícil carrera de licenciado en las *cortes de abajo*, y en tan honorosa como distinguida profesión hace más ruido que un muerto en penas, y mayores fueran sus penas si no hiciera ruido.

Pancho que antes de ir a la legislatura no conocía ni la O por lo redondo, ahora ya masca las letras que es un primor, y de aquí le viene el nombre de *cogotinta* [sic], como anillo en dedo.

Pancho es bastante modesto y en su modestía confiese que es incapaz (bueno es que lo diga con boca propia).

Pancho, ya sea por un atributo [ilegible] de la naturaleza, o ya sea que lo vaya aprendido de sus burros (porque dice un dicho que "quien como lobos anda a aullar se aprende") tiene una voz como un trueno y cuando esta alegando en una corte con su voz hace temblar la casa, atemoriza al juez alcalde, confunde a los testigos, no deja dormir a los del jurado y pone cual la basura a la parte contraria.

Pancho en la práctica de las leyes ha sido muy afortunado, todos los pleitos que lo [ilegible] los gana, porque el juez acalde es de su partido, el alguacil es de su partido y de consiguiente le preparan un jurado de su partido: de aquí se sigue que esta haciendose muy popular y progresando en su política que nunca la pierde [ilegible].

Pancho en cuanto a principios políticos no sabe si él es radical o demócrata; pero esta por hay de piones [sic] . . . y en el año del 1861 y 62 simpatizaba con los insurgentes del sur; pues cuando los Tejanos entraron al territorio, Pancho abandonó casa, Pipiana, y burros para irse a los montes a esconderse para no pelear contra los rebeldes.

Pancho ha dado prueba que no es anti-americano porque está de acuerdo y armonía con dos gobernadores *ad interín*; uno que ha dicho que los *grisos* y los Indios son iguales de ladrones; y otro que abroga la ley de elecciones que ha hecho Pancho para su gobierno.

En fin Pancho desde ahora está haciendo partido para que lo envíen otra vez a la legislatura, y asegura que lo consigue, y más se atreve a decir que mientras el pueblo está en las tinieblas de la ignorancia y entorprecido con el capricho de los partidos, no escojerán hombres propios para legislar ni administrar las leyes; y en ese caso él ocupará su puesto.

Ahora, ya oyen algo de Pancho y con el tiempo oirán más, y también sobran de Chepe, aunque de Chepe nadie ha hecho memorias.

Anónimo, *Gaceta Semanaria de Santa Fé*, 27 de Junio de 1868

Appendix 11

Los Republicanos disputando entre si mismos la candidatura para Delegado al Congreso este año de 1871

José (con arrogancia)
Soy Republicano
Quiero ir al congreso,
(Santiago le arrebata la palabra)
Yo también lo soy,
Y propio para eso;
Cualidades tengo—
Que me recomiendan.
¿Pues que no recuerdan
Que el republicano
Debe de ser negro?
A más, yo diciendo
De una Buena sangre
Soy hijo de fraile
"Así yo me atendo,
A mi *tata padre.*"

¡Qué bien se imita!
Para ganar votos;
Bien puedo engañar
Mi compadre Pedro
Me podra ayudar
Con los pontentes,
Que hay en su lugar
Y la sociedad
Que tiene á su mando,
Bien comprometida
Y juramentando;
Es hombre que entiende,
Y sabe servir,

Don Leandro, (con autoridad)
No se esten alborotando.
Ni empiesen con ambición
Pues ya saben que yo mando
Y me deben sumisión,
Los Franciscos, mis sobrinos
(Y Bonifacio también)
Uno de ellos ha de ser,
Para ellos es el destino;
El que manda no se turba,
Y si se turba, es lo mismo,
Y ya que esta desprendido
Que vaya Francisco el *mismo.*

―――――――

Los de San Miguel (como si
Fueran independientes
y hablando
En terminos parlamentarios).
"Nosotros queremos
Uno de los nuestros,
Abreu Francisco,
O, a Perea Demetrio
O, a Sena José—
Si más no podemos."
Don Leandro, (con enfado)
Ustedes silencio
Tienen que guardar,
Bien saben que a mi—
Me han de respetar
Quedense contentos

Y no tiene rey—
En cuanto a mentir;
El merecería
Ir a Washington.
Que allí engañaría
Al más copetón
Con su hipocrecía
Porque es . . . . . taleg—
———

Con la prefectura,
La secretaría
Y legislatura;
La alguacería
(Que es cosa segura)
Cualquier alcaldía
Mientras que nos dura
El palo y el mando,
Y buena ventura.

Elkins (sonriéndose)
Dejen las disputas
Y no alboroten,
Que al cabo y al fin
Tocarán coyote;
Yo soy uno de tantos,
Que al congreso—
Ir quiero,
Pero yo prefiero
Cuando fuere estado,
Y si se pudiera
También delegado.
Soy un abogado
Que gano dinero,
Y del Territorio
Muchos bonos tengo,
Que compré baratos
Y caros los vendo;
La legislatura
Que el invierno venga
Si, son como han sido
De baja ralea

Haré que me ayuden
A imponer más rentas,
Bien podré comprarlos
Con poca moneda

———

    Anónimo, *El Fronterizo* (Las Cruces NM), 18 de Mayo de 1871

Appendix 12

Manifestación al Pueblo del Territorio de Nuevo México

Caros conciudadanos: Me tomo la libertad de llamar hoy la seria atención de Vdes., en un asunto de grande importancia que se verse sobre vuestro honor, sobre vuestros intereses y sobre vuestro brillante futuro de progreso en la serie de los tiempos venideros.

La convención Democrática que tuvo lugar el día 24 de Junio pasado unánimamente me nombró candidato para Delegado al Congreso nacional; y hoy como hombre público tengo el honor de presentarme ante la faz del pueblo Nuevo Mexicano para impetrar sus honestos sufragios no solamente a nombre mío, sino de la masa respectable del pueblo que nombró é instruyó á los miembros de la convención que me elijió.

Yo, el humilde conciudadano de Vdes., he sido en otras épocas el sirviente del pueblo de este país, y hoy por la soberana voluntad de una grande masa del mismo pueblo, que me ha honrado con escojerme como candidato, me veo en el deber imperativo de manifestar a Veds. mis sentimientos políticos, lejos de mis sentimientos bastardos de hostilidad personal, lejos de mis miras particulares de engrandecimiento personal, y lejos de mí, el traicionar los justos derechos a que Vdes., como un pueblo libre, estan intitulados, y en bajo la sagrada letra de la Constitución general, o el sabio tratado nacional de Guadalupe Hidalgo, por las leyes generales y especialmente por las leyes locales de nuestro Territorio. Conozco muy bien vuestro carácter, conozco prácticamente vuestras necesidades en todos respectos, y el sentimiento vital que oscila y palpita patrióticamente en vuestros corazones generosos, y estos atributos esencialmene me compelen en consagrar en mis últimos años la ofrenda de mis pequeños servicios al pueblo de mi nacimiento, ahora y todas las veces que sea llamado al servicio por la mayoría de la comunidad de mis caros compatriotas.

Cumpliendo, pues, con este sagrado deber, decenderé gustoso un día no muy lejano a la tumba del descanso en la larga noche de los siglos, con el dulce placer de haber satisfecho los positivos deseos de Vdes.

Mis conciudadanos y Buenos amigos: la material pública no es propiamente mía, no lo es de mi honorable competidor, el señor José F. Chávez, ni de ninguna otra persona que preocupada se hinche con ilusiones entretenidas de criminal orgullo; repito que en esta misma material se versan intereses generales correspondientes a la comunidad del pueblo para segurar el bienestar y progreso.

El día señalada por la ley, el día memorable de la elección Territorial, el pueblo en ejercicio libre de su soberanía, resolverá enfáticamente el problema que hoy agitado llama la atención de todas las clases de nuestro Territorio, sin distinción de sexo o condición; y entonces la sabia providencia que rige y gobierna los destinos de los mortales, bendecirá para siempre la obra de sus hijos predilectos.

Conciudadanos, confiad vuestro voto a la persona que merezca vuestro aprecio y confianza y desechad para siempre la nube opresora que eclipsa nuestros libres derechos que empreñada, infesta y estorba nuestro progreso.

Todos, todos somos iguales en el nacimiento, todos iguales en la suerte final de la muerte y también iguales en la garantía libre de nuestros derechos. El divino sol que gira sobre nuestras cabezas hace fructificar y admirablemente nutrir la tierra del globo que nos formó y llegó el divino criador para nuestra utilidad y sustento; los vegetales y animales de todos géneros libremente son iluminados y alimentados por el astro resplandeciente.

Así nosotros como entes racionales y superiores, somos iluminados por el astro magnífico del Ser divino para proceder como hombres independientes y libres en al ejercicio de todas nuestras acciones espirituales y temporales.

Esta ha sido y es la doctrina Cristiana que nos enseñó nuestro Señor Jesucristo, autor de la Iglesia militante y triunfante, que edificó la tierra para nuestro beneficio en la serie de los siglos.

En fin, mis caros conciudadanos: Yo, y mi parte, tenemos nuestros reclamos legales para pedir vuestros sufragios, mirad y considerar las obras públicas, fruto de mis trabajos como sirviente público del pueblo; mirad y considerar con justicia imparcial y preguntad; ¿Que cosa ha hecho en nuestro beneficio mi amigo y competidor, el Sr. Chávez? Yo entiendo que todos Vds. saben muy bien que nada ha hecho por nuestro país; que en la capital de la Unión ha levantado su bandera de guerra contra sus compatriotas, debiendo de haber eregido su bandera de paz en honor y beneficio de todo el pueblo que representaba.

El abandono criminal que ha tenido el señor Chávez en el cumplimiento de su deber público, jamás lo acreditan en sus reclamos para pedir vuestros sufragios. Pero si vosotros prácticamente, conociendolo por los colores de sus obras, y si a sabiendas deseais colocarlo otra vez en la posición que sin fruto público ha desempeñado por largo espacio de seis años, vosotros mismos sufriréis en tiempo las tristes consecuencias que hoy llenan de pobreza y luto nuestro caro país.

En conclusión, conciudadanos, os suplico que juiciosamente consideréis la materia, entre tanto quedo con gusto sujeto a vuestra deliberación soberana.

JOSÉ M. GALLEGOS

El Fronterizo (Las Cruces NM), 26 de Julio de 1871

Notes

Abbreviations

Arrott Collection	James W. Arrott's Fort Union Collection, Thomas C. Donnelly Library, New Mexico Highlands University, Las Vegas
Chávez letters	Letters from J. Francisco Chávez, Carl Hayden Papers, Arizona Historical Society, Tucson
Gaceta	*Gaceta Semanaria de Santa Fe*, Spanish section of *Santa Fe Weekly Gazette*
Gazette	*Santa Fe Weekly Gazette*
Insurrection	United States War Department, *Insurrection against the Military Government in New Mexico and California, 1847 and 1848*, Senate Doc. no. 442, 56th Congress, 1st session
JANM	Journal of the Assembly of New Mexico, Mexican Archives of New Mexico
MANM	Mexican Archives of New Mexico, 1821–1846
New Mexican	*Santa Fe New Mexican*; later *Santa Fe Daily New Mexican*
Nuevo-Mejicano	*El Nuevo-Mejicano,* Spanish section of the *Santa Fe New Mexican*; later *Nuevo-Mejicano Diário*
"Procedimientos," 1853	Facundo Pino and José Gutierrez, "Procedimientos de la Co[n]vención Demócrata del Territorio de Nuevo Mexico," *Santa Fe Weekly Gazette*, August 20, 1853
"Procedimientos," 1857	Diego Archuleta et al., "Procedimientos de la junta Demócrata,

	habida en el Condado de Rio Arriba," *Santa Fe Weekly Gazette*, March 7, 1857
Republican	*Santa Fe Republican*
Republicano	*El Republicano*, Santa Fe
Review	*Semi-Weekly Review*; later *Republican Review*, Albuquerque
RG 46	Record Group 46, Territorial Papers—New Mexico, National Archives
RTG	Records of the Territorial Governors, in Territorial Archives of New Mexico
TANM	Territorial Archives of New Mexico, 1846–1912
Weekly Press	*Rio Abajo Weekly Press*, Albuquerque

Introduction

1. Quoted in Larson, *New Mexico's Quest*, 30; Ganaway, *New Mexico and Sectional Controversy*, 46–47.

2. One historian notes with respect to American Indians that the U.S. expansion into the frontier of the North American continent legitimated force, land fraud, physical assault, the denial of sovereignty, removal from ancestral lands, war, and genocidal decimation before any process of effective structural integration; in Ringer, *"We the People": Duality and America's Treatment of its Racial Minorities*, 120. Among the exceptions are the Pueblo Indians of New Mexico, who were exempted from a trajectory of violence at their immediate incorporation by the United States.

3. Hechter, *Internal Colonialism*, 30. Hechter analyzes internal colonialism in the case of Northern Ireland. For an application of the cultural division of labor concept to the Quebecois, see McRoberts, *Quebec*, 25–27.

4. González, *Refusing the Favor*; Montoya, *Translating Property*; Vizenor, *Survivance*. The idea of "forced" annexation implies that the annexation of foreign lands can also occur through peaceful means, through contractual purchase, for example, as in the cases of Louisiana and Florida.

5. Gómez, "Race, Colonialism, and Criminal Law," 1192–93.

6. Farrand, *Legislation for Government of the Organized Territories*, 50.

7. For Nuevomexicano representation in the assemblies of the territorial period, see Padilla and Ramírez, "Patterns of Chicano Representation," 213.

8. Unless otherwise indicated, all translations are by the author. Throughout this volume minor faulty grammar in quoted material has been corrected to correspond to accepted prose usage. Missing diacritical marks have been inserted where necessary.

9. Chaves, *Papers in the Case of J. Francisco Chaves vs. Charles P. Clever, Delegate from the Territory of New Mexico*, 40th Congress, House of Representatives, 2nd session, Misc. Doc. no. 154 (Washington: Government Printing Office, 1867), 121.

10. William Lee Harper, "A History of New Mexico Election Laws," 9.

11. Gómez, *Manifest Destinies*, 9–10; also Zeleny, "Relations between the Spanish-Americans and Anglo-Americans," 221.
12. Gómez, "Race, Colonialism, and Criminal Law," 1192.
13. Theorists of hegemonic colonialism claim that the colonized retain a right to autonomy or independent self-determination. Native cultural heritage forms the basis for a politics of opposition, secession, or irredentism (return to the former sovereign). Puerto Rico is analyzed as such. Since its U.S. annexation in the late nineteenth century, and despite its conversion from a federal territory to a free associated commonwealth, Puerto Ricans have "professed attachment" to the U.S. legal-economic-political system despite the island's dependence on multinational corporations and a stumbling government bereft of appreciable sovereignty; Rivera Ramos, *Legal Construction of Identity*.
14. Gómez, "Race, Colonialism, and Criminal Law," 1192–93.
15. Rivera Ramos, *Legal Construction of Identity*, 5–16, 19.
16. Shalhope, "Toward a Republican Synthesis," 65; Shalhope, *John Taylor of Caroline*, quote 4–5; Johannsen, *To the Halls of the Montezumas*, 47–48; Kekes, *Against Liberalism*, 2.
17. For a recent review of the literature, see Keith Thomas, "The Great Fight over the Enlightenment," 72.
18. Wallerstein, *Centrist Liberalism Triumphant*.
19. Israel, *Revolution of the Mind*, 37–38.
20. Coronado, *A World Not to Come*, 147.
21. Israel, *A Revolution of the Mind*, 48, 87; Pocock, *The Machiavellian Moment*; Rahe, *Machiavelli's Liberal Republican Legacy*.
22. See Zafirovski, *The Enlightenment and Its Effects*. Liberal philosophers such as John Quincy Adams did not universally regard the procedures of the wild French Revolution as a healthy historical trend shortly after they were reported. See von Gentz and Possony, *Three Revolutions*, 3–5.
23. Loughran, *The Republic in Print*, 37.
24. McCarthy, *Race, Empire*, 166–77.
25. Schermerhorn, *Comparative Ethnic Relations*, 82–83.
26. Mehta, *Liberalism and Empire*, 115.
27. Tocqueville, *Democracy in America*, 837–38.
28. Israel, *Revolution of the Mind*, viii, xii, 5, 6, 11, 21, 27, 33, 34, 36, 46, 48.
29. Horton, *Race and the Making of American Liberalism*, 6.
30. Israel, *Revolution of the Mind*, 36.
31. Shalhope, "Republicanism and Early American Historiography," 335–36, quote 335.
32. Harrison, "America: The Struggle to Be Reborn," 64.
33. Israel, *Revolution of the Mind*, 44, 48, 53, 86.
34. Allen, *Our Declaration*, 166.
35. McClain and Stewart, *"Can We All Get Along?"* 10–11.
36. Lieven, *America Right or Wrong*, 50–51, 52; see definitions of the Creed in Lipset, *American Exceptionalism*, 19; Lind, *The Next American Nation*, 90–91, 219–

33; McClosky, "Consensus and Ideology in American Politics"; for "the American Proposition," see *USA: The Permanent Revolution*, by the editors of *Fortune* magazine (1951), quoted in Hartz, *Liberal Tradition in America*, 305.

37. Frederick Jackson Turner, "Western State Making in the Revolutionary Era." On the Turner thesis, see Fernlund, "American Exceptionalism or Atlantic Unity?"; Doob, *Patriotism*, 117–18; Potter, *People of Plenty*, 152.

38. Nichols, "The Territories," 159.

39. Deutsch, *Nationalism and Social Communication*, 104; Doob, *Patriotism*, 40–41, 244.

40. Fox and Guglielmo, "Defining America's Racial Boundaries."

41. Blauner, *Racial Oppression in America*, 51–75.

42. Leopold, "A Cautious Embrace," 11.

43. McWilliams, *North from Mexico*, 81.

44. Pitt, *Decline of the Californios*, 197–201; Almaguer, *Racial Faultlines*, 54–57.

45. Ramos, *Beyond the Alamo*, 169–77.

46. León, *Tejano Community*, 23–24; Ramos, *Beyond the Alamo*, 209–10, 227–29; Montejano, *Anglos and Mexicans*, 39–41.

47. Paquette, "Introduction, in *Enlightened Reform*, 4.

48. Thomas D. Hall, *Social Change in the Southwest*, 242–43.

49. This tendency was not inconsistent with the prejudice and racialism of some major Enlightenment philosophers; Keith Thomas, "The Great Fight over the Enlightenment," 72

50. Dunbar-Ortiz, *Roots of Resistance*, 122–13. The case of the settled Pueblo nations of New Mexico varied from the peripatetic Plains tribes, the question of their citizenship status not settled until New Mexico gained statehood in 1912.

51. Shalhope, *John Taylor of Caroline*, 11, and "Toward a Republican Synthesis," 62.

52. Waldron, "How Politics Are Haunted by the Past."

53. Pombeni, "Problem of Political Parties in Western Liberalism," 119. The second and third quotes are those of Michael Freeden.

54. Eisenstadt, *Modernization: Protest and Change*, 12–13.

55. Pombeni, "Problem of Political Parties in Western Liberalism," 120.

56. LaPalombara and Weiner, "Origin and Development of Political Parties," 3–6.

57. Neumann, "Toward a Comparative Study of Political Parties," 403–4.

58. Scott, "Political Parties and Policy-Making in Latin America," 334–35.

59. Huston, *Stephen A. Douglas*, 8–9.

60. Deutsch, *Nationalism and Its Alternatives*, 104.

61. Jack E. Holmes, *Politics in New Mexico*, 20.

62. Correia, *Properties of Violence*, 32.

63. Benedict Anderson, *Imagined Communities*, 75; Merry, *Human Rights and Gender Violence*, 219.

64. Coronado, *A World Not to Come*, 29.

65. Sztompka, *The Sociology of Social Change*, 140.

66. Alexander, "Theorizing the 'Modes of Incorporation,'" 242.

67. Smelser, *Sociology*, 77; Schumpeter *Capitalism, Socialism, and Democracy*, 289.

68. Valdes, "A Sociological Analysis and Description," 63.

69. Resolutions of the Legislative Assembly of the Territory of New Mexico in favor of the removal of Robert B. Mitchell from the position of Governor of that Territory, March 7, 1868, National Archives, Territorial Papers—New Mexico, Record Group 46 (hereafter RG 46), tray 2, folder 5.

70. Rosenbaum, "Mexicano versus Americano," 63.

71. Valdes, "A Sociological Analysis and Description," 63.

72. W.E.B. Du Bois, "The African Roots of War," 28.

73. Jordan, *Imperial Democracy*, 108–9.

74. Horton, *Race and the Making of American Liberalism*, 4, 5, 9.

Part 1. Initializing Annexation

1. Schermerhorn, *Comparative Ethnic Relations*, 72–73, quote 137; Deutsch, *Nationalism and Social Communication*, 156–57; also Hechter, *Internal Colonialism*, 43.

2. Lamar, *Far Southwest*, 21–29.

3. Thomas D. Hall, *Social Change in the Southwest*, 157–58, 164. For a comprehensive history of the colonial Southwest, see Kessel, *Spain in the Southwest*; on the revolt, see J. Manuel Espinosa, *The Pueblo Indian Revolt of 1696*.

4. Breuilly, *Nationalism and the State*, 158.

5. Henderson, *Glorious Defeat*, 7.

6. Reséndez, *Changing National Identities*, 93.

7. Reséndez, *Changing National Identities*, 93.

8. Henderson, *Glorious Defeat*, 71; for a sanguine view of class in early Mexico, see Gómez-Quiñones, *Roots of Chicano Politics*, 91, 98.

9. Henderson, *Glorious Defeat*, 4, 5, 12.

10. Coronado, *A World Not to Come*, 265; Brading, "Patriotism and the Nation in Colonial Spanish America," 31; Gómez-Quiñones, *Roots of Chicano Politics*, 70–74, 99; Scott, "Political Parties and Policy-Making in Latin America," 76.

11. Cocker, *Rivers of Blood, Rivers of Gold*, 16; Henderson, *Glorious Defeat*, 12–13, 18–19, 21–23; Gómez-Quiñones, *Roots of Chicano Politics*, 86–87.

12. For the study of these factions, see Brading, *The Origins of Mexican Nationalism*, 64, 92–93; Santoni, *Mexicans at Arms*, 2–4; Cress, "Introduction," in *Dispatches from the Mexican War*, 101.

13. Joseph P. Sánchez, *Between Two Rivers*, 106; Henderson, *Glorious Defeat*, 85; Gómez-Quiñones, *Roots of Chicano Politics*, 149.

14. Henderson, *Glorious Defeat*, 118.

15. For the argument that the *internas provincias* would have had every reason to break off from the newly established Mexican state after 1821 as did the territories that became the Central American countries in 1823, see Tenenbaum, "Making of a Fait Accompli," 92.

16. Gellner, *Nationalism*, 30; also Gellner, *Nations and Nationalism*, 10.

17. Deutsch, *Nationalism and Its Alternatives*, 8; also on the spoke wheel metaphor, Pye, *Communications and Political Development*, 27.

18. Tenenbaum, "Making of a Fait Accompli," 96. It overstates the case to say that "frontier society and culture, which possessed characteristics that distinguished it

from central Mexico in the Spanish era, grew even more distinctive and separate in the Mexican era"; David J. Weber, *Mexican Frontier*, 241.

19. Parraga, "Santa Fe de Nuevo Mexico," 7.

20. Harry Harootunian, quoted in Coronado, *A World Not to Come*, 24. On the Spanish colonial roots of the Mexican political and institutional systems, see Blackmar, *Spanish Institutions of the Southwest*.

21. Peceny, *Democracy at the Point of Bayonets*, 1–2. As Peceny notes, "The phrase 'at the point of bayonets' was used by Warren Harding during the 1920 presidential election campaign to criticize Woodrow Wilson's Haitian policies," 1n1.

22. Peceny, *Democracy at the Point of Bayonets*, 5.

23. O'Donnell and Schmitter, *Transitions from Authoritarian Rule*, 37.

24. Michael Burton et al., "Introduction: Elite Transformations and Democratic Regimes," 14; Diamond, "Introduction" to *Democracy in Developing Countries*, 49.

25. Montejano, *Anglos and Mexicans*, 34.

26. Charles Taylor, "A Different Kind of Courage," *New York Review of Books*, April 26, 2007, 8.

27. See the discussion in Breuilly, *Nationalism and the State*, 158–61.

28. Oomen, "Social Movements," 112.

29. For a dramatic account of American social and civic replication on the frontier, see Devoto, *Year of Decision*, 520.

1. Nuevomexicano Politics and Society

1. Chambers, *Political Parties in a New Nation*, 15.

2. González de la Vara, "Política," 85, 87–88; Joseph P. Sánchez, *Between Two Rivers*, 108; Wayne Harper, "Juan Bautista Vigil y Alarid," 2, 27, 139.

3. González de la Vara, "Política"; Gómez-Quiñones, *Roots of Chicano Politics*, 122. The first session met in April 1822, a year after Mexico's independence from Spain. Who constituted the assembly's full membership is not known. Three names are in the assembly Journal as members of one committee and three others of another committee; Read, *Illustrated History*, 366.

4. Sánchez, *Between Two Rivers*, 107–7; also, González de la Vara, "Política," 85.

5. In Journal of the Assembly of New Mexico (hereafter JANM), microfilm, reel 42, frames 751–868, Mexican Archives of New Mexico, Center for Southwest Research and Special Collections, University of New Mexico, Albuquerque, "Seción," "Seción ordinaria," or "Seción extraordinaria," dates and frames as follows: June 5, 1845 (frame 751); July 7, 1845 (764); October 27, 1845 (805–6); November 3, 1845 (806–7); January 3, 27, and 29, 1846 (824–25, 845, 849); February 3, 1846 (849); March 2, 21, and 26, 1846 (861–64, 865–66, 867–68).

6. Gómez-Quiñones, *Roots of Chicano Politics*, 89.

7. Sánchez, *Between Two Rivers*, 107; Gómez-Quiñones, *Roots of Chicano Politics*, 124.

8. See JANM, reel 42.

9. JANM, reel 42, "Seción del dia 22 de Diciembre de 1845," frames 818–19.

10. JANM, reel 42, "Seción del dia 31 de Diciembre de 1845, frames 821–22, and "Seción del dia 29 de Diciembre de 1845," frames 819–20; Gómez-Quiñones, *Roots of Chicano Politics*, 92.

11. The origin of this office lay in an 1810 Royal Statute authorizing the election of a provincial deputy to the Cortes of Spain; Read, *Illustrated History*, 351–52; Simmons, *Spanish Government in New Mexico*, 203–4.

12. González de la Vara, "Política," 83, 84–85; Wayne Harper, "Juan Bautista Vigil y Alarid," 21–22.

13. Bloom, *New Mexico under Mexican Administration 1821–1846*, pt. III, ch. VI: "Constitutional Government Re-established, 1843–1844," 157.

14. JANM, reel 42, "Seción del día 8 de Noviembre de 1830," frame 644.

15. González de la Vara, "Política," 86.

16. JANM, reel 42, "Seción extraordinaria 1 de enero de 1846," frame 822; Bloom, *New Mexico under Mexican Administration 1821–1846*, pt. II, ch. XII: "Changing to the Departmental System," 9–11; Sánchez, *Between Two Rivers*, 107.

17. González de la Vara, "Política," 81, 83–84; Weber, *Mexican Frontier*, 35–42; Sánchez, *Between Two Rivers*, 100–101; Wayne Harper, "Juan Bautista Vigil y Alarid," 20, 23.

18. Fray Angélico Chávez, *But Time and Chance: The Story of Padre Martínez of Taos, 1793–1867*, 41; Gómez-Quiñones, *Roots of Chicano Politics*, 75.

19. Cutts, *Conquest*, 22.

20. Pomeroy, *The Territories*, xi.

21. Thomas D. Hall, *Social Change in the Southwest*, 205–6.

22. Henderson, *Glorious Defeat*, 11–12.

23. Santoni, *Mexicans at Arms*, 232; Henderson, *Glorious Defeat*, 12.

24. Sánchez, *Between Two Rivers*, 101.

25. Henderson, *Glorious Defeat*, 65–66, 18, 123–24; Lecompte, *Rebellion*, 17; Reséndez, *Changing National Identities*, 153.

26. Transl. in McMurtrie, *El Payo de Nuevo Mejico*, 6–9.

27. JANM, reel 42, "Seción ordinaria del día 21 de Mayo de 1845," frames 747–49, and "Seción extraordinaria del día 18 de Enero del 1846," frames 836–37; Bloom, *New Mexico under Mexican Administration*, pt III, ch. VIII: "Six Months under the Senior Deputy," 242. That the lack of supplies went back a while is indicated in JANM, reel 42, "Seción del día 8 de Noviembre de 1830," frames 643–49.

28. JANM, reel 42, "Seción extraordinaria de 1.o de Octubre del 1845," frames 801–1; Bloom, *New Mexico under Mexican Administration*, pt. III, ch. IV: "A One-Man Administration, 1838 to 1844," 130–31.

29. JANM, reel 42, "Seción del día 28 de Junio de 1845," frames 760–61; Bloom, *New Mexico under Mexican Administration*, pt. III, ch.1: "New Mexico in 1838," 37–38; Bieber, "Introduction," *Journal of a Soldier*, 62.

30. JANM, reel 42, "Seción Ordinaria del día 5 de Enero de 1846," frames 825–26; "Ordinaria del día 9 de Enero de 1846," frame 830; "Seción extraordinaria del día 22 de Enero del 1846," frames 840–41.

31. Bloom, *New Mexico under Mexican Administration*, pt. III, ch. VII: "A Year Under an Alien Governor," 228–29, 231.

32. JANM, reel 42, "Seción del día 22 de Diciembre de 1845," frames 818–19, and "Seción extraordinaria del día 6 de Agosto de 1845," frames 772–73.

33. González de la Vara, "Política," 86–87.

34. Sánchez, *Between Two Rivers*, 109.

35. Reséndez, *Changing National Identities*, 79–80, 175–80; Sánchez, *Between Two Rivers*, 110–11; Gómez-Quiñones, *Roots of Chicano Politics*, 156–57; on the rebellion, see Gregg, *Commerce of the Prairies*, 122–29; Lecompte, *Rebellion*.

36. Sánchez, *Between Two Rivers*, 113; Gómez-Quiñones, *Roots of Chicano Politics*, 157–58.

37. Reséndez, *Changing National Identities*, 177–80.

38. Sánchez, *Between Two Rivers*, 112–13; Bancroft, *History of Arizona and New Mexico*, 316–19; Lecompte, *Rebellion*, 21–40, 56, 68–69; Reséndez, *Changing National Identities*, 184; Chávez, *But Time*, 239; Weber, *Mexican Frontier*, 262.

39. Lecompte, *Rebellion*, 44–45, 70; Reséndez, *Changing National Identities*, 184–6.

40. Lecompte, *Rebellion*, 47; Reséndez, *Changing National Identities*, 189–94; Gómez-Quiñones, *Roots of Chicano Politics*, 158–60.

41. Sánchez, *Between Two Rivers*, 114.

42. Coronado, *A World Not to Come*, 22.

43. González, *Refusing the Favor*, 86.

44. Frazer, "The New Mexican Scene," 40–41.

45. Boyle, *Los Capitalistas*, 36–37; Charles, "Development of the Partido System," 19–20; Sunseri, *Seeds of Discord*, 31. Gregg, *Commerce of the Prairies*, 61–62); Twitchell, *Leading Facts*, 493; Brooks, *Captives and Cousins*, 208; Frazer, "The New Mexican Scene," 89n12; Adrian Herminio Bustamante, "Los Hispanos," 80.

46. Reséndez (*Changing National Identities*, 192, inter alia) calls this segment *vecinos*, citizen-neighbors of the New Mexico countryside, but *vecino* more accurately includes *pobladores*, the economically midlevel ranchers who settled the territorial outback.

47. Costeloe, *Central Republic*, first quote 17, second quote 17–18; Henderson, *Glorious Defeat*, 21, 82, 143, 153.

48. Santoni, *Mexicans at Arms*, 6, 116–17; Henderson, *Glorious Defeat*, 64.

49. Henderson, *Glorious Defeat*, 21.

50. Santoni, *Mexicans at Arms*, 21, 101, 116–17.

51. Anonymous, "Pancho y Chepe en su tercer encuentro," *Santa Fe Weekly Gazette* (hereafter *Gazette*), July 27, 1867; Un Amigo de Pepe, untitled, *Gazette*, August 17, 1867; Juan de J. Trujillo, Cura de Santa Cruz, to editor, *Gazette*, August 17, 1867; La Verdad (The Truth) to editor, *Gazette*, March 21, 1868; "Atentados Criminales," *El Nuevo-Mejicano* (Santa Fe), June 22, 1866; Lecompte, *Rebellion*, 31–32; Henderson, *Glorious Defeat*, 27; Bancroft, *History of Arizona and New Mexico*, 312n5; Gregg, *Commerce of the Prairies*, 222, 233–38.

52. Donaciano Vigil, "La Convención," *El Republicano* (Santa Fe), January 29, 1848 (hereafter *Republicano*).

53. As Weber concludes (*Mexican Frontier*, 265), "In general, the New Mexico upper class displayed little understanding of the grievances of the *pobres* [poor people]"; also Thomas D. Hall, *Social Change in the Southwest*, 90–192; Baxter, *Las Carneradas*, 106–7; Thomas E. Chávez, *Manuel Álvarez*, 17–18.

54. Reséndez, *Changing National Identities*, 242–44; Sánchez, *Between Two Rivers*, 117.

55. "Proclamation of Manuel Armijo, January 7, 1838 [?], in Lecompte, *Rebellion*, 142–45, quotes 143–44. For similar statements reproduced in Lecompte, *Rebellion*, see "Letter of Manuel Armijo, September 12, 1837," 104–8, esp. 107, and "Letter of Manuel Armijo [to Minister of War and Navy], October 11, 1837," 136–42, esp. 137.

56. "Obituary," *Santa Fe Weekly Press*, November 26, 1870.

57. The Río Abajo township was originally spelled Alburquerque, and by the late 1870s had informally shifted to Albuquerque. The original spelling is retained for most of the narrative in this book until the final chapter, when the story enters the era when the new spelling became customary.

58. Lecompte, *Rebellion*, first quote 10; Bancroft, *History of Arizona and New Mexico*, 313; Cooke, *The Conquest*, 33. Second quote, Donaciano Vigil, Address to the New Mexico Assembly, 18 June 1846 (publ. and transl. as "Vigil on Arms, Munitions, Trade, North Americans, and 'Barbaric Indians," 1–8, and "Vigil opina sobre armas, municiones, comercio, norteamericanos, y indios bárbaras," 9–17), in Vigil, *Arms, Indians*, 6; also in Lecompte, *Rebellion*, 83–89. Parraga, "Santa Fe de Nuevo Mexico," 10–11; González de la Vara, "Política," 98.

59. Gómez-Quiñones, *Roots of Chicano Politics*, 98–99.

60. Lomnitz, "Nationalism as a Practical System, 350. On Chacón, see, "El Mayor Rafael Chacón Nació en Santa Fe," *Nuevo Mexicano*, June 15, 1912.

61. "New Mexico Centenarian Dies," *El Combate* (Wagon Mound NM), December 6, 1902.

62. González de la Vara, "Política," 96–97; Lecompte, *Rebellion*, 21–22, 35; Gómez-Quiñones, *Roots of Chicano Politics*, 94.

63. Chaves, *Papers in the Case of J. Francisco Chaves vs. Charles P. Clever*, 144; Salazar, *The Military Career of Donaciano Vigil*; Stanley, *Giant*; Lecompte, *Rebellion*, 40; Reséndez, *Changing National Identities*, 190.

64. Diego Archuleta to editors, *Nuevo Mexicano*, March 12, 1872; Reséndez, *Changing National Identities*, 251, 255.

65. González de la Vara, "Política," 96–97; Lecompte, *Rebellion*, 21–22, 35; Gómez-Quiñones, *Roots of Chicano Politics*, 94.

66. Some states continued to provide support to churches. On the founding separation of church and state in the United States, see Waldman, *Founding Faith*; Meacham, *American Gospel*; David L. Holmes, *Faiths of the Founding Fathers*.

67. For a strategic journalistic essay, see "The True State of the Case," *Gazette*, August 27, 1853.

68. Coronado, *A World Not to Come*, 28; González, *Refusing the Favor*, 26; Santoni, *Mexicans at Arms*, 15.

69. First quote, Lomnitz, "Nationalism as a Practical System, 350; second quote, Henderson, *Glorious Defeat*, 15.

70. Rodriguez-O., "The Conflict between Church," 93–96.

71. Manuel Armijo to President of the Esteemed Assembly, January 19, 1846, JANM, reel 42, "Seción extraordinaria del día 20 de Enero del 1846," frames 838–40;

Trinidad Barceló legal report to Gov. D. Donaciano Vigil, October 23, 1846, Governor's Papers, Bent, reel 1, frame 10, Records of the Territorial Governors, 1846–1912 (hereafter RTG), microfilm, Territorial Archives of New Mexico, 1846–1912 (hereafter TANM); "Letter of Antonio Lopez de Santa Anna to Manuel Reyes Veramendi," ed. Robert S. Chamberlain, in *Hispanic American Historical Review*; Chávez, *But Time*, 30, 73, 75.

72. Reséndez, *Changing National Identities*, 76–78, quote 79, 79–80; González de la Vara, "Política," 103, 104, 107–8; on three vicars in the 1820s and 1830s, see Martínez, "Apología," 337–38.

73. Theisen, "José Manuel Gallegos," 24; Chávez and Chávez, *Wake*, 39.

74. "Obituario," *El Nuevo-Mejicano* (Santa Fe, hereafter *Nuevo-Mejicano*), August 17, 1867; Chávez, *But Time*, 23–24.

75. Chávez, *But Time*, 41; quote, Gómez-Quiñones, *Roots of Chicano Politics*, 75.

76. Weber, "Failure of a Frontier Institution," 142.

77. Martínez "Apologia," 340.

78. Martínez, "Apología," 344–45; Bloom, *New Mexico under Mexican Administration*, pt. II, ch. XII: "Changing to the Department System," 9–11.

79. Martínez, "Apología," 340–41; "Obituario," *Nuevo-Mejicano*, August 17, 1867; Lecompte, *Rebellion*, 47.

80. Reséndez, *Changing National Identities*, 74.

81. Thiesen, "Jose Manuel Gallegos," 24.

82. Chávez and Chávez, *Wake*, 59; for the claim of 11 clergy, see Weber, "Failure of a Frontier Institution," 131.

83. González, *Refusing the Favor*, 26; Lamar, *Far Southwest*, 77.

84. JANM, reel 42, "Seción extraordinario de 18 de Junio de 1845," frames 754–55.

85. JANM, reel 42, "Seción extraordinario del 16 de Agosto de 1845," frames 790–91.

86. JANM, reel 42, "Seción ordinaria del 23 de Abril de 1846," frame 881; "Seción ordinaria del dia 13 de Noviembre del 1845," frames 810–11; "Seción ordinaria del dia 7 de Noviembre del 1845," frames 809–10; for a slightly differing list, see Twitchell, *Old Santa Fe*, 245n485.

87. Bloom, *New Mexico under Mexican Administration*, pt. III, ch. IX: "A Third and Last Chance for Manuel Armijo," 251–52; González, *Refusing the Favor*, 20.

88. Monroy, "Creation and Re-Creation," 180–81.

89. Coronado, *A World Not to Come*, 68.

90. JANM, reel 42, "Seción ordinaria del 5 de Enero de 1846," frames 825–26 and "Seción extraordinaria del día 18 de Enero del 1846, frames 836–37; Bloom, *New Mexico under Mexican Administration*, pt. III, ch. IX: "A Third and Last Chance for Manuel Armijo," 256–57, 259; also Donaciano Vigil, Address to the New Mexico Assembly, 22 June 1846 (publ. and transl. as "Vigil on the Maladministration of New Mexico under Governors Perez and Martinez and under Commanding General Garcia Conde," 17–40, and "Vigil opina"), in Vigil, *Arms, Indians*, 17, 28, 40; Reséndez, *Changing National Identities*, 244. Californios used *hijos del país* as they made themselves into a regional elite; Salomon, "California Son," 50. The phrase was used by the citizens of the other Mexican departments maintaining

their autonomy, which Nuevomexicano assemblymen endorsed, in JANM, reel 42, "Seción extraordinaria del día 26 de Enero del 1846, frames 842–43"; "Seción ordinaria del día 29 de Enero de 1846," frame 849; "Seción ordinaria del día 5 de Febrero del 1846," frame 850; "Seción ordinaria del día 3 de Febrero del 1846," frame 849.

91. Weber, *Mexican Frontier*, 230.

92. Wagner, "New Mexico Spanish Press," 3; also Chávez, *But Time*, 49.

93. Horgan, *Lamy of Santa Fe*, 48–49, 50; Gómez-Quiñones, *Roots of Chicano Politics*, 127.

94. Stanley, *Giant*, 131–32; McMurtrie, *El Payo de Nuevo-Mejico*, 5n6. Two issues of *El Payo* survive; it is uncertain how long it lasted. Wagner, "New Mexico Spanish Press," 8–40; Weber, *Mexican Frontier*, 230–31; Stratton, *Territorial Press of New Mexico*, 2; Grove et al., *New Mexico Newspapers*, 442, 463, 489. JANM, reel 42, "Seción del día 2 de Junio de 1845," frame 750, and "Seción extraordinaria del día 28 de Marzo 1846," frames 868–70.

95. González de la Vara, "Política," 95; Governor Mariano Martínez, Assembly President Jesús María Gallegos, Assembly Secretary Juan Bautista Vigil y Maris, Department Secretary José Félix Jubia, "Division of the Department," June 17, 1844, in Abert, *Report*, 476–77 (the translator mistakenly calls the Southwestern District the Southeastern); Bancroft, *History of Arizona and New Mexico*, 311; Baxter, *Dividing New Mexico's Waters*, 44; Sánchez, *Between Two Rivers*, 101–2.

96. Grivas, *Military Governments*, 152–53, 158–59; Jenkins, *County Boundaries of New Mexico*, 26; James S. Calhoun to [Cmdr. of Ind. Affrs.], Orlando Brown, January 25, 1850, in Abel, *Official Correspondence*, 103.

97. Coronado, *A World Not to Come*, 210–11; Poldervaart, "Black Robed Justice in New Mexico," 29–36.

98. This general picture pieced together from Bloom, *New Mexico under Mexican Administration*, serialized in *Old Santa Fe*, vols. 1–2, 1913–15: from pt. II, ch. IV, "New Mexico Becomes a Territory," 165–68, and ch. XII, "Changing to the Departmental System," 6–12; from pt. III, ch. IV, "A One-Man Administration," 130–31, 140; ch. VI, "Constitutional Government Re-established, 1843–1844," 162–63; ch. VII, "A Year Under an Alien Governor," 224, 227–28; ch. VIII, "Six Months Under the Senior Deputy," 240, 248; and ch. IX, "A Third and Last Chance for Manuel Armijo," 257. See also Read, *Illustrated History*, 328, 374; Baxter, *Dividing New Mexico's Waters*, 32, 44; Abert, *Report*, 571; Poldervaart, "Black Robed Justice in New Mexico," 18–50; Wayne Harper, "Juan Bautista Vigil y Alarid," 80–81.

99. Harper, "Juan Bautista Vigil y Alarid," 16–17; Read, *Illustrated History*, 415, 444–45.

100. Mondragón and Stapleton, *Public Education*, 9, 10, 13.

101. "The New Mexican Correspondent of the New York Times," *Gazette*, June 17, 1854; Chávez, *But Time*, 43–44.

102. Martínez, "Apología," 341–42; Theisen, "José Manuel Gallegos," 6, 8, 12, 13, 15, 24; González de la Vara, "Política," 106.

103. JANM, reel 42, "Sesíon de día 27 de Abril de 1822," frame 14; Mondragón and Stapleton, *Public Education*, 8; Chávez, *But Time*, 30.

104. JANM, reel 42, "Seción del día de 29 de Febrero de 1830," frames 633-34; "Seción del día de 4 de Marzo de 1830," frames 635-37; "Seción del día de 6 de Marzo de 1830," frames 639-40; "Seción del día 8 de Noviembre de 1830," frames 643-49.

105. Read, *Illustrated History*, 366; Bloom, *New Mexico under Mexican Administration*, pt. III, ch. IX: "A Third and Last Chance for Manuel Armijo," 254; Theisen, "José Manuel Gallegos," 7.

106. Mondragón and Stapleton, *Public Education*, 10.

107. Bloom, *New Mexico under Mexican Administration*, pt. II, ch. XII: "Changing to the Departmental System," 14-15; Allison, "Colonel Francisco Perea," 210, 211; Bloom, *New Mexico under Mexican Administration*, pt. III, ch. IX, "A Third and Last Chance for Manuel Armijo," 254; Weber, *Mexican Frontier*, 233; Chávez, *But Time*, 44.

108. Wayne Harper, "Juan Bautista Vigil y Alarid," 97-98.

109. Martínez, "Apología," 329-35; Twitchell, *History of the Military Occupation*, 208; Hall, "Giant Before the Surveyor-General," 67-68; Stanley, *Giant*, 24-25.

110. Chávez, *But Time*, 17-18, quote 20; Chávez and Chávez, *Wake*, 25-26.

111. Twitchell, *History of the Military Occupation*, 361-62.

112. Leandro Sánchez to editors, *Nuevo-Mejicano*, June 30, 1865.

113. Gómez-Quiñones, *Roots of Chicano Politics*, 91.

114. Calvin, "Introduction," in *Lieutenant Emory Reports*, 14-15.

115. Gómez-Quiñones, *Roots of Chicano Politics*, 119.

116. First quote, Cutts, *Conquest*, 56; second quote, Garrard, *Wah-to-yah and the Taos Trail*, 233.

117. McCall, *New Mexico in 1850*, 96-97; Gregg, *Commerce of the Prairies*, 151; McCall, *New Mexico in 1850*, 87; Cooke, *The Conquest*, 49, quote 73.

118. Gibson, *Journal of a Soldier*, quote 194; on the Indian-Mexican-Pueblo relations, see Frazer, "The New Mexican Scene," 88-89, 98-109; also, Read, *Illustrated History*, 501-2.

119. Johnston, *Journal of Captain A. R. Johnston*, 567.

120. Gibson, *Journal of a Soldier*, 194.

121. Kiser, "A 'charming name,'" 60-61.

122. Charles, "Development of the Partido System," 22; Parish, *Charles Ilfeld*, 150-52.

123. Johnston, *Journal of Captain A. R. Johnston*, 567.

124. Baxter, *Las Carneradas*, 28-31; Calvin, "Introduction," 15; Cutts, *Conquest*, Kiser, "A 'charming name,'" 174.

125. Weber, *Mexican Frontier*, 212; see also, Calvin, "Introduction," 14; Cooke, *The Conquest*, 47-48; Garrard, *Wah-to-Yah and the Taos Trail*, 233.

126. Montoya, *Translating Property*, 63-65; Bustamante, "Los Hispanos," 85-88.

127. Quoted in Kiser, "A 'charming name,'" 172.

128. Gellner, *Encounters with Nationalism*, 35; also Gellner, *Nationalism*, 24.

129. Nostrand, *Hispano Homeland*, 44; Thomas D. Hall, *Social Change in the Southwest*, 75-109; Cooke, *The Conquest*, 103.

130. An extensive literature on the New Mexican land grants exists. Among the most authoritative, see Ebright, *Land Grants and Lawsuits*, 21-28, and Correia, *Properties of Violence*. For excellent ethnohistorical discussions of community grants,

long-lots, and irrigation in the Río Arriba, see Carlson, *Spanish American Homeland*, chapter 2; Van Ness, *Hispanos*.

131. Lamar, "Land Policy in the Spanish Southwest."

132. A major point of Correia's *Properties of Violence*.

133. Lamar, "Land Policy in the Spanish Southwest," 500.

134. For the authoritative discussion of the empresario and Mexican law, see Montoya, *Translating Property*, 161, 163–65, 168, 174–75, 179–89.

135. González, *Refusing the Favor*, 29; Hall and Weber, "Mexican Liberals and the Pueblo Indians," 8–9; Wayne Harper, "Juan Bautista Vigíl y Alarid," 160–63.

136. Van Ness, *Hispanos*; Parish, *Charles Ilfeld*, 151; Bustamante, "Los Hispanos," 83–85.

137. Thomas D. Hall, *Social Change in the Southwest*, 190.

138. Swadesh, *Primeros Pobladores*; Frank, *From Settler to Citizen*; Calvin, "Introduction," 14.

139. Garrard, *Wah-to-yah and the Taos Trail*, 169; Twitchell, *Leading Facts*, 174–76.

140. McCall, *New Mexico in 1850*, 85–86.

141. Nostrand, *Hispano Homeland*, 73; Rosenbaum, "Mexicano versus Americano," 16–17; Van Ness, *Hispanos*, 255; Baxter, *Las Carneradas*, 42–43; 59–63; 94–95; Perrigo, *American Southwest*, 75; Charles, "Development of the Partido System," 19; Mosk, "The Influence of Tradition on Agriculture."

142. Ríos-Bustamante, "New Mexico in the Eighteenth Century."

143. Brooks, *Captives and Cousins*, 214–16; Swadesh, *Primeros Pobladores*, 58, 69; Thomas D. Hall, *Social Change in the Southwest*, 157; DeLay, *War of a Thousand Deserts*; Durwood Ball, "Fort Craig, New Mexico," 154.

144. Cutts, *Conquest*, 14; Magoffin, *Down the Santa Fe Trail*, 163; Gómez-Quiñones, *Roots of Chicano Politics*, 91.

145. Cooke, *The Conquest*, 80.

146. Brooks, *Captives and Cousins*, 125; for the Spanish etymology of *genizaro*, see 127–28.

147. Moises Gonzales, "The Genizaro Land Grant Settlements," 584; Brooks, *Captives and Cousins*, 129–30, 133, 135; also Horvath, "The Genizaro." The phrase "raiding and revenge" comes from a study of Californio life and its own tradition of hostilities with native tribes; Monroy, "Creation and Re-Creation," 191.

148. Moises Gonzales, "The Genizaro Land Grant Settlements," 595; Van Ness, *Hispanos*, 203; Bloom, *New Mexico under Mexican Administration*, pt. III, ch. I: "New Mexico in 1838," 40. On the growth of the "free, yet socially marginal, mixed-blood population," see Brooks, *Captives and Cousins*, 143–47.

149. Brooks, "Violence, Justice, and State Power," 39.

150. Gellner, *Encounters with Nationalism*; also Gellner, *Nationalism*, 24.

151. Cooke, *The Conquest*, 60–61, 80.

152. Gellner, *Encounters with Nationalism*, 38–39; Gellner, *Nationalism*, 77.

153. Hordes, *To the End of the Earth*, 199–201. An 1850 census has seven-eighths of the adults not able to read and write; Vaughn, *New Mexico History and Government*, 213; cf. Larson, *New Mexico's Quest*, 65.

154. For documented cases of such petitioning, see Ebright, *Land Grants and Lawsuits*.

155. See Gallegos, *Literacy, Education, and Society*; also, Ebright, *Land Grants and Lawsuits*.

156. Bloom, *New Mexico under Mexican Administration*, pt. III, ch. I: "New Mexico in 1838," 45; Weber, *Mexican Frontier*, 2, 231; Arellano, "Through Thick and Thin," 56.

157. Wayne Harper, "Juan Bautista Vigil y Alarid," 109–10.

158. "The pure Spanish blood, favored with wealth and honors, preserved its caste, education, intelligence and refinement, and to this day, is as clear to the discriminating observer as it was one hundred and fifty years ago"; "Revolution of 1837," *Santa Fe New Mexican*, December 24, 1863; Meinig, *Shaping of America*, 133–34.

159. Donaciano Vigil, Address to the New Mexico Assembly, 18 June 1846 (trans. as "Vigil on Arms, Munitions, Trade, North Americans, and Barbaric Indians," 1–8, and "Vigil opina sobre armas, municiones, comercio, norteamericanos, y indios bárbaras," 9–17), in Vigil, *Arms, Indians, and the Mismanagement of New Mexico*, 7, 15; Gregg, *Commerce of the Prairies*, 76; also Horgan, *Lamy of Santa Fe*, 234.

160. Nieto-Phillips, *Language of Blood*, 38.

161. Florescano, *Étnia, Estado y Nación*, 314. For a review of the literature on Los Hermanos in New Mexico, see Pulido, *Sacred World of the Penitentes*, 53–56.

162. Theisen, "José Manuel Gallegos," 9.

163. Steele and Rivera, *Penitente Self-Government*, 1, 4; Van Ness, *Hispanos*, 193–94.

164. Florescano, *Étnia, Estado y Nación*, 314–16; quotation, Weigle, *Brothers of Light*, 24–25, 22; Fray Angélico Chávez, "The Penitentes of New Mexico"; Chávez, *But Time*, 45–46; Lamar, *Far Southwest*, 30; Steele and Rivera, *Penitente Self-Government*, 5; quotation Chávez and Chávez, *Wake*, 34; Reséndez, *Changing National Identities*, 79–80.

165. Weigle, *Brothers of Light*, 142; Steele and Rivera, *Penitente Self-Government*, 8, 14–15. The statement that 95 percent of Hispano men of the villages were penitentes is clearly an overestimate; Montgomery, *Spanish Redemption*, 209.

166. Weigle, *Brothers of Light*, 140. For an essay premised on the distinction between penitente and non-penitente elements, see Chávez, *My Penitente Land*.

167. Steele and Rivera, *Penitente Self-Government*, 50; Weigle, *Brothers of Light*, 7.

168. For evidence, see the literature review in Weigle, *Brothers of Light*, 140–43; Kutsche, and Van Ness, *Cañones*, 2.

169. Nostrand (*Hispano Homeland*, 109, fn) finds sixteen clergy in 1850 who were born in New Mexico. Carlson, *Spanish American Homeland*, 146; Weigle, *Brothers of Light*, 25; Van Ness, *Hispanos*, 204; Nostrand, *Hispano Homeland*, 73. One researcher claims that Father Martínez was a member of the brotherhood; Aragon, *Padre Martinez*, 134–36. Martinez was granted sponsorship over the brotherhood, but would have been an honorary rather than an initiated member; Chávez, *But Time*, 35–37, 45–47. Primary evidence proves that Martínez sought to sustain a universal Roman Catholicism to parishioners; see Martinez's circular titled "Iglesia Cristiana, Católica, Apostólica," box 1, LeBaron Prince Papers, Center for Southwest Research, University of New Mexico.

170. Steele and Rivera, *Penitente Self-Government*, 23–25, 40; Weigle, *Brothers of Light*, 92.

171. Richard D. Meyers, "'From Hell Itself'"; Lamar, *Far Southwest*, 51; Reséndez, *Changing National Identities*, 106.

172. Ake, *A Theory of Political Integration*, 118.

173. One historian cautions against considering the U.S. acquisition of the Mexican territories in the nineteenth century as "inevitable," seeing it more as "a series of fortuitous events"; Griswold del Castillo, *The Treaty of Guadalupe Hidalgo*, 172.

174. Meinig, *Shaping of America*, 4.

175. Craver, *Impact of Intimacy*, 80.

176. Lamar, *Far Southwest*, 47, 48.

177. Stanley, *Giant*, 103–4.

178. Pratt, *Imperial Eyes*, 7; Bloom, *New Mexico under Mexican Administration*, pt. II, ch. IV: "New Mexico Becomes a Territory," 173.

179. Sunseri, *Seeds of Discord*, 38; Cooke, *The Conquest*, 17; Emory, *Notes of a Reconnaisance*, 47; Henderson, *Glorious Defeat*, 38.

180. Craver, *Impact of Intimacy*, 19, 36; Weber, *Mexican Frontier*, 190–94; Ebright, *Land Grants and Lawsuits*, 27; Chavez, "Manuel Álvarez," 25; Lamar, "Land Policy in the Spanish Southwest," 501, 502.

181. Reséndez, *Changing National Identities*, 34–37; Hall, "Giant Before the Surveyor General," 64.

182. JANM, reel 42, "Seción ordinaria del 1 de Mayo de 1846," frames 882–83, and "Seción ordinaria del 25 de Mayo de 1846," frame 886.

183. Sunder, "Introduction," in *Matt Field*, xxvi.

184. Reséndez, *Changing National Identities*, 88.

185. Beachum, *William Becknell*, 29–30; Calvin, "Introduction," 15; Sobel, *Conquest and Conscience*, 37.

186. Vigil, *Arms, Indians*, 4–5; Stanley, *Giant*, 103.

187. Matt Field, "A Cool Greeting," *Picayune* (New Orleans), May 16, 1840, in Sunder, *Matt Field*, 278–81; Pike, *Prose Sketches and Poems*, 35–36.

188. Boyle, *Los Capitalistas*, 47–49; Lamar, *Far Southwest*, 47, 48; Moorhead, *New Mexico's Royal Road*, 102–16; Thomas Chávez, *Manuel Álvarez*, 10; Nostrand, *Hispano Homeland*, 100; Thomas D. Hall, *Social Change in the Southwest*, 148–50; Tenenbaum, "Making of a Fait Accompli," 96.

189. Crutchfield, *Tragedy at Taos*, 31; also Weber, *Mexican Frontier*, 132–33.

190. Reséndez, *Changing National Identities*, first quote 93–94, second quote 96; cf. Sobel, *Conquest and Conscience*, 37–38.

191. For comprehensive treatments, see Lavender, *Bent's Fort*; Comer, *Ritual Ground*.

192. Reséndez, *Changing National Identities*, 98.

193. Reséndez, *Changing National Identities*, 98–99; Weber, *Mexican Frontier*, 239; Bloom, *New Mexico under Mexican Administration*, pt. II, ch. IV: "New Mexico Becomes a Territory," 169–72; Boyle, *Los Capitalistas*, 35, 61.

194. Quoted in Reséndez, *Changing National Identities*, 103; and *Daily Missouri Republican*, January 1, 1846, quoted in Bieber, "Introduction," *Journal of a Soldier*, 61–63; Sandovál, "Gnats, Goods and Greasers," 25.

195. Sobel, *Conquest and Conscience*, 37.

196. Reséndez, *Changing National Identities*," shrewdly," 100–101, "no longer found," 99; Cotner, *Career of José Joaquín De Herrera*, 133; Weber, *Mexican Frontier*, 125–29; Chávez, *Manuel Álvarez*, 3, 81–82; Van Ness, *Hispanos*, 203–6.

197. Edwards, "Journal of Marcellus Ball Edwards," 211; Sunder, "Introduction," in *Matt Field*, xxiv; Reséndez, *Changing National Identities*, 101.

198. Groom, *Kearny's March*, 64.

199. Reséndez, *Changing National Identities*, 101.

200. See, for example, the account of officer José Romero and son Miguel in Maurilio E. Vigil, *Los Patrones*, 63; cf. Chávez, *Manuel Álvarez*; Lamar, *Far Southwest*, 65.

201. Weber, "Introduction," in Donaciano Vigil, *Arms, Indians*, xvi; Twitchell, *History of the Military Occupation*, 149.

202. González, "Gertrudis Barceló, 42, 45; Magoffin, *Down the Santa Fe Trail*, 119–20; Twitchell, *Old Santa Fe*, 338; Reséndez, *Changing National Identities*, 103.

203. Chávez, *Manuel Álvarez*, 61–62; González, "Gertrudis Barceló, 42–43.

204. Ruxton, *Adventures in Mexico*, 152; Reséndez, *Changing National Identities*, 120; González de la Vara, "Política," 89.

205. Sobel, *Conquest and Conscience*, 37.

206. Gregg, *Commerce of the Prairies*, 226; Coan, *A History of New Mexico*, 1: 306–7; Emory, *Notes of a Reconnaissance*, 61; Sunder, "Introduction," in *Matt Field*, xii–xxiii; Chávez, *Manuel Álvarez*, 38, 57–58. For a review of the negative view that Americans had of Armijo, see Lecompte, *Rebellion*, 59–60.

207. Manuel Álvarez to Daniel Webster, in Chávez, ed., *Conflict and Acculturation: Manuel Álvarez's 1842 Memorial*, 41; Sunder, *Matt Field*, 281n125.

208. Bieber, "Introduction," *Journal of a Soldier*, 62; also Bloom, *New Mexico under Mexican Administration*, pt. II, ch. IV: "New Mexico Becomes a Territory," 17.

209. Holtby, *Forty-Seventh Star*, "a new ethic" 134; Cooke, *The Conquest*, 43; Groom, *Kearny's March*, 64; Devoto, *Year of Decision*, "glassware" 24–25.

210. Reséndez, *Changing National Identities*, 107–8, 112–13, 113–14.

211. Kenneth R. Weber, "Ecology, Economy, and Demography, "while stimulating" 59; Garrard, *Wah-to-yah and the Taos Trail*, "something from" 169.

212. Gregg, *Commerce of the Prairies*, 22–23; Crutchfield, *Tragedy at Taos*, 33; Sandoval, "Gnats, Goods and Greasers" 26; Bloom, *New Mexico under Mexican Administration*, pt. II, ch. IV: "New Mexico Becomes a Territory," "It is small wonder" 171; Craver, *Impact of Intimacy*, "Mexican commercial," 20; González, "Gertrudis Barceló," 50.

213. David J. Weber, *Mexican Frontier*, 231–32, 234; Henry Nash Smith, *Virgin Land*, "assumptions and aspirations" 124.

214. Devoto, *Year of Decision*, 125; Reséndez, *Changing National Identities*, 270; see also Thomas D. Hall, *Social Change in the Southwest*, 190.

215. Stanley, *Giant*, 31, 32–34; Weber "Introduction," in Vigil, *Arms, Indians*, xvi. Similar social ties were established between Mexican and Anglo Tejanos in the 1830s; Ramos, *Beyond the Alamo*, 151.

216. Reséndez, *Changing National Identities*, "far more supportive" 118–19, 120; Bieber, "Introduction," *Journal of a Soldier*, "learned to respect" 62.

217. Deutsch, *Nationalism and Social Communication*, 109.

218. González, *Refusing the Favor*, 74; also Gómez, "Race, Colonialism, and Criminal Law," 1160–61n74; Nieto-Phillips, *Language of Blood*, 134.

219. Craver, *Impact of Intimacy*, 6, 17, 36. Craver (*Impact of Intimacy*, 4, 6, 16–17) found 122 Mexican females marrying foreigners in the Río Arriba between 1821 and 1846. The first group of outsiders involved French Canadians. By the conquest, American citizens formed the majority of the husbands with Europeans a distant third. Among the many discussions, see González, *Refusing the Favor*, 114–15; Nostrand, *Hispano Homeland*, 103–4.

220. González, *Refusing the Favor*, 113–14; Craver, *Impact of Intimacy*, 27–28; Weber (*Mexican Frontier*, 240) invokes Owen Lattimore's notion of "marginal" borderlands peoples to make this point. González (*Refusing the Favor*, 72) minimizes the consensus importance of American men–Nuevomexicano women intermarriage and relationships, calling it trivial in relation to the Spanish-Mexican society. However, that it was even possible would seem to be a statement on the order of colonialism that arose in nineteenth-century New Mexico.

221. Among the many references to families in the literature, see Ritch, *New Mexico Bluebook*, Appendix, 46; Sunseri, *Seeds of Discord*, 134; Horgan, *Lamy of Santa Fe*, passim; Otero, *My Nine Years as Governor*, 99; Craver, *Impact of Intimacy*, 20; Allison, "Colonel Francisco Perea," 212–13.

222. Chávez, *Manuel Álvarez*, 3; Woodward and Feth, *New Mexico, Land of Enchantment*, 31–33.

223. Comer, *Ritual Ground*, "new identities" 18; Reséndez, *Changing National Identities*, 106. In 1845 just prior to the outbreak of war, President Polk had already dispatched a diplomat to see if the United States could purchase Mexico's northern provinces; Larson, *New Mexico's Quest*, 1–2.

224. Weber, *Mexican Frontier*, 240; Reséndez, *Changing National Identities*, 123; Theisen, "José Manuel Gallegos," "exhibited patriotism" 27.

225. Quoted in Weber, *Mexican Frontier*, 240.

226. Craver, *Impact of Intimacy*, "collusion," 30, 20–22; Stanley, *Giant*, "abominable" 104; *Daily Missouri Republican*, January 1, 846, in Bieber, "Introduction," *Journal of a Soldier*, "no fighting" 61–63.

227. Weber, *Mexican Frontier*, "ambivalent loyalties" 240–1; Ramos, *Beyond the Alamo*, 134–37; Craver's phrase in *Impact of Intimacy*, "cooperative fusion" 2–3.

228. Chávez, *Manuel Álvarez*, 23–24.

229. Bancroft, *History of Arizona and New Mexico*, 316–17; Chávez and Chávez, *Wake*, 53; Chávez, *But Time*, "different breed" 71, 72.

230. Chávez, *Manuel Álvarez*, 72–76.

231. A first-person journalistic account of the 1841 Texas Expedition is George Wilkins Kendall, *Narrative of the Texan Santa Fe Expedition*, 1929 [1884]. Also Loomis, *The Texan-Santa Fe Pioneers*; Bloom, *New Mexico under Mexican Administration*, pt. III, ch. V: "Texan Aggressions 1841–1843," *Old Santa Fe* 2, no. 2 (1914): 143–156; Arellano, "Through Thick and Thin," 42; Joseph P. Sánchez, *Between Two Rivers*, 118–19; Reséndez, *Changing National Identities*, 235.

232. Chávez and Chávez, *Wake*, 56–57; Chávez, *But Time*, 72; Sánchez, *Between Two Rivers*, 120.

233. Chávez, *Manuel Álvarez*, 97; Lamar, *Far Southwest*, 52–53; Arellano, "Through Thick and Thin," 145–46. Chávez, *But Time*, 72.

234. Lecompte, *Rebellion*, 14; Garrard, *Wah-to-Yah and the Taos Trail*, "the Mexican" 188; Chávez, *Manuel Álvarez*, 52–54.

235. Reséndez, *Changing National Identities*, quote 123; Lamar, "Land Policy in the Spanish Southwest," 501; Sánchez, *Between Two Rivers*, 122; González de la Vara, "Política," 108–9; Chávez, *Manuel Álvarez*, 98; Lamar, *Far Southwest*, 47, 52.

236. Reséndez, *Changing National Identities*, first quote 140; Chávez, *But Time*, second quote 73.

237. Weber, *Mexican Frontier*, 193; Rosenbaum, *Mexicano Resistance in the Southwest*, 71; Montoya, *Translating Property*, 32–36; Read, *Illustrated History*, 408–9; Murphy, "The Beaubien and Miranda Land Grant."

238. Chávez, *But Time*, 76.

239. Theisen, "José Manuel Gallegos," 29–30; Wayne Harper, "Juan Bautista Vigil y Alarid," quote 129.

240. Martínez, *Esposición Que el Presbitero Antonio José Martínez*, 5–15; on Martínez's concerns for Indians, see Weber, *Mexican Frontier*, 98.

241. Chávez, *But Time*, quote 66–67; Chávez, *Manuel Álvarez*, 49, 51–52.

242. Chávez, *But Time*, 75–76.

243. Chávez and Chávez, *Wake*, 58; Chávez, *But Time*, 66, 77.

244. Chávez, *But Time*, 68–69.

245. Sunder, *Matt Field*, 206–n93; Gregg, *Commerce of the Prairies*, 79; Ferguson, "Diary of Philip Gooch Ferguson," 325; Drumm, "Introduction," in *Down the Santa Fe Trail*, 96n35; Henderson, *Glorious Defeat*, 79.

246. Thomas D. Hall, *Social Change in the Southwest*, 190; Weber, *Mexican Frontier*, 207–8, 210; Moorhead, *New Mexico's Royal Road*, 65.

247. Vigil, Address to the New Mexico Assembly, 18 June 1846 (publ. and transl. as "Vigil on Arms, Munitions, Trade, North Americans, and 'Barbaric Indians,'" 1–8), in Vigil, *Arms, Indians*, 3–6.

248. Reséndez, *Changing National Identities*, 140, 233. For a list of Nuevomexicanos who tended to support this aspect of resistance, see 234n106.

249. Reséndez, *Changing National Identities*, 115; also Chávez, *Manuel Álvarez*, 91–93, 65–66; Craver, *Impact of Intimacy*, 39–40; Lamar, *Far Southwest*, 54.

2. Bloodless and Bloody Conquests

1. Quoted in Chávez, *Manuel Álvarez*, 98.

2. Polk, *Diary*, 1: 223–25, 226, 227–30, 305–13; Henderson, *Glorious Defeat*, 139; Chávez, *Manuel Álvarez*, 102; Stegmaier, *Texas*, 14–15, 17; Sobel, *Conquest and Conscience*, 247–49; Haas, "War in California, 1846–1848," 336.

3. Santoni, *Mexicans at Arms*, 3, 36–37.

4. International tensions grew out of attempts in Mexico City and among Tejanos to take Texas back from the control of Anglo-Texans in the Republic of Texas; Ramos, *Beyond the Alamo*, 177–91.

5. Polk, *Diary*, 1: 351; Cotner, *Career of José Joaquín De Herrera*, 127–130, 136; Santoni, *Mexicans at Arms*, 37–41, 50–67.

6. Henderson, *Glorious Defeat*, 144–47, 150–52, 188; Santoni, *Mexicans at Arms*, 81–99.

7. Chávez, *Manuel Álvarez*, 98–99.

8. JANM, reel 42, "Seción ordinaria del día 9 de Febrero del 1846," frames 851–52; "Seción extraordinaria del día 25 de Febrero 1846," frames 859–61. New Mexicans may not have voted for the plan had Paredes not delayed in revealing his monarchist intentions. For Armijo's proclamation see Twitchell, *Old Santa Fe*, 102–3.

9. Polk, *Diary*, 1: 306–7. On Parades's regime, see Santoni, *Mexicans at Arms*, 105–28.

10. Chávez, *Manuel Álvarez*, 105, 107; Sandoval, "American Invasion," 62; Bieber, "Introduction," *Journal of a Soldier*, 27–28.

11. Devoto, *Year of Decision*, 8–9, "no war hawk" 216; Polk, *Diary*, 1: 230, 233–34.

12. Polk, *Diary* 1: 316–17, 319, 325, 327–28, 337–38, 354–55, 375–77, 382; 2: 156–57.

13. Polk, *Diary*, 1: 397, 437–38.

14. Polk, *Diary*, 1: 365, 379, 384–85, 387–89, 391, 392, 394, 395–97; Devoto, *Year of Decision*, 244–45, 214; also Groom, *Kearny's March*, 26; Henderson, *Glorious Defeat*, 154–55.

15. Polk, *Diary*, 1: 438–39, 408–10, 411; 2: 188–89; 3: "ferocity & fanaticism"104.

16. Benton quoted in Bieber, "Introduction," *Journal of a Soldier*, 27.

17. Polk, *Diary*, 1: 474–75; Bieber, "Introduction," *Journal of a Soldier*, 17–113; Gibson, *Journal of a Soldier*, 55–56; cf. Twitchell, *History of the Military Occupation*, 376–77.

18. W. L. Marcy to Col. S. W. Kearny, June 3, 1846, in Polk, *Occupation*, 6–9.

19. W. L. Marcy to Col. S. W. Kearny, June 3, 1846, in Polk, *Occupation*, 8–9; Grivas, *Military Governments*, 18–19. Secretary of the Navy George Bancroft issued similar injunctions to Capt. John Sloat to effect friendly relations in his occupation of San Francisco and encourage the Californios to adopt neutrality in the war at least; George Bancroft to John D. Sloat, June 24, 1845, in Cutts, *Conquest*, 252–53, and George Bancroft to John D. Sloat, June 8, 1846, in Cutts, *Conquest*, 255–56. Commodore Thomas Jones attempted the same operation of making that department an American territory by decree and a proclamation to the citizens of Monterey guaranteeing them the exercise of their full civil liberties and protection by the United States. It occurred before there was any credible information whether it and Mexico were even at war. Thomas was temporarily recalled for his unwarranted aggression; Haas, "War in California, 1846–1848," 335.

20. Polk, *Diary*, 1: 408–10; Bieber, "Introduction," *Journal of a Soldier*, "a person" 25, 30; Grivas, *Military Governments*, 19.

21. Emory, *Notes of a Reconnaissance*, 30–31; Hughes, *Doniphan's Expedition*, 18; Twitchell, *History of the Military Occupation*, 38, 41; Bieber, "Introduction," to "Diary of Philip Gooch Henderson," in *Marching with the Army of the West*, 26.

22. Devoto, *Year of Decision*, 286; Sandoval, "American Invasion," 65.

23. Sandovál, "American Invasion," 65.

24. Clarke, *Stephen Watts Kearny*, 120–21; Cooke, *The Conquest*, 6; quoted in Bieber, *Marching with the Army of the West*, 92n115; "Diary of Philip Gooch Henderson," *Marching the Army of the West*, 283–361.

25. Cooke, *The Conquest*, 6, 14, 22; see also Bieber, "Introduction," *Journal of a Soldier*, 55, and Devoto, *Year of Decision*, 270–71.

26. Magoffin, *Down the Santa Fe Trail*, 159.

27. W. L. Marcy to Colonel S.W. Kearny, June 18, 1846, in Magoffin, *Down the Santa Fe Trail*, 263–64; Drumm, "Introduction," in Magoffin, *Down the Santa Fe Trail*, xii–xiii; Devoto, *Year of Decision*, 286; Bieber, "Introduction," *Journal of a Soldier*, 28–29, 50–51.

28. Chávez, *Manuel Álvarez*, 107.

29. See the proclamation in Twitchell, *Old Santa Fe*, 249–50; cf. Bieber, "Introduction," *Journal of a Soldier*, 63–64.

30. JANM, reel 42, "Seción extraordinária del 1 de Julio del 1846, frame 896; Twitchell, *Old Santa Fe*, 248–49.

31. Ugarte to Armijo (transl.), 369–70 in Gibson, *Journal of a Soldier*, 369; for Gibson's commentary on the letter, see 232–33; Bieber, "Introduction," *Marching with the Army of the West*, 45; Bieber, "Introduction," *Journal of a Soldier*, 72–73; Sandoval, "American Invasion," 65, 66; Stanley, *Giant*, 110; Clarke, *Stephen Watts Kearny*, 129–30.

32. JANM, reel 42, "Seción extraordinaria del 1 de Julio del 1846," frame 896; Twitchell, *History of the Military Occupation*, 57, 60; Chávez and Chávez, *Wake*, 62; Bieber, "Introduction," *Journal of a Soldier*, 64–65.

33. Henderson, *Glorious Defeat*, 128.

34. JANM, reel 42, "Seción ordinaria del 13 de Julio del 1846," frames 906–7; "Sección extraordinaria del 16 de Julio del 1846," frames 908–10; Twitchell, *Old Santa Fe*, 251.

35. For Armijo's proclamation see Manuel Armijo and Juan Bautista Vigil y Alarid to President of the Departmental Assembly, "Comunicación Official," *Santa Fe Republican* (hereafter *Republican*), May 3, 1848, 3; Twitchell, *History of the Military Occupation*, 60–63; Twitchell, *Old Santa Fe*, 251–52.

36. JANM, reel 42, "Seción extraordinaria del 8 de Agosto de 1846," frames 916–18; Crutchfield, *Tragedy at Taos*, 65–66. According to David Weber ("Introduction" to Vigil, *Arms, Indians*, xvi–xvii), Vigil joined in the preparations for defending New Mexico against the invading American army even though "he knew that resistance might be futile."

37. JANM, reel 42, "Seción ordinaria del día 10 de Agosto de 1846," frames 918–20; Manuel Armijo and Juan Bautista Vigil y Alarid official communication to the New Mexico legislative assembly, August 10, 1846, published retrospectively in "Comunicación Oficial," *Republican*, May 3, 1848, 3. Chávez and Chávez (*Wake*, 62) record that Ortiz promised 261 pesos of his cash and said he could possibly raise more by

selling silver objects, 1,300 sheep, and 150 head of cattle, donations meant for the "independence and the liberty of the Mexican nation."

38. "Decreto de la Asamblea," *Republican*, May 3, 1848, 3; JANM, reel 42, "Seción ordinaria del día 10 de Agosto de 1846," frames 918–20; Twitchell, *Old Santa Fe*, 252.

39. Emory, *Notes of a Reconnaissance*, 42, 44; Bieber, "Introduction," *Journal of a Soldier*, 69.

40. Twitchell, *History of the Military Occupation*, 46, 48; Devoto, *Year of Decision*, 288.

41. W. L. Marcy to Col. S. W. Kearny, June 3, 1846, in Polk, *Occupation*. Viewing war developments against the political backdrop of the United States, Devoto (*Year of Decision*, 247) indicates that this was because Kearny was not known to be a Whig.

42. Cooke, *The Conquest*, 7; Twitchell, *History of the Military Occupation*, 65; Bieber, "Introduction," *Journal of a Soldier*, 27, 52–53; Spruce M. Baird to Colonel John M. Washington, September 23, 1849, in Binkley, "Reports from a Texan Agent," 164–69.

43. Edrington, "Military Influence," 373; Binkley, "Reports from a Texan Agent," 165n21.

44. S. W. Kearny, "Proclamation to the Citizens of New Mexico by Col. Kearny, Commanding the United States Forces," 20–21, in Polk, *Occupation*; also Twitchell, *Leading Facts*, 201; Cutts, *Conquest*, 42; Bieber, "Introduction," *Journal of a Soldier*, 51–52.

45. Hughes, *Doniphan's Expedition*, 29.

46. Col. Stephen W. Kearny to Governor Manuel Armijo, August 1, 1846, transl. in Moorhead, "Notes and Documents," 80.

47. Baird to Washington, in Cooke, *The Conquest*, 6; Bieber, *Marching with the Army of the West*, 92n115, 152–53; Bieber, "Introduction," *Journal of a Soldier*, 53–55, 56–57; Emory, *Notes of a Reconnaissance*, 37; Horn, *New Mexico's Troubled Years*, 95–96; Thompson, introduction to "An Indian Superintendent," 218.

48. Groom, *Kearny's March*, 81; Twitchell, *History of the Military Occupation*, 43.

49. Edwards, "Journal of Marcellus Ball Edwards," 141–42; Bieber, ed., *Journal of a Soldier*, 187n330; Clarke, *Stephen Watts Kearny*, 124–25. For Kearny's order to Leitensdorfer see Bieber, *Marching with the Army of the West*, 91n113, and 142n140; Bieber, "Introduction," *Journal of a Soldier*, 51–52.

50. Clarke, *Stephen Watts Kearny*, 124, 133; Johnston, "Journal of Abraham Robinson Johnston," 90, 91; Gibson, *Journal of a Soldier*, 166–67; Hughes, *Doniphan's Expedition*, 32.

51. Bieber, "Introduction," *Journal of a Soldier*, 60–61; Twitchell, *The History*, 384.

52. Edwards, "Journal of Marcellus Ball Edwards," 149–50.

53. Governor Manuel Armijo to Stephen W. Kearny, August 12, 1846, transl. in Moorhead, "Notes and Documents," 81–82; Henry Connelly to General Manuel Armijo, August 18, 1846, transl. in Moorhead, "Notes and Documents," 82; Hughes, *Doniphan's Expedition*, 42; Edwards, "Journal of Marcellus Ball Edwards," 152–53, 158–59; Emory, *Notes of a Reconnaissance*, 55, 47, 48; Abert, *Report*, 419, 420; Henry Smith Turner, *The Original Journals of Henry Smith Turner with Stephen Watts Kearny*, 71; Johnston, "Journal of Abraham Robinson Johnston," 99, 103; Gibson,

Journal of a Soldier, 196; Anonymous staff officer of the Army of the West, *St. Louis Republican*, September 24, 1846, and *Washington Union*, October 2, 1846, in Cutts, *Conquest*, 52 (hereafter cited as Anonymous Officer; Army of the West Second Lieutenant George Gibson may have been the anonymous officer). For published treatments of these events, see Edrington, "Military Influence," 374–75; Twitchell, *History of the Military Occupation*, 48; Bieber, "Introduction," *Journal of a Soldier*, 74; Clarke, *Stephen Watts Kearny*, 133; Sandoval, "American Invasion," 66; Lamar, *Far Southwest*, 52–55.

54. Gibson, *Journal of a Soldier*, 194; Edwards, "Journal of Marcellus Ball Edwards," 153; Groom, *Kearny's March*, 83–84; Twitchell, *History of the Military Occupation*, 48.

55. U.S. Congress, Senate, Notes of a Military Reconnaissance, Senate Exec. Doc. 7 (Serial 505), 30th Cong., 1st Sess., 1847, 27; Emory, *Notes of a Reconnaissance*, 49–50; Twitchell, *History of the Military Occupation*, 49–50; Turner, *Original Journals*, 71; Twitchell, *Old Santa Fe*, 259–60; Clarke, *Stephen Watts Kearny*, 134–35.

56. Emory, *Notes of a Reconnaissance*, 50; Johnston, "Journal of Abraham Robinson Johnston," 99–100; Clarke, *Stephen Watts Kearny*, 135–36.

57. Hughes, *Doniphan's Expedition*, 40; Cooke, *The Conquest*, 37; Turner, *Original Journals*, 72; also Emory, *Notes of a Reconnaissance*, 50–51, 52; Gibson, *Journal of a Soldier*, 195, 199; Groom, *Kearny's March*, 85–86; Alexander B. Dyer to My dear friend (R. Johnston), February 14, 1847 (transcribed typed copy), Alexander B. Dyer, Mexican War Journal, 1846–1848, manuscript AC 070-P, Digitized Collection Archives, Museum of New Mexico, Fray Angélico Chávez History Library.

58. Anonymous Officer, 49. "Unfortunately . . . on the American occupation we have practically nothing of real value from Mexican sources"; Bancroft, *History of Arizona and New Mexico*, 434n31.

59. Johnston, "Journal of Abraham Robinson Johnston," 98–99, 100.

60. Hechter, *Internal Colonialism*, 19–20n3.

61. Edwards, "Journal of Marcellus Ball Edwards," 155.

62. Emory, *Notes of a Reconnaissance*, 50; Clarke, *Stephen Watts Kearny*, 135–36.

63. Cooke, *The Conquest*, 37; Twitchell, *History of the Military Occupation*, 52.

64. Johnston, "Journal of Abraham Robinson Johnston," 101; also Gibson, *Journal of a Soldier*, 201.

65. Anonymous Officer, 48–50, also 47–48.

66. Johnston, "Journal of Abraham Robinson Johnston," 100.

67. Emory, *Notes of a Reconnaissance*, 50; Groom, *Kearny's March*, 86.

68. Gibson, *Journal of a Soldier*, "a thing not dreamed of" 194n336 (also in Anonymous Officer, 47); Gibson, *Journal of a Soldier*, "The poorer natives" 193n335; Edwards, "Journal of Marcellus Ball Edwards," "perfectly friendly" 153; Hughes, *Doniphan's Expedition*, "drained most" 41.

69. Henderson, *Glorious Defeat*, 31–32; Cooke, *The Conquest*, 34–35, 59.

70. Cooke, *The Conquest*, 37–38; Bieber, "Introduction," *Journal of a Soldier*, 72, 73; Anonymous Officer, 50; Johnston, "Journal of Abraham Robinson Johnston," 99, 101–2; Emory, *Notes of a Reconnaissance*, 52–53, 54; Edwards, "Journal of Marcellus Ball Edwards," 155, 157, 158–59; Anonymous Officer, 50–51; Twitchell, *History*

of the Military Occupation, 53, 214–15; Clarke, *Stephen Watts Kearny*, 136; Devoto, *Year of Decision*, 291–92.

71. Carlos María de Bustamante, *El Nuevo Bernal Díaz del Castillo*, 270; Ruxton, *Adventures in Mexico*, 156–57.

72. Manuel Armijo, "Report of Gov. Manuel Armijo to the Minister of Foreign Relations, Interior and Police," September 8, 1846, transl. in Moorhead, "Notes and Documents," 76–78; Manuel Armijo to Colonel Mauricio Ugarte, September 10, 1846, in Bieber, ed., *Journal of a Soldier*, 201–2n345; Mauricio Ugarte to Cuilty, August 23, 1846, in Bieber, ed., *Journal of a Soldier*, 204n347; Bustamante, *El Nuevo Bernal Díaz del Castillo*, 269–71; Emory, *Notes of a Reconnaissance*, 50–51, 52; Cooke, *The Conquest*, 42; Gibson, *Journal of a Soldier*, 201, 203–4; Ruxton, *Adventures in Mexico*, 110; also Twitchell, *History of the Military Occupation*, 67; Larson, *New Mexico's Quest*, 3–4; Lamar, *Far Southwest*, 55–56; Sandoval "American Invasion," 70–71.

73. Hughes, *Doniphan's Expedition*, 42, 52.

74. Amado Chávez address before the New Mexico Historical Society, in "Walks and Talks," *New Mexican Review* (Santa Fe), July 26, 1883. Chávez is said to have based his remarks on an original historical document.

75. Edwards, "Journal of Marcellus Ball Edwards," 157; Emory, *Notes of a Reconnaissance*, 52; Clarke, *Stephen Watts Kearny*, 140–41.

76. Turner, *Original Journals*, 70; see also Johnston, "Journal of Abraham Robinson Johnston," 96.

77. Emory, *Notes of a Reconnaissance*, 53; Clarke, *Stephen Watts Kearny*, 133.

78. Cooke, *The Conquest*, 32–33; Turner, *Original Journals*, 63, 65.

79. Hughes, *Doniphan's Expedition*, 19; Twitchell, *Old Santa Fe*, 250–51; Bieber, "Introduction," *Journal of a Soldier*, 41–44, 65–66.

80. Cooke, *The Conquest*, 32.

81. Twitchell, *The Bench and Bar of New Mexico*, 10; Twitchell, *History of the Military Occupation*, 243; Bieber, "Introduction," *Journal of a Soldier*, 71; Clarke, *Stephen Watts Kearny*, 126.

82. For example, Groom, *Kearny's March*, 79, 80, 87. For an effective critique of Kendall's undeserved influence on the historical view of Armijo, see Lecompte, "Manuel Armijo, George Wilkins Kendall, and the Baca-Caballero Conspiracy."

83. For example, Twitchell, *History of the Military Occupation*, 57; Crutchfield, *Tragedy at Taos*, 57; Drumm, "Introduction," 96–97n35; Devoto, *Year of Decision*, 291.

84. Clarke, *Stephen Watts Kearny*, 126–27, 137.

85. P. St. George Cooke to J. W. Magoffin, February 21, 1849, in Magoffin, *Down the Santa Fe Trail*, 264–65; also Bieber, "Introduction," *Journal of a Soldier*, 69–72, 87–88; Clarke, *Stephen Watts Kearny*, 127.

86. Devoto, *Year of Decision*, 270–71, 538n8, 291; Twitchell, *History of the Military Occupation*, 240, 243; Chávez, *Manuel Álvarez*, 108. Historian Winston Groom (*Kearny's March*, 89) records that Cooke's family up to the mid-twentieth century believed that Armijo had been bribed.

87. Bieber, "Introduction," *Journal of a Soldier*, 79–80; Devoto, *Year of Decision*, 291–92.

88. Emory, *Notes of a Reconnaissance,* 70.

89. Magoffin, *Down the Santa Fe Trail,* 109.

90. Cooke, *The Conquest,* 80–81.

91. Antonio Sandoval et al., "Report of the Citizens of New Mexico to the President of Mexico," September 26, 1846, in Moorhead, "Notes and Documents," 69–76; also as "We Would Have Made Some Kind of Resistance," in David J. Weber, ed., *Foreigners in Their Native Land,* 121–25; see also, Hughes, *Doniphan's Expedition,* 80–81.

92. For discussions of Vigil's signing of the petition, see Weber, "Introduction" to Vigil, *Arms, Indians,* xviii; and E. Bennett Burton, "The Taos Rebellion," 176.

93. Brigadier-General S. W. Kearny, "Order Number 13," H. S. Turner, A.A.A. General Headquarters, Army of the west, Camp near Old Pecos, on Pecos River, August 17, 1846, in Gibson, *Journal of a Soldier,* 370, also 209; Bustamante, *El Nuevo Bernal Díaz del Castillo,* 270.

94. Twitchell, *History of the Military Occupation,* 57; Wayne Harper, "Juan Bautista Vigil y Alarid,", 148–49; Bieber, "Introduction," *Marching with the Army of the West,* 26.

95. Anonymous Officer, 54; Cooke, *The Conquest,* 38.

96. Edwards, "Journal of Marcellus Ball Edwards," 159; see Bieber, "Introduction," *Journal of a Soldier,* starting 81.

97. Anonymous Officer, 53.

98. Anonymous Officer, 53. For a reprint of Kearny's announcement, see Twitchell, *History of the Military Occupation,* 73–74, and Johnston, "Journal of Abraham Robinson Johnston," 104.

99. Gibson, *Journal of a Soldier,* 204–5; Ugarte to Cuilty, in Bieber, ed., *Journal of a Soldier*; Johnston, "Journal of Abraham Robinson Johnston," 104; Clarke, *Stephen Watts Kearny,* 142, 143; Anonymous Officer, "There" 53; Twitchell, *History of the Military Occupation,* 72.

100. Emory, *Notes of a Reconnaissance,* 55, 56; Juan Bautista Vigil y Alarid, "Reaction to Defeat," in Weber, *Foreigners,* 128–29; Crutchfield, *Tragedy at Taos,* 81–82.

101. Thomas D. Hall, *Social Change in the Southwest,* 193.

102. Genaro Padilla, *My History, Not Yours,* 51.

103. Sisneros, "'She Was Our Mother,'" 280–81.

104. Vigil y Alarid's remarks in Twitchell, *History of the Military Occupation,* 74–75; Twitchell, *Old Santa Fe,* 265–66; and Bieber, "Introduction," *Journal of a Soldier,* 85–86.

105. Turner, *Original Journals,* 73; Clarke, *Stephen Watts Kearny,* 146–47; Mangusso, "Citizenship Provisions of the Treaty of Guadalupe Hidalgo," 18–19.

106. S.W. Kearny to Brigadier General R. [Roger] Jones, August 24, 1846, in Polk, *Occupation,* 21–22; also Cutts, *Conquest,* 59–60; S. W. Kearny to General John E. Wool, August 22, 1846, in Polk, *Occupation,* 23.

107. S. W. Kearny, "Proclamation to the Inhabitants of New Mexico by Brig. Gen. S.W. Kearny, Commanding the Troops of the United States in the Same," in Polk, *Occupation,* 22–23; also Twitchell, *History of the Military Occupation,* 78–80; Hughes, *Doniphan's Expedition,* 43, 46; George B. Anderson, *History of New Mexico,*

80; Twitchell, *Old Santa Fe*, 264–65; also Anonymous Officer, 54; Edwards, "Journal of Marcellus Ball Edwards," 160; Cutts, *Conquest*, 57–58; Kearny to Wool, in Polk, *Occupation*; Gibson, *Journal of a Soldier*, 212; Clarke, *Stephan Watts Kearny*, 143.

108. Cooke, *The Conquest*, 62; Anonymous Officer, 54.

109. "Proclamation to the inhabitants of New Mexico by Brigadier General S. W. Kearny, commanding the troops of the United States in the same," *Santa Fe Daily New Mexican*, March 16, 1870; also Twitchell, *Old Santa Fe*, 267–68; Edrington, "Military Influence," 375.

110. Hughes, *Doniphan's Expedition*, 73, 74.

111. Hughes, *Doniphan's Expedition*, 42–43, 65, 64, 69; also Cutts, *Conquest*, 55–56.

112. Cooke, *The Conquest*, 70.

113. Edwards, "Journal of Marcellus Ball Edwards," 158.

114. Anonymous Officer, 55.

115. Cooke, *The Conquest*, 60–61.

116. Anonymous Officer, 53.

117. Gibson, *Journal of a Soldier*, 210.

118. Magoffin, *Down the Santa Fe Trail*, 103; Twitchell, *History of the Military Occupation*, 82.

119. Emory, *Notes of a Reconnaissance*, 58, 63–65; Gibson, *Journal of a Soldier*, 210, 213; Cooke, *The Conquest*, 40–41, 54–55; Cutts, *Conquest*, 57; Clarke, *Stephen Watts Kearny*, 147, 155; Hughes, *Doniphan's Expedition*, 44; Simpson, *Journal of a Military Reconnaissance from Santa Fe*, 23; Twitchell, *History of the Military Occupation*, 82; Twitchell, *Old Santa Fe*, 266; Groom, *Kearny's March*, 91.

120. Allison, "Colonel Francisco Perea," 213; "The Late Pedro Perea," *Santa Fe New Mexican*, January 12, 1906, 2.

121. Emory, *Notes of a Reconnaissance*, 58.

122. Turner, *Original Journals*, 73, 74.

123. Chávez, *But Time*, 79.

124. Gibson, *Journal of a Soldier*, 214–15, "get the shut" and "good friends" 218; Emory, *Notes of a Reconnaissance*, 59; Turner, *Original Journals*, 73; Anonymous Officer, 55; Cooke, *The Conquest*, 43–44; Clarke, *Stephen Watts Kearny*, 147–48, 150–51; Chávez and Chávez, *Wake*, 63, 65.

125. Hughes, *Doniphan's Expedition*, 52.

126. Theisen, "José Manuel Gallegos," 56; Fray Angélico Chávez, *Très Macho*, 20.

127. Cooke, *The Conquest*, 49–50.

128. Gibson, *Journal of a Soldier*, 224–25; also, Turner, *Original Journals*, 74; Clarke, *Stephen Watts Kearny*, 151–52.

129. Kearny to Jones, in Polk, *Occupation*, 21; Cooke, *The Conquest*, 4; Hughes, *Doniphan's Expedition*, 63.

130. Turner, *Original Journals*, 76; Allison, "Don Francisco Perea."

131. Edwards, "Journal of Marcellus Ball Edwards," 167; Gibson, *Journal of a Soldier*, 238–39.

132. First quote, Emory, *Notes of a Reconnaissance*, 69; Clarke, *Stephen Watts Kearny*, 156; Bieber, "Introduction," *Marching with the Army of the West*, 27, and

165n49; Edwards, "Journal of Marcellus Ball Edwards," 168–69; Hughes, *Doniphan's Expedition*, 61; second quote, Cooke, *The Conquest*, 57–58.

133. Theisen, "José Manuel Gallegos," 60–61.

134. Secretary of War William Marcy, in "Six Per Cent Duty," *Republican*, September 6, 1848.

135. S. W. Kearny, "Order of Gen. Kearny Abolishing the Use of Stamp Paper," and "Order of Gen. Kearny Regulating Licenses," in Polk, *Occupation*, 25; S. W. Kearny proclamation appointing Francisco Armijo y Ortiz the prefect of the Southwest district and Miguel Romero alcalde at Placeya; Gibson, *Journal of a Soldier*, 221; Cutts, *The Conquest*, 63; Twitchell, *Old Santa Fe*, 268–69.

136. Hughes, *Doniphan's Expedition*, 65.

137. Hurst, *Growth of American Law*, 224–25.

138. S. W. Kearny to Adjutant General, U.S. Army, September 22, 1846, in Polk, *Occupation*, 27; Baird to Washington, in Cooke, *The Conquest*, 6; Twitchell, *History of the Military Occupation*, 85–86; Cutts, *Conquest*, 64; Bancroft, *History of Arizona and New Mexico*, 426; Lamar, *Far Southwest*, 56–57.

139. Hughes, *Doniphan's Expedition*, 64.

140. For the following discussion, see S. W. Kearny, "Laws for the Government of the Territory of New Mexico, September 22, 1846, in Polk, *Occupation*, 34–76; Cooke, *The Conquest*, 66.

141. Peceny, *Democracy at the Point of Bayonets*, 15.

142. Henderson, *Glorious Defeat*, 6; Devoto, *Year of Decision*, 220–21. Democrats and Whigs provided common support for public education; Howe, *Political Culture of American Whigs*, 16.

143. S. W. Kearny, "Organic Law of the Territory of New Mexico," in Polk, *Occupation*, 28–34; *Organic Law, Session Laws of New Mexico, 1st and 2nd Sessions*, Records of the States of the United States, microfilm, 1846–1861, N.M. B. 2, reel 1, 3–15, Center for Southwest Research and Special Collections, University of New Mexico, Albuquerque.

144. S. W. Kearny, "Laws for the Government of the Territory of New Mexico," September 22, 1846, in Polk, *Occupation*, 34–76; also Cooke, *The Conquest*, 66.

145. Hughes, *Doniphan's Expedition*, 64; Gibson, *Journal of a Soldier*, 221; Chávez, *But Time*, 79; Clarke, *Stephen Watts Kearny*, 150.

146. Clarke, *Stephen Watts Kearny*, 149.

147. "Appointment, by Gen. Kearny, of Civil Officers," in Polk, *Occupation*, 27–28; Chaves, *Papers in the Case of J. Francisco Chaves vs. Charles P. Clever*, 144; Hughes, *Doniphan's Expedition*, 64–65; Twitchell, *The Bench and Bar of New Mexico*, 17–18.

148. Ortiz took ill and could not fulfill the post; S. W. Kearny, "Appointment by Gen. Kearny of Treasurer of Santa Fe," in Polk, *Occupation*, 23–24; S. W. Kearny, "Appointment of Gen. Kearny of Collector of Santa Fe," in Polk, *Occupation*, 24.

149. Twitchell, *History of the Military Occupation*, 215–16; Clarke, *Stephen Watts Kearny*, 160.

150. Gómez, *Manifest Destinies*, 10–11.

151. As noted in Lamar, *Far Southwest*, 58; Wayne Harper, "Juan Bautista Vigil y Alarid," 155, 160–62, 166–67. Vigil y Alarid returned to New Mexico in the late 1850s after a stormy political career in Mexico; Sisneros, "'She Was Our Mother,'" 2.

152. Allison, "Don Francisco Perea"; also Espinosa and Chávez, *El Río Abajo*, 111–12. That Kearny did not tap Juan Bautista Vigil y Alarid for interim governor may have stemmed from the fact that he was imprisoned for political corruption; see González de la Vara, "Política," 90. Vigil y Alarid was one of the few upper-class members of Mexican New Mexico who did not become an American citizen as New Mexico became a permanent part of the United States; Sisneros, "'She Was Our Mother,'" 289, and McCall, *New Mexico in 1850*, 82–83.

153. Twitchell, *The Bench and Bar of New Mexico*, 10; Cutts, *Conquest*, 64–65. Bent apparently lived with the Nuevomexicana Ignacia Jaramillo and was not married to her; Gómez, *Manifest Destinies*, 24.

154. Cooke, *The Conquest*, 54; Bieber, "Introduction," *Marching with the Army of the West*, 45.

155. Anonymous Officer, 53.

156. Edwards, "Journal of Marcellus Ball Edwards," 158–59; Devoto, *Year of Decision*, 293.

157. Bieber, *Journal of a Soldier*, 87–88.

158. S. W. Kearny to Brigadier Gen. R. [Roger] Jones, September 16, 1846, 25–27, in Polk, *Occupation*, 26; Cutts, *Conquest*, 65–66; Crutchfield, *Tragedy at Taos*, 95.

159. Clarke, *Stephen Watts Kearny*, 159.

160. Clarke, *Stephen Watts Kearny*, 190; also Comer, *Ritual Ground*, 18; Cutts, *Conquest*, 38, 39.

161. Grivas, *Military Governments*, 18–19. These terms were permanently set out in *Downes v. Bidwell* 182, U.S. 244, 1901. The case involved the treaty that ceded the Louisiana Territory, which declared an immediate incorporation of the native inhabitants "with the usual advantages and privileges accorded to citizens of the United States." It was determined that rights of citizens were not to be fulfilled until after Louisiana became a federal territory.

162. Twitchell, *The Bench and Bar of New Mexico*, 3.

163. See Grivas, *Military Governments*, 30–32.

164. Winfield Scott to S.W. Kearny, November 3, 1846, in Polk, *Occupation*, 16–18, esp. 17; also Grivas, *Military Governments*, 36–37.

165. Pinheiro, *Manifest Ambition*, 116.

166. Polk, *Occupation*; also in Cutts, *Conquest*, 60–62; extracted in Twitchell, *History of the Military Occupation*, 91, 93; Polk, *Diary*, 2: 282, 285; cf. Chávez, *Manuel Álvarez*, 117–18; Stegmaier, *Texas*, 21–24.

167. W. L. Marcy to Brig. Gen. S. W. Kearny, January 11, 1847, in Cutts, *Conquest*, 260–61. On consideration of the Kearny documents, orders were dispatched to the military leaders occupying California that they were to consider the right of possession temporary, "unless made absolute by subsequent events," or peace declared by international treaty, and that "No political right can be conferred on the inhabitants thus situated, emanating from the Constitution of the United

States." J. Y. Mason to Commodore R. F. Stockton, January 11, 1847, in Cutts, *Conquest*, 261-63.

168. Clarke, *Stephen Watts Kearny*, 150; Crutchfield, *Tragedy at Taos*, 143.

169. Devoto, *Year of Decision*, 430.

170. Dyer to Johnston, Dyer, Mexican War Journal, 1846-1848; Twitchell, *History of the Military Occupation*, 330-31.

171. Ruxton, *Adventures in Mexico*, 107.

172. Lamar, *Far Southwest*, 58; Twitchell, *History of the Military Occupation*, 122-23.

173. Wayne Harper, "Juan Bautista Vigil y Alarid," 131-32, 134; Sisneros, "'She Was Our Mother,'" 287-88.

174. In the *Missouri Statesman*, December 25, 1846, cited in Gibson, *Journal of a Soldier*, "a good deal" 242; Lamar, *Far Southwest*, 58.

175. Ruxton, *Adventures in Mexico*, 107; Clarke, *Stephen Watts Kearny*, 155. On the undisciplined and untrained volunteers during the Mexican War, see Johannsen, *To the Halls of the Montezumas*, 28-37.

176. Devoto, *Year of Decision*, 430, 249-50; Magoffin, *Down the Santa Fe Trail*, 228-29, 201, 130; Green, "James S. Calhoun," 331; Groom, *Kearny's March*, 157-58.

177. Devoto, *Year of Decision*, 430, 249-50.

178. On the racism against Mexicans in the American ranks during the war, see Johannsen, *To the Halls of the Montezumas*, 22; Greenberg, *A Wicked War*, 131-32.

179. Magoffin, *Down the Santa Fe Trail*, 130.

180. Gibson, *Journal of a Soldier*, 259-60.

181. Cooke, *The Conquest*, 102-03; Dyer to Johnston, Dyer, Mexican War Journal, 1846-1848.

182. "Report of Colonel Price on the hostilities in vicinity of Santa Fe," February 15, 1847 (hereafter Sterling Price Report), in United States War Department, *Insurrection against the Military Government in New Mexico* (hereafter *Insurrection*), 8-13, quote 8; Twitchell, *History of the Military Occupation*, 122; Twitchell, *Old Santa Fe*, 277.

183. Cooke, *The Conquest*, 111; Twitchell, *History of the Military Occupation*, 313-14; Twitchell, *Leading Facts* 2: 232; Twitchell, *Old Santa Fe*, 276, 278.

184. Twitchell, *History of the Military Occupation*, 122; Twitchell, *Leading Facts*, 2: 232; Crutchfield, *Tragedy at Taos*, 98; Magoffin, *Down the Santa Fe Trail*, 188; Craver, *Impact of Intimacy*, 42; McNierney, *Taos 1847*, 4; Larson, *New Mexico's Quest*, 6-7; Lamar, *Far Southwest*, 61. Against frequent claims of researchers, Chávez and Chávez dispute that Father Martínez had anything to do with the insurgencies against the American occupation (*But Time*, 82-3, and *Wake*, 76). However, it can be noted that Martínez had the only press in Taos. It must have been used in the insurgents' communications.

185. Theisen, "José Manuel Gallegos," 52-53.

186. Sterling Price Report, in *Insurrection*. Twitchell identifies the informant as José María Sanches, who named Archuleta and Ortiz as the leaders of the revolutionary meetings (*History of Military Occupation*, 315, and *Leading Facts*, 2: 232).

187. Twitchell, *History of the Military Occupation*, 313-14; Twitchell, *Leading Facts*, 2: 232; Twitchell, *Old Santa Fe*, 276, 278.

188. Chávez address before the New Mexico Historical Society, in "Walks and Talks," *New Mexican Review* (Santa Fe), July 26, 1883; Twitchell, *History of the Military Occupation*, 238; Drumm, "Introduction," xiii, 183–86n77–78; "Tomás Pino Descendant of N. M. Delegate to the Cortes of Spain," *Santa Fe New Mexican,* May 24, 1921, 3.

189. Horgan, *Centuries of Santa Fe*, 205.

190. Twitchell, *History of the Military Occupation*, 240; Bieber, "Introduction," *Journal of a Soldier*, 69–71; Clarke, *Stephen Watts Kearny*, 127, 136–39, 148; Crutchfield, *Tragedy at Taos*, 74, 98; Devoto, *Year of Decision*, 291, 429.

191. Twitchell, *History of the Military Occupation*, 244.

192. Americans accused him of torturing 1841 Texas prisoners; Drumm, "Introduction," 186n186.

193. Abert, *Report*, 511; Twitchell, *Old Santa Fe,* 277.

194. Magoffin, *Down the Santa Fe Trail*, 188.

195. Twitchell, *Leading Facts*, 2: 233; on her political influence, González, "Gertrudis Barceló," 45.

196. C. Bent to James Buchanan, December 26, 1846, in *Insurrection*, 6; Edwards, "Journal of Marcellus Ball Edwards," 241–42; Cooke, *The Conquest*, 111; Twitchell, *History of the Military Occupation*, 298–301, 312, 314, 315–16, 318–20 (claiming that Chaves was indicted and tried for treason and acquitted in January 1847, 299–300). For a detailed oral history of Ortíz's escape, see Twitchell, *Old Santa Fe,* 278–80.

197. Abert, *Report*, 511; Meketa, *Legacy of Honor*, 66.

198. Bent to James Buchanan, in *Insurrection*, 6; Crutchfield, *Tragedy at Taos*, 100–102.

199. Twitchell, *History of the Military Occupation*, 124–25. For the suggestion of a Chihuahua military offensive, see Angel Frías, *Los Chihuahenses van a ocupar la vanguardia contra las fuerzas enemigas*, Chihuahua, August 29, 1846, New Mexico, manuscript letter, 2 pp. folio and 2 printed small folio documents (four pages each), all in Spanish, cloth bound into a small folio volume regarding the invasion of New Mexico by American troops, listed in W. J. Holliday, *Western Americana Many of Great Rarity: The Distinguished Collection Formed by W. J. Holliday* (New York: Parke-Bernet Galleries, 1954), 177, catalogue of items sold at auction from the W. J. Holliday collection, Arizona Historical Society, Tucson. The Frías letter is followed by printed "Boletín N.1." dated "Chihuahua, Domingo 30 de Agosto de 1846" and headed "Noticias de la Guerra exterior en los Departamentos del Norte y Occidente de la República Mexicana" (ending: "Imprenta del Gobierno"); the second printed piece is "Alcance al Num. 32 del Provisional. Chihuahua, Jueves 27 de Agosto de 1846" (ending: "Imprenta del Gobierno").

200. Abert, *Report*, 512–13.

201. Charles Bent to Fellow Citizens, January 5, 1847, in Twitchell, *Old Santa Fe,* 284–85.

202. Juan Antonio García, Dn. Pedro Vigil, and Antonio Maria Trujillo, "To the Defenders of Their Country," in Twitchell, *History of the Military Occupation*, 139–40 ; Twitchell, *Leading Facts*, 2: 252; Twitchell, *Old Santa Fe,* 302; Twitchell, *The Bench and the Bar,* 16.

203. Dyer to Johnston, Dyer, Mexican War Journal, 1846–1848, 2. For Bent's proclamation calling for peace issued two days before his departure for Taos, see Twitchell, *Leading Facts*, 2: 233–34.

204. S. W. Kearny to Brigadier General R. [Roger] Jones, September 1, 1846, 24, in Polk, *Occupation*; Cutts, *Conquest*, 63–64.

205. "Official Public Proclamation Regarding Insurrection, Records War Department" (hereafter Public Proclamation), Santa Fe, February 15, 1846, 24–26 in *Insurrection*, 24; Sterling Price Report, in *Insurrection*, 8; Ruxton, *Adventures in Mexico*, 201; Twitchell, *Leading Facts*, 2: 233–34; Twitchell, *Old Santa Fe*, 289. A popular account depicts a horrific, bloody rampage fueled by alcohol; Groom, *Kearny's March*, 158–60.

206. Captain I. R. Hendly to Colonel Sterling Price, January 23, 1847, in *Insurrection*, 18; Lamar, *Far Southwest*, 60; Coan, *A History of New Mexico*, 1: 342.

207. Sterling Price Report, in *Insurrection*, 8; Price, "From Colonel Sterling Price's Report to the Adjutant General," in *Insurrection*, 9. For an overview of the Taos Rebellion based on the documents contained in *Insurrection*, see Charles E. Magoon to the U.S. Secretary of War, May 31, 1900, in *Insurrection*, 1–5.

208. Cooke, *The Conquest*, 110; Dyer to Johnston, Mexican War Journal, 1846–1848, 1.

209. Cooke, *The Conquest*, 110.

210. Lamar, *Far Southwest*, 60; Craver, *Impact of Intimacy*, 44–45; Larson, *New Mexico's Quest*, 6–7; Crutchfield, *Tragedy at Taos*, 105–6. For the motivations of the Taos Indians for the Bent assassination, see Chávez, *Manuel Álvarez*, 114–15.

211. Garrard, *Wah to-yah and the Taos Trail*, 175–76.

212. Magoffin, *Down the Santa Fe Trail*, 192.

213. Donaciano Vigil to James Buchanan, February 16, 1847, in *Insurrection*, 6–7, esp. 7; Sterling Price Report, in *Insurrection*, 8; Hendly to Price, January 23, 1847, in *Insurrection*, 19; Cooke, *The Conquest*, 122.

214. Public Proclamation, in *Insurrection*, 24; Sterling Price Report, in *Insurrection*, 8; Ruxton, *Adventures in Mexico*, 227–29; Crutchfield, *Tragedy at Taos*, 107–9.

215. For the full Turley story, see Ruxton, *Adventures in Mexico*, 234–38, also Twitchell, *Leading Facts*, 2: 236–37; Sterling Price Report, in *Insurrection*, 8.

216. Captain I. R. Hendly to Colonel Sterling Price, January 23, 1847, in *Insurrection*, 18.

217. Captain W. S. Murphy to Colonel Sterling Price, January 25, 1847, in *Insurrection*, 20; Hendly to Price, January 23, 1847, in *Insurrection*, 20, 18; Lt. T. C. McKamey to Colonel Price, January 25, 1847, in *Insurrection*, 19–20; Twitchell, *History of the Military Occupation*, 127–28, 330, 332; Twitchell, *Old Santa Fe*, 290–91.

218. Hendly to Price, January 23, 1847, in *Insurrection*, 18.

219. Hendly to Price, January 23, 1847, in *Insurrection*, 19; Public Proclamation, in *Insurrection*, 24–26; Crutchfield, *Tragedy at Taos*, 110; Coan, *A History of New Mexico*, 1: 342–43.

220. Soni, *Mourning Happiness*; Coronado, *A World Not to Come*, 106–7.

221. Donaciano Vigil to Fellow Citizens, January 22, 1847, in *Insurrection*, 27–28, Senate Document no. 442, 56th Congress, 1st session; Crutchfield, *Tragedy at Taos*, 116–17.

222. *Truinfo de los Principios Contra la Torpeza!: El Governador Interino del Territorio a los Habitantes del Mismo*, January 25, 1847, reel 1, frame 193, RTG, Donaciano Vigil Papers. The original Donaciano Vigil Papers are in the Southwest Collection, New Mexico State Records Center and Archives, Santa Fe, but all citations of the Vigil papers in this volume are from Records of the Territorial Governors, 1846–1912, microfilm, TANM. *Truinfo de los Principios* is also in box 1, LeBaron Prince Papers, Center for Southwest Research, University of New Mexico; also transl. as "Triumph of Principles over Turpitude," in *Insurrection*, 27; Twitchell, *Leading Facts*, 2: 248–49.

223. Dyer to Johnston, Dyer, Mexican War Journal, 1846–1848, 1–2. For a roster of officers and men, and St. Vrain's biographical sketch, see Twitchell, *Old Santa Fe*, 282, 298–99.

224. In *Insurrection*, see Public Proclamation, 25; Sterling Price Report, 9–11; Captain William N. Grier to Lt. W. H. Staunton, Acting Adjutant First Dragoons, February 15, 1847, 15–16, esp. 15; and Lieutenant Rufus Ingalls to Lieut. Col. C. Wharton, Feb. 16, 1847, 16–17, esp. 16. See also Dyer to Johnston, Dyer, Mexican War Journal, 1846–1848, 1–2; Cooke, *The Conquest*, 115; Twitchell, *History of the Military Occupation*, 128, 332; Twitchell, *Old Santa Fe*, 291–97; Groom, *Kearny's March*, 161.

225. In *Insurrection*, see Public Proclamation, 26, and Major D. B. Edmonson to Col. S. Price, June 14, 1847, 21–23, esp. 22; see also Twitchell, *History of the Military Occupation*, 136, 138, 331, 333, and *Leading Facts*, 2: 239–45.

226. Dyer to Johnston, Dyer, Mexican War Journal, 1846–1848, 2; Vigil to Buchanan, February 16, 1847, in *Insurrection*, 7.

227. Dyer to Johnston, Dyer, Mexican War Journal, 1846–1848, 3. In *Insurrection*, see Sterling Price Report, 11–13; Murphy to Price, 20; Edmonson to Price, June 14, 1847, 22; Captain Woldemar Fischer to the Adjutant General, February 16, 1847; Grier to Staunton, 16; and Ingalls to Wharton, 17. See also Abert, *Report*, 457; Cooke, *The Conquest*, 120–21; Twitchell, *History of the Military Occupation*, 129, 131–33; Groom, *Kearny's March*, 162–64.

228. Twitchell, *Old Santa Fe*, 299.

229. Dyer to Johnston, Dyer, Mexican War Journal, 1846–1848, 3; Edwards, "Journal of Marcellus Ball Edwards," 215, 222–23, 244–45.

230. Donaciano Vigil, "Circular. Gobierno Superior del Territorio," Santa Fe, February 12, 1847, box 1, LeBaron Prince Papers, Center for Southwest Research, University of New Mexico; also transl. in *Insurrection*, 29–30, and Twitchell, *Leading Facts*, 2: 250–51.

231. Vigil to Buchanan, February 16, 1847, in *Insurrection*, 7.

232. Cheetham, "First Term"; Lavender, *Bent's Fort*, 295–97.

233. Garrard, *Wah-to-yah and the Taos Trail*, 163.

234. F. P. Blair indictment against Antonio María Trujillo, March 1847, in Twitchell, *The Bench and Bar of New Mexico*, 14.

235. Garrard, *Wah-to-yah and the Taos Trail*, 162, 171.

236. Cheetham, "First Term," 27. In addition seventeen individuals were indicted for larceny, of whom six were convicted, three found not guilty, seven discharged by *nolle prosque*, and one case continued. Again, it is not clear whether these cases were part of the political trials.

237. Pronouncement in Twitchell, *The Bench and Bar of New Mexico*, 15.

238. Magoon to the U.S. Secretary of War, in *Insurrection*, 4–5; for a reprint of the sentence of Trujillo, see Twitchell, *Leading Facts*, 2: 252–53.

239. Cheetham, "First Term," 27. For a vivid description of the hanging procession, see Garrard, *Wah-to-yah and the Taos Trail*, 182–83, 185–91. For secondary treatments, the best is Gómez, *Manifest Destinies*, 31–41; also, Groom, *Kearny's March*, 165–66; McNierney, *Taos 1847*; Lamar, *Far Southwest*, 60–61; Rosenbaum, "Mexicano versus Americano," 26; Coan, *A History of New Mexico*, 1: 343–44; Lavender, *Bent's Fort*, 296; Read, *Illustrated History*, 445.

240. Garrard, *Wah-to-yah and the Taos Trail* 188–89.

241. Chávez, *Manuel Álvarez*, 77, 113; Donaciano Vigil to Secretary of State James Buchanan, in Twitchell, *Old Santa Fe*, 304–5.

242. Marcy to Price, June 26, 1847, extracted in Magoon to the U.S. Secretary of War, in *Insurrection*, 5; Chávez, *Manuel Álvarez*, 113–14.

243. Message of President Polk, July 24, 1848, in Twitchell, *History of the Military Occupation*, 144; also Magoon to the U.S. Secretary of War, in *Insurrection*, 5.

244. Gómez, *Manifest Destinies*, 39.

245. Donaciano Vigil to James Buchanan, March 1847, in *Insurrection*, 30–31.

3. Integrative Conquest

1. Emory, *Notes of a Reconnaissance*, 59; Abert, *Report*, 485; Sterling Price to the Adjutant-General of the Army, July 20, 1847, in *Insurrection*, 20–21; Twitchell, *History of the Military Occupation*, 145–46; Magoon to the U.S. Secretary of War, in *Insurrection*, 4; Brooks, *Captives and Cousins*, 291; Dyer, Mexican War Journal, 1846–1848 (transcribed typed copy), 81-b, 82, 85, 98.

2. Untitled, *Republicano*, October 16, 1847, 3.

3. Quoted in Cooke, *The Conquest*, 124; Twitchell, *Leading Facts*, 2: 246–48; Sterling Price to the Adjutant-General of the Army, July 20, 1847, in *Insurrection*, 21; Crutchfield, *Tragedy at Taos*, 65–66, 155.

4. Twitchell, *Leading Facts*, 2: 264; Weber, "Introduction" to Vigil, *Arms, Indians*, xviii.

5. José María Miera y Pino to Donaciano Vigil, April 18, 1847, reel 1, frames 62–63; María de la Cruz Ulibarri to Donaciano Vigil, n.d., frames 51–52; María Antonio Baca to Governor Donaciano Vigil, May 11, 1847, frames 67–68, Records of the Territorial Governors (hereafter RTG), microfilm, Territorial Archives of New Mexico, 1846–1912 (hereafter TANM); Larry D. Ball, *Desert Lawmen*, 2–3.

6. Comer, *Ritual Ground*, 18–20.

7. Donaciano Vigil to Carlos Beaubien, September [14], 1847, reel 1, frames 181–82, RTG, Donaciano Vigil Papers; original Donaciano Vigil Papers in the Southwest Collection, New Mexico State Records Center and Archives, Santa Fe.

8. Chávez, *Manuel Álvarez*, 121–22.

9. Donaciano Vigil to Fellow Citizens, January 22, 1847, in United States War Department, *Insurrection*, 27–28, Senate Document No. 442, 56th Congress, 1st Session. For translations see RTG, reel 1, Donaciano Vigil to Antonio

Jose Otero, January 21, 1848, frames 184–186, TRG, TANM; Donaciano Vigil to [Antonio Jose Otero?], n.d., frame 188; and Donaciano Vigil to [Antonio Jose Otero?], n.d., frame 188. See also Cooke, *The Conquest*, 80–81; Crutchfield, *Tragedy at Taos*, 116–17; Zuckert, *Natural Rights Republic*, 4. For the origins of natural law in twelfth century canon law, see Siedentop, *Inventing the Individual*, 213–15.

10. Donaciano Vigil to [Antonio Jose Otero?], n.d., reel 1, frame 188, RTG.

11. Donaciano Vigil to Thomas H. Benton, October 3, 1847, reel 1, frames 182–83, RTG. On the military trampling on judicial and civil terrain, see Twitchell, *History of the Military Occupation*, 148–49.

12. Donaciano Vigil to James Buchanan, March 26, 1847, in *Insurrection*, 31–32; also, Crutchfield, *Tragedy at Taos*, 153–55; Clarke, *Stephen Watts Kearny*, 158–59; Bieber, "Introduction," *Journal of a Soldier*, 41; Calvin, "Introduction," in *Lieutenant Emory Reports* 10–11.

13. Donaciano Vigil to [Antonio Jose Otero?], n.d., reel 1, frame 188, RTG.

14. Dyer, Mexican War Journal, 1846–1848, 97; "New Mexico," *Santa Fe Republican* (hereafter *Republican*), January 18, 1848, 2; Twitchell, *The Bench and Bar of New Mexico*, 4–5. Gibson appears the most exercised by the military; Frazer, ed., *Over the Chihuahua and Santa Fe Trails*, 57–58.

15. Theisen, "José Manuel Gallegos," 52–53, 56.

16. Francisco Sarracino to Donaciano Vigil, February 8, 1847, frames 38–39, RTG.

17. Donaciano Vigil to [Antonio Jose Otero?], n.d., reel 1, frame 188, RTG. On the frontier value of independence and self-government, see Nash, *Wilderness and the American Mind*, 146–47, and Jacobson, *Place and Belonging*, 64, 67–69.

18. Dyer, Mexican War Journal, 1846–1848, 98; "Donaciano Vigil, Gobernador Interino del Territorio de Nuevo Mejico a Los Habitantes del Mismo," Santa Fe, July 1, 1847, reel 1, frame 194, RTG; also Donaciano Vigil to Carlos Beaubien, October 27, 1847, frames 183–84, RTG, and Donaciano Vigil to Antonio José Otero, August 28, 1848, frames 186–87, RTG.

19. Donaciano Vigil, Gobernador Interino, "Condado del Río Arriba Dividido en Dies y Siete Precinto Eletorales [sic]," July 1, 1847, reel 1, frame 196, RTG.

20. Francisco Sarracino to Donaciano Vigil, September 27, 1848, reel 1, frame 170, RTG.

21. Weber, "Introduction" to Vigil, *Arms, Indians*, xviii.

22. For prefects' field reports of the election, see Francisco Sarracino to Governor Donaciano Vigil, August 10, 1847, reel 1, frames 85–86, RTG, Donaciano Vigil Papers; Manuel Antonio Baca to Governor Donaciano, August 23, 1847, reel 1, frame 89, RTG, Donaciano Vigil Papers.

23. Hoover, "History of the Republican Party," 13–14, 14.

24. Donaciano to Antonio José Otero, August 28, 1848, reel 1, frames 186–87, RTG.

25. The names are listed in Stanley, *Giant*, 154.

26. Donaciano to Carlos Beaubien, October 27, 1847, reel 1, frames 183–84, RTG.

27. "Diversiones del Hinbierno," *Republicano*, December 4, 1847, 2.

28. Reséndez, *Changing National Identities*, 201, 206.

29. Coronado, *A World Not to Come*, 267–69; Reséndez, *Changing National Identities,* 200–201; also Spencer, *Yellow Journalism*; and Brazeal, "Precursor to Modern Media Hype."

30. Johannsen, *To the Halls of the Montezumas*, 16.

31. [Johnson], "'Art Preservative,'" 1–2; Grove et al., *New Mexico Newspapers*, 446; Towne, "Printing in New Mexico, 112–13; Stratton, *Territorial Press of New Mexico*, 2–3; Frazer, *Over the Chihuahua*, 53–54.

32. Alexander, "Core Solidarity," 272, "they themselves" 279–82.

33. Donaciano to Antonio José Otero, August 20, 1847, reel 1, frame 180, RTG; Donaciano to Antonio Jose Otero, September [?], 1847, frames 180–81, RTG; Donaciano to Cura José Manuel Gallegos, September 1, 1847, frames 180–81, RTG; Donaciano to Carlos Beaubien, September 12[?], 1847, frames 180–81, RTG. Masthead, editorial page, *Republican*, January 15, 1848.

34. "To the Public," editorial, *Republican*, September 10, 1847.

35. For an evident Whig statement, see Mann, "The Necessity of Education," 148–58. For a discussion of Whig views on education, see Howe, *Political Culture of American Whigs*, 3, 13, 16, 22, 36–37, 200–201.

36. "Escuelas," *Republican*, September 10, 1847.

37. J. Manuel Gallegos to Donaciano Vigil, October 1, 1847, reel 1, frame 92, RTG; Juan C. Armijo to Donaciano Vigil, October 7, 1847, frame 94, RTG; Carlos Beaubien to Donaciano, September 12, 1847, frame 95–96, RTG; Lamar, *Far Southwest*, 71.

38. Habermas, *Structural Transformation of the Public Sphere*. For a review of the literature and a proposed expansion of the concept of the public sphere, see Adut, "A Theory of the Public Sphere."

39. Warner, *Letters of the Republic*, 34–72.

40. Warner, *Letters of the Republic*, 43.

41. Galileo Galilei, *Dialogue Concerning the Two Chief World Systems,* transl. by Stillman Drake (University of California Press, 1967 [1953]).

42. Inocencio may have been Inocencio Martínez, nephew and student of the Taos priest José Antonio Martínez; Pedro Sánchez, *Memories of Antonio José Martínez*, 41. There was also Inocencio Valdez Jr., likewise a friend of Padre Martínez, who later edited *El Monitor* (Taos), one of New Mexico's early territorial Spanish-language weeklies (see, e.g., June 25, 1891).

43. Un Labrador to editor, *Republicano*, January 15, 1848.

44. El Cristiano de Estos Tiempos, "Nullus represensor formidandus est amarforis veridatis," *Republicano*, June 17, 1848, 2; El Amigo de los Pueblos to editors, *Republicano*, June 17, 1848, 2.

45. Un Minero to editor, *Republicano*, January 15, 1848, 3.

46. Anonymous, "Sres. Editores del Republicano de Ste. Fe," *Republican,* November 13, 1847. On the Illinois Volunteers see Bieber, "Introduction," *Journal of a Soldier*, 58, 59–60.

47. Bieber, "Introduction," *Journal of a Soldier*, 329n208.

48. Quoted in Henderson, *Glorious Defeat*, 32.

49. Johannsen, *To the Halls of the Montezumas*, 23–24.

50. Reséndez, *Changing National Identities*, 207–8.
51. "To the Public," editorial, *Republican*, September 10, 1847, 3.
52. Johannsen, *To the Halls of the Montezumas*, 21–22.
53. Untitled, *Republican*, November 13, 1847, 2.
54. Johannsen, *To the Halls of the Montezumas*, 47–48.
55. Frazer, *Over the Chihuahua*, 55.
56. "The Government of Santa Fe," *Republican*, September 24, 1847, 3; "El Gobierno de Santa Fe," *Republicano*, September 24, 1847.
57. Interpretations of the speech here are based on Donaciano Vigil, *Mensage del Gobernador*, Santa Fe, December 6, 1847, *Republicano*, December 11, 1847, 3; transl. as "Governor's Message Delivered to the Senate and House of Representatives," *Republican*, December 11, 1847; also in Twitchell, *History of the Military Occupation*, 150–51; Twitchell, *Old Santa Fe*, 311–12; Prince, *New Mexico's Struggle for Statehood*, 8.
58. For the Whig call, see Marvin Meyers, *Jacksonian Persuasion*, 10, 13–15, 212–21; Hanyan and Hanyan, *De Witt Clinton*, 15.
59. Hanyan and Hanyan, *De Witt Clinton*, 67.
60. "Viva el Gobernador" and "Mensage," *Republicano*, December 11, 1847.
61. "Asamblea," *Republicano*, December 11, 1847, 3; "Consejo Legislativo," *Republicano*, December 11, 1847, 2; cf. Twitchell, *The Bench and Bar of New Mexico*, 6–7.
62. "Legislatura," *Republicano*, December 11, 1847. For allusions to the December 1847 legislative assembly, see Larson, *New Mexico's Quest*, 5, and Coan, *A History of New Mexico*, 1: 306–7.
63. The council members were Antonio Sandoval (president), Henry Henrie (secretary), James Hubbell (porter), José Francisco Baca, Nicolás Lucero, Pascual Martínez, Juan Otero y Chávez, José Sandoval, and Juan Telles; in the house were William C. Angney (president), James Giddings (secretary), E. J. Vaughn (porter), Manuel Álvarez, Rafael Armijo Maestas, Tomás Cabeza de Baca, Juan Cristobal Chávez, Juan Cruz Baca, Gerald Gold, Levi J. Keithly, Mariano Lucero, Rafael Luna, Antonio José Manzanares, Antonio Martínez, Jose Martínez, Antonio José Ortiz, Juan Perea, José Ramon, Antonio Saiz, Miguel Sánchez, Juan Sanchez y Carrillo; Jesús Sandoval, and William Skinner; Twitchell, *Leading Facts*, 2: 265.
64. *Laws Passed by the General Assembly of the Territory of New Mexico in the Session of December, 1847,* Records of the States of the United States, microfilms, 1846–1861, N.M. B. 2, reel 1; "Annexation" and "Legislature," *Republican*, December 18, 1847; "New Mexico," *Republican*, January 22, 1848, 2; Twitchell, *History of the Military Occupation*, 151–52, and *Leading Facts*, 2: 264–65; Stegmaier, *Texas*, 25–26.
65. David Yancey Thomas, *History of Military Government*, 129; Secretary of War William Marcy, quoted in "Six Per Cent Duty," *Republican*, September 6, 1848; also Twitchell, *History of the Military Occupation*, 152.
66. Antonio José Martines [sic] and 28 others, to "Fellow Citizens," Taos, December 17, 1847, in Spanish, *Republicano*, January 8, 1848, 3; in English, *Republican*, January 15, 1848.
67. Reséndez, *Changing National Identities*, 212.
68. Martines et al. to "Fellow Citizens."

69. Un Conciudadano to editor, *Republicano*, January 15, 1848.
70. Un Labrador and Un Minero to editor, *Republicano*, January 15, 1848.
71. Don Simplício to *Republicano*, December 25, 1847.
72. Inocencio to editor, *Republicano*, January 8, 1848.
73. Inocencio to editor, *Republicano*, January 8, 1848.
74. Stanley, *Giant*, 157.
75. Inocencio to editor, *Republicano*, January 8, 1848.
76. Hennesey, *American Catholics*, 117–19.
77. Reséndez, *Changing National Identities*, 213.
78. Stratton, *Territorial Press of New Mexico*, 135–36.
79. Reséndez, *Changing National Identities*, 74.
80. Alexander, *Performance of Politics*, 90, 91.
81. "Gobierno Civil," anonymous to *Republican*, January 1, 1848, 3; transl. "Civil Government."
82. Conciudadano, "To the Citizens of this Territory," *Republican*, January 1, 1848.
83. El Azote de los Reveldes to editor, *Republicano*, January 15, 1848.
84. "The Priests," *Republican*, January 15, 1848; "Los Eclesiástices," *Republicano*, January 15, 1848.
85. "Sacado del Hermano Jesusuita de Nueva York," *Republicano*, January 15, 1848.
86. Huston, *Stephen A. Douglas*, 11; Hanyan and Hanyan, *De Witt Clinton*, 12–13.
87. Conciudadano, "To the Citizens of this Territory," *Republican*, January 1, 1848.
88. Johannsen, *To the Halls of the Montezumas*, 49.
89. "New Mexico," *Republican*, January 22, 1848.
90. Untitled editorial, *Republican*, January 15, 1848, 2; Un Conciudadano to editor, *Republicano*, January 15, 1848.
91. "The Annexation of New Mexico," *Republican*, January 22, 1848; "La Agregación del N. Mejico," *Republicano*, January 29, 1848.
92. Untitled editorial, *Republican*, January 29, 1848.
93. CEMAPA to editor, *Republicano*, January 15, 1848.
94. CEMAPA, "La Convención," *Republicano*, January 29, 1848.
95. Carlos Beaubien to Donaciano Vigil, January 16, 1848, frames 119–20, RTG.
96. "The Annexation of New Mexico," *Republican*, January 22, 1848; "La Agregación del N. Mejico," *Republicano*, January 29, 1848.
97. Donaciano Vigil to Antonio Jose Otero, January 21, 1848, frames 184–86, RTG.
98. W to editor, *Republican*, January 22, 1848.
99. "Sterling Price to the delegates of the People of New Mexico in Convention assembled," and "A los Delegados del Pueblo de Nuevo Mejico reunidos en Convención," February 8, 1848, in *Republican*, March 11, 1848, 2, 3; Twitchell, *The Bench and Bar of New Mexico*, 7–8; cf. Twitchell, *History of the Military Occupation*, 153, and *Leading Facts*, 2: 277n191.
100. Carlos Beaubien to Donaciano Vigil, January 16, 1848, frames 119–20, RTG
101. El Amigo de los Pueblos, "Annexation," *Republicano*, March 11, 1848, 4; cf. Stegmaier, *Texas*, 32.

102. Antonio José Otero to Donaciano Vigil, March 5, 1848, frames 123–24, RTG; Antonio Jose Otero and Francisco Sarracino to Donaciano Vigil, March 6, 1848, frames 127–28; RTG; Chávez, *But Time*, 87.

103. Rives, *United States and Mexico*, 649; Twitchell, *Bench and Bar of New Mexico*, 8–9.

104. "The War," *Republican*, March 18, 1848.

105. "Prospecto del Tratado de Paz," *Republicano*, May 3, 1848; cf. Stegmaier, *Texas*, 32. Parts of the treaty appeared in "Párrafos del Mensaje del Presidente de los E. Unidos al Congreso," *Republicano*, October 29, 1848.

106. Dyer, Mexican War Journal, 1846–1848, 143; Rives, *United States and Mexico*, 649.

107. "Dato Histórico," *El Independiente* (Las Vegas NM), December 22, 1894.

108. Twitchell, *The Bench and Bar of New Mexico*, 6.

109. Bancroft, *History of Arizona and New Mexico*, 442.

110. José Felix Benavides to Governor Donaciano, April 11, 1848, Governor's Papers, reel 1, frames 132–33, RTG, TANM; Twitchell, *History of the Military Occupation*, 222. Vigil has not yet received the sort of classic monument that his friend envisioned, although in 1972 the Santa Fe home where he lived was listed on the National Register of Historic Places.

111. Donaciano Vigil to Cura Francisco Leyva, September 4, 1848, reel 6 (no frame designated), RTG, Donaciano Vigil Papers.

Part 2. Política in the Ante Bellum

1. Griswold del Castillo, *The Treaty of Guadalupe Hidalgo*, xii.

2. "J. M. Washington to the people of New Mexico," April 21, 1849, in *U.S. Gov. Doc.*, House Misc. Doc. no. 5, 34th Congress, 1st session, 15, 114; *U.S. Gov. Doc.*, House. Misc. Report 90, 34th Congress, 1st session, 3; Chaves, *Papers in the Case of J. Francisco Chaves vs. Charles P. Clever*, 144, 147–48; Hernández, *Mexican American Colonization*, 101, 104, 112; Sisneros, "'She was Our Mother,'" 289.

3. Hernández, *Mexican American Colonization*, 104, 105–6.

4. Mora, *Border Dilemmas*, 73–74; Mangusso, "Citizenship Provisions of the Treaty of Guadalupe Hidalgo," 62–64; Frazer, ed., *Over the Chihuahua and Santa Fe Trails*, 80–81n2; "Politics in New Mexico," *Santa Fe Weekly Gazette* (hereafter *Gazette*), September 30, 1857. For Ortiz's reports to the governor of Chihuahua State, see Carroll and Haggard, transl., *Three New Mexico Chronicles*, 141–52.

5. González de la Vara "El Traslado de Familias de Nuevo México," 15.

6. Sisneros, "*Los emigrantes nuevomexicanos*," 29–32; Hernández, *Mexican American Colonization*, 110; Mora, *Border Dilemmas*, 73–74; Mary Daniels Taylor, *A Place as Wild*, 25–26. Earlier work has Ortiz exaggerating the number of Mexicans wishing to remain to keep his job going; Mangusso, "Citizenship Provisions of the Treaty of Guadalupe Hidalgo," 62–64; Frazer, "The New Mexico Scene," 80–81n2; "Politics in New Mexico," *Gazette*, September 30, 1857.

7. Sisneros, "'She Was Our Mother,'" 289; Sisneros, "*Los emigrantes nuevomexicanos*," 28–29.

8. Hernández, *Mexican American Colonization*, 106.

9. McCall, *New Mexico in 1850*, 82–83. For the account of the Nuevomexicano expatriates' fortunes in the state of Chihuahua, see Hernández, *Mexican American Colonization*, 114–35.

10. Donaciano Vigil, "El Gobernador al Pueblo del Territorio," September 23, 1848, *Republicano*, September 23, 1848; also Chaves, *Papers in the Case of J. Francisco Chaves vs. Charles P. Clever*, 144, 146.

11. Chaves, *Papers in the Case of J. Francisco Chaves vs. Charles P. Clever*, 146–47; Theisen, "José Manuel Gallegos," 60, 57; Griswold del Castillo, *Treaty*, 64–66; Mangusso, "Citizenship Provisions of the Treaty of Guadalupe Hidalgo," 60, 290.

12. Joseph P. Sánchez, *Between Two Rivers*, 134.

13. Glenn, *Unequal Freedom*, 24, 54, 261.

14. Orum and Dale, *Political Sociology*, 145–46.

15. Nichols, "The Territories," 159–60.

16. Patterson, "Relation of the Federal Government," 46.

17. See Patterson, "Relation of the Federal Government," 47; also Alden, "Evolution of the American System," 81.

18. Patterson, "Relation of the Federal Government," 47–48.

19. "It is by their sovereign will, alone, that the State comes into existence"; Joy, *Right of the Territories*, 7–8.

20. The "equal footing" clause came under continual erosion with the federal imposition of special conditions on new states, producing de facto inequality among states; see Alden, "Evolution of the American System," 88–89.

21. Pomeroy, *The Territories*, xii.

22. Chambers, *Political Parties in a New Nation*, 12–13.

23. Pomeroy, *The Territories*, 97.

24. Pomeroy, *The Territories*, 80.

25. Grupo de Investigadores Puertoriqueños (hereafter Grupo), *Breakthrough from Colonialism: An Interdisciplinary Study of Statehood*. I am grateful to John Nieto-Phillips for calling this important work to my attention.

26. Republican to editors ("Washington Correspondence"), *Santa Fe Daily New Mexican*, July 7, 1871, 1.

27. Grupo, *Breakthrough*, 47.

28. Grupo, *Breakthrough*, 48, "necessarily involved," and "to a community," 49.

29. Grupo, *Breakthrough*, 13.

30. Neil, "The American Territorial System," 219, 222.

31. Grupo, *Breakthrough*, "in spite of" 55, "the political power" 61–62.

32. Pomeroy, *The Territories*, 2.

33. On New Mexico's final battle to gain statehood, see Holtby, *Forty-Seventh Star*.

34. Grupo, *Breakthrough*, 55.

35. Patterson, "Relation of the Federal Government," 56.

36. Jack E. Holmes, *Politics in New Mexico*, 51–52.

37. Gómez, "Off-White in an Age of White Supremacy"; cf. Ganaway, *New Mexico and Sectional Controversy*, 43.

38. Hechter, *Internal Colonialism*, 26.
39. Stegmaier, "'Imaginary Negro'" 265.
40. Holtby, *Forty-Seventh Star*, 133.
41. William Lee Harper, "A History of New Mexico Election Laws," 6, 8; Coan, "County Boundaries," 255–56; George P. Anderson, *History of New Mexico*, 523; Lamar, *Far Southwest*, 132.
42. Larry D. Ball, *Desert Lawmen*, 2–3; Anonymous, *Inventory of County Archive*, 71.
43. Lamar, *Far Southwest*, 77; William Lee Harper, "A History of New Mexico Election Laws," 4.
44. Weigle, *Brothers of Light*, 82.
45. Pomeroy, *The Territories*, 98.
46. "Registrars," *Gazette*, August 15, 1868, 2.
47. William Lee Harper, "A History of New Mexico Election Laws," 3; Thomas D. Hall, *Social Change in the Southwest*, 85.
48. Harper, "A History of New Mexico Election Laws," 6; Chapter 21: "An Act Creating the precinct of Picuris in the county of Taos," New Mexico Session laws of 1857–58, 78, in *Laws of the Territory of New Mexico . . . 1859–60*, Records of the States of the United States, microfilms, 1846–1861, N.M. B. 2, reel 1; Coan, "County Boundaries," 268.
49. Lipset, *The First New Nation*, 45–60.
50. Vaughn, *New Mexico History and Government*, 155; Hepler, "William Watts Hart Davis in New Mexico," 22–23; Mangusso, "Citizenship Provisions of the Treaty of Guadalupe Hidalgo," 68–9; "Governments in the Territories: New Mexico," *Semi-Weekly Review* (Santa Fe), March 30, 1869.
51. "La Legislatura," *Nuevo-Mejicano*, February 6, 1864, 3.
52. On citizen mobilization, see Deutsch, *Nationalism and Its Alternatives*, 21–22, 109, 126.
53. "Public Meeting at Albuquerque," *Gazette*, February 5, 1859.
54. Ramos, *Beyond the Alamo*, 133–34.
55. "Junta Pública," *La Gaceta de Santa Fe*, October 15, 1864, 3; "Public Meeting," *Republican Review* (Santa Fe), March 4, 1871.
56. Billington, *America's Frontier Heritage*, 134–35.
57. "Convención Republicana del Condado de Valencia," *Revista Republicana* (Santa Fe), August 26, 1871.
58. Wallerstein, *Centrist Liberalism Triumphant*; Flores and Benmayor, *Latino Cultural Citizenship*.
59. American institutions formally applied ascriptive criteria based on the superiority of the white Anglo-Saxon male, alongside liberal and democratic republican standards, as criteria for national inclusion, producing widespread second-class inequality for others; Rogers Smith, *Civic Ideals*.
60. Chaves, *Papers in the Case of J. Francisco Chaves vs. Charles P. Clever*, 147.
61. Memorial of the Legislature of the Territory of New Mexico to the Senate and House of Representatives of the Congress of the United States, July 28, 1851, National Archives, Territorial Papers—New Mexico, RG 46, tray 1, folder 8, 229; *The Second Annual*

Message of acting Governor Arny to the Legislative Assembly of New Mexico, Delivered December 1866 (Santa Fe: Manderfield & Tucker, 1866), 8–10, in Governor's Papers, reel 1, frames 355–56, RTG, TANM; *Laws of the Territory of New Mexico . . . 1859–60*, Records of the States of the United States, microfilms, 1846–1861, N.M. B. 2, reel 1, 30, 32.

62. Mangusso, "Citizenship Provisions of the Treaty of Guadalupe Hidalgo," 66–68; Davis, *El Gringo*, 332–33; Griswold del Castillo, *Treaty of Guadalupe Hidalgo*, 66.

63. Lawson, *Patriot Fires*, 68–69.

64. Among leading interests were individual state governments, small freehold farmers, slave plantation owners, domestic merchants, ship owners and builders, struggling manufactures, importers/exporters, and artisan mechanics; Chambers, *Political Parties in a New Nation*, 3.

65. Schlesinger, "Introduction," in *History of U.S. Political Parties*, 1: xxiv–xxxv; Bibby and Maisel, *Two Parties*, 21.

66. Ostrogorski, *Democracy*, 3–24.

67. Schlesinger, "Introduction," xxxiv–xxxv; Aldrich, *Why Parties?*, 68–70; cf. Hofstadter, *The Idea*, viii–ix, 2–21, 49.

68. Chambers, *Political Parties in a New Nation*, 49.

69. Kerber, "The Federalist Party," 6–8.

70. Hofstadter, *The Idea*, 47.

71. Shalhope, "Toward a Republican Synthesis," 74.

72. For essential histories, see Kerber, "The Federalist Party"; Main, "The Antifederalist Party"; Cunningham, "The Jeffersonian Republican Party."

73. Remini, *Martin Van Buren*, 3, 10.

74. Cole, *Martin Van Buren*, 95–98; also Ray, *Introduction to Political Parties*, 89–90; Chambers, *Political Parties in a New Nation*, 18, 206–08; Hofstadter, *The Idea*, 42; Formisano, *Birth of Mass Political Parties*, 67.

75. Ostrogorski, *Democracy*, 49.

76. Aldrich, *Why Parties?*, 97.

77. Frymer, *Uneasy Alliances*, 121–22.

78. Kohl, *Politics of Individualism*, 130; Cole, *Martin Van Buren*, 4.

79. Kohl, *Politics of Individualism*, 130. That Whigs had a disproportionate share of anti-party members is attributed to the prevalence among its members of Yankee Protestantism and pietism; Formisano, *Birth of Mass Political Parties*, 58, 72.

80. Formisano, *Birth of Mass Political Parties*, 67; Kohl, *Politics of Individualism*, 5, 14, 130; Hanyan and Hanyan, *De Witt Clinton*, 62.

81. Lawson, *Patriot Fires*, 69.

82. Bibby and Maisel, *Two Parties*, 25; Ladd, *American Political Parties*, 99.

83. Warren, "Elections and Popular Political Participation," 30–31, 35, 44.

84. Formisano, *Birth of Mass Political Parties*, 4.

85. Lomnitz, "Nationalism as a Practical System," 350 (see also Brading, *The Origins of Mexican Nationalism*, 92–3); quote, Costeloe, *Central Republic*, 2. In congratulating José Joaquín de Herrera on being elected president in 1844, General Anastasio Bustamante, the exiled former revolutionary, opined unrealistically that the time was "ripe to compose party differences"; Cotner, *José Joaquín De Herrera*, 120.

86. Huston, *Stephen A. Douglas*, 8, 10, 11, 13.

87. Hoover, "History of the Republican Party."

88. Lamar, *Far Southwest*, 88.

89. Roberts, *Death Comes for the Chief Justice*, 6–7, 9; also Kellogg, "Lincoln's New Mexico Patronage," 522; Weber, "Samuel Ellison on the Election of 1857," 215; Westphall, *Thomas Benton Catron*, 24.

90. Lamar, *Far Southwest*, 116–17.

91. Bancroft, *History of Arizona and New Mexico*, 650; Ganaway, *New Mexico and Sectional Controversy*, 54.

92. Alexander, *Performance of Politics*, 89–90.

93. Political historians have noted this in the development of a viable two-party system in the nineteenth century; Huston, *The Panic of 1857*, 203; Holt, *Political Crisis*, 3–5, 235–36; Kruman, *Parties and Politics*, 140–42.

94. Stinchcombe, *Constructing Social Theories*, 80.

95. Scher, *Modern Political Campaign*.

96. Alexander, *Performance of Politics*, 89–90.

97. That it involved a wholly voluntary process speaks to Alexander's key point that democracy draws from the public space of civil society; *Performance of Politics*, 1, 9–11.

98. Bauer, "Sticking With It," 3. Reviewing the literature on the theory of party loyalty, Bauer notes that political scientists have yet to develop a comprehensive model to explain affective factional attachment.

99. Joseph A. Schlesinger, *Ambition and Politics*, 5.

100. Aldrich, *Why Parties?*, 19–21, 28.

101. On the stabilizing role of modern party competition, see Lipset and Rokkan, *Party Systems and Voter Alignments*, 4; Nielsen, "Ethnic Solidarity," 142.

102. See, for example, Kaplan, *Politics and the American Press*, 22–55; Chambers, *Political Parties in a New Nation*, 60–61.

103. Stratton, *Territorial Press of New Mexico*, 81.

104. "Discurso Inaugural del General Pierce," *Nuevo-Mejicano*, May 28, 1853, 4.

105. Coronado, *A World Not to Come*, 141; Anonymous to the editors, *Nuevo-Mejicano*, June 22, 1867; "Thanks," *Borderer* (Las Cruces), March 16, 1871; Untitled, *Borderer*, July 19, 1871.

106. See Mora, *Border Dilemmas*, 20.

107. Schermerhorn, *Comparative Ethnic Relations*, 68, 72–73, 73–74.

108. For settler colonialism as a master determinant of racial inequality, see Glenn, "Settler Colonialism as Structure." Colonizers may turn on their country's imperial project, becoming independence fighters themselves at the expense of the natives; Emmanuel, "White-Settler Colonialism," 38–39. They may form a power grouping to work its appropriation of materiel and labor "to the benefit of both the imperial power and the settler minority at the expense of the colonized"; Utete, *Road to Zimbabwe*, 3. Or they may displace/replace the indigenous for their land; Wolfe, *Settler Colonialism*, 1–7, and the collection in Goldstein and Lubin, *Settler Colonialism*.

109. Utete, *Road to Zimbabwe*, 10.

110. Gómez, "Off-White in an Age of White Supremacy."
111. Schermerhorn, *Comparative Ethnic Relations*, 23.
112. Schermerhorn, *Comparative Ethnic Relations*, 192–94, 106, 134.
113. Walzer, *On Toleration*, 28.
114. For a review of the literature, see Thomas D. Hall, *Social Change in the Southwest*, 161–63.
115. Quintana, *Los Primeros Pobladores*, 64; Hall, *Social Change in the Southwest*, 204.
116. One historian reports on the bitterness felt by Indian fighter Raphael Chacón over the Navajo killings of his family members and Nuevo Mexicano officers. The U.S. policy of clearing the West of Indian problems intensified the violence. The U.S. Army tried treaty negotiations with individuals they considered chiefs, only to find such "leaders" could not always command obedience from the rest of their people. U.S. agents acted contradictorily, often violating the terms of treaties themselves or exacerbating the problems by selling liquor and weapons to the Indians. Important were the ecological pressures placed by the establishment of military posts in the middle of regions occupied by nomadic peoples; Meketa, *Legacy of Honor*, 303.
117. Quintana, *Los Primeros Pobladores*, 65. For a report of Nuevo Mexicano sheep herders "wantonly" murdering Utes, see Bonneville to L. Thomas, February 28, 1857, box 31, Frank Driver Reeve Papers, Center for Southwest Research, University of New Mexico; for an interpretation of the literature on Apache hatred of Mexicans, see Hall, *Social Change in the Southwest*, 228.
118. Steinmetz, "Colonial State as a Social Field," 589.
119. Wolf, *Peasant Wars*, 276, 279, 149, 278, 279, 280.
120. Hechter, "Dynamics of Secession," 267–83.
121. Alexander, "Core Solidarity" 268–84.
122. Stratton, *Territorial Press of New Mexico*, 90.
123. Barth, "Introduction," *Ethnic Groups and Boundaries*; Nagel, "Political Construction of Ethnicity," 98–107; Olzak, *Dynamics of Ethnic Competition*, 2–3, 162–64.
124. Gans, *Limits of Nationalism*, 2.
125. Suzman, *Ethnic Nationalism*, 29.
126. Ash, "Freedom and Diversity," "hard grind" 34.

4. A Budding Binary

1. David Yancey Thomas, *History of Military Government*, 133.
2. "Agrecación de este Territorio a los Estados Unidos," *Republicano*, May 15, 1848.
3. Donaciano Vigil, "El Gobernador al Pueblo del Territorio, *Republicano*, September 23, 1848.
4. Untitled editorial, *Republicano*, November 15, 1848; "To the Public," *Republican*, June 17, 1848; "Our Civil Government," *Republican*, May 13, 1848; "Has New Mexico a Government," *Republican*, November 15, 1848.
5. Thomas, *History of Military Government*, 130–32.
6. Lamar, *Far Southwest*, 61, 62; also Vaughn, *New Mexico History and Government*, 149, 155; and Chávez, *Manuel Álvarez*, 119.

7. Wm. S. Messervy et al., "Petition to General Price," *Republican*, August 16, 1848; "Six Per Cent Duty," September 6, 1848; W. E Prince [Price] to Mr. Messervy, Brent and others," *Republican*, August 16, 1848; Thomas, *History of Military Government*, 130–31.

8. See Stegmaier, *Texas*, 33; Edrington, "Military Influence."

9. "Inesperada Llegada," *Republicano*, November 15, 1848.

10. Thomas, *History of Military Government*, 129–30.

11. Donaciano Vigil, "Un Proclamo," *Republicano*, September 25, 1848; cf. Stegmaier, *Texas*, 31–33; on the confusion regarding the origins of the proceedings, see Larson, *New Mexico's Quest*, 14.

12. E. J. Vaughn, "Justice to Whom Justice Is Due," *Republican*, September 25, 1848; "Candidatos," *Republicano*, September 25, 1848; R. H. Weightman, "Al Público," *Republicano*, November 2, 1848.

13. Santiago Hubbell and Francisco Sarracino to Señores Editores, *Republican*, September 25 and October 29, 1848.

14. Francisco Sarracino et al. to editors, *Republicano*, October 15, 1848.

15. Election," *Republican*, October 19, 1848, 2. For accounts, see Bancroft, *Works*, 17: 443–44; Chávez, *Manuel Álvarez*, 127; Coan, *A History of New Mexico*, 1: 344–45; Ganaway, *New Mexico and Sectional Controversy*, 39; Lamar, *Far Southwest*, 72; Larson, *New Mexico's Quest*, 14–15; "Little Scrap of History," *Albuquerque Journal-Democrat*, December 29, 1902; Prince, *New Mexico's Struggle for Statehood*, 9–11; Twitchell, *History of the Military Occupation*.

16. "The Convention," *Republican*, October 19, 1848; "La Convención," *Republicano*, November 2, 1848.

17. Antonio J. Martínez et al., "Petition of the People of New Mexico Assembled in Convention, praying the organization of a territorial government," December 13, 1848, National Archives, Territorial Papers—New Mexico, RG 46, tray 1, folder 2; *U.S. Gov. Doc.*, 30th Congress, 2nd session, *Senate Misc. Doc no. 5*; *Republican*, October 19, 1848, 2; cf. Spruce M. Baird to W. D. Miller, September 23, 1849, in Binkley, "Reports from a Texan Agent," 164–66; Spruce M. Baird to W. D. Miller, September 30 1849, in Binkley, "Reports from a Texan Agent," 169–70; Thomas, *History of Military Government*, 131; Lamar, *Far Southwest*, 64; Twitchell, *History of the Military Occupation*, 154–55, 162; Bancroft, *History of Arizona and New Mexico*, 443; also Larson, *New Mexico's Quest*, 14–18; Chávez, *Manuel Álvarez*, 127–28; Ganaway, *New Mexico and Sectional Controversy*, 40–41.

18. Thomas, *History of Military Government*, 131–32; Baird to Miller, September 23, 1849.

19. Secretary of State James Buchanan repealed the tax subsequently; Thomas, *History of Military Government*, 131.

20. "Petition to General Price" and W. E. Prince to Gentlemen, *Republican*, August 16, 1848; Ganaway, *New Mexico and Sectional Controversy*, 38–39, 57; Gorenfeld, "Taos Mutiny of 1855," 296–97.

21. Abel, *Official Correspondence*, 133; Durwood Ball, *Army Regulars*, 7–8; Durwood Ball, "By Right of Conquest"; Westphall, *Thomas Benton Catron*, 310–12; McCall, *New Mexico in 1850*, 65; Twitchell, *Old Santa Fe*, 314–16.

22. Lena Dingman Dargan, "James S. Calhoun in New Mexico," 17; Davis, *El Gringo*, 111–12; Green, "James S. Calhoun," 331–32, 336–37. On the evidence as to whether Calhoun was a Taylor plant, see Larson, *New Mexico's Quest*, 27–28.

23. Dargan, "James S. Calhoun in New Mexico," 21.

24. Lamar, *Far Southwest*, 64.

25. Westphall, *Thomas Benton Catron*, 310–12; Frazer, "The New Mexican Scene," 65; Gómez-Quiñones, *Roots of Chicano Politics*, 239; Chávez, *Manuel Alvarez*, 130.

26. Larson, *New Mexico's Quest*, 48–49; Twitchell, *History of the Military Occupation*, 158–59; Twitchell, *Old Santa Fe*, 280.

27. Twitchell, *Old Santa Fe*, 254, 341; Abel, *Official Correspondence*, 133; Larson, *New Mexico's Quest*, 29; Stegmaier, *Texas*, 50–51; Twitchell, *History of the Military Occupation*, 175–80; Jordan et al., "Notorious as the Noonday Sun," 462–63. Weightman is described as an "expansive temperamental Washingtonian ... versed in the Spanish language, a defender of the Catholic church, and a great favorite of the native New Mexicans"; Lamar, *Far Southwest*, 64.

28. Weightman, *To the Congress*, 3; Chávez, *Manuel Álvarez*, 133–34; Twitchell, *Old Santa Fe*, 321n565.

29. Twitchell, *History of the Military Occupation*, 161; Lamar, *Far Southwest*, 65; Abel, *Official Correspondence*, 133.

30. For Weightman's complaints about Houghton and response, see Twitchell, *History of the Military Occupation*, 165–75; Chávez, *Manuel Álvarez*, 134–35; Stegmaier, *Texas*, 48–49, 64.

31. Twitchell, *History of the Military Occupation*, 156–57; Larson, *New Mexico's Quest*, 29; Thomas, *History of Military Government*, 134.

32. James S. Calhoun to T. Ewing (Sec. of Int.), October 16, 1849, in Abel, *Official Correspondence*, 58–59; the anonymous letter was reprinted in "Para el Republicano, Al Sr. Weightman," in *Nuevo-Mejicano*, November 28, 1849; Spruce M. Baird to W. D. Miller, October 9, 1849, Binkley, "Reports from a Texan Agent," 172–73; Stegmaier, *Texas*, 51–52; Twitchell, *History of the Military Occupation*, 176–78, and *Old Santa Fe*, 345–46; Chávez, *But Time*, 140.

33. Martínez, *Journal and Proceedings of a Convention of Delegates Elected by the people of New Mexico, held at Santa Fe on the 24th of September, 1849, presenting a plan for a civil government of said territory of New Mexico*. For discussion, see Larson, *New Mexico's Quest*, 18; Stegmaier, *Texas*, 53.

34. Martínez, *Journal and Proceedings*, 7; Larson, *New Mexico's Quest*, 19, 20; Chávez, *Manuel Álvarez*, 130–31, 132; Ganaway, *New Mexico and Sectional Controversy*, 42; Thomas, *History of Military Government*, 134; Lamar, *Far Southwest*, 63–64; muster roll, St.Vrain volunteer company, in "Walks and Talks," *New Mexican Review* (Santa Fe), July 26, 1883.

35. Martínez, *Journal and Proceedings*, 13–17, 18; Larson, *New Mexico's Quest*, 19; Meriwether, *My Life in the Mountains*, 155.

36. Martínez, *Journal and Proceedings*, 9–10, 13, 17; Larson, *New Mexico's Quest*, 19.

37. Lamar, *Far Southwest*, 66–67.

38. Martínez, *Journal and Proceedings*, 19-21; Frazer, "New Mexican Scene," 22; Stegmaier, *Texas*, 53; Ganaway, *New Mexico and the Sectional Controversy*, 42-43; Larson, *New Mexico's Quest*, 18-19.

39. Antonio José Otero to Donaciano Vigil, May 15, 1848, frame 136, RTG; Larson, *New Mexico's Quest*, 18-20; Jordan et al., "'Notorious as the Noonday Sun,'" 463-64.

40. Dargan, "James S. Calhoun in New Mexico," "incite the people" 18; Larson, *New Mexico's Quest*, 20, 22, 23-24; Stegmaier, *Texas*, 92-93, 141-42, 175-76; Chávez, *Manuel Alvarez*, 132, 133-34; Lamar, *Far Southwest*, 65, 67; Twitchell, *History of the Military Occupation*, 156-58; Thomas, *History of Military Government*, "a large tract" 135.

41. Lamar, *Far Southwest*, 65.

42. Thomas, *History of Military Government*, 136-37; Lamar, *Far Southwest*, 65-66; Chávez, *Manuel Alvarez*, 134.

43. Stegmaier, *Texas*, 65.

44. Stegmaier (*Texas*, 75-76) finds Crawford wanting McCall to support statehood passively, unaware of the colonel's White House special orders to actively foment statehood activity.

45. Thomas, *History of Military Government*, 136; Larson, *New Mexico's Quest*, 26-27; Abel, *Official Correspondence*, 133. The Crawford statement is in Frazer, "The New Mexican Scene," 66-67; see Larson, *New Mexico's Quest*, 29; Twitchell, *History of the Military Occupation*, 156-57; Ganaway, *New Mexico and Sectional Controversy*, 46.

46. Chávez, *Manuel Álvarez*, 140; also Stegmaier, *Texas*, 68-69.

47. Thomas, *History of Military Government*, 136; Green, "James S. Calhoun," 338-39.

48. Stegmaier, *Texas*, 76-77, 79; Ganaway, *New Mexico and Sectional Controversy*, 47-48.

49. Thomas, *History of Military Government*, "people's leaders" 137; John Munroe, "Proclamation," April 23, 1850, in Weightman, *To the Congress*, 5-6; see Stegmaier, *Texas*, 80; Larson, *New Mexico's Quest*, 29, 30-31; Chávez, *Manuel Álvarez*, 136-37; Twitchell, *History of the Military Occupation*, 165, 181; Frazer, "The New Mexican Scene," 68-69; Ganaway, *New Mexico and Sectional Controversy*, 49.

50. Thomas, *History of Military Government*, 138-39; Lamar, *Far Southwest*, 67, 68.

51. Cyrus Choice to J. S. Calhoun, May 8, 1850, in Abel, *Official Correspondence*, 194-95.

52. James S. Calhoun to Orlando Brown, February 2, 1850, in Abel, *Official Correspondence*, 132-33.

53. Thomas, *History of Military Government*, 139; Larson, *New Mexico's Quest*, 31-32; Prince, *New Mexico's Struggle for Statehood*, 17-18.

54. Larson, *New Mexico's Quest*, 32-33; Stegmaier, *Texas*, 117; Ganaway, *New Mexico and Sectional Controversy*, 49-50.

55. Thomas, *History of Military Government*, 139-40; Rosen, "Pueblo Indians and Citizenship," 6; Larson, *New Mexico's Quest*, 33-36; Stegmaier, *Texas*, 117-18; Chávez, *Manuel Álvarez*, 138; Prince, *New Mexico's Struggle for Statehood*, 3-4.

56. Stegmaier, *Texas*, 152-53; see Twitchell's discussion, *Old Santa Fe*, 317-19.

57. John Munroe, *Proclamación*, May 28, 1850, Governor's Papers, reel 1, frame 206, RTG, TANM; also in Weightman, *To the Congress*, 5-6; and Abel, *Official Cor-*

respondence, 219–20; see also Thomas, *History of Military Government*, 140; Larson, *New Mexico's Quest*, 36; Chávez, *Manuel Álvarez*, 138; Stegmaier, *Texas*, 119.

58. Larson, *New Mexico's Quest*, 36–37; Chávez, *Manuel Álvarez*, 138–39; Ganaway, *New Mexico and Sectional Controversy*, 51; Lamar errs in the names on the respective tickets, *Far Southwest*, 67.

59. Michael Les Benedict, *Preserving the Constitution*, 56.

60. Larson, *New Mexico's Quest*, 37–38, 40; Chávez, *Manuel Álvarez*, 139–40; Lamar, *Far Southwest*, 68; Twitchell, *History of the Military Occupation*, 164; Ganaway, *New Mexico and Sectional Controversy*, 51–52.

61. Stegmaier, *Texas*, 121–22.

62. J. H. Whittlesey to Lt. L. McLaws, June 10, 1850, in Abel, *Official Correspondence*, 210.

63. Capt. Wm. N. Grier to Lt. L. McLaws, June 18, 1850, in Abel, *Official Correspondence*, 210.

64. Lamar, *Far Southwest*, 68.

65. J. S. Calhoun to Orlando Brown, June 19, 1850, and John Munroe, A LOS INDIOS DE PUEBLO DE NUEVO MEJICO, June 6, 1850, in Abel, *Official Correspondence*, 213–14. James Collins argued that the Pueblos were citizens of the United States, in "The Pueblo Indians of New Mexico," *Gazette*, April 12, 1856. For a cogent argument against the position that neither the Treaty of Guadalupe Hidalgo nor the 1850 Organic Act granted citizenship to the Pueblos, see La Verdad to editor, *Gazette*, April 19, 1856 (the *Gazette* named W. W. H. Davis the author); see also "The Pueblo Indian Again," *Gazette*, April 19, 1856, 2.

66. J. S. Calhoun to Orlando Brown, July 31, 1850, in Abel, *Official Correspondence*, 231–32.

67. James S. Calhoun to Col. W. Medill (Cmdr. of Ind. Affairs), October 15, 1849, in Abel, *Official Correspondence*, 53.

68. See the table in McCall, *New Mexico in 1850*, 109.

69. James S. Calhoun to Orlando Brown, July 15, 1850, in Abel, *Official Correspondence*, 218; McCall, *New Mexico in 1850*, 109; Weightman, *To the Congress*, 7–8; also Thomas, *History of Military Government*, 140; Larson, *New Mexico's Quest*, 38; Chávez, *Manuel Álvarez*, 139–41; Twitchell, *History of the Military Occupation*, 161–62, 181; Frazer, "The New Mexican Scene," 69; Stegmaier, *Texas*, 123; Ganaway, *New Mexico and Sectional Controversy*, 52; but see Lamar's variant narrative, *Far Southwest*, 68.

70. J. S. Calhoun to Orlando Brown, July 31, 1850, in Abel, *Official Correspondence*, 231–32.

71. Weightman, *To the Congress*, 7; Kiser, "A 'charming name,'" 176–77; Thomas, *History of Military Government*, 14–41; Stegmaier, *Texas*, 124–25; Chávez, *Manuel Álvarez*, 140, 141–43, "sovereign guide" 142.

72. James S. Calhoun to Orlando Brown, July 15, 1850, in Abel, *Official Correspondence*, 218; Bancroft, *History of Arizona and New Mexico*, 448; Frazer, "The New Mexican Scene," 69–70; Lamar, *Far Southwest*, 68; Larson, *New Mexico's Quest*, 39–40, 42; Chávez, *Manuel Álvarez*, 242.

73. Memorial of the Legislature of New Mexico to the Congress of the United States, National Archives, Territorial Papers—New Mexico, RG 46, tray 1, folder 2; also in Weightman, *To the Congress*, 7; Twitchell, *History of the Military Occupation*, 163–64, and *Old Santa Fe*, 322n566; Thomas, *History of Military Government of Military Government*, 143–44.

74. James S. Calhoun to Orlando Brown, July 15, 1850, in Abel, *Official Correspondence*, 218.

75. Quoted in Larson, *New Mexico's Quest*, 42–43; also David Miller to *Gazette*, May 22, 1858, and Stegmaier, *Texas*, 128.

76. Thomas, *History of Military Government*, 141–42; Larson, *New Mexico's Quest*, 43–44; Chávez, *Manuel Álvarez*, 143.

77. The Álvarez-Munroe exchange appears verbatim in Twitchell, *History of the Military Occupation*, 181–90; see also Thomas, *History of Military Government*, 142–43; Lamar, *Far Southwest*, 68–69.

78. Munroe, PROCLAMATION, May 28, 1850, in Abel, *Official Correspondence*, 219–20.

79. Larson, *New Mexico's Quest*, 41.

80. Lamar, *Far Southwest*, 66–69.

81. For the memorial see Twitchell, *History of the Military Occupation*, 191–92; see Thomas, *History of Military Government*, 143; Lamar, *Far Southwest*, 69; Chávez, *Manuel Álvarez*, 143–46; Larson, *New Mexico's Quest*, 43–44; Stegmaier, *Texas*, 128.

82. Thomas, *History of Military Government*, 145; Larson, *New Mexico's Quest*, 44–46; Chávez, *Manuel Álvarez*, 143–46; Frazer, "The New Mexican Scene," 71; Stegmaier, *Texas*, 129.

83. James Munroe to Major General R. Jones, July 16, 1850, in Twitchell, *History of the Military Occupation*, 192–94; cf. Thomas, *History of Military Government*, 145; Stegmaier, *Texas*, 129–30.

84. Abel, *Official Correspondence*, 133.

85. Weightman, *To the Congress*, 21, 22; Ganaway, *New Mexico and Sectional Controversy*, 52–54; cf. Thomas, *History of Military Government*, 143–44.

86. Stegmaier, *Texas*, 212–13; Chávez, *Manuel Álvarez*, 146, 148; Lamar, *Far Southwest*, 69; Frazer, "The New Mexican Scene," 71–72.

87. J. S. Calhoun to Orlando Brown, July 31, 1850, in Abel, *Official Correspondence*, 231–32.

88. Winfield Scott to Col. John Munroe, August 6, 1850, in Abel, *Official Correspondence*, 164–65.

89. J. S. Calhoun to Orlando Brown, July 31, 1850, in Abel, *Official Correspondence*, 231–32.

90. S. M. Baird, "ELECTION NOTICE," July 20, 1850, in Abel, *Official Correspondence*, 233.

91. Lewis D. Sheetz (Secretary of State), PROCLAMA, July 20, 1850, and Manuel Álvarez, PROCLAMATION n.d., in Abel, *Official Correspondence*, 254, 234.

92. John Munroe, Al Prefecto del Condado de ____ [n d.], and To the prefect of the County of ____ [sic], in Abel, *Official Correspondence*, 234–35.

93. James S. Calhoun to Orlando Brown, August 13, 1850, in Abel, *Official Correspondence,* 252–53.

94. Larson, *New Mexico's Quest,* 52–57, 58; Chávez, *Manuel Álvarez,* 147; Lamar, *Far Southwest,* 69–70; Twitchell, *History of the Military Occupation,* 161. For details of the Omnibus compromise battle in Congress, see Stegmaier, *Texas,* 135–65; for Conrad's correspondence of September 10, 1850 to Munroe, see Twitchell, *History of the Military Occupation,* 195–96.

95. C. M. Conrad to John Munroe, September 10, 1850, in Abel, *Official Correspondence,* 220–21; Thomas, *History of Military Government,* 146.

96. Dargan, "James S. Calhoun in New Mexico," vi; [Secretary of State] Daniel Webster to James S. Calhoun, January 9, 1851, in Abel, *Official Correspondence,* 296; Chávez, *Manuel Álvarez,* 148–52; Stegmaier, *Texas,* 315; "Little Scrap of History," *Albuquerque Journal Democrat,* December 29, 1902, 3; Green, "James S. Calhoun," 339; J. S. Calhoun to Daniel Webster, June 30, 1851, in Abel, *Official Correspondence,* 361–63; Edward H. Wingfield to Luke Lea, May 22, 1852, in Abel, *Official Correspondence,* 538.

97. Abel, *Official Correspondence,* 296; Murphy, *Frontier Crusader,* 133.

98. James S. Calhoun to all whom it may concern, August 8, 1851, Executive Records, Book #1, June 26, 1851–July 18, 1867 (hereafter Executive Records), reel 21, frame 3, TANM; 1st Lt. L. McLaws, Special Order no. 12, March 2, 1851, in Abel, *Official Correspondence,* 296–97; John Munroe to [Secretary of War] C. M. Conrad, March 3, 1851, in Abel, *Official Correspondence,* 297; Green, "James S. Calhoun," 339–40; Horn, *New Mexico's Troubled Years,* 25–26, 28.

99. Green, "James S. Calhoun," 310–11, 325, 327; on "ardent," see Abel, *Official Correspondence,* xii; Larson, *New Mexico's Quest,* 76; Horn, *New Mexico's Troubled Years,* 22, 39; Kellogg, "Lincoln's New Mexico Patronage," 523.

100. Ellison, "History of New Mexico," 7.

101. "'El Demócrata' and National Democracy," *Gazette,* August 22, 1857, 2; Kellogg, "Lincoln's New Mexico Patronage," 523, 524; Whiting, "Minutes of the Historical Society," 253; Hall, "Giant Before the Surveyor General," 67; Kirby Benedict, *Journey through New Mexico's First Judicial District,* 53n18; Twitchell, *Leading Facts,* 2: 411.

102. Formisano (*Birth of Mass Political Parties,* 56–57, 60–74, 77) attributes much to the anti-Masonry movement in the formation of political parties. To the anti-Masons, "the Masonic Order looked like a secret organization whose members were placing themselves above the law"; Howe, *Political Culture of the American Whigs,* 55–56.

103. Zachary Taylor, for example, successfully posed to "stand above party"; Howe, *Political Culture of American Whigs,* 50, also 52–53, 244; also Formisano, *Birth of Mass Political Parties,* 73.

104. Howe (*Political Culture of American Whigs,* 53) cautions against viewing it only in terms of Whig slowness to set up political organization according to standards of party success that they rejected.

105. "The approaching Election.–The Necessity of Organizing the Democratic Party," *Gazette,* July 15, 1854. The editor at the time was W. W. H. Davis.

106. R. T. Brent, "Public Meeting" and untitled editorial, *Gazette,* April 26, 1851; untitled, *Gazette,* April 26, 1851.

107. Brent, "Public Meeting" and untitled editorial, *Gazette*, April 26, 1851.

108. "A List of the Members of the Legislative Assembly of the Territory of New Mexico, 1851-52," in *Laws of the Territory of New Mexico . . . 1851*, Records of the States of the United States, microfilms, 1846-1861, N.M. B. 2, reel 1, 152-54).

109. Green, "James S. Calhoun," 341-42; Ganaway, *New Mexico and Sectional Controversy*, 55-56.

110. Thomas, *History of Military Government*, 147; Twitchell, *Old Santa Fe*, 319-20.

111. "An Act Declaring and establishing the Rights of the People of the Territory of New Mexico," July 12, 1851, "Memorial and Joint Resolution," in *Laws of the Territory of New Mexico . . . 1851, Second Session*, Records of the States of the United States, microfilms, 1846-1861, N.M. B. 2, reel 1, 405; Twitchell, *Leading Facts*, 2: 291; Horn, *New Mexico's Troubled Years*, 44.

112. In 1861 a judge described to the U.S. attorney general the need of Americans to speak Spanish in order to function properly professionally in New Mexico; Kirby Benedict to Hon. Edward Bates, June 16, 1861, in Hunt, *Kirby Benedict*, 145-50. For other statements on the importance of the Spanish language currency in the territory, see H. H. Heath to Edward Scoe, Consul of Belgium, September 12, 1867, and H. H. Heath to Register Treasury, September 15, 1867, box 1, folder 4, Clinton P. Anderson Papers, Center for Southwest Research, University of New Mexico.

113. J. S. Calhoun to Luke Lea, June 30 1851, in Abel, *Official Correspondence*, 368-70.

114. Shalhope, "Toward a Republican Synthesis," 72.

115. The interpretation of the circular in what follows is based on Antonio Sandoval et al., "TO THE PEOPLE OF NEW MEXICO," n.d., in Abel, *Official Correspondence*, 370-75; see also Dargan, "James S. Calhoun in New Mexico," 66-67.

116. "The Santa Fe Tragedy," *Semi-Weekly Review* (Santa Fe), June 6, 1869; Keleher, *Turmoil in New Mexico*, 300; Hunt, *Kirby Benedict*, 149n15; Thompson, introduction to "An Indian Superintendent," 217; Whiting, "Minutes of the Historical Society," 270.

117. C. H. Merritt to [Interior Secretary] H. H. Stuart, April 30, 1852, in Abel, *Official Correspondence*, 533.

118. Lamar, *Far Southwest*, 76-77.

119. Caleb Sherman to Grafton Baker, August 30, 1851, in Abel, *Official Correspondence*, 406-11; Grafton Baker to Millard Fillmore, December 24, 1851, in Abel, *Official Correspondence*, 412.

120. Dargan, "James S. Calhoun in New Mexico," 49.

121. J. S. Calhoun to Daniel Webster, June 30, 1851, in Abel, *Official Correspondence*, 362-64.

122. J. S. Calhoun to Luke Lea, June 30 1851, in Abel, *Official Correspondence*, 368-70.

123. J. S. Calhoun to L. Lea, October 29, 1851, in Abel, *Official Correspondence*, 442.

124. Dargan, "James S. Calhoun in New Mexico," 51, 54, 130-31.

125. The interpretation in what follows of the legislators' response is based on Antonio Jose Martines et al., MANIFESTACIÓN ACORDADA EN JUNTA AMISTOSA, COMPUESTA DE LOS MIEMBROS DE LA LEGISLATURA TERRITORIAL, PARA CONOCIMIENTO DE LOS HABITANTES DEL TERRITORIO, June 13, 1851, in Abel, *Official Correspondence*, 375-78.

126. Lamar, *Far Southwest*, 76–77.

127. J. S. Calhoun to L. Lea, July 25, 1851, in Abel, *Official Correspondence*, 388.

128. Jordan et al., "'Notorious as the Noonday Sun,'" 464–65, 468. An active military officer, Reynolds apparently had a right to run for office, but the action was not liked by his commanding officer, Col. E. V. Sumner, who with limited success tried curtailing Reynolds's political activity, assigning him to field duty; E. V. Sumner to C. M. Conrad, December 22, 1852, in Abel, *Official Correspondence*, 144–45.

129. J. S. Calhoun to Daniel Webster, June 30, 1851, in Abel, *Official Correspondence*, 362–64.

130. Jordan et al., "'Notorious as the Noonday Sun,'" 469–70.

131. Quoted in Bieber, ed., *Letters of William Carr Lane*, 186.

132. In Abel, *Official Correspondence*: Charles Beaubien to James S. Calhoun, June 11, 1851, 357–58; John Munroe to [Adjutant General] R. Jones, June 30, 1851, 358–59; James S. Calhoun to Col. Munroe, June 14, 1851, 361.

133. The major's view was mentioned in Lt. L. McLaws to Maj. W. H. Gordon, June 24, 1851, in Abel, *Official Correspondence*, 360–61.

134. Larson, *New Mexico's Quest*, 67–69, "he must protect" 68; Jordan et al., "Notorious as the Noonday Sun," 472–73.

135. Jordan et al., "Notorious as the Noonday Sun," 474–75; see Horn, *New Mexico's Troubled Years*, 29; Larson, *New Mexico's Quest*, 66, 69; Stegmaier, *Texas*, 315.

136. Weightman, *To the Congress*, "colonial dependencies" 22, 8–10, 13, 11–12, 17–18; Jordan et al., "Notorious as the Noonday Sun," 474–75.

137. Larson, *New Mexico's Quest*, 42.

138. Twitchell, *History of the Military Occupation*, 386–91, and *Old Santa Fe*, 342.

139. Richard Weightman to Miguel Pino and Hilario Gonzales, March 20, 1852, in Twitchell, *History of the Military Occupation*, 386–91, and Twitchell, *Old Santa Fe*, 342–43n620.

140. J. S. Calhoun to D. Webster, September 23, 1851, in Abel, *Official Correspondence*, 428–29.

141. Green, "James S. Calhoun," all quotes 345–46; Larson, *New Mexico's Quest*, 63–64, 65, 71–72; Weightman, *To the Congress*, 7.

142. Richard Weightman, speech made in Congress, March 15, 1852, in Read, *Illustrated History*, 470–86, "reckless and unscrupulous" 470–71; also Larson, *New Mexico's Quest*, 67.

5. Mexican Democratic Party

1. Marcelino Vigil to Col. [John] Munroe, March 10, 1851, Series 02, National Archives, microfilm, Record Group 393, M1103, roll 2, frame 980, and M1102, roll 3, frame 973.

2. W. H. Gordon to SIR [Col. John Munroe], June 21, 1851, Series 02, National Archives, microfilm, Record Group 393, M1102, roll 4, frame 597.

3. E. V. Summer to J. S. Calhoun, April 14, 1852, in Abel, *Official Correspondence*, "some ill will" 526–27; J. S. Calhoun to W. C. Dawson, April 12, 1852, in Abel, *Official Correspondence*, "angry condition" 523–24.

4. J. S. Calhoun to E. V. Sumner, April 12, 1852, in Abel, *Official Correspondence* 524–25.

5. E. V. Sumner to [Maj. Gen.] R. Jones, April 9, 1852, in Abel, *Official Correspondence*, "justly and properly" 521–22; E. V. Sumner to [Maj. Gen.] R. Jones, April 22, 1852, in Abel, *Official Correspondence*, "several desperadoes" 525–26.

6. C. H. Merritt to [Interior Secretary] H. H. Stuart, April 30, 1852, in Abel, *Official Correspondence*, 533.

7. E. V. Sumner to Major General K. Jones, Adjutant General, April 28, 1852, in Abel, *Official Correspondence*, 532.

8. Green, "James S. Calhoun," 347.

9. Edward H. Wingfield to Luke Lea, May 22, 1852, in Abel, *Official Correspondence*, 538.

10. E. V. Sumner to R. Jones, May 8, 1852, in Abel, *Official Correspondence*, 535.

11. Ganaway, *New Mexico and Sectional Controversy*, 56.

12. Horn, *New Mexico's Troubled Years*, 32–33, 37, 44–45; Larson, *New Mexico's Quest*, 75.

13. J. S. Calhoun to Daniel Webster, September 15, 1851, in Abel, *Official Correspondence*, 425–26.

14. For example, Petition of the Citizens of Socorro County to His Excellency the Governor of N. M., signed by 143 residents of Socorro County, n.d., in Abel, *Official Correspondence,* 481–82; J. S. Calhoun to Hon. Danl. Webster, October 1, 1851, in Abel, *Official Correspondence*, 430–31.

15. Celedonio Valdes et al., Legislative Assembly Memorial to Governor J. S. Calhoun, July 9, 1851, in Abel, *Official Correspondence*, 386–87.

16. "El Discurso del Hon. J. E. Ottiz [Ortiz]," and "Speech of Hon. Eulogio Ortiz," *Gazette*, December 18, 1852, 3, 2; *Laws of the Territory of New Mexico . . . 1852*, Records of the States of the United States, microfilms, 1846–1861, N.M. B. 2, reel 1.

17. The interpretation of Lane's message below takes from Message of William Carr Lane, Governor of the Territory of New Mexico to the Legislative Assembly of the Territory at Santa Fe, December 7, 1852 (Santa Fe: *Santa Fe Weekly Gazette*), Governor's Papers, reel 1, frames 246–47, RTG, TANM (original copy of the message in Benjamin Read Collection, New Mexico State Records Center and Archives, Santa Fe); also Read, *Illustrated History*, 492–93.

18. On Adams, Whiggery, and his political philosophy of freedom, see Formisano, *Birth of Mass Political Parties*, 77, and on social harmony, 77–78; Howe, *Political Culture of the American Whigs*, 52–53, 59, 66, 67.

19. Formisano, *Birth of Mass Political Parties*, 81–101, 87; 93; also Gerring, *Party Ideologies in America*, 11.

20. See Loughran, *The Republic in Print*, 37–38.

21. Message of William Carr Lane; also, Larson, *New Mexico's Quest*, 76–77.

22. "Our Territory," *Gazette*, February 12, 1853.

23. W.G.K. [Kephart], "Letters from the Editor," *Gazette*, April 30, 1853.

24. Quote, W. G. K. [Kephart], "Letters from the Editor," *Gazette*, April 30, 1853; "The Assembly," *Gazette*, December 18, 1852, 2; "Mr. Otero's Defense," and Miguel

Antonio Otero, statement with regard to his ejection ("Mr. Otero's Defense"), *Gazette*, January 15, 1853; "Legislative Assembly. House of Representatives," *Gazette*, January 1, 1853, 4; "Legislative Assembly. House of Representatives," *Gazette*, January 15, 1853.

25. "Legislative Assembly," *Gazette*, January 15, 1853.

26. Untitled editorial, *Gazette*, April 23, 1853.

27. The interpretation of this report is from "Legislative Assembly," *Gazette*, January 15, 1853.

28. "The House of Representatives Journal for this session is not in official custody and if extant, its location is not known"; TANM, reel 1, frame 2. The bill's contents are evidenced in the press reports cited in the following notes.

29. "The Mexican Policy, Its Effects Upon the Mexican People, Etc.," *Gazette*, January 22, 1853; "La Política del H. Facundo Pino y Otros,–Su Efecto Sobre el Pueblo Mejicano &c.," *Gaceta Semanaria de Santa Fe* (Spanish section of the *Gazette*, hereafter *Gaceta*), February 5, 1853.

30. Stewart, *Nature's God*, 274. For Stewart's exegesis on the founding incorporation of Epicurean philosophy, see 273–313. As Stewart notes regarding the spread of the founder's ideas, "By book, sermon, and anti-sermon, the ideas tucked between the covers of Jefferson's book ultimately spread across all geographic boundaries in revolutionary America," 30.

31. The Editor, "To Our Readers," *Gazette*, January 29, 1853.

32. The pundit's column is Anonymous, "Review &c.: The Capacity of the Mexican People for Self-Government," *Gazette*, January 29, 1853.

33. Shalhope, "Toward a Republican Synthesis," 80, 66; Bailyn, *Pamphlets of the American Revolution*, 38–39.

34. E. V. Sumner to C. M. Conrad, March 27, 1852, in Abel, *Official Correspondence*, 516.

35. Sumner to Conrad, May 27, 1852, in *Gazette*, March 5, 1853, 3; "Review &c.: The Capacity of the Mexican People for Self-Government," *Gazette*, January 29, 1853; untitled and "Tocante a Aquella Carta," *Gazette*, March 12, 1853; Analogisma to *Gaceta*, April 23, 1853, 3; Lamar, *Far Southwest*, 83; Larson, *New Mexico's Quest*, 78, 72–73.

36. Joseph Nangle and Charles Spencer, untitled report of mass meeting, *Gazette*, April 9, 1853; for Sumner's inability to work with New Mexico's leadership, see Horn, *New Mexico's Troubled Years*, 29–30.

37. Justitia [sic] to editor, *Gazette*, March 5, 1853, 2–3.

38. Anonymous, *Gazette*, March 12, 1853; "Tocante a Aquella Carta," *Gaceta*, March 12, 1853.

39. Analogisma to *Gaceta*, April 23, 1853.

40. Stegmaier, *Texas*, 319–20.

41. J.D.R, "New Mexican Appointments," *Missouri Democrat*, in *Gazette*, July 23, 1853; Larson, *New Mexico's Quest*, 9, 20.

42. Ganaway, *New Mexico and Sectional Controversy*, 58; David Miller to editor, *Gazette*, May 22, 1858; "Democratic Organization," *Gazette*, December 31, 1853.

43. J. L. Collins, "To the Readers of the Gazette," *Gazette*, December 24, 1853, and "A Los Lectores de la Gaceta," *Gaceta*, December 31, 1853.

44. Ganaway, *New Mexico and Sectional Controversy*, 58.

45. "New Mexico—the Past and Future—Democracy and Whiggery," *Gazette*, February 5, 1853; "New Mexico and the United States Government," *Gazette*, February 19, 1853.

46. "Our Territory," *Gazette*, February 12, 1853.

47. On the inclusive wing of the party, see Formisano, *Birth of Mass Political Parties*, 44–46, 85–86. On grievance #7 in the Declaration of Independence demanding the right to naturalize immigrants in the thirteen colonies, see Allen, *Our Declaration*, 222–23. On the Democratic support of Texas Mexicans, see Ramos, *Beyond the Alamo*, 210–12, 215–19; Tejano incorporation in the Texas Democratic Party was very limited at the state level, rarely extending "to significant participation in elective bodies," 219.

48. "Maj. Weightman's Manifesto," *Gazette*, May 21, 1853.

49. "Major Weightman Against N. Mexico," *Gazette*, April 9, 1853.

50. Larson, *New Mexico's Quest*, 48.

51. "The Democrat," *Gazette*, April 18, 1857; "El Demócrata," *Gaceta*, April 25, 1857; "Democratic Meeting," *Gazette*, July 2, 1853; "Junta Democrática," *Gaceta*, July 2, 1853.

52. "Sovereign guide," "The Democrat," *Gazette*, July 2, 1853; also "Democratic Meeting," *Gazette*, July 2, 1853; "Junta Democrática," *Gaceta*, July 2, 1853.

53. Francis John Thomas to editors, *Gazette*, July 2, 1853; J. L. Collins, "To the Readers of the Gazette," *Gazette*, December 24, 1853; "A Los Lectores de la Gaceta," *Gazette*, December 31, 1853, 3.

54. "The Democrat," *Gazette*, April 18, 1857; "El Demócrata," *Gaceta*, April 25, 1857.

55. [Johnson], "'Art Preservative'"; for contemporary references to the Weightman-controlled *Amigo del Pais*, see the editorials in the *Gazette*, December 3, 1853, and December 10, 1853; "The Democrat," *Gazette*, April 18, 1857; "El Demócrata," *Gaceta*, April 25, 1857; Chávez, *Très Macho*, 66; also Larson, *New Mexico's Quest*, 35n4. *El Amigo del Pais* (Friend of the [New Mexican] country), was pronounced "pays" with a short *a*, a regional colloquialism distinct from the modern *país*.

56. Facundo Pino, Presidente de la convención, and José Gutierrez, Secretario primero de la convención, "Procedimientos de la Co[n]vención Demócrata del Territorio de Nuevo Mexico," *Gazette*, August 20, 1853 (hereafter "Procedimientos," 1853); "The Democratic Convention at Algodones in 1853," *Gazette*, April 11, 1857; cf. Chávez, *Très Macho*, 63.

57. Pino and Gutierrez, "Procedimientos," 1853.

58. C. H. Merritt to [Interior Secretary] H. H. Stuart, April 30, 1852, in Abel, *Official Correspondence*, 533; James S. Calhoun to Luke Lea, March 21, 1851, in Abel, *Official Correspondence*, 312.

59. See the series of letters by Baird in Binkley, "Reports from a Texan Agent," 158–83; also Weber, "Samuel Ellison on the Election of 1857," 215; Larson, *New Mexico's Quest*, "Many early" 48–49, 17–18, 47–49.

60. "Bases del Partido Demócrata Para el Territorio de Nuevo Méjico, *Gaceta*, August 13, 1853; "Convención Demócrata," *Gazette*, August 13, 1853. Hispancized, the founding father's name required a *G*.

61. On "party principle," Cole, *Martin Van Buren*, 151–52; Michael Les Benedict, *Preserving the Constitution*, 84.

62. "Bases del Partido Demócrata"; Formisano, *Birth of Mass Political Parties*, 60.

63. Pino and Gutierrez, "Procedimientos," 1853.

64. Chávez, *Très Macho*, 92.

65. Donaciano Vigil to Antonio Jose Otero, January 28, 1848, reel 1, frames 186–87, RTG; Twitchell, *History of Military Occupation*, 221. For a critical account of Vigil's admonishment of Ortiz, see Fray Angélico Chávez, "A Nineteenth-Century New Mexico Schism," 43–44; Chávez and Chávez, *Wake*, 79–80.

66. Twitchell, *History of the Military Occupation*, 175–80; Chávez, "A Nineteenth-Century New Mexico Schism," 35–54, 43–44; Chávez and Chávez, *Wake*, 79–80. For a defense of Father Benigno Cárdenas, one of the priests installed in a church by an alcalde, and a criticism of Weightman, see Anonymous, "Para el Republicano, Al Sr. Weightman," *Nuevo-Mejicano*, November 28, 1849.

67. Chávez, *Très Macho*, 25, 38; Chávez, *But Time*, 93–94.

68. Steele, *Archbishop Lamy*, 43.

69. Horgan, *Lamy of Santa Fe*, 149–50.

70. Bridgers, *Death's Deceiver*, 84, 86.

71. Pulido, *Sacred World of the Penitentes*, 45.

72. Chávez, *But Time*, 141–42.

73. Steele, *Archbishop Lamy*, 30.

74. Steele, *Archbishop Lamy*, 59, 73; Horgan, *Lamy of Santa Fe*, 127, 131, 153, 170; Chávez, *But Time*, 101, 102; Bridgers, *Death's Deceiver*, 99, 118; "A Celebration," *Gazette*, June 25, 1853.

75. Chávez, *But Time*, 99–100.

76. Chávez and Chávez, *Wake*, 90, "zealous" 92.

77. Chávez and Chávez, *Wake*, 92, 159, 165–67; Bridgers, *Death's Deceiver*, 99; Aragón, *Padre Martínez and Bishop Lamy*, 140.

78. Horgan, *Lamy of Santa Fe*.

79. Aragón, *Padre Martínez*, iv, v.

80. Chávez and Chávez, *Wake*, 142.

81. Steele, *Archbishop Lamy*, 49.

82. Steele, *Archbishop Lamy*, 33; Bridgers, *Death's Deceiver*, "revered" 95–96; Chávez, *But Time*, "puritanical" 95–96.

83. Steele, *Archbishop Lamy*, 43.

84. Chávez, *Très Macho*, 41; Un Católico to editors, *Republicano*, June 8, 1848.

85. Steele, *Archbishop Lamy*, 43–44. A Mexican liberal accused the New Mexico priests of not sermonizing at Mass; Anonymous para *Nuevo-Mejicano*, November 28, 1849; Chávez and Chávez, *Wake*, 184.

86. Bridgers, *Death's Deceiver*, 92–93.

87. Chávez, *But Time*, 94–96; Chávez, *Très Macho*, 25; Chávez and Chávez, *Wake*, 95.

88. Chávez and Chávez, *Wake*, 126–27; Chávez, *Très Macho*, 31, 33–34, 39.

89. Horgan, *Lamy of Santa Fe*, 108–10; Chávez and Chávez, *Wake*, 84–91; Chávez, *But Time*, 92; Bridgers, *Death's Deceiver*, 86–87; Steele, *Archbishop Lamy*, 71; Twitchell, *Old Santa Fe*, 362.

90. Horgan, *Lamy of Santa Fe*, 114–16; Bridgers, *Death's Deceiver*, 88–89; Chávez and Chávez, *Wake*, 97–98, 104–6.

91. Horgan, *Lamy of Santa Fe*, 113–14. As Horgan documents, the lapse occurred because Rome sent the orders of transfer to the wrong Mexican bishop, 141–42.

92. Bridgers, *Death's Deceiver*, 90, 99, 101, 102, 110; Chávez and Chávez, *Wake*, 126–27.

93. Chávez, *Très Macho*, 33–34, 42.

94. Chávez, *But Time*, 98–99, 102; Chávez and Chávez, *Wake*, 118–19, 123, 127; Bridgers, *Death's Deceiver*, 98; Chávez, *Très Macho*, 31; Horgan, *Lamy of Santa Fe*, 150.

95. Bridgers, *Death's Deceiver*, 101; on Machebeuf's failed travels, see 102 and 110.

96. Chávez and Chávez, *Wake*, 126, 108, 117–18; Chávez, *But Time*, 103; Chávez, *Très Macho*, 31, 39; Horgan, *Lamy of Santa Fe*, 128.

97. Chávez, *But Time*, 98–99; Lamar, *Far Southwest*, 77–78.

98. Chávez, *Très Macho*, 45.

99. Horgan, *Lamy of Santa Fe*, 128–29; Chávez, *But Time*, 101–2; Theisen, "José Manuel Gallegos," 85. Steele (*Archbishop Lamy*, 67) verifies the truth of Gallegos's "scandalous and flagrantly public affair with the widow María de Jesús Trujillo de Hinojós," while Chávez (*Très Macho*, 47) and Chávez and Chávez (*Wake*, 129) argue that there is no indisputable proof that Gallegos engaged in any untoward relationship with his house mate.

100. Horgan, *Lamy of Santa Fe*, 190.

101. Chávez, *Très Macho*, "typically Mexican" 45, 43, 44–45; Chávez, *But Time*, 103; Chávez and Chávez, *Wake*, 129; Horgan, *Lamy of Santa Fe*, 190–91.

102. The interpretation of the pastoral letter that follows is from "Carta Pastoral," *Gazette*, January 1, 1853.

103. Chávez, *But Time*, 103–5; Chávez, *Très Macho*, 47. Chávez and Chávez (*Wake*, 130) argue that Lamy stepped outside the bounds of his constituted authority in declaring that parishioners who failed to pay their tithes were no longer to be treated as members of the Catholic Church.

104. Horgan, *Lamy of Santa Fe*, 169.

105. "Carta Pastoral"; Chávez, *But Time*, 104; Steele, *Archbishop Lamy*, 68–69; Chávez and Chávez, *Wake*, 111; González de la Vara, "Política," 105, 106; Horgan, *Lamy of Santa Fe*, 170–72.

106. See Steele, *Archbishop Lamy*, 68.

107. Horgan, *Lamy of Santa Fe*, 173, 175.

108. Chávez, *But Time*, 105–7; Chávez and Chávez, *Wake*, 134–35; Chávez, *Très Macho*, 42, 49, 52; on the charge of the confessional violation, see also Steele, *Archbishop Lamy*, 71; Horgan, *Lamy of Santa Fe*, 176–80; Bridgers, *Death's Deceiver*, 109–12.

109. Theisen, "José Manuel Gallegos," 85–88; Horgan, *Lamy of Santa Fe*, 190–91, 226–27; Fergusson, *Río Grande*, 236.

110. Horgan, *Lamy of Santa Fe*, 177; Steele, *Archbishop Lamy*, 71; Bridgers, *Death's Deceiver*, 109–12; Chávez, *But Time*, 108–9; Chávez, *Très Macho*, 52–53.

111. Chávez, *Très Macho*, 54; Chávez, *But Time*, 109; Steele, *Archbishop Lamy*, 68–69; Chávez and Chávez, *Wake*, 159; Horgan, *Lamy of Santa Fe*, 191.

112. Chávez and Chávez, *Wake*, 135; Horgan, *Lamy of Santa Fe*, 177; Steele, *Archbishop Lamy*, 71; Bridgers, *Death's Deceiver*, 109–12; Chávez, *But Time*, 109; Chávez, *Très Macho*, 54–55.

113. Chávez and Chávez, *Wake*, 135; Steele, *Archbishop Lamy*, 71; Horgan, *Lamy of Santa Fe*, 178; Bridgers, *Death's Deceiver*, 109–12, 165; Chávez, *But Time*, 110–13.

114. Horgan, *Lamy of Santa Fe*, 178–79, "judicial" and "null," 182; Chávez, *But Time*, 111–13; Chávez and Chávez, *Wake*, 135–36.

115. Chávez, *But Time*, 114–15; Chávez and Chávez, *Wake*, 136; Horgan, *Lamy of Santa Fe*, 191.

116. Chávez, *But Time*, 115–16; Chávez and Chávez, *Wake*, 136–37, 139–40.

117. Horgan, *Lamy of Santa Fe*, 192–94.

118. Theisen, "José Manuel Gallegos," 65–66, 89; Chávez, *Très Macho*, 63–64; Chávez, *But Time*, 114–21.

119. Pino and Gutierrez, "Procedimientos," 1853.

120. Pino and Gutierrez, "Procedimientos," 1853.

121. Kiser, *Turmoil on the Rio Grande*, 79–80; Meriwether, *My Life in the Mountains*, 131; also Horn, *New Mexico's Troubled Years*, 46–48, 165–66; Meriwether, "Inaugural Address of Governor Meriwether," in Meriwether, *My Life*, 157; David Meriwether, "Ciudadanos de Nuevo Mejico," *Gaceta*, August 13, 1853.

122. Meriwether, *My Life*, 166; Howe, *Political Culture of American Whigs*, 59.

123. [Johnson], "'Art Preservative'"; "A New Paper," *Gazette*, August 20, 1853; Stratton, *Territorial Press of New Mexico*, 84.

124. J. E. Sabine et al., "A Card," *Gazette*, August 13, 1853, 3.

125. "The Late Political Events—Our Course," *Gazette*, August 20, 1853, 2; "Eventos Recientes Políticos—Nuestro Curso," *Gaceta*, August 13, 1853.

126. "Padre Gallegos Nominated for Congress," *Gazette*, August 13, 1853, 2; Spanish version in "Nombramiento del Padre Gallegos Para Delegado al Congreso," *Gaceta*, 3; see also, Chávez, *Très Macho*, 64.

127. "Padre Gallegos Nominated."

128. Formisano, *Birth of Mass Political Parties*, 81–83.

129. As scholars point out, at some minimum level, natives need to learn a new language among other acculturations. The sheer experience of learning a new language, adopting another culture, and shedding old ways can be slow, changes counted in decades and generations. See Rosaldo and Flores, "Identity, Conflict"; Deutsch, *Nationalism and Social Communication*, 120, 126, 163, 162, 174–45; Lipset and Rokkan, "Cleavage Structures, Party Systems, and Voter Alignments," 1–64, in Lipset and Rokkan *Party Systems and Voter Alignments*, 42.

130. "Padre Gallegos Nominated;" see Chávez, *Très Macho*, 64, and "Padre Gallegos."

131. Unos Amigos del Señor Gallegos, "Respuesta al artículo número 9 con título 'Nombramiento del Padre Gallegos para Delegado al Congreso,'" *Gazette*, August 27, 1853; also, Chávez, *Trés Macho*, 64–65.

132. Anglo-Saxon settlers argued that New Mexico should establish secular public schools. Collins stood by Lamy's parochial primary; see, for example, "A Celebration," *Gazette*, June 25, 1853.

133. "A Celebration," *Gazette*, June 25, 1853.

134. "The Defense of Padre Gallegos," *Gazette*, August 27, 1853.

135. "The Defense" and "The True State of the Case," *Gazette*, August 27, 1853.

136. "The Defense."

137. Lamar, *Far Southwest*, 89, 90.

138. Un Observador to *Gaceta*, February 14, 1857.

139. Chávez, *Trés Macho*, 63–64; also Twitchell, *Leading Facts*, 2: 309, and Larson, *New Mexico's Quest*, 82.

140. J. L. Collins et al., April 11, 1853, in *Gazette*, May 14, 1853; untitled report of the Bernalillo County Convention, *Gazette*, June 25, 1853; "The Next Delegate," *Gazette*, April 23, 1853; A. Armijo to J. L. Collins, J. Houghton, and others, May 6, 1853, *Gazette*, May 14, 1853.

141. On the People's Party in New York and the 1824 election, see Hanyan and Hanyan, *De Witt Clinton*; Cornog, *Birth of Empire*, 149–57, "revolutionary republicanism," 149.

142. Well before the People's Party of the 1890s agrarian Populist Movement, factions in various states organized oppositional people's parties. In Michigan, Indiana, Pennsylvania, Texas, and elsewhere People's Parties formed key anti-slavery, anti-Democratic, and anti-Know Nothing nuclei that would soon coalesce into the second Republican party; Huston, *The Panic of 1857*, 144–45, 147, 153, 160, 166; Formisano, *Birth of Mass Political Parties*, 237, 238, 284; Reséndez, *Changing National Identities*, 165.

143. The interpretation of the convention that follows is from Murray F. Tuley et al., untitled proceedings of convention, *Gazette*, August 27, 1853.

144. "Legislative Assembly," *Gazette*, December 11, 1852.

145. For a tribute to Vigil because of this fact, see Twitchell, *History of the Military Occupation*, 224.

146. F. Tuley et al., untitled proceedings.

147. Guillermo Carr Lane, "Conciudadanos de Nuevo Méjico," August 13, 1853, in *Gazette*, August 20, 1853.

148. Lane, "Conciudadanos de Nuevo Méjico."

149. "National Prejudice," editorial, *Gazette*, August 20, 1853.

150. See, for example, Barnard, "The Social System."

151. "National Prejudice," *Gazette*, August 20, 1853.

152. Lamar, *Far Southwest*, 90; Theisen, "José Manuel Gallegos," 105–6.

153. "Campaña Demócrata," *Gazette*, September 10, 1853.

154. Meriwether, *My Life*, 166, 167; Horgan, *Lamy of Santa Fe*, 193.

155. "Chief Justice Deavenport," *Gazette*, August 15, 1857, 3; also "Judge S. M. Baird and Hon. M. A. Otero," *Gazette*, January 9, 1858.

156. "New Mexico-Gov. Meriwether," *Gazette*, January 7, 1854; Meriwether, *My Life*, 167-68, 169; "Chief Justice Deavenport," *Gazette*, August 15, 1857; "Judge S. M. Baird and Hon. M. A. Otero," *Gazette*, January 9, 1858. Meriwether erroneously recalled that the *Gazette* had reported on the incident shortly after it happened, when it was actually *El Amigo del Pais*. It was only later, when W. W. H. Davis took over the editorship of the *Gazette*, that the paper reproduced a story in the *Washington Union* that had described the incident based on copies of the *Pais* column that Meriwether had mailed in.

157. William Carr Lane to Mary Lane (My Dear & Excellent Wife), August 26, 1853, and William Carr Lane to Mary Lane (My good wife), August 30, 1853, in Bieber, ed., *Letters of William Carr Lane*, 197, 198.

158. Meriwether, *My Life*, 170-72; Twitchell, *Leading Facts*, 2: 309; William Carr Lane to Mary Lane (My Friend), December 24, 1853, in Bieber, ed., *Letters of William Carr Lane*, 200-201.

159. "Election Frauds," *Gazette*, September 17, 1853; also untitled editorial, *Gazette*, September 24, 1853.

160. "Padre Gallegos' Democracy and Our Position," *Gazette*, September 10, 1853.

161. "Election Frauds," *Gazette*, September 17, 1853; also untitled, *Gazette*, September 24, 1853.

162. Meriwether, *My Life*, 172.

163. "Legislative Acts or Legal Proceedings," *Daily National Era* (Washington DC), January 26, 1854, n.p. [6].

164. J. Manuel Gallegos to Governor David Meriwether, December 21, 1853, published in "Carta Interesante del Sr. Gallegos," *Gazette*, March 11, 1854, 3.

165. "Contested Election—New Mexico," February 24, 1854, in United States Congress, House, Report 121, 33rd Congress, 1st session; Twitchell, *Leading Facts*, 2: 309; Horn, *New Mexico's Troubled Years*, 48; Larson, *New Mexico's Quest*, 82; Horgan, *Lamy of Santa Fe*, 193.

166. Gallegos garnered an appropriation to renew the Santa Fe Capitol and one for a penitentiary. On New Mexico's difficult land question, he introduced legislation to have the public lands surveyed and helped establish the office of Surveyor General to begin the process of settling the disposition of the territory's immense community land grants; Larson, *New Mexico's Quest*, 82; Ellison, "History of New Mexico," 8; "The Survey of Public Lands in New Mexico—a Bill Before Congress for that Purpose," *Gazette*, June 3, 1854, 2; Meriwether, *My Life*, 172; Theisen, "José Manuel Gallegos," 104-6.

167. Theisen, "José Manuel Gallegos," 106-7, 116.

168. On the western philosophers' discourse on Epicurean happiness, pleasure, and the good, see Stewart, *Nature's God*, 274-87, and its adoption by American founders, 307-13.

169. J. L. Collins, "To the Readers of the Gazette," *Gazette*, December 24, 1853, 2; "A Los Lectores de la Gaceta," *Gaceta*, December 31, 1853.

170. "Minnesota and New Mexico," *Gazette*, January 7, 1854; "New Mexico-Gov. Meriwether," *Gazette*, January 7, 1854; cf. Chávez, *Très Macho*, 69-70.

6. American Democratic Party

1. "The Approaching Election.—The Necessity of Organizing the Democratic Party," *Gazette*, July 15, 1854.

2. [Johnson], "'Art Preservative.'"

3. For the story, see Twitchell, *Leading Facts*, 2: 305–9; Wyman, "F. X. Aubrey," 9–11; Hunt, *Kirby Benedict*, 63–64; also Ganaway, *New Mexico and Sectional Controversy 1846–1861*, 59.

4. "The Adjournment of the Legislature—Disgraceful Proceedings," and, "La Prorroga de la Legislatura—Procederes Vergonzosos," *Gazette*, February 25, 1854; "The Question of Public Printing," *Gazette*, January 28, 1854; Horn, *New Mexico's Troubled Years*, 57–58.

5. José Serafín Ramírez y Casanoba to the Representatives of the Council, December 19, 1853 ("Discurso Pronunciado en la Camara de Representantes por el Hon. José Serafín Ramírez y Casanoba"), *Gazette*, December 31, 1853, 3; Formisano, *Birth of Mass Political Parties*, 77.

6. The *Gazette* from March 1855 to the eve of the election is missing. The duties of editor Davis as territorial secretary may have led to its suspension for a block of the election season.

7. See J. L. Collins, "To the Public," *Gazette*, February 23, 1856; W. W. H. Davis, "To the Readers of the Santa Fe Gazette," *Gazette*, February 16 , 1856; P. E. Brocchus, address at a public dinner in Santa Fe given in his honor, October 4, 1855, in *Gazette*, October 20, 1855.

8. "'Partidos,'" *Río Abajo Weekly Press*, July 14, 1863 (hereafter *Weekly Press*).

9. Lamar, *Far Southwest*, 90; Ganaway, *New Mexico and Sectional Controversy*, 61; Otero, *My Life on the Frontier*, 3.

10. Chávez and Chávez, *Wake*, 195.

11. Horgan, *Lamy of Santa Fe*, 233.

12. "Taking of the Poll Books of Río Arriba County," *Gazette*, September 22, 1855.

13. "Taking of the Poll Books of Rio Arriba County" and "Letter of Judge Watts," *Gazette*, September 29, 1855; James A. Watts to editor, *Gazette*, September 22, 1855; Chávez, *Très Macho*, 75–76.

14. Governor David Meriwether certification of election, September 18, 1855, Records of the Secretary of the Territory, 1851–1911, reel 21, frames 140–41, TANM; "The Election," *Gazette*, September 8, 1855; "Result of the Late Election," *Gazette*, September 15, 1855; "Local Items: Result of the election for Delegate," *Gazette*, September 22, 1855; Chávez, *Très Macho*, 75–76.

15. P. E. Brocchus, address at a public dinner in Santa Fe given in his honor, October 4, 1855, in *Gazette*, October 20, 1855; "Article of Judge Brocchus," *Gazette*, November 10, 1855.

16. Justice to the editor, *Gazette*, February 2, 1856.

17. "Article of Judge Brocchus"; P. E. Brocchus to Editor, *Gazette*, November 10, 1855; W. W. H. Davis to Elias T. Clark, October 4, 1855, Executive Records, reel 21, frame 144, TANM.

18. *Laws of the Territory of New Mexico . . . 1855–56*, 116; "Joint Resolution of the Legislative Assembly Asking the President to Remove Judge Brocchus," *Gazette*, January 26, 1856.

19. Governor's Acts and Commissions, December 31, 1855, Executive Records, reel 21, frame 161, TANM; A. G. Mayers and R.W. Stephens, "Public Meeting," *Gazette*, and "Junta Pública," *Gaceta*, January 5, 1856.

20. Diego Archuleta, Manuel Garcia, and Juan Isidro Lucero, report of proceedings ("Junta de indignación en el Condado del Río Arriba"), *Gazette*, January 26, 1856.

21. Rosen, "Pueblo Indians and Citizenship," 2; Reeve, "The Federal Indian Policy," 52; Horn, *New Mexico's Troubled Years*, 62.

22. See Diego Archuleta et al., "Procedimientos de la junta Demócrata, habida en el Condado de Rio Arriba," in *Gazette*, March 7, 1857 (hereafter "Procedimientos," 1857); Horn, *New Mexico's Troubled Years*, 63; for the greater disgruntlement over Meriwether's Indian policy, see Alburquerque to *Gazette*, March 15, 1856; "Our Indian Affairs," *Gazette*, March 1, 1856; "Preamble and Joint Resolution" (of the Legislative Assembly protesting the governor's message that we are at peace with the Indians), *Gazette*, March 8, 1856, 3; "Proceedings of a mass meeting in Fernando de Taos protesting Governor Meriwether's treaty-promise of land to the Yutas and Jicarillas," in *Gazette*, May 3, 1856; on Meriwether's Indian policies and practices, see Twitchell, *Leading Facts*, 2: 298–304.

23. "Our Indian Affairs," *Gazette*, March 1, 1856; also "Los Nabajoes," *Gaceta*, May 24, 1856; "The Indians of New Mexico," *Gazette*, October 18, 1856; "¿Quién tiene la culpa?," *Gaceta*, November 15, 1856; Santa Fe to editor, *Gazette*, November 29, 1856.

24. "Reception of Judge Brocchus," *Gazette*, May 31, 1856.

25. See A.C. to *Gazette*, August 22, 1857.

26. Horgan, *Lamy of Santa Fe*, "under the sponsorship" 220; Chávez, *But Time*, 125–28, "crassly ignorant" 126; Chávez and Chávez, *Wake*, 175–80, "corrupt" 180; Chávez, *Très Macho*, 77–79, 81–85.

27. United States Congress, House Committee on Elections, *New Mexico Contested Election*.

28. Miguel A. Otero to José Manuel Gallegos, October 16, 1855, in "Contested Election—New Mexico, Memorial of Miguel A. Otero contesting the seat of Hon. José Manuel Gallegos as Delegate from the Territory of New Mexico," in *U.S. Gov. Doc.*, House Misc. Doc. no. 5, 34th Congress, 1st session; "New Mexico Contested Election," May 10, 1856, in *U.S. Gov. Doc.*, House Misc. Report 90, 34th Congress, 1st session, 6–13; cf. Twitchell, *Leading Facts*, 2: 309n234.

29. "New Mexico Contested Election," May 10, 1856, in House Misc. Report 90, 15.

30. "Contested Election—New Mexico," May 23, 1856, in House Misc. Doc. no. 114, 3–4; House Misc. Report 90, 3–6, 11–13, 6–10, 14–15. For a different treatment of the Gallegos and Otero statements, see Horgan, *Lamy of Santa Fe*, 233–36.

31. See Hennesey, *American Catholics*, 136–38, and Gómez-Quiñones, *Roots of Chicano Politics*, 238.

32. Anthony D. Smith, *Theories of Nationalism*, 242, 243–44.

33. "Contested Election—New Mexico," May 10, 1856, in House Misc. Report 90, 1–3; cf. Chávez, *Très Macho*, 90.

34. W. W. H. Davis to José Manuel Gallegos, June 8, 1856, in U.S. Congress, House, *Congressional Globe*, 34th Congress, 1st session, 1856, 1732; "Secretary Davis," *Gazette*, March 28, 1857, 2.

35. Chávez, *Très Macho*, 90–92; Theisen, "José Manuel Gallegos," 107–9.

36. Proceedings on the contest in the House, July 25, 1856, U.S. Congress, House, *Congressional Globe*, 34th Congress, 1st session, 1856, 1733–36; "Address of Hon. Miguel Antonio Otero to his Fellow Citizens of New Mexico," December 16, 1856, *Gazette*, March 7, 1857.

37. Chávez, *Très Macho*, 85–86; cf. Chávez and Chávez, *Wake*, 197. Otero's son, who served as territorial governor of New Mexico at close of the nineteenth century, enshrined his father's point of view, referring to the Otero, Chaves, and Armijo families who were "all for the American party as against the Mexican party"; Otero, *My Life on the Frontier*, 282.

38. Theisen, "José Manuel Gallegos," 110–14; Horgan, *Lamy of Santa Fe*, 239.

39. W. W. H. Davis, "To the Readers of the Santa Fe Gazette," *Gazette*, February 16, 1856.

40. J. L. Collins, "To the Public," *Gazette*, February 23, 1856.

41. Davis, "To the Readers," 2.

42. "La Convención Nacional Democrática—principio de pretensores," *Gaceta*, May 3, 1856.

43. Macmillan Information Now Encyclopedia, "The Confederacy," www.civilwarhome.com/statesrights.htm.

44. *Official Proceedings, National Democratic Party . . . 1856*, 25, 26, available from Library of Princeton University; also "National Democracy—Gov. Floyd," *Gazette*, August 29, 1857, 2.

45. *Official Proceedings, National Democratic Party . . . 1856*, 25, 69.

46. "Politics in New Mexico," *Gazette*, September 30, 1857; James L. Collins, editorial, *Gazette*, October 4, 1856.

47. "Politics in New Mexico," *Gazette*, September 30, 1857.

48. "Democratic Platform" and "Plataforma Democrática," *Gazette*, February 7, 1857; "Junta Demócrata," *Gazette*, February 21, 1857.

49. "Legislative Assembly," *Gazette*, February 7, 1857.

50. "Democratic Platform" and "Plataforma Democrática"; also Archuleta et al., "Procedimientos," 1857; Juan Benabides et al., "Junta Demócrata," *Gaceta*, February 21, 1857; Carlos Beaubien et al., "Proceedings of the Taos Democratic Party Convention," February 25, 1857, in *Gazette*, March 7, 1857; Santiago L. Collins, Proceedings, "Junta Demócrata," *Gaceta*, February 7, 1857.

51. "Democratic Platform" and "Plataforma Democrática," 2, 3.

52. Huston, *Stephen A. Douglas*, 133, 152–53; Foner, *Fiery Trial*, 63, 67, 95, 96, 97, 106.

53. Santiago L. Collins, Proceedings, "Junta Demócrata," *Gaceta*, February 7, 1857; also "Franklin Pierce," *Gazette*, April 19, 1856.

54. Collins, Proceedings. The value appeared in 1855, for example in *Official Proceedings, National Democratic Party . . . 1856*, 25, 27; "El Nuevo Partido Político," *Gazette*, September 1, 1855.

55. Collins, Proceedings.

56. "Democratic Platform" and "Plataforma Democrática"; Archuleta et al., "Procedimientos," 1857.

57. Collins, Proceedings.

58. "The Message of Governor Meriwether," *Gazette*, December 20, 1856; F. Repito to *Gaceta*, February 7, 1857; untitled, *Gazette*, December 20, 1856, incl. extract from an anonymous citizen's letter to a territorial legislator.

59. Collins, Proceedings; Alburquerque to *Gazette*, March 15, 1856; Un Veterano to *Gaceta*, March 15, 1856; Beaubien et al., Proceedings; "Consejos Piadosos," *Gaceta*, August 15, 1857; "Kit Carson and W. W. H. Davis," *Gazette*, August 15, 1857.

60. Meriwether resigned on October 31, 1857, and left New Mexico on May 1; Davis left on October 15 (Executive Records, reel 21, frames 172, 175, TANM); Observador to *Gaceta*, March 22, 1856; Observer to *Gaceta*, May 17, 1856; Observer to *Gaceta*, October 4, 1856.

61. "Chief Justice Deavenport," *Gazette*, August 15, 1857; "Two of You Hold Brown, One can Hold Me," *Gazette*, August 22, 1857; "Deavenport, the Duellist," *Gazette*, August 29, 1857.

62. Archuleta et al., "Procedimientos," 1857; Collins, "Proceedings."

63. Beaubien et al., Proceedings; Archuleta et al., "Procedimientos," 1857; S to *Gazette*, March 28, 1857; "Honorable M. A. Otero," *Gazette*, February 28, 1857.

64. "Address of Hon. Miguel Antonio Otero to his Fellow Citizens of New Mexico," December 16, 1856, *Gazette*, March 7, 1857.

65. Michael Les Benedict, *Preserving the Constitution*, 56.

66. "Hon. Miguel Antonio Otero," *Gazette*, March 14, 1857.

67. Diego Archuleta, President, et al., Proceedings, "General Convention of the National Democracy of the Territory of New Mexico," *Gazette*, March 21, 1857; "The Convention of National Democrats of New Mexico," *Gazette*, March 21, 1857; "The National Democracy of New Mexico," *Gazette*, March 28, 1857; "La Democracia Nacional del Nuevo Mejico," *Gaceta*, April, 11, 1857.

68. "Politics in New Mexico," *Gazette*, September 30, 1857.

69. Collins, Proceedings; Archuleta et al., Proceedings, "General Convention"; "The Democratic Convention at Algodones in 1853," *Gazette*, April 11, 1857; "The Democrat," *Gazette*, April 18, 1857; "El Demócrata," *Gaceta*, April 25, 1857.

70. "The National Democracy of New Mexico," *Gazette*, March 28, 1857; "La Democracia Nacional del Nuevo Mejico," *Gazette*, April 11, 1857.

71. "National Democracy," *Gazette*, July 11, 1857; "La Democracia Nacional," *Gaceta*, July 11, 1857.

72. J. L. Collins, "To the Public," *Gazette*, February 23, 1856.

73. Archuleta et al., "Procedimientos," 1857.

74. *El Demócrata/The Democrat* (Santa Fe), October 1, 1857, National Archives, Record Group 59, Miscellaneous Letters, October 1857, Santa Fe, New Mexico; "A Fizzle," *Gazette*, August 29, 1857.

75. Un Demócrata Nacional to editor, *Gazette*, March 28, 1857.

76. Twitchell, *Old Santa Fe*, 280.

77. "Anuncio," *The Democrat*, October 1, 1857; Stratton, *Territorial Press of New Mexico*, 285; "Politics in New Mexico," *Gazette*, September 30, 1857; Sydney A. Hubble to *Gazette*, August 8, 1857; "Una Palabra Personal," *Gaceta*, August 15, 1857; C. P. Clever, "'¡Keep Cool!,'" *Gazette*, August 22, 1857; Uno Con Cola to *Gaceta*, August 29, 1857; "Chief Justice Deavenport," *Gazette*, August 15, 1857, 3. Some claim that Padre Martínez actively supported Otero (e.g., A.C. to *Gazette*, August 22, 1857), but Chávez (*But Time*, 144–45) claims that he played no political role in this election.

78. James L. Collins, untitled editorial, *Gazette*, October 4, 1856.

79. Thomas H. Hopkins to James Buchanan, Santa Fe, July 11, 1857, in Ganaway, *New Mexico and Sectional Controversy*, 63.

80. "El Nativismo Triunfante," *El Demócrata*, October 1, 1857.

81. Kass, *Politics in New York State*, 116.

82. Ryan, "'The Puritans of Today,'" 219.

83. Simmons, *Witchcraft in the Southwest*, 40; chapter 3 is "The Devil's Domain on the Rio Grande."

84. "Trampled on" is from "El Nativismo Triunfante," *El Demócrata*, October 1, 1857; "Toing the Mark," *El Demócrata*, October 1, 1857, 3; "the aristocrat," "The Democrat," *Gazette*, April 18, 1857; "El Demócrata," *Gaceta*, April 25, 1857; also "El Demócrata and National Democracy," *Gazette*, August 22, 1857; "Politics in New Mexico," *Gazette*, September 30, 1857; "National Democracy—Gov. Floyd," *Gazette*, August 29, 1857; on "Rich Man's party," see "Nonconflicting Interests," *Weekly Press*, November 24, 1863.

85. "El Nativismo Triunfante"; "El Sr. Obispo Lamy," *Gaceta*, September 30, 1858; untitled, *Gaceta*, August 22, 1857; Anonymous to *Gazette*, August 29, 1857; Clever, "'¡Keep Cool!'"

86. Hopkins to Buchanan, July 11, 1857, in Ganaway, *New Mexico and Sectional Controversy*, 63; "Politically Bewildered" and "Políticamente Atolondrado," *Gazette*, September 20, 1858.

87. "It won't do, Mr. Davis," *Gazette*, August 29, 1857; "Politics in New Mexico," *Gazette*, September 30, 1857.

88. Miguel E. Pino, "Proclamación," and "Procedimientos de la Junta de Educación," *Gaceta*, May 17, 1856; "Procedimientos de la Junta de Educación," *Gaceta*, November 29, 1856; "Officiales de Batallón de Voluntarios Montados," *Gaceta*, March 17, 1855.

89. "Fourth of July Proceedings Today," *Gazette*, July 4, 1857; "The Celebration of the Fourth," *Gazette*, July 11, 1857.

90. Manuel Chávez to Juan Montoya, February 25, 1857, in Un Demócrata Nacional to editor, *Gazette*, March 28, 1857. For Chávez's role in the revolts of 1846 and the resistance to the Texas invasions of 1841, see Crutchfield, *Tragedy at Taos*, 98, 162–63.

91. Un Demócrata Nacional to *Gaceta*, July 4, 1857.
92. "The Next Delegate for New Mexico," *Gazette*, February 21, 1857.
93. "Aclaración de un misterio de la Demócrata Reservada," *Gaceta*, July 4, 1857.
94. "Judge Baird Candidate for Delegate," *Gazette*, pril 4, 1857, 2; "El Juez Baird Candidato para Delegado," *Gaceta*, April 11, 1857.
95. Miller, "Finis" and "Ridiculous," *Gazette*, August 22, 1857; "Baird and Otero," *Gazette*, July 11, 1857.
96. Rick Hendricks, "David J. Miller, Biographical Sketch," http://newmexicohistory.org/people/david-j-miller, accessed January 3, 2015.
97. "Padre Gallegos," *Gaceta*, September 12, 1857; David Miller to editor, *Gazette*, May 22, 1858; also Stratton, *Territorial Press of New Mexico*, 90; Theisen, "José Manuel Gallegos," 122–23.
98. "Aclaración de un misterio de la Demócrata Reservada," *Gaceta*, July 4, 1857; "The Democratic Convention at Algodones in 1853," *Gazette*, April 11, 1857; Antoine Leroux to *Gaceta*, August 29, 1857; Lino Trujillo to *Gaceta*, August 29, 1857.
99. Theisen, "José Manuel Gallegos," 123–24.
100. "Judge Baird and Taxes," *Gazette*, July 4, 1857; "El Juez Baird y Tasaciones," *Gaceta*, July 11, 1857.
101. "El Nativismo Triunfante," *Demócrata*, October 1, 1857.
102. "El Chino Tejano," *Gaceta*, August 15, 1857"; "Can the Editor of El Demócrata Answer?," Preguntón to *Gazette*, August 29, 1857.
103. Preguntón, "Can the Editor"; "The Late Canvass," *Gazette*, September 12, 1857; "Politics in New Mexico," *Gazette*, September 30, 1857; also "'El Demócrata' and National Democracy, *Gazette*, August 22, 1857.
104. Juan Benavides et al., "Junta Pública de los Demócratas Nacionales," *Gaceta*, April 3, 1857.
105. Preston Beck et al., "Convención del Condado de Santa Fe de los Demócratas Nacionales," *Gaceta*, August 15, 1857; "The Convention Nominees," *Gazette*, August 15, 1857.
106. Howe, *Political Culture of the American Whigs*, 65.
107. Carlos Beaubien et al., "Convención del Condado de Taos," *Gaceta*, August 15, 1857.
108. Juan C Armijo et al., "Convención del condado de Bernalillo," *Gaceta*, August 22, 1857; untitled, *Gazette*, August 22, 1857.
109. Anonymous to *Gazette*, August 29, 1857.
110. Clever, "'¡Keep Cool!'"; Hunt, *Kirby Benedict*, 155n26.
111. J. Perea to the Central Committee of the national Democrats of the County of Santa Fe, *Gazette*, August 22, 1857; Preston Beck, "La Convención del Condado de Santa Fe," *Gaceta*, August 29, 1857; "Nominación para Alcalde y Alguacil," *Gaceta*, August 22, 1857.
112. Untitled, *Gazette*, August 22, 1857; "The Meeting of the 'Bobtails'" Tomorrow," *Gazette*, August 22, 1857; "La Junta de los 'Descolados' el Domingo Próximo Pasado," *Gaceta*, August 29, 1857.

113. Samuel Ellison to J. J. Webb, September 30, 1857, Santa Fe, in Weber, "Samuel Ellison on the Election of 1857," 217–18.

114. Uno con Cola to Santa Fe, *Gaceta*, August 29, 1857.

115. F. Repito to *Gaceta*, February 7, 1857.

116. Francisco Gonzales, El Repito, to editor and to Señor Don José Antonio Martínez, *Gaceta,* August 15, 1857. Angélico Chávez states that Martínez was not the one to have started this fight, but rather Vicente Ferrer Romero, a younger nativo priest whom Chávez claims was in open schism with Bishop Lamy's church in New Mexico. The translation of "chuchos y alcahuetes" as "foot-licking pimps and minions" is by Chávez, *But Time*, 144–45.

117. Un Demócrata Nacional to *Gaceta*, July 4, 1857.

118. "Respuesta del ignorante, Expectador a un Ignorante Preguntón," *Gaceta*, August 29, 1857.

119. "Muerte con sus Propias Armas," *Gaceta*, August 22, 1857.

120. Clever, "'¡Keep Cool!'"

121. L., "José Antonio Otero," *Gaceta*, August 22, 1857. For an explicitly anti-Baird verse, see "Otero en Taos," *Gaceta*, August 22, 1857.

122. "Mas Claro no Canta un Gallego," anonymous to *Gaceta*, August 29, 1857.

123. Dav. J. Miller, "Finis," *Gazette*, September 30, 1857; "Ridiculous," *Gazette*, August 22, 1857.

124. "'El Demócrata' and National Democracy, *Gazette*, August 22, 1857. For other essays with references to patriotism, the Jeffersonian roots of the National party and the significance of Buchanan's cabinet appointments, see "National Democracy," and "La Democracia Nacional," *Gazette*, July 11, 1857; "National Democracy—Gov. Floyd," *Gazette*, August 29, 1857.

125. Ganaway, *New Mexico and Sectional Controversy*, 58; W. W. H. Davis, "To the Readers of the Santa Fe Gazette," *Gazette*, February 16, 1856; "At his old Tricks," *Gazette*, August 15, 1857; "Alert, National Democrats!," *Gazette*, April 25, 1857.

126. "¡Lean, Nuevo Mejicanos!," *Gazette*, August 8, 1857; also August 15, 1857; August 22, 1857.

127. El Espectador, "Respuesta del ignorante Expectador a un Ignorante Preguntón," *Gaceta*, August 29, 1857; "Mas Claro no Canta un Gallego," anonymous to *Gaceta*, August 29, 1857.

128. "Additional Extracts from 'El Gringo,'" *Gazette*, August 8, 1857.

129. "W. W. H. Davis, President of the Peña Blanca Baird Convention," *Gazette*, July 4, 1857.

130. "Judge Baird and 'El Gringo' Days Again," *Gazette,* August 22, 1857; also untitled, *Gazette*, August 15, 1857; untitled in Spanish, August 22, 1857; August 29, 1857.

131. Sydney A. Hubble to *Gazette*, August 8, 1857.

132. W. W. H. Davis, "To the Readers of the Santa Fe Gazette," *Gazette*, February 16, 1856.

133. W. W. H. Davis to the *Doylestown Democrat*, August 23, 1859, and March 29, 1859, in Hepler, "William Watts Hart Davis in New Mexico," 172–73, 180. Davis gained recognition for his writing on New Mexico from scholars and pop-

ular authorities; Christine M. Van Ness and John R. Van Ness, "W. W. H. Davis: Neglected Figure of New Mexico's Early Territorial Period," *Journal of the West* 16, no. 3 (1977): 68–74.

134. "Mr. Otero in the Rio Arriba," *Gazette*, July 11, 1857.

135. Jno. F. Hutchinson, "Mr. Otero's Reception in the Mora Valley," *Gazette*, August 29, 1857.

136. "Mr. Otero in the Rio Abajo," *Gazette*, July 11, 1857.

137. "Judge Baird at Santa Clara," *Gazette*, August 15, 1857; "El Juez Baird en Santa Clara," *Gaceta*, August 22, 1857.

138. "Otero en Taos," *Gaceta*, August 22, 1857.

139. Un Observador to *Gaceta*, February 14, 1857; Chávez and Chávez, *Wake*, 175; Chávez, *Très Macho*, 74.

140. Samuel Ellison to J. J. Webb, September 30, 1857, Santa Fe, in "Samuel Ellison on the Election of 1857," 219.

141. Ellison to Webb, 219; untitled, *Gazette* August 22, 1857.

142. Mr. Otero in the Rio Arriba," *Gazette*, July 11, 1857.

143. Anonymous to *Gazette*, August 29, 1857; see also Jno. F. Hutchinson, "Mr. Otero's Reception in the Mora Valley," *Gazette*, August 29, 1857; "Otero en Taos," *Gazette*, August 22, 1857.

144. "Mr. Otero in the Rio Abajo," *Gazette*, July 11, 1857; also "Judge Baird at Santa Clara," *Gazette*, August 15, 1857; "El Juez Baird en Santa Clara," *Gaceta*, August 22, 1857.

145. "Ley de Educación," *Gaceta*, August 22, 1857.

146. "¡Atención Demócratas Descolados!," *Gaceta*, August 15, 1857; "Attention, 'Demócratas Descolados!," *Gaceta*, August 22, 1857.

147. "A la Democracia Nacional de Nuevo Mejico," *Gaceta*, August 15, 1857; also "Los Jueces de la Elección—Imparcialidád," *Gaceta*, August 15, 1857.

148. W. W. H. Davis certificate of election, September 8, 1857, Records of the Secretary of the Territory, 1851–1911, reel 21, frames 180–81, TANM; untitled, *Gazette*, September 30, 1858; Miller to editor, May 22, 1858; "News From New Mexico," *St. Louis Leader*, in *Gazette*, January 2, 1858; "Politics in New Mexico," *Gazette*, September 30, 1857; "Overwhelming Rebuke!," *Gazette*, September 12, 1857; "Judge Deavenport Repudiated," *Gazette*, September 12, 1857. Official election canvasses for New Mexico prior to 1888 are not extant.

149. David Miller to editor, *Gazette*, May 22, 1858.

150. "Padre Gallegos," *Gazette*, September 12, 1857; Theisen, "José Manuel Gallegos," 125.

151. "The Legislature of New Mexico," and untitled editorial, *Gazette*, December 12, 1857.

152. "Politics in New Mexico," *Gazette*, September 310, 1857.

153. "Overwhelming Rebuke!," *Gazette*, September 12, 1857.

154. "A Suggestion to Honest Men" and "Una Sugestión a Hombres Honestos," *Gazette/Gaceta*, September 30, 1857.

155. "Judge S. M. Baird and Hon. M. A. Otero," *Gazette*, January 9, 1858; "Politics in New Mexico," *Gazette*, September 30, 1857.

156. Joint Resolution VI, approved December 29, 1857, in *Laws of the Territory of New Mexico, 1857–58*, 88; C. P. Clever, "Joint Resolutions," *Gazette*, December 12, 1857; "Hon. Perry S. Brocchus," *Gazette*, December 12, 1857.

157. Untitled editorial, *Gazette*, January 2, 1858.

158. F. G. to the editor, *Gazette*, December 19, 1857.

159. Q. S. M. B. to *Gazette*, January 23, 1858.

160. "The Rio Arriba Contested Election Case," *Gazette*, December 19, 1857; Un Chimayo to *Gaceta* ("La Contesta de la Elección del Condado de Río Arriba"), December 19, 1857.

161. "To the Public," *Gazette*, December 5, 1857.

162. Untitled editorial, *Gazette*, December 12, 1857.

163. "The Legislature of New Mexico," *Gazette*, December 5, 1857.

164. "To the Public," "Territorial Secretary," *Gazette*, December 5, 1857; also S. M. Yost, "Salutory," *Gazette*, December 5, 1857; Dav. J. Miller, "Finis," *Gazette*, September 30, 1857; Ganaway, *New Mexico and Sectional Controversy*, 65; "guarded," Horn, *New Mexico's Troubled Years*, 74; "The New Territorial Administration," *Gazette*, January 9, 1958; "La Nueva Administración Territorial," *Gaceta*, January 16, 1858.

165. "El Nativismo Triunfante," *El Demócrata*, October 1, 1857.

166. "A Territory without a Government," *Gazette*, October 31, 1857; "An Insidious Attack," *Gazette*, September 30, 1858; "The New Territorial Administration," *Gazette*, January 9, 1858.

167. "A Territory without a Government"; "¡Ho! For Salt River!," *Gazette*, September 12, 1857; Samuel Ellison to J. J. Webb, September 30, 1857, Santa Fe, in Weber, "Samuel Ellison on the Election of 1857," 217–18.

168. "Un Epitafo para 'El Gringo' Davis," *Gaceta*, August 15, 1857.

169. Gonzales, "La Junta de Indignación."

170. Executive Records, reel 21, frame 175, TANM.

171. David Miller to editor, *Gazette*, May 22, 1858.

172. Anonymous to Mr. Editor, *Gazette*, May 1, 1858; "El Discurso del Hon. M. A. Otero," *Gaceta*, August 21, 1858.

173. "Democratic Convention" and José María Valdez et al., "Convención de los Demócratas," *Gaceta*, July 24, 1858; also "José M. Martínez et al., "Junta de los Demócratas Nacionales," *Gaceta*, August 7, 1858; Jesús Pacheco, untitled, *Gazette*, August 7, 1858.

174. "Elección," *Gaceta*, August 21, 1858; also untitled, *Gazette*, August 21, 1858.

175. Untitled editorial, *Gazette*, August 21, 1858.

176. "Representates Elegidos," *Gaceta*, October 2, 1858; untitled, *Gazette*, December 11, 1858.

177. "Civil Appointments for New Mexico," *Gazette*, November 1, 1856.

178. "Lorenzo Martínez et al., "Meeting of the National Democracy," *Gazette*, May 21, 1859; "Junta Pública en el Río de Tesuque," *Gaceta*, August 10, 1859, and August 28, 1859; "Junta del Condado de Santa Fe," *Gazette*, August 10, 1859, 3, and August 28, 1859; "Junta Pública en Santa Fe," *Gaceta*, August 10, 1859, and August 28, 1859; "La Democracia Nacional del Cuarto Precinto," *Gaceta*, August 10, 1859; "County

Convention of National Democrats," *Gazette*, August 20, 1859; "Junta Demócrata Nacional," August 10, 1859; "County Meeting of Santa Fe," *Gazette*, August 28, 1859; "Convención Demócrata Nacional," *Gaceta*, September 3, 1859.

179. As Hezekiah Johnson recalled in "Nonconflicting Interests," *Weekly Press*, November 24, 1863.

180. "Hon. Miguel Antonio Otero," *Gazette*, January 22, 1859; "Our Territorial Convention and Its Nominee," *Gazette*, July 30, 1859; "National Democracy of New Mexico, Proceedings of the Territorial Convention of National Democracy of New Mexico held at Albuquerque on the first Monday of June 1859, *Gazette*, July 30, 1859.

181. Theisen, "José Manuel Gallegos," 125.

182. H. Connelly, "National Democracy of New Mexico, Proceedings of the Territorial Convention of National Democracy of New Mexico held at Albuquerque on the first Monday of June 1859, published in *Gazette*, July 30, 1859; "The Two Candidates," *Gazette*, August 10, 1859; "National Democratic Politics in New Mexico, *Gazette*, August 20, 1859.

183. "The Two Candidates," *Gazette*, August 28, 1859; Connelly, "National Democracy."

184. Bancroft, *History of Arizona and New Mexico*, 650n22; Twitchell, *Leading Facts*, 2: 283, 310; Theisen, "José Manuel Gallegos," 125–26.

185. "Bonita Dilegencia," *Gaceta*, August 10, 1859; untitled, *Gazette*, August 20, 1859; untitled editorial, *Gazette*, August 28, 1859; "Trabajo con Engaño," *Gazette*, August 28, 1859.

186. "National Democratic Politics in New Mexico," *Gazette*, August 20, 1859; untitled, *Gazette*, August 28, 1859; also "¡Alerta! ¡Alerta!," *Gaceta*, August 28, 1859; "Los Descolados Acesan Pecados Agenos y los Suyos los Esconden!," *Gaceta*, August 28, 1859; "La Verdád es como el Maíz: Siempre Sale," *Gaceta*, August 28, 1859.

187. "Hon. M. A. Otero," *Gazette*, September 3, 1859.

188. Two anonymous letters and one from Q.S.M.B. to *Gazette*, August 28, 1859.

189. "The Result," *Gazette*, September 24, 1859; Theisen, "José Manuel Gallegos," 130–31.

190. Executive Records, reel 21, frame 190, TANM.

191. Miguel Antonio Otero to Alexander M. Jackson, December 16, 1858, in Hunt, *Kirby Benedict*, 113, and 113–19; Whiting, "Minutes of the Historical Society," 271, 292; Kellogg, "Lincoln's New Mexico Patronage," 514; Ganaway, *New Mexico and Sectional Controversy*, 66–76; Lamar, *Far Southwest*, 91; Larson, *New Mexico's Quest*, 64–65; Theisen, "José Manuel Gallegos," 121–22; Brooks, *Captives and Cousins*, 329–30; Gómez, "Off-White in an Age of White Supremacy," 44–46; Horn, *New Mexico's Troubled Years*, 86.

192. "New Mexico and Her Situation," *Santa Fe New Mexican*, December 19, 1863.

193. "Governor's Message to the Legislature," December 14, 1859, Executive Records, reel 21, frame 241, TANM.

Part 3. Party Modalities in the Time of Civil War

1. S. B. Watrous to editors, August 1, 1865 ("Letter from S.B. Watrous"), *Santa Fe New Mexican* (hereafter *New Mexican*), August 11, 1865; "An Historical Item," *New Mexican*, December 24, 1963.

2. See S. P. Chase, Charles Sumner, J. R. Giddings, Edward Wade, Gerritt Smith, and Alexander De Witt, "Appeal of the Independent Democrats," January 19, 1854, http://civilwarcauses.org/kansas.htm.

3. "Latest News from the States," *Gazette*, January 9, 1858; Huston, *The Panic of 1857*, 140, 163, 166, 167; "Senator Douglas," *Gazette*, August 21, 1858; New Mexico, "Letter from Washington," *Gazette*, November 27, 1858.

7. Low Tide in the Partisan Divide

1. Huston, *Stephen A. Douglas*, 162–64.

2. Stratton, *Territorial Press of New Mexico*, 8; "The Presidential Campaign," *Gazette*, October 27, 1860; untitled editorial, *Gazette*, September 22, 1860.

3. As New Mexicans could see; "The Presidential Election," *Albany Argus*, in *Gazette*, January 5, 1861.

4. Miguel A. Otero to James Collins, November 9, 1860, in *Gazette*, December 8, 1860.

5. "From the States," *Gazette*, January 12, 1861; Stegmaier, "New Mexico's Delegate," 513–14.

6. New Mexico readers encountered the proposal in "The Crittenden Resolutions," *Gazette*, February 16, 1861.

7. Larson, *New Mexico's Quest*, 84.

8. Stegmaier, "'Imaginary Negro,'" 266–70; Ganaway, *New Mexico and Sectional Controversy*, 77–78; Crofts and Cress, *Reluctant Confederates*, 204.

9. Stegmaier, "'Imaginary Negro,'" 270; "Shall New Mexico Become a State?," *Gazette*, January 12, 1861; quote from "A State Government," *Gazette*, January 19, 1861; "Procedimientos de la Legislatura: Consejo," *Gaceta*, December 22, 1860.

10. Stegmaier, "New Mexico's Delegate," 387–88.

11. Stegmaier, "New Mexico's Delegate," 388; Stegmaier, "'Imaginary Negro,'" 270; Ganaway, *New Mexico and Sectional Controversy*, 80–81.

12. Horace Greeley, "New Mexico," *New York Tribune*, December 31, 1860, in Ganaway, *New Mexico and Sectional Controversy*, 80.

13. Bilotta, *Race and the Rise*, 12; see also Stegmaier, "'Imaginary Negro,'" 274.

14. Greeley, "New Mexico."

15. This account of Otero's extended response is based on Miguel A. Otero to the Editor of the *Constitution*, Washington DC, January 5, 1861, in *Gazette*, February 16, 1861; Otero, *An Abolition Attack upon New Mexico and a Reply by Hon. M. A. Otero* (Santa Fe: Santa Fe Gazette Office, 1861); Stegmaier, "New Mexico's Delegate," 515–21; cf. Ganaway, *New Mexico and Sectional Controversy*, 82; Kiser, "A 'charming name,'" 172; Stegmaier, "'Imaginary Negro,'" 280–81.

16. Bilotta, *Race and the Rise*, 28

17. For the definitive study, see Brooks, *Captives and Cousins*.

18. Stegmaier, "New Mexico's Delegate," 388–89.

19. Crofts and Cress, *Reluctant Confederates*, 241–42, 243, 250; Stegmaier, "'Imaginary Negro,'" 283–84.

20. For example, "The National Crisis," *Gazette*, January 2, 1861; "Late from the States," *Gazette*, January 19, 1861; "About Dissolution," *Gazette*, January 19, 1861; "Latest from the States," *Gazette*, January 19, 1861.

21. Horn, *New Mexico's Troubled Years*, 87.

22. Enquirer to Mr. Editor, *Gazette*, January 19, 1861, 1; S. M. Baird to Mr. Editor, *Gazette*, January 12, 1861, 2; cf. Larson, *New Mexico's Quest*, 84.

23. Kellogg, "Lincoln's New Mexico Patronage," 521–22; also Kirby Benedict to Hon. Edward Bates, June 25, 1861, in Hunt, *Kirby Benedict*, 150–53; Larson, *New Mexico's Quest*, 84; Hunt, *Major General James Henry Carleton*, 208, 260–62.

24. Juan M. Baca, Faustín Baca y Ulivarri, A. Morrison, and Severo Baca, "Union Meeting," proceedings of a meeting held in Las Vegas NM, March 27, 1861, *Gazette*, April 13, 1861.

25. New Mexico readers beheld the start of the Civil War in "The Attack on Fort Sumter!" and "War Commenced," *Gazette*, May 4, 1861.

26. Lamar, *Far Southwest*, 90; Colton, *The Civil War*, 192; Ganaway, *New Mexico and Sectional Controversy*, 92–94; Horn, *New Mexico's Troubled Years*, 86.

27. Kirby Benedict to His Excellency Abraham Lincoln, June 2, 1861, in Hunt, *Kirby Benedict*, 136–38; Kirby Benedict to Hon. Edward Bates, June 16 and 25, 1861, in Hunt, *Kirby Benedict*, 145–50, 150–53; Colton, *Civil War*, 191; Horn, *New Mexico's Troubled Years*, 87; Murphy, *Frontier Crusader*, 115.

28. Horn, *New Mexico's Troubled Years*, 89.

29. Horn, *New Mexico's Troubled Years*, 87, 89; Colton, *Civil War*, 191–92.

30. Kirby Benedict to His Excellency Abraham Lincoln, June 2, 1861, in Hunt, *Kirby Benedict*, 136; Kirby Benedict to Hon. Edward Bates, June 16, 1861, in Hunt, *Kirby Benedict*, 145–50.

31. Larson, *New Mexico's Quest*, 86.

32. Jon. R. Baylor (Lt. Col. Com. Mid. R Flea, C.S.A.), "Proclamation: To the People of the Territory of Arizona," August 2, 1861, in *Gazette*, August 17, 1861; "being little short," untitled, *Gazette*, August 31, 1861.

33. Thompson, "Brave Christian Soldiers," 266; Ganaway, *New Mexico and Sectional Controversy*, 92–93.

34. Kellogg, "Lincoln's New Mexico Patronage," 514–15; Twitchell, *Leading Facts*, 2: 392n317, 283.

35. Kellogg, "Lincoln's New Mexico Patronage," 513–15, 522–23, 529.

36. Murphy, "William F. M. Arny," 325; Kellogg, "Lincoln's New Mexico Patronage," 523.

37. "Death of Ex. Governor Henry Connelly," *Gazette*, August 18, 1866, 2; Kellogg, "Lincoln's New Mexico Patronage," 514; Horn, *New Mexico's Troubled Years*, 93–94.

38. "Gov. Connelly's Reception," *Gazette*, August 31, 1861.

39. Henry Connelly, "Inaugural Address of Gov. Connelly," in *Gazette*, September 7, 1861; Henry Connelly, "Proclamation by the Governor," September 9, 1861, Governor's Papers, Connelly, reel 1, frame 343, RTG, TANM; also in *Gazette*, September 14, 1861; [NM Governor] Enrique Connelly, "Requisición Militar," October

29, 1861, Governor's Papers, Connelly, reel 1, frame 344, RTG, TANM; Horn, *New Mexico's Troubled Years*, 98–100; see also Colton, *Civil War*, 191–92; Twitchell, *Leading Facts*, 2: 381–92; Murphy, "William F.M. Arny," 325–26; Kellogg, "Lincoln's New Mexico Patronage," 517–18.

40. "Nombramientos Para Nuevomexico, *Gaceta*, May 25, 1861; Kellogg, "Lincoln's New Mexico Patronage," 516–17.

41. Kellogg, "Lincoln's New Mexico Patronage," 523–24; Ganaway, *New Mexico and Sectional Controversy*, 92–94.

42. Quoted in Kellogg, "Lincoln's New Mexico Patronage," 519, 521; the "half-breed Hidalgo" aspersion quoted in Stegmaier, "New Mexico's Delegate," 522.

43. Kellogg, "Lincoln's New Mexico Patronage," 514–15; Murphy, *Frontier Crusader*, 117; Colton, *Civil War*, 192; Theisen, "José Manuel Gallegos," 31–32.

44. Colton, *Civil War*, 272.

45. Kellogg, "Lincoln's New Mexico Patronage," 519; Brooks, *Captives and Cousins*, 330; Gómez, "Off-White in an Age of White Supremacy," 39; Lamar, *Far Southwest*, 91; Theisen, "José Manuel Gallegos," 127–28.

46. Russell says he proposed the convention, "Judge Watts for Delegate," *Gazette*, July 6, 1861.

47. Foner, *Fiery Trial*, 171–74.

48. Michael Les Benedict, *A Compromise of Principle*.

49. "About Dissolution," *Gazette*, January 19, 1861.

50. Bancroft, *History of Arizona and New Mexico*, 650n22; Twitchell, *Leading Facts*, 2: 283, 305, 310; Theisen, "José Manuel Gallegos," 125–26.

51. Thompson, *The Army and the Navajo*, 84.

52. Joab Houghton, President, and Nicolás Quintana, Secretary, "Public Meeting," *Gazette*, July 6 1861, including John S. Watts to Gentlemen, July 3, 1861; cf. Theisen, "José Manuel Gallegos," 127–29; Lamar, *Far Southwest*, 91, 101.

53. "Judge Watts for Delegate," *Gazette*, July 6, 1861.

54. "Election for Delegate," *Gazette*, July 13, 1861.

55. Untitled editorial, *Gazette*, July 13, 1861.

56. "Judge Watts for Delegate," *Gazette*, July 6, 1861.

57. Francisco Tomás Cabeza de Baca to the people of the Territory of New Mexico, and to my friends, July 2, 1861, published in *Gazette*, July 13, 1861.

58. "County Candidates," *Gazette*, August 17, 1861.

59. Francisco Tomás Cabeza de Baca to the people of the Territory of New Mexico, and to my friends, July 2, 1861, in *Gazette*, July 13, 1861.

60. Untitled editorial, *Gazette*, July 13, 1861.

61. "County Candidates," *Gazette*, August 17, 1861; Colton, *Civil War*, 193.

62. Torrez, "San Juan Gold Rush," 263–64.

63. "Misrepresentations," *Gazette*, December 8, 1860; James L. Collins, "A Statement in Reference to Diego Archuleta," *Gazette*, December 15, 1860; "Indian Depredations," *Gazette*, January 18, 1862.

64. "The Election," *Gazette*, July 17, 1861.

65. Theisen, "José Manuel Gallegos," 128.

66. José M. Gallegos (President), Santiago Baca, and J. M. Edger, "County Convention," *Gazette*, July 17, 1861; "Procedimientos," *Gaceta*, August 17, 1861.

67. "County Candidates," *Gazette*, August 17, 1861.

68. "Procedimientos," *Gaceta*, August 17, 1861.

69. "The Election," *Gazette*, July 17, 1861; see also "The Election," *Gazette*, August 31, 1861; "La Elección," *Gaceta*, August 31, 1861, 3; "County Candidates," *Gazette*, August 17, 1861.

70. "County Candidates," *Gazette*, August 17, 1861; Twitchell, *Leading Facts*, 2: 392n317.

71. Untitled, *Gazette*, September 28, 1861; "Election for Delegate, *Gazette*, September 21, 1861.

72. "La Elección," *Gaceta*, September 14, 1861.

73. "The Legislative Assembly," *Gazette*, September 21, 1861; Chávez, *Très Macho*, 95; Theisen, "José Manuel Gallegos," 127.

74. Kellogg, "Lincoln's New Mexico Patronage," 516; Hunt, *Kirby Benedict*, 15, 24, 44, 50, 71; Murphy, "William F. M. Arny," 332.

75. Kirby Benedict to His Excellency Abraham Lincoln, June 2, 1861, in Hunt, *Kirby Benedict*, 135–36, 149n16; Kirby Benedict to Hon. Edward Bates, October 5, 1861, in Hunt, *Kirby Benedict*, 153–54.

76. Kirby Benedict to His Excellency Abraham Lincoln, February 17, 1861, in Hunt, *Kirby Benedict*, 134.

77. Facundo Pino (Presidente del Consejo Legislativo), and J. M. Gallegos (Presidente de la Camara de Representates), "Preamble and Resolutions of the Council and House of Representatives of the Legislative Assembly of the Territory of New Mexico in relation to the Hon. Kirby Benedict, Chief Justice," in *Gazette*, February 1, 1862.

78. Kellogg, "Lincoln's New Mexico Patronage," 516; Hunt, *Kirby Benedict*, 15, 24, 44; "El Juez Superior Kirby Benedict," *Gaceta*, June 28, 1862.

79. Kellogg, "Lincoln's, New Mexico Patronage" 517–18; quote, Horn, *New Mexico's Troubled Years*, 98–100; Theisen, "José Manuel Gallegos," 128–29; Colton, *Civil War*, 193–94.

8. Republican Toehold and the Partisan Normal

1. Glenn, *Unequal Freedom*, 54.

2. Rivera Ramos, *Legal Construction of Identity*, 164–65.

3. "Proclamation. James S. Calhoun, Governor of the Territory of New Mexico, to the People of Said Territory," March 18, 1851, Governor's Papers, reel 1, frame 219, RTG, TANM.

4. "Proclamation. James S. Calhoun, Governor and Commander-in-Chief of the Territory of New Mexico," October 24, 1851, Governor's Papers, reel 1, frame 221, RTG, TANM.

5. Bieber, "Introduction," *Journal of a Soldier*, 37–39; Devoto, *Year of Decision*, 248–49, 253; Edwards, "Journal of Marcellus Ball Edwards," 177, 210; Gibson, *Journal of a Soldier*, 240; S.W. Kearny to Captain James Allen, June 19, 1846, in Cooke, *The Conquest*, iv.

6. See, for example, "An Act Amendatory of the Militia Law of this Territory," in *Laws of the Territory of New Mexico . . . 1859-60*, Records of the States of the United States, microfilms, 1846-1861, N.M. B. 2, reel 1, 8-10. Also the 1855 militia organized to fight the Jicarillas and Capote Yutas; Memorial II, Session Laws of New Mexico, 1856-57, 98-100.

7. "An Act Authorizing the Loan of Public Arms," Session Laws of New Mexico, 1856-57, 44-47.

8. "The Militia Called into Active Service," *Gazette*, June 10, 1854; "Local Items," *Gazette*, June 17, 1854; "New Mexico Centenarian Dies," *El Combate* (Wagon Mound NM), December 6, 1902.

9. "An Act Amendatory of the Militia Law of this Territory," in *Laws of the Territory of New Mexico . . . 1859-60*, Records of the States of the United States, Microfilms, 1846-1861, N.M. B. 2, reel 1, 8-10; Lamar, *Far Southwest*, 99.

10. Thompson, "Brave Christian Soldiers," 266; [NM Governor] Enrique Connelly, "Requisición Militar," October 29, 1861, Governor's Papers, Connelly, reel 1, frame 344, RTG, TANM.

11. Colton, *Civil War*, 193-94; "Drive off," Larson, *New Mexico's Quest*, 85.

12. Thompson, "Brave Christian Soldiers," 265-87; George P. Anderson, *History of New Mexico*, 817.

13. Twitchell, *Leading Facts*, 2: 357-58, 359n284; Colton, *Civil War*, 191-92; Thompson, introduction to "An Indian Superintendent," 221.

14. Meketa, *Louis Felsenthal*, 29-31; Twitchell, *History of the Military Occupation*, 306-7; "Honor to whom honor is due," *Gazette*, 1 July 1865, 2.

15. Peters, *Kit Carson's Life*, 487-88.

16. Davis, *El Gringo*, 219. Historian Jerry Thompson observes that because of poor record keeping and lack of care in preserving documents, the exact number of men serving in the militia during the Civil War may never be known "with any degree of certainty"; Thompson, "Brave Christian Soldiers," 269. Estimates range from 2,500 to 4,000 Mexicans enlisting in the New Mexico Volunteers; see Miller, "Hispanos and the Civil War," 116, 106-7, 112; Meketa, *Legacy of Honor*, 191. One estimate is that 6,000 New Mexico citizens enlisted in the Union cause, but this exaggerated claim may have been made to help Congress see that New Mexico deserved statehood; L. Bradford Prince to editor ("The People of New Mexico: The Hon. L. Bradford Prince"), *New York Times*, February 28, 1882.

17. Thompson, "Brave Christian Soldiers," 266-67, 268, 272, 274.

18. A. B. Curry to Captain B. C. Cutter, February 28, 1864, box 31, Frank Driver Reeve Papers, Center for Southwest Research, University of New Mexico.

19. Thompson, "Brave Christian Soldiers," 266, 277, 288; also Peters, *Kit Carson's Life*, 487; Meketa, *Legacy of Honor*, 98. For one territorial legislature's attempts to get payment to the militiamen, see "An Act to Amend an Act entitled 'Militia,'" in *Laws of the Territory of New Mexico . . . 1866-67*, Records of the States of the United States, microfilms, 1862-1875, N.M. B. 2, reel 2, 56-66.

20. Miller, "Hispanos and the Civil War," 116, 106-7; Thompson, "Brave Christian Soldiers," 292-93.

21. Meketa, *Legacy of Honor*, quote 247, 275, 246–47, 274.

22. Thompson, "Brave Christian Soldiers," 266–67, 290, 291, 292–96.

23. Returning from the battlefield, Gov. Connelly "wrote to Secretary of State Seward, describing the battle at Valverde and the progress of the Texans who were moving toward Santa Fe and Fort Union. . . . He wrote: 'I am sorry to say that the Texans have not behaved with the moderation that was expected and that desolation has marked their program on the Rio Grande from Craig to Bernalillo." Horn, *New Mexico's Troubled Years*, 101; see, "Military Events in New Mexico," *Gazette*, April 4, 1862. Spruce Baird, former Mexican Party activist, had returned to Texas and was commissioned a colonel for the South, charged with recruiting men for his Fourth Arizona Brigade, Confederate Army. He was pulled off this duty before it could be fulfilled. After the war, he would be charged with disloyalty and his property was confiscated; Hunt, *Major General James Henry Carleton*, 244–45, 268.

24. Thompson, "Brave Christian Soldiers," 296–98; "New Mexican Invasions," *Gazette*, April 26, 1862; Horn, *New Mexico's Troubled Years*, 102; Colton, *Civil War*, 194–95.

25. "¡Honrad a el que lo Merece!," *Gaceta*, April 26, 1862; for accounts of Collins's military participation in the Civil War, see Kosmider, "Samuel B. Watrous," 58–61, and Thompson, ed. "An Indian Superintendent."

26. "Celebration of the Anniversary of our National Independence," *Gazette*, 28 June 1862, 2; "The Fourth," *Gazette*, July 5, 1862; quote, Un Observador to editors ("Correspondencia de Taos"), *New Mexican*, July 11, 1871; "Disurso del Honorable José Manuel Gallegos," *El Republicano*, July 12, 1862.

27. "True Blue Loyal Man," *Gazette*, May 3, 1862.

28. For a recent interpretation of these events see Foner, *Fiery Trial*, 171–75.

29. Untitled, *Gazette*, September 13, 1862.

30. On the buildup of criticism of the Lincoln administration's conduct of war and the rise of the Copperhead movement, see Jennifer L. Weber, *Copperheads*, 47–60; for the negative reaction to the Emancipation Proclamation, 58.

31. "Unity of Spirit," *National Intelligencer*, in *Gazette*, April 18, 1863; "The New Territory of Arizona," *New York Journal of Commerce*, in *Gazette*, April 18, 1863, 1.

32. "Prospectus of the Santa Fe *Republican*," *Republican* (Santa Fe), July 5 and July 12, 1862; [Johnson], "'Art Preservative.'"

33. Kellogg, "Lincoln's New Mexico Patronage," 516–17, 525; Colton, *Civil War*, 192; "True Blue Loyal Man," *Gazette*, May 3, 1862; "The New Mexican," *Gazette*, November 2, 1867; quotes, "Desperadoes," *New Mexican*, January 16, 1864.

34. "Watrous," Shirley Cushing Flint and Richard Flint, Courtesy of the New Mexico State Records Center and Archives webpage.

35. "Fort Building in New Mexico," *Republican*, July 5, 1862; "Is It Necessary," *Republican*, July 12, 1862; first quote, "Suppression of the Only Republican Paper in New Mexico," *Republican*, July 12, 1862; second quote, "James H. Holmes, Special notice to the Patrons of the *Republican*," *Republican*, July 12, 1862; untitled, *Republican*, July 12, 1862; "A Good Job Office in Santa Fe," *Republican*, July 12, 1862; "Notice to the Patrons of the Santa Fe *Republican*," August 17, 1862, in *Gazette*, August 30, 1862.

36. Emmett, *Fort Union*, 254-55; [Johnson], "'Art Preservative'"; untitled, *Gazette*, July 19, 1862; "The New Mexican," *Gazette*, November 2, 1867.

37. Quoted in Kellogg, "Lincoln's New Mexico Patronage," 525.

38. "The Public Printing," *Gazette*, July 19, 1862; "Holmes Drafts Protested," *Gazette*, October 18, 1862;"The Public Printing," *Gazette*, December 27, 1862; "The New Mexican," *Gazette*, November 2, 1867; "Desperadoes," *New Mexican*, January 16, 1864; Kellogg, "Lincoln's New Mexico Patronage," 524-25; Pioneer Women on the Santa Fe Trail, www.sangres.com/history/santafetrail/womenoftrail01.htm.

39. Henry Connelly, "To the People of New Mexico," *Gazette*, September 20, 1862; "Al Pueblo de Nuevo Mejico," *Gaceta*, September 20, 1862. Arny famously attended an 1861 reception at the White House dressed as a Mountain Man to plead the cause of his destitute Indian charges. Murphy, "William F. M. Arny," 323-24 ; Reeve, "The Federal Indian Policy," 56; Colton, *Civil War*, 192; Kellogg, "Lincoln's New Mexico Patronage," 528-29.

40. *Organic Law, Session Laws of New Mexico, 1st and 2nd Sessions*, Records of the States of the United States, microfilms, 1846-1861, N.M. B. 2, reel 1, 19.

41. Kiser, "A 'charming name,'" 184; Kellogg, "Lincoln's New Mexico Patronage," 528-29; Arny, *Executive message of his excellency, William F.M. Arny*, 12-13; Murphy, *Frontier Crusader*, 117-18; Murphy, "William F. M. Arny," 326-27; Murphy, "Reconstruction in New Mexico," 99-100. On the importance of free labor for the early Republican Party, see Foner, *Free Soil, Free Labor, Free Men*, 11-39.

42. Facundo Pino, President of the Legislative Council, and J. M. Gallegos, Speaker of the House of Representatives, "Preamble and Joint Resolution," *Gazette*, December 20, 1862; untitled, *Gazette*, December 20, 1862. According to Col. Thomas L. Fauntleroy, commander of the New Mexico Military Department, the Mexican militia companies often took the form of "free-booting, plundering parties" against the Navajo from 1860 when the New Mexico legislature passed a law permitting any individual "of experience and good character" to raise volunteer campaigns against warring Indians; Bailey, *Bosque Redondo*, 47-48.

43. Dispatch of the executive to the Honorable House of Representatives, Santa Fe, N.M., December 6, 1862, in *Gazette*, December 20, 1862.

44. "Our New Secretary," *Gazette*, September 6, 1862; "The Governor and Legislature," *Gazette*, December 20, 1862.

45. "The Public Printing," *Gazette*, December 27, 1862.

46. "Perea, the Young and the Jealousy," *New Mexican*, August 22, 1863.

47. "Perea, the Young and the Jealousy," *New Mexican*, August 22, 1863; "The New Mexican," *Gazette*, November 2, 1867; Hunt, *Kirby Benedict*, 209; Kirby Benedict to Hon. Edward Bates, January 3, 1864, in Hunt, *Kirby Benedict*, 166; Kirby Benedict to His Excellency Andrew Johnson, May 10, 1865, in Hunt, *Kirby Benedict*, 169. Rodney O. Davis, "Dr. Charles Leib: Lincoln's Mole?," *Journal of the Abraham Lincoln Association*, Summer 2003, 21, 32-33, http://www.historycooperative.org/journals/jala/24.2/davis.html, accessed February 4, 2011.

48. Collins is quoted to this effect in W.F.M. Arny to editors, *New Mexican*, September 15, 1865, 2; cf. Theisen, "José Manuel Gallegos," 145-46.

49. For the story of the Watrous-Collins feud, see Kosmider, "Samuel B. Watrous," ch. 3.

50. Murphy, "William F. M. Arny," 329.

51. The host of specific charges included receiving a rental fee from the government to pay for his office building; failure to carry out the laws of the New Mexico government; erecting an expensive house for the superintendency; charging the government exorbitant rent for use of a dwelling; depositing a note instead of cash with the receiver of the Land Office; and securing vouchers and blank receipts for the money going to the Indian Affairs office without making purchases. Kosmider, "Samuel B. Watrous," 68;

52. Untitled extract of a *Gazette* editorial of June 4, 1864, in "The Gazette's Demurrer," *Weekly Press*, June 14, 1864.

53. Murphy, "William F. M. Arny," 328–29; Murphy, *Frontier Crusader*, 120–21; Kosmider, "Samuel B. Watrous," 68–71; Reeve, "The Federal Indian Policy," 56, 59; Rodney O. Davis (see note 47), "Dr. Charles Leib," 32–33; Keleher, *Turmoil in New Mexico*, 410; Dailey, "Michael Steck," 136, 143–45, 146; "The Gazette's Demurrer," *Weekly Press*, June 14, 1864.

54. Pomeroy, *The Territories*, 111; Murphy, *Frontier Crusader*, 121; Murphy, "William F.M. Arny," 330.

55. Stone, *The Albion Press*.

56. "Our Enlargement, and Our Platform," *Weekly Press*, August 11, 1863. Johnson intended to initiate a bilingual paper, but the Spanish language type cast from the manufacturer was delivered late. He could not institute it until July. H. S. Johnson, "Prospecto de la Prensa Semanaria," *Weekly Press*, February 10, 1863; untitled, *Weekly Press*, March 32, 1863; "Our Paper's Prospects," *Weekly Press*, April 14, 1863.

57. Stratton, *Territorial Press of New Mexico*, 206n23; Bullis, *New Mexico: A Biographical Dictionary*, 127; Hezekiah S. Johnson, "Salutatory," *Weekly Press*, January 20, 1863; J. B. Hogan, "Last Rider: Sedalia, Missouri," *Frontier Tales*, frontiertales.com, accessed February 17, 2011; Murphy, "Reconstruction in New Mexico," 528; "General Carleton," *Weekly Press*, April 21, 1863; Bernalillo County Post Office History, rootsweb.ancestry.com/~nma/bernalillo/postoffice_bernalillo.htm-28k.

58. Johnson, "Prospecto de la Prensa Semanaria"; "Harmonious Elements," *Weekly Press*, April 21, 1863.

59. Hunt, *Kirby Benedict*, 208.

60. "A Glimpse at the Prospect," *Weekly Press*, June 23, 1863; "The New Mexican 'Versus' the Administration," *Weekly Press*, June 16, 1863.

61. "Brag," *Gazette*, August 15, 1863; Johnson, "Prospecto de la Prensa Semanaria"; "Misrepresentation," *Weekly Press*, March 24, 1863.

62. For example, "Copperhead Plot," *Weekly Press*, May 19, 1863; untitled editorial, *Crawford Journal*, n.d., in *Weekly Press*, April 21, 1863, 3; "Bold Words by the Democrats of Wisconsin," *Madison Patriot*, n.d., in *Weekly Press*, June 23, 1863; "Artemus Ward on Copperheads," *Weekly Press*, July 7, 1863; "Rebel Views of Northern Copperheads," *Weekly Press*, July 18, 1863.

63. *New Mexican* quoted in "Padre Gallegos is in favor of a State Government," *Gazette*, August 8, 1863.

64. "Padre Gallegos is in favor of a State Government," *Gazette*, August 8, 1863, 2.

65. "Gobierno de Estado," *Novo-Mejicano*, August 22, 1863 (see reference to name change of El Nuevo Mejicano later in the chapter); "The June-bug Convention," *Weekly Press*, reprinted in *Gazette*, May 16, 1863; "State Government," *Gazette*, July 18, 1863; "Politics in Santa Fe County this week," *Gazette*, June 6, 1863; "Some of that 'Will,'" *Weekly Press*, June 2, 1863; "Inharmonious Elements," *Weekly Press*, April 21, 1863; Theisen, "José Manuel Gallegos," 137–38.

66. "State Government," *Weekly Press*, March 3, 1863.

67. "Something to the Point," *Weekly Press*, March 10, 1863.

68. Menchaca, *Recovering History, Constructing Race*, 71. Father Ramón Ortiz settled Nuevomexicano expatriates there in 1848, in conflict with settled Euroamericans; see Hernández, *Mexican American Colonization*, 169–70.

69. Bartlett, *Personal Narrative of Explorations*, 212–13.

70. Charles A. Hoppin to James L. Collins, *Gazette*, April 11, 1857.

71. "Proclama del gobernador interino de Nuevo Méjico," W.F.M. Arny, Gobernador interino de N.M., *Nuevo-Mejicano*, April 25, 1863; in English, "Proclamation," *Gazette*, April 25, 1863; "Doña Ana County Reorganized," *Weekly Press*, April 21, 1863.

72. Nepumoceno Y. Ancheta (Presidente de la convención), and J. M. Taylor (Secretario de la convención), "Procedimientos de la convención tenida en el condado de Doña Ana de N. Méjico," *El Nuevo Mexicano*, April 25, 1863; "Proceedings of Convention held in Doña Ana County, New Mexico," in *Gazette*, April 25, 1863; "The Dona Ana Resolution," *New Mexican*, April 25, 1863.

73. "Some of that 'Will,'" *Weekly Press*, June 2, 1863; "More Exposure of Humbuggery," *Weekly Press*, June 9, 1863; "Padre Gallegos is in favor of a State Government," *Gazette*, August 8, 1863.

74. In his major accomplishment, Watts arranged for New Mexico to be relieved from federal taxation at least temporarily, in no small part because of the Indian curtailment of economic development in the settlements; untitled, *Gazette*, May 3, 1862.

75. Rio Abajo, "Communication: "More Democratic Absurdity," *Republican Review* (Santa Fe), July 22, 1871.

76. Cf. Twitchell, *Leading Facts*, 2: 392n317

77. "Perea Triumphant," *Gazette*, September 12, 1863.

78. Theisen, "José Manuel Gallegos," 130–32; Chávez, *Très Macho*, 98. Under the Confiscation Act of 1862, several Nuevomexicanos had property confiscated for the treason of supporting the rebellion; Hunt, *Major General James Henry Carleton*, 265, 268–69, 270.

79. "Inharmonious Elements," *Weekly Press*, April 21, 1863.

80. "How It Is," *Weekly Press*, April 14, 1863; also "More About It," *Weekly Press*, May 17, 1864; cf. Waldrip, "New Mexico during the Civil War" 84–85; Allison, "Colonel Francisco Perea," 219; Theisen, "José Manuel Gallegos," 132.

81. Francisco Perea to Fellow Citizens, *Gazette*, June 13, 1863; untitled, *Weekly Press*, January 27, 1863; Allison, "Colonel Francisco Perea," 219; "Muere en Albuquerque,"

El Nuevo Mexicano, March 29, 1913; Waldrip, "New Mexico during the Civil War," 84. For documentation on the economic fortunes of Nuevomexicano sheep tycoons and mercantilists after 1848, see Baxter, *Las Carneradas*; Boyle, *Los Capitalistas*; "New Mexico Sheep for California," *Gazette*, October 9, 1858; Colton, *Civil War*, 193.

82. "More About It" *Weekly Press*, May 17, 1864; "Perea Triumphant," *Gazette*, September 12, 1863; "Perea, the Young and the Jealousy," *New Mexican*, August 22, 1863; Francisco Perea to Fellow Citizens; "Politics in Santa Fe County This Week," *Gazette*, June 6, 1863; cf. Waldrip, "New Mexico during the Civil War," 84–85; Rio Abajo, "Communication: "More Democratic Absurdity," *Republican Review* (Santa Fe), July 22, 1871.

83. "Hon. Facundo Pino," *Weekly Press*, February 3, 1863; Joint Resolutions Honoring and lamenting the passing of Facundo Pino, lauding him, Approved January 29, 1863, in *Laws of the Territory of New Mexico . . . 1862–63*, Records of the States of the United States, microfilms, 1862–1875, N.M. B. 2, reel 2, 108–9; Hunt, *Kirby Benedict*, 131.

84. Facts gleaned from allusions in "Padre Gallegos is in favor of a State Government," *Gazette*, August 8, 1863; "The Will of The People," *Weekly Press*, May 19, 1863, 2; untitled, *Weekly Press*, June 9, 1863; "Our Paper's Prospects," *Weekly Press*, April 14 1863. Unfortunately, only a handful of issues of the *New Mexican* for 1863 survive, so it is not possible to know of its whole campaign in this year. Fortunately, to give their critiques credibility, both the *Gazette* and the *Press* quoted extensively from the *New Mexican* columns.

85. "Doña Ana County," *Gazette*, April 25, 1863; for Baca y Ulivarri's county provenance, "Noticias Locales," *Nuevo-Mejicano*, April 25, 1863; for Baca as a San Miguel County leader, untitled, *New Mexican,* January 31, 1864, and "Died," *New Mexican,* May 27, 1864.

86. "Padre Gallegos is in favor of a State Government," *Gazette*, August 8, 1863.

87. "The Movement," *Weekly Press*, March 24, 1863; "How It Is," *Weekly Press*, April 14, 1863; Theisen, "José Manuel Gallegos," 145–46, 131–32.

88. "Padre Gallegos is in favor of a State Government," *Gazette*, August 8, 1863.

89. "Doña Ana County," *Gazette*, April 25, 1863; "Politics in Santa Fe County This Week," *Gazette*, June 6, 1863.

90. "Our Paper's Prospects," *Weekly Press*, April 14, 1863.

91. "Right Views," *Weekly Press*, April 28, 1863.

92. "Inharmonious Elements," *Weekly Press*, April 21, 1863; also "The State of Utopia," *Weekly Press*, May 19, 1863; "The June-bug convention," *Weekly Press*, in *Gazette*, May 16, 1863.

93. Anonymous ("For the Santa Fe *Gazette*"), "The State Government," *Gazette*, May 30, 1863.

94. "The June-bug convention," *Weekly Press*, in *Gazette*, May 16, 1863.

95. "Independent Candidate for Delegate in Congress, Joab Houghton," *Weekly Press*, March 17, 1863.

96. "How It Is," *Weekly Press*, April 14, 1863.

97. "The Will of the People," *Weekly Press*, May 19, 1863.

98. "Honor to whom honor is due," *Gazette,* July 1, 1865.

99. "Discurso pronunciado por el Senor Nicolás Quintana en la ciudád de Santa Fe, el día 4 de Julio de 1863," *Gazette,* July 11, 1863.

100. Miguel E. Pino et al., "Procedimientos de una junta pública tenida en la ciudad de Santa Fe el domingo 17 de mayo de 1863," *Gazette,* May 23, 1863; "Inharmonious Elements," *Weekly Press,* April 21, 1863; the flier was included in "The Meeting Last Sunday," *Gazette,* May 23, 1863; also "La Junta el Domingo Pasado," *Gaceta,* May 23, 1863; "Young New Mexico Versus Fogyism," *Weekly Press,* June 2, 1863; "Some of that 'Will,'" *Weekly Press,* June 2, 1863.

101. "Politics in Santa Fe County this week," *Gazette,* June 6, 1863; "State Government," *Gazette,* July 18, 1863; Theisen, "José Manuel Gallegos," 135.

102. "Tit for Tat," *Gazette,* December 24, 1864; "Kirby Benedict," *Gazette,* August 5, 1865. For other suggestions of Benedict's ambition to be delegate, see "Judge Benedict," *Gazette,* December 12, 1857; Theisen, "José Manuel Gallegos," 135–36; Allison, "Colonel Francisco Perea," 2; Hunt, *Kirby Benedict,* 184; "Politics in Santa Fe County this Week," *Gazette,* June 6, 1863.

103. "Politics in Santa Fe County this week," *Gazette,* June 6, 1863; "Kirby Benedict," *Gazette,* August 5, 1865.

104. "People's Union Candidate," *Weekly Press,* June 16, 1863, reprinted in *Gazette,* June 27, 1863; "The Canvass for Delegate," *Weekly Press,* June 30, 1863, reprinted in *Gazette,* July 4, 1863; "Judge Benedict," *Gazette,* December 12, 1857; Theisen, "José Manuel Gallegos," 135–36; Allison, "Don Francisco Perea," 2; "Politics in Santa Fe County this week," *Gazette,* June 6, 1863; "N. Quintana to the People of New Mexico," *Gazette,* June 20, 1863.

105. "Politics in Santa Fe County this week," *Gazette,* June 6, 1863.

106. "N. Quintana to the People of New Mexico," *Gazette,* June 20, 1863.

107. "Multum in Parvo," *Weekly Press,* July 28, 1863.

108. "Politics in Santa Fe County this week," *Gazette,* June 6, 1863.

109. "Multum in Parvo," *Weekly Press,* July 28, 1863.

110. "Politics in Santa Fe County this week," *Gazette,* June 6, 1863; "State Government," *Gazette,* July 18, 1863; "Look out for the Fraud," *Gazette,* August 1, 1863; "Padre Gallegos is in favor of a State Government," *Gazette,* August 8, 1863; "He says so," *Gazette,* August 22, 1863; Theisen, "José Manuel Gallegos," 137–38.

111. "More Exposure of Humbuggery," *Weekly Press,* June 9, 1863.

112. "'The people he loves,'" *Gazette,* July 11, 1863.

113. "'The people he loves.'"

114. "Padre Gallegos as a Plunderer," *Gazette,* July 4, 1863; "His Charity," *Gazette,* August 1, 1863; cf. Theisen, "José Manuel Gallegos," 140.

115. Santiago L. Hubbell to editor, *New Mexican,* August 20, 1863, in *Weekly Press,* August 25, 1863.

116. "The Meeting Last Sunday," *Gazette,* May 23, 1863; "La Junta el Domingo Pasado," *Gaceta,* May 23, 1863; "Repudiated," *Gazette,* May 23, 1863; "No Hair on his Head, &c," *Gazette,* May 23, 1863; untitled, *Gazette,* May 23, 1863; cf. Theisen, "José Manuel Gallegos," 133–34.

117. "Young New Mexico Versus Fogyism," *Weekly Press*, June 2, 1863.
118. "In behalf of the young men of New Mexico," *Gazette*, June 27, 1863.
119. "People's Union Candidate," *Weekly Press*, June 16, 1863, reprinted in *Gazette*, June 27, 1863; "'El Candidato Unionista del Pueblo Para Delegado Al Congreso," *Gaceta*, June 27, 1863; Theisen, "José Manuel Gallegos," 142–43.
120. Theisen, "José Manuel Gallegos," 163–64; untitled, *Gazette*, July 18, 1863, 3; also anonymous paean to Gallegos's immorality, "El pequeño Padre," *Gazette*, August 29, 1863; also Chávez, *Très Macho*, 99–101.
121. "Multum in Parvo," *Weekly Press*, July 28, 1863.
122. "People's Union Candidate," *Weekly Press*, June 16, 1863, reprinted in *Gazette*, June 27, 1863; "'El Candidato Unionista del Pueblo Para Delegado Al Congreso," *Gaceta*, June 27, 1863.
123. "Nothing to do with his Private Character," *Gazette*, July 25, 1863.
124. "The Canvass for Delegate," *Weekly Press*, in *Gazette*, July 4, 1863; Theisen, "José Manuel Gallegos," 154n36.
125. "'Partidos,'" *Weekly Press*, July 14, 1863.
126. The quote actually has *no me espanten*, which would have meant the imperative "don't scare me." Given the context, I suggest it is a misprint and that the declarative *no me espantan*, "you don't scare me," is correct. "Don Miguel Pino," *Novo-Mejicano*, August 22, 1863.
127. "A Specialist," *Weekly Press*, February 3, 1863.
128. "'Partidos,'" *Weekly Press*, July 14, 1863.
129. "More About Prejudice," *Weekly Press*, July 21, 1863.
130. La Verdad to Fellow Citizens [Para el *Novo-Mejicano*], Agosto 18 de 1863, *Novo-Mejicano*, August 22, 1863.
131. Francisco Perea to Fellow Citizens, published in *Gazette*, June 13, 1863.
132. Untitled, *Gazette*, June 27, 1863.
133. Untitled, *Gazette*, June 27, 1863.
134. Untitled, *Weekly Press*, June 9, 1863.
135. This appears in a disparaging editorial referring to "certain demagogues" who believed that the counties of Santa Fe, Río Arriba, and Taos "should be the Territory"; "How It Is," *Weekly Press*, April 14, 1863; see also the reference to the "sectional" predispositions of Gallegos's politics in "The Next Legislature," *Weekly Press*, June 23, 1863.
136. Diego Archuleta to Don José Ignacio Cruz, August 28, 1863, in *New Mexican*, August 25, 1865; A Friend of the Country ("From Washington City"), *Gazette*, July 23, 1864.
137. "More About It," *Gazette*, May 17, 1864.
138. See, for example, *Weekly Press*, July 21, 1863; "Our Position on the Delegacy," *Weekly Press*, July 14, 1863.
139. "Withdrawal," *Gazette*, July 4, 1863; cf. Theisen, "José Manuel Gallegos," 135–36.
140. After months without a paycheck and questions raised about the propriety of his traveling to Washington without formally taking leave, Arny appealed to President Lincoln to authorize payment of his salary, as the expense of moving his

family to New Mexico and the expenses of government he paid out of pocket had taken a toll on the means for providing for his family. W.F.M. Arny to His Excellency Abraham Lincoln, May 12, 1864, New Mexico: Board of Commssioners Letterbook (second set of letters), William G. Ritch Papers, microfilm, reel 10, frames 54–55 (original in the Huntington Library, San Marino CA), Center for Southwest Research, University of New Mexico.

141. "Juntita," *Gazette*, August 15, 1863; "Gallegos as drawn by Clever," *New Mexican*, July 27, 1867; "Honor to whom honor is due," *Gazette*, July 1, 1865.

142. "Don Miguel Pino," *Novo-Mejicano*, August 22, 1863; "Don Diego Archuleta," *Novo-Mejicano*, August 22, 1863; "Boleta de Gallegos Para el Condado," *Novo-Mejicano*, August 22, 1863, 3; "Los Señores Jesús María Baca y Salazar y Victor Garcia," *Novo-Mejicano*, August 22, 1863; "An Explanation," *Gazette*, November 26, 1864.

143. C. P. Clever, "Valedictory," *New Mexican*, November 7, 1863; "Dr. Charles Leib," *New Mexican*, November 7, 1863; cf. Rodney O. Davis (see note 47 to this chapter), "Dr. Charles Leib," 32–33; "Juntita," *Gazette*, August 15, 1863; "The *New Mexican*," *Gazette*, November 2, 1867; Allison, "Don Francisco Perea," 2; Hunt, *Kirby Benedict*, 207–8; Theisen, "José Manuel Gallegos," 138, 158n67; "Tit for Tat," *Gazette*, 31 December 1864, 2; "Gobierno de Estado," *Nuevo-Mejicano*, August 22, 1863, 3; Hunt, *Kirby Benedict*, 208–10.

144. M. Ashurst et al., "Santa Fe County Convention," *Gazette*, July 25, 1863, and "Santa Fe Resolutions," *Weekly Press*, August 4, 1863, 1; "Union ticket," *Gazette*, July 25, 1863; untitled, *Weekly Press*, August 4, 1863.

145. "The Convention," *Gazette*, July 25, 1863; Joab Houghton et al., "Junta Pública," *Gazette*, July 18, 1863.

146. Ashurst et al., "Santa Fe County Convention."

147. "Who's to Blame?–Compromise," *Weekly Press*, August 4, 1863; untitled, *Gazette*, August 29, 1863.

148. "Who's to Blame?–Compromise," *Weekly Press*, August 4, 1863; "For the *Río Abajo Weekly Press*," *Gazette*, August 22, 1863.

149. "For the *Río Abajo Weekly Press*," *Gazette*, August 22, 1863.

150. "Etiquette and Truth," *Weekly Press*, August 25, 1863.

151. Untitled editorial, *Gazette*, September 5, 1863.

152. Untitled, *Weekly Press*, August 4, 1863.

153. William H. Henrie, "Proceedings," *Weekly Press*, August 11, 1863; "Bernalillo County Ticket," *Gazette*, August 22, 1863.

154. Untitled, *Gazette*, July 11, 1863.

155. Looker on to Mr. Editor, July 29, 1863, *Gazette*, August 8, 1863.

156. Ceran St. Vrain et al. to Mr. Editor, *Gazette*, August 15, 1863.

157. "How it Works," *Weekly Press*, August 11, 1863.

158. "More About It," *Weekly Press*, May 17, 1864.

159. El Mágico, La Venganza [Señor Editor], *Novo-Mejicano*, August 22, 1863.

160. "Juntita," *Gazette*, August 15, 1863, 2; "Declined," *Gazette*, July 25, 1863, 2.

161. "Perea, the Young and the Jealousy," *New Mexican*, August 22, 1863.

162. "County Meeting," *Gazette*, July 18, 1863; untitled, *Gazette*, July 18, 1863.

163. "Don Miguel Pino," *Novo-Mejicano*, August 22, 1863; "Juntita," *Gazette*, August 15, 1863.

164. "Gallegos Usurping the Powers of the President of the United States," *New Mexican*, August 22, 1863.

165. "The Prospects," *Gazette*, August 29, 1863.

166. "Perea Triumphant," *Gazette*, September 12, 1863.

167. "Frauds," *Gazette*, September 19, 1863; "Violadores de Elecciones Arrestados," *Novo-Mexicano*, November 7, 1863.

168. "The Election in Santa Fe Co.," *Gazette*, September 12, 1863.

169. Allison, "Don Francisco Perea," 2; Murphy, *Frontier Crusader*, 124–25; Murphy, "William F.M. Arny," 332–34; Theisen, "José Manuel Gallegos," 139–40, 143.

170. "The Certificate of Election," *Gazette*, September 26, 1863.

171. "Padre Gallegos and his Partizans," *Gazette*, September 26, 1863; cf. Theisen, "José Manuel Gallegos," 134.

172. "The Legislative Assembly," *New Mexican*, December 19, 1863; Murphy, *Frontier Crusader*, 124–25; Murphy, "William F.M. Arny," 332–34; Theisen, "José Manuel Gallegos," 144–45; "Gallegos and his Contest," *New Mexican*, May 21, 1864.

173. "The Next Legislature," *Gazette*, June 27, 1863.

174. "The Legislature Organized on Monday," *New Mexican*, December 5, 1862; "Don Diego Archuleta," *New Mexican*, December 5, 1863; "The Legislative Assembly," *New Mexican*, December 19 1863; "Don Diego Archuleta," and "Representative Gutierres [*sic*] of Bernalillo County," *New Mexican*, January 31, 1864; "Election Returns," *Weekly Press*, September 8, 1863; "More About It," *Weekly Press*, May 17 1864; Theisen, "José Manuel Gallegos," 146.

175. C. P. Clever, "Valedictory" and "The New Mexican, the Press," *New Mexican*, November 7, 1863.

9. Bosque Redondo and José Francisco Chávez

1. Franco to Francisco Perea, September 23, 1864, two installments: "Chavez and the Reservation Question," Santa Fe *Weekly Gazette* [hereafter Gazette], August 5, 1865, and "The Balance of the Letter," *Gazette*, August 26, 1865.

2. At some point the spelling of José Francisco's surname changed from Chávez to "Chaves." He retained the original in his signature; see, for example, José Francisco Chavez to R. E. Twitchell, October 14, 1892, Thomas B. Catron Papers, box 401, folder 3, Center for Southwest Research, University of New Mexico. The original spelling is retained in this book.

3. "José Francisco Chávez," *New Mexican*, November 21, 1863; "Col. Francisco Chavez," *New Mexican*, October 20, 1865. For more evidence of Chávez's assimilated conversational English, see J. Francisco Chávez to Felipe Chávez, December 4, 1865, in Steve C. Martinez, "The Political Life of Colonel Jose Francisco Chaves y Perea," 33. Chávez too was known as "Frank," for example in J. L. Collins to S. B. Watrous, *New Mexican*, August 25, 1865.

4. The other two were his grandfather Francisco Xavier Chávez (1822–23) and great uncle José Antonio Chavez (1828–31).

5. "Bosquejos Biográficos: Hon. J. Francisco Chaves," *Boletín Popular* (Santa Fe), February 7, 1895. "José Francisco Chávez," *New Mexican*, November 21, 1863; "Sketch of Colonel Chaves," *El Combate* (Wagon Mound NM), December 24, 1904; Allison, "Colonel Francisco Perea," 212–18; Twitchell, *Leading Facts*, 2: 400–401; Walter et al., *Colonel José Francisco Chaves*, 2–3; Frank W. Clancy, "Paper at Unveiling of Bust in New Mexico Senate," in Walter et al., *Colonel José Francisco Chaves*, 4–11, 5; Julyan, *Place Names of New Mexico*, 77.

6. Noted in J.M.H. Alarid to editors, Santa Fe, June 30, 1865, *Nuevo-Mejicano*, July 7, 1865. Perea's father was brother to Chávez's mother; "José Francisco Chávez," *New Mexican*, November 21, 1863.

7. "Justice at Last," *New Mexican*, September 16, 1864.

8. "The Balance of the Letter," *Gazette*, August 26, 1865.

9. See S. B. Watrous to editors, July 11, 1865, *New Mexican*, July 21, 1865.

10. S. B. Watrous to editors, July 24, 1865, *New Mexican*, August 4, 1865.

11. Bailey, *Bosque Redondo*; Thompson, *The Army and the Navajo*; Keleher, *Turmoil in New Mexico*; McNitt, *Navajo Wars*; Sides, *Blood and Thunder*, 471–82; Hunt, *Major General James Henry Carleton*; Dailey, "Michael Steck." For a critique of much of this literature for underplaying the brutality of the Bosque Redondo experience for the Navajos, see Denetdale, *Reclaiming Diné History*, 76–78.

12. "Sketch of Colonel Chaves," *El Combate* (Wagon Mound NM), December 24, 1904; James H. Carleton to J. Francisco Chaves, October 1, 1864, James W. Arrott's Fort Union Collection, Department of New Mexico, Letters, Reports and Orders, vol. 17, p. 009, Thomas C. Donnelly Library, Special Collections, New Mexico Highlands University, 15–068 (hereafter Arrott Collection).

13. James H. Carleton testimony before the Doolittle Commission, July 3, 1865, Arrott Collection, 17–009; Colonel Willis testimony before the Doolittle Commission, July 2, 1865, Arrott Collection, 17–008; James H. Carleton to [Capt.] Allen S. Anderson, October 13, 1864, Arrott Collection, 15–096. That Carleton ended up with mining claims and interest in a mill, see Miller, "William Logan Rynerson," 102–3.

14. James H. Carleton to Brigadier General Lorenzo Thomas, September 6, 1863, in *Gazette*, December 1, 1863.

15. Arny, *Executive message of his excellency*, 16–17; Bailey, *Bosque Redondo*, 67–68; Dailey, "Michael Steck," 142–43.

16. Henry Connelly, Governor, "Proclamation," and "The Proclamation of the Governor," *New Mexican*, November 7, 1863; Henry C. Connelly, "The Governor's Message," *New Mexican*, December 12, 1863; untitled, *New Mexico Press*, December 8, 1863; Henry Connelly, "Proclamation," in Henry Connelly testimony before the Doolittle Commission, n.d., Arrott Collection, 16–386; Denetdale, *Reclaiming Diné History*, 70–71.

17. "From Washington City," *Gazette*, July 23, 1864; "Appropriations for New Mexico," *Gazette* July 30, 1864, 2; cf. Bailey, *Bosque Redondo*, 121; "How Mighty Smart," *New Mexican*, October 28, 1864; on Russell, see "How Mighty Smart," *New Mexican*, October 28, 1864.

18. [Title blotched in original], *New Mexican*, February 13, 1864; also in the *New Mexican*, see "The Governor's Message," December 19, 1863; "Military Officers in New Mexico Value their Honor," January 9, 1864; "The Indians," January 23, 1864; "When Carleton Came," March 5, 1864; "More than Two Hundred Years of Indian Murders and Robberies Drawing to a Close," April 2, 1864.

19. "The Voice of the People," *New Mexico Press* (Albuquerque), March 1, 1864.

20. Harris, *Lincoln and the Border States*, 7, 249, 280.

21. "Gazette Belles-Lettres," *New Mexico Press*, July 26, 1864, 1. The entire Knapp affair is given in rich detail in Keleher, *Turmoil in New Mexico*, 400–408; cf. Murphy, *Frontier Crusader*, 126, and "William F.M. Arny," 334–35; for early press reports, see, for example, J. G. Knapp to H.S. Johnson, editor, *New Mexico Press* (Albuquerque), April 12, 1864; untitled, *Gazette*, June 14, 1864; "Knapp to Knapp," *Gazette*, July 9, 1864; untitled, *Gazette*, July 30, 1864; untitled, *Gazette*, July 30, 1864; "Supreme Court," *New Mexican*, January 9, 1864; "Supreme Court," *New Mexican*, January 16, 1864.

22. "Wm. H. Manderfield, Tho. S. Tucker, "Salutatory," *New Mexican*, May 27, 1864; Fierman, "The Career of Clever," 4. At one point Manderfield and Tucker found themselves needing to explain, against the accusation that Justice Benedict still ran the paper's editorial policies, that they and they alone were responsible for it; "A Todos Los Interesados," *Nuevo-Mejicano*, December 9, 1864; "An Explanation," *Gazette*, November 26, 1864; Hunt, *Kirby Benedict*, 208.

23. "The Knapp-Military Imbroglio," *Weekly Press*, April 5, 1864; "Military License," *National Intelligencer*," February 26, 1864, in *Weekly Press*, April 25, 1864; Hunt, *Major General James Henry Carleton*, 299–301.

24. J. G. Knapp to H. S. Johnson, editor, *Weekly Press*, April 12, 1864.

25. John M. Kerr, "California Volunteers vs. General James H. Carleton," *New Mexican*, January 6, 1865; cf. Keleher, *Turmoil in New Mexico*, 453–54.

26. Un Peón, "El Interés Propio vs. El Interés Público," *Nuevo-Mejicano*, September 1, 1865.

27. The affair is given in rich detail in Keleher, *Turmoil in New Mexico*, 400–408; cf. Murphy, *Frontier Crusader*, 126, and "William F.M. Arny," 334–35. For samples of the early press reports, see the *Gazette*, untitled editorial, June 14, 1864; "Knapp to Knapp," July 9, 1864; untitled, July 30, 1864. See also the *New Mexican*, "Supreme Court," January 9 and 16, 1864; Observer to Messrs Editors and Publisher, March 26, 1864; "Gen. Carleton and the New York 'World,'" April 30, 1864; "Hatred Against the Military," May 7, 1864; "Judge Knapp's Attacks," May 7, 1864; "The Government and the Navajoes," May 14, 1864; "The Military again upon the 'War Path,'" May 14, 1864.

28. Henry Connelly et al., "Public Meeting," *New Mexican*, February 27, 1864; "Santa Fe Public Meeting," *New Mexico Press*, March 1, 1864.

29. Public Meeting," *New Mexico Press*, March 15, 1864.

30. "Socorro County Meeting," *New Mexico Press*, March 29, 1864.

31. John Lemon and Jose De J. Baca, to editor ("The Policies and Official Acts of Carleton vindicated by the citizens of the county of Dona Ana"), *Gazette*, April 22, 1865.

32. Joshua S. Sledd, "Judge Knapp at Home," *New Mexican*, November 4, 1864; "Judge Knapp's Reply," October 19, 1864, *New Mexican*, November 4, 1864.

33. "Gen. Carleton's Indian Policy," *New Mexican*, November 4, 1864. The litany noted in the *New Mexican* and *Nuevo-Mejicano* of 1864–65 also included accusations of fraud in the Fort Sumner commissary; exorbitant costs to the government of maintaining the reservation, including the feeding of internees; Carleton's prime motivation of personally profiteering from investments in the mining operations he was seeking to protect in western New Mexico; sloughing off on New Mexico the responsibility for managing Indian tribes belonging to the newly created Territory of Arizona; interfering in elections; and choosing a faulty location on which to put his reservation, where the water was too brackish and wood fuel extremely wanting.

34. "The Reservation Question," *New Mexican*, October 28, 1864.

35. "Scarcity of Provisions—High Prices," *New Mexican*, November 4, 1864; "Navajoe Policy—Starving Poor," *New Mexican*, November 11, 1864; "More Consistencies!," *New Mexican*, November 18, 1864.

36. "Gen. Carleton's Indian Policy," *New Mexican*, November 11, 1864.

37. Evangelista Pérez to His Excellency Henry Connelly, April 28, 1864, in *New Mexican*, June 22, 1864; "Rio Abajo," *New Mexican*, November 11, 1864.

38. "Brigadier Carleton's Abuse of New Mexican People," *New Mexican*, December 9, 1864. For a large extract of the disparaging remarks, see "Carleton's Abuse of New Mexican People," *New Mexican*, July 27, 1867.

39. See, for example, James H. Carleton to Matthew [sic] Steck, November 8, 1864, Arrott Collection, 15–166.

40. Lester, "Michael Steck," 192–94; Keleher, *Turmoil in New Mexico*, 422–25.

41. See, for example, S. to Messrs. Manderfield & Tucker, *New Mexican*, November 25, 1864.

42. Miguel Romero y Baca to editor, *New Mexican*, August 26, 1864; cf. Keleher, *Turmoil in New Mexico*, 438–39; Anselmo F. Arellano, "Through Thick and Thin," 92–94; "The Reservation Question," *New Mexican*, October 28, 1864; "The Colorado Chiquito," *Weekly Press*, May 17, 1864; Lester, "Michael Steck," 202–3.

43. "The Navajo Reservation," *New Mexico Press*, September 6, 1864.

44. "Navajo Depredations," *Gazette*, September 17, 1864.

45. Lorenzo Labadí to editor, September 17, 1864 ("Del Fuerte Sumner"), *Gazette*, October 1, 1864.

46. Observer, "A Letter from San Miguel," *Gazette*, September 24, 1864.

47. M. Desmarais et al., "El condado de San Miguel y la Reservación," *Gazette*, October 1, 1864; cf. Arellano, "Through Thick and Thin," 194–95.

48. "Territory of New Mexico, County of San Miguel, October 20, 1864," *New Mexican*, November 25, 1864; San Miguel to editor, *New Mexican*, October 14, 1864; in English, *New Mexican*, October 21, 1864.

49. Lawrence G. Murphy, testimony before the Doolittle Commission, June 27, 1865, Arrott Collection, 16–390.

50. Arellano, "Through Thick and Thin," 195–97.

51. Gómez, *Manifest Destinies;* Miguel Romero y Baca to Editors of New Mexican ("Letter from Hon. Romero y Baca"), October 19, 1864 *New Mexican*, November 25, 1864.

52. "Territory of New Mexico, County of San Miguel, October 20, 1864," *New Mexican*, November 25, 1864, 2–3; San Miguel to editor, *New Mexican*, October 14, 1864; in English, *New Mexican*, October 21, 1864.

53. "The Letter of Hon. Romero y Baca," *New Mexican*, December 2, 1864.

54. Untitled editorial, *Gazette*, October 22, 1864.

55. Untitled, *Gazette*, October 1, 1864; also, "Let us Have the Proof," *Gazette*, January 23, 1865.

56. For Carleton's statement, see Keleher, *Turmoil in New Mexico*, 409–10; "La Primera Epistola de Santiago a Los Nuevo Mejicanos," *New Mexican*, January 27, 1865.

57. "The Reservation Question," *New Mexican*, October 28, 1864.

58. Lester, "Michael Steck," 198, 232; Keleher, *Turmoil in New Mexico*, 409–10; "'Make a Choice!,'" *New Mexico Press*, April 12, 1864; Erastus W. Wood to [Lieut. Col.] Nelson H. Davis, June 20, 1865, Arrott Collection, 16–357; Erastus W. Wood to [Lieut. Col.] Julius Shaw, June 20, 1865, Arrott Collection, 16–358.

59. Keleher, *Turmoil in New Mexico*, 417–21; "Agua Negra, & C.," *New Mexico Press*, October 4, 1864.

60. Wood to Davis and Wood to Shaw, June 20, 1865, Arrott Collection, 16–357, 16–358.

61. Kosmider, "Samuel B. Watrous," 86–87, 88; Keleher, *Turmoil in New Mexico*, 422–27.

62. Lester, "Michael Steck," 199; Rev. Eleazer Slingsby, "A Reprint of 'Fair Carletonia,' with Notes and something more," *New Mexican*, July 14, 1865; Sides, *Blood and Thunder*, 477.

63. Lester, "Michael Steck," 205; Ciudadano to editors, *Nuevo-Mejicano*, January 20, 1865; and several items in the *New Mexican*: "Consistency," September 16, 1864; "Governor's Message," December 9, 1864, and January 6, 1865; "The Whys and Wherefores," December 16, 1864; Apache, "More Indian Robberies," November 4, 1864, 1; Ibex to editor, January 20, 1865; Gringo, "Letter from Mesilla," April 14, 1865; X.Y.Z. to editors, August 18, 1865. One researcher agrees with Carleton that "a large number of the complaints were probably exaggerated and that the Navajo were often blamed for depredations that other Indians committed"; Osburn, "The Navajo at the Bosque Redondo," 405.

64. New Mexico, "Our Late and Present Congressman," *New Mexican*, November 18, 1864.

65. "I Shot the Turkey. Who? Mose," *New Mexican*, August 4, 1865; "Extracts from Gen. Orders No. 11," *New Mexican*, September 1, 1865; "Carleton and Flunkies," *New Mexican*, December 23; A Chávez Gringo to editor, August 7, 1865 ("From Fort Union"), *New Mexican*, August 25, 1865; untitled, *New Mexican*, August 18, 1865; W.F.M. Arny, "TO THE PUBLIC," *New Mexican*, September 1, 1865.

66. For Lincoln's expert manipulation of the press to promote his career, see Holzer, *Lincoln and the Power of the Press*; also Paludan, *Presidency*, 222–23; Foner, *Fiery Trial*, 296–98; "Extract from the President's Message," *New Mexican*, January 9, 1864; "President's Message," *New Mexican*, January 13, 1865.

67. Trefousse, "The Republican Party," 1170; Paludan, *Presidency*, 224–25.

68. The story ran in "The Cleveland Convention," *New Mexican*, June 24, 1864.

69. "The Presidential Canvass," *Weekly Press*, July 5, 1864.

70. "Abraham Lincoln," *New Mexican*, July 8, 1864.

71. "Territorial Convention," *Weekly Press*, April 12, 1864.

72. "UNCONDITIONAL UNION MEN, Albuquerque, April 7, 1864, National Convention!," *New Mexico Press*, May 3, 1864.

73. Paludan, *Presidency*, 6, 308, 324, 334, 338.

74. Crofts and Cress, *Reluctant Confederates*, 104, 348; Harris, *Lincoln and the Border States*, 6.

75. Paludan, *Presidency*, 225.

76. "Unconditional Union," *Weekly Press*, April 19, 1864; also "Territorial Convention," *Weekly Press*, April 12, 1864.

77. "The Governor is sternly opposed to the rebellion and with the government to destroy the rebellious opposition. He was so when the Texans were here. He is for such a 'reconstruction as will give security in the future' against other similar attempt to destroy the union. The territorial executive is thoroughly union"; "The Governor's Message," *New Mexican*, December 19, 1863; "The Governor's Message," *New Mexican*, December 12, 1863.

78. Vindex to editor, *Gazette*, June 17, 1865; "Cat's Paw," *Gazette*, August 26, 1865.

79. "Territorial Convention," *Weekly Press*, April 12, 1864.

80. "UNCONDITIONAL UNION MEN. Albuquerque, April 7, 1864. National Convention!," *Weekly Press*, May 12, 1864; "National Convention!," *Weekly Press*, May 3, 1864. "Underground Plotting," *New Mexico Press*, May 3, 1864.

81. Untitled, *New Mexican*, May 27, 1864.

82. "Unconditional Union," *New Mexico Press*, May 10, 1864.

83. Chase, who was Lincoln's treasury secretary, had been clearly running for president to the extent of using his patronage powers to build a base. His chances were undercut by a manifesto that mentioned him, and which had drawn so much negative reaction among Republicans that he was forced to withdraw from the race; see, for example, Foner, *Fiery Trial*, 297.

84. "Administration Party," *Gazette*, February 18, 1865.

85. "The Gazette still Continues its Abuse of our Civil Officers," *New Mexican*, March 17, 1865; "'The Mountain Labored, and brought forth a Mouse,'" *New Mexican*, March 17, 1865; untitled, *New Mexican*, February 24, 1864. New Mexicans' strong support for Lincoln is evident in the *New Mexican*: see "The Public Printing" and "The President's Proclamation," January 2, 1864; "Extract from the President's Message" and "The End of the War," January 9, 1864; untitled, February 24, 1864.

86. "The 'Opposite Party,'" *Weekly Press*, May 31, 1864; untitled, *New Mexican*, February 24, 1864; "'The Mountain Labored, and brought forth a Mouse,'" *New Mexican*, March 17, 1865; "The Gazette still Continues its Abuse of our Civil Officers," *New Mexican*, March 17, 1865.

87. "A Friend of the Country, "From Washington City," *Gazette*, July 23, 1864.

88. "Resolutions of the Baltimore Convention," *New Mexican*, July 8, 1864; Paludan, *Presidency*, 271–72; "President Lincoln," *New Mexican*, May 14, 1864.

89. "The withdrawal of Gen. Fremont," *New Mexican*, October 21, 1864.

90. "Old Abe," *New Mexican*, October 14, 1864.

91. "Presidential Election," *New Mexican*, December 9, 1864; "President Lincoln," *New Mexican*, May 14, 1864.

92. Alan Holmes, "Major General James H. Carleton," 59.

93. "The Whys and Wherefores," *New Mexican*, December 16, 1864.

94. "The Whys and Wherefores." An informant for the charge that Carleton favored anti-Lincoln contractors was probably Capt. Amos F. Garrison, district commissary officer, who openly criticized Carleton for mismanaging government contracts; Lester, "Michael Steck," 201.

95. Francisco Perea to the Editor, *Gazette*, January 14, 1865.

96. "For Delegate, Hon. Francisco Perea," *Gazette*, January 14, 1865.

97. A Friend of the Country, "From Washington City," *Gazette*, January 23, 1864.

98. "Can't Co-operate with the Superintendent," *New Mexican*, November 18, 1864; James H. Carleton to Matthew [sic] Steck, November 8, 1864, Arrott Collection, 15-166.

99. Dailey, "Michael Steck"; Keleher, *Turmoil in New Mexico*, 434; Murphy, *Frontier Crusader*, 130; but compare Bailey, *Bosque Redondo*, 183. According to Thompson (*The Army and the Navajo*, 83), Steck resigned "perhaps at the request of Commissioner Dole"; Bloom, ed., "Historical Society Minutes," 274; Thompson, *The Army and the Navajo*, 107, http://rancho.pancho.pagesperso_orange.fr/Indian.htm.

100. Vindex to editor, *Gazette*, 17 June 1865, 2; "Judge J. G. Knapp," *New Mexican*, July 7, 1865; J. G. Knapp to editors, *New Mexican*, August 4, 1865.

101. Bailey, *Bosque Redondo*, 179-80; untitled, *New Mexican*, March 17, 1865; "The Congressional Committee," *New Mexican*, July 7, 1865.

102. Twitchell, *Leading Facts*, 2: 400.

103. "José Francisco Chávez," *New Mexican*, November 21, 1863.

104. TARA to editor ("Letter from Navajo"), February 15, 1864, in *Weekly Press*, March 22, 1864; "Our Regiments," *Weekly Press*, February 2, 1864.

105. Thompson, "Brave Christian Soldiers," 291, 292.

106. Meketa, *Legacy of Honor*, 273-75.

107. Emmett, *Fort Union*, 250-54.

108. Bailey, *Bosque Redondo*, 91; Alpha to Dear Press ("Press Correspondence"), March 27, 1864, in *New Mexico Press*, April 26, 1864; "The Chavez Cut-Off," *Arizona Miner*, in *New Mexico Press*, May 17, 1864.

109. Franco to Francisco Perea, in "The Balance of the Letter," *Gazette*, August 26, 1865.

110. "Lieut. Colonel Chaves," *New Mexican*, November 25, 1864; cf. Keleher, who wrote, "Chaves and Gen. Carleton, Commander of the Department of New Mexico, differed on military and political matters, and Chaves resigned from the army"; *Turmoil in New Mexico*, 480n1.

111. [Capt.] Cyrus H. DeForrest to [Lt. Col.] J. Francisco Chaves, April 27, 1864, and James H. Carleton to J. Francisco Chaves, October 1, 1864, Arrott Collection, 15-062, 15-068.

112. "The Petition from San Miguel County," *New Mexican*, January 27, 1865, 2. Collins questioned the validity of the petition, as no names were associated with it; "Chávez and the Reservation Question," *Gazette*, August 5, 1865.

113. Diego Archuleta to editor ("Asuntos Politicos"), *Gazette*, June 3, 1865, 3; James H. Carleton to [Brig. Gen.] Marcellus M. Crocker, January 22, 1864, Arrott Collection, 16–023; Theisen, "José Manuel Gallegos," 161, 169–70.

114. "Carleton's Resolutions of Last Winter," *New Mexican*, January 26, 1866.

115. "The Issue," *Gazette*, June 10, 1865.

116. "Carleton's Resolutions of last Winter," *New Mexican*, January 26, 1866; James H. Carleton to [Brig. Gen.] Marcellus M. Crocker, October 31, 1864, Arrott Collection, 15–159; Diego Archuleta, President of the Council, and Pedro Valdez, Speaker of the House of Representatives, "Joint Resolutions of the Legislative Assembly of New Mexico," approved January 30, 1865, published in *Gazette*, February 4, 1865.

117. "The Issue," *Gazette*, June 10, 1865.

118. R. Ranchero to editors, February 12, 1865, *New Mexican*, February 24, 1865, 1.

119. "Mr. Chávez on the Stump," *Gazette*, July 22, 1865, 2; "Mr. Chavez as a Campaigner," *Gazette*, 22 July 1865, 2; for support of this interpretation, see also A Voter to editor ("The Canvass in Taos County"), *Gazette*, August 5, 1865; "The Campaign for Delegate," *Gazette*, August 19, 1865; Rio Abajo to editors, *New Mexican*, November 11, 1864; Ranchero to editors, March 25, 1865 ("Letter from 'Ranchero'"), *New Mexican*, April 7, 1865.

120. However, only Nevada became a state in 1864, internal politics leading to rejection in the others; Berwanger, *Rise of the Centennial State*, 41–42.

121. Llamada de Una Convención Para Nominar un Candidato de Administración Para Delegado al Congreso," *Nuevo-Mexicano*, February 10, 1865; "Call For a Convention to Nominate an Administration Candidate for Delegate to Congress," *New Mexican*, February 17, 1865; "Miembros del Consejo Legislativo," *Nuevo-Mexicano*, December 23, 1864; "The Election," *New Mexican*, September 9, 1864.

122. Untitled, *Nuevo-Mejicano*, February 10, 1865.

123. "Administration Party," *Gazette*, February 18, 1865.

124. Untitled, *New Mexican*, February 24, 1864.

125. "Copper-heads—Traitors," *Gazette*, June 10, 1865.

126. Untitled, *New Mexican*, February 24, 1864; "Copper-heads—Traitors," *Gazette*, June 10, 1865. For a run-down of the public positions held by Collins's family, see Un Peón, "El Interés Propio vs. El Interés Público," *Nuevo-Mejicano*, September 1, 1865.

127. "That Administration Party," *Gazette*, March 4, 1865.

128. References to the convention are taken from Tomás C. de Baca et al., 'Proceedings of the Convention," *New Mexican*, April 21, 1865.

129. Emmett, *Fort Union*, 250–54.

130. "El Mayor Rafael Chacón Nació en Santa Fe," *Nuevo-Mejicano*, June 15, 1912; untitled, *New Mexico Press*, December 8, 1863.

131. Meketa, *Legacy of Honor*, 242, quote 247.

132. Chaves, *Papers in the Case of J. Francisco Chaves vs. Charles P. Clever,* 57; Quien tu sabes, "La luz de la razón," *Gazette,* July 13, 1867; "Our Sheriff, Major Sena," *New Mexican,* October 21, 1864.

133. C. de Baca et al., 'Proceedings of the Convention," 2; "Un Desembarazo," *Nuevo-Mejicano,* April 28, 1865, including "eloquent address," which was greeted "throughout with the utmost enthusiasm"; "Platform &c.," *Gazette,* April 29, 1865; A. Cutler to editor, *Gazette,* April 22, 1865; "to declare those general principles...," Un Miembro to editors, April 25, 1865 ("Replica a una tarjeta"), *Nuevo-Mejicano,* April 28, 1865; "The Plot and its Success," *New Mexican,* April 28, 1865.

134. "The Convention and the Nominee," *New Mexican,* April 21, 1865; on "*Gazette* clique," "How Mighty Smart," *New Mexican,* October 28, 1864.

135. "How the People Accept the Nomination of Col. Chavez," *New Mexican,* May 19, 1865.

136. El Neofito to editors, *New Mexican,* May 19, 1865, 2.

137. A Voter to editors, May 2, 1865, *New Mexican,* May 19, 1865.

138. A Citizen to editors, *New Mexican,* May 19, 1865.

139. "Parties and the Reservation," *Gazette,* May 20, 1865; on McCook, see untitled, *New Mexican,* June 9, 1865.

140. "Assassination of President Lincoln," *Denver News,* April 14, 1865, in *New Mexican,* May 5, 1865; untitled, *New Mexican,* May 5, 1865; Henry Connelly, "Public Meeting," *Gazette,* May 26, 1865; but see "The Assassination of President Lincoln," *Gazette,* May 26, 1865.

141. "The Assassination of President Lincoln," *Gazette,* May 26, 1865.

142. Untitled, *New Mexican,* May 5, 1865; Ben C. Cutler to Commanding Officer, April 29, 1865, Arrott Collection, 16–241.

143. "The Assassination of President Lincoln," *Gazette,* May 26, 1865.

144. Untitled, *New Mexican,* May 5, 1865; also "Abraham Lincoln," *New Mexican,* May 5, 1865.

145. Untitled, *New Mexican,* May 5, 1865; Henry Connelly, "Public Meeting," *Gazette,* May 26 , 1865; "Col. O. M. Brown's Speech," *Gazette,* May 26, 1865.

146. Juan Salazar y Jimenes et al., "Public Meeting at Peralta, N.M.," *Gazette,* May 13, 1865.

147. "C. Carson et al., "Public Meeting," *Gazette,* May 13, 1865.

148. Diego Archuleta, Chairman, *Public Notice,* Santa Fe, May 22, 1865, in *Gazette,* June 10, 1865.

149. Diego Archuleta to editor ("Asuntos Politicos"), *Gazette,* June 3, 1865; "Of the New Mexican People," *New Mexican,* January 9, 1864.

150. Miguel E. Pino to editors ("Archuleta in Politics"), *New Mexican,* June 9, 1865.

151. Diego Archuleta to editor ("¡Pino en la política en busca de una torta!"), *Gazette,* July 1, 1865.

152. Miguel E. Pino to editors ("¡El Ocho Hijos de Diego Archuleta Fiel a la Torta!"), *Nuevo-Mejicano,* August 25, 1865.

153. El Major Chacón to Diego Archuleta, Peñasco, June 12, 1865, in *New Mexican* ("¡El Hombre de influjo!"), June 22, 1865.

154. Leandro Sánchez to editors, *Nuevo-Mejicano,* June 30, 1865.
155. Diego Archuleta, Chairman, *Public Notice,* Santa Fe, May 22, 1865, in *Gazette,* June 10, 1865.
156. Antonio Joseph et al., "Junta Pública en Taos," *Gazette,* June 24, 1865.
157. "A Notable Event," *New Mexican,* June 16, 1865.
158. Pablo Gallegos et al., "Proceedings of the Union Convention," *Gazette,* June 21, 1865.
159. Francisco Ortíz y Delgado, Nasario Gonzales, Merrill Ashurst, committee, to Hon. Francisco Perea, Santa Fe, July 5, 1865, "Col. Perea's Acceptance," *Gazette,* July 8, 1865.
160. Francisco Perea to Messrs. Nasario Gonzales, M. Ashurst, and Francisco Ortíz y Delgado, Committee &c., July 5, 1865, in *Gazette,* July 8, 1865.
161. Untitled, *New Mexican,* June 22, 1865; "The Union Convention," *New Mexican,* June 30, 1865.
162. "I Shot the Turkey. Who? Mose," *New Mexican,* August 4, 1865.
163. "The Reservation," *Gazette,* July 1, 1865.
164. "'One More Reliable Witness," *New Mexican,* July 7, 1865.
165. José Manuel Gallegos, "Santa Fe County Meeting," *Gazette,* August 19, 1865; Theisen, "José Manuel Gallegos," 160–62.
166. "Obstructing the Governor in his Duties," *New Mexican,* March 26, 1864; "The Fraudulent Uses of Public Seals," *New Mexican,* March 26, 1864; "Secretary Arny," *New Mexican,* May 21, 1864; "Official Breaches of Law," *New Mexico Press,* April 5, 1864; Murphy, *Frontier Crusader,* 124, 129–30; Murphy, "William F.M. Arny," 334; Horn, *New Mexico's Troubled Years,* 109.
167. "The Public Printing," *Gazette,* June 4, 1864; "Arny on the Brain," *New Mexican,* October 28, 1864.
168. W.F.M. Arny, "TO THE PUBLIC," *New Mexican,* September 1, 1865.
169. "How it was," *Gazette,* May 28, 1864; "How Is It?," *New Mexico Press,* September 20, 1864; "More About It," *New Mexico Press,* May 17, 1864.
170. "'The Opposite Party!,'" *New Mexico Press,* May 24, 1864.
171. "Save the Pieces!," *New Mexico Press,* April 26, 1864.
172. "'How It Was,'" *New Mexico Press,* June 7, 1864; "The Absolute Veto," *New Mexico Press,* June 21, 1864.
173. Untitled, *New Mexican,* August 18, 1865.
174. "Mr. Chaves on the Stump," *Gazette,* July 22, 1865; "Mr. Chavez as a Campaigner," *Gazette,* July 22, 1865.
175. "The Issue to be Decided," *Gazette,* August 26, 1865.
176. "Chávez and the Reservation Question," *Gazette,* August 5, 1865; "Two Faces," *Gazette,* July 22, 1865.
177. "Contentment at the Bosque," *New Mexican,* April 28, 1865; "Our Indian Affairs," *New Mexican,* May 19, 1865; "More Navajoes," *New Mexican,* July 28, 1865; "Justice at Last," *New Mexican,* September 16, 1864.
178. "Honor to whom honor is due," *Gazette,* July 1, 1865.
179. C. to editors, *New Mexican,* July 21, 1865.

180. "The Comanche Peace," *New Mexican*, April 28, 1865.

181. "Martial Law Abolished in New Mexico," *New Mexican*, August 11, 1865.

182. "Who Shall We Believe?," *New Mexican*, June 9, 1865; "Indian News," *New Mexican*, July 14, 1865; untitled, *New Mexican*, July 21, 1865; "Look out for False Reports" *Gazette*, August 26, 1865.

183. Untitled, *New Mexican*, March 3, 1865; "Our Late and Present Congressman," *New Mexican*, November 18, 1864; "Watts on the Rampage for Perea," *New Mexican*, August 18, 1865.

184. "Shame, where is thy blush?," *Gazette*, March 11, 1865; "Ingratitude," *Gazette*, November 26, 1864; "Why Perea should be Defeated," *New Mexican*, July 28, 1865. The *Gazette* mistakenly thought Kirby Benedict was the author of the *New Mexican* editorials flailing at Perea and Watts.

185. Francisco Perea to Hon. Jas. M. Ashley, Chairman of the Committee on Territories of the House of Representatives, January 1, 1865, in *Gazette*, February 18, 1865; and "The Conejos," *Gazette*, February 18, 1865.

186. Untitled, *New Mexican*, March 3, 1865.

187. "Shame, where is thy blush?," *Gazette*, March 11, 1865.

188. "The Conejos," *Gazette*, July 1, 1865.

189. W.F.M. Arny, "TO THE PUBLIC," *New Mexican*, September 1, 1865.

190. Untitled, *New Mexican*, March 3, 1865, 2; "Our Territorial Capitol," *New Mexican*, June 2, 1865.

191. "Shame, where is thy blush?," *Gazette*, March 11, 1865.

192. S.B. Watrous to editors, July 11, 1865 ("Letter from S.B. Watrous"), *New Mexican*, July 21, 1865; Kosmider, "Samuel B. Watrous," 88–89.

193. See, inter alia, S.B. Watrous letters to editors in the *New Mexican*, August 4, 11, and 25, and September 1, 8, and 22, 1865.

194. Pablo Gallegos et al., "Proceedings of the Union Convention," *Gazette*, June 21, 1865.

195. "Desperation," *New Mexican*, August 4, 1865.

196. A Voter to editor ("The Canvass in Taos County"), *Gazette*, August 5, 1865; Stranger to editor ("Public Meeting in Taos"), *Gazette*, July 8, 1865; "Meeting in Taos," *New Mexican*, July 7, 1865; Vicente St. Vrain, "Junta Pública," *Gazette*, July 1, 1865; untitled, *New Mexican*, July 28, 1865; Joaquín Chávez et al., "Procedimientos de una junta pública tenida en Galisteo el día 28 de Julio de 1865," *Nuevo-Mejicano*, August 4, 1865; Pablo Melendrez et al., "Junta Pública," *Nuevo-Mejicano*, August 18, 1865.

197. V. Vásquez et al., "Convención del partido Unionista," *Nuevo-Mejicano*, August 11, 1865.

198. Un Peón, "El Interés Propio Vs. El Interés Público," *Nuevo-Mejicano*, September 1, 1865.

199. "The Election—the Result," *New Mexican*, October 6, 1865.

200. *New Mexican*, October 13, 1865. For a negative account of a pro-Carleton meeting run by sutlers, see "The Mesilla Meeting," *New Mexican*, April 28, 1865.

201. Annon to William Manderfield, April 15, 1864, in Kirby Benedict, *Journey through New Mexico's First Judicial District*, 54; quote, Arellano, "Through Thick and Thin," 203–4.

202. "The Election—the Result," *New Mexican*, October 6, 1865; in Santa Fe County the election "passed off in an orderly manner and with very little excitement, each party exerting itself to advance the interests of its candidates, but neither attempting to interfere with the other; "The election in Santa Fe County," *Gazette*, September 9, 1865.

203. "Official Returns of the Election," *New Mexican*, September 29, 1865; "The election in Santa Fe County," *Gazette*, September 9, 1865; "Vote in Santa Fe County," *Gazette*, September 30, 1865; "Col. Francisco Chavez," *New Mexican*, October 20, 1865; "Miguel Pino and the Poor," *Gazette*, August 26, 1865; "La Administración del Condado de Santa Fe," *Nuevo-Mejicano*, September 1, 1866.

204. "Col. Francisco Chavez," *New Mexican*, October 20, 1865.

205. José Francisco Chávez, "To the People of New Mexico," *New Mexican*, October 20, 1865, and "Al Pueblo de Nuevo Mejico," *Nuevo-Mejicano*, October 20, 1865.

206. W.F.M. Arny to editors, *New Mexican*, September 15, 1865. In a report of the friends and backers of Perea engaging in "petty and contemptible revenge," Juan José Sánchez of Valencia County had been receiving commissary rations for having lost a leg in the war, but was told to contact Chávez, for whom he had voted, "if he wanted anything"; "A Contemptible Revenge," *New Mexican*, September 15, 1865.

Part 4. Political Agonism under Reconstruction

1. Unreadable byline, *Gazette*, August 17, 1867.
2. Un Ranchero to editor, *Gaceta*, July 27, 1867, 4.

10. Party Definitions of the Colonizer

1. Yngacio Gonzalez, foreman, et al., "Presentment of the Grand Jury of Doña Ana County in Reference to General Carleton and the Corn Question," *New Mexican*, December 22, 1865, 2.

2. CAXY to editor, December 16, 1865, *New Mexican*, December 29, 1865.

3. "Indian News," *New Mexican*, June 22, 1866, 2.

4. "Indian News," *New Mexican*, June 29, 1866, 2; also "Indian Matters," *New Mexican*, July 7, 1866, 2.

5. Untitled, *New Mexican*, January 26, 1866.

6. Keleher, *Turmoil in New Mexico*, 454; untitled, *New Mexican*, February 9, 1866.

7. Untitled, *Nuevo-Mejicano*, January 26, 1866; Miguel E. Pino, President Council and Samuel Ellison, speaker House of Representatives, "Joint Resolution of the Legislative Assembly," certified by W.F.M. Arny, Secretary of the Territory of New Mexico, *Gazette*, December 30, 1865, and *New Mexican*, December 29, 1865; Bailey, *Bosque Redondo*, 185; "Memorial," *New Mexican*, August 17, 1867; Keleher, *Turmoil in New Mexico*, 455–56.

8. "Carleton and the Legislature," *New Mexican*, January 26, 1866.

9. Felipe Sánchez and Tomás Salazar, untitled report, *Gazette*, January 27, 1866, 3.

10. "The Legislature Again," *Gazette*, December 30, 1865; Henry Connelly et al., "Public Meeting," *Gazette*, December 30, 1865.

11. Pedro Valdez, Pres., Juan Rodriguez, Vice Pres., Severiano Martinez and Marcelino Rivera, secretaries, "Public Meeting in Mora," *Gazette*, January 20, 1866.

12. "A Legislative Leader," *Gazette,* January 20, 1866.

13. Un Ciudadano Libre, "El Amor y el Interés," *Nuevo-Mejicano*, January 26, 1866.

14. Jose Luterio Garcia et al., "Public Meeting at El Rito," *Gazette,* January 27, 1866; Ramón Sanchez et al., "Public Meeting at Cubero," *Gazette,* January 27, 1866; untitled, *Gazette,* January 27, 1866; "attend to," Ambrosio Armijo et al., "Public Meeting in Albuquerque," *Gazette,* January 27, 1866.

15. James H. Carleton to Edwin M. Stanton, Secretary of War, December 27, 1865, *Gazette,* December 30, 1865, 2; Hunt, *Major General James Henry Carleton,* 299–30; untitled, *Nuevo-Mejicano,* January 26, 1866.

16. Hunt, *Major General James Henry Carleton,* 301.

17. J. K. Graves to Henry Connelly, January 9, 1866, *New Mexican,* January 19, 1866; "A Los Ciudadanos De Nuevo Mejico," *Nuevo-Mejicano,* July 7, 1866; "Agent Graves and the legislature," *New Mexican,* February 16, 1866; "The Replies of the Legislature to the Interrogatories of Mr. J. K. Graves," *New Mexican,* February 16, 1866.

18. Hunt, *Major General James Henry Carleton,* 290–91.

19. "Carleton and the Senate," *New Mexican,* January 19, 1867; "Peonage in New Mexico," *New Mexican,* January 26, 1867; "Carleton and Peonage," *New Mexican,* March 16, 1867; "General Carleton and Peonage," *New Mexican,* February 23, 1867.

20. "Carleton's Administration to be Investigated," *New Mexican,* January 19, 1867; "Congress and Carleton," *New Mexican,* February 2, 1867.

21. "Speech of Hon. J. F. Chaves, of New Mexico, in the House of Representatives, March 2, 1867," *New Mexican,* April 6, 1867; "Discurso del Hon. J. Francisco Chaves, Hechoen la Camara de Representantes de los Estados Unidos de America, Marzo 2 de 1867," *Nuevo-Mejicano,* March 30, 1867.

22. "Speech of Hon. J. F. Chaves," *New Mexican,* March 30, 1867.

23. Thompson, *The Army and the Navajo,* 132–33.

24. Oman, "The Beginning of the End," 44–45.

25. Thompson, *The Army and the Navajo,* 133.

26. Bailey, *Bosque Redondo,* 185; Keleher, *Turmoil in New Mexico,* 458.

27. "Carleton Removed," *New Mexican,* October 27, 1866; also Keleher, *Turmoil in New Mexico,* 457; Kosmider, "Samuel B. Watrous," 94–95; Arellano, "Through Thick and Thin," 207; Keleher, *Turmoil in New Mexico,* 466.

28. Arellano, "Through Thick and Thin," 205–7.

29. Thompson, *The Army and the Navajo,* 133.

30. Denetdale, *Reclaiming Diné History,* 76. The Mescalero Apaches would not receive their reservation for another four years.

31. "The House of Representatives," *Gazette,* January 5, 1867.

32. Bendix, "Industrialization, Ideologies, and Social Structure," 617.

33. "The Legislature," *New Mexican,* February 9, 1866; "Un Acto, Abrogando un acto intitulado enmendando la ley relativa a contratos entre amos y sirvientes,"

Nuevo-Mejicano, March 2, 1866; "An act to repeal an act amendatory of the law relative to contracts between masters and servants, approved January 26, 1859," *New Mexican*, March 9, 1866; untitled, *New Mexican*, September 8, 1866; Larson, *New Mexico's Quest*, 91.

34. Kiser, "A 'charming name,'" 184–85; Roberts, *Death Comes for the Chief Justice*, 3–4.

35. Murphy, "Reconstruction in New Mexico," 101; "The legislature," *New Mexican*, February 9, 1866.

36. "Benedict as Mexican Official," including Kirby Benedict to W. P. Dole, June 12, 1865, *Gazette*, February 17, 1866.

37. Legislative Resolution, in "Legislative Mendacity," *Gazette*, December 23, 1865.

38. "Legislative Mendacity," *Gazette*, December 23, 1865; "Joint Resolutions, Council and House of Representatives of the Territory of New Mexico," *New Mexican*, December 22, 1865; Murphy, *Louis Felsenthal*, 132.

39. La Verité, "Refutandolas Calumnias Hechas a los Legisladores de N.M.," *Nuevo-Mejicano*, January 5, 1866.

40. Anonymous, "¡¡Cuidado!! ¡¡Cuidado!! ¡¡De El Alarcán Colorado!!," *Nuevo-Mejicano*, January 5, 1866.

41. La Verité, "Refutando las Calumnias Hechas a los Legisladores de N.M."

42. Miguel E. Pino, "¡El Son Que le Tocan Baila!," *Nuevo-Mejicano*, January 26, 1866.

43. Un Anciano to editors, January 15, 1866, *Nuevo-Mejicano*, January 26, 1866.

44. Miguel E. Pino, "¡El Son Que le Tocan Baila!," *Nuevo-Mejicano*, January 26, 1866.

45. Henry Connelly, "Governor's Message," given December 1865, Governor's Papers, Connelly, reel 1, frame 346, RTG, TANM; Larson, *New Mexico's Quest*, 86–89.

46. W.F.M. Arny, "An Act authorizing the Governor to call a Convention to frame a Constitution for a Government of State," *New Mexican*, February 9, 1866; Enrique Connelly, *Proclama por el Gobernador de Nuevo Mejico*, and Un Acto, Asamblea Legislativa, February 2, 1866, Governor's Papers, Connelly, reel 1, frame 346, RTG, TANM; "Proclamation by the Governor of New Mexico," *New Mexican*, February 9, 1866.

47. Untitled, *New Mexican*, March 30, 1866, 2; Larson, *New Mexico's Quest*, 90.

48. Larson, *New Mexico's Quest*, 91.

49. "The Legislature," *New Mexican*, February 9, 1866.

50. "The State Question," *Weekly Gazette*, December 16, 1865.

51. "A Constitutional Convention," *Gazette*, February 3, 1866.

52. "He can't do it," *Gazette*, February 10, 1866.

53. "The Constitutional Convention," *Gazette*, February 10, 1866.

54. Untitled, *Gazette*, February 17, 1866.

55. "The State," *New Mexican*, March 2, 1866.

56. "The County Convention," *New Mexican*, March 2, 1866; "La Convención del Condado de Santa Fe," *Nuevo-Mejicano*, March 2, 1866.

57. "The Election," *New Mexican*, March 9, 1866.

58. Sydney A. Hubbell and Wm. Zeckendorf, "Junta Pública," *Nuevo-Mejicano*, March 2, 1866.

59. Pedro A. Baca, Robert Stapleton, and Isaac P. Hirshfield, "Junta Pública en el condado del Socorro," *Nuevo-Mejicano*, March 16, 1866; José de Jesús Baca, Marcelino Gallegos, and F. Buchner, untitled, *Nuevo-Mejicano*, March 9, 1866.

60. "Election in San Miguel," *Gazette*, March 24, 1866; Rafael Romero report on the San Miguel Convention, *Gazette*, March 31, 1866.

61. "State Government," *New Mexican*, March 23, 1860.

62. "Who are opposed to a State?," *Gazette*, March 31, 1866.

63. The following review of Chávez's statement is based on J. Francisco Chávez, Washington DC, March 28, 1866, in "A los ciudadanos de Nuevo Mejico," *Nuevo-Mejicano*, May 4, 1866.

64. Indian raiding and settlement retaliation continued to affect the territory. Reports of the frontier violence began to run continually in the *New Mexican* beginning in October 1865.

65. Miguel E. Pino and Demetrio Perea, "The Constitutional Convention," *New Mexican*, May 4, 1866.

66. Larson, *New Mexico's Quest*, 92.

67. Anonymous, "¡Explosión!," *Gaceta*, June 8, 1867.

68. "That Terrible Scheme," *Gazette*, September 22, 1866; "Aquel Atentado Terrible," *Gaceta*, September 29, 1866.

69. "The Removals," *New Mexican*, February 16, 1866; Thompson, *The Army and the Navajo*, 107.

70. "The Removals."

71. Roberts, *Death Comes for the Chief Justice*, "No one understood" 17–18; "warm and personal" is from "The Removals," *New Mexican*, February 16, 1866; cf. Thompson, *The Army and the Navajo*, 107.

72. Horn, *New Mexico's Troubled Years*, 92; Roberts, *Death Comes for the Chief Justice*, 18.

73. "Death of Ex. Governor Henry Connelly," *Gazette*, August 18, 1866; Santiago L. Collins, Simon Delgado, W.F.M. Arny, and Carlos Emilio Wesche, untitled, *Nuevo-Mejicano*, August 18, 1866; James L. Collins, president; Simon Delgado, WFM Arny, vice presidents; Charles Emile Wesche, Sec," untitled, *New Mexican*, August 18, 1866; "Ex-Governor Connelly," *New Mexican*, August 18, 1866; Horn, *New Mexico's Troubled Years*, 110–11, 116.

74. "Governor Mitchell," *New Mexican*, August 11, 1866.

75. "The Removals," *New Mexican*, February 16, 1866.

76. On settling in, see Horn, *New Mexico's Troubled Years*, 117–18; "The Future New Mexico," *New Mexican*, September 15, 1866; "The Memorial Asking for Troops," *New Mexican*, December 1, 1866; Jno. D. Henderson to the editors ("A Card"), *New Mexican*, July 6, 1867. On the extractive fever, see, for example, W.F.M. Arny to editors, "Resources of New Mexico, Railroads etc.," *New Mexican*, June 22, 1867; "Al Público," *Nuevo-Mejicano*, April 13, 1867; "Sign of Progress," *New Mexican*, March 30, 1867; Severo Baca et al., "Procedimientos de la Convención General del Partido Nacionál Unionista del Territorio de Nuevo Mejico," *Nuevo-Mejicano*, April 6, 1867.

77. Untitled, *New Mexican*, December 15, 1866; "Principle in our Leaders is the Palladium of our Liberties," *New Mexican*, December 15, 1866; untitled, *New Mexican*, June 22, 1867; "'False Certificate,'" *New Mexican*, August 10 , 1867.

78. Horn, *New Mexico's Troubled Years*, 116.

79. "Gov. Mitchell," *New Mexican*, December 1, 1866; untitled, *New Mexican*, December 15, 1866; "Principle in our Leaders is the Palladium of our Liberties"; Horn, *New Mexico's Troubled Years*, 116, 118.

80. "Governor Arny and the Gazette," *New Mexican*, December 29, 1866; W.F.M. Arny to Dear Sirs, *New Mexican*, April 20, 1867.

81. "The Removals," *New Mexican*, February 16, 1866, 2; "In a Nutshell," *New Mexican*, December 29, 1866; Hasta Otra Vista, "Los Sediciosos y el Gobernador Interino Arny," *Nuevo-Mejicano*, December 29, 1867; "Wherefore?," *New Mexican*, December 22, 1866; Horn, *New Mexico's Troubled Years*, 118; Murphy, *Frontier Crusader*, 133.

82. Fierman, "The Career of Clever," 5.

83. Murphy, *Frontier Crusader*, 132–33; Horn, *New Mexico's Troubled Years*, 119. "Governor Arny and the *Gazette*," *New Mexican*, December 29, 1866; "The 'Unprecedented, Unauthorized and Illegal' acts of Governor Mitchell," *New Mexican*, July 20, 1867; S. B. Elkins to Robert B. Mitchell, "The Correspondence between Governor Mitchell and S. B. Elkins, Esq., in relation to the Attorney Generalship," *New Mexican*, March 9, 1867.

84. "The 'Unprecedented, Unauthorized and Illegal' acts of Governor Mitchell," *New Mexican*, July 20, 1867.

85. Pascual Martinez et al., *Gazette*, January 26, 1867; "The House of Representatives," *Gazette*, January 5, 1867; "The Legislature," *New Mexican*, January 19, 1867; untitled, *New Mexican*, February 9, 1867.

86. Hasta Otra Vista, "Los Sediciosos y el Gobernador Interino Arny," *Nuevo-Mejicano*, December 29, 1867."

87. "Rafael Chacon," *Gazette*, January 26, 1867.

88. "The Legislature," *New Mexican*, January 19, 1867.

89. Hasta Otra Vista, "Los Sediciosos."

90. Pascual Martínez et al., *Gazette*, January 26, 1867.

91. "Governor Arny and the *Gazette*," *New Mexican*, December 29, 1866; quote, "In a Nutshell," *New Mexican*, December 29, 1866; "The Legislature," *New Mexican*, January 19, 1867; "Query?," *New Mexican*, January 5, 1867.

92. *The Second Annual Message of the Acting Governor Arny to the Legislative Assembly of New Mexico, Delivered December 1866* (Santa Fe: Manderfield & Tucker, 1866), Governor's Papers, reel 1, frame 354, "Governor Arny's Message," RTG, TANM; "Governor Arny's Message," *New Mexican*, December 15, 1866; "The Proclamation of Acting Governor Arny," *New Mexican*, November 24, 1866. W.F.M. Arny, "Proclamation," *New Mexican*, November 24, 1866; Centinela to editors, "Distribución de la Herencia," *Nuevo-Mejicano*, March 16, 1867; reprinted March 30, 1867.

93. "The Gazette vs. Truth," *New Mexican*, February 9, 1867; J. K. Graves to Henry Connelly, January 9, 1866, in *New Mexican*, January 19, 1866; "An Act Relative to Involuntary Servitude, " appvd. January 26, 1867, in *Laws of the Territory of New*

Mexico . . . 1866–67, Records of the States of the United States, microfilms, 1862–1875, N.M. B. 2, reel 2, 44–46; Robt. B. Mitchell, "Proclamation," *Gazette*, April 20, 1867; Lamar, *Far Southwest*, 79, also 113–14.

94. Keleher, *Turmoil in New Mexico*, 470; cf. Murphy, "Reconstruction in New Mexico," 101.

95. "The Gazette vs. Truth," *New Mexican*, February 9, 1867; Keleher, *Turmoil in New Mexico*, 467–69.

96. Rob'to B. Mitchell, "Proclama," April 14, 1867, Governor's Papers, Mitchell, reel 1, frame 398, RTG, TANM; Keleher, *Turmoil in New Mexico*, 470.

97. W.F.M. Arny to Dear Sirs, *New Mexican*, April 20, 1867; S. B. Elkins to Robert B. Mitchell, "The Correspondence between Governor Mitchell and S. B. Elkins, Esq., in relation to the Attorney Generalship," *New Mexican*, March 9, 1867; untitled, S. B. Watrous to editors, August 1, 1865 ("Letter from S. B. Watrous"), *New Mexican*, August 25, 1865; "Trinidad Alarid, Old Resident of Capital, is Dead," *Albuquerque Morning Journal*, December 24, 1919.

98. W.F.M. Arny to Legislative Council, December 14, 1866, and January 28, 1867, in "The 'Unprecedented, Unauthorized and Illegal' acts of Governor Mitchell," *New Mexican*, July 20, 1867; cf. Murphy, *Frontier Crusader*, 133; W.F.M. Arny to Dear Sirs, *New Mexican*, April 20, 1867; Elkins to Mitchell, "Correspondence . . . Attorney Generalship."

99. Anastacio Sandobal, President of the Senate, and Francisco P. Abreu, Speaker of the House, "Resolutions of the Legislative Assembly of the Territory of New Mexico, in favor of the removal of Robert B. Mitchell from the position of Governor of that Territory," March 7, 1868, National Archives, Territorial Papers—New Mexico, RG 46, tray 2, folder 5; W.F.M. Arny to editors, "'Facts which are not Falsehoods,'" *New Mexican*, July 6, 1867; "Facts for the People," *New Mexican*, May 25, 1867; the law is reproduced in "'False Certificate,'" *New Mexican*, August 10, 1867; untitled, *New Mexican*, June 22, 1867.

100. Elkins to Mitchell, "Correspondence . . . Attorney Generalship."

101. "Facts for the People," *New Mexican*, May 25, 1867.

102. Robert B. Mitchell to S. B. Elkins, and Robert B Mitchell to John Gwyn, March 6, 1867, in "The Correspondence between Governor Mitchell and John Gwyn, Jr. in relation to the Adjutant Generalship," *New Mexican*, March 16, 1867; Robert B. Mitchell to Anastacio Sandoval, March 5, 1867, in "Correspondencia Entre el Gobernador Mitchell y Anastacio Sandoval en Relación al Empleo de Intendente de Cuentas Públicas del Territorio de Nuevo Mejico," *Nuevo-Mejicano*, March 23, 1867.

103. "The 'Unprecedented, Unauthorized and Illegal' acts of Governor Mitchell," *New Mexican*, July 20, 1867; Anastacio Sandobal, President of the Senate, and Francisco P. Abreu, Speaker of the House, "Resolutions of the Legislative Assembly of the Territory of New Mexico, in favor of the removal of Robert B. Mitchell from the position of Governor of that Territory," March 7, 1868, National Archives, Territorial Papers—New Mexico, RG 46, tray 2, folder 5; Horn, *New Mexico's Troubled Years*, 118–19.

104. "EL GOBERNADOR MITCHELL SACA LAS UÑAS," *Nuevo-Mejicano*, March 9, 1867.

105. Centinela to editors, "Distribución de la Herencia," *Nuevo-Mejicano*, March 16, 1867, and March 30, 1867.

106. "Ultraje Brutal," *Nuevo-Mejicano*, May 11, 1867.

107. Un Ranchero to editor, *Gazette*, June 1, 1867.

108. El Bibliotecario to editor ("Esta Mula es muy Macho"), *Gaceta*," May 18, 1867; Roberts, *Death Comes for the Chief Justice*, 28–29.

109. Centinela to editors, "Distribución de la Herencia," *Nuevo-Mejicano*, March 30, 1867; S. B. Elkins to Robert B. Mitchell, "The Correspondence between Governor Mitchell and S. B. Elkins, Esq., in relation to the Attorney Generalship," *New Mexican*, March 9, 1867, 1; "The Removals," *New Mexican*, February 16, 1866, 2.

110. John Gwyn Jr. to Gov. Robert T Mitchell, March 9, 1867, in "The Correspondence between Governor Mitchell and John Gwyn, Jr. in relation to the Adjutant Generalship," *New Mexican*, March 16, 1867, 2; cf. Horn, *New Mexico's Troubled Years*, 120–21.

111. Robert B. Mitchell to Anastacio Sandoval, March 5, 1867, and Anastacio Sandoval to Robert B. Mitchell, both in "Correspondencia Entre el Gobernador Mitchell y Anastacio Sandoval en Relación al Empleo de Intendente de Cuentas Públicas del Territorio de Nuevo Mejico," *Nuevo-Mejicano*, March 23, 1867.

112. John Gwyn Jr. to Gov. Robert T Mitchell, March 9, 1867, in "The Correspondence between Governor Mitchell and John Gwyn, Jr. in relation to the Adjutant Generalship," *New Mexican,* March 16, 1867.

113. "Resolution No. 14," *New Mexican*, June 1, 1867; R. F. Chew, Chief Clerk, Department of State, "Public Resolution 14," March 30, 1867, in *New Mexican*, April 20, 1867, and *Gazette*, April 27, 1867; H. H. Heath to editors, *New Mexican*, April 20, 1867; B. to editor, Washington, March 12, 1867 ("Governor Arny Sustained"), *New Mexican*, April 6, 1867; Horn, *New Mexico's Troubled Years*, 119–20; Fireman, "The Frontier Career," 6.

114. Untitled, *New Mexican*, March 30, 1867.

115. Horn, *New Mexico's Troubled Years,* 120–21.

116. "How Congress fixed it," *Gazette*, April 27, 1867.

117. "Resolution No. 14," *New Mexican*, June 1, 1867; "Governor Mitchell," *New Mexican*, March 9, 1867; "Gov. W.M.F. Arny," *New Mexican*, April 13, 1867; WFM Arny to Dear Sirs, *New Mexican*, April 20, 1867.

118. "Slander and vituperation," *Gazette*, March 16, 1867.

119. "La Verdad personifacada," *Gazette*, July 13, 1867.

120. "Circular No. 4," *New Mexican*, June 1, 1867.

121. "Facts for the People," *New Mexican*, May 25, 1867.

122. W.F.M. Arny to editors, "'Facts which are not Falsehoods," *New Mexican*, July 6, 1867.

123. "'False Certificate,'" *New Mexican*, August 10, 1867; also untitled, *New Mexican*, June 22, 1867, and Anonymous, "La Verdád personifacada."

124. Thompson, *The Army and the Navajo*, 107; Opler and Opler, "Mescalero Apache History," 20; Felipe Delgado to W. P. Dole, July 16, 1865, http://rancho.pancho.pagesperso_orange.fr/Indian.htm.

125. J. L. Collins to Hon. Commissioner of Indian Affairs, February 5, 1866, "A Protest," *Gazette*, March 17, 1866.

126. J. Francisco Chávez to editor, March 28, 1866, in *Nuevo-Mejicano*, April 27, 1866. Denman had lived in New Mexico three years; "H. B. Denman, Esq.," *New Mexican*, July 28, 1866.

127. "Hon. J. Francisco Chavez," *New Mexican*, September 8, 1866.

128. Robert B Mitchell to the speaker of the House of Representatives," March 18, 1867, in "Mitchell's Delegate—How Congress disposed of Watts and Rebuked Mitchell," *New Mexican*, August 31, 1867.

129. "Delegate Watts," *New Mexican*, May 25, 1867; "The Beggar on Horseback," *New Mexican*, May 4, 1867; Buckeye to editors, Mora, July 20, 1867, *New Mexican*, August 10, 1867.

130. "Delegate Watts," *New Mexican*, May 25, 1867; "The 'Unprecedented, Unauthorized and Illegal' acts of Governor Mitchell," *New Mexican*, July 20, 1867; "Watts in Congress," *New Mexican*, July 27, 1867; "Mitchell's Delegate—How Congress disposed of Watts and Rebuked Mitchell," *New Mexican*, August 31, 1867; Davis quoted in Reynolds, "The Commander of Civil War History," 41.

131. Untitled editorial, *Gazette*, September 5, 1866.

132. Untitled, *New Mexican*, September 22, 1866.

133. "Strategy," *Gazette*, September 29, 1866.

134. Untitled, *New Mexican*, March 30, 1866.

135. "Col. Norton," *New Mexican*, December 15, 1866; Un Ranchero to editor, *Gaceta*, July 27, 1867; Thompson, *The Army and the Navajo*, 107.

136. "Slander and vituperation," *Gazette*, March 16, 1867.

137. Un Ranchero to editor, *Gaceta*, July 27, 1867.

138. Untitled, *New Mexican*, February 16, 1867; "Arrivals," *New Mexican*, March 2, 1867.

139. "Officiousness," *New Mexican*, March 2, 1867.

140. "General H. H. Heath," *New Mexican*, July 20, 1867; untitled, *New Mexican*, February 2, 1867; untitled, *Gazette*, October 12, 1867; Murphy, *Frontier Crusader*, 133; "General H. H. Heath," *New Mexican*, July 20, 1867; "General H. H. Heath," *New Mexican*, July 20, 1867; "Impudence," *New Mexican*, April 13, 1867; untitled, *Gazette*, October 12, 1867; quotes, Roberts, *Death Comes for the Chief Justice*, 31.

141. Un Ranchero to editor, *Gaceta*, July 27, 1867.

142. "That Terrible Scheme," *Gazette*, September 22, 1866; "Aquel Atentado Terrible," *Gazeta*, September 29, 1866.

143. Untitled, *New Mexican*, December 8, 1866. On the national politics, see Michael Les Benedict, *Impeachment and Trial of Andrew Johnson*, 14–15, and *Preserving the Constitution*, 23–27, 34; Ferrell, *Reconstruction*, 19–27, and Mantell, *Johnson, Grant*, 17–18.

144. "Radical Tactics," *National Republic*, in *Gazette*, July 28, 1866.

145. "National Union Convention," *New Mexican*, July 28, 1866.

146. Merrill Ashurst, Dan C. Cutler, and George T. Beale, "Public Meeting," *New Mexican*, July 28, 1866.

147. "National Convention," *Gazette*, August 11, 1866; "The Southern Loyalist Convention," *National Intelligencer*, in *New Mexican*, September 29, 1866; the delegates are named in "A little of the Gazette Politically, in contradistinction with Loyalty," *New Mexican*, November 19, 1867.

148. "The Philadelphia Convention," *Gazette*, September 8, 1866; "The Convention," *Gazette*, September 8, 1866; "Address of the Philadelphia Convention, the President," in *Gazette,* September 15, 1866.

149. "The Philadelphia Convention," *Gazette*, September 8, 1866.

150. Robert B. Mitchell et al. to His Excellency, Andrew Johnson, September 7, 1866, National Archives, Territorial Papers—New Mexico, RG 46, tray 2, folder 1; untitled, *New Mexican*, June 15, 1866.

151. Charles Emil Wesche et al., "County Convention," *Gazette*, August 25, 1866.

152. See, for example, "Public Meeting," *New Mexican*, August 25, 1866; untitled, *New Mexican*, August 25, 1866; "The Election," *New Mexican*, September 1, 1866.

153. "Election News," *New Mexican*, October 27, 1866.

154. McKitrick, *Andrew Johnson*, 13.

155. "The Election," *New Mexican*, September 8, 1866; untitled, *New Mexican*, September 8, 1866; "Election News," *New Mexican*, September 15, 1866.

156. "¡¡¡HORRIBLE ATENTADO!!!," *Nuevo-Mejicano*, September 15, 1866.

157. "That Terrible Scheme," *Gazette*, September 22, 1866; "Aquel Atentado Terrible," *Gazeta Semanaria*, September 29, 1866.

158. John T. Russell to Senator Charles Sumner ("Peonage in New Mexico"), *Gazette*, February 2, 1867.

159. McKitrick, *Andrew Johnson*, 357.

160. José M. Gallegos et al., "Convention to nominate a Candidate for Delegate," *Gazette*, January 26, 1867; F. Perea et al., "To the People of the Territory of New Mexico," January 28, 1867, *Gazette*, February 2, 1867.

161. Arny's term ended in mid-February 1867. Benedict stepped down on March 10, 1866, replaced as chief justice by Judge John P. Slough. He had served in the territorial judiciary for twelve years. At a public meeting the members of the New Mexico bar expressed their appreciation for his service, regretting the "disposition of government officials" to remove him. The *New Mexican* noted that the "hardships of mountain travel, the rigors of winter, and danger from hostile Indians," had never deterred him from the discharge of his official duties. "The Removals," *New Mexican*, February 16, 1866; untitled, M. Ashurst, H. Thompkins, Theodore S. Greiner, C. P. Cleaver, Attorney General, and S. B. Elkins, *New Mexican*, March 16, 1866; Hunt, *Kirby Benedict*, 188, 190.

162. "Convention," *Gazette*, January 26, 1867; "Convention," *Gazette*, March 2, 1867.

163. "Slander and vituperation," *Gazette*, March 16, 1867.

164. Kirby Benedict et al., *New Mexican*, February 2, 1867; "Junta Pública de los Amigos del Partido de Chavez," *Nuevo-Mejicano*, February 2, 1867; Ferrell, *Reconstruction*, 29.

165. La Comisión Central, March 4, 1867 ("Llamada de Convención General"), *Nuevo-Mejicano*, March 9, 1867.

166. Mora to editor, *Gaceta*, January 19, 1867.

167. Taosonian to editor, *Gazette*, March 2, 1867.

168. Taoseño to editor, March 11, 1867, in *Gazette*, March 16, 1867.

169. Untitled editorial, *Gaceta*, January 19, 1867.

170. "The Carleton-Mitchell Convention," *New Mexican*, March 23, 1867.

171. "Frank Perea—Secretary Heath," *New Mexican*, March 30, 1867; "The Convention," *Gazette*, March 23, 1867; "C. P. Clever to José Manuel Gallegos," Santa Fe, April 11, 1867, in *Gazette*, April 20, 1867.

172. According to one historian, he was "one of the early settlers, prominent in the business community, and reputation as an able attorney. Roberts, *Death Comes for the Chief Justice*, 44.

173. "The Ratification," *Gazette*, April 20, 1867.

174. "Mariano Larragoite," *La Voz del Pueblo* (Las Vegas NM), December 19, 1908.

175. Mariano Larragoiti to editor, *Gaceta*, March 2, 1867. The correct spelling was Larragoite.

176. Lorenzo Labadie et al., "Junta Especial," in "Junta Pública de los Ciudadanos del Condado de San Miguel con el fin de Llamar la Convención del Condado," *Nuevo-Mejicano*, April 20, 1867.

177. Francisco Lopez et al., "Convención," in "Junta Pública de los Ciudadanos."

178. Severo Baca et al., "Procedimientos de la Convención General del Partido Nacionál Unionista del Territorio de Nuevo Mejico," *Nuevo-Mejicano*, April 6, 1867; "The Convention and the Nominee," *New Mexican*, April 6, 1867; J. Francisco Chaves [sic] to Major Jose D. Sena, April 19, 1867, in "Col. Chaves' Letter of Acceptance," *New Mexican*, April 27, 1867; "Special Correspondence of the *Herald*," New York *Herald*, April 22, 1867, transl. in José Francisco Chávez folder, Carl Hayden Papers, Arizona Historical Society, Tucson.

179. "Discurso de José D. Sena a la Convención General Reunida en Santa Fe el Primer Lunes de Abríl, 1867," *Nuevo-Mejicano*, April 27, 1867.

180. Bormann, "Fantasy and Rhetorical Vision," 396; Devine, "Race as Poverty," 2.

11. *Política Judaica e Literaria*

1. Bein, *Jewish Question*, 206–11, 212–17.

2. Carlos María de Bustamante, *El Nuevo Bernal Díaz del Castillo*, 34.

3. Religious freedom was established in Mexico in 1865; Krause, *Los Judíos en México*, 41, 47–48.

4. Korn, *American Jewry*, 1–14.

5. Michael, *Concise History of American Antisemitism*, 69.

6. Sarna, *When General Grant Expelled the Jews*, 4–23.

7. Michael, *Concise History of American Antisemitism*, 90–92; Jaher, *A Scapegoat*, 179, 196–97, 198–99; Korn, *American Jewry*, 22–23.

8. Jaher, *A Scapegoat*, 206; Korn, *American Jewry*, 158–88. The effects of General Order No. 11 lingered to Grant's two presidential terms, coming to haunt him to the

end of his life; on the aftermath impact of General Order No. 11, see Sarna, *When General Grant Expelled the Jews.*

9. Lomnitz, "Anti-Semitism."

10. Clever first hired on in the store of Eugene Leitensdorfer and later became a charter member of Seligman & Clever; Fierman, "The Career of Clever," 2–5, 34–35; Charles Clever, "Address," *Republican* (Santa Fe), July 12, 1862.

11. Tobias, *History of the Jews*, 86.

12. Juan de J. Trujillo, Cura de Santa Cruz, to editor, *Gazette*, August 17, 1867.

13. As a critic emphasized during the campaign; untitled, *New Mexican*, August 17, 1867.

14. Fierman, "The Career of Clever," 2, 3; Roberts, *Death Comes for the Chief Justice*, 44.

15. "A Political Sky-Rocket," *New Mexican*, May 4, 1867.

16. "Clever's Pretensions," *New Mexican*, August 17, 1867.

17. Marx, *A World without Jews*, introduction by Dagobert D. Runes, 41.

18. J.A.M. Y MEDINA [José Durán] to editors, *Nuevo-Mejicano*, August 3, 1867.

19. Juan 6:61–63 Palabra de Dios para Todos (PDT). © 2005, 2008, 2012 Centro Mundial de Traducción de La Biblia © 2005, 2008, 2012 World Bible Translation Center, https://www.biblegateway.com/passage/?search=Juan+6%3A61–63&version=PDT.

20. One military officer left seventeen Spanish-era novels and nineteen nonfiction works to his Nuevomexican heirs. Manuel Delgado, settlement of estate, Santa Fe, 1815, Spanish Archives of New Mexico, ser. I, no. 252, History File, no. 42, New Mexico State Records Center and Archives, Santa Fe; see discussion in Hordes, *To the End of the Earth*, 199–201.

21. Marx, *World without Jews*, 37; Bein, *Jewish Question*, 217.

22. Socorroeño to editors, *Nuevo-Mejicano*, June 15, 1867.

23. Lomnitz, "Anti-Semitism," 21. On the debate in the gospels whether Judas was a traitor to Jesus or Jesus' most "trusting and "trustworthy" disciple, see Pagels and King, *Reading Judas.*

24. Un Pastor de Ovejas to editor, *Gazette*, August 10, 1867.

25. El Valle del Tulquillo to my dear sister, August 15, 1867, *Nuevo-Mejicano*, August 17, 1867; La Vega de Mora to My dear brother, *Nuevo-Mejicano*, August 17, 1867. On the value of the thirty coins in the legend of Judas in the Passion, see Pagels and King, *Reading Judas*, 17–20.

26. Un Votante to editors, *Nuevo-Mejicano*, July 13, 1867.

27. "The *New York Tribune, Herald,* and *Commercial,* the Patterson Press, and the Detroit Commercial Advertiser were only a few of the papers which alleged that Jews were responsible for the speculation in gold: 'all Jews are gold speculators,' 'those hook-nosed wretches speculate on disasters'"; Korn, *American Jewry*, 161.

28. Un Ex-Voluntario to editors ("Regalo 2do."), *Nuevo-Mejicano*, August 17, 1867.

29. Bein, *Jewish Question*, 219.

30. Fierman, "The Career of Clever," 2, 3; Roberts, *Death Comes for the Chief Justice*, 44.

31. "The Democrat," *Gazette*, April 18, 1857; "El Demócrata," *Gaceta*, April 25, 1857.

32. Un Ranchero, "Procedimientos de una Convención," *Nuevo-Mejicano*, June 29, 1867. This pseudonym was similar to the pen name "Ranchero" that José Francisco Chávez had adopted in his plan for running for delegate in 1865. It is unlikely that the incumbent delegate participated in actually calling Clever a Jew in the campaign of 1867.

33. For "pound of flesh" see Cuando Mande, "A Nuestro Amigo 'Nada,'" *Nuevo-Mejicano*, May 18, 1867. President Johnson called his former political allies "a common gang of cormorants and blood-suckers, who have been fattening upon the country"; Michael Les Benedict, *Impeachment and Trial of Andrew Johnson*, 13.

34. Korn, *American Jewry*, 161.

35. For a recent discussion of the trope of melancholia in the eighteenth-century Baroque expressions, see Coronado, *A World Not to Come*, 104–6, 136–37, 167, 170–74, 353, 386.

36. Gracián y Morales, *Oráculo manual, y arte de prudencia* (1647), 17–18; translated into English by Abel Swalle, *The Courtiers Manual Oracle: or, The Art of Prudence* (London, 1685), 16.

37. Zorrilla, *Traidor, Inconfeso y Mártir*.

38. The entire dialogue appears in a column in which the title may have been cut off from the saved edition and which has no byline, in *Nuevo-Mejicano*, June 8, 1867.

39. On "homeless wandering" see Bein, *Jewish Question*, 211.

40. Boyle, *Los Capitalistas*, 71–72. On the middle merchant role played by Jews throughout the world in the nineteenth century, see Bonacich, "Class Approaches to Ethnicity and Race," 66–67, and Bein, *Jewish Question*, 217–20.

41. Tobias, *History of the Jews*, 44–45, 51, 55–56, 72, quote 37; Parish, *German Jew*, 318, 319.

42. Parish, *German Jew*, 319; for a discussion on the visible Jew in the modern age and its portents for ethnic hostility, see Bein, *Jewish Question*, 220–21.

43. Parish, *German Jew*, 321; Parish, *Charles Ilfeld*, 37–38.

44. Un Ranchero, "Procedimientos de una Convención," *Nuevo-Mejicano*, June 29, 1867.

45. Rothschild, *Ethnopolitics*, 74–75.

46. Tobias, *History of the Jews*, 45.

47. Hasta Otra Vista, "El que Dice lo Quiere, Oye, lo Que No Quiere," *Nuevo-Mejicano*, May 4, 1867, 3. On the "New Jerusalem" in Revelations and its relation to Judaism, see Pagels, *Revelations*, 163; cf. 2, 7, 103, 132, 165, 171.

48. "Junta Pública Tenida en Alburquerque, N.M. el Día Domingo, de Abríl 19, A.D., 1867," *Nuevo-Mejicano*, June 1, 1867.

49. Alburquereño, untitled, *Nuevo-Mejicano*, June 1, 1867.

50. A fragmentary report suggests that Chávez walked into the convention shortly after Sena delivered his nomination speech; Tomás C. de Baca et al., "Proceedings of the Convention," *New Mexican*, April 21, 1865.

51. Un Ex-Voluntario for the Nuevo-Mejicano ("El Regalo"), *Nuevo-Mejicano*, July 27, 1867; Un Ranchero, "Procedimientos de una Convención," *Nuevo-Mejicano*, June 29, 1867.

52. Lomnitz, "Modes of Citizenship in Mexico," 282-83; Cubereño to editors, June 10, 1867, *Nuevo-Mejicano*, June 29, 1867.
53. Primeriso, Socorro, "Opinión Política de un Joven Nuevo Mejicano," *Nuevo-Mejicano*, July 13, 1867.
54. Un Ex-Voluntario for the Nuevo-Mejicano ("El Regalo"), *Nuevo-Mejicano*, July 27, 1867.
55. Fidelio, "The True Policy for New Mexico," *New Mexican*, June 8, 1867.
56. Untitled, *Gazette*, August 10, 1867.
57. Un Albuquerqueño Libre, "De Alburquerque," to editor, June 7, 1867, *Gazette*, June 22, 1867.
58. Verdad to editor, *Gazette*, July 6, 1867.
59. "Manifiesto," *Gaceta*, July 13, 1867.
60. Yanos Veremos to editor, *Gaceta*, May 11, 1867.
61. Anonymous to Querida Gazeta, *Gaceta*, May 11, 1867.
62. Anonymous to Dear Sir, *Gazette*, August 17, 1867.
63. "Clever Triumphant!," *Gazette*, September 14, 1867.
64. Un Tauseño to John T. Russell, Fernando de Taos, July 9, 1867, *Gazette*, July 20, 1867; "Chaves in Doña Ana County," *New Mexican*, August 31, 1867; "The Ball opened in Dona Ana County," *New Mexican*, June 15, 1867; Trinidad Lopez to editor, *Gaceta*, August 17, 1867; Un Espectador Imparcial, "Chavez en Mora," *Gaceta*, August 3, 1867; Q.B.S.M., Q. Esperanza to editor, *Gaceta*, August 24,1867; J. Francisco Chavez to General H. H. Heath, September 5, 1867, and J. Francisco Chavez to H. H. Heath, August 29, 1867, Carl Hayden Papers, MS 0585: Herman H. Heath Papers, 1867–1869, Arizona Historical Society, Tucson.
65. José de Jesús García to editor ("Contesta al Cubereño"), *Gaceta*, July 13, 1867.
66. Un Miembro de la Convención del 20 de Marzo to editor, *Gazette*, May 18, 1867.
67. "The Issue," *Gazette*, August 10, 1867.
68. Anonymous, "'La Nada, es Nada,'" April 15, 1867, in *Gazette*, April 27, 1867.
69. Hasta Otra Vista, "El que Dice lo Quiere, Oye lo Que No Quiere," *Nuevo-Mejicano*, May 4, 1867.
70. Pagels and King, *Reading Judas*, 53–54.
71. Tobias, *History of the Jews*, 73, 74; Parish, *German Jew*, 315.
72. Wm. Zeckendorf to editor, June 4, 1867, *Gazette*, June 22, 1867.
73. Un Americano de Nacimiento y no Judío, untitled, *Nuevo-Mejicano*, July 13, 1867.
74. Unreadable byline, *Gazette*, August 17, 1867.
75. Fidelio, "The True Policy for New Mexico," *New Mexican*, June 8, 1867.
76. "How Chavez opens the Campaign," *Gazette*, April 27, 1867.
77. "Clever's Friendship for Americans," *New Mexican*, July 27, 1867.
78. Un Miembro de la Convención del 20 de Marzo to editor, *Gaceta*, May 18, 1867.
79. Anonymous to Querida Gazeta, *Gaceta*, May 11, 1867.
80. Un Ciudadano, untitled essay, *Gazette*, August 31, 1867.
81. Un Escuelero, "El Pitillo," Rio Arriba, *Gazette*, August 10, 1867.
82. The use of *pais* (country) at this time among the Nuevomexicanos reflected the old use and pronunciation (*pays*) of the more modern and formally correct *país*.

83. Un Hijo del Pais to editor, *Gaceta*, July 27, 1867.
84. "The Dunghill odor," *Gazette*, May 11, 1967.
85. "Manifiesto," *Gazette*, July 13, 1867; the Canadian connection is mentioned in Un Ciudadano, untitled, *Gazette*, August 31, 1867. The name of Chávez's wife was Mary Bowie.
86. Amigo del Pueblo to editor, *Gazette*, June 8, 1867.
87. Un Ranchero to editor, *Gazette*, June 15, 1867.
88. Un Ranchero to editor, *Gaceta*, July 27, 1867.
89. Formisano, *Birth of Mass Political Parties*, 105.
90. Untitled, *Gazette*, July 6, 1867.
91. La Revelación to editor, May 30, 1867, *Gaceta*, June 15, 1867.
92. Pepe to editor, *Gaceta*, July 27, 1867.
93. Untitled, *Gazette*, July 20, 1867.
94. Un Navajoe, "Delegados," *Gaceta*, June 22, 1867.
95. Anonymous, "The Duty of the Hour," *Gazette*, August 17, 1867.
96. Un Ranchero to editor, *Gaceta*, August 17, 1867; [Putnam], "En Route for Arizona," *Hartford Evening Press*, January 5, 1864, transcribed in José Francisco Chávez folder, Carl Hayden Papers, Arizona Historical Society, Tucson.
97. Un Miembro de la Convención del 20 de Marzo to editor, *Gazette*, May 18, 1867; José D. Sena, "Al Mono de la Convención del 20 de Abríl de 1867," *Nuevo-Mejicano*, May 25, 1867.
98. Tobias, *History of the Jews*, 34, 37, 73.
99. Joseph Hersch to editor, *Gazette*, June 8, 1867.
100. Hughes, *Doniphan's Expedition*, 61–62. Lamy apparently considered the comedic theater rather sinful; Horgan, *Lamy of Santa Fe*, 190. Early in the next election cycle, however, the *New Mexican* would comment that it had very little to commend in the pages of the *Gazette*: "But when the question of amusement arises, we can say with a great degree of truth, that in the absence of theatres with comedians and circuses and clowns, the *Gazette* furnishes a remarkably good substitute"; "A little of the Gazette Politically, in contradistinction with Loyalty," *New Mexican*, November 19, 1867.
101. Zavala, "La Prensa Exaltada," 366.
102. "Chicote," *Gaceta*, August 24, 1867.
103. Un Pirata, "Los Dos Compadres," *Gaceta*, May 18, 1867.
104. Miguel E. Pino [to editors], *Nuevo-Mejicano*, June 1, 1867.
105. Anonymous to editor, March 26, 1867, *Gazette*, April 6, 1867; anonymous to editors, *Nuevo-Mejicano*, May 11, 1867.
106. Anonymous to *Gazette*, June 1, 1867; Eugenio Romero to editors ("¿A Que Puerta Tocan, Que no Responden?"), *Nuevo-Mejicano*, June 29, 1867; Daniel a Eugenio Romero, June 1867, *Gaceta*, July 6, 1867; Valentín Vásquez to editors, *Nuevo-Mejicano*, July 6, 1867; anonymous, "Que Rueda la Bola," *Gazette*, June 1, 1867.
107. Anonymous to editors, *Nuevo-Mejicano*, June 1, 1867.
108. Zurriago, "Penúltimo diálogo entre Pancho y Juan, proveido, que el cotera Morbus no estorbe los pasos," *Gazette*, August 3, 1867. The sequence of motions plays off the Spanish *agregar*.

109. 2, "Diálogo Entre Juan y Pedro," *Gazette*, June 29, 1867; "Diálogo 30 entre Juan y Pedro," *Gazette*, August 24, 1867.

110. Un Ranchero to editor ("Un Enigma"), *Gazette*, June 8, 1867. It is possible that Un Ranchero was Donaciano Vigil, who as an entrepreneurial rancher in Pecos tended to take up "rancher" as his identity in his land dealings; see Hall, "Giant Before the Surveyor-General," 67.

111. La Revelación to editor, May 30, 1867, *Gazette*, June 15, 1867.

112. Un Hijo del Pais to editor, *Gazette*, July 27, 1867.

113. The *Gazette* took note of the volume of expressions coming in from the Mexicans but published only the ones coming into its offices by the "more intelligent and educated portion of our Territory, by men who, collectively, certainly have the true interests of the country at heart—men who must live and die here and whose private fortunes for good or bad must rise and fall in exact proportion as those of the Territory are properly cared for or suffered to be neglected. They know this, and are beginning to make it tell." Of course, in the *Gazette*'s slant, it was intelligence and education that led this portion of the Nuevomexicanos, as well as the "Americans," to see Clever making a better delegate than Chávez; "A Short Comment," *Gazette* June 22, 1867.

114. El Trueno, "Al Pueblo del condado de Doña Ana especialmente, y en general, al Territorio de Nuevo Mejico," *Nuevo-Mejicano*, December 24, 1867.

115. Un Ranchero to editor, *Gazette*, June 1, 1867.

116. José D. Sena, "Al Ranchero," *Nuevo-Mejicano*, June 8, 1867.

117. Jesús Ma. H. Alarid to José D. Sena, June 19, 1867, *Gazette*, June 15, 1867.

118. El Ranchero to editor, *Gazette*, June 22, 1867.

119. José D. Sena to J.M.H. Alarid, *Nuevo-Mejicano*, June 22, 1867.

120. Anonymous to the editors, *Nuevo-Mejicano*, June 22, 1867.

121. Quien tu sabes, "La luz de la razón," *Gazette*, July 13, 1867.

122. Zavala, "La Prensa Exaltada," 365–88.

123. Adios, "Reto," *Gazette*, June 22, 1867.

124. "Santa Fe County Convention," *New Mexican*, August 10, 1867; Kirby Benedict et al., "Public Meeting," *New Mexican*, August 10, 1867.

125. José M. Gallegos et al., "Convención tenida por el partido Unionista en el condado de Santa Fe, en la casa de Don Albino Roibal, el día 28 de Julio 1867," *Gazette*, August 3, 1867.

126. "Gen'l. Clever's Reception," *Gazette*, July 27, 1867.

127. Theisen, "José Manuel Gallegos," 162–63; "Gallegos as drawn by Clever," *New Mexican*, July 27, 1867; Perfecto Armijo to editors ("Tulerosa"), *New Mexican*, August 24, 1867.

128. For Chávez's National Union ballots, see, for example, "Socorro County Ticket," *New Mexican*, June 15, 1867; "Santa Ana County Ticket," *New Mexican*, July 13, 1867; W. R. McCormick, "Doña Ana County," *New Mexican*, July 13, 1867.

129. "The Canvass," *Gazette*, July 20, 1867; anonymous, "From Valencia County," *New Mexican*, August 24, 1867; Antonio S. Baca to editors, *New Mexican*, June 29, 1867, Socorro County Ticket," *New Mexican*, June 15, 1867; Un Curioso Espectador,

"El Coronel Chavez en Taos," *Nuevo-Mejicano*, August 3, 1867; Observador in Taos County to editors ("From Taos"), *New Mexican*, August 24, 1867; Truth to editors, May 21, 1867 ("The Taos Meeting"), *New Mexican*, May 25, 1867; Miller, "William Logan Rynerson," 101–2.

130. W. L. Rynerson and Nepomuceno Ancheta, "Proceedings of the People of Doña Ana County Assembled in Mass Convention at Las Cruces N.M. on the 30th Day of June 1867 in Pursuance of Public Notice and Call of Committee," *New Mexican*, July 13, 1867; W. R. McCormick, "Doña Ana County," *New Mexican*, July 13, 1867; Roberts, *Death Comes for the Chief Justice*, 58.

131. "Chaves in Doña Ana County," *New Mexican*, August 31, 1867; untitled, *Nuevo-Mejicano*, August 31, 1867.

132. Chaves, *Papers in the Case of J. Francisco Chaves vs. Charles P. Clever*, 157–58.

133. "The Ball opened in Dona Ana County," *New Mexican*, June 15, 1867.

134. Perfecto Armijo, "From Las Cruces," *New Mexican*, July 13, 1867.

135. A. Miner, "Pinos Altos," *New Mexican*, July 27, 1867.

136. "The Canvass," *Gazette*, May 18, 1867.

137. "Enthusiastic Public Meeting in Albuquerque," *Gazette*, August 24, 1867.

138. Juan Armijo et al., "Junta pública tenida el 16 de Julio 1867, en el condado del Socorro, precinto dos y en la casa del coronel R. H. Stapleton," *Gazette*, August 3, 1867; Pedro A. Baca et al. to editor ("Junta pública en el condado del Socorro"), *Gazette*, June 15, 1867.

139. D. to editor, July 16, 1867, *Gazette*, July 27, 1867. On the lineage, see "A Notable Family," *Daily Herald* (Phoenix), February 8, 1899, transcribed in José Francisco Chávez folder, Carl Hayden Papers, Arizona Historical Society, Tucson.

140. "Reflecciones de un Labrador," *Gazette*, July 20, 1867.

141. Pablo Pino et al., "Junta Pública Tenida en Cubero Precinto No. 9 del Condado de Valencia el Domingo Día 9 del Mes de Junio 1867," *Nuevo-Mejicano*, June 29, 1867.

142. "The Demonstration Sunday Night," *Gazette*, April 27, 1867.

143. "Splendid 'Splay," *New Mexican*, April 27, 1867.

144. "Discussion," *Gazette*, August 3, 1867; "Public Meeting," *New Mexican*, August 3, 1867.

145. Untitled, *Gazette*, August 10, 1867.

146. Un Tauseño, "Desengaño Glorioso," *Gaceta*, August 24, 1867.

147. Untitled, *New Mexican*, July 13, 1867; "The Canvass," *New Mexican*, July 20, 1867; Observador in Taos County to editors ("From Taos"), *New Mexican*, August 24, 1867.

148. Un Espectador to editor, *Gaceta*, July 6, 1867; Teófilo Chavez and Fred Bradford, "Public Meeting," *Gazette*, July 6, 1867.

149. Antonio G. Cordova et al., untitled, *Nuevo-Mejicano*, August 31, 1867.

150. Taos to editor, May 5, 1867, *Gazette*, May 11, 1867; Un Tauseño to *Gaceta*, May 11, 1867.

151. Un Curioso Espectador, "El Coronel Chávez en Taos," *Nuevo-Mejicano*, August 3, 1867.

152. Truth to editors, May 21, 1867 ("The Taos Meeting"), *New Mexican*, May 25, 1867.

153. La Verdad to J. T. Russell, *Gaceta*, July 20, 1867; Public Meeting," *New Mexican*, August 3, 1867; Un Tausense, "Desengaño Glorioso," *Gazette*, August 24, 1867; Un Curioso Espectador, "El Coronel Chávez en Taos," *Nuevo-Mejicano*, August 3, 1867.

154. Incognito, "Recepción del Hon. J. Francisco Chavez en los Rincones, Condado de Taos," *Nuevo-Mejicano*, July 27, 1867; Un Curioso Espectador, "El Coronel Chavez en Taos," *Nuevo-Mejicano*, August 3, 1867.

155. "The Canvass," *Gazette*, July 20, 1867.

156. Un Curioso Espectador, "El Coronel Chavez en Taos," *Nuevo-Mejicano*, August 3, 1867.

157. Un Tausense, "Desengaño Glorioso," *Gaceta*, August 24, 1867; Un Tauseno to John T. Russell, Fernando de Taos, July 9, 1867, *Gaceta*, July 20, 1867.

158. Un Curioso Espectador, "El Coronel Chavez en Taos," *Nuevo-Mejicano*, August 3, 1867.

159. Un Curioso Espectador, "El Coronel Chavez en Taos."

160. Un Testigo de Vista to editor, *Gaceta*, August 31, 1867. A present-day descendant of J. Leandro Perea identifies him as having been a crypto-Jew (Hordes, *To the End of the Earth*, 197–99). But this means a good chance of José Francisco Chávez, Perea's nephew, also being one. No hint of this association ever arose in the anti-Semitic discourse of 1867.

161. Un Tauseño to John T. Russell, Fernando de Taos, July 9, 1867, *Gaceta*, July 20, 1867; La Verdad to J. T. Russell, *Gaceta*, July 20, 1867.

162. Fernandeño to editors, *Nuevo-Mejicano*, August 3, 1867.

163. Un Testigo de Vista to editor, *Gaceta*, August 31, 1867.

164. Un Espectador Imparcial, "Chavez en Mora," *Gaceta*, August 3, 1867.

165. Trinidad López to editor, *Gaceta*, August 17, 1867.

166. Serie Pensador, "Presinto No. 7 del Condado de Mora," *Nuevo-Mejicano*, July 27, 1867; Santiago Abreu et al., "Junta Pública," *Nuevo-Mejicano*, August 3, 1867.

167. Trinidad López to editor, *Gaceta*, August 17, 1867.

168. Q.B.S.M., Q. Esperanza to editor, *Gaceta*, August 24, 1867. Note that the Jewish prophet Amos announced that God rejected the pagan worships of the Jews, "the offerings of well-being of your fatted animals"; Pagels, *Reading Judas*, 69.

169. Chaves, *Papers in the Case of J. Francisco Chaves vs. Charles P. Clever*, 46–48, 66–67, 70, 93–99, 103–4, 112–15, 123–34, 129–31, 137–38; Chaves, *Additional Papers in the Case of J. Francisco Chaves against Charles P. Clever, of New Mexico*, Misc. Doc. no. 14, 40th Congress, 3rd session, 13–14, 18–22, 31–32, 36–37.

170. "Vote for Delegate in New Mexico," *Gazette*, November 9, 1867.

171. J. Francisco Chávez to General H. H. Heath, September 5, 1867, Carl Hayden Papers, MS 0585: Herman H. Heath Papers, 1867–1869, Arizona Historical Society, Tucson (hereafter Chávez letters); Roberts, *Death Comes for the Chief Justice*, 47.

172. "The Official Vote," *Gazette*, September 21, 1867. For different figures (i.e., 17,606 votes cast, 540 majority for Clever, 9,073 v. 8,533 for Chávez), see *J. Francisco Chaves vs. Charles P. Clever*, Report, February 9, 1869, 40th Congress, 3rd session, House of Representatives, Report No. 18, 1.

173. Bormann, "Fantasy and Rhetorical Vision," 102; Foss, *Rhetorical Criticism*, 97.

174. "Justification," *Gazette*, September 21, 1867.
175. "Clever Triumphant!," *Gazette*, September 14, 1867.
176. "Diálogo conclusivo entre Pedro y Juan," *Gaceta*, September 21, 1867.
177. "About Election Frauds," *Gazette*, September 28, 1867.

12. A Contest for the Ages

1. Roberts, *Death Comes for the Chief Justice*, 45.
2. H. H. Heath to Henry Dawes, October 4, 1867, in Proceedings of the House of Representatives relative to the admission of the Delegate from New Mexico, *Daily Globe*, December 20, 1868, in "Delegate From New Mexico," *Gazette*, January 11, 1868; H. H. Heath, "Official Returns of the Territory of New Mexico for the Election held September 2d, 1867," Carl Hayden Papers, folder 4, MS 0585: Herman H. Heath Papers, 1867–1869, Arizona Historical Society, Tucson.
3. Heath to Dawson, October 4, 1867, in Proceedings; J. Francisco Chavez to H. H. Heath, October 26, 1867, Chávez letters; *Daily Globe*, December 20, 1868, in "New Mexico Contested Election," *Gazette*, January 11, 1868.
4. "Heath," *Gazette*, December 14, 1867.
5. Untitled editorial, *Gazette*, October 12, 1867; untitled editorial, *Gazette*, October 19, 1867.
6. J. Francisco Chavez to H. H. Heath, December 1, 1867, Chávez letters.
7. Roberts, *Death Comes for the Chief Justice*, 46–47.
8. H. H. Heath to Schuyler Colfax, October 1, 1867, in "Heath," *Gazette*, December 14, 1867; Roberts, *Death Comes for the Chief Justice*. For the reports on the Chávez party winning the territorial legislature, see "Santa Fe County Election," *New Mexican*, September 14, 1867; anonymous, "Pancho y Chepe ya son compadres!!!," *Gaceta*, October 12, 1867; "Peonage and Indian Slavery," *Gazette*, May 23, 1868; "Copperheads," *Gazette*, February 8, 1868.
9. H. H. Heath to Henry S. [sic] Dawes, October 23, 1867, box 1, folder 4, Clinton P. Anderson Papers, Center for Southwest Research, University of New Mexico.
10. Untitled, *Gazette*, January 18, 1868.
11. "The Gazette as a Loyal Paper," *New Mexican*, October 26, 1867; "The Loyalty of the Gazette," *New Mexican*, November 5, 1867; "The Gazette as a Loyal Paper," *New Mexican*, November 12, 1867; "A little of the Gazette Politically, in contradistinction with Loyalty," *New Mexican*, November 19, 1867; cf. Roberts, *Death Comes for the Chief Justice*, 48. For attempts by the *Gazette* and allies to answer to the *New Mexican*'s onslaught, see, untitled *Gazette*, October 12, 1867; Zurriago, "Cabezas de Cobre," October 12, 1867, *Gazette*, October 19, 1867; "The New Mexican," *Gazette*, November 2, 1867.
12. "The Result," *New Mexican*, September 21, 1867. The charges of fraud included wild increases of voters in Mora, Río Arriba, and Socorro counties, attributed to Governor Mitchell illegally creating new precincts to bolster chances for Clever; fraudulent counts in Río Arriba County; making the poll site at Fort Union inaccessible so that the sutler, quartermaster's men, and government employees could sweep the votes with money and have military officers vote illegally; directing individuals to

vote in more than one precinct; an interfering probate judge in Doña Ana County; illegal voters from the mines in Colorado paid to come in to vote; the stealing of ballot boxes in Río Arriba and Santa Fe counties; perjury as to the number of legal voters in Tierra Amarilla; and ironically, noncitizens voting; see *New Mexican,* "The Election," September 7, 1867; "The Election," September 14, 1867; "Santa Fe County Election," September 14, 1867; "The Result," September 21, 1867, 2.

13. "The Result," *New Mexican*, September 21, 1867.

14. "Santa Fe County Election," *New Mexican*, September 14, 1867.

15. For the part of Clever's supporters, "The Result," *Gazette*, September 14, 1867; Dos Tauseños to editor, *Gaceta*, September 14, 1867; "Frauds," *Gazette*, September 14, 1867.

16. "About Election Frauds," *Gazette*, September 28, 1867.

17. "Vote for Delegate in New Mexico," *Gazette*, November 9, 1867.

18. H. H. Heath to William L. Rynerson, November 10, 1867, Carl Hayden Papers, folder 4, MS 0585: Herman H. Heath Papers, 1867–1869, Arizona Historical Society, Tucson; W. H. Henrie, "Report of the Committee of the two Houses of Territorial Legislature of New Mexico on the subject of frauds perpetrated at the general election held in this Territory on the 2d day of September, A.D. 1867, under the Joint Resolution of the Legislature, passed January 18th, 1868," "Report," *New Mexican*, February 4, 1868; Sam J. Jones to the people of the Territory of New Mexico and particularly of the voters of the County of Doña Ana, *Gazette*, December 14, 1867; El Trueno, "Al Pueblo del condado de Doña Ana especialmente, y en general, al Territorio de Nuevo Mejico," *Nuevo-Mejicano*, December 24, 1867; cf. Roberts, *Death Comes for the Chief Justice*, 48, 57–58, and Miller, "William Logan Rynerson," 103.

19. J. Francisco Chavez to H. H. Heath, December 11, 1867, Chávez letters.

20. "Gen'l Clever," *Gazette*, January 4, 1868; cf. "Chavez and Clever," *New Mexican*, January 7, 1868.

21. Un Taoseño, "¡¡¡Una Gran Demostración en Taos!!!," *Gazette*, January 25, 1868.

22. Annon to William Manderfield, April 15, 1864, in Kirby Benedict, *Journey through New Mexico's First Judicial District*, 54.

23. Vicente Romero et al., "Procedimientos de una junta pública," *Gazette*, January 18, 1868.

24. Un Nuevo Mejicano to the *Gazette*, February 22, 1868.

25. H. H. Heath to José Francisco Chávez, December 30, 1867, box 1, folder 2, Clinton P. Anderson Papers, Center for Southwest Research, University of New Mexico.

26. H. H. Heath to F. N. Seward, Asst. Secretary of State, Washington DC, December 23, 1867, box 1, folder 4, Anderson Papers.

27. H. H. Heath to José Francisco Chávez, December 30, 1867, box 1, folder 2, Anderson Papers.

28. "Governor's Message," *New Mexican*, December 10, 1867.

29. *Organic Law, Session Laws of New Mexico, 1st and 2nd Sessions,* Records of the States of the United States, microfilms, 1846–1861, N.M. B. 2, reel 1, 22.

30. Suggested in the letter Heath wrote to a friend stating that Nebraska customarily gave the swearing in responsibility to the secretary; H. H. Heath to Gen.

N. P. Chipman, December 24, 1867, box 1, folder 4, Anderson Papers; also "Postscript," *New Mexican*, December 3, 1867; Roberts, *Death Comes for the Chief Justice*, 53–54, 77.

31. "Postscript" *New Mexican*, December 3, 1867; "The Legislature," *Gazette*, December 7, 1867; cf. Roberts, *Death Comes for the Chief Justice*, 48; for a brief account of this episode, see Miller, "William Logan Rynerson," 103–5.

32. See, for example, the detailed complaint of a Nuevomexicano in the precinct of Albuquerque that the justice of the peace decided on civil court cases based on the partisan memberships of the disputed principals; Rancho Seco to editor ("El Partido de Chavez en contra de la ley en el Precinto de Albuquerque del condado de Bernalillo"), *Gazette*, July 11, 1868.

33. Roberts, *Death Comes for the Chief Justice*, 20–21, quote 27, 36–37, 40–41, 51.

34. Roberts, *Death Comes for the Chief Justice*, 36; cf. "Laying of the Corner Stone of the Monument," *New Mexican*, November 5, 1867.

35. "An Official Excitement," *New Mexican*, December 3, 1867; untitled, *Gazette*, January 4, 1868; Roberts, *Death Comes for the Chief Justice*, 20–23; Horn, *New Mexico's Troubled Years*; *Organic Law*, 19. Roberts (37–39) also claims unconvincingly that Slough's attack on the institution of peonage was another factor generating Republican opposition to him.

36. Roberts, *Death Comes for the Chief Justice*, 54–55; "Postscript" *New Mexican*, December 3, 1867; H. H. Heath to Gen. N. P. Chipman

37. "A Finale to Judge Slough," *New Mexican*, December 10, 1867; Roberts, *Death Comes for the Chief Justice*, 60–61.

38. J. Ma. Pacheco notarized affidavit, February 5, 1868, in J. Ma. Pacheco to editor ("¡ . . . Granizo! ¡Granizo!"), *Gazette*, May 3, 1868; H. H. Heath to Gen. N. P. Chipman; "¿Quién será el Embustero?," *Gazette*, May 23, 1868; Roberts, *Death Comes for the Chief Justice*, 61–63.

39. Including J. Ma. H. Alarid, Aniceto Abeytia, Diego Archuleta, Merrill Ashurst, James Edgar, Herman Ilfeld, Fernando Nolan, Nicolás Quintana, and Manuel Spiegelberg; James Edgar et al., "Junta Pública," *Gazette*, January 18, 1868.

40. Merrill Ashurst et al., untitled, *Gazette*, January 18, 1868. Roberts (*Death Comes for the Chief Justice*, 82–83) calls the resolutions "bipartisan."

41. "The Santa Fe Gazette," *New Mexican*, December 24, 1867.

42. Roberts, *Death Comes for the Chief Justice*, 69–74, 77–78; Horn, *New Mexico's Troubled Years*, 127–28; "Muerte del Juez Slough en Nuevo Mejico," *Herald* (Dubuque), in *Gaceta*, January 25, 1868; "A Sad Occurrence," *New Mexican*, December 17, 1867; untitled, *Gazette*, January 4, 1868.

43. Manuel Romero to Aniceto Salazar, December 2, 1867, in *Gazette*, January 18, 1868; cf. Roberts, *Death Comes for the Chief Justice*, 142–43; Tobias, *History of the Jews*, 86–87.

44. Jesús M. Baca y Salazar to editor, *Gazette*, January 18, 1868.

45. "Fiendish Letter," *Gazette*, January 25, 1868; also untitled editorial, *Gazette*, January 18, 1868.

46. In another communication, Baca y Salazar sought to absolve Nolan of the rumor that Nolan had provided him with the letter, explaining that he had picked it up himself from the floor of a gambling den, where Aniceto Salazar dropped it in a fit of frustration over his losses; Jesús M. Baca y Salazar to editor, *Gazette*, January 18, 1868.

47. Aniceto Salazar to editors, *Nuevo-Mejicano*, January 28, 1868.

48. Roberts, *Death Comes for the Chief Justice*, 75.

49. H. H. Heath to Gen. N. P. Chipman.

50. H. H. Heath to José Francisco Chávez, December 30, 1867, box 1, folder 2, Anderson Papers.

51. "An 'Army officer' writes a Letter," *New Mexican*, January 21, 1868.

52. "Muerte del Juez Slough en Nuevo Mejico," *Herald* (Dubuque), in *Gaceta*, January 25, 1868; "Procedimientos de una junta pública tenida en el Condado de Taos, en el Precinto número 9 en la plaza de Chamizal en la casa de Don Jose Gregorio Belarde," *Nuevo-Mejicano*, March 3, 1868, 3; Roberts, *Death Comes for the Chief Justice*, 75–76.

53. Roberts, *Death Comes for the Chief Justice*, 75.

54. As reported in H. H. Heath to Wm. H. Seward, March 11, 1868, box 1, folder 5, Anderson Papers.

55. Anastasio Sandovál, president of the Council, *Resolutions of the Legislative Council of New Mexico approving the official acts of Gen. H.H. Heath, Secretary of that Territory*, 40th Congress, 2nd session, January 6, 1868, Referred to Committee on Territories.

56. S . . . to editors, *Gaceta*, January 18, 1868.

57. X.X.X., *Gazette*, January 4, 1868.

58. "Examination of Hon. Wm. L. Rynerson for Shooting Judge John P. Slough, Chief Justice of New Mexico," *New Mexican*, January 14, 1868; "The case of Captain Rynerson and Judge Slough," *New Mexican*, January 14, 1868.

59. Untitled, *Gazette*, January 18, 1868.

60. Anastacio Sandoval, "Informe del Intendente de Cuentas Públicas," *Nuevo-Mejicano*, January 7, 1868; Trinidad Alarid to the Honorable Anastacio Sandoval, President of the Legislative Council ("Informe del Bibliotecario"), *Nuevo-Mejicano*, January 7, 1868; John Gwyn Jr., Attorney General to the Legislative Assembly of the Territory of New Mexico, November 29, 1867, in *Nuevo-Mejicano*, January 14, 1868.

61. "Territorial Officers," *New Mexican*, December 24, 1867; "Oficiales Territoriales," *Nuevo-Mejicano*, January 7, 1868; "The Gazette as a Loyal Paper," *New Mexican*, October 26, 1867.

62. Farrand, *Legislation for Government of the Organized Territories*, 38–41.

63. Untitled, *Gazette*, December 28, 1867.

64. Farrand, *Legislation for Government of the Organized Territories*, 27.

65. "The *Gazette* on the Legislature," *New Mexican*, December 31, 1867.

66. Farrand, *Legislation for Government of the Organized Territories*, 41, 42.

67. Robert B. Mitchell to President of the Council and the House of Representatives, December 30, 1867, Governor's Papers, Mitchell, reel 1, frames 394–95, RTG, TANM; also

in "Despacho del Ejecutivo," *Nuevo-Mejicano*, January 14, 1868; "The Territories in Congress," *New Mexican*, August 18, 1868; "The Bill Restricting the Veto of the Governor of New Mexico," *New Mexican*, August 25, 1868, and September 1, 1868; "Veto del Gobernador," *Nuevo-Mejicano Diário* (hereafter still cited as *Nuevo-Mejicano* though its name now included *Diário*), August 27, 1868; cf. Roberts, *Death Comes for the Chief Justice*, 75–76.

68. "Preámbulo y Resolución Introducido por Don Celso Baca," *Nuevo-Mejicano*, January 14, 1868; *Nuevo-Mejicano*, January 28, 1868; "Gov. Mitchell and the Veto," *New Mexican*, February 4, 1868.

69. "Russell's idea of the qualifications of the Members of the Legislature," *New Mexican*, January 7, 1868.

70. "Governor Mitchell vetoes a Memorial of the Legislature to Congress," *New Mexican*, January 7, 1868; "El Gobernador Mitchell desaprueba un Memorial de la Legislatura al Congreso," *Nuevo-Mejicano*, January 14, 1868; cf. Horn, *New Mexico's Troubled Years*, 122.

71. Progresistas, "¡Hurrah! ¡Hurrah! ¡Hurrah!: La Constitución Enmendada por el Consejo," *Gazette*, January 25, 1868.

72. "Our Organic Act," *New Mexican*, December 17, 1867.

73. "Gov. Mitchell and the Veto," *New Mexican*, February 4, 1868.

74. Un miembro de la Legislatura to editors, *Nuevo-Mejicano*, March 3, 1868.

75. Wm. H. Henrie, Chairman of Committee, "Resolutions of the Legislative Assembly of the Territory of New Mexico, in favor of the removal of Robert B. Mitchell from the position of Governor of that Territory," March 7, 1868, National Archives, Territorial Papers—New Mexico, RG 46, tray 2, folder 5; also in "Preamble and Joint Resolutions," *New Mexican*, January 21, 1868; H. H. Heath to J. F. Chaves, March 17, 1868, box 1, folder 5, Anderson Papers.

76. "An 'Army Officer' writes a Letter," *New Mexican*, January 21, 1868; "Troubles in New Mexico," *Leavenworth Times*, in *New Mexican*, May 5, 1868; "'Bob' Mitchell in Trouble," *Leavenworth Times*, in *New Mexican*, May 5, 1868.

77. "The Legislature and Governor Mitchell," *Gazette*, January 18, 1868.

78. Merrill Ashurst et al., "Mass Meeting," *Gazette*, January 25, 1868; untitled, *Gazette*, January 25, 1868.

79. "The Great Mass Meeting," *Gazette*, January 25, 1868, 2; cf. Horn, *New Mexico's Troubled Years*, 124–25.

80. "Another Scandalous Junta of Copperheads," *New Mexican*, February 4, 1868.

81. Manuel Armijo et al., "Enthusiastic Public Meeting at Albuquerque on the 3d of Feb," *Gazette*, February 8, 1868.

82. J. Francisco Chavez to H. H. Heath, December 1, 1867, Chávez letters; Roberts, *Death Comes for the Chief Justice*, 48.

83. Antonio Martínez y Medina, Gregorio Velarde, Mariano Lucero, Eulogio Romero, and Eugenio Domingues, "Procedimientos de una junta pública tenida en el Condado de Taos, en el Precinto número 9 en la plaza de Chamizal en la casa de Don Jose Gregorio Belarde," *Nuevo-Mejicano*, March 3, 1868.

84. W. H. Henrie, "Report of the Committee of the two Houses of Territorial Legislature of New Mexico on the subject of frauds perpetrated at the general election

held in this Territory on the 2d day of September, A.D. 1867, under the Joint Resolution of the Legislature, passed January 18th, 1868," published in "Report," *New Mexican*, February 4, 1868; "Preamble and Joint Resolution of Both Houses of the Legislative Assembly of New Mexico," *New Mexican*, February 4, 1868.

85. "[Communicated] Bobby's Device," *New Mexican,* February 18, 1868.
86. "Appointments by the Governor," *Gazette,* February 8, 1868.
87. Untitled editorial, *Gazette*, February 1, 1868.
88. "The Legislature," *New Mexican*, February 4, 1868.

13. Republican Party Debut

1. "General Grant for President," *New Mexican*, November 5, 1867.
2. Mantell, *Johnson, Grant*, 32, 34–35.
3. Mantell, *Johnson, Grant*, 30–31, 35, 68.
4. Simpson, *"Let Us Have Peace,"* 219–24, quote, 223; Mantell, *Johnson, Grant*, 63–70.
5. Michael Les Benedict, *Preserving the Constitution*, 26–31; Simpson, *"Let Us Have Peace,"* 225; Mantell, *Johnson, Grant*, 64–68.
6. "The Republican National Convention—Gen. Grant in Possession," *New York Herald*, in *New Mexican,* December 31, 1867.
7. "New York—Republican Rally," *New Mexican*, November 12, 1867.
8. "Changing Again," *New Mexican*, November 12, 1867.
9. "Grant for the Presidency," *New Mexican*, November 19, 1867.
10. "General Grant for President," *New Mexican*, November 5, 1867; "The New Motto for our Paper," *New Mexican*, November 5, 1867.
11. "Gen. Grant a Radical," *New Mexican*, November 26, 1867.
12. "True Republicanism is True Patriotism," *New Mexican*, November 26, 1867; "How the Rebels Talk," *New Mexican*, December 3, 1867.
13. "Juarez Re-Elected president of old Mexico," *New Mexican*, November 12, 1867.
14. "A Good Joke—Clever a Radical," *New Mexican*, November 19, 1867.
15. "The legislature—its approaching session," *New Mexican*, November 26, 1867.
16. "The Legislature," *New Mexican*, December 3, 1867.
17. Julyan, *Place Names of New Mexico*, 153–54; "Grant County," *New Mexican*, February 25, 1868.
18. "Col. J. F. Chaves," *Missouri Democrat*, in *New Mexican*, November 5, 1867.
19. "To be Subsidized," *New Mexican*, November 5, 1867.
20. San Miguel to editors ("They won't Face the Music"), November 4, 1867, *New Mexican*, November 12, 1867.
21. Una Voz del Pueblo to editors ("Felicitación"), November 16, 1867, *Nuevo-Mejicano*, November 19, 1867.
22. Vox Populi to Fellow Citizens ("A Card to the People of New Mexico"), *Gazette*, December 14, 1867. Suggesting that John Russell was Vox Populi is "Valedictory," *Gazette*, September 25, 1869.
23. William Breeden, "Relative Strength," *Weekly New Mexican Review and Live Stock Journal*, July 31, 1884; H. H. Heath to [U.S. Senator] Richard Yates, February 28, 1868, box 1, folder 4, Clinton P. Anderson Papers, Center for Southwest Research,

University of New Mexico; "Gen'l Clever," *Gazette*, January 4, 1868; Zurriago, "¡Apocalipsis Cumplida!," *Gaceta*, June 27, 1868.

24. Untitled, *Nuevo-Mejicano*, December 31, 1867.

25. "Declaration of Principles of the Union Republican Association of New Mexico," *New Mexican*, January 7, 1868.

26. "Platform of the Union Republican Association of New Mexico," *New Mexican*, January 7, 1868.

27. "Rules and Regulations of the Union Republican Association of New Mexico," *New Mexican*, January 7, 1868.

28. "Correction," *New Mexican*, January 14, 1868.

29. "List of the Officers," *New Mexican*, January 21, 1868.

30. The rest of the members included Sebero Baca, San Miguel County; José Lerrue, Mora County; Francisco Salazar, Río Arriba County; Tomás C. de Baca, Santa Ana County; Tomás C. Gutierres, Bernalillo County; Jesús Ma. Luna, Valencia County; Luis Ma. Baca, Socorro County; and José de Jesús Baca, Doña Ana County. Francisco P. Abreu to President, Union Republican Association of New Mexico, January 28, 1868, transl. in *Nuevo-Mejicano*, February 4, 1868.

31. Untitled, *New Mexican*, January 21, 1868; "A Good Joke—Clever a Radical," *New Mexican*, November 19, 1867; "Clever Abroad," *New Mexican*, November 26, 1867; "Mitchell, Collins and Clever pledge their Support to Andrew Johnson," *New Mexican*, March 24, 1868.

32. H. H. Heath to Maj. L. B. Fleah, February 2, 1868, box 1, folder 4, Anderson Papers.

33. W. H. Henrie, "Report of the Committee of the two Houses of Territorial Legislature of New Mexico on the subject of frauds perpetrated at the general election held in this Territory on the 2d day of September, A.D. 1867, under the Joint Resolution of the Legislature, passed January 18th, 1868," in "Report," *New Mexican*, February 4, 1868.

34. "The Legislature," *New Mexican*, February 4, 1868.

35. H. H. Heath to Gen. John A. Logan, Grand Commander of GAR, Washington DC, January 30, 1868, box 1, folder 4, Anderson Papers.

36. Chaves, *Papers in the Case of J. Francisco Chaves vs. Charles P. Clever*, 46.

37. Anonymous to editors, *Nuevo-Mejicano*, March 3, 1868.

38. J. Francisco Chavez to H. H. Heath, October 26, 1867, Chávez letters, Carl Hayden Papers. See Anderson Papers, box 1, folder 4: H. H. Heath to Gen. N. P. Chipman, December 24, 1867; H. H. Heath to Dear Governor, January 29, 1868; and H. H. Heath to Gen. John A. Logan, Grand Commander of GAR, Washington DC, January 30, 1868; and folder 5: H. H. Heath to N. P. Chipman, March 9, 1868; H. H. Heath to Wm. T. Collins, March 9, 1868. Cf. Roberts, *Death Comes for the Chief Justice*, 32–33.

39. Pancho, "Correspondencia entre los Compadres Hon. Pancho y Don Chepe," *Gazette*, January 25, 1868, 3.

40. Zurriago, "¡Apocalipsis Cumplida!," *Gaceta*, June 27, 1868.

41. "Gen'l Clever," *Gazette*, January 4, 1868; cf. "Chavez and Clever," *New Mexican*, January 7, 1868.

42. PS, Commander, and Zurriago, Assistant, "Sorcito de Operaciones [Little Soldier of Operations]: Especial No. 1," *Gaceta*, January 25, 1868.

43. Gaspar Ortiz y Alarid to editor, *Gazette*, January 18, 1868.

44. "How is it, and why is it?," *Gazette*, January 25, 1868, 2; Kiser, "A 'charming name,'" 188.

45. "Copperheads," *Gazette*, February 8, 1868.

46. "Peonage and Indian Slavery," *Gazette*, March 14, 1868; Kiser, "A 'charming name,'" 185–86, 186–87.

47. "Col. J. F. Chaves," *Missouri Democrat*, in *New Mexican*, November 5, 1867.

48. Untitled, *New Mexican*, March 31, 1868.

49. Un Observador Imparcial to editors ("Clever denunciado a Nuevo Mejico"), *Nuevo-Mejicano*, April 14, 1868.

50. William W. Griffin to Charles Sumner, U.S. Senate, March 18, 1869, National Archives, Territorial Papers—New Mexico, RG 46, tray 2, folder 4; Bvt. Lt. Col. Edward McVale to Acting Assistant Adjutant General, District of New Mexico, April 21, 1869, National Archives, Territorial Papers—New Mexico, RG 46, tray 2, folder 4; Kiser, "A 'charming name,'" 188.

51. "Peonage and Indian Slavery," *Gazette*, May 23, 1868.

52. "Peonage in New Mexico," *New Mexican*, May 26, 1868.

53. "Peonage and Indian Slavery," *Gazette*, May 30, 1868.

54. The story is told in Horn, *New Mexico's Troubled Years*, 126; also Anderson Papers, box 1, folder 4: H. H. Heath to Dear Governor [Arny], January 29, 1868; H. H. Heath to Col. J. Franco. Chaves, January 30, 1868; H. H. Heath to Wm. H. Seward, March 8, 1868.

55. Anderson Papers, box 1, folder 5: H. H. Heath to Dear [William] Henrie, March 21, 1868; H. H. Heath to Dear Colonel [J. F. Chávez], March 8 1868; H. H. Heath to Col. R. McAllister, March 8, 1868; H. H. Heath to N. P. Chipman, March 9, 1868; Horn, *New Mexico's Troubled Years*, 126.

56. Herman H. Heath, *Proclamation of the Acting Governor of the Territory of New Mexico in relation to holding Peons in bondage and involuntary servitude in violation of the laws*, July 3, 1868, National Archives, Territorial Papers—New Mexico, RG 46, tray 2, folder 5; "A Proclamation by the Acting Governor of New Mexico on the Subject of Peonage in New Mexico and the abolition thereof by Law," *New Mexican*, June 16, 1868; "Proclamation by Acting Governor Heath on the Subject of Peonage," *New Mexican*, June 16, 1868; Herman H. Heath, "Proclamation," *Gazette*, June 20, 1868.

57. "Proclamation," *Gazette*, June 20, 1868.

58. Untitled, *New Mexican*, June 23, 1868.

59. William Breeden, clerk of the New Mexico Territorial Supreme Court, "Extract Report of the U.S. Grand Jury, U.S. District Court, 1st Judicial District Territory of New Mexico Territorial Papers," 1868, National Archives, Territorial Papers—New Mexico, RG 46, tray 2, folder 4; "Court," *Gazette*, August 1, 1868.

60. "'Navajo Captives,'" *New Mexican*, August 11, 1868.

61. Untitled announcement, *Semi-Weekly Review* (Albuquerque, hereafter *Review*), January 21, 1868.

62. As he explained later in "Cause and Effect," *Review*, December 4, 1868; "Claims on Grant," *Review*, May 29, 1868.

63. "Where are They?," *Review*, May 29, 1868. For Heath's checkered political associations, see Roberts, *Death Comes for the Chief Justice*, 30–32.

64. J. Francisco Chavez to H. H. Heath, January 4, 1868, Chávez letters; J. Francisco Chávez to H. H. Heath, January 8, 1868, Chávez letters.

65. Anderson Papers, box 1, folder 5: H. H. Heath to Dear [William] Henrie, March 21, 1868; H. H. Heath to Dear Colonel [J. F. Chávez], March 8, 1868; H. H. Heath to Col. R. McAllister, March 8, 1868; H. H. Heath to N. P. Chipman, March 9, 1868.

66. H. H. Heath to J. F. Chaves, March 30, 1868, box 1, folder 5, Anderson Papers.

67. H. H. Heath to W. H. Henry, March 2, 1868, box 1, folder 4, Anderson Papers.

68. H. H. Heath to Col. R. McCallister, February 27, 1868, box 1, folder 4, Anderson Papers.

69. H. H. Heath to J. F. Chaves, February 28, 1868, box 1, folder 4, Anderson Papers.

70. Anderson Papers, box 1, folder 5: H. H. Heath to P. E. Brocchus, March 19, 1868; H. H. Heath to J. Franco. Chaves, March 19, 1868; H. H. Heath to Dear [William] Henrie, March 21, 1868; H. H. Heath to P. E. Brocchus, March 22, 1868; H. H. Heath to Messrs. Benedict & Elkins, March 22, 1868; H. H. Heath to W. H. Henrie, March 24, 1868; H. H. Heath to J. F. Chaves, March 24, 1868.

71. "New Mexico, I assure you, is truly loyal"; H. H. Heath to Lucious Fairchild, April 11, 1868, box 1, folder 5, Anderson Papers.

72. H. H. Heath to J. F. Chaves, March 17, 1868, box 1, folder 5, Anderson Papers.

73. H. H. Heath to Col. Chas. E. Moss, April 11, 1868, box 1, folder 5, Anderson Papers; "New Mexican Translations," *New Mexican*, July 14, 1868.

74. "It is really glorious to see how you have outstripped & whipped Clever in the matter of appointments. It looks to me as if Watts, Clever, Mitchell & Collins have lost ground materially in Washington"; H. H. Heath to J. F. Chaves, February 28, 1868, box 1, folder 4, Anderson Papers; also J. Francisco Chávez to H. H. Heath, June 13, 1868, Chávez letters.

75. H. H. Heath to Dear [William] Henrie, March 21, 1868, box 1, folder 5, Anderson Papers. For a detailed account of the trial, see Roberts, *Death Comes for the Chief Justice*, 104–9.

76. See, for example, H. H. Heath to Wm. L. Rynerson, March 19, 1868, box 1, folder 5 Anderson Papers.

77. See, for example, H. H. Heath to P. E. Brocchus, March 22, 1868, box 1, folder 5, Anderson Papers.

78. http://history.house.gov/Map/Mapping-Congress.

79. J. Francisco Chávez to H. H. Heath, February 11, 1868, Chávez letters; H. H. Heath to Col. Wm. H. Russell, W. H. March 8, 1868, box 1, folder 5, Anderson Papers.

80. "H. H. Heath to W. L. Rynerson, April 12, 1868, box 1, folder 5, Anderson Papers.

81. H. H. Heath to [U.S. Senator] Henry Wilson, March 24, 1868, box 1, folder 5, Anderson Papers; also H. H. Heath to Col. R. McAllister, April 5, 1868, box 1, folder 5, Anderson Papers; Roberts, *Death Comes for the Chief Justice*, 78, 111.

82. Anderson Papers, box 1, folder 5: H. H. Heath to [U.S. Senator] James Harlan, April 8, 1868; H. H. Heath to [U.S. Senator] L. W. Lipton, April 8, 1868.

83. H. H. Heath to [U.S. Senator] John M. Thayer, April 8, 1868, box 1, folder 5, Anderson Papers; "John S. Watts et al.," *New Mexican*, April 14, 1868.

84. Roberts, *Death Comes for the Chief Justice*, 112–18.

85. "Jottings and Gleanings: Judge Brocchus," *Review*, April 24, 1868.

86. J. Francisco Chávez to H. H. Heath, June 15, 1868, Chávez letters.

87. "A Copperhead," *Review*, April 10, 1868.

88. H. H. Heath to editors ("A Card"), *New Mexican*, April 23, 1870; J. Francisco Chávez to H. H. Heath, June 23, 1868, Chávez letters.

89. "A Leader Wanted," *Gazette*, July 18, 1868.

90. "The New Chief Justice," *New Mexican*, August 11, 1868.

91. Untitled, *Gazette*, January 25, 1868; Wm. Breeden, "A Card," *New Mexican*, February 4, 1868; "Great Success of Clever," *New Mexican*, April 7, 1868; J. Francisco Chávez to H. H. Heath, June 13, 1868, Chávez letters; Roberts, *Death Comes for the Chief Justice*, 118.

92. "Col. Chavez," *New Mexican*, April 7, 1868.

93. Anderson Papers, box 1, folder 5: H. H. Heath to Hawkins Taylor, March 24, 1868; H. H. Heath to J. F. Chaves, March 24, 1868; H. H. Heath to W. L. Rynerson, April 12, 1868.

94. "The Impeachment," *New Mexican*, April 21, 1868; also "Impeachment," *New Mexican*, April 7, 1868.

95. "The Approaching Close of the Impeachment," *Review*, May 8, 1868; "The Impeachment," *Review*, May 26, 1868.

96. "El Juzgar," *Review*, April 21, 1868.

97. "'The Country,'–The *Gazette* at last defines its Position," *New Mexican*, March 24, 1868.

98. Hearn, *Impeachment of Andrew Johnson*, 195–98; Simpson, "Let Us Have Peace," 244; "Hon. S. B. Elkins," *New Mexican*, June 23, 1868.

99. Hearn, *Impeachment of Andrew Johnson*, 199.

100. "Republican Territorial Convention," *New Mexican*, April 14, 1868; Kirby Benedict, "Republican Mass Territorial Convention," *Review*, April 17, 1868.

101. J. Francisco Chávez to H. H. Heath, June 23, 1868, Chávez letters.

102. A 'Fizzle,'" *Review*, May 5, 1868; untitled, *Review*, May 1, 1868.

103. Extract of a story in the Chicago *Tribune*, in "Presidential," *New Mexican*, January 7, 1868.

104. Hearn, *Impeachment of Andrew Johnson*, 200; "The National Republican Platform," *Review*, July 5, 1868; "Platform of the National Republican party of the United States," *New Mexican*, June 9, 1868.

105. "Gen. Grant for President," *New Mexican*, April 7, 1868.

106. Anastacio Sandoval et al., "Grant and Colfax-Ratification Meeting," *New Mexican*, June 30, 1868; "Grant y Colfax—Junta de Ratificación," *Nuevo-Mejicano*, June 30, 1868; Junta Pública," *Nuevo-Mejicano*, June 30, 1868; "The New Mexico Republican Platform," *Review*, December 1, 1868. On the Democratic Party's suc-

cess with European immigrants up through the 1860s, see Friedman, "The Democratic Party 1860–1884," 897–98.

107. "The Chicago Convention," *New Mexican*, June 9, 1868; also, "Grant and Colfax," *New Mexican*, June 30, 1868; "General Grant," *New Mexican*, September 1, 1868.

108. "The *Gazette* Admits to an Anti-Grant Party in New Mexico," *New Mexican*, June 30, 1868.

109. "The Ticket," *Review*, June 2, 1868; also reinforcing Republicanism were "Grant and Colfax," *Review*, July 5, 1868, and "Grant and the Presidency," *Review*, July 9, 1868.

110. J. Francisco Chávez to H. H. Heath, June 15, 1868, Chávez letters.

111. Hearn, *Impeachment of Andrew Johnson*, 200–201.

112. Michael Les Benedict, *Impeachment and Trial of Andrew Johnson*, 143; cf. Ferrell, *Reconstruction*, 42–45.

113. Untitled, *New Mexican*, July 14, 1868; "Another Telegram from Clever," *New Mexican*, January 28, 1869; "The Governor's Message," *Review*, December 15, 1868.

114. "Proceedings of the National Democratic Convention," *New Mexican*, July 14, 1868.

115. Simpson, "Let Us Have Peace," 247–48; Hearn, *Impeachment of Andrew Johnson*, 204–6; "Proceedings of the National Democratic Convention," *Gazette*, July 10, 1868, 2.

116. Quote from untitled, *New Mexican*, October 26, 1867; also on Pomeroy, "The Democracy," *Review*, June 26, 1868; "Brick Pomeroy," *Kansas City Journal*, May 29, 1868, in *Review*, June 23, 1868; Brick Pomeroy to editor *Kansas City Journal*, May 29, 1868, in *Review*, June 23, 1868.

117. Hearn, *Impeachment of Andrew Johnson*, 204; Mantell, *Johnson, Grant*, 10; "Amnesty Proclamation by the President," *New Mexican*, July 17, 1868.

118. Hearn, *Impeachment of Andrew Johnson*, 204–5; untitled, *New Mexican*, July 14, 1868; "Democratic Platform," *Gazette*, July 25, 1868; untitled, *New Mexican*, September 5, 1868.

119. "The Presidential Ticket," *Gazette*, July 18, 1868; also "Important Documents," *Gazette*, July 25, 1868; untitled editorial, *Gazette*, July 25, 1868.

120. Frank B. Blair to James O. Broadhead, June 30, 1868, in "The Democratic Candidate for Vice President," *Review*, August 14, 1868.

121. "A Difference with a Distinction," *New Mexican*, July 30, 1868.

122. "The Daily New Mexican," *New Mexican*, July 9, 1868; "The Daily New Mexican," *New Mexican*, July 14, 1868; also "The Telegraph Completed," *New Mexican*, July 14, 1868.

123. "Registrars," *Gazette*, August 15, 1868.

124. "Jottings and Gleanings: In Town," *Review*, April 24, 1868.

125. "To our Friends throughout the Territory," *New Mexican*, April 7, 1868.

126. "The Next Legislature," *New Mexican*, July 27, 1868.

127. Anonymous, "He Aquí a Pancho," *Gazette*, June 27, 1868.

128. Farrand, *Legislation for Government of the Organized Territories*, 42; J. Francisco Chávez to H. H. Heath, January 8, 1868, Chávez letters; "in all respects," H. H. Heath to Hon. Schuyler Colfax, February 26, 1868, box 1, folder 4, Anderson Papers;

"Amendment to Organic Act of New Mexico," *New Mexican*, July 9, 1868; "The Governor's Veto," *New Mexican*, August 5, 1868.

129. "Santa Fe," *New Mexican*, July 11, 1868; "Improvement—Enterprise—The Daily New Mexican," *New Mexican*, July 28, 1868.

130. Tecolote to editor ("¡Nuestro Ex-Delegado en Washington!"), *Gaceta*, August 22, 1868.

131. Un Mejicano to *La Gaceta*, August 8, 1868.

132. Untitled, *New Mexican*, August 11, 1868; "Mistaken," *Review*, September 22, 1868; "The *Gazette* and the Election," *New Mexican*, October 1, 1868; "The Election in Bernalillo," *New Mexican*, September 12, 1868; "Take Him!," *Review*, September 29, 1868.

133. For Bernalillo, see John E. Murphy, "Proceedings of the Meeting," *Review*, August 25, 1868; John E. Murphy, "Procederes de la Junta," *Review*, August 28, 1868; Hezek. S. Johnson to the electors of Albuquerque and Duranes ("Aviso de Elección"), *Review*, August 28, 1868; untitled, *New Mexican*, August 11, 1868; untitled, *New Mexican*, August 22, 1868. For San Miguel, see "Convención del Condado de San Miguel," *Nuevo-Mejicano*, August 24, 1868.

134. "Republican Convention," *New Mexican*, August 17, 1868; Antonio Ortiz y Salazar et al., "Proceedings of a Republican Convention of the county of Santa Fe," *New Mexican*, September 5 1868, 1; "Resoluciones Adoptadas por la Convención del Condado de Santa Fe el Domingo de 30 Agosto de 1868," *Nuevo-Mejicano*, September 8, 1868.

135. "Nominaciones," *Nuevo-Mejicano*, September 2, 1868; "Nominations," *New Mexican*, September 8, 1868.

136. Once the Brocchus nomination for chief justice fell through, Chávez had Tompkins in mind for the position; J. Francisco Chávez to H. H. Heath, January 8, 1868, Chávez letters.

137. José M. Gallegos et al., "Democratic County Convention," *Gazette*, September 5, 1868; see, for example, G.T.C. to the *Round Table* (Far Rockaway), in *Gazette*, September 5, 1868.

138. José M. Gallegos et al., "Democratic County Convention," *Gazette*, September 5, 1868; "New Mexico Democratic Platform," *Review*, November 17, 1868; "father," *New Mexican*, November 14, 1868.

139. Diego Archuleta, "Convention," *Gazette*, August 29, 1868.

140. "A New Party," *Review*, September 1, 1868.

141. "The Santa Fe Democracy and the Negro," *Review*, September 11, 1868.

142. *Laws of the Territory of New Mexico . . . 1867–68*, Records of the States of the United States, microfilms, 1862–1875, N.M. B. 2, reel 2, 110–20; "The Registration of Voters," *New Mexican*, August 17, 1868; "Enregistración de Votantes," *New Mexican*, August 11, 1868; "Registration of Voters," *New Mexican*, August 13, 1868.

143. "New Mexico is Republican," *New Mexican*, September 22, 1868.

144. Un Enfermo to editor, *New Mexican*, September 23, 1868, and in "Reprensión a los Republicanos de Valencia," *New Mexican*, September 29, 1868.

145. "Col. J. F. Chavez," *New Mexican*, September 1, 1868; "New Mexico is Republican," *New Mexican*, September 22, 1868; "The *Gazette* and the Election," *New Mexican*, October 1, 1868; also, "Election Returns," *New Mexican*, September 15, 1868.

146. "Santa Fe," *Review*, September 15, 1868; "Accounted For," *Review*, September 18, 1868.

147. "Working," *Review*, September 15, 1868.

148. Un Mejicano, "La Ley de Registración," *Gaceta*, October 3, 1868.

149. "New Mexico is Republican," *New Mexican*, September 22, 1868.

150. "Election Returns," *New Mexican*, September 10, 1868, and untitled, *New Mexican*, September 15, 1868.

151. "The Election," *New Mexican*, September 8, 1868.

152. "Mistaken," *Review*, September 22, 1868.

153. "Party Lines Drawn," *Review*, October 6, 1868.

154. Donald, "The Republican Party 1864–1876," 1283.

155. William Breeden, 'Programme of Arrangements for the Demonstration in Honor of the Election of Grant and Colfax," *New Mexican*, November 11, 1868; "The Grant and Colfax Demonstration last Night," *New Mexican*, November 13, 1868; *Address of General H. H. Heath, at Santa Fe, New Mexico, of the Night of the 12th of Nov., '68 on the Occasion of the Republican Jubilee and Torchlight Procession in Honor of Grant's Election to the Presidency* (Santa Fe: Manderfield & Tucker, 1869), 5, 7, 10; also in "Santa Fé," *Review*, November 17, 1868.

156. Anastacio Sandoval, "Rally to the Loyal Standard!," *New Mexican*, November 6, 1868, 1; "Grant & Colfax Jubilee," *New Mexican*, November 6, 1868; "Attention Grant Men!!," *New Mexican*, November 10, 1868; Breeden, 'Programme of Arrangements.'

157. "Here," *Review*, November 17, 1868.

158. "Junta Republicana" and "The Republican Meeting," *Review*, November 17, 1868; "The Republican Meeting," *New Mexican*, November 23, 1868.

159. Extract of a letter from an anonymous correspondent to the *Missouri Democrat*, in "How are you now!," *New Mexican*, January 7, 1869.

14. Steady Republicans, Hazy Democrats

1. "The Legislature," *New Mexican*, December 8, 1868; also "The Legislative Republican Caucus Last Night," *New Mexican*, December 7, 1868; "The Republican Association," *New Mexican*, December 8, 1868; "Olla Podrida: Legislative," *Review*, January 15, 1869.

2. "Olla Podrida: Don't Connect," *Review*, January 15, 1869.

3. "The Governor's Message," *Review*, December 15, 1868.

4. Untitled, *New Mexican*, December 21, 1868; "Is a Change Necessary!," *New Mexican*, January 4, 1869.

5. "Why the Legislature Did It," *Review*, March 16, 1869; "The People in Power," *New Mexican*, January 13, 1869; "Olla Podrida: Legislative," *Review*, January 15, 1869.

6. Pablo Melendres et al., "La Prefectura en Doña Ana," *Review*, February 16, 1869.

7. "Olla Podrida: Legislative," *Review*, January 15, 1869; "anywhere," untitled, *New Mexican*, January 22, 1869; J. Francisco Chávez to H. H. Heath, January 16,

1869, Chávez letters, Carl Hayden Papers; J. Francisco Chávez to H. H. Heath, January 23, 1869, Chávez letters.

8. "Schools in New Mexico," *New Mexican*, October 3, 1868; "wild system," "The Legislature," *New Mexican*, December 5, 1868; Horn, *New Mexico's Troubled Years*, 129.

9. "Gov. Arny's Speech," *New Mexican*, December 15, 1868.

10. Untitled, *New Mexican*, January 21, 1869.

11. "General H. H. Heath," *Review*, January 22, 1869; "Olla Podrida: Gazette Vagaries," *Review*, February 9, 1869; untitled, *New Mexican*, February 2, 1869; J. Francisco Chávez to H. H. Heath, January 29, 1869, Chávez letters.

12. "Pancho y Chepe. Diálogo," *Gazette*, January 9, 1869.

13. Los Dichos Expectadores, "¡El Limosnero Desahuciado!"; Jesús María Pacheco to editor; Jesús María Pacheco to La Asociación Republicanos de la Unión, all in *Gaceta,* January 2, 1869.

14. Un Mejicano, "¡Oremos, Oremos, Oremos!," *Gaceta*, February 13, 1869.

15. "Adjourned," *Gazette*, February 6, 1869; Horn, *New Mexico's Troubled Years,* 129.

16. "A New Adjutant General," *New Mexican*, January 29, 1869, 1; untitled, *New Mexican* January 30, 1869.

17. Untitled editorial, *New Mexican* January 30, 1869; untitled, *New Mexican*, April 10, 1869.

18. "New Mexicans at Washington," *New Mexican*, March 27, 1869; "Olla Podrida: On Dit," *Review*, December 25, 1868.

19. "Asociación Republicana" and "Republican Association," *Review*, December 22, 1868.

20. "Cause and Effect," *Review*, December 4, 1868.

21. "At it again," *Review*, December 8, 1868.

22. "Our Choice for Delegate," *Review*, December 15, 1868. Johnson put the name of Chávez on the *Review*'s masthead for delegate, "Subject to the action of the Republican Territorial Convention"; "For Delegate in Congress," *Review*, December 29, 1868.

23. "Olla Podrida: Legislature," *Review*, December 18, 1868; "Change of Election Day," *Review*, December 25, 1868; "Change of Election Day," *Review*, January 1, 1869.

24. Untitled editorial, *New Mexican*, January 5, 1869.

25. "Plain Talk!," *Review*, January 8, 1869.

26. "'Powerfully Weak!,'" *Review*, January 26, 1869.

27. "Reported for the Review: Congratulatory," *Review*, April 20, 1869; "A Townsman in Luck," *Review*, May 11, 1869; "frequent and sustained," untitled, *New Mexican*, April 20, 1869; "Appointments," *New Mexican*, April 21, 1869; Pomeroy, *The Territories*, 113.

28. H. H. Heath, "Convención Republicana de Delegados Territoriales," *Review*, January 19, 1869; H. H. Heath, "Republican Territorial Delegate Convention," *New Mexican,* January 25, 1869.

29. "County Convention," *Review*, January 22, 1869, and Salvador Armijo et al., "Convención Republicana," *Review*, January 19, 1869.

30. "Republican Nomination for Delegate," *Review*, February 2, 1869.

31. H. H. Heath, Chairman of the Committee, to editors, *New Mexican*, January 25, 1869; H. H. Heath, "Republican Territorial Delegate Convention," *New Mexican*, January 23, 1869; "Tomás Cabeza de Baca et al., "Proceedings of the Republican Territorial Convention," *Review*, February 5, 1869; "Our Nomination for Congress," *New Mexican*, February 1, 1869; "Republican Platform of New Mexico," *New Mexican*, February 9, 1869; "Republican Platform," *New Mexican*, February 9, 1869.

32. "Chaves the Candidate," *Gazette*, February 6, 1869, 2.

33. "Frauds," *Gazette*, February 27, 1869.

34. "In Straightened Circumstances," *Review*, January 12, 1869.

35. "No Name Yet!," *Review*, February 2, 1869.

36. "Olla Podrida: Not Yet," *Review*, January 12, 1869; "Olla Podrida: Conservative," *Review*, January 19, 1869; "Olla Podrida: Doubtful," *Review*, January 22, 1869; "'Powerfully Weak!,'" *Review*, January 26, 1869; "anti-Republicans," "The *Gazette* on a Beader," *New Mexican*, January 30, 1869.

37. J. Francisco Chávez to H. H. Heath, January 23, 1869, Chávez letters.

38. C. P. Clever to Diego Archuleta, January 20, 1869, in "Interesting from Clever," *New Mexican*, January 27, 1869; C. P. Clever to José Manuel Gallegos, "Another Telegram from Clever," *New Mexican*, January 28, 1869; "No Name Yet!," *Review*, February 2, 1869.

39. "A more precious," "Interesting from Clever," *New Mexican*, January 27, 1869; "genuine Republicans," "No Name Yet!," *Review*, February 2, 1869.

40. "Clever's Politics and Party," *New Mexican*, February 13, 1869.

41. "Hon. J. Francisco Chaves," *New Mexican*, November 19, 1868.

42. J. Francisco Chávez to Manderfield & Tucker, February 9, 1869, in "Good News from Washington!," *New Mexican*, February 10, 1869; Report: J. Francisco Chaves vs. Charles P. Clever, February 9, 1869, House of Representatives, Report no. 18, 40th Congress, 3rd session, 1–5.

43. "Tardy Justice," *Washington Sunday Herald*, in *New Mexican*, March 4, 1869; J. Francisco Chaves to Manderfield & Tucker, February 20, 1869, in *New Mexican*, February 22, 1869.

44. *National Intelligencer*, in *New Mexican*, March 16, 1869.

45. "Tardy Justice," *Sunday Herald* (Washington DC), in *New Mexican*, March 4, 1869.

46. "The Delegate from New Mexico," *Chronicle* (Washington DC), in *Review*, March 9, 1869.

47. J. Francisco Chaves to my fellow citizens of New Mexico ("Address"), *New Mexican*, March 9, 1869; also in "Mr. Chavez to his Constituents," *Review*, March 12, 1869.

48. Charity noted in "Olla Podrida: Gazettical," *Review*, March 2, 1869.

49. "The Manifesto," *Gazette*, March 13, 1869; untitled, *Gaceta*, March 20, 1869; "Not at all!," *Review*, March 19, 1869.

50. "Great Rejoicing," *Review*, February 12, 1869.

51. "Republicanos, Alerta!!!," *Review*, February 26, 1869.

52. "Col. Chaves in his seat," *New Mexican*, February 11, 1869.

53. "Col. Chaves in his seat—Clever Ousted from Congress," *New Mexican*, February 22, 1869.

54. "Col. Chaves in his seat," *New Mexican*, February 11, 1869;" "¡Chavez en su Asiento!," *New Mexican*, February 13, 1869; "The Result in Congress," *New Mexican*, February 23, 1869.

55. Anonymous, untitled, *New Mexican*, March 1, 1869.

56. Anonymous, untitled, *New Mexican*, March 24, 1869, 3.

57. "Olla Podrida: Jollification," *Review*, February 16, 1869; Un Demócrata Convertido y Gran Sostenedor de Los Republicanos, "Demostración pública en Taos," *New Mexican,* March 6, 1869.

58. "Comunicados," *New Mexican*, February 15, 1869.

59. Anonymous, "Al Señor Don Franco. Chavez," *Review*, April 16, 1869.

60. "Convención," *Review*, January 26, 1869.

61. "Olla Podrida: Special Election," *Review*, February 26, 1869; untitled, *New Mexican*, February 27, 1869; "Special Election," *Review*, January 26, 1869; "For Probate Judge," *Review*, January 29, 1869; "For Probate Judge, Nestor Montoya," *Review*, March 2, 1869; "Republican Victory," *Review*, March 5, 1869; anonymous to editors ("The Bernalillo Election"), *New Mexican*, March 6, 1869; "Un Borracho," *New Mexican*, March 9, 1869.

62. Juan Santisteban, "Procedimientos de una junta pública republicana tenida en Don Fernando de Taos, el día 28 de Febrero de 1869," *New Mexican*, March 19, 1869; Uno de los de la Junta to editors ("Correción de Yerro Tipográfico"), *New Mexican*, April, 3, 1869.

63. Un Republicano to editors ("Los Republicanos del Peñasco"), *New Mexican*, April 19, 1869.

64. "The Manifesto," *Gazette*, March 13, 1869.

65. Un Mejicano, "¡Oremos, Oremos, Oremos!," *Gaceta*, February 13, 1869.

66. "Progreso," *Gaceta*, February 13, 1869; Juan P. Romero et al., "Junta Pública General," *New Mexican*, March 2, 1869; also untitled, *New Mexican*, March 4, 1869; Juan P. Romero et al., "(Las Trampas)," *New Mexican*, March 5, 1869; see also, J.A.M. y Martinez to editors ("Un Republicano a Dos de Sus Colegas y a un Fugitivo Audaz"), *New Mexican*, March 13, 1869, and Un Pradito to editors, *New Mexican*, April 10, 1869.

67. Veritás to *Gazette*, November 14, 1868.

68. G. Sape, "Décima," *Gaceta*, May 22, 1869.

69. Nuevo Mejicano, "El Nuevo Mejico Vendido," *Gaceta*, April 3, 1869.

70. "County Property Sale Again," *Gazette*, April 17, 1869.

71. "Frauds," *Gazette*, February 27, 1869; "New Mexico sold out," *New Mexican*, April 6, 1869.

72. "The Delegate," *Gazette*, January 30, 1869.

73. Felipe Delgado et al., *Gaceta*, January 30, 1869.

74. "Olla Podrida: Who's He," *Review*, February 9, 1869.

75. "Clever's Politics and Party," *New Mexican*, February 13, 1869.

76. "Olla Podrida: Delegate," *Review*, December 25, 1868; "Political Summary," *Review*, February 16, 1869; "Olla Podrida: On Dit," *Review*, March 23, 1896; Un Observador to editors ("¡Y de los Demócratas quien sera!"), *Nuevo-Mejicano*, April 3, 1869.

77. A point effectively made in anonymous, "Comunicado," *Nuevo-Mejicano*, February 12, 1869.

78. John Symington, "Salutory," *Review*, May 4, 1869; "Introductorio," *Review*, May 4, 1869; "'Another Richmond in the Field,'" *Review*, June 6, 1869; "The 'Elements' Candidate," *Review*, June 12, 1869.

79. Anonymous, "Los Pescamos," *Nuevo-Mejicano*, February 15, 1869.

80. As the administrator of the U.S. depository in New Mexico, Collins was transporting $100,000 when he was robbed and murdered; N.Q., "A la muerte del Coronel James L. Collins," *Gaceta*, June 12, 1869; "The Santa Fe Tragedy," *Review*, June 11, 1869; see Hunt, *Kirby Benedict*, 149n15. Ironically, Chávez, while in Washington, tried to have Collins removed as director of the depository; J. Francisco Chávez to H. H. Heath, April 10, 1869, Chávez letters.

81. Jesús Ma. Samora, Juan Sánchez, and Encarnación Medina, "La Muerte de Merrill Ashurst.–Procedimientos de Respecto &c.," *Gaceta*, July 17, 1869.

82. Quote, Annon to William Manderfield, April 9, 1864, in Kirby Benedict, *A Journey Through New Mexico's First Judicial District*, 51; "County Officers," *New Mexican*, July 10, 1868, 2; Chaves, *Papers in the Case of J. Francisco Chaves vs. Charles P. Clever*, 87; Vicente Romero et al., "Procedimientos de una junta pública," *Gazette*, January 18, 1868; Jose M. Gallegos et al., "Convención tenida por el partido Unionista en el condado de Santa Fe, en la casa de Don Albino Roibal, el día 28 de Julio 1867," *Gazette*, August 3, 1867.

83. "Don Vicente Romero," *Gazette*, July 3, 1869.

84. Rincón to General John T. Russell ("Don Vicente Romero for Delegate"), *Gazette*, July 17, 1869.

85. "Judge Antonio Jose Otero," *Gazette*," July 10, 1869.

86. "Rio Abajo" [sic] to editor ("Judge Antonio Jose Otero"), *Gazette*, July 17, 1869.

87. Diego Archuleta et al., "Territorial Convention," *Gazette*, July 24, 1869; "The Convention," *Gazette*, July 17, 1869; Theisen, "José Manuel Gallegos," 176–77.

88. "The Nominee," *Gazette*, July 24, 1869.

89. Vicente Romero to Diego Archuleta, President of the Convention ("Letter of Acceptance"), *Gazette*, July 31, 1869.

90. "Mr. Romero's Letter of Acceptance," *Gazette*, July 31, 1869.

91. "The Nominee of the 'Elements' for Delegate—Signs of the Times," *Review*, July 20, 1869.

92. "How is it to be?," *Review*, July 30, 1869.

93. Zurriago, "La Nominación del Hon. Vicente Romero," *Gaceta*, July 31, 1869.

94. "Why Col. J. Francisco Chaves should be Elected," *Review*, August 10, 1869.

95. "Romeroisms," *Review*, August 20, 1869.

96. "Como Estará Si Electo?," *Review*, August 17, 1869.

97. Jesús M. Pacheco, extracts of an address delivered in Mora, New Mexico, July 25, 1869, published in Amigo, "Extractos," *Gaceta*, July 31, 1869.

98. "Why Col. J. Francisco Chaves should be Elected," *Review*, August 10, 1869.

99. "Why Col. J. Francisco Chaves should be Elected"; "political sneaks," "Political Sneaks in New Mexico," *Review*, August 3, 1869.

100. "Where Are They?," *Review*, July 30, 1869.

101. "County Convention," *Gazette*, August 7, 1869; "Our County Ticket," *Gazette*, August 21, 1869.

102. "Republican Ticket in Santa Fe," *Review*, August 20, 1869. Robert Mitchell's dismissal was due sooner or later. He submitted a resignation in the spring of 1869 but had to stay on because his replacement did not qualify. Mitchell hastened his own demise by single-handedly declaring war on the Gila Apaches and Navajos, prompting outcry from Congress, the State Department, the U.S. Army, and New Mexicans. One of the first actions of his successor was to rescind his Indian war proclamation; Horn, *New Mexico's Troubled Years*, 129–31; untitled, *Gazette*, August 7, 1869; "General Pile," *Review*, June 25, 1869.

103. "Frauds, Corruption, &c.," *Review*, August 17, 1869.

104. "Election Frauds," *Gazette*, August 21, 1869.

105. "Santa Fe," *Gazette*, August 21, 1869.

106. Veritás to editor, *Gaceta*, September 4, 1869.

107. Un Espectador, "Antogonismo [sic] Politico," *Review*, August 13, 1869.

108. "Territorial Finances," *Gazette*, July 31, 1869.

109. "Olla Podrida: Opposition Nominations," *Review*, August 17, 1869.

110. "From Socorro County," *Review*, September 3, 1869.

111. "For Chaves," *Review*, September 3, 1869.

112. "Our County Ticket," *Gazette*, September 4, 1869, 2.

113. Untitled, *Review*, August 20, 1869; "Republican Nominations," *Review*, August 27, 1869.

114. "Grant County," *Review*, August 27, 1869.

115. See in *Gaceta*, September 4, 1869: J. Miguel Dominguez," Junta Pública"; Juan C. Romero, "Junta Tenida en el precincto de Pojoaque"; Francisco Quintana, "Junta tenida en San Ildefonso"; Francisco E. Valdez, "Procedimientos de una convención tenida en el precinto no. 2 del condado de Santa Fe."

116. "The Election in Bernalillo County," *Review*, September 10, 1869.

117. "The Finality of our Delegate Election," *New Mexican*, September 24, 1869.

118. "The Finality of our Delegate Election"; "Result of the Election," *Review*, September 24, 1869; "Result of the Election," *Review*, September 21, 1869; "Bernalillo," *Gazette*, September 11, 1869.

119. "The Finality of our Delegate Election," *New Mexican*, September 24, 1869.

120. "Suspicious," *Review*, September 21, 1869.

121. "Santa Fe County," *Gazette*, September 11, 1869.

122. "The Election," *Gazette*, September 18, 1869.

123. "The Election in Socorro," *Review*, September 21, 1869.

124. See in *Review*, September 10, 1869: "Election News"; "Our Senator and Representatives"; "The Republican County Ticket"; "The Justices of the Peace"; "The Vote for Delegate in Bernalillo County"; also Theisen, "Jose Manuel Gallegos," 176–77.

125. "Results of the Election," *Gazette*, September 11, 1869.

126. Precursor de la Justicia, "¡Contesten Después veremos!," *Gaceta*, September 18, 1869.

127. "The Gazette Mourneth," *New Mexican*, September 17, 1869.

128. "The Republican Triumph in New Mexico," *Review*, September 24, 1869.

129. Anonymous, "Lamentaciones de la Gazeta," *Nuevo-Mejicano*, September 21, 1869, in *Review*, September 24, 1869.

15. Realized Political Parties

1. "The Finality of our Delegate Election," *New Mexican*, September 24, 1869; "Our New Governor," *New Mexican*, August 10, 1869; http://en.wikipedia.org/wiki/William_A._Pile.

2. "The Legislature," *New Mexican*, February 4, 1870; "The Governor's Message," *Weekly Post* (Santa Fe), December 11, 1869. (The *Post* was published daily and weekly; the former was called the *Santa Fe Post* and the latter the *Weekly Post;* hereafter both are cited as *Post*.) See in *New Mexican*: "Advantages of an Equitable Tax Law," December 15, 1869; "Grand Army of the Republic," January 3, 1870; "Installation of Officers of the G. A. R.," January 10, 1870, including Joseph LaGrand address; "The Tax Law Passed," January 15, 1870.

3. John T. Russell, "Valedictory," *Gazette*, September 5, 1869; "The Gazette defunct—The New Mexican still lives," *New Mexican*, September 27, 1869.

4. "The Post," and untitled, *Post*, October 2, 1869; "The Fifteenth Amendment," *Post*, October 9, 1869. 1869.

5. *Argus*, quoted in *Post*, April, 1, 1871; "The Cimarron News," *Post*, October 1, 1870; "Progressive," *New Mexican*, November 23, 1870; Price, *Pioneers of the Mesilla Valley*, 37.

6. Jean Edward Smith, *Grant*, 469, 479–80, 490, 504; McFeely, *Grant: A Biography*, 328–29.

7. For a review of the literature on intra-party factionalism, see Michael Les Benedict, *Preserving the Constitution*, 69–71.

8. "A.P. Sullivan, late Internal Revenue Collector for New Mexico; his removal and his course as a Republican Official," *New Mexican*, December 4, 1869.

9. "The Post," *New Mexican*, September 4, 1869.

10. A. P. Sullivan, "The Post and the Cliques," *Post*, October 2, 1869.

11. Untitled, *Post*, December 4, 1869.

12. For a focused treatment of Elkins and Catron in New Mexico, see Turo, "An Empire of Dust."

13. Untitled, *New Mexican*, May 18, 1871; untitled, *Post*, May 20, 1871.

14. "What of '72," *Review*, December 10, 1870; untitled, *New Mexican*, July 13, 1871; untitled, May 20, 1871.

15. "The opposition to Governor Pile," *New Mexican*, September 26, 1870.

16. A. P. Sullivan, "The Post and the Cliques," *Post*, October 2, 1869.

17. "The Post," *Post*, October 2, 1869.

18. "New Mexican Wealth–What is Needed to Develope [sic] It," *Post*, November 6, 1869.

19. "A Word of Warning to the Business Men of New Mexico," *Post*, November 6, 1989.

20. "Sullivan Removed!," *New Mexican*, December 3, 1869; "A.P. Sullivan, late Internal Revenue Collector for New Mexico; his removal and his course as a Republican Official," *New Mexican*, December 4, 1869; reprinted in *Post*, December 11, 1869; "A. P. Sullivan, ultimamente Colector de rentas Internas, su remoción y su curso como Oficial Republicano," *Nuevo-Mejicano*, December 4, 1869.

21. "The Editor of the POST Removed from the Collectorship of New Mexico," *Post*, December 4, 1869.

22. "A.P. Sullivan, late Internal Revenue Collector," *New Mexican*, reprinted in *Post*, December 11, 1869.

23. Untitled, *New Mexican*, December 17, 1869.

24. "The New Mexican endorsed as the Organ of the Republican Party in New Mexico," *New Mexican*, January 4, 1870.

25. Larson, *New Mexico's Quest*, 94; José Leandro Perea to José Manuel Gallegos, January 17, 1870, in *Nuevo-Mejicano*, January 22, 1870.

26. Special Committee to Leandro Sanches, *New Mexican*, January 24, 1870; "The Legislature," *New Mexican*, February 4, 1870.

27. "The Constitution," *New Mexican*, March 10, 1870.

28. Special Committee to Leandro Sanches, *New Mexican*, January 24, 1870; "The Constitution," *New Mexican*, 10 March 1870, 1; anonymous to editor ("Gov. Pile."), *Post*, October 22, 1870.

29. Untitled, *New Mexican*, February 3, 1870, 1; "The Enabling Act for New Mexico," *New Mexican*, February 9, 1870; untitled, *New Mexican*, February 1, 1870.

30. "The Constitution," *New Mexican*, March 10, 1870; "New Mexico in Congress," *New Mexican*, February 23, 1870; "Junta en Masa," *Nuevo-Mejicano*, March 2, 1870.

31. "Shall New Mexico become a State?," *New Mexican*, February 11, 1870; also "Sera bien que Nuevo Mejico sea hecho un Estado?," *Nuevo-Mejicano*, February 14, 1870.

32. "Shall New Mexico become a State?," *New Mexican*, February 15, 1870.

33. State, "A few words on State Government," *New Mexican*, February 19, 1870; Estado, "Unas pocas Palabras sobre el Gobierno de Estado," *Nuevo-Mejicano*, February 22, 1870; untitled, *New Mexican*, February 7, 1870.

34. Jornada to editors ("Why are our Mines not Worked?"), *New Mexican*, August 31, 1870.

35. G.W.O., "State Government," *New Mexican*, March 19, 1870, 1.

36. Benjamin Stevens to editors ("Hon. Benjamin Stevens on the State Question"), *New Mexican*, March 11, 1870.

37. "Who is to Blame?–What is the Remedy?," *Post*, December 31, 1870.

38. "State Peonage," *New Mexican*, April 13, 1870.

39. "Who is to Blame?–What is the Remedy?," *Post*, December 31, 1870.

40. Desiderio Romero et al., "Junta de la Sociedad Progresiva de Las Vegas," *El Correo* (Santa Fe; hereafter *Correo*), January 14, 1871.

41. "The State Question," *New Mexican*, March 2, 1870; "The opposition to Governor Pile," *New Mexican*, September 26, 1870.

42. Amigo to editors ("State Question"), *New Mexican*, February 17, 1870.

43. "Comments by the New Mexican," *New Mexican*, February 17, 1870. Sullivan later said that Governor Pile was the author of this editorial; "Convicted by His Associates," *Post*, October 8, 1870.

44. "The State Question," *New Mexican*, February 22, 1870; "Asuntos de Estado," *Nuevo-Mejicano*, February 24, 1870.

45. "The State Question"; "Asuntos de Estado," *Nuevo-Mejicano*, February 24, 1870; "The State Meeting," *New Mexican*, February 28, 1870; The Secretaries, "Mass Meeting for a State," *New Mexican*, March 2, 1870; "Call for a Convention to be held at Santa Fe, New Mexico, on Monday, June 6th, 1870," *New Mexican*, March 19, 1870.

46. The Secretaries, "Mass Meeting for a State," *New Mexican*, March 2, 1870.

47. "Junta en Masa," *Nuevo-Mejicano*, March 2, 1870; for a short biography of Santiago Baca, see untitled, *Nuevo-Mexicano*, [December] 1877 (n.d. on the reel).

48. Untitled, *New Mexican*, March 1, 1870; "La Junta," *Nuevo-Mejicano*, March 2, 1870; "The State Question," *New Mexican*, March 2, 1870; untitled and José D. Sena to W. H. Manderfield, *New Mexican*, September 27, 1870.

49. Untitled, *New Mexican*, March 7, 1870.

50. Amigo to editors ("Albuquerque Correspondence"), March 4, 1870, in *New Mexican*, March 9, 1870.

51. "Or Alliance," *Republican Review* (Albuquerque, formerly *Semi-Weekly Review*, hereafter *Review*), April 9, 1870; "The Convention," *Review*, May 6, 1871; "Our Opposition," *Review*, December 17, 1870; also Gen. G. to the Decatur *Daily Magnet*, in untitled, *New Mexican*, December 15, 1870.

52. William A. Pile et al., "Call for a Convention to be held at Santa Fe, New Mexico, on Monday, June 6th, 1870," *New Mexican*, March 19, 1870.

53. Untitled, *New Mexican*, April 14, 1870; untitled, *N.Y. Tribune*, in *New Mexican*, April 23, 1870; untitled, *New Mexican*, April 29, 1870, 1; "New Mexico," *Exchange*, in *New Mexican*, July 29, 1870, 1; untitled, *New Mexican*, June 13, 1870.

54. "The Enabling Act—Let the June Convention be postponed," *New Mexican*, April 30, 1870; "The Convention Postponed," *New Mexican*, May 3, 1870; "The Enabling Act," *New Mexican*, June 29, 1870.

55. Larson, *New Mexico's Quest*, 94; also, "The State Movement," *Post*, July 2, 1870; "The Enabling Act," *New Mexican*, June 20, 1870; "The Proposed State of Lincoln," *New York Times*, in *New Mexican*, February 10, 1871; "The Enabling Act," *Post*, July 2, 1870.

56. "The Enabling Act," *New Mexican*, June 29, 1870; "The Enabling Act," *Post*, July 2, 1870.

57. "The Enabling Act," *Post*, July 2, 1870.

58. "Consistency," *Post*, July 9, 1870; "The State Movement," *Post*, July 2, 1870; untitled, *New Mexican*, July 1, 1870; untitled, *New Mexican*, July 11, 1870; quote, untitled, *New Mexican*, July 12, 1870; untitled, *New Mexican*, June 30, 1870; untitled, *Post*, July 9, 1870.

59. "Republican County Committee," *Review*, August 20, 1870; "That Invisible Committee," *Review*, August 27, 1870; untitled *Review*, March 11, 1871, 1. Sullivan needled the Central Committee to "be prepared for a contest at any time," not to

postpone until the opposition was in the field "endeavoring to defeat us; "Organization," *Post*, February 25, 1871.

60. "Republican Congressional Convention," *New Mexican*, March 9, 1871; "Convención Congressional Republicano," *Nuevo-Mejicano*, March 10, 1871.

61. "The Convention," *Post*, March 11, 1871; also "Republican Territorial Convention," *Review*, March 11, 1871; Administration Republican to editor, *Post*, March 11, 1871.

62. "Organization," *Post*, February 25, 1871, 2; "The Election," *New Mexican*, September 6, 1870; anonymous to editors ("The Election in Valencia County"), *New Mexican*, September 14, 1870; anonymous to editors ("From Valencia County"), *New Mexican*, September 21, 1870.

63. Friedman, "The Democratic Party 1860–1884," 899.

64. Friedman, "The Democratic Party 1860–1884," 898–99.

65. Not clear is where the Bennett brothers, including Joseph, came from; perhaps Texas. Nehemiah went to New Mexico for his health and had journalism experience; Stratton, *Territorial Press of New Mexico*, 7–8.

66. "Our Platform!," *Borderer* (La Cruces NM), March 16, 1871.

67. Untitled, *Borderer*, March 23, 1871; "The Bayonet Bill," *Borderer*, March 30, 1871.

68. "Salutatory," *Borderer*, March 16, 1871; "Grant and Bribery," *New York Sun*, in *Borderer*, April 6, 1871, 1; "Free, Gratis, for Nothing," *Borderer*, April 13, 1871.

69. Price, *Pioneers of the Mesilla Valley*, 91.

70. "Thanks," *Borderer*, March 16, 1871.

71. Untitled, *Borderer*, July 19, 1871.

72. Anthony Joseph to editor, *Borderer*, July 13, 1871.

73. "Blazing," *Review*, September 3, 1869; untitled, *New Mexican*, September 4, 1869.

74. Untitled, *El Fronterizo* (Las Cruces NM, hereafter *Fronterizo*), April 20, 1871.

75. Untitled, *Fronterizo*, April 20, 1871.

76. Anonymous, "Los Republicanos disputando entre si mismos la candidatura para Delegado al Congreso este año de 1871," *Fronterizo*, May 18, 1871.

77. Untitled, *Borderer*, March 23, 1871.

78. Untitled, *New Mexican*, April 14, 1871.

79. J. Francisco Chaves to Lyman Trumbull, March 4, 1870, in *Elizabethtown Argus* and *Post*, April, 1, 1871, and *Borderer*, April 13, 1871.

80. "Chaves' Strictures on the Santa Fe Bar," *Borderer*, April 13, 1871.

81. *Nuevo-Mejicano*, March 10, 1871.

82. "The Convention," *New Mexican*, March 17, 1871.

83. "A Plain Talk," *New Mexican*, March 30, 1871.

84. Henry Hilgert, "To the People of New Mexico," *New Mexican*, April 21, 1871.

85. Republican to editors ("Washington Correspondence"), *New Mexican*, August 7, 1871.

86. Untitled, *New Mexican*, April 14, 1871.

87. Untitled, *Review*, April 8, 1871.

88. Untitled, *Review*, April 8, 1871; untitled, *Review*, April 9, 1870.

89. "Rio Arriba County Convention," *New Mexican*, April 25, 1871.

90. Salvador Armijo et al., "The Republican County Convention," *New Mexican*, April 8, 1871; "Convención republicana de condado," *Nuevo-Mejicano*, April 10, 1871; "Convención del Condado del Socorro," *Correo*, April 22, 1871; Manuel Vigil et al., "Junta Pública," *Nuevo-Mejicano*, April 26, 1871; Antonio Jose Luna et al., "Republican Convention held at the town of Tomé, Valencia County," *Post*, August 24, 1871; Antonio José Luna et al., "Proceedings of the Republican Convention of the County of Valencia," *Review*, August 26, 1871.

91. "Correspondence," *Post*, April 1, 1871.

92. Desiderio Romero et al., "San Miguel County Resolutions Adopted by the Republican County Convention Assembled at Las Vegas, on Monday, April 10, 1871, in *Post*, April 15, 1871; untitled, *New Mexican*, April 14, 1871.

93. Desiderio Romero et al., "San Miguel County. Resolutions Adopted by the Republican County Convention Assembled at Las Vegas, on Monday, April 10, 1871," in *Post*, April 15, 1871; untitled, *New Mexican*, April 14, 1871; "A word to the convention," *Post*, in "To the People," *Borderer*, August 16, 1871. Julius Hayden Pardee was appointed to West Point from New Mexico; *Official Register of the Officers and Cadets of the U.S. Military Academy* (West Point, New York, June 1867, 17), http://digital-library.usma.edu/libmedia/archives/oroc/v1867.pdf.

94. Desiderio Romero et al., "San Miguel County. Resolutions . . . April 10, 1871," in *Post*, April 15, 1871; untitled, *New Mexican*, April 14, 1871.

95. J. Francisco Chaves to Kirby Benedict, May 1, 1871 ("Col. Chaves in Reply,"), *Post*, May 4 and 6, 1871; Doña Ana to editor ("Elkins and Catron"), *Borderer*, May 18, 1871; "Benedict and Chaves—The Trumbull Letter," *Borderer*, May 18, 1871.

96. Republican to editors ("Washington Correspondence"), *New Mexican*, August 7, 1871.

97. Desiderio Romero et al., "San Miguel County. Resolutions . . . April 10, 1871," in *Post*, April 15, 1871; untitled, *New Mexican*, April 14, 1871.

98. "Convención del Condado de Mora," *Correo*, April 29, 1871; Santiago Valdes et al., "Convención de Condado," *Nuevo-Mejicano*, April 27, 1871; Celso Baca et al., "Junta Pública," *Nuevo-Mejicano*, August 14, 1871; "The Republican Meeting at Las Vegas," *New Mexican*, August 17, 1871.

99. "The Convention," *New Mexican*, April 18, 1871; W. W. Griffin et al., "Republican County Convention," untitled, *New Mexican*, April 18, 1871.

100. Untitled, *Post*, April 22, 1871; "The County Convention," *Post*, April 22, 1871. This last story first appeared on April 20, but that issue may not be available.

101. Michael Les Benedict, *Preserving the Constitution*, 88.

102. Untitled, *Post*, April 22, 1871; "The County Convention."

103. Anonymous to editors, *New Mexican*, April 26, 1871.

104. Untitled, *Post*, April 22, 1871; untitled ("[From Wednesday's Daily]"), *Post*, April 22, 1871. This report first appeared on April 19, but may not be available.

105. Untitled ("[From Wednesday's Daily]"), *Post*, April 22, 1871.

106. Untitled, *Post*, April 22, 1871, 1; "Republican County Convention," *Post*, April 22, 1871; "En una Convención del Partido Republicano tenida en Santa Fe día 20

de Abríl de 1871," *Correo*, April 24, 1871; Anastacio Sandoval et al., untitled report, *Nuevo-Mejicano*, April 21, 1871.

107. "The 'Bolters' Convention,'" *New Mexican*, April 21, 1871.
108. Untitled, *Post*, April 29, 1871.
109. "The Bolters Repenting," *New Mexican*, April 22, 1871.
110. *New Mexican* quoted in untitled, *Post*, April 29, 1871.
111. Untitled, *Post*, April 29, 1871.
112. Pascual Martinez et al., "Junta Pública del condado de Taos," *Nuevo-Mejicano*, April 20, 1871.
113. S. W. Lloyd, "Convención del Condado de Lincoln," *Correo*, April 29, 1871; untitled, *Post*, April 29, 1871; untitled, *New Mexican*, April 25, 1871.
114. "A Word to the Convention," *Post*, April 29, 1871, in "To the People," *Borderer*, August 16, 1871; "Republican Nomination for Delegate to Congress," *Borderer*, May 11, 1871; "Nominación Republicana para Delegado al Congreso," *Fronterizo*, May 11, 1871.
115. Untitled, *Post*, April 29, 1871.
116. "The Territorial Convention," *Review*, May 6, 1871; "The Territorial Convention," *New Mexican*, April 29, 1871, 1; "Proceedings of a Republican Convention Assembled at Santa Fe, N.M., April 29th, 1871, pursuant to a published Call," *Post*, May 6, 1871 . Well after the election, the *New Mexican* questioned Sullivan's authority to act on behalf of the Doña Ana delegation as the county's caucus had met in a "rebel's house." Sullivan defended the proxy role. The issue seems not have arisen in the convention; untitled, *Post*, September 23, 1871, 1; untitled, *Post*, September 23, 1871.
117. "The Territorial Convention," *New Mexican*, May 1, 1871; "The Territorial Convention," *New Mexican*, April 29, 1871; "Proceedings of a Republican Convention Assembled at Santa Fe, N.M., April 29th, 1871, pursuant to a published Call," *Post*, May 6, 1871; untitled, *New Mexican*, May 13, 1871; "Organize," *Post*, May 6, 1871.
118. Untitled, *New Mexican*, May 9, 1871; "The Convention," *Review,* May 6, 1871; "Our Opposition," *Review*, December 17, 1870.
119. "The Nomination," *Post*, May 6, 1871; untitled, *Argus*, in *New Mexican*, May 13, 1871.
120. "The Nomination," *New Mexican*, May 1, 1871.
121. "County Committees," *New Mexican*, May 13, 1871.
122. "To the Democrats of New Mexico," *Borderer*, May 11, 1871; "Organization of Democratic Central Committee," *Borderer*, May 11, 1871.
123. R. H. Tompkins et al., "Democratic Convention," *New Mexican*, May 22, 1871.
124. "Democrats of New Mexico," *Borderer*, May 11, 1871.
125. "Territorial Democratic Convention," *Borderer*, May 25, 1871; "The New Mexico *Democrat*," *New Mexican*, May 22, 23 1871; "*El Demócrata, Nuevo-Mejicano*, May 22, 1871.
126. "New Democratic Paper in Santa Fe," *Borderer,* June 15, 1871.
127. Untitled, *New Mexican*, June 7, 1871.
128. "Glory Enough for One Day!," *Borderer*, May 4, 1871.

129. José Ma. Pino to editor and Jesús Ma. Gonzales to editor, *Fronterizo,* May 18, 1871.

130. Jose M. De Cámara to editor, in "Democracia en Chamberino," *Fronterizo,* May 18, 1871.

131. Anonymous to editors, *New Mexican,* June 2, 1871.

132. "Democratic Baile at Chamberino," *Borderer,* July 19, 1871.

133. Francisco Perea et al., "Proceedings of Bernalillo County Democratic Convention at the Court House Albuquerque N.M, June 16th, 1871," *Borderer,* June 29, 1871; untitled, *New Mexican,* June 20, 1871.

134. Untitled, *New Mexican,* May 29, 1871.

135. Don Pedro A. Baca et al., "Grand Democratic Meeting! In the County of Socorro," *Borderer,* June 22, 1871.

136. "Will the Radical Party Heed the Lesson?," *Borderer,* September 6, 1871; "Darán Atención los Radicales a Esta Lección," *Fronterizo,* September 6, 1871.

137. "Gallegos and Victory!!," *Borderer,* June 29, 1871; untitled, *New Mexican,* June 26, 1871; "Gallegos y la Victoria," *Fronterizo,* June 29, 1871; "Democratic Territorial Convention," *Borderer,* July 13, 1871, 1; "Convención Demócrata Territorial," *Fronterizo,* July 13, 1871; untitled, *New Mexican,* June 24, 1871; "Democratic Territorial Convention," *Post,* July 1, 1871; *el ingrato,* "Hon. J. Manuel Gallegos, como Delegado al Congreso por la Convención Demócrata de Santa Fe, el 24 del pasado," *Fronterizo,* July 13, 1871; "Destruction of the Archives of New Mexico," *Borderer,* July 26, 1871; Horn, *New Mexico's Troubled Years,* 137–42.

138. José Manuel Gallegos to Manuel García, June 29, 1871, in *Nuevo-Mejicano,* July 26, 1871; "Our Candidate," *Borderer,* August 30, 1871; "Hon. S. B. Elkins, Radical Candidate for Delegate to Congress," *Borderer,* August 16, 1873.

139. José Manuel Gallegos, "Manifestación al Pueblo del Territorio de Nuevo Mexico," *Fronterizo,* July 26, 1871.

140. Untitled, *New Mexican,* June 26, 1871; "The Republican Party," *New Mexican,* July 12, 1871.

141. Republican to editors ("Washington Correspondence"), *New Mexican,* July 24, 1871.

142. Untitled, *Post,* July 1, 1871.

143. Untitled, *New Mexican,* July 15, 1871; "Political Consistency," *New Mexican,* July 29, 1871.

144. Untitled, *Post,* July 1, 1871.

145. Untitled, *Denver News,* in *New Mexican,* August 4, 1871.

146. Republican to editors ("Washington Correspondence"), *New Mexican,* August 7, 1871.

147. Untitled, *New Mexican,* July 22, 1871.

148. Untitled, *New Mexican,* May 25, 1871.

149. "Influence of Chaves in Washington," *Borderer,* August 16, 1871.

150. "Plataforma del Candidato Republicano Independiente," *Fronterizo,* August 16, 1871; Varón Votador to editors ("El Sufragio Feminíl en Nuevo Mejico"), *Nuevo-Mejicano,* January 11, 1870.

151. Adolph Guttman to editor, in "Interesting Letter," *Borderer*, August 2, 1871; "Interesante Carta," *Fronterizo*, August 2, 1871; "The Public Meeting of Sunday Disgraceful Proceeding," *Review*, August 26, 1871; untitled, *New Mexican*, July 22, 1871.

152. "A New and Singular Sickness," *Borderer*, July 26, 1871; "Peace Commissioner From Washington to New Mexico and Arizona!," *Borderer*, July 26, 1871.

153. "The 'New Departure,'" *New Mexican*, June 10, 1871; also, "The Republican Party," *New Mexican*, July 12, 1871.

154. "To the People," *Borderer*, August 16, 1871.

155. W. F. Arny to editor, July 25, 1871 ("Correspondencia"), *Correo*, August 12, 1871. Oddly, the *New Mexican* (untitled, June 17, 1871), argued in a debate with the *Democrat* that since New Mexico had no vote in Congress, the subject had "not the slightest interest to our people in determining party lines in New Mexico." On the rise of free labor ideology post Civil War, see Shalhope, *John Taylor of Caroline*, 6-7.

156. Michael Les Benedict, *Preserving the Constitution*, 100.

157. Untitled, *New Mexican*, June 15, 1871; last quote, untitled, *New Mexican*, June 8, 1871.

158. "Out Among our Friends—The People," *Borderer*, May 4, 1871.

159. Untitled editorial, *Review*, August 19, 1871.

160. Río Abajo to the *Review* ("Democratic Prescriptions"), *Review*, July 15, 1871.

161. "Gallegos' Cadet Appointment," *New Mexican*, August 1, 1871; untitled, *New Mexican*, August 5, 1871; untitled, *Correo*, August 12, 1871.

162. Untitled, *New Mexican*, September 2, 1871; untitled, *Borderer*, August 23, 1871.

163. Rio Abajo, "Communication: More Democratic Absurdity," *Review*, July 22, 1871; "Political Misrepresentations," *New Mexican*, September 2, 1871; Republican to editors ("Washington Correspondence"), *New Mexican*, July 20, 1871.

164. Republican to editors ("Washington Correspondence"), *New Mexican*, July 14, 1871; Republican to editors ("Washington Correspondence"), *New Mexican*, July 10, 1871.

165. Farrand, *Legislation for Government of the Organized Territories*, 46; Wm. A. Pile, "Proclamation," *New Mexican*, June 22, 1871; untitled, *New Mexican*, May 3, 1871. The act produced confusion as to whether New Mexico's legislature should meet in 1870, as a previous territorial law called for an election and a session. A kind of stunted rump session convened but disbanded immediately. Many accounts in the *New Mexican* tell the story of the elections and the response in New Mexico to the congressional shift.

166. Anonymous, "La Política en el condado de Rio Arriba," *Nuevo-Mejicano*, August 30, 1871.

167. Untitled, *New Mexican*, August 27, 1870; quote, "'Let us have Peace,'" *New Mexican*, August 30, 1870; untitled, *New Mexican*, August 31, 1870; untitled, *New Mexican*, October 27, 1870.

168. Anonymous to editors, *New Mexican*, July 17, 1871; anonymous to editors ("From Dona Ana County"), *New Mexican*, July 18, 1871; anonymous to editors ("Political News"), *New Mexican*, July 18, 1871; also Anonymous to *New Mexican*, July 21, 1871.

169. 33 to editors, *Nuevo-Mejicano*, August 5, 1871.

170. Anonymous, "Dispatches by Pony Express," *Borderer*, July 13, 1871; Miller, "William Logan Rynerson," 109.

171. "Cheering for the Party," *Borderer*, July 19, 1871.

172. "Los Amenazas del Partido Radical," *Fronterizo*, June 29, 1871; Mary Daniels Taylor, *A Place as Wild*, 152.

173. Republican to editors ("From Doña Ana County"), *New Mexican*, July 8, 1871; Taylor, *A Place as Wild*, 151.

174. Pablo Melendres to the people, published in "Threats of the Radicals to Carry the Election with Bullets, Clubs, Rocks and Blows," Borderer, July 19, 1871; Miller, "William Logan Rynerson," 109–10; Taylor, A Place as Wild, 153–54.

175. "Threats of the Radicals to Carry the Election with Bullets, Clubs, Rocks and Blows," *Borderer*, July 19, 1871.

176. "The Open Threat of the Radical Leaders Carried out by Midnight Assassins," *Borderer*, August 2, 1871.

177. For a prominent parody of Heath as a high-pitched turncoat representative of Radicalism, see untitled, *Borderer*, July 26, 1871; for another that made Heath out as a *chicuelo* (child) with a "very high voice," see Votador to editors, *Fronterizo*, June 29, 1871.

178. Untitled, *New Mexican*, June 17, 1871.

179. "Interesting Love Feast," *Borderer*, June 22, 1871.

180. Anonymous to editor, *Borderer*, August 2, 1871, 1; "Hefty Statesmanship," *Borderer*, August 16, 1871.

181. Anonymous, "Dispatches by Pony Express," *Borderer*, July 13, 1871.

182. "Dona Ana County Republican Convention," *Borderer*, June 15, 1871; that the monkey is H. H. Heath, see anonymous, "Dispatches by Pony Express," *Borderer*, July 13, 1871.

183. "It's Proof you want, is it, Mr. Republican?" *Borderer*, August 23, 1871.

184. Untitled, *Borderer*, August 23, 1871.

185. Anonymous, "Grand Democratic Demonstration," *Borderer*, July 26, 1871; "Gran Demostración Democrática," *Fronterizo*, July 26, 1871.

186. Verdad to editors, *New Mexican*, August 31 and September 1, 1871. S. N. Ashenfelter, untitled, *Silver City Independent*, date not cited, in Griggs, *History of the Mesilla Valley*, 90–91; Ashenfelter was U.S. attorney and editor of a Silver City weekly. See also Theisen, "José Manuel Gallegos,"178–79; Siemers, "Campaigning, New Mexico Style," 5–6; Freitze, *History of La Mesilla*, 123–24.

187. Discussed in Freitze, *History of La Mesilla*, 129.

188. Sessame to editors, August 28 1871, *New Mexican*, August 31and September 1, 1871; "The Mesilla Riot," *New Mexican*, August 31, September 1, 1871; Freitze, *History of La Mesilla*, 125.

189. Ashenfelter, untitled, 92; Siemers, "Campaigning, New Mexico Style," 5–6; Freitze, *History of La Mesilla*, 123, 127; Ygnacio to editor ("Another Report"), *Post*, September 2, 1871.

190. "It is no," anonymous correspondent to editor ("Riot at la Mesilla"), *Post*, September 2, 1871; Verdad to editors, *New Mexican*, August 31 and September 1, 1871; Sessame to editors, August 28 1871, *New Mexican*, August 31 and September 1, 1871; Verdad to editors, *New Mexican*, August 31 and September 1, 1871; Ashenfelter, untitled, 92; Taylor, *A Place as Wild*, 161–63.

191. Ashenfelter, untitled, 92–93; Larson, *New Mexico's Quest*, 94; Twitchell, *Leading Facts*, 2: 400. Besides Felicito Arroyo y Lueras, the others were Sotelo Lopez, Francisco Rodriguez, Fabián Cortez, someone identified as a Chihuahuense, and an innocent young bystander; Freitze, *History of La Mesilla*, 125.

192. Ashenfelter, untitled, 93; Larson, *New Mexico's Quest*, 94; Taylor, *A Place as Wild*, 164–65.

193. "The Mesilla Riot," *New Mexican*, August 31 and September 1, 1871.

194. Untitled, *New Mexican*, July 15, 1871; also Ashenfelter, untitled, 93; Freitze, *History of La Mesilla*, 133.

195. Untitled, *Post*, September 30, 1871, 2.

196. "Injusto," *Correo*, September 23, 1871.

197. "Distortions of the Eastern Press," *Borderer*, September 20, 1871.

198. Untitled, *New Mexican*, July 15, 1871; "New York Riot," *Borderer*, August 2, 1871.

199. Untitled, *New Mexican*, October 4, 1869; untitled, *New Mexican*, October 13, 1869.

200. "Terrible Scene at Sunrise," *Borderer*, October 4, 1871.

201. On how the Mesilla Riot led scores of Nuevomexicanos to repatriate to Chihuahua, see Hernández, *Mexican American Colonization*, 181–201.

202. "Col. Chaves," *Borderer*, September 6, 1871; untitled, *Fronterizo*, September 6, 1871.

203. Untitled, *Borderer*, September 6, 1871; Republican to editors ("Doña Ana County Politics"), *New Mexican*, August 31, 1871; Republicano to editors, *Nuevo-Mejicano*, September 1, 1871.

204. "To the Voters of New Mexico," *New Mexican*, August 29, 1871.

205. "To the Voters of New Mexico," *New Mexican*, August 29, 1871.

206. "Official Vote for Delegate," *New Mexican*, September 19, 1871.

207. Untitled, *New Mexican*, September 5, 1871.

208. "Official Vote of the Territory for Delegate," *Post*, September 23, 1871.

209. Untitled, *New Mexican*, September 9, 1871.

210. Untitled, *New Mexican*, September 11, 1871.

211. Untitled, *New Mexican*, September 8, 1871.

212. "Official Vote of the Territory for Delegate," *Post*, September 23, 1871; "Official Vote for Delegate," *New Mexican*, September 18, 1871; untitled, *New Mexican*, September 8, 1871; *Borderer*, September 27, 1871; "Voto Oficiál de Nuevo Mejico," *Fronterizo*, September 27, 1871.

213. "Official Vote of the Territory for Delegate," *Post*, September 23, 1871; "Election Returns," *Borderer*, September 20, 1871; untitled, *New Mexican*, September 8, 1871.

214. "Election in Doña Ana," *Borderer*, September 6, 1871; "Elección en Doña Ana," *Fronterizo*, September 6, 1871; "Una Buena Elección," *Fronterizo*, September 6,

1871; "Official Vote of the Territory for Delegate," *Post*, September 23, 1871; "Election Returns," *Borderer*, September 20, 1871; untitled, *New Mexican*, September 8, 1871.

215. Freitze, *History of La Mesilla*, 127.

216. "Will the Radical Party Heed the Lesson?," *Borderer*, September 6, 1871; "Darán Atención los Radicales a Esta Lección," *Fronterizo*, September 6, 1871.

217. Quoted in untitled, *Borderer*, October 4, 1871.

218. Untitled, *Post*, September 9, 1871.

219. "The Election," *New Mexican*, September 7, 1871; untitled, *New Mexican*, September 8, 1871; also untitled, *New Mexican*, September 22, 1871.

220. Untitled, *Review*, September 9, 1871.

221. "Party Responsibility," *New Mexican*, September 27, 1871.

Conclusions

1. José M. Gallegos to the People of New Mexico, *Review*, March 15, 1873 and March 22, 1873; "Party Fealty, Party Discipline and Loyalty to Principle," *Borderer*, July 5, 1873; "Letter of José M. Gallegos to Hon. Rafael Romero, Explaining his Position," *Borderer*, August 9, 1873; untitled, *Borderer*, August 9, 1873; Michael Cronin to editor, *Borderer*, August 17, 1873.

2. "Let the Cannon Roar!," *Review*, September 6, 1873.

3. "Address of the Executive Committee," *Review*, September 23, 1876; Pedro Valdes to editors, *Revista Republicana* (Albuquerque, hereafter *Revista*), October 28, 1876.

4. "Convención Republicana del Condado de San Miguel," *La Beliota* (Las Vegas NM), May 25, 1875.

5. Lamar, *Far Southwest*, 142–43; Twitchell, *Leading Facts*, 464; Marion Dargan, "New Mexico's Fight for Statehood," 136; "¡Que Descaro!," *El Guía de Santa Fe*, September 2, 1886.

6. Report of the Republican Territorial Nominating Convention, *New Mexican*, extracted in the *Acorn* (Las Vegas NM), June 8, 1875; William Breeden, "Relative Strength," *Weekly New Mexican Review and Live Stock Journal* (Santa Fe), July 31, 1884; Hoover, "History of the Republican Party," 119.

7. Untitled, *Review*, July 5, 1873.

8. "Lista de leyes decreiadas en la sesión de 1871–2 de la Asamblea Legislativa de Nuevo Mexico," *Revista*, February 17, 1872.

9. See, for example, "Republican Convention of Bernalillo County, held at Albuquerque, September 4, 1876," *Review*, September 9, 1876, 2.

10. Hoover, "History of the Republican Party," 34, 36, 37; "Thomas B. Catron, Esq.," *New Mexican*, February 20, 1872, 1.

11. "Bosquejos Biográficos: Hon. J. Francisco Chaves," *El Boletín Popular* (Santa Fe), February 7, 1895.

12. "The Presiding Officers," *New Mexican*, January 3, 1882; Walter et al., *Colonel Jose Francisco Chaves*, 3, 5, 12, 16; "Assassination," *El Combate* (Wagon Mound NM), December 3, 1904.

13. "Appointments by the Governor," *New Mexican*, February 20, 1872; untitled, *Gazette*, January 16, 1858.

14. "Address of the Executive Committee," *Review,* September 23, 1876; "Discurso de la Comisión," *Revista,* September 23, 1876.

15. See, for example, "The Coming Campaign," *Borderer,* May 31, 1873; "The New Mexican and the Ring," *Review,* September 23,1876; "Plataforma Democrática," *Revista,* September 23,1876; *Revista,* October 7, 1876; "The Santa Fe 'Ring,'" *Review,* January 26, 1877; "La 'Rueda' de Santa Fe," *Revista,* January 26, 1878.

16. Hoover, "History of the Republican Party," 30; Stratton, *Territorial Press of New Mexico,* 27.

17. Territorial Archives of New Mexico, reel 39, frame 62, TANM; Frymer, *Uneasy Alliances,* 122–23.

18. "Territorial Newspapers," *Combate,* September 12, 1903; Stratton, *Territorial Press of New Mexico,* 2.

19. Untitled, *Review,* August 12, 1873; Stratton, *Territorial Press of New Mexico,* 285.

20. Stratton, *Territorial Press of New Mexico,* 36, 59; "Territorial Newspapers," *Combate,* September 12, 1903.

21. On the Nuevomexicano press see Meyer, *Speaking for Themselves,* and Meléndez, *So All Is Not Lost.*

22. Stratton, *Territorial Press of New Mexico,* 26, 36–37, 288.

23. Hoover, "History of the Republican Party," 119–21.

24. Phillip B. Gonzales, "El Jefe," 77–78.

25. Maurilio E. Vigil, *Los Patrones,* 166.

26. "Junta de los Demócratas y Liberales en Favor de Greeley y Brown," *Fronterizo,* September 14, 1872.

27. Frymer, *Uneasy Alliances,* 61–62; "Platform of the Liberal Republicans," *New Mexican,* May 21, 1872.

28. "The Republican Party," *New Mexican,* January 3, 1882.

29. See Tucker, *Mugwumps.*

30. Lamar, *Far Southwest,* 142–43.

31. "Assassination," *Combate,* December 3, 1904.

32. "Democratic Convention," *Review,* September 2, 1876.

33. Phillip B. Gonzales, "Race, Party, Class," 98–101.

34. United States Bureau of the Census, *Thirteenth Census of the United States,* 158. In one projection, the percentage of Euroamericans in New Mexico prior to the 1880s did not go beyond 10 percent and shot up to one-third by 1900; Valdes, "A Sociological Analysis and Description," 65.

35. *Diario del Consejo, Procedimientos del Consejo Legislativo del Territorio de Nuevo Mexico, Sesión Vigesima-Octava,* 1889, 3–4, and subsequent editions up to 1909, available at the Center for Southwest Research and Special Collections, University of New Mexico.

36. Hoover, "History of the Republican Party," 39–40; William Breeden, "To the Voters of New Mexico," Republican Party, New Mexico Territory, Central Executive Committee [1876], Rare Books Collection 82036, Huntington Library, San Marino, California.

37. "Republican Territorial Convention," *Review,* April 15, 1871.

38. Edmund F. Dunne to Conciudadanos de Nuevo Mejico ("Discurso de la Comisión Ejecutiva de la Democracia de Nuevo Mejico"), *Revista,* September 23, 1876; Lamar, *Far Southwest,* 144–45; "H. B. Fergusson," *El Labrador* (Las Cruces NM), October 6, 1896.

39. Territory of New Mexico, *Proceedings of the Constitutional Convention of the Proposed State of New Mexico*; Gómez-Quiñones, *Roots of Chicano Politics,* 258.

40. See Phillip B. Gonzales, "New Mexico Statehood and Political Inequality."

41. Wolf, *Peasant Wars,* 276, 278, 279.

42. Rosenbaum, *Mexicano Resistance in the Southwest,* 42; David J. Weber, *Mexican Frontier,* 81, 98, 193.

43. Phillip B. Gonzales, "Struggle for Survival"; Newman, "The Santa Fe Ring." For a recent treatment of the Santa Fe Ring, see Caffey, *Chasing the Santa Fe Ring.*

44. Westphall, *Mercedes Reales,* 102–5; Ebright, *Land Grants and Lawsuits,* 40–41, "With this network" 43.

45. Blackmar, *Spanish Institutions of the Southwest,* 326–27; Benavides, "Lawyer-Induced Partitioning of New Mexican Land Grants," 15; Ebright, "Land Grant Community Associations," 1, and, *Land Grants and Lawsuits,* 44, 155; Van Ness, *Hispanos,* 228, 229–30, 242; Westphall, *Mercedes Reales,* 139, 143.

46. On the formation, personnel, and process of the court, see Westphall, *Mercedes Reales,* 236–68.

47. Ebright, *Land Grants and Lawsuits,* 46; Natural Resources Center, *Remote Claims Impact Study: Lot II-A; Study of Problems that Result from Spanish and Mexican Land Grant Claims* (Albuquerque: Natural Resources Center, 1980), ii; Malcolm Ebright, Testimony in *Status of Community Land Grants in Northern New Mexico,* Oversight Hearing before the Subcommittee on General Oversight and Investigations of the House Committee on Interior and Insular Affairs (Washington DC: Government Printing Office, 1989), 9; Westphall, *Mercedes Reales,* 255.

48. Natural Resources Center, *Remote Claims,* ii. Meyer and Brescia, "The Treaty of Guadalupe Hidalgo," 325; "single most," Ebright, Testimony, 11. Ebright, *Land Grants and Lawsuits,* 48–49. Westphall, *Mercedes Reales,* 138–39, 256. Not all legal researchers disagree with this assessment of *Sandoval*; see, for example, Gilberto Espinosa, "New Mexico Land Grants."

49. Ebright, *Land Grants and Lawsuits,* 46–47.

50. Westphall, *Mercedes Reales,* 265; "Modern scholars," Ebright, Testimony, 6.

51. General Accounting Office, *Treaty of Guadalupe Hidalgo,* 9; Ebright, *Land Grants and Lawsuits,* 37; Van Ness, *Hispanos,* 220–21; Westphall, *Mercedes Reales,* 144.

52. Montoya, *Translating Property,* 38–39, 71–75, 96–113, 121–38, 143–56, 192–206; Pearson, *Maxwell Land Grant,* 119–32; Rosenbaum, *Mexicano Resistance in the Southwest,* 75; Lamar, "Land Policy in the Spanish Southwest," quote 510.

53. Utley, *High Noon in Lincoln,* 10–13.

54. Correia, *Properties of Violence.*

55. Knowlton, "The Study of Land Grants," 3–4; Larson, "The White Caps of New Mexico," 176–77.

56. Van Ness, *Hispanos,* 245–46.

57. Carlson, *Spanish American Homeland*, 83.

58. Allan Harper et al., *Man and Resources in the Middle Rio Grande Valley*, 56–65, quote, 64; Montgomery, *Spanish Redemption*, 40–53.

59. Sánchez, *Forgotten People*.

60. Turo, "An Empire of Dust," 162.

61. Zeleny, "Relations between the Spanish-Americans and Anglo-Americans," 225–26. For a general treatment on political parties competing with ethnic solidarity, see Nielsen, "Ethnic Solidarity," 142–43.

62. Hechter, "Nationalism as Group Solidarity," 419; Gellner, *Thought and Change*, 174.

63. "Death of General Armijo," *Gazette*, January 28, 1854; untitled, *Gazette*, October 4, 1856; "Death of Juan Felipe Ortiz," *Gazette*, January 23, 1858; "Necrología del sr. Vicario Don Juan Felipe Ortiz, *Gaceta*, January 30, 1858; "Hon. Facundo Pino," *Río Abajo Weekly Press* (Albuquerque NM), February 3, 1863; "Deceased," *Gazette*, June 22, 1867; untitled, *Nuevo-Mejicano*, June 25, 1869; Wayne Harper, "Juan Bautista Vigíl y Alarid," 175; Hall, "Giant Before the Surveyor-General," 64.

64. "Deceased," *Gazette*, June 22, 1867 ¡FALLESIMIENTOS!," *Nuevo-Mejicano*, June 22, 1867; "Junta pública tenida en la casa de Don Ventura Lovato," *Gazette*, August 10, 1867; "Proceedings," *Gazette*, June 29, 1867; *Nuevo-Mejicano*, June 29, 1867; "Salvador Armijo et al., "Junta Pública," *Gazette,* July 6, 1867; Cristóval Sanches y Baca et al., "Procedimientos de una Junta Pública," *Nuevo-Mejicano*, July 27, 1867; Sebero Baca et al., Proceedings, *Nuevo-Mejicano*, July 27, 1867.

65. Twitchell, *History of the Military Occupation*, 226–28.

66. "Enthusiastic Welcome," *New Mexican*, April 27, 1867; "How Chavez opens the Campaign," *Gazette*, April 27, 1867; "The Canvass," *Gazette*, May 18, 1867; anonymous to Querida Gazeta, *Gaceta*, May 11, 1867.

67. "Death of Simón Delgado and Miguel E. Pino," *New Mexican*, June 29, 1867; "Obituario," *Nuevo-Mejicano*, June 29, 1867.

68. Twitchell, *History of the Military Occupation*, 247–48.

69. "The Angel of Death," *Weekly New Mexico Review and Legislative Journal* (Santa Fe), March 27, 1884, 2; also "Diego Archuleta," *Weekly New Mexico Review and Legislative Journal,* March 27, 1884.

Bibliography

Archives

Arizona Historical Society, Tucson, Arizona.
    Angel Frías, *Los Chihuahenses van a ocupar la vanguardia contra las fuerzas enemigas.*
    Carl Hayden Papers.
Center for Southwest Research and Special Collections, University of New Mexico, Albuquerque.
    Clinton P. Anderson Papers.
    Frank Driver Reeve Papers.
    LeBaron Prince Papers.
    Mexican Archives of New Mexico, 1821–1846, microfilm.
        Journal of the Assembly of New Mexico.
    Records of the States of the United States, microfilm.
        1846–1861, N.M. B. 2, reel 1
        1862–1875, N.M. B. 2, reel 2
    William G. Ritch Papers, microfilm.
    Thomas B. Catron Papers.
    Territorial Archives of New Mexico, 1846–1912, microfilm.
        Executive Records.
        Records of the Territorial Governors.
Thomas C. Donnelly Library, New Mexico Highlands University, Las Vegas.
    James W. Arrott's Fort Union Collection.
Huntington Library, San Marino, California.
Museum of New Mexico, Fray Angélico Chávez History Library.
    Alexander B. Dyer, Mexican War Journal, 1846–1848, manuscript AC 070-P, Digitized Collection Archives.
    Palace of the Governors Photo Archives, Digitized Collection Archives.
National Archives.
    Record Group 46, Territorial Papers—New Mexico.
    Record Group 59, Miscellaneous Letters, October 1857, Santa Fe, New Mexico.
    Record Group 393, Series 02, microfilm.
New Mexico State Records Center and Archives, Santa Fe.
    Benjamin Read Collection.

Governor Henry Connelly Papers, 1861–1866, microfilm.
Mexican Archives of New Mexico, 1821–1846, microfilm.
   Journal of the Assembly of New Mexico.
Spanish Archives of New Mexico.
Southwest Collection, Donaciano Vigil Papers.
Territorial Archives of New Mexico, 1846–1912, microfilm.
   Executive Records.
   Records of the Territorial Governors.

Published Works

Abel, Annie Heloise, ed. *The Official Correspondence of James S. Calhoun*. Washington DC: Government Printing Office, 1915.

Abert, J. W. *Report of Lieut. J. W. Abert, of his Examination of New Mexico, in the Years 1846–47*. In Exec. Doc. no. 41, 30th Congress, 1st session, 417–548. Washington DC: Wendell and Van Benthuysen, 1848.

Adut, Ari. "A Theory of the Public Sphere." *Sociological Theory*, 30, no. 4 (2012): 238–62.

Ake, Claude. *A Theory of Political Integration*. Homewood IL: Dorsey Press, 1967.

Alden, George H. "The Evolution of the American System of Forming and Admitting New States into the Union." *Annals of the American Academy of Political and Social Science* 18, no. 4 (1901): 79–89.

Aldrich, John Herbert. *Why Parties?: The Origin and Transformation of Political Parties in America*. Chicago: University of Chicago Press, 1995.

Alexander, Jeffrey. "Core Solidarity, Ethnic Out-Groups, and Social Differentiation." In *Differentiation Theory and Social Change*, edited by Jeffrey Alexander and Paul Colomy, 267–93. New York: Columbia University Press, 1990.

———. "Differentiation Theory: Problems and Prospects." In *Differentiation Theory and Social Change*, edited by Jeffrey Alexander and Paul Colomy, 268–84. New York: Columbia University Press, 1990.

———. *The Performance of Politics: Obama's Victory and the Democratic Struggle for Power*. New York: Oxford University Press, 2010.

———. "Theorizing the 'Modes of Incorporation': Assimilation, Hyphenation, and Multiculturalism as Varieties of Civil Participation." *Sociological Theory* 19, no. 3 (2001): 237–49.

Allen, Danielle S. *Our Declaration: A Reading of the Declaration of Independence in Defense of Equality*. New York: Liveright Publishing Corporation, 2014.

Allison, W. H. H. "Colonel Francisco Perea." *Old Santa Fe* 1, no. 2 (1913): 210–22.

———. "Don Francisco Perea, Delegado al Congreso 38vo., Muere en Albuquerque." *El Nuevo Mexicano* (Santa Fe), May 29, 1913.

Almaguer, Tomás. *Racial Faultlines: The Historical Origins of White Supremacy in California*. Berkeley: University of California Press, 1994.

Anderson, Benedict. *Imagined Communities: Reflections on the Origin and Spread of Nationalism*. London: Verso, 1983.

Anderson, George B. *History of New Mexico: Its Resources and People*. Los Angeles: Pacific States Publishing, 1907.

Anonymous. *Inventory of County Archives of San Miguel County, New Mexico*. Albuquerque: New Mexico Historical Records Survey, 1937.

Aragón, John Ray de. *Padre Martínez and Bishop Lamy*. Las Vegas NM: Pan American Publishing Company, 1978.

———. *Padre Martínez: New Perspectives from Taos*. Taos NM: Millicent Rogers Museum, 1988.

Archuleta, Diego, et al. "Procedimientos de la junta Demócrata, habida en el Condado de Rio Arriba." *Santa Fe Weekly Gazette*, March 7, 1857.

Arellano, Anselmo F. "Through Thick and Thin: Evolutionary Transitions of Las Vegas Grandes and Its Pobladores." PhD diss., University of New Mexico, 1990.

Arny, William F. M. *Executive message of his excellency, William F. M. Arny, acting governor of New Mexico, to the Legislative Assembly of the Territory Delivered the 2d Day of December 1862*. Santa Fe: Santa Fe Gazette, 1862.

Ash, Timothy Garton. "Freedom and Diversity: A Liberal Pentagram for Living Together." *New York Review of Books*, November 22, 2012: 33–36.

Bailey, Lynn R. *Bosque Redondo: The Navajo Internment at Fort Sumner, New Mexico, 1863–1868*. Tucson: Westernlore Press, 1998.

Bailyn, Bernard. *Pamphlets of the American Revolution, 1750–1776*. Cambridge MA: Harvard University Press, 1965.

Ball, Durwood. *Army Regulars on the Western Frontier, 1848–1861*. Norman: University of Oklahoma Press, 2001.

———. "By Right of Conquest: Military Government in New Mexico and California, 1846–1851." *Journal of the West* 41 (summer 2001): 8–16.

———. "Fort Craig, New Mexico, and the Southwest Indian Wars, 1854–1884." *New Mexico Historical Review* 73, no. 2 (1998): 153–73.

Ball, Larry D. *Desert Lawmen: The High Sheriffs of New Mexico and Arizona, 1846–1912*. Albuquerque: University of New Mexico Press, 1996.

Bancroft, Hubert Howe. *History of Arizona and New Mexico, 1530–1888*. Albuquerque: Horn and Wallace, 1962 [1889].

Barnard, Daniel D. "The Social System: An Address Pronounced Before the House of Convocation of Trinity College," Hartford CT, 1848. In *The American Whigs: An Anthology*, edited by Daniel Walker Howe, 106–20. New York: John Wiley and Sons, 1973.

Barth, Fredrik. "Introduction." In *Ethnic Groups and Boundaries: The Social Organization of Culture Difference*, edited by Fredrik Barth, 9–38. Prospect Heights IL: Waveland Press, 1998.

Bartlett, John Russell. *Personal Narrative of Explorations and Incidents in Texas, New Mexico, California, Sonora, and Chihuahua, Connected with the United States and Mexican Boundary Commission, During the Years 1850, 1851, 1852, and 1853*, vol. 1 New York: D. Appleton and Company, 1854.

Bauer, Nichole. "Sticking With It: How Loyalty Explains Political Party Identification." Y673 Mini Conference, Indiana University, Spring 2010.

Baxter, John O. *Las Carneradas: Sheep Trade in New Mexico, 1700–1860*. Albuquerque: University of New Mexico Press, 1987.

———. *Dividing New Mexico's Waters, 1700–1912*. Albuquerque: University of New Mexico Press, 1997.

Beachum, Larry M. *William Becknell, Father of the Santa Fe Trade*. El Paso: Texas Western Press, 1982.

Bein, Alex. *The Jewish Question: Biography of a World Problem*. Rutherford NJ: Farleigh Dickinson University Press, 1990.

Benavides, David. "Lawyer-Induced Partitioning of New Mexican Land Grants: An Ethical Travesty." Guadalupita NM: Paper, Center for Land Grant Studies, 1994.

Bendix, Reinhard. "Industrialization, Ideologies, and Social Structure." *American Sociological Review*, 24, no. 4 (1959): 613–23.

———. *Nation-Building and Citizenship: Studies of Our Changing Social Order* Berkeley: University of California Press, 1977.

Benedict, Kirby. *A Journey through New Mexico's First Judicial District in 1864*. Los Angeles: Westernlore Press, 1956.

Benedict, Michael Les. *A Compromise of Principle: Congressional Republicans and Reconstruction, 1863–1869*. New York: W. W. Norton, 1974.

———. *The Impeachment and Trial of Andrew Johnson*. New York: W. W. Norton and Company, 1973.

———. *Preserving the Constitution: Essays on Politics and the Constitution in the Reconstruction Era*. New York: Fordham University, 2006.

Berwanger, Eugene H. *The Rise of the Centennial State: Colorado Territory, 1861–76*. Urbana: University of Illinois Press, 2007.

Bibby, John F., and L. Sandy Maisel. *Two Parties–Or More?* Boulder CO: Westview Press, 2003.

Bieber, Ralph P. "Introduction." In George Rutledge Gibson, *Journal of a Soldier under Kearny and Doniphan, 1846–1847*, edited by Ralph P. Bieber, 17–105. Philadelphia: Porcupine Press, 1974.

———. "Introduction" to Philip Gooch Henderson, "Diary of Philip Gooch Henderson." In Abraham Robinson Johnston, Marcellus Ball Edwards, and Philip Gooch Ferguson, *Marching with the Army of the West 1846–1848*, edited by Ralph P. Bieber, 283–361. Glendale CA: Arthur H. Clark Company, 1936.

Bieber, Ralph P., ed. *Letters of William Carr Lane, 1852–1854*. Santa Fe NM: El Palacio Press, 1928.

Biege, Bernd. "The Easter Rising of 1916–a New Dawn for Irish Independence." About.com.

Billington, Ray Allen. *America's Frontier Heritage*. Albuquerque NM: University of New Mexico Press, 1974.

Bilotta, James A. *Race and the Rise of the Republican Party, 1848–1865*. Philadelphia: Xlibris, 2002.

Binkley, William Campbell. "Reports from a Texan Agent in New Mexico, 1849." In *New Spain and the Anglo American West*, vol. 2, edited by George P. Hammond, 157–83. Lancaster PA: Privately printed, 1932.

Blackmar, Frank Wilson. *Spanish Institutions of the Southwest*. Glorieta NM: The Grande Press, 1976 [1891].

Blauner, Bob. *Racial Oppression in America*. New York: Harper and Row, 1972.
Bloom, Lansing Bartlett. *New Mexico under Mexican Administration 1821–1846*, serialized in *Old Santa Fe* vol. 1, no. 1 (July 1913)–vol. 2, no. 4 (April 1915):
Pt. II: *Narrative History of the Years 1821–1837*
ch. IV: "New Mexico Becomes a Territory." *Old Santa Fe* 1, no. 2 (1913): 166–75.
ch. XII: "Changing to the Departmental System." *Old Santa Fe* 2, no. 1 (1914): 3–18.
Pt. III: *New Mexico as a Department 1837–1846*
ch. I: "New Mexico in 1838." *Old Santa Fe* 2, no. 1 (1914): 37–46.
ch. IV: "A One-Man Administration, 1838–1844." *Old Santa Fe* 2, no. 2 (1914): 127–42.
ch. V: "Texan Aggressions 1841–1843." *Old Santa Fe* 2, no. 2 (1914): 143–56.
ch. VI: "Constitutional Government Re-established, 1843–1844." *Old Santa Fe* 2, no. 2 (1914): 157–69.
ch. VII: A Year under an Alien Governor." *Old Santa Fe* 2, no. 3 (1915): 223–37.
ch. VIII: "Six Months under the Senior Deputy." *Old Santa Fe* 2, no. 3 (1915): 238–48.
ch. IX: "A Third and Last Chance for Manuel Armijo." *Old Santa Fe* 2, no. 3 (1915): 249–62.
Bloom, Lansing P., ed. "Historical Society Minutes, 1859–1863." *New Mexico Historical Review* 18, no. 3 (1943): 247–311.
Bonacich, Edna. "Class Approaches to Ethnicity and Race." In *Majority and Minority: The Dynamics of Race and Ethnicity in American Life*, edited by Norman Y. Yetman, 59–75. Boston: Allyn and Bacon, 1991.
Bormann, E. G. "Fantasy and Rhetorical Vision: The Rhetorical Criticism of Social Reality." *Quarterly Journal of Speech*, 58, no. 4 (1972): 396–407.
Boyle, Susan Calafate. *Los Capitalistas: Hispano Merchants and the Santa Fe Trade*. Albuquerque: University of New Mexico Press, 1997.
Brading, David. *The Origins of Mexican Nationalism*. Cambridge: Cambridge University Press, 1985
———. "Patriotism and the Nation in Colonial Spanish America." In *Constructing Collective Identities and Shaping Public Spheres*, edited by Luis Roniger and Mario Sznajder, 13-45. Brighthon UK: Sussex Academic Press, 1998.
Brazeal, Donald K. "Precursor to Modern Media Hype: The 1830s Penny Press." *Journal of American Culture* 28, no. 4 (2005): 405–14.
Breuilly, John. *Nationalism and the State*. Manchester UK: Manchester University Press, 1993.
Bridgers, Lynn. *Death's Deceiver: The Life of Joseph P. Machebeuf*. Albuquerque: University of New Mexico Press, 1997.
Brooks, James F. *Captives and Cousins: Slavery, Kinship, and Community in the Southwest Borderlands*. Chapel Hill: University of North Carolina Press, 1996.
———. "Violence, Justice, and State Power in the New Mexican Borderlands, 1780–1880." In *Power and Place in the North American West*, edited by Richard White and John M. Findlay, 23–60. Seattle: Center for the Study of the Pacific Norwest, University of Washington, 1999.
Bullis, Don. *New Mexico: A Biographical Dictionary 1540–1980*. Los Ranchos de Albuquerque: Rio Grande Books, 2007.

Burton, E. Bennett. "The Taos Rebellion." *Old Santa Fe* 1, no. 2 (1913): 176–209.

Burton, Michael, Richard Gunther, and John Higley, "Introduction: Elite Transformations and Democratic Regimes." In *Elites and Democratic Consolidation in Latin America and Southern Europe*, edited by John Higley and Richard Gunther, 1–37. Cambridge UK: Cambridge University Press, 1992.

Bustamante, Adrian Herminio. "Los Hispanos: Ethnicity and Social Change in New Mexico." PhD diss., University of New Mexico, 1982.

Bustamante, Carlos María de. *El Nuevo Bernal Díaz del Castillo, ó sea, Historia de la invasión de los Anglo-Americanos en México*. Mexico City: V. Garcia Torres, 1847.

Caffey, David L. *Chasing the Santa Fe Ring: Power and Privilege in Territorial New Mexico* Albuquerque: University of New Mexico Press, 204.

Calvin, Ross, ed. "Introduction." In *Lieutenant Emory Reports: A Reprint of Lieutenant W. H. Emory's Notes of a Military Reconnoissance*, edited by Ross Calvin, 1–16. Albuquerque: University of New Mexico Press, 1951.

Carlson, Alvar. *The Spanish American Homeland*. Baltimore: Johns Hopkins University Press, 1990.

Carroll, H. Bailey, and J. Villasaña Haggard, transl. *Three New Mexico Chronicles: The Exposición of Don Pedro Bautista Pino 1812; the Ojeada of Lic. Antonio Barrriro 1832; and the additions by Don José Agustín de Escudero, 1849*. Albuquerque: Quivira Society, 1942.

Chambers, William Nisbet. *Political Parties in a New Nation: The American Experience, 1776–1809*. New York: Oxford University Press, 1963.

Charles, Ralph. "Development of the Partido System in the New Mexico Sheep Industry." MA thesis, University of New Mexico, 1940.

Chaves, J. Francisco. *Papers in the Case of J. Francisco Chaves vs. Charles P. Clever, Delegate from the Territory of New Mexico*. House of Representatives, Misc. Doc. no. 154, 40th Congress, 2nd session. Washington: Government Printing Office, 1867.

———. *Additional Papers in the Case of J. Francisco Chaves against Charles P. Clever, of New Mexico*. Misc. Doc. no. 14, 40th Congress, 3rd session. Washington: Government Printing Office, 1868.

Chávez, Fray Angélico. *But Time and Chance: The Story of Padre Martínez of Taos, 1793–1867*. Santa Fe: Sunstone Press, 1981.

———. *My Penitente Land: The Soul Story of Spanish New Mexico*. Santa Fe: William Gannon, 1979.

———. "A Nineteenth-Century New Mexico Schism." *New Mexico Historical Review* 58, no. 1 (1983): 35–54.

———. "The Penitentes of New Mexico." *New Mexico Historical Review* 29, no. 2 (1954): 97–132.

———. *Très Macho–He Said: Padre Gallegos of Albuquerque: New Mexico's First Congressman*. Santa Fe: William Gannon, 1985.

Chávez, Fray Angélico, and Thomas E. Chávez. *Wake for a Fat Vicar: Father Juan Felipe Ortiz, Archbishop Lamy, and the New Mexican Catholic Church in the Middle of the Nineteenth Century*. Albuquerque: LPD Press, 2004.

Chávez, Thomas E. *Manuel Álvarez 1794–1856: A Southwestern Biography.* Niwot: University Press of Colorado, 1990.

Chávez, Thomas E., ed. *Conflict and Acculturation: Manuel Álvarez's 1842 Memorial.* Santa Fe: Museum of New Mexico Press, 1989.

———. "Manuel Álvarez, Empire Builder of the Southwest." MA thesis, University of New Mexico, 1976.

Cheetham, Francis T. "The First Term of the American Court in Taos, New Mexico." *New Mexico Historical Review* 1, no. 1 (1926): 23–41.

Clarke, Dwight L. *Stephen Watts Kearny: Soldier of the West.* Norman: University of Oklahoma Press, 1961.

Coan, Charles F. "The County Boundaries of New Mexico." *Southwestern Political Science Quarterly* 3, no. 4 (1922): 252–75.

———. *A History of New Mexico.* Chicago: American Historical Society, 1925.

Cocker, Mark. *Rivers of Blood, Rivers of Gold: Europe's Conquest of Indigenous Peoples.* New York: Grove Press, 1998.

Cole, Donald B. *Martin Van Buren and the American Political System.* Princeton NJ: Princeton University Press, 1984.

Colton, Ray C. *The Civil War in the Western Territories: Arizona, Colorado, New Mexico, and Utah.* Norman: University of Oklahoma Press, 1959.

Comer, Douglas C. *Ritual Ground: Bent's Old Fort, World Formation, and the Annexation of the Southwest.* Berkeley: University of California Press, 1996.

Cooke, Philip St. George. *The Conquest of New Mexico and California: An Historical and Personal Narrative.* Albuquerque: Horn and Wallace, 1964 [1878].

Cornog, Evan. *The Birth of Empire: DeWitt Clinton and the American Experience, 1769–1828* New York: Oxford University Press, 1998.

Coronado, Raúl. *A World Not to Come: A History of Latino Writing and Print Culture.* Cambridge MA: Harvard University Press, 2013.

Correia, David. *Properties of Violence: Law and Land Grant Struggle in Northern New Mexico.* Athens: University of Georgia Press, 2013.

Costeloe, Michael P. *The Central Republic in Mexico, 1835–1846: "Hombres de Bien" in the Age of Santa Anna.* Cambridge UK: Cambridge University Press, 1993.

Cotner, Thomas E. *The Military and Political Career of José Joaquín De Herrera.* Austin: University of Texas Press, 1949.

Craver, Rebecca McDowell. *The Impact of Intimacy: Mexican-Anglo Intermarriage in New Mexico, 1821–1846.* El Paso: Texas Western Press, 1982.

Cress, Lawrence Delbert. "Introduction." In George Wilkins Kendall, *Dispatches from the Mexican War*, 3–33. Norman: University of Oklahoma Press, 1999.

Crofts, Daniel W., and Lawrence Delbert Cress. *Reluctant Confederates: Upper South Unionists in the Secession Crisis.* Chapel Hill: University of North Carolina Press, 1989.

Crutchfield, James A. *Tragedy at Taos: The Revolt of 1847.* Plano: Republic of Texas Press, 1995.

Cunningham, Noble E. "The Jeffersonian Republican Party." In *History of U.S. Political Parties*, vol.1: *1789–1860, From Factions to Parties*, ed. Arthur M. Schlesinger Jr., 239–72. New York: Chelsea House Publishers, 1973.

Cutts, James Madison. *The Conquest of California and New Mexico, by the Forces of the United States, in the Years 1846 & 1847.* Philadelphia: Carey and Hart, 1847.

Dailey, Martha Lacroix. "Michael Steck: A Prototype of Nineteenth Century Individualism." PhD diss., University of New Mexico, 1989.

Dargan, Lena Dingman. "James S. Calhoun in New Mexico." MA thesis, University of New Mexico, 1932.

Dargan, Marion. "New Mexico's Fight for Statehood, 1895–1912, III: The Opposition within the Territory (1888–1890)." *New Mexico Historical Review* 15, no. 2 (1940): 133–87.

Davis, W. W. H. *El Gringo; or, New Mexico and Her People.* New York: Harper and Brothers, 1857.

DeLay, Brian. *War of a Thousand Deserts: Indian Raids and the U.S.-Mexican War.* New Haven: Yale University Press, 2008.

Denetdale, Jennifer Nez. *Reclaiming Diné History: The Legacies of Navajo Chief Manuelito and Juanita.* Tucson: University of Arizona Press, 2007.

Deutsch, Karl W. *Nationalism and Its Alternatives.* New York: Alfred A. Knopf, 1969.

——. *Nationalism and Social Communication.* Cambridge MA: MIT Press, 1966.

Devine, Jaclyn R. "Race as Poverty: A Fantasy-Theme Analysis of Paul Ryan's Poverty Speech." Unpublished paper, University of New Mexico, 1911.

Devoto, Bernard. *The Year of Decision: 1846.* New York: Book-of-the Month Club, 1984.

Diamond, Larry. "Introduction: Persistence, Erosion, Breakdown, and Renewal." In *Democracy in Developing Countries: Asia*, vol. 3, edited by Larry Diamond, Juan J. Linz, and Seymour Martin Lipset, 1–52. Boulder CO: L. Rienner; London: Adamantine, 1988.

Diario del Consejo, Procedimientos del Consejo Legislativo del Territorio de Nuevo Mexico, Sesión Vigésima-Octava. Santa Fe: New Mexican, 1889, 1891, 1895, 1899, 1901, 1904, 1905, 1907, 1909.

Donald, David Herbert. "The Republican Party 1864–1876." In *History of U.S. Political Parties*, vol. 2: *1860–1910, The Gilded Age of Politics*, edited by Arthur M. Schlesinger Jr., 1281–94. New York: Chelsea House Publishers, 1973.

Doob, Leonard W. *Patriotism and Nationalism: Their Psychological Foundations.* New Haven: Yale University Press, 1964.

Drumm, Stella M. "Introduction." In Susan Shelby Magoffin, *Down the Santa Fe Trail and into Mexico: The Diary of Susan Shelby Magoffin, 1846–1847,* edited by Stella M. Drumm, xi–xxv. New Haven: Yale University Press, 1926.

Du Bois, W.E.B. "The African Roots of War." *Monthly Review,* 24, no. 2 (1973): 28–40.

Dunbar-Ortiz, Roxanne. *Roots of Resistance: A History of Land Tenure in New Mexico.* Norman: University of Oklahoma Press, 2007.

Ebright, Malcolm. *Land Grants and Lawsuits in Northern New Mexico.* Albuquerque: University of New Mexico, 1993.

———. *Land Grant Community Associations in New Mexico.* Guadalupita NM: Center for Land Grant Studies, 1994.
Edrington, Thomas S. "Military Influence on the Texas–New Mexico Boundary Settlement." *New Mexico Historical Review* 59, no. 3 (1984): 371–93.
Edwards, Marcellus Ball. "Journal of Marcellus Ball Edwards." In Abraham Robinson Johnston, Marcellus Ball Edwards, and Philip Gooch Ferguson, *Marching with the Army of the West 1846–1848*, edited by Ralph P. Bieber, 106–280. Glendale CA: Arthur H. Clark Company, 1936.
Eisenstadt, S. N. *Modernization: Protest and Change.* Englewood Cliffs: Prentice-Hall, 1966.
Ellison, Samuel. "History of New Mexico." In "Memoir of a Kentuckian in New Mexico, 1848–1884," edited by J. Manuel Espinosa. *New Mexico Historical Review* 13, no. 1 (1938): 1–13.
Emmett, Chris. *Fort Union and the Winning of the Southwest.* Norman: University of Oklahoma Press, 1965.
Emmanuel, Arghiri. "White-Settler Colonialism and the Myth of Investment Imperialism." *New Left Review* 73 (May–June 1972): 35–57.
Emory, W. H. *Notes of a Reconnaissance from Fort Leavenworth, in Missouri, to San Diego, in California.* In *Lieutenant Emory Reports: A Reprint of Lieutenant W. H. Emory's Notes of a Military Reconnaissance*, edited by Ross Calvin. Albuquerque: University of New Mexico Press, 1951.
Espinosa, Gilberto. "New Mexico Land Grants." *State Bar of New Mexico Journal* 1, no. 3 (1962): 3–13.
Espinosa, Gilberto, and Tibo J. Chavez. *El Río Abajo.* Pampa TX: Pampa Print Shop, n.d.
Espinosa, J. Manuel. *The Pueblo Indian Revolt of 1696 and the Franciscan Missions in New Mexico.* Norman: University of Oklahoma Press, 1988.
Farrand, Max. *The Legislation of Congress for the Government of the Organized Territories of the United States: 1789–1895.* Newark NJ: Wm. A. Baker, 1896.
Fergusson, Harvey. *Río Grande.* New York: Morrow, 1967.
Fernlund, Kevin Jon. "American Exceptionalism or Atlantic Unity? Frederick Jackson Turner and the Enduring Problem of American Historiography." *New Mexico Historical Review* 89, no. 3 (2014): 359–99.
Ferrell, Claudine L. *Reconstruction.* Westport CN: Greenwood Press, 2003.
Fierman, Floyd S. "The Career of Clever." *El Palacio* 85, no. 4 (Winter 1979–80): 2–5, 34–35.
Flores, William V., and Rina Benmayor, eds. *Latino Cultural Citizenship: Claiming Identity, Space and Rights.* Boston: Beacon Press, 1997.
Florescano, Enrique. *Étnia, estado y nación: Los indigenas y la sociedad colonial.* Aguilar, Mexico: Nuevo Siglo, 1997.
Foner, Eric. *The Fiery Trial: Abraham Lincoln and American Slavery.* New York: W. W. Norton, 2010.
———. *Free Soil, Free Labor, Free Men: The Ideology of the Republican Party Before the Civil War.* New York: Alfred A. Knopf, 1970.

Formisano, Ronald P. *The Birth of Mass Political Parties: Michigan, 1827–1861*. Princeton NJ: Princeton University Press, 1971.

Foss, S. *Rhetorical Criticism: Exploration and Practice*. Long Grove IL: Waveland Press, 2009.

Fox, Cybelle, and Thomas A. Guglielmo. "Defining America's Racial Boundaries: Blacks, Mexicans, and European Immigrants, 1890–1945." *American Journal of Sociology* 118, no. 2 (2012): 327–79.

Frank, Ross. *From Settler to Citizen: New Mexican Economic Development and the Creation of Vecino Society, 1750–1820*. Berkeley: University of California Press, 2000.

Frazer, Robert W. "The New Mexican Scene." In George Archibald McCall, *New Mexico in 1850: A Military View*. Norman: University of Oklahoma Press, 1968.

Frazer, Robert W. ed. *Over the Chihuahua and Santa Fe Trails 1847–1848: George Rutledge Gibson's Journal*. Albuquerque: University of New Mexico Press, 1981.

Freitze, Lionel Cajen. *History of La Mesilla and Her Mesilleros*. Las Cruces: ig Printing, 1995.

Friedman, Leon. "The Democratic Party 1860–1884." In *History of U.S. Political Parties, vol. 2: 1860–1910, The Gilded Age of Politics*, edited by Arthur M. Schlesinger Jr., 885–905. New York: Chelsea House Publishers, 1973.

Frymer, Paul. *Uneasy Alliances: Race and Party Competition in America*. Princeton NJ: Princeton University Press, 1999.

Galilei, Galileo. *Dialogue Concerning the Two Chief World Systems*, transl. by Stillman Drake. Berkeley: University of California Press, 1967 [1953].

Gallegos, Bernardo P. *Literacy, Education, and Society in New Mexico, 1693–1821*. Albuquerque: University of New Mexico Press, 1992.

Ganaway, Loomis Morton. *New Mexico and the Sectional Controversy, 1846–1861*. Albuquerque: University of New Mexico Press, 1944.

Gans, Chaim. *The Limits of Nationalism*. Cambridge UK: Cambridge University Press, 2003.

Garrard, Lewis H. *Wah-to-yah and the Taos Trail*. Norman: University of Oklahoma Press, 1968.

Gellner, Ernest. *Encounters with Nationalism*. Oxford: Blackwell, 1994.

———. *Nationalism*. Washington Square NY: New York University Press, 1997.

———. *Nations and Nationalism*. Oxford: Blackwell, 1983.

———. *Thought and Change*. Chicago: University of Chicago Press, 1964.

General Accounting Office: *Treaty of Guadalupe Hidalgo: Findings and Possible Options* Washington DC: United States Government, 2004.

Gerring, John. *Party Ideologies in America, 1828–1996*. Cambridge UK: Cambridge University Press, 1998.

Gibson, George Rutledge. *Journal of a Soldier under Kearny and Doniphan, 1846–1847*, edited by Ralph P. Bieber. Philadelphia: Porcupine Press, 1974.

Glenn, Evelyn Nakano. "Settler Colonialism as Structure: A Framework for Comparative Studies of U.S. Race and Gender Formation." *Sociology of Race & Ethnicity* 1, no. 1 (2015): 52–72.

———. *Unequal Freedom: How Race and Gender Shaped American Citizenship and Labor.* Cambridge MA: Harvard University Press, 2002.

Goldstein, Alyosha, and Alex Lubin, eds., *Settler Colonialism.* Durham NC: Duke University Press, 2008.

Gómez, Laura E. *Manifest Destinies: The Making of the Mexican Race.* New York: New York University Press, 2007.

———. "Off-White in an Age of White Supremacy: Mexican Elites and the Rights of Indians and Blacks in Nineteenth-Century New Mexico." *Chicano-Latino Law Review* 25, no. 2 (2005): 9–59.

———. "Race, Colonialism, and Criminal Law: Mexicans and the American Criminal Justice System in Territorial New Mexico." *Law & Society Review* 34, no. 4 (2000): 1192–93.

Gómez-Quiñones, Juan. *Roots of Chicano Politics, 1600–1940.* Albuquerque: University of New Mexico, 1994.

Gonzales, Moises. "The Genizaro Land Grant Settlements of New Mexico." *Journal of the Southwest* 56, no. 4 (2014): 583–602.

Gonzales, Phillip B. "El Jefe: Bronson Cutting and the Politics of Hispano Interests in New Mexico, 1920–1935." *Aztlán*, 25, no. 2 (2000): 67–108.

———. "La Junta de Indignación: Hispano Repertoire of Collective Protest in New Mexico, 1884–1933." *Western Historical Quarterly* 31, no. 2 (2000): 161–86.

———. "Mexican Party, American Party, Democratic Party: Establishing the American Political Party in New Mexico, 1848–1853." *New Mexico Historical Review* 88, no. 3 (2013): 253–85.

———. "New Mexico Statehood and Political Inequality: The Case of Nuevomexicanos." *New Mexico Historical Review* 90, no. 1 (2015): 31–52.

———. "Race, Party, Class: The Contradictions of Octaviano Larrazolo." In *Noble Purposes: Nine Champions of the Rule of Law*, edited by Norman Gross, 95–109. Athens: Ohio University Press, 2007.

———."Struggle for Survival: The Hispanic Land Grants of New Mexico." *Agricultural History* 77, no. 2 (2003): 293–324.

González, Deena, J. "Gertrudis Barceló: La Tules of Image and Reality." In *Latina Legacies: Identity, Biography, and Community*, edited by Vicki L. Ruiz and Virginia Sánchez Korrol, 39–58. Oxford: Oxford University Press, 2005.

———. *Refusing the Favor: The Spanish-Mexican Women of Santa Fe, 1829–1880.* New York: Oxford University Press, 1999.

González de la Vara, Martín. "El Traslado de Familias de Nuevo México al Norte de Chihuahua y la Conformación de Una Región Fronteriza, 1848–1864." *Frontera Norte* 6, no. 11 (1994): 9–22.

———. "La Política del Federalismo en Nuevo México (1821–1836)." *Historia Mexicana* 36 (July–September 1986): 81–112.

Gorenfeld, Will. "The Taos Mutiny of 1855." *New Mexico Historical Review* 88, no. 3 (2013): 287–319.

Gracián y Morales, Baltasar. *Oráculo manual, y arte de prudencia.* Amsterdam: D. Vivencio de Lastanosa, 1647.

Green, Fletcher M. "James S. Calhoun: Pioneer Georgia Leader and First Governor of New Mexico." *Georgia Historical Quarterly* 39, no. 4 (1955): 309–47.

Greenberg, Amy S. *A Wicked War: Polk, Clay, Lincoln, and the 1846 Invasion of Mexico.* New York: Knopf, 2012.

Gregg, Josiah. *Commerce of the Prairies.* New York: Henry G. Langley, 1926 [1844].

Griggs, George. *History of the Mesilla Valley or the Gadsden Purchase.* Las Cruces NM: Bronson Print Company, 1930.

Griswold del Castillo, Richard. *The Treaty of Guadalupe Hidalgo: A Legacy of Conflict.* Norman: University of Oklahoma Press, 1990.

Grivas, Theodore. *Military Governments in California, 1846–1850: With a Chapter on Their Prior Use in Louisiana, Florida, and New Mexico.* Glendale CA: Arthur H. Clark Company, 1963.

Groom, Winston. *Kearny's March: The Epic Creation of the American West, 1846–1847.* New York: Alfred A. Knopf, 2011.

Grove, Pearce S., Becky J. Barnett, and Sanra J. Hansen, eds. *New Mexico Newspapers: A Comprehensive Guide to Bibliographical Entries and Locations.* Albuquerque: University of New Mexico Press, 1975.

Grupo de Investigadores Puertoriqueños. *Breakthrough from Colonialism: An Interdisciplinary Study of Statehood.* 2 vols. Rio Piedras, P.R.: University of Puerto Rico, 1984.

Haas, Lisbeth. "War in California, 1846–1848." In *Contested Eden: California before the Gold Rush*, edited by Ramón A. Gutiérrez and Richard J. Orsi, 331–55. Berkeley: University of California Press, 1998.

Habermas, Jurgen. *The Structural Transformation of the Public Sphere.* Cambridge MA: MIT Press, 1997.

Hall, G. Emlen. "Giant before the Surveyor General: The Land Career of Donaciano Vigil." *Journal of the West* 19 (July 1980): 64–73.

Hall, Emlen, and David J. Weber. "Mexican Liberals and the Pueblo Indians, 1821–1829." *New Mexico Historical Review* 59, no. 1 (1984): 5–32.

Hall, Thomas D. *Social Change in the Southwest, 1350–1880.* Lawrence: University Press of Kansas, 1989.

Hammond, George P., ed. *New Spain and the Anglo American West*, vol. 2. Lancaster PA: Privately printed, 1932.

Hanyan, Craig, with Mary L. Hanyan. *De Witt Clinton and the Rise of the People's Men* Montreal: McGill-Queen's University Press, 1996.

Harper, Allan G., Andrew R. Cordova, and Kalervo Oberg. *Man and Resources in the Middle Rio Grande Valley.* Albuquerque: University of New Mexico Press, 1943.

Harper, Wayne A. "Juan Bautista Vigil y Alarid, a New Mexico Bureaucrat, 1792–1866." MA thesis, Brigham Young University, 1985.

Harper, William Lee. "A History of New Mexico Election Laws." MA thesis, University of New Mexico, 1927.

Harris, William C. *Lincoln and the Border States: Preserving the Union.* Lawrence: University Press of Kansas, 2011.

Harrison, Robert Pogue. "America: The Struggle to Be Reborn." *New York Review of Books* 59 (October 25, 2012): 64–65.

Hartz, Louis. *The Liberal Tradition in America: An Interpretation of American Political Thought since the Revolution.* New York: Harcourt Brace, 1955.

Hearn, Chester G. *The Impeachment of Andrew Johnson.* Jefferson NC: McFarland and Company, 2000.

Hechter, Michael. "The Dynamics of Secession." *Acta Sociologica* 35, no. 4 (1992): 267–83.

———. *Internal Colonialism: The Celtic Fringe in British National Development.* New Brunswick NJ: Transaction Publishers, 1999.

———. "Nationalism as Group Solidarity." *Ethnic and Racial Studies* 10 (1987): 415–26.

Henderson, Timothy J. *A Glorious Defeat: Mexico and Its War with the United States.* New York: Hill and Wang, 2007.

Hennesey, James. *American Catholics: A History of the Roman Catholic Community in the United States.* New York: Oxford University Press, 1981.

Hepler, Robert D. "William Watts Hart Davis in New Mexico." MA thesis, University of New Mexico, 1941.

Hernández, José Angel. *Mexican American Colonization during the Nineteenth Century: A History of the U.S.-Mexico Borderlands.* Cambridge UK: Cambridge University Press, 2012.

Hofstadter, Richard. *The Idea of a Party System: The Rise of Legitimate Opposition in the United States, 1780–1840.* Berkeley: University of California Press, 1969.

Hogan, J. B. "Last Rider: Sedalia, Missouri." *Frontier Tales,* no. 17 (February 2011), frontiertales.com.

[Holliday, W. J.] *Western Americana Many of Great Rarity: The Distinguished Collection Formed by W. J. Holliday.* New York: Parke-Bernet Galleries, 1954.

Holmes, Alan. "Major General James H. Carleton: New Mexico's Controversial Civil War Commander." *Journal of Southern New Mexico* 1, no. 1 (1994): 47–61.

Holmes, David L. *The Faiths of the Founding Fathers.* Oxford: Oxford University Press, 2006.

Holmes, Jack E. *Politics in New Mexico.* Albuquerque: University of New Mexico Press, 1967.

Holt, Michael F. *The Political Crisis of the 1850s.* New York: Wiley, 1978.

Holtby, David V. *Forty-Seventh Star: New Mexico's Struggle for Statehood.* Norman: University of Oklahoma Press, 2012.

Holzer, Harold. *Lincoln and the Power of the Press: The War for Public Opinion.* New York: Simon and Schuster, 2014.

Hoover, Herbert Theodore. "History of the Republican Party in New Mexico." PhD diss., University of Oklahoma, 1966.

Hordes, Stanley M. *To the End of the Earth: A History of the Crypto-Jews of New Mexico.* New York: Columbia University Press, 2005.

Horgan, Paul. *The Centuries of Santa Fe.* Albuquerque: University of New Mexico Press, 1994.

———. *Lamy of Santa Fe, His Life and Times.* New York: Farrar, Straus and Giroux, 1975.

Horn, Calvin. *New Mexico's Troubled Years: The Story of the Early Territorial Governors.* Albuquerque: Horn and Wallace, 1963.

Horton, Carol A. *Race and the Making of American Liberalism.* Oxford: Oxford University Press, 2005.

Horvath, Steven M. Jr. "The Genízaro of Eighteenth-Century New Mexico: A Reexamination." *Discovery: School of American Research* (1977): 25–40.

Howe, Daniel Walker. *The Political Culture of American Whigs.* Chicago: University of Chicago Press, 1979.

Hughes, John T. *Doniphan's Expedition.* Cincinnati: U. P. James, 1847.

Hurst, James Willard. *The Growth of American Law: The Law Makers.* Boston: Little, Brown, 1950.

Hunt, Aurora. *Kirby Benedict: Frontier Federal Judge.* Glendale CA: Arthur H. Clark Company, 1961.

———. *Major General James Henry Carleton, 1814–1873, Western Frontier Dragoon.* Glendale CA: Arthur H. Clark Company, 1958.

Huston, James L. *The Panic of 1857 and the Coming of the Civil War.* Baton Rouge: Louisiana State University Press, 1987.

———. *Stephen A. Douglas and the Dilemmas of Democratic Equality.* Lanham MD: Rowman and Littlefield, 2007.

Israel, Jonathan. *A Revolution of the Mind: Radical Enlightenment and the Intellectual Origins of Modern Democracy.* Princeton NJ: Princeton University Press, 2010.

Jacobson, David. *Place and Belonging in America.* Baltimore: Johns Hopkins University Press, 2002.

Jaher, Frederic Cople. *A Scapegoat in the New Wilderness: The Origins and Rise of Anti-Semitism in America.* Cambridge MA: Harvard University Press, 1994.

Jenkins, Myra Ellen. *The County Boundaries of New Mexico.* Santa Fe: New Mexico Legislative Council Service, 1965.

"J. M. Washington to the people of New Mexico," April 21, 1849. *U.S. Gov. Doc.,* House Misc. Doc. no. 5, 34th Congress, 1st session.

Johannsen, Robert W. *To the Halls of the Montezumas: The Mexican War and the American Imagination.* New York: Oxford University Press, 1985.

[Johnson, Hezekiah]. "The 'Art Preservative of all Arts' in New Mexico." *Río Abajo Weekly Press* (Albuquerque), January 20, 1863.

Johnston, A. R. *Journal of Captain A. R. Johnston, First Dragoons.* In Exec. Doc. no. 41, 30th Congress, 1st session, 566–614. Washington DC: Wendell and Van Benthuysen, 1848.

———. "Journal of Abraham Robinson Johnston." In Abraham Robinson Johnston, Marcellus Ball Edwards, and Philip Gooch Ferguson, *Marching with the Army of the West 1846–1848,* edited by Ralph P. Bieber, 73–104. Glendale CA: Arthur H. Clark Company, 1936.

Jordan, David Starr. *Imperial Democracy.* New York, Garland Publishing, 1972 [1899].

Jordan, Weymouth T. Jr., John. D. Chapla, and Shann C. Hutton. "Notorious as the Noonday Sun." *New Mexico Historical Review* 75, no. 4 (2000): 457–508.

Joy, Edmund Steele. *The Right of the Territories to Become States of the Union.* Newark: Advertiser Printing House, 1892.

Julyan, Robert. *The Place Names of New Mexico.* Albuquerque: University of New Mexico Press, 1996.

Kaplan, Richard L. *Politics and the American Press: The Rise of Objectivity, 1865–1920.* Cambridge UK: Cambridge University Press, 2002.

Kass, Alvin. *Politics in New York State, 1800–1830.* Syracuse NY: Syracuse University, 1965.

Kekes, John. *Against Liberalism.* Ithaca NY: Cornell University Press, 1997.

Keleher, William. *Turmoil in New Mexico 1846–68.* Albuquerque: University of New Mexico Press, 1982 [1952].

Kellogg, Deren Earl. "Lincoln's New Mexico Patronage: Saving the Far Southwest for the Union." *New Mexico Historical Review* 75, no. 4 (2000): 511–33.

Kendall George Wilkins. *Narrative of the Texan Santa Fe Expedition.* Chicago: Donnelley and Sons Company, 1929 [1844].

Kerber, Linda K. "The Federalist Party." *History of U.S. Political Parties,* vol. 1: *1789–1860, From Factions to Parties,* ed. Arthur M. Schlesinger Jr., 3–29. New York: Chelsea House Publishers, 1973.

Kessel, John L. *Spain in the Southwest: A Narrative History of Colonial New Mexico, Arizona, Texas, and California.* Norman: University of Oklahoma Press, 2002.

Kiser, William S. "A 'charming name for a species of slavery': Political Debate on Debt Peonage in the Southwest, 1840s–1860s." *Western Historical Quarterly* 45, no. 2 (2014): 169–89.

———. *Turmoil on the Rio Grande: History of the Mesilla Valley, 1846–1865.* College Station: Texas A&M University Press, 2011.

Kohl, Lawrence Frederick. *The Politics of Individualism: Parties and the American Character in the Jacksonian Era.* New York: Oxford University Press, 1989.

Kosmider, Alexia M. "Samuel B. Watrous: New Mexico Pioneer." MA thesis, University of New Mexico, 1983.

Knowlton, Clark S. "The Study of Land Grants as an Academic Discipline." *Social Science Journal* 13, no. 3 (1976): 3–7.

Korn, Bertram Wallace. *American Jewry and the Civil War.* Philadelphia: Jewish Publication Society, 1951.

Krause, Corinne. *Los Judíos en México: Una Historia con énfasis en el periodo de 1857 a 1930* Mexico City: Universidad Iberoamericana, 1987.

Kruman, Marc W. *Parties and Politics in North Carolina, 1836–1865.* Baton Rouge: Louisiana State University, 1983.

Kutsche, Paul, and John R. Van Ness. *Cañones.* Albuquerque: University of New Mexico Press, 1981.

Ladd, Everett Carll. *American Political Parties: Social Change and Response.* New York: W. W. Norton, 1970.

Lamar, Howard Roberts. *The Far Southwest, 1846–1912.* New York: W. W. Norton, 2000.

———. "Land Policy in the Spanish Southwest, 1846–1891: A Study in Contrasts." *Journal of Economic History* 22, no. 4 (1962): 498–515.

LaPalombara, Joseph, and Myron Weiner. "The Origin and Development of Political Parties." In *Political Parties and Political Development*, edited by Joseph LaPalombara and Myron Weiner, 3–42. Princeton NJ: Princeton University Press, 1966.

Larson, Robert W. *New Mexico's Quest for Statehood*. Albuquerque: University of New Mexico Press, 1968.

———. "The White Caps of New Mexico: A Study of Ethnic Militancy in the Southwest." *Pacific Historical Review* 44, no. 2 (1975): 171–85.

Lavender, David. *Bent's Fort*. Garden City NJ: Doubleday and Company, 1954.

Laws Passed by the General Assembly of the Territory of New Mexico in the Session of December, 1847. Santa Fe: Hovey and Davis, 1848. Records of the States of the United States, microfilms, 1846–1861. N.M. B. 2, reel 1.

Laws of the Territory of New Mexico, Passed by the First Legislative Assembly in the City of Santa Fe, at a Session begun on the Third Day of June 1851. Santa Fe: James L. Collins and Company, 1853. Records of the States of the United States, microfilms, 1846–1861. N.M. B. 2, reel 1.

Laws of the Territory of New Mexico Passed by the Legislative Assembly 1855–56. Santa Fe: *Santa Fe Weekly Gazette*, 1856. Records of the States of the United States, microfilms, 1846–1861. N.M. B. 2, reel 1.

Laws of the Territory of New Mexico Passed by the Legislative Assembly 1856–57. Santa Fe: Office of the Democrat, 1857. Records of the States of the United States, microfilms, 1846–1861. N.M. B. 2, reel 1.

Laws of the Territory of New Mexico, 1857–58. Santa Fe: Santa Fe Weekly Gazette, 1858.

Laws of the Territory of New Mexico, Passed by the Legislative Assembly, Session of 1859–60. Santa Fe: O. P. Hovey, 1860. New Mexico Session laws of 1857–58. Records of the States of the United States, microfilms, 1846–1861. N.M. B. 2, reel 1.

Laws of the Territory of New Mexico, passed by the Legislative Assembly, Session of 1862–63. Santa Fe: Charles Lieb, 1863. Records of the States of the United States, microfilms, 1862–1875. N.M. B. 2, reel 2.

Laws of the Territory of New Mexico, Passed by the Legislative Assembly, Session 1867–68. Santa Fe NM: Manderfield and Tucker, 1867 [sic]. Records of the States of the United States, microfilms, 1862–1875. N.M. B. 2, reel 2.

Lawson, Melinda. *Patriot Fires: Forging a New American Nationalism in the Civil War North*. Lawrence: University Press of Kansas, 2002.

Lecompte, Janet. "Manuel Armijo, George Wilkins Kendall, and the Baca-Caballero Conspiracy." *New Mexico Historical Review* 59, no. 1 (1984): 49–65.

———. *Rebellion in Río Arriba, 1837*. Albuquerque: University of New Mexico Press, 1985.

León, Arnoldo De. *The Tejano Community, 1836–1900*. Albuquerque: University of New Mexico Press, 1982.

Leopold, David. "A Cautious Embrace: Reflections on (Left) Liberalism and Utopia." In *Liberalism as Ideology: Essays in Honour of Michael Freeden*, edited by Ben Jackson and Marc Stears, 9–33. Oxford: Oxford University Press, 2012.

Lester, Paul Arnold. "Michael Steck and New Mexico Indian Affairs, 1852–1865." PhD diss., University of Oklahoma, 1986.

"Letter of Antonio López de Santa Anna to Manuel Reyes Veramendi, President of the Ayuntamiento of Mexico City, Guadalupe, September 15, 1847." Edited by Robert S. Chamberlain. *Hispanic American Historical Review* 24, no. 4 (1944): 614-17.

Lieven, Anatol. *America Right or Wrong: An Anatomy of American Nationalism.* New York: Oxford University Press, 2004.

Lind, Michael. *The Next American Nation: The New Nationalism and the Fourth American Revolution.* New York: Free Press, 1995.

Lipset, Seymour Martin. *American Exceptionalism: A Double-Edged Sword.* New York: W. W. Norton, 1996.

———. *The First New Nation: The United States in Historical and Comparative Perspective.* New York: Basic Books, 1963.

Lipset, Seymour H., and Stein Rokkan. *Party Systems and Voter Alignments.* New York: Free Press, 1967.

Lomnitz, Claudio. "Modes of Citizenship in Mexico," *Public Culture* 11, no. 1 (1999), 269-293.

———. "Anti-Semitism and the Ideology of the Mexican Revolution." *Representations* 110, no. 1 (2010): 1–28.

———. "Nationalism as a Practical System: Benedict Anderson's Theory of Nationalism from the Vantage Point of Spanish America." In *Miguel Angel Centeno and Fernando López-Alves, The Other Mirror: Grand Theory through the Lens of Latin America*, 329-59, Princeton NJ: Princeton University Press, 2001.

Loomis, N. M. *The Texan-Santa Fe Pioneers.* Norman: University of Oklahoma Press, 1958.

Loughran, Trish. *The Republic in Print: Print Culture in the Age of U.S. Nation Building, 1770-1870.* New York: Columbia University Press, 2007.

Magoffin, Susan Shelby. *Down the Santa Fe Trail and into Mexico: The Diary of Susan Shelby Magoffin, 1846-1847.* New Haven: Yale University Press, 1926.

Main, Jackson T. "The Antifederalist Party." In *History of U.S. Political Parties*, vol. 1: *1789-1860, From Factions to Parties*, ed. Arthur M. Schlesinger Jr., 135–69. New York: Chelsea House Publishers, 1973.

Mangusso, Mary Childers. "A Study of the Citizenship Provisions of the Treaty of Guadalupe Hidalgo." MA thesis, University of New Mexico, 1966.

Mann, Horace. "The Necessity of Education in a Republican Government" [1838]. In *The American Whigs: An Anthology*, edited by Daniel Walker Howe, 148–58. New York: John Wiley and Sons, 1973.

Mantell, Martin E. *Johnson, Grant and the Politics of Reconstruction.* New York: Columbia University Press, 1973.

Martínez, Antonio José. "Apología of Presbyter Antonio J. Martinez." *New Mexico Historical Review* 3, no. 3 (1928): 325–346.

———. *Esposición Que el Presbitero Antonio José Martínez, Cura de Taos en Nuevo México, Dirije al Gobierno del Exmo. Sor. General D. Antonio López de Santa Anna Proponiendo la Civilización de las Naciones Bárbaras Que son al Contorno del Departamento de Neuvo México.* Taos: J.M.B. 1843. Imprint no. 5, in *Rare Imprints Concerning California, Arizona, New Mex-*

ico, and Texas, 1821–1846, edited by David J. Weber, 5–15. New York: Arno Press, 1976.

———. *Journal and Proceedings of a Convention of Delegates Elected by the people of New Mexico, held at Santa Fe on the 24th of September, 1849, presenting a plan for a civil government of said territory of New Mexico, and asking the action of Congress thereon.*" In "Journal of New Mexico Convention of Delegates to Recommend a Plan of Civil Government," *Historical Society of New Mexico*, no. 10. Santa Fe: New Mexican Printing Company, 1907.

Martinez, Steve C. "The Political Life of Colonel Jose Francisco Chaves y Perea 1833–1904." New Mexico Highlands University, Las Vegas NM, 1997.

Marx, Karl. *A World without Jews.* New York: Philosophical Library, 1959 [1844].

McCall, Colonel George Archibald. *New Mexico in 1850: A Military View,* edited by Robert W. Frazer. Norman: University of Oklahoma Press, 1968.

McCarthy, Thomas. *Race, Empire, and the Idea of Human Development.* Cambridge UK: Cambridge University Press, 2009.

McClain, Paula D., and Joseph Stewart Jr. *"Can We All Get Along?": Racial and Ethnic Minorities in American Politics.* Boulder CO: Westview Press, 2006.

McClosky, Herbert. "Consensus and Ideology in American Politics." *American Political Science Review* 58, no. 2 (1964): 361–82.

McFeely, William S. *Grant: A Biography.* New York: W. W. Norton, 1981.

McKitrick, Eric L. *Andrew Johnson and Reconstruction.* Chicago: University of Chicago Press, 1960.

McMurtrie, Douglas C. *El Payo de Nuevo-Mejico.* Albuquerque: Privately printed, 1933.

McNierney, Michael. *Taos 1847: The Revolt in Contemporary Accounts.* Boulder CO: Johnson Publishing Company, 1980.

McNitt, Frank. *Navajo Wars: Military Campaigns, Slave Raids, and Reprisals.* Albuquerque: University of New Mexico Press, 1972.

McRoberts, Kenneth. *Quebec: Social Change and Political Crisis.* Toronto: McClelland and Stewart, 1988.

McWilliams, Carey. *North from Mexico: The Spanish-Speaking People of the United States.* Philadelphia: J. B. Lippincott Company, 1949.

Meacham, Jon. *American Gospel: God, the Founding Fathers, and Making of a Nation.* New York: Random House, 2006.

Mehta, Uday Singh. *Liberalism and Empire: A Study in Nineteenth Century British Liberal Thought.* Chicago: University of Chicago Press, 1999.

Meinig, D. W. *The Shaping of America: A Geographical Perspective on 500 Years of History,* vol. 2: *Continental America 1800–1867.* New Haven: Yale University Press, 1993.

Meketa, Jacqueline Dorgan. *Legacy of Honor: The Life of Rafael Chacón, a Nineteenth-Century New Mexican.* Albuquerque: University of New Mexico Press, 1986.

———. *Louis Felsenthal: Citizen-Soldier of Territorial New Mexico.* Albuquerque: University of New Mexico Press, 1982.

Meléndez, A. Gabriel. *So All Is Not Lost: The Poetics of Print in Nuevomexicano Communities, 1834–1958.* Albuquerque: University of New Mexico Press, 1997.

Menchaca, Martha. *Recovering History, Constructing Race: The Indian, Black, and White Roots of Mexican Americans*. Austin: University of Texas Press, 2001.

Meriwether, David. *My Life in the Mountains and on the Plains: The Newly Discovered Autobiography*. Edited and with an introduction by Robert A. Griffen. Norman: University of Oklahoma Press, 1965.

Merry, Sally Engle. *Human Rights and Gender Violence: Translating International Law into Local Justice*. Chicago: University of Chicago Press, 2006.

Meyer, Doris. *Speaking for Themselves: Neomexicano Cultural Identity and the Spanish-Language Press, 1880–1920*. Albuquerque: University of New Mexico Press, 1996.

Meyer, Michael C., and Michael Brescia. "The Treaty of Guadalupe Hidalgo as a Living Document: Water and Land Use Issues in Northern New Mexico." *New Mexico Historical Review* 73, no. 3 (1998): 321–46.

Meyers, Marvin. *The Jacksonian Persuasion: Politics and Belief*. Stanford: Stanford University Press, 1960.

Meyers, Richard D. "'From Hell Itself': The Americanization of Mexico's Northern Frontier, 1821–1846." *Cochise Quarterly* 16, no. 2 (1986): 3–11.

Michael, Robert. *A Concise History of American Antisemitism*. Lanham MD: Rowman and Littlefield, 2005.

Miller, Darlis A. "Hispanos and the Civil War in New Mexico: A Reconsideration," *New Mexico Historical Review*, no. 2 (1979): 106–23.

———. "William Logan Rynerson in New Mexico, 1862–1893." *New Mexico Historical Review* 48, no. 2 (1973): 101–32.

Mondragón, John B., and Ernest S. Stapleton. *Public Education in New Mexico*. Albuquerque: University of New Mexico Press, 2005.

Monroy, Douglas. "The Creation and Re-Creation of Californio Society." *California History* 76, nos. 2–3 (1997): 173–95.

Montejano, David. *Anglos and Mexicans in the Making of Texas*. Austin: University of Texas Press, 1987.

Montgomery, Charles. *The Spanish Redemption: Heritage, Power, and Loss on New Mexico's Upper Rio Grande*. Berkeley: University of California Press, 2002.

Montoya, Maria E. *Translating Property: The Maxwell Land Grant and the Conflict over Land in the American West, 1840–1900*. Berkeley: University of California Press, 2002.

Moorhead, Max L. *New Mexico's Royal Road: Trade and Travel on the Chihuahua Trail*. Norman: University of Oklahoma Press, 1958.

———. "Notes and Documents." *New Mexico Historical Review* 26, no. 1 (1951): 68–82.

Mora, Anthony. *Border Dilemmas: Racial and National Uncertainties in New Mexico, 1848–1912*. Durham NC: Duke University Press, 2011.

Mosk, Sanford A., "The Influence of Tradition on Agriculture in New Mexico." *Journal of Economic History* 2, no. 4 (1942): 34–51.

Murphy, Lawrence R. "The Beaubien and Miranda Land Grant, 1841–46." *New Mexico Historical Review* 42, no. 1 (1967): 27–47.

———. *Frontier Crusader–William F. M. Arny*. Tucson: University of Arizona Press, 1972.

———. *Louis Felsenthal: Citizen-Soldier of Territorial New Mexico.* Albuquerque: University of New Mexico Press, 1982.

———. "Reconstruction in New Mexico." *New Mexico Historical Review* 43, no. 2 (1968): 99–115

———. "William F. M. Arny 1862–1867." *Arizona and the West* 8, no. 4 (1966): 323–38.

Nagel, Joane. "The Political Construction of Ethnicity." In *Competitive Ethnic Relations,* edited by Susan Olzak and Joane Nagel, 93–112. Orlando FL: Academic Press, 1986.

Nash, Roderick. *Wilderness and the American Mind.* New Haven: Yale University Press, 1973.

Neil, William M. "The American Territorial System since the Civil War: A Summary Analysis." *Indiana-Magazine of History* 60 (1964): 219–40.

Neumann, Sigmund. "Toward a Comparative Study of Political Parties." In *Modern Political Parties,* edited by Sigmund Neumann, 395–421. Chicago: University of Chicago Press, 1956.

Newman, Simeon H. III. "The Santa Fe Ring: A Letter to the New York *Sun.*" *Arizona and the West* 12, no. 3 (1970): 269–88.

Nichols, Roy F. "The Territories: Seedbeds of Democracy." *Nebraska History* 35, no. 3 (1954): 159–72.

Nielsen, François. "Ethnic Solidarity in Modern Societies." *American Sociological Review* 50, no. 2 (1985): 133–45.

Nieto-Phillips, John. *The Language of Blood: The Making of Spanish-American Identity in New Mexico, 1880s–1930s.* Albuquerque: University of New Mexico Press, 2004.

Nostrand, Richard L. *The Hispano Homeland.* Norman: University of Oklahoma Press, 1992.

O'Donnell, Guillermo, and Philippe C. Schmitter. *Transitions from Authoritarian Rule: Tentative Conclusions about Uncertain Democracies.* Baltimore: Johns Hopkins University Press, 1986.

Official Proceedings, National Democratic Party National Convention, Held in Cincinnati, June 2–6, 1856. Cincinnati OH: Enquirer Company, 1856.

Olzak, Susan. *The Dynamics of Ethnic Competition and Conflict.* Stanford: Stanford University Press, 1992.

Oman, Kerry R. "The Beginning of the End: The Indian Peace Commission of 1867–1868." *Great Plains Quarterly* 22, no. 4 (2002): 35–51.

Oomen, T. K. "Social Movements in a Comparative Perspective: Situating Alain Touraine." In *Alain Touraine,* edited by Jon Clark and Marco Diani, 127–43. London: Falmer Press, 1996.

Opler, Morris Edward, and Catherine H. Opler. "Mescalero Apache History in the Southwest." *New Mexico Historical Review* 25, no. 1 (1950): 1–36.

Organic Law, Session Laws of New Mexico, 1st and 2nd Sessions. Santa Fe: James L. Collins, 1852. Records of the States of the United States, microfilms, 1846–1861. N.M. B. 2, reel 1.

Orum, Anthony M., and John G. Dale. *Political Sociology.* New York: Oxford University Press, 2009.

Osburn, Katherine Marie Birmingham. "The Navajo at the Bosque Redondo: Cooperation, Resistance, and Initiative, 1864–1868." *New Mexico Historical Review*, 60, no. 4 (1985): 399–413.

Ostrogorski, Moisei. *Democracy and the Organization of Political Parties*, vol. 2: *The United States*. Chicago: Quadrangle Books, 1964 [1904].

Otero, Miguel Antonio, II. *An Abolition Attack upon New Mexico and a reply by Hon. M. A. Otero*. Santa Fe: Santa Fe Gazette Office, 1861.

———. *My Life on the Frontier, 1864–1882*. New York: Press of the Pioneers, 1935; repr. Albuquerque: University of New Mexico Press, 1987.

———. *My Nine Years as Governor of the Territory of New Mexico, 1897–1906*. Albuquerque: University of New Mexico Press, 1940.

Padilla, Fernando V., and Carlos B. Ramírez. "Patterns of Chicano Representation in California, Colorado and Nuevo Mexico." *Aztlan* 5, no. 3 (1974): 189–234.

Padilla, Genaro. *My History, Not Yours: The Formation of Mexican American Autobiography*. Madison: University of Wisconsin Press, 1993.

Pagels, Elaine. *Revelations: Visions, Prophecy, and Politics in the Book of Revelation*. New York: Viking, 2012.

Pagels, Elaine, and Karen L. King. *Reading Judas: The Gospel of Judas and the Shaping of Christianity*. New York: Viking Penguin, 2007.

Paludan, Phillip Shaw. *The Presidency of Abraham Lincoln*. Lawrence: University Press of Kansas, 1994.

Paquette, Gabriel. "Introduction." In *Enlightened Reform in Southern Europe and its Atlantic Colonies, c. 1750–1830*, edited by Gabriel Paquette, 1–20. Farnham, England: Ashgate, 2009.

Parish, William J. *The Charles Ilfeld Company: A Study in the Rise and Decline of Mercantile Capitalism in New Mexico*. Cambridge MA: Harvard University Press, 1961.

———. *The German Jew and the Commercial Revolution in Territorial New Mexico 1850–1900*. Albuquerque: University of New Mexico Press, 1959.

Parraga, Charlotte Marie Nelson. "Santa Fe de Nuevo Mexico: A Study of a Frontier City Based on an Annotated Translation of Selected Documents (1825–1832) from the Mexican Archives of New Mexico." PhD diss., Ball State University, Muncie IN, 1976.

Patterson, C. Perry. "The Relation of the Federal Government to the Territories and the States in Landholding." *Texas Law Review* 28, no. 1 (1949): 43–73.

Pearson, Jim Berry. *The Maxwell Land Grant*. Norman: University of Oklahoma Press, 1961.

Peceny, Mark. *Democracy at the Point of Bayonets*. University Park: Pennsylvania State University Press, 1999.

Perrigo, Lynn I. *The American Southwest: Its Peoples and Cultures*. New York: Rinehart and Winston, 1971.

Peters, Dewitt C. *Kit Carson's Life and Adventures*. Hartford CT: Dustin Gilman and Company, 1875.

Pike, Abert. *Prose Sketches and Poems, Written in the Western Country*. Albuquerque: Calvin Horn, 1967.

Pinheiro, John C. *Manifest Ambition: James K. Polk and Civil-Military Relations during the Mexican War*. Westport CT: Praeger Security International, 2007.

Pino, Facundo, and José Gutierrez. "Procedimientos de la Co[n]vención Demócrata del Territorio de Nuevo Mexico." *Santa Fe Weekly Gazette*, August 20, 1853.

Pitt, Leonard. *The Decline of the Californios*. Berkeley: University of California Press, 1971.

Pocock, J. G. A. *The Machiavellian Moment: Florentine Political Thought and the Atlantic Republican Tradition*. Princeton NJ: Princeton University Press, 1975.

Poldervaart, Arie. "Black Robed Justice in New Mexico, 1846–1912." *New Mexico Historical Review* 23, no. 2 (1948): 18–50.

Polk, James K. *The Diary of James K. Polk during His Presidency, 1845 to 1849*. 3 vols. Chicago: A. C. Clurg, 1910.

———. *Occupation of Mexican Territory. Message from the President of the United States in Answer to a Resolution of the House of Representatives of the 15th Instant Relative to the Occupation of Mexican Territory*, December 22, 1846. House Exec. Doc. no. 60, 30th Congress, 1st session.

Pombeni, Paolo. "The Problem of Political Parties in Western Liberalism, 1868–1968." In *Liberalism as Ideology: Essays in Honour of Michael Freeden*, edited by Ben Jackson and Marc Stears, 119–36. Oxford: Oxford University Press, 2012.

Pomeroy, Earl S. *The Territories and the United States, 1861–1890: Studies in Colonial Administration*. Seattle: University of Washington Press, 1969 [1947].

Potter, David M. *People of Plenty*. Chicago: University of Chicago Press, 1954.

Pratt, Mary Louise. *Imperial Eyes: Travel Writing and Transculturation*. London: Routledge. 1992.

Price, Paxton P. *Pioneers of the Mesilla Valley*. Las Cruces NM: Yucca Tree Press, 1995.

Prince, L. Bradford. *New Mexico's Struggle for Statehood*. Santa Fe: New Mexican Printing Company, 1910.

Pulido, Alberto López. *The Sacred World of the Penitentes*. Washington DC: Smithsonian Institution Press, 2000.

Pye, Lucian. *Communications and Political Development*. Princeton NJ: Princeton University Press, 1963.

Quintana, Frances Leon. *Los Primeros Pobladores Hispanic Americans on the Ute Frontier*. Notre Dame IN: Notre Dame University, 1974.

Rahe, Paul A. *Machiavelli's Liberal Republican Legacy*. Cambridge: Cambridge University Press, 2006.

Ramírez, Carlos B. "The Hispanic Political Elite in Territorial New Mexico." PhD diss., University of California, Santa Barbara, 1979.

Ramos, Raúl A. *Beyond the Alamo: Forging Mexican Ethnicity in San Antonio, 1821–1862*. Chapel Hill: University of North Carolina Press, 2008.

Ray, P. Orman. *An Introduction to Political Parties and Practical Politics*. New York: Charles Scribner's Sons, 1924.

Read, Benjamin. *Illustrated History of New Mexico*. Santa Fe: New Mexican Print Company, 1912.

Reeve, Frank D. "The Federal Indian Policy in New Mexico, 1858–1880," II. *New Mexico Historical Review* 13, no. 1 (1938): 14–62.

Remini, Robert V. *Martin Van Buren and the Making of the Democratic Party*. New York: Columbia University, 1959.

Reséndez, Andrés. *Changing National Identities at the Frontier: Texas and New Mexico, 1800–1850*. Cambridge UK: Cambridge University Press, 2005.

Reynolds, David S. "The Commander of Civil War History." *New York Review of Books*, November 19, 2015: 41–43.

Ringer, Benjamin B. *"We the People": Duality and America's Treatment of its Racial Minorities* New York: Tavistock Publications, 1983.

Ríos-Bustamante, Antonio. "New Mexico in the Eighteenth Century: Life and Trade in La Villa de San Felipe de Albuquerque, 1706–790." *Aztlan* 3, no. 3 (1976): 357–89.

Ritch, W. G. *New Mexico Bluebook*. Albuquerque: University of New Mexico Press, 1968 [1882].

Rivera Ramos, Efrén. *The Legal Construction of Identity: The Judicial and Social Legacy of American Colonialism in Puerto Rico*. Washington DC: American Psychological Association, 2001.

Rives, George Lockhart. *The United States and Mexico, 1821–1848*. New York: Charles Scribner's Sons, 1913.

Roberts, Gary L. *Death Comes for the Chief Justice: The Slough-Rynerson Quarrel and Political Violence in New Mexico*. Niwot: University Press of Colorado, 1990.

Rodriguez-O., Jaime E. "The Conflict between Church and State in Early Republican Mexico." *New World* 2, nos. 1 & 2 (1987): 93–112.

Rosaldo, Renato. "Cultural Citizenship, Inequality, and Multiculturalism." In *Latino Cultural Citizenship: Claiming Identity, Space and Rights*, edited by William V. Flores and Rina Benmayor, 27–38. Boston: Beacon, 1997.

Rosaldo, Renato, and William V. Flores, "Identity, Conflict, and Evolving Latino Communities." In *Latino Cultural Citizenship: Claiming Identity, Space and Rights*, edited by William V. Flores and Rina Benmayor, 57–96. Boston: Beacon, 1997.

Rosen, Deborah. "Pueblo Indians and Citizenship in Territorial New Mexico." *New Mexico Historical Review*, 78, no. 1 (2003): 1–28.

Rosenbaum, Robert J. *Mexicano Resistance in the Southwest*. Austin: University of Texas Press, 1981.

———. "Mexicano versus Americano: A Study of Hispanic-American Resistance to Anglo-American Control in New Mexico Territory, 1870–1900." PhD diss., University of Texas, Austin, 1972.

Rothschild, Joseph. *Ethnopolitics: A Conceptual Framework*. New York: Columbia University Press, 1981.

Ruxton, George F. A. *Adventures in Mexico and the Rocky Mountains*. Glorieta NM: Rio Grande Press, 1973 [1847].

Ryan, Michael. "'The Puritans of Today': The Anti-Whig Argument of The Scarlet Letter," *Canadian Review of American Studies/Revue canadienne d'étudesaméricaines* 38, no. 2 (2008): 201-25.

Salazar, J. Richard. *The Military Career of Donaciano Vigil*. Guadalupita NM: Center for Land Grant Studies, 1994.

Salomon, Carlos. "California Son: The Life of Pío Pico." PhD diss., University of New Mexico, 2002.

Sánchez, George I. *Forgotten People: A Study of New Mexicans*. Albuquerque: University of New Mexico Press, 1940; repr. Albuquerque: Calvin Horn, 1967.

Sánchez, Joseph P. *Between Two Rivers: The Atrisco Land Grant in Albuquerque History, 1692-1968*. Norman: University of Oklahoma Press, 2008.

Sánchez, Pedro. *Memories of Antonio José Martínez*. Transl. by Guadalupe Baca-Vaughn. Santa Fe: Rydal Press, 1978 [1903].

Sandoval, David A. "The American Invasion of New Mexico and Mexican Merchants." *Journal of Popular Culture* 35, no. 2 (2001): 61-72.

———. "Gnats, Goods and Greasers: Mexican Merchants on the Santa Fe Trail." *Journal of the West* 28, no. 2 (1989): 22-31.

Santoni, Pedro. *Mexicans at Arms: Puro Federalists and the Politics of War, 1845-1848*. Fort Worth: Texas Christian University Press, 1996.

Sarna, Jonathan D. *When General Grant Expelled the Jews*. New York: Schocken Books, 2012.

Scher, Richard K. *The Modern Political Campaign: Mudslinging, Bombast, and the Vitality of American Politics*. Armonk NY: M.E. Sharpe, 1997.

Schermerhorn, R. A. *Comparative Ethnic Relations: A Framework for Theory and Research*. Chicago: University of Chicago Press, 1978.

Schlesinger, Arthur M. Jr. "Introduction." In *History of U.S. Political Parties*, vol. 1: *1789-1860, From Factions to Parties*, edited by Arthur M. Schlesinger Jr., xxxiii-liv. New York: Chelsea House Publishers, 1973.

Schlesinger, Joseph A. *Ambition and Politics: Political Careers in the United States*. Chicago: Rand McNally and Company, 1966.

Schumpeter, Joseph. *Capitalism, Socialism, and Democracy*. New York: Harper and Row, 1942.

Scott, Robert E. "Political Parties and Policy-Making in Latin America." In *Political Parties and Political Development*, edited by Joseph LaPalombara and Myron Weiner, 331-68. Princeton NJ: Princeton University Press, 1966.

Shalhope, Robert E. *John Taylor of Caroline: Pastoral Republican*. Columbia SC: University of South Carolina, 1980.

———. "Republicanism and Early American Historiography." *William and Mary Quarterly* 39, no. 2 (1982): 334-56.

———. "Toward a Republican Synthesis: The Emergence of an Understanding of Republicanism in American Historiography." *William and Mary Quarterly* 29, no. 1 (1972): 49-80.

Sides, Hampton. *Blood and Thunder: The Epic Story of Kit Carson and the Conquest of the American West*. New York: Anchor Books, 2006.

Siedentop, Larry. *Inventing the Individual: The Origins of Western Liberalism.* Cambridge MA: Belknap Press, 2014.
Siemers, Vesta. "Campaigning, New Mexico Style: The Mesilla Riot of 1871." *Journal of Southern New Mexico* 2, no. 1 (1995): 5–8.
Simmons, Marc. *Witchcraft in the Southwest: Spanish and Indian Supernaturalism on the Rio Grande.* Lincoln: University of Nebraska Press, 1980.
———. *Spanish Government in New Mexico.* Albuquerque: University of New Mexico Press, 1968.
Simpson, Brooks D. *"Let Us Have Peace": Ulysses S. Grant and the Politics of War and Reconstruction, 1861–1868.* Chapel Hill: University of North Carolina Press, 1991.
Simpson, James H. *Journal of a Military Reconnaissance from Santa Fe, New Mexico to the Navajo Country Made with the Troops under the Command of Brevet Lieutenant Colonel John M. Washington, Chief of Ninth Military Department, and Governor of New Mexico, in 1849.* Philadelphia: Lippincott, Grambo and Company, 1852.
Sisneros, Samuel E. "*Los emigrantes nuevomexicanos*: The 1849 Repatriation to Guadalupe and San Ignacio, Chihuahua, Mexico." MA thesis, University of Texas, El Paso, 2001.
———. "'She Was Our Mother,' New Mexico's Change of National Sovereignty and Juan Bautista Vigil y Alarid, the Last Mexican Governor of New Mexico." In *All Trails Lead to Santa Fe: An Anthology Commemorating the 400th Anniversary of the Founding of Santa Fe, New Mexico in 1610*, no editor, 279–316. Santa Fe: Sunstone Press, 2010.
Smelser, Neil J. *Sociology.* Cambridge MA: Blackwell, 1994.
Smith, Anthony D. *Theories of Nationalism.* London: Duckworth, 1971.
Smith, Henry Nash. *Virgin Land: The American West as Symbol and Myth.* Cambridge MA: Harvard University Press, 1950.
Smith, Jean Edward. *Grant.* New York: Simon and Schuster, 2001.
Smith, Rogers. *Civic Ideals: Conflicting Visions of Citizenship in U.S. History.* New Haven: Yale University Press, 1997.
Sobel, Robert. *Conquest and Conscience in the 1840s.* New York: Thomas Y. Crowell Company, 1971.
Soni, Vivasvan. *Mourning Happiness: Narrative and the Politics of Modernity.* Ithaca: Cornell University Press, 2010.
Spencer, David R. *The Yellow Journalism: The Press and America's Emergence as a World Power.* Evanston IL: Northwestern University Press, 2007.
Stanley, F. (pseud.). *Giant in Lilliput: The Story of Donaciano Vigil.* Pampa TX: Pampa Print Shop, 1963.
Steele, Thomas J. *Archbishop Lamy: In His Own Words.* Albuquerque: LPD Press, 2000.
Steele, Thomas J., and Rowena A. Rivera. *Penitente Self-Government: Brotherhoods and Councils, 1797–1947.* Santa Fe NM: Ancient City Press, 1985.
Stegmaier, Mark J. "New Mexico's Delegate in the Secession Winter Congress, Part 1." *New Mexico Historical Review* 86, no. 3 (2011): 385–92.

———. "New Mexico's Delegate in the Secession Winter Congress, Part 2." *New Mexico Historical Review* 86, no. 4 (2011): 513–23.

———. "'An Imaginary Negro in an Impossible Place'?: The Issue of New Mexico Statehood in the Secession Crisis, 1860–1861." *New Mexico Historical Review* 84, no. 2 (2009): 263–90.

———. *Texas, New Mexico, and the Compromise of 1850: Boundary Dispute and Sectional Crisis*. Kent OH: Kent University Press, 1996.

Steinmetz, George. "The Colonial State as a Social Field: Ethnographic Capital and Native Policy in the German Overseas Empire before 1914." *American Sociological Review* 73, no. 4 (2008): 589–612.

Stewart, Matthew. *Nature's God: The Heretical Origins of the American Republic*. New York: W. W. Norton, 2014.

Stinchcombe, Arthur. *Constructing Social Theories*. New York: Harcourt, Brace and World, 1978.

Stone, Reynolds. *The Albion Press*. London: Printing Historical Society, 2005.

Stratton, Porter A. *The Territorial Press of New Mexico, 1834–1912*. Albuquerque: University of New Mexico Press, 1969.

Sunder, John E., ed. *Matt Field on the Santa Fe Trail*. Norman: University of Oklahoma Press, 1995.

Sunseri, Alvin. *Seeds of Discord: New Mexico in the Aftermath of the American Conquest, 1846–1861*. Chicago: Nelson-Hall, 1979.

Suzman, Mark. *Ethnic Nationalism and State Power: The Rise of Irish Nationalism, Afrikaner Nationalism, and Zionism*. New York: Macmillan, 1999.

Swadesh, Frances. *Los Primeros Pobladores*. Notre Dame IN: University of Notre Dame Press, 1974.

Sztompka, Piotr. *The Sociology of Social Change*. Oxford UK: Blackwell, 1994.

Taylor, Charles. "A Different Kind of Courage." *New York Review of Books*, April 26, 2007.

Taylor, Mary Daniels. *A Place as Wild as the West Ever Was: Mesilla, New Mexico, 1848–1872*. Las Cruces: New Mexico State University Museum Press, 2004.

Tenenbaum, Barbara A. "The Making of a Fait Accompli: Mexico and the Provincias Internas, 1776–1846." In *The Origins of Mexican National Politics, 1808–1847*, edited by Jaime E. Rodríguez, 85–109. Wilmington DE: SR Books, 1997.

Territory of New Mexico. *Proceedings of the Constitutional Convention of the Proposed State of New Mexico Held at Santa Fe, New Mexico*. Albuquerque: Press of the Morning Journal, 1910.

Theisen, Gerald Arthur. "José Manuel Gallegos (1815–75): The First Mexican American in the United States Congress." PhD diss., University of New Mexico, 1985.

Thomas, David Yancey. *A History of Military Government in Newly Acquired Territory of the United States*. New York: Columbia University Press, 1904.

Thomas, Keith. "The Great Fight over the Enlightenment." *New York Review of Books*. April 3, 2014.

Thompson, Gerald. *The Army and the Navajo: The Bosque Redondo Reservation Experiment 1863–1868*. Tucson: University of Arizona Press, 1982.

Thompson, Jerry. "Brave Christian Soldiers: The New Mexico Territorial Militia in the Civil War." *New Mexico Historical Review* 89, no. 3 (2014): 263–320.

———. Introduction to "An Indian Superintendent at the Battle of Valverde: The Civil War Letters of James L. Collins." Edited by Jerry Thompson. *Southwestern Historical Quarterly* 103, no. 2 (1999): 214–29.

Tobias, Henry. *A History of the Jews in New Mexico.* Albuquerque: University of New Mexico Press, 1990.

Tocqueville, Alexis de. *Democracy in America,* vol. 2. Edited by Eduardo Nolla, translated by James T. Schliefer. Indianapolis: Liberty Fund, 2012.

Torrez, Robert J. "The San Juan Gold Rush of 1860 and Its Effect on the Development of Northern New Mexico." *New Mexico Historical Review* 63, no. 3 (1988): 257–72.

Towne, Jackson E. "Printing in New Mexico beyond Santa Fe and Taos 1848–1875." *New Mexico Historical Review* 35, no. 2 (1960): 109–17.

Trefousse, Hans L. "The Republican Party 1854–1864." In *History of U.S. Political Parties,* vol. 2, edited by Arthur M. Schlesinger Jr., 1141–72. New York: Chelsea House Publishers, 1973.

Tucker, David M. *Mugwumps: Public Moralists of the Gilded Age.* Columbia: University of Missouri Press, 1998.

Turo, Bryan W. "An Empire of Dust: Thomas Benton Catron and the Age of Capital in the Hispano Borderlands, 1840–1921." PhD diss., University of New Mexico, 2015.

Turner, Frederick Jackson. "Western State Making in the Revolutionary Era." *American Historical Review* 1, no. 2 (1896): 251–69.

Turner, Henry Smith. *The Original Journals of Henry Smith Turner with Stephen Watts Kearny to New Mexico and California, 1846–1847.* Edited by Dwight L. Clarke. Norman, University of Oklahoma Press, 1966.

Twitchell, Ralph Emerson. *The Bench and Bar of New Mexico during the American Occupation, A. D. 1846–1850.* Santa Fe: New Mexican Printing, 1891.

———. *The History of the Military Occupation of New Mexico from 1846 to 1851 by the Government of the United States.* Chicago: Rio Grande Press, 1963 [1909].

———. *The Leading Facts of New Mexican History,* vol. 2. Cedar Rapids IA: Torch Press. 1912.

———. *Old Santa Fe: The Story of New Mexico's Ancient Capital.* Santa Fe: Sunstone, 2007 [1925].

United States Bureau of the Census. *Thirteenth Census of the United States Taken in the Year 1910,* vol. 3. Washington: Government Printing Office, 1913.

United States Congress, House. *Congressional Globe,* 34th Congress, 1st session, 1856.

United States Congress, House. Report 121. 33rd Congress, 1st session.

United States Congress, House Committee on Elections. *New Mexico Contested Election: Papers and testimony in the case of Miguel A. Otero, contesting the seat of José M. Gallegos, delegate from the Territory of New Mexico: Feb. 18, 1856, referred to the Committee of Elections, Feb. 18, 1856, ordered to be printed* [Washington, D.C., 1856].

United States War Department. *Insurrection against the Military Government in New Mexico and California, 1847 and 1848: Letter from the Secretary of War transmitting, in response to resolution of the Senate of June 5, 1900, a report on the insurrection against the military government in New Mexico and California in the years 1847 and 1848.* 1900. Senate Doc. no. 442, 56th Congress, 1st session.

U.S. Gov. Doc. 30th Congress, 2nd session, *Senate Misc. Doc no. 5.*

U.S. Gov. Doc. 34th Congress, 1st session, *H. Miscl. Doc. 5.*

U.S. Gov. Doc. 34th Congress, 1st session, *H. Miscl. House Report 90.*

Utley, Robert Marshall. *High Noon in Lincoln: Violence on the Western Frontier.* Albuquerque: University of New Mexico Press, 1987.

Utete, C. Munhamu Botsio. *The Road to Zimbabwe: The Political Economy of Settler Colonialism, National Liberation and Foreign Intervention.* Washington: University Press of America, 1979.

Valdes, Daniel Tapia. "A Sociological Analysis and Description of the Political Role, Status, and Voting Behavior of Americans with Spanish Names." PhD diss., University of Colorado, 1964.

Van Ness, Christine M., and John R. Van Ness. "W. W. H. Davis: Neglected Figure of New Mexico's Early Territorial Period." *Journal of the West* 16, no. 3 (1977): 68-74.

Van Ness, John R. *Hispanos in Northern New Mexico: The Development of Corporate Community and Multicommunity.* Philadelphia: University of Pennsylvania Press, 1979.

Vaughn, John H. *New Mexico History and Government.* Las Cruces NM: State College, 1931.

Vigil, Donaciano. *Arms, Indians, and the Mismanagement of New Mexico.* Edited and translated by David J. Weber. El Paso: Texas Western Press, 1846.

Vigil, Maurilio E. *Los Patrones: Profiles of Hispanic Political Leaders in New Mexico History.* Washington DC: University Press of America, 1980.

Vizenor, Gerald, editor. *Survivance: Narratives of Native Presence.* Lincoln: University of Nebraska Press, 2008.

von Gentz, Friedrich, and Stefan Thomas Possony. *Three Revolutions.* Westport CN: Greenwood, 1976.

Wagner, Henry R. "New Mexico Spanish Press." *New Mexico Historical Review* 12, no. 2 (1937): 1-12.

Waldman, Steven. *Founding Faith: Providence, Politics, and the Birth of Religious Freedom in America.* New York: Random House, 2008.

Waldrip, William I. "New Mexico during the Civil War." Master's thesis, University of New Mexico, 1950.

Waldron, Jeremy. "How Politics Are Haunted by the Past." *New York Review of Books.* February 21, 2013, 42.

Wallerstein, Immanuel. *Centrist Liberalism Triumphant, 1789-1914.* Berkeley: University of California Press, 2011.

Walter, Paul, A. F. Frank, W. Clancy, and M. A. Otero. *Colonel José Francisco Chaves, 1833-1924.* Publication no. 31. Santa Fe: Historical Society of New Mexico, 1926.

Walzer, Michael. *On Toleration.* New Haven: Yale University Press, 1997.

Warner, Michael. *The Letters of the Republic: Publication and the Public Sphere in Eighteenth-Century America*. Cambridge: Harvard University Press, 1990.

Warren, Richard. "Elections and Popular Political Participation in Mexico, 1808–1836." In *Liberals, Politics and Power: State Formation in Nineteenth-Century Latin America*, edited by Vincent C. Peloso and Barbara Tenenbaum, 30–58. Athens: University of Georgia Press, 1996.

Weber, David J. "Failure of a Frontier Institution: The Secular Church in the Borderlands under Independent Mexico, 1821–1846." *Western Historical Quarterly* 12, no. 2 (1981): 125–43.

———. "Introduction." In Donaciano Vigil, *Arms, Indians, and the Mismanagement of New Mexico*, edited and translated by David J. Weber, ix–xx. El Paso: Texas Western Press, 1986 [1846].

———. *The Mexican Frontier 1821–1846*. Albuquerque: University of New Mexico Press, 1982.

———. "Samuel Ellison on the Election of 1857." *New Mexico Historical Review* 44, no. 3 (1969): 215–21.

Weber, David J., ed. *Foreigners in Their Native Land: Historical Roots of the Mexican Americans*. Albuquerque: University of New Mexico Press, 1973.

Weber, Jennifer L. *Copperheads: The Rise and Fall of Lincoln's Opponents in the North*. New York: Oxford University Press, 2006.

Weber, Kenneth R. "Ecology, Economy, and Demography: Some Parameters of Social Change in Hispanic New Mexico." *Social Science Journal* 17, no. 1 (1980): 53–64.

Weightman, R. H. *To the Congress of the United States Requesting the Passage of a Bill Declaring New Mexico One of the United States of America on Certain Conditions*. Washington DC: Gideon and Company, 1851.

Weigle, Marta. *Brothers of Light, Brothers of Blood: The Penitentes of the Southwest*. Santa Fe: Ancient City Press, 1976.

Westphall, Victor. *Mercedes Reales: Hispanic Land Grants of the Upper Rio Grande Region* Albuquerque: University of New Mexico Press, 1983.

———. *Thomas Benton Catron and His Era*. Tucson: University of Arizona Press, 1973.

Whiting, David V. "Minutes of the Historical Society of New Mexico." *New Mexico Historical Review* 18, no. 3 (1943): 252–311.

Wolf, Eric. R. *Peasant Wars of the Twentieth Century*. New York: Harper and Row, 1968.

Wolfe, Patrick. *Settler Colonialism and the Transformation of Anthropology: The Politics and Poetics of an Ethnographic Event*. London: Cassell, 1999.

Woodward Dorothy, and J. H. Feth. *New Mexico, Land of Enchantment*. Washington DC: Government Printing Office, 1941.

Wyman, Walker D. "F. X. Aubrey: Santa Fe Freighter, Pathfinder an Explorer." *New Mexico Historical Review* 7, no. 1 (1932): 1–31.

Zafirovski, Milan. *The Enlightenment and Its Effects on Modern Society*. New York: Springer 2011.

Zavala, I. M. "La Prensa Exaltada en el Trienio Constitucional: El Zurriago." *Bulletin Hispanique* 69, nos. 3–4 (1967): 365–88.

Zeleny, Carolyn "Relations between the Spanish-Americans and Anglo-Americans in New Mexico: A Study of Conflict and Accommodation in a Dual-Ethnic Situation." PhD diss., Yale University, 1944.

Zorrilla, José. *Traidor, Inconfeso y Mártir*. Madrid: Cátedra, 2009.

Zuckert, Michael P. *The Natural Rights Republic: Studies in the Foundation of the American Political Tradition*. Notre Dame IN: University of Notre Dame Press, 1996.

Index

In this index, NM *is used for New Mexico and* URA *is used for Union Republican Association. Page numbers in italic indicate illustrations.*

Abert, J. W., 124–25
Abeytia, Antonio, 381
Abreu, Francisco P., 381, 455, 614, 651, 751
Abreu, Ramón, 57
Abreu, Santiago, 76
Adams, John Quincy, 253, 291, 851n22
Administration Party: in the 1865 election, 453–59, 470, 481–83, 485; in the 1865–66 legislature, 497–98; in the 1866 election, 534–35; and the 1866 statehood proposal, 508; in the 1866–67 legislature, 514–17; and the Archuleta-Pino verbal duel, 462–69; position on statehood, 502–3; on racial prejudice, 481
African Americans, 236, 359–60, 683. *See also* slavery
agrarian societies, 38, 63, 67
agricultural industry: benefits of annexation in, 166–67; limiting factors in, 61–62; and the peonage system, 62; railroads' impact on, 801; and social hierarchies, 49–50
Alarid, Jesús María: during the 1867 election, 542; administrative appointments of, 518, 519, 520–21, 637; and José D. Sena, 587–88; role in the Democratic Party, 680; voiding of warrants of, 693
Alarid, Trinidad: during the 1868 presidential election, 688; during the 1871 election, 752–54; administrative appointments of, 519, 787; on Governor Mitchell's appointments, 627; image of, *513*; as URA charter member, 651
Albany Regency, 189
Albert, J. J., 94

alcalde mayor position, 58, 185
alcaldías (townships), 57–58
Aldrich, John, 196–97
Alexander, Jeffrey, 27, 147, 158, 193, 195
Algodones Democratic Convention (1853), 266–69, 285–87, 289–90, 300
allegiance citizenship, 379–83
Allen, Ethan, 259
Allen, William, 229–30
Allison, William H., 424
Álvarez, Manuel: during the 1850 elections, 219, 222; as acting governor, 222, 223–25, 226–27; and Charles Bent, 85; on contraband at Bent's Fort, 81–82; death of, 803; financial records of, 74; during the Mexican-American War, 86, 89–90; political affiliations, 229; as potential delegate, 140; role in the Mexican Party, 211
Álvarez Mexican Party. *See* Mexican Party
ambition theory, 196–97
American Creed, 14
American Party: in the 1850 election, 219–22; in the 1851 election, 232, 242–45; in the 1852–53 legislature, 255–58; in the 1853 election, 290–91; in the 1855 election, 300–302; in the 1863 election, 397, 403, 426; in the 1866 Philadelphia convention, 532; advocating territorial status, 213–14; anti-legislative protests of, 306–7; assimilation views of, 204–5, 255, 473; and the Catholic Church, 271; circular criticizing Governor Calhoun, 234–38; criticizing the Algodones convention, 285–87, 289–90; demographics of, 193; development of, 193–97; on ethnocentrism in politics,

American Party (*continued*)
312; members of, 234, 807; and the National Democratic Party, 319; opposing racial prejudice, 260–61; role in forming the Democratic Party, 262, 263–65, 317; on slavery, 359; in statehood movements, 205–6, 216–17, 217–19, 502–3, 509; Whig presence in, 300; on the William Skinner shooting, 244. *See also* National Union Democratic Party; People's Independent Party

El Amigo del País (newspaper), 266, 285, 299

Ancheta, Nepomuceno, 394, 594

Anderson, Benedict, 24

Andrews, William H., 794

Angeny, William, 220, 262

Anglo-Saxonism: as basis for racial hierarchies, 887n59; and imperial democracy, 28–29, 149–50; in Manifest Destiny, 199–200; and providential messianism, 163; and U.S. economic development, 36. *See also* racism

Angney, William, 153, 232

annexation: CEMAPA's justifications for, 164–67; cross-ethnic connections in, 39; and Euroamerican emigration rates, 793; multiple narratives of, 16–18; Nuevomexicanos legitimizing, 26, 154; and political participation, 2–3, 8, 203–4; and racism, 29, 199–201; sociracial impacts of, 801; types of, 850n4

annexation convention (1848), 154, 161, 167–69

annexation proclamation (Kearny), 93–98

anti-Catholicism, 158

anti-Semitism, 549–50; during the 1867 election, 564, 569–71, 572–73, 581, 613, 825–29, 952n32; 1867 election criticism of, 566–69, 571–72, 573–74, 579, 581–82; in the *diálogos*, 584–86; General Order No. 11, 550, 950n8; global circulation of, 553; Jewish greed stereotype, 553–55, 557, 951n27; in literature, 554; surrounding Jewish economic success, 562–63

Apache Canyon fortification, 101

Apaches, 59, 62, 308, 380, 431, 477, 495, 942n30. *See also* Bosque Redondo reservation

Aragón, Diego, 147
Aragón, Francisco, 383
Aragón, José María, 460
Aragón, Pedro, 343–44
Aragón, Ray John de, 273
Archuleta, Diego: in the 1850 statehood movement, 218; in the 1857 election, 323, 345; in the 1861 election, 374–76; in the 1863 election, 398, 415–16, 423, 426; in the 1865 election, 471–72, 481; in the 1866 statehood movement, 509; in the 1867 election, 538, 542, 597, 598–602; during the 1868 election, 682; during the 1869 election, 700, 710; during the 1870 statehood movement, 740, 741; during the 1871 election, 761; in the American Party, 234; and Bosque Redondo, 452; criticism of, 470–71; death of, 804–5; defending Judge Brocchus, 308; in the Democratic Party, 682; at the Durango seminary, 61; image of, 526; and James Collins, 374, 391; language barrier, 375–76; during the Mexican-American War, 103, 104, 123–25, 133, 139; in the Mexican Party, 193, 266–67; during the Mexican period, 52, 56; and Miguel Pino, 462–69; military service of, 52, 381; in the National Democracy, 320, 321, 323; political appointments of, 637; political impact of, 374, 804–5; in the Union Party, 471–72

Archuleta, Felipe, 599
Archuleta, Pantaleón, 381
Archuleta, Santiago, 210
Arizona: land grants in, 797; statehood movement of, 502
Armijo, Ambrosio: in the 1853 election, 293–94; during the 1867 election, 595; during the 1871 election, 761; in the American Party, 290; in the Bishop Lamy controversy, 282–83; on General Carleton, 494; as hombre de bien, 51; role in political organization, 186
Armijo, Juan Cristóval, 56, 244, 266–67, 345
Armijo, Manuel: on Americanization, 77–78; business ventures of, 73, 76, 82; as complicated figure, 83–84; death of, 803; duty fee controversy, 74; following the

Chimayó Revolt, 49, 50–51; as hombre de bien, 50–51, 56; image of, *91*; and land grants, 70, 80, 82; during the Mexican-American War, 78, 86, 90–93, 95–97, 101–4, 139; and the Texan invasion, 79
Armijo, Salvador, 545, 688, 758–59
Armijo, Santiago, 56, 534
Armijo y Maestas, Rafaél, 154
Armijo y Ortiz, José, 688
Arny, William Frederick Milton: during the 1863 election, 424, 425–26; at the 1863 People's Convention, 401, 402; and the 1863 statehood petition, 395, 407; during the 1865 election, 454; and the 1866 statehood movement, 502–3; during the 1867 election, 539, 593, 599, 665; during the 1868 election, 673; during the 1871 election, 758, 760; as acting governor, 388–92, 514–18; administrative appointments controversy, 518–25; as agent for the Utes, 531; appointed territorial secretary, 387–88; and Bosque Redondo, 433–34, 442, 497; and the Conejos region, 479; criticism of, 463, 465–66, 475, 486, 537; on federal appointments, 511; on government finances, 693; on H. H. Heath as governor, 667; on Justice Slough, 619–21; land speculation of, 802; Mountain Man costume incident, 923n39; Pino's defense of, 464; removal from office, 530; salary issues, 928n140; securing the border region, 394–95; on slave laws, 498; in the URA, 651, 673
Arroyo y Lueras, Felicito, 777
Articles of Confederation, 178
Ashley, James, 678
Ashurst, Merrill: during the 1851 election, 232; during the 1857 election, 330, 341; during the 1861 election, 371; during the 1863 election, 403; during the 1865 election, 472; and the 1866 Philadelphia Convention, 532; during the 1867 election, 542, 593, 666; and the 1867 swearing-in controversy, 620; administrative appointment controversy, 521; in the American Party, 234; death of, 708; as James Collins' lawyer, 391; political appointments of, 637; on Reconstruction, 534; and the Slough shooting, 621; supporting General Carleton, 435; supporting Governor Mitchell, 632; in the Union Party, 472; voiding of warrants of, 693; in the Whig Party, 231
assimilation: as American Party platform, 204; and bilingualism, 904n129; and citizenship, 297; and colonialism, 12, 202–3; and the Conejos region, 478; factors in success of, 35; integration theory, 15, 19; of Jews, 549; and liberalism, 11–12, 13–16, 202–3; Miguel Otero as example of, 303–4; of Navajo captives, 664–65; and political systems, 27; and racism, 15–17; through military service, 379; types of, 310, 312; Whig Party position on, 255
Aurora (newspaper), 197

Baca, Bartolomé, 72, 76, 83
Baca, Benito, 786
Baca, Celso, 630–31, 698
Baca, Jesús, 281
Baca, José de Jesús, 435, 556, 964n30
Baca, Juan Antonio, 599, 601
Baca, Juan M., 363
Baca, Manuel, 168
Baca, Pedro, 763
Baca, Román, 718
Baca, Severo, 363, 545, 964n30
Baca y Pino, Juan Antonio, 218
Baca y Salazar, Jesús María: during the 1857 election, 4, 324; during the 1867 election, 622–23, 961n46; and Bosque Redondo, 477; military service of, 455; public service of, 6, 187
Baca y Salazar, José María, 383, 384, 402
Baca y Sena, Francisco, 741
Baca y Sena, Jesús María: during the 1863 election, 422; and Bosque Redondo, 477; during the Civil War, 382; on Reconstruction, 534
Baca y Ulivarrí, Faustín, 363, 398, 422
Bache, Benjamin Franklin, 197
Baird, Spruce M.: in the 1851 election, 232; and the 1851 legislative manifesto, 239; at the 1853 Algodones convention, 266–67; during the 1853 election, 285, 286; in the 1857 election, 328–30, 341–42;

Baird, Spruce M. (*continued*)
and the *Campaña Demócrata*, 293; during the Civil War, 922n23; in the Independent Democratic Party, 324–25, 347; in the Mexican Democratic Party, 284; potential administrative appointments of, 252; resignation of, 346; on secession, 363
Baker, Grafton, 237
Bancroft, George, 867n19
Bancroft, Hubert H., 192
Barbe, J. L., 695
Barceló, Gertrudis, 73–74, 75, 124
Barceló, Trinidad, 60
Barela, Anastasio, 291
Barela, Apolonio, 777
Barela, Mariano, 775
Barreiro, Antonio, 47, 57, 78
Bates, Edward, 365
Battle of Glorieta Pass, 384
Bautista y Vigil, Juan, 56
Baylor, John, 365
Beall, Benjamin, 213
Beall, George P., 532
Beaubien, Charles "Carlos": and the 1857 election, 330; on annexation, 167, 168; marriage of, 117; on possible insurrections, 243–44; and the *Republican*, 147; and the Taos Revolt, 134
Beaubien, Narciso, 126
Beck, Preston, Jr., 231
Becknell, William, 71
Benavides, José Félix, 170
Benedict, Kirby: during the 1861 election, 373, 375; during the 1863 election, 402, 403, 416–17, 426; at the 1866 statehood convention, 508; during the 1867 election, 539, 593, 599, 614, 665, 666; during the 1868 election, 680; during the 1870 statehood movement, 741; during the 1871 election, 780; abolitionist editorials of, 390; and Bosque Redondo, 497; during the Civil War, 365; criticism of, 386, 748; following Lincoln's assassination, 460; image of, *753*; and José Francisco Chávez, 751–52; judicial service, 376–77, 949n161; on Nuevomexicano Indian agents, 498–99; at President Grant's inauguration, 694; replacement of, 618; role in the Republican party, 651, 680
Benedict, Michael Les, 370, 754
Benitez, Federico, 615
Bennett, Joseph, 761, 763, 979n65
Bennett, Nehemiah V.: during the 1871 election, 761–64, 769, 772–73, 781–82; on the 1871 Republican convention, 747–48; background of, 979n65; on Democratic renewal, 744–45
Bent, Alfred, 421
Bent, Charles: appointed governor, 117, 120–21; assassination of, 126, 156; conflict with Juan Vigil y Alarid, 120–21; image of, *127*; on the Polk presidency, 85; and the resistance movements, 122, 124–26; during the Texas invasion, 79; in the trade system, 72, 81; wife of, 77, 117, 126, 875n153
Bent, George, 84, 134
Bent, William, 72
Benton, Thomas Hart: and the annexation convention, 169; and the Mexican-American War, 86, 87–88, 103–4; and military oppression, 142; and New Mexican statehood, 210, 211; on New Mexico's territorial government, 208–9; role in party system creation, 293
Bent's Fort, 72
Bermudes, Rafael, 773
Bieber, Ralph, 103
bilingualism: and acculturation, 904n129; importance in NM politics, 375–76, 714, 897n112; legislation concerning, 233; and territorial appointments, 526–27
Bilotta, James, 358, 359
binary political system. *See* political system (two-party/binary)
bishops, 272. *See also* priests
Black Legend, 276
Blackwood, William G., 706
Blaine, James, 791
Blair, Francis, 84, 135, 676–77
bolts (political), 755–57, 791–92
Bond, Ira M., 741
Borderer (newspaper): during the 1871 election, 748, 761–63, 768–69; on 1871 election results, 781–82; on 1871 election violence, 772–79; as Democratic organ, 744–46, 788; establishment of, 744; on José Chávez's

1024 INDEX

appointment-giving, 767
Bosque Redondo reservation: in the 1864–65 legislature, 452–53, 464; as 1865 election issue, 430, 448, 458–59, 474–75, 476–77; background of, 431–34; binary formed around, 434–42, 464; congressional hearings on, 494–96; criticism of General Carleton over, 491–92, 933n33; General Carleton's plan for, 430, 433; public opinions on, 493–94; resolution of controversy, 497
Boston (MA) political clubs, 188
Bowie, Mary, 954n85
Breckinridge, John, 355, 370
Breeden, William: during the 1867 election, 546, 593, 665; during the 1868 election, 673, 679, 687–88; during the 1869 election, 698–99; during the 1871 election, 759; as assessor, 530, 670; criticism of, 670, 717; image of, 649; role in the Republican Party, 648, 679, 795; role in the URA, 651, 673, 695
Breuilly, John, 41
Brocchus, Perry E., 302–8, 343; and the 1867 election, 666; judicial reassignment of, 692; possible federal appointment of, 668; and the Slough shooting, 668, 669
Brooks, James F., 65
Brown, Nicholas, 274
Brown, Oscar M., 460
Browning, Orville, 496
Buchanan, James: in the 1856 presidential election, 318; and Indian raiding, 143; and the Mexican-American War, 86, 122, 124; and Miguel Otero, 321; opposition to, 353; political appointments of, 376; as president, 319; repeal of duty tax, 891n19
Bustamante, Anastasio, 888n85
Bustamante, Carlos María de, 549

Cabeza de Baca, Tomás: in the 1850 election, 219, 222; in the 1851 election, 232; and the 1851 manifesto, 239; in the 1852–53 legislature, 255; during the 1857 election, 324, 334–35; in the 1861 election, 373, 376; during the 1867 election, 607; during the 1869 election, 698; during the 1870 statehood movement, 741; during the 1871 election, 759; and the Administration Party, 456; challenging Bishop Lamy, 282–83; image of, 278; during the Mexican-American War, 123; petitioning for Brocchus's removal, 306; in the Republican Party, 698, 964n30
Calderón, Magadaleno, 596
Calhoun, James Silas: and the 1850 election, 217, 220–22; and the 1850 statehood movement, 223; during the 1851 election, 242–43, 244–45; address to the 1851 legislature, 232–33; appointed governor, 230; circular criticizing, 234–38; death of, 251–52; image of, 212; as Indian agent, 211, 217; militias formed by, 379; on NM's contested condition, 226–29; on possible rebellions, 249–50; praise for, 237–38; racism of, 233, 238–39; and the Skinner shooting, 244; on state rights, 317
California: American incorporation experience, 16; established as a state, 228; political rights, 875n167; repatriation campaign, 175; statehood movement in, 224; U.S. occupation of, 85, 87, 118, 867n19
California Volunteers (military unit), 431, 434
Campaña Demócrata (campaign weekly), 293–94
Campbell, Alexander, 388
Canby, Stephen: during the Civil War, 380, 384, 386–87; racial prejudice of, 383, 450–51, 457; reservation proposal of, 413, 431; work with the Navajo, 495
capitalism: negative impacts of, 796; in partisan politics, 25–26. *See also* economy
Cárdenas, Benigno, 300
Carey, Robert, 218
Carleton, James H.: during the 1865 election, 458, 472, 474, 485; during the 1867 election, 599; and Bosque Redondo, 431–34, 440–42, 448, 449, 452, 477; business ventures of, 512, 551; and Charles Leib, 416; congressional hearings, 494–96; criticism of, 434–36, 438–39, 447–49, 451, 491–94, 933n33, 936n94; defending James Collins, 391; image of, 432; Indian policy of, 413, 475; on Indian slavery, 517; on peonage, 517; racial prejudice of, 435–36, 480–81;

INDEX 1025

Carleton, James H. (*continued*)
removed from command, 497; reservation project of, 430; response to Lincoln's assassination, 460, 461; supporters of, 434–35, 437–38, 462–63, 492; and the Union Party, 472

Carson, Kit: and Bosque Redondo, 434, 437, 438; feud with Secretary Davis, 321; as Indian agent, 388; marriage of, 77; military service of, 381, 453, 455; response to Lincoln's assassination, 461

Cary, Robert, 421

cathedral (St. Francis), 272, *274*, *275*, *276*

Catholic Church: and anti-Semitism, 555; Bishop Lamy's Christmas Pastoral letter, 281; during the Chimayó Revolt, 48; and citizenship rights, 549; conversion requirement, 71; differentiation within, 68–69; fears of political control by, 157–61; Jansenism in, 273–74; during the Mexican-American War, 88, 97, 111–12; in New Mexico, 274–76, 279; opposing settler colonialism, 80–82; and the political binary, 271; political power during the Mexican period, 52–56; and religious freedom, 215, 271–72; role in education, 60. *See also* priests

Catron, Thomas: during the 1870 statehood movement, 741; during the 1871 election, 759; during the 1896 election, 792; as congressional delegate, 794; José Chávez's denouncement of, 748; land acquisitions of, 796–97; role in the Republican Party, 727, 791, 795

cattle industry: limiting factors in, 61–62; and the peonage system, 62; railroads' impact on, 801; and social hierarchies, 49–50

Cayetano (Navajo chief), 495

C. de Baca, Domingo, 123

C. de Baca, Ezequiel, 789, 790

CEMAPA (pen name), 164–67

cemetery measure (1847), 157–60

centrifugal colonialism, 11

centripetal colonialism, 11

Chacón, Albino, 79

Chacón, Rafael: during the 1865 election, 469–70; during the 1867 election, 539, 605; during the 1869 election, 706; on the Arny controversy, 515; and Indian conflicts, 890n116; military service of, 52, 381, 383, 457

Chase, Salmon, 445, 454, 644, 935n83

Chaves, Bonifacio, 187

Chávez, Amado, 123

Chávez, Angélico, 80–81, 82, 112, 269, 273, 276–77, 280, 290, 309, 316

Chávez, Dionicio, 460

Chávez, Felipe, 595, 707

Chávez, Jesús María, 763

Chávez, José, 113

Chávez, José Antonio, 77

Chávez, José Bonifacio, 673

Chávez, José Felipe, 460

Chávez, José Francisco: in the 1863 election, 484; in the 1865 election, 458–59, 463–65, 473, 476, 480–81, 483–86; and the 1866 statehood movement, 502–3, 505–9; 1867 campaigning, 594–606; in the 1867 election, 540, 545–46; 1867 election results, 4–6, 607–8, 611–18, 636–37, 701–3, 780–81, 782; as 1867 native son candidate, 5, 564–66, 574–77, 702; in the 1869 election, 695, 698–99, 713–14, 719–22; and the 1870 statehood movement, 732; in the 1871 election, 748, 750–52, 760, 770–71; in the 1884 election, 791; advocating for Nuevomexicano rights, 450, 496, 751–52; Americanization of, 77; and anti-Semitism, 564, 957n160; appointments by, 767, 770; assassination of, 791–92; background of, 429–30, 449–50; and Bosque Redondo, 430–31, 436, 452–53; controversies addressed by, 491; criticism of, 527–31, 537, 538–39, 574; and cross-ethnic consensus, 22; defending H. H. Heath, 667, 748; and Felipe Delgado's dismissal, 527; following Lincoln's assassination, 460; on General Carleton's mismanagement, 491, 495–96; image of, *482*; and Indian slavery, 517; and James Collins, 974n80; and José Francisco Perea, 429–30, 931n6; during the Mexican-American War, 89; military service of, 381, 429–30, 431, 450–51; and the Offutt letter, 669–70; and Perry Brocchus, 668, 966n74; political impact of, 787;

at President Grant's inauguration, 694; Radical Republican affiliation of, 646; on Republican differences, 674–75; role in Nuevomexicano political integration, 530–31, 802–3; spelling variations, 930n2; and the veto controversy, 678; wife of, 954n85. *See also* election of 1867

Chávez, José María, 52, 380

Chávez, Manuel: during the 1857 election, 328; during the Civil War, 381, 384, 396; during the Mexican-American War, 123, 124, 130; during the Texas invasion, 79; work stoppage incident, 457

Chávez, Mariano, 57, 73, 367

Chávez, Miguel, 193

Chávez, Pablo, 130–31, 133

Chávez, Rafael, 255, 693, 718

Chávez, Teófilo, 688

Chávez, Thomas, 273, 277, 280

Chávez y Castillo, José, 51

Chávez y Castillo, Tomás, 73

Chimayó Revolt (1837), 48–49, 50–51, 52, 55

church-state separation, 52–53, 157–58, 280, 286–87

citizenship: in the 1849 territorial constitution, 214; exclusions in, 187; in integration theory, 15; of Jews, 549; in Kearny's Code, 114, 118; in Kearny's proclamation, 98; and Mexican repatriation, 175–77; of Native Americans, 235–36, 852n50, 894n65; and political participation, 18–19, 177–78, 180; rights for Mexican citizens, 177, 187, 218, 232–33, 304–6, 314–15; rights in territories, 118–20, 875n161, 875n167; through military service, 379–83

civic citizenship, 15, 177, 187

civil marriage bill (1847), 157–60

Civil War, 353–54; as 1863 election issue, 414–15, 418–20; and the 1864 election, 447; anti-Semitism during, 550; beginning of, 365; militias formed during, 380–83, 921n16; NM's position on, 363–65, 367; political positions regarding, 384–86; racism directed toward Nuevomexicanos during, 450–51; Texas invasion of NM during, 365–66, 383–84, 922n23

El Clarín Mejicano (newspaper), 788

Clark, Elias T., 266–67, 300–302, 306

Clarke, Dwight, 103, 124

Clay, Henry, 228

Clayton, John M., 169, 210

clergy. *See* priests

Cleveland, Grover, 791

Clever, Charles P.: during the 1857 election, 331, 333, 341; during the 1863 election, 403, 418, 422, 425, 426–27; and the 1866 Philadelphia Convention, 532; 1867 contested results, 611–17, 636–37, 646, 666; during the 1867 election, 542, 563–66, 574–77, 593–606; 1867 results, 607–8, 701–3; during the 1869 election, 700, 707; during the 1870 statehood movement, 741; during the 1871 election, 763; administrative appointments controversy, 518, 519, 521, 522, 524; in the American Party, 556–57; anti-peonage act of, 657–58; anti-Semitic attacks on, 551–56, 558–62, 702, 817–24, 952n32; on Arny as acting governor, 514–15; background of, 416; and Bosque Redondo, 477; business ventures of, 512, 550, 551, 951n10; during the Civil War, 365, 382, 384; criticism of, 505, 547; and cross-ethnic consensus, 22; endorsing Reconstruction, 533; image of, 552; military service of, 455; and the *New Mexican*, 416; political offices held by, 551; religion of, 550–51; and the Slough shooting, 622, 624; and William Breeden, 670. *See also* election of 1867; *Gazette* (newspaper)

Colfax, Schuyler: and the 1867 contested election, 612; during the 1868 election, 645, 673, 687; and the veto controversy, 678

Collins, James L.: during the 1851 election, 232; during the 1853 election, 295; during the 1857 election, 322, 323–24, 328; during the 1861 election, 371; during the 1863 election, 395, 397, 403, 426; during the 1864 election, 445–46; during the 1865 election, 449, 454–56, 458–59, 473, 476; and the 1866 Philadelphia Convention, 532; during the 1867 election, 542, 593; in the American Party, 234; background of, 234; and Bosque Redondo, 433, 437, 442; campaign against, 390–91, 924n51; during the Civil War, 384; on the Conejos region, 479;

Collins, James L. (*continued*)
criticisms of, 326; criticizing the Algodones convention, 286–87, 289–90; death of, 708, 974n30; as depository director, 498; endorsing Reconstruction, 533; and Felipe Delgado's dismissal, 527; feud with Davis, 336; feud with Diego Archuleta, 374; on Governor Meriwether's treaty signing, 308; impact of the National Democracy on, 318–19; as Indian agent, 329; on land surveying, 479–80; military contracts of, 434–35; military service of, 455; opposing racial prejudice, 261, 293, 526–27; on patriotism, 327; on the peonage system, 498; political affiliations of, 688–89; on Pueblo citizenship status, 894n65; quitting as *Gazette* editor, 297; recommended as governor, 323; role in the Democratic party, 262–64, 316–17; and Sam Watrous, 480; on the Skinner shooting, 244; and the Slough shooting, 621; and the Whig Party, 231. See also *Gazette* (newspaper)

colonialism: differentiation in, 147; hegemonic, 8–9, 11, 116–17, 851n13; impact of railroads on, 793; inequalities in, 27–29, 199–203; and intermarriages, 865n220; legitimation during, 98, 116–17; and native cultural heritage, 851n13; negative economic impacts of, 796; and Nuevomexicano political participation, 2–3, 41; and racial inequality, 889n108; reasons for power-sharing in, 8–9; replicative, 41; and resistance politics, 203–6, 204; retreatist, 41; settler, 199–203, 204, 889n108; and the statehood process, 181–82; territorial double colonialism, 199, 203. See also race colonialism

Colorado Territory: and the Conejos region, 415–16, 477–79; land grants in, 797; statehood movement of, 453, 502, 937n120

Comanches, 59, 62, 65, 238, 477

comedic theater, 582

Comer, Douglas, 77

Conejos region, 415–16, 477–79

Confiscation Act (1862), 925n78

Congress (Mexican): departmental delegates to, 45; and departmental legislatures, 43, 47; and the Treaty of Guadalupe Hidalgo, 169

Congress (U.S.): abolishing the peonage system, 518; and the administrative appointments controversy, 522–25; and the annexation convention, 169; and the Bosque Redondo controversy, 494–97; and the Conejos region, 415–16, 478–79; on federal territorial appointments, 516; following the Mexican-American War, 207–8; formalizing 1848 military government, 210–11; formalizing 1850 territorial government, 228–29; and the Fourteenth Amendment, 532–33; funding changes for territorial legislature, 771, 983n165; governor veto controversy, 629–32, 678; impeachment proceedings against Johnson, 670–72, 675; on interim delegates, 372; on John Watts as special delegate, 528; and Kearny's Code, 114; and land grants, 479–80, 797; and the Mexican-American War, 86–87; petitions for citizenship, 187; and Reconstruction, 643–44; rejecting Miguel Otero's nomination, 369; role in territorial governance, 28, 177–79, 180; role of territorial delegate in, 3–4, 180, 183–84; and southern secession, 356, 363, 370; and statehood movements, 191, 225–26, 228, 453, 732, 742–43; and the Texas border dispute, 215–16; and the Treaty of Guadalupe Hidalgo, 169; and voting fraud, 309–16, 426, 611–13, 614, 616, 701–2

congressional delegate (office): Euroamerican dominance in, 794–95; importance of, 3–4, 180, 183–84; in the Mexican period, 45–46; Nuevomexicanos as, 4–6, 785–86, 794–95; Organic Law provision on, 372; origins of office, 855n11; post-1897 Republican dominance of, 789; process for contesting results, 701; proposed election date change, 695–96. See also Congress (U.S.); *specific elections*

Conklin, Charles, 534

Connelly, Henry B.: during the 1850 election, 219, 222; during the 1861 election, 371; during the 1863 election, 403, 424, 425–26; during the 1864 election, 444; and the 1866 statehood movement, 501–2; appointed governor, 366–67; and

1028 INDEX

the Arny controversy, 466; and Bosque Redondo, 434, 442, 477; during the Civil War, 365, 380, 383, 384, 922n23; criticism of, 386; death of, 511; following Lincoln's assassination, 460; illness of, 388; image of, 368; during the Mexican-American War, 95, 96; military service of, 455; on the peonage system, 498, 517; political appointments by, 551; political impact of, 511–12; removed from office, 511; and the Slave Act, 377; vetoing General Carleton's dismissal, 492; in the Whig Party, 231
Conness, John, 494–95
Conrad, Charles, 228–29, 260
Conservative Party, 532
Constitutional Convention (1910), 795–96
Constitutional Party: during the 1867 election, 564; dialogues mocking, 558–62, 817–24
Constitutional Union Party, 538–39, 540–44, 593–94
contact zones, 70
continental liberalism, 11–17
conventions (national): during the 1852 election, 268; during the 1856 election, 317; during the 1864 election, 443, 446; during the 1868 election, 645, 675–77
conventions (statehood): in 1848, 209–10; in 1849, 213–15; in 1850, 217–19; in 1866, 502, 504–5; in 1870, 732
conventions (territorial): during the 1853 election, 265–66, 284–87, 291–92; during the 1855 election, 300; during the 1857 election, 321–22, 328–29; during the 1861 election, 373–74; during the 1863 election, 398–402, 403; during the 1865 election, 471–75; during the 1867 election, 538–42, 544–48, 593–95, 598; during the 1868 election, 679–82; during the 1869 election, 697–99, 707, 710–12, 716; 1871 bolter's convention, 755–57; 1871 Democratic county, 762–63; 1871 Democratic territorial, 761, 763–66; 1871 Republican county, 749–58; 1871 Republican territorial, 747–49, 758–60, 981n116; for annexation, 154, 161, 167–69
Cook, George W., 675, 694
Cooke, Philip St. George: on the international border line, 93; on the invasion's success, 109–10; during the Mexican-American War, 89, 95; on resistance movements, 102–3, 122, 126; on responses to invasion, 99, 100–101, 104, 105; on the Santa Fe ball, 112; and the trade system, 76
Copperhead Democrats. *See* Democratic Party (Copperheads)
Coronado, Raul, 26
Correia, David, 23
Cortez, Manuel, 129, 131, 133, 332
county offices (territorial): governmental structure of, 184–86; Nuevomexicano participation in, 6–7; post-1897 Republican dominance of, 789
Court of Private Land Claims, 797–99
Coyotero Apaches, 59, 495
Craver, Rebecca, 77, 78
Crawford, George, 216, 217, 893n44
El Crepúsculo de la Libertad (newspaper), 57, 78
Crist, Jacob, 795
Crittenden, John J., 356
Crittenden Compromise, 356, 363
cross-ethnic marriages. *See* intermarriage
Cruz, Juan Ignacio, 415
Cunningham, Francis A., 222
Cutler, Abraham, 457–58, 472
Cutler, Ben C., 532
Cutting, Bronson, xiv–xv

Davies, Edward T., 146
Davis, Henry Winter, 356
Davis, Jefferson, 525, 669
Davis, William Watts Hart: during the 1855 election, 302, 314; during the 1857 election, 324, 328, 333; on charges against Clark, 306; criticism of, 321, 336–38; on Democratic Party development, 299–300; *El Gringo*, 336–38, 341, 346; leaving the *Gazette*, 316–17; opposition to Bishop Lamy, 308–9; political positions of, 296; resignation of, 346, 910n60. *See also Gazette* (newspaper)
Dawes, Henry, 528, 612
Deavenport, J. J., 294, 324, 336, 346
debt peonage. *See* peonage system
DeCámara, José M., 762–63

Declaration of Independence, 13–14
delegate to Congress. *See* congressional delegate (office)
Delgado, Felipe: during the 1857 election, 330; during the 1861 election, 371; during the 1863 election, 403; at the 1863 People's Convention, 401, 402; during the 1867 election, 538, 593; during the 1868 election, 680; during the 1871 election, 761; defense of Indian slavery, 525; in the Democratic Party, 680; dismissal of, 525–26; following Lincoln's assassination, 460; image of, 526; military service of, 380; political appointments of, 449, 637; in the URA, 695
Delgado, Fernando, 741
Delgado, Pablo: during the 1868 election, 673, 680; during the 1871 election, 756; following Lincoln's assassination, 460; political appointments of, 787; role in the Republican Party, 651, 673, 680, 695
Delgado, Simón: at the 1863 People's Convention, 402; at the 1866 statehood convention, 508; during the 1867 election, 539; administrative appointments controversy, 518, 519
Democrat (campaign weekly), 762, 769–70, 983n155
El Demócrata (campaign weekly), 324–25, 332–37, 348
Democratic Party (Copperheads): in the 1863 election, 417–20; in the 1864 election, 447; in the 1867–68 legislature, 646; in national politics, 643; in New Mexico, 645; position on the Civil War, 384–85
Democratic Party (national): during the 1860 election, 355; 1868 election impact on, 644–45; 1868 national convention, 675–77; dissension in, 353, 355; formal recognition of territorial party, 295–96; impact on territorial party, 686–87; lack of party identification in, 710; New Departure resolutions, 744; platform of, 691; political riots, 779; positions on slavery, 285; and Republican bolts, 791; in the two-party system, 188
Democratic Party (NMT): during the 1868 election, 680–82; 1869 election impact on, 723; during the 1870 statehood movement, 739–42; 1871 county conventions, 762–63; 1871 election impacts, 785; 1871 election results, 779–83; 1871 election violence, 771–79; 1871 territorial nominating convention, 761, 763–66; and the *Borderer*, 744–46; challenges to formally organizing, 699–700; contention over ownership of, 350; development of, 20–23; dissension in, 792; dominance in delegate races, 786; erosion of Nuevomexicano power in, 795; formal recognition of, 295–96; impact of national party on, 686–87; need to reorganize, 712; New Departure resolutions, 744; newspapers of, 788–89; Nuevomexicano leaders in, 790; post-1868 weakening of, 688–89; post-1871 organization of, 786–88; racist platform of, 681; Republican dissension's impact on, 746
Democratic Party (proto-party): during the 1853 election, 284–85, 297–98; during the 1864 election, 447; in the 1867 election, 612–13; in the 1868 election, 684–86; in the 1869 election, 706, 716; attachment to national party, 191–92; development of, 189–90, 262–69, 299–300; division in, 370; and the Holmes controversy, 387; Johnson impeachment trial's impact on, 671–72; naturalization policy of, 305; racial inequality in platform of, 683; unconditional unionism in, 443–44. *See also* Mexican Democratic Party
Denetdale, Jennifer Nez, 497
Denman, H. B., 527, 948n126
"devil" characterizations, 325, 393
Devoto, Bernard, 103–4, 117, 120
diálogos, 528–87, 557; anti-Republican caricatures, 693–94; Bartolo's dream, 625–26, 830–32; Despotism-Worrywart (parody), 583–86; *Oráculo manual*, 557–58; Pancho-Chepe, 653–54, 678, 833–35, 840–41; Pancho-Juan, 608–9; *Servil-Adulón*, 583; *Traidor*, 558–62, 817–24
Díaz, Porfirio, 550
Dole, William: and Bosque Redondo, 436, 441–42; and Felipe Delgado's firing, 526; on Indian slavery, 525; Judge Benedict's letter to, 498–99; and Michael Steck, 449
Domínguez, Matías, 679

1030 INDEX

Doña Ana County (NM): 1871 campaign violence in, 771–79; desire for secession, 414; lawlessness in, 394–95; national provenance disputes, 394
Doniphan, Alexander, 118, 121
Doolittle, James, 449
Doolittle Commission, 449, 494, 525
Douglas, Stephen A.: during the 1860 election, 355; death of, 370; and Democratic dissension, 353; and Kirby Benedict, 376; on the Know-Nothing Party, 326; on political parties, 20, 191; on slavery, 319; state rights philosophy of, 317, 349
Downes v. Bidwell, 875n161
drafts (military), 382
Dred Scott v. Sandford, 319, 349
Dryden, William, 81
Dubois, W. E. B., 28
Dunn, John W., 545
Dunne, Edmund F., 795
Durán, Anastasio, 384
Durán, Augustín, 56
Durán, José, 232, 383, 553–54
Durán, Ramón, 330
Durango diocese, 272
duty levy, 74, 208
Dwyer, J. W., 794
Dyer, Alexander, 98, 120, 122, 125, 126, 131, 143, 144

Ebright, Malcolm, 797
economy: benefits of annexation for, 166–67; development in Mexico, 36, 38; development in the U.S., 36; Euroamerican dominance of, 80, 801–2; impacts of capitalism on, 796; Jewish success in, 562–63; land grant loss impacts on, 801; limits on growth in, 61–62; during the Mexican period, 71–78, 83; in partisan politics, 25–26; railroads' impact on, 801; and the Santa Fe Trail, 70–76; social hierarchies in, 49–50, 62–66. See also agricultural industry
Edrington, Thomas, 93, 109
education: as 1863 campaign issue, 412; anti-Semitism in, 549; under Kearny's code, 115; liberalism's focus on, 13; during the Mexican period, 60–61; Miguel Otero's defense of, 361–62; during the occupation period, 147, 152; priests' traditional roles in, 272–73
Edwards, Marcellus, 98, 100, 105, 109, 131–32
election of 1847, 115, 144–45
election of 1848, 209
election of 1849, 213–15
election of 1850, 217, 219–22
election of 1851, 5, 232, 233–34, 242–45
election of 1853: Algodones convention, 266–69, 285–87, 289–90, 300; campaigning during, 293–95; candidates in, 269, 291–93; failed Santa Fe meeting, 265–66; mudslinging during, 285–90; People's Party convention, 290–91; results, 295; voting fraud in, 295, 296–97
election of 1855: campaigning during, 299–302; contested results of, 302, 309–16; contrasting cultural profiles in, 712–13; *Gazette* coverage during, 907n6; results of, 302, 310, 316
election of 1856, 318
election of 1857: campaigning during, 340–42; ethnicity of candidates, 328–31; impacts of, 342–45; Independent Democrats during, 325–26, 328–32; Mexican Democrats in, 320, 324–25; National Democracy during, 318–21, 326–28; National Democratic nominating convention, 321–24; results of, 342; role of newspapers in, 332–37
election of 1858, 346–47
election of 1859, 347–49
election of 1860, 355, 370
election of 1861, 370–76
election of 1863: campaigning during, 402–10, 413–14, 420–22; candidates in, 395–402, 416–18; nominating conventions, 398–402, 417–20; racism in, 410–12; results of, 423, 426, 484; voting fraud during, 424–25
election of 1864, 442–47
election of 1865: Bosque Redondo controversy in, 430–31, 447–49, 492; campaigning during, 481–83; candidates in, 458; conventions during, 453–58, 471–75; reproduction of the binary during, 486, 941n206; results of, 484, 485; topic of racism in, 480–81

election of 1866, 531–35
election of 1867: anti-Semitic attacks during, 564, 569–71, 572–73, 581, 613, 825–29, 952n32; campaigning during, 594–606; congressional ruling on, 701–2; contested results of, 636–37, 646–48, 651–53, 665–66; conventions during, 538–42, 544–48, 593–95, 598; criticism of anti-Semitism during, 566–69, 571–72, 573–74, 579, 581–82; criticism of José Sena during, 587–93; cross-ethnic consensus in, 22; debates during, 596–97; *diálogos* discussing, 558–62, 582–87, 608–9, 653–54, 817–24, 833–35; election day, 606–7; Jewish involvement in, 563–64; nativo *vs.* outsider issue, 574–77, 608–9; and Nuevomexicano political incorporation, 3–6; reactions to congressional ruling on, 701–4; results of, 607–8; *rico* class issue during, 542–44, 577–80, 608–9; voting fraud in, 70, 611–18, 686, 958n12
election of 1868: *diálogos* during, 678, 840–41; impact of national election on NM, 686–89; nominating conventions during, 672–73, 679–82; presidential candidates, 643, 644–45; for territorial legislature, 677–84; territorial results, 684–86
election of 1869: anti-Republican "party" during, 700, 707–12; campaigning during, 717; candidates in, 708–11; contrasting cultural profiles in, 713–15; conventions during, 697–99, 707, 710–12, 716; impact of 1867 election on, 704; popular commentary on results, 721–23; popular debates during, 717–19; results of, 719–21; *Review-New Mexican* feud during, 695–97; voting fraud claimed in, 720
election of 1871: anti-Republican parody, 746–47, 842–43; bolter's convention, 755–57; campaign issues, 768–71; candidates in, 760, 764, 766–68; Democratic county conventions, 762–63; Democratic territorial nominating convention, 761, 763–66; impact of third candidate in, 779–82; impacts of, 785; Republican county conventions during, 749–58; Republican dissension during, 748–58; Republican territorial nominating convention, 743–44, 747–49, 758–60, 981n116; results of, 780–82; violence during, 771–79, 985n191
election of 1872, 791
election of 1884, 791
elections: 1868 registration law, 684, 685–86; for the annexation convention, 167; in civilian militias, 379–80; electoral process, 21; under Kearny's Code, 115; during the Mexican period, 45; Nuevomexicano participation in, 6; and political incorporation, 19; post-1871 expansion of electoral base, 788; post-1871 precinct organization in, 786; and representational citizenship, 180; scheduling for territorial, 677; use of stories in, 562. *See also* voting fraud; *specific elections*
elite class. *See rico* class
Elkins, Stephen B.: during the 1867 election, 539, 665, 666; during the 1870 statehood movement, 741; during the 1871 election, 752–54, 755, 758–60; and the administrative appointments controversy, 518, 519, 521, 522–23; as congressional delegate, 785; at Johnson's impeachment trial, 672; José Chávez's denouncement of, 748; role in the Republican Party, 727
Ellison, Samuel, 389–90, 435, 539
Emancipation Proclamation, 385, 442
Emory, William H., 94, 98–99, 100, 102
empresarios (land grants), 62, 63–64
Enlightenment liberalism: ideologies of, 12–13; and Nuevomexicano political integration, 793; Nuevomexicanos invoking, 9–10, 23–26; roots of, 9–10
Epicurean philosophy, 258–59, 900n30
Espinosa, Julián, 421
Everett, Eben, 694
expansionism: impact on Native Americans, 850n2; as leading to Mexican-American War, 85–87; and liberalism, 14; of President Polk, 85, 865n223; of the U.S., 69–70
expansionist nationalism, 310

Fauntleroy, Thomas L., 923n42
Federalist Party, 188–89
federal territorial appointments: by Abraham Lincoln, 366–69, 376; by Andrew

Johnson, 511, 530–31; complaints regarding, 506, 520; Congress's criticism of absences from, 516; inequality of, 27–28; by Millard Fillmore, 229–31; Nuevomexicano representation in, 473, 526–27, 530–31, 751–52, 787; Republicans' 1868 plan for, 667–69, 699
Felsenthal, Louis, 597
Ferguson, Harvey, 792
Fillmore, Millard, 217, 226, 230, 252, 318, 469
Foos, William, 421
forced annexation: compared to peaceful annexation, 850n4; cross-ethnic connections in, 39; multiple narratives of, 16–18; and political participation, 2–3, 8, 203–4; socioracial impacts of, 801
Fort Sumner, 431–33, 439, 442
Fort Sumter, 365
Fourteenth Amendment, 531, 532–33, 538, 643
Fourth of July (1857) celebration, 327
Freeden, Michael, 15–16
Freedman's Bureau Act, 676
Freemasons, 190–91, 896n102
Free Soil Party, 353
Frémont, John C., 318, 442–43, 447
Freneau, Philip, 197
Fresquis, Esquipula, 706
Friedman, Julius, 461
el Fronterizo (newspaper), 745–46, 773. See also *Borderer* (newspaper)
Fuenteovejuna (tragicomedy), 555–56
Fuller, L. D., 752
functional causal imagery, 194
Furnier, C. John, 70
fusion tickets, 718, 720

Gadsden Treaty (1854), 394
Gallegos, José Manuel: in the 1850 statehood movement, 217–18; and the 1851 manifesto, 239; in the 1853 election, 5, 266–67, 269, 285, 286–90, 294–95; in the 1855 election, 300–302, 310–12; 1855 letter to the pope, 309; in the 1857 election, 328–29, 332, 333, 341, 342; in the 1857 Fourth of July celebration, 327; in the 1859 election, 347–48; in the 1861 election, 374, 376; in the 1863 election, 396, 398, 399, 402, 406–11, 413, 420–26, 484; at the 1863 People's Convention, 401, 402; 1863 statehood petition, 393; during the 1865 election, 463, 466, 474–75; in the 1866 statehood movement, 504, 508; during the 1867 election, 538, 541, 542, 593, 597; during the 1868 election, 680–81; during the 1869 election, 700, 707, 710; in the 1870 statehood movement, 731–32, 741; in the 1871 election, 764–66, 780–81, 845–47; and Bishop Zubiría, 60; and Bosque Redondo, 452, 474–75; business of, 280–81, 283, 452; during the Civil War, 384, 396; claimed romantic relationship of, 903n99; as congressional delegate, 295–97, 906n166; criticisms of, 304, 312–15, 322, 464–65, 770; death of, 803; in the Democratic Party, 680–81; image of, *270*; and José Sena, 768; language barrier, 287, 297, 304, 310–11, 322; during the Mexican-American War, 92, 112, 123, 143; on Mexican patriotism, 55, 80–82; military service of, 380, 381; opposing William Arny, 390; party loyalty gaffe, 785; patronage appointments of, 770; political career of, 56, 280; role in Nuevomexicano political integration, 297, 802–3; supporting Governor Mitchell, 632; suspension of, 281, 282–84; on the value of the press, 148
Gallegos, José Pablo, 114, 217–18, 239, 381
Gallegos, Pablo, 380, 472
Gallegos, Pedro Ignacio, 113–14
Ganaway, Loomis, 262
Gans, Chaim, 205
GAR (Grand Army of the Republic), 653, 654–55
García, Esteban, 601–2
García, José, 116
García, José de Jesús, 567–68
García, Juan, 597, 679
García, Juan Antonio, 125
García, Manuel, 704
García, Pedro, 331, 515
García, Vicente: during the 1865 election, 454; during the 1867 election, 539; during the 1868 presidential election, 688; during the 1870 statehood movement, 741; role in the URA, 651, 694

INDEX 1033

Garrard, Lewis H., 64, 75, 128, 134–35
Garrison, Amos F., 936n94
Gazette (newspaper): during the 1852–53 session, 255–59; during the 1853 election, 265, 267; during the 1855 election, 907n6; during the 1857 election, 332–37; during the 1863 election, 397, 406–12, 415, 423; during the 1864 election, 445–46; during the 1865 election, 454–55, 474–77, 479–80, 485–86; and 1865–66 legislature partisanship, 497–98; and the 1866 statehood movement, 503–4, 505, 509; during the 1867 election, 574–76, 595, 607–9, 611–14; on the 1867–68 legislature, 632–34, 637–38; during the 1868 election, 674, 676–77; during the 1869 election, 706–7, 708, 710–11, 718–19, 720–21; and the administrative appointments controversy, 523–25; and the Arny governorship controversy, 514–16; and the Bosque Redondo controversy, 434, 439–40, 492–93; Charles Clever's purchase of, 551; during the Civil War, 383; criticizing José Chávez, 527–31; criticizing the Algodones convention, 286–90; under David Miller, 329; and the Democratic Party, 682–83; establishment of, 245; under James Collins, 316–17, 445; under John Russell, 498; and Nuevomexicano participation, 260–61; on the peonage system, 657, 659–63; political positions of, 262–63, 318, 336, 445, 725; publishing Nuevomexicanos's opinions, 955n113; racialized attacks of, 498–501; refuting "Horrible Atentado" article, 536–37; rivalries, 392–93; under Samuel Yost, 345; on the Slough shooting, 621–23; tribute to Miguel E. Pino, 804; under W. W. H. Davis, 296. See also *Post* (newspaper)
Gellner, Ernest, 38, 63, 66–67
genízaros class, 65–66
Gibson, George Rutledge, 100, 110, 112, 122, 146–48, 150
Giddings, James, 153
Giddings, Marsh, 787
Gilded Age Republicans, 727, 751–52, 768, 782–83, 787, 796–97
Gildersleeve, C. H., 795

Glenn, Evelyn Nakano, 177, 379
Glorieta Pass battle, 384
Gómez, Laura, 2–3, 8, 136, 439
Gómez-Quiñones, Juan, 44–45
Gonzales, Fabián, 777
Gonzales, Francisco Repito, 332–33
Gonzales, Hilario, 232, 239, 246
Gonzales, José, 48, 49, 89, 95
Gonzales, Manuel, 752
Gonzales, Nasario, 330
Gonzales, Santiago, 291
Gonzales, Teodoro, 330
González, Deena, 75
government contracts: in the 1865 election, 483; criticism of, 438–40, 474, 936n94; under General Carleton, 434–35; partisan control through, 389–90, 455–56, 788
governor (office), 43, 627–29, 692
Gracián y Morales, Baltasar, 557–58
Grand Army of the Republic (GAR), 653, 654–55
Grant, Ulysses S.: in the 1868 election, 643, 644–45, 687; in the 1872 election, 791; anti-Semitism of, 550, 950n8; appointed interim secretary of war, 644; federal appointments of, 697; inauguration of, 694; and Republican dissension, 726
Grayson, John B., 327
Greeley, Andrew, 645
Greeley, Horace: in the 1872 election, 791; on the Civil War's cause, 385; and Miguel Otero, 358–63, 369; on political parties, 231; racism of, 355, 358
Gregg, Josiah, 57, 75
Greiner, John, 230, 243, 392, 402
Greiner, Theodore: during the 1863 election, 424, 425, 426; during the 1865 election, 454; and the administrative appointments controversy, 518, 519; and the Bosque Redondo controversy, 442; in the Republican Party, 392
Griego, Luis, 330
Griego, Miguel, 706
Griffin, W. W., 532, 727, 752–54
El Gringo (Davis), 336–37, 341, 346
Guadalupe, Antonio, 652
Gutierres, Rafael, 256
Gutierrez, José, 266–67

Gutierrez, Román, 688
Gutierrez, Tomás, 421–22, 688, 964n30
Guttmann, Adolph, 741
Gwyn, John: during the 1867 election, 539; and the administrative appointments controversy, 519, 521, 522, 524; on Governor Mitchell's appointments, 627

Habermas, Jurgen, 148
Hall, Thomas, 17, 36, 105, 108
Hamilton, Alexander, 188–89
Hays v. United States, 798–99
Heath, H. H.: during the 1867 election, 611–15, 616–18, 636–37, 647–48, 665–66; and the 1867 swearing-in controversy, 620; during the 1868 election, 673, 680, 687–88; during the 1869 election, 698–99; during the 1871 election, 772, 775; as acting governor, 662–63; appointed territorial secretary, 531; Clever's attempts to dismiss, 693; establishing GAR chapter, 653; feud with A. P. Sullivan, 730, 771; on Johnson's impeachment trial, 671; and the Offutt letter, 669–70; on the peonage system, 662–63; political ambitions of, 666–67; on the Republican legislative majority, 652; role in the Republican Party, 648, 651, 673, 680; Russell's criticism of, 537; and the Slough shooting, 623–24; U.S. marshal position, 748; and the veto controversy, 629–32, 678
Hechter, Michael, 2, 98, 184, 203
hegemonic colonialism, 8–9, 11, 116–17, 851n13
Hendly, I. R., 128, 130
Henrie, William Henry, 153, 631, 666, 719
herencia (heritage), xiii–xiv, xv–xvi
Los Hermanos (lay brotherhood), 68–69, 862n169
Hernández, José Angel, 176
Herrera, Joaquín, 47
Herrera, José Joaquín de, 85, 888n85
Herrera, Juan de, 602
Hersch, Joseph, 581–82
Hidalgo, José Miguel, 55
hijo del país (native son), 56, 613, 858n90
Hilgert, Henry, 750
Hinojós, María de Jesús Trujillo de, 903n99

hispanidad, 67–68, 862n158
Historias de Nuevo México conference, xii–xiv
Hockenhull, A. W., xiv
Holmes, James H., 22–23, 384, 386–87
Holtby, David, 184
hombres de bien class, 50, 56. *See also* sociо-racial hierarchies
Hoover, Herbert T., 191, 789
Horgan, Paul, 124, 273, 281
"Horrible Atentado" (article), 535–36, 814–16
Horton, Carol A., 29
Houghton, Joab: in the 1848 election, 209; and the 1850 statehood movement, 216–17, 218; during the 1861 election, 371; during the 1863 election, 396, 400–401, 416; in the American Party, 213, 234, 246; business ventures of, 556–57; during the Civil War, 384; endorsing Reconstruction, 533; and the *Gazette*, 345; during the Mexican-American War, 85–86, 102, 117, 134; opposing racial prejudice, 261; political appointments of, 117; and the Skinner shooting, 244; and the Slough shooting, 626; supporting General Carleton, 435; and the Taos Revolt trials, 134
Houghton party. *See* American Party
Hovey, Oliver, 146, 455
Hubbell, James "Santiago," 366, 407
Hubbell, Sydney, 337, 357, 367–69, 457, 508, 533
Hughes, John, 94–95, 100, 101, 109, 112, 113, 114
Hunt, Aurora, 392
Hunter, James, 532

immigration: and anti-Catholicism, 158; and assimilation, 13–15; Democratic resolutions on, 264; in the Mexican period, 70–71; and political offices, 573–74; and racism, 15–17; reasons for, 1–2; Republican resolutions on, 674
imperial democracy, 28–29, 88, 149–50, 162–63
imperialism: justified by liberalism, 11, 199–201; and republican enlightenment, 162–63; and sociopolitical inclusion, 793; theories regarding, 35. *See also* colonialism

Independent Democratic Party: in the 1857 election, 325–26, 328–32, 340–42; in the 1858 election, 347; in the 1859 election, 347–49; in the 1861 election, 374–75; establishment of, 325; following the 1857 election, 343–45; leadership changes in, 345–46; on slavery, 353
Independent Party, 353, 371–76, 392
El Independiente (newspaper), 789
Indian raiding. *See* raiding (Native American)
Indians. *See* Native Americans
Indian slavery. *See* slavery (Native American)
Inquisition, 549
integration. *See* assimilation
integrative colonialism, 27, 177, 205
intermarriage: and colonialism, 865n220; integration through, 76–77; and land grants, 70; between Nuevomexicanos and Indians, 361, 658–59; in partisan attacks, 359–60; statistics on, 865n219; Vicar Ortiz's concerns regarding, 83
internal colonialism, 2
Irish immigration, 158
Israel, Jonathan, 10
Iturbide y Arámburu, Agustín Cosme Damián de, 37, 46

Jackson, Alexander M., 345, 349
Jackson, Andrew, 189
James, Horace, 158
Jansenism, 273–74
Jaramillo, Ignacia, 126, 875n153
Jaramillo, Pablo, 126
Jaramillo, Venceslao, xiv, xv
Jefferson, Thomas, 140, 149, 178–79, 189, 259, 900n30
Jewish communities, 549–50, 562–63. *See also* anti-Semitism
Jicarilla Apaches, 62, 308, 380
Johnson, Andrew: in the 1864 election, 446; during the 1868 election, 675–76; on abolitionists, 445; federal appointments of, 511, 530–31; and Felipe Delgado's dismissal, 527; following Lincoln's assassination, 461; and the Fourteenth Amendment, 538; impeachment trial of, 670–72, 675; on Indian slavery, 525; loyalty to Lincoln, 443; and the National Union Party, 532–34; and Reconstruction, 531–32, 643–44; "swing around the circle" tour, 533–34
Johnson, Henry C. "Spectacle," 264–65
Johnson, Hezekiah S.: during the 1863 election, 396, 399–401, 406–12, 415, 416, 418–22, 426; during the 1864 election, 443–45; during the 1865 election, 475–76; during the 1868 election, 685, 688, 971n22; associate judge appointment, 697; and Bosque Redondo, 436; criticizing General Carleton, 434; criticizing Governor Mitchell, 691; criticizing John Fremont, 443; on the Democratic Party, 682–83; on developing political parties, 686–87; establishing the *Semi-Weekly Review*, 665; feud with the *New Mexican*, 695–97; on Johnson's impeachment trial, 671; possible federal appointment of, 668; praise for Facundo Pino, 398; and the *Weekly Press*, 392–93, 924n56
Johnson, James L., 402, 532, 727, 741
Johnson, Thomas, 218, 246
Johnston, Abraham, 98, 99
Jones, Andrieus, xiv
Jones, Joshua R., 444
Jones, R., 225
Jones, Thomas, 867n19
Jordan, David Starr, 28–29
Joseph, Antonio: during the 1867 election, 599; in the 1884 election, 791; background of, 786; and the *Borderer*, 745; as congressional delegate, 786, 794; Democratic Party work of, 787–88
Juárez, Benito, 646
judicial system: attempts to politicize, 237; in the border region, 394; charges of corruption in, 235; desire for home rule in, 252; Justice Slough's criticism of, 618–19; and land grants, 797–99; in the Mexican period, 57–58; Nuevomexicano participation in, 3, 6–7; prosecution of peonage, 663–64

Kansas-Nebraska Act, 319, 353
Kearny, Stephen Watts, 193; annexation proclamation of, 93–98; Code of Law

of, 114–16, 118–20; images of, *106, 107*; invading Santa Fe, 104–13; journey to Río Abajo, 113–14; and militia suffrage, 379; occupation instructions, 87–89, 118–20; occupying Las Vegas, 97–100; political appointments by, 116–17, 120–21, 875n152; political incorporation of Nuevomexicanos, 41; and resistance movements, 101–4; success of invasion, 117–18
Kearny Code, 114–16, 119–20, 129, 144, 184
Keithly, Levi, 218, 353
Kellner, Anthony, 45
Kelly, I. N., 777
Kendall, George W., 103
Kephart, W. G.: during the 1851 election, 245; abolitionist work of, 226; on Baird as potential governor, 252; continental liberalism of, 255; fomenting the binary, 246–47, 256–59; political party of, 262, 263
Ker, Crohan, 266–67
Kitchen, Charles W., 472
Knapp, Joseph G., 386, 392, 434–35, 448, 449
Know-Nothing Party, 16–17, 318, 326

Labadí, Lorenzo, 437
Lamar, Howard Roberts, 35, 191, 197, 208, 211, 224, 237
Lamar, Mirabeau, 79
Lamy, Jean Baptiste: 1852 Christmas Pastoral letter of, 281; 1855 legislative petition criticizing, 308–9; during the 1857 election, 341; during the 1859 election, 348; appointed New Mexico's first bishop, 271; conflicts with native priests, 272–84; electioneering charges against, 290; and Governor Connelly's funeral, 511; image of, *275*; Independent Democrats' criticisms of, 326; James Collins's defense of, 289; Miguel Otero's defense of, 314; New Mexico project of, 272–73; on tithes, 903n103; transfer orders mix up, 903n91
land grants (*mercedes*), 761, 796–802; economic impacts of losses, 801; and Euroamerican settlers, 80–81; during the Mexican period, 63–64; through intermarriage, 70
Lane, William Carr, 252–55, 290, 291–95; image of, *254*

Laroux, Juan B., 599, 601
Larragoiti, Mariano, 542–44, 598, 599, 682
Larrazolo, Octaviano, 790, 792, 794
Larson, Robert, 264, 267, 508
Las Gorras Blancas movement, 800
law enforcement (territorial), 184–85
Leal, James, 126
Lee, Louis Stephen, 126
legislature (NMD): 1847 session, 151–54, 169–70; first session of, 854n3; under Kearny's Code, 114–15, 169; requesting autonomy, 56; response to U.S. invasion, 90–93; responsibilities of, 43–45; role in education system, 60; tensions with Congress, 47–48
legislature (NMT): 1850 presumptive session, 222–23; 1851 manifesto, 239–42; 1851 session, 232–33; 1868 voter registration law, 684; administrative appointments controversy, 518–25; Administrative Party dominance in, 497–98; anti-Brocchus memorial of, 306–7; Arny's acting governorship controversy, 514–16; Arny-Slough conflict, 619–21; balance of power in, 694; bipartisan harmony during, 725; Bosque Redondo controversy, 452–53; during the Civil War, 376–77; condemning Bishop Lamy, 308–9; congressional funding changes for, 771, 983n165; and the contested 1867 delegate election, 636–37; delegate election date change proposal, 695–96; electoral process for, 21; Euroamerican dominance in, 795; following the 1857 election, 342–44; framework for, 6, 180; Governor Calhoun's address to, 232–33; Governor Lane's address to, 252–55; investigating James Collins, 391; under Kearny's Code, 114–15; mourning Governor Calhoun's death, 251–52; Nuevomexicano political participation in, 6; political parties demographics (1867–68), 646; post-1871 precinct organization by, 786; post-1897 Republican dominance in, 789; power conflicts with governor, 626–32, 637–38, 678, 692–94; public criticism of 1867–68 session, 632–35; race conflict in, 200; repealing the Slavery Act, 353, 377; Republican dominance in, 686, 691–94; requesting General Carleton's removal, 492–93; salaries of, 185–86;

legislature (NMD) (*continued*)
on slavery and peonage systems, 353, 498, 516–18, 659–63; on the Slough shooting, 624–25; and statehood movements, 356–57, 501–3, 731, 732; swearing-in controversy, 618–20; veto controversy, 629–32, 678, 692; Whig presence in, 300; and William Arny's reform agenda, 388–90. *See also specific elections*

legislature (occupation period): 1847 elections for, 144–45; 1847 session, 151–54, 169–70, 883n63; under Kearny's Code, 114–15, 169; public debates on 1847 proceedings, 154–58

Leib, Charles: during the 1863 election, 396, 409–12; at the 1863 People's Convention, 401, 402; and the 1863 statehood petition, 393, 395, 398; background of, 390; establishing the *New Mexican*, 390; leaving the *New Mexican*, 416; and William Arny, 391, 392

Leitensdorfer, Eugene, 95, 951n10
Lejanza, Mariano Martínez de, 82
Lemon, John, 692, 775–78
Leopold, David, 15–16
Leroux, John, 420, 421
Lesinsky, Henry, 773
levy, 74, 208
Leyva, José Francisco: in the 1851 election, 232; and the 1851 manifesto, 239; factionalism fueled by, 171; political career of, 56; suspension of, 279
liberal colonialism, 289, 304
liberal imperialism, 199–201
liberalism, 269–71; and assimilation, 11–12, 202; clashes with traditional culture, 26; and differentiation, 146–47; ideologies of, 12–13; and imperial democracy, 28–29; and imperialism, 11; and Nuevomexicano political integration, 793; Nuevomexicanos invoking, 9–10, 23–26; political parties in, 19–20; republican government in, 13–14; roots of, 9–10; through coercion, 40–41

Lincoln, Abraham: in the 1860 election, 370; in the 1864 election, 442–47; and anti-Semitism, 550; and the Bosque Redondo controversy, 442; during the Civil War, 365; election of, 355; Emancipation Proclamation, 385; federal territorial appointments by, 366–69, 376, 385–91; impact of assassination, 459–61; opposing the Crittenden Compromise, 356; removing James Collins, 391; on slavery, 442, 446; on southern secession, 364

Lipset, Seymour Martin, 185
literacy: impact of Americanization on, 75–76; increase in Spanish, 788; and print culture, 198; rates of (1850 census), 861n153; and social segmentation, 67. *See also* education

literature: anti-Semitism in, 554; fictional dialogue technique, 557; as property inheritance, 554, 951n20

loans (wartime), 90, 92–93
Lomnitz, Claudio, 550
Lope de Vega, Félix Carpio, 555–56, 582
López, Juan B., 598
López, Trinidad, 604–5
Loughran, Trish, 10–11
Louisiana Territory, 166, 875n161
Lovato, Buenaventura, 515
Lovato, Miguel Antonio, 291
Lovato, Ventura, 599
Lucero, Antonio, 789, 790
Lucero, Gabriel, 461, 599
Lucero, Jesús, 599
Luján, José de Jesús, 186, 232, 280, 281, 604–6
Luna, Ramón, 210, 217–18
Luna, Tranquilino, 786

Machebeuf, J. Projectus: allegations against, 281–83, 309, 316; conflicts with native priests, 273–77, 279–84; and Lamy's modernizing project, 272
Madison, James, 189
Magoffin, James, 57, 88, 89, 95, 103–4, 123
Magoffin, Susan, 89, 104, 121, 124, 128
Mail (newspaper), 745
Manderfield, William H.: during the 1867 election, 539; during the 1870 statehood movement, 741; during the 1871 election, 752–54, 755, 759; on Governor Connelly, 511; and the *New Mexican*, 426, 788; possible federal appointment of, 668

Manifest Destiny, 2, 109, 187, 199–200
Mansfield, William, 645
Manuelito (Navajo chief), 497
Manzanares, Francisco A., 727, 786
Manzanares, José Antonio, 218, 380
maps: geopolitical districts, 59; of New Mexico, 94; of precinct stops, 339
Marcy, William, 88, 93, 119–20, 135, 136, 208
Marle, Augustine de, 552
marriage bill (1847), 157–60
Martín, Juan de Reyes, 706
Martínez, Antonio José: in the 1848 statehood convention, 210; in the 1849 statehood convention, 214; in the 1851 election, 232; and the 1851 manifesto, 239; during the 1857 election, 332–33; allegations against Vicar Machebeuf, 281–83; conflicts with Bishop Lamy, 279, 913n116; conflict with Charles Bent, 120; as departmental legislator, 47; education of, 61; endorsing the 1847 legislature, 154–56; and land grants, 796; and *Los Hermanos*, 68, 862n169; during the Mexican-American War, 111–12, 123, 126, 135, 140, 876n184; Mexican patriotism of, 80–82; political activity of, 55, 56, 280; role in education, 60, 273; role in the press, 57
Martínez, Félix, 789
Martínez, Inocencio, 461, 598
Martínez, José Antonio, 193, 381
Martinez, José Benito, 421
Martínez, José María, 217–18, 330
Martínez, Pascual, 497, 514, 515, 538
Martínez, Santiago, 599
Martínez, Severiano, 615
Martínez, Vicente, 51, 56, 239, 599
Martínez y Medina, José Antonio, 515, 553–54, 635
Marx, Karl, 553, 554
Masonic organizations, 190–91, 896n102
Mata, Blas, 671
Maxwell, Ferdinand, 421, 541
Maxwell, Lucien, 541
McCall, George Archibald, 1–2, 61, 176, 216, 223, 893n44
McClellan, George B., 447

McGuiness, William: and the 1870 statehood movement, 742; during the 1871 election, 744, 750, 770, 782–83; and the *Republican Review*, 725
McWilliams, Carey, 16
Mehta, Uday Singh, 11–12
Melendres, Pablo, 614, 763, 774–75, 781
Melgares, Facundo, 45, 46, 71
Meriwether, David: and the 1853 election, 285, 294, 295, 906n156; and the 1855 election, 302, 314; criticism of, 320–21; inaugural address, 284–85; Indian policies of, 308; and Judge Brocchus, 305–6; resignation of, 346, 910n60
Merry, Sally Engle, 24
Mescalero Apaches, 62, 433, 441, 942n30
Mesilla Valley: 1871 campaign violence in, 771–79; Democratic emergence from, 744; maps of, 339; national provenance disputes, 394; sympathy for Confederacy in, 363
Messervy, William, 242, 295
mestizaje, 66, 664
Mexican-American War: American patriotism during, 162–63; ending of, 164, 169; events leading to, 85–87; Kearny's annexation proclamation, 93–98; Kearny's Code, 114–16, 118–20; Kearny's Río Abajo journey, 113–14; occupation of Las Vegas, 97–100; occupation of Santa Fe, 104–13; partisanship during, 20–21; resistance movements during, 101–4, 120–31, 139–40; responses to U.S. invasion, 90–93, 94–96, 98–101, 110–13; response to Taos rebellion, 131–37; success of invasion, 117–18; troop conduct orders, 97, 104–5; troop deployment, 89; U.S. preparations for, 87–90. *See also* Treaty of Guadalupe Hidalgo
Mexican Colonization Decree, 70–71, 77
Mexican Democratic Party, 317; 1853 Algodones convention, 266–69, 285–87, 289–90, 300; 1853 Santa Fe rally, 294; in the 1855 election, 300–302; in the 1857 election, 324–25; condemning Bishop Lamy, 308–9; criticized by the National Democrats, 320–21; decline following 1853 election, 299; identifying with National Democracy, 318; Judge Brocchus' criticism of, 302–3

INDEX 1039

Mexican Party: in the 1850 election, 219–22; in the 1851 election, 232, 233–34, 242–45; during the 1852–53 session, 252, 255–58; in the 1853 election, 266–69, 284–85; in the 1863 election, 398; and the Administration Party, 456; anti-Semitism in, 564; demographics of membership, 193, 211–13, 807; development of, 193–97, 211–13; partisan attacks against, 264; race-critical approach of, 473; resistance politics of, 204–6; role in forming the Democratic Party, 266, 317; and statehood movements, 205–6, 213–14, 216–17, 217–19. *See also* Mexican Democratic Party

Mexico: and American expansionism, 69–70, 85–87, 865n223; Catholic Church's power in, 53–56; identifying with Spanish heritage, 67–68; independence from Spain, 37, 46, 53; Inquisition in, 549; modernization process in, 36–39; political conflicts in, 37–38; political power bases, 46–56; political structure of, 43–46, 190–91; religious exclusions in, 549; repatriation campaign of, 175–77; under Spanish rule, 53. *See also* Mexican-American War; Treaty of Guadalupe Hidalgo

military: and citizenship, 379–83; complaints of abuse, 121, 142–43, 149, 214–15, 223, 249, 434, 435; in the Mexican period, 51–52; problems with Navajo, 494–97; racism in, 121, 383, 450–51, 457; and the Santa Fe trade, 73, 76. *See also* Mexican-American War

military contracts. *See* government contracts

military drafts, 382

militias: during the Civil War, 365–66, 376, 380–84, 921n16; democracy in, 379–80; during the Mexican period, 52; against the Navajo, 923n42; payment processing delays for, 519, 525; purposes of, 379

Miller, David: during the 1857 election, 341, 342–43; at the 1863 People's Convention, 402; on Democratic tensions, 330, 335–36; on *El Gringo*, 337; in the National Party, 329, 346; possible federal appointment of, 668; on Reconstruction, 534. *See also Gazette* (newspaper)

Miller, Edward, 695
Miller, Morris, 634
Mills, W. W., 527
mining industry, 61, 394, 512, 796, 800
Mink, John, 266–67
Miranda, Guadalupe, 82
miscegenation. *See* intermarriage
Mitchell, Robert B.: and the 1866 Philadelphia Convention, 532; during the 1867 election, 547, 599, 611, 612, 958n12; and the 1867 swearing-in controversy, 620; and the 1867–68 legislature, 618; during the 1868 election, 675; administrative appointments controversy, 518–25; appointed governor, 511; background of, 511; business ventures of, 512–13, 551; criticism of, 544, 545, 547, 635–36, 958n12; declaring war on Native Americans, 975n102; dismissal of, 716, 975n102; endorsing Reconstruction, 533; image of, *510*; and John Watts as delegate, 528; and Justice Slough, 619; leave of absence, 662, 665; legislature's opposition to, 626–29; and the peonage system, 518; political affiliations of, 688–89; power conflicts with legislature, 626–29, 691–94; at President Grant's inauguration, 694; public support for, 632–35; and the Slough shooting, 622; and the spring election bill, 700–701; territorial appointments of, 637; veto controversy, 629–32, 692

modernization theory, 35–36, 205
Money, George P., 794
Montejano, David, 40
Montezuma Territory, 395
Montoya, Abad, 48
Montoya, Andrés, 763
Montoya, Candelaria, 408
Montoya, Desiderio, 48
Montoya, Juan Francisco, 706
Montoya, Nestor, 291, 688, 704–5, 719, 790
Montoya, Pablo, 48, 126, 129, 130–31, 133, 139–40
Mora, Gertrudis, 331
moradas (chapels), 68–69
Moreno, Ylario, 775
Moreno Lantern (newspaper), 745
Mormons, 343–44, 379–80

Morrison, A., 363, 455
Moss, Charles, 667, 668
Muller, Frederick, 330, 461
municipal elections (Mexico), 190
Muñiz, Santos, 515
Munroe, John: and the 1850 election, 219; handling military abuse complaints, 244, 249; as military governor, 217, 230–31; on Pueblo Indian voting rights, 221; on the statehood movement, 223–25, 227–28; and the Texas invasion, 226–27
Murphy, Lawrence, 230, 391

Nangle, Joseph, 261
National Democratic Party: in the 1857 election, 321–24, 329–32, 340–42; in the 1858 elections, 346–47; in the 1859 election, 347–49; characterized by Independent Democrats, 325–27; division in, 370; following the 1857 election, 343–45; founding of, 317–18; growing identification with, 318–19; platform of, 319–21; on slavery, 349–50
National Gazette (newspaper), 197
National Intelligencer (newspaper), 701
National Republican Association, 730–31
National Union Democratic Party, 426, 514–17
National Union Party: in the 1865–66 legislature, 497–98; 1866 Philadelphia convention, 532–34; during the 1867 election, 539–40, 544–48, 593, 594–95; anti-Semitism in, 564; formation of, 446, 532; relation to Republican Party, 446, 453. *See also* Republican Party (national)
Native Americans: American policy toward, 413, 431, 596; citizenship status of, 235–36, 238, 241, 852n50, 894n65; Governor Mitchell's war proclamation on, 975n102; impact of expansionism on, 850n2; impact on economy, 62; ineffectiveness of U.S. policies toward, 308, 890n116; and intermarriage, 361; map of homelands, 59; during the Mexican-American War, 95; militias formed as defense against, 379–80; as outside the republican system, 18; proposed impact of statehood on, 506–7; racism experienced by, 441; reservation proposals for, 430, 942n30; response to U.S. occupation, 111; in socioracial hierarchies, 65–66, 238–39; during Spanish period, 35; trade system's impact on, 81–82; violence between Nuevomexicanos and, 201–2; and voting fraud, 217, 221, 296; voting rights, 218, 241. *See also* Bosque Redondo reservation; raiding (Native American); slavery (Native American)
Navajos: American policy toward, 413, 431, 596; Kit Carson's campaigns against, 453; map of homelands, 59; militias formed against, 380, 923n42; peace settlements, 65; reservation proposals for, 430; violence between Nuevomexicanos and, 201–2, 658–59. *See also* Bosque Redondo reservation; raiding (Native American); slavery (Native American)
Nebraska statehood movement, 453, 502, 937n120
New Departure resolutions, 744
New Mexican (newspaper): during the 1863 election, 396, 398–99, 406–12, 415, 426, 926n84; during the 1864 election, 445, 447; during the 1865 election, 454–55, 457–58, 474–75, 477, 479–81, 485–86; on 1865–66 legislature partisanship, 497–98; during the 1866 statehood movement, 503, 504, 505, 509; during the 1867 election, 574–76, 594, 613, 703; during the 1868 election, 645–46, 674, 676–77; during the 1869 election, 700, 719–20, 722; and the 1870 statehood movement, 732–34, 737, 739–43; on 1871 as a binary race, 779–80; during the 1871 election, 744, 748–49, 754–57, 760–61, 768–69, 981n116, 983n155; on 1871 election results, 781–82; on 1871 election violence, 778; and the administrative appointments controversy, 520, 522–25; and the Arny governorship controversy, 514–16; and Bosque Redondo, 434, 439–41, 492–93, 497, 933n33; under Bronson Cutting, xiv; criticizing Charles Clever, 551–53; criticizing the *Post*'s policies, 728–31; defending José Chávez, 527–31; on executive-legislative powers, 627–31, 632; feud with the *Review*, 695–97;

New Mexican (newspaper) (*continued*)
on frontier violence, 944n64; on Governor Mitchell, 512–13; on impeachment, 671; John Russell's criticism of, 537; and Nuevomexicano political participation, 198; on the peonage system, 657, 660–63; politics of, 677, 730–31; purchased by Charles Clever, 416; rivalries, 392; selling of, 788; on the Slough shooting, 621–22; under William Manderfield, 426–27. See also *Republican* (newspaper)

New Mexico (occupation period): 1847 legislature during, 151–58; Donaciano Vigil's role in, 139–45; impact of print culture in, 146–48; under Kearny's Code, 114–20; and Mexican repatriation, 175–77; military governance during, 140–45, 150–51, 183; partisanship during, 20–21; preparations for 1847 legislature, 144–45

New Mexico (Spanish colonial period), 35–36, 63

New Mexico Department (NMD): Americanization of, 69–78; Catholic Church's role in, 54–56; economy of, 61–62; education in, 60–61; judicial system in, 57–59; justifications for annexation of, 164–67; under Kearny's Code, 114–20; local governance systems in, 57–59; maps of, 59, 94; occupation governmental organization, 140–45; political power bases in, 46–56; political structure of, 38, 43–46; print culture in, 57; resistance to Americanization, 78–84; response to Taos Revolt, 131–37; sociocultural structure of, 39, 62–66. See also Mexican-American War

New Mexico Territory (NMT): border dispute, 208–9, 210–11, 218, 226–27, 228; citizen mobilization efforts, 186–87; civil *vs.* military government debate (1850), 223–28; governmental structure in, 43–46, 184–86; incorporation of, 183, 228–29; and Mexican repatriation, 175–77; under military control, 207–9, 210, 214–15, 228–29; political binary development in, 192–97; power-sharing in, 8–9

newspapers: during the American occupation, 146–48; and citizen involvement, 587; and comedic theater, 582–83;

covering 1867 delegate contest, 701–3; feuds among Republican press, 728–31; on impact of Lincoln's death, 459–60; during the Mexican period, 57; post-1871 increase in, 788–89; Republican dominance of, 725–26; role in partisan development, 192, 197–99, 392; role of pseudonymity, 332–37; Spanish-language, 788–89

New York Tribune (newspaper), 737
Nichols, Roy, 178
Nolan, Fernando, 623, 761, 961n46
Northern New Mexico College, xiii–xiv, xv
Northwest Ordinance (1787), 179, 183
Norton, Daniel S., 529
el Nuevo-Mejicano (newspaper): caricatures of Charles Clever in, 557; criticism of *Gazette*'s racism in, 809–13; "Horrible Atentado!" article, 535–36, 814–16; *Traidor* dialogue, 558–62, 817–24. See also *New Mexican* (newspaper)

oaths of allegiance, 98–99, 108, 214
O'Brien, Putnam, 386–87
Odin, Jean-Marie, 276–77
Offutt letter, 669–70
Old Line Democrats, 296
Oñate, Juan de, 35
Oomen, T. K., 41
Oráculo manual (Gracián), 557–58
Ordinance of 1784, 179, 886n20
Organic Act, 183; acting governor provisions, 388; on administrative appointments, 518; on congressional delegate terms, 372; Kearny's Code as, 114; legislators' oath of loyalty in, 618; misuse of, 235; on Native American citizenship, 241; territorial secretary's responsibilities under, 611; veto provision in, 629–32
Orrantia, Ignacio, 614, 636, 745, 774
Ortiz, Abrán, 620
Ortiz, Ambrosio, 695
Ortiz, Antonio, 752
Ortiz, Antonio Matías, 330, 618
Ortiz, Cándido, 232, 255, 256, 306, 347
Ortiz, Clemente P., 545
Ortiz, Fernando, 61
Ortiz, Francisco, 116, 330, 874n148
Ortíz, José E., 269, 651, 694, 752

Ortiz, Juan Felipe: in the 1851 election, 232; and the 1851 manifesto, 239; in the 1852–53 legislature, 255; 1855 letter to the pope, 309; during the 1857 election, 324; autonomy of, 272; and Bishop Lamy, 277–79, 280, 290, 903n91; and Bishop Zubiría, 54, 271; death of, 803; education of, 61; during the Mexican-American War, 90, 92, 112, 123, 868n37; Mexican patriotism of, 80, 83; political activity of, 55, 56, 280; suspensions of priests by, 168–69; on the Texan invasion, 79

Ortiz, Rafael, 61

Ortiz, Ramón, 175–76, 925n68

Ortiz, Tomás: in the 1851 election, 232; accusations of torture by, 877n192; in the American Party, 234; during the Mexican-American War, 123, 124; political career of, 56

Ortiz y Alarid, Gaspar, 655, 680, 741, 755, 756

Ortiz y Delgado, Francisco, 218

Ortiz y Salazar, Antonio: during the 1865 election, 457–58; during the 1868 election, 679; during the 1870 statehood movement, 741; during the 1871 election, 752, 755, 758–59; political appointments of, 485, 787; role in the URA, 694; supporting H. H. Heath, 693

Otero, Antonio José: in the 1857 election, 323, 345; during the 1869 election, 707; in the American Party, 193, 213, 234; business ventures of, 73; death of, 803; following Lincoln's assassination, 460; during the Mexican-American War, 104, 116–17, 134; in the National Democratic Party, 323; political impact of, 51; political offices during Mexican period, 56; political offices during the occupation, 116–17; protesting priests' suspensions, 168, 281; suppressing priests, 271

Otero, Gregorio, 508, 596

Otero, Manuel A., 187, 210, 218, 727

Otero, Mariano, 759, 786, 794

Otero, Miguel Antonio, I: in the 1855 election, 300–304, 309–10, 312–16; in the 1857 election, 321–23, 332, 333, 340–41; in the 1859 election, 342, 347–49; during the 1861 election, 371, 374; in the 1863 election, 397; in the 1880 election, 786; Americanization of, 77, 329–30; appointed territorial secretary, 369; challenges to eligibility of, 256; and Charles Clever, 557; as congressional delegate, 316, 357–63; criticism of, 326, 338; as *hombre de bien*, 51; image of, 301; and land speculation, 326; military service of, 381; political career of, 369–70; role in Nuevomexicano political integration, 802–3; on slavery, 319, 349, 377; on southern secession, 355–56, 363

Otero, Miguel Antonio, II, 789, 909n37

Otero, Vicente, 460

Overman, Charles, 218

Pacheco, Antonio María, 331

Pacheco, Jesús María: and the 1867 swearing-in controversy, 620; during the 1869 election, 710, 714–15; during the 1870 statehood movement, 741; during the 1871 election, 752; and the Slough shooting, 625; taunting Radicals, 707; and the veto controversy, 630–31

Pacheco, Juan Rafael, 601

Padilla, Genaro, 108

Page, William Tyler, 14

Paine, Thomas, 10

Palace of the Governors, 44, 45

Pardee, Julius Hayden, 751

Paredes y Arrillaga, Mariano, 85–86, 867n8

parochial school, 272

partido system. *See* peonage system

patronage appointments. *See* federal territorial appointments

Patterson, C. Perry, 178–79

El Payo de Nuevo Méjico (newspaper), 47

Pearce, James A., 228

Peceny, Mark, 40

Pelham, William, 341

Pendleton, George H., 447

peonage system: as 1870 statehood issue, 737; legislation regarding, 350, 388, 516–18, 657–58, 662–63; Miguel Otero's defense of, 360; partisan debate on, 655–56, 659–63, 836–39; portrayed in parodies, 583; prosecution of, 663–64; reformation of, 498; in socioracial hierarchies, 62–66. *See also* slavery

peón class, 62–63
People's Convention (1863), 398–402, 403
People's Independent Party, 290–95
People's Party: in the 1869 election, 716, 718, 720–23; early national factions of, 905n142
Perea, Felipe, 710
Perea, Joaquín, 330
Perea, José Francisco: during the 1863 election, 397, 402–3, 406, 413–16, 420–26, 484; during the 1864 election, 444, 446; during the 1865 election, 448–49, 454, 458, 472, 481–85; during the 1866 election, 535; during the 1867 election, 538, 541–42, 595; during the 1871 election, 763; Americanization of, 77; on the Arny controversy, 515; background of, 397; and Bosque Redondo, 434, 442, 477; during the Civil War, 381, 382; and the Conejos region, 478–79; criticism of, 477, 479–80, 505; as *hombre de bien*, 51; image of, *404*; and José Francisco Chávez, 429–30, 931n6; Nuevomexicano appointees of, 530; and Sam Watrous, 480
Perea, José Leandro: at the 1853 Algodones convention, 266–67; in the 1870 statehood movement, 731–32, 741; alliances with Euroamerican businessmen, 727; and anti-Semitism, 957n160; during the Civil War, 381, 382; defense against the Navajo, 380; image of, *733*; during the Mexican-American War, 113, 117; in the National Democratic Party, 323; response to U.S. invasion, 111; and Stephen Elkins, 785
Perea, José S., 381
Perea, Juan, 51, 56, 92, 113, 210, 218
Perea, Pedro, 794
Pérez, Albino, 48, 79
Peters, Dewitt, 382
Pettis, S. Newton, 775–76
Pfeiffer, James, 455
Phillips, Wendell, 445
Pierce, Franklin, 191, 198, 262, 263, 284, 317, 376
Pile, William A., 716, 725, 732, 741
Pillans, Palmer, 213, 232
Pino, Facundo: in the 1852–53 legislature, 255, 256; at the 1853 Algodones convention, 266–67; during the 1853 election, 285; during the 1859 election, 347, 348; during the 1861 election, 375, 376; during the Civil War, 381, 384, 396; criticized by James Collins, 318–19; death of, 397–98, 803; during the Mexican-American War, 104, 123, 130; in the Mexican Party, 211; petitioning for Judge Brocchus's removal, 306
Pino, José María, 762
Pino, Manuel, 123, 124, 381
Pino, Miguel E.: during the 1853 election, 285; during the 1857 election, 324, 327–28, 331, 333; during the 1861 election, 375; during the 1863 election, 410, 422, 423, 424; at the 1863 People's Convention, 401, 402; during the 1865 election, 454; in the 1865–66 legislature, 497; at the 1866 statehood convention, 508; in the 1866–67 legislature, 514; during the 1867 election, 539, 542–43, 546, 568, 585–86; and the Administration Party, 456; administrative appointments controversy, 518; and Bosque Redondo, 475; during the Civil War, 381, 383; death of, 614, 803–4; following Lincoln's assassination, 460; on John Russell's racism, 501; in the legislature, 485; during the Mexican-American War, 123; military service of, 380, 381, 457; petitioning for Judge Brocchus's removal, 306; political impact of, 803–4; verbal duel with Diego Archuleta, 462–69
Pino, Nicolás: at the 1863 People's Convention, 402; during the 1871 election, 755, 756; death of, 803; during the Mexican-American War, 123, 124, 130
Pino, Pablo, 596
Pius IX (pope), 161, 282
Pley, José, 210, 340, 345
poblador class, 63–65, 68–69, 796, 856n46. *See also* sociracial hierarchies
political parties: and the anti-Masonic movement, 896n102; development in Mexico, 190–91; development in New Mexico, 208, 641; development in U.S., 188–90; development of principles, 267–68; factionalism in, 170–71, 189, 191–93, 726; integrative functions of, 19–20; personalism in, 617, 618; role of ambitious politicians in, 196–97; theories on faction-

alism in, 726. *See also individual parties*
political riots, 779
political system (two-party/binary): cross-ethnic consensus in, 22–23; development in New Mexico, 192–97, 641; development of, 188; development of in New Mexico, 20–24; impact of statehood movements on, 228; Nuevomexicano roles in establishing, 22–26; role of the press in forming, 197–99
political verse, 333–34
Polk, James K.: defending Kearny's instructions, 119–20; expansionism of, 85, 865n223; instructions to Magoffin, 103; and the Mexican-American War, 86–88, 117; and the Taos Revolt trials, 136; on Texas imperialism, 208; and the Treaty of Guadalupe Hidalgo, 207. *See also* Mexican-American War
Pomeroy, Earl, 183
Pope, John, 494
Post (newspaper): and the 1870 statehood movement, 737, 740–43; during the 1871 election, 755–56, 760, 778; establishment of, 725; names of, 976n2; political position of, 731; role in the Republican Party, 726–31
postal system (NMD), 58
Pratt, Mary Louise, 70
prefects (territorial office), 185
press. *See* newspapers
Press (newspaper). *See Weekly Press* (newspaper)
Price, John T., 461
Price, Sterling: and the 1847 legislature, 154; at the annexation convention, 167–68; duty levy of, 208; and Indian raiding, 143; military command of, 118; political appointments of, 145; replaced by John Washington, 210; and resistance movements, 120, 122, 124, 126, 128, 130–31, 139
priests: during the 1867 elections, 567; and the annexation convention, 168–69; Bishop Lamy's conflict with nativo, 272–84, 314; isolation of New Mexico's, 274–77, 279; negative stereotypes of, 158–61, 276–77, 279, 286–87; opposing settler colonialism, 80–82; political activity of, 52, 55–56, 280; and the political binary, 269–71; role in education, 60, 61; traditional role in education, 272–73. *See also* Catholic Church
Prince, L. B., 794
print culture. *See* newspapers
printing contracts, 389–90, 514, 788
Private Land Claims court, 797–99
probate judge (territorial office), 7, 184–85
Protestant Christianity, 52–53, 549
providential messianism, 162–63
pseudonymity, 148, 332
public cemetery measure (1847), 157–60
Puebloan tribes: citizenship status of, 235–36, 238, 241, 852n50, 894n65; during the Mexican-American War, 95; response to U.S. occupation, 111; during Spanish period, 35; and voting fraud, 221, 296; voting rights, 218, 241
Puerto Rico, 851n13

querencia (cultural identity), xiii–xiv, xv–xvi, 799
Quinn, James, 218, 266–67
Quintana, Nicolás: during the 1863 election, 403–6, 407, 408, 418, 422; at the 1863 People's Convention, 401, 402; during the 1867 election, 538, 597; during the 1871 election, 761, 770; and Bosque Redondo, 477; and the *Democrat*, 762; following Lincoln's assassination, 460; military service of, 382, 455; role in the Democratic Party, 680, 682; supporting Governor Mitchell, 632
Quintana v. Thompkins, 305–6, 315

race colonialism: and the 1866 statehood movement, 505, 509; and the 1870 statehood movement, 737–38; in governance structure, 28; James Collins's stance against, 526–27; Nuevomexicanos' fight against, 496, 499–501, 809–11
racism: in the 1863 election, 410–12, 425; and the 1870 statehood movement, 735–38; during the 1871 election, 768; of abolitionists, 358; American Party position on, 204–5; in annexation, 199–201; in the Democratic platform, 681, 683; experienced by Native Americans, 441; experienced by Nuevomexicanos, 259–61, 358;

INDEX 1045

racism (*continued*)
of Governor Calhoun, 238–39; and immigration, 15; and imperial democracy, 28–29, 182; in the military, 121, 383, 450–51, 457; Radical position on, 705; of Russell's *Gazette*, 499–501, 809–11; and settler colonialism, 889n108; and sociopolitical inclusion, 793; Union Party position on, 472–73. *See also* anti-Semitism; socioracial hierarchies
Radical Democratic Party, 442–43
Radical Republican Party: during the 1864 election, 442–43; during the 1868 election, 672–73; charges of slavery among, 660–61; and Johnson's impeachment proceeding, 672, 675; in national politics, 643; in New Mexico, 396, 645; on racial equality, 705; on Reconstruction, 531–32, 643–44; on slavery, 385, 388; unconditional unionism in, 443–44
raiding (Native American): American policy's impact on, 308; and the Bosque Redondo controversy, 436–38, 491–92; economic impact of, 62; Kearny's attempts to control, 142–43; mutual nature of, 201–2; partisan debate on, 320–21, 391; prevalence of, 65, 477, 944n64
railroads, 769, 793–94, 796
Ramirez y Casanoba, Serafín: during the 1853 election, 292; during the 1853–54 legislative session, 300; during the 1863 election, 422; during the 1867 election, 595; in the American Party, 234; death of, 803; political career of, 56
ranch industry: benefits of annexation in, 166–67; limiting factors in, 61–62; and the peonage system, 62; railroads' impact on, 801; and social hierarchies, 49–50
Reconstruction, 525, 531–33, 643–44
registrars (territorial office), 185
registration law (1868), 684, 685–86
religion: and Jewish civil rights, 549; separation of church and state, 52–53, 157–58, 280, 286–87
religious freedom: established in Mexico, 950n3; under Kearny's Code, 115; during the Mexican-American War, 97; and multiple Christian sects, 53; in Organic laws, 215; in the Treaty of Guadalupe

Hidalgo, 271
Rencher, Abraham, 345, 349–50, 365
Rencher, William, 761, 762
repatriation programs (Mexican), 175–77
replicative colonialism, 41
representational citizenship, 180
Republican (newspaper): during the Civil War, 383; cross-ethnic consensus portrayed in, 146; differentiating agenda of, 146–47; ending of, 387; establishment of, 386; founding of, 146; pseudonymic commentaries in, 148–49, 156–62. *See also New Mexican* (newspaper)
Republican Party (national): in the 1856 election, 318; in the 1868 election, 672–73; 1868 election impact, 644–45; dissension within, 726, 790–92; formation of, 353–54; impact on NMT's politics, 686–87, 705–6, 716; during Johnson's impeachment trial, 671–72; platform of, 691, 716; political riots, 779; role of the People's Party in, 905n142; and the URA, 650
Republican Party (NMT): during the 1865 election, 673–75; 1867 election impact, 652, 704–5; during the 1868 election, 677–80; 1868 presidential election's impact on, 687–88; in the 1868–69 legislature, 691–94; in the 1869 election, 695, 697–99, 715, 716, 720–23; and the 1870 statehood movement, 732–34, 739–43; in the 1871 election, 766; 1871 election results, 779–83; 1871 election violence, 771–79; 1871 territorial nominating convention, 743–44, 747–49, 758–60; adopting national agenda, 686–87, 705–6, 715; desired federal appointments, 667–69; development of, 20–23; dissension within, 746–48, 790–92; dominance in delegate races, 785–86; erosion of Nuevomexicano power in, 795; formal organization of, 648–51; Gilded Age clique in, 727, 768, 787, 796–97; newspapers of, 728–31, 788–89; Nuevomexicano roles in, 698, 789–90; platform of, 698; post-1869 dominance of, 725–26; post-1871 organization of, 786–87; post-1897 dominance of, 789–90
Republican Party (proto-party): in the 1864 election, 442–47; in the 1866 election, 534;

in the 1867 election, 612–13; in the 1867–68 legislature, 646; in the 1868 election, 684–86; creation of, 189; and federal appointments, 386–92, 511, 530–31; increased power during Civil War, 370; role of the press in, 197, 665; on slavery, 446, 662; and statehood movements, 393

Republican Review (newspaper): during the 1870 statehood movement, 742; during the 1871 election, 750, 760, 770; replacing the *Weekly Review*, 725

Reséndez, Andrés, 49, 50, 71, 72, 76, 84, 146

reservations (Native American), 430, 431–34, 472, 942n30. *See also* Bosque Redondo reservation

Resolve of 1780, 178–79

Restoration (1815–1848), 273–74

retreatist colonialism, 41

Review (newspaper): during the 1868 election, 676–77, 971n22; on the 1868 election results, 685; on the 1868 URA rally, 674; establishment of, 665; feud with the *New Mexican*, 695–97; on impeachment, 671

Reynolds, A. W., 242–43, 244–45, 898n128

rico class: as 1867 election issue, 577–80; in the American conquest, 8–9; Americanization of, 77–78; economic power of, 49–50, 83; and Indian slavery, 65; political power of, 50–51, 184; in the Santa Fe trade, 72–73; social segmentation of, 66–67; W. W. H. Davis' disdain for, 338. *See also* sociracial hierarchies

The Rights of Man (Paine), 10

Riley, Bennet, 76, 224

Río Abajo (district): maps of, 59, 339; partitioning of, 58

Río Abajo Weekly Press (newspaper). *See Weekly Press* (newspaper)

Río Arriba (district): maps of, 59, 339; partitioning of, 58

riots (political), 779

Roberts, Gary L., 192, 511, 611, 618, 619

Roberts, Thomas, 532

Roddy, Edward G., 385

Rodey, Bernard S., 794

Rodriguez, Rafael, 694

Roibal, Albino, 402, 403

Roival, Antonio, 343–44, 637, 682, 761

Roman Catholicism. *See* Catholic Church

Romero, Benito, 679

Romero, Bonifacio, 455

Romero, Felipe, 615

Romero, Juan, 601

Romero, Juan Cristóval, 534

Romero, Manuel, 622–23

Romero, Rafael, 505

Romero, Secundino, 790

Romero, Trinidad, 381, 786

Romero, Vicente: during the 1867 election, 541–42, 593, 603, 615; during the 1869 election, 708–11, 713–15, 720, 722; during the 1871 election, 761

Romero, Vicente Ferrer, 913n116

Romero y Baca, Miguel, 436–40

Ronquillo, José María, 52

Russell, John T.: during the 1861 election, 370–71, 372, 375–76; during the 1863 election, 399, 402, 415, 417, 418–20, 424–25; during the 1865 election, 472; during the 1867 election, 538, 608–9, 611; during the 1869 election, 699, 706, 707, 717, 721; on abolition, 355, 385; administrative appointments controversy, 523–25; on the Arny controversy, 515; criticizing José F. Chávez, 528–29; criticizing the URA, 655–56; declining health of, 725; defending Miguel Otero, 369; defending William Arny, 389; on executive-legislative power, 627–29; Governor Mitchell's nomination of, 627; on the Holmes controversy, 387; on Johnson's impeachment, 671–72; military contracts of, 434; as owner/editor of *Gazette*, 498; on the peonage system, 517, 537–38, 659–63; political appointments of, 637; racism of, 499–501, 628, 809–13; on Reconstruction, 534; resignation of, 694; on statehood, 357, 371, 503–4, 505; and the Union Party, 472, 533; voiding of warrants of, 693. *See also Gazette* (newspaper)

Ruxton, George, 120, 121

Rynerson, William L.: during the 1867 election, 594, 614, 636; in the 1869 election, 719; during the 1871 election, 772, 775; in the 1884 election, 791, 794; on Governor Mitchell's veto, 692; and Justice Slough, 620–21, 626, 668, 669

INDEX 1047

Saavedra, Norberto, 714
Saenz, Antonio, 210
salaries (public service), 185–86
Salazar, Aniceto, 623
Salazar, Antonio de Jesús, 280
Salazar, Francisco, 597–98, 599, 964n30
Salazar, Ramón, 279
Salazar, Tomás, 759
Salazar y Jimenes, Juan, 187, 460
Sánchez, George I., 802
Sánchez, José de Merced, 383
Sánchez, Joseph, 43–44, 46, 177
Sánchez, Juan José, 460, 941n206
Sánchez, Leandro, 470–71
Sánchez, Pedro: during the 1863 election, 398, 415, 420; during the 1867 election, 545, 599, 615; during the Civil War, 381
Sánchez Vergara, Vincente, 51, 56
Sandoval, Anastacio: during the 1865 election, 454; at the 1866 statehood convention, 508; during the 1867 election, 539, 593, 614; during the 1868 election, 673, 679, 680, 687–88; in the 1868–69 legislature, 691; during the 1870 statehood movement, 741; during the 1871 election, 755, 756, 758–59; and the administrative appointments controversy, 518–19, 522; following Lincoln's assassination, 460; on Governor Mitchell's appointments, 627; political appointments of, 694, 787; resignation of, 637; role in the Republican Party, 651, 673, 680, 694; and the Slough shooting, 625
Sandoval, Antonio, 153, 234, 291, 384, 407
Sandoval, Francisco, 508
Santa Anna, Antonio Lopez de, 47, 81
Santa Fe (NM): as government headquarters, 43; image of plaza, *274*, *405*; images of, *276*; U.S. invasion of, 104–13
Santa Fe New Mexican (newspaper). See *New Mexican* (newspaper)
Santa Fe Post (newspaper). See *Post* (newspaper)
Santa Fe Republican (newspaper). See *Republican* (newspaper)
Santa Fe trade, 70–76; and the Mexican-American War, 88, 89, 102, 121
Santa Fe Weekly Gazette (newspaper). See *Gazette* (newspaper)
Santa Fe Weekly Post (newspaper). See *Post* (newspaper)
Santistevan, Jesús, 461
Santistevan, Juan, 705
Sarracino, Francisco, 51, 143, 145, 147, 168
Sarracino, Rafael, 46
Schenck, Robert, 528
Schermerhorn, Richard, 11, 199
Schlesinger, Joseph, 196
Schock, John, 461
schools. *See* education
Scott, Winfield, 117, 118
Seligman, A., 741
seminaries, 60
Semi-Weekly Review (newspaper). See *Review* (newspaper)
Sena, Antonio, 92, 383, 534
Sena, Felipe, 56, 318, 330, 534
Sena, José D.: during the 1867 election, 539, 544, 546–48, 568, 581, 587–93; during the 1868 election, 679, 680, 687–88; during the 1869 election, 698; during the 1870 statehood movement, 741; during the 1871 election, 750, 752, 756–57, 766–68, 780–81, 782; on Charles Clever, 551; during the Civil War, 381; following Lincoln's assassination, 460; image of, *584*; and military abuses, 457; possible federal appointment of, 667; role in the Republican Party, 648, 698; role in the URA, 651, 694; and the Slough shooting, 621
Sena, Ramón, 755
Sena y Armijo, Felipe, 92
Sena y Baca, Jesús María: in the 1857 election, 330; during the 1863 election, 403, 408, 418; at the 1863 People's Convention, 401; following Lincoln's assassination, 460; military service of, 455
Sena y Quintana, José, 147
Sena y Quintana, Miguel, 239
Sena y Romero, Jesús, 255
Sena y Romero, Miguel, 232
separation of church and state, 52–53, 157–58, 280, 286–87
settler colonialism, 199–203, 204, 889n108
Seward, F. N., 616–17
Seward, William H., 365, 442, 619, 922n23

Seymour, Horatio, 676
sheep industry: benefits of annexation in, 166–67; limiting factors in, 61–62; and the peonage system, 62; railroads' impact on, 801; and social hierarchies, 49–50
Sheridan, Philip, 644
sheriff (territorial office), 184–85
Sherman, Caleb, 237, 266–67
Sherman, John, 357
Sherman, William T., 496–97
Shurz, Carl, 646
Sibley, Henry H., 383–84
Sigel, Franz, 646
Simmons, Marc, 325
Sisneros, Agustín, 598
Sisneros, Samuel, 108, 176
Skinner, William, 244, 250
slavery: Administration Party's position on, 456; and the Civil War, 353–54; in the Crittenden Compromise, 356; National Democracy's position on, 349–50; NM's laws on, 349–50, 353, 377, 498, 516–18; partisan debate on, 246–47, 317, 319, 385; President Lincoln's vetoing bills prohibiting, 442; prosecution of, 663–64; Republican position on, 446; role in statehood debate, 210–11, 226, 236
slavery (Native American): accusations of, 388, 517, 537–38; legislation on, 350, 516–18; Nuevomexicano justification of, 525, 658–59, 663–65; partisan debate on, 659–63; and sociracial hierarchies, 65–66
Slough, John, 521, 618–22, 626, 668
Smith, Anthony, 310
Smith, Hugh N., 214, 215–16, 231, 261, 326
Smith, Thomas W., 460
sociracial hierarchies: based on Anglo-Saxonism, 887n59; cultural segmentation in, 66–69; and economic power, 49–50; forced annexation's impact on, 801; impact of market revolution on, 73–74, 83; and literacy, 67; Native Americans in, 238–39, 361; and the *partido* system, 62–66; political integration in, 25; in post-conquest New Mexico, 2–3; in power-sharing systems, 8–9; in territorial politics, 184
Spain: and the Catholic Church, 53; colonizing New Mexico, 35–36; Inquisition in, 549; Mexico's independence from, 37, 46, 53; Nuevomexicano identification with, 67–68
Spencer, Charles, 261, 266–67
Speyer, Albert, 102
Spiegelberg, Lehman, 741, 755, 756
Spiegelberg, Manuel, 597
Stanberry, Henry, 522
standing citizenship, 177
Stanton, Edwin, 492, 643–44
Stanton, Henry, 433
Stapleton, R. H., 508, 763
statehood: 1848 congressional debate on, 210; benefits of, 506–7; Civil War's impact on, 371; colonialism as impetus for, 181–82; partisan debate on, 21, 205–6; process for, 180–81; requirements for, 179; slavery issue's impact on, 210, 356–58; as territorial goal, 178–79, 183
statehood citizenship, 178
statehood movement (1848), 211–19
statehood movement (1850): Governor Munroe's tamping down of, 223–28; June elections, 219–22
statehood movement (1861): opposition to, 393–95; proposal for, 356–57
statehood movement (1863): opposition to, 399–400, 402, 413–14; and the People's Convention, 398–400; petition for, 383–95
statehood movement (1866), 501–9
statehood movement (1870): abandonment of, 743; bipartisanship in, 731–32, 739–42; February 26th meeting on, 741–42; planned conventions for, 742; race-based concerns during, 734–38
statehood movement (1910), 795–96
Statehood Revolution thesis, 180–83, 205, 210, 216, 224, 315–16, 393
Steck, Michael: during the 1867 election, 539; during the 1868 election, 688; appointed Indian superintendent, 391–92; and Bosque Redondo, 436, 441–42; conflicts with General Carleton, 449, 495; Diego Archuleta's criticism of, 465; resignation of, 936n99
Steele, Thomas, 281
Stegmaier, Mark, 184, 356, 357

Steinmetz, George, 202
Stephens, A. J., 310
Stephens, R. M., 679, 694, 700, 741
Stevens, Benjamin, 736–37
Stevens, Thaddeus, 357, 359–60, 645
Stewart, Matthew, 259, 900n30
St. Francis Cathedral, 272, *274*, *275*, *276*
Stinchcombe, Arthur, 194
Strachan, W. T., 532
Stuart, Alexander, 251
St. Vrain, Ceran: during the 1863 election, 421; in the American Party, 234; during the Mexican-American War, 130; military service of, 455; in the trade system, 72
St. Vrain, Vincent, 218, 345
subscription schools, 60
suffrage. *See* voting
Sullivan, A. P.: during the 1870 statehood movement, 737–39, 740, 741; during the 1871 election, 752–60, 766, 782, 978n59, 981n116; feud with H. H. Heath, 771; and José F. Chávez, 727; postmaster appointment of, 767; removed from federal post, 728; and Republican dissension, 726–31; and the *Weekly Post*, 725
Sumner, Charles, 494–95, 517, 537, 726
Sumner, E. V., 431; on officers' political activities, 898n128; on possible rebellions, 249–51; racism of, 260–61; as territorial commander, 249, 252
Sumner, Fort, 431–33, 439, 442
Supreme Court (NM), 305
Supreme Court (U.S.), 798–99
surrogate Jew phenomenon, 550
surveyor general (office), 797–98
Sutler's Store, *440*
Symington, John: during the 1869 election, 711–12, 718, 719; as editor of the *Review*, 707; leaving the *Review*, 722; on political sneaks, 715–16

Tafolla, Jesús, 125, 130–31, 133
Taos Revolt (1847), 125–28; trials and executions, 134–37, 879n236
Tapia, Juan, 327
Tappan, Samuel F., 496–97
taxation: as 1869 campaign issue, 718; as 1871 campaign issue, 769; addressed by the legislature, 256–57, 693; Delegate Watts's work on, 925n74; duty levy, 74, 208; and statehood, 508; and territorial salaries, 185–86
Taylor, James M., 519
Taylor, Nathanial, 496
Taylor, Zachary: death of, 226; in the Mexican-American War, 87; on New Mexican statehood, 210–11, 216; on slavery, 359; and Texas aggression, 217
Tenorio, Rafael, 601
Tenure of Office Act, 643–44, 670, 726
territorial secretary (office), 611
territories: colonialism as impetus for, 181–82; goal of statehood for, 178–79; governance system in, 28; legalities in forming, 118; legislatures in, 6; path to statehood, 179, 180–81, 191, 230; political rights for, 177, 875n161, 875n167; political status of, 177–79
Texas: American incorporation experience, 16–17; during the Civil War, 365–66, 380–81, 383–84, 922n23; invading New Mexico, 78–80, 215–16, 217; and land grant disputes, 800; map of, *94*; NM border dispute, 208–9, 210–11, 218, 226–27, 228; and U.S. expansionism, 85–87
Theisen, Gerald, 374, 408
Third Party system, 790
Thomas, Francis J., 261, 264–66
Thomasson, Nelson, 460
Thompson, Jerry, 381, 382–83, 921n16
Thornton, William T., 787–88
Tipton, Thomas, 631
Tipton, William, 386
Tobias, Henry, 563
Tomasito (Taos Puebloan), 126, 131
Tompkins, R. H. (Richard): at the 1866 statehood movement, 504, 508; during the 1868 election, 680, 682; during the 1871 election, 763; and American party, 391; supporting General Carleton, 435; as URA charter member, 651
torreón, 106
trade system: as contact zone, 71–78; debated impacts of, 83; impacts on Native Americans, 81–82; during the Mexican-American War, 88, 89, 102, 121. *See also*

economy
Traidor (dialogue), 558–62, 817–24
treaties: ineffectiveness of, 890n116; with the Navajo, 497
Treaty of Guadalupe Hidalgo, 1; citizenship rights in, 16, 175; expectation of statehood, 183; land grants in, 798, 799; map errors in, 394; and military government, 207; religious freedom in, 271; signing of, 169
Trujillo, Antonio María, 125, 135, 147
Trujillo, Juan de J., 550–51
Trujillo de Hinojós, María de Jesús, 903n99
Tucker, Thomas S.: during the 1865 election, 455–56; and the 1866 statehood movement, 505; during the 1868 election, 645, 688; during the 1870 statehood movement, 737, 741; during the 1871 election, 752–54, 766–67, 782; and the administrative appointments controversy, 523–24; and Bosque Redondo, 439, 492; feud with the *Review*, 695–96; on Governor Connelly, 511; on peonage, 660–61, 737; on political appointments, 530; possible federal appointment of, 668; on President Lincoln's assassination, 459–60; selling the *New Mexican*, 788; as URA charter member, 651
Tully, Murray, 218, 291
Turley, Simeon, 128
Turner, Frederick Jackson, 14
Turner, Henry, 111, 112
Twitchell, Ralph Emerson, 122–23, 124, 170, 803
two-party political system. *See* political system (two-party/binary)

Ugarte, Mauricio, 117
Unconditional Union Party, 443–45, 456, 462–69, 471
Union Administration Party, 534–35
Union Party, 471–75, 480–81. *See also* American Party
Union Republican Association (URA): on the 1867 contested election, 651–53; 1869 nominating convention, 697–99; charter members of, 964n30; criticized by Russell, 655–56; formal organizing of, 648–51; officers in (1868), 694–95; ratifying meeting (1868 election), 673–74. *See also* Republican Party (NMT)
Union Republican Party, 674
United States: church-state separation in, 52–53, 157–58, 280, 286–87; modernization process in, 36–37; westward expansionism of, 69–70, 85–87. *See also* Mexican-American War; Treaty of Guadalupe Hidalgo
United States v. Sandoval et al., 798
URA (Union Republican Association). *See* Union Republican Association (URA)
Usher, J. P., 433
usury Jewish stereotype, 554–55
Utah, 228
Utes, 62, 308, 320, 431

Valdez, Aniceto, 330
Valdez, Celedonio, 330
Valdez, José María, 421, 455, 615
Valdez, Juan Benito, 659–60
Valdez, Pedro: during the 1863 election, 420; during the 1867 election, 603, 615; during the 1875 election, 785; and the Bosque Redondo controversy, 452; slavery laws, 349
Valdez, Santiago, 420, 637, 706
Valencia, Nicolás, 168, 214
Vallandigham, Clement, 447, 744
Van Buren, Martin, 189, 291, 370
Vargas, Diego de, 35
Vasquez, Valentín, 363
Vatican, 271, 309, 316
Vaughn, E. J., 232
La Verdad (newspaper), 57
vernacularization, 24
veterans citizenship, 401
veto power, 629–32, 678, 692
Vigil, Antonio, 48, 455
Vigil, Cornelio, 126, 128
Vigil, Daniel, 599
Vigil, Donaciano: at the 1847 legislative assembly, 151–54; in the 1850 constitutional convention, 218; in the 1851 election, 232; in the 1853 election, 291; in the 1857 election, 323, 342, 345; during the 1863 election, 426; during the 1871 election, 761; in the American Party, 193, 204, 213, 234;

Vigil, Donaciano (*continued*)
on annexation, 167, 168–69; on benefits of citizenship, 207; during the Civil War, 381; death of, 803; educational background of, 60–61; *hispanidad* of, 67–68; on *hombres de bien*, 50; image of, *141*; as interim occupational governor, 128, 139–45, 170–71; and Kearny's Code, 116; on mercantile capitalism, 72; during the Mexican-American War, 90, 92, 124, 128–30, 132–34, 135, 137; on Mexican liberal principles, 78; in the National Democratic Party, 323; political appointments of, 116–17; political career of, 52, 56; political impact of, 803; possible pseudonyms of, 955n110; recognition of, 885n110; and the repatriation campaign, 176–77; and the *Republican*, 147; role in the press, 57; suspension of clergy, 271; as territorial secretary, 210; during the Texas invasion, 79; and the trade system, 73, 76, 83

Vigil, Epifanio: administrative appointments controversy, 518–19; and the administrative appointments controversy, 518–19, 522; Democratic Party work of, 787; political appointments of, 637; voiding of warrants of, 693

Vigil, Gregorio, 210
Vigil, José, 460
Vigil, Marcelino, 249
Vigil, Maurilio, 790
Vigil, Pedro, 125
Vigil, Trinidad, 381
Vigil y Alarid, Juan Bautista: and Americanization, 82; conflict with Charles Bent, 121; death of, 803; during the Mexican-American War, 105–8, 117; repatriation of, 176, 875n152; and the Santa Fe trade, 81
Viscarra, Antonio, 76
vocales (assemblymen), 45
voting: 1868 registration law, 684, 685–86; in civilian militias, 379–80; in Kearny's Code, 144–45; racial inequality in, 683; rationalized conceptions of, 158–59; and representational citizenship, 180; requirements, 235. *See also* elections
voting fraud: in the 1853 election, 295, 296–97; in the 1855 election, 300–302, 309–16; in the 1863 election, 424–25; in the 1867 election, 611–14, 636–37, 666, 701, 958n12; in the 1869 election, 720
La Voz del Pueblo (newspaper), 789

Wade, Benjamin F., 502, 644
Waldo, David, 72, 116
Waldo, Lawrence, 120, 128
Wallerstein, Immanuel, 9–10
Walzer, Michael, 200
Warner, Michael, 148
wartime loans, 90, 92–93
Washburn, Cadwallader, 357
Washington, George, 188
Washington, John M., 175–76, 210, 271
Washington Chronicle (newspaper), 702
Washington Sunday Herald (newspaper), 701–2
Watrous, Sam, 386, 390–91, 480, 497
Watts, John S.: during the 1859 election, 348; in the 1861 election, 371–76, 375; during the 1864 election, 444; in the 1865 election, 458; and attacks on William Arny, 475; and the Bosque Redondo controversy, 442; and the Conejos region, 479; as congressional delegate, 395, 925n74; criticism of, 477, 505; defending James Collins, 391; and Felipe Delgado's dismissal, 527; on Judge Benedict's reappointment, 377; judicial appointments of, 230, 668–69, 670, 692; and Lincoln's territorial appointments, 366–69, 387, 449; military service of, 455; as possible special delegate, 528
Webb, James J., 232
Weber, David, 77
Webster, Daniel, 229–30
Weekly Gazette (newspaper). See *Gazette* (newspaper)
Weekly Post (newspaper). See *Post* (newspaper)
Weekly Press (newspaper): during the 1863 election, 396, 406–12, 416; during the 1864 election, 445; and Bosque Redondo, 434; establishment of, 392, 924n56; rivalries, 392–93
Weekly Review (newspaper): on 1867 contested election, 703; during the 1869 election, 711–12, 715–16, 719–20, 722; political affiliations of, 707–8; replaced by

Republican Review, 725
Weightman, Richard: and the 1848 convention, 209; during the 1850 election, 219–20; in the 1850 statehood movement, 217; in the 1851 election, 5, 242, 244–45; background of, 211; and *Campaña Demócrata*, 293; as congressional delegate, 5, 225–26, 245–47; defending the traditional church, 214, 271; departing New Mexico, 299; description of, 892n27; as designated U.S. senator, 222; and the *El Amigo del País*, 266, 285, 299; endorsing Diego Archuleta, 308; on Governor Calhoun's replacement, 252; in the Mexican Party, 211–14, 264; role in federal appointments, 229–30
Welch, Y. B., 107
Wesche, Charles, 534
West, Elias P., 257
Wheaton, Theodore, 220, 239, 328
Wheelock, John E., 651
Wheelock, S. B., 695, 727
Whig Party: in the 1851 election, 231–32, 233; in the American Party, 300; anti-party members in, 888n79; assimilation views, 255; characterized as devils, 325; criticism of, 263; decline of, 262, 353; on Kearny's Code, 119; mistrust of political organization, 190, 231; and the National Democracy, 335, 346; in national politics, 188; in New Mexican politics, 191–92, 230–32, 330; on public education, 147; on slavery, 285; and social harmony, 253
Whiting, David, 293
Whiting, Harry R., 719, 722
Whittredge, Thomas Worthington, 276
Wilbar, A. P., 327, 330
Wolf, Eric, 796, 799
women: in the 1857 campaign, 330–31; education of, 147, 152; impact of economic modernization on, 73–74
"working the binaries," 193
Workmen, William, 81

Yates, Richard, 678
Yost, Samuel, 336, 345, 348. See also *Gazette* (newspaper)
Yrizarri, Mariano, 234, 595

Zeckendorf, William, 571–72
Zeleny, Carolyn, 802
Zorrilla, José, 558
Zubiría, José Antonio Laureano de, 48, 54, 68, 158, 271, 272, 279

Other works by Phillip B. Gonzales

Expressing Culture: Nuevomexicana/o Creativity, Everyday Ritual, Collective Remembrance

Forced Sacrifice as Ethnic Protest: The Hispano Cause in New Mexico and the Racial Attitude Confrontation of 1933

Sunbelt Working Mothers: Reconciling Family and Factory (with Louise Lamphere and Patricia Zavella)

CPSIA information can be obtained
at www.ICGtesting.com
Printed in the USA
LVOW01*2234080916

503841LV00015B/58/P

9 780803 284654